D0993616

IMPORTANT

HERE IS YOUR REGISTRATION CODE TO ACCESS MCGRAW-HILL PREMIUM CONTENT AND MCGRAW-HILL ONLINE RESOURCES

For key premium online resources you need THIS CODE to gain access. Once the code is entered, you will be able to use the web resources for the length of your course.

Access is provided only if you have purchased a new book.

If the registration code is missing from this book, the registration screen on our website, and within your WebCT or Blackboard course will tell you how to obtain your new code. Your registration code can be used only once to establish access. It is not transferable.

To gain access to these online resources

1. **USE** your web browser to go to: **http://www.mhhe.com/dess2e**

2. **CLICK** on "First Time User"

3. **ENTER** the Registration Code printed on the tear-off bookmark on the right

4. After you have entered your registration code, click on "Register"

5. **FOLLOW** the instructions to setup your personal UserID and Password

6. **WRITE** your UserID and Password down for future reference. Keep it in a safe place.

If your course is using WebCT or Blackboard, you'll be able to use this code to access the McGraw-Hill content within your instructor's online course.

To gain access to the McGraw-Hill content in your instructor's WebCT or Blackboard course simply log into the course with the user ID and Password provided by your instructor. Enter the registration code exactly as it appears to the right when prompted by the system. You will only need to use this code the first time you click on McGraw-Hill content.

These instructions are specifically for student access. Instructors are not required to register via the above instructions.

The McGraw-Hill Companies

McGraw-Hill
Irwin

Thank you, and welcome to your McGraw-Hill/Irwin Online Resources.

REGISTRATION CODE
CT28-RSRE-4PQN-Q1DI-DY7H

REGISTRATION CODE

The McGraw-Hill Companies

McGraw-Hill
Irwin

ISBN 0-07-313283-7 DESS: TITLE: STRATEGIC MANAGEMENT: TEXT AND CASES, 2/E

Strategic Management

text and cases

second edition

Gregory G. Dess
University of Texas at Dallas

G. T. Lumpkin
University of Illinois at Chicago

Alan B. Eisner
Pace University

McGraw-Hill Irwin

Boston   Burr Ridge, IL   Dubuque, IA   Madison, WI   New York
San Francisco   St. Louis   Bangkok   Bogotá   Caracas   Kuala Lumpur
Lisbon   London   Madrid   Mexico City   Milan   Montreal   New Delhi
Santiago   Seoul   Singapore   Sydney   Taipei   Toronto

The McGraw·Hill Companies

McGraw-Hill
Irwin

STRATEGIC MANAGEMENT: TEXT AND CASES
Published by McGraw-Hill/Irwin, a business unit of The McGraw-Hill Companies, Inc.,
1221 Avenue of the Americas, New York, NY, 10020. Copyright © 2006, 2004 by The McGraw-Hill
Companies, Inc. All rights reserved. No part of this publication may be reproduced or distributed
in any form or by any means, or stored in a database or retrieval system, without the prior written
consent of The McGraw-Hill Companies, Inc., including, but not limited to, in any network or
other electronic storage or transmission, or broadcast for distance learning.
Some ancillaries, including electronic and print components, may not be available to customers
outside the United States.

This book is printed on acid-free paper.

1 2 3 4 5 6 7 8 9 0 WCK/WCK 0 9 8 7 6 5 4

ISBN 0-07-111576-5

www.mhhe.com

To my family, Margie and Taylor; my parents, Bill and Mary Dess; and Professor Donald Beard
–Greg

To my wife, Vicki; and my colleagues at the University of Illinois at Chicago
–Tom

To my family, Helaine, Rachel, and Jacob
–Alan

dedication

brief contents

Strategic Analysis 1

1 Strategic Management: *Creating Competitive Advantages* 4

2 Analyzing the External Environment of the Firm 36

3 Assessing the Internal Environment of the Firm 68

4 Recognizing a Firm's Intellectual Assets 114

Strategic Formulation 2

5 Business-Level Strategy: *Creating and Sustaining Competitive Advantages* 146

6 Corporate-Level Strategy: *Creating Value through Diversification* 182

7 International Strategy: *Creating Value in Global Markets* 218

8 Digital Business Strategy: *Leveraging Internet and E-Business Capabilities* 250

Strategic Implementation 3

9 Strategic Control and Corporate Governance 288

10 Creating Effective Organizational Designs 328

11 Strategic Leadership: *Creating a Learning Organization and an Ethical Organization* 360

12 Managing Innovation and Fostering Corporate Entrepreneurship 394

13 Recognizing Opportunities and Creating New Ventures 428

Case Analysis 4

14 Analyzing Strategic Management Cases 470

Cases 500

Indexes 919

contents

1 Strategic Analysis

Chapter 1
Strategic Management: Creating Competitive Advantages 4

What Is Strategic Management? **8**
Defining Strategic Management 9
The Four Key Attributes of Strategic Management 10
The Strategic Management Process **11**
Strategy Analysis 12
Strategy Formulation 14
Strategy Implementation 15
The Role of Corporate Governance and Stakeholder Management **17**
Zero Sum or Symbiosis? Two Alternate Perspectives of Stakeholder Management 19
Social Responsibility: Moving Beyond the Immediate Stakeholders 19
The Strategic Management Perspective: An Imperative Throughout the Organization **21**
Some Key Driving Forces 21
Enhancing Employee Involvement in the Strategic Management Process 24
Ensuring Coherence in Strategic Direction **26**
Organizational Vision 26
Mission Statements 28
Strategic Objectives 29
Summary 31

Chapter 2
Analyzing the External Environment of the Firm 36

Creating the Environmentally Aware Organization **39**
The Role of Scanning, Monitoring, Competitive Intelligence, and Forecasting 39
SWOT Analysis 45
The General Environment **45**
The Demographic Segment 45
The Sociocultural Segment 48
The Political/Legal Segment 48
The Technological Segment 49
The Economic Segment 51
The Global Segment 52
Relationships among Elements of the General Environment 52

The Competitive Environment **53**
Porter's Five-Forces Model of Industry Competition 54
Strategic Groups within Industries 61
Summary 64

Chapter 3
Assessing the Internal Environment of the Firm 68

Value-Chain Analysis **71**
Primary Activities 73
Support Activities 76
Interrelationships among Value-Chain Activities within and across Organizations 81
Resource-Based View of the Firm **81**
Types of Firm Resources 82
Firm Resources and Sustainable Competitive Advantages 84
The Generation and Distribution of a Firm's Profits: Extending the Resource-Based View of the Firm 89
Evaluating Firm Performance: Two Approaches **91**
Financial Ratio Analysis 91
Integrating Financial Analysis and Stakeholder Perspectives: The Balanced Scorecard 94
Summary 97
Appendix to Chapter 3: Financial Ratio Analysis 102

Chapter 4
Recognizing a Firm's Intellectual Assets 114

The Central Role of Knowledge in Today's Economy **117**
Human Capital: The Foundation of Intellectual Capital **120**
Attracting Human Capital 121
Developing Human Capital 123
Retaining Human Capital 126
The Vital Role of Social Capital **129**
How Social Capital Helps Attract and Retain Talent 130
The Potential Downside of Social Capital 132
Using Technology to Leverage Human Capital and Knowledge **133**

Using Networks to Share Information
 and Develop Products and Services 133
Codifying Knowledge for Competitive Advantage 134
Retaining Knowledge When Employees Leave 135

**The Central Role of Leveraging Human
Capital in Strategy Formulation 137**
Leveraging Human Capital and
 Business-Level Strategy 137
Leveraging Human Capital and
 Corporate-Level Strategy 137
Leveraging Human Capital and
 International-Level Strategy 139
Leveraging Human Capital and
 Internet Strategies 139
Summary 139

Strategic Formulation

Chapter 5
Business-Level Strategy: Creating and
Sustaining Competitive Advantages 146

**Types of Competitive Advantage
and Sustainability 150**
Overall Cost Leadership 151
Differentiation 157
Focus 162
Combination Strategies: Integrating Overall
 Low Cost and Differentiation 164

**Industry Life Cycle Stages:
Strategic Implications 169**
Strategies in the Introduction Stage 170
Strategies in the Growth Stage 171
Strategies in the Maturity Stage 172
Strategies in the Decline Stage 173
Relating Generic Strategies to Stages of the
 Industry Life Cycle: The Personal
 Computer Industry 175
Turnaround Strategies 175
Summary 177

Chapter 6
Corporate-Level Strategy:
Creating Value through Diversification 182

Making Diversification Work: An Overview 186
**Related Diversification: Economies of Scope
and Revenue Enhancement 187**
Leveraging Core Competencies 188
Sharing Activities 189

Related Diversification: Market Power 190
Pooled Negotiating Power 190
Vertical Integration 192

**Unrelated Diversification: Financial
Synergies and Parenting 195**
Corporate Parenting and Restructuring 197
Portfolio Management 198
Caveat: Is Risk Reduction a Viable Goal of
 Diversification? 201

The Means to Achieve Diversification 201
Mergers and Acquisitions 202
Strategic Alliances and Joint Ventures 203
Internal Development 206

Real Options Analysis: A Useful Tool 207
**How Managerial Motives Can Erode
Value Creation 208**
Growth for Growth's Sake 209
Egotism 210
Antitakeover Tactics 212
Summary 212

Chapter 7
International Strategy: Creating
Value in Global Markets 218

The Global Economy: A Brief Overview 220
Factors Affecting a Nation's Competitiveness 221
Factor Conditions 222
Demand Conditions 223
Related and Supporting Industries 223
Firm Strategy, Structure, and Rivalry 224
Concluding Comment on Factors Affecting
 a Nation's Competitiveness 226

**International Expansion: A Company's
Motivations and Risks 226**
Motivations for International Expansion 226
Potential Risks of International Expansion 228

**Achieving Competitive Advantage
in Global Markets 232**
Two Opposing Pressures: Reducing Costs
 and Adapting to Local Markets 232
International Strategy 234
Global Strategy 235
Multidomestic Strategy 236
Transnational Strategy 238

Entry Modes of International Expansion 239
Exporting 240
Licensing and Franchising 242
Strategic Alliances and Joint Ventures 242
Wholly Owned Subsidiaries 244
Summary 246

Chapter 8
Digital Business Strategy: Leveraging Internet and E-Business Capabilities 250

How the Internet Is Affecting the Five Competitive Forces **257**
  The Threat of New Entrants *257*
  The Bargaining Power of Buyers *258*
  The Bargaining Power of Suppliers *259*
  The Threat of Substitutes *260*
  The Intensity of Competitive Rivalry *262*
How the Internet Adds Value **263**
  Search Activities *263*
  Evaluation Activities *265*
  Problem-Solving Activities *265*
  Transaction Activities *266*
  Other Sources of Competitive Advantage *267*
  Business Models *268*
How the Internet Is Affecting the Competitive Strategies **270**
  Overall Cost Leadership *272*
  Differentiation *273*
  Focus *275*
Are Internet-Based Advantages Sustainable? **278**
  Are Combination Strategies the Key to E-Business Success? *278*
Leveraging Internet Capabilities **280**
Summary 281

Strategic Implementation 3

Chapter 9
Strategic Control and Corporate Governance 288

Ensuring Informational Control: Responding Effectively to Environmental Change **291**
  A Traditional Approach to Strategic Control *291*
  A Contemporary Approach to Strategic Control *292*
Attaining Behavioral Control: Balancing Culture, Rewards, and Boundaries **295**
  Building a Strong and Effective Culture *296*
  Motivating with Rewards and Incentives *297*
  Setting Boundaries and Constraints *299*
  Behavioral Control in Organizations: Situational Factors *302*
  Evolving from Boundaries to Rewards and Culture *303*

Linking Strategic Control to Business-Level and Corporate-Level Strategies **304**
  Business-Level Strategy and Strategic Control *305*
  Corporate-Level Strategy and Strategic Control *306*
The Role of Corporate Governance **307**
  The Modern Corporation: The Separation of Owners (Shareholders) and Management *309*
  Governance Mechanisms: Aligning the Interests of Owners and Managers *311*
  External Governance Control Mechanisms *317*
Summary 321

Chapter 10
Creating Effective Organizational Designs 328

Traditional Forms of Organizational Structure **330**
  Patterns of Growth of Large Corporations *331*
  Simple Structure *332*
  Functional Structure *333*
  Divisional Structure *334*
  Matrix Structure *338*
  International Operations: Implications for Organizational Structure *339*
  How an Organization's Structure Can Influence Strategy Formulation *341*
Boundaryless Organizational Designs **341**
  The Barrier-Free Organization *343*
  The Modular Organization *347*
  The Virtual Organization *348*
  Boundaryless Organizations: Making Them Work *352*
Summary 355

Chapter 11
Strategic Leadership: Creating a Learning Organization and an Ethical Organization 360

Leadership: Three Interdependent Activities **363**
  Setting a Direction *365*
  Designing the Organization *365*
  Nurturing a Culture Dedicated to Excellence and Ethical Behavior *367*
  Overcoming Barriers to Change and the Effective Use of Power *367*
Emotional Intelligence: A Key Leadership Trait **370**
Developing a Learning Organization **374**
  Empowering Employees at All Levels *375*
  Accumulating and Sharing Internal Knowledge *376*

Gathering and Integrating External Information 378
Challenging the Status Quo and Enabling
   Creativity 380
Creating an Ethical Organization 381
Individual Ethics versus Organizational Ethics 381
Integrity-Based versus Compliance-Based
   Approaches to Organizational Ethics 383
Role Models 387
Corporate Credos and Codes of Conduct 387
Reward and Evaluation Systems 388
Summary 390

Chapter 12
Managing Innovation and Fostering
Corporate Entrepreneurship 394

Managing Innovation 397
Types of Innovation 398
Challenges of Innovation 400
Defining the Scope of Innovation 401
Managing the Pace of Innovation 402
Collaborating with Innovation Partners 402
Corporate Entrepreneurship 404
Focused Approaches to Corporate
   Entrepreneurship 405
Dispersed Approaches to Corporate
   Entrepreneurship 408
Measuring the Success of Corporate
   Entrepreneurship Activities 410
Entrepreneurial Orientation 414
Autonomy 414
Innovativeness 416
Proactiveness 418
Competitive Aggressiveness 419
Risk Taking 421
Summary 423

Chapter 13
Recognizing Opportunities
and Creating New Ventures 428

New Ventures and Small Businesses 431
Categories of Entrepreneurial Ventures 431
Opportunity Recognition: Identifying
and Developing Market Opportunities 435
The Opportunity Recognition Process 438
Characteristics of Good Opportunities 440
Entrepreneurial Resources 442
New-Venture Financing 443
Other Entrepreneurial Resources 447
Entrepreneurial Leadership 450
Vision 450

Dedication and Drive 451
Commitment to Excellence 453
Entrepreneurial Strategy 454
Entry Strategies 455
Generic Strategies 459
Combination Strategies 462
Summary 463

Case Analysis 4

Chapter 14
Analyzing Strategic
Management Cases 470

Why Analyze Strategic Management Cases? 472
How to Conduct a Case Analysis 473
Become Familiar with the Material 475
Identify Problems 477
Conduct Strategic Analyses 477
Propose Alternative Solutions 478
Make Recommendations 480
How to Get the Most from Case Analysis 480
Using Conflict-Inducing Decision-Making
Techniques in Case Analysis 483
Symptoms of Groupthink and How to Prevent It 485
Using Conflict to Improve Decision Making 485
Following the Analysis-Decision-Action Cycle
in Case Analysis 487
Summary 491
Appendix to Chapter 14: Sources of Company and Industry
   Information 493

Cases

1. Adolph Coors in the Brewing Industry 500
2. American Red Cross to 2002 (A) 514
3. American Red Cross, 2002–2004 (B) 525
4. Atari and InfoGrames Entertainment SA 530
5. Ben & Jerry's Homemade, Inc.: Passing
   the Torch 540
6. The Best-Laid Incentive Plans 555
7. Carly Fiorina: The Reinvention
   of Hewlett-Packard 559

8. Challenges Brewing
   at Breckenridge Brewery 576
9. Chiquita's Global Turnaround 589
10. Crown Cork and Seal in 1989 597
11. Dippin' Dots Ice Cream 615
12. eBay: King of the Online Auction Industry 621
13. Edward Marshall Boehm, Inc. 640
14. Ford Motor Company in 2004: Entering
    a Second Century of Existence 641
15. FreshDirect 650
16. General Motors 660
17. Go Global—or No? 666
18. Green Mountain Coffee Roasters 670
19. Growing for Broke 679
20. Heineken 683
21. Jay's Foods, LLC 689
22. JetBlue Airways 700
23. Johnson & Johnson 710
24. The Lincoln Electric Company, 1989 716
25. McDonald's 730
26. Microsoft's Battle for the Living Room:
    The Trojan Horse—The Xbox 736
27. Nokia's Strategic Intent for the
    21st Century 751
28. Outback Steakhouse Goes International 764

29. Panera Bread Company 783
30. Pixar Animation Studios 793
31. Procter & Gamble 799
32. Robin Hood 805
33. Samsung Electronics 806
34. Schoolhouse Lane Estates 811
35. Segway: A New Dimension
    in Human Transportation 825
36. The Skeleton in the Corporate Closet 834
37. Southwest Airlines: How Much Can
    "LUV" Do? 837
38. Starbucks Corporation: Competing
    in a Global Market 846
39. Toys "R" Us Moving into 2004 866
40. Trouble in Paradise 872
41. Wal-Mart's Strategy for the 21st Century:
    Sustaining Dominance 876
42. World Wrestling Entertainment 895
43. Yahoo! 901
44. Yum! Brands, Pizza Hut, and KFC 907

Indexes

Company *919*
Name *926*
Subject *936*

about the authors

Gregory G. Dess is the Andrew R. Cecil Endowed Chair in Management at the University of Texas at Dallas. His primary research interests are in strategic management, organization-environment relationships, and knowledge management. He has published numerous articles on these subjects in both academic and practitioner-oriented journals. In August 2000, he was inducted into the Academy of Management's Journals Hall of Fame as one of its charter members. Professor Dess has conducted executive programs in the United States, Europe, Africa, Hong Kong, and Australia. During 1994 he was a Fulbright Scholar in Oporto, Portugal. He received his PhD in Business Administration from the University of Washington (Seattle).

G. T. (Tom) Lumpkin is Associate Professor of Management and Entrepreneurship at the University of Illinois at Chicago. He received his PhD in management from the University of Texas at Arlington and MBA from the University of Southern California. His research interests include entrepreneurial orientation, opportunity recognition, strategy-making processes, and innovative forms of organizing work. He has published numerous research articles and book chapters. He is a member of Editorial Review Boards of *Entrepreneurship Theory & Practice* and the *Journal of Business Venturing.* Professor Lumpkin also conducts executive programs in strategic and entrepreneurial applications of e-commerce and digital business technologies.

Alan B. Eisner is Associate Professor of Management and Graduate Management Program Chair at the Lubin School of Business, Pace University. He received his PhD in management from the Stern School of Business, New York University. His primary research interests are in strategic management, technology management, organizational learning, and managerial decision making. He has published research articles and cases in journals such as *Advances in Strategic Management, International Journal of Electronic Commerce, International Journal of Technology Management, American Business Review, Journal of Behavioral and Applied Management,* and *Journal of the International Academy for Case Studies.* He is the Associate Editor of the Case Association's peer reviewed journal, *The CASE Journal.*

Highlights of the Second Edition

Welcome to the Second Edition of *Strategic Management: Text and Cases!* We are very pleased with the positive response to our initial edition, and we were gratified and appreciative of the extensive and valuable feedback that we received from the many individuals who took the time to review and critique our work. Much of this input has been invaluable and has led to many of the improvements that we'll summarize below. We, of course, acknowledge these professionals later in the Preface.

With this edition of *Strategic Management: Text and Cases,* we are truly excited to welcome Alan B. Eisner (Pace University) to the author team as our Case Editor. Alan is a very experienced case writer and the authors as well as our colleagues at McGraw-Hill/Irwin were very impressed by his professionalism and judgment in every aspect of putting together what we consider to be a "best in class" case package. Alan has assembled an excellent set of cases that emphasize well-known organizations; provide up-to-date financial data and information of strategic importance; create a superb match with the conceptual material in the 13 text chapters; and include excellent teaching notes. We also greatly appreciate Alan's responsiveness to suggestions and deadlines throughout the process.

We would also like to thank Marilyn L. Taylor (University of Missouri at Kansas City) for the many contributions that she has made, as Case Editor, to our first edition. We look forward to receiving valuable insights and case materials from this superb case writer who, in senior leadership roles, has made significant contributions to so many case research organizations.

Based on the many useful insights from our reviewers as well as reflecting on the changes that have occurred in the field of strategic management and the "real world," we have made many improvements in the Second Edition. These occur throughout the entire book in each of the major sections: strategic analysis (Chapters 1–4), strategic formulation (Chapters 5–8), strategic implementation (Chapters 9–13), case analysis (Chapter 14), and the cases. To make these changes and still keep the chapters of roughly the same length, we strove to tighten the writing style, remove a few redundant examples, and keep things as crisp and to the point as possible.

Before we briefly discuss the key changes that we've made to improve *Strategic Management* and keep it up-to-date, let's briefly discuss many of the exciting features that remain from the first edition.

♦ Crisply written chapters cover all of the strategy bases as well as address contemporary topics. We divide the chapters logically into the traditional sequence: strategic analysis, strategic formulation, and strategic implementation. In addition, we provide chapters on such timely topics as the Internet and digital strategies, intellectual capital/knowledge management, and entrepreneurship. (As you'll see below, we now have two separate chapters on entrepreneurship. Chapter 12 addresses innovation within the corporation, and Chapter 13 focuses on new ventures.)

♦ Key strategic concepts are introduced in a clear and concise manner and are followed by timely and interesting examples from business practice. These concepts include SWOT analysis, the resource-based view of the firm, competitive advantage, boundaryless organizations, digital strategies, corporate governance, and, entrepreneurship.

♦ The text provides a thorough grounding in ethics, globalization, and technology. These concepts are central themes throughout the book and form the basis for many of the sidebars, called "Strategy Spotlights," in the chapters.

◆ Many of the key concepts are applied to start-up firms and smaller businesses. This is particularly important since many students have professional plans to work in such firms.

◆ *Strategic Management* features the best chapter teaching notes available today. Rather than just summarize key points, we focus on "value-added" material to enhance the teaching (and learning) experience. Each chapter includes dozens of questions to spur discussion as well as many examples from business practice to provide further illustrations of key concepts.

Now, we'll briefly summarize some of the things we've done in the Second Edition to enhance the value of our book for both instructors and students.

◆ Nine of the opening "minicases" that lead off each of the chapters are new. Again, we feel that it is better to analyze things that can go wrong when strategy concepts aren't followed than to observe perfection.

◆ In Chapter 1, we have further reinforced the key role of corporate governance in the strategic management process—clearly this is one of the "hottest" and most controversial topics in today's business organizations. Also, the relationships between intended and realized strategies as well as the distinction between operational performance and strategy—two central issues in strategic management—have been clarified.

◆ Chapter 2 (external analysis) has been strengthened by providing a more detailed discussion of competitive intelligence—both from the perspective of how it can be enhanced as well as many of the ethical considerations that must be addressed. In addition, we incorporate into our analysis of forces that drive competition the key role of products and services that might impact the value of a firm's own products and services.

◆ Chapter 3 (internal analysis) incorporates a discussion of the "appropriation of value," a process whereby the profits of a business may be appropriated or retained by employees or other stakeholders. Such an issue becomes important when addressing competitive advantage, since profits may not, in all cases, be retained by the owners of the firm. We address what factors determine when this, in fact, will likely be the case.

◆ Chapter 4 (analysis of intellectual assets) has been improved by further discussing how knowledge is shared within firms. We also address some of the dysfunctional outcomes that firms may experience by participating in the "war for talent" and how firms can effectively control human resource costs without eroding their base of human capital.

◆ Chapter 5 (business-level strategy) has addressed how firms use a variety of "turnaround strategies" to reverse their fortunes. Here, we explain why some turnarounds fail and others succeed by drawing on key concepts as well as examples from business practice.

◆ Chapter 6 (corporate-level strategy) has been strengthened by a pragmatic, nontechnical discussion of real options analysis (ROA). ROA enables managers to decide whether to invest additional funds to grow or accelerate a course of action; delay, perhaps to learn more; shrink the scale of the activity; or even abandon it. We provide examples of the application of ROA for both an internal development decision as well as a decision to enter into a strategic alliance. In addition, a more detailed discussion is included to address the various types of restructuring activities that firms may undertake: asset, capital structure, and management. We also address in more detail one of the most frequently addressed (and emotional) topics in the business press: how managerial motives can erode the creation of value.

♦ In Chapter 7 (international strategy), we offer a more detailed discussion of one of the key challenges that managers face when moving beyond their geographic boundaries—dealing with unfamiliar cultures and their implications for the firm. We also address the increasing impact of political risk for Western businesses that are doing business in the Middle East. We expand our discussion of achieving competitive advantages in global markets by addressing "international strategies" which are recommended when firms face rather low pressures for both local adaptation and lowering costs.

♦ Chapter 8 (digital business strategy) widens our discussion beyond the Internet to include the implications of wireless technologies and the digital economy. We have also added a new section that addresses how the Internet and digital technologies are being used to add value. Four value-adding activities are discussed—search, evaluation, problem solving, and transaction—as well as business models used by Web-based businesses to create competitive advantages.

♦ In Chapter 9 (effective strategic controls), we incorporate a detailed discussion of the role of corporate governance in today's organization. We address both key internal governance mechanisms (committed and involved boards of directors; shareholder activism; and managerial rewards and incentives) as well as five external control mechanisms (e.g., market for corporate control, government, and auditors). As we all know, few topics have generated as much heated discussion as well as extensive legislative attention in the United States. We have also provided guidelines for relating the proper form of behavioral controls (culture, boundaries, and rewards) to types of organizations.

♦ Chapter 10 (organizational structure and design) has been improved by a more detailed discussion of organizational designs that foster teamwork—a valuable means of enhancing coordination across organizational units. We also address how a firm's structure can significantly affect its strategy.

♦ In Chapter 11 (strategic leadership, learning organizations, and ethics), we address one of the current leadership topics that has created a lot of interest—both in the academic and practitioner circles: emotional intelligence (EI). We address the components of EI and how it can play a key role in a leader's effectiveness. In addition, we discuss the importance of the bases of a leader's power and how its effective use can overcome barriers to change. Our discussion of a leader's role in shaping an ethical organization has also been expanded by articulating the need for organizations to become more proactive and move from compliance-based models to integrity-based models.

♦ Chapter 12 (managing innovation and corporate entrepreneurship) addresses the issues that incumbent firms face in their efforts to pursue venture opportunities and strategically renew themselves. This chapter includes a new section on managing innovation that discusses methods firms use to achieve innovativeness and the difficulties associated with effective innovation. There is also an expanded discussion of corporate entrepreneurship that addresses both focused and dispersed approaches to corporate venturing.

♦ Chapter 13 (creating new ventures) is a new chapter that focuses on venture creation by young and small firms. It addresses several types of entrepreneurial firms and includes an expanded discussion of opportunity recognition. The chapter discusses the importance of entrepreneurial leadership and how entrepreneurial firms obtain and use various types of resources. The section on entrepreneurial strategies presents three types of entry strategies—pioneering, imitative, and adaptive—and the use of generic and combination strategies by entrepreneurial firms.

- ◆ Chapter 14 (case analysis) contains a new section on the role of conflict-inducing decision-making techniques. It draws on the research using dialectical inquiry and devil's advocate approaches and discusses how better decisions can emerge in the process of reconciling conflicting views.

- ◆ We have brought together an exciting collection of current and classic cases for this edition, carefully selecting a wide variety of cases that are matched to key strategic concepts and organized to create maximum flexibility. We now have a selection of shorter-length cases including five new *Harvard Business Review* minicases and the classics, Robin Hood and Edward Marshall Boehm. We have also increased the currency and name recognition of our cases with brand-new, classroom-tested cases on Ford, General Motors, JetBlue, Pixar, Toys "R" Us, World Wrestling Entertainment, and many others. We offer a balance of short, medium-length, and comprehensive cases that offer a variety of classic and contemporary industry settings. Teaching notes for all cases are available on the Instructor's Resource CD-ROM. And finally, several cases have supplemental student and teacher resources to cultivate research skills, provide additional background, and encourage critical thinking. These "enhanced" case studies have a variety of features such as case PowerPoint slides, Web links, discussion questions, and videos with teaching notes.

Introduction

The most obvious question we need to address is: Why did we write the book? This was a question that we pondered for some time. After all, there were already some good strategy textbooks on the market. We decided that there was still a need for a book that students find to be highly relevant and readable—as well as rigorous. To this end, we worked hard both to "cover all of the traditional bases" and to integrate key themes throughout the book that are vital to an understanding of strategic management. These include such topics as globalization, technology, ethics, and entrepreneurship. To bring strategy concepts to life, we incorporated short examples from business practice to illustrate virtually every concept in the book and provided 100 "Strategy Spotlights"—more detailed examples—to drive home key points. We also included four separate chapters which other strategy texts lack that address timely subjects about which all business students should have a solid understanding: the role of intellectual assets and knowledge in value creation; the importance of the Internet and digital business strategies in creating competitive advantage; the value of fostering entrepreneurship in established organizations; and a new chapter on creating new venture start-ups. And we provide an excellent set of cases to help you analyze, integrate, and apply strategic management concepts.

In developing *Strategic Management* and the support materials, we did not, of course, forget the instructors. You have a most challenging job, and we want to do our best to help you. In addition to providing a total package that students should find attractive and valuable, we also provide you with a variety of supplementary materials that should aid you in class preparation and delivery. Our focus was not on reviewing what we have in the text; rather, our efforts were centered on where we can "add value" to your pedagogy. In short, we have worked hard to provide a complete package that should make your classes relevant, rigorous, and rewarding for you and your students.

Let's now discuss in some detail why we find strategic management to be such a relevant and worthwhile topic along with some of the attractive features and benefits of *Strategic Management*. Strategic management seeks to answer a simple and basic question: How and why do some firms outperform others? Stated differently, Why are some firms able to enjoy the benefits of developing and maintaining competitive advantages in the marketplace while others are not? *Strategic Management: Text and Cases,* Second Edition, was written to address this question. To do so, we examine the three interrelated and principal activities that are part of the overall strategic management process: analysis, formulation, and implementation. *Strategy analysis* involves the careful consideration of an organization's goals as well as a thorough analysis of its external and internal environment. *Strategy formulation* focuses on developing strategies to attain competitive advantages in the marketplace that are difficult for competitors to imitate. *Strategy implementation* addresses the challenge of making sure that the desired strategies are effectively carried out. This involves such things as creating the necessary action plans, incentive and control systems, and organizational structures. After all, without effective implementation, the whole process becomes the proverbial "academic exercise" and nothing is accomplished except frustration and wasted resources.

Why is strategic management relevant for students at the early stages of their business careers? The answer is that in today's organization, there is a far greater need for broad involvement throughout the organization in the strategic management process. One of the biggest reasons is the unprecedented rate of change. As noted by former AOL Time Warner chairman Steven M. Case:

> I sometimes feel like I'm behind the wheel of a race car . . . One of the biggest challenges is there are no road signs to help navigate. And in fact . . . no one has yet determined which side of the road we're supposed to be on.*

*Quoted in J. E. Garten, *The Mind of the C.E.O* (New York: Basic Books, 2001).

There are many forces driving change in modern business that we address throughout the book. Primary among these are the accelerating role of globalization and technology, and the emergence of knowledge as the primary source of value creation in today's economy. Within many organizations, the ongoing process of downsizing and delayering has streamlined firms and required more people to get involved in anticipating and responding to changing customer demands. As a result, employees with multiple functional responsibilities now share responsibilities that were once compartmentalized. Accordingly, the need has increased for empowering employees throughout the organization. Peter Senge, one of the leading writers in strategic management, articulated this need:

> In an increasingly dynamic, interdependent, and unpredictable world, it is simply no longer possible for anyone to "figure it all out at the top." The old model, "the top thinks and the local acts," must now give way to integrating and acting at all levels.†

That is, *everyone* must be involved in integrating—seeing how different parts of the organization fit together—and acting at all levels.

So how does a course in strategic management fit in? For students this course is one of the most important—and useful—that you will take in your business curriculum. Up to now, your classes have focused on a variety of functional areas such as marketing, accounting, finance, and operations. What we do in this course is to bring it all together by asking you to take the perspective of a senior executive with responsibility for an entire organization. To be successful (in this course and in your future business endeavors), you will need to further develop many skills and abilities considered to be the essence of a strategic management perspective. These include (1) integrating the functional areas in a firm to attain the organization's overall goals and objectives, (2) incorporating the needs of multiple stakeholders, (3) recognizing the dual objectives—and sometimes inevitable trade-offs—between effectiveness ("doing the right thing") and efficiency ("doing things right"), and (4) reconciling the potential conflicts between short-term and long-term horizons. In this course, you will build on your areas of expertise such as finance or marketing by incorporating a wide variety of perspectives in deciding what course of action a firm should take and how it should implement its strategies.

Throughout your career, incorporating these elements of a strategic management perspective will be essential to your success. In the more immediate term, such an orientation will help you to see how your role and activities fit into the overall mission and strategies of your organization. Such awareness enhances your potential to make a significant contribution.

In writing *Strategic Management,* we have tried to create a strong blend of rigor and relevance. The material is not "watered down." If it were, students (and instructors!) would lose interest. At the same time, we did not want to have the book infiltrated with academic jargon—terminology about which many academics themselves have significant differences. Instead, we have worked to address the most important (and sometimes complex) issues and concepts in a stimulating and engaging manner that both challenges the reader and enhances student enthusiasm for the understanding and application of course material. Accordingly, concepts are explained in a direct and straightforward manner and illustrated with thought-provoking and contemporary examples from business practice. In many instances, these examples come from knowledge-intensive industries, such as computer software and services, pharmaceuticals, and biotechnology, where substantial wealth is being created today.

---

†P. Senge, "The Leader's New Work: Building Learning Organizations," *Sloan Management Review* 32, no. 1 (1990), p. 7.

We have carefully researched the concepts and topics in this book from a wide variety of sources. These include both academic- and practitioner-oriented journals. This research was combined with a thorough search through many publications in the popular business press such as *BusinessWeek, Fortune, Forbes, Inc., Fast Company,* and the *Wall Street Journal.* In addition, we collected some "primary data" by writing to the CEOs of about 100 of the "Most Admired Firms" in *Fortune* magazine's annual survey as well as many of *Inc.* magazine's "Fastest Growing Firms" to request material that they felt would be helpful in illustrating sound strategy concepts. We were pleased to obtain excellent responses both in terms of "quality" and "quantity" and received a wide variety of annual reports, 10-K forms, executive speeches, internal company publications, and videos which were very useful in driving home key concepts and ideas.

Our goal is to have a timely, readable book that accomplishes many things. First, we "cover the bases" of the traditional concepts—SWOT (strengths-weaknesses-opportunities-threats) and five-forces analysis; value-chain analysis; competitive advantage; and portfolio analysis—in a thorough and integrative manner. Second, we incorporate the latest thinking on contemporary topics such as e-commerce strategies, empowerment, network organizations, entrepreneurship, corporate governance, and the role of human and social capital in value creation. Third, we bring these concepts to life with examples from organizations that encompass a wide range in size, industry type, and geographic scope. It is our hope that students and instructors have a challenging and rewarding experience in a discipline to which we, the authors, have devoted our professional careers.

We would now like to go into more detail and point out some of the key features and benefits of *Strategic Management.* This helps to explain how we have tried to achieve our goals in writing this book.

Key Features of Strategic Management

We believe the features we discuss below add value to our book for both instructors and students.

- *Variety, currency, and familiar company names.* The cases are up-to-date in terms of both financial data and strategic issues. We have selected a group of cases that give both instructors and students unparalleled quality and variety. At the same time, we have chosen a combination of comprehensive and shorter-length cases about well-known companies.

- *Traditional organizing framework.* We have organized the book around the traditional sequence of topics and concepts in strategic management. The text is divided into three major sections that address analysis, formulation, and implementation. All of the topics that form the core of the discipline are covered, including SWOT analysis, five-forces analysis, value-chain analysis, competitive advantage, portfolio analysis, corporate governance, and organization structure. Such concepts are time-tested and have proven their value and relevance through research and managerial practice.

- *Integrative themes.* Several integrative themes that recur throughout the book add timeliness and integration to the text material. Among these themes are ethics and social responsibility, globalization, technology, and entrepreneurship. Such topics are essential to gaining a full understanding of the strategies that a firm formulates and implements.

- *Extensive use of sidebars.* As noted above, we will use sidebars—detailed examples of business practice—to drive home important points in the book. All 100 Strategy

Spotlights (roughly seven per chapter) are written in a way to enhance student interest in learning and applying key concepts in strategic management.

♦ *Separate chapters that focus on key contemporary issues.* In addition to "covering the bases" with our traditional organizing framework, we include four separate chapters that focus on important, timely issues facing today's strategic managers. These are:

Chapter 4: "Recognizing a Firm's Intellectual Assets" discusses the importance of knowledge and intangible assets as the key driver of wealth creation in today's economy.

Chapter 8: "Digital Business Strategy: Leveraging Internet and E-Business Capabilities" addresses the critical role that digital technologies and the Internet have played in creating and enhancing competitive advantages as well as developing new business opportunities.

Chapter 12: "Managing Innovation and Fostering Corporate Entrepreneurship" discusses the role of innovation in creating new business opportunities and the importance of internal corporate venturing in creating value for incumbent firms.

Chapter 13: "Recognizing Opportunities and Creating New Ventures" examines the role of opportunity recognition, entrepreneurial leadership, and access to resources to the new venture creation process and how entrepreneurial strategies create competitive advantages for young and small firms.

♦ *Chapter opening cases—What can go wrong?* To enhance student interest, we begin each chapter with a case that depicts an organization that has suffered a dramatic performance drop—or outright failure—by failing to adhere to sound strategic management concepts and principles. This feature serves to underline the value of the concepts in the course. We believe this is the preferred teaching approach to one of merely providing examples of outstanding companies that always seem to get it right! After all, isn't it better to diagnose problems than admire perfection? Some examples: We discuss how Dick Brown, CEO of EDS, ignored the economic environment and the intensity of competition, set unrealistically high goals, and eroded his firm's competitive position (and lost his job); how Charles Schwab and Company's acquisition of U.S. Trust, a financial services firm that caters to wealthy clients, has not worked out as planned; and some of the problems experienced by Volkswagen as it tries to enter the luxury segment of the U.S. automobile industry.

♦ *Consistent chapter format and features to reinforce learning.* We have included several features in each chapter to "add value" and, we hope, create an enhanced learning experience. First, each chapter begins with an overview and a set of "bullets" pointing to the key learning objectives. Second, as noted previously, the opening case describes a situation in which a company's performance eroded because of the lack of proper application of strategy concepts. Third, at the end of each chapter there are four different types of questions/exercises that should help students assess their understanding and application of material: (1) experiential exercises, (2) summary review questions, (3) application questions and exercises, and (4) ethics questions. Given the emergence of the Internet and e-commerce, each chapter contains at least one exercise that involves the use of the Internet.

♦ *BusinessWeek subscription.* Students can subscribe to *BusinessWeek* for a special rate in addition to the price of the text. Students will receive a pass code card shrink-wrapped with their new text. The card directs students to a website where they enter the code and then gain access to *BusinessWeek*'s registration page to enter their address information and also set up their print and online subscription. Please ask your rep for more info.

Acknowledgments

Strategic Management represents far more than just the joint efforts of the three coauthors. Rather, it is the product of the collaborative inputs and contributions of many individuals. Some of these people are academic colleagues, others are the outstanding team of professionals at McGraw-Hill/Irwin, and still others are those individuals who are closest to us—our families. It is time to express our sincere gratitude.

First, we'd like to acknowledge the thorough, constructive reviews that we received from our superb team of reviewers. Their input was very helpful in both pointing out errors in the manuscript and suggesting areas that needed further development as additional topics. We sincerely believe that the incorporation of their ideas was critical to improving the final product. These professionals and their affiliations are:

Second Edition Reviewers

Larry Alexander, *Virginia Polytechnic Institute*
Jay Azriel, *Illinois State University*
Brent D. Beal, *Louisiana State University*
Dusty Bodie, *Boise State University*
William Bogner, *Georgia State University*
Radha Chaganti, *Rider University*
Michael Fathi, *Georgia Southwestern University*
Paula Harveston, *Berry College*
Dana M. Johnson, *Michigan Technical University*
Franz Kellermanns, *Mississippi State University*
Donna Kelley, *Babson College*
Theresa Lant, *New York University*
Wanda Lester, *North Carolina A&T State University*

John M. Mezias, *University of Miami*
Michael Michalisin, *Southern Illinois University at Carbondale*
Stephen Mueller, *Northern Kentucky University*
Karen Page, *University of Wyoming*
Kira Reed, *Syracuse University*
Barbara Ribbens, *Western Illinois University*
Ken Robinson, *Kennesaw State University*
Patrick R. Rogers, *North Carolina A&T State University*
Jamal Shamsie, *Michigan State University*
Herbert Sherman, *Long Island University*
Roy Suddaby, *University of Iowa*
Justin Tan, *Creighton University*
Robert Trumble, *Virginia Commonwealth University*

Developmental Reviewers

Dave Arnott, *Dallas Baptist University*
Bruce Barringer, *University of Central Florida*
Dusty Bodie, *Boise State University*
Gary Carini, *Baylor University*
Gary J. Castrogiovanni, *University of Tulsa*
Jeffrey Covin, *Indiana University*
Deepak Datta, *University of Texas at Arlington*

Jim Davis, *University of Notre Dame*
Rocki-Lee DeWitt, *University of Vermont*
Tom Douglas, *Clemson University*
Matt Gilley, *Oklahoma State University*
Gordon Holbein, *Northern Kentucky University*
Jay J. Janney, *University of Dayton*
Lawrence Jauch, *University of Louisiana–Monroe*

Dave Ketchen, *Florida State University*

Stan Kowalczyk, *San Francisco State University*

Ted Legatski, *Texas Christian University*

Benyamin Lichtenstein, *University of Massachusetts at Boston*

Doug Lyon, *Fort Lewis College*

Stephanie Newport, *Austin Peay State University, Tennessee*

Abdul Rasheed, *University of Texas at Arlington*

Lois Shelton, *Chapman University*

Mark Simon, *Oakland University, Michigan*

Rob Singh, *Morgan State University*

Bruce Skaggs, *University of Kentucky*

Timothy Stearns, *California State University, Fresno*

Beverly Tyler, *North Carolina State University*

Bruce Walters, *Louisiana Tech University*

Monica Zimmerman, *Temple University*

Part Reviewers

Abagail McWilliams, *University of Illinois, Chicago*

V. K. Narayanan, *Drexel University*

Bill Norton, *University of Louisville*

Laura Poppo, *Virginia Tech*

Nandini Rajagopalan, *University of Southern California*

Kenneth Robinson, *Kennesaw State University*

Justin Tan, *Creighton University*

Larry Watts, *Stephen F. Austin University*

Anne York, *University of North Carolina*

Chapter Reviewers

Allen C. Amason, *The University of Georgia*

Peter H. Antoniou, *California State University, San Marcos*

Jeffrey J. Bailey, *University of Idaho*

Eldon Bernstein, *Lynn University*

Samuel D. Cappel, *Southeastern Louisiana State University*

Betty S. Coffey, *Appalachian State University*

James J. Cordeiro, *SUNY Brockport*

Jon Down, *Oregon State University*

Clare Engle, *Concordia University*

Vance Fried, *Oklahoma State University*

Kim Hester, *Arkansas State University*

Alan Hoffman, *Bentley College*

James G. Ibe, *Morris College*

Daniel Kraska, *North Central State College*

Subodh P. Kulkarni, *Howard University*

Dan Lockhart, *University of Kentucky*

Santo D. Marabella, *Moravian College*

Larry McDaniel, *Alabama A&M University*

John Mezias, *University of Miami*

John Mullane, *Middle Tennessee State University*

Anil Nair, *Old Dominion University*

Maria L. Nathan, *Lynchburg College*

Julie Palmer, *University of Missouri, Columbia*

Gerald Parker, *Saint Louis University*

Douglas K. Peterson, *Indiana State University*

Clint Relyea, *Arkansas State University*

Barbara A. Ribbens, *Western Illinois University*

Patrick R. Rogers, *North Carolina A&T State University*

Yolanda Sarason, *Colorado State University*

Alice Stewart, *Ohio State University*

Ram Subramanian, *Grand Valley State University*

Bing-Sheng Teng, *George Washington University*
Jay A. Vora, *St. Cloud State University*
Edward Ward, *St. Cloud State University*

Paula Weber, *St. Cloud State University*
Diana J. Wong, *Bowling Green State University*

Previous Revision Reviewers

Todd Alessandri, *Syracuse University*
Jay Azriel, *Illinois State University*
Mikelle A. Calhoun, *Valparaiso University*
Shawn M. Carraher, *Texas A&M University, Commerce*
Don Caruth, *Amberton University*
Gary Castrogiovanni, *University of Tulsa*
Theresa Cho, *Rutgers University*
Wade Coggins, *Webster University, Fort Smith Metro Campus*
Joseph Coombs, *University of Richmond*
James Davis, *University of Notre Dame*
Helen Deresky, *State University of New York, Plattsburgh*
Kristen Bell DeTienne, *Brigham Young University*
Michael E. Dobbs, *Arkansas State University*
Jonathan Doh, *Villanova University*
William A. Evans, *Troy State University, Dothan*
Frances H. Fabian, *University of North Carolina, Charlotte*
Angelo Fanelli, *Warrington College of Business*
Carolyn J. Fausnaugh, *Florida Institute of Technology*
Tamela D. Ferguson, *University of Louisiana at Lafayette*
Isaac Fox, *University of Minnesota*
Steven A. Frankforter, *Winthrop University*
Diana L. Gilbertson, *California State University, Fresno*
Debbie Gilliard, *Metropolitan State College of Denver*
Sanjay Goel, *University of Minnesota, Duluth*
Niran Harrison, *University of Oregon*
John Hironaka, *California State University, Sacramento*

Allan Hoffman, *Bentley College*
Jill Hough, *University of Tulsa*
John Humphreys, *Eastern New Mexico University*
James Katzenstein, *California State University, Dominguez Hills*
Craig Kelley, *California State University, Sacramento*
John A. Kilpatrick, *Idaho State University*
Donald E. Kreps, *Kutztown University*
Subodh P. Kulkarni, *Howard University*
Peter Ping Li, *California State University, Stanislaus*
Hao Ma, *Bryant College*
James Maddox, *Friends University*
Paul Mallette, *Colorado State University*
John E. Merchant, *California State University, Sacramento*
Debra Moody, *University of North Carolina, Charlotte*
Gregory A. Moore, *Middle Tennessee State University*
James R. Morgan, *Dominican University and UC Berkeley Extension–International Partnerships*
John Mullane, *Middle Tennessee State University*
Gerry Nkombo Muuka, *Murray State University*
Maria L. Nathan, *Lynchburg College*
Yusuf A. Nur, *SUNY–Brockport*
Jacquelyn W. Palmer, *University of Cincinnati*
Daewoo Park, *Xavier University*
Edward Petkus, *Mary Baldwin College*
Michael C. Pickett, *National University*
Laura Poppo, *Virginia Tech*
Scott A. Quatro, *Grand Canyon University*
Barbara Ribbens, *Western Illinois University*
Maurice Rice, *University of Washington*

Violina P. Rindova, *University of Maryland, College Park*

John K. Ross III, *Texas State University, San Marcos*

Robert Rottman, *Kentucky State University*

Carol M. Sánchez, *Grand Valley State University*

Marguerite Schneider, *New Jersey Institute of Technology*

Roger R. Schnorbus, *University of Richmond*

Wayne Smeltz, *Rider University*

Ram Subramanian, *Grand Valley State University*

Michael Sullivan, *UC Berkeley Extension*

Tracy Thompson, *University of Washington, Tacoma*

Paula S. Weber, *St. Cloud State University*

Kenneth E. A. Wendeln, *Indiana University*

Robert R. Wharton, *Western Kentucky University*

Beth Woodard, *Belmont University*

Focus Group Participants

Cynthia Lengnick-Hall, *University of Texas at San Antonio*

Dave Ketchen, *Florida State University*

John Mezias, *University of Miami*

Barbara Ribbens, *Western Illinois University*

Second, the authors would like to thank several faculty colleagues who were particularly helpful in the review, critique, and development of the book and supplementary materials. While Greg was at the University of Kentucky, faculty in the strategic management area were extremely generous with their time. They provided many excellent ideas and contributions. Accordingly, he would like to thank Wally Ferrier, Gordon Holbein, Dan Lockhart, and Bruce Skaggs. His colleagues at the University of Texas at Dallas have also been very helpful and supportive. These include Joe Picken, Paul Gaddis, Seung-Hyun Lee, Tev Dalgic, and Jane Salk. His administrative assistant, Yung Hua, has been extremely helpful, and an MBA student—Naga Damaraju—has provided many useful inputs and ideas. He also appreciates the support of his dean and associate dean, Hasan Pirkul and Varghese Jacob, respectively. Tom would like to thank Gerry Hills, Abagail McWilliams, Darold Barnum, Sheila Goins, Mike Miller, Rod Shrader, James Thompson, Cindy Atchley, Joel Warady, and Lou Coco, colleagues at the University of Illinois at Chicago, for their support and patience throughout the process. Tom also extends a special thanks to Benyamin Lichtenstein for his support and encouragement. Both Greg and Tom wish to thank a special colleague, Abdul Rasheed at the University of Texas at Arlington, who certainly has been a valued source of friendship and ideas for us for many years. He provided many valuable contributions to the second edition—both in the text and the Instructor's Manual. Alan thanks his colleagues at Pace University and the Case Association for their support in developing these fine case selections. Special thanks to Jamal Shamsie at Michigan State University for his support in developing the case selections for this edition.

Third, we would like to thank the team at McGraw-Hill/Irwin for their outstanding support throughout the process. This begins with John Biernat, Editorial Director, who signed us to the contract. John was always available to provide support and valued input during the entire process. In "editorial," Ryan Blankenship and Natalie Ruffatto kept things on track, responded quickly to our never-ending needs and requests, and offered insights and encouragement. Once the manuscript was completed and revised, Harvey Yep, as project manager, expertly guided the manuscript through the production process. The authors were very impressed by the superb final copyediting talents of Charles Olsen. Cathy Tepper did an outstanding job in helping the authors with the supplementary materials. Pam Verros provided excellent design and art work. And, finally, we thank Ellen Cleary for her energetic, competent, and thorough marketing efforts.

Last, we would like to thank our families. For Greg this includes his parents, William and Mary Dess, who have always been there for him. And his wife, Margie, and daughter, Taylor, have been a constant source of love and companionship. He promises to have more family time and take Taylor to parks and shopping more often. Greg would also like to acknowledge the invaluable contribution that Professor Donald W. Beard (University of Washington) has made to his career. Don has been a constant source of support and was very helpful with Greg's dissertation and the many papers on which they worked together. Greg will always be indebted to Don for his many intellectual contributions, enthusiasm, good humor, and patience. Tom thanks his wife Vicki for her constant love and companionship. Tom also thanks Lee Hetherington and Thelma Lumpkin for their inspiration and his mom, Katy, and his sister, Kitty, for a lifetime of support. Alan thanks his family, Helaine, Rachel, and Jacob for their love and support. He also thanks his parents, Gail Eisner and the late Marvin Eisner, for their support and encouragement.

Strategic Management

text and cases

2e

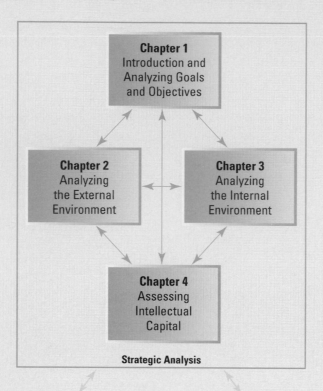

Chapter 1
Introduction and
Analyzing Goals
and Objectives

Chapter 2
Analyzing
the External
Environment

Chapter 3
Analyzing
the Internal
Environment

Chapter 4
Assessing
Intellectual
Capital

Strategic Analysis

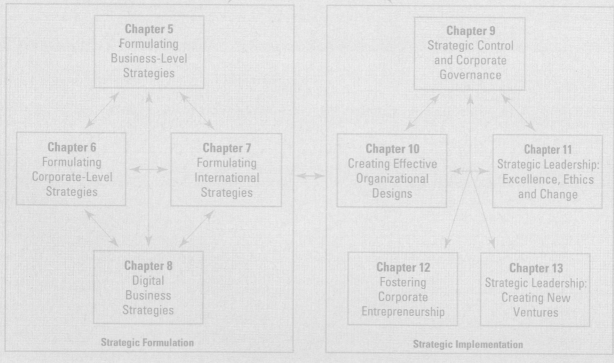

Chapter 5
Formulating
Business-Level
Strategies

Chapter 9
Strategic Control
and Corporate
Governance

Chapter 6
Formulating
Corporate-Level
Strategies

Chapter 7
Formulating
International
Strategies

Chapter 10
Creating Effective
Organizational
Designs

Chapter 11
Strategic Leadership:
Excellence, Ethics
and Change

Chapter 8
Digital
Business
Strategies

Chapter 12
Fostering
Corporate
Entrepreneurship

Chapter 13
Strategic Leadership:
Creating New
Ventures

Strategic Formulation

Strategic Implementation

Chapter 14
Case
Analysis

Strategic Analysis

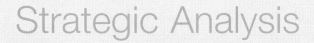

Strategic Management: Creating Competitive Advantages 1

Analyzing the External Environment of the Firm 2

Assessing the Internal Environment of the Firm 3

Recognizing a Firm's Intellectual Assets: Moving beyond a Firm's Tangible Resources 4

part One

Strategic Analysis

chapter 1

Strategic Management:

Creating Competitive Advantages

*After
reading this
chapter, you should
have a good understanding of:*

- The definition of strategic management and its four key attributes.

- The strategic management process and its three interrelated and principal activities.

- The vital role of corporate governance and stakeholder management as well as how "symbiosis" can be achieved among an organization's stakeholders.

- The key environmental forces that are creating more unpredictable change and requiring greater empowerment throughout the organization.

- How an awareness of a hierarchy of strategic goals can help an organization achieve coherence in its strategic direction.

We define strategic management as consisting of the analysis, decisions, and actions an organization undertakes in order to create and sustain competitive advantages. At the heart of strategic management is the question: How and why do some firms outperform others? Thus, the challenge to managers is to decide on strategies that provide advantages that can be sustained over time. There are four key attributes of strategic management. It is directed at overall organizational goals, includes multiple stakeholders, incorporates short-term as well as long-term perspectives, and recognizes trade-offs between effectiveness and efficiency. We discuss the above definition and the four key attributes in the first section.

The second section addresses the strategic management process. The three major processes are strategy analysis, strategy formulation, and strategy implementation. These three components parallel the analyses, decisions, and actions in the above definition. We discuss how each of the 13 chapters addresses these three processes and provide examples from each chapter.

The third section discusses two important and interrelated concepts: corporate governance and stakeholder management. Corporate governance addresses the issue of who "governs" the corporation and determines its direction. It consists of three primary participants: stockholders (owners), management (led by the chief executive officer), and the board of directors (elected to monitor management). Stakeholder management recognizes that the interests of various stakeholders, such as owners, customers, and employees, can often conflict and create challenging decision-making dilemmas for managers. However, we will also discuss how some firms have been able to achieve "symbiosis" among stakeholders wherein their interests are considered interdependent and can be achieved simultaneously.

The fourth section addresses three interrelated factors in the business environment—globalization, technology, and intellectual capital—that have increased the level of unpredictable change for today's leaders. These factors have also created the need for a greater strategic management perspective and reinforced the role of empowerment throughout the organization.

The final section focuses on the need for organizations to ensure consistency in their vision, mission, and strategic objectives which, collectively, form a hierarchy of goals. While visions may lack specificity, they must evoke powerful and compelling mental images. Strategic objectives are much more specific and are essential for driving toward overall goals.

One of the things that makes the study of strategic management so interesting is that struggling firms can become stars, while high flyers can become earthbound very rapidly. During the stock market slump beginning in 2000, many technology firms were particularly ravaged. Let's look at one such firm that experienced a hard fall from grace: EDS.

Electronic Data Systems (EDS), with $22 billion in revenues, is one of the giants in the $140 billion computer services outsourcing industry.[1] Prior to the hiring of Richard Brown as CEO in December 1998, the firm's shares were trading at $35. Unfortunately, when Brown was removed on March 20, 2003, the shares had shrunk to $16. About 55 percent of the firm's market capitalization (or $9 billion) had vanished. In addition, EDS's reputation had been sullied by investigations by the Securities and Exchange Commission, and its competitive position had eroded.

In a sense, such a reversal may appear as a rather surprising turn of events. Founded by Ross Perot in 1962, EDS had been well-known for its technical competence, steady growth, and Perot's conservative culture—symbolized by crisp white shirts and military-issue haircuts. However, by 1998 Brown's gung-ho style seemed to be needed to revitalize a company that had become bureaucratic and inefficient. Early in his tenure, Brown assured security analysts: "The EDS you see one year from now will be very different from the company you know now."

To spur growth, Brown pushed executives to win prized "megadeals," which were multi-billion-dollar contracts in which corporations or government agencies outsourced a wide range of computing operations. While such deals ensured a steady stream of revenues, EDS and its rivals had to make bigger up-front investments in equipment and labor. EDS enjoyed some early success: EDS signed $24.9 billion in new contracts in 1999, up a dramatic 111 percent from 1998. In 1999, EDS's stock reached its all-time high of $76.68. Brown was rewarded very well—by 2001 he received $52 million in total compensation.

As time went on, however, EDS had to take some "megarisks" to win the megadeals. For example, in the fall of 2000, the firm won a $6.9 billion Navy contract to overhaul its computer systems. Unfortunately, Brown ignored the warnings of two senior executives who had cautioned Brown that the firm wouldn't make any profit from the deal after inflation was taken into account. EDS's winning bid built in only a 4 percent margin, roughly half of the 7 percent margin that was typical of such huge contracts, according to an analyst. The Navy contract ran into a myriad of problems that held up payment, and by the end of 2002, the deal had drained $1.9 billion in cash from EDS.

Other huge bets went south, as well. In June 1999, Brown signed an enormous $12.4 billion contract with WorldCom, Inc., that required EDS to resell more than $400 million of the telco's services each year to other customers. Even before WorldCom's bankruptcy, EDS was having difficulties finding customers and was forced to set up $118 million in reserves and write-downs.

As time went on, Brown failed to recognize and heed warning signs. The world faced a deepening recession and the level of technology-related spending began to decline sharply. Furthermore, EDS was having more difficulty keeping its expenses in line. Despite such trends, Brown assured the investment community that EDS would grow core revenues by 13 to 16 percent in 2002, with higher year-over-year margins. The downdraft, however, was becoming clearer. When EDS reported first and second quarter 2002 results, core revenues had grown only 8 percent each quarter. EDS only did that well by landing a $200 million prepayment from an unidentified customer, according to analysts. Long after rivals IBM and Computer Services Corporation had warned of slumps in 2002, Brown remained positive, saying repeatedly: "We're the fastest horse on a muddy track." At a meeting in June 2002 with EDS's executives, he ignored their grim financial outlooks and told them that there was, in effect, "gold in the hills and to go look for it." Executives made little effort to rein in Brown's expectations. They feared they would be publicly humiliated, according to former senior executives in attendance. According to one: "You'd be singled out as a quitter." Another asserted: "Delivering bad news was not a good thing. So you postponed it as long as you could."

To shore up confidence, Brown went on a six-city trip to meet with investors to respond to concerns about client bankruptcies (such as WorldCom and United Airlines) and questions about EDS's accounting. He assured investors that EDS's huge backlog and pipeline of potential deals would permit the company to meet expectations.

Despite Brown's rosy projections, things soon came to a head. On September 18, 2002, EDS announced that it would earn only $74 million in its third quarter. This was a stunning 80 percent less than consensus estimates. In a conference call, Brown said that a host of unforeseen problems "hit us with a force that was unexpected." But, given the magnitude of the fall, Brown clearly appeared out of touch with his company's performance. EDS's stock plunged 53 percent the next day. A few days later it tumbled another 29 percent to $11.68 when a Wall Street analyst revealed that EDS had made a $225 million payment to settle put options and purchase agreements on its own stock that had been entered into months earlier when the shares were near their peak. The SEC began investigating this payment as well as management's failure to properly disclose the severe earnings shortfall in advance of the September 2002 announcement.

EDS had a disastrous 2002. By March 2003, EDS's board lost patience and pushed Brown out. Despite EDS's woes, Brown came out very well! According to his 20-page employment contract, he could have been terminated "with cause" only by outright dishonesty or "willful repeated violations" of his obligations. Thus, terminated "without cause," Brown is collecting $37 million in total severance, including retirement benefits and stock options.

A closing comment: In late 2001, Brown (in a speech at Southern Methodist University in Dallas, Texas) stated: "Pay for performance. Differentiate performance-reward based on achievement, not organizational level . . . make difficult choices. Some people aren't good enough to stay at EDS." Perhaps, to recall the old cliché: "Do as I say, not as I do . . ."

Today's leaders—such as those at EDS—face a large number of complex challenges in today's global marketplace. In considering how much credit (or blame) they deserve, two perspectives of leadership come immediately to mind: the "romantic" and "external control" perspectives.[2] First, let's look at the romantic view of leadership. Here, the implicit assumption is that the leader is the key force in determining an organization's success—or lack thereof. This view dominates the popular press in business magazines such as *Fortune, BusinessWeek,* and *Forbes,* wherein the CEO is either lauded for his or her firm's success or chided for the organization's demise. Consider, for example, the credit that has been bestowed on leaders such as Jack Welch, Andrew Grove, and Herb Kelleher for the tremendous accomplishments of their firms, General Electric, Intel, and Southwest Airlines, respectively. In the world of sports, managers and coaches, such as Joe Torre of the New York Yankees, get a lot of the credit for their team's outstanding success on the field. On the other hand, when things don't go well, much of the failure of an organization can also, rightfully, be attributed to the leader. After all, EDS's Richard Brown, in his enthusiasm to pump up revenues, aggressively bid on huge contracts that left little margin for error. Such risks are generally not advised, especially as market and economic conditions erode. Nonetheless, he repeatedly ignored such negative signals and continued to make rosy forecasts. Profits and the firm's stock price eventually took a big hit.

However, this gives only part of the picture. Another perspective of leadership is called the "external control" perspective. Here, rather than making the implicit assumption that the leader is the most important factor in determining organizational outcomes, the focus is on external factors that may positively or negatively affect a firm's success. One doesn't have to look far to support this perspective. Clearly, EDS was negatively impacted by the worldwide recession that began in 2000 that cut the demand for computer services. Other rivals, such as IBM and Computer Services Corporation, were also negatively affected.

The point, of course, is that, while neither the romantic nor the external control perspective is entirely correct, we must acknowledge both in the study of strategic management.

strategy spotlight

September 11, Terrorism, and U.S. Business: The Aftermath

The terrorist attacks on September 11, 2001, paralyzed the U.S. economy for a few days. Its aftermath can still be felt in several industries, including airlines and tourism. Consumers, businesses, schools, and colleges have all significantly cut their technology spending. There is, however, a major purchaser of Silicon Valley's latest technology: the federal government.

With the 2003 Iraq War and the creation of a new Department of Homeland Security, government spending has become one of the few bright spots in tech-land. The Feds have recently spent $47 billion on publicly disclosed tech projects and up to $15 billion on off-the-record projects, and these expenditures are expected to grow in the coming years. The beneficiaries include both long-time suppliers and start-ups. For many of them, almost 20 to 40 percent of their business comes from government purchases. Military computing needs also present a lucrative opportunity. Network Associates, for instance, landed its largest order ever from the Defense Information Systems Agency—a $16 million contract for antivirus protection software.

Sources: J. Kerstetter, S. Crock, and R. D. Hof, "More Bang for the Bite," *BusinessWeek,* April 7, 2003, pp. 39–40; J. Rae-Dupree, "A Target for Tech," *U.S. News & World Report,* January 13, 2003, pp. 30–32; S. Lawrence, "Defense Spending May Be the Mother of All Invention," *Red Herring,* December 11, 2001, pp. 17–18; and www.sgi.com.

Not all tech firms do business with the government directly. When Lockheed Martin became the prime contractor on the $200 billion Joint Strike Fighter program, it chose Silicon Graphics, Inc., (SGI) to design, evaluate, and simulate the aircraft. Similarly, when General Dynamics was asked to develop the Navy's Area Air Defense Commander Capability System—a real-time, three-dimensional view of the tactical area around the ship—high-end SGI computers were a natural fit. Apart from this, SGI now does ballistic missile defense; training systems, command, control, and surveillance systems; and weather and climate forecasting. All this has meant that for SGI, which traditionally had less than 28 percent of its revenues selling supercomputing defense systems, government contracts now represent 35 percent of its $1.3 billion annual revenue.

At times, high-profile success on the battlefield can provide a powerful boost for new technology that carries over to the commercial world. For example, in 1990 tiny Trimble Navigation Ltd., based in Sunnyvale, California, sold 10,000 handheld devices with global positioning systems to the military for the first Gulf War. The devices were a success in the war and a boon to Trimble and the commercial GPS market. Now Trimble is a $466 million firm, with just 3 percent of its sales from the military.

Our premise is that leaders can make a difference, but they must be constantly aware of the opportunities and threats that they face in the external environment as well as have a thorough understanding of their firm's resources and capabilities.

Before we move on, we'd like to provide a rather dramatic example of the external control perspective at work: the terrorist attack on the twin towers of the World Trade Center in New York City and the Pentagon building in Arlington, Virginia, on September 11, 2001. The loss of life and injuries to innocent people were immense, and the damage to property was enormous. Wall Street suffered a loss of about $1.4 trillion in the five trading sessions after the market opened on September 17. The effect on many industries was devastating. Strategy Spotlight 1.1 looks at some high-technology industries that have recognized opportunities and benefited from the terrorist attacks and from subsequent developments such as the creation of the Department of Homeland Security and the Iraq War in 2003.

What Is Strategic Management?

Given the many challenges and opportunities in the global marketplace, today's managers must do more than set long-term strategies and hope for the best.[3] They must go beyond what some have called "incremental management," whereby they view their job as making a series of small, minor changes to improve the efficiency of their firm's operations.[4] That is fine if your firm is competing in a very stable, simple, and unchanging industry.

But there aren't many of those left. As we shall discuss in this chapter and throughout the book, the pace of change is accelerating and the pressure on managers to make both major and minor changes in a firm's strategic direction is increasing.

Rather than see their role as merely custodians of the status quo, today's leaders must be proactive, anticipate change, and continually refine and, when necessary, make significant changes to their strategies. The strategic management of the organization must become both a process and a way of thinking throughout the organization.

Defining Strategic Management

As we stated at the beginning of this chapter, strategic management consists of the analysis, decisions, and actions an organization undertakes in order to create and sustain competitive advantages. This definition captures two main elements that go to the heart of the field of strategic management.

First, the strategic management of an organization entails three ongoing processes: *analysis, decisions,* and *actions.* That is, strategic management is concerned with the *analysis* of strategic goals (vision, mission, and strategic objectives) along with the analysis of the internal and external environment of the organization. Next, leaders must make strategic decisions. These *decisions,* broadly speaking, address two basic questions: What industries should we compete in? How should we compete in those industries? These questions also often involve an organization's domestic as well as its international operations. And last are the *actions* that must be taken. Decisions are of little use, of course, unless they are acted on. Firms must take the necessary actions to implement their strategies. This requires leaders to allocate the necessary resources and to design the organization to bring the intended strategies to reality. As we will see in the next section, this is an ongoing, evolving process that requires a great deal of interaction among these three processes.

Second, the essence of strategic management is the study of why some firms outperform others.[5] Thus, managers need to determine how a firm is to compete so that it can obtain advantages that are sustainable over a lengthy period of time. That means focusing on two fundamental questions: *How should we compete in order to create competitive advantages in the marketplace?* For example, managers need to determine if the firm should position itself as the low-cost producer, or develop products and services that are unique which will enable the firm to charge premium prices—or some combination of both.

Managers must also ask how to make such advantages sustainable, instead of highly temporary, in the marketplace. That is: *How can we create competitive advantages in the marketplace that are not only unique and valuable but also difficult for competitors to copy or substitute?*[6,7]

Ideas that work are almost always copied by rivals immediately. In the 1980s, American Airlines tried to establish a competitive advantage by introducing the frequent flyer program. Within weeks, all the airlines did the same thing. Overnight, instead of competitive advantage, frequent flyer programs became a necessary tool for competitive parity, not competitive advantage. The challenge, therefore, is to create competitive advantages that are sustainable.

Michael Porter argues that sustainable competitive advantage cannot be achieved through operational effectiveness alone.[8] Most of the popular management innovations of the last two decades—total quality, just-in-time, benchmarking, business process reengineering, outsourcing—all are about operational effectiveness. Operational effectiveness means performing similar activities better than rivals. Each of these is important, but none lead to sustainable competitive advantage, for the simple reason that everyone is doing them. Strategy is all about being different from everyone else. Sustainable competitive advantage is possible only through performing different activities from rivals or performing similar activities in different ways. Companies such as Wal-Mart, Southwest Airlines, and

**Exhibit 1.1
Strategic
Management
Concepts**

> **Definition:** Strategic management consists of the analysis, decisions, and actions an organization undertakes in order to create and sustain competitive advantages.
>
> **Key attributes of strategic management**
>
> ♦ Directs the organization toward overall goals and objectives.
> ♦ Includes multiple stakeholders in decision making.
> ♦ Needs to incorporate short-term and long-term perspectives.
> ♦ Recognizes trade-offs between efficiency and effectiveness.

IKEA have developed unique, internally consistent, and difficult to imitate activity systems that have provided them with sustained competitive advantage. A company with a good strategy must make clear choices about what it wants to accomplish. Trying to do everything that your rivals do eventually leads to mutually destructive price competition, not long-term advantage.

The Four Key Attributes of Strategic Management

Before discussing the strategic management process in more detail, let's briefly talk about four attributes of strategic management.[9] In doing so, it will become clear how this course differs from other courses that you have had in functional areas, such as accounting, marketing, operations, and finance. Exhibit 1.1 provides a definition and the four attributes of strategic management.

First, strategic management is *directed toward overall organizational goals and objectives.* That is, effort must be directed at what is best for the total organization, not just a single functional area. Some authors have referred to this perspective as "organizational versus individual rationality."[10] That is, what might look "rational" or most appropriate for one functional area, such as operations, may not be in the best interest of the overall firm. For example, operations may decide to schedule long production runs of similar products in order to lower unit costs. However, the standardized output may be counter to what the marketing department needs in order to appeal to a sophisticated and demanding target market. Similarly, research and development may "overengineer" the product in order to develop a far superior offering, but the design may make the product so expensive that market demand is minimal. Therefore, in this course you will look at cases and strategic issues from the perspective of the organization rather than that of the functional area(s) in which you have had the most training and experience.

Second, strategic management *includes multiple stakeholders in decision making.* Managers must incorporate the demands of many stakeholders when making decisions.[11] Stakeholders are those individuals, groups, and organizations who have a "stake" in the success of the organization, including owners (shareholders in a publicly held corporation), employees, customers, suppliers, the community at large, and so on. We'll discuss this in more detail later in this chapter. Managers will not be successful if they continually focus on a single stakeholder. For example, if the overwhelming emphasis is on generating profits for the owners, employees may become alienated, customer service may suffer, and the suppliers may become resentful of continual demands for pricing concessions. As we will see, however, many organizations have been able to satisfy multiple stakeholder needs simultaneously. For example, financial performance may actually be greater because employees who are satisfied with their jobs make a greater effort to enhance customer satisfaction, thus leading to higher profits.

Third, strategic management *requires incorporating both short-term and long-term perspectives.* Peter Senge, a leading strategic management author at the Massachusetts Institute of Technology, has referred to this need as a "creative tension."[12] That is, managers must maintain both a vision for the future of the organization as well as a focus on its present operating needs. However, as one descends the hierarchy of the organization from executive to middle-level managers to lower level managers at the level of operations, there tends to be a narrower, short-term perspective. Nonetheless, all managers throughout the organization must maintain a strategic management perspective and assess how their actions impact the overall attainment of organizational objectives. For example, laying off several valuable employees may help to cut costs and improve profits in the short term, but the long-term implications for employee morale and customer relationships may suffer—leading to subsequent performance declines.[13]

Fourth, strategic management *involves the recognition of trade-offs between effectiveness and efficiency.* Closely related to the third point above, this recognition means being aware of the need for organizations to strive to act effectively and efficiently. Some authors have referred to this as the difference between "doing the right thing" (effectiveness) and "doing things right" (efficiency).[14] While managers must allocate and use resources wisely, they must still direct their efforts toward the attainment of overall organizational objectives. Managers who are totally focused on meeting short-term budgets and targets may fail to attain the broader goals of the organization. Consider the following amusing story told by Norman Augustine, formerly CEO of defense giant, Martin Marietta (now Lockheed Martin):

> I am reminded of an article I once read in a British newspaper which described a problem with the local bus service between the towns of Bagnall and Greenfields. It seemed that, to the great annoyance of customers, drivers had been passing long queues of would-be passengers with a smile and a wave of the hand. This practice was, however, clarified by a bus company official who explained, "It is impossible for the drivers to keep their timetables if they must stop for passengers."[15]

Clearly, the drivers who were trying to stay on schedule had ignored the overall mission. As Augustine noted: "Impeccable logic but something seems to be missing!"

The Strategic Management Process

We've identified three ongoing processes—analysis, decisions, and actions—that are central to strategic management. In practice, these three processes—often referred to as strategy analysis, strategy formulation, and strategy implementation—are highly interdependent. Further, these three processes do not take place one after the other in a sequential fashion in most companies.

Henry Mintzberg, a very influential management scholar at McGill University, argues that conceptualizing the strategic management process as one in which analysis is followed by optimal decisions and their subsequent meticulous implementation neither describes the strategic management process accurately nor prescribes ideal practice.[16] In his view, the business environment is far from predictable, thus limiting our ability for analysis. Further, decisions in an organization are seldom based on optimal rationality alone, given the political processes that occur in all organizations.

Taking into consideration the limitations discussed above, Mintzberg proposed an alternative model of strategy development. As depicted in Exhibit 1.2, decisions following from analysis, in this model, constitute the *intended* strategy of the firm. For a variety of reasons, the intended strategy rarely survives in its original form. Unforeseen environmental developments, unanticipated resource constraints, or changes in managerial preferences

Exhibit 1.2 Realized Strategy and Intended Strategy: Usually Not the Same

Source: H. Mintzberg and J. A. Waters, "Of Strategies, Deliberate and Emergent," *Strategic Management Journal* 6 (1985), pp. 257–72.

may result in at least some parts of the intended strategy remaining *unrealized*. On the other hand, good managers will want to take advantage of a new opportunity presented by the environment even if it was not part of the original set of intentions. For example, the 2002 SARS crisis in Southeast Asia was a completely unexpected environmental development. If managers of a pharmaceutical firm redeployed their R&D capabilities to develop a drug to fight SARS, that would be an *emergent* strategy. The final *realized* strategy of any firm is thus a combination of deliberate and emergent strategies.

In the next three subsections, we will address each of the three key strategic management processes: strategy analysis, strategy formulation, and strategy implementation. We also highlight brief examples from business practice that are based on the opening vignettes for each chapter. Throughout the book, they serve to demonstrate that effective strategic management poses complex challenges and that sometimes things can go wrong.

Exhibit 1.3 depicts the strategic management process and indicates how it ties into the chapters in the book. Consistent with our discussion above, we use two-way arrows to convey the interactive nature of the processes.

Strategy Analysis

Strategy analysis may be looked upon as the starting point of the strategic management process. It consists of the "advance work" that must be done in order to effectively formulate and implement strategies. Many strategies fail because managers may want to formulate and implement strategies without a careful analysis of the overarching goals of the organization and without a thorough analysis of its external and internal environment.

Analyzing Organizational Goals and Objectives (Chapter 1)   Later in this chapter, we will address how organizations must have clearly articulated goals and objectives in order to channel the efforts of individuals throughout the organization toward common ends. Goals and objectives also provide a means of allocating resources effectively. A firm's vision, mission, and strategic objectives form a hierarchy of goals that range from broad statements of intent and bases for competitive advantage to specific, measurable strategic objectives.

As indicated in Exhibit 1.3, this hierarchy of goals is not developed in isolation. Rather, it is developed in concert with a rigorous understanding of the opportunities and threats in the external environment (Chapter 2) as well as a thorough understanding of the firm's strengths and weaknesses (Chapters 3 and 4). The opening incident in Chapter 1 describes how Richard Brown, CEO of EDS, ignored the economic and competitive landscape and set unrealistically high growth targets. The result was an erosion of his firm's competitive position.

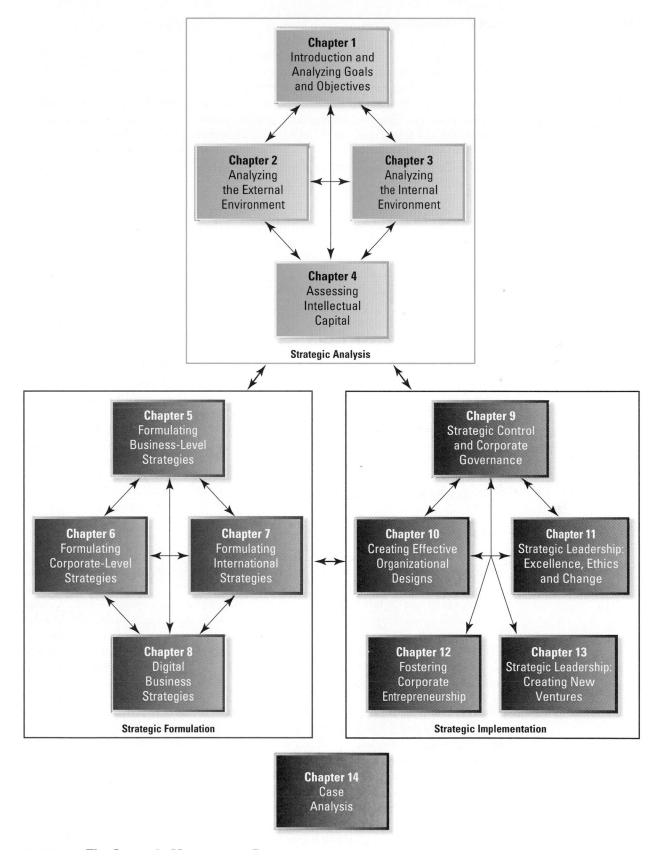

Exhibit 1.3 The Strategic Management Process

Analyzing the External Environment of the Firm (Chapter 2)   Managers must monitor and scan the environment as well as analyze competitors. Such information is critical in determining the opportunity and threats in the external environment. We provide two frameworks of the external environment. First, the general environment consists of several elements, such as demographic, technological, and economic segments, from which key trends and events can have a dramatic impact on the firm. Second, the industry environment consists of competitors and other organizations that may threaten the success of a firm's products and services. We discuss how Motorola misread the evolution toward digital cell phones and lost its leading position in the industry.

Assessing the Internal Environment of the Firm (Chapter 3)   We provide some useful frameworks for analyzing a firm's internal environment. Such analysis helps to identify both strengths and weaknesses that can, in part, determine how well a firm will succeed in an industry. Analyzing the strengths and relationships among the activities that constitute a firm's value chain (e.g., operations, marketing and sales, and human resource management) can be a means of uncovering potential sources of competitive advantage for the firm. We discuss how Oracle's aggressive approach to generating sales resulted in some undesirable outcomes.

Assessing a Firm's Intellectual Assets (Chapter 4)   The knowledge worker and a firm's other intellectual assets (e.g., patents, trademarks) are becoming increasingly important as the drivers of competitive advantages and wealth creation in today's economy. In addition to human capital, we assess how well the organization creates networks and relationships among its employees as well as its customers, suppliers, and alliance partners. We also address the need for organizations to use technology to enhance collaboration among employees as well as provide a means of accumulating and storing knowledge. We describe how one of America's greatest corporate icons, Xerox, botched its lead in technology through poor relationships among its top executives and by mismanaging its intellectual assets.

Strategy Formulation

A firm's strategy formulation is developed at several levels. First, business-level strategy addresses the issue of how to compete in given business environments to attain competitive advantage. Second, corporate-level strategy focuses on two issues: (1) what businesses to compete in and (2) how businesses can be managed to achieve synergy—that is, create more value by working together than if they operate as stand-alone businesses. Third, a firm must determine the best method to develop international strategies as it ventures beyond its national boundaries. Finally, the growing importance of the Internet has increased the necessity for firms to explore the ramifications of this new strategic platform and formulate Internet and e-business strategies.

Formulating Business-Level Strategy (Chapter 5)   The question of how firms compete and outperform their rivals and how they achieve and sustain competitive advantages goes to the heart of strategic management. Successful firms strive to develop bases for competitive advantage. These can be achieved through cost leadership and/or differentiation as well as by focusing on a narrow or industrywide market segment. We'll also discuss why some advantages can be more sustainable (or durable) over time and how a firm's business-level strategy changes with the industry life cycle—that is, the stages of introduction, growth, maturity, and decline. We discuss how a fast-growing competitor, Food Lion, overextended its cost leadership strategy in its attempt to get ahead.

Formulating Corporate-Level Strategy (Chapter 6)   Whereas business-level strategy is concerned with how to create and sustain competitive advantage in an individual business, corporate-level strategy addresses issues concerning a firm's portfolio (or group) of businesses. That is, it asks (1) What business (or businesses) should we compete in? and (2) How can we manage this portfolio of businesses to create synergies among the businesses? In this chapter, we explore the relative advantages and disadvantages of firms pursuing strategies of related or unrelated diversification. In addition, we discuss the various means that firms can employ to diversify—internal development, mergers and acquisitions, and joint ventures and strategic alliances—as well as their relative advantages and disadvantages. We describe how a leading discount broker, Charles Schwab and Company, erred when it acquired U.S. Trust, a financial services firm that catered to wealthy clients.

Formulating International Strategy (Chapter 7)   When firms expand their scope of operations to include foreign markets, they encounter many opportunities and potential pitfalls. They must decide not only on the most appropriate entry strategy but also how they will go about attaining competitive advantages in international markets. Many successful international firms have been able to attain both lower costs and higher levels of differentiated products and services through the successful implementation of a "transnational strategy." We describe some of the problems experienced by Volkswagen as it tried to enter the luxury segment of the U.S. market.

Formulating Digital Business Strategy (Chapter 8)   Digital technologies such as the Internet and wireless communications are changing the way business is conducted. These capabilities present both new opportunities and new threats for virtually all businesses. We believe that when firms formulate strategies, they should give explicit consideration to how digital technologies add value and impact their performance outcomes. The effective use of the Internet and digital business strategies can help an organization improve its competitive position and enhance its ability to create advantages by enhancing both cost leadership and differentiation strategies. We describe how Agillion, Inc., an application service provider founded in 1999, went bankrupt in just three years not because the Internet bubble burst, but because its product could easily be imitated. Further, it did not use digital technologies in a way that customers valued.

Strategic Implementation

As we have noted earlier in the chapter, effective strategies are of no value if they are not properly implemented. Strategy implementation involves ensuring that a firm has proper strategic controls and organizational designs. Of particular importance is ensuring that the firm has established effective means to coordinate and integrate activities within the firm as well as with its suppliers, customers, and alliance partners. In addition, leadership plays a central role. This involves many things, including ensuring that the organization is committed to excellence and ethical behavior, promotes learning and continuous improvement, and acts entrepreneurially in creating and taking advantage of new opportunities.

Strategic Control and Corporate Governance (Chapter 9)   To implement strategies, firms must exercise effective strategic control. This consists of two types. First, informational control requires that organizations continually monitor and scan the environment and respond effectively to threats and opportunities. Second, behavioral control involves the proper balance of rewards and incentives, cultures and boundaries (or constraints). In addition to effective informational and behavioral controls, successful firms (those that are incorporated) practice effective corporate governance. That is, mechanisms must be created to ensure that the interests of the managers are consistent with those of the owners (shareholders) of the firm. These include an effective board of directors, actively engaged shareholders, and proper managerial reward and incentive systems. We also discuss the important role played by various external mechanisms such as the market for corporate control, auditors, banks, analysts, and the financial press in ensuring good governance. Chapter 9 explains what can happen when a firm, Tyco International, has a strong reward system but few other controls.

Creating Effective Organizational Designs (Chapter 10)   To succeed, firms must have organizational structures and designs that are consistent with their strategy. For example, firms that diversify into related product-market areas typically implement divisional structures. In today's rapidly changing competitive environments, firms must design their companies to ensure that their organizational boundaries—those internal to the firm and external—are more flexible and permeable. In many cases, organizations should consider creating strategic alliances in order to capitalize on the capabilities of other organizations. We describe how Ford had to write off $1 billion of the value of its stockpile of precious metals because of poor decisions by its purchasing department.

Creating a Learning Organization and an Ethical Organization (Chapter 11)   Effective leaders must engage in several ongoing activities: setting a direction, designing the organization, and developing an organization that is committed to excellence and ethical behavior. In addition, given the rapid and unpredictable change in today's competitive environments, leaders need to create a "learning organization." This ensures that the organization can benefit from individual and collective talents throughout the organization. We describe how one leader's mismanagement, Morrison Knudsen's Bill Agee, almost caused a world-class company to go under.

Fostering Corporate Entrepreneurship (Chapter 12)   Today's successes do not guarantee success in the future. With rapid and unpredictable change in the global marketplace, firms must continually improve and grow as well as find new ways to renew their organizations. Corporate entrepreneurship and innovation provide firms with new opportunities, and strategies should be formulated that enhance a firm's innovative capacity. Within corporations, proactiveness and autonomous entrepreneurial behavior by product champions and other organizational members are needed to turn new ideas into corporate ventures. We present the case of Polaroid, a company that grew from a revolutionary technology—instantly developing film. However, it fell behind when it was slow to adapt to a new way of developing pictures instantly—digital photography.

Creating New Ventures (Chapter 13)   New ventures and small businesses represent a major engine of economic growth. Although the challenges they face are unique, especially for start-up firms entering into business for the first time, many of the concepts that we address in the text can be applied to new ventures and small businesses. Viable opportunities must be recognized, effective strategies must be implemented, and entrepreneurial leadership skills are needed to successfully launch and sustain these enterprises. We discuss the fate of Rosen Motors, a young firm with an innovative, hybrid automobile drive train that could save millions in energy costs. However, Rosen did not recognize critical market forces when implementing its start-up strategy—including the power of its most important buyers, the big automakers—and failed as a result.

We've discussed the strategic management process. In addition, Chapter 14, "Analyzing Strategic Management Cases," provides guidelines and suggestions on how to evaluate cases in this course. Thus, the concepts and techniques discussed in these 13 chapters can be applied to real-world organizations.

Let's now address two concepts, corporate governance and stakeholder management, that are critical to the strategic management process.

The Role of Corporate Governance and Stakeholder Management

Most business enterprises that employ more than a few dozen people are organized as corporations. As you recall from your finance classes, the overall purpose of a corporation is to maximize the long-term return to the owners (shareholders). Thus, one may ask: Who is really responsible for fulfilling this purpose? Robert Monks and Neil Minow, in addressing this issue, provide a useful definition of corporate governance as "the relationship among various participants in determining the direction and performance of corporations. The primary participants are (1) the shareholders, (2) the management (led by the chief executive officer), and (3) the board of directors."[17] This relationship is illustrated in Exhibit 1.4.

The directors on the board of directors (BOD) are the elected representatives of the shareholders. They are charged with ensuring that the interests and motives of management are aligned with those of the owners (i.e., shareholders). In many cases, the BOD is diligent in fulfilling its purpose. For example, Intel Corporation, the giant $27 billion maker of microprocessor chips, is widely recognized as an excellent example of sound governance practices. For example, the BOD has established guidelines to ensure that its members are independent (i.e., not members of the executive management team nor having close personal ties to top executives) so that they can provide proper oversight; it has explicit guidelines on the selection of director candidates (to avoid "cronyism"); and it provides detailed procedures for formal evaluations of both directors and the firm's top officers.[18] Such guidelines serve to ensure that management is acting in the best interests of shareholders.

Recently, there has been much criticism as well as cynicism by both citizens and the business press about the poor job by management and the BODs of large corporations. One only has to look at the recent scandals at such firms as Arthur Andersen, WorldCom, Enron, Tyco, and ImClone Systems.[19] Such malfeasance has led to an erosion of the public's trust in the governance of corporations. For example, a recent Gallup poll found that

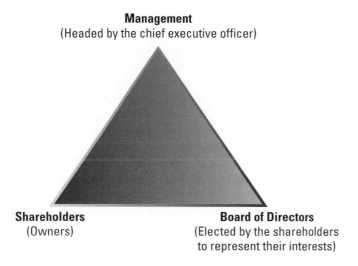

Management
(Headed by the chief executive officer)

Shareholders
(Owners)

Board of Directors
(Elected by the shareholders
to represent their interests)

Exhibit 1.4 The Key Elements of Corporate Governance

Sprint Corporation: A Reputation for Poor Corporate Governance

Sprint has had a long reputation for weak corporate governance. One former Sprint executive described its board of directors as clubby, entrenched, and passive. In fact, Sprint's name was synonymous with many things shareholders love to hate. These include enormous executive pay resulting from massive stock option grants and repriced options. For example, when the company spun off its PCS tracking stock, the board awarded options that gave the seven top executives a total of $185 million. Some felt it was only a matter of time before the board's weak oversight caught up with the company.

It did on February 2, 2003, and it was ugly. Sprint announced that both CEO William Esrey and President Ronald T. LeMay were vacating their posts. Why? Their careers were cut short by a highly questionable tax shelter set up by Sprint's auditors, Ernst & Young, that helped the two executives shield more than $130 million in stock option gains. However, even if the board finally acted deci-

sively in ousting them, the board itself also needs to be reformed. The tax-shelter tale is simply one more mistake made by a board that was too close to senior management to properly monitor management and represent the best interests of shareholders.

Let's take a look at the makeup of Sprint's board of directors. This will help us get at the root cause of the above problems. It consisted of only eight members, and two of them, CEO Esrey and President LeMay, were the firm's top two executives. And other directors hardly met standards for independence. For example, Director DuBose Ausley's Florida law firm received $723,292 in legal fees from Sprint in 2001, and Irvine O. Hockaday, Jr., the former CEO of Hallmark Cards, Inc., who sits on the compensation committee, was Esrey's next-door neighbor and close friend. Further, the other two members on the compensation committee have been on the board for more than two decades. The board lacked anyone with auditing or CFO experience. Hardly a formula for close monitoring and objective evaluation of Sprint's management, compensation, and strategies! As noted by Ned Regan, Baruch College president and ex-New York State Comptroller: "The board is too cozy."

Sources: L. Lavelle, "Sprint's Board Needs a Good Sweeping, Too," *BusinessWeek*, February 24, 2003, p. 40; "Another Nail in the Coffin," *The Economist*, February 15, 2003, pp. 69–70; and N. Byrnes, P. Dwyer, and M. McNamee, "Hacking Away at Tax Shelters," *BusinessWeek*, February 24, 2003, p. 41.

90 percent of Americans felt that people leading corporations could not be trusted to look after the interests of their employees, and only 18 percent thought that corporations looked after their shareholders. Forty-three percent, in fact, believed that senior executives were in it only for themselves. In Britain, that figure, according to another poll, was an astonishing 95 percent.[20]

At times, BODs have become complacent and, in many cases, incompetent. They have often been accused of rubber stamping strategies and actions proposed by top management, and they have clearly not acted in a manner consistent with shareholder interests. Strategy Spotlight 1.2 provides an example of a corporation, Sprint, which has failed to exercise sound corporate governance.

Clearly, there is a strong need for improved corporate governance, and we will address this topic in greater detail in Chapter 9. We focus on three important mechanisms to help ensure effective corporate governance: an effective and engaged board of directors, shareholder activism, and proper managerial rewards and incentives. In addition to these internal controls, a key role is played by various external control mechanisms. These include the auditors, banks, analysts, an active financial press, as well as the threat of hostile takeovers.

Generating long-term returns for the shareholders is the primary goal of a publicly held corporation. As noted by former Chrysler vice chairman Robert Lutz: "We are here to serve the shareholder and create shareholder value. I insist that the only person who owns the company is the person who paid good money for it."[21]

Despite the primacy of generating shareholder value, managers who focus solely on the interests of the owners of the business will often make poor decisions that lead to negative, unanticipated outcomes. For example, decisions such as mass layoffs to increase profits, ignoring issues related to conservation of the natural environment to save money, and exerting excessive pressure on suppliers to lower prices can certainly harm the firm in the long run. Such actions would likely lead to negative outcomes such as alienated employees, increased governmental oversight and fines, and disloyal suppliers.

Clearly, in addition to *shareholders,* there are other *stakeholders* that must be explicitly taken into account in the strategic management process.[22] A stakeholder can be defined as an individual or group, inside or outside the company, that has a stake in and can influence an organization's performance. Although companies can have different stakeholders, each generally has five prominent stakeholder groups: customers, employees, suppliers (of goods, services, and capital), the community at large, and, of course, the owners.[23]

Zero Sum or Symbiosis? Two Alternate Perspectives of Stakeholder Management

There are two opposing ways of looking at the role of stakeholder management in the strategic management process.[24] The first one can be termed "zero sum." In this view, the role of management is to look upon the various stakeholders as competing for the attention and resources of the organization. In essence, the gain of one individual or group is the loss of another individual or group. That is, employees want higher wages (which drive down profits), suppliers want higher prices for their inputs and slower, more flexible delivery times (which drive up costs), customers want fast deliveries and higher quality (which drive up costs), the community at large wants charitable contributions (which take money from company goals), and so on. This zero-sum thinking is rooted, in part, in the traditional conflict between workers and management, leading to the formation of unions and sometimes ending in adversarial union-management negotiations that can lead to long, bitter strikes.

Although there will always be some conflicting demands placed on the organization by its various stakeholders, there is value in exploring how the organization can achieve mutual benefit through *stakeholder symbiosis,* which recognizes that stakeholders are dependent upon each other for their success and well-being.[25] That is, managers acknowledge the interdependence among employees, suppliers, customers, shareholders, and the community at large, as we will discuss in Chapter 3 in more detail. Sears, for example, has developed a sophisticated quantitative model that demonstrates symbiosis. With this model, Sears can predict the relationship between employee satisfaction, customer satisfaction, and financial results.[26] The Sears model found that a 5 percent improvement in employee attitudes led to a 1.3 percent improvement in customer satisfaction, which, in turn, will drive a 0.5 percent improvement in revenue.

Social Responsibility: Moving Beyond the Immediate Stakeholders

Organizations must acknowledge and act upon the interests and demands of stakeholders such as citizens and society in general that are beyond its immediate constituencies—customers, owners, suppliers, and employees. That is, they must consider the needs of the broader community at large and act in a socially responsible manner.[27]

Social responsibility is the expectation that businesses or individuals will strive to improve the overall welfare of society.[28] From the perspective of a business, this means that managers must take active steps to make society better by virtue of the business being in

Measuring More Than Just Financial Performance

It is in an organization's best interest to look beyond just the numbers. Financial performance alone will not create a sustainable enterprise. A company needs to know what its ecological and social impact is and what changes it should make to reduce the size of the impact.

The Gap Corporation's response to these issues is reflected in its recently constructed corporate campus in San Bruno, California. The roof of the building is a giant undulating meadow that absorbs storm water and supports local birds, while the interior is designed so that people feel as if they were working outdoors under giant clouds.

Cool nighttime air is stored in the flooring material and reused to cool the building during the daytime. This reduces the need for mechanical heating and cooling equipment by over 50 percent and energy consumption by over 60 percent. Employees breathe fresh air and spend their day in natural light.

Dow Chemical Corporation addressed environmental issues by embarking on a two-year collaboration with its traditional adversaries—five local environmental groups—to find effective ways to reduce toxic waste at its Midland, Michigan, complex. The company invested $3.1 million in making changes that cut production of several toxic chemicals by 37 percent and reduced the release of chemicals to water and air by 43 percent.

Sources: J. E. Austin, "Principles of Partnership," *Leader to Leader,* Fall 2000, pp. 44–52; and www.nrdc.org/cities/manufacturing/msri/intro.asp.

existence. Similar to norms and values, actions that constitute socially responsible behavior tend to change over time. In the 1970s affirmative action was a high priority and firms responded. During the 1990s and up to the present time, the public has been concerned about the quality of the environment. Many firms have responded to this by engaging in recycling and reducing waste. Today, in the wake of terrorist attacks on New York City and the Pentagon, and the continuing threat from terrorists worldwide, a new kind of priority has arisen: the need to be responsible and vigilant concerning public safety.

To remain viable in the long run, many companies are measuring what has been called a "triple bottom line." This technique involves assessing environmental, social, and financial performance.[29] Shell, NEC, and Procter & Gamble, along with other corporations, have recognized that failing to account for the environmental and social costs of doing business poses risks to the company and the community in which it operates.

In the new "triple bottom line" accounting model, the first bottom line presents the financial measures with which all leaders are familiar.[30] The second bottom line assesses ecological and material capital. And the third bottom line measures human and social capital. In a recent annual report, for example, BP Amoco reported on such performance indicators as annual sales and operating costs (bottom line #1); levels of hydrocarbon emissions, greenhouse emissions, and oil spills compared to the prior year (bottom line #2); and its workforce safety record, training delivered to employees, and philanthropic contributions (bottom line #3).

The approach is "a revolution in the way we conceptualize corporate responsibility," according to Thomas Gladwin, professor of sustainable enterprise at the University of Michigan. He has helped corporations develop new ways of assessing performance. He sees a shift in the attitudes and assumptions of even the most established companies. "Literally hundreds of companies are taking in-depth, serious looks at what sustainability means."

Gladwin proposed that companies continue to build and manage capital but widen the definition to include all the resources they depend on, not just financial capital. He distinguished four additional types of capital:

- *Ecological.* Renewable resources generated by living systems, such as wood or animal by-products.
- *Material.* Nonrenewable or geological resources such as mineral ores and fossil fuels.
- *Human.* People's knowledge, skills, health, nutrition, safety, security, and motivation.
- *Social.* Assets of civil society, such as social cohesion, trust, reciprocity, equity, and other values that provide mutual benefit.

Strategy Spotlight 1.3 discusses how two well-known companies—The Gap and Dow Chemical—go beyond just financial considerations in their strategic actions.

The Strategic Management Perspective: An Imperative Throughout the Organization

As we have noted in this chapter, strategic management requires managers to take an integrative view of the organization and assess how all of the functional areas and activities "fit together" to help an organization achieve its goals and objectives. This cannot be accomplished if only the top managers in the organization take an integrative, strategic perspective of issues facing the firm and everyone else "fends for themselves" in their independent, isolated functional areas. Marketing and sales will generally favor broad, tailor-made product lines, production will demand standardized products that are relatively easy to make in order to lower manufacturing costs, research and development will design products to demonstrate technical elegance, and so on. Instead, people throughout the organization need to be striving toward overall goals.

The above argument clearly makes sense. However, the need for such a perspective is accelerating in today's increasingly complex, interconnected, ever-changing, global economy. In this section, we will address some major trends that are making the need for a strategic perspective throughout the organization even more critical. As noted by Peter Senge of MIT, the days when Henry Ford, Alfred Sloan, and Tom Watson (top executives at Ford, General Motors, and IBM, respectively) "learned for the organization are gone." He goes on to say:

> In an increasingly dynamic, interdependent, and unpredictable world, it is simply no longer possible for anyone to "figure it all out at the top." The old model, "the top thinks and the local acts," must now give way to integrating thinking and acting at all levels. While the challenge is great, so is the potential payoff. "The person who figures out how to harness the collective genius of the people in his or her organization," according to former Citibank CEO Walter Wriston, "is going to blow the competition away."[31]

In this section we will first address some of the key forces that are driving the need for a strategic perspective at all levels as well as greater participation and involvement in the strategic management process throughout the organization. Then, we will provide examples of how firms are engaging people throughout the organization to these ends.

Some Key Driving Forces

There are many driving forces that are increasing the need for a strategic perspective and greater involvement throughout the organization.[32] Among the most important of these are globalization, technology, and intellectual capital.[33] These forces are inherently interrelated and, collectively, they are accelerating the rate of change and uncertainty with which managers at all levels must deal. The implication of such unpredictable change was probably best captured by former AOL Time Warner Chairman Stephen M. Case, in a talk to investors and analysts:

> I sometimes feel like I'm behind the wheel of a race car. . . . One of the biggest challenges is there are no road signs to help navigate. And . . . no one has yet determined which side of the road we're supposed to be on.[34]

Globalization   The defining feature of the global economy is not the flow of goods—international trade has existed for centuries—but the flow of capital, people, and information worldwide. With globalization, time and space are no longer a barrier to making deals anywhere in the world. Computer networks permit instantaneous transactions, and the market watchers operate around the clock on a 24/7 basis.

Along with the increasing speed of transactions and global sourcing of all forms of resources and information, managers must address the paradoxical demand to think globally and act locally. They have to move resources and information rapidly around the world to meet local needs. They also face new challenges when formulating strategies: volatile political situations, difficult trade issues, ever-fluctuating exchange rates, unfamiliar cultures, and gut-wrenching social problems.[35] Today, managers must be more literate in the ways of foreign customers, commerce, and competition than ever before.

As markets become more open—as evidenced by free trade agreements between nations—more foreign firms are likely to enter domestic markets. This increases the amount of competition. Further, since firms are operating in global markets, competitive moves in a domestic economy may negatively impact the firm in another segment of the international market. This places pressure on firms to move into international markets in order to maintain their competitiveness in areas where they already operate. Clearly, globalization requires that organizations increase their ability to learn and collaborate and to manage diversity, complexity, and ambiguity. Top-level managers can't do it all alone.

Technology   Technological change and diffusion of new technologies are moving at an incredible pace. Such development and diffusion accelerates the importance of innovation for firms if they are to remain competitive. David de Pury, former cochair of the board of Asea Brown Boveri, claimed that "innovate or die" is the first rule of international industrial competition. Similarly, continuous technological development and change have produced decreasing product life cycles. Andrew Grove, chairman of Intel, explained the introduction of a new product at his company. Recently, the firm introduced a sophisticated product in which it had invested considerable funds. However, later in the same year, Intel introduced a new product that would cannibalize its existing product. Thus, the firm had only 11 months to recoup that significant investment. Such time-intensive product development involves the efforts and collaboration of managers and professionals throughout the organization.

From videoconferencing to the Internet, technology has made our world smaller and faster moving. Ideas and huge amounts of information are in constant movement. The challenge for managers is to make sense of what technology offers. Not all technology adds value. In the coming years, managers in all organizations will be charged with making technology an even more viable, productive part of the work setting. They will need to stay ahead of the information curve and learn to leverage information to enhance business performance. If not, they risk being swallowed in a tidal wave of data—not ideas.

In addition to its potential benefits, technology can raise some important ethical issues that need to be addressed. Strategy Spotlight 1.4 raises the issue of "designer babies."

Intellectual Capital   Knowledge has become the direct source of competitive advantage(s) for companies selling ideas and relationships (e.g., professional services, soft-

Designer Babies

No one would dispute that it's all right to custom-design some products and services. With individual tastes, it's only natural to desire to bring customization into the plan. But customization, and the associated technology, can go too far.

Since James D. Watson and Francis H. C. Crick's discovery of the DNA molecule in 1954, customization possibilities regarding human children have become technologically feasible. Watson and Crick probably never foresaw this. But nearly a half century later, the potential to genetically alter babies before birth is actually here.

Source: E. Licking, "Ten Technologies That Will Change Our Lives," *BusinessWeek*, Spring 2000.

This raises a host of ethical questions. Imagine designer babies, children that are born to parents that have the financial resources to create the "perfect" child. Without a doubt, DNA experimentation has led to scientific advances, such as treatment of certain diseases, that are valuable and ethical. But when it comes to customizing a human being, the line between right and wrong can become blurry. For example, some may believe it is ethical for parents to choose the color of their baby's eyes, but not the baby's gender. Others may find an ethical dilemma in artificially raising a baby's potential for a high IQ, but believe that it is ethical to genetically enhance a baby's overall health. Technology, with all its benefits, must also be considered in light of these and other ethical considerations.

ware, and technology-driven companies) as well as an indirect source of competitive advantage for all companies trying to differentiate themselves from rivals by how they create value for their customers. As we will note in Chapter 4, Merck, the $52 billion pharmaceutical company, has become enormously successful because its scientists discover medicines, not because of their skills in producing pills in an efficient manner. As noted by Dr. Roy Vagelos, Merck's former CEO: "A low-value product can be made by anyone anywhere. When you have knowledge no one else has access to—that's dynamite. We guard our research even more carefully than our financial assets."[36]

Exhibit 1.5 displays some interesting figures on the importance of knowledge or "brainpower," in the creation of value. What's behind the numbers? While manufactured goods have steadily accounted for a shrinking proportion of the total economy, their value has risen substantially. Why? In the information age, manufactured goods have increasingly become what can be called "congealed brainpower." Intel, for example, turns something of less value than metal—sand (which becomes silicon)—into something far more valuable than gold, Pentium III chips. Geoffrey Colvin, the *Fortune* magazine writer, noted that the "magic ingredient, brainpower, can work in many ways. Sometimes, it takes the form of ultrahigh technology, as in the Pentium chip. Sometimes it's brand power, as in the Hermès scarf. Most often it's both, as in the Mercedes-Benz."[37]

Creating and applying knowledge to deliver differentiated products and services of superior value for customers requires the acquisition of superior talent, as well as the ability to develop and retain that talent.[38] However, successful firms must also create an environment with strong social and professional relationships, where people feel strong "ties" to their colleagues and their organization. Gary Hamel, one of today's leading strategic management writers, noted: "As the number and quality of interconnections between individuals and ideas go up, the ability to combine and recombine ideas accelerates as well."[39]

Technologies must also be used effectively to leverage human capital to facilitate collaboration among individuals and to develop more sophisticated knowledge management systems.[40] The challenge and opportunity of management is not only to acquire and retain

Exhibit 1.5
Brainpower
Weighs In

Product	Price	Weight in Pounds	Price per Pound
Pentium III 800MHz microprocessor	$ 851.00	0.01984	$42,893.00
Viagra (tablet)	8.00	0.00068	11,766.00
Gold (ounce)	301.70	0.0625	4,827.20
Hermès scarf	275.00	0.14	1,964.29
Palm V	449.00	0.26	1,726.92
Saving Private Ryan on DVD	34.99	0.04	874.75
Cigarettes (20)	4.00	0.04	100.00
Who Moved My Cheese? by Spencer Johnson	19.99	0.49	40.80
Mercedes-Benz S-class four-door sedan	78,445.00	4,134.00	18.98
The Competitive Advantage of Nations by Michael Porter	40.00	2.99	13.38
Chevrolet Cavalier four-door sedan	17,770.00	2,630.00	6.76
Hot-rolled steel (ton)	370.00	2,000.00	0.19

Source: G. Colvin, "We're Worth Our Weight in Pentium Chips," *Fortune,* March 20, 2000, p. 68. © 2001 Time Inc. All rights reserved.

human capital but also to ensure that they develop and maintain a strategic perspective as they contribute to the organization. This is essential if management is to use its talents to effectively help the organization attain its goals and objectives.

Strategy Spotlight 1.5 discusses the global market for talent. It illustrates how forces of globalization, technology, and intellectual capital can be related.

Let's now look at what some companies are doing to increase the involvement of employees throughout the organization in the strategic management process.

Enhancing Employee Involvement in the Strategic Management Process

Today's organizations increasingly need to anticipate and respond to dramatic and unpredictable changes in the competitive environment. With the emergence of the knowledge economy, human capital (as opposed to financial and physical assets) has become the key to securing advantages in the marketplace that persist over time.

To develop and mobilize people and other assets in the organization, leaders are needed throughout the organization.[41] No longer can organizations be effective if the top "does the thinking" and the rest of the organization "does the work." Everyone needs to be involved in the strategic management process. Peter Senge noted the critical need for three types of leaders.

◆   Local line leaders who have significant profit and loss responsibility.
◆   Executive leaders who champion and guide ideas, create a learning infrastructure, and establish a domain for taking action.

strategy spotlight

The Global Market for Talent

Globalization today involves the movement of people and information across borders, not just goods and investment. Many American technology-strategy consultants, who make about $150,000 annually, today are blissfully unaware of the challenge posed by the likes of Ganesh Narasimhaiya.

Ganesh is a 30-year-old Indian who enjoys cricket, R&B music, and bowling. He has a bachelor's degree in electronics and communications, and he can spin out code in a variety of languages: COBOL, Java, and UML (Unified Modeling Language), among others. Ganesh has worked on high-profile projects for Wipro, a $903 million Indian software giant, all over the world. He has helped GE Medical Systems roll out a logistics application throughout Southeast Asia. He proposed a plan to consolidate and synchronize security solutions across a British client's e-business applications. He developed a strategy for transferring legacy system applications onto the Web for a company in Norway. He works up to 18 or 19 hours a day at a customer site and for that he may earn as much as $7,000 a month. When he's home in Bangalore, his pay is about one-quarter of that—$21,000 a year. But by Indian standards, this is a small fortune.

Ganesh is part of Wipro's strategy of amassing a small force of high-level experts who are increasingly focused on specific industries and can compete with anyone for a given consulting project. Wipro's Trojan horse is the incredibly cheap offshore outsourcing solution that it can provide. The rise of a globally integrated knowledge economy is a blessing for developing nations. What it means for the U.S. skilled labor force is less clear. This is something strategy consultants working for Accenture or EDS in the United States need to think about. Why? Forrester Research has predicted that at least 3.3 million white-collar jobs and $136 billion in wages will shift from the U.S. to low-cost countries by 2015. With dramatically lower wage rates and the same level of service, how is the American technology professional going to compete with the likes of Ganesh and his colleagues?

Sources: K. H. Hammonds, "Smart, Determined, Ambitious, Cheap: The New Face of Global Competition," *Fast Company*, February 2003, pp. 91–97; P. Engardio, A. Bernstein; and M. Kripalani, "Is Your Job Next?" *BusinessWeek*, February 3, 2003, pp. 50–60.

- ◆ Internal networkers who, although having little positional power and formal authority, generate their power through the conviction and clarity of their ideas.[42]

Sally Helgesen, author of *The Web of Inclusion: A New Architecture for Building Great Organizations*, made a similar point regarding the need for leaders throughout the organization. She asserted that many organizations "fall prey to the heroes-and-drones syndrome, exalting the value of those in powerful positions while implicitly demeaning the contributions of those who fail to achieve top rank."[43] Culture and processes in which leaders emerge at all levels, both up and down as well as across the organization, typify today's high-performing firms.[44]

Now we will provide examples of what some firms are doing to increase the involvement of employees throughout the organization. Top-level executives are key in setting the tone. Consider Richard Branson, founder of the Virgin Group, whose core businesses include retail operations, hotels, communications, and an airline. He is well known for creating a culture and informal structure where anybody in the organization can be involved in generating and acting upon new business ideas. In an interview, he stated:

> [S]peed is something that we are better at than most companies. We don't have formal board meetings, committees, etc. If someone has an idea, they can pick up the phone and talk to me. I can vote "done, let's do it." Or, better still, they can just go ahead and do it. They know that they are not going to get a mouthful from me if they make a mistake. Rules and regulations are

not our forte. Analyzing things to death is not our kind of thing. We very rarely sit back and analyze what we do.[45]

To inculcate a strategic management perspective throughout the organization, many large traditional organizations often require a major effort in transformational change. This involves extensive communication, training, and development to strengthen a strategic perspective throughout the organization. Ford Motor Company is one such example.

Ford instituted a major cultural overhaul and embarked on a broad-based attempt to develop leaders throughout the organization. It wanted to build an army of "warrior-entrepreneurs"—people who have the courage and skills to reject old ideas and who believe in change passionately enough to make it happen. A few details:

> Recently, Ford sent about 2,500 managers to its Leadership Development Center during the year for one of its four programs—Capstone, Experienced Leader Challenge, Ford Business Associates, and New Business Leader—instilling in them not just the mind-set and vocabulary of a revolutionary but also the tools necessary to achieve a revolution. At the same time, through the Business Leaders Initiative, all 100,000 salaried employees worldwide will participate in business-leadership "cascades," intense exercises that combine trickle-down communications with substantive team projects.[46]

We'd like to close with our favorite example of how inexperience can be a virtue. It further reinforces the benefits of having broad involvement throughout the organization in the strategic management process (see Strategy Spotlight 1.6)

Ensuring Coherence in Strategic Direction

To be successful, employees and managers throughout the organization must be striving for common goals and objectives. By specifying desired results, it becomes much easier to move forward. Otherwise, when no one knows what the firm is striving to accomplish, they have no idea of what to work toward. As the old nautical expression puts it: "No wind favors the ship that has no charted course."

Organizations express priorities best through stated goals and objectives that form a *hierarchy of goals*. The hierarchy of goals for an organization includes its vision, mission, and strategic objectives. What visions may lack in specificity, they make up for in their ability to evoke powerful and compelling mental images. On the other hand, strategic objectives tend to be more specific and provide a more direct means of determining if the organization is moving toward broader, overall goals. We will now address visions, missions, and strategic objectives in the next subsections.[47]

Organizational Vision

The starting point for articulating a firm's hierarchy of goals is the company vision. It is often described as a goal that is "massively inspiring, overarching, and long-term."[48] A vision represents a destination that is driven by and evokes passion. A vision may or may not succeed; it depends on whether everything else happens according to a firm's strategy.

Developing and implementing a vision is one of a leader's central roles. In a survey of 1,500 senior leaders, 870 of them CEOs (from 20 different countries), respondents were asked what they believed were the key traits that leaders must have. Ninety-eight percent responded that "a strong sense of vision" was the most important. Similarly, when asked about the critical knowledge skills, the leaders cited "strategy formulation to achieve a vision" as the most important skill. In other words, managers need to have not only a vision but also a plan to implement it. Regretfully, 90 percent reported a lack of confidence in their own skills and ability to conceive a vision for their organization. For example, T. J.

strategy spotlight

Strategy and the Value of Inexperience

Peter Gruber, chairman of Mandalay Entertainment, explained how his firm benefited from the creative insights of an inexperienced intern.

Sometimes life is all about solving problems. In the movie business, at least, there seems to be one around every corner. One of the most effective lessons I've learned about tackling problems is to start by asking not "How to?" but rather "What if?" I learned that lesson from a young woman who was interning on a film I was producing. She actually saved the movie from being shelved by the studio.

The movie, *Gorillas in the Mist,* had turned into a logistical nightmare. We wanted to film at an altitude of 11,000 feet, in the middle of the jungle, in Rwanda—then on the verge of a revolution—and to use more than 200 animals. Warner Brothers, the studio financing the movie, worried that we would exceed our budget. But our biggest problem was that the screenplay required the gorillas to do what we wrote—in other words, to "act." If they couldn't or wouldn't, we'd have to fall back on a formula that the studio had seen fail before: using dwarfs in gorilla suits on a soundstage.

We called an emergency meeting to solve these problems. In the middle of it, a young intern asked, "What if you let the gorillas write the story?" Everyone laughed and wondered what she was doing in the meeting with experienced filmmakers. Hours later, someone casually asked her what she had meant. She said, "What if you sent a really good cinematographer into the jungle with a ton of film to shoot the gorillas. Then you could write a story around what the gorillas did on film." It was a brilliant idea. And we did exactly what she suggested: We sent Alan Root, an Academy Award–nominated cinematographer, into the jungle for three weeks. He came back with phenomenal footage that practically wrote the story for us. We shot the film for $20 million—half of the original budget!

This woman's inexperience enabled her to see opportunities where we saw only boundaries. This experience taught me three things. First, ask high-quality questions, like "what if?" Second, find people who add new perspectives and create new conversations. As experienced filmmakers, we believed that our way was the only way—and that the intern lacked the experience to have an opinion. Third, pay attention to those with new voices. If you want unlimited options for solving a problem, engage the what if before you lock onto the how to. You'll be surprised by what you discover.

Source: P. Gruber, "My Greatest Lesson," *Fast Company* 15 (1998), pp. 88, 90.

Rogers, CEO of Cypress Semiconductor, an electronic chipmaker that faced some difficulties in 1992, lamented that his own shortsightedness caused the danger: "I did not have the 50,000-foot view, and got caught."[49]

One of the most famous examples of a vision is from Disneyland: "To be the happiest place on earth." Other examples are:

◆ "Restoring patients to full life." (Medtronic)
◆ "We want to satisfy all of our customers' financial needs and help them succeed financially." (Wells Fargo)
◆ "Our vision is to be the world's best quick service restaurant." (McDonald's)

Although such visions cannot be accurately measured by a specific indicator of how well they are being achieved, they do provide a fundamental statement of an organization's values, aspirations, and goals. Such visions go well beyond narrow financial objectives, of course, and strive to capture both the minds and hearts of employees.

The vision statement may also contain a slogan, diagram, or picture—whatever grabs attention.[50] The aim is to capture the essence of the more formal parts of the vision in a few words that are easily remembered, yet evoke the spirit of the entire vision statement. In its 20-year battle with Xerox, Canon's slogan—or battle cry—was "Beat Xerox." Motorola's slogan is "Total Customer Satisfaction." Outboard Marine Corporation's slogan is "To Take the World Boating." And Chevron strives "To Become Better than the Best."

Clearly, vision statements are not a cure-all. Sometimes they backfire and erode a company's credibility. Visions fail for many reasons, including those discussed in the following paragraphs.[51]

The Walk Doesn't Match the Talk   An idealistic vision can arouse employee enthusiasm. However, that same enthusiasm can be quickly dashed if employees find that senior management's behavior is not consistent with the vision. Often, vision is a sloganeering campaign of new buzzwords and empty platitudes like "devotion to the customer," "teamwork," or "total quality" that aren't consistently backed by management's action.

Irrelevance   A vision that is created in a vacuum—unrelated to environmental threats or opportunity or an organization's resources and capabilities—can ignore the needs of those who are expected to buy into it. When the vision is not anchored in reality, employees will reject it.

Not the Holy Grail   Managers often search continually for the one elusive solution that will solve their firm's problems—that is, the next holy grail of management. They may have tried other management fads only to find that they fell short of their expectations. However, they remain convinced that one exists. Visions support sound management, but they require everyone to walk the talk and be accountable for their behavior. A vision simply cannot be viewed as a magic cure for an organization's illness.

An Ideal Future Irreconciled with the Present   Although visions are not designed to mirror reality, they do need to be anchored somehow in it. People have difficulty identifying with a vision that paints a rosy picture of the future but takes no account of the often hostile environment in which the firm competes or ignores some of the firm's weaknesses. As we will see in the next section, many of these same issues can apply to mission statements.

Mission Statements

A company's mission differs from vision in that it encompasses both the purpose of the company as well as the basis of competition and competitive advantage.

Exhibit 1.6 contains the vision statement and mission statement of WellPoint Health Networks, a $17 billion managed health care organization. Note that while the vision statement is broad based, the mission statement is more specific and focused on the means by which the firm will compete. This includes providing branded products that will be tailor-made to customers in order to create long-term customer relationships.

**Exhibit 1.6
Comparing
WellPoint Health
Network's Vision
and Mission**

Vision
WellPoint *will redefine our industry:*
Through a new generation of consumer-friendly products that put individuals back in control of their future.

Mission
The WellPoint companies provide health *security* by offering a *choice* of quality branded health and related financial services *designed* to meet the *changing* expectations of individuals, families, and their sponsors throughout a *lifelong* relationship.

Source: WellPoint Health Network company records.

Effective mission statements incorporate the concept of stakeholder management, suggesting that organizations must respond to multiple constituencies if they are to survive and prosper. Customers, employees, suppliers, and owners are the primary stakeholders, but others may also play an important role in a particular corporation. Mission statements also have the greatest impact when they reflect an organization's enduring, overarching strategic priorities and competitive positioning. Mission statements can also vary in length and specificity. The two mission statements below illustrate these issues:

- To produce superior financial returns for our shareholders as we serve our customers with the highest quality transportation, logistics, and e-commerce. (Federal Express)
- To be the very best in the business. Our game plan is status go . . . we are constantly looking ahead, building on our strengths, and reaching for new goals. In our quest of these goals, we look at the three stars of the Brinker logo and are reminded of the basic values that are the strength of this company . . . People, Quality and Profitability. Everything we do at Brinker must support these core values. We also look at the eight golden flames depicted in our logo, and are reminded of the fire that ignites our mission and makes up the heart and soul of this incredible company. These flames are: Customers, Food, Team, Concepts, Culture, Partners, Community and Shareholders. As keeper of these flames, we will continue to build on our strengths and work together to be the best in the business. (Brinker International, whose restaurant chains include Chili's and On the Border)[52]

Few mission statements identify profit or any other financial indicator as the sole purpose of the firm. Indeed, many do not even mention profit or shareholder return.[53] Employees of organizations or departments are usually the mission's most important audience. For them, the mission should help to build a common understanding of purpose and commitment to nurture.

Profit maximization not only fails to motivate people but also does not differentiate between organizations. Every corporation wants to maximize profits over the long term. A good mission statement, by addressing each principal theme, must communicate why an organization is special and different. Two studies that linked corporate values and mission statements with financial performance found that the most successful firms mentioned values other than profits. The less successful firms focused almost entirely on profitability.[54] In essence, profit is the metaphorical equivalent of oxygen, food, and water that the body requires. They are not the point of life, but without them, there is no life.

Although vision statements tend to be quite enduring and seldom change, a firm's mission can and should change when competitive conditions dramatically change or the firm is faced with new threats or opportunities. Strategy Spotlight 1.7 provides an example of a firm, NextJet, that changed its mission in order to realize new opportunities.

Strategic Objectives

Thus far, we have discussed both visions and missions. Statements of vision tend to be quite broad and can be described as a goal that represents an inspiring, overarching, and emotionally driven destination. Mission statements, on the other hand, tend to be more specific and address questions concerning the organization's reason for being and the basis of its intended competitive advantage in the marketplace. Strategic objectives are used to operationalize the mission statement. That is, they help to provide guidance on how the organization can fulfill or move toward the "higher goals" in the goal hierarchy—the mission and vision. As a result, they tend to be more specific and cover a more well-defined time frame.

NextJet's Change of Mission

The dot-com crash was only the first blow to NextJet, Inc., a Dallas-based business launched in 1999 to ship packages overnight. The bigger blow came with the September 11 terrorist attacks, when passenger airlines were forced to add security and reduce flights. One of NextJet's strengths was its nationwide network of local courier services that got packages to and from airports, all coordinated through their proprietary software that could determine the optimal routing. However, the company's business model fell apart when it could not rely on the airlines to get packages between cities quickly enough to make the added cost for same-day delivery worthwhile.

Rather than give up, NextJet reinvented the business around the idea that its most important asset was the software itself. The company's new mission received almost immediate validation when its software was deployed successfully at United Parcel Service. NextJet's software provides Atlanta-based UPS with tools for setting online rates and tracking packages. While a lot of same-day business did evaporate when corporations tightened the reins on spending, some things can't wait overnight to be shipped. For example, makers of hospital equipment may need to ship critical parts within a few hours. NextJet's software can help shippers make important decisions in less than a second, finding the fastest and most economical route among air, truck, and courier operations.

NextJet, Inc., currently has 40 employees and seems to be on the right track with its new mission. Although executives at the privately held company will not disclose financial results, they say they are about to complete their third consecutive profitable quarter.

Sources: A. Goldstein, "NextJet Is Hoping That Its Software Can Deliver," *Dallas Morning News,* December 4, 2002, pp. 1–3; industry.java.sun.com/javanews/stories/story2/0,1072,34986,00.html; and M. G. Nelson, "NextJet Network Adds Wireless," *Information Week,* April 30, 2001, p. 34.

Setting objectives demands a yardstick to measure the fulfillment of the objectives.[55] If an objective lacks specificity or measurability, it is not very useful, simply because there is no way of determining whether it is helping the organization to move toward the organization's mission and vision.

Exhibit 1.7 lists several strategic objectives of corporations, divided into financial and nonfinancial categories. While most of these strategic objectives are directed toward generating greater profits and returns for the owners of the business, others are directed at customers or society at large.

For objectives to be meaningful, they need to satisfy several criteria. They must be:

- *Measurable.* There must be at least one indicator (or yardstick) that measures progress against fulfilling the objective.
- *Specific.* This provides a clear message as to what needs to be accomplished.
- *Appropriate.* It must be consistent with the vision and mission of the organization.
- *Realistic.* It must be an achievable target given the organization's capabilities and opportunities in the environment. In essence, it must be challenging but doable.
- *Timely.* There needs to be a time frame for accomplishing the objective. After all, as the economist John Maynard Keynes once said, "In the long run, we are all dead!"

When objectives satisfy the above criteria, there are many benefits for the organization. First, they help to channel employees throughout the organization toward common goals. This helps to concentrate and conserve valuable resources in the organization and to work collectively in a more timely manner.

Second, challenging objectives can help to motivate and inspire employees throughout the organization to higher levels of commitment and effort. A great deal of research has

Exhibit 1.7
Strategic
Objectives

Strategic Objectives (Financial)

- Increase sales growth 6% to 8% and accelerate core net earnings growth to 13% to 15% per share in each of the next five years. (Procter & Gamble)
- Generate Internet-related revenue of $1.5 billion. (Automation)
- Increase the contribution of Banking Group earnings from investments, brokerage, and insurance from 16% to 25%. (Wells Fargo)
- Cut corporate overhead costs by $30 million per year. (Fortune Brands)

Strategic Objectives (Nonfinancial)

- We want a majority of our customers, when surveyed, to say they consider Wells Fargo the best financial institution in the community. (Wells Fargo)
- We want to operate 6,000 stores by 2010—up from 3,000 in the year 2000. (Walgreen's)
- Develop a smart card strategy that will help us play a key role in shaping online payments. (American Express)
- Reduce greenhouse gases by 10 percent (from a 1990 base) by 2010. (BP Amoco)

Sources: Company documents and annual reports.

supported the notion that individuals work harder when they are striving toward specific goals instead of being asked simply to "do their best."

Third, as we have noted earlier in the chapter, there is always the potential for different parts of an organization to pursue their own goals rather than overall company goals. Although well intentioned, these may work at cross-purposes to the organization as a whole. Meaningful objectives thus help to resolve conflicts when they arise.

Finally, proper objectives provide a yardstick for rewards and incentives. Not only will they lead to higher levels of motivation by employees but also they will help to ensure a greater sense of equity or fairness when rewards are allocated.

There are, of course, still other objectives that are even more specific. These are often referred to as short-term objectives—essential components of "action plans" that are critical in implementing a firm's chosen strategy. We will discuss these issues in Chapter 9.

summary

We began this introductory chapter by defining strategic management and articulating some of its key attributes. Strategic management is defined as "consisting of the analysis, decisions, and actions an organization undertakes to create and sustain competitive advantages." The issue of how and why some firms outperform others in the marketplace is central to the study of strategic management. Strategic management has four key attributes: It is directed at overall organizational goals, includes multiple stakeholders, incorporates both short-term and long-term perspectives, and incorporates trade-offs between efficiency and effectiveness.

The second section discussed the strategic management process. Here, we paralleled the above definition of strategic management and focused on three core activities in the strategic management process—strategy analysis, strategy formulation, and strategy implementation. We noted how each of these activities is highly interrelated to and interdependent on the others. We also discussed how each of the 13 chapters fits into the three core activities and provided a summary of the opening vignettes in each chapter.

Next, we introduced two important concepts, corporate governance and stakeholder management, which must be taken into account throughout the strategic management process. Governance mechanisms can be broadly divided into two groups: internal and external. Internal governance mechanisms include shareholders (owners), management (led by the chief executive officer), and the board of directors. External control is exercised by auditors, banks, analysts, and an active business press as well as the threat of takeovers. We identified five key stakeholders in all organizations: owners, customers, suppliers, employees, and society at large. Successful firms go beyond an overriding focus on satisfying solely the interests of owners. Rather, they recognize the inherent conflicts that arise among the demands of the various stakeholders as well as the need to endeavor to attain "symbiosis"—that is, interdependence and mutual benefit—among the various stakeholder groups.

In the fourth section, we discussed three interrelated factors—globalization, technology, and intellectual capital—that have accelerated the rate of unpredictable change that managers face today. These factors, and the combination of them, have increased the need for managers and employees throughout the organization to have a strategic management perspective and to become more empowered.

The final section addressed the need for consistency between a firm's vision, mission, and strategic objectives. Collectively, they form an organization's hierarchy of goals. Visions should evoke powerful and compelling mental images. However, they are not very specific. Strategic objectives, on the other hand, are much more specific and are vital to ensuring that the organization is striving toward fulfilling its vision and mission.

summary review questions

1. How is "strategic management" defined in the text, and what are its four key attributes?

2. Briefly discuss the three key activities in the strategic management process. Why is it important for managers to recognize the interdependent nature of these activities?

3. Explain the concept of "stakeholder management." Why shouldn't managers be solely interested in stockholder management, that is, maximizing the returns for owners of the firm—its shareholders?

4. What is corporate governance? What are its three key elements and how can it be improved?

5. How can "symbiosis" (interdependence, mutual benefit) be achieved among a firm's stakeholders?

6. What are some of the major trends that now require firms to have a greater strategic management perspective and empowerment in the strategic management process throughout the firm?

7. What is meant by a "hierarchy of goals"? What are the main components of it and why must consistency be achieved among them?

experiential exercise

Using the Internet or library sources, select four organizations—two in the private sector and two in the public sector. Find their Mission Statements. Complete the following exhibit by identifying the stakeholders that are mentioned. Evaluate the differences between firms in the private sector and those in the public sector.

	Private Sector #1	Private Sector #2	Public Sector #1	Public Sector #2
Name				
Mission Statement				
Stakeholders (√ = mentioned)				
1. Customers				
2. Suppliers				
3. Managers/employees				
4. Community-at-large				
5. Owners				
6. Others?				
7. Others?				

application questions & exercises

1. Go to the Internet and look up one of these company sites: www.walmart.com, www.ge.com, or www.fordmotor.com. What are some of the key events that would represent the "romantic" perspective of leadership? What are some of the key events that depict the "external control" perspective of leadership?

2. Select a company that competes in an industry in which you are interested. What are some of the recent demands that stakeholders have placed on this company? Can you find examples of how the company is trying to develop "symbiosis" (interdependence and mutual benefit) among its stakeholders? (Use the Internet and library resources.)

3. Provide examples of companies that are actively trying to increase the amount of empowerment in the strategic management process throughout the organization. Do these companies seem to be having positive outcomes? Why? Why not?

4. Look up the vision statements and/or mission statements for a few companies. Do you feel that they are constructive and useful as a means of motivating employees and providing a strong strategic direction? Why? Why not? (*Note:* Annual reports, along with the Internet, may be good sources of information.)

ethics questions

1. A company focuses solely on short-term profits to provide the greatest return to the owners of the business (i.e., the shareholders in a publicly held firm). What ethical issues could this raise?
2. A firm has spent some time—with input from managers at all levels—in developing a vision statement and a mission statement. Over time, however, the behavior of some executives is contrary to these statements. Could this raise some ethical issues?

references

1. This example draws on Park, A., 2003, EDS: What went wrong, *BusinessWeek,* April 7: 60–63; Loomis, C. J., 2003, EDS: Executives don't suffer, *Fortune,* April 14: 56; I own this problem, 2003, *Fortune,* February 3: 45–47; The best and worst managers, 2003, *BusinessWeek,* January 13: 78–79; and Revell, J., 2003, CEO pensions: The latest way to hide millions, *Fortune,* April 28: 68–70.
2. For a discussion of the "romantic" versus "external control" perspective, refer to Meindl, J. R., 1987, The romance of leadership and the evaluation of organizational performance, *Academy of Management Journal* 30:92–109; and Pfeffer, J., & Salancik, G. R., 1978, *The External Control of Organizations: A Resource Dependence Perspective* (New York: Harper & Row).
3. For an interesting perspective on the need for strategists to maintain a global mind-set, refer to Begley, T. M., & Boyd, D. P., 2003, The need for a global mind-set, *MIT Sloan Management Review* 44 (2): 25–32.
4. Porter, M. E., 1996, What is strategy? *Harvard Business Review* 74 (6): 61–78.
5. See, for example, Barney, J. B., & Arikan, A. M., 2001, The resource-based view: Origins and implications, in Hitt, M. A., Freeman, R. E., & Harrison, J. S., eds., *Handbook of Strategic Management* (Malden, MA: Blackwell), 124–89.
6. Barney, J., 1991, Firm resources and sustained competitive advantage, *Journal of Management* 17 (1): 99–120.
7. Much of Gary Hamel's work advocates the importance of not focusing on incremental change. For example, refer to Hamel, G., & Prahalad, C. K., 1994, *Competing for the Future* (Boston: Harvard Business School Press); see also Christensen, C. M., 2001, The past and future of competitive advantage, *Sloan Management Review* 42 (3): 105–9.
8. Porter, M. E., 1996, What is strategy? *Harvard Business Review* 74 (6): 61–78; and Hammonds, K. H., 2001, Michael Porter's big ideas, *Fast Company,* March: 55–56.
9. This section draws upon Dess, G. G., & Miller, A., 1993, *Strategic Management* (New York: McGraw-Hill).
10. See, for example, Hrebiniak, L. G., & Joyce, W. F., 1986, The strategic importance of managing myopia, *Sloan Management Review* 28 (1): 5–14.
11. For an insightful discussion on how to manage diverse stakeholder groups, refer to Rondinelli, D. A., & London, T., 2003, How corporations and environmental groups cooperate: Assessing cross-sector alliances and collaborations, *Academy of Management Executive* 17 (1): 61–76.
12. Senge, P., 1996, Leading learning organizations: The bold, the powerful, and the invisible, in Hesselbein, F., Goldsmith, M., & Beckhard, R., eds., *The Leader of the Future* (San Francisco: Jossey Bass), 41–58.
13. For another interesting perspective on this issue, refer to Abell, D. F., 1999, Competing today while preparing for tomorrow, *Sloan Management Review* 40 (3): 73–81.
14. Loeb, M., 1994, Where leaders come from, *Fortune,* September 19: 241 (quoting Warren Bennis).
15. Address by Norman R. Augustine at the Crummer Business School, Rollins College, Winter Park, FL, October 20, 1989.
16. Mintzberg, H., 1985, Of strategies: Deliberate and emergent, *Strategic Management Journal* 6:257–72.
17. Monks, R., & Minow, N., 2001, *Corporate Governance,* 2nd ed. (Malden, MA: Blackwell).
18. Intel Corp., www.intel.com/intel/finance/corp_gov.html.
19. For example, see The best (& worst) managers of the year, 2003, *BusinessWeek,* January 13: 58–92; and Lavelle, M., 2003, Rogues of the year, *Time,* January 6: 33–45.
20. Handy, C., 2002, What's a business for? *Harvard Business Review* 80 (12): 49–55.
21. Stakeholder symbiosis. 1998. *Fortune,* March 30: S2.
22. For a definitive, recent discussion of the stakeholder concept, refer to Freeman, R. E., & McVae, J., 2001, A stakeholder approach to strategic management, in Hitt, M. A., Freeman, R. E., & Harrison, J. S., eds., *Handbook of Strategic Management* (Malden, MA: Blackwell), 189–207.
23. Atkinson, A. A., Waterhouse, J. H., & Wells, R. B., 1997, A stakeholder approach to strategic performance measurement, *Sloan Management Review* 39 (3): 25–38.
24. For an insightful discussion on the role of business in society, refer to Handy, op. cit.
25. Stakeholder symbiosis. op. cit., p. S3.

26. Rucci, A. J., Kirn, S. P., & Quinn, R. T., 1998, The employee-customer-profit chain at Sears, *Harvard Business Review* 76 (1): 82–97.

27. An excellent theoretical discussion on stakeholder activity is Rowley, T. J., & Moldoveanu, M., 2003, When will stakeholder groups act? An interest- and identity-based model of stakeholder group mobilization, *Academy of Management Review* 28 (2): 204–19.

28. Thomas, J. G., 2000, Macroenvironmetal forces, in Helms, M. M., ed., *Encyclopedia of Management,* 4th ed. (Farmington Hills, MI: Gale Group), 516–20.

29. This discussion draws upon Austin, J. E., 2000, Measuring a triple bottom line, *Leader to Leader,* Fall: 51.

30. Funk, K., 2003, Sustainability and performance, *MIT Sloan Management Review* 44 (2): 65–70.

31. Senge, P. M., 1990, The leader's new work: Building learning organizations, *Sloan Management Review* 32 (1): 7–23.

32. Barkema, G. G., Baum, A. C., & Mannix, E. A., 2002, Management challenges in a new time, *Academy of Management Journal* 45 (5): 916–30.

33. This section draws upon a variety of sources, including Tetenbaum, T. J., 1998, Shifting paradigms: From Newton to chaos, *Organizational Dynamics* 26 (4): 21–33; Ulrich, D., 1998, A new mandate for human resources, *Harvard Business Review* 76 (1): 125–35; and Hitt, M. A., 2000, The new frontier: Transformation of management for the new millennium, *Organizational Dynamics* 28 (2): 7–17.

34. Garten, J. E., 2001, *The Mind of the C.E.O.* (New York: Basic Books).

35. An interesting discussion on the impact of AIDS on the global economy is found in Rosen, S., 2003, AIDS *is* your business, *Harvard Business Review* 81 (2): 80–87.

36. Weber, J., 1996, Mr. nice guy with a mission, *BusinessWeek,* November 25: 137.

37. Colvin, G., 2000, We're worth our weight in Pentium chips, *Fortune,* March 20: 68.

38. Ulrich, D., 1998, Intellectual capital: Competence × commitment, *Strategic Management Journal* 39 (2): 15–26.

39. Stewart, T. A., 2000, Today's companies won't make it, and Gary Hamel knows why, *Fortune,* September 4: 390.

40. Rivette, K. G., & Kline, D., 2000, Discovering new value in intellectual property, *Harvard Business Review* 78 (1): 54–66.

41. For an interesting perspective on the role of middle managers in the strategic management process, refer to Huy, Q. H., 2001, In praise of middle managers, *Harvard Business Review* 79 (8): 72–81.

42. Senge, 1996, op. cit., pp. 41–58.

43. Helgesen, S., 1996, Leading from the grass roots, in Hesselbein, F., Goldsmith, M., & Beckhard, R., eds., *The Leader of the Future* (San Francisco: Jossey-Bass), 19–24.

44. Wetlaufer, S., 1999, Organizing for empowerment: An interview with AES's Roger Sant and Dennis Blake, *Harvard Business Review* 77 (1): 110–26.

45. Kets de Vries, M. F. R., 1998, Charisma in action: The transformational abilities of Virgin's Richard Branson and ABB's Percy Barnevik, *Organizational Dynamics* 26 (3): 7–21.

46. Hammonds, K. H., 2000, The next agenda, *Fast Company,* April: 140.

47. Our discussion draws on a variety of sources. These include Lipton, M., 1996, Demystifying the development of an organizational vision, *Sloan Management Review* 37 (4): 83–92; Bart, C. K., 2000, Lasting inspiration, *CA Magazine,* May: 49–50; and Quigley, J. V., 1994, Vision: How leaders develop it, share it, and sustain it, *Business Horizons,* September–October: 37–40.

48. Lipton, op. cit.

49. Quigley, op. cit.

50. Ibid.

51. Lipton, op. cit. Additional pitfalls are addressed in this article.

52. Company records.

53. Lipton, op. cit.

54. Sexton, D. A., & Van Aukun, P. M., 1985, A longitudinal study of small business strategic planning, *Journal of Small Business Management,* January: 8–15, cited in Lipton, op. cit.

55. Ibid.

chapter 2

Analyzing the External Environment of the Firm

*After
reading this
chapter, you should
have a good understanding of:*

- The importance of developing forecasts of the business environment.

- Why environmental scanning, environmental monitoring, and collecting competitive intelligence are critical inputs to forecasting.

- Why scenario planning is a useful technique for firms competing in industries characterized by unpredictability and change.

- The impact of the general environment on a firm's strategies and performance.

- How forces in the competitive environment can affect profitability and how a firm can improve its competitive position by increasing its power vis-à-vis these forces.

- How trends and events in the general environment and forces in the competitive environment are interrelated and affect performance.

- The concept of strategic groups as well as their strategy and performance implications.

Strategies are not and should not be developed in a vacuum. They must be responsive to the external business environment. Otherwise, your firm could become, in effect, the most efficient producer of buggy whips, leisure suits, or slide rules. To avoid such strategic mistakes, firms must become knowledgeable about the business environment. One tool for analyzing trends is forecasting. In the development of forecasts, environmental scanning and environmental monitoring are important in detecting key trends and events. Managers must aggressively collect and disseminate competitor intelligence. The information gleaned from these three activities is invaluable in developing forecasts and scenarios to minimize present and future threats as well as to exploit opportunities. We address these issues in the first part of this chapter. We also introduce a basic tool of strategy analysis—the concept of SWOT analysis (Strengths, Weaknesses, Opportunities, and Threats).

In the second part of the chapter, we present two frameworks for analyzing the external environment: the general environment and the competitive environment. The general environment consists of six segments—demographic, sociocultural, political/legal, technological, economic, and global. Trends and events in these segments can have a dramatic impact on your firm. The competitive environment is closer to home. It consists of five industry-related factors that can dramatically affect the average level of industry profitability. An awareness of such factors is critical in making decisions such as which industries to enter and how to improve your firm's current position within an industry. This is helpful in neutralizing competitive threats and increasing power over customers and suppliers. In the final part of this section, we place firms within an industry into strategic groups on the basis of similarities of resources and strategies. As we will see, the concept of strategic groups has important implications for the intensity of rivalry and how the effects of a given environmental trend or event differ across groups.

Let's begin by considering the case of Motorola—a company that lost its leadership position because of its failure to keep pace with changes in its external environment.

Motorola, founded in the 1930s as a maker of car radios, expanded into international markets in the 1960s and began shifting its focus away from consumer electronics.[1] Its color television receiver business was sold in the mid-1970s, allowing Motorola to concentrate its energies on high-technology markets in commercial, industrial, and government fields. By the end of the 1980s, Motorola had become the leading supplier of cellular telephones in the world. Its flip phone had been adopted by many cellular phone services, including McCaw Cellular, the predecessor to AT&T Wireless. Eighty-five percent of the cell phones that McCaw sold to its customers were made by Motorola. Motorola's dominant position and the strong performance of its stock led *Fortune* magazine in 1994 to claim that Motorola was "the company that almost everyone loves to love." A Malcolm Baldrige National Quality Award winner and a pioneer of Six-Sigma for Quality Excellence, Motorola has been a company par excellence in integrated communication systems.

Recently, however, Motorola fell out of step with cutting-edge trends in wireless communications. The company made a series of critical strategic errors. The wireless communications industry was shifting its attention away from analog technology, where Motorola had a strong lead. Nearly every major wireless player had switched to the digital technology. Motorola's customers told the company that in the near future they would need digital phones, and lots of them. In 1996, not long after AT&T Wireless rolled out its digital network, Motorola released its newest model—the StarTAC. It was sleek and beautiful . . . and analog. AT&T had no choice but to turn to Nokia and Ericsson for digital phones. Motorola missed the technology trend. Further, consumer tastes and preferences vary in different parts of the world. In the global markets, "one-size-fits-all" was not the winning strategy. Motorola continued to develop its products based on the customers and technologies in its home market without tracking the changing consumer tastes and preferences around the world. It failed to recognize the potential to turn the phone into a fashion icon and was slow to recognize that a broader but more fragmented user base required a more segmented approach to marketing.

At the same time, Nokia, a Finland-based company that transformed itself from being a diaper and rubber boot maker to a high-tech company leading in cutting-edge technologies, has overtaken Motorola in mobile phones. Nokia has been more sensitive to the changing trends in the environment. It was among the first to recognize the power of digital technology in improving the functionality of mobile phones by observing pilot users across Scandinavia. Nokia discovered the need for customized handsets and the potential of the mobile phone as a fashion accessory from its knowledge of working with diverse consumer groups in Asia and Europe and its constant search for promising technologies around the world. Not surprisingly, Nokia's global market share is currently over twice that of Motorola's (38 percent versus 17 percent).

What Went Wrong at Motorola?   Motorola missed the key trends. Rather than maintaining its dominant position by embracing the shift to digital technology, Motorola stuck with analog phones because they were a key to its past success. It ignored the digital wave that was rushing toward it and also ignored the new rules of the global game. Because it was not willing to respond to changing trends, its actions lacked speed and decisiveness. As a result, today they are lagging in an industry that they once practically owned.

To be a successful manager, you must recognize opportunities and threats in your firm's external environment. You must be aware of what's going on outside your company. If you focus exclusively on the efficiency of internal operations, your firm may degenerate into the world's most efficient producer of buggy whips or carbon paper. But if you miscalculate the market, opportunities will be lost—hardly an enviable position for you or your firm.

In their award-winning book *Competing for the Future,* Gary Hamel and C. K. Prahalad suggest that "every manager carries around in his or her head a set of biases, assumptions, and presuppositions about the structure of the relevant 'industry,' about how one makes money in the industry, about who the competition is and isn't, about who the customers are and aren't, and so on."[2] Environmental analysis requires you to continually question these assumptions. Peter Drucker labeled these interrelated sets of assumptions the "theory of the business."[3]

Your firm's strategy may be good at one point in time, but it may go astray when management's frame of reference gets out of touch with the realities of the actual business situation. This results when management's assumptions, premises, or beliefs are incorrect or when internal inconsistencies among them render the overall "theory of the business" invalid. As Warren Buffett, investor extraordinaire, colorfully notes, "Beware of past performance 'proofs.' If history books were the key to riches, the Forbes 400 would consist of librarians." And Arthur Martinez, former chairman of Sears, Roebuck & Co., states: "Today's peacock is tomorrow's feather duster."

In the business world, many peacocks have become feather dusters, or at least had their plumage dulled. Consider the high-tech company Novell, which has undergone hard times.[4] Novell went head-to-head with Microsoft and bought market-share loser Word-Perfect to compete with Microsoft Word. The result: a $1.3 billion loss when Novell sold WordPerfect to Corel. And today we may wonder who will be the next Wang, Kmart, or Encyclopaedia Britannica.

Creating the Environmentally Aware Organization

So how do managers become environmentally aware?[5] We will now address three important processes—scanning, monitoring, and gathering competitive intelligence—which managers must use to develop forecasts. Exhibit 2.1 illustrates relationships among these important activities. We also discuss the importance of scenario planning in anticipating major future changes in the external environment as well as the role of SWOT analysis.[6]

The Role of Scanning, Monitoring, Competitive Intelligence, and Forecasting

Environmental Scanning Environmental scanning involves surveillance of a firm's external environment to predict environmental changes to come and detect changes already under way.[7] Successful environmental scanning alerts the organization to critical trends and events before the changes have developed a discernible pattern and before competitors recognize them.[8] Otherwise, the firm may be forced into a reactive mode instead of being proactive.[9]

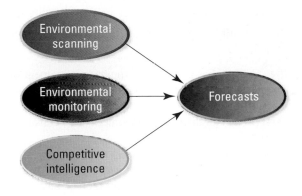

Exhibit 2.1 Inputs to Forecasting

Sir John Browne, chief executive officer of petroleum company BP Amoco, described in a speech the kind of environmental changes his company was experiencing.

> The next element of the change we've experienced is the growth in demand, and the changing nature of that demand. The world uses eight million more barrels of oil and 30 billion more cubic feet of natural gas every day than it did in the spring of 1990. The growth of natural gas in particular has been and continues to be spectacular, and I believe that change can legitimately be seen as part of a wider, longer-term shift to lighter, cleaner, less carbon-intensive fuels.[10]

Consider how difficult it would be for BP Amoco to develop strategies and allocate resources if it did not scan the external environment for such emerging changes in demand.

At times, your company may benefit from studies conducted by outside experts in a particular industry. A. T. Kearney, a large international consulting company, identified several "key issues" in the automobile industry, including:[11]

◆ *Globalization.* This is not a new trend but it has intensified, with enormous opportunities opening up in Asia, central and eastern Europe, and Latin America.

◆ *Time to Market.* Although some improvements have been made, there's still a gap between product development cycles in the United States and Europe compared to Japan. This gap may be widening as Japanese companies continue to make improvements.

◆ *Shifting Roles and Responsibilities.* Design responsibility, purchasing, even project management and systems engineering, are shifting from original equipment manufacturer to integrator/supplier.

Consider how disadvantaged you would be as an executive in the global automobile industry if you were unaware of such trends.

Environmental Monitoring   Environmental monitoring tracks the evolution of environmental trends, sequences of events, or streams of activities. These are often uncovered during the environmental scanning process. They may be trends that the firm came across by accident or were brought to its attention from outside the organization. Consider the automobile industry example. While environmental scanning may make you aware of the trends, they require close monitoring, which involves closer ongoing scrutiny. For example, you should closely monitor sales in Asia, central and eastern Europe, and Latin America. You should observe how fast Japanese companies and other competitors bring products to market compared with your firm. You should also study trends with your own suppliers/integrators in purchasing, project management, and systems engineering. Monitoring enables firms to evaluate how dramatically environmental trends are changing the competitive landscape.

One of the authors recently conducted on-site interviews with executives from several industries. The goal was to identify indicators that firms monitor as inputs to their strategy process. Examples included:

◆ *A Motel 6 executive.* The number of rooms in the budget segment of the industry in the United States, and the difference between the average daily room rate and the Consumer Price Index (CPI).

◆ *A Pier 1 Imports executive.* Net disposable income (NDI), consumer confidence index, and housing starts.

◆ *A Johnson & Johnson medical products executive.* Percentage of gross domestic product (GDP) spent on health care, number of active hospital beds, and the size and power of purchasing agents (indicates the concentration of buyers).

Such indices are critical for managers in determining each firm's strategic direction and resource allocation.

Competitive Intelligence *Is* . . .	Competitive Intelligence *Is Not* . . .
1. **Information** that has been analyzed to the point where you can make a decision.	1. **Spying.** Spying implies illegal or unethical activities. It is a rare activity, since most corporations do not want to find themselves in court or to upset shareholders.
2. **A tool** to alert management to early recognition of both threats and opportunities.	2. **A crystal ball.** CI gives corporations good approximations of reality, short and long term. It does not predict the future.
3. **A means to deliver reasonable assessments.** CI offers approximations of the market and competition. It is not a peek at a rival's financial books. Reasonable assessments are what modern entrepreneurs need and want on a regular basis.	3. **Database search.** Databases offer just that—data. They do not massage or analyze the data in any way. They certainly don't replace human beings, who make decisions by examining the data and applying their common sense, experience, and intuition.
4. **A way of life, a process.** If a company uses CI the way it should be used, it becomes everyone's job—not just the strategic planning or marketing staff's. It is a process by which critical information is available to those who need it.	4. **A job for one smart person.** A CEO may appoint one person as the CI ringmaster, but one person cannot do it all. At best, the ringmaster can keep management informed and ensure that others become trained to apply this tool within their business units.

Sources: G. Imperato, "Competitive Intelligence—Get Smart!" *Fast Company*, April 1998, p. 269; and F. M. Fuld, "What Competitive Intelligence Is and Is Not!" www.fuld.com/whatCI.html.

Exhibit 2.2
What Competitive Intelligence (CI) Is and Is Not!

Competitive Intelligence   Competitive intelligence (CI) helps firms define and understand their industry and identify rivals' strengths and weaknesses.[12] This includes the intelligence gathering associated with the collection of data on competitors and interpretation of such data for managerial decision making. Done properly, competitive intelligence helps a company avoid surprises by anticipating competitors' moves and decreasing response time.[13]

Examples of competitive analysis are evident in daily newspapers and periodicals such as *The Wall Street Journal, BusinessWeek,* and *Fortune.* For example, banks continually track home loan, auto loan, and certificate of deposit (CD) interest rates charged by peers in a given geographic region. Major airlines change hundreds of fares daily in response to competitors' tactics. Car manufacturers are keenly aware of announced cuts or increases in rivals' production volume, sales, and sales incentives (e.g., rebates and low interest rates on financing). They use this information to plan their own marketing, pricing, and production strategies. Exhibit 2.2 provides some insights on what CI is (and what it isn't).

The Internet has dramatically accelerated the speed at which firms can find competitive intelligence. Leonard Fuld, founder of the Cambridge, Massachusetts, training and consulting firm Fuld & Co., specializes in competitive intelligence.[14] His firm often profiles top company and business group managers and considers these issues: What is their background? Style? Are they marketers? Are they cost cutters? Fuld has found that the

Ethical Guidelines on Competitive Intelligence: United Technologies

United Technologies (UT) is a $28 billion global conglomerate composed of world-leading businesses with rich histories of technological pioneering, such as Otis Elevator, Carrier Air Conditioning, and Sikorsky (helicopters). It was founded in 1853 and has an impressive history of technological accomplishments. UT built the first working helicopter, developed the first commercially available hydrogen cells, and designed complete life support systems for space shuttles. UT believes strongly in a robust code of ethics. In the last decade, they have clearly articulated their principles governing business conduct. These include an antitrust guide, an ethics guide when contracting with the U.S. government and foreign governments, a policy on accepting gifts from suppliers, and guidelines for proper usage of e-mail. One such document is the Code of Ethics Guide on Competitive Intelligence. This encourages managers and workers to ask themselves these five questions whenever they have ethical concerns.

Sources: B. Nelson, "The Thinker," *Forbes,* March 3, 2003, pp. 62–64; and "The Fuld War Room—Survival Kit 010," Code of Ethics (printed 2/26/01).

1. Have I done anything that coerced somebody to share this information? Have I, for example, threatened a supplier by indicating that future business opportunities will be influenced by the receipt of information with respect to a competitor?

2. Am I in a place where I should not be? If, for example, I am a field representative with privileges to move around in a customer's facility, have I gone outside the areas permitted? Have I misled anybody in order to gain access?

3. Is the contemplated technique for gathering information evasive, such as sifting through trash or setting up an electronic "snooping" device directed at a competitor's facility from across the street?

4. Have I misled somebody in a way that the person believed sharing information with me was required or would be protected by a confidentiality agreement? Have I, for example, called and misrepresented myself as a government official who was seeking some information for some official purpose?

5. Have I done something to evade or circumvent a system intended to secure or protect information?

more articles he collects and the more biographies he downloads, the better he can develop profiles.

One of Fuld & Co.'s clients needed to know if a rival was going to start competing more aggressively on costs. Fuld's analysts tracked down articles from the Internet and a local newspaper profile of the rival firm's CEO. The profile said the CEO had taken a bus to a nearby town to visit one of the firm's plants. Fuld claimed, "Those few words were a small but important sign to me that this company was going to be incredibly cost-conscious." Another client retained Fuld to determine the size, strength, and technical capabilities of a privately held company. Initially, it was difficult to get detailed information. Then one analyst used Deja News (www.dejanews.com), now part of Google, to tap into some online discussion groups. The analyst's research determined that the company had posted 14 job openings on one Usenet group. That posting was a road map to the competitor's development strategy.

At times, a firm's aggressive efforts to gather competitive intelligence may lead to unethical or illegal behaviors.[15] Strategy Spotlight 2.1 provides an example of a company, United Technologies, that has set clear guidelines to help prevent unethical behavior.

A word of caution: Executives must be careful to avoid spending so much time and effort tracking the competitive actions of traditional competitors that they ignore new competitors. Further, broad changes and events in the larger environment may have a dramatic impact on a firm's viability. Peter Drucker, whom many consider the father of modern management, wrote:

> Increasingly, a winning strategy will require information about events and conditions outside the institution: noncustomers, technologies other than those currently used by the company and its present competitors, markets not currently served, and so on.[16]

Consider the fall of the once-mighty Encyclopaedia Britannica.[17] Its demise was not caused by a traditional competitor in the encyclopedia industry. It was caused by new technology. CD-ROMs came out of nowhere and devastated the printed encyclopedia industry. Why? A full set of the *Encyclopaedia Britannica* sells for about $2,000, but an encyclopedia on CD-ROM, such as Microsoft *Encarta,* sells for about $50. To make matters worse, many people receive *Encarta* free with their personal computers.

Environmental Forecasting   Environmental scanning, monitoring, and competitive intelligence are important inputs for analyzing the external environment. However, they are of little use unless they provide raw material that is reliable enough to help managers make accurate forecasts. Environmental forecasting involves the development of plausible projections about the direction, scope, speed, and intensity of environmental change.[18] Its purpose is to predict change. It asks: How long will it take a new technology to reach the marketplace? Will the present social concern about an issue result in new legislation? Are current lifestyle trends likely to continue?

Some forecasting issues are much more specific to a particular firm and the industry in which it competes. Consider how important it is for Motel 6 to predict future indicators, such as the number of rooms, in the budget segment of the industry. If its predictions are low, it will build too many units, creating a surplus of room capacity that would drive down room rates. Similarly, if Pier 1 Imports is overly optimistic in its forecast of future net disposable income and U.S. housing starts, it will order too much inventory and later be forced to discount merchandise drastically.

A danger of forecasting is that managers may view uncertainty as black and white and ignore important gray areas. Either they assume that the world is certain and open to precise predictions, or they assume it is uncertain and completely unpredictable.[19] The problem? Underestimating uncertainty can lead to strategies that neither defend against threats nor take advantage of opportunities. In 1977 one of the colossal underestimations in business history occurred. Kenneth H. Olsen, then president of Digital Equipment Corp., announced: "There is no reason for individuals to have a computer in their home." The explosion in the personal computer market was not easy to detect in 1977, but it was clearly within the range of possibilities that industry experts were discussing at the time. And, historically, there have been underestimates of the growth potential of new telecommunication services. The electric telegraph was derided by Ralph Waldo Emerson, and the telephone had its skeptics. More recently, an "infamous" McKinsey study in the early 1980s predicted that there would be fewer than 1 million cellular users in the United States by the year 2000. Actually, there were nearly 100 million.[20]

At the other extreme, if managers assume the world is unpredictable, they may abandon the analytical rigor of their traditional planning process and base strategic decisions on gut instinct. Such a "just do it" approach may cause executives to place misinformed bets on emerging products or markets that result in record write-offs. Entrepreneurs and venture capitalists who took the plunge and invested in questionable Internet ventures in the late 1990s provide many examples.

A more in-depth approach to forecasting involves scenario analysis. Scenario analysis draws on a range of disciplines and interests, among them economics, psychology, sociology, and demographics. It usually begins with a discussion of participants' thoughts on

Scenario Planning at Shell Oil Company

Preparing to cope with uncertainty is one of the biggest strategic challenges faced by most businesses. There are few tools for coping with strategic uncertainty, especially over medium- to long-term horizons. One technique that has proved its usefulness is scenario planning.

Scenario planning is different from other tools for strategic planning such as trend analysis or high and low forecasts. The origins of scenario planning lie with the military, which used it to cope effectively with multiple challenges and limited resources.

In the 1960s and 1970s, Shell combined analytical tools with information to create scenarios of possible outcomes. The result of the 1973 oil embargo was a sharp increase in crude oil prices, short supplies of gasoline for consumers, and a depressed world economy. However, Shell's strategic planning, including the use of scenarios, had strongly suggested that a more unstable environment was coming, with a shift of power from oil companies to oil producers. As a result of the precautionary actions it took, Shell was in a better position than most oil companies when the 1973 embargo occurred. Shell also uses scenario planning to plan major new oil field investments. This is because elements of risk can be identified and explored over a considerable period of time.

The Shell process of scenario planning involves the following stages:

1. Interviews with people both inside and outside the business, using an open-ended questioning technique to encourage full and frank answers.

2. Analysis of interviews by issue in order to build a "natural agenda" for further processing.

3. Synthesis of each agenda so as to draw out underlying areas of uncertainty/dispute and possible interrelationships among issues.

4. A small number of issues workshops to explore key issues to improve understanding and identify gaps for further research. These generate a wide range of options for strategy.

5. A scenario workshop to identify and build a small number of scenarios which may occur in some 10 to 15 years time or even later.

6. A testing of strategy options against the scenarios in order to assess robustness (i.e., whether or not a given strategy is effective under more than one scenario).

Other practitioners of scenario planning include Levi Strauss, which uses scenario planning to consider potential impacts of everything from cotton deregulation to the total disappearance of cotton from this planet. Also, a German insurance company anticipated the fall of the Berlin wall and made plans to expand in central Europe. And in 1990 when Nelson Mandela was released from a South African prison, he met with a panel that helped him create scenarios to chart out the country's future. Scenario planning helps by considering not just trends or forecasts but also how they could be upset by events and the resulting outcomes.

Sources: R. Martin, "The Oracles of Oil," *Business 2.0,* January 2002, pp. 35–39; www.touchstonerenard.co.uk/Expertise/Strategy/Scenario_Planning/scenario_planning.htm; and J. Epstein, "Scenario Planning: An Introduction," *The Futurist,* September 1998, pp. 50–52.

ways in which societal trends, economics, politics, and technology may affect the issue under discussion. For example, consider Lego. The popular Danish toy manufacturer has a strong position in its market for "construction toys." But what would happen if its market, broadly defined, should change dramatically? After all, Lego is competing not only with producers of similar products. Instead, it is competing on a much broader canvas for a share of children's playtime. In this market, Lego has a host of competitors, many of them computer based; still others have not yet been invented. Lego may end up with an increasing share of a narrow, shrinking market (much like IBM in the declining days of the mainframe computer). To avoid such a fate, managers must consider their future in a wider context than their narrow, traditional markets. They need to lay down guidelines for at least 10 years in the future to anticipate rapid change. Strategy Spotlight 2.2 provides an example of scenario analysis at Shell Oil Company.

SWOT Analysis

To understand the business environment of a particular firm, you need to analyze both the general environment and the firm's industry and competitive environment. Generally, firms compete with other firms in the same industry. An industry is composed of a set of firms that produce similar products or services, sell to similar customers, and use similar methods of production. Gathering industry information and understanding competitive dynamics among the different companies in your industry is key to successful strategic management.

One of the most basic techniques for analyzing firm and industry conditions is SWOT analysis. SWOT stands for strengths, weaknesses, opportunities, and threats. SWOT analysis provides a framework for analyzing these four elements of a company's internal and external environment. It provides "raw material," a basic listing of conditions both inside and surrounding your company. The strengths and weaknesses portion of SWOT refers to the internal conditions of a firm where your firm excels (strengths) and where it may be lacking relative to similar competitors (weaknesses). We will address strengths and weaknesses again in Chapter 3. Opportunities and threats are environmental conditions external to the firm. These could be factors in the general environment, such as improving economic conditions that cause lower borrowing costs, or trends that benefit some companies and harm others. An example is the heightened concern with fitness, which is a threat to some companies (e.g., tobacco) and an opportunity to others (e.g., health clubs). Opportunities and threats are also present in the competitive environment among firms competing for the same customers.

The General Environment

The general environment is composed of factors that can have dramatic effects on firm strategy.[21] Typically, a firm has little ability to predict trends and events in the general environment, and even less ability to control them. When listening to CNBC, for example, one can hear many experts espouse totally different perspectives on what action the Federal Reserve Board may take on short-term interest rates—an action that can have huge effects on the valuation of entire economic sectors. Also, it's difficult to predict future political events such as the ongoing Middle East peace negotiations and tensions on the Korean peninsula. In addition, who would have guessed the Internet's impact on national and global economies in the past decade or two? Such dramatic innovations in information technology (e.g., the Internet) have helped keep inflation in check by lowering the cost of doing business in the United States at the beginning of the 21st century.

We divide the general environment into six segments: demographic, sociocultural, political/legal, technological, economic, and global. First, we discuss each segment and provide a summary of the segment and examples of how events and trends can impact industries. Second, we address relationships among the general environment segments. Third, we consider how trends and events can vary across industries. Exhibit 2.3 provides examples of key trends and events in each of the six segments of the general environment.

The Demographic Segment

Demographics are the most easily understood and quantifiable elements of the general environment. They are at the root of many changes in society. Demographics include elements such as the aging population,[22] rising or declining affluence, changes in ethnic composition, geographic distribution of the population, and disparities in income level.

The impact of a demographic trend, like all segments of the general environment, varies across industries. The aging of the U.S. population has had a positive effect on the health care industry but a negative impact on the industry that produces diapers and baby

**Exhibit 2.3
General
Environment: Key
Trends and Events**

Demographic

- Aging population
- Rising affluence
- Changes in ethnic composition
- Geographic distribution of population
- Greater disparities in income levels

Sociocultural

- More women in the workforce
- Increase in temporary workers
- Greater concern for fitness
- Greater concern for environment
- Postponement of family formation

Political/Legal

- Tort reform
- Americans with Disabilities Act (ADA) of 1990
- Repeal of Glass-Steagall Act in 1999 (banks may now offer brokerage services)
- Deregulation of utility and other industries
- Increases in federally mandated minimum wages
- Taxation at local, state, federal levels
- Legislation on corporate governance reforms in bookkeeping, stock options, etc. (Sarbanes-Oxley Act of 2002)

Technological

- Genetic engineering
- Emergence of Internet technology
- Computer-aided design/computer-aided manufacturing systems (CAD/CAM)
- Research in synthetic and exotic materials
- Pollution/global warming
- Miniaturization of computing technologies
- Wireless communications
- Nanotechnology

Economic

- Interest rates
- Unemployment
- Consumer Price Index
- Trends in GDP
- Changes in stock market valuations

Global

- Increasing global trade
- Currency exchange rates
- Emergence of the Indian and Chinese economies
- Trade agreements among regional blocs (e.g., NAFTA, EU, ASEAN)
- Creation of WTO (leading to decreasing tariffs/free trade in services)

strategy spotlight

Americans Are Living Longer . . . and the Funeral Home Industry Is Ailing

It would appear that everyone would welcome the fact that Americans are living longer because of such factors as better health care and nutrition. But this is not good news for one industry: the funeral home industry. The number of Americans who died during the 12 months prior to January 31, 2003, was 2 percent less than the number of Americans who died in the previous 12-month period—which was 5.3 percent less than the previous one-year period. These figures are provided by the Centers for Disease Control.

In addition to a declining death rate, people are spending less on funerals. This is due, in part, to difficult

Source: B. Grow, "What's Killing the Undertakers," *BusinessWeek,* March 24, 2003, p. 16.

economic times as well as the trend toward a stronger preference for cremations—which start at about $2,000, compared to about $5,000 for a coffin and burial. Rather colorfully (at least given the industry), Kenneth Budde claims: "It's killing our margins." Mr. Budde is chief financial officer of Stewart Enterprises in Metarie, Louisiana, the nation's third largest funeral home and cemetery operator. Stewart has reduced its earnings estimates, and Houston's Service Corporation International claims that its sales are down one percent for the year.

Things aren't likely to get better any time soon. According to the Funeral Directors Association and Census Bureau data, U.S. death rates are expected to remain flat until about 2020.

food. Rising levels of affluence in many developed countries bode well for brokerage services, as well as upscale pets and supplies. However, these same trends may have an adverse effect on fast foods because people can afford to dine at higher-priced restaurants. Fast-food restaurants depend on minimum-wage employees to operate efficiently, but the competition for labor intensifies as more attractive employment opportunities become prevalent, thus threatening the employment base for restaurants. Let's look at the details of some of these trends.

The aging of the population in the United States and other developed countries has important implications. With the graying of baby boomers, the demand for homes for "active elders" (as home developers refer to retirees) is bound to soar. The National Association of Home Builders estimates that people in the 55–74 age group will buy 281,000 homes in 2010, up from 189,000 in 1995.[23] This provides an opportunity for developers who focus on that segment of the construction industry. Another long-term projection is that by the year 2025, nearly one-fifth of the American population will be 65 or older. This may be good news for baby boomers, because there is always strength in numbers (especially in the political arena). It's also good news for drugstores, which see older patients seven times more often than younger ones.[24] Strategy Spotlight 2.3 discusses one industry that is clearly not benefiting from the increasing life expectancy of Americans: the funeral home industry.

Another demographic trend is the shift in the geographic population of the United States. Although the population increased by about 13 percent (from 248 million to 281 million) during the 1990s, this growth was not evenly distributed.[25] Strong growth in the South and West—spurred in large part by an increase in the Hispanic population and relocation to economic hot spots such as Atlanta and Las Vegas—was offset by slowing growth in the North and Midwest. The resulting redistribution affects two other environmental segments: the economic well-being of those regions and the political/legal population-based representation in the U.S. House of Representatives.

The Sociocultural Segment

Sociocultural forces influence the values, beliefs, and lifestyles of a society. Examples include a higher percentage of women in the workforce, dual-income families, increases in the number of temporary workers, greater concern for healthy diets and physical fitness, greater interest in the environment, and postponement of having children. Such forces enhance sales of products and services in many industries but depress sales in others. The increased number of women in the workforce has increased the need for business clothing merchandise but decreased the demand for baking product staples (since people would have less time to cook from scratch). A greater concern for health and fitness has had differential effects. This trend has helped industries that manufacture exercise equipment and healthful foods but harmed industries that produce unhealthful foods.

The trend toward increased educational attainment of women in the workplace has led to the increased participation of women in upper management positions. U.S. Department of Education statistics show that women have become the dominant holders of college degrees. Based on figures of a recent graduating class, women with bachelor's degrees will outnumber their male counterparts by 27 percent. By the class of 2006–2007, the gap should surge to 38 percent. Additionally, throughout the 1990s the number of women earning MBAs increased by 29 percent compared to only 15 percent for men.[26] Given these educational attainments, it is hardly surprising that companies owned by women have been one of the key drivers of the U.S. economy; these companies (now more than 9 million in number) account for 40 percent of all U.S. businesses and have generated more than $3.6 trillion in annual revenue.

The Political/Legal Segment

Political processes and legislation influence the environmental regulations with which industries must comply.[27] Some important elements of the political/legal arena include tort reform, the Americans with Disabilities Act (ADA) of 1990, the repeal of the Glass-Steagall Act in 1999 (banks may now offer brokerage services), deregulation of utilities and other industries, and increases in the federally mandated minimum wage.

As with many factors in the general environment, changes that benefit one industry may damage others. For example, tort reform (legislation designed to limit the liability of defendants in the litigation process) may be good for industries such as automobile and tire manufacturers. Witness the litigation associated with Firestone tires and Ford Explorers, for example. However, tort reform will be bad for law firms, whose fees are often linked to the size of a settlement. Many have argued that without significant tort reform, large jury awards are a constant threat to companies and lead to higher consumer prices. On the other hand, the possibility of large judgments influences companies to act in a more ethical manner. The Americans with Disabilities Act has had a profound impact on industries. Companies with more than 15 employees must provide reasonable accommodations for employees and customers, which increases their construction and maintenance costs, but companies manufacturing elevators, escalators, and ramps have benefited from such legislation.

Government legislation can also have a significant impact on the governance of corporations. The U.S. Congress passed the Sarbanes-Oxley Act in 2002, which greatly increases the accountability of auditors, executives, and corporate lawyers. This act was a response to the widespread perception that existing governance mechanisms have failed to protect the interests of shareholders, employees, and creditors. It also helps companies in the high-tech sector of the economy by expanding the number of temporary visas available for highly skilled foreign professionals. For example, a bill passed in October 2000 allows 195,000 H-1B visas in each of the next three years, up from the cap of only 115,000 in

strategy spotlight

Airline Bailout Legislation: A Highly Controversial Political Issue

Recently, the United States government was planning to give the airlines $5 billion in cash and an additional $10 billion in loan guarantees. This has stirred considerable controversy. Some feel that it is Congress's way of paying back the airlines for their soft money contributions. Without government help, many airlines will go bankrupt. But "so what?" ask the critics. They will be reorganized and the profitable flights will continue to be flown—if not by existing carriers, then by new carriers who will step in to fill any breach. All those jumbo jets will still be out there, and as long as enough people want to fly, someone will be flying them.

It is also argued that an airline bailout essentially enriches the millions of people who own airline stocks at the expense of the millions of others who do not. It isn't fair to the taxpayer who will foot the bill and not get a share of the bounty when the airline has a year of windfall profits. There has always been some risk that air travel would reduce dramatically. However, it is one of those risks that the capitalist system can handle. If you are willing to bear the risk, you buy the airline stock; otherwise you buy something else. Risky investments usually yield high returns. The mix of risk and return in airline stocks may be

attractive to some investors. But if the risky industries are bailed out, then both the risk of the stock market investing and the high returns that are associated with it are reduced. This limits the range of options available to everyone. The risk-averse are forced to (through the tax system) bear the very risks they are averse to, and the risk-preferring are prevented from shouldering other people's risk burdens and earning a fair reward for their courage. So what's the argument for bailing out airlines? Is it just payback for political donations or are there significant social benefits from it?

The supporters of the airline industry point out several reasons why the industry should be helped by the government. The decline in air travel, especially by business travelers who pay full fare, was caused by the terrorist attacks of September 2001. Subsequently, a whole host of additional factors, such as the Iraq War, the SARS epidemic, and higher oil prices, did severe damage to the airline industry. These were all environmental developments over which the industry had no control. For example, in March 2003, the Air Transport Association, in making its case for help, claimed that the aviation industry had been hit by a "perfect economic storm" for which it could not be blamed: terrorism, war, high fuel prices, higher security costs, deflation, and a weak economy. Moreover, the airline industry is a basic infrastructure industry. The United States has no alternative comprehensive public transport system. Thus, the traveling public will be greatly hurt by the collapse of the airlines.

Sources: www.airlineinvestigationunit.com/aiu/msn010928.htm; C. Murphy, "A No-Fly Zone," *Fortune*, April 14, 2003, p. 56; E. Torbenson, "The Airlines' DC connection," *Dallas Morning News*, November 17, 2002, p. 1H; and M. Arndt, N. Byrnes, and L. Woellert, "An Airline Bailout—with Strings Attached," *BusinessWeek*, October 8, 2001, p. 17.

2000. The allotment for the year 2000 was used up by March and the cap decreased to 107,500 for 2001 and a mere 65,000 each year thereafter. Almost half of the visas are for professionals from India, and most of them are computer or software specialists.[28] For U.S. labor and workers' rights groups, however, the issue was a political hot potato.

Strategy Spotlight 2.4 discusses the controversy surrounding governmental assistance to ailing airlines.

The Technological Segment

Developments in technology lead to new products and services and improve how they are produced and delivered to the end user. Innovations can create entirely new industries and alter the boundaries of existing industries.[29] Examples of technological developments and trends are genetic engineering, Internet technology, computer-aided design/computer-aided manufacturing (CAD/CAM), research in artificial and exotic materials, and, on the

Sequencing the Human Genome

Researchers are quickly approaching the day when they can identify the "genetic bad actors" that are responsible for conditions from arthritis to Alzheimer's disease. Soon, it is predicted, we will know who has an aptitude for math and who has a low pain threshold. We will understand the way genes have "taught themselves" to develop nervous systems. How soon will this occur?

In 2010 your physician will scan a malignancy to determine the type of cell causing the tumor. Since the genome can be specifically identified, it will take only one round of therapy to fire a "magic bullet" and decimate the tumor. Researchers at the Whitehead Institute in Cambridge, Massachusetts, have already genotyped different forms of leukemia using DNA arrays from Affymetrix of Santa Clara, California.

By 2020 pharmaceutical firms will use vastly different techniques to develop new drugs, according to Joshua Boger, CEO of Vertex Pharmaceuticals. Drugs that are specific to each individual patient's genetic structure will be available for switching off the autoimmune defenses

Source: David Stipp, "From the Book of Life," *Fortune,* March 6, 2000, pp. 22–28.

that plague sufferers of rheumatoid arthritis and lupus. The root cause of psychiatric disorders such as schizophrenia will be known, and pharmaceutical agents will be available to provide complete cures. A host of "lifestyle drugs" will be available to treat the effects of aging, such as slowed metabolism, baldness, and wrinkles.

When we reach 2040, the average life span will exceed 90 years. Antiaging drugs will be on the way, with life insurance companies as major financial contributors to research. We will be clinically testing drugs to enhance IQ and memory. Endangered species will be cryogenically frozen for future reproduction as a backup to prevent extinction. Cardiac cells that have been growing in a laboratory for years will replace yours once age has taken its toll on your heart. As for preventive medicine, some of your biomolecules will be replaced with hardier synthetic molecules to eliminate the possibility of developing a multitude of illnesses.

When you turn 70 and think about the future, you will be faced with a number of new questions—How should you spend the next two decades of your life? A second career? Back to school for another college degree?

downside, pollution and global warming. Firms in the petroleum and primary metals industries incur significant expenses to reduce the amount of pollution they produce. Engineering and consulting firms that work with polluting industries derive financial benefits from solving such problems.

Another important technology development is the combination of information technology (IT) and the Internet. By the end of 2000, productivity in the United States was increasing at an annual rate of 5.7 percent. This represents the fastest pace in 35 years, double the historical average of 2 to 3 percent per year. According to a study conducted jointly by Harvard University and the Federal Reserve, IT is responsible for almost half of the rapid productivity gains in recent years. It has also helped offset the inflationary effects of wage increases.[30]

The Internet has reduced the cost of getting information and increased its availability, boosting company profits. How are these costs reduced? Consider two examples. The National Association of Purchasing Managers pinpoints the cost of an average in-store purchase to be $79. However, Commerce One believes the proper use of the Internet can cut it to $6. Similarly, Fidelity Investments has found that it costs $15 to handle a transaction over the phone, but less than a cent to perform that same transaction on the Web.

Strategy Spotlight 2.5 addresses a fascinating issue—some of the biotechnology miracles that may result from the decoding of the human genome and forecasts for the years 2010, 2020, and 2040.

strategy spotlight

The Relationship between Stock Market Drops and Consumer Spending

The relationship between the performance of a nation's equity markets and its key economic indicators can be dramatic. For example, during the six months following the March 2000 peak of the Nasdaq, investors lost approximately $2 trillion. Economists say that this erosion of wealth will hurt consumer confidence and spending, especially with personal savings in negative territory. With

Source: L. Cohn and D. Lindorff, "Cancel My Boxster: My Portfolio Has Been Pummeled," *BusinessWeek,* October 3, 2000, p. 56.

nearly 50 percent of U.S. households owning stock—a historical high—consumer spending is increasingly tied to the fluctuations of Wall Street. Economists estimate that every $1 gain in stock-market wealth increases consumer spending by 3 to 7 cents after a lag of 12 to 36 months. This phenomenon is known as the "wealth effect."

Not surprisingly, the effect can work in reverse. For example, discretionary spending for big-ticket items like boats and luxury cars is the first to be adversely affected. (Note the *BusinessWeek* source for this Spotlight: "Cancel my Boxster. My portfolio has been pummeled!")

There are downsides to technology. In addition to ethical issues in biotechnology, there are threats to our environment associated with the emission of greenhouse gases. To combat such problems, some firms in the petroleum industry take a proactive approach. BP Amoco plans to decrease its greenhouse gas emissions by giving each of its 150 business units a quota of emission permits and encouraging the units to trade them. If a unit cuts emissions and has leftover permits, it can sell them to other units that are having difficulty in meeting their goals. For example, Julie Hardwick, manager at the Naperville, Illinois, petrochemical division, saved up permits by fast-tracking a furnace upgrade that allowed elimination of a second furnace.[31]

The Economic Segment

The economy has an impact on all industries, from suppliers of raw materials to manufacturers of finished goods and services, as well as all organizations in the service, wholesale, retail, government, and nonprofit sectors. Key economic indicators include interest rates, unemployment rates, the consumer price index, the gross domestic product (GDP), and net disposable income. Interest-rate increases have a negative impact on the residential home construction industry but a negligible (or neutral) effect on industries that produce consumer necessities such as prescription drugs or common grocery items.

Other economic indicators are associated with equity markets. Perhaps the most watched is the Dow Jones Industrial Average (DJIA), which is composed of 30 large industrial firms. When stock market indexes increase, consumers' discretionary income rises and there is often an increased demand for luxury items such as jewelry and automobiles. But when stock valuations decrease, demand for these items shrinks. Strategy Spotlight 2.6 looks at relationships between stock market fluctuations and economic indicators.

Despite the recent mediocre stock market and overall economic performance in the United States, the housing sector continued to be one of the bright spots. This is mainly due to a series of interest rate cuts by the Federal Reserve which, by mid-2003, led to the lowest mortgage rates since World War II.

The Global Segment

There is an increasing trend for firms to expand their operations and market reach beyond the borders of their "home" country. Globalization provides both opportunities to access larger potential markets and a broad base of factors of production such as raw materials, labor, skilled managers, and technical professionals. However, such endeavors also carry many political, social, and economic risks.

Examples of important elements in the global segment include currency exchange rates, increasing global trade, the economic emergence of China, trade agreements among regional blocs (e.g., North American Free Trade Agreement, European Union), and the GATT Agreement (lowering of tariffs). Increases in trade across national boundaries also provide benefits to air cargo and shipping industries but have a minimal impact on service industries such as bookkeeping and routine medical services. The emergence of China as an economic power has benefited many industries, such as construction, soft drinks, and computers. However, it has had a negative impact on the defense industry in the United States as diplomatic relations between the two nations improve.

Few industries are as global as the automobile industry. Consider just a few examples of how some of the key players expanded their reach into Latin America during the 1990s. Fiat built a new plant in Argentina, Volkswagen retooled a plant in Mexico to launch the New Beetle, DaimlerChrysler built a new plant as a joint venture with BMW to produce engines in Brazil, and General Motors built a new car factory in Brazil. Why the interest? In addition to the region's low wage rates and declining trade barriers, the population of 400 million is very attractive. But the real bonus lies in the 9-to-1 ratio of people to cars in the region compared to a 2-to-1 ratio in developed countries. With this region's growth expected to be in the 3 to 4 percent range for the first part of the century, sales should increase at a healthy rate.[32]

The extent of globalization is illustrated by the Norwegian shipping industry. Despite a small population of only 4.5 million, Norway developed the world's third-largest merchant fleet. And as the world's second-largest oil exporter, it has the vessels and equipment needed to service oil fields off its storm-swept coast. When the warship *USS Cole* was severely damaged by terrorists on October 12, 2000, it was returned to the United States from Yemen aboard a giant Norwegian-owned transport ship, the *Blue Marlin*. According to Frederik Steenbuch, manager of Oslo-based Offshore Heavy Transport, which owns the *Blue Marlin:* "This has nothing to do with Norway. It is purely international. The *Blue Marlin* was built in Taiwan, flies a Panamanian flag, and has a crew from Latvia. The key machinery on board was built in Korea under a Danish license."[33]

Relationships among Elements of the General Environment

In our discussion of the general environment, we see many relationships among the various elements.[34] For example, two demographic trends in the United States, the aging of the population and regional population shifts, have important implications for the economic segment (in terms of tax policies to provide benefits to increasing numbers of older citizens) and the political segment (because the redistribution of seats in the U.S. House of Representatives among the states increases the power of some states and reduces the power of others). Another example is the emergence of information technology as a means to increase the rate of productivity gains in the United States and other developed countries. Such use of IT results in lower inflation (an important element of the economic segment) and helps offset costs associated with higher labor rates. Strategy Spotlight 2.7 provides the perspective of Honeywell's CEO, Michael R. Bonsignore.

The effects of a trend or event in the general environment vary across industries. Governmental legislation (political/legal event) to permit the importation of prescription drugs

strategy spotlight

Global Connectivity: For Every Action There Is a Chain Reaction

The following is an excerpt from a speech by Michael R. Bonsignore, former chairman and CEO of Honeywell.

In the new information age, we operate in a matrix. When CEOs make decisions, we do more than initiate a sequence of actions over time. Rather, we witness an immediate exponential result as these actions affect global economic, political, and social relationships. When you turn a Rubik's cube, you're making a single move, but you're also rearranging the pattern of as many as 21 squares. Solving the puzzle requires the ability to see the effect of more than one simple move at a time. Similarly, the better a company is at anticipating the global effects of its actions, the more successful it's likely to be.

One of the great lessons of the 1990s is the realization that while the global economy is interconnected,

it is not a zero-sum game. We have moved from the win-lose paradigm of the industrial age to the win-win paradigm of the information age. The diverse stakeholders trying to solve the problems of the global economy—business, government, special-interest groups—are inextricably connected.

Go back to Rubik's cube for a moment. Imagine each side as a global impact point. Business is the economic engine of the world. Government is the political engine. Technology is the change engine of the world. Culture sets values for society. Trade policy sets the rules of the economic game, and the people of the world (who must be our foremost concern) win or lose depending on our ability to anticipate and understand the effect of our actions.

So, as a CEO charged with leading a global corporation, when I make a decision—when I turn Honeywell's cube—it may be in the best interests of my shareholders, but it could upset a government or conflict with a culture on the other side of the globe.

Source: Michael R. Bonsignore, speech delivered to the Economic Strategy Institute Global Forum 2000, Washington, DC, July 15, 2000.

from foreign countries is a very positive development for drugstores but a very negative event for drug manufacturers in the United States. Exhibit 2.4 provides other examples of how the impact of trends or events in the general environment can vary across industries.

The Competitive Environment

In addition to the general environment, managers must also consider the competitive environment (also sometimes referred to as the task or industry environment). The nature of competition in an industry, as well as the profitability of a firm, is more directly influenced by developments in the competitive environment.

The competitive environment consists of many factors that are particularly relevant to a firm's strategy. These include competitors (existing or potential), customers, and suppliers. Potential competitors may include a supplier considering forward integration, such as an automobile manufacturer acquiring a rental car company, or a firm in an entirely new industry introducing a similar product that uses a more efficient technology.

In the following sections, we will discuss key concepts and analytical techniques that managers should use to assess their competitive environments. First, we examine Michael Porter's five-forces model that illustrates how these forces can be used to explain low profitability in an industry.[35] Then, we address the concept of strategic groups. This concept demonstrates that even within an industry it is often useful to group firms on the basis of similarities of their strategies. As we will see, competition tends to be more intense among firms *within* a strategic group than between strategic groups.

**Exhibit 2.4
The Impact of
General
Environmental
Trends on Various
Industries**

Segment/Trends and Events	Industry	Positive	Neutral	Negative
Demographic				
Aging population	Health care	✓		
	Baby products			✓
Rising affluence	Brokerage services	✓		
	Fast foods			✓
	Upscale pets and supplies	✓		
Sociocultural				
More women in the workforce	Clothing	✓		
	Baking products (staples)			✓
Greater concern for health and fitness	Home exercise equipment	✓		
	Meat products			✓
Political/legal				
Tort reform	Legal services			✓
	Auto manufacturing	✓		
Americans with Disabilities Act (ADA)	Retail			✓
	Manufacturers of elevators, escalators, and ramps	✓		
Technological				
Genetic engineering	Pharmaceutical	✓		
	Publishing		✓	
Pollution/global warming	Engineering services	✓		
	Petroleum			✓
Economic				
Interest rate increases	Residential construction			✓
	Most common grocery products		✓	
Global				
Increasing global trade	Shipping	✓		
	Personal service		✓	
Emergence of China as an economic power	Soft drinks	✓		
	Defense			✓

Porter's Five-Forces Model of Industry Competition

The "five-forces" model developed by Michael E. Porter has been the most commonly used analytical tool for examining the competitive environment. It describes the competitive environment in terms of five basic competitive forces.[36]

1. The threat of new entrants.
2. The bargaining power of buyers.

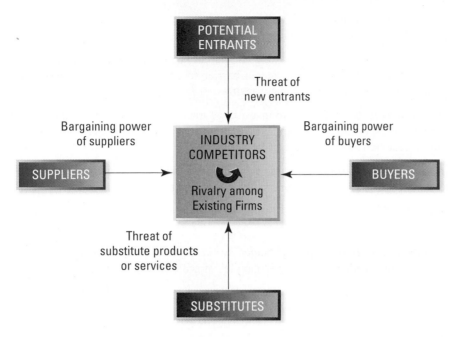

Exhibit 2.5 Porter's Five-Forces Model of Industry Competition

Source: Reprinted with permission of The Free Press, a division of Simon & Schuster Adult Publishing Group, from *Competitive Strategy: Techniques for Analyzing Industries and Competitors* by Michael E. Porter. Copyright © 1980, 1998 by The Free Press. All rights reserved.

3. The bargaining power of suppliers.
4. The threat of substitute products and services.
5. The intensity of rivalry among competitors in an industry.

Each of these forces affects a firm's ability to compete in a given market. Together, they determine the profit potential for a particular industry. The model is shown in Exhibit 2.5. As a manager, you should be familiar with the five-forces model for several reasons. It helps you decide whether your firm should remain in or exit an industry. It provides the rationale for increasing or decreasing resource commitments. The model helps you assess how to improve your firm's competitive position with regard to each of the five forces. For example (and looking ahead a bit), you can use insights provided by the five-forces model to create higher entry barriers that discourage new rivals from competing with you.[37] Or you may develop strong relationships with your distribution channels. You may decide to find suppliers who satisfy the price/performance criteria needed to make your product or service a top performer.

The Threat of New Entrants   The threat of new entrants refers to the possibility that the profits of established firms in the industry may be eroded by new competitors. The extent of the threat depends on existing barriers to entry and the combined reactions from existing competitors. If entry barriers are high and/or the newcomer can anticipate a sharp retaliation from established competitors, the threat of entry is low. These circumstances discourage new competitors. There are six major sources of entry barriers:

Economies of Scale   Economies of scale refers to spreading the costs of production over the number of units produced. The cost of a product per unit declines as the absolute volume per period increases. This deters entry by forcing the entrant to come in at a large scale and risk strong reaction from existing firms or come in at a small scale and accept a cost disadvantage. Both are undesirable options.

Product Differentiation   When existing competitors have strong brand identification and customer loyalty, differentiation creates a barrier to entry by forcing entrants to spend heavily to overcome existing customer loyalties.

Capital Requirements   The need to invest large financial resources to compete creates a barrier to entry, especially if the capital is required for risky or unrecoverable up-front advertising or research and development (R&D).

Switching Costs   A barrier to entry is created by the existence of one-time costs that the buyer faces when switching from one supplier's product or service to another.

Access to Distribution Channels   The new entrant's need to secure distribution for its product can create a barrier to entry.

Cost Disadvantages Independent of Scale   Some existing competitors may have advantages that are independent of size or economies of scale. These derive from:

- Proprietary product
- Favorable access to raw materials
- Government subsidies
- Favorable government policies

In an environment where few, or none, of these entry barriers are present, the threat of new entry is high. For example, if a new firm can launch its business with a low capital investment and operate efficiently despite its small scale of operation, it is likely to be a threat. One company that failed because of low entry barriers in an industry is ProCD.[38] You probably never heard of this company. It didn't last very long. ProCD provides an example of a firm that failed because it entered an industry with very low entry barriers.

The story begins in 1986 when Nynex (a Baby Bell company) issued the first electronic phone book, a compact disk containing all listings for the New York City area. It charged $10,000 per copy and sold the CDs to the FBI, IRS, and other large commercial and government organizations. James Bryant, the Nynex executive in charge of the project, smelled a fantastic business opportunity. He quit Nynex and set up his own firm, ProCD, with the ambitious goal of producing an electronic directory covering the entire United States.

As expected, the telephone companies, fearing an attack on their highly profitable Yellow Pages business, refused to license digital copies of their listings to this upstart. Bryant was not deterred. He traveled to Beijing and hired Chinese workers at $3.50 a day to type every listing from every U.S. telephone book into a database. The result contained more than 70 million phone numbers and was used to create a master disk that enabled ProCD to make hundreds of thousands of copies. Each CD sold for hundreds of dollars and cost less than a dollar each to produce.

A profitable business indeed! However, success was fleeting. Competitors such as Digital Directory Assistance and American Business Information quickly launched competing products with the same information. Since customers couldn't tell one product from the next, the players were forced to compete on price alone. Prices for the CD soon plummeted to a few dollars each. A high-priced, high-margin product just months earlier, the CD phone book became little more than a cheap commodity.

The Bargaining Power of Buyers   Buyers threaten an industry by forcing down prices, bargaining for higher quality or more services, and playing competitors against each other. These actions erode industry profitability.[39] The power of each large buyer group depends on attributes of the market situation and the importance of purchases from that group compared with the industry's overall business. A buyer group is powerful under the following conditions:

- *It is concentrated or purchases large volumes relative to seller sales.* If a large percentage of a supplier's sales are purchased by a single buyer, the importance of the buyer's business to the supplier increases. Large-volume buyers also are powerful in industries with high fixed costs (e.g., steel manufacturing).
- *The products it purchases from the industry are standard or undifferentiated.* Confident they can always find alternative suppliers, buyers play one company against the other, as in commodity grain products.
- *The buyer faces few switching costs.* Switching costs lock the buyer to particular sellers. Conversely, the buyer's power is enhanced if the seller faces high switching costs.
- *It earns low profits.* Low profits create incentives to lower purchasing costs. On the other hand, highly profitable buyers are generally less price sensitive.
- *The buyers pose a credible threat of backward integration.* If buyers are either partially integrated or pose a credible threat of backward integration, they are typically able to secure bargaining concessions.
- *The industry's product is unimportant to the quality of the buyer's products or services.* When the quality of the buyer's products is not affected by the industry's product, the buyer is more price sensitive.

At times, a firm or set of firms in an industry may increase its buyer power by using the services of a third party. FreeMarkets Online is one such third party.[40] Pittsburgh-based FreeMarkets has developed software enabling large industrial buyers to organize online auctions for qualified suppliers of semistandard parts such as fabricated components, packaging materials, metal stampings, and services. By aggregating buyers, FreeMarkets increases the buyers' bargaining power. The results are impressive. In its first 48 auctions, most participating companies saved over 15 percent; some saved as much as 50 percent. Exhibit 2.6 provides some examples of how much money some companies have saved by using FreeMarkets' auctions.

The Bargaining Power of Suppliers   Suppliers can exert bargaining power over participants in an industry by threatening to raise prices or reduce the quality of purchased goods and services. Powerful suppliers can squeeze the profitability of firms in an

**Exhibit 2.6
What Buyers Have Saved on FreeMarkets' Auctions**

Item	Buyer	Expected Outlay (in millions)	Actual Outlay (in millions)	Savings (%)
Semiconductors, metal stampings, etc.	Delpi Automotive	$420 (yearly total)	$360	14
Aluminum	Commonwealth of Pennsylvania	$ 2.8	$ 2.5	9
Packing materials, etc.	Owens Corning	$129 (yearly total)	$120	7
Circuit boards	United Technologies	$ 74	$ 42	43

Source: From Shawn Tully, "Going, Going, Gone: The B2B Tool That Really is Changing the World." *Fortune*, March 20, 2000. © 2000 Time Inc. All rights reserved.

industry so far that they can't recover the costs of raw material inputs.[41] The factors that make suppliers powerful tend to mirror those that make buyers powerful. A supplier group will be powerful in the following circumstances:

◆ ***The supplier group is dominated by a few companies and is more concentrated (few firms dominate the industry) than the industry it sells to.*** Suppliers selling from fragmented industries influence prices, quality, and terms.

◆ ***The supplier group is not obliged to contend with substitute products for sale to the industry.*** The power of even large, powerful suppliers can be checked if they compete with substitutes.

◆ ***The industry is not an important customer of the supplier group.*** When suppliers sell to several industries and a particular industry does not represent a significant fraction of its sales, suppliers are more prone to exert power.

◆ ***The supplier's product is an important input to the buyer's business.*** When such inputs are important to the success of the buyer's manufacturing process or product quality, the bargaining power of suppliers is high.

◆ ***The supplier group's products are differentiated or it has built up switching costs for the buyer.*** Differentiation or switching costs facing the buyers cut off their options to play one supplier against another.

◆ ***The supplier group poses a credible threat of forward integration.*** This provides a check against the industry's ability to improve the terms by which it purchases.

When considering supplier power, we focus on companies that supply raw materials, equipment, machinery, and associated services. But the supply of labor is also an important input to businesses, and labor's power varies over time and across occupations and industries. As we enter the 21st century, the outlook is not very good for semiskilled and unskilled laborers. Annual wage gains before inflation is taken into account—typically a good measure of workers' bargaining clout in the labor market—have remained in the 3 percent range for much of the 1990s.[42] When the CPI averaged around 2 percent, that provided employees with pay increases that exceeded inflation. With higher consumer prices, however, real wage gains (wage increases above the inflation rate) have been virtually nonexistent recently.

Workers with the right skills and jobs have enjoyed the spoils of the New Economy and will likely continue to do so. However, many other employees face the same forces that kept wages flat in the early 1990s: high immigration, deunionization, and globalization. For example, steel imports surged in 2000, threatening the jobs of many U.S. steelworkers. Not surprisingly, members of the United Steel Workers (USW) have been forced to accept below-inflation pay increases. On September 1, 2000, 900 USW members at AK Steel Corp.'s Ashland, Kentucky, facility approved a pay hike of only 2.6 percent a year for the next five years. Said Roy Murray, a USW official, "We didn't want to be out there demanding more money when the industry is on its heels."

The Threat of Substitute Products and Services   All firms within an industry compete with industries producing substitute products and services. Substitutes limit the potential returns of an industry by placing a ceiling on the prices that firms in that industry can profitably charge. The more attractive the price/performance ratio of substitute products, the tighter the lid on an industry's profits.

Identifying substitute products involves searching for other products or services that can perform the same function as the industry's offerings. This is a subtle task, one that leads a manager into businesses seemingly far removed from the industry. For example, the airline industry might not consider video cameras much of a threat. But as digital technology has improved and wireless and other forms of telecommunication have become more efficient, teleconferencing has become a viable substitute for business travel for many executives.

Teleconferencing can save both time and money, as IBM found out with its "Manager Jam" idea.[43] Currently, with 319,000 employees scattered around six continents, it is one of the world's largest businesses (including 32,000 managers) and can be a pretty confusing place. The shift to an increasingly mobile workplace means many managers supervise employees they rarely see face-to-face. To enhance coordination, Samuel Palmisano, IBM's new CEO, launched one of his first big initiatives: a two-year program exploring the role of the manager in the 21st century. "Manager Jam," as the project was nicknamed, was a 48-hour real-time Web event in which managers from 50 different countries swapped ideas and strategies for dealing with problems shared by all of them, regardless of geography. Some 8,100 managers logged on to the company's intranet to participate in the discussion forums.

The Intensity of Rivalry among Competitors in an Industry   Rivalry among existing competitors takes the form of jockeying for position. Firms use tactics like price competition, advertising battles, product introductions, and increased customer service or warranties. Rivalry occurs when competitors sense the pressure or act on an opportunity to improve their position.

Some forms of competition, such as price competition, are typically highly destabilizing and are likely to erode the average level of profitability in an industry. Rivals easily match price cuts, an action that lowers profits for all firms. On the other hand, advertising battles expand overall demand or enhance the level of product differentiation for the benefit of all firms in the industry. Rivalry, of course, differs across industries. In some instances it is characterized as warlike, bitter, or cutthroat, whereas in other industries it is referred to as polite and gentlemanly. Intense rivalry is the result of several interacting factors, including the following:

- *Numerous or equally balanced competitors.* When there are many firms in an industry, the likelihood of mavericks is great. Some firms believe they can make moves without being noticed. Even when there are relatively few firms, and they are nearly equal in size and resources, instability results from fighting among companies having the resources for sustained and vigorous retaliation.
- *Slow industry growth.* Slow industry growth turns competition into a fight for market share, since firms seek to expand their sales.
- *High fixed or storage costs.* High fixed costs create strong pressures for all firms to increase capacity. Excess capacity often leads to escalating price cutting.
- *Lack of differentiation or switching costs.* Where the product or service is perceived as a commodity or near commodity, the buyer's choice is typically based on price and service, resulting in pressures for intense price and service competition. Lack of switching costs, described earlier, has the same effect.
- *Capacity augmented in large increments.* Where economies of scale require that capacity must be added in large increments, capacity additions can be very disruptive to the industry supply/demand balance.
- *High exit barriers.* Exit barriers are economic, strategic, and emotional factors that keep firms competing even though they may be earning low or negative returns on their investments. Some exit barriers are specialized assets, fixed costs of exit, strategic interrelationships (e.g., relationships between the business units and others within a company in terms of image, marketing, shared facilities, and so on), emotional barriers, and government and social pressures (e.g., governmental discouragement of exit out of concern for job loss).

Rivalry between firms is often based solely on price, but it can involve other factors. Take Pfizer's market position in the impotence treatment market. Pfizer was the first pharmaceutical firm to develop Viagra, a drug that treats impotence. International sales of Viagra were $332 million during a recent quarter. There are currently 30 million prescriptions for the drug. Pfizer would like to keep competitors from challenging this lucrative position.

In several countries, the United Kingdom among them, Pfizer faced a lawsuit by Eli Lilly & Co. and Icos Corp. challenging its patent protection. These two pharmaceutical firms recently entered into a joint venture to market Cialis, a drug to compete with Viagra. The U.K. courts agreed and lifted the patent.

This opened the door for Eli Lilly and Icos to proceed with challenging Pfizer's market position. Because Cialis has fewer side effects than Viagra, the drug has the potential to rapidly decrease Pfizer's market share in the United Kingdom—if physicians switch prescriptions from Viagra to Cialis. If future patent challenges are successful, Pfizer may see its sales of Viagra erode rapidly. With projected annual sales of Cialis of $1 billion, Pfizer has reason to worry. With FDA approval, sales of Cialis could cause those of Viagra to plummet in the United States, further eroding Pfizer's market share.[44] But Pfizer is hardly standing still. It recently doubled its advertising expenditures on Viagra.

Using Industry Analyses: A Few Caveats   For industry analyses to be valuable, a company must collect and evaluate a wide variety of information from many sources. As the trend toward globalization accelerates, information on foreign markets as well as on a wider variety of competitors, suppliers, customers, substitutes, and potential new entrants becomes more critical. Industry analysis helps a firm not only to evaluate the profit potential of an industry, but also to consider various ways to strengthen its position vis-à-vis the five forces.

Five-forces analysis implicitly assumes a zero-sum game, determining how a firm can enhance its position relative to the forces. Yet such an approach can often be shortsighted; that is, it can overlook the many potential benefits of developing constructive win–win relationships with suppliers and customers. Establishing long-term mutually beneficial relationships with suppliers improves a firm's ability to implement just-in-time (JIT) inventory systems, which let it manage inventories better and respond quickly to market demands. A recent study found that if a company exploits its powerful position against a supplier, that action may come back to haunt the company if the position of power changes.[45] Further, by working together as partners, suppliers and manufacturers can provide the greatest value at the lowest possible cost. Later chapters address such collaborative relationships and how they can be made most effective.

The five-forces analysis has also been criticized for being essentially a static analysis. External forces as well as strategies of individual firms are continually changing the structure of all industries. The search for a dynamic theory of strategy has led to greater use of game theory in industrial organization economics research and strategy research. Based on game-theoretic considerations, Brandenburger and Nalebuff recently introduced the concept of the value net,[46] which in many ways is an extension of the five-forces analysis. It is illustrated in Exhibit 2.7. The value net represents all the players in the game and analyzes how their interactions affect a firm's ability to generate and appropriate value. The vertical dimension of the net includes suppliers and customers. The firm has direct transactions with them. On the horizontal dimension are substitutes and complementors, players with whom a firm interacts, but may not necessarily transact. The concept of complementors is perhaps the single most important contribution of value net analysis and hence is explained in more detail in the next paragraph.

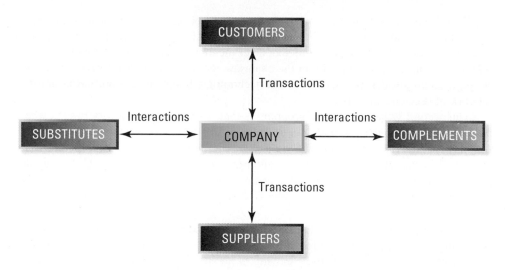

Exhibit 2.7 The Value Net

Source: Adapted and reprinted by permission of Harvard Business Review, exhibit from "The Right Game: Use Game Theory to Shape Strategy," by A. Brandenburger and B. J. Nalebuff, July–August 1995. Copyright © 1995 by the Harvard Business School Publishing Corporation. All rights reserved.

Complementors typically are products or services that have a potential impact on the value of a firm's own products or services. Those who produce complements are usually referred to as complementors. Powerful hardware is of no value to a user unless there is software that runs on it. Similarly, new and better software is possible only if the hardware on which it can be run is available. This is equally true in the video game industry, where the sales of game consoles and video games complement each other. Nintendo's success in the early 1990s was a result of their ability to manage their relationship with their complementors. They built a security chip into the hardware and then licensed the right to develop games to outside firms. These firms paid a royalty to Nintendo for each copy of the game sold. The royalty revenue enabled Nintendo to sell game consoles at close to their cost, thereby increasing their market share, which in turn caused more games to be sold and more royalties to be generated.

Strategic Groups within Industries

In an industry analysis, two assumptions are unassailable: (1) No two firms are totally different and (2) no two firms are exactly the same. The issue becomes one of identifying groups of firms that are more similar to each other than firms that are not, otherwise known as strategic groups.[47] This is important because rivalry tends to be greater among firms that are alike. Strategic groups are clusters of firms that share similar strategies. After all, is Kmart more concerned about Nordstrom or Wal-Mart? Is Mercedes more concerned about Hyundai or BMW? The answers are straightforward.[48]

These examples are not meant to trivialize the strategic groups concept. Classifying an industry into strategic groups involves judgment. If it is useful as an analytical tool, one must exercise caution in deciding what dimensions to use to map these firms. Dimensions include breadth of product and geographic scope, price/quality, degree of vertical integration, type of distribution (e.g., dealers, mass merchandisers, private label), and so on. Dimensions should also be selected to reflect the variety of strategic combinations in an industry. For example, if all firms in an industry have roughly the same level of product differentiation (or R&D intensity), this would not be a good dimension to select.

What value is the strategic groups concept as an analytical tool? First, strategic groupings help a firm identify barriers to mobility that protect a group from attacks by other groups.[49] Mobility barriers are factors that deter the movement of firms from one strategic position to another. For example, in the chainsaw industry, the major barriers protecting the high-quality/dealer-oriented group are technology, brand image, and an established network of servicing dealers.

The second value of strategic grouping is that it helps a firm identify groups whose competitive position may be marginal or tenuous. One may anticipate that these competitors may exit the industry or try to move into another group. This has been the case in recent years in the retail department store industry, where firms such as J. C. Penney and Sears have experienced extremely difficult times because they were stuck in the middle, neither an aggressive discount player like Wal-Mart nor a prestigious upscale player like Neiman Marcus.

Third, strategic groupings help chart the future directions of firms' strategies. Arrows emanating from each strategic group can represent the direction in which the group (or a firm within the group) seems to be moving. If all strategic groups are moving in a similar direction, this could indicate a high degree of future volatility and intensity of competition. In the automobile industry, for example, the competition in the minivan and sport utility segments has intensified in recent years as many firms have entered those product segments.

Fourth, strategic groups are helpful in thinking through the implications of each industry trend for the strategic group as a whole. Is the trend decreasing the viability of a group? If so, in what direction should the strategic group move? Is the trend increasing or decreasing entry barriers in a given group? Will the trend decrease the ability of one group to separate itself from other groups? Such analysis can help in making predictions about industry evolution. A sharp increase in interest rates, for example, would tend to have less impact on providers of higher-priced goods (e.g., Porsches) than on providers of lower-priced goods (e.g., Dodge Neons). The Dodge Neon customer base is much more price sensitive.

Exhibit 2.8 provides a strategic grouping of the worldwide automobile industry.[50] The firms in each group are representative; not all firms are included in the mapping. We have identified four strategic groups. In the top left-hand corner are high-end luxury automakers who focus on a very narrow product market. Most of the cars produced by the members of this group cost well over $100,000. Some cost many times that amount. The Ferrari F50 costs roughly $550,000 and the Lamborghini L147 $300,000[51] (in case you were wondering how to spend your employment signing bonus). Players in this market have a very exclusive clientele and face little rivalry from other strategic groups. At the other extreme, in the lower left-hand corner is a strategic group that has low-price/quality attributes and targets a narrow market. These players, Hyundai and Kia, limit competition from other strategic groups by pricing their products very low. The third group (near the middle) consists of firms high in product pricing/quality and average in their product-line breadth. The final group (at the far right) consists of firms with a broad range of products and multiple price points. These firms have entries that compete at both the lower end of the market (e.g., the Ford Focus) and the higher end (e.g., Chevrolet Corvette).

The auto market has been very dynamic and competition has intensified in recent years. Many firms in different strategic groups compete in the same product markets, such as minivans and sport utility vehicles. In the late 1990s Mercedes entered the fray with its M series, and Porsche now has an entry as well with its Cayenne, a 2004 model. Some players are also going more upscale with their product offerings. Recently, Hyundai intro-

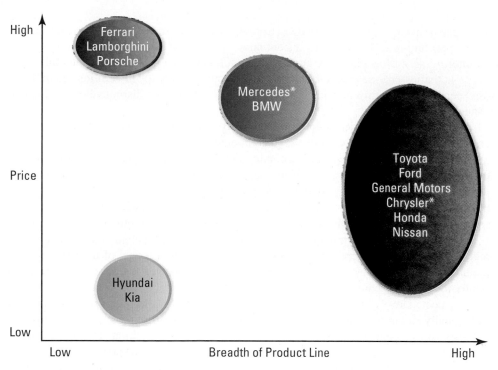

Exhibit 2.8 The World Automobile Industry: Strategic Groups

* Chrysler and Mercedes (part of DaimlerChrysler) are separated for purposes of illustration.

Note: Members of each strategic group are not inclusive, only illustrative.

duced its XG300, priced at over $25,000 for a fully loaded model. This brings Hyundai into direct competition with entries from other strategic groups—Toyota's Camry and Honda's Accord, for example. Hyundai is offering an extensive warranty (ten years, 100,000 miles) in an effort to offset customer perceptions of their lower quality. Perhaps Ford has made the most notable efforts to go upscale. Not content to rely solely on the Lincoln nameplate to attract high-ticket buyers, Ford, like other large players, has gone on an acquisition binge. It recently acquired Volvo, Land Rover, Jaguar, and Aston Martin. Ford is aggressively accelerating its forecasted sales for each of these brands.[52] To further intensify competition, some key automakers are providing offerings in lower-priced segments. Mercedes and BMW, with their C-class and 3-series, respectively, are well-known examples. Such cars, priced in the low $30,000s, compete more directly with products from broad-line manufacturers like Ford, General Motors, and Toyota.

These new products are competing in an industry that has experienced relatively flat sales in the early part of this decade. U.S passenger car and truck volume should be only 16.9 million units in 2004—which is only slightly up from the 16.5 million units in 2003. Overall, such figures represent a slight decline from the 16.8 million units in 2002 and the 17.4 million units in 1999.[53] In addition, high-incentive–laden offerings appear to be losing some of their appeal to consumers, and there are higher levels of inventory at dealerships. Further, since manufacturers have maintained, if not increased, production schedules, overall competition should intensify. Don't be surprised, therefore, if rebates and discounting continue on most models.

summary

Managers must analyze the external environment to minimize or eliminate threats and exploit opportunities. This involves a continuous process of environmental scanning and monitoring as well as obtaining competitive intelligence on present and potential rivals. These activities provide valuable inputs for developing forecasts. In addition, many firms use scenario planning to anticipate and respond to volatile and disruptive environmental changes.

We identified two types of environment: the general environment and the competitive environment. The six segments of the general environment are demographic, sociocultural, political/legal, technological, economic, and global. Trends and events occurring in these segments, such as the aging of the population, higher percentages of women in the workplace, governmental legislation, and increasing (or decreasing) interest rates, can have a dramatic effect on your firm. A given trend or event may have a positive impact on some industries and a negative or neutral impact or none at all on others.

The competitive environment consists of industry-related factors and has a more direct impact than the general environment. Porter's five-forces model of industry analysis includes the threat of new entrants, buyer power, supplier power, threat of substitutes, and rivalry among competitors. The intensity of these factors determines, in large part, the average expected level of profitability in an industry. A sound awareness of such factors, both individually and in combination, is beneficial not only for deciding what industries to enter but also for assessing how a firm can improve its competitive position. The limitations of five-forces analysis include its static nature and its inability to acknowledge the role of complementors. Although we discussed the general environment and competitive environment in separate sections, they are quite interdependent. A given environmental trend or event, such as changes in the ethnic composition of a population or a technological innovation, typically has a much greater impact on some industries than on others.

The concept of strategic groups is also important to the external environment of a firm. No two organizations are completely different nor are they exactly the same. The question is how to group firms in an industry on the basis of similarities in their resources and strategies. The strategic groups concept is valuable for determining mobility barriers across groups, identifying groups with marginal competitive positions, charting the future directions of firm strategies, and assessing the implications of industry trends for the strategic group as a whole.

summary review questions

1. Why must managers be aware of a firm's external environment?

2. What is gathering and analyzing competitive intelligence and why is it important for firms to engage in it?

3. Discuss and describe the six elements of the external environment.

4. Select one of these elements and describe some changes relating to it in an industry that interests you.

5. Describe how the five forces can be used to determine the average expected profitability in an industry.

6. What are some of the limitations (or caveats) in using five-forces analysis?

7. Explain how the general environment and industry environment are highly related. How can such interrelationships affect the profitability of a firm or industry?

8. Explain the concept of strategic groups. What are the performance implications?

Select one of the following industries: personal computers, airlines, or automobiles. For this industry, evaluate the strength of each of Porter's five forces as well as complementors.

Industry Force	High? Medium? Low?	Why?
1. Threat of new entrants		
2. Power of buyers		
3. Power of suppliers		
4. Power of substitutes		
5. Rivalry among competitors		
6. Complementors		

1. Imagine yourself as the CEO of a large firm in an industry in which you are interested. Please (1) identify major trends in the general environment, (2) analyze their impact on the firm, and (3) identify major sources of information to monitor these trends. (Use Internet and library resources.)
2. Analyze movements across the strategic groups in the U.S. retail industry. How do these movements within this industry change the nature of competition?
3. What are the major trends in the general environment that have impacted the U.S. pharmaceutical industry?
4. Go to the Internet and look up www.kroger.com. What are some of the five forces driving industry competition that are affecting the profitability of this firm?

1. What are some of the legal and ethical issues involved in collecting competitor intelligence in the following situations?
   a. Hotel A sends an employee posing as a potential client to Hotel B to find out who Hotel B's major corporate customers are.
   b. A firm hires an MBA student to collect information directly from a competitor while claiming the information is for a course project.
   c. A firm advertises a nonexistent position and interviews a rival's employees with the intention of obtaining competitor information.
2. What are some of the ethical implications that arise when a firm tries to exploit its power over a supplier?

references

1. Crockett, R. O., & Reinhardt, A., 2003, Can Mike Z work more magic at Motorola? *BusinessWeek,* April 14: 58–60; Crockett, R. O., 2001, Motorola, *BusinessWeek,* July 16: 73–78; Cusumano, M., Finkelstein, S., & Sanford, S. H., 2000, Learning from corporate mistakes: The rise and fall of Iridium, *Organizational Dynamics* 29 (2): 138–48; Roth, D., 1998, Burying Motorola, *Fortune,* July 6: 28–29; and Doz, Y. L., dos Santos, J. F. P., & Williamson, P. J., 2002, The metanational advantage, *Optimize Magazine,* May: 16–20.

2. Hamel, G., & Prahalad, C. K., 1994, *Competing for the Future* (Boston: Harvard Business School Press).

3. Drucker, P. F., 1994, Theory of the business, *Harvard Business Review* 72:95–104.

4. The examples of Novell and Silicon Graphics draw on Pickering, C. I., 1998, Sorry . . . Try again next year, *Forbes ASAP,* February 23: 82–83.

5. For an insightful discussion on managers' assessment of the external environment, refer to Sutcliffe, K. M., & Weber, K., 2003, The high cost of accurate knowledge, *Harvard Business Review* 81 (5): 74–86.

6. Charitou, C. D., & Markides, C. C., 2003, Responses to disruptive strategic innovation, *MIT Sloan Management Review* 44 (2): 55–64.

7. Our discussion of scanning, monitoring, competitive intelligence, and forecasting concepts draws on several sources. These include Fahey, L., & Narayanan, V. K., 1983, *Macroenvironmental Analysis for Strategic Management* (St. Paul, MN: West); Lorange, P., Scott, F. S., & Ghoshal, S., 1986, *Strategic Control* (St. Paul, MN: West); Ansoff, H. I., 1984, *Implementing Strategic Management* (Englewood Cliffs, NJ: Prentice Hall); and Schreyogg, G., & Stienmann, H., 1987, Strategic control: A new perspective, *Academy of Management Review* 12: 91–103.

8. Elenkov, D. S., 1997, Strategic uncertainty and environmental scanning: The case for institutional influences on scanning behavior, *Strategic Management Journal* 18: 287–302.

9. For an interesting perspective on environmental scanning in emerging economies, see May, R. C., Stewart, W. H., & Sweo, R., 2000, Environmental scanning behavior in a transitional economy: Evidence from Russia, *Academy of Management Journal* 43 (3): 403–27.

10. Browne, Sir John, The new agenda, Keynote speech delivered to the World Petroleum Congress in Calgary, Canada, June 13, 2000.

11. Bowles, J., 1997, Key issues for the automotive industry CEOs, *Fortune,* August 18: S3.

12. Walters, B. A., & Priem, R. L., 1999, Business strategy and CEO intelligence acquisition, *Competitive Intelligence Review* 10 (2): 15–22.

13. Prior, V., 1999, The language of competitive intelligence, Part 4, *Competitive Intelligence Review* 10 (1): 84–87.

14. Zahra, S. A., & Charples, S. S., 1993, Blind spots in competitive analysis, *Academy of Management Executive* 7 (2): 7–27.

15. Wolfenson, J., 1999, The world in 1999: A battle for corporate honesty, *Economist* 38: 13–30.

16. Drucker, P. F., 1997, The future that has already happened, *Harvard Business Review* 75 (6): 22.

17. Evans, P. B., & Wurster, T. S., 1997, Strategy and the new economics of information, *Harvard Business Review* 75 (5): 71–82.

18. Fahey & Narayanan, op. cit., p. 41.

19. Courtney, H., Kirkland, J., & Viguerie, P., 1997, Strategy under uncertainty, *Harvard Business Review* 75 (6): 66–79.

20. Odlyzko, A., 2003, False hopes, *Red Herring,* March: 31.

21. Dean, T. J., Brown, R. L., & Bamford, C. E., 1998, Differences in large and small firm responses to environmental context: Strategic implications from a comparative analysis of business formations. *Strategic Management Journal* 19: 709–28.

22. Colvin, G., 1997, How to beat the boomer rush, *Fortune,* August 18: 59–63.

23. Grant, P., 2000, Developing plans to serve a graying population, *Wall Street Journal,* October 18: B12.

24. Walgreens, Inc., 2000, annual report, 20.

25. Armas, G. C., 2000, Census figures point to changes in Congress, washingtonpost.com/wpdyn/articles/A58952 Dec28.html.

26. Challenger, J., 2000, Women's corporate rise has reduced relocations, *Lexington* (KY) *Herald-Leader,* October 29: D1.

27. Watkins, M. D., 2003, Government games, *MIT Sloan Management Review* 44 (2): 91–95.

28. Davies, A., 2000, The welcome mat is out for nerds, *BusinessWeek,* October 16: 64.

29. Business ready for Internet revolution, 1999, *Financial Times,* May 21: 17.

30. The Internet example draws on Bernasek, A., 2000, How the broadband adds up, *Fortune,* October 9: 28, 30; and Kromer, E., B2B or not B2B? *UW Alumni Magazine:* 10–19.

31. Ginsburg, J., 2000, Letting the free market clear the air, *BusinessWeek,* November 6: 200, 204.

32. Smith, G., Wheatley, J., & Green, J., 2000, Car power, *BusinessWeek,* October 23: 72–80.

33. Mellgren, D., 2000, Norwegian ships relied on in global disasters, *Lexington* (KY) *Herald-Leader,* November 6: A8.

34. Goll, I., & Rasheed, M. A., 1997, Rational decision-making and firm performance: The moderating role of environment, *Strategic Management Journal* 18: 583–91.

35. This discussion draws heavily on Porter, M. E., 1980, *Competitive Strategy* (New York: Free Press), (chap. 1).

36. Ibid.

37. Fryer, B., 2001, Leading through rough times: An interview with Novell's Eric Schmidt, *Harvard Business Review* 78 (5): 117–23.

38. The ProCD example draws heavily upon Shapiro, C., & Varian, H. R., 2000, Versioning: The smart way to sell information, *Harvard Business Review* 78 (1): 106–14.

39. Wise, R., & Baumgarter, P., 1999, Go downstream: The new profit imperative in manufacturing, *Harvard Business Review* 77 (5): 133–41.

40. Salman, W. A., 2000, The new economy is stronger than you think, *Harvard Business Review* 77 (6): 99–106.

41. Mudambi, R., & Helper, S., 1998, The "close but adversarial" model of supplier relations in the U.S. auto industry, *Strategic Management Journal* 19: 775–92.

42. Bernstein, A., 2000, Workers are doing well, but will it last? *BusinessWeek,* October 9: 48.

43. Tischler, L., 2002, IBM: Manager Jam, *Fast Company,* October: 48.

44. Marcial, G., 2000, Giving Viagra a run for its money, *BusinessWeek,* October 23: 173.

45. Kumar, N., 1996, The power of trust in manufacturer-retailer relationship, *Harvard Business Review* 74 (6): 92–110.

46. Brandenburger, A., & Nalebuff, B. J., 1995, The right game: Use game theory to shape strategy, *Harvard Business Review* 73 (4): 57–71.

47. Peteraf, M., & Shanly, M., 1997, Getting to know you: A theory of strategic group identity, *Strategic Management Journal* 18 (Special Issue): 165–86.

48. An interesting scholarly perspective on strategic groups may be found in Dranove, D., Perteraf, M., & Shanly, M., 1998, Do strategic groups exist? An economic framework for analysis, *Strategic Management Journal* 19 (11): 1029–44.

49. This section draws on several sources, including Kerwin, K. R., & Haughton, K., 1997, Can Detroit make cars that baby boomers like? *BusinessWeek,* December 1: 134–48; and Taylor, A., III, 1994, The new golden age of autos, *Fortune,* April 4: 50–66.

50. Csere, C., 2001, Supercar supermarket, *Car and Driver,* January: 118–27.

51. Healey, J. R., 1999, Groomed so as not to marry, *USA Today,* August 6: B1.

52. Csere, op. cit.

53. Flint, J., 2003, The outlook for 2003, www.forbes.com, October 28.

chapter 3

Assessing the Internal Environment of the Firm

chapter objectives

*After
reading this
chapter, you should
have a good understanding of:*

- The benefits and limitations of SWOT analysis in conducting an internal analysis of the firm.

- The primary and support activities of a firm's value chain.

- How value-chain analysis can help managers create value by investigating relationships among activities within the firm and between the firm and its customers and suppliers.

- The resource-based view of the firm and the different types of tangible and intangible resources, as well as organizational capabilities.

- The four criteria that a firm's resources must possess to maintain a sustainable advantage and how value created can be appropriated by employees.

- The usefulness of financial ratio analysis, its inherent limitations, and how to make meaningful comparisons of performance across firms.

- The value of recognizing how the interests of a variety of stakeholders can be interrelated.

*t*wo firms compete in the same industry and both have many strengths in a variety of functional areas: marketing, operations, logistics, and so on. However, one of these firms outperforms the other by a wide margin over a long period of time. How can this be so? This chapter endeavors to answer that question.

We begin with two sections that include frameworks for gaining key insights into a firm's internal environment: value-chain analysis and the resource-based view of the firm. In value-chain analysis, we divide a firm's activities into a series of value-creating steps. We then explore how individual activities within the firm add value, and also how *interrelationships* among activities within the firm, and between the firm and its suppliers and customers, create value.

In the resource-based view of the firm, we analyze the firm as a collection of tangible and intangible resources as well as organizational capabilities. Advantages that tend to be sustainable over time typically arise from creating *bundles* of resources and capabilities that satisfy four criteria: they are valuable, rare, difficult to imitate, and difficult to substitute. Not all of the value created by a firm will necessarily be kept (or appropriated) by the owners. We discuss the four key factors that determine how profits will be distributed between owners and employees.

In the closing sections, we discuss how to evaluate a firm's performance and make comparisons across firms. We emphasize both the inclusion of financial resources and the interests of multiple stakeholders. Central to our discussion of this concept is the balanced scorecard, which recognizes that the interests of different stakeholders can be interrelated. We also consider how a firm's performance evolves over time as well as how it compares with industry norms and key competitors.

Oracle is a giant database and applications software company with annual revenues of $10 billion. However, it seems to have earned the wrath of the customers more than anybody in its industry. Oracle has made quite a name for itself with its aggressive sales tactics, "bug-laden" software, and poor customer service. Today, customers are not sure whether they can trust this aggressive seller. What went wrong?[1]

Oracle has a long history of aggressive selling. Its salespeople go to nearly any extent to make a deal. Establishing personal relationships with executives who make purchasing decisions in companies, slipping personal notes under the front door of a prospective customer's home, and offering airport rides to CEOs for just an opportunity to talk are just a small part of the story. Oracle salespeople go much beyond that. "I even knew of a guy who went to the same church as one customer who was Irish Catholic—and he was Jewish," said one former Oracle manager.

If such a "personal approach" does not work, Oracle offers steep discounts, with money as a powerful incentive. A former Siebel employee says, "Oracle will never lose a deal on price, they will just give away their stuff and make it up with services later." According to a former Oracle manager, Arvindh Balakrisnan, who is now CEO of software maker MetricStream.com: "I myself was involved in selling a product for $25 million with consulting costs of $80 million." He adds, "This is nothing new. A one-to-one consulting ratio would be considered extremely good." What this meant to customers was that the cost of after-the-fact consulting often exceeded the price of the original product. Golfsmith International, the golf equipment retailer, is a case in point. It experienced so many difficulties with Oracle's software that it had to spend millions of dollars over and above the original licensing fees to solve the problems. Golfsmith International was in such a bad position that it felt compelled to send a letter to its customers explaining business problems caused by complications with Oracle's software.

In their zeal to get the sale and under pressure to make the deal, Oracle's salespeople sold software that their customers really did not need, often described features of products that were not yet developed, and lured customers with deep discounts. This often meant misrepresentation of the products' functionality, performance, and expected savings to the customer. Several of Oracle's customers are complaining about such strong-arm sales tactics. In many cases, this seems to have backfired very badly. California state officials testified in a legislative investigation that they rushed into signing the contract with Oracle without a thorough evaluation. This is because the terms of the deal (including steep discounts) expired on May 31, the final day of Oracle's 2001 fiscal year. California's state auditor alleged in an April 16, 2002, report that Oracle Corporation had talked the state into spending $41 million more than it needed to on software. After a spate of criticism and political uproar, Oracle had to work with the state of California to make the deal void. The state of California is only one of such dissatisfied customers. From Georgia to Canada, several public and private companies are complaining that Oracle misled them. The state of Georgia forced Oracle to renegotiate a major software deal after its officials found that the software would not save as much money as Oracle promised. An Ohio jury, in May 2002, ordered Oracle to pay $13 million for selling software that did not work to a firm that makes auto trim.

As a result of all these problems, Oracle seems to have suffered considerable erosion of its credibility as a reliable partner, the necessary qualification for success in the industry. Technology analysts have stepped up warnings to software buyers that they should be careful in dealing with Oracle and its high-pressure sales teams. Oracle does not still qualify as a "mature company" on the "maturity scale" for software companies developed by Ted Schadler, group director of research at prestigious Forrester Research of Cambridge, Massachusetts. According to him, mature companies are those which assist their clients with due diligence, are straightforward about additional costs, and are realistic about implementation time frames. On the other hand, immature companies are recklessly aggressive and do anything to get the sale before the competitor does, even if it means deceiving the customers. Schadler says, diplomatically, that Oracle is maturing or, alternatively, is being forced to mature.

Such aggressive selling techniques and consequent customer aversion is also supposed to be one of the causes of why Oracle is losing market share to IBM and other competitors. Not only this, Oracle is getting led into its own trap of selling at a discount. Customers are learning to hold out until Oracle sells for a discount at quarter end to meet its own sales targets. This means lesser revenues being realized than otherwise would have been the case.

Confusing "overselling" with an effective approach to sales seems to be the problem with Oracle. Effective sales professionals make win–win deals by keeping customers' best interests in mind while making a deal. Oracle is learning this lesson the hard way.

As you learned in Chapter 2, a SWOT analysis consists of a careful listing of a firm's strengths, weaknesses, opportunities, and threats. Despite its many strengths and strong competitive position, Oracle's sales operations have hurt the firm. Before moving ahead to value-chain analysis, let's briefly revisit SWOT to discuss some of its benefits and limitations. While we believe SWOT analysis is very helpful as a starting point, it should not form the sole basis for evaluating a firm's internal strengths and weaknesses or the opportunities and threats in the environment. Strategy Spotlight 3.1 elaborates on the limitations of the traditional SWOT approach.

We will now turn to value-chain analysis. As you will see, it provides greater insights into analyzing a firm's competitive position than SWOT analysis does by itself.

Value-Chain Analysis

Value-chain analysis views the organization as a sequential process of value-creating activities. The approach is useful for understanding the building blocks of competitive advantage. Value-chain analysis was described in Michael Porter's seminal book *Competitive Advantage*.[2] In competitive terms, value is the amount that buyers are willing to pay for what a firm provides them. Value is measured by total revenue, a reflection of the price a firm's product commands and the quantity it can sell. A firm is profitable to the extent that the value it receives exceeds the total costs involved in creating its product or service. Creating value for buyers that exceeds the costs of production (i.e., margin) is a key concept used in analyzing a firm's competitive position.

Porter described two different categories of activities. First, five primary activities—inbound logistics, operations, outbound logistics, marketing and sales, and service—contribute to the physical creation of the product or service, its sale and transfer to the buyer, and its service after the sale. Second, support activities—procurement, technology development, human resource management, and firm infrastructure—either add value by themselves or add value through important relationships with both primary activities and other support activities. Exhibit 3.1 illustrates Porter's value chain.

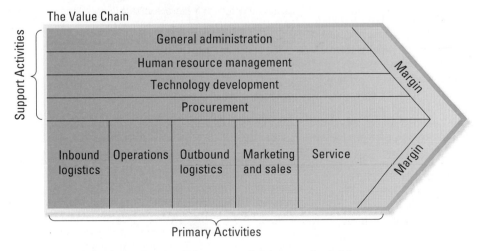

Exhibit 3.1 The Value Chain: Primary and Support Activities

Source: Adapted with the permission of The Free Press, a division of Simon & Schuster Adult Publishing Group, from *Competitive Advantage: Creating and Sustaining Superior Performance* by Michael E. Porter. Copyright © 1985, 1998 by Michael E. Porter. All rights reserved.

The Limitations of SWOT Analysis

SWOT analysis is a tried-and-true tool of strategic analysis. SWOT (strengths, weaknesses, opportunities, threats) analysis is used regularly in business to initially evaluate the opportunities and threats in the business environment as well as the strengths and weaknesses of a firm's internal environment. Top managers rely on SWOT to stimulate self-reflection and group discussions about how to improve their firm and position it for success.

But SWOT has its limitations. It is just a starting point for discussion. By listing the firm's attributes, managers have the raw material needed to perform more in-depth strategic analysis. However, SWOT cannot show them how to achieve a competitive advantage. They must not make SWOT analysis an end in itself, temporarily raising awareness about important issues but failing to lead to the kind of action steps necessary to enact strategic change.

Consider the ProCD example from Chapter 2, page 56. A brief SWOT analysis might include the following:

Strengths	Opportunities
First-mover advantage	Demand for electronic phone books
Low cost of labor	Sudden growth in use of digital technology

Weaknesses	Threats
Inexperienced new company	Easily duplicated product
No proprietary information	Market power of incumbent firms

The combination of low costs of production and an early-mover advantage in an environment where demand for CD-based phone books was growing rapidly seems to indicate that ProCD founder James Bryant had a golden opportunity. But the SWOT analysis did not reveal how to turn those strengths into a competitive advantage, nor did it highlight how rapidly the environment would change, allowing imitators to come into the market and erode his first-mover advantage. Let's look at some of the limitations of SWOT analysis.

Strengths May Not Lead to an Advantage

A firm's strengths and capabilities, no matter how unique or impressive, may not enable it to achieve a competitive advantage in the marketplace. It is akin to recruiting a concert pianist into a gang of thugs—even though such an ability is rare and valuable, it hardly helps the organiza-

tion attain its goals and objectives! Similarly, the skills of a highly creative product designer would offer little competitive advantage to a firm that produces low-cost commodity products. Indeed, the additional expense of hiring such an individual could erode the firm's cost advantages. If a firm builds its strategy on a capability that cannot, by itself, create or sustain competitive advantage, it is essentially a wasted use of resources. ProCD had several key strengths, but it did not translate them into lasting advantages in the marketplace.

SWOT's Focus on the External Environment Is Too Narrow

Strategists who rely on traditional definitions of their industry and competitive environment often focus their sights too narrowly on current customers, technologies, and competitors. Hence they fail to notice important changes on the periphery of their environment that may trigger the need to redefine industry boundaries and identify a whole new set of competitive relationships. Reconsider the example from (Chapter 2) of Encyclopaedia Britannica, whose competitive position was severely eroded by a "nontraditional" competitor—CD-based encyclopedias (e.g., Microsoft *Encarta*) that could be used on home computers.

SWOT Gives a One-Shot View of a Moving Target

A key weakness of SWOT is that it is primarily a static assessment. It focuses too much of a firm's attention on one moment in time. Essentially, this is like studying a single frame of a motion picture. You may be able to identify the principal actors and learn something about the setting, but it doesn't tell you much about the plot. Competition among organizations is played out over time. As circumstances, capabilities, and strategies change, static analysis techniques do not reveal the dynamics of the competitive environment. Clearly, ProCD was unaware that its competitiveness was being eroded so quickly.

SWOT Overemphasizes a Single Dimension of Strategy

Sometimes firms become preoccupied with a single strength or a key feature of the product or service they are offering and ignore other factors needed for competitive success. For example, Food Lion, a large grocery retailer, paid a heavy price for its excessive emphasis on cost control. The resulting problems with labor and the negative publicity led to its eventual withdrawal from several markets.

SWOT analysis has much to offer, but only as a starting point. By itself, it rarely helps a firm develop competitive advantages that it can sustain over time.

Sources: C. Shapiro and H. R. Varian, "Versioning: The Smart Way to Sell Information," *Harvard Business Review* 78, no. 1 (2000), pp. 99–106; and J. C. Picken and G. G. Dess, *Mission Critical* (Burr Ridge, IL: Irwin Professional Publishing, 1997).

To get the most out of value-chain analysis, you need to view the concept in its broadest context, without regard to the boundaries of your own organization. That is, place your organization within a more encompassing value chain that includes your firm's suppliers, customers, and alliance partners. Thus, in addition to thoroughly understanding how value is created within the organization, you must become aware of how value is created for other organizations that are involved in the overall supply chain or distribution channel in which your firm participates.[3]

Next, we'll describe and provide examples of each of the primary and support activities. Then, we'll provide examples of how companies add value by means of relationships among activities within the organization as well as activities outside the organization, such as those activities associated with customers and suppliers.[4]

Primary Activities

Five generic categories of primary activities are involved in competing in any industry, as shown in Exhibit 3.2. Each category is divisible into a number of distinct activities that depend on the particular industry and the firm's strategy.[5]

Exhibit 3.2
The Value Chain: Some Factors to Consider in Assessing a Firm's Primary Activities

Inbound Logistics	Operations	Outbound Logistics	Marketing and Sales	Service
• Location of distribution facilities to minimize shipping times. • Excellent material and inventory control systems. • Systems to reduce time to send "returns" to suppliers. • Warehouse layout and designs to increase efficiency of operations for incoming materials.	• Efficient plant operations to minimize costs. • Appropriate level of automation in manufacturing. • Quality production control systems to reduce costs and enhance quality. • Efficient plant layout and workflow design.	• Effective shipping processes to provide quick delivery and minimize damages. • Efficient finished goods warehousing processes. • Shipping of goods in large lot sizes to minimize transportation costs. • Quality material handling equipment to increase order picking.	• Highly motivated and competent sales force. • Innovative approaches to promotion and advertising. • Selection of most appropriate distribution channels. • Proper identification of customer segments and needs. • Effective pricing strategies.	• Effective use of procedures to solicit customer feedback and to act on information. • Quick response to customer needs and emergencies. • Ability to furnish replacement parts as required. • Effective management of parts and equipment inventory. • Quality of service personnel and ongoing training. • Appropriate warranty and guarantee policies.

Source: Adapted with permission of The Free Press, a division of Simon & Schuster Adult Publishing Group, from *Competitive Advantage: Creating and Sustaining Superior Performance* by Michael E. Porter. Copyright © 1985, 1998 by Michael E. Porter. All rights reserved.

Inbound Logistics   Inbound logistics is primarily associated with receiving, storing, and distributing inputs to the product. It includes material handling, warehousing, inventory control, vehicle scheduling, and returns to suppliers.

Just-in-time (JIT) inventory systems, for example, were designed to achieve efficient inbound logistics. In essence, Toyota epitomizes JIT inventory systems, in which parts deliveries arrive at the assembly plants only hours before they are needed. JIT systems will play a vital role in fulfilling Toyota's commitment to fill a buyer's new car order in just five days.[6] This standard is in sharp contrast to most competitors that require approximately 30 days' notice to build vehicles. Toyota's standard is three times faster than even Honda Motors, considered to be the industry's most efficient in order follow-through. The five days represent the time from the company's receipt of an order to the time the car leaves the assembly plant. Actual delivery may take longer, depending on where a customer lives. How can Toyota achieve such fast turnaround?

- Its 360 key suppliers are now linked to the company by way of computer on a virtual assembly line.
- Suppliers load parts onto trucks in the order in which they will be installed.
- Parts are stacked on trucks in the same place each time to help workers unload them quickly.
- Deliveries are required to meet a rigid schedule: with as many as 12 trucks a day and no more than four hours between trucks.

Operations   Operations include all activities associated with transforming inputs into the final product form, such as machining, packaging, assembly, testing, printing, and facility operations.

Creating environmentally friendly manufacturing is one way a firm can use operations to achieve competitive advantage. Shaw Industries (now part of Berkshire Hathaway), a world-class competitor in the floor-covering industry, is well known for its strong concern for the environment.[7] It has been successful in reducing the expenses associated with the disposal of dangerous chemicals and other waste products from its manufacturing operations. Its environmental endeavors have multiple payoffs. Shaw has received numerous awards for its recycling efforts—awards that enhance its corporate reputation.

Some examples: EcoSolution Q®, the industry's first nylon covering containing recycled content, was the most successful product launch in the company's history. Shaw's residential staple polyester carpet, made from virtually 100 percent petroleum-based materials, keeps one billion plastic containers out of landfills each year through recycling. Shaw is also pioneering other innovative recycling solutions, including recycled nylon for automotive under-hood applications and ground-up carpet as an ingredient in road materials and fiber-reinforced concrete.

Outbound Logistics   The activities of outbound logistics are associated with collecting, storing, and distributing the product or service to buyers. They include finished goods, warehousing, material handling, delivery vehicle operation, order processing, and scheduling.

Campbell Soup uses an electronic network to facilitate its continuous-replenishment program with its most progressive retailers.[8] Each morning, retailers electronically inform Campbell of their product needs and of the level of inventories in their distribution centers. Campbell uses that information to forecast future demand and to determine which products require replenishment (based on the inventory limits previously established with each retailer). Trucks leave Campbell's shipping plant that afternoon and arrive at the retailers' distribution centers the same day. The program cuts the inventories of participating retailers from about a four- to a two-weeks' supply. Campbell Soup achieved this improvement because it slashed delivery time and because it knows the inventories of key retailers and can deploy supplies when they are most needed.

The Campbell Soup example also illustrates the win–win benefits of exemplary value-chain activities. Both the supplier (Campbell) and its buyers (retailers) come out ahead. Since the retailer makes more money on Campbell products delivered through continuous replenishment, it has an incentive to carry a broader line and give the company greater shelf space. Campbell found that after it introduced the program, sales of its products grew twice as fast through participating retailers as through all other retailers. Not surprisingly, supermarket chains love such programs. For example, Wegman's Food Markets in upstate New York has augmented its accounting system to measure and reward suppliers whose products cost the least to stock and sell.

Marketing and Sales   Marketing and sales activities are associated with purchases of products and services by end users and the inducements used to get them to make purchases.[9] They include advertising, promotion, sales force, quoting, channel selection, channel relations, and pricing.[10] It is not always enough to have a great product. The key is to convince your channel partners that it is in their best interests not only to carry your product but also to market it in a way that is consistent with your strategy. Consider Monsanto's efforts at educating distributors to improve the value proposition of its line of Saflex® windows.[11] The products introduced in the early 1990s had a superior attribute: The window design permitted laminators to form an exceptional type of glass by sandwiching a plastic sheet interlayer between two pieces of glass. Not only is this product stronger and offers better ultraviolet protection than regular glass, but when cracked, it adheres to the plastic sheet—an excellent safety feature for both cars and homes.

Despite these benefits, Monsanto had a hard time convincing laminators and window manufacturers to carry products made with Saflex. According to Melissa Toledo, brand manager at Monsanto, "Saflex was priced at a 30 percent premium above traditional glass, and the various stages in the value chain (distributors and retailers) didn't think there would be a demand for such an expensive glass product." Monsanto's solution? Subsequently, it reintroduced Saflex as KeepSafe® and worked to coordinate the product's value propositions. By analyzing the experiences of all of the players in the supply chain, it was able to create marketing programs that helped each build a business aimed at selling its products. Said Toledo, "We want to know how they go about selling those types of products, what challenges they face, and what they think they need to sell our products. This helps us a lot when we try to provide them with these needs." Thus, marketing is often a key element of competitive advantage.

Strategy Spotlight 3.2 discusses how Staples redirected its marketing efforts.

At times, a firm's marketing initiatives may become overly aggressive and lead to actions that are both unethical and illegal.[12] For example:

◆ *Burdines.* This department store chain is under investigation for allegedly adding club memberships to its customers' credit cards without prior approval.

◆ *Fleet Mortgage.* This company has been accused of adding insurance fees for dental coverage and home insurance to its customers' mortgage loans without the customers' knowledge.

◆ *HCI Direct.* Eleven states have charged this direct-mail firm with charging for panty hose samples that customers did not order.

◆ *Juno Online Services.* The Federal Trade Commission brought charges against this Internet service provider for failing to provide customers with a telephone number to cancel service.

Service   This primary activity includes all activities associated with providing service to enhance or maintain the value of the product, such as installation, repair, training, parts supply, and product adjustment.

Redirecting Marketing Efforts at Staples

On his first day as CEO of Staples, the nation's largest office supply chain, Ron Sargent put on the black pants, black shoes, and red shirt that associates wear and headed to the Staples store in Brighton, Massachusetts. This is Staples's first store (opened in May 1986), and by going there he was trying to rally the Staples troops around a concept called "Back to Brighton." It was a symbolic message to the members of the organization that they were going to improve service and refocus on their core customer base: the small-business customer. After growing rapidly for most of its 16 years, Staples encountered a decline in performance during the economic slowdown. To make matters worse,

its main rival, Office Depot, was experiencing a competitive rebound. Thus, Staples was forced to reexamine every aspect of its business.

For example, the company's catering to the casual customer had not proved to be profitable. So Ron removed 600 items that appealed to the casual customer and replaced them with 700 items that appealed to the small-business customer. The chain improved the quality of the merchandise it offered, because businesses have more demanding needs than the casual customer. It stopped advertising in the Sunday newspapers, which businesses do not read, and put more money into direct marketing. Staples also upgraded its Web site and doubled its direct sales force. Taking the money that was originally allocated to advertising, Ron invested it in training for associates and added more staff to stores to provide better service.

Sources: M. Roman, "Ronald Sargent: Straightening Out Staples," *BusinessWeek,* September 17, 2001, pp. 9–11; and A. Overholt, "New Leaders, New Agenda," *Fast Company,* June 2002, p. 52.

Internet-based retailers (e-tailers) provide many examples of how superb customer service is critical for adding value. Nearly all e-tailers have faced a similar problem: They figured that the Web's self-service model would save them millions in customer service costs. But that was the last place they could afford to shave costs.[13] According to market researcher Datamonitor, 7.8 percent of abandoned online shopping carts could be salvaged through an effective customer service solution—an impressive $6.1 billion in lost annual sales. Bill Bass, senior vice president of e-commerce at catalog retailer Lands' End, Inc., claimed, "If there's a train wreck to happen, it's going to be around customer service."

Let's see what two retailers are doing to provide exemplary customer service. At Sephora.com, a customer service representative taking a phone call from a repeat customer has instant access to, for example, what shade of lipstick the customer likes best. This will help the rep cross-sell by suggesting a matching shade of lip gloss. CEO Jim Wiggett expects such personalization to build loyalty and boost sales per customer. Nordstrom, the Seattle-based department store chain, goes even a step further. It offers a cyber-assist: A service rep can take control of a customer's Web browser and literally lead her to just the silk scarf that she is looking for. CEO Dan Nordstrom believes that such a capability will close enough additional purchases to pay for the $1 million investment in software.

Support Activities

Support activities in the value chain are involved with competing in any industry and can be divided into four generic categories, as shown in Exhibit 3.3. As with primary activities, each category of the support activity is divisible into a number of distinct value activities that are specific to a particular industry. For example, technology development's discrete activities may include component design, feature design, field testing, process en-

Exhibit 3.3
The Value Chain:
Some Factors to
Consider in
Assessing a Firm's
Support Activities

General Administration

- ◆ Effective planning systems to attain overall goals and objectives.
- ◆ Ability of top management to anticipate and act on key environmental trends and events.
- ◆ Ability to obtain low-cost funds for capital expenditures and working capital.
- ◆ Excellent relationships with diverse stakeholder groups.
- ◆ Ability to coordinate and integrate activities across the "value system."
- ◆ Highly visible to inculcate organizational culture, reputation, and values.

Human Resource Management

- ◆ Effective recruiting, development, and retention mechanisms for employees.
- ◆ Quality relations with trade unions.
- ◆ Quality work environment to maximize overall employee performance and minimize absenteeism.
- ◆ Reward and incentive programs to motivate all employees.

Technology Development

- ◆ Effective research and development activities for process and product initiatives.
- • Positive collaborative relationships between R&D and other departments.
- ◆ State-of-the art facilities and equipment.
- ◆ Culture to enhance creativity and innovation.
- ◆ Excellent professional qualifications of personnel.
- ◆ Ability to meet critical deadlines.

Procurement

- ◆ Procurement of raw material inputs to optimize quality and speed, and to minimize the associated costs.
- ◆ Development of collaborative "win–win" relationships with suppliers.
- ◆ Effective procedures to purchase advertising and media services.
- ◆ Analysis and selection of alternate sources of inputs to minimize dependence on one supplier.
- ◆ Ability to make proper lease versus buy decisions.

Source: Adapted with permission of The Free Press, a division of Simon & Schuster Adult Publishing Group, from *Competitive Advantage: Creating and Sustaining Superior Performance* by Michael E. Porter. Copyright © 1985, 1998 by Michael E. Porter. All rights reserved.

gineering, and technology selection. Similarly, procurement may be divided into activities such as qualifying new suppliers, purchasing different groups of inputs, and monitoring supplier performance.

Procurement Procurement refers to the function of purchasing inputs used in the firm's value chain, not to the purchased inputs themselves. Purchased inputs include raw materials, supplies, and other consumable items as well as assets such as machinery, laboratory equipment, office equipment, and buildings.

Microsoft is a company that has enhanced its procurement process (and the quality of its suppliers) by providing formal reviews of its suppliers. One of Microsoft's divisions has extended the review process used for employees to its outside suppliers.[14] The employee services group, which is responsible for everything from travel to 401(k) programs to the on-site library, outsources more than 60 percent of the services it provides. Despite all the business it was doing with suppliers, the employee services group was not providing them with enough feedback on how well Microsoft thought they were doing. This was feedback that the suppliers wanted to get and that Microsoft wanted to give. The evaluation system that Microsoft developed helped clarify its expectations to suppliers. An executive noted: "We had one supplier—this was before the new system—that would have scored a 1.2 out of 5. After we started giving this feedback, and the supplier understood our expectations, its performance improved dramatically. Within six months, it scored a 4. If you'd asked me before we began the feedback system, I would have said that was impossible."

Technology Development   Every value activity embodies technology.[15] The array of technologies employed in most firms is very broad, ranging from technologies used to prepare documents and transport goods to those embodied in processes and equipment or the product itself. Technology development related to the product and its features supports the entire value chain, while other technology development is associated with particular primary or support activities.

The 2000 merger of Allied Signal and Honeywell brought together roughly 13,000 scientists and an $870 million R&D budget that promises to lead to some innovative products and services in two major areas: performance materials and control systems. Some of the possible innovations:

- ***Performance materials.*** The development of uniquely shaped fibers with very high absorption capability. When employed in the company's Fram oil filters, they capture 50 percent more particles than ordinary filters. This means that cars can travel further with fewer oil changes.
- ***Control systems.*** Working with six leading oil companies, Honeywell developed software using "self-learning" algorithms that predict when something might go wrong in an oil refinery before it actually does. Examples include a faulty gas valve or hazardous spillage.[16]

Human Resource Management   Human resource management consists of activities involved in the recruiting, hiring, training, development, and compensation of all types of personnel.[17] It supports both individual primary and support activities (e.g., hiring of engineers and scientists) and the entire value chain (e.g., negotiations with labor unions).

Like all great service companies, JetBlue Airways Corporation is obsessed with hiring superior employees.[18] But they found it difficult to attract college graduates to commit to a career as flight attendants. JetBlue developed a highly innovative recruitment program for flight attendants—a one-year contract that gives them a chance to travel, meet lots of people, and then decide what else they might like to do. They also introduced the idea of training a friend and employee together so that they could share a job. With such employee-friendly initiatives, JetBlue has been very successful in attracting talent.

Employees often leave a firm because they reach a plateau and begin to look for new opportunities and challenges.[19] AT&T strives to retain such people with Resource Link, an in-house temporary service that enables employees with diverse management, technical, or professional skills to market their abilities to different departments for short-term assignments. This not only enables professionals to broaden their experience base but also provides a mechanism for other parts of the organization to benefit from new sources of ideas.

strategy spotlight

SAS and Employee Turnover

Jeffrey Pfeffer, professor of organizational behavior at Stanford University, asked a managing partner at a San Francisco law firm about its employee turnover rate. Turnover had increased from 25 percent to 30 percent over the last few years. The law firm's solution: Increase recruitment of new employees. Pfeffer's response: "What kind of doctor would you be if your patient was bleeding faster and faster, and your only response was to increase the rate of transfusion?"

It's not difficult to calculate the cost of a new hire, but what does it cost a firm when employees leave? Software developer SAS Institute puts the cost at around $50 million. David Russo, director of human resources at SAS, suggested that keeping employees is not just about caring for your employees—it also provides a strong economic advantage to the company.

Consider Russo's example: Average employee turnover in the software business is 20 percent per year. SAS's turnover rate is 4 percent. SAS has 5,000 employees earning an average of $60,000 a year. The difference between turnover in the industry and turnover at SAS is 16 percent. Multiplying 16 percent by SAS's 5,000 employees at $60,000 a year, SAS has a cost savings of nearly $50 million. (SAS estimates the total cost of turnover per employee to equal the employee's annual salary.)

What can a firm do with an extra $50 million? SAS spends a large portion of this sum on its employees. The SAS gym, cafeteria (with pianist), on-site medical and child care, flexible work schedules, employer retirement contributions of 15 percent of an employee's pay, and a host of other family-friendly programs help keep SAS's employee turnover level well below the industry average. Even after all these perks, SAS still has money left over.

Russo's message? "This is not tree-huggery. This is money in the bank." Bottom line: It pays to retain employees.

Sources: R. Levering and M. Moskowitz, "The 100 Best Companies to Work For," *Fortune*, January 20, 2003, pp. 127–52; and A. M. Webber, "Danger: Toxic Company," *Fast Company*, November 1998, pp. 152–61.

Strategy Spotlight 3.3 describes how SAS Institute's innovative approach to human resources provides an insightful financial justification for the broad array of benefits it provides to employees.

General Administration General administration consists of a number of activities, including general management, planning, finance, accounting, legal, government affairs, quality management, and information systems. Administration (unlike the other support activities) typically supports the entire value chain and not individual activities.

Although general administration is sometimes viewed only as overhead, it can be a powerful source of competitive advantage. In a telephone operating company, for example, negotiating and maintaining ongoing relations with regulatory bodies can be among the most important activities for competitive advantage. In a similar vein, effective information systems can contribute significantly to cost position, while in some industries top management plays a vital role in dealing with important buyers.[20]

The strong symbolic leadership of CEOs such as Carly Fiorina of Hewlett-Packard (HP) shows exemplary management of general administration. Many would argue that top executives have a strong impact on the core values of an organization. A symbolic act by a CEO can have an important effect on an organization's culture. Recently, Fiorina said that she would repay the $625,000 second-half bonus that was part of the pay package she received when she came to HP in mid-1999. Although she was within the range of the goals specified in her contract, she took the action when HP missed its fourth-quarter 2000 earnings target by 25 percent. She had earlier told employees, "If you miss your numbers, there are going to be consequences—and that means everyone." Not surprisingly, her seven-person executive committee followed suit, forgoing about $1 million in bonuses.

How a Firm's General Administration Can Create Value

A firm's general administration can significantly impact a firm's performance. Southwest Airlines's chief financial officer, Gary Kelly, is a key contributor to the airline's solid financial performance. He drives a red Porsche, which might lead one to believe that the 48-year-old CFO likes speed and recklessness. But he drives the car carefully and conscientiously, the very model of maturity on the road. He takes a similar approach to managing Southwest's finances.

While the rest of the airline industry was laying off workers by the thousands, Southwest did not furlough anyone. Its ability to shine in dire times is a result of its conservative financial culture that values a large cash balance and low debt. Southwest began conserving funds in 2000, when it saw a recession on the horizon. After installing a new computer system and renegotiating contracts with vendors, it managed to boost its cash on hand from $600 million to about $1 billion.

Sources: W. Zellner and M. Arnadt, "Holding Steady," *BusinessWeek*, February 3, 2003; and I. Mount, "Southwest's Gary Kelly: A Tip of the Hat to the CFO at the One Airline Still Making Money," *Business 2.0*, February 12, 2002, pp. 5–7.

Through the years, Wall Street analysts have criticized Kelly's conservative approach and goaded him to use the extra cash to make acquisitions or buy back stock. Goldman Sachs's airline analyst actually calls the balance sheet "too strong." Yet it is such fiscal preparedness that has kept the company's debt-to-capital ratio at around 40 percent (compared to the industry average of about 70 percent), which allows for more flexibility during tough times.

Kelly has also come up with some creative measures to get through the recent slumping economy and terrorism threats. For example, he rescheduled the delivery of 19 planes from Boeing by developing an arrangement between Boeing and a collection of banks. This arrangement, whereby the banks formed a group called the Amor Trust, allowed the trust to take delivery from Boeing as scheduled and store the planes in the Mojave Desert until Southwest needed them. The idea was to strike a balance between maintaining the good relationship with Boeing, its only supplier of planes, and holding off spending the cash on the planes it does not yet need. Darryl Jenkins, director of the Aviation Institute at George Washington University, attributes Southwest's success to two things: "Consistency, and the fact that they don't listen to other people."

Information systems can also play a key role in increasing operating efficiencies and enhancing a firm's performance.[21] Consider Walgreen Co.'s introduction of Intercom Plus, a computer-based prescription management system. Linked by computer to both doctors' offices and third-party payment plans, the system automates telephone refills, store-to-store prescription transfers, and drug reordering. It also provides information on drug interactions and, coupled with revised workflows, frees up pharmacists from administrative tasks to devote more time to patient counseling.

Lawyers often receive a "bad rap"—even in the corporate world! However, legal services can be a source of significant competitive advantage. One example is ensuring the protection of a firm's intellectual property through patents, trademarks, and copyrights. Although many companies are not aware of the earnings potential of their patent holdings, Texas Instruments (TI) is one notable exception.[22] In essence, TI began investing the income-generation potential of its patent portfolio in the mid-1980s, when, out of desperation, it faced bankruptcy. Since then, TI has earned an impressive $4 billion in patent royalties; its licensing revenues are estimated to be $800 million per year. In May 1999 TI signed yet another licensing pact for its semiconductor patents with Hyundai, an agreement that is expected to generate a total of $1 billion in additional royalties over seven years.

Strategy Spotlight 3.4 discusses how Gary Kelly, Southwest Airlines's chief financial officer, adds value for his company.

Interrelationships among Value-Chain Activities within and across Organizations

We have defined each of the value activities separately for clarity of presentation, but this approach implicitly understates the importance of relationships among value activities. There are two levels that must be addressed: (1) interrelationships among activities within the firm and (2) relationships among activities within the firm and with other organizations (e.g., customers and suppliers) that are part of the firm's expanded value chain.[23]

With regard to the first level, recall AT&T's innovative Resource Link program wherein employees who have reached their plateau may apply for temporary positions in other parts of the organization. Clearly, this program has the potential to benefit all activities within the firm's value chain because it creates opportunities for top employees to lend their expertise to all of the organization's value-creating activities.

With regard to the second level, Campbell Soup's use of electronic networks enabled it to improve the efficiency of outbound logistics. However, it also helped Campbell manage the ordering of raw materials more effectively, improve its production scheduling, and help its customers better manage their inbound logistics operations.

An example of how a firm's value-creating activity can enhance customer value is provided by Ciba Specialty Chemicals (which merged with Sandoz in 1996 to form Novartis), a Swiss manufacturer of textile dyes.[24] The firm's research and development experts have created dyes that fix more readily to the fabric and therefore require less salt. How does this innovation add value for Ciba's customers? There are three ways. First, it lowers the outlays for salt. Textile companies using the new dyes are able to reduce their costs for salt by up to 2 percent of revenues, a significant drop in an industry with razor-thin profit margins. Second, it reduces manufacturers' costs for water treatment. Used bathwater—full of salt and unfixed dye—must be treated before it is released into rivers or streams (even in low-income countries where environmental standards are typically lax). Simply put, less salt and less unfixed dye mean lower water-treatment costs. Third, the higher fixation rates of the new dyes make quality control easier, lowering the costs of rework.

We conclude this section with Strategy Spotlight 3.5. It addresses how Cardinal Health expertly integrates several value activities to create value for its suppliers and customers.

Resource-Based View of the Firm

The resource-based view (RBV) of the firm combines two perspectives: (1) the internal analysis of phenomena within a company and (2) an external analysis of the industry and its competitive environment.[25] It goes beyond the traditional SWOT (strengths, weaknesses, opportunities, threats) analysis by integrating internal and external perspectives. It is a very useful framework for gaining insights on why some competitors are more profitable than others. As we will see later in the book, the RBV is also helpful in developing strategies for individual businesses and diversified firms by revealing how core competencies embedded in a firm can help it exploit new product and market opportunities.

In the two sections that follow, we will discuss the three key types of resources (summarized in Exhibit 3.4) that firms possess: tangible resources, intangible resources, and organizational capabilities. Then we will address the conditions under which such assets and capabilities can enable a firm to attain a sustainable competitive advantage.

It is important to note that resources by themselves typically do not yield a competitive advantage. Even if a basketball team recruited an all-star center, there would be little chance of victory if the other members of the team were continually outplayed by their opponents or if the coach's attitude were so negative that everyone, including the center, became unwilling to put forth their best efforts. And imagine how many World Series titles

Cardinal Health: Creating Value through the Extended Value Chain

Cardinal Health is a wholesale drug distributor that buys sprays, pills, and capsules from pharmaceutical companies and puts them on the shelves in pharmacies or into the hands of emergency-room nurses. Profitability is a problem in this business, because the company is caught between powerful manufacturers and cost-conscious customers. Cardinal, for example, buys pharmaceuticals from the likes of Pfizer (its biggest supplier) and sells them to the likes of CVS (its largest customer).

Cardinal responded to the profitability challenge by trying to add value for both customers and suppliers. It understood how urgent it was for one of its customers (hospitals) to control costs. So it began to offer services to hospital pharmacies. Rather than shipping medications to the hospitals' front door, it "followed the pill" into the hospital and right to the patient's room, offering pharmacy-management services—and extending those services to customized surgical kits.

As the knowledgeable intermediary, Cardinal realized it could bring significant value to its suppliers (the pharmaceutical manufacturers) by providing services in drug formulation, testing, manufacturing, and packaging—freeing those companies to concentrate on the discovery of the next round of blockbuster medicines. Cardinal even used its position to develop new services for commercial pharmacies. Cardinal's drug-chain customers depend on third-party payments for most of the prescriptions it fills. It worked with a number of leading chains to develop a system called ScriptLINE that automates the reimbursement process for pharmacies and updates rates daily.

The result of this stream of innovations is a wave of growth and profits. Cardinal, with annual sales of $51 billion, has registered compound annual earnings growth of approximately 20 percent or better for the past 15 years.

The Cardinal Health story is a powerful example of extending the value chain and adding value to the many players involved—from the suppliers to the customers. The company found opportunities in an unpromising business landscape by identifying new customer needs related to the activities that surround the products that it sells.

Sources: A. Slywotzky and R. Wise, "Double Digit Growth in No-Growth Times," *Fast Company,* April 2003, pp. 66–70; T. Stewart, "Fueling Drug Growth during an Economic Drought," *Business 2.0,* May 2002, pp. 17–21; and A. Lashinsky, "Big Man in the Middle," *Fortune,* April 14, 2003, pp. 161–62.

Joe Torre would have won as manager of the New York Yankees if none of the players he signed could throw fastballs over 70 miles per hour. Although the all-star center and the baseball manager are unquestionably valuable resources, they would *not* enable the organization to attain advantages under these circumstances.

In a business context, Cardinal Health's excellent value-creating activities (e.g., logistics, drug formulation) would not be a source of competitive advantage if those activities were not integrated with other important value-creating activities. Thus, a central theme of the resource-based view of the firm is that competitive advantages are created (and sustained) through the bundling of several resources in unique combinations.

Types of Firm Resources

We define firm resources to include all assets, capabilities, organizational processes, information, knowledge, and so forth, controlled by a firm that enable it to develop and implement value-creating strategies.

Tangible Resources   Assets that are relatively easy to identify are called tangible resources. They include the physical and financial assets that an organization uses to create value for its customers. Among them are financial resources (e.g., a firm's cash and accounts receivable as well as its ability to borrow funds); physical resources (e.g., the

Tangible Resources		
Financial	◆	Firm's cash account and cash equivalents.
	◆	Firm's capacity to raise equity.
	◆	Firm's borrowing capacity.
Physical	◆	Modern plant and facilities.
	◆	Favorable manufacturing locations.
	◆	State-of-the-art machinery and equipment.
Technological	◆	Trade secrets.
	◆	Innovative production processes.
	◆	Patents, copyrights, trademarks.
Organizational	◆	Effective strategic planning processes.
	◆	Excellent evaluation and control systems.

Intangible Resources		
Human	◆	Experience and capabilities of employees.
	◆	Trust.
	◆	Managerial skills.
	◆	Firm-specific practices and procedures.
Innovation and creativity	◆	Technical and scientific skills.
	◆	Innovation capacities.
Reputation	◆	Brand name.
	◆	Reputation with customers for quality and reliability.
	◆	Reputation with suppliers for fairness, non-zero-sum relationships.

Organizational Capabilities

◆ Firm competences or skills the firm employs to transfer inputs to outputs.
◆ Capacity to combine tangible and intangible resources, using organizational processes to attain desired end.

Examples:
◆ Outstanding customer service.
◆ Excellent product development capabilities.
◆ Innovativeness of products and services.
◆ Ability to hire, motivate, and retain human capital.

Source: Adapted from J. B. Barney, "Firm Resources and Sustained Competitive Advantage," *Journal of Management* 17 (1991), p. 101; R. M. Grant, *Contemporary Strategy Analysis* (Cambridge, England: Blackwell Business, 1991), pp. 100–102; M. A. Hitt, R. D. Ireland, and R. E. Hoskisson, *Strategic Management: Competitivenesss and Globalization*, 4th ed. (Cincinnati, OH: South-Western College Publishing, 2001).

company's plant, equipment, and machinery as well as its proximity to customers and suppliers); organizational resources (e.g., the company's strategic planning process; employee development, evaluation, and reward systems); and technological resources (e.g., trade secrets, patents, and copyrights).

Many firms are finding that high-tech, computerized training has dual benefits: It develops more effective employees and reduces costs at the same time. Employees at FedEx take computer-based job competency tests every 6 to 12 months.[26] The 90-minute computer-based tests identify areas of individual weakness and provide input to a computer database of employee skills—information the firm uses in promotion decisions.

Intangible Resources   Much more difficult for competitors (and, for that matter, a firm's own managers) to account for or imitate are intangible resources, which are typically embedded in unique routines and practices that have evolved and accumulated over time. These include human resources (e.g., experience and capability of employees, trust, effectiveness of work teams, managerial skills), innovation resources (e.g., technical and scientific expertise, ideas), and reputation resources (e.g., brand name, reputation with suppliers for fairness and with customers for reliability and product quality). A firm's culture may also be a resource that provides competitive advantage.[27]

For example, one might not think that motorcycles, clothes, toys, and restaurants have much in common. Yet Harley-Davidson has entered all of these product and service markets by capitalizing on its strong brand image, a valuable intangible resource.[28] It has used that image to sell accessories, clothing, and toys, and it has licensed the Harley-Davidson Café in New York City to provide further exposure for its brand name and products.

Organizational Capabilities   Organizational capabilities are not specific tangible or intangible assets, but the competencies or skills that a firm employs to transform inputs into outputs. In short, they refer to an organization's capacity to deploy tangible and intangible resources over time, generally in combination, and to leverage those capabilities to bring about a desired end. Examples of organizational capabilities are outstanding customer service, excellent product development capabilities, superb innovation processes, and flexibility in manufacturing processes.[29]

Gillette's capability to combine several technologies has been one of the keys to its unparalleled success in the wet-shaving industry. Technologies that are central to its product development efforts include its expertise concerning the physiology of facial hair and skin, the metallurgy of blade strength and sharpness, the dynamics of a cartridge moving across skin, and the physics of a razor blade severing the hair—highly specialized areas for which Gillette has unique capabilities. Combining these technologies has helped the company to develop innovative products such as the Excel, Sensor Excel, and MACH 3 shaving systems.

Marks & Spencer is one of the best-known department store chains in the United Kingdom. Exhibit 3.5 shows how Marks & Spencer's resources have enabled it to retain its competitive advantage in the British retailing industry. In the past few decades the company has devoted huge sums to renovate stores, develop new store locations, and update its procurement and distribution systems.

Firm Resources and Sustainable Competitive Advantages

As we have mentioned, resources alone are not a basis for competitive advantages, nor are advantages sustainable over time. In some cases, a resource or capability helps a firm to increase its revenues or to lower costs but the firm derives only a temporary advantage because competitors quickly imitate or substitute for it. Many e-commerce businesses in the

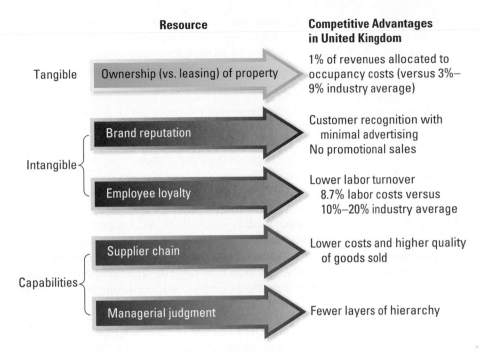

Exhibit 3.5 Marks & Spencer: How Resources and Capabilities Lead to Advantages

Source: Adapted and reprinted by permission of *Harvard Business Review*. Exhibit from "Competing on Resources: Strategy in the 1990's" by D. J. Collis and C. Montgomery, July–August 1995. Copyright © 1995 by the Harvard Business School Publishing Corporation; all rights reserved.

early 2000s have seen their profits seriously eroded because new (or existing) competitors easily duplicated their business model. One noteworthy example is Priceline.com, which expanded its offerings from enabling customers to place bids online for airline tickets and a wide variety of other products. It was simply too easy for competitors (e.g., a consortium of major airlines) to duplicate Priceline's products and services. By the end of 2001, its market capitalization had plummeted roughly 98 percent from its 52-week high.

For a resource to provide a firm with the potential for a sustainable competitive advantage, it must have four attributes.[30] These criteria are summarized in Exhibit 3.6. First,

Is the resource or capability . . .	Implications
Valuable	◆ Neutralize threats and exploit opportunities
Rare	◆ Not many firms possess
Difficult to imitate	◆ Physically unique
	◆ Path dependency (how accumulated over time)
	◆ Causal ambiguity (difficult to disentangle what it is or how it could be recreated)
	◆ Social complexity (trust, interpersonal relationships, culture, reputation)
Difficult to substitute	◆ No equivalent strategic resources or capabilities

**Exhibit 3.6
Four Criteria for Assessing Sustainability of Resources and Capabilities**

the resource must be valuable in the sense that it exploits opportunities and/or neutralizes threats in the firm's environment. Second, it must be rare among the firm's current and potential competitors. Third, the resource must be difficult for competitors to imitate. Fourth, the resource must have no strategically equivalent substitutes. Let's examine each of these criteria.

Is the Resource Valuable?   Organizational resources can be a source of competitive advantage only when they are valuable. Resources are valuable when they enable a firm to formulate and implement strategies that improve its efficiency or effectiveness. The SWOT framework suggests that firms improve their performance only when they exploit opportunities or neutralize (or minimize) threats.

The fact that firm attributes must be valuable in order to be considered resources (as well as potential sources of competitive advantage) reveals an important complementary relationship among environmental models (e.g., SWOT and five-forces analyses) and the resource-based model. Environmental models isolate those firm attributes that exploit opportunities and/or neutralize threats. Thus, they specify what firm attributes may be considered as resources. The resource-based model then suggests what additional characteristics these resources must possess if they are to develop a sustained competitive advantage.

Is the Resource Rare?   If competitors or potential competitors also possess the same valuable resource, it is not a source of a competitive advantage because all of these firms have the capability to exploit that resource in the same way. Common strategies based on such a resource would give no one firm an advantage. For a resource to provide competitive advantages, it must be uncommon, that is, rare relative to other competitors.

This argument can apply to bundles of valuable firm resources that are used to formulate and develop strategies. Some strategies require a mix of multiple types of resources—tangible assets, intangible assets, and organizational capabilities. If a particular bundle of firm resources is not rare, then relatively large numbers of firms will be able to conceive of and implement the strategies in question. Thus, such strategies will not be a source of competitive advantage, even if the resources in question are valuable.

Can the Resource Be Imitated Easily?   Inimitability (difficulty in imitating) is a key to value creation because it constrains competition.[31] If a resource is inimitable, then any profits generated are more likely to be sustainable. Having a resource that competitors can easily copy generates only temporary value. This has important implications. Since managers often fail to apply this test, they tend to base long-term strategies on resources that are imitable. IBP (Iowa Beef Processors) became the first meatpacking company in the United States to modernize by building a set of assets (automated plants located in cattle-producing states) and capabilities (low-cost "disassembly" of carcasses) that earned returns on assets of 1.3 percent in the 1970s. By the late 1980s, however, ConAgra and Cargill had imitated these resources, and IBP's profitability fell by nearly 70 percent, to 0.4 percent.

Strategy Spotlight 3.6 discusses Monster.com, which entered the executive recruiting market by providing, in essence, a substitute for traditional bricks-and-mortar headhunting firms. Although Monster.com's resources are rare and valuable, they are subject to imitation by new rivals—other dot-com firms. It would be difficult for any firm to attain a sustainable advantage in this industry.

Clearly, an advantage based on inimitability won't last forever. Competitors will eventually discover a way to copy most valuable resources. However, managers can forestall them—and sustain profits for a while—by developing strategies around resources that have at least one of the following four characteristics.[32]

strategy spotlight

Monster.com: The Godzilla of Recruiters

Traditionally, managers and other professionals have been recruited by "headhunters," firms specializing in the recruitment of executives. Recently, however, a new type of company has appeared on the scene to challenge the competitive position of recruitment firms. Companies like Monster.com, CareerPath.com, and CareerMosaic.com have challenged traditional recruitment firms by offering a substitute service. Using the wide reach of the Internet, employer access to potential employees, and employee access to employers, the new companies have turned the tables and threatened the $17 billion-a-year traditional executive search agencies.

What caused this challenge? By connecting employees and employers, dot-coms supplant the need for more expensive recruitment agencies. In 1998, 17 percent of Fortune 500 companies were involved in Internet recruiting. One year later, that figure had risen to 45 percent. According to projections by Forrester Research in Cambridge, Massachusetts, online recruiting will grow from a $1.2 billion industry in 2000 to a $7.4 billion industry by 2005. For example, Cisco Systems hires about two-thirds of its employees from résumés submitted online.

Sources: S. Bolton, "Online recruiting," *iQ Magazine,* May–June 2002, (www.business.cisco.com); J. Useem, "For Sale Online: You," *Fortune,* July 5, 1999, pp. 67–78; D. H. Pink, "The Talent Market," *Fast Company,* August 1998, pp. 87–103; D. Leonard, "They're Coming to Take You Away," *Fortune,* May 29, 2000, pp. 89–106.

There are very low entry barriers for firms wanting to try their hand at recruitment. For proof, just look at the prevalence of job search dot-coms that have emerged recently. In addition to the firms previously cited, there are Jobsearch.com, HeadHunter.com, Nationjob.com, and Hotjobs.com, to name a few. In all, some 28,500 online job boards are available to job seekers. The leading site, Monster.com, had over 2 million new visitors in a recent year. If you add up the new visitors to the top 10 sites, they total nearly 7.5 million visitors each month.

Some of the executive search agencies are deciding that if you can't beat 'em, join 'em. Jeff Christian of Christian and Timbers, an executive search firm in Cleveland, has recently started an Internet-based service. Christian says, "Online recruiting is ready to just step on the executive search industry. Personally, I don't want to be stepped on."

With low entry barriers and the availability of substitutes, it's easy to see why the traditional services are nervous. Even though the services provided by traditional executive search firms have rarity and value (two requirements for sustainability of competitive advantage), the threat of a substitute defies their entrenchment.

But what about the new dot-coms? Is their position secure? With low entry barriers, it will not be difficult for new firms to enter the market, which, in turn, will drive down profits. The sustainability of the substitutes, the new Internet services themselves, must be questioned.

Physical Uniqueness The first source of inimitability is physical uniqueness, which by definition is inherently difficult to copy. A beautiful resort location, mineral rights, or Merck & Co.'s pharmaceutical patents simply cannot be imitated. Many managers believe that several of their resources may fall into this category, but on close inspection, few do.

Path Dependency A greater number of resources cannot be imitated because of what economists refer to as path dependency. This simply means that resources are unique and therefore scarce because of all that has happened along the path followed in their development and/or accumulation. Competitors cannot go out and buy these resources quickly and easily; they must be built up over time in ways that are difficult to accelerate.

The Gerber Products Co. brand name for baby food is an example of a resource that is potentially inimitable. Re-creating Gerber's brand loyalty would be a time-consuming process that competitors could not expedite, even with expensive marketing campaigns. Similarly, the loyalty and trust that Southwest Airlines employees feel for their firm and its cofounder, Herb Kelleher, is the result of a resource that has been built up over a long period of time. Also, a crash R&D program generally cannot replicate a successful technology when research findings cumulate. Clearly, these path-dependent conditions build protection for the original resource. The benefits from experience and learning through trial and error cannot be duplicated overnight.

Causal Ambiguity The third source of inimitability is termed causal ambiguity. This means that would-be competitors may be thwarted because it is impossible to disentangle the causes (or possible explanations) of either what the valuable resource is or how it can be re-created. What is the root of 3M's innovation process? You can study it and draw up a list of possible factors. But it is a complex, unfolding (or folding) process that is hard to understand and would be hard to imitate.

In many cases, causally ambiguous resources are organizational capabilities. They often involve a complex web of social interactions that may even depend on particular individuals. When Continental and United tried to mimic the successful low-cost strategy of Southwest Airlines, the planes, routes, and fast gate turnarounds were not the most difficult aspects for them to copy. Those were all rather easy to observe and, at least in principle, easy to duplicate. However, they could not replicate Southwest's culture of fun, family, frugality, and focus since no one can clearly specify exactly what that culture is or how it came to be.

Social Complexity A final reason that a firm's resources may be imperfectly inimitable is that they may reflect a high level of social complexity. Such phenomena are typically beyond the ability of firms to systematically manage or influence. When competitive advantages are based on social complexity, it is difficult for other firms to imitate them.

A wide variety of firm resources may be considered socially complex. Examples include interpersonal relations with the managers in a firm, its culture, and its reputation with its suppliers and customers. In many of these cases, it is easy to specify how these socially complex resources add value to a firm. Hence, there is little or no causal ambiguity surrounding the link between them and competitive advantage. But an understanding that certain firm attributes, such as quality relations among managers, can improve a firm's efficiency does not necessarily lead to systematic efforts to imitate them. Such social engineering efforts are beyond the capabilities of most firms.

Although complex physical technology is not included in this category of sources of imperfect inimitability, the exploitation of physical technology in a firm typically involves the use of socially complex resources. That is, several firms may possess the same physical technology, but only one of them may have the social relations, culture, group norms, and so on to fully exploit the technology in implementing its strategies. If such complex social resources are not subject to imitation (and assuming they are valuable and rare and no substitutes exist), this firm may obtain a sustained competitive advantage from exploiting its physical technology more effectively than other firms.

Are Substitutes Readily Available?   The fourth requirement for a firm resource to be a source of sustainable competitive advantage is that there must be no strategically equivalent valuable resources that are themselves not rare or inimitable. Two valuable firm resources (or two bundles of resources) are strategically equivalent when each one can be exploited separately to implement the same strategies.

Substitutability may take at least two forms. First, though it may be impossible for a firm to imitate exactly another firm's resource, it may be able to substitute a similar resource that enables it to develop and implement the same strategy. Clearly, a firm seeking to imitate another firm's high-quality top management team would be unable to copy the team exactly. However, it might be able to develop its own unique management team. Though these two teams would have different ages, functional backgrounds, experience, and so on, they could be strategically equivalent and thus substitutes for one another.

Second, very different firm resources can become strategic substitutes. For example, Internet booksellers such as Amazon.com compete as substitutes for bricks-and-mortar

Is a resource or capability . . .					Exhibit 3.7 Criteria for Sustainable Competitive Advantage and Strategic Implications
Valuable	**Rare**	**Difficult to Imitate**	**Without Substitutes**	**Implications for Competitiveness**	
No	No	No	No	Competitive disadvantage	
Yes	No	No	No	Competitive parity	
Yes	Yes	No	No	Temporary competitive advantage	
Yes	Yes	Yes	Yes	Sustainable competitive advantage	

Source: Adapted from J. Barney, "Firm Resources and Sustained Competitive Advantage," *Journal of Management* 17 (1991), pp. 99–120.

booksellers such as B. Dalton. The result is that resources such as premier retail locations become less valuable. In a similar vein, several pharmaceutical firms have seen the value of patent protection erode in the face of new drugs that are based on different production processes and act in different ways, but can be used in similar treatment regimes. The coming years will likely see even more radical change in the pharmaceutical industry as the substitution of genetic therapies eliminates certain uses of chemotherapy.[33]

To recap this section, recall that resources and capabilities must be rare and valuable as well as difficult to imitate or substitute in order for a firm to attain competitive advantages that are sustainable over time.[34] Exhibit 3.7 illustrates the relationship among the four criteria of sustainability and shows the competitive implications.

In firms represented by the first row of Exhibit 3.7, managers are in a difficult situation. When their resources and capabilities do not meet any of the four criteria, it would be difficult to develop any type of competitive advantage, in the short or long term. The resources and capabilities they possess enable the firm neither to exploit environmental opportunities nor neutralize environmental threats. In the second and third rows, firms have resources and capabilities that are valuable as well as rare, respectively. However, in both cases the resources and capabilities are not difficult for competitors to imitate or substitute. Here, the firms could attain some level of competitive parity. They could perform on a par with equally endowed rivals or attain a temporary competitive advantage. But their advantages would be easy for competitors to match. It is only in the fourth row, where all four criteria are satisfied, that competitive advantages can be sustained over time.

The Generation and Distribution of a Firm's Profits: Extending the Resource-Based View of the Firm

Many scholars would agree that the resource-based view of the firm has been useful in determining when firms will create competitive advantages and enjoy high levels of profitability. However, it has not been developed to address how a firm's profits (often referred to as "rents" by economists) will be distributed to a firm's management and employees.[35] This becomes an important issue because firms may be successful in creating competitive advantages that can be sustainable for a period of time but much of the profits can be retained (or "appropriated") by its employees and managers—instead of flowing to the owners of the firm (i.e., the stockholders).*

---

* Economists define rents as profits (or prices) in excess of what is required to provide a normal return.

For a simple illustration, let's first consider Viewpoint DataLabs International, a Salt Lake City–based company that makes sophisticated three-dimensional models and textures for film production houses, video games, and car manufacturers. This example will help to show how employees are often able to obtain (or "appropriate") a high proportion of a firm's profits:

> Walter Noot, head of production, was having trouble keeping his highly skilled Generation X employees happy with their compensation. Each time one of them was lured away for more money, everyone would want a raise. "We were having to give out raises every six months—30 to 40 percent—then six months later they'd expect the same. It was a big struggle to keep people happy."[36]

At Viewpoint DataLabs, it is apparent that much of the profits are being generated by the highly skilled professionals working together on a variety of projects. They are able to exercise their power by successfully demanding more financial compensation. In part, management has responded favorably because they are united in their demands, and their work involves a certain amount of social complexity and causal ambiguity—given the complex, coordinated efforts that their work entails.

Four factors help explain the extent to which employees and managers will be able to obtain a proportionately high level of the profits that they generate.[37] These include:

- ◆ *Employee Bargaining Power.* If employees are vital to forming a firm's unique capability, they will earn disproportionately high wages. For example, marketing professionals may have access to valuable information which helps them to understand the intricacies of customer demands and expectations, or engineers may understand unique technical aspects of the products or services. Additionally, in some industries such as consulting, advertising, and tax preparation, clients tend to be very loyal to individual professionals employed by the firm, instead of to the firm itself. This enables them to "take the clients with them" if they leave. This enhances their bargaining power.

- ◆ *Employee Replacement Cost.* If employees' skills are idiosyncratic and rare (a source of resource-based advantage), they should have high bargaining power based on the high cost required by the firm to replace them. For example, Raymond Ozzie, the software designer who was critical in the development of Lotus Notes, was able to dictate the terms under which IBM acquired Lotus.

- ◆ *Employee Exit Costs.* This factor may tend to reduce an employee's bargaining power. An individual may face high personal costs when leaving the organization. Thus, that individual's threat of leaving may not be credible. In addition, some of an employee's expertise may be firm-specific. Thus, it would be of limited value to other firms. A related factor is that of causal ambiguity, which would make it difficult for the employee to explain his or her specific contribution to a given project. Thus, a rival firm might be less likely to pay a high wage premium since it would be unsure of the employee's unique contribution to the firm's success.

- ◆ *Manager Bargaining Power.* Like other members of the firm, managers' power would be based on how well they create resource-based advantages. They are generally charged with creating value through the process of organizing, coordinating, and leveraging employees as well as other forms of capital such as plant, equipment, and financial capital (issues that we will address in more detail in Chapter 4). Such activities provide managers with sources of information that may not be readily available to others. Thus, although managers may not know as much about the specific nature of customers and technologies, they are in a position to have a more thorough, integrated understanding of the total operation.

We will discuss in Chapter 9 the conditions under which top-level managers (such as CEOs) of large corporations have been, at times, able to obtain levels of total compensation that would appear to be significantly disproportionate to their contributions to wealth generation as well as to top executives in peer organizations. Here, corporate governance becomes a critical control mechanism. For example, as we discussed in Spotlight 1.2, William Esrey and Ronald T. LeMay (the former two top executives at Sprint Corporation) were able to earn more than $130 million in stock options primarily because of "cozy" relationships with members of their board of directors, who tended to approve with little debate huge compensation packages. Such diversion of profits from the owners of the business to top management is far less likely when the board does not consist of a high proportion of the firm's management and board members are truly independent outsiders (i.e., do not have close ties to management). In general, given the external market for top talent, the level of compensation that executives receive is based on factors similar to the ones discussed above that determine the level of their bargaining power.[38]

Evaluating Firm Performance: Two Approaches

This section addresses two approaches to use when evaluating a firm's performance. The first is financial ratio analysis, which, generally speaking, identifies how a firm is performing according to its balance sheet and income statement. As we will discuss, when performing a financial ratio analysis, you must take into account the firm's performance from a historical perspective (not just at one point in time) as well as how it compares with both industry norms and key competitors.[39]

The second perspective may be considered a broader stakeholder perspective. Firms must satisfy a broad range of stakeholders, including employees, customers, and owners, to ensure their long-term viability. Central to our discussion will be a well-known approach, the balanced scorecard, which has been popularized by Robert Kaplan and David Norton.[40]

Financial Ratio Analysis

The beginning point in analyzing the financial position of a firm is to compute and analyze five different types of financial ratios:

- Short-term solvency or liquidity
- Long-term solvency measures
- Asset management (or turnover)
- Profitability
- Market value

The Appendix to this chapter provides detailed definitions for and discussions of each of these types of ratios as well as examples of how each is calculated.

A meaningful ratio analysis must go beyond the calculation and interpretation of financial ratios.[41] It must include an analysis of how ratios change over time as well as how they are interrelated. For example, a firm that takes on too much long-term debt to finance operations will see an immediate impact on its indicators of long-term financial leverage. The additional debt will also have a negative impact on the firm's short-term liquidity ratio (i.e., current and quick ratios) since the firm must pay interest and principal on the additional debt each year until it is retired. Additionally, the interest expenses must be deducted from revenues, reducing the firm's profitability.

A firm's financial position should not be analyzed in isolation. Important reference points are needed. We will address some issues that must be taken into account to make

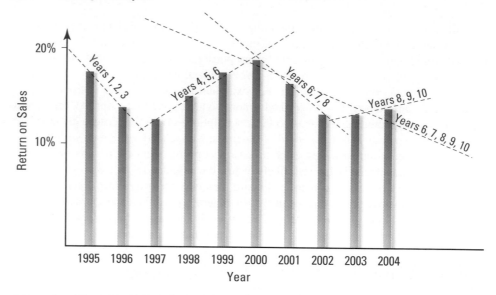

Exhibit 3.8 Historical Trends: Return on Sales (ROS) for a Hypothetical Company

financial analysis more meaningful: historical comparisons, comparisons with industry norms, and comparisons with key competitors.

Historical Comparisons   When you evaluate a firm's financial performance, it is very useful to compare its financial position over time. This provides a means of evaluating trends. For example, Nissan Motors's profit for the first half of fiscal 2000 was $1.6 billion.[42] This is quite impressive given that Nissan suffered a $2.9 billion loss during the previous year. This is evidence that the Nissan Revival Plan launched in October 1999 was quite successful. Nissan's performance, however, is significant only in its own historical context. If General Motors had made a profit of $1.6 billion during the same period, it would have been very disappointing. Its profit for 1999, for example, was $6.2 billion. Similarly, the time period that is selected for determining trends can have important implications.[43] Exhibit 3.8 illustrates a 10-year period of return on sales (ROS) for a hypothetical company. As indicated by the dotted trend lines, the rate of growth (or decline) differs substantially over time periods.

Comparison with Industry Norms   When you are evaluating a firm's financial performance, remember also to compare it with industry norms. A firm's current ratio or profitability may appear impressive at first glance. However, it may pale when compared with industry standards or norms.

By comparing your firm with all other firms in your industry, you can calculate relative performance. Banks and other lending institutions often use such comparisons when evaluating a firm's creditworthiness. Exhibit 3.9 includes a variety of financial ratios for three industries: semiconductors, grocery stores, and skilled-nursing facilities. Why is there such variation among the financial ratios for these three industries? There are several reasons. With regard to the collection period, grocery stores operate mostly on a cash basis, so they have a very short collection period. Semiconductor manufacturers sell their output to other manufacturers (e.g., computer makers) on terms such as 2/15 net 45, which means they give a 2 percent discount on bills paid within 15 days and start charging interest after 45 days. Skilled-nursing facilities would also have a longer collection period than grocery stores because they typically rely on payments from insurance companies.

Exhibit 3.9
How Financial
Ratios Differ
across Industries

Financial Ratio	Semiconductors	Grocery Stores	Skilled-Nursing Facilities
Quick ratio (times)	1.8	0.4	1.1
Current ratio (times)	3.8	1.5	1.8
Total liabilities to net worth (%)	32.6	118.8	191.4
Collection period (days)	42.7	2.6	36.9
Assets to sales (%)	138.7	20.7	107.8
Return on sales (%)	3.1	0.6	1.3

Source: Dun & Bradstreet, *Industry Norms and Key Business Ratios, 2002–2003,* One Year Edition, SIC #2000-3999 (Semiconductors); SIC #5200-5499 (Grocery Stores); SIC #6100-8999 (Skilled-Nursing Facilities); New York: Dun & Bradstreet Credit Services.

The industry norms for return on sales also highlight some differences among these industries. Grocers, with very slim margins, have a lower return on sales than either skilled-nursing facilities or semiconductor manufacturers. But how might we explain the differences between skilled-nursing facilities and semiconductor manufacturers? Health care facilities, in general, are limited in their pricing structures by Medicare/ Medicaid regulations and by insurance reimbursement limits, but semiconductor producers have pricing structures determined by the market. If their products have superior performance, semiconductor manufacturers can charge premium prices.

Comparison with Key Competitors Recall from Chapter 2 that firms with similar strategies are considered members of a strategic group in an industry. Furthermore, competition tends to be more intense among competitors within groups than across groups. Thus, you can gain valuable insights into a firm's financial and competitive position if you make comparisons between a firm and its most direct competitors. Consider Procter & Gamble's ill-fated efforts to enter the highly profitable pharmaceutical industry. Although P&G is a giant in consumer products, its efforts over two decades have produced nominal profits at best. In 1999 P&G spent $380 million on R&D in drugs—22 percent of its total corporate R&D budget. However, its drug unit produced only 2 percent of the company's $40 billion sales. The reason: While $380 million is hardly a trivial amount of capital, its key competitors dwarf P&G. Consider the drug revenues and R&D budgets of P&G compared to its main rivals as shown in Exhibit 3.10. *BusinessWeek's* take on P&G's chances

Exhibit 3.10
Comparison of
Procter &
Gamble's and Key
Competitors' Drug
Revenues and
R&D Expenditures

Company (or division)	Sales* ($ billions)	R&D budget ($ billions)
P&G Drug Division	$ 0.8	$0.38
Bristol-Myers Squibb	20.2	1.80
Pfizer	27.4	4.00
Merck	32.7	2.10

*Most recently completed fiscal year. Data: Lehman Brothers, Procter & Gamble Co.

Source: R. Berner, "Procter & Gamble: Just Say No to Drugs," *BusinessWeek,* October 9, 2000, p. 128; data courtesy of Lehman Brothers and Procter & Gamble.

in an article entitled "Just Say No to Drugs" was this: "Don't bet on it. P&G may be a giant in detergent and toothpaste, but the consumer-products maker is simply outclassed by the competition."[44]

Integrating Financial Analysis and Stakeholder Perspectives: The Balanced Scorecard

In the previous section, we focused on what may be considered a good starting point in assessing a firm's performance. Clearly, it is useful to see how a firm is performing over time in terms of the several ratios. However, such traditional approaches to performance assessments can be a double-edged sword.[45] Many important transactions that managers make—investments in research and development, employee training and development, advertising and promotion of key brands, and new product development—may greatly expand a firm's market potential and create significant long-term shareholder value. But such critical investments are not reflected positively in short-term financial reports. Why? Because financial reports typically measure expenses, not the value created. Thus, managers may be penalized for spending money in the short term to improve their firm's long-term competitive viability!

Now consider the other side of the coin. A manager may be destroying the firm's future value by operating in a way that makes customers dissatisfied, depletes the firm's stock of good products coming out of R&D, or damages the morale of valued employees. Such budget cuts, however, may lead to very good short-term financials. The manager may look good in the short run and even receive credit for improving the firm's performance. In essence, such a manager has mastered denominator management, whereby decreasing investments makes the return on investment (ROI) ratio larger, even though the actual return remains constant or shrinks.

To provide a meaningful integration of the many issues that come into evaluating a firm's performance, Kaplan and Norton developed a "balanced scorecard."[46] This is a set of measures that provide top managers with a fast but comprehensive view of the business. In a nutshell, it includes financial measures that reflect the results of actions already taken, but it complements these indicators with operational measures of customer satisfaction, internal processes, and the organization's innovation and improvement activities—operational measures that drive future financial performance.

The balanced scorecard enables managers to consider their business from four key perspectives:

*   How do customers see us? (customer perspective)
*   What must we excel at? (internal perspective)
*   Can we continue to improve and create value? (innovation and learning perspective)
*   How do we look to shareholders? (financial perspective)

Customer Perspective   Clearly, how a company is performing from its customers' perspective is a top priority for management. The balanced scorecard requires that managers translate their general mission statements on customer service into specific measures that reflect the factors that really matter to customers. For the balanced scorecard to work, managers must articulate goals for four key categories of customer concerns: time, quality, performance and service, and cost. For example, lead time may be measured as the time from the company's receipt of an order to the time it actually delivers the product or service to the customer. Also, quality measures may indicate the level of defective incoming products as perceived by the customer, as well as the accuracy of the company's delivery forecasts.

Internal Business Perspective Although customer-based measures are important, they must be translated into indicators of what the firm must do internally to meet customers' expectations. Excellent customer performance results from processes, decisions, and actions that occur throughout organizations in a coordinated fashion, and managers must focus on those critical internal operations that enable them to satisfy customer needs. The internal measures should reflect business processes that have the greatest impact on customer satisfaction. These include factors that affect cycle time, quality, employee skills, and productivity. Firms also must identify and measure the key resources and capabilities they need to ensure continued strategic success.

Innovation and Learning Perspective The customer and internal business process measures on the balanced scorecard identify the parameters that the company considers most critical to success. However, given the rapid rate of markets, technologies, and global competition, the criteria for success are constantly changing. To survive and prosper, managers must make frequent changes to existing products and services as well as introduce entirely new products with expanded capabilities. A firm's ability to improve, innovate, and learn is tied directly to its value. Simply put, only by developing new products and services, creating greater value for customers, and increasing operating efficiencies can a company penetrate new markets, increase revenues and margins, and enhance shareholder value.

Financial Perspective Measures of financial performance indicate whether the company's strategy, implementation, and execution are indeed contributing to bottom-line improvement. Typical financial goals include profitability, growth, and shareholder value. Periodic financial statements remind managers that improved quality, response time, productivity, and innovative products benefit the firm only when they result in improved sales, increased market share, reduced operating expenses, or higher asset turnover.

Exhibit 3.11 provides an example of the balanced scorecard for a semiconductor manufacturer, ECI (a disguised name). Its managers saw the scorecard as a way to clarify, simplify, and then operationalize the vision at the top of the firm. The scorecard was designed to focus the attention of top executives on a short list of critical indicators of current and future performance. For example, to track the specific goal of providing a continuous stream of attractive solutions, ECI measured the percent of sales from new products and the percent of sales from proprietary products (customer perspective). After deciding that manufacturing excellence was critical to their success, managers determined that cycle time, unit costs, and yield would be the most viable indicators (internal business perspective). Like many companies, ECI has determined that the percent of sales from new products is a key measure of innovation and improvement (innovation and learning perspective). Finally, ECI decided on three key financial goals—survive, succeed, and prosper—with the corresponding measures of cash flow, quarterly sales growth/operating income by division, and increased market share and return on equity, respectively.

Before ending our discussion of the balanced scorecard, we would like to provide another example that illustrates the causal relationships among the multiple perspectives in the model. Sears, the huge retailer, found a strong causal relationship between employee attitudes, customer attitudes, and financial outcomes.[47] Through an ongoing study, Sears developed (and continues to refine) what it calls its total performance indicators, or TPI—a set of indicators that shows how well the company is doing with customers, employees, and investors. Sears's quantitative model has shown that a 5.0 percent improvement in employee attitudes leads to a 1.3 percent improvement in customer satisfaction, which in turn will drive a 0.5 percent improvement in revenue. Thus, if a single store improved its employee attitude by 5.0 percent on a survey scale, Sears could predict with confidence that

**Exhibit 3.11
ECI's Balanced
Business
Scorecard**

Financial Perspective	
Goals	**Measures**
◆ Survive	◆ Cash flow
◆ Succeed	◆ Quarterly sales growth and operating income by division
◆ Prosper	◆ Increased market share and ROE

Customer Perspective	
Goals	**Measures**
◆ New products	◆ Percent of sales from new products
◆ Responsive supply	◆ On-time delivery (defined by customer)
◆ Customer partnership	◆ Number of cooperative engineering efforts

Internal Business Perspective	
Goals	**Measures**
◆ Manufacturing excellence	◆ Cycle time
	◆ Unit cost
	◆ Yield
◆ Design productivity	◆ Silicon efficiency
	◆ Engineering efficiency
◆ New product introduction	◆ Actual introduction schedule versus plan

Innovation and Learning Perspective	
Goals	**Measures**
◆ Technology leadership	◆ Time to develop next generation
◆ Manufacturing learning	◆ Process time to maturity
◆ Product focus	◆ Percent of products that equal 80% of sales
◆ Time to market	◆ New product introduction versus competition

Source: Adapted and reprinted by permission of *Harvard Business Review,* Exhibit from "The Balanced Scorecard: Measures that Drive Performance," by R. S. Kaplan and D. P. Norton, January–February 1992. Copyright © 1992 by the Harvard Business School Publishing Corporation; all rights reserved.

if the revenue growth in the district as a whole were 5.0 percent, the revenue growth in this particular store would be 5.5 percent. Interestingly, Sears's managers consider such numbers as rigorous as any others that they work with every year. The company's accounting firm audits management as closely as it audits the financial statements.

One final implication of the balanced scorecard is that managers do not need to look at their job as primarily balancing stakeholder demands. They need to avoid the following mind-set: "How many units in employee satisfaction do I have to give up to get some additional units of customer satisfaction or profits?" Instead, when done properly, the balanced scorecard provides a win–win approach, a means of simultaneously increasing satisfaction among a wide variety of organizational stakeholders—employees (at all levels), customers, and stockholders. And, as we shall see in Chapter 4, indicators of employee satisfaction have become more important in a knowledge economy, where intellectual capital (as opposed to labor and financial capital) is the primary creator of wealth.

summary

In the traditional approaches to assessing a firm's internal environment, the primary goal of managers would be to determine their firm's relative strengths and weaknesses. Such is the role of SWOT analysis, wherein managers analyze their firm's strengths and weaknesses as well as the opportunities and threats in the external environment. In this chapter, we discussed why this may be a good starting point but hardly the best approach to take in performing a sound analysis. There are many limitations to SWOT analysis, including its static perspective, its potential to overemphasize a single dimension of a firm's strategy, and the likelihood that a firm's strengths do not necessarily help the firm create value or competitive advantages.

We identified two frameworks that serve to complement SWOT analysis in assessing a firm's internal environment: value-chain analysis and the resource-based view of the firm. In conducting a value-chain analysis, first divide the firm into a series of value-creating activities. These include primary activities such as inbound logistics, operations, and service as well as support activities such as procurement and human resources management. Then analyze how each activity adds value as well as how *interrelationships* among value activities in the firm and among the firm and its customers and suppliers add value. Thus, instead of merely determining a firm's strengths and weaknesses per se, you analyze them in the overall context of the firm and its relationships with customers and suppliers, the value system.

The resource-based view of the firm considers the firm as a bundle of resources: tangible resources, intangible resources, and organizational capabilities. Competitive advantages that are sustainable over time generally arise from the creation of bundles of resources and capabilities. For advantages to be sustainable, four criteria must be satisfied: value, rarity, difficulty in imitation, and difficulty in substitution. Such an evaluation requires a sound knowledge of the competitive context in which the firm exists. The owners of a business may not capture all of the value created by the firm. The appropriation of value created by a firm between the owners and employees is determined by four factors: employee bargaining power, replacement cost, employee exit costs, and manager bargaining power.

An internal analysis of the firm would not be complete unless you evaluate its performance and make the appropriate comparisons. Determining a firm's performance requires an analysis of its financial situation as well as a review of how well it is satisfying a broad range of stakeholders, including customers, employees, and stockholders. We discussed the concept of the balanced scorecard, in which four perspectives must be addressed: customer, internal business, innovation and learning, and financial. Central to the balanced scorecard is the idea that the interests of various stakeholders can be interrelated. We provide examples of how indicators of employee satisfaction lead to higher levels of customer satisfaction, which in turn lead to higher levels of financial performance. Thus, improving a firm's performance does not need to involve making trade-offs among different stakeholders. Assessing the firm's performance is also more useful if it is evaluated in terms of how it changes over time, compares with industry norms, and compares with key competitors.

summary review questions

1. SWOT analysis is a technique to analyze the internal and external environment of a firm. What are its advantages and disadvantages?
2. Briefly describe the primary and support activities in a firm's value chain.
3. How can managers create value by establishing important relationships among the value-chain activities both within their firm and between the firm and its customers and suppliers?
4. Briefly explain the four criteria for sustainability of competitive advantages.
5. Under what conditions are employees and managers able to appropriate some of the value created by their firm?
6. What are the advantages and disadvantages of conducting a financial ratio analysis of a firm?
7. Summarize the concept of the balanced scorecard. What are its main advantages?

experiential exercise

Dell Computer is a leading firm in the personal computer industry, with annual revenues of $35 billion during its 2003 fiscal year. Dell has created a very strong competitive position via its "direct model," whereby it manufactures its personal computers to detailed customer specifications.

Below we address several questions that focus on Dell's value-chain activities and interrelationships among them as well as whether they are able to attain sustainable competitive advantage(s).

1. Where in Dell's value chain are they creating value for their customer?

Value Chain Activity	Yes/No	How Does Dell Create Value for the Customer?
Primary:		
Inbound logistics		
Operations		
Outbound logistics		
Marketing and sales		
Service		
Support:		
Procurement		
Technology development		
Human resource management		
General administration		

2. What are the important relationships among Dell's value-chain activities? What are the important interdependencies? For each activity, identify the relationships and interdependencies.

	Inbound logistics	Operations	Outbound logistics	Marketing and sales	Service	Procurement	Technology development	Human resource management	General administration
Inbound logistics									
Operations									
Outbound logistics									
Marketing and sales									
Service									
Procurement									
Technology development									
Human resource management									
General administration									

3. What resources, activities, and relationships enable Dell to achieve a sustainable competitive advantage?

Resource/Activity	Is It Valuable?	Is It Rare?	Are There Few Substitutes?	Is It Difficult to Make?
Inbound logistics				
Operations				
Outbound logistics				
Marketing and sales				
Service				
Procurement				
Technology development				
Human resource management				
General administration				

application questions & exercises

1. Using published reports, select two CEOs who have recently made public statements regarding a major change in their firm's strategy. Discuss how the successful implementation of such strategies requires changes in the firm's primary and support activities.
2. Select a firm that competes in an industry in which you are interested. Drawing upon published financial reports, complete a financial ratio analysis. Based on changes over time and a comparison with industry norms, evaluate the firm's strengths and weaknesses in terms of its financial position.
3. How might exemplary human resource practices enhance and strengthen a firm's value-chain activities?
4. Using the Internet, look up your university or college. What are some of its key value-creating activities that provide competitive advantages? Why?

ethics questions

1. What are some of the ethical issues that arise when a firm becomes overly zealous in advertising its products?
2. What are some of the unethical issues that may arise from a firm's procurement activities? Are you aware of any of these issues from your personal experience or businesses you are familiar with?

references

1. Kerstetter, J., 2002, Oracle: When strong-arm tactics backfire, *BusinessWeek,* June 17: 34; Levey, N., 2002, Oracle tactics draw ire, *Mercury News,* May 29; www.bayarea.com/mld/bayarea/business/3363163.htm; Hellweg, E., 2002, Oracle's California scandal problem, *Business 2.0,* May 13; www.business2.com/articles/web/0,1653,40464,00.html; Kawamoto, D., & Wong, W., 2001, Oracle's hard sell illustrates industrywide problems, *CNET News.com,* June 29, news.com/2009-1017-269001.html; Gilbert, A., 2002, Oracle cuts rewards for last-minute deals, *CNET News.com,* June 19, news.com/2100-1017-937593.html.
2. Our discussion of the value chain will draw on Porter, M. E., 1985, *Competitive Advantage* (New York: Free Press), chap. 2.
3. Dyer, J. H., 1996, Specialized supplier networks as a source of competitive advantage: Evidence from the auto industry, *Strategic Management Journal* 17: 271–91.
4. For an insightful perspective on value-chain analysis, refer to Stabell, C. B., & Fjeldstad, O. D., 1998, Configuring value for competitive advantage: On chains, shops, and networks, *Strategic Management Journal* 19: 413–37. The authors develop concepts of value chains, value shops, and value networks to extend the value-creation logic across a broad range of industries. Their work builds on the seminal contributions of Porter, 1985, op. cit., and others who have addressed how firms create value through key interrelationships among value-creating activities.
5. Ibid.
6. Maynard, M., 1999, Toyota promises custom order in 5 days, *USA Today,* August 6: B1.
7. Shaw Industries, 1999, annual report, 14–15.
8. Fisher, M. L., 1997, What is the right supply chain for your product? *Harvard Business Review* 75 (2): 105–16.
9. Jackson, M., 2001, Bringing a dying brand back to life, *Harvard Business Review* 79 (5): 53–61.
10. Anderson, J. C., & Nmarus, J. A., 2003, Selectively pursuing more of your customer's business, *MIT Sloan Management Review* 44 (3): 42–50.
11. Berggren, E., & Nacher, T., 2000, Why good ideas go bust, *Management Review,* February: 32–36.
12. Haddad, C., & Grow, B., 2001, Wait a second—I didn't order that! *BusinessWeek,* July 16: 45.
13. Brown, J., 2000, Service, please, *BusinessWeek* E. Biz, October 23: EB 48–50.
14. Imperato, G., 1998, How to give good feedback, *Fast Company,* September: 144–56.
15. Bensaou, B. M., & Earl, M., 1998, The right mindset for managing information technology, *Harvard Business Review* 96 (5): 118–28.
16. Donlon, J. P., 2000, Bonsignore's bid for the big time, *Chief Executive,* March: 28–37.
17. Ulrich, D., 1998, A new mandate for human resources, *Harvard Business Review* 96 (1): 124–34.
18. Wood, J., 2003, Sharing jobs and working from home: The new face of the airline industry, *AviationCareer.net,* February 21.
19. Follow AT&T's lead in this tactic to retain "plateaued" employees, n.d., *Recruitment & Retention*: 1.

20. For a cautionary note on the use of IT, refer to McAfee, A., 2003, When too much IT knowledge is a dangerous thing, *MIT Sloan Management Review* 44 (2): 83–90.

21. Walgreen Co., 1996, *Information Technology and Walgreen's: Opportunities for Employment,* January; and Dess, G. G., & Picken, J. C., 1997, *Beyond Productivity* (New York: AMACOM).

22. Rivette, K. G., & Kline, D., 2000, Discovering new value in intellectual property, *Harvard Business Review* 78 (1): 54–66.

23. Day, G. S., 2003, Creating a superior customer-relating capability, *MIT Sloan Management Review* 44 (3): 77–82.

24. Reinhardt, F. L., 1999, Bringing the environment down to earth, *Harvard Business Review* 77 (4): 149–57.

25. Collis, D. J., & Montgomery, C. A., 1995, Competing on resources: Strategy in the 1990's, *Harvard Business Review* 73 (4): 119–28; and Barney, J., 1991, Firm resources and sustained competitive advantage, *Journal of Management* 17 (1): 99–120.

26. Henkoff, R., 1993, Companies that train the best, *Fortune,* March 22: 83; and Dess & Picken, *Beyond Productivity,* p. 98.

27. Barney, J. B., 1986, Types of competition and the theory of strategy: Towards an integrative framework, *Academy of Management Review* 11 (4): 791–800.

28. Harley-Davidson, 1993, annual report.

29. Lorenzoni, G., & Lipparini, A., 1999, The leveraging of interfirm relationships as a distinctive organizational capability: A longitudinal study, *Strategic Management Journal* 20: 317–38.

30. Barney, J., 1991, Firm resources and sustained competitive advantage, *Journal of Management* 17 (1): 99–120.

31. Barney, 1986, op. cit. Our discussion of inimitability and substitution draws upon this source.

32. Deephouse, D. L., 1999, To be different, or to be the same? It's a question (and theory) of strategic balance, *Strategic Management Journal* 20: 147–66.

33. Yeoh, P. L., & Roth, K., 1999, An empirical analysis of sustained advantage in the U.S. pharmaceutical industry: Impact of firm resources and capabilities, *Strategic Management Journal* 20: 637–53.

34. Robins, J. A., & Wiersema, M. F., 2000, Strategies for unstructured competitive environments: Using scarce resources to create new markets, in Bresser, R. F., et al., eds., *Winning Strategies in a Deconstructing World* (New York: John Wiley), 201–20.

35. Amit, R., & Schoemaker, J. H., 1993, Strategic assets and organizational rent, *Strategic Management Journal* 14 (1): 33–46; Collis, D. J., & Montgomery, C. A., 1995, Competing on resources: Strategy in the 1990's, *Harvard Business Review* 73 (4): 118–28; Coff, R. W., 1999, When competitive advantage doesn't lead to performance: The resource-based view and stakeholder bargaining power, *Organization Science* 10 (2): 119–33; and Blyler, M., & Coff, R. W., 2003, Dynamic capabilities, social capital, and rent appropriation: Ties that split pies, *Strategic Management Journal* 24: 677–686.

36. Munk, N., 1998, The new organization man, *Fortune,* March 16: 62–74.

37. Coff, op. cit.

38. We have focused our discussion on how internal stakeholders (e.g., employees, managers, and top executives) may appropriate a firm's profits (or rents). For an interesting discussion of how a firm's innovations may be appropriated by external stakeholders (e.g., customers, suppliers) as well as competitors, refer to Grant, R. M., 2002, *Contemporary Strategy Analysis,* 4th ed. (Malden, MA: Blackwell), 335–40.

39. Luehrman, T. A., 1997, What's it worth? A general manager's guide to valuation, *Harvard Business Review* 45 (3): 132–42.

40. See, for example, Kaplan, R. S., & Norton, D. P., 1992, The balanced scorecard: Measures that drive performance, *Harvard Business Review* 69 (1): 71–79.

41. Hitt, M. A., Ireland, R. D., & Stadter, G., 1982, Functional importance of company performance: Moderating effects of grand strategy and industry type, *Strategic Management Journal* 3: 315–30.

42. Nissan Motor Company, 2001, annual report.

43. Rigby, D., 2001, Moving up in a downturn, *Harvard Business Review* 79 (6): 98–105.

44. Berner, R., 2000, Procter & Gamble: Just say no to drugs, *BusinessWeek,* October 9: 128.

45. Kaplan & Norton, op. cit.

46. Ibid.

47. Rucci, A. J., Kirn, S. P., & Quinn, R. T., 1998, The employee-customer-profit chain at Sears, *Harvard Business Review* 76 (1): 82–97.

Appendix to Chapter 3

Financial Ratio Analysis

Standard Financial Statements

One obvious thing we might want to do with a company's financial statements is to compare them to those of other, similar companies. We would immediately have a problem, however. It's almost impossible to directly compare the financial statements for two companies because of differences in size.

For example, Oracle and IBM are obviously serious rivals in the computer software market, but IBM is much larger (in terms of assets), so it is difficult to compare them directly. For that matter, it's difficult to even compare financial statements from different points in time for the same company if the company's size has changed. The size problem is compounded if we try to compare IBM and, say, SAP (of Germany). If SAP's financial statements are denominated in German marks, then we have a size *and* a currency difference.

To start making comparisons, one obvious thing we might try to do is to somehow standardize the financial statements. One very common and useful way of doing this is to work with percentages instead of total dollars. The resulting financial statements are called *common-size statements.* We consider these next.

Common-Size Balance Sheets

For easy reference, Prufrock Corporation's 2002 and 2003 balance sheets are provided in Exhibit 3A.1. Using these, we construct common-size balance sheets by expressing each item as a percentage of total assets. Prufrock's 2002 and 2003 common-size balance sheets are shown in Exhibit 3A.2.

Notice that some of the totals don't check exactly because of rounding errors. Also notice that the total change has to be zero since the beginning and ending numbers must add up to 100 percent.

In this form, financial statements are relatively easy to read and compare. For example, just looking at the two balance sheets for Prufrock, we see that current assets were 19.7 percent of total assets in 2003, up from 19.1 percent in 2002. Current liabilities declined from 16.0 percent to 15.1 percent of total liabilities and equity over that same time. Similarly, total equity rose from 68.1 percent of total liabilities and equity to 72.2 percent.

Overall, Prufrock's liquidity, as measured by current assets compared to current liabilities, increased over the year. Simultaneously, Prufrock's indebtedness diminished as a percentage of total assets. We might be tempted to conclude that the balance sheet has grown "stronger."

Common-Size Income Statements

A useful way of standardizing the income statement, shown in Exhibit 3A.3, is to express each item as a percentage of total sales, as illustrated for Prufrock in Exhibit 3A.4.

This income statement tells us what happens to each dollar in sales. For Prufrock, interest expense eats up $.061 out of every sales dollar and taxes take another $.081. When all is said and done, $.157 of each dollar flows through to the bottom line (net income), and that amount is split into $.105 retained in the business and $.052 paid out in dividends.

Source: Adapted from S. A. Ross, R. W. Westerfield, & B. D. Jordan, *Essentials of Corporate Finance,* 2nd ed. (New York: McGraw-Hill, 1999), chap. 3.

Exhibit 3A.1
Prufrock
Corporation
Balance Sheets as of
December 31, 2002
and 2003
($ in millions)

	2002	2003
Assets		
Current assets		
Cash	$ 84	$ 98
Accounts receivable	165	188
Inventory	393	422
Total	$ 642	$ 708
Fixed assets		
Net plant and equipment	$2,731	$2,880
Total assets	$3,373	$3,588
Liabilities and Owners' Equity		
Current liabilities		
Accounts payable	$ 312	$ 344
Notes payable	231	196
Total	$ 543	$ 540
Long-term debt	$ 531	$ 457
Owners' equity		
Common stock and paid-in surplus	$ 500	$ 550
Retained earnings	1,799	2,041
Total	$2,299	$2,591
Total liabilities and owners' equity	$3,373	$3,588

These percentages are very useful in comparisons. For example, a relevant figure is the cost percentage. For Prufrock, $.582 of each $1.00 in sales goes to pay for goods sold. It would be interesting to compute the same percentage for Prufrock's main competitors to see how Prufrock stacks up in terms of cost control.

Ratio Analysis

Another way of avoiding the problems involved in comparing companies of different sizes is to calculate and compare *financial ratios*. Such ratios are ways of comparing and investigating the relationships between different pieces of financial information. We cover some of the more common ratios next, but there are many others that we don't touch on.

One problem with ratios is that different people and different sources frequently don't compute them in exactly the same way, and this leads to much confusion. The specific definitions we use here may or may not be the same as others you have seen or will see elsewhere. If you ever use ratios as a tool for analysis, you should be careful to document how you calculate each one, and, if you are comparing your numbers to those of another source, be sure you know how its numbers are computed.

Exhibit 3A.2
Prufrock
Corporation
Common-Size Balance
Sheets as of
December 31, 2002
and 2003 (%)

	2002	2003	Change
Assets			
Current assets			
Cash	2.5%	2.7%	+ .2%
Accounts receivable	4.9	5.2	+ .3
Inventory	11.7	11.8	+ .1
Total	19.1	19.7	+ .6
Fixed assets			
Net plant and equipment	80.9	80.3	− .6
Total assets	100.0%	100.0%	.0%
Liabilities and Owners' Equity			
Current liabilities			
Accounts payable	9.2%	9.6%	+ .4%
Notes payable	6.8	5.5	− 1.3
Total	16.0	15.1	− .9
Long-term debt	15.7	12.7	− 3.0
Owners' equity			
Common stock and paid-in surplus	14.8	15.3	+ .5
Retained earnings	53.3	56.9	+ 3.6
Total	68.1	72.2	+ 4.1
Total liabilities and owners' equities	100.0%	100.0%	.0%

Exhibit 3A.3
Prufrock
Corporation
2003 Income
Statement
($ in millions)

Sales		$2,311
Cost of goods sold		1,344
Depreciation		276
Earnings before interest and taxes		$ 691
Interest paid		141
Taxable income		$ 550
Taxes (34%)		187
Net income		$ 363
Dividends	$121	
Addition to retained earnings	242	

For each of the ratios we discuss, several questions come to mind:

1. How is it computed?
2. What is it intended to measure, and why might we be interested?
3. What is the unit of measurement?

Sales		100.0%
Cost of goods sold		58.2
Depreciation		11.9
Earnings before interest and taxes		29.9
Interest paid		6.1
Taxable income		23.8
Taxes (34%)		8.1
Net income		15.7%
Dividends	5.2%	
Addition to retained earnings	10.5	

Exhibit 3A.4
Prufrock
Corporation
2003 Common-Size
Income Statement (%)

4. What might a high or low value be telling us? How might such values be misleading?
5. How could this measure be improved?

Financial ratios are traditionally grouped into the following categories:

1. Short-term solvency, or liquidity, ratios.
2. Long-term solvency, or financial leverage, ratios.
3. Asset management, or turnover, ratios.
4. Profitability ratios.
5. Market value ratios.

We will consider each of these in turn. In calculating these numbers for Prufrock, we will use the ending balance sheet (2003) figures unless we explicitly say otherwise. The numbers for the various ratios come from the income statement and the balance sheet.

Short-Term Solvency, or Liquidity, Measures

As the name suggests, short-term solvency ratios as a group are intended to provide information about a firm's liquidity, and these ratios are sometimes called *liquidity measures*. The primary concern is the firm's ability to pay its bills over the short run without undue stress. Consequently, these ratios focus on current assets and current liabilities.

For obvious reasons, liquidity ratios are particularly interesting to short-term creditors. Since financial managers are constantly working with banks and other short-term lenders, an understanding of these ratios is essential.

One advantage of looking at current assets and liabilities is that their book values and market values are likely to be similar. Often (though not always), these assets and liabilities just don't live long enough for the two to get seriously out of step. On the other hand, like any type of near cash, current assets and liabilities can and do change fairly rapidly, so today's amounts may not be a reliable guide to the future.

Current Ratio

One of the best-known and most widely used ratios is the *current ratio*. As you might guess, the current ratio is defined as:

$$\text{Current ratio} = \frac{\text{Current assets}}{\text{Current liabilities}}$$

For Prufrock, the 2003 current ratio is:

$$\text{Current ratio} = \frac{\$708}{\$540} = 1.31 \text{ times}$$

Because current assets and liabilities are, in principle, converted to cash over the following 12 months, the current ratio is a measure of short-term liquidity. The unit of measurement is either dollars or times. So, we could say Prufrock has $1.31 in current assets for every $1 in current liabilities, or we could say Prufrock has its current liabilities covered 1.31 times over.

To a creditor, particularly a short-term creditor such as a supplier, the higher the current ratio, the better. To the firm, a high current ratio indicates liquidity, but it also may indicate an inefficient use of cash and other short-term assets. Absent some extraordinary circumstances, we would expect to see a current ratio of at least 1, because a current ratio of less than 1 would mean that net working capital (current assets less current liabilities) is negative. This would be unusual in a healthy firm, at least for most types of businesses.

The current ratio, like any ratio, is affected by various types of transactions. For example, suppose the firm borrows over the long term to raise money. The short-run effect would be an increase in cash from the issue proceeds and an increase in long-term debt. Current liabilities would not be affected, so the current ratio would rise.

Finally, note that an apparently low current ratio may not be a bad sign for a company with a large reserve of untapped borrowing power.

Quick (or Acid-Test) Ratio

Inventory is often the least liquid current asset. It's also the one for which the book values are least reliable as measures of market value, since the quality of the inventory isn't considered. Some of the inventory may later turn out to be damaged, obsolete, or lost.

More to the point, relatively large inventories are often a sign of short-term trouble. The firm may have overestimated sales and overbought or overproduced as a result. In this case, the firm may have a substantial portion of its liquidity tied up in slow-moving inventory.

To further evaluate liquidity, the *quick,* or *acid-test, ratio* is computed just like the current ratio, except inventory is omitted:

$$\text{Quick ratio} = \frac{\text{Current assets} - \text{Inventory}}{\text{Current liabilities}}$$

Notice that using cash to buy inventory does not affect the current ratio, but it reduces the quick ratio. Again, the idea is that inventory is relatively illiquid compared to cash.

For Prufrock, this ratio in 2003 was:

$$\text{Quick ratio} = \frac{\$708 - 422}{\$540} = .53 \text{ times}$$

The quick ratio here tells a somewhat different story than the current ratio, because inventory accounts for more than half of Prufrock's current assets. To exaggerate the point, if this inventory consisted of, say, unsold nuclear power plants, then this would be a cause for concern.

Cash Ratio

A very short-term creditor might be interested in the *cash ratio:*

$$\text{Cash ratio} = \frac{\text{Cash}}{\text{Current liabilities}}$$

You can verify that this works out to be .18 times for Prufrock.

Long-Term Solvency Measures

Long-term solvency ratios are intended to address the firm's long-run ability to meet its obligations, or, more generally, its financial leverage. These ratios are sometimes called *financial leverage ratios* or just *leverage ratios.* We consider three commonly used measures and some variations.

Total Debt Ratio

The *total debt ratio* takes into account all debts of all maturities to all creditors. It can be defined in several ways, the easiest of which is:

$$\text{Total debt ratio} = \frac{\text{Total assets} - \text{Total equity}}{\text{Total assets}}$$

$$= \frac{\$3,588 - 2,591}{\$3,588} = .28 \text{ times}$$

In this case, an analyst might say that Prufrock uses 28 percent debt.[1] Whether this is high or low or whether it even makes any difference depends on whether or not capital structure matters.

Prufrock has $.28 in debt for every $1 in assets. Therefore, there is $.72 in equity ($1 − .28) for every $.28 in debt. With this in mind, we can define two useful variations on the total debt ratio, the *debt-equity ratio* and the *equity multiplier:*

$$\text{Debt-equity ratio} = \text{Total debt/Total equity}$$

$$= \$.28/\$.72 = .39 \text{ times}$$

$$\text{Equity multiplier} = \text{Total assets/Total equity}$$

$$= \$1/\$.72 = 1.39 \text{ times}$$

The fact that the equity multiplier is 1 plus the debt-equity ratio is not a coincidence:

$$\text{Equity multiplier} = \text{Total assets/Total equity} = \$1/\$.72 = 1.39$$

$$= (\text{Total equity} + \text{Total debt})/\text{Total equity}$$

$$= 1 + \text{Debt-equity ratio} = 1.39 \text{ times}$$

The thing to notice here is that given any one of these three ratios, you can immediately calculate the other two, so they all say exactly the same thing.

Times Interest Earned

Another common measure of long-term solvency is the *times interest earned* (TIE) *ratio.* Once again, there are several possible (and common) definitions, but we'll stick with the most traditional:

---

[1]Total equity here includes preferred stock, if there is any. An equivalent numerator in this ratio would be (Current liabilities + Long-term debt).

$$\text{Times interest earned ratio} = \frac{\text{EBIT}}{\text{Interest}}$$

$$= \frac{\$691}{\$141} = 4.9 \text{ times}$$

As the name suggests, this ratio measures how well a company has its interest obligations covered, and it is often called the interest coverage ratio. For Prufrock, the interest bill is covered 4.9 times over.

Cash Coverage

A problem with the TIE ratio is that it is based on earnings before interest and taxes (EBIT), which is not really a measure of cash available to pay interest. The reason is that depreciation, a noncash expense, has been deducted out. Since interest is most definitely a cash outflow (to creditors), one way to define the *cash coverage ratio* is:

$$\text{Cash coverage ratio} = \frac{\text{EBIT} + \text{Depreciation}}{\text{Interest}}$$

$$= \frac{\$691 + 276}{\$141} = \frac{\$967}{\$141} = 6.9 \text{ times}$$

The numerator here, EBIT plus depreciation, is often abbreviated EBDIT (earnings before depreciation, interest, and taxes). It is a basic measure of the firm's ability to generate cash from operations, and it is frequently used as a measure of cash flow available to meet financial obligations.

Asset Management, or Turnover, Measures

We next turn our attention to the efficiency with which Prufrock uses its assets. The measures in this section are sometimes called *asset utilization ratios*. The specific ratios we discuss can all be interpreted as measures of turnover. What they are intended to describe is how efficiently, or intensively, a firm uses its assets to generate sales. We first look at two important current assets: inventory and receivables.

Inventory Turnover and Days' Sales in Inventory

During the year, Prufrock had a cost of goods sold of $1,344. Inventory at the end of the year was $422. With these numbers, *inventory turnover* can be calculated as:

$$\text{Inventory turnover} = \frac{\text{Cost of goods sold}}{\text{Inventory}}$$

$$= \frac{\$1,344}{\$422} = 3.2 \text{ times}$$

In a sense, we sold off, or turned over, the entire inventory 3.2 times. As long as we are not running out of stock and thereby forgoing sales, the higher this ratio is, the more efficiently we are managing inventory.

If we know that we turned our inventory over 3.2 times during the year, then we can immediately figure out how long it took us to turn it over on average. The result is the average *days' sales in inventory:*

$$\text{Days' sales in inventory} = \frac{365 \text{ days}}{\text{Inventory turnover}}$$

$$= \frac{365}{3.2} = 114 \text{ days}$$

This tells us that, roughly speaking, inventory sits 114 days on average before it is sold. Alternatively, assuming we used the most recent inventory and cost figures, it will take about 114 days to work off our current inventory.

For example, we frequently hear things like "Majestic Motors has a 60 days' supply of cars." This means that, at current daily sales, it would take 60 days to deplete the available inventory. We could also say that Majestic has 60 days of sales in inventory.

Receivables Turnover and Days' Sales in Receivables

Our inventory measures give some indication of how fast we can sell products. We now look at how fast we collect on those sales. The *receivables turnover* is defined in the same way as inventory turnover:

$$\text{Receivables turnover} = \frac{\text{Sales}}{\text{Accounts receivable}}$$

$$= \frac{\$2,311}{\$188} = 12.3 \text{ times}$$

Loosely speaking, we collected our outstanding credit accounts and reloaned the money 12.3 times during the year.[2]

This ratio makes more sense if we convert it to days, so the *days' sales in receivables* is:

$$\text{Days' sales in receivables} = \frac{365 \text{ days}}{\text{Receivables turnover}}$$

$$= \frac{365}{12.3} = 30 \text{ days}$$

Therefore, on average, we collect on our credit sales in 30 days. For obvious reasons, this ratio is very frequently called the *average collection period* (ACP).

Also note that if we are using the most recent figures, we can also say that we have 30 days' worth of sales currently uncollected.

Total Asset Turnover

Moving away from specific accounts like inventory or receivables, we can consider an important "big picture" ratio, the *total asset turnover ratio.* As the name suggests, total asset turnover is:

$$\text{Total asset turnover} = \frac{\text{Sales}}{\text{Total assets}}$$

$$= \frac{\$2,311}{\$3,588} = .64 \text{ times}$$

In other words, for every dollar in assets, we generated $ .64 in sales.

A closely related ratio, the *capital intensity ratio,* is simply the reciprocal of (i.e., 1 divided by) total asset turnover. It can be interpreted as the dollar investment in assets needed to generate $1 in sales. High values correspond to capital intensive industries (e.g., public utilities). For Prufrock, total asset turnover is .64, so, if we flip this over, we get that capital intensity is $1/.64 = $1.56. That is, it takes Prufrock $1.56 in assets to create $1 in sales.

---

[2]Here we have implicitly assumed that all sales are credit sales. If they were not, then we would simply use total credit sales in these calculations, not total sales.

Profitability Measures

The three measures we discuss in this section are probably the best known and most widely used of all financial ratios. In one form or another, they are intended to measure how efficiently the firm uses its assets and how efficiently the firm manages its operations. The focus in this group is on the bottom line, net income.

Profit Margin

Companies pay a great deal of attention to their *profit margin:*

$$\text{Profit margin} = \frac{\text{Net income}}{\text{Sales}}$$

$$= \frac{\$363}{\$2,311} = 15.7\%$$

This tells us that Prufrock, in an accounting sense, generates a little less than 16 cents in profit for every dollar in sales.

All other things being equal, a relatively high profit margin is obviously desirable. This situation corresponds to low expense ratios relative to sales. However, we hasten to add that other things are often not equal.

For example, lowering our sales price will usually increase unit volume, but will normally cause profit margins to shrink. Total profit (or, more importantly, operating cash flow) may go up or down; so the fact that margins are smaller isn't necessarily bad. After all, isn't it possible that, as the saying goes, "Our prices are so low that we lose money on everything we sell, but we make it up in volume!"[3]

Return on Assets

Return on assets (ROA) is a measure of profit per dollar of assets. It can be defined several ways, but the most common is:

$$\text{Return on assets} = \frac{\text{Net income}}{\text{Total assets}}$$

$$= \frac{\$363}{\$3,588} = 10.12\%$$

Return on Equity

Return on equity (ROE) is a measure of how the stockholders fared during the year. Since benefiting shareholders is our goal, ROE is, in an accounting sense, the true bottom-line measure of performance. ROE is usually measured as:

$$\text{Return on equity} = \frac{\text{Net income}}{\text{Total equity}}$$

$$= \frac{\$363}{\$2,591} = 14\%$$

For every dollar in equity, therefore, Prufrock generated 14 cents in profit, but, again, this is only correct in accounting terms.

---

[3]No, it's not; margins can be small, but they do need to be positive!

Because ROA and ROE are such commonly cited numbers, we stress that it is important to remember they are accounting rates of return. For this reason, these measures should properly be called *return on book assets* and *return on book equity*. In addition, ROE is sometimes called *return on net worth*. Whatever it's called, it would be inappropriate to compare the results to, for example, an interest rate observed in the financial markets.

The fact that ROE exceeds ROA reflects Prufrock's use of financial leverage. We will examine the relationship between these two measures in more detail below.

Market Value Measures

Our final group of measures is based, in part, on information not necessarily contained in financial statements—the market price per share of the stock. Obviously, these measures can only be calculated directly for publicly traded companies.

We assume that Prufrock has 33 million shares outstanding and the stock sold for $88 per share at the end of the year. If we recall that Prufrock's net income was $363 million, then we can calculate that its earnings per share were:

$$\text{EPS} = \frac{\text{Net income}}{\text{Shares outstanding}} = \frac{\$363}{33} = \$11$$

Price-Earnings Ratio

The first of our market value measures, the *price-earnings,* or PE, *ratio* (or multiple), is defined as:

$$\text{PE ratio} = \frac{\text{Price per share}}{\text{Earnings per share}}$$

$$= \frac{\$85}{\$11} = 8 \text{ times}$$

In the vernacular, we would say that Prufrock shares sell for eight times earnings, or we might say that Prufrock shares have, or "carry," a PE multiple of 8.

Since the PE ratio measures how much investors are willing to pay per dollar of current earnings, higher PEs are often taken to mean that the firm has significant prospects for future growth. Of course, if a firm had no or almost no earnings, its PE would probably be quite large; so, as always, care is needed in interpreting this ratio.

Market-to-Book Ratio

A second commonly quoted measure is the *market-to-book ratio:*

$$\text{Market-to-book ratio} = \frac{\text{Market value per share}}{\text{Book value per share}}$$

$$= \frac{\$88}{(\$2,591/33)} = \frac{\$88}{\$78.5} = 1.12 \text{ times}$$

Notice that book value per share is total equity (not just common stock) divided by the number of shares outstanding.

Since book value per share is an accounting number, it reflects historical costs. In a loose sense, the market-to-book ratio therefore compares the market value of the firm's investments to their cost. A value less than 1 could mean that the firm has not been successful overall in creating value for its stockholders.

Conclusion

This completes our definition of some common ratios. Exhibit 3A.5 summarizes the ratios we've discussed.

Exhibit 3A.5

I. Short-term solvency, or liquidity, ratios

$$\text{Current ratio} = \frac{\text{Current assets}}{\text{Current liabilities}}$$

$$\text{Quick ratio} = \frac{\text{Current assets} - \text{Inventory}}{\text{Current liabilities}}$$

$$\text{Cash ratio} = \frac{\text{Cash}}{\text{Current liabilities}}$$

II. Long-term solvency, or financial leverage, ratios

$$\text{Total debt ratio} = \frac{\text{Total assets} - \text{Total equity}}{\text{Total assets}}$$

$$\text{Debt-equity ratio} = \text{Total debt/Total equity}$$

$$\text{Equity multiplier} = \text{Total assets/Total equity}$$

$$\text{Times interest earned ratio} = \frac{\text{EBIT}}{\text{Interest}}$$

$$\text{Cash coverage ratio} = \frac{\text{EBIT} + \text{Depreciation}}{\text{Interest}}$$

III. Asset utilization, or turnover, ratios

$$\text{Inventory turnover} = \frac{\text{Cost of goods sold}}{\text{Inventory}}$$

$$\text{Days' sales in inventory} = \frac{365 \text{ days}}{\text{Inventory turnover}}$$

$$\text{Receivables turnover} = \frac{\text{Sales}}{\text{Accounts receivable}}$$

$$\text{Days' sales in receivables} = \frac{365 \text{ days}}{\text{Receivables turnover}}$$

$$\text{Total asset turnover} = \frac{\text{Sales}}{\text{Total assets}}$$

$$\text{Capital intensity} = \frac{\text{Total assets}}{\text{Sales}}$$

IV. Profitability ratios

$$\text{Profit margin} = \frac{\text{Net income}}{\text{Sales}}$$

$$\text{Return on assets (ROA)} = \frac{\text{Net income}}{\text{Total assets}}$$

$$\text{Return on equity (ROE)} = \frac{\text{Net income}}{\text{Total equity}}$$

$$\text{ROE} = \frac{\text{Net income}}{\text{Sales}} \times \frac{\text{Sales}}{\text{Assets}} \times \frac{\text{Assets}}{\text{Equity}}$$

V. Market value ratios

$$\text{Price-earnings ratio} = \frac{\text{Price per share}}{\text{Earnings per share}}$$

$$\text{Market-to-book ratio} = \frac{\text{Market value per share}}{\text{Book value per share}}$$

chapter 4

Recognizing a Firm's Intellectual Assets:

Moving beyond a Firm's
Tangible Resources

After
reading this
chapter, you should
have a good understanding of:

- Why the management of knowledge professionals and knowledge itself are so critical in today's organizations.

- The importance of recognizing the interdependence of attracting, developing, and retaining human capital.

- The key role of social capital in leveraging human capital within and across the firm.

- Why teams are critical in combining and leveraging knowledge in organizations and how they can be made more effective.

- The vital role of technology in leveraging knowledge and human capital.

- How technology can help to retain knowledge even when employees cannot be retained by the organization.

- How leveraging human capital is critical to strategy formulation at the business, corporate, international, and Internet levels.

One of
the most
important trends that
managers must consider is the
significance of the knowledge worker in today's economy.
Managers must both recognize the importance of top talent as well as
provide mechanisms to enhance the leveraging of human capital to innovate and, in
the end, develop products and services that create value.

The first section addresses the increasing role of knowledge as the primary
means of wealth generation in today's economy. A company's value is not derived
solely from its physical assets, such as plant, equipment, and machinery. Rather, it
is based on knowledge, know-how, and intellectual assets—all embedded in
people.

The second section discusses the key resource itself, human capital, the
foundation of intellectual capital. We explore ways in which the organization can
attract, develop, and retain top talent—three important, interdependent activities.
With regard to attracting human capital, we address issues such as "hiring for
attitude, training for skill." One of the issues regarding developing human capital is
encouraging widespread involvement throughout the organization. Our discussion of
retaining human capital addresses issues such as the importance of having
employees identify with an organization's mission and values.

The attraction, development, and retention of human capital are necessary but
not sufficient conditions for organizational success. In the third section we address
social capital—networks of relationships among a firm's members. This is especially
important where collaboration and sharing information are critical. In this section we
address why social capital can be particularly important in attracting human capital
as well as in making teams effective.

The fourth section addresses the role of technology in leveraging human
capital. Examples range from e-mail and the use of networks to facilitate
collaboration among individuals to more complex forms of technologies, such as
sophisticated knowledge management systems. We also address how technology
can help to retain knowledge.

The fifth and final section discusses how leveraging human capital is vital to
each of the levels of strategy formulation. These include the business, corporate,
international, and Internet levels.

Some companies excel at leveraging their human capital. Strong human capital often leads to useful relationships among others within the firm, promoting a social infrastructure that is often vital for gaining consensus on major decisions, integrating multiple administrative levels, promoting cooperation, and sharing information across departmental boundaries. Xerox is *not* such a company. Rather, Xerox is a better example of the *mis*management of human capital and social relationships. Despite its famous Palo Alto Research Center, Xerox's breakthroughs in technology have sometimes remained dormant as the company struggled to integrate its human resources in bringing new technology to market. Xerox's stock price was not much higher in late 2004 than it was in 1961. How do human and social capital figure in this?

The story begins when Xerox hired Paul Allaire as CEO in 1990.[1] Allaire was charged with reinventing Xerox to become the major technology player it had once been. Allaire enjoyed early success. He had just taken over the company's helm when it launched the lucrative digital printer. Five years later, Xerox introduced the digital copier with its $3 billion annual revenues. By 1999 Xerox stock had soared to its all-time high of $64.

But subtle politics were working behind the scenes to derail these successes. Xerox had hired Rick Thoman from IBM in 1997 to become chief operating officer. All was well early on. In 1999 Thoman took over as Allaire's successor and Allaire was named chairman. Together, they developed a strategic plan to propel Xerox into the new millennium. Their plan couldn't have been more mistaken. In the end the plan failed, not from strategic misdirection or failed technology, but from poor management of the human and social capital inherent in Xerox's executive ranks that seemingly spread throughout the organization.

Thoman had worked previously at Intel, where the climate encouraged open disagreement when problems arose. But that's not how things were done at Xerox. Despite its ability for technological innovation, Xerox had little imagination for challenging the status quo in executive-level discussions. With a bureaucratic style and a formality reminiscent of a military barracks, Xerox had come to be known as "Burox."

Thoman badly needed to shake things up in the executive suite. Barry Romeril, vice president and chief financial officer, had done a poor job of overseeing corporate finances. "Creative accounting" made Xerox's Mexican subsidiary look stellar until someone noticed just how creative this had been! The result: a $119 million write-off from a subsidiary with only $400 million in revenues, a Securities and Exchange Committee lawsuit for overstating earnings $3 billion between 1997 and 2000 (that eventually cost Xerox $10 million to settle), a downgrade of Xerox's bonds to junk status, and numerous shareholder lawsuits. Romeril had also dangerously exposed the company to the turbulent Brazilian economy by failing to hedge against currency exchange rates. After Xerox incurred a 13 percent loss in net worth in 1999, Thoman wanted Romeril fired. But things weren't that simple. Romeril was a friend of Allaire's. With Allaire serving as chairman, Thoman couldn't get rid of Romeril.

Thomas Dolan, president of Xerox's global sales, also contributed to the Burox inertia. Thoman wanted to restructure Xerox's global sales force to make the company more competitive with Japanese firms. Dolan disagreed. Dolan, also a friend of Allaire's, was able to wield Allaire's power over Thoman and resist the restructuring. And as it turned out, another Xerox executive, Anne Mulcahy, was Dolan's sister. Thoman's disagreements with Dolan put Thoman at odds with Mulcahy.

Such in-fighting affected not just those in the executive office. The sales force too began to feel the impact of the negative relationships and lack of direction. The sales force had previously served as experts on one or just a few of Xerox's products, marketing to a wide market. Thoman's vision included a sales force that was limited geographically, but had broad product depth. Rather than service a wide market, the sales force would concentrate on developing relationships with customers. Customers would benefit by having closer access to the expertise of the sales reps. But as tensions within the sales force grew, the negativity spilled over to Xerox's customers. Customers grew increasingly dissatisfied with the service they were receiving. This only further strengthened the competitive intensity brought about by stiff price pressure from Japanese manufacturers.

Naturally, all of this adversely affected the morale of the sales force. The uncertainty surrounding their job duties had a negative impact on how the reps viewed the company. It became increasingly difficult for them to portray the positive image of the firm that's so necessary to increase sales revenues. As the reps began considering their options, many of them quit to join other firms that had more stability. When they left, they took with them valuable product knowledge that often took years to acquire, as well as their relationships with customers that had been built through time. So as sales reps left Xerox, the firm lost not only employees but also vast amounts of product knowledge and valuable social relationships with clients. Although new reps could be trained to regain product knowledge, many of the client relationships were permanently scarred.

With Xerox's stock tumbling, one would have thought that a strong leader like Thoman would be valued. But not at Xerox. The end result? In May 2001 Thoman was fired. Mulcahy was promoted to president and chief operating officer. Romeril kept his job. For a while, Xerox was facing possible Chapter 11 bankruptcy.

The Xerox case addresses many key issues for today's organizations. Here is a firm that has consistently developed leading-edge technology, but recently its financial performance and competitive position have severely eroded. Over a four-year period—from 1999 to 2003—its market valuation has dropped nearly 90 percent! Historically, Xerox hasn't suffered from a shortage of talent or technological innovation. Rather, it has experienced problems leveraging its talent and technologies into successful products and services. Also, the dysfunctional organizational politics at the top of the organization eroded human and social capital throughout the company. As we will see below, in today's knowledge economy, it doesn't matter too much how big your stock of resources is—whether it be top-level talent, physical resources such as buildings and machinery, or financial capital. Rather, the question becomes: How good is the company in attracting top talent and leveraging that talent to produce a stream of products and services valued by the marketplace?

The Central Role of Knowledge in Today's Economy

Central to our discussion is an enormous change that has accelerated over the past few decades and its implications for the strategic management of organizations.[2] That is, for most of the 20th century, managers were primarily concerned with tangible resources such as land, equipment, and money as well as intangibles such as brands, image, and customer loyalty. Most efforts were directed more toward the efficient allocation of labor and capital—the two traditional factors of production.

How times have changed. Today, more than 50 percent of the gross domestic product (GDP) in developed economies is knowledge-based; that is, it is based on intellectual assets and intangible people skills.[3] In the United States, intellectual and information processes create most of the value for firms in large service industries (e.g., software, medical care, communications, and education), which provide 76 percent of all U.S. GDP. In the manufacturing sector, intellectual activities like R&D, process design, product design, logistics, marketing, or technological innovation produce the preponderance of value added.[4] To drive home the point, consider the perspective of Gary Hamel and C. K. Prahalad, two leading writers in strategic management:

> The machine age was a physical world. It consisted of things. Companies made and distributed things (physical products). Management allocated things (capital budgets); management invested in things (plant and equipment).
>
> In the machine age, people were ancillary, and things were central. In the information age, things are ancillary, knowledge is central. A company's value derives not from things, but from knowledge, know-how, intellectual assets, competencies—all embedded in people.[5]

In the knowledge economy, wealth is increasingly created through the effective management of knowledge workers instead of by the efficient control of physical and financial assets. The growing importance of knowledge, coupled with the move by labor markets to reward knowledge work, tells us that someone who invests in a company is, in essence, buying a set of talents, capabilities, skills, and ideas—intellectual capital—not physical and financial resources.[6]

Let's provide a few examples. People don't buy Microsoft's stock because of its software factories; it doesn't own any. Rather, the value of Microsoft is bid up because of its ability to set standards for personal-computing software, exploit the value of its name, and forge alliances with other companies. Similarly, Merck didn't become the "Most Admired" company, for seven consecutive years in *Fortune*'s annual survey, because it can manufacture pills, but because its scientists can discover medicines. P. Roy Vagelos, who was CEO of Merck during its long run atop the "Most Admired" survey, said: "A low-value product can be made by anyone anywhere. When you have knowledge no one else has access to—that's dynamite. We guard our research even more carefully than our financial assets."[7]

To apply some numbers to our arguments, let's ask: What's a company worth?[8] Start with the "big three" financial statements: income statement, balance sheet, and statement of cash flow. If these statements tell a story that investors find useful, then a company's market value* should roughly (but not precisely, because the market looks forward and the books backward) be the same as the value that accountants ascribe to it—the book value of the firm. However, such is not the case. A study compared the market value with the book value of 3,500 U.S. companies over a period of two decades. In 1978 the two were pretty well matched: Book value was 95 percent of market value. However, the gap between market values and book values has widened significantly. Twenty years later, book value was just 28 percent of market value. A colorful commentary comes from Robert A. Howell, an expert on the changing role of finance and accounting: "The big three financial statements . . . are about as useful as an 80-year-old Los Angeles road map."

As one might expect based on the above discussion, the gap between a firm's market value and book value is far greater for knowledge-intensive corporations than for firms with strategies based primarily on tangible assets. Exhibit 4.1 shows the ratio of market-to-book value for a selected set of companies. In firms where knowledge and the management of knowledge workers are relatively important contributors to developing products and services—and physical resources are less critical—the ratio of market-to-book value tends to be much higher. Many writers have defined intellectual capital as the difference between a firm's market value and book value, that is, a measure of the value of a firm's intangible assets.[9] This admittedly broad definition includes assets such as reputation, employee loyalty and commitment, customer relationships, company values, brand names, and the experience and skills of employees.[10] Thus, simplifying, we have:

Intellectual capital = Market value of the firm − Book value of the firm

The issue becomes: How do companies create value in the knowledge-intensive economy? As we stated above, the general answer is to attract and leverage human capital effectively through mechanisms that create products and services of value over time. Let's articulate a few of the basic concepts that we will be talking about in this chapter.

First, consider human capital. Human capital is the "*individual* capabilities, knowledge, skills, and experience of the company's employees and managers." This is knowl-

---

*The market value of a firm is equal to the value of a share of its common stock times the number of shares outstanding. The book value of a firm is primarily a measure of the value of its tangible assets. It can be calculated by the formula: total assets − total liabilities.

Exhibit 4.1
Ratio of Market
Value to Book
Value for Selected
Companies

Company	Annual Sales ($ billions)	Market Value ($ billions)	Book Value ($ billions)	Ratio of Market to Book Value
eBay	2.2	54.5	4.9	11.1
Intel	30.1	170.9	33.5	5.1
Microsoft	32.2	286.2	57.5	5.0
Nucor (Steel)	6.3	4.8	2.3	2.1
J. C. Penney	32.3	10.0	6.4	1.6
General Motors Corporation	185.5	27.3	25.3	1.1

Note: The data on market valuations are as of April 28, 2004. All other financial data is based on the most recently available balance sheets and income statements.

edge that is relevant to the task at hand, as well as the capacity to add to this reservoir of knowledge, skills, and experience through learning.[11]

Second, social capital can be defined as "the network of relationships that individuals have throughout the organization." Such relationships are critical in sharing and leveraging knowledge and in acquiring resources. Social capital can also extend beyond the organizational boundaries to include relationships between the firm and its suppliers, customers, and alliance partners.[12]

Third is the concept of "knowledge," which comes in two different forms. On the one hand, there is explicit knowledge that is codified, documented, easily reproduced, and widely distributed. Examples include engineering drawings, software code, sales collateral, and patents. The other type of knowledge is tacit knowledge.[13] This is knowledge that is, in essence, in the minds of employees and is based on their experiences and backgrounds. Tacit knowledge is shared only with the consent and participation of the individual.

New knowledge is constantly being created in organizations. It involves the continual interaction of explicit and tacit knowledge. Consider, for example, two software engineers working together on a computer code. The computer code itself is the explicit knowledge. However, through their sharing of ideas based on each individual's experience—that is, their tacit knowledge—new knowledge is created when they make modifications to the existing code. Another important issue is the role of "socially complex processes," which include leadership, culture, and trust.[14] These processes play a central role in the creation of knowledge. They represent the "glue" that holds the organization together and helps to create a working environment where individuals are more willing to share their ideas, work in teams, and, in the end, create products and services of value. In a later section, we will address the importance of social capital in the value creation process.

Numerous books have been written on the subject of knowledge management and the central role that it has played in creating wealth in organizations and countries throughout the developed world.[15] Here, we focus on some of the key issues that organizations must address to compete through knowledge.

We will now turn our discussion to the central resource itself, human capital, and some guidelines on how it can be attracted/selected, developed, and retained. Tom Stewart, editor of the *Harvard Business Review,* noted that organizations must also undergo significant efforts to protect their human capital. A firm may "diversify the ownership of vital knowledge by emphasizing teamwork, guard against obsolescence by developing learning programs, and shackle key people with golden handcuffs."[16] In addition, people are less likely to leave an organization if there are effective structures to promote teamwork and information sharing, strong leadership that encourages innovation, and cultures that demand excellence and ethical behavior. Such issues are also central to the topic of this chapter. Although we touch on these issues throughout this chapter, we provide more detail in later chapters. We discuss organizational controls (culture, rewards, and boundaries) in Chapter 9, organization structure and design in Chapter 10, and a variety of leadership and entrepreneurship topics in Chapters 11, 12, and 13.

Human Capital: The Foundation of Intellectual Capital

To be successful, organizations must recruit talented people—employees at all levels with the proper sets of skills and capabilities coupled with the right values and attitudes. Such skills and attitudes must be continually developed, strengthened, and reinforced, and each employee must be motivated and his or her efforts focused on the organization's goals and objectives.

The rise to prominence of the knowledge worker as a vital source of competitive advantage is changing the balance of power in today's organization. Knowledge workers place professional development and personal enrichment (financial and otherwise) above company loyalty. Attracting, recruiting, and hiring the "best and the brightest," is a critical first step in the process of building intellectual capital. At a symposium for CEOs, Bill Gates said, "The thing that is holding Microsoft back . . . is simply how [hard] we find it to go out and recruit the kind of people we want to grow our research team."[17]

But hiring is only the first of three vital processes in which all successful organizations must engage to build and leverage their human capital. Firms must also *develop* employees at all levels and specialties to fulfill their full potential in order to maximize their joint contributions. Finally, the first two processes are for naught if firms can't provide the working environment and intrinsic and extrinsic rewards to *retain* their best and brightest.

These three activities are highly interrelated. We would like to suggest the imagery of a three-legged stool (see Exhibit 4.2).[18] If one leg is weak or broken, the stool collapses.

To illustrate such interdependence, poor hiring impedes the effectiveness of development and retention processes. In a similar vein, ineffective retention efforts place additional burdens on hiring and development. Consider the following anecdote, provided by Jeffrey Pfeffer of the Stanford University Business School:

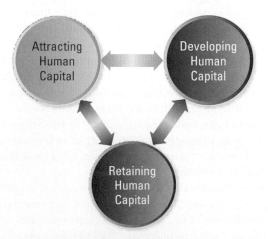

Exhibit 4.2 Human Capital: Three Interdependent Activities

Not long ago, I went to a large, fancy San Francisco law firm—where they treat their associates like dog doo and where the turnover is very high. I asked the managing partner about the turnover rate. He said, "A few years ago, it was 25 percent, and now we're up to 30 percent." I asked him how the firm had responded to that trend. He said, "We increased our recruiting." So I asked him, "What kind of doctor would you be if your patient was bleeding faster and faster, and your only response was to increase the speed of the transfusion?"[19]

Clearly, stepped-up recruiting is a poor substitute for weak retention. Although there are no simple, easy-to-apply answers, we can learn from what leading-edge firms are doing to attract, develop, and retain human capital in today's highly competitive and rapidly changing marketplace. Let's begin by discussing hiring and selection practices.

Attracting Human Capital

All we can do is bet on the people we pick. So my whole job is picking the right people.

Jack Welch, former chairman, General Electric Company[20]

As we have noted, the first step in the process of building superior human capital is input control: attracting and selecting the right person. Many human resource professionals still approach employee selection from a "lock and key" mentality—that is, fit a key (a job candidate) into a lock (the job). Such an approach involves a thorough analysis of both the person and the job. Only then can the right decision be made as to how well the two will fit together. How can you fail, the theory goes, if you get a precise match of knowledge, ability, and skill profiles? Frequently, however, the precise matching approach places its primary emphasis on task-specific skills (e.g., motor skills, specific information gathering and processing capabilities, and communication skills) and puts less emphasis on the broad general knowledge and experience, social skills and values, beliefs, and attitudes of employees.

Many have questioned the precise matching approach. Instead, they argue that firms can identify top performers by focusing on key employee mind-sets, attitudes, social skills, and general orientations that lead to success in nearly all jobs. These firms reason that if they get these elements right, the task-specific skills can be learned in relatively short order. (This does not imply, however, that task-specific skills are unimportant; rather, it suggests that the requisite skill sets must be viewed as a necessary but not sufficient condition.) This leads us to a phrase that is popular with many organizations today and serves as the title of the next section.

"Hire for Attitude, Train for Skill"   Organizations are increasingly placing their emphasis on the general knowledge and experience, social skills, values, beliefs, and attitudes of employees. Consider Southwest Airlines's hiring practices, with their strong focus on employee values and attitudes. Given its strong team orientation, Southwest uses an "indirect" approach. For example, the interviewing team asks a group of employees to prepare a five-minute presentation about themselves. During the presentations, the interviewers observe which candidates are enthusiastically supporting their peers and which candidates are focused on polishing their own presentations while the others are presenting.[21] The former are, of course, favored.

Social skills are also important. You need to be both pleasant and collegial to be hired by Rosenbluth International, a travel-management company based in Philadelphia, with annual revenues over $5 billion. Here, job applicants are asked to play a trial game of softball with the company team. Potential executives are frequently flown to the firm's North Dakota ranch to help repair fences or drive cattle. Do athletic ability or ranching skills matter? Not at all. According to Keami Lewis, Rosenbluth's diversity manager, "You can teach a person

Cooper Software's "Bozo Filter"

Hiring is often easier than firing. Even when unemployment rates are low and labor is scarce, it's still easier to find employees than it is to get them out the door if they don't work out. Not only do poor employees affect the morale of better talent, but they also cost the company money in lost productivity.

Cooper Software has found an innovative way to prevent the problem of hiring bad employees. CEO Alan Cooper asks job applicants to visit the company's Web site, where the applicants will find a short test. The test asks questions designed to see how prospective employees approach problem-solving tasks. For example, one key question asks software engineer applicants to design a new table-creation software program for Microsoft Word.

Sources: R. Cardin, "Make Your Own Bozo Filter," *Fast Company,* October–November, 1997, p. 56; A. Cooper, "Getting Design Across," unpublished manuscript, November 23, 1997, pp. 1–8.

Candidates provide pencil sketches and a description of the new user interface. Another question is used for design communicators. They are asked to develop a marketing strategy for a new touch-tone phone—directed at consumers in the year 1850. Candidates e-mail their answers back to the company, and the answers are circulated around the firm to solicit feedback. Only candidates with the highest marks get interviews.

Jonathan Korman, a design communicator, suggested that the test "told me more about real job duties than any description could." Josh Seiden, a software designer, is even more positive: "It was a fun puzzle—much more engaging than most of what I was doing at my previous job."

That's exactly the kind of attitude Cooper wants. "We get e-mail from some people saying, 'Before I take this test, is the position still open?' I say no, because I don't want anybody who sees it as an effort," claims Cooper. "People who really care take the test and love it. Other people say it's hard. We don't want those people."

almost anything. But you can't teach him or her how to be nice."[22] Or, as Tom Stewart has suggested, "You can make a leopard a better leopard, but you can't change its spots."[23]

Alan Cooper, president of Cooper Software, Inc., in Palo Alto, California, goes a few steps further. He cleverly *uses technology* to hone in on the problem-solving ability of his applicants, as well as their attitudes before an interview even takes place. He has devised a "Bozo Filter," a test administered online (see Strategy Spotlight 4.1) that can be applied to any industry: Before you spend time figuring out whether job candidates will work out satisfactorily, find out how their minds work. Cooper advised: "Hiring was a black hole. I don't talk to bozos anymore because 90 percent of them turn away when they see our test. It's a self-administering bozo filter."[24]

The central point is what some have called the Popeye Principle, "I y'am what I y'am," borrowing from the famous cartoon sailor. Many have argued that the most common—and fatal—hiring mistake is to select individuals with the right skills but the wrong mind-set on the theory that "we can change them." According to Alan Davidson, an industrial psychologist in San Diego whose clients include Chevron, Merrill Lynch, and the Internal Revenue Service, "The single best predictor of future behavior is past behavior. Your personality (largely reflecting values, beliefs, attitudes, and social skills) is going to be essentially the same throughout your life."[25]

Sound Recruiting Approaches and Networking Companies that take hiring seriously must also take recruiting seriously. The number of jobs that successful knowledge-intensive companies must fill is astonishing. Ironically, many companies still have no shortage of applicants. Southwest Airlines typically gets 150,000 résumés a year, yet hires only about 5,000. And Netscape (now part of Time Warner) reviews 60 résumés for every hire.[26] The challenge becomes having the right job candidates, not the greatest number of them.

Few firms are as thorough as Microsoft when it comes to recruiting. Each year the firm scans the entire pool of 25,000 U.S. computer-science graduates and identifies the 8,000 in which they are interested. After further screening, 2,600 are invited for on-campus interviews at their universities. Out of these, only 800 are invited to the company's Redmond, Washington, headquarters. Of these, 500 receive offers, and usually 400 accept. These massive efforts, however, provide less than 20 percent of the company's hiring needs. To find the other talent, Microsoft maintains a team of 300 recruiting experts whose full-time job is to locate the best and brightest in the industry.[27]

GE Medical Systems, which builds CT scanners and magnetic resonance imaging (MRI) systems, relies extensively on networking. They have found that current employees are the best source for new ones. Recently, Steven Patscot, head of staffing and leadership development, made a few simple changes to double the number of referrals. First, he simplified the process—no complex forms, no bureaucracy, and so on. Second, he increased incentives. Everyone referring a qualified candidate received a gift certificate from Sears. For referrals who were hired, the "bounty" was increased to $2,000 (or $3,000 if the referral was a software engineer). Although this may sound like a lot of money, it is "peanuts" compared to the $15,000 to $20,000 fees that GE typically pays to headhunters for each person hired.[28] Also, when someone refers a former colleague or friend for a job, his or her credibility is on the line. Thus, employees will tend to be careful in recommending people for employment unless they are reasonably confident that these people will turn out well. This provides a good "screen" for the firm in deciding whom to hire. After all, hiring the right people makes things a lot easier: fewer rules and regulations, less need for monitoring and hierarchy, and greater internalization of organizational norms and objectives.

Before moving on, it is useful to point out an important caveat. While it is important to strive to attract "top talent," managers must avoid a mind-set where they engage in "war for talent." We address this issue in Strategy Spotlight 4.2.

Developing Human Capital

It is not enough to hire top-level talent and expect that the skills and capabilities of those employees remain current throughout the duration of their employment. Rather, training and development must take place at all levels of the organization. For example, Solectron assembles printed circuit boards and other components for its Silicon Valley clients.[29] Its employees receive an average of 95 hours of company-provided training each year. Chairman Winston Chen observed, "Technology changes so fast that we estimate 20 percent of an engineer's knowledge becomes obsolete each year. Training is an obligation we owe to our employees. If you want high growth and high quality, then training is a big part of the equation." Although the financial returns on training may be hard to calculate, most experts believe it is not only real, but also essential. One company that has calculated the benefit from training is Motorola. This high-technology firm has calculated that every dollar spent on training returns $30 in productivity gains over the following three years.

Cinergy, the $12 billion Cincinnati-based gas, electric, and energy services company, is another firm that recognizes that all employees must be the prime investors and beneficiaries of learning.[30] Gone is the focus on executive leadership. In its place is "talent development"—available to everyone. Elizabeth Lanier, the legal chief of staff, stated, "The premise is that we want to have the smartest people in every layer of the job. If it's the janitor in a power plant, I want him smarter than any other janitor." Lanier is convinced that if you only recruit and train your best talent, you run the risk of having that talent take your investment to the competition.

The "War for Talent": Possible Downsides

Various organizational processes and dynamics arise when organizations adopt a "war for talent" mind-set that can lead to many adverse outcomes. Dr. Jeffrey Pfeffer, a professor at Stanford University's Business School, cautions that not only should a firm *not* try to "win" the war for talent but also that even adopting this imagery to guide recruiting initiatives can be hazardous to an organization's health.

When a firm engages in a war for talent, there is:

- An inevitable emphasis on individual performance (rewarding "stars"). This tends to erode teamwork, increase internal competition, and reduce learning and the spread of best practices within the firm.

- A tendency to become enamored with the talents of those outside the firm and discount the talents and abilities of insiders. This generally leads to less motivation of the firm's existing employees as well as greater turnover. This often causes greater

difficulties in future recruiting as the company tries to replace those who left.

- A self-fulfilling prophecy. Those labeled as less capable become less able because they are often asked to do less and given fewer resources, training, and mentoring. In the process, the organization has far too many people who are in the process of dropping out of the competitive fray.

- A reduced emphasis on repairing the systemic, cultural, and business process issues that are typically much more important for enhanced performance. Why? The company seeks success solely by getting the right people into the company.

- The creation of an elitist, arrogant attitude. After all, once a firm has successfully completed the war for talent, it develops an attitude that makes building a wise organization extremely difficult. In wise organizations, people know what they know and what they don't know. However, companies that believe they have won the war for talent think they are so full of smart people that they know everything!

Source: J. Pfeffer, "Fighting the War for Talent Is Hazardous to Your Organization's Health," *Organizational Dynamics* 29, no. 4 (2001), pp. 248–59.

In addition to the importance of training and developing human capital throughout the organization, let's now discuss three other related topics: encouraging widespread involvement, monitoring and tracking employee development, and evaluating human capital.

Encouraging Widespread Involvement The development of human capital requires the active involvement of leaders at all levels throughout the organization. It won't be successful if it is viewed only as the responsibility of the human resources department. Each year at General Electric, 200 facilitators, 30 officers, 30 human resource executives, and many young managers actively participate in GE's orientation program at the firm's impressive Crotonville training center outside New York City. Topics include global competition, winning on the global playing field, and personal examination of the new employee's core values vis-à-vis GE's values. As a senior manager once commented, "There is nothing like teaching Sunday school to force you to confront your own values."

The "cascade approach" is another way that managers at multiple levels in an organization become actively involved in developing human capital. For example, Robert Galvin, former chairman of Motorola, requested a workshop for more than 1,000 Motorola senior executives to help them understand the market potential of selected Asian countries. However, rather than bringing in outside experts, participants were asked to analyze the existing competition and to determine how Motorola could compete in these markets. After researching their topics, the executives traveled around the world to directly observe local market developments. Then they taught the concepts of globalization to the next level of 3,000 Motorola managers. By doing so, they not only verified their impressions with first-hand observations, but they also reinforced their learning and shared it by teaching others.

Monitoring Progress and Tracking Development   Whether a firm uses on-site formal training, off-site training (e.g., universities), or on-the-job training, tracking individual progress—and sharing this knowledge with both the employee and key managers—becomes essential. At Citibank (part of Citigroup, the large financial services organization), a talent inventory program keeps track of roughly 10,000 employees world-wide—how they're doing, what skills they need to work on, and where else in the company they might thrive. Larry Phillips, head of human resources, considers the program critical to the company's global growth.[31]

Like many leading-edge organizations, GlaxoSmithKline places increasingly greater emphasis on broader experiences over longer periods of time. Dan Phelan, senior vice president and director of human resources, explained, "We ideally follow a two-plus-two-plus-two formula in developing people for top management positions." The formula reflects the belief that SmithKline's best people should gain experience in two business units, two functional units (such as finance and marketing), in two countries. Interestingly, when vacancies occur among the firm's top 300 positions, the company will consider looking outside for talent. According to CEO Jan Leschly, "A little new blood doesn't hurt. If you're not the best person for the job, we'll show no hesitancy to go outside."

Evaluating Human Capital   In today's competitive environment, collaboration and interdependence have become vital to organizational success. Individuals must share their knowledge and work together constructively to achieve collective, not just individual, goals. However, traditional evaluation systems evaluate performance from a single perspective (i.e., "top down") and generally don't address the "softer" dimensions of communications and social skills, values, beliefs, and attitudes.

To address the limitations of the traditional approach, many organizations have begun to use 360-degree evaluation and feedback systems.[32] In these systems, superiors, direct reports, colleagues, and even internal and external customers rate a person's skills. Managers also rate themselves in order to have a personal benchmark. The 360-degree feedback system complements teamwork, employee involvement, and organizational flattening. As organizations continue to push responsibility downward, traditional top-down appraisal systems become insufficient. For example, a manager who previously managed the performance of 3 supervisors might now be responsible for 10, and less likely to have the in-depth knowledge needed to appraise and develop each sufficiently and fairly. Exhibit 4.3 provides a portion of GE's 360-degree evaluation system.

In addition to being more accurate, companies are also adopting multirater feedback systems to shorten the process for developing human capital. "What might have taken four or five years for people to realize about themselves before can happen in much less time," claimed Stella Estevez of Warner-Lambert (now merged into Pfizer), a pharmaceutical firm that uses 360-degree feedback. Similarly, Jerry Wallace of Saturn (a division of General Motors) learned that, although he considered himself as flexible, his subordinates did not. Instead they felt that he used excessive control. Wallace claimed, "I got a strong message that I need to delegate more. I thought I'd been doing it. But I need to do it more and sooner."

Finally, evaluation systems must ensure that a manager's success does not come at the cost of compromising the organization's core values. Clearly, such behavior generally leads to only short-term wins for both the manager and the organization. The organization typically suffers long-term losses in terms of morale, turnover, productivity, and so on. Accordingly, Merck's chairman, Ray Gilmartin, told his employees, "If someone is achieving

**Exhibit 4.3
An Excerpt from
General Electric's
360-Degree
Leadership
Assessment Chart**

Vision
- Has developed and communicated a clear, simple, customer-focused vision/direction for the organization.
- Forward-thinking, stretches horizons, challenges imaginations.
- Inspires and energizes others to commit to Vision. Captures minds. Leads by example.
- As appropriate, updates Vision to reflect constant and accelerating change affecting the business.

Customer/Quality Focus

Integrity

Accountability/Commitment

Communication/Influence

Shared Ownership/Boundary-less

Team Builder/Empowerment

Knowledge/Expertise/Intellect

Initiative/Speed

Global Mind-Set

Note: This evaluation system consists of 10 "characteristics"—Vision, Customer/Quality Focus, Integrity, and so on. Each of these characteristics has four "performance criteria." For illustrative purposes, the four performance criteria of "Vision" are included.

Source: Adapted from R. Slater, *Get Better or Get Beaten* (Burr Ridge, IL: Irwin Professional Publishing, 1994), pp. 152–55.

results but not demonstrating the core values of the company, at the expense of our people, that manager does not have much of a career here."

Retaining Human Capital

It has been said that talented employees are like "frogs in a wheelbarrow."[33] They can jump out at any time. By analogy, the organization can either try to force employees to stay in the firm, or try to keep them from wanting to jump out by creating incentives. In other words, today's leaders can either provide the work environment and incentives to keep productive employees and management from wanting to bail out, or rely on legal means such as employment contracts and noncompete clauses.[34] Clearly, firms must provide mechanisms that prevent the transfer of valuable and sensitive information outside the organization. Failure to do so would be, among other things, the neglect of a leader's fiduciary responsibility to shareholders. Clearly, greater efforts should be directed at the former (e.g., good work environment and incentives), but, as we all know, the latter (e.g., employment contracts and noncompete clauses) have their place.

Let's now discuss the importance of an individual's identification with the organization's mission and values, challenging work and stimulating environment, and financial and nonfinancial rewards and incentives in retaining a firm's human capital.

Identifying with an Organization's Mission and Values   People who identify with and are more committed to the core mission and values of the organization are less likely to stray or bolt to the competition. Consider Medtronic, Inc., an $8 billion medical products firm based in Minneapolis.[35] CEO Bill George stated: "Shareholder value is a hollow notion as the sole source of employee motivation. If you do business that way, you'll end up like ITT." What motivates its workers to go well beyond Medtronic's 34 percent total return to shareholders? Simply put, it's helping sick people get well. The company's motto is "Restoring patients to full life," and its symbol is an image of a supine human rising toward upright wellness. Sounds good, but how does the "resurrection" imagery come to life?

> Each December, at the company's holiday party, patients, their families, and their doctors are flown in to tell their survival stories. It's for employees—who are moved to tears year after year—and journalists are generally not invited. President Art Collins, a strapping guy with a firm handshake who is not prone to crying fits, said, "I remember my first holiday party and someone asked me if I had brought my Kleenex. I assumed I'd be fine, but these parents got up with their daughter who was alive because of our product. Even surgeons who see this stuff all the time were crying."

So much for the all-consuming emphasis on profits.

Employees can also form strong alliances to organizations that create simple and straightforward missions—"strategic intents"—that channel efforts and generate intense loyalties.[36] Examples include Canon's passion to "beat Xerox" and Honda's early quest to become a second Ford. Likewise, leaders can arouse passions and loyalty by reinforcing the firm's quest to "topple Goliath" or by constantly communicating a history of overcoming adversity and life-threatening challenges.[37] For example, CEO Richard Branson of the Virgin Group constantly uses the "David and Goliath" imagery, pitting his company against such powerful adversaries as British Airways and Coca-Cola. A key part of Southwest Airlines's folklore is its struggle for survival in the Texas courts against such entrenched (and now bankrupt) rivals as Braniff and Texas Air. Southwest does not exist because of regulated or protected markets, but despite them; during its first three years of existence, no planes left the ground!

Challenging Work and a Stimulating Environment Arthur Schawlow, winner of the 1981 Nobel Prize in physics, was once asked what he believed made the difference between highly creative and less creative scientists. His reply: "The labor of love aspect is very important. The most successful scientists often are not the most talented. But they are the ones impelled by curiosity. They've got to know what the answer is."[38]

Such insights highlight the importance of intrinsic motivation: the motivation to work on something because it is interesting, exciting, satisfying, or personally challenging. Consider the perspective of Jorgen Wedel, executive vice president of Gillette's international division, on the relative importance of pay compared with the meaningfulness of work: "I get calls from headhunters who offer bigger salaries, signing bonuses, and such. But the excitement of what I am doing here is equal to a 30 percent pay raise."

To keep competitors from poaching talent, organizations must keep employees excited about the challenges and opportunities available. Scott Cook, chairman of Intuit, understands this reality: "I wake up every morning knowing that if my people don't sense a compelling vision and a big upside, they'll simply leave."[39]

One way successful firms keep highly mobile employees motivated and challenged is through an internal market for opportunities, to lower the barriers to an employee's mobility within a company. For example, Shell Oil Company has created an "open sourcing" model for talent. Jobs are listed on Shell's intranet, and, with a two-month notice, employees can go to work on anything that interests them. Monsanto[40] has developed a similar approach. According to one executive:

Because we don't have a lot of structure, people will flow toward where success and innovation are taking place. We have a free-market system where people can move, so you have an outflow of people in areas where not much progress is being made. Before, the HR function ran processes like management development and performance evaluation. Now it also facilitates this movement of people.

Financial and Nonfinancial Rewards and Incentives   Without a doubt, financial rewards are a vital organizational control mechanism (as we will discuss in Chapter 9). Money—whether in the form of salary, bonus, stock options, and so forth—can mean many different things to people. For some it might mean security, to others recognition, and to still others, a sense of freedom and independence.

In an article in *Organizational Dynamics,* the point was raised that there is little evidence that simply paying people more is the most important factor in attracting and retaining human capital.[41] Most surveys show that money is not the most important reason why people take or leave jobs and that money, in some surveys, is not even in the top 10. Consistent with these findings, Tandem Computers (now part of Hewlett-Packard) never used to tell people being recruited what their salaries would be. People who asked were told that their salaries were competitive. If they persisted along this line of questioning, they would not be offered a position. Why? Tandem realized a rather simple idea: People who come for money will leave for money. Clearly, money can't be ignored, but it shouldn't be the primary mechanism to attract and retain talent.

Without the proper retention mechanisms (and as we all know, there are no easy answers), organizations can commit time and resources to inadvertently helping the competition develop their human capital.[42] And, given the importance of networking and teams, losses tend to multiply and intensify. The exodus of talent can erode a firm's competitive advantages in the marketplace. Let's now consider what some firms are doing to improve flexibility and amenities.

When discussing firms with an impressive array of amenities to retain (and attract) employees, few compare with USAA, the San Antonio–based insurance and financial services company.

> If you're not keen on driving to work, the company sponsors a van pool. A run in your hose? Pick up a pair at the on-site store. There's also a dry cleaning service, a bank, and several ATMs. Even the cafeteria food is so tasty that several years ago employees began demanding dinner to go. The athletic facilities are striking. The three gyms rival those of many upscale health clubs and one is open 24 hours a day. Outside, employees compete in intramural leagues in basketball and tennis as well as on the softball and tennis courts. Into golf? There's also a driving range.
>
> Many return to campus on weekends with their families. Donna Castillo, a sales manager in consumer finance and auto service, said, "There are playgrounds where they can run around, and it's nice to take pictures when the bluebonnets come out in the spring." USAA also scores high on the emerging trend for on-site child care. The facility can handle 300 children. Raul Navarez, a security officer, said, "My wife and I visited 10 or 12 day care facilities . . . there was no competition."[43]

Another nonfinancial reward involves accomodating working families with children. Coping with the conflicting demands of family and work is a problem at some point for virtually all employees. After all, women represent 44 percent of today's U.S. workforce, and mothers of children under age six represent the fastest-growing segment. Mothers are often the primary caregivers in a family. It is estimated that 60 percent of working-age women are employed outside the home. And, according to a recent study, 13 percent of women with preschoolers indicated that they would work more hours if additional or better child care were provided.[44]

strategy spotlight

Controlling HR Costs without Eroding Human Capital

HR managers are striving to increase the return on investment (ROI) in human capital. With labor costs accounting for more than 60 percent of the cost of sales, they are under increasing pressure to control costs without negatively affecting morale.

With the help of sophisticated statistical modeling tools, innovative firms are trying to analyze employee data to predict employee behavior and to ascertain how to cut costs without alienating employees. Such techniques will also help companies identify which incentives would enhance employee productivity. Could they pay an employee 20 percent less but give a three-month sabbatical every two years, cementing allegiance? Could they substitute flexible work hours for reduced pay? Does a boss's

managerial touch inspire an employee or undermine the employee's ability to produce? Finding answers to such questions will provide firms with the information they need to customize the hitherto standard compensation packages to give employees what they value. Such a practice helps in creating a more customized workplace in which the ROI of human capital can be increased.

Mercer Human Resources Consulting is pioneering its employee data statistical modeling technology with clients including Quest Diagnostics, Fleet Boston Financial, and First Tennessee. A larger number of blue chip companies are ascertaining the ROI they are attaining on their human capital investment and how they can improve it by creating more personalized reward systems. They are finding that employee productivity can be enhanced by tailoring salary and benefit packages to suit the employee's individual needs.

Source: M. Comlin, "Now It's Getting Personal," *BusinessWeek,* December 16, 2002, pp. 90–93; and B. Pfau and I. Kay, "The Hidden Human Resource: Shareholder Value," *Optimize,* June 2002, pp. 50–54.

Strategy Spotlight 4.3 discusses some innovative approaches to motivating and retaining human capital in a cost-effective model.

The Vital Role of Social Capital

Successful firms are well aware that the attraction, development, and retention of talent *is a necessary but not sufficient condition* for creating competitive advantages.[45] In the knowledge economy, it is not the stock of human capital that is important, but the extent to which it is combined and leveraged. In a sense, developing and retaining human capital becomes less important as key players (talented professionals, in particular) take the role of "free agents" and bring with them the requisite skill in many cases. Rather, the development of social capital (that is, the friendships and working relationships among talented individuals) gains importance, because it helps tie knowledge workers to a given firm.[46] Knowledge workers often exhibit greater loyalties to their colleagues and their profession than their employing organization, which may be "an amorphous, distant, and sometimes threatening entity."[47] Thus, a firm must find ways to create "ties" among its knowledge workers.

To illustrate, let's look at a hypothetical example. Two pharmaceutical firms are fortunate enough to hire Nobel Prize–winning scientists to work in their laboratories.[48] In one case, the scientist is offered a very attractive salary, outstanding facilities and equipment, and told to "go to it"! In the second case, the scientist is offered approximately the same salary, facilities, and equipment plus one additional ingredient. He or she will be working in a laboratory with 10 highly skilled and enthusiastic scientists. Part of the job is to collaborate with these peers and jointly develop promising drug compounds. There is little doubt as to which scenario will lead to a higher probability of retaining the scientist. Clearly, the interaction, sharing, and collaboration will create a situation in which the

How Nucor Shares Knowledge within and between Its Manufacturing Plants

Nucor, with 2003 revenues of $6.3 billion, is the most efficient steel producer in the world. A key aspect of its strategy is to develop strong social relationships and a team-based culture throughout the firm. It is effectively supported by a combination of work-group, plant-level, and corporate-wide financial incentives and rewards, wherein knowledge and best practices are eagerly shared by everyone in the organization. How does Nucor do it?

Within Plant Knowledge Transfers. Nucor strives to develop a social community within each plant that promotes trust and open communication. People know each other very well throughout each plant, and they are encouraged to interact. To accomplish this, the firm's policy is to keep the number of employees at each plant between 250 and 300. Such a relatively small number, combined with employees' long tenure, fosters a high degree of interpersonal familiarity. Additionally, each plant's general manager regularly holds dinner meetings for groups of 25

to 30, inviting every employee once a year. The format is free and open and includes a few ground rules: All comments are to remain business-related and are not to be directed to specific individuals. In turn, managers guarantee that they will carefully consider and respond to all suggestions and criticisms.

Between Plant Knowledge Transfers. Nucor uses several mechanisms to transfer knowledge among its plants. First, detailed performance data on each mill are regularly distributed to all of the plant managers. Second, all plant general managers meet as a group three times a year to review each facility's performance and develop formal plans on how to transfer best practices. Third, plant managers, supervisors, and machine operators regularly visit each other's mills. These visits enable operations personnel to go beyond performance data in order to understand firsthand the factors that make particular practices superior or inferior. After all, they are the true possessors of process knowledge. Fourth, given the inherent difficulties in transferring complex knowledge, Nucor selectively assigns people from one plant to another on the basis of their expertise.

Source: A. K. Gupta and V. Govindarajan, "Knowledge Management's Social Dimension: Lessons from Nucor Steel," *Organizational Dynamics,* Fall 2000, pp. 71–80.

scientist will develop firm-specific ties and be less likely to "bolt" for a higher salary offer. Such ties are critical because knowledge-based resources tend to be more tacit in nature, as we mentioned early in this chapter. Therefore, they are much more difficult to protect against loss (i.e., the individual quitting the organization) than other types of capital, such as equipment, machinery, and land.

Another way to view this situation is in terms of the resource-based view of the firm that we discussed in Chapter 3. That is, competitive advantages tend to be harder for competitors to copy if they are based on "unique bundles" of resources.[49] So, if employees are working effectively in teams and sharing their knowledge and learning from each other, not only will they be more likely to add value to the firm, but they also will be less likely to leave the organization, because of the loyalties and social ties that they develop over time. Strategy Spotlight 4.4 discusses how Nucor, a highly successful steel manufacturer, develops social capital among its employees and managers. This promotes the sharing of ideas within and across its manufacturing plants.

Next, we'll address a key concept in the New Economy—the Pied Piper Effect. Here, groups of professionals join (or leave) organizations en masse, not one at a time.

How Social Capital Helps Attract and Retain Talent

The importance of social ties among talented professionals is creating an important challenge (and opportunity) for organizations today. In the *Wall Street Journal,* Bernard Wysocki described the increasing prevalence of a type of "Pied Piper Effect," in which teams or networks of people are leaving one company for another.[50] The trend is to recruit job candidates at the crux of social networks in organizations, particularly if they are seen as having the potential to bring with them a raft of valuable colleagues. This is a process that is referred to as "hiring via personal networks." Let's look at one instance of this practice.

Gerald Eickhoff, founder of an electronic commerce company called Third Millennium Communications, tried for 15 years to hire Michael Reene. Why? Mr. Eickhoff says that he has "these Pied Piper skills." Mr. Reene was a star at Andersen Consulting in the 1980s and at IBM in the 1990s. He built his businesses and kept turning down overtures from Mr. Eickhoff.

However, in early 2000, he joined Third Millennium as chief executive officer, with just a $120,000 salary—but a 20 percent stake in the firm. Since then, he has brought in a raft of former IBM colleagues and Andersen subordinates. One protégé from his time at Andersen, Mary Goode, was brought on board as executive vice president. She promptly tapped her own network and brought along a half-dozen friends and former colleagues.

Wysocki considers the Pied Piper effect as one of the underappreciated factors in the war for talent today. This is because one of the myths of the New Economy is rampant individualism, wherein individuals find jobs on the Internet career sites and go to work for complete strangers. Perhaps, instead of Me Inc., the truth is closer to We Inc.[51]

Another example of social networks causing human capital mobility is the emigration of talent from an organization to form start-up ventures. Microsoft is perhaps the best-known example of this phenomenon.[52] Professionals have frequently left Microsoft—en masse—to form venture capital and technology start-ups built around teams of software developers. One example is Ignition Corporation, of Bellevue, Washington, which was formed by Brad Silverberg, a former Microsoft senior vice president. Eight former Microsoft executives, among others, founded the company. Exhibit 4.4 provides a partial listing of other companies that have been formed by groups of former Microsoft employees.

The importance of the Pied Piper Effect for today's firms is rather self-evident. Leaders must be aware of social relationships among professionals as important recruiting and retention mechanisms. Some good advice for professionals would be to not invest all their

Company	What It Does	Defectors from Microsoft
Crossgain	Builds software around XML computer language	23 of 60 employees
ViAir	Makes software for wireless providers	Company declines to specify
CheckSpace	Builds online payment service for small businesses	Company says "a good chunk" of its 30 employees
digiMine	Sells data mining service	About 15% of 62 employees in addition to the 3 founders
Avogadro	Builds wireless notification software	8 of 25 employees
Tellme Networks	Offers information like stock quotes and scores over the phone	About 40 of 250 employees; another 40 from the former Netscape

Exhibit 4.4 Microsoft Employees Who Have Left the Company for Other Businesses

Source: From the *Wall Street Journal*, Eastern Edition by Rebecca Buckman. Copyright © 2000 by Dow Jones & Company, Inc. Reproduced with permission of Dow Jones & Company, Inc., via Copyright Clearance Center.

Silicon Valley has been a breeding ground for entrepreneurial talent. But where does this talent come from? Perhaps a few entrepreneurial firms in this unique area have tried traditional routes such as help wanted ads, but for the most part Silicon Valley finds new talent by tapping the social contacts of existing owners and employees.

The Valley has a vast network of interwoven relationships. New firms develop from previous experience; previous experience involves contact with prior employers and co-workers. As professionals expand these contacts over time, a web of relationships develops. Silicon Valley relies on this intricate network for finding new talent. Rather than posting ads on Internet job service bulletin boards, firms needing new talent rely on the social

network. This enables companies to prescreen potential candidates. Those who have reputations for 30-hour work weeks and 40-hour golf weeks are excluded. Candidates who are known for off-the-wall ideas that just might work are included.

Shared values characterize Silicon Valley. Individuals often have more loyalty to their peers—including those in competing firms—than they do to their current employer. This makes the social network even more crucial; if individuals are known for undermining others, even contacts in rival firms, their future job mobility becomes limited. Thus, the network of talent is more cooperative than competitive.

Individuals in Silicon Valley typically do not work for the same company for a lifetime. Job changes are frequent and common. John Doerr of Kleiner Perkins (a top venture capital firm) is fond of saying that the Silicon Valley is the only place you can change jobs and keep your parking space!

Sources: W. Swap and D. Leonard, "Gurus in the Garage," *Harvard Business Review* 78, no. 6 (2000), pp. 71–82; G. Hamel, "Bringing Silicon Valley Inside," *Harvard Business Review* 77, no. 5 (1999), pp. 71–84; J. Aley, "Silicon Valley Is the Intellectual Incubator of the Digital Age," *Fortune,* July 7, 1997, pp. 67–74.

time and effort in enhancing their human capital (skills and competences). Rather, they should be sure to also develop their social networks.[53]

Social networks can provide an important mechanism for obtaining both resources and information from individuals and organizations outside the boundary of a firm.[54] Also, to be a valued member of a social network, one typically has to have the requisite human capital, that is, knowledge and capabilities that can add value to other members of the network. Strategy Spotlight 4.5 is an example of how social networks allow exchange of resources and information in the technology-intensive Silicon Valley in Northern California.

The Potential Downside of Social Capital

Some companies have been damaged by high social capital that breeds "groupthink"—a tendency not to question shared beliefs.[55] When people identify strongly with a group, they sometimes support ideas that are suboptimal or simply wrong. Too great a degree of warm and fuzzy feelings among group members prevents people from challenging one another with tough questions as well as discourages them from engaging in the "creative abrasion" that Dorothy Leonard of Harvard University described as a key source of innovation.[56] Two firms well known for their collegiality, strong sense of employee membership, and humane treatment—Digital Equipment (now part of Hewlett-Packard Co.) and Polaroid—suffered greatly from market misjudgments and strategic errors. The aforementioned aspects of their culture contributed to their problems.

Additionally, some have argued that socialization processes whereby individuals are "socialized in the norms, values, and ways of working inherent to the workgroup and the organization" can be potentially expensive in terms of financial resources and managerial commitment.[57] Such expenses may represent a significant opportunity cost that should be evaluated in terms of the potential costs and benefits. Clearly, if such expenses become excessive, profitability may be eroded.

In general, however, the effects of high social capital are strongly positive. Engagement, collaboration, loyalty, persistence, and dedication are important benefits.[58] Firms such as United Parcel Service, Hewlett-Packard, and SAS Institute have made significant investments in social capital that enable them to attract and retain talent and help them to do their best work. Few of such companies seem to face any imminent danger from an overdose of a good thing.

Using Technology to Leverage Human Capital and Knowledge

Sharing knowledge and information throughout the organization can be a means of conserving resources, developing products and services, and creating new opportunities. In this section we will discuss how technology can be used to leverage human capital and knowledge within organizations as well as with customers and suppliers beyond their boundaries. We will start with simple applications, such as the use of e-mail and networks for product development, and then we will discuss how technology can help to enhance the competitive position of knowledge-intensive firms in industries such as consulting, health care, and personal computers. We will close by discussing how technology can help firms to retain employees' knowledge—even when they leave, because, even in the most desirable workplaces, people will leave. Technology can help us to make sure they don't take all of the valuable knowledge with them.

Using Networks to Share Information and Develop Products and Services

As we all know, e-mail is an effective means of communicating a wide variety of information. It is quick, easy, and almost costless. Of course, it can become a problem when employees use it extensively for personal reasons and it detracts from productivity. Consider how fast jokes or rumors can spread within and across organizations! For example, at Computer Associates, the $3 billion software giant, e-mail is banned from 10 a.m. to noon and again from 2 p.m. to 4 p.m. because the firm's chairman, Charles Wang, believes that it detracts from productivity.[59]

E-mail can, however, be a means for top executives to communicate information efficiently. For example, Martin Sorrell, chairman of WPP Group PLC, a $3.2 billion advertising and public relations firm, is a strong believer in the use of e-mail.[60] He writes to all of his employees once a month by means of e-mail. He discusses how the company is doing, addresses specific issues, and offers his perspectives on hot issues, such as new business models for the Internet. He believes that it is a great way to keep people abreast of what he is working on.

As one might expect, the idea of top executives sharing ideas with many or all individuals in their company is hardly new.[61] In the 1800s at British American Tobacco (BAT), the chief executive would write a monthly report to all of BAT's country managers. The executive used a fountain pen, and it generally took about three months for the report to reach India. With e-mail the message gets out in seconds—an enormous difference. Clearly, e-mail can be an effective tool, but it must be used judiciously.

The use of technology has also enabled professionals to work as part of virtual teams to enhance the speed and effectiveness with which products are developed. For example,

Microsoft has concentrated much of its development around virtual teams that are networked together throughout the company.[62] This helps accelerate design and testing of new software modules that use the Windows-based framework as their central architecture. Microsoft is able to foster specialized technical expertise while sharing knowledge rapidly throughout the organization. This helps the firm learn how its new technologies can be applied rapidly to new business ventures such as cable television, broadcasting, travel services, and financial services.

Codifying Knowledge for Competitive Advantage

As we discussed early in this chapter, there are two different kinds of knowledge. Tacit knowledge is embedded in personal experience and shared only with the consent and participation of the individual. Explicit (or codified) knowledge, on the other hand, is knowledge that can be documented, widely distributed, and easily replicated. One of the challenges of knowledge-intensive organizations is to capture and codify the knowledge and experience that, in effect, resides in the heads of its employees. Otherwise, they will have to constantly "reinvent the wheel," which is both expensive and inefficient. Also, the "new wheel" may not necessarily be superior to the "old wheel."[63]

Once a knowledge asset (e.g., a software code or processes/routines for a consulting firm) is developed and paid for, it can be reused many times at very low cost, assuming that it doesn't have to be substantially modified each time. Let's take the case of a consulting company, such as Accenture (formerly Andersen Consulting).[64] Since the knowledge of its consultants has been codified and stored in electronic repositories, it can be employed in many jobs by a huge number of consultants. Additionally, since the work has a high level of standardization (i.e., there are strong similarities across the numerous client engagements), there generally tends to be a rather high ratio of consultants to partners. For example, the ratio of consultants to partners is roughly 30, which is quite high. As one might expect, there must be extensive training of the newly hired consultants for such an approach to work. The recruits are trained at Accenture's Center for Professional Education, a 150-acre campus in St. Charles, Illinois. Using the center's knowledge-management respository, the consultants work through many scenarios designed to improve business processes. In effect, the information technologies enable the consultants to be "implementers, not inventors."

Access Health, a call-in medical center, also uses technology to capture and share knowledge. When someone calls the center, a registered nurse uses the company's "clinical decision architecture" to assess the caller's symptoms, rule out possible conditions, and recommend a home remedy, doctor's visit, or trip to the emergency room. The company's knowledge repository contains algorithms of the symptoms of more than 500 illnesses. According to CEO Joseph Tallman, "We are not inventing a new way to cure disease. We are taking available knowledge and inventing processes to put it to better use." At Access Health, the codified knowledge is in the form of software algorithms. They were very expensive to develop, but the investment has been repaid many times over. The first 300 algorithms that Access Health developed have each been used an average of 8,000 times a year. Further, the company's paying customers—insurance companies and provider groups —save money because many callers would have made expensive trips to the emergency room or the doctor's office had they not been diagnosed over the phone.

The use of information technology in codifying knowledge can also help a firm to integrate activities among its internal value-chain activities, customers, and suppliers. Strategy Spotlight 4.6 shows how Dell Computer's sophisticated knowledge-management system is an integral part of its widely admired business model.

Dell Computer's Knowledge Management

A company that can successfully assemble and sell 11 million personal computers (PCs) a year, using 40,000 possible configurations (compared with about 100 for competitors), is clearly one that has learned something about knowledge management. Dell Computer Corporation has recruited talented engineers to design these processes, but the company's real strength is found in the way it has codified these processes.

By investing heavily in the ability to determine the necessary configurations up front, Dell is able to reuse this knowledge to its advantage. Although each configuration is used on average only about 275 times each year, Dell has captured the knowledge of its talented engineers in the

Sources: M. T. Hansen, N. Nohria, and T. Tierney, "What's Your Strategy for Managing Knowledge?" *Harvard Business Review* 77, no. 2 (1999), pp. 106–17; J. Magretta, "The Power of Virtual Integration: An Interview with Dell Computer's Michael Dell," *Harvard Business Review* 76, no. 2 (1998), pp. 73–84.

processes used to custom assemble PCs en masse. Key to Dell's knowledge-management system is a repository that contains a list of available components. Dell uses this system to its competitive advantage through cost containment that is passed on, in part, to consumers. This low-cost advantage provides Dell with a 25 percent share of the U.S. personal computer market.

Dell effectively uses its knowledge-management system to integrate assembly activities from the initial customer order to product delivery. The company's external supply chain is linked to the assembly process by an elaborate inventory-control system that enables the firm to know what parts are currently available, matching these to possible configurations. This enhances Dell's link with customers by giving customers the flexibility to order PCs to their desired specifications. By integrating the entire value chain with its knowledge-management system, Dell has given itself an edge in the intensely competitive PC market.

Retaining Knowledge When Employees Leave

All organizations—with few exceptions, such as prisons and the military during periods of conscription—suffer the adverse consequences of voluntary turnover. As we noted in Chapter 3, even SAS Institute, consistently one of *Fortune* magazine's "Most Desirable Places to Work," has a 4 percent turnover (far below the software industry's average of 20 percent). So, turnover—to a high, moderate, or low degree—is simply an organizational fact of life. However, many leading firms are devising ways to minimize the loss of knowledge when employees leave.

Information technology can often help employers cope with turnover by saving some tacit knowledge that the firm would otherwise lose.[65] Customer relationship software, for example, automates sales and provides salespeople with access to client histories, including prior orders and complaints. This enables salespeople to quickly become familiar with client accounts (about which they might otherwise know nothing). Similarly, groupware applications such as Lotus Notes can standardize interactions and keep records of decisions and crucial contextual information, providing something like an electronic record of employee knowledge. Other programs, such as Open Text's Livelink, enable all employees to track and share documents on their firm's intranet. New simulation software for team-based project management, such as Thinking Tools's Project Challenge, enables new teams to learn how to work together much more rapidly than on-the-job experience alone would permit.

Even a simple technology such as e-mail can help when key employees leave an organization. For example, Pamela Hirshman, a project manager at Young & Rubicam, a large international advertising firm, was asked to take over a project after the entire original project team bolted.[66] Noted Hirshman: "The project file had a record of all the e-mails between the team and the client, and after reviewing about 50 of these, I was up to speed on the problems of the client and where the project was headed."

Capturing Employee Knowledge

The rules have changed in the increasingly competitive game of recruiting and retaining IT professionals at health care organizations. People with the right technical skills are in high demand, and they are demanding even more. As a result, employee turnover rates have increased.

What happens to the knowledge that these employees take with them? The problem is more serious for organizations that lose tacit knowledge when an employee leaves. "If an employee is going to leave, the organization has to be prepared," says Debra Speight, CIO of Harvard Pilgrim Healthcare. The Brookline, Massachusetts–based health plan has come up with the creative idea of paying a

bonus for departing IT employees to leave behind the knowledge they have about the health plan's technical systems. It pays a bonus anywhere between $1,000 and $5,000, depending on the quality of information that is given to the organization. A committee reviews the information and pays out the bonus. It is clearly recognized that retaining knowledge is vital to ongoing operations.

There are also added benefits. Speight claimed that "the process itself has been priceless. It may even cause our turnover rate to go down. When people understand exactly how much you value their knowledge, they're less like to leave." Organizations that are knowledge-intensive need to have such strategies in place for capturing and retaining as much knowledge as possible.

Sources: P. Labarre, "People Go, Knowledge Stays," *Fast Company,* September 1998, 48; and www.healthcare-informatics.com/issues/1992/02_99/money.htm.

A key issue in such knowledge-management systems becomes one of motivation. That is, what are the incentives for people to contribute their knowledge? Some organizations have found that such systems work best when they are incorporated into the firm's evaluation and reward system. For example, Bruce Strong, founder and CEO of Context Integration, a Web consulting firm, decided to develop a knowledge-management system to help employees unlock their thoughts and, collectively, help them to be more productive.[67] Six months and a half-million dollars later, he unveiled IAN (Intellectual Assets Network). The objective was to provide a medium for his consultants to share ideas, ask questions, and trace earlier journeys on similar projects. The theory was fine, but Strong was disappointed with the lack of involvement by his employees. This is not surprising. Carla O'Dell, president of the American Productivity and Quality Center, said that of the companies trying knowledge management, fewer than 10 percent succeeded in making it part of their culture.

Why didn't the consultants embrace IAN? There were many reasons:

- Consultants saw depositing notes or project records into the database as one more task in a busy day.
- The task didn't appear to have any urgency.
- Consultants generally did not like to admit they couldn't solve a problem.
- They resented management trying to impose what consultants perceived as a rigid structure on their work.

What was Strong to do? He began to reinforce the many benefits of the system, such as providing better and more consistent service. He also publicly recognized people who stood out as strong IAN contributors, and he made this part of everyone's job description. Perhaps most important, he began paying people to use it. He assigned points when people used the system—for example, one point for posting a résumé on the system, five points for creating a project record, and so on. The results were tallied every three months and the score accounted for 10 percent of a consultant's quarterly bonus. Over a two-month period, overall IAN usage almost doubled. However, more important, many consultants became enthusiastic converts once they had a positive experience with IAN. Not only does IAN continue to help many of them to provide excellent service to their clients, but also some of their knowledge remains in the firm when they leave.

Strategy Spotlight 4.7 discusses Harvard Pilgrim Health Care's innovative approach to capturing employees' knowledge—an especially important challenge when people leave the organization.

We close this section with a series of questions managers should consider in determining (1) how effective their organization is in attracting, developing, and retaining human capital and (2) how effective they are in leveraging human capital through social capital and technology. These questions, included in Exhibit 4.5, summarize some of the key issues addressed in this chapter.

The Central Role of Leveraging Human Capital in Strategy Formulation

In this chapter we have emphasized the importance of human capital and how such intangible assets can create the greatest value in today's successful organizations. As we have noted throughout the chapter, attracting top talent is a necessary but not sufficient condition for competitive advantage. It must be not only developed and retained, but also leveraged through effective use of social capital and technology. In this section we will discuss how leveraging human capital is vital to each of the levels of strategy that we will address in the next four chapters (5, 6, 7, and 8) of the book.

Leveraging Human Capital and Business-Level Strategy

At the business level (Chapter 5), firms strive to create advantages that are sustainable over time. To do this, managers must integrate the primary and support activities in their firm's value chain (discussed in Chapter 3). In Chapter 5 we will lead off with the problems that Food Lion had with its employees because of the company's overemphasis on cost reduction. This alienated employees, leading to lowered productivity, legal action, and a "we versus them" attitude—causing the erosion of social relations among Food Lion employees. On a more positive note, we will discuss how much of Siebel Systems's success can be attributed to its excellent customer relationships, fostered by the firm's insistence on having customer input before the software is written. And FedEx has provided its drivers with handheld computers—a valuable technology—to help them effectively track customer packages. The examples of Siebel Systems and FedEx point out how social capital and technology can help a firm enhance business-level strategies by leveraging its human capital.

Leveraging Human Capital and Corporate-Level Strategy

In Chapter 6 on corporate-level strategy, we will discuss how firms can create value by managing their business to create synergy; that is, how more value can be created by working together across business units than if they were freestanding units. Managers must determine what important relationships (products, markets, technologies) exist across businesses and how they can be leveraged. We will discuss how Procter & Gamble is able to reapply its customer knowledge and understanding of technologies across many different product markets. For example, P&G's knowledge in oral hygiene and bleaching agents enabled it to develop a special film technology that whitened teeth within 14 days. For such knowledge transfer to occur, managers must be aware of not only their human capital (tacit

Exhibit 4.5

Issues to Consider in Creating Value through Human Capital, Social Capital, and Technology

Human Capital

Recruiting "Top-Notch" Human Capital

- Does the organization assess attitude and "general makeup" instead of focusing primarily on skills and background in selecting employees at all levels?
- How important is creativity and problem solving ability? Are they properly considered in hiring decisions?
- Do people throughout the organization engage in effective networking activities to obtain a broad pool of worthy potential employees? Is the organization creative in such endeavors?

Enhancing Human Capital through Employee Development

- Does the development and training process inculcate an "organizationwide" perspective?
- Is there widespread involvement—including top executives—in the preparation and delivery of training and development programs?
- Is the development of human capital effectively tracked and monitored?
- Are there effective programs for succession at all levels of the organization—especially the top-most levels?
- Does the firm effectively evaluate its human capital? Is a 360-degree evaluation used? Why? Why not?
- Are mechanisms in place to assure that a manager's success does not come at the cost of compromising the organization's core values?

Retaining the Best Employees

- Are there appropriate financial rewards to motivate employees at all levels?
- Do people throughout the organization strongly identify with the organization's mission?
- Are employees provided a stimulating and challenging work environment that fosters professional growth?
- Are valued amenities provided (e.g., flextime, child-care facilities, telecommuting) that are appropriate given the organization's mission, strategy, and how work is accomplished?
- Is the organization continually devising strategies and mechanisms to retain top performers?

Social Capital

- Are there positive personal and professional relationships among employees?
- Is the organization benefiting (or being penalized) by hiring (or by voluntary turnover) en masse?
- Does an environment of caring and encouragement rather than competition enhance team performance?
- Does the organization minimize the adverse effects of excessive social capital—such as excessive costs and "groupthink"?

Technology

- Does the organization effectively use technology to transfer best practices across the organization?
- Does the organization use technology to leverage both human capital and knowledge both within the boundaries of the organization as well as among its suppliers and customers?
- Has the organization used technologies such as e-mail and networks to develop products and services?
- Has the organization effectively used technology to codify knowledge for competitive advantage?
- Does the organization try to retain some of the knowledge of employees when they decide to leave the firm?

Source: Adapted from G. G. Dess and J. C. Picken, *Beyond Productivity* (New York: AMACON, 1999), pp. 63–64.

knowledge), but also their organization's codified knowledge and relationships among key professionals and business units.

Leveraging Human Capital and International-Level Strategy

In Chapter 7 we will address how companies create value by leveraging resources and knowledge across national boundaries. Here firms are faced with two opposing forces: how to achieve economies of scale and how to adapt to local market needs. We will discuss how some leading-edge firms are able to successfully attain a "transnational strategy" wherein not only do the firms achieve lower costs through economies of scale, but also are able to adapt successfully to local markets. To do so, firms must facilitate the flow of information and knowledge between business units in different countries. This requires not only attracting, developing, and retaining superior talent, but also leveraging their knowledge and skills through effective working relationships (i.e., social capital) and use of technology.

Leveraging Human Capital and Internet Strategies

Chapter 8 addresses the role of digital and Internet-based technologies in creating competitive advantages. These technologies have enormous strategic implications for managers who use them to lower costs, enhance customer service, and improve performance. We provide the example of BP Amoco, a company that has pursued an aggressive policy of implementing Internet-based capabilities. Managers are able to tap into the company's reservoir of knowledge by using the personalized Web pages that all BP Amoco employees use to report on their areas of expertise. In one example, engineers drilling for oil in the Caribbean saved $600,000 by using a process that had been developed in Norway just a few days earlier. To make such technologies effective, of course, requires both talented professionals to develop and apply knowledge as well as strong, positive working relationships between managers and technology experts.

summary

Firms throughout the industrial world are recognizing that the knowledge worker is the key to success in the marketplace. However, we also recognize that human capital, although vital, is still only a necessary but not a sufficient condition for creating value. We began the first section of the chapter by addressing the importance of human capital and how it can be attracted, developed, and retained. Then we discussed the role of social capital and technology in leveraging human capital for competitive success. We pointed out that intellectual capital—the difference between a firm's market value and its book value—has increased significantly over the past few decades. This is particularly true for firms in knowledge-intensive industries, especially where there are relatively few tangible assets, such as software development.

The second section of the chapter addressed the attraction, development, and retention of human capital. We viewed these three activities as a "three-legged stool"—that is, it is difficult for firms to be successful if they ignore or are unsuccessful in any one of these activities. Among the issues we discussed in *attracting* human capital were "hiring for attitude, training for skill" and the value of using social networks to attract human capital. In particular, it is important to attract employees who can collaborate with others, given the importance of collective efforts such as teams and task forces. With regard to *developing* human capital, we discussed the need to encourage widespread involvement throughout the organization, monitor progress and track the development of human capital, and evaluate human capital. Among the issues that are widely practiced in evaluating human capital is the 360-degree evaluation system. Employees are evaluated by their superiors, peers, direct reports, and even internal and external customers. Finally, some mechanisms for retaining human capital are employees' identification with the organization's mission and values, providing challenging work and a stimulating environment, the importance of financial and nonfinancial rewards and incentives, and providing flexibility and amenities. A key issue here is that a firm should not overemphasize financial rewards. After all, if individuals join an organization for money, they also are likely to leave for money. With money as the primary motivator, there is little chance that employees will develop firm-specific ties to keep them with the organization.

The third section of the chapter discussed the importance of social capital in leveraging human capital. Social capital refers to the network of relationships that individuals have throughout the organization as well as with customers and suppliers. Such ties can be critical in obtaining both information and resources. With regard to recruiting, for example, we saw how some firms are able to hire en masse groups of individuals who are part of social networks. Social relationships can also be very important in the effective functioning of groups. Finally, we discussed some of the potential downsides of social capital. These include the expenses that firms may bear when promoting social and working relationships among individuals as well as the potential for "groupthink," wherein individuals are reluctant to express divergent (or opposing) views on an issue because of social pressures to conform.

The fourth section addressed the role of technology in leveraging human capital. We discussed relatively simple means of using technology, such as e-mail and networks where individuals can collaborate by way of personal computers. We also addressed more sophisticated uses of technology, such as sophisticated management systems. Here knowledge can be codified and reused at very low cost, as we saw in the examples of firms in the consulting, health care, and high-technology industries. Also, given that there will still be some turnover—voluntary or involuntary—even in the most desirable places to work, technology can be a valuable means of retaining knowledge when individuals terminate their employment with a firm.

The final section addressed how the leveraging of human capital is critical in strategy formulation at all levels. This includes the business, corporate, international, and Internet levels.

summary review questions

1. Explain the role of knowledge in today's competitive environment.

2. Why is it important for managers to recognize the interdependence in the attraction, development, and retention of talented professionals?

3. What are some of the potential downsides for firms that engage in a "war for talent"?

4. Discuss the need for managers to use social capital in leveraging their human capital both within and across their firm.

5. Discuss the key role of technology in leveraging knowledge and human capital.

experiential exercise

Johnson & Johnson, a leading health care firm with $42 billion in 2003 revenues, is often rated as one of *Fortune*'s "Most Admired Firms." It is also considered an excellent place to work and has generated high return to shareholders. Clearly, they value their human capital. Using the Internet and/or library resources, identify some of the actions/strategies Johnson & Johnson has taken to attract, develop, and retain human capital. What are their implications?

Activity	Actions/Strategies	Implications
Attracting human capital		
Developing human capital		
Retaining human capital		

1. Look up successful firms in a high-technology industry as well as two successful firms in more traditional industries such as automobile manufacturing and retailing. Compare their market values and book values. What are some implications of these differences?
2. Select a firm for which you believe its social capital—both within the firm and among its suppliers and customers—is vital to its competitive advantage. Support your arguments.
3. Choose a company with which you are familiar. What are some of the ways in which it uses technology to leverage its human capital?
4. Using the Internet, look up a company with which you are familiar. What are some of the policies and procedures that it uses to enhance the firm's human and social capital?

1. Recall an example of a firm that recently faced an ethical crisis. How do you feel the crisis and management's handling of it affected the firm's human capital and social capital?
2. Based on your experiences or what you have learned in your previous classes, are you familiar with any companies that used unethical practices to attract talented professionals? What do you feel were the short-term and long-term consequences of such practices?

1. Gunning for KPMG, 2003, *The Economist*, February 1: 63; Bianco, A., & Moore, P. L., 2001, Downfall: The inside story of the management fiasco at Xerox, *Business-Week*, May 5: 82–92; Deutsch, C. H., 2000, Moody's puts Xerox below investment grade, *New York Times*, December 2: A1; Deutsch, C. H., 2000, The fading copier king: Xerox has failed to capitalize on its own innovations, *New York Times*, October 19: B6.
2. This chapter draws upon some of the ideas and examples from Dess, G. G., & Picken, J. C., 1999, *Beyond Productivity* (New York: AMACOM).
3. An acknowledged trend: The world economic survey, 1996, *Economist*, September 28: 25–28.
4. Quinn, J. B., Anderson, P., & Finkelstein, S., 1996, Leveraging intellect, *Academy of Management Executive* 10 (3): 7–27.

5. Hamel, G., & Prahalad, C. K., 1996, Competing in the new economy: Managing out of bounds, *Strategic Management Journal* 17:238.

6. Stewart, T. A., 1997, *Intellectual Capital: The New Wealth of Organizations* (New York: Doubleday/Currency).

7. Leif Edvisson and Michael S. Malone have a similar, more detailed definition of *intellectual capital:* "the combined knowledge, skill, innovativeness, and ability to meet the task at hand." They consider intellectual capital to equal human capital plus structural capital. *Structural capital* is defined as "the hardware, software, databases, organization structure, patents, trademarks, and everything else of organizational capability that supports those employees' productivity—in a word, everything left at the office when the employees go home." Edvisson, L., & Malone, M. S., 1997, *Intellectual Capital: Realizing Your Company's True Value by Finding Its Hidden Brainpower* (New York: HarperBusiness), especially pp. 10–14.

8. Stewart, T. A., 2001, Accounting gets radical, *Fortune*, April 16: 184–94.

9. Thomas Stewart has suggested this formula in his book *Intellectual Capital.* He provides an insightful discussion on pages 224–25, including some of the limitations of this approach to measuring intellectual capital. We recognize, of course, that during the late 1990s and in early 2000, there were some excessive market valuations of high-technology and Internet firms. For an interesting discussion of the extraordinary market valuation of Yahoo!, an Internet company, refer to Perkins, A. B., 2001, The Internet bubble encapsulated: Yahoo! *Red Herring,* April 15: 17–18.

10. Roberts, P. W., & Dowling, G. R., 2002, Corporate reputation and sustained superior financial performance, *Strategic Management Journal* 23 (12): 1077–95.

11. One of the seminal contributions on knowledge management is Becker, G. S., 1993, *Human Capital: A Theoretical and Empirical Analysis with Special Reference to Education,* 3rd ed. (Chicago: University of Chicago Press).

12. For an excellent discussion of social capital and its impact on organizational performance, refer to Nahapiet, J., & Ghoshal, S., 1998, Social capital, intellectual capital, and the organizational advantage, *Academy of Management Review* 23: 242–66.

13. Polanyi, M., 1967, *The Tacit Dimension* (Garden City, NY: Anchor Publishing).

14. Barney, J. B., 1991, Firm resources and sustained competitive advantage, *Journal of Management* 17: 99–120.

15. Some of the notable books on this topic include Edvisson & Malone, op. cit.; Stewart, op. cit.; and Nonaka, I., & Takeuchi, I., 1995, *The Knowledge Creating Company* (New York: Oxford University Press).

16. Stewart, T. A., 2000, Taking risk to the marketplace, *Fortune,* March 6: 424.

17. Dutton, G., 1997, Are you technologically competent? *Management Review,* November: 54–58.

18. Dess & Picken, op. cit., p. 34.

19. Webber, A. M., 1998, Danger: Toxic company, *Fast Company,* November: 152–61.

20. Key to success: People, people, people, 1997, *Fortune,* October 27: 232.

21. Martin, J., 1998, So, you want to work for the best . . . , *Fortune,* January 12: 77.

22. Carbonara, P., 1997, Hire for attitude, train for skill, *Fast Company,* August–September: 66–67.

23. Stewart, T. A., 1996, Why value statements don't work, *Fortune,* June 10: 138.

24. Cardin, R., 1997, Make your own Bozo Filter, *Fast Company,* October–November: 56.

25. Carbonara, op. cit.

26. Martin, op. cit.; Henkoff, R., 1993, Companies that train best, *Fortune,* March 22: 53–60.

27. Bartlett, C. A., & Ghoshal, S., 2002, Building competitive advantage through people, *MIT Sloan Management Review* 43 (2): 34–41.

28. Ibid.

29. Stewart, T. A., 1998, Gray flannel suit? moi? *Fortune,* March 18: 80–82.

30. Ibid.

31. Keys to success: People, people, people, 1997, *Fortune,* October 27: 232.

32. The discussion of the 360-degree feedback system draws on UPS, 1997, 360-degree feedback: Coming from all sides, *Vision* (a UPS Corporation internal company publication), March: 3; Slater, R., 1994, *Get Better or Get Beaten: Thirty-one Leadership Secrets from Jack Welch* (Burr Ridge, IL: Irwin); Nexon, M., 1997, General Electric: The secrets of the finest company in the world, *L'Expansion,* July 23: 18–30; and Smith, D., 1996, Bold new directions for human resources, *Merck World* (internal company publication), October: 8.

33. Kets de Vries, M. F. R., 1998, Charisma in action: The transformational abilities of Virgin's Richard Branson and ABB's Percy Barnevik, *Organizational Dynamics,* Winter: 20.

34. One has only to consider the most celebrated case of industrial espionage in recent years, wherein José Ignacio Lopez was indicted in a German court for stealing sensitive product planning documents from his former employer, General Motors, and sharing them with his executive colleagues at Volkswagen. The lawsuit was dismissed by the German courts, but Lopez and his colleagues were investigated by the U.S. Justice Department. Also consider the recent litigation involving noncompete employment contracts and confidentiality clauses of *International Paper v. Louisiana-Pacific, Campbell Soup v. H. J. Heinz Co.,* and *PepsiCo v. Quaker Oats's Gatorade.* In addition to retaining valuable human resources and often their valuable network of customers, firms must also protect proprietary infor-

mation and knowledge. For interesting insights, refer to Carley, W. M., 1998, CEO gets hard lesson in how not to keep his lieutenants, *Wall Street Journal,* February 11: A1, A10; and Lenzner, R., & Shook, C., 1998, Whose Rolodex is it, anyway? *Forbes,* February 23: 100–103.

35. Lieber, R. B., 1998, Why employees love these companies, *Fortune,* January 12: 72–74.

36. The examples in this section draw upon a variety of sources, including Lubove, S., 1998, New age capitalist, *Forbes,* April 6: 42–43; Kets de Vries, op. cit.; Pfeffer, J., 1995, Producing sustainable competitive advantage through the effective management of people, *Academy of Management Executive* 9 (1): 55–69. The concept of strategic intent is generally credited to Hamel, G., & Prahalad, C. K., 1989, Strategic intent, *Harvard Business Review* 67: 63–76.

37. Kets de Vries, op. cit., pp. 73–92.

38. Amabile, T. M., 1997, Motivating creativity in organizations: On doing what you love and loving what you do, *California Management Review,* Fall: 39–58.

39. The discussion of internal markets for human capital draws on Hamel, G., 1999, Bringing Silicon Valley inside, *Harvard Business Review* 77 (5): 71–84.

40. Monsanto has been part of Pharmacia since 2002. *Hoover's Handbook of Am. Bus. 2004,* p. 562.

41. Pfeffer, J., 2001, Fighting the war for talent is hazardous to your organization's health, *Organizational Dynamics* 29 (4): 248–59.

42. For an insightful discussion on strategies for retaining and developing human capital, refer to Coff, R. W., 1997, Human assets and management dilemmas: Coping with hazards on the road to resource-based theory, *Academy of Management Review* 22 (2): 374–402.

43. The examples in this section draw upon the following sources: Stewart, *Intellectual Capital;* and Fisher, A., 1998, The 100 best companies to work for in America, *Fortune,* January 12: 69–70.

44. The statistics on child care trends are drawn from Bubbar, S. E., & Aspelin, D. J., 1998, The overtime rebellion: Symptom of a bigger problem? *Academy of Management Executive* 12:68–76. The other examples in this section are drawn from various sources, including Munk, N., 1998, The new organization man, *Fortune,* March 16: 68–72; and Hammonds, K. H., Furchgott, R., Hamm, S., & Judge, P. C., 1997, Work and family, *BusinessWeek,* September 15: 96–104.

45. This discussion draws on Dess, G. G., & Lumpkin, G. T., 2001, Emerging issues in strategy process research, in Hitt, M. A., Freeman, R. E., & Harrison, J. S., eds., *Handbook of Strategic Management* (Malden, MA: Blackwell), 3–34.

46. Adler, P. S., & Kwon, S.-W., 2002, Social capital: Prospects for a new concept, *Academy of Management Review* 27 (1): 17–40.

47. Capelli, P., 2000, A market-driven approach to retaining talent, *Harvard Business Review* 78 (1): 103–13.

48. This hypothetical example draws on Peteraf, M., 1993, The cornerstones of competitive advantage, *Strategic Management Journal* 14: 179–91.

49. Wernerfelt, B., 1984, A resource-based view of the firm, *Strategic Management Journal* 5:171–80.

50. Wysocki, B., Jr., 2000, Yet another hazard of the new economy: The Pied Piper Effect, *Wall Street Journal,* March 20: A1–A16.

51. Ibid.

52. Buckman, R. C., 2000, Tech defectors from Microsoft resettle together, *Wall Street Journal,* October: B1–B6.

53. For an insightful discussion on the creation of social capital, see Bolino, M. C., Turnley, W. H., & Bloodgood, J. M., 2002, Citizenship behavior and the creation of social capital in organizations, *Academy of Management Review* 27 (4): 505–22.

54. An insightful discussion of the interorganizational aspects of social capital can be found in Dyer, J. H., & Singh, H., 1998, The relational view: Cooperative strategy and sources of interorganizational competitive advantage, *Academy of Management Review* 23:66–79.

55. Prusak, L., & Cohen, D., 2001, How to invest in social capital, *Harvard Business Review* 79 (6): 86–93.

56. Leonard, D., & Straus, S., 1997, Putting your company's whole brain to work, *Harvard Business Review* 75 (4): 110–22.

57. Leana, C. R., & Van Buren, H. J., III, 1999, Organizational social capital and employment practices, *Academy of Management Review* 24: 538–55.

58. Prusak & Cohen, op. cit., pp. 86–93.

59. Teitelbaum, R., 1997, Tough guys finish first, *Fortune,* July 21: 82–84.

60. Taylor, W. C., 1999, Whatever happened to globalization? *Fast Company,* December: 228–36.

61. Ibid.

62. Lei, D., Slocum, J., & Pitts, R. A., 1999, Designing organizations for competitive advantage: The power of unlearning and learning, *Organizational Dynamics,* Winter: 24–38.

63. For an innovative study on how firms share knowledge with competitors and the performance implications, read Spencer, J. W., 2003, Firms' knowledge sharing strategies in the global innovation system: Empirical evidence from the flat panel display industry, *Strategic Management Journal* 24 (3): 217–35.

64. The examples of Andersen Consulting and Access Health draw upon Hansen, M. T., Nohria, N., & Tierney, T., 1999, What's your strategy for managing knowledge? *Harvard Business Review* 77 (2): 106–18.

65. Capelli, op. cit.

66. Ibid.

67. Koudsi, S., 2000, Actually, it is brain surgery, *Fortune,* March 20: 233.

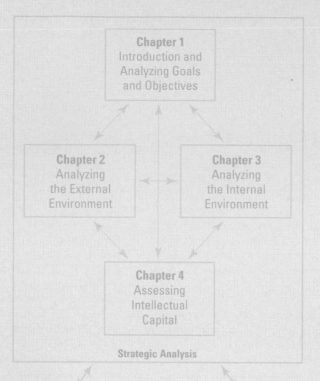

Chapter 1
Introduction and Analyzing Goals and Objectives

Chapter 2
Analyzing the External Environment

Chapter 3
Analyzing the Internal Environment

Chapter 4
Assessing Intellectual Capital

Strategic Analysis

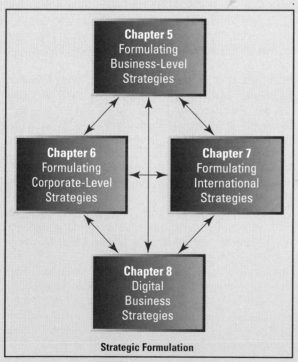

Chapter 5
Formulating Business-Level Strategies

Chapter 6
Formulating Corporate-Level Strategies

Chapter 7
Formulating International Strategies

Chapter 8
Digital Business Strategies

Strategic Formulation

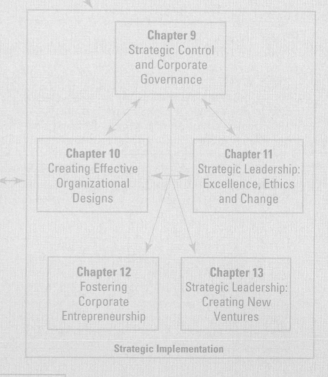

Chapter 9
Strategic Control and Corporate Governance

Chapter 10
Creating Effective Organizational Designs

Chapter 11
Strategic Leadership: Excellence, Ethics and Change

Chapter 12
Fostering Corporate Entrepreneurship

Chapter 13
Strategic Leadership: Creating New Ventures

Strategic Implementation

Chapter 14
Case Analysis

Strategic Formulation

5 Business-Level Strategy: Creating and Sustaining Competitive Advantages

6 Corporate-Level Strategy: Creating Value through Diversification

7 International Strategy: Creating Value in Global Markets

8 Digital Business Strategies: Leveraging Internet and E-Business Capabilities

part**TWO**

Strategic Formulation

Business-Level Strategy:

Creating and Sustaining Competitive Advantages

*After
reading this
chapter, you should
have a good understanding of:*

- The central role of competitive advantage in the study of strategic management.

- The three generic strategies: overall cost leadership, differentiation, and focus.

- How the successful attainment of generic strategies can improve a firm's relative power vis-à-vis the five forces that determine an industry's average profitability.

- The pitfalls managers must avoid in striving to attain generic strategies.

- How firms can effectively combine the generic strategies of overall cost leadership and differentiation.

- The importance of considering the industry life cycle to determine a firm's business-level strategy and its relative emphasis on functional area strategies and value-creating activities.

- The need for turnaround strategies which enable a firm to reposition its competitive position in an industry.

*h*ow firms
compete with each
other as well as how they attain
and sustain competitive advantages go to
the heart of strategic management. In short, the key issue becomes:
Why do some firms outperform others and enjoy such advantages over time?
This subject, business-level strategy, is the focus of Chapter 5.

The first part of the chapter draws on Michael Porter's framework of generic strategies. He identifies three strategies—overall cost leadership, differentiation, and focus—that firms may apply to outperform their rivals in an industry. We begin by describing each of these strategies and provide examples of firms that have successfully attained them as a means of outperforming competitors in their industry. Next, we address how these strategies help a firm develop a favorable position vis-à-vis the "five forces" (Chapter 2). We then suggest some of the pitfalls that managers must avoid if they are to successfully pursue these generic strategies. We close this section with a discussion of the conditions under which firms may effectively combine generic strategies to outperform rivals. Firms that fail to consider carefully the potential downsides associated with the generic strategies—separately and in combination—will have the most difficulty in either creating or sustaining competitive advantages over time.

The second part of Chapter 5 discusses a vital consideration in the effective use of business-level strategies: industry life cycles. The four stages of the industry life cycle—introduction, growth, maturity, and decline—are indicative of an evolving management process that affects factors such as the market growth rate and the intensity of competition. Accordingly, the stages of an industry's life cycle are an important contingency that managers should take into account when making decisions concerning the optimal overall business-level strategies and the relative emphasis to place on functional capabilities and value-creating activities. At times, firms are faced with performance declines and must find ways to revitalize their competitive positions. The actions followed to do so are referred to as turnaround strategies, which may be needed at any stage of the industry life cycle. However, they occur more frequently during the maturity and decline stages.

> Success doesn't breed success. Success begets failure because the more you know a
> thing works, the less likely you are to think that it won't work. When you've had a long
> string of victories, it's harder to foresee your own vulnerabilities.
>
> **Leslie Wexner,** CEO, The Limited, Inc.[1]

This quote by a well-respected business leader reflects, to a large extent, human nature. We all tend to work to improve in areas where we excel and to shortchange our weak areas. Such a mind-set also applies to organizations. The Limited, Inc., enjoyed great success throughout its history. However, it floundered in the early 1990s because of ineffective merchandising strategies and store overexpansion. But let's look at another firm—Food Lion—that generated a great deal of "bad press" during the same time period. As you read this example, ask yourself: What are the underlying problems (versus the more "visible" symptoms) at this large retail grocery chain?

In the 1990s, few firms were ridiculed as much as Food Lion.[2] Starting with the exposé on ABC's *PrimeTime Live* charging employee exploitation, false package dating, and unsanitary meat-handling practices, Food Lion faced an avalanche of bad press. This caused a harsh blow to its reputation, as well as sharp declines in sales and earnings. What makes the Food Lion story so fascinating is its astonishing change in fortune. Few corporations have rewarded their initial investors as richly as Food Lion's original 100-odd backers. A single share of stock bought for $10 in 1957 split into more than 12,000 shares by 1991 with a value of over $200,000. Food Lion's employees have not fared nearly so well and their discontent is one major source—but certainly not the only one—of the firm's problems.

Three former Winn-Dixie employees—Wilson Smith and brothers Ralph and Brown Ketner—formed Food Lion in 1957 in Salisbury, North Carolina. They peddled stock at $10 a share to any takers. Food Lion wasn't an overnight success, struggling during its first 10 years. Nothing seemed to work. Trading stamps, contests, and drawings all failed to draw customers. However, 1967 marked a turning point.

That year, Ralph Ketner pored over six months of receipts and determined that if Food Lion lowered its prices on all 3,000 items and sales increased by 50 percent, the firm might survive. The strategy paid off, the company was reborn as a resolute cost cutter, and the slogan LFPINC ("Lowest Food Prices in North Carolina") soon appeared on bumper stickers. By 1983 annual sales topped $1 billion. Over the next nine years, sales grew by $7.2 billion and net income by $178 million—more than a 22 percent growth rate annually. Buoyed by its success in the Southeast, Food Lion opened 100 stores in Texas, Louisiana, and Oklahoma in the early 1990s. Then disaster struck, and the downside of Food Lion's fervent quest for cost control became strikingly evident.

The first blow came November 5, 1992, when ABC's *PrimeTime Live* news program uncovered unsanitary meat-handling practices and false package dating. Jean Bull, a meat wrapper who had worked in 12 different Food Lion stores over a 13-year period, charged:

> I have seen my supervisor take chicken back out of the bone can, make us wash it and put it back in, and it was rotten. It's just unreal what they'll do to save a dime. They take that pork that's already starting to get a slime to it, it gets what they call a halo to it, a kind of green tinge to it, and take and put that into a grinder with sausage mixture, and they put it back out for anywhere from 7 to 10 days, as fresh, home-made sausage. And it's rotten.

Throughout its history, Food Lion's nonunion status and labor practices have not endeared the firm to its employees nor to the United Food and Commercial Workers (UFCW) union. In efforts to organize Food Lion's employees, the UFCW applied pressure by bringing violations to the attention of the Department of Labor and mailing more than a million brochures to consumers to remind them of the *PrimeTime Live* exposé. Shortly after the *PrimeTime Live* broadcast, the Labor Department began investigating violations of child safety laws and pressures by management for employees to work after quitting time without pay. In August 1993 the firm agreed to pay $16.3 million to settle charges of more than 1,000 violations. This was the largest settlement ever by a private employer over wage and work-hour violations.

Unfortunately, timing is everything! These problems surfaced shortly after Food Lion had begun its major expansion into the Southwest, where it faced strong, entrenched competition. In Dallas–Fort Worth, for example, the company planned to open 54 new stores. However, Kroger, Albertson's, and Winn-Dixie were well-established national players, and regional grocers such as Tom Thumb, Minyard's, and IGA were already strong competitors. These stores fine-tuned their market analysis to the point where they offered a product mix tailored to the economics and demographics of local neighborhoods. Into this foray, Food Lion's stringent cost-control strategy dictated smaller stores (33,000 square feet compared with the 45,000–70,000 square-foot stores of competitors), limited product selection, and fewer employees. Store managers, operating within the confines of stringent cost controls, lacked the resources and flexibility to respond effectively to the competitive environment. Whatever competitive position Food Lion had hoped to build quickly disappeared with the *PrimeTime Live* report and surrounding controversy.

What Went Wrong at Food Lion?   What were Food Lion's underlying problems? Was it worker exploitation? A management team out of touch with operations? Failure to adapt to new markets? Too much focus on the bottom line or, for that matter, the top line?

Clearly, Food Lion's ruthless cost cutting backfired. Its small stores, limited selection, and rigid cost and manpower control procedures contributed to a spartan atmosphere—long on efficiency but short on product selection and customer service amenities—an approach that fell flat in new markets.

Referring back to the value-chain concept (Chapter 3), Food Lion effectively reduced costs in *upstream activities* such as inbound logistics, warehousing, and outbound logistics to deliver products from wholesalers to retail stores. But the overwhelming emphasis on cost control spilled over to the *downstream activities*—marketing, sales, and customer service—at the retail level. Here, Food Lion's management and employees interacted directly with customers and they came up far short. Forced to retreat, by the end of 1994 Food Lion had closed more than half the stores it had opened in the Southwest in 1991.

Food Lion's fundamental problem was that it based its strategy on an organizational strength that did not create a sustainable competitive advantage.[3] The company's principal strength lay in its ability to drive down costs—the foundation of its success as it came to dominate Southeastern markets. As Food Lion expanded into the Southwest, the narrowly focused generic strategy of overall cost leadership fell apart. Differences in the competitive environment dictated a different approach. By continuing to blindly pursue its traditional cost-cutting approach, Food Lion missed the message: The essence of competition in the Dallas–Fort Worth market called for greater product variety and a high level of customer service. Even in traditional markets, Food Lion's high-pressure management tactics and hard-nosed employee practices came home to roost when *PrimeTime Live* offered employees a chance to vent their frustrations.

This example shows that the single-minded pursuit of a narrowly defined source of competitive advantage is often insufficient to guarantee success. In fact, it can lead to failure. This is why the topic of competitive advantages is critical for effective strategic management. Without competitive advantages, firms are doomed to earn no more than "normal returns"—the level of profits that they could expect from other investments that have the same level of risk.[4] Over time, firms that perform below that level will have difficulty attracting and maintaining the level of investments needed to continue operations.

Since all firms endeavor to enjoy above-average returns (or profits), the question of how management should go about this is a core issue in strategic management. Organizations that have created sustainable competitive advantages don't rely on a single strength, as Food Lion did initially, but strive for well-rounded strategies. This increases the chances that advantages will be more lasting, or sustainable, instead of temporary.

These avenues of competitive advantage take several forms known as generic strategies. There are three major types: overall low cost, differentiation, and focus. In the next section, we discuss how Michael Porter's three generic strategies contribute to a firm's competitive advantage and how firms can successfully combine multiple strategies.

Types of Competitive Advantage and Sustainability

Michael Porter presented three generic strategies that a firm can use to overcome the five forces and achieve competitive advantage.[5] Each of Porter's generic strategies has the potential to allow a firm to outperform rivals within the same industry. The first, *overall cost leadership*, is based on creating a low-cost-position relative to a firm's peers. With this strategy, a firm must manage the relationships throughout the entire value chain and be devoted to lowering costs throughout the entire chain. On the other hand, *differentiation* requires a firm (or business unit) to create products and/or services that are unique and valued. Here, the primary emphasis is on "nonprice" attributes for which customers will gladly pay a premium. Finally, a firm following a *focus* strategy must direct its attention (or "focus") toward narrow product lines, buyer segments, or targeted geographic markets. A firm emphasizing a focus strategy must attain advantages either through differentiation or a cost leadership approach. Whereas the overall cost leadership and differentiation strategies strive to attain advantages industrywide, focusers build their strategy with a narrow target market in mind. Exhibit 5.1 illustrates these three strategies on two dimensions: competitive advantage and strategic target.

Before moving on to each generic strategy, it is important to note that both casual observation and research support the notion that firms that identify with one or more of the forms of competitive advantage that Porter identified outperform those that do not. There has been a rich history of strategic management research addressing this topic. One study analyzed 1,789 strategic business units and found that businesses combining multiple forms of competitive advantage (differentiation and overall cost leadership) outperformed businesses that used only a single form. The lowest performers were those that did not

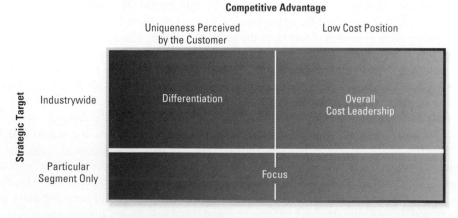

Exhibit 5.1 Three Generic Strategies

Source: Reprinted with the permission of The Free Press, a division of Simon & Schuster Adult Publishing Group, from *Competitive Strategy: Techniques for Analyzing Industries and Competitors* by Michael E. Porter. Copyright © 1980, 1998 by The Free Press. All rights reserved.

Exhibit 5.2
Competitive Advantage and Business Performance

	Competitive Advantage					
	Differentiation and Cost	Differentiation	Cost	Differentiation Focus	Cost Focus	Stuck in the Middle
Performance						
Return on investment (%)	35.5	32.9	30.2	17.0	23.7	17.8
Sales growth (%)	15.1	13.5	13.5	16.4	17.5	12.2
Gain in market share (%)	5.3	5.3	5.5	6.1	6.3	4.4
Sample size	123	160	100	141	86	105

identify with even a single type of advantage. They were classified as "stuck in the middle." Results of this study are presented in Exhibit 5.2.[6]

Overall Cost Leadership

The first generic strategy is overall cost leadership. Cost leadership requires a tight set of interrelated tactics that include:

- Aggressive construction of efficient-scale facilities.
- Vigorous pursuit of cost reductions from experience.
- Tight cost and overhead control.
- Avoidance of marginal customer accounts.
- Cost minimization in all activities in the firm's value chain, such as R&D, service, sales force, and advertising.

Exhibit 5.3 draws on the value-chain concept (see Chapter 3) to provide examples of how a firm can attain an overall cost leadership strategy in its primary and support activities.

An important concept related to an overall cost leadership strategy is the experience curve, which refers to how business "learns" how to lower costs as it gains experience with production processes. That is, with experience, unit costs of production decline as output increases in most industries. The experience curve concept is discussed in Strategy Spotlight 5.1 and Exhibit 5.4.

To generate above-average performance, a firm following an overall cost leadership position must attain parity on the basis of differentiation relative to competitors. In other words, a firm achieving parity is similar to its competitors, or "on par," with respect to differentiated products.[7] Parity on the basis of differentiation permits a cost leader to translate cost advantages directly into higher profits than competitors. Thus, the cost leader earns above-average returns.[8]

The failure to attain parity on the basis of differentiation is another lesson from Food Lion, Inc., our opening case. Its "blind" application of overall cost leadership strategies and tactics throughout the entire value chain caused much of the firm's troubles. Failure to adapt strategies to new markets, such as the Dallas–Fort Worth area, where many of its rivals competed on the basis of both cost and differentiation, caused a disadvantage rather than an advantage.

In recent years, Food Lion has maintained its primary emphasis on cost-leadership strategies. However, it has placed more effort than before on differentiation—focusing on

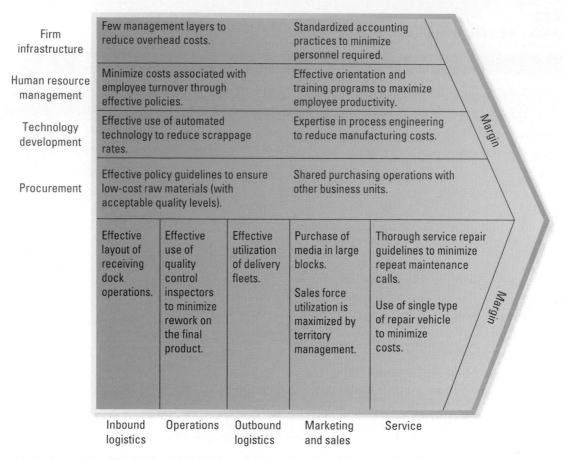

Firm infrastructure	Few management layers to reduce overhead costs.	Standardized accounting practices to minimize personnel required.			
Human resource management	Minimize costs associated with employee turnover through effective policies.	Effective orientation and training programs to maximize employee productivity.			
Technology development	Effective use of automated technology to reduce scrappage rates.	Expertise in process engineering to reduce manufacturing costs.			
Procurement	Effective policy guidelines to ensure low-cost raw materials (with acceptable quality levels).	Shared purchasing operations with other business units.			
	Effective layout of receiving dock operations.	Effective use of quality control inspectors to minimize rework on the final product.	Effective utilization of delivery fleets.	Purchase of media in large blocks. Sales force utilization is maximized by territory management.	Thorough service repair guidelines to minimize repeat maintenance calls. Use of single type of repair vehicle to minimize costs.
	Inbound logistics	Operations	Outbound logistics	Marketing and sales	Service

Exhibit 5.3 Value-Chain Activities: Examples of Overall Cost Leadership

Source: Adapted with the permission of The Free Press, a division of Simon & Schuster Adult Publishing Group, from *Competitive Advantage: Creating and Sustaining Superior Performance* by Michael E. Porter. Copyright © 1985, 1998 by Michael E. Porter. All rights reserved.

the downstream activities of sales, marketing, and service. For example, it is updating and enlarging its current stores, offering extended operating hours, such as being open 24 hours a day, to improve shoppers' convenience, as well as experimenting with new formats, such as larger "store-within-a-store" nonfood departments like photofinishing. It has also developed a partnership with another company to create a program called "Homestyle Meals to Go!" which features hot and cold entrees with side dishes that can be prepared in minutes.[9]

Below, we discuss some examples of how firms enhance cost leadership position in their industries.

While other managed care providers were having a string of weak years, WellPoint, based in Thousand Oaks, California, has had a number of banner years and recently enjoyed a profit growth of 22 percent to approximately $340 million.[10] CEO Leonard Schaeffer credits the company's focus on innovation for both expanding revenues and cutting costs. Recently, for example, WellPoint asked the Food and Drug Administration (FDA) to make the allergy drug Claritin available over the counter. Surprisingly, this may be the first time that an insurer has approached the FDA with this type of request. Schaeffer claimed, "They were kind of stunned," but the FDA agreed to consider it. It was a smart move for WellPoint. If approved as an over-the-counter drug, Claritin would reduce patient visits to

strategy spotlight

The Experience Curve

The experience curve, developed by the Boston Consulting Group in 1968, is a way of looking at efficiencies developed through a firm's cumulative experience. In its basic form, the experience curve relates production costs to production output. As output doubles, costs decline by 10 percent to 30 percent. For example, if it costs $1 per unit to produce 100 units, the per unit cost will decline to between 70 to 90 cents as output increases to 200 units.

What factors account for this increased efficiency? First, the success of an experience curve strategy depends on the industry life cycle for the product. Early stages of a product's life cycle are typically characterized by rapid gains in technological advances in production efficiency. Most experience curve gains come early in the product life cycle.

Second, the inherent technology of the product offers opportunities for enhancement through gained experience. High-tech products give the best opportunity for gains in production efficiencies. As technology is developed, "value engineering" of innovative production processes is implemented, driving down the per unit costs of production.

Third, a product's sensitivity to price strongly affects a firm's ability to exploit the experience curve. Cutting the price of a product with high demand elasticity—where demand increases when price decreases—rapidly creates consumer purchases of the new product. By cutting prices, a firm can increase demand for its product. The increased demand in turn increases product manufacture, thus increasing the firm's experience in the manufacturing process. So by decreasing price and increasing demand, a firm gains manufacturing experience in that particular product, which drives down per unit production costs.

Fourth, the competitive landscape factors into whether or not a firm might benefit from an experience curve strategy. If other competitors are well positioned in the market, have strong capital resources, and are known to promote their product lines aggressively to gain market share, an experience curve strategy may lead to nothing more than a price war between two or more strong competitors. But if a company is the first to market with the product and has good financial backing, an experience curve strategy may be successful.

In an article in the *Harvard Business Review,* Pankaj Ghemawat recommended answering several questions when considering an experience curve strategy.

- Does my industry exhibit a significant experience curve?
- Have I defined the industry broadly enough to take into account interrelated experience?
- What is the precise source of cost reduction?
- Can my company keep cost reductions proprietary?
- Is demand sufficiently stable to justify using the experience curve?
- Is cumulated output doubling fast enough for the experience curve to provide much strategic leverage?
- Do the returns from an experience curve strategy warrant the risks of technological obsolescence?
- Is demand price-sensitive?
- Are there well-financed competitors who are already following an experience curve strategy or are likely to adopt one if my company does?

Michael Porter suggested, however, that the experience curve is not useful in all situations. Whether or not to base strategy on the experience curve depends on what specifically causes the decline in costs. For example, if costs drop from efficient production facilities and not necessarily from experience, the experience curve is not helpful. But as Sharon Oster pointed out in her book on competitive analysis, the experience curve can help managers analyze costs when efficient learning, rather than efficient machinery, is the source of cost savings.

Sources: P. Ghemawat, "Building Strategy on the Experience Curve," *Harvard Business Review,* March–April 1985, pp. 143–49; M. E. Porter, *On Competition* (Boston: Harvard Business Review Press, 1996); S. M. Oster, *Modern Competitive Analysis,* 2d ed. (New York: Oxford University Press, 1994).

the doctor and eliminate the need for prescriptions—two reimbursable expenses for which WellPoint would otherwise be responsible.

Stephen Sanger, CEO of General Mills, recently came up with an idea that helped his firm cut costs.[11] To improve productivity, he sent technicians to watch pit crews during a NASCAR race. That experience inspired the techies to figure out how to reduce the time

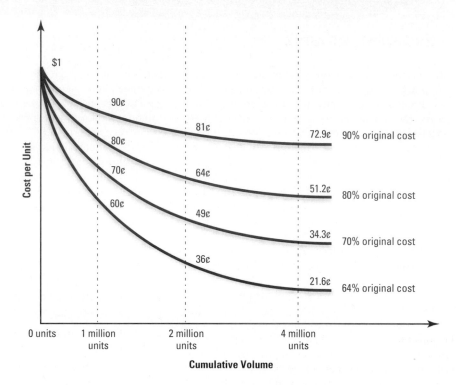

Exhibit 5.4 Comparing Experience Curve Effects

it takes to switch a plant line from five hours to 20 minutes. An important lesson: Many interesting benchmarking examples can take place far outside of one's industry. Often, process improvements involve identifying the best practices in other industries and adapting them for implementation in one's own firm. After all, when firms benchmark competitors in their own industry, the end result is often copying and playing catch-up.[12]

IKEA achieves competitive advantage in different ways and at different points in its value chain. A business that strives for a low-cost advantage must attain an absolute cost advantage relative to its rivals. This is typically accomplished by offering a no-frills product or service to a broad target market using standardization to derive the greatest benefits from economies of scale and experience. However, such a strategy may fail if a firm is unable to attain parity on important dimensions of differentiation such as quick responses to customer requests for design changes. Strategy Spotlight 5.2 describes how IKEA, a global furniture retailer based in Sweden, achieves a successful cost-leadership strategy. At the same time, it avoids perceptions of poor quality or "cheap" merchandise—thus achieving relative parity on differentiation.

Overall Cost Leadership: Improving Competitive Position vis-à-vis the Five Forces   An overall low-cost position enables a firm to achieve above-average returns despite strong competition. It protects a firm against rivalry from competitors, because lower costs allow a firm to earn returns even if its competitors eroded their profits through intense rivalry. A low-cost position also protects firms against powerful buyers. Buyers can exert power to drive down prices only to the level of the next most efficient producer. Also, a low-cost position provides more flexibility to cope with demands from powerful suppliers for input cost increases. The factors that lead to a low-cost position also

strategy spotlight

IKEA's Successful Overall Cost Leadership Strategy

IKEA began in 1943 as a one-person mail-order company in a small farming village in the southern part of Sweden. The founder, Ingvar Kamprad, only a 17-year-old boy at the time, initially arranged for the local county milk van to transport the goods to the nearby train station. This cost-effective way of thinking has guided IKEA's success. Today, through its unique, low-cost strategy, IKEA Group has 70,000 employees and revenues of $11 billion. And Interbrand, a marketing research firm, recently rated IKEA 44th on its list of the top 100 most valuable global brands, ahead of Pepsi, Harley-Davidson, and Apple.

How is IKEA different? Most furniture stores have elaborate showrooms with expensive display samples, several salespeople, and third-party manufacturers who may require up to eight weeks to deliver an order. In contrast, IKEA takes a totally different approach and has been very successful.

Sources: K. Kling and I. Goteman, "IKEA CEO Anders Dahlvig on International Growth and IKEA's Unique Corporate Culture and Brand Identity," *Academy of Management Executive* 17, no. 1 (2003), pp. 31–37; L. Margonelli, "How Ikea Designs Its Sexy Price Tags," *Business 2.0,* October 2002, pp. 45–50; and M. E. Porter, "What Is Strategy?" *Harvard Business Review* 74, no. 4 (1996), p. 65.

IKEA serves customers who are happy to trade off service for lower prices. Rather than have a salesperson follow customers around the store, IKEA uses a self-service model based on clear, in-store displays. IKEA doesn't rely on third-party manufacturers. Instead, they design their own low-cost, modular, ready-to-assemble furniture. In their huge stores, IKEA displays every product in roomlike settings. Thus, customers don't need a decorator to help them imagine what the pieces would look like together. Next to the finished showrooms is a warehouse section where the products are in boxes on pallets. Customers are expected to do their own pickup and delivery. IKEA will even sell you a roof rack for your car that you can return for a refund during your next visit.

What's central to IKEA's strategy? Good quality at a low price. They sell furniture that is cheap but not "cheapo," at prices that are generally 30 to 50 percent below that of the competition. While rivals' prices tend to rise over time, IKEA says that it has reduced its retail prices by a total of 20 percent over the past four years. At IKEA the process of driving down costs starts the moment a new item is conceived and continues relentlessly throughout its production run.

provide substantial entry barriers from economies of scale and cost advantages. Finally, a low-cost position puts the firm in a favorable position with respect to substitute products introduced by new and existing competitors.

A few examples will illustrate these points. IKEA's close attention to costs helps to protect them from buyer power and intense rivalry from competitors. They design their own furniture and order in large quantities. Thus, they are able to drive down unit costs and enjoy relatively high power over their suppliers. By increasing its productivity and lowering unit costs, General Mills (and its competitors in that industry) enjoy greater scale economies and erect higher entry barriers for others who want to enter the industry. Finally, as competitors such as WellPoint lower costs through means such as petitioning the FDA to make certain drugs available over the counter, they become less vulnerable to substitutes such as Internet-based competitors.

Potential Pitfalls of Overall Cost Leadership Strategies   There are many benefits from following a strategy of overall cost leadership. However, there are some pitfalls to avoid:

- ◆ *Too much focus on one or a few value-chain activities.* Would you consider a person to be astute if he cancelled his newspaper subscription and quit eating out to save money, but then "maxed out" several credit cards, requiring him to pay hundreds of dollars a month in interest charges? Of course not. Similarly, firms need to pay attention to all activities in the value chain to manage their overall costs. Too often managers make big cuts in operating expenses, but don't question year-to-year spending on capital projects. Or managers may decide to cut selling and marketing expenses but leave manufacturing expenses untouched. Managers should explore *all* value-chain activities—including relationships among them—as candidates for cost reductions.

- *All rivals share a common input or raw material.* Firms that compete on overall low-cost strategies are vulnerable to price increases in the factors of production. Since they're competing on costs, they are less able to pass on price increases, because customers can easily take their business to competitors who have lower prices. Consider the hardship experienced by fertilizer producers in early 2001 when energy prices spiked.[13] The dramatic increase—a quadrupling of prices to $10 per thousand cubic feet of natural gas—forced firms to shut down nearly half of their production capacity. Why? Natural gas accounts for over 70 percent of the fertilizer's cost. According to Betty-Ann Hegge, senior vice president of Potash Corporation of Saskatchewan, Inc., North America's second largest producer, "Many companies are not even covering their cash costs at these prices."

- *The strategy is imitated too easily.* One of the common pitfalls of a cost-leadership strategy is that a firm's strategy may consist of value-creating activities that are easy to imitate.[14] Such was the case with online brokers in recent years.[15] As of early 2001, there were about 140 online brokers, hardly symbolic of an industry where imitation is extremely difficult. But according to Henry McVey, financial services analyst at Morgan Stanley, "We think you need five to ten" online brokers.

  What are some of the dynamics? First, although online brokers were geared up to handle 1.2 million trades a day by early 2001, volume had shrunk to about 834,000—a 30 percent drop. Thus, competition for a smaller pool of business is increasingly intense. Second, when the stock market is down, many investors trust their instincts less and seek professional guidance from brokerages that offer differentiated services. Eric Rajendra of A. T. Kearney, an international consulting company, claimed, "The current (online broker) model is inadequate for the pressures the industry is facing now."

- *A lack of parity on differentiation.* As noted earlier, firms endeavoring to attain cost leadership advantages need to obtain a level of parity on differentiation. Food Lion illustrates a firm that had its cost advantages eroded because of this strategic oversight. Another example is organizations providing online degree programs to adults working full-time. Although such firms may offer low prices, they may not be successful unless they can offer instruction that is perceived as comparable to traditional providers. For them, parity can be achieved on differentiation dimensions such as reputation and quality and through signaling mechanisms such as national and regional accreditation agencies.

- *Erosion of cost advantages when the pricing information available to customers increases.* This is becoming a more significant challenge as the Internet dramatically increases both the quantity and volume of information available to consumers about pricing and cost structures. Life insurance firms offering whole life insurance provide an interesting example.[16] One study found that for each 10 percent increase in consumer use of the Internet, there is a corresponding reduction in insurance prices to consumers of 3 to 5 percent. Recently, the nationwide savings (or, alternatively, reduced revenues to providers) was between $115 and $125 million annually.

Differentiation

As the name implies, the strategy of differentiation consists of creating differences in the firm's product or service offering by creating something that is perceived *industrywide* as unique and valued by customers. Differentiation can take many forms:

- Prestige or brand image (Adam's Mark hotels, BMW automobiles).
- Technology (Martin guitars, Marantz stereo components, North Face camping equipment).
- Innovation (Medtronic medical equipment, Nokia cellular phones).
- Features (Cannondale mountain bikes, Honda Goldwing motorcycles).
- Customer service (Nordstrom department stores, Sears lawn equipment retailing).
- Dealer network (Lexus automobiles, Caterpillar earth-moving equipment).

Exhibit 5.5 draws on the concept of the value chain as an example of how firms may differentiate themselves in primary and support activities.

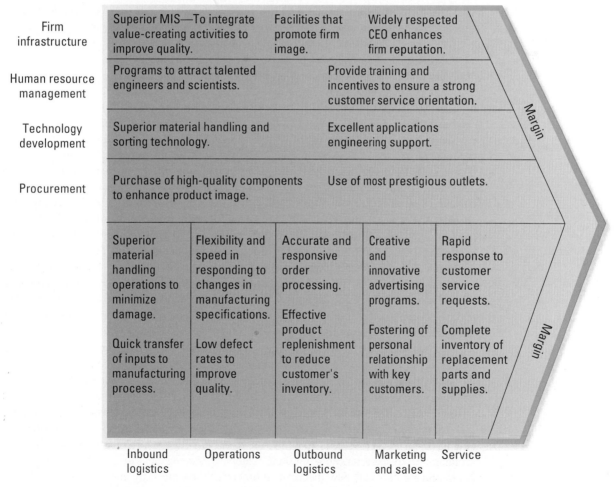

Exhibit 5.5 Value-Chain Activities: Examples of Differentiation

Source: Adapted with the permission of The Free Press, a division of Simon & Schuster Adult Publishing Group, from *Competitive Advantage: Creating and Sustaining Superior Performance* by Michael E. Porter. Copyright © 1985, 1998 by Michael E. Porter. All rights reserved.

Firms may differentiate themselves along several different dimensions at once. For example, BMW is known for its high prestige, superior engineering, and high-quality automobiles. Another example is Harley-Davidson, which differentiates on image and dealer services.[17]

Firms achieve and sustain differentiation advantages and attain above-average performance when their price premiums exceed the extra costs incurred in being unique.[18] For example, both BMW and Harley-Davidson must increase consumer costs to offset added marketing expenses. Thus, a differentiator will always seek out ways of distinguishing itself from similar competitors to justify price premiums greater than the costs incurred by differentiating. Clearly, a differentiator cannot ignore costs. After all, its premium prices would be eroded by a markedly inferior cost position. Therefore, it must attain a level of cost *parity* relative to competitors. Differentiators can do this by reducing costs in all areas that do not affect differentiation. Porsche, for example, invests heavily in engine design—an area in which its customers demand excellence—but it is less concerned and spends fewer resources in the design of the instrument panel or the arrangement of switches on the radio.[19]

Many companies successfully follow a differentiation strategy.[20] For example, some firms have been able to appeal to a very upscale and discriminating segment of the market by offering products with an excellent image and strong brand identification. If you are interested in one of Ferrari's lower-priced models, the 360 Modena, be prepared to pay about $160,000. But it might take more than money; you'll need patience. Recently, there was a 50-person, 18-month waiting list for the all-aluminum, 400-horsepower V8-powered model.[21] And if you want the top-of-the-line Destiny yacht, a 135 footer, be prepared to spend around $13 million. If that is a little steep, a 94-foot model is only $6 million.[22]

Siebel Systems, a leader in software that manages customer relations, is well known for its customer service.[23] No software is written until the customer has significant input. Outside consultants routinely poll clients on satisfaction; the compensation of managers and technical professionals is heavily based on such reports. How successful is Siebel? In just seven years from its founding, its sales have exceeded $1 billion—faster than any other software maker, including Microsoft. CEO Tom Siebel is confident the firm will sustain its growth rate as long as the company, as he expressed it, "shows respect for the customer."

FedEx's CEO and founder, Fred Smith, claims that the key to his firm's success is innovation.[24] He contends his management team didn't understand their real goal when they started the firm in 1971: "We thought that we were selling the transportation of goods; in fact, we were selling peace of mind." To that end, they now provide each driver with a handheld computer and a transmitting device that makes it possible for customers to track their packages right from their desktop PCs.

Lexus, a division of Toyota, provides an example of how a firm can strengthen its differentiation strategy by *achieving integration at multiple points along the value chain.*[25] Although the luxury car line was not introduced until the late 1980s, by the early 1990s the cars had already soared to the top of J. D. Power & Associates's customer satisfaction ratings.

In the spirit of benchmarking, one of Lexus's competitors hired Custom Research Inc. (CRI), a marketing research firm, to find out why Lexus owners were so satisfied. CRI conducted a series of focus groups in which Lexus drivers eagerly offered anecdotes about the special care they experienced from their dealers. It became clear that, although Lexus was manufacturing cars with few mechanical defects, it was the extra care shown by the sales and service staff that resulted in satisfied customers. Such pampering is reflected in the feedback from one customer who claimed she never had a problem with her Lexus. However, upon further probing, she said, "Well, I suppose you could call the four times they had to replace the windshield a 'problem.' But frankly, they took care of it so well and always gave me a loaner car, so I never really considered it a problem until you mentioned

Roberts Express

Roberts Express—the name itself may appear to be less than inspiring in today's knowledge economy. The image may be of trucks lumbering down the interstate, carefree drivers listening to all-night radio talk shows interrupted occasionally by static from the CB radio, and dispatchers who start at 9 a.m. and leave at 5 p.m. What doesn't get done today can always wait until tomorrow. Not always! Roberts Express is more about action, rapid response, information technology, and satellite communications than it is about truck stops and greasy food.

Any trucking company can haul a load of freight, but how many can do it the same day the order is placed? Roberts Express is "as much an information company as we are a transportation company," according to Roberts's president, Bruce Simpson. The nerve center of Roberts Express is a software system developed at Princeton University—Dynamic Vehicle Allocation—that continually tracks all 1,600 trucks in Roberts's fleet. What's impressive is that not only does the software track the company's fleet, it actually projects where the trucks will most likely be needed over the next four days. Taking into account previous shipments, day of the week (Friday is the busiest; Sunday is the slowest), time of year (October is busiest; January is slowest), and 20 other factors, Roberts Express anticipates where its trucks will be needed and routes them accordingly. They pick up most of their loads within 90 minutes of the time a customer calls in an order.

Interestingly, when Roberts's customers talk about the company, it's not the technology that they mention. It's the speed, service, and peace of mind knowing that their shipment will arrive on time. For example, when a load was on its way to a critical destination with only hours to spare, the truck got stuck in traffic and couldn't move. Roberts dispatched a Huey helicopter to pick up the load and fly it to its destination. The result? A very satisfied customer!

Joe Greulich is manager of Management Information Systems (MIS) for Roberts. Although deeply involved with the technological side of the business, he realizes that it's not the technology per se that causes customers to keep coming back. "Customers don't say, 'Hey, we use you because of your fancy computers and your satellites.' They say, 'It's because you get there on time.'"

In 1998, FedEx acquired Roberts Express, and it was renamed FedEx Custom Critical in 2000. That year it won the TechKnow Award from *Inside Business* for its superb integration of satellite trucking technology, computers, and telephony.

Sources: C. Salter, "Roberts Rules the Road," *Fast Company,* September 1998, pp. 114–28; C. Trimble, "Roberts Express Offers QUALCOMM's CabCARD Communications Services to Its Independent Fleets," QUALCOMM press release, May 6, 1999; and www.customercritical.fedex.com.

it now." An insight gained in CRI's research is that perceptions of product quality (design, engineering, and manufacturing) can be strongly influenced by downstream activities in the value chain (marketing and sales, service).

Let's take a closer look at the Lexus example to reiterate some of the key points of a successful differentiation strategy.[26] The example illustrates how strong relationships among value activities reinforce and strengthen the customer's total perception of value. Value activity integration creates value for the end user. Clearly, Lexus must establish and maintain close ties with its dealers by providing resources such as advertising materials, training, parts, supplies, and automobile inventories. Yet one could easily imagine the futility of Lexus's superb marketing, sales, and service efforts if the company could not maintain high production quality or if procurement were unable to acquire high-quality components. Superb marketing and service alone would be inadequate to support Lexus's strategy. Thus, successful differentiation requires attention to and integration with all parts of a firm's value chain.

An important aspect of differentiation in today's competitive marketplace is speed or, alternatively, quick response. Strategy Spotlight 5.3 provides the example of how Roberts Express (now FedEx Custom Critical) has increased its competitive position through speed and quick response to customers.

Differentiation: Improving Competitive Position vis-à-vis the Five Forces   Achieving differentiation is a viable strategy for earning above-average returns by creating a defensible position for overcoming Porter's five competitive forces. Differentiation provides protection against rivalry since brand loyalty lowers customer sensitivity to price and raises customer switching costs. By increasing a firm's margins, differentiation also avoids the need for a low-cost position. Higher entry barriers result because of customer loyalty and the firm's ability to provide uniqueness in its products or services. Differentiation also provides higher margins that enable a firm to deal with supplier power. And it reduces buyer power, because buyers lack comparable alternatives and are therefore less price sensitive. Supplier power is also decreased because there is a certain amount of prestige associated with being the supplier to a producer of highly differentiated products and services. Last, a firm that uses differentiation will enjoy high customer loyalty, thus experiencing less threat from substitutes than its competitors.

The examples in this section will be used to illustrate the above points. Lexus has enjoyed enhanced power over buyers because its top J. D. Power ranking makes buyers more willing to pay a premium price. This lessens rivalry, since buyers become less price-sensitive. The prestige associated with these upper-crust brand names such as Destiny yachts and Ferrari automobiles also lowers supplier power since margins are high. Suppliers would probably desire to be associated with prestige brands, thus lessening their incentives to drive up prices. Finally, the loyalty and "peace of mind" associated with a service provider such as FedEx or Siebel Systems makes these firms less vulnerable to rivalry or substitute products and services.

Potential Pitfalls of Differentiation Strategies   Along with the benefits of differentiation, there are also pitfalls:

- ◆ *Uniqueness that is not valuable.* A differentiation strategy must provide unique bundles of products and/or services that customers value highly. It's not enough just to be "different." An example is Gibson's Dobro bass guitar. Gibson came up with a unique idea: Design and build an acoustic bass guitar with sufficient sound volume so that amplification wasn't necessary. The problem with other acoustic bass guitars was that they did not project enough volume because of the low-frequency bass notes. By adding a resonator plate on the body of the traditional acoustic bass, Gibson increased the sound volume. Gibson believed this product would serve a particular niche market—bluegrass and folk artists who played in small group "jams" with other acoustic musicians. Unfortunately, Gibson soon discovered that its targeted market was content with their existing options: an upright bass amplified with a microphone or an acoustic electric guitar. Thus, Gibson developed a unique product, but it was not perceived as valuable by its potential customers.[27]
- ◆ *Too much differentiation.* Firms may strive for quality or service that is higher than customers desire. Thus, they are vulnerable to competitors who provide an appropriate level of quality at a lower price. For example, the release of Windows 2000 was delayed for over a year because of the 35 million lines of code necessary to accommodate its extensive list of features.[28] By contrast, Sun Microsystems's Solaris 7 operating system consisted of only 11 million lines of code (with other features found in Windows 2000 sold separately by Sun). This made Microsoft more vulnerable. Although Microsoft once boasted about its number of lines of code, chairman Bill Gates commented that if it doesn't keep its code base under control, Microsoft might be stymied from adding features and improving quality.
- ◆ *Too high a price premium.* This pitfall is quite similar to too much differentiation. Customers may desire the product, but they are repelled by the price premium compared to that of competitors. For example, Duracell (a division of Gillette)

recently charged too high a price for batteries.[29] The firm tried to sell consumers on its superior quality products, but the mass market wasn't convinced. Why? The price differential was simply too high. At a CVS drugstore just one block from Gillette's headquarters, a four-pack of Energizer AA batteries was on sale at $2.99 compared with a Duracell four-pack at $4.59. Not only did Duracell's market share drop 2 percent in a recent two-year period, but its profits declined over 30 percent. Clearly, the price/performance proposition Duracell offered customers was not being accepted.

♦ ***Differentiation that is easily imitated.*** As we noted in Chapter 3, resources that are easily imitated cannot lead to sustainable advantages. Similarly, firms may strive for—and even attain—a differentiation strategy that is successful for a time. However, the advantages are eroded through imitation. L.A. Gear, a maker of high-end fashion sneakers and shoes, shows what can happen when a firm creates a product that is easy to imitate.[30] At one time, L.A. Gear enjoyed rapid success. Its revenues increased from $36 million in 1986 to $902 million in 1990. But by the early 1990s, intense competition eroded L.A. Gear's competitive position. Sales dropped to $416 million by 1994, but L.A. Gear failed to cut back its investments.

Several problems plagued L.A. Gear. First, there was increasing price competition. Given low switching costs, rivals were able to attract L.A. Gear's customers with lower prices. Second, L.A. Gear had specialized assets and inventories that locked the company into its position. Thus, as competition intensified, the firm could not exit the industry without walking away from valuable assets.

♦ ***Dilution of brand identification through product-line extensions.*** Firms may erode their quality brand image by adding products or services with lower prices and less quality. Although this can increase short-term revenues, it may be detrimental in the long run. Profits don't necessarily follow revenues. Consider the case of Gucci.[31] In the 1980s Gucci was determined to capitalize on its prestigious brand name by launching an aggressive strategy of revenue growth. It added a set of lower-priced canvas goods to its product line. It also pushed goods heavily into department stores and duty-free channels and allowed its name to appear on a host of licensed items such as watches, eyeglasses, and perfumes. In the short term, this strategy worked. Sales soared. However, the strategy carried a high price. Gucci's indiscriminate approach to expanding its products and channels tarnished its sterling brand. Sales of its high-end goods (with higher profit margins) fell, causing profits to decline.

♦ ***Perceptions of differentiation may vary between buyers and sellers.*** The issue here is that "beauty is in the eye of the beholder." Companies must realize that although they may perceive their products and services as differentiated, their customers may view them as commodities. Indeed, in today's marketplace, many products and services have been reduced to commodities.[32] Thus, a firm could overprice its offerings and lose margins altogether if it has to lower prices to reflect market realities.

Exhibit 5.6 contains a list of products and services that Geoffrey Colvin, an editor for *Fortune* magazine, claimed are now commodities and some that may become commodities in the near future. Why? The items in the left-hand column in the exhibit include all products and services, with two exceptions, that have been sold on FreeMarkets (an online business-to-business auction site), where several competing sellers fought for big pieces of business on exactly one criterion: price. That means, according to Colvin, that the products had become commoditized. The two exceptions were bandwidth and ocean shipping. But these two items have recently been sold at Enron Online where these and other items are continually priced. Colvin claimed that all of these items have been "as utterly commoditized as pork bellies and soybeans." This does not mean that it is impossible for a firm to achieve successful differentiation strategies in these industries. However, with the

Exhibit 5.6
The Erosion of
Product and
Service
Differentiation

What Are the Raw Commodities?	
Now	**Next?**
Personal computers	Servers
Hotel rooms	Car rentals
Legal services	Credit
Police cars	Generic drugs
Ocean shipping	Insurance
Bandwidth	Pharmacy services
Network hosting	Data storage capacity
Manufacturing capacity	Multibillion-dollar infrastructure projects

Source: From Geofrey Colvin, "You Could Be Selling Soybeans," *Fortune,* November 13, 2000. Copyright © 2000 *Time* Inc. All rights reserved.

emergence of online auctions featuring readily available information about competing products and services, differentiation is becoming more difficult.

Focus

The third generic strategy, focus, is based on the choice of a narrow competitive scope within an industry. A firm following this strategy selects a segment or group of segments and tailors its strategy to serve them. The focuser achieves competitive advantages by dedicating itself to these segments exclusively. The essence of focus is the exploitation of a particular market niche that is different from the rest of the industry. As you might expect, narrow focus itself (like merely "being different" as a differentiator) is simply not sufficient for above-average performance. The focus strategy, as indicated in Exhibit 5.1, has two variants. In a cost focus, a firm strives to create a cost advantage in its target segment. In a differentiation focus, a firm seeks to differentiate in its target market. Both variants of the focus strategy rely on providing better service than broad-based competitors who are trying to serve the focuser's target segment. Cost focus exploits differences in cost behavior in some segments, while differentiation focus exploits the special needs of buyers in other segments.

Let's look at examples of two firms that have successfully implemented focus strategies. Network Appliance (NA) has developed a more cost-effective way to store and distribute computer files.[33] Its larger rival, EMC, makes mainframe-style products priced over $1 million that store files and accommodate Internet traffic. NA makes devices that cost under $200,000 for particular storage jobs such as caching (temporary storage) of Internet content. Focusing on such narrow segments has certainly paid off for NA; it has posted a remarkable 20 straight quarters of revenue growth.

The above example was drawn from the high-technology industry. Our next example, Bessemer Trust, competes in the private banking industry.[34] A differentiation focuser, Bessemer targets families with a minimum of $5 million in assets, who desire both capital preservation and wealth accumulation. In other words, these are not people who want to put all their "eggs in a dot-com basket." Bessemer configures its activities for highly personalized service by assigning one account officer for every 14 families. Meetings are more likely to be held at a client's ranch or yacht than in Bessemer's office. Bessemer offers a wide range of customized services, such as investment management, estate admin-

strategy spotlight

Porsche: Winning through Differentiation Focus

After nearly filing for bankruptcy in the 1990s, Porsche has emerged as a company in a class by itself. It embodies the essence of a differentiation focus strategy. Porsche has one manufacturing plant in Stuttgart, Germany, and the entire company employs only 8,200 employees—fewer than just two or three Detroit automobile factories. And the worst thing (or best?) is that no one *needs* a Porsche.

What's their secret? The answer lies in Porsche's very specific market niche. In fact, their Cayenne, a new sport utility vehicle that was introduced in late 2002, is a "very expensive toy that caters to the person who wants everything," according to Ron Pinelli, an analyst with Autodata Corporation in Woodcliff Lake, New Jersey. Target marketing to a focal segment is Porsche's key to success. Current sales of 40,000 cars a year pales in comparison to the Big Three automakers. To illustrate, General Motors stopped making the Pontiac Fiero when sales fell below 40,000. By contrast, Porsche's sales of 40,000 units give it enough room to profitably restructure its operations and pull itself out of potential bankruptcy without merging or being acquired by a larger firm. With a breakeven point of only 12,000 to 14,000 unit sales, Porsche certainly has a comfortable cushion. Further, with growth in its traditional products and the successful launch of the Cayenne, it hopes to increase annual sales to about 80,000 units.

Their differentiation focus strategy has successfully positioned the company as a producer of highly sought-after luxury sports cars. As noted by CEO Wendelin Wiedekig: "Porsche wants to grow and we want to have exclusive products. That means we will keep following the niche strategy." A recent research report from Deutsche Bank states, "It is the design, the technology, and the brand that make a Porsche stand out." If you can't afford to buy a Porsche, but still want to enjoy the experience, take heart: You can rent a Porsche 996 for a day for *only* $749 at the Driven Image agency in Las Vegas, Nevada.

Sources: A. Taylor, III, "Porsche's Risky Recipe," *Fortune,* February 17, 2003, pp. 90–94; A. Curry, "Dude, Where's My Porsche," *U.S. News & World Report,* November 25, 2002, p. D8; J. Suhr, 2001, "Porsche Has High Hopes for SUV in '02," *Lexington* (KY) *Herald-Leader,* February 2001, p. B10; and J. Healey, "Groomed so as Not to Marry," *USA Today,* August 6, 1999, pp. B1–B2.

istration, oversight of oil and gas investments, and accounting for race horses and aircraft. Despite the industry's most generous compensation of account officers and the highest personnel cost as a percentage of operating expenses, Bessemer's focused differentiation strategy is estimated to yield the highest return on equity in the industry.

Strategy Spotlight 5.4 provides an example of a well-known company that has a successful differentiation focus strategy—Porsche. Here's a firm that thrives by making products nobody needs but everyone seems to want!

Focus: Improving Competitive Position vis-à-vis the Five Forces As we have seen, firms pursuing a focus strategy can earn above-average returns. Focus requires that a firm either have a low-cost position with its strategic target, high differentiation, or both. As we discussed with regard to cost and differentiation strategies, these positions provide defenses against each competitive force. Focus is also used to select niches that are least vulnerable to substitutes or where competitors are weakest.

Let's look at our examples to illustrate some of these points. First, Bessemer Trust and Porsche experienced less rivalry and lower bargaining power of buyers by providing products and services to a targeted market segment that was less price-sensitive. New rivals would have difficulty attracting customers away from these firms based only on lower prices. Similarly, the brand image and quality that these brands evoked heightened the entry barriers for rivals trying to gain market share. Additionally, one could reasonably speculate that these two firms enjoyed some protection against substitute products and services because of their relatively high reputation, brand image, and customer loyalty. With regard to the strategy of cost focus, Network Appliances, the successful rival to EMC in the computer storage industry, was better able to absorb pricing increases from suppliers as a result of its lower cost structure. Thus, the effects of supplier power were lessened.

Potential Pitfalls of Focus Strategies   Along with the benefits, managers must be aware of the pitfalls of a focus strategy:

- *Erosion of cost advantages within the narrow segment.* The advantages of a cost focus strategy may be fleeting if the cost advantages are eroded over time. For example, Dell's pioneering direct selling model in the personal computer industry—while still the industry standard—is constantly being challenged by competitors as other computer makers gain experience with Dell's distribution method. Similarly, other firms have seen their profit margins drop as competitors enter their product segment.

- *Even product and service offerings that are highly focused are subject to competition from new entrants and from imitation.* Some firms adopting a focus strategy may enjoy temporary advantages because they select a small niche with few rivals. However, their advantages may be short-lived as rivals invade their market niche. A notable example is the multitude of dot-com firms that specialize in very narrow segments such as pet supplies, ethnic foods, and vintage automobile accessories. The entry barriers tend to be low, there is little buyer loyalty, and competition becomes intense. And since the marketing strategies and technologies employed by most rivals are largely nonproprietary, imitation is easy. Over time, revenues fall, profits margins are squeezed, and only the strongest players survive the shakeout.

- *Focusers can become too focused to satisfy buyer needs.* Some firms attempting to attain competitive advantages through a focus strategy may have too narrow a product or service. Examples include many retail firms. Hardware chains such as Ace and True Value are losing market share to rivals such as Lowe's and Home Depot who offer a full line of home and garden equipment and accessories. Similarly, many specialty ethnic and gourmet food stores may see their sales and profits shrink as large, national grocers such as Kroger's expand their already broad product lines to include such items. And given the enormous purchasing power of the national chains, it would be difficult for such specialty retailers to attain parity on costs.

Combination Strategies: Integrating Overall Low Cost and Differentiation

There has been ample evidence—in the popular press and in research studies—about the strategic benefits of combining generic strategies. In the beginning of this section, we provided some evidence from nearly 1,800 strategic business units (see Exhibit 5.2) to support this contention. As you will recall, the highest performers were businesses that attained both cost and differentiation advantages, followed by those that had either one or the other. Those strategic business units that had the lowest performance identified with neither generic strategy; that is, they were "stuck in the middle." Results from other studies are consistent with these findings across a wide variety of industries including low-profit industries, the paints and allied products industry, the Korean electronics industry, the apparel industry, and the screw machine products industry.[35]

Perhaps the primary benefit to be enjoyed by firms that successfully integrate low-cost and differentiation strategies is that it is generally harder for competitors to duplicate or imitate. An integrated strategy enables a firm to provide two types of value to customers: differentiated attributes (e.g., high quality, brand identification, reputation) and lower prices (because of the firm's lower costs in value-creating activities). The goal becomes one of providing unique value to customers in an efficient manner.[36] Some firms are able to attain both types of advantages simultaneously. For example, superior quality can lead to lower costs because of less need for rework in manufacturing, fewer warranty claims, a reduced need for customer service personnel to resolve customer complaints, and so forth. Thus, the benefits of combining advantages can be additive, instead of merely involving trade-offs. Next, we consider three approaches to combining overall low-cost and differentiation competitive strategies.

Automated and Flexible Manufacturing Systems   Given the advances in manufacturing technologies such as CAD/CAM (computer aided design and computer aided manufacturing) as well as information technologies, many firms have been able to manufacture unique products in relatively small quantities at lower costs—a concept known as "mass customization."[37]

Let's consider the case of Andersen Windows of Bayport, Minnesota—a $1 billion manufacturer of windows for the building industry.[38] Until about 15 years ago, Andersen was a mass producer, in small batches, of a variety of standard windows. However, to meet changing customer needs, Andersen kept adding to its product line. The result: catalogs of ever-increasing size and a bewildering set of choices for both homeowners and contractors. Over a six-year period, the number of products tripled, price quotes took several hours, and the error rate increased—not only damaging the company's reputation, but also adding to its manufacturing expenses.

To bring about a major change, Andersen developed an interactive computer version of its paper catalogs that it sold to distributors and retailers. Salespersons can now customize each window to meet the customer's needs, check the design for structural soundness, and provide a price quote. The system is virtually error free, customers get exactly what they want, and the time to develop the design and furnish a quotation has been cut by 75 percent. Each showroom computer is connected to the factory and customers are assigned a code number that permits them to track the order. The manufacturing system has been developed to use some common finished parts (e.g., mullions, the vertical or horizontal strips separating window panes and sashes) but it also allows considerable variation in the final products. Despite its huge investment in time and money, Andersen has found that the new system has lowered costs, enhanced quality and variety, and improved its response time to customers.

Exploiting the Profit Pool Concept for Competitive Advantage   A profit pool can be defined as the total profits in an industry at all points along the industry's value chain.[39] Although the concept is relatively straightforward, the structure of the profit pool can be complex. The potential pool of profits will be deeper in some segments of the value chain than in others, and the depths will vary within an individual segment. Segment profitability may vary widely by customer group, product category, geographic market, or distribution channel. Additionally, the pattern of profit concentration in an industry is very often different from the pattern of revenue generation.

Consider the automobile industry profit pool in Exhibit 5.7. Here we see little relationship between the generation of revenues and capturing of profits. While manufacturing generates most of the revenue, this value activity is far smaller profit-wise than other value activities such as financing and extended warranty operations. Thus, while a car manufacturer may be under tremendous pressure to produce cars efficiently, much of the profit (at least proportionately) can be captured in the aforementioned downstream operations. Thus, a carmaker would be ill-advised to focus solely on manufacturing while leaving downstream operations to others through outsourcing.

The profit pool concept helps explain U-Haul's success in the truck rental business. Its 10 percent operating margin is far superior to the industry average of less than 3 percent. U-Haul's largest competitor, Ryder, even abandoned the consumer rental business and sold off its fleet in 1996.

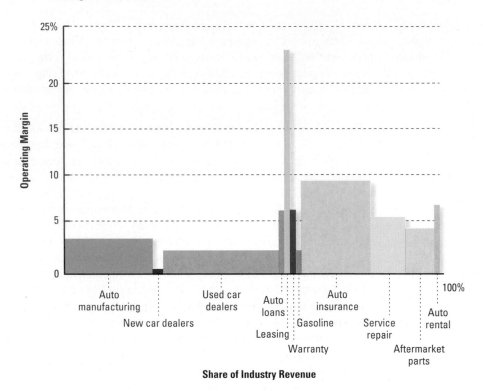

Exhibit 5.7 The U.S. Auto Industry's Profit Pool

Source: Adapted and reprinted by permission of Harvard Business Review, Exhibit from "Profit Pools: A Fresh Look at Strategy," by O. Gadiesh and J. L. Gilbert, May–June 1998. Copyright © 1998 by the Harvard Business School Publishing Corporation; all rights reserved.

What is the key to U-Haul's outstanding performance? Unlike its competitors, U-Haul looked past its core truck rental business and found an untapped source of profit. That source was the accessories business—the sale of boxes and insurance, rentals of trailers and storage space—all the ancillary products and services customers need to complete the moving job that begins when they rent the truck. Profit margins for moving-truck rentals are small; customers shop for the lowest daily rate. But accessories are a different story. With virtually no competition in this part of the value chain, the accessories business enjoys attractive margins. And once a customer signs a rental agreement for a truck, his or her comparison shopping ends. Although the accessory business requires a greater variety of offerings, customers are largely "a captive market" and are, therefore, less price-sensitive. Thus, U-Haul's strategy became one of tightly managing its costs and prices to consumers in the low-profit truck rental part of the business. This enabled them to attract more customers to whom they sold high-margin accessories.

Coordinating the "Extended" Value Chain by Way of Information Technology   Many firms have achieved success by integrating activities throughout the "extended value chain" by using information technology to link their own value chain with the value chains of their customers and suppliers. As noted in Chapter 3, this approach enables a firm not only to add value through its own value-creating activities, but also for its customers and suppliers.

Such a strategy often necessitates redefining the industry's value chain. A number of years ago, Wal-Mart took a close look at its industry's value chain and decided to reframe the competitive challenge.[40] Although its competitors were primarily focused on retailing—merchandising and promotion—Wal-Mart determined that it was not so much in the retailing industry as in transportation logistics and communications. Here, linkages in the extended value chain became central. That became Wal-Mart's chosen battleground. By redefining the rules of competition that played to its strengths, Wal-Mart has attained competitive advantages and dominates its industry.

Strategy Spotlight 5.5 provides some details of how Wal-Mart was able to combine differentiation and overall cost leadership to become the dominant retailer in the world. We also discuss why the company's strategy is highly sustainable; competitors would have a very difficult time to imitate it or find substitutes.

Integrated Overall Low-Cost and Differentiation Strategies:
Improving Competitive Position vis-à-vis the Five Forces   Firms that successfully integrate both differentiation and cost advantages create an enviable position relative to industry forces. For example, Wal-Mart's integration of information systems, logistics, and transportation helps it to drive down costs and provide outstanding product selection. This dominant competitive position, along with its excellent reputation, serves to erect high entry barriers to potential competitors that have neither the financial nor physical resources to compete head-to-head. Wal-Mart's size—$259 billion in 2003 sales—provides the chain with enormous bargaining power over suppliers. Its low pricing and wide selection reduce the power of buyers (its customers), because there are relatively few competitors that can provide a comparable cost/value proposition. This reduces the possibility of intense head-to-head rivalry, such as protracted price wars. Finally, Wal-Mart's overall value proposition makes potential substitute products (e.g., Internet competitors) a less viable threat.

Pitfalls of Integrated Overall Cost Leadership and Differentiation
Strategies   Firms that attain both types of competitive advantage enjoy high returns. However, as with each generic strategy taken individually, there are some pitfalls to avoid:

- *Firms that fail to attain both strategies may end up with neither and become "stuck in the middle."* A key issue in strategic management is the creation of competitive advantages that enable a firm to enjoy above average returns. Some firms may become "stuck in the middle" if they try to attain both cost and differentiation advantages. J. C. Penney Co., for example, has become, in the words of a *BusinessWeek* writer, "trapped in no-man's land . . . its fashions are tired, its prices unreasonable . . . and [it has] lost . . . cachet with customers."[41] Why? Penney's tried to achieve differentiation and cost control at the same time, but succeeded in neither. It struggled to fend off discounters such as Wal-Mart and Target on one front, and upscale department stores such as Macy's on the other. Not surprisingly, Penney's stock dropped about 80 percent between 1998 and 2000. As one might expect, the key elements of J. C. Penney's CEO Allen Questrom's turnaround plan include elements of both differentiation and cost control:
  - Improve store presentations.
  - Radically rethink merchandise.
  - Market the company brand more effectively.
  - Slash costs, including closing 44 stores and cutting 5,000 jobs.
  - Overhaul management ranks, including more outside recruitment.
- *Underestimating the challenges and expenses associated with coordinating value-creating activities in the extended value chain.* Successfully integrating activities across a firm's value chain with the value chain of suppliers and customers involves a significant investment in financial and human resources. Managers must not underestimate the expenses linked to technology investment, managerial time and commitment, and the involvement and investment required by the firm's customers and suppliers. The firm must be confident that it can generate a sufficient scale of operations and revenues to justify all associated expenses.

How Wal-Mart Combines Advantages

One of the most successful retailers of all time, Wal-Mart has trounced its competitors by combining competitive advantages. With net income of $9 billion from total revenues of $259 billion in 2003, Wal-Mart continued to post very impressive performance numbers. During the four-year period from 2000 to 2003, it experienced annual growth rates in revenues and net income of 10 percent and 13 percent, respectively. Wal-Mart has broadened its product offerings in recent years and now offers a diverse product line, including groceries, deli items, pharmaceuticals, and fast food. It has expanded internationally by exporting its data systems and models of efficiency to international markets, including Canada, Mexico, China, Indonesia, the United Kingdom, and Brazil.

Much of Wal-Mart's success can be attributed to its strategic focus, emphasis on key value-chain activities, and combination of competitive advantages. The value chains of merchandise retailers such as Kmart and Target have been much like that of grocery retailers. These value chains focused on cost control, efficiency in distribution and purchasing, and low-overhead facilities. Rivalry in this sector has centered around store location, pricing, and promotion.

Sources: J. Useem, "One nation under Wal-Mart. *Fortune,* March 3, 2003, pp. 65–78; G. G. Dess and J. C. Picken, "Creating Competitive (Dis)Advantage: Learning from Food Lion's Freefall," *Academy of Management Executive 13,* no. 3 (1999), pp. 97–111; R. Berner, "Too Many Retailers, Not Enough Shoppers," *BusinessWeek,* February 12, 2001, pp. 36–42.

Over the past decade, Wal-Mart has left its competitors behind by differentiating itself. In addition to the diverse product lines previously mentioned, Wal-Mart has distinguished itself from competitors by offering optical shops and photofinishing. By moving into such nontraditional areas, Wal-Mart challenges competitors in industries other than traditional discount retailers. Grocery chains, optical shops, fast-food restaurants, photofinishing stores, and pharmacies must now be concerned with the impact on market share each time Wal-Mart opens a new store in their town.

What is Wal-Mart's secret? We'll look at how Wal-Mart competes successfully on multiple forms of competitive advantage. A central feature of Wal-Mart's strategy is the logistics technique of cross-docking. Goods are continuously delivered to the company's warehouses, where they are selected, repacked, and then distributed to stores, often without placement in inventory. Instead of wasting valuable time in warehouses, merchandise moves across one loading dock to another in 48 hours or less. This lets Wal-Mart achieve economies associated with full-truckload purchasing while avoiding the usual inventory and handling costs. Impressively, this reduces Wal-Mart's cost of sales by 2 to 3 percent compared to its competitors.

The benefits to Wal-Mart and its customers multiply. Lower costs help make possible the re-

(continued)

+ ***Miscalculating sources of revenue and profit pools in the firm's industry.*** Firms may fail to accurately assess sources of revenue and profits in their value chain. This can occur for several reasons. For example, a manager's bias may be due to his or her functional area background, work experiences, and educational background. If the manager's background is in engineering, he or she might perceive that proportionately greater revenue and margins were being created in manufacturing, product, and process design than a person whose background is in a "downstream" value-chain activity such as marketing and sales. Or politics could make managers "fudge" the numbers to put their area of operations in a more favorable light. This would make them responsible for a greater proportion of the firm's profits, thus improving their bargaining position for their share of the firm's internal resources.

A related problem is directing an overwhelming amount of managerial time, attention, and resources to value-creating activities that create the greatest margins—to the detriment of other important, albeit less profitable, activities. For example, an automobile manufacturer may focus too much on downstream activities, such as warranty fulfillment and financing operations, to the detriment of differentiation and cost of the automobiles them-

tailer's everyday low prices. This, in turn, saves money with less frequent promotions. Stable prices lead to more predictable sales, thus reducing stockouts and excess inventory. Fewer stockouts increase customer loyalty, while inventory control allows quick response to changing customer preferences. Everyday low prices bring in more customer traffic, which translates into more sales.

These economies allow Wal-Mart to staff stores with greeters and additional checkout clerks and to reward employees with stock ownership through a profit-sharing plan. Loyal, dedicated employees and enhanced customer service are elements of differentiation that translate into more customer loyalty and increased sales.

Despite the value of cross-docking, it's not easily copied by competitors. If it were, Wal-Mart's advantage would have long since vanished. The key is that cross-docking is complicated to manage. Wal-Mart made strategic investments in a variety of interlocking support systems that are difficult to imitate. The systems involve:

- Continuous contact between Wal-Mart's distribution centers, suppliers, and every point of sale in each store, so that orders can be executed within hours.

- Fast, responsive transportation, including 19 distribution centers serviced by nearly 2,000 company-owned trucks.

- Fundamental changes in managerial control that allow the stores to pull products when and where they need them rather than having suppliers push products into the system. With less centralized control, a premium is placed on frequent, informed cooperation between stores, distribution centers, and suppliers.

- Information systems that provide store managers detailed information about customer behavior and a fleet of airplanes that regularly ferry store managers to Wal-Mart's Bentonville, Arkansas, headquarters for training on market trends and merchandising.

- A video link connecting each store.

- Profit sharing for employees, to encourage high customer responsiveness.

The cross-docking logistics strategy and sophisticated information systems reduce costs in a number of ways. By reducing inventories and shortening procurement cycle times, Wal-Mart can increase its flexibility and responsiveness to changing customer preferences. Wal-Mart has understood the business as a process and expanded its boundaries to include customers and suppliers. It has identified its strengths, added value to multiple activities in new and innovative ways, and leveraged its capabilities to enhance the flexibility of operations through close integration and coordination of interdependent activities. As the company broadens its product offerings and expands into new markets, it's likely that the benefits will only grow, entrenching Wal-Mart as the dominant player in the retail merchandise market and preserving the sustainability of its competitive edge.

selves. Or, as described earlier in the case of the truck rental industry, management might let the quality of rental trucks deteriorate while directing the lion's share of attention to the more profitable accessory side of the business.

Industry Life Cycle Stages: Strategic Implications

The life cycle of an industry refers to the stages of introduction, growth, maturity, and decline that occur over the life of an industry. In considering the industry life cycle, it is useful to think in terms of broad product lines such as personal computers, photocopiers, or long-distance telephone service. Yet the industry life cycle concept can be explored from several levels, from the life cycle of an entire industry to the life cycle of a single variation or model of a specific product or service.

Why is it important to consider industry life cycles? The emphasis on various generic strategies, functional areas, value-creating activities, and overall objectives varies over the course of an industry life cycle. Managers must become even more aware of their firm's strengths and weaknesses in many areas to attain competitive advantages. For example, firms depend on their research and development (R&D) activities in the introductory stage of the life cycle. R&D is the source of new products and features that everyone hopes will appeal to customers. Firms develop products and services to stimulate consumer demand. Later, during the maturity phase, the functions of the product have been defined, more competitors have entered the market, and competition is intense. Managers then place greater emphasis on production efficiencies and process (as opposed to the product) engineering in order to lower manufacturing costs. This helps to protect the firm's market position and extends the product life cycle because the firm's lower costs can be "passed on" to consumers in the form of lower prices, and price-sensitive customers will find the product more appealing.

Exhibit 5.8 illustrates the four stages of the industry life cycle and how factors such as generic strategies, market growth rate, intensity of competition, and overall objectives change over time. As we noted earlier, managers must strive to emphasize the key functional areas during each of the four stages, as well as to attain a level of "parity" in all functional areas and value-creating activities. For example, even though controlling production costs may be a primary concern during the maturity stage, managers should not totally ignore other functions such as marketing and R&D. If they do, they can become so focused on lowering costs that they miss market trends or fail to incorporate important product or process designs. In such cases, the firm may attain low-cost products that have limited market appeal.

It is important to point out a caveat. While the life cycle idea is analogous to a living organism (i.e., birth, growth, maturity, and death), the comparison does have limitations.[42] Products and services go through many cycles of innovation and renewal. For the most part, only fad products have a single life cycle. Maturity stages of an industry can be "transformed" or followed by a stage of rapid growth if consumer tastes change, technological innovations take place, or new developments occur in the general environment. The cereal industry is a good example. When medical research indicated that oat consumption reduced a person's cholesterol, sales of Quaker Oats increased dramatically.[43]

We will next discuss each stage of the industry life cycle. Then we will summarize how each stage poses important implications for a firm's generic strategies. To do this, we will briefly discuss the evolution of the personal computer industry. Finally, we discuss turnaround strategies, that is, strategies that are necessary in order to reverse performance erosion and regain competitive position.

Strategies in the Introduction Stage

In the introduction stage, products are unfamiliar to consumers.[44] Market segments are not well defined, and product features are not clearly specified. The early development of an industry typically involves low sales growth, rapid technological change, operating losses, and the need for strong sources of cash to finance operations. Since there are few players and not much growth, competition tends to be limited.

Success in the introduction stage requires an emphasis on research and development and marketing activities to enhance awareness of the product or service. The challenge becomes one of (1) developing the product and finding a way to get users to try it, and (2) generating enough exposure so the product emerges as the "standard" by which all other competitors' products are evaluated.

There's an advantage to being the "first mover" in a market.[45] Consider Coca-Cola's success in becoming the first soft-drink company to build a recognizable global brand. Moving first enabled Caterpillar to get a lock on overseas sales channels and service capabilities. Being a first mover allowed Matsushita to establish Video Home Source (VHS) as the global standard for videocassette recorders.

However, there can also be a benefit to being a "late mover." Target carefully thought out the decision to delay its Internet strategy. Compared to its competitors Wal-Mart and

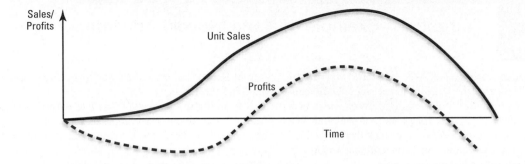

Stage / Factor	Introduction	Growth	Maturity	Decline
Generic strategies	Differentiation	Differentiation	Differentiation Overall cost leadership	Overall cost leadership Focus
Market growth rate	Low	Very large	Low to moderate	Negative
Number of segments	Very few	Some	Many	Few
Intensity of competition	Low	Increasing	Very intense	Changing
Emphasis on product design	Very high	High	Low to moderate	Low
Emphasis on process design	Low	Low to moderate	High	Low
Major functional area(s) of concern	Research and development	Sales and marketing	Production	General management and finance
Overall objective	Increase market awareness	Create consumer demand	Defend market share and extend product life cycles	Consolidate, maintain, harvest, or exit

Exhibit 5.8 Stages of the Industry Life Cycle

Kmart, Target was definitely the industry laggard. Strategy Spotlight 5.6 explains why its strategy paid off.

Examples of products currently in the introductory stages of the industry life cycle include electric vehicles, digital cameras, and high-definition television (HDTV).

Strategies in the Growth Stage

The second stage of the industry life cycle, growth, is characterized by strong increases in sales. The potential for strong sales (and profits) attracts other competitors who also want to benefit. As products enter the growth stage, the primary key to success is to build consumer preferences for specific brands. This requires strong brand recognition, differentiated products, and the financial resources to support a variety of value-chain activities such

Target: An Example of "Late Mover" Advantage

All cutting-edge retailers have Web sites. The first retailer with a Web site gains the largest market share. Only technologically inept stores don't rush to reach customers though the Internet. At least that's the conventional wisdom. Looking back on the success (or lack thereof) gained from these strategies shows that conventional wisdom is sometimes conventional thoughtlessness.

Two of the first movers in Web-based retailing were Kmart and Wal-Mart. While Kmart faltered with BlueLight.com and Wal-Mart struggled with Walmart.com, Target patiently waited. Electronic retailing, or "e-tailing," was a new area for low-cost retailers. Target's strategy was to learn from the mistakes of the first movers. Target waited until it understood *how* to attract customers with a website before it actually tried to attract customers with one. It seems like the conventional wis-

dom of Kmart and Wal-Mart was just a little too unconventional for Target.

By waiting, Target gained a "late mover" advantage. The store was able to use competitors' mistakes as its own learning curve. This saved money, and customers didn't seem to mind the wait: When Target finally opened its website, it quickly captured market share from both Kmart and Wal-Mart Internet shoppers. Forrester Research Internet analyst Stephen Zrike commented, "There's no question, in our mind, that Target has a far better understanding of how consumers buy online."

"I think the first mover advantage was grossly overrated on the Web," according to Jerry Storch, president of financial services and new business for Target. The conventional wisdom says that the first to market will capture the largest market share. This is often true, but only if the company that is first to market has the ability to do things right. Otherwise, customers become disgruntled; this affects not only the firm's Web store, but also the reputation of its bricks-and-mortar facilities. By waiting until it could do things right, Target now has more Web market share than either of its early mover rivals.

Sources: S. Stoughton, "Target Aimed Carefully at Web Sales, Then Stepped Up and Hit the Bull's-Eye," *Lexington* (KY) *Herald-Leader,* November 20, 2000, Business Monday, p. 2; E. Neuborne, "E-tailers Hit the Relaunch Key," *BusinessWeek,* October 17, 2000, p. 62.

---

as marketing and sales, customer service, and research and development. Whereas marketing and sales initiatives were mainly directed at spurring *aggregate* demand—that is, demand for all such products in the introduction stage—efforts in the growth stage are directed toward stimulating *selective* demand, in which a firm's product offerings are chosen instead of those of its rivals.

Revenues in the growth stage increase at an accelerating rate because (1) new consumers are trying the product and (2) a growing proportion of satisfied consumers are making repeat purchases.[46] In general, as a product moves through its life cycle, the proportion of repeat buyers to new purchasers increases. Conversely, new products and services often fail if there are relatively few repeat purchases. This is especially true with many consumer products that are characterized by relatively low price and frequent purchase. For example, Alberto-Culver introduced Mr. Culver's Sparklers, which were solid air fresheners that looked like stained glass. Although the product quickly went from the introductory to the growth stage, sales then plummeted. Why? Unfortunately, there were few repeat purchasers because buyers treated them as inexpensive window decorations, left them there, and felt little need to purchase new ones. Examples of products currently in the growth stage of the industry life cycle include Internet servers and personal digital assistants (e.g., Palm Pilots).

Strategies in the Maturity Stage

In the third stage, maturity, aggregate industry demand begins to slow. Since markets are becoming saturated, there are few opportunities to attract new adopters. It's no longer possible to "grow around" the competition, so direct competition becomes predominant.[47] With few attractive prospects, marginal competitors begin to exit the market. At the same time, rivalry among existing competitors intensifies because there is often fierce price competition at the same time that expenses associated with attracting new buyers are rising. Advantages based on efficient manufacturing operations and process engineering become more important for keeping costs low as customers become more price sensitive. It also becomes more difficult for firms to differentiate their offerings, because users have a greater understanding of products and services.

An article in *Fortune* magazine that addressed the intensity of rivalry in mature markets was aptly titled: "A Game of Inches." It stated: "Battling for market share in a slowing industry can be a mighty dirty business. Just ask laundry soap archrivals Unilever and Procter & Gamble."[48] These two firms have been locked in a battle for market share since 1965. Why is the competition so intense? There is not much territory to gain. In 2000 total sales for the industry were flat at $6 billion a year. A Lehman Brothers analyst noted, "People aren't getting any dirtier." Thus, the only way to win is to take market share from the competition. To increase its share, Procter & Gamble (P&G) spends $100 million a year promoting its Tide brand on television, billboards, subways, buses, magazines, and the Internet. But Unilever isn't standing still. Armed with a new $80 million budget, it recently launched a soap tablet product named Wisk Dual Action Tablets. On January 7, 2001, it delivered samples of this product to 24 million U.S. homes in Sunday newspapers, followed by a series of TV ads. P&G launched a counteroffensive: Tide Rapid Action Tablets ads showed side-by-side comparisons of the two products dropped into beakers of water. In the promotion, P&G claimed that its product is superior because it dissolves faster than Unilever's product. A minor point—but Unilever is challenging P&G in court. And the beat goes on . . .

Although the above is only one example, many product classes and industries, including consumer products such as beer, automobiles, and televisions, are in the maturity stage.

Strategies in the Decline Stage

Although all decisions in the phases of an industry life cycle are important, they become particularly difficult in the decline stage. Hard choices must be made, and firms must face up to the fundamental strategic choices of either exiting or staying and attempting to consolidate their position in the industry.[49]

The decline stage occurs when industry sales and profits begin to fall. Typically, changes in the business environment are at the root of an industry or product group entering this stage.[50] Changes in consumer tastes or a technological innovation can push a product into decline. Typewriters have entered into the decline stage because of the word processing capabilities of personal computers. Compact disks have forced cassette tapes into decline in the prerecorded music industry, and digital video disks (DVDs) may soon replace compact disks. About 20 years earlier, of course, cassette tapes had led to the demise of long-playing records (LPs).

When a product enters the decline stage, it often consumes a large share of management time and financial resources relative to its potential worth. Not only are sales and profits declining, but also competitors may start drastically cutting their prices to raise cash and remain solvent in the short term. The situation is further aggravated by the wholesale liquidation of assets, including inventory, of some of the competitors that have failed. This further intensifies price competition.

In the decline stage, a firm's strategic options become dependent on the actions of rivals. If many competitors decide to leave the market, sales and profit opportunities increase.

On the other hand, prospects are limited if all competitors remain.[51] If some competitors merge, their increased market power may erode the opportunities for the remaining players. Managers must carefully monitor the actions and intentions of competitors before deciding on a course of action.

Four basic strategies are available in the decline phase: *maintaining, harvesting, exiting,* or *consolidating.*[52]

♦   *Maintaining* refers to keeping a product going without significantly reducing marketing support, technological development, or other investments, in the hope that competitors will eventually exit the market. Many offices, for example, still use typewriters for filling out forms and other purposes that cannot be completed on a personal computer. In some rural areas, rotary (or dial) telephones persist because of the older technology used in central switching offices. Thus, if a firm remains in the business and others exit, there may still be the potential for revenues and profits.

♦   *Harvesting* involves obtaining as much profit as possible and requires that costs in the decline stage be reduced quickly. Managers should consider the firm's value-creating activities and cut associated budgets. Value-chain activities to consider are primary (e.g., operations, sales and marketing) and support (e.g., procurement, information systems, technology development). The objective is to wring out as much profit as possible.

♦   *Exiting the market* involves dropping the product from a firm's portfolio. Since a residual core of consumers may still use the product, eliminating it should be considered carefully. If the firm's exit involves product markets that affect important relationships with other product markets in the corporation's overall portfolio, an exit could have repercussions for the whole corporation. For example, it may involve the loss of valuable brand names or human capital with a broad variety of expertise in many value-creating activities such as marketing, technology, and operations.

♦   *Consolidation* involves one firm acquiring at a reasonable price the best of the surviving firms in an industry. This enables firms to enhance market power and acquire valuable assets. One example of a consolidation strategy took place in the defense industry in the early 1990s. As the cliché suggests, "peace broke out" at the end of the Cold War and overall U.S. defense spending levels plummeted.[53] Many companies that make up the defense industry saw more than 50 percent of their market disappear. Only one-quarter of the 120,000 companies that once supplied the Department of Defense still serve in that capacity; the others have shut down their defense business or dissolved altogether. But one key player, Lockheed Martin, became a dominant rival by pursuing an aggressive strategy of consolidation. During the 1990s, it purchased 17 independent entities, including General Dynamics's tactical aircraft and space systems divisions, GE Aerospace, Goodyear Aerospace, and Honeywell ElectroOptics. These combinations enabled Lockheed Martin to emerge as the top provider to three governmental customers: the Department of Defense, the Department of Energy, and NASA. Despite several downsizing initiatives, the firm was ranked for the first time in the Fortune 25 (the largest 25 industrial concerns in the United States). Clearly, the prospects for industry prosperity have increased in the aftermath of the September 11, 2001, terrorist attacks.

Examples of products currently in the decline stage of the industry life cycle include automotive spark plugs (replaced by electronic fuel ignition), videocassette recorders (replaced by digital video disk recorders), and personal computer zip drives (replaced by compact disk read-write drives). As we mentioned previously, compact disks may soon be replaced by digital video disks (DVDs).

Relating Generic Strategies to Stages of the Industry Life Cycle: The Personal Computer Industry

The personal computer (PC) industry provides an example of how a firm's generic strategies can vary over stages of the industry life cycle. In the introduction and growth stages, there were many players, such as IBM, Compaq, and others, who endeavored to create brand recognition and build loyal followings for their entries. To do so required well-developed and executed differentiation strategies. Apple was further differentiated because it was the only player to have a graphical user interface (GUI). However, well within a decade the market matured, particularly when the "Wintel" standard (Microsoft's *Wind*ows operating system and In*tel*'s microprocessor units) was widely adopted. This, in effect, eroded Apple's unique feature. Price competition then quickly intensified. Why? Consumer awareness and sophistication with personal computers quickly accelerated and the market became saturated with similar products. Here, overall low-cost strategies became the dominant form of competition. However, some firms, such as Dell Computer, were still able to make differentiation a key part of their business-level strategy by offering superior service and rapid fulfillment of customer orders. It now appears that many Web appliances, such as Oracle TalkBack and Intel's Dot.Station (each priced at approximately $200), may become viable substitute products. These products provide many features similar to those of personal computers: Internet access, e-mail delivery, and personal calendars. Thus, demand for these products may drive the personal computer industry into the decline stage by significantly lowering aggregate consumer demand. If, faced with the decline stage, the personal computer companies have to intensify their cost-reduction initiatives as well as to develop focus strategies in order to seek out niches in the market, that may prove more viable than exiting the industry altogether.

Turnaround Strategies

One problem with the life cycle analogy is that we tend to think that decline is inevitably followed by death. In the case of businesses, however, decline can be reversed by strategies that lead to turnaround and rejuvenation. Such a need for turnaround may occur at any stage in the life cycle. However, it is more likely to occur during the maturity or decline stage.

Most turnarounds require a firm to carefully analyze the external and internal environments. The external analysis leads to identification of market segments or customer groups who may still find the product attractive. Internal analysis results in actions aimed at reduced costs and higher efficiency. Typically, a firm needs to undertake a mix of both internally and externally oriented actions to effect a turnaround.

A study of 260 mature businesses in need of a turnaround identified three strategies used by successful companies.[54]

- *Asset and cost surgery.* Very often, mature firms tend to have assets that do not produce any returns. These include real estate, buildings, etc. Outright sales or sale and leaseback free up considerable cash and improve returns. Investment in new plants and equipment can be deferred. Firms in turnaround situations try to aggressively cut administrative expenses and inventories and speed up collection of receivables. Costs can also be reduced by outsourcing production of various inputs for which market prices may be cheaper than in-house production costs.

- *Selective product and market pruning.* Most mature or declining firms have many product lines that are losing money or only marginally profitable. One strategy is to discontinue these product lines and focus all resources on a few core profitable areas. For example, in the early 1980s, faced with possible bankruptcy, Chrysler Corporation sold off all their nonautomotive businesses as well as all their

Caswell-Massey: A Failed Turnaround

When Anne Robinson joined Caswell-Massey in 1995 as head of marketing, she assumed that the nation's oldest luxury soap company was in good shape. Far from it, she learned nine months later. The company was losing $3 million on sales of $13 million and its credit lines were overextended. The company had $2.5 million worth of returned goods in their warehouse that were the leftovers from an unsuccessful launch of a cheaper line in 20,000 mass-market outlets. The business continued to decline during the next four years.

But Anne Robinson's ambition exceeded her judgment. She decided to buy the company in 1999 despite glaring internal problems and an increasingly competitive arena with companies like Bath & Body Works and The Gap entering the luxury soap market. She pooled $1 million from friends (including $200,000 of her life savings) and took out a second mortgage on her Manhattan co-op to buy Caswell. American Capital Strategies, a publicly traded buyout firm, put in $4.2 million in debt plus warrants for a 24 percent stake, with the rest belonging to Robinson and other investors. Robinson needed all the knowledge she gained from her Harvard MBA and 16 years of work experience at Filene's Basement and Lord & Taylor to try to get this company back on track.

She studied the company's operations quickly to determine where it was making money and where it was hemorrhaging cash and then took steps to preserve cash. She started with cost-cutting measures. In the next few months, as part of product and market pruning, she shuttered 15 stores (out of 28) and cut one-third of the product line. Her asset and cost surgery moves included a 25 percent reduction in a 70-person staff (mostly midlevel managers) and liquidation of old inventory. On the productivity front, she changed the demand forecasting system, which led to increased inventory turnover, fine-tuned

deals with vendors giving manufacturers three months of lead time, and saved 20 percent on expenses. These initiatives increased sales by 15 percent to $20 million. In the very first year after Anne Robinson took charge, Caswell-Massey made a small profit.

But sales have not grown beyond $20 million since 1999 and have dropped recently. What went wrong?

She failed to have any clear strategies for growth. A quick-fix solution in a turnaround has to be followed by a more sound long-term strategy. This includes assessing survival chances by determining whether there are any parts of the company that are worth saving and prescribing a cure. After implementing a strategy to cut overhead costs, one must sell noncore assets, boost revenues, and improve liquidity. And if all these fail, arrange for a quick sale.

These are areas in which Anne Robinson failed. Perhaps the survival chances were overestimated because of her ambition to keep the company alive. Competitors such as Bath & Body Works were expanding by aggressively opening about 42 new stores in year 2002 for a total of 1,642 stores. Another competitor, Crabtree and Evelyn, added 10 stores to a base of 145. Competitors were also aggressive in new product launches by introducing new products every 90 days or so. At Caswell, however, the vital element for growth—namely, liquidity—has been a problem. Anne Robinson was cash-strapped and had a depleted credit line. Thus, she could support neither expansion of stores nor new product introductions. Added to this was the poor image of existing stores, which made expansion virtually impossible. The one way to drive up sales per square foot was through markdowns. But even this did not help. After a 50 percent markdown, Caswell's products were still priced higher than competitors'.

One might ask: Why hasn't Robinson tried to sell the business, given its failed turnaround? "It's my job to keep this company alive," says Robinson. "It's been around for 250 years, and I don't want it to die on my watch." But some businesses, like failed marriages, just can't be saved. And the sooner it is realized, the better.

Sources: V. Murphy, "Will It Stay Afloat?" *Forbes,* August 12, 2002, pp. 104–5; and J. Muller, "When the Going Gets Tough, Alix Gets Busy," *BusinessWeek,* September 23, 2002, pp. 69–70.

production facilities abroad. Focus on the North American market and identification of a profitable niche, namely, minivans, were keys to their eventual successful turnaround.

- ◆ *Piecemeal productivity improvements.* There are hundreds of ways in which a firm can eliminate costs and improve productivity. Although individually these are small gains, they cumulate over a period of time to substantial gains. Improving business processes by reengineering them, benchmarking specific activities against industry leaders, encouraging employee input to identify excess costs, reducing R&D and marketing expenses, increasing capacity utilization, and improving employee productivity lead to a significant overall gain.

The turnaround of software maker Intuit is an interesting case of a quick but well-implemented turnaround strategy. After stagnating and stumbling during the dot-com boom, Intuit, which is known for its Quickbook and Turbotax software, hired Stephen M. Bennett, a 22-year GE veteran, in 1999. He immediately discontinued Intuit's online finance, insurance, and bill-paying operations that were losing money. Instead, he focused on software for small businesses that employ less than 250 people. He also instituted a performance-based reward system that greatly improved employee productivity. By the end of 2002, Intuit was once again making substantial profits and its stock was up 42%.[55]

Even when an industry is in overall decline, pockets of profitability remain. These are segments with customers who are relatively price insensitive. For example, the replacement demand for vacuum tubes affords its manufacturers an opportunity to earn above normal returns although the product itself is technologically obsolete. Surprisingly, within declining industries, there may still be segments that are either stable or growing. Cigars and chewing tobacco are examples of profitable segments within the tobacco industry. Although fountain pens ceased to be the writing instrument of choice a long time ago, the fountain pen industry has successfully reconceptualized the product as a high margin luxury item that signals accomplishment, success, and appreciation of the finer things in life. In the final analysis, every business has the potential for rejuvenation. But it takes creativity, persistence, and most of all a clear strategy to translate that potential into reality.

Strategy Spotlight 5.7 describes a failed turnaround attempt at Caswell-Massey, a luxury soap maker. Clearly, Anne Robinson failed to develop a long-term turnaround strategy for her company, although she took many of the actions necessary for a turnaround.

summary

How and why firms outperform each other goes to the heart of strategic management. In this chapter, we identified three generic strategies and discussed how firms are able not only to attain advantages over competitors, but also to sustain such advantages over time. Why do some advantages become long-lasting while others are quickly imitated by competitors?

The three generic strategies—overall cost leadership, differentiation, and focus—form the core of this chapter. We began by providing a brief description of each generic strategy (or competitive advantage) and furnished examples of firms that have successfully implemented these strategies. Successful generic strategies invariably enhance a firm's position vis-à-vis the five forces of that industry—a point that we stressed and illustrated with examples. However, as we pointed out, there are pitfalls to each of the generic strategies. Thus, the sustainability of a firm's advantage is always challenged because of imitation or substitution by new or existing rivals. Such competitor moves erode a firm's advantage over time.

We also discussed the viability of combining (or integrating) overall cost leadership and differentiation generic strategies. If successful, such integration can enable a firm to enjoy superior performance and improve its competitive position. However, this is challenging, and managers must be aware of the potential downside risks associated with such an initiative.

The concept of the industry life cycle is a critical contingency that managers must take into account in striving to create and sustain competitive advantages. We identified the four stages of the industry life cycle—introduction, growth, maturity, and decline—and suggested how these stages can play a role in decisions that managers must make at the business level. These include overall strategies as well as the relative emphasis on functional areas and value-creating activities.

When a firm's performance severely erodes, turnaround strategies are needed to reverse its situation and enhance its competitive position. We have discussed three approaches—asset cost surgery, selective product and market pruning, and piecemeal productivity improvements.

summary review questions

1. Explain why the concept of competitive advantage is central to the study of strategic management.

2. Briefly describe the three generic strategies: overall cost leadership, differentiation, and focus.

3. Explain the relationship between the three generic strategies and the five forces that determine the average profitability within an industry.

4. What are some of the ways in which a firm can attain a successful turnaround strategy?

5. Describe some of the pitfalls associated with each of the three generic strategies.

6. Can firms combine the generic strategies of overall cost leadership and differentiation? Why or why not?

7. Explain why the industry life cycle concept is an important factor in determining a firm's business-level strategy.

experiential exercise

What are some examples of primary and support activities that enable Nucor, a $5 billion steel manufacturer, to achieve a low-cost strategy?

Value Chain Activity	Yes/No	How Does Nucor Create Value for the Customer?
Primary:		
Inbound logistics		
Operations		
Outbound logistics		
Marketing and sales		
Service		
Support:		
Procurement		
Technology development		
Human resource management		
General administration		

1. Go to the Internet and look up www.walmart.com. How has this firm been able to combine overall cost leadership and differentiation strategies?
2. Choose a firm with which you are familiar in your local business community. Is the firm successful in following one (or more) generic strategies? Why or why not? What do you think are some of the challenges it faces in implementing these strategies in an effective manner?
3. Think of a firm that has attained a differentiation focus or cost focus strategy. Are their advantages sustainable? Why? Why not? (*Hint:* Consider its position vis-à-vis Porter's five forces.)
4. Think of a firm that successfully achieved a combination overall cost leadership and differentiation strategy. What can be learned from this example? Are these advantages sustainable? Why? Why not? (*Hint:* Consider its competitive position vis-à-vis Porter's five forces.)

application questions exercises

1. Can you think of a company (other than the opening case of Food Lion) that suffered ethical consequences as a result of an overemphasis on a cost leadership strategy? What do you think were the financial and nonfinancial implications?
2. In the introductory stage of the product life cycle, what are some of the unethical practices that managers could engage in to enhance their firm's market position? What could be some of the long-term implications of such actions?

ethics questions

references

1. Davis, J. E., 1994, Can The Limited fix itself? *Fortune,* October 17: 161–72.
2. The discussion of Food Lion draws on Dess, G. G., & Picken, J. C., 1997, *Mission Critical* (Burr Ridge, IL: Irwin); and Dess, G. G., & Picken, J. C., 1999, Creating competitive (dis)advantage: Learning from Food Lion's freefall, *Academy of Management Executive* 13 (3): 97–111.
3. For a perspective on the need for adapting competitive strategies to competitive conditions, refer to Christenson, C. M., 2001, The past and the future of competitive strategy, *Harvard Business Review* 42 (2): 105–9; and D'Aveni, R. A., 1999, Strategic supremacy through disruption and dominance, *Sloan Management Review* 40 (3): 117–35.
4. Porter, M. E., 1980, *Competitive Strategy* (New York: McGraw-Hill).
5. For a recent perspective by Porter on competitive strategy, refer to Porter, M. E., 1996, What is strategy? *Harvard Business Review* 74 (6): 61–78.
6. Miller, A., & Dess, G. G., 1993, Assessing Porter's model in terms of its generalizability, accuracy, and simplicity, *Journal of Management Studies* 30 (4): 553–85.
7. For a scholarly discussion and analysis of the concept of competitive parity, refer to Powell, T. C., 2003, Varieties of competitive parity, *Strategic Management Journal* 24 (1): 61–86.

8. Rao, A. R., Bergen, M. E., & Davis, S., 2000, How to fight a price war, *Harvard Business Review* 78 (2): 107–20.
9. Peterson, T., 1999, Is Food Lion biting off more than it can chew? *BusinessWeek Online,* August 19.
10. Whalen, C. J., Pascual, A. M., Lowery, T., & Muller, J., 2001, The top 25 managers, *BusinessWeek,* January 8: 63.
11. Ibid.
12. For an interesting perspective on the need for creative strategies, refer to Hamel, G., & Prahalad, C. K., 1994, *Competing for the Future* (Boston: Harvard Business School Press).
13. Symonds, W. C., Arndt, M., Palmer, A. T., Weintraub, A., & Holmes, S., 2001, Trying to break the choke hold, *BusinessWeek,* January 22: 38–39.
14. For a perspective on the sustainability of competitive advantages, refer to Barney, J., 1995, Looking inside for competitive advantage, *Academy of Management Executive* 9 (4): 49–61
15. Thornton, E., 2001, Why e-brokers are broker and broker, *BusinessWeek,* January 22: 94.
16. Koretz, G., 2001, E-commerce: The buyer wins, *BusinessWeek,* January 8: 30.
17. MacMillan, I., & McGrath, R., 1997, Discovering new points of differentiation, *Harvard Business Review* 75 (4): 133–45; Wise, R., & Baumgarter, P., 1999, Beating the clock: Corporate responses to rapid change in the

PC industry, *California Management Review* 42 (1): 8–36.

18. For a discussion on quality in terms of a company's software and information systems, refer to Prahalad, C. K., & Krishnan, M. S., 1999, The new meaning of quality in the information age, *Harvard Business Review* 77 (5): 109–18.

19. Taylor, A., III, 2001, Can you believe Porsche is putting its badge on this car? *Fortune,* February 19: 168–72.

20. Ward, S., Light, L., & Goldstine, J., 1999, What high-tech managers need to know about brands, *Harvard Business Review* 77 (4): 85–95.

21. Zesiger, S., 1999, Silicon speed, *Fortune,* September 13: 120.

22. Blank, D., 2001, Down to the sea in mega-yachts, *BusinessWeek,* October 30: 18.

23. Whalen et al., op. cit.

24. Rosenfeld, J., 2000, Unit of one, *Fast Company,* April: 98.

25. Markides, C., 1997, Strategic innovation, *Sloan Management Review* 38 (3): 9–23.

26. Dess & Picken, *Mission Critical,* p. 84.

27. The authors would like to thank Scott Droege, a faculty member at Mississippi State University, for providing this example.

28. Mardesich, J., 1999, What's weighing down Microsoft? *Fortune,* January 11: 147–84.

29. Symonds, W. C., 2000, Can Gillette regain its voltage? *BusinessWeek,* October 16: 102–4.

30. McGahan, A. M., 1999, Competition, strategy, and business performance, *California Management Review* 41 (3): 74–102.

31. Gadiesh, O., & Gilbert, J. L., 1998, Profit pools: A fresh look at strategy, *Harvard Business Review* 76 (3): 139–58.

32. Colvin, G., 2000, Beware: You could soon be selling soybeans, *Fortune,* November 13: 80.

33. Whalen et al., op. cit., p. 63.

34. Porter, M. E., 1996, What is strategy? *Harvard Business Review* 74 (6): 61–78.

35. Hall, W. K., 1980, Survival strategies in a hostile environment, *Harvard Business Review* 58:75–87; on the paint and allied products industry, see Dess, G. G., & Davis, P. S., 1984, Porter's (1980) generic strategies as determinants of strategic group membership and organizational performance, *Academy of Management Journal* 27:467–88; for the Korean electronics industry, see Kim, L., & Lim, Y., 1988, Environment, generic strategies, and performance in a rapidly developing country: A taxonomic approach, *Academy of Management Journal* 31: 802–27; Wright, P., Hotard, D., Kroll, M., Chan, P., & Tanner, J., 1990, Performance and multiple strategies in a firm: Evidence from the apparel industry, in

Dean, B. V., & Cassidy, J. C., eds., *Strategic Management: Methods and Studies* (Amsterdam: Elsevier-North Holland), 93–110; and Wright, P., Kroll, M., Tu, H., & Helms, M., 1991, Generic strategies and business performance: An empirical study of the screw machine products industry, *British Journal of Management* 2:1–9.

36. Gilmore, J. H., & Pine, B. J., II, 1997, The four faces of customization, *Harvard Business Review* 75 (1): 91–101.

37. Ibid.

38. Goodstein, L. D., & Butz, H. E., 1998, Customer value: The linchpin of organizational change, *Organizational Dynamics,* Summer: 21–34.

39. Gadiesh & Gilbert, op. cit., pp. 139–58.

40. This example draws on Dess & Picken, 1999, op. cit.

41. Forest, S. A., 2001, Can an outsider fix J. C. Penney? *BusinessWeek,* February 12: 56, 58.

42. Dickson, P. R., 1994, *Marketing Management* (Fort Worth, TX: Dryden Press), 293; Day, G. S., 1981, The product life cycle: Analysis and application, *Journal of Marketing Research* 45: 60–67.

43. Bearden, W. O., Ingram, T. N., & LaForge, R. W., 1995, *Marketing Principles and Practices* (Burr Ridge, IL: Irwin).

44. MacMillan, I. C., 1985, Preemptive strategies, in Guth, W. D., ed., *Handbook of Business Strategy* (Boston: Warren, Gorham & Lamont), 9-1–9-22; Pearce, J. A., & Robinson, R. B., 2000, *Strategic Management,* 7th ed. (New York: McGraw-Hill); Dickson, op. cit., pp. 295–96.

45. Bartlett, C. A., & Ghoshal, S., 2000, Going global: Lessons for late movers, *Harvard Business Review* 78 (2): 132–42.

46. Berkowitz, E. N., Kerin, R. A., & Hartley, S. W., 2000, *Marketing,* 6th ed. (New York: McGraw-Hill).

47. MacMillan, op. cit.

48. Brooker, K., 2001, A game of inches, *Fortune,* February 5: 98–100.

49. MacMillan, op. cit.

50. Berkowitz et al., op. cit.

51. Bearden et al., op. cit.

52. The discussion of these four strategies draws on MacMillan, op. cit.; Berkowitz et al., op. cit.; and Bearden et al., op. cit.

53. Augustine, N. R., 1997, Reshaping an industry: Lockheed Martin's survival story, *Harvard Business Review* 75 (3): 83–94.

54. Hambrick, D. C., & Schecter, S. M., 1983, Turnaround strategies for mature industrial product business units, *Academy of Management Journal* 26 (2): 231–48.

55. Mullaney, T. J., 2002, The wizard of Intuit, *BusinessWeek,* October 28: pp. 60–63.

chapter 6

Corporate-Level Strategy:

Creating Value through Diversification

After reading this chapter, you should have a good understanding of:

- How managers can create value through diversification initiatives.

- The reasons for the failure of many diversification efforts.

- How corporations can use related diversification to achieve synergistic benefits through economies of scope and market power.

- How corporations can use unrelated diversification to attain synergistic benefits through corporate restructuring, parenting, and portfolio analysis.

- The various means of engaging in diversification—mergers and acquisitions, joint ventures/strategic alliances, and internal development.

- The value of real options analysis (ROA) in making resource allocation decisions under conditions of high uncertainty.

- Managerial behaviors that can erode the creation of value.

Corporate-level strategy addresses two related issues: (1) what businesses should a corporation compete in, and (2) how can these businesses be managed so they create "synergy"—that is, more value by working together than if they were freestanding units? As we will see, these questions present a key challenge to today's managers. Many diversification efforts fail or, in many cases, provide only marginal returns to shareholders. Thus, determining how to create value through entering new markets, introducing new products, or developing new technologies is a vital issue in strategic management.

We begin by discussing why diversification initiatives, in general, have not yielded the anticipated benefits. Then, in the next three sections of the chapter, we explore the two key alternative approaches: related and unrelated diversification. With related diversification, corporations strive to enter product markets that share some resources and capabilities with their existing business units or increase their market power. Here, we suggest four means of creating value: leveraging core competencies, sharing activities, pooled negotiating power, and vertical integration. With unrelated diversification, there are few similarities in the resources and capabilities among the firm's business units but value can be created in multiple ways. These include restructuring, corporate parenting, and portfolio analysis approaches. Whereas the synergies to be realized with related diversification come from *horizontal relationships* among the business units, the synergies from unrelated diversification are derived from *hierarchical relationships* between the corporate office and the business units.

The last three sections address (1) the various means that corporations can use to achieve diversification; (2) real options analysis; and (3) managerial behaviors (e.g., self-interest) that serve to erode shareholder value. We address merger and acquisitions (M&A), joint ventures/strategic alliances, and internal development. Each of these involves the evaluation of important trade-offs. We also discuss real options analysis (ROA)—an increasingly popular technique for making resource allocation decisions. Detrimental managerial behaviors—often guided by a manager's self-interest—are "growth for growth's sake," egotism, and antitakeover tactics. Some of these behaviors raise ethical issues because managers, in some cases, are not acting in the best interests of a firm's shareholders.

The pioneering discount broker Charles Schwab and Company became the industry leader through its focus on the customer and the innovative use of information technology. Faced with intense competition from deep-discount Internet brokerages in the late 1990s, Schwab tried to greatly expand its services to wealthy clientele by acquiring U.S. Trust. Below, we discuss why things didn't work out as planned.

"Clicks and mortar" broker Charles Schwab Corp. bought U.S. Trust Corp. in mid-2000, joining a 147-year-old private-client wealth management firm with a leading provider of discount investor services.[1] Schwab paid a premium of 63.5 percent to U.S. Trust shareholders. The steep premium for U.S. Trust reflects the broker's deep pockets as well as its interest in becoming a full-service investment firm. At the time of the acquisition, Schwab was the nation's number one Internet and discount broker and number four financial services company overall.

Several synergies were expected from this acquisition. According to Schwab, the move expanded on its already developed offerings for wealthy clientele, including Schwab's Advisor Source and Signature Services. Schwab saw great potential for growth in the market represented by high-net-worth individuals and hoped its combination of Internet savvy and U.S. Trust's high-touch business lines would be tailor-made for that segment. In all, Schwab expected to leverage on its core competency in investor services to build greater market power.

But the news out of Charles Schwab and Co. has not been good. The bear market took a big bite out of Schwab's trading volume, revenues, and profits. With investment returns eroding, customers were much more sensitive to brokerage and commission fees. The management shake-up at U.S. Trust Corp. in October 2002 also raised serious questions. In its eagerness to tap upscale markets and become more than the people's broker, did the normally savvy Schwab miss serious warning signs at U.S. Trust? What went wrong?

The apparent synergies have not worked out, and deeper incompatibilities surfaced. Former U.S. Trust employees claimed that Schwab was overly enamored by the glossy brand and pedigreed clients of U.S. Trust. The company was too optimistic about Schwab's ability to direct their high-end clients to U.S. Trust, but very few Schwab customers have $2 million in assets, the minimum for U.S. Trust's pricey hand holding. Even those referred were often turned down by the subsidiary. Therefore, the main hope for the acquisition—stopping Schwab's richest customers from defecting to full-service brokerages such as Merrill Lynch—has not panned out. Also, many key managers left when their retention agreements expired in May 2002, taking their clients with them.

A major problem has been the technology. Despite reports of federal regulators' hinting at system-related problems, Schwab thought it was manageable and was content with its inspection of U.S. Trust's system. However, it eventually discovered the magnitude of the problem when the computer systems failed to detect suspicious patterns of cash transactions. The bank had to pay $10 million in July 2001 to settle charges by the New York State Banking Department and Federal Reserve that it was not complying with anti-money laundering rules. (The bank did not admit or deny fault.) The severity of the technology problem is illustrated by the fact that U.S. Trust did not even use the standard Windows operating system until the late 1990s. Furthermore, its 30 branches are not on a single computer system, hindering back-office operations such as order processing.

Compounding the problems after the compliance fiasco, U.S. Trust started screening clients so closely that it alienated them. This consumed time and money that could otherwise have been spent in generating new business. Cost cutting has been another area of concern. U.S. Trust's executives dragged their feet on consolidating their numerous bank charters and cutting costs at offices outside New York, adding to the disappointing performance. Several weak branches will likely be closed.

With problems mounting, Schwab replaced U.S. Trust CEO Jeffrey S. Maurer and the president, Amribeth S. Rahe. They named Alan J. Weber, former head of Citibank's international operations, to be CEO and president. Weber faces the Herculean task of making things work. "The wild card is whether Schwab can transform a high-net-worth business from (one of) steady earnings growth to more dynamic earnings growth," says a Wall Street analyst. Seems marrying up has not been the ticket to wealth it was supposed to be.

strategy spotlight

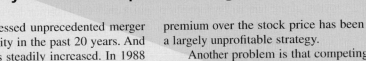

Why the M&A Party Causes Corporate Hangovers

Corporate America has witnessed unprecedented merger and acquisition (M&A) activity in the past 20 years. And the rate of M&A activity has steadily increased. In 1988 there were $378.9 billion of mergers and acquisitions—a total of 4,066 deals. This had ballooned to $1.63 *trillion* in 1998, with 12,356 deals, and approximately $3 trillion and 30,000 deals in 2000. Mergers aren't limited to small companies; the past two decades have seen unprecedented megamergers. Why are companies rushing to the M&A party? The conventional wisdom says that M&A is the quickest route to growth by gaining access to new markets and expertise. This is a worthwhile goal, but does it work? Let's look at the evidence.

Two times out of three, the stock price of the acquiring company falls once the deal is made public. Since the acquiring firm usually pays a 30 to 40 percent premium for the target company, the acquirer must create synergies and scale economies resulting in sales and market gains exceeding the premium price. Firms paying higher premiums set the performance hurdle even higher. For example, Household International paid an 82 percent premium to buy Beneficial, and Conseco paid an 83 percent premium to acquire Green Tree Financial. Historically, paying a premium over the stock price has been a largely unprofitable strategy.

Another problem is that competing firms can imitate any advantages realized or copy synergies that result from the M&A. So a firm that plans to achieve competitive advantage through M&A activity can see its advantages quickly evaporate. Unless the advantages are sustainable and difficult to copy, investors will not be willing to pay a premium for the stock. Similarly, the time value of money must be factored into the stock price. M&A costs are paid up front. Conversely, firms pay for research and development, ongoing marketing, and capacity expansion over time. This stretches out the payments needed to gain new competencies. The M&A argument is that a large initial investment is worthwhile because it creates long-term advantages. But stock analysts want to see immediate results from such a large cash outlay. If the acquired firm does not produce results quickly, investors often sell the stock, driving the price down.

Managers' credibility and ego can sometimes get in the way of sound business decisions. If the M&A does not perform as planned, managers who pushed for the deal find their reputation at stake. At times, this can lead these managers to protect their credibility by funneling more money—or escalating their commitment—into an inevitably doomed operation. Further, when all hope is lost and the firm tries to unload the acquisition, managers often find they must sell at a discount. These problems further compound the costs and weaken the stock price.

Sources: A. Rappaport and M. L. Sirower, "Stock or Cash? The Trade-offs for Buyers and Sellers in Mergers and Acquisitions," *Harvard Business Review,* November–December, 1999, pp.147–58; S. Lipin and N. Deogun, "Big Mergers of 90s Prove Disappointing to Shareholders," *Wall Street Journal,* October 30, 2000, p. C1.

Schwab is not alone in having a disappointing experience with an acquisition. Some large multinational firms and recent big acquirers—including NationsBank, First Union, and AOL—have failed to effectively integrate their acquisitions, paid too high a premium for the target's common stock, or were unable to understand how the acquired firm's assets would fit with their own business lines. Thus, many high-flying firms have been grounded, largely because of ill-fated deals that were developed by some of Wall Street's top investment banking firms. Strategy Spotlight 6.1 provides an interesting perspective on the extent of mergers and acquisitions in the United States in recent years as well as some of the reasons for their less than stellar outcomes.

Some years ago, a writer for *Fortune* magazine lamented, "Studies show that 33 percent to 50 percent of acquisitions are later divested, giving corporate marriages a divorce rate roughly comparable to that of men and women."[2] Despite such pessimism, we'll now discuss the rationales for diversification.

Making Diversification Work: An Overview

Admittedly, we've been pretty negative thus far and may have overstated the downside of diversification strategies. Clearly, not all diversification moves, including those involving mergers and acquisitions, erode performance. For example, acquisitions in the oil industry such as British Petroleum PLC's purchases of Amoco and Arco are performing well, as is the merger of Exxon and Mobil. Similarly, many leading high-tech firms, such as Microsoft and Intel, have dramatically increased their revenues, profits, and market values through a wide variety of diversification moves, including mergers and acquisitions, strategic alliances and joint ventures, and internal development.

So, the question becomes: Why do some diversification efforts pay off and others produce disappointing results? In this chapter we will address this question. Whereas Chapter 5 focused on business-level strategy, that is, how to achieve sustainable advantages in a given business or product market, this chapter addresses two related issues: (1) What businesses should a corporation compete in? and (2) How should these businesses be managed to jointly create more value than if they were freestanding units?

Diversification initiatives—whether through mergers and acquisitions, strategic alliances and joint ventures, or internal development—must be justified by the creation of value for shareholders. But this is not always the case. For example, as noted earlier and in Strategy Spotlight 6.1, acquiring firms typically pay high premiums when they acquire a target firm. However, you and I, as private investors, can diversify our portfolio of stocks very cheaply. With the advent of the intensely competitive online brokerage industry, we can acquire hundreds (or thousands) of shares for a transaction fee of as little as $10.00 or less—a far cry from the 30 to 40 percent (or higher) premiums that corporations typically must pay to acquire companies.

Given the seemingly high inherent downside risks and uncertainties, it might be reasonable to ask why companies should even bother with diversification initiatives. The answer, in a word, is *synergy,* derived from the Greek word *synergos,* which means "working together." This can have two different, but not mutually exclusive, meanings. First, a firm may diversify into *related* businesses. Here, the primary potential benefits to be derived come from *horizontal relationships,* that is, businesses sharing intangible resources (e.g., core competences) and tangible resources (e.g., production facilities, distribution channels). Additionally, firms can enhance their market power through pooled negotiating power and vertical integration. As we will see in this chapter, Procter & Gamble enjoys many synergies from having businesses that share distribution resources.

Second, a corporation may diversify into *unrelated* businesses. In these instances, the primary potential benefits are derived largely from *hierarchical relationships,* that is, value creation derived from the corporate office. Examples of the latter would include leveraging some of the support activities in the value chain that we discussed in Chapter 3, such as information systems or human resource practices. Cooper Industries, another firm we will discuss, has followed a successful strategy of unrelated diversification. There are few similarities in the products it makes or the industries in which it competes. However, the corporate office adds value through such activities as superb human resource practices as well as planning and budgeting systems.

It is important to note that the aforementioned horizontal (derived from related diversification) and hierarchical (derived from related and unrelated diversification) relationships are not mutually exclusive. Many firms that diversify into related areas benefit from information technology expertise in the corporate office and firms diversifying into unrelated areas often benefit from "best practices" of sister businesses even though their products, markets, and technologies may differ dramatically.

Exhibit 6.1
Creating Value through Related and Unrelated Diversification

Related Diversification: Economies of Scope

Leveraging core competences

- 3M leverages its competencies in adhesives technologies to many industries, including automotive, construction, and telecommunications.

Sharing activities

- McKesson, a large distribution company, sells many product lines, such as pharmaceuticals and liquor, through its superwarehouses.

Related Diversification: Market Power

Pooled negotiating power

- The Times Mirror Company increases its power over customers by providing "one-stop shopping" for advertisers to reach customers through multiple media—television and newspapers—in several huge markets such as New York and Chicago.

Vertical integration

- Shaw Industries, a giant carpet manufacturer, increases its control over raw materials by producing much of its own polypropylene fiber, a key input to its manufacturing process.

Unrelated Diversification: Parenting, Restructuring, and Financial Synergies

Corporate restructuring and parenting

- The corporate office of Cooper Industries adds value to its acquired businesses by performing such activities as auditing their manufacturing operations, improving their accounting activities, and centralizing union negotiations.

Portfolio management

- Novartis, formerly Ciba-Geigy, uses portfolio management to improve many key activities, including resource allocation and reward and evaluation systems.

Exhibit 6.1 provides an overview of how we will address the various means by which firms create value through both related and unrelated diversification.[3] We also include an overview of some examples that we will address in this chapter.

Related Diversification: Economies of Scope and Revenue Enhancement

As discussed earlier, related diversification enables a firm to benefit from horizontal relationships across different businesses in the diversified corporation by leveraging core competencies and sharing activities (e.g., production facilities and distribution facilities). This enables a corporation to benefit from economies of scope. *Economies of scope* refers to cost savings from leveraging core competencies or sharing related activities among businesses in the corporation. A firm can also enjoy greater revenues if two businesses attain higher levels of sales growth combined than either company could attain independently.

For example, a sporting goods store with one or several locations may acquire other stores. This enables it to leverage, or reuse, many of its key resources—favorable reputation, expert staff and management skills, efficient purchasing operations—the basis of its competitive advantage(s), over a larger number of stores.[4] Let's next address how to create value by leveraging core competencies.

Leveraging Core Competencies

The concept of core competencies can be illustrated by the imagery of the diversified corporation as a tree.[5] The trunk and major limbs represent core products; the smaller branches are business units; and the leaves, flowers, and fruit are end products. The core competencies are represented by the root system, which provides nourishment, sustenance, and stability. Managers often misread the strength of competitors by looking only at their end products, just as one can fail to appreciate the strength of a tree by looking only at its leaves. Core competencies may also be viewed as the "glue" that binds existing businesses together or as the engine that fuels new business growth.

Core competencies reflect the collective learning in organizations—how to coordinate diverse production skills, integrate multiple streams of technologies, and market and merchandise diverse products and services. The theoretical knowledge necessary to put a radio on a chip does not in itself assure a company of the skill needed to produce a miniature radio approximately the size of a business card. To accomplish this, Casio, a giant electronic products producer, must synthesize know-how in miniaturization, microprocessor design, material science, and ultrathin precision castings. These are the same skills that it applies in its miniature card calculators, pocket TVs, and digital watches.

For a core competence to create value and provide a viable basis for synergy among the businesses in a corporation, it must meet three criteria.[6]

- ◆   ***The core competence must enhance competitive advantage(s) by creating superior customer value.*** It must enable the business to develop strengths relative to the competition. Every value chain activity has the potential to provide a viable basis for building on a core competence. At Gillette, for example, scientists developed the Mach 3 and Sensor Excel after the introduction of the tremendously successful Sensor System through a thorough understanding of several phenomena that underlie shaving. These include the physiology of facial hair and skin, the metallurgy of blade strength and sharpness, the dynamics of a cartridge moving across skin, and the physics of a razor blade severing hair. Such innovations are possible only with an understanding of such phenomena and the ability to combine such technologies into innovative products. Customers have consistently been willing to pay more for such technologically differentiated products.
- ◆   ***Different businesses in the corporation must be similar in at least one important way related to the core competence.*** It is not essential that the products or services themselves be similar. Rather, at least one element in the value chain must require similar skills in creating competitive advantage if the corporation is to capitalize on its core competence. At first glance one might think that motorcycles, clothes, and restaurants have little in common. But at Harley-Davidson, they do.[7] Harley-Davidson has capitalized on its exceptionally strong brand image as well as merchandising and licensing skills to sell accessories, clothing, and toys, and has licensed the Harley-Davidson Café in New York City—further evidence of the strength of its brand name and products.
- ◆   ***The core competencies must be difficult for competitors to imitate or find substitutes for.*** As we discussed in Chapter 5, competitive advantages will not be sustainable if the competition can easily imitate or substitute them. Similarly, if the skills associated with a firm's core competencies are easily imitated or replicated, they are not a sound basis for sustainable advantages. Consider Sharp Corporation, a $17 billion consumer electronics giant.[8] It has a set of specialized core competencies

in optoelectronics technologies that are difficult to replicate and contribute to its competitive advantages in its core businesses. Its most successful technology has been liquid crystal displays (LCDs) that are critical components in nearly all of Sharp's products. Its expertise in this technology enabled Sharp to succeed in videocassette recorders (VCRs) with its innovative LCD viewfinder and led to the creation of its Wizard, a personal electronic organizer.

Sharing Activities

As we saw above, leveraging core competencies involves transferring accumulated skills and expertise across business units in a corporation. When carried out effectively, this leads to advantages that can become quite sustainable over time. Corporations can also achieve synergy by sharing tangible activities across their business units. These include value-creating activities such as common manufacturing facilities, distribution channels, and sales forces. As we will see, sharing activities can potentially provide two primary payoffs: cost savings and revenue enhancements.

Deriving Cost Savings through Sharing Activities   Typically, this is the most common type of synergy and the easiest to estimate. Peter Shaw, head of mergers and acquisitions at the British chemical and pharmaceutical company ICI refers to cost savings as "hard synergies" and contends that the level of certainty of their achievement is quite high. Cost savings come from many sources, including elimination of jobs, facilities, and related expenses that are no longer needed when functions are consolidated, or from economies of scale in purchasing. Cost savings are generally highest when one company acquires another from the same industry in the same country. Shaw Industries, recently acquired by Berkshire Hathaway, is the nation's largest carpet producer. Over the years, it has dominated the competition through a strategy of acquisition which has enabled Shaw, among other things, to consolidate its manufacturing operations in a few, highly efficient plants, and lower costs through higher capacity utilization.

It is important to note that sharing activities inevitably involve costs that the benefits must outweigh. One often overlooked cost is the greater coordination required to manage a shared activity. Even more important is the need to compromise the design or performance of an activity so that it can be shared. For example, a salesperson handling the products of two business units must operate in a way that is usually not what either unit would choose were it independent. If the compromise erodes the unit's effectiveness, then sharing may reduce rather than enhance competitive advantage.

Enhancing Revenue and Differentiation through Sharing Activities
Often an acquiring firm and its target may achieve a higher level of sales growth together than either company could on its own. Shortly after Gillette acquired Duracell, it confirmed its expectation that selling Duracell batteries through Gillette's existing channels for personal care products would increase sales, particularly internationally. Gillette sold Duracell products in 25 new markets in the first year after the acquisition and substantially increased sales in established international markets. In a similar vein, a target company's distribution channel can be used to escalate the sales of the acquiring company's product. Such was the case when Gillette acquired Parker Pen. Gillette estimated that it could gain an additional $25 million in sales of its own Waterman pens by taking advantage of Parker's distribution channels.

Firms can also enhance the effectiveness of their differentiation strategies by means of sharing activities among business units. A shared order-processing system, for example, may permit new features and services that a buyer will value. Also, sharing can reduce the cost of differentiation. For instance, a shared service network may make more advanced, remote service technology economically feasible. To illustrate the potential for enhanced differentiation though sharing, consider $5.1 billion VF Corporation—producer of such well-known brands as Lee, Wrangler, Vanity Fair, and Jantzen.

> VF's acquisition of Nutmeg Industries and H. H. Cutler provided it with several large customers that it didn't have before, increasing its plant utilization and productivity. But more importantly, Nutmeg designs and makes licensed apparel for sports teams and organizations, while Cutler manufactures licensed brand-name children's apparel, including Walt Disney kid's wear. Such brand labeling enhances the differentiation of VF's apparel products. According to VF President Mackey McDonald, "What we're doing is looking at value-added knitwear, taking our basic fleece from Basset-Walker [one of its divisions], embellishing it through Cutler and Nutmeg, and selling it as a value-added product." Additionally, Cutler's advanced high-speed printing technologies will enable VF to be more proactive in anticipating trends in the fashion-driven fleece market. Claims McDonald, "Rather than printing first and then trying to guess what the customer wants, we can see what's happening in the marketplace and then print it up."[9]

As a cautionary note, managers must keep in mind that sharing activities among businesses in a corporation can have a negative effect on a given business's differentiation. For example, with the merger of Chrysler and Daimler-Benz, many consumers may lower their perceptions of Mercedes's quality and prestige if they feel that common production components and processes are being used across the two divisions. And the Jaguar division of Ford Motor Company may be adversely affected as consumers come to understand that it shares many components with its sister divisions at Ford, including Lincoln.

Strategy Spotlight 6.2 illustrates how Walt Disney Company leverages its core competencies and shares activities across many business units.

Related Diversification: Market Power

In the previous section, we explained how leveraging core competencies and sharing activities help firms create economies of scale and scope through related diversification. In this section, we discuss how companies achieve related diversification through market power. We also address the two principal means by which firms achieve synergy through market power: *pooled negotiating power* and *vertical integration.* It is important to recognize that managers have limits on their ability to use market power for diversification, because government regulations can sometimes restrict the ability of a business to gain very large shares of a particular market.

When General Electric (GE) announced a $41 billion bid for Honeywell, the European Union stepped in. GE's market clout would have expanded significantly as a result of the deal, with GE supplying over one-half the parts needed to build several aircraft engines. The commission's concern, causing them to reject the acquisition, was that GE could use its increased market power to dominate the aircraft engine parts market and crowd out competitors.[10] Thus, while managers need to be aware of the strategic advantages of market power, they must at the same time be aware of regulations and legislation.

Pooled Negotiating Power

Similar businesses working together or the affiliation of a business with a strong parent can strengthen an organization's bargaining position in relation to suppliers and customers as well as enhance its position vis-à-vis competitors. Compare, for example, the position of an independent food manufacturer with the same business within Nestlé. Being part of Nestlé Corporation provides the business with significant clout—greater bargaining power with suppliers and customers—since it is part of a firm that makes large purchases from suppliers and provides a wide variety of products to their customers. Access to the parent's

strategy spotlight

How Walt Disney Company Leverages Its Core Competencies and Shares Activities

One plus one can equal more than two when firms leverage core competencies and share activities. Disney is a prime example. CEO Michael Eisner credited Disney's success to several factors. Among these, diversity leads the list. Eisner attributed the company's creativity to the diversity of ideas generated by its employees. Although diversity of opinion can cause friction, this "creative friction" is the foundation of Disney's idea generation success.

The company harnesses this creative friction through synergies among business units. For example, Disney recently reorganized its structure from a hierarchical to a hybrid form. With the hierarchical structure, an employee writing a movie in Italy would report directly to the movie division. But this keeps the knowledge gained from the Italian movie production within the movie production division. So now the Italian movie producer reports to someone outside the movie division in addition to the producer's own work unit. This gives others access to information that would otherwise remain isolated, creating the chance that knowledge gained in one division can be used elsewhere. In other words, Disney arranges "chance accidents" in which synergies can develop and duplication of efforts can decrease.

Disney also has expertise in sharing activities. Consider the box office hit *The Lion King*. Disney was not satisfied to sit back and collect the box office revenues. After the movie's success, it developed more than 150 different *Lion King* products. Disney based the soundtrack, *Rhythm of the Pride Lands,* on the music from *The Lion King. Simba's Pride* is a video spawned from *The Lion King.* By leveraging *The Lion King*'s success and sharing activities among different business divisions, Disney turned a $600 million movie success into a $3 billion revenue stream. Other examples abound at Disney. Disney World works with a cruise line to sell joint vacations. *The Little Mermaid* became a popular television production. *Toy Story* was leveraged with a video game based on the movie's animated characters. A successful Broadway play was the result of *Beauty and the Beast.* EuroDisney managers share their knowledge and expertise with Disney's other resort managers.

The result? Three movie studios; theme parks in the United States, France, and Japan and a future development in Hong Kong; two Disney cruise ships in addition to joint efforts with other cruise lines; 725 Disney stores; and ownership of major media outlets including ABC, ESPN, Lifetime, and E! Entertainment Television. With $25 billion in annual revenues, Disney is an exemplar of the benefits of leveraging core competencies and sharing activities.

Sources: K. Eisenhardt and D. C. Galunic, "Coevolving: At Last, a Way to Make Synergies Work," *Harvard Business Review* 78, no. 1 (2000), pp. 91–101; S. Wetlaufer, "Common Sense and Conflict: An Interview with Disney's Michael Eisner," *Harvard Business Review* 78, no. 1 (2000), pp. 115–24.

deep pockets increases the business's strength relative to rivals. Further, the Nestlé unit enjoys greater protection from substitutes and new entrants. Not only would rivals perceive the unit as a more formidable opponent, but the unit's association with Nestlé would also provide greater visibility and improved image.

Consolidating an industry can also increase a firm's market power. This is clearly an emerging trend in the multimedia industry.[11] All of these mergers and acquisitions have a common goal: to control and leverage as many news and entertainment channels as possible. In total, more than $261 billion in mergers and acquisitions in the media industry were announced in 2000—up 12 percent from 1999. For example, consider the Tribune Company's $8 billion purchase of the Times Mirror Company.

> The merger doubled the size of the Tribune and secured its position among the top tier of major media companies. The enhanced scale and scope helped it to compete more effectively and grow more rapidly in two consolidating industries—newspaper and television broadcasting. The combined company would increase its power over customers by providing a "one-stop shop" for advertisers desiring to reach consumers through multiple media in enormous markets

such as Chicago, Los Angeles, and New York. The company has estimated its incremental revenue from national and cross-media advertising to grow from $40–50 million in 2001 to $200 million by 2005. The combined company should also increase its power relative to its suppliers. The company's enhanced size is expected to lead to increased efficiencies when purchasing newsprint and other commodities.[12]

When acquiring related businesses, a firm's potential for pooled negotiating power vis-à-vis its customers and suppliers can be very enticing. However, managers must carefully evaluate how the combined businesses may affect relationships with actual and potential customers, suppliers, and competitors. For example, when PepsiCo diversified into the fast-food industry with its acquisitions of Kentucky Fried Chicken, Taco Bell, and Pizza Hut (since spun off as Tricon, Inc.), it clearly benefited from its position over these units that served as a captive market for its soft-drink products. However, many competitors such as McDonald's have refused to consider PepsiCo as a supplier of its own soft-drink needs because of competition with Pepsi's divisions in the fast-food industry. Simply put, McDonald's did not want to subsidize the enemy! Thus, although acquiring related businesses can enhance a corporation's bargaining power, it must be aware of the potential for retaliation.

Vertical Integration

Vertical integration represents an expansion or extension of the firm by integrating preceding or successive productive processes.[13] That is, the firm incorporates more processes toward the original source of raw materials (backward integration) or toward the ultimate consumer (forward integration). For example, an automobile manufacturer might supply its own parts or make its own engines to secure sources of supply. Or it might control its own system of dealerships to ensure retail outlets for its products. Similarly, an oil refinery might secure land leases and develop its own drilling capacity to ensure a constant supply of crude oil. Or it could expand into retail operations by owning or licensing gasoline stations to guarantee customers for its petroleum products.

Clearly, vertical integration can be a viable strategy for many firms. Strategy Spotlight 6.3 discusses Shaw Industries, a carpet manufacturer. It has attained a dominant position in the industry via a strategy of vertical integration. Shaw has successfully implemented strategies of both forward and backward integration.

Benefits and Risks of Vertical Integration   Although vertical integration is a means for an organization to reduce its dependence on suppliers or its channels of distribution to end users, it represents a major decision that an organization must carefully consider. The benefits associated with vertical integration—backward or forward—must be carefully weighed against the risks.[14]

The *benefits* of vertical integration include (1) a secure source of supply of raw materials or distribution channels that cannot be "held hostage" to external markets where costs can fluctuate over time, (2) protection and control over assets and services required to produce and deliver valuable products and services, (3) access to new business opportunities and new forms of technologies, and (4) simplified procurement and administrative procedures since key activities are brought inside the firm, eliminating the need to deal with a wide variety of suppliers and distributors.

The *risks* of vertical integration include (1) the costs and expenses associated with increased overhead and capital expenditures to provide facilities, raw material inputs, and distribution channels inside the organization, (2) a loss of flexibility resulting from the inability to respond quickly to changes in the external environment because of the huge investments in vertical integration activities that generally cannot be easily deployed else-

strategy spotlight

Vertical Integration at Shaw Industries

Shaw Industries (now part of Berkshire Hathaway) is an example of a firm that has followed a very successful strategy of vertical integration. By relentlessly pursuing both backward and forward integration, Shaw has become the dominant manufacturer of carpeting products in the United States. According to CEO Robert Shaw, "We want to be involved with as much of the process of making and selling carpets as practical. That way, we're in charge of

Sources: J. White, "Shaw to Home in on More with Georgia Tufters Deal," *HFN: The Weekly Newspaper for the Home Furnishing Network*, May 5, 2003, p. 32; Shaw Industries, annual reports, 1993, 2000; and A. Server, "How to Escape a Price War," *Fortune*, June 13, 1994, p. 88.

costs." For example, Shaw acquired Amoco's polypropylene fiber manufacturing facilities in Alabama and Georgia. These new plants provide carpet fibers for internal use and for sale to other manufacturers. With this backward integration, fully one-quarter of Shaw's carpet fiber needs are now met in-house. In early 1996 Shaw began to integrate forward, acquiring seven floor-covering retailers in a move that suggested a strategy to consolidate the fragmented industry and increase its influence over retail pricing. Exhibit 6.2 provides a simplified depiction of the stages of vertical integration for Shaw Industries.

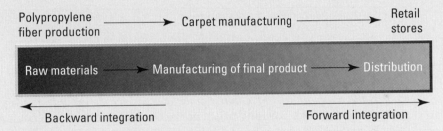

Exhibit 6.2 Simplified Stages of Vertical Integration: Shaw Industries

where, (3) problems associated with unbalanced capacities or unfilled demand along the value chain, and (4) additional administrative costs associated with managing a more complex set of activities. Exhibit 6.3 summarizes the benefits and risks of vertical integration.

In making decisions associated with vertical integration, four issues should be considered.[15]

1. *Are we satisfied with the quality of the value that our present suppliers and distributors are providing?* If the performance of organizations in the vertical chain—both suppliers and distributors—is satisfactory, it may not, in general, be appropriate to perform these activities ourselves. Firms in the athletic footwear industry such as Nike and Reebok have traditionally outsourced the manufacture of their shoes to countries such as China and Indonesia where labor costs are low. Since the strengths of these companies are typically in design and marketing, it would be advisable to continue to outsource production operations and continue to focus on where they can add the most value.

2. *Are there activities in our industry value chain presently being outsourced or performed independently by others that are a viable source of future profits?* Even if a firm is outsourcing value-chain activities to companies that are doing a credible job, it may be missing out on substantial profit opportunities. To illustrate, consider the automobile industry's profit pool. As you may recall from Chapter 5, there is much more potential profit in many downstream activities (e.g., leasing, warranty,

**Exhibit 6.3
Benefits and Risks
of Vertical
Integration**

Benefits
◆   A secure source of raw materials or distribution channels.
◆   Protection of and control over valuable assets.
◆   Access to new business opportunities.
◆   Simplified procurement and administrative procedures.

Risks
◆   Costs and expenses associated with increased overhead and capital expenditures.
◆   Loss of flexibility resulting from large investments.
◆   Problems associated with unbalanced capacities along the value chain.
◆   Additional administrative costs associated with managing a more complex set of activities.

insurance, and service) than in the manufacture of automobiles. Not surprising, carmakers such as Ford and General Motors are undertaking forward integration strategies to become bigger players in these high-profit activities.

3. *Is there a high level of stability in the demand for the organization's products?* High demand or sales volatility would not be conducive to a vertical integration strategy. With the high level of fixed costs in plant and equipment as well as operating costs that accompany endeavors toward vertical integration, widely fluctuating sales demand can either strain resources (in times of high demand) or result in unused capacity (in times of low demand). The cycles of "boom and bust" in the automobile industry are a key reason why the manufacturers have increased the amount of outsourced inputs in recent years.

4. *How high is the proportion of additional production capacity actually absorbed by existing products or by the prospects of new and similar products?* The smaller the proportion of production capacity to be absorbed by existing or future products, the lower is the potential for achieving scale economies associated with the increased capacity—either in terms of backward integration (toward the supply of raw materials) or forward integration (toward the end user). Alternatively, if there is excess capacity in the near term, the strategy of vertical integration may be viable if there is the anticipation of future expansion of products.

Analyzing Vertical Integration: The Transaction Cost Perspective

Another approach that has proved very useful in understanding vertical integration is the *transaction cost perspective.*[16] According to this perspective, every market transaction involves some *transaction costs.* First, a decision to purchase an input from an outside source leads to *search* costs (i.e., the cost to find where it is available, the level of quality, etc.). Second, there are costs associated with *negotiating.* Third, a *contract* needs to be written spelling out future possible contingencies. Fourth, parties in a contract have to *monitor* each other. Finally, if a party does not comply with the terms of the contract, there are *enforcement* costs. Transaction costs are thus the sum of search costs, negotiation costs, contracting costs, monitoring costs, and enforcement costs. These transaction costs can be avoided by internalizing the activity, in other words, by producing the input in-house.

A related problem with purchasing a specialized input from outside is the issue of *transaction-specific investments.* For example, when an automobile company needs an input specifically designed for a particular car model, the supplier may be unwilling to make the investments in plant and machinery necessary to produce that component for two reasons. First, the investment may take many years to recover but there is no guarantee the automobile company will continue to buy from them after the contract expires, typically in one year. Second, once the investment is made, the supplier has no bargaining power. That is, the buyer knows that the supplier has no option but to supply at ever-lower prices because the investments were so specific that they cannot be used to produce alternative products. In such circumstances, again, vertical integration may be the only option.

Vertical integration, however, gives rise to a different set of costs. These costs are referred to as *administrative costs*. Coordinating different stages of the value chain now internalized within the firm causes administrative costs to go up. Decisions about vertical integration are, therefore, based on a comparison of transaction costs and administrative costs. If transaction costs are lower than administrative costs, it is best to resort to market transactions and avoid vertical integration. For example, McDonald's may be the world's biggest buyer of beef, but they do not raise cattle. The market for beef has low transaction costs and requires no transaction-specific investments. On the other hand, if transaction costs are higher than administrative costs, vertical integration becomes an attractive strategy. Most automobile manufacturers produce their own engines because the market for engines involves high transaction costs and transaction-specific investments.

Vertical Integration: Further Considerations   As many companies would attest, successfully executing strategies of vertical integration can be very difficult. For example, Unocal, a major petroleum refiner, which once owned retail gas stations, was slow to capture the potential grocery and merchandise side business that might have resulted from customer traffic to its service stations. Unocal lacked the competencies to develop a separate retail organization and culture. The company eventually sold the assets and brand to Tosco (now part of Phillips Petroleum Co.). Eli Lilly, the pharmaceutical firm, tried to achieve forward integration by acquiring a pharmaceutical mail-order business in 1994, but it was unsuccessful in increasing market share because it failed to integrate its operations. Two years later, Lilly wrote off the venture.

Last, as with our earlier discussion of pooled negotiating power, managers must carefully consider the impact that vertical integration may have on existing and future customers, suppliers, and competitors. After Lockheed Martin, a dominant defense contractor, acquired Loral Corporation, an electronics supplier, for $9.1 billion, it had an unpleasant and unanticipated surprise. Loral, as a captive supplier of Lockheed, is now perceived and treated as a competitor by many of its previous customers. McDonnell Douglas (MD), for example, announced that it would switch its business from Loral to other suppliers of electronic systems such as Litton Industries or Raytheon. Thus, before Lockheed Martin can realize any net synergies from this acquisition, it must make up for the substantial lost business resulting from MD's (now part of Boeing) decision to switch suppliers.

In these two sections we have addressed four means by which firms can achieve synergies through related diversification: leveraging core competences, sharing activities, pooled negotiating power, and vertical integration. In Strategy Spotlight 6.4, we address how Procter & Gamble strengthened its competitive position by combining all four means. We next turn our attention to unrelated diversification.

Unrelated Diversification: Financial Synergies and Parenting

With unrelated diversification, unlike related diversification, few benefits are derived from *horizontal relationships*—that is, the leveraging of core competencies or the sharing of activities across business units within a corporation. Instead, potential benefits can be gained from *vertical (or hierarchical) relationships*—the creation of synergies from the interaction of the corporate office with the individual business units. There are two main sources

strategy spotlight

Procter & Gamble: Using Multiple Means to Achieve Synergies

To accomplish successful related diversification, a company must combine multiple facets of its business to create synergies across the organization. Procter & Gamble (P&G) is a prime example of such a firm. Using related diversification, it creates synergies by leveraging core competencies, sharing activities, pooling negotiating power, and vertically integrating certain product lines as part of its corporate-level strategy. The following excerpt from a speech by Clayt Daley, Procter & Gamble's chief financial officer, illustrates how the company has done this.

Remarks to Financial Analysts

Today, we already sell 10 brands with sales of one billion dollars or more. Seven of these 10 brands surpassed the billion-dollar sales mark during the '90s. And, in total, these 10 brands accounted for more than half of our sales growth during the decade. Beyond these 10, there are several brands with the potential to achieve a billion dollars in sales by 2005. Olay could surpass a billion dollars in sales in 2001, Iams by 2002.

P&G's unmatched lineup of billion-dollar leadership brands generates consistently strong returns. In virtually every case, P&G's leading brands achieve higher margins and deliver consistently strong shareholder returns. Having a stable of such strong global brands creates significant advantages for P&G—and our total company scale multiplies those advantages.

We can obviously take advantage of our purchasing power for things as varied as raw materials and advertising media. We can leverage the scale of our manufacturing and logistics operations. But we can do far more.

We have the scale of our intellectual property—the knowledge and deep insight that exists throughout our organization. We have scale in our technologies—the enormous breadth of expertise we have across our product categories. There is scale in our go-to-market capabilities and our global customer relationships.

Source: C. Daley, "Remarks to Financial Analysts," speech excerpt, Procter & Gamble Company, September 28, 2000.

Let me give you three quick examples. First, scale of consumer knowledge. We are able to learn, reapply, and multiply knowledge across many brands with a similar target audience. For example, teens. The teen market is global. Teens in New York, Tokyo, and Caracas wear the same clothes, listen to the same music, and have many of the same attitudes. We have categories they buy and use: cosmetics, hair care, skin care, personal cleansing and body products, feminine protection, snacks and beverages, oral care, and others. Our scale enables us to develop unique insights on teens—like how to identify teen chat leaders—and then reapply that across all our teen-focused businesses.

Another way we can leverage scale is through the transfer of product technologies across categories. We can connect seemingly unrelated technologies to create surprising new products. Our new Crest White Strips are a great example of the innovation that can result. This new product provides a major new tooth-whitening benefit that can be achieved in the home. We have combined our knowledge in oral hygiene, and our knowledge of bleaching agents, with a special film technology to provide a safe and effective product that can whiten teeth within 14 days.

Another important source of scale is our go-to-market capability. No other consumer products company works with retailers the way we do. Our Customer Business Development approach is a fundamentally different way of working with our trade partners. We seek to build businesses across common goals.

We bring a philosophy that encourages a simple, transparent shopping experience—with simple, transparent pricing, efficient assortment, efficient in-store promotion, and efficient replenishment. This approach has helped us build extremely strong relationships with our customers. For example, in the annual Cannondale "Power-Ranking Survey," U.S. retailers consistently ranked P&G at the top on brands, consumer information, supply-chain management, category management, and more.

of such synergies. First, the corporate office can contribute to "parenting" and restructuring of (often acquired) businesses. Second, the corporate office can add value by viewing the entire corporation as a family or "portfolio" of businesses and allocating resources to optimize corporate goals of profitability, cash flow, and growth. Additionally, the corporate office enhances value by establishing appropriate human resource practices and financial controls for each of its business units.

Corporate Parenting and Restructuring

So far, we have discussed how corporations can add value through related diversification by exploring sources of synergy *across* business units. In this section, we will discuss how value can be created *within* business units as a result of the expertise and support provided by the corporate office. Thus, we look at these as *hierarchical* sources of synergy.

The positive contributions of the corporate office have been referred to as the "parenting advantage."[17] Many firms have successfully diversified their holdings without strong evidence of the more traditional sources of synergy (i.e., horizontally across business units). Diversified public corporations such as BTR, Emerson Electric, and Hanson and leveraged buyout firms such as Kohlberg, Kravis, Roberts & Company and Clayton, Dublilier & Rice are a few examples.[18] These parent companies create value through management expertise. How? They improve plans and budgets and provide especially competent central functions such as legal, financial, human resource management, procurement, and the like. Additionally, they help subsidiaries to make wise choices in their own acquisitions, divestitures, and new internal development decisions. Such contributions often help business units to substantially increase their revenues and profits. Consider Texas-based Cooper Industries's acquisition of Champion International, the spark plug company, as an example of corporate parenting.[19]

Cooper applies a distinctive parenting approach designed to help its businesses improve their manufacturing performance. New acquisitions are "Cooperized"—Cooper audits their manufacturing operations; improves their cost accounting systems; makes their planning, budgeting, and human resource systems conform with its systems; and centralizes union negotiations. Excess cash is squeezed out through tighter controls and reinvested in productivity enhancements, which improve overall operating efficiency. As one manager observed, "When you get acquired by Cooper, one of the first things that happens is a truckload of policy manuals arrives at your door." Such active parenting has been effective in enhancing the competitive advantages of many kinds of manufacturing businesses.

Restructuring is another means by which the corporate office can add substantial value to a business.[20] The central idea can be captured in the real estate phrase "buy low and sell high." Here, the corporate office tries to find either poorly performing firms with unrealized potential or firms in industries on the threshold of significant, positive change. The parent intervenes, often selling off parts of the business, changing the management, reducing payroll and unnecessary sources of expenses, changing strategies, and infusing the company with new technologies, processes, reward systems, and so forth. When the restructuring is complete, the firm can either "sell high" and capture the added value or keep the business in the corporate family and enjoy the financial and competitive benefits of the enhanced performance.[21]

For the restructuring strategy to work, the corporate management must have both the insight to detect undervalued companies (otherwise the cost of acquisition would be too high) or businesses competing in industries with a high potential for transformation.[22] Additionally, of course, they must have the requisite skills and resources to turn the businesses around, even if they may be in new and unfamiliar industries.

Restructuring can involve changes in assets, capital structure, or management. *Asset restructuring* involves the sale of unproductive assets, or even whole lines of businesses, that are peripheral. In some cases, it may even involve acquisitions that strengthen the core business. *Capital restructuring* involves changing the debt-equity mix, or the mix between different classes of debt or equity. Although the substitution of equity with debt is more common in buyout situations, occasionally the parent may provide additional equity capital. *Management restructuring* typically involves changes in the composition of the top management team, organizational structure, and reporting relationships. Tight financial control, rewards based strictly on meeting short- to medium-term performance goals, and reduction in the number of middle-level managers are common steps in management restructuring. In some cases, parental intervention may even result in changes in strategy as well as infusion of new technologies and processes.

Hanson, plc, a British conglomerate, made numerous such acquisitions in the United States in the 1980s, often selling these firms at significant profits after a few years of successful restructuring efforts. Hanson's acquisition and subsequent restructuring of the SCM group is a classic example of the restructuring strategy. Hanson acquired SCM, a diversified manufacturer of industrial and consumer products (including Smith-Corona typewriters, Glidden paints, and Durkee Famous Foods), for $930 million in 1986 after a bitter takeover battle. In the next few months, Hanson sold SCM's paper and pulp operations for $160 million, the chemical division for $30 million, Glidden paints for $580 million, and Durkee Famous Foods for $120 million, virtually recovering the entire original investment. In addition, Hanson also sold the SCM headquarters in New York for $36 million and reduced the headquarters staff by 250. They still retained several profitable divisions, including the titanium dioxide operations and managed them with tight financial controls that led to increased returns.[23]

Portfolio Management

During the 1970s and early 1980s, several leading consulting firms developed the concept of portfolio matrices to achieve a better understanding of the competitive position of an overall portfolio (or family) of businesses, to suggest strategic alternatives for each of the businesses, and to identify priorities for the allocation of resources. Several studies have reported widespread use of these techniques among American firms.[24]

The key purpose of portfolio models was to assist a firm in achieving a balanced portfolio of businesses.[25] This consisted of businesses whose profitability, growth, and cash flow characteristics would complement each other, and add up to a satisfactory overall corporate performance. Imbalance, for example, could be caused either by excessive cash generation with too few growth opportunities or by insufficient cash generation to fund the growth requirements in the portfolio. Monsanto, for example, used portfolio planning to restructure its portfolio, divesting low-growth commodity chemicals businesses and acquiring businesses in higher-growth industries such as biotechnology.

The Boston Consulting Group's (BCG) growth/share matrix is among the best known of these approaches.[26] In the BCG approach, each of the firm's strategic business units (SBUs) is plotted on a two-dimensional grid in which the axes are relative market share and industry growth rate. The grid is broken into four quadrants. Exhibit 6.4 depicts the BCG matrix. A few clarifications:

1.   Each circle represents one of the corporation's business units. The size of the circle represents the relative size of the business unit in terms of revenues.
2.   Relative market share, measured by the ratio of the business unit's size to that of its largest competitor, is plotted along the horizontal axis.
3.   Market share is central to the BCG matrix. This is because high relative market share leads to unit cost reduction due to experience and learning curve effects and, consequently, superior competitive position.

Each of the four quadrants of the grid has different implications for the SBUs that fall into the category:

◆   SBUs competing in high-growth industries with relatively high market shares are labeled "stars." These firms have long-term growth potential and should continue to receive substantial investment funding.

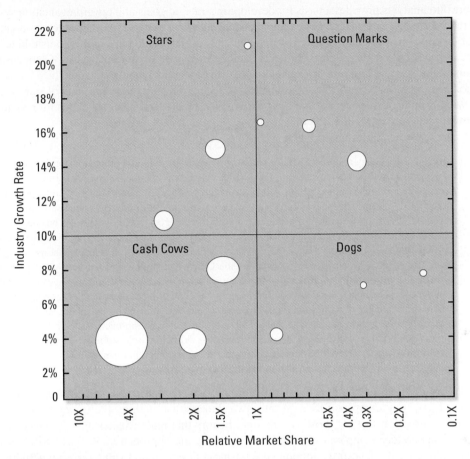

Exhibit 6.4 The Boston Consulting Group (BCG) Portfolio Matrix

- SBUs competing in high-growth industries but having relatively weak market shares are labeled "question marks." Resources should be invested in them to enhance their competitive positions.
- SBUs with high market shares in low-growth industries are labeled "cash cows." These units have limited long-run potential but represent a source of current cash flows to fund investments in "stars" and "question marks."
- SBUs with weak market shares in low-growth industries are called "dogs." Because they have weak positions and limited potential, most analysts recommend that they be divested.

In using portfolio strategy approaches, a corporation tries to create synergies and shareholder value in a number of ways.[27] Since the businesses are unrelated, synergies that develop are those that result from the actions of the corporate office with the individual units (i.e., hierarchical relationships) instead of among business units (i.e., horizontal relationships). First, portfolio analysis provides a snapshot of the businesses in a corporation's portfolio; therefore, the corporation is in a better position to allocate resources among the business units according to prescribed criteria (e.g., use cash flows from the "cash cows" to fund promising "stars"). Second, the expertise and analytical resources in the corporate office provide guidance in determining what firms may be attractive (or unattractive) acquisitions. Third, the corporate office is able to provide financial resources to the business units on favorable terms that reflect the corporation's overall ability to raise funds. Fourth, the corporate office can provide high-quality review and coaching for the individual businesses. Fifth, portfolio analysis provides a basis for developing strategic goals and reward/evaluation systems for business managers. For example, managers of cash cows would have lower targets for revenue growth than managers of stars, but the former would have higher threshold levels of profit targets on proposed projects than the managers of star businesses. Compensation systems would also reflect such realities: Cash cows understandably would be rewarded more on the basis of cash that their businesses generate than would managers of star businesses. Similarly, managers of star businesses would be held to higher standards for revenue growth than managers of cash cow businesses.

To see how companies can benefit from portfolio approaches, consider Ciba-Geigy.

> In 1994 Ciba-Geigy adopted portfolio planning approaches to help it manage its business units, which competed in a wide variety of industries, including chemicals, dyes, pharmaceuticals, crop protection, and animal health.[28] It placed each business unit in a category corresponding to the BCG matrix. The business unit's goals, compensation programs, personnel selection, and resource allocation were strongly associated with the category within which the business was placed. For example, business units classified as "cash cows" had much higher hurdles for obtaining financial resources (from the corporate office) for expansion than "question marks" since the latter were businesses for which Ciba-Geigy had high hopes for accelerated future growth and profitability. Additionally, the compensation of a business unit manager in a cash cow would be strongly associated with its success in generating cash to fund other businesses, whereas a manager of a question mark business would be rewarded on his or her ability to increase revenue growth and market share. The portfolio planning approaches appear to be working. In 2003, Ciba-Geigy's (now Novartis) revenues and net income stood at $19.0 billion and $5.3 billion, respectively. This represents a rather modest 23 percent increase in revenues but a most impressive 160 percent growth in net income over a seven-year period.

Despite the potential benefits of portfolio models, there are also some notable downsides. First, they compare SBUs on only two dimensions, making the implicit but erroneous assumption that (1) those are the only factors that really matter and (2) every unit can be accurately compared on that basis. Second, the approach views each SBU as a stand-alone entity, ignoring common core business practices and value-creating activities that may hold promise for synergies across business units. Third, unless care is exercised, the process becomes largely mechanical, substituting an oversimplified graphical model for the important contributions of the CEO's (and other corporate managers's) experience and judgment. Fourth, the reliance on "strict rules" regarding resource allocation across SBUs can be detrimental to a firm's long-term viability. For example, according to one study, over one-half of all the businesses that should have been cash users (based on the BCG matrix) were instead cash providers.[29] Finally, while colorful and easy to comprehend, the imagery of the BCG matrix can lead to some troublesome and overly simplistic prescriptions. According to one author:

> The dairying analogy is appropriate (for some cash cows), so long as we resist the urge to oversimplify it. On the farm, even the best-producing cows eventually begin to dry up. The farmer's solution to this is euphemistically called "freshening" the cow: The farmer arranges a date for the cow with a bull, she has a calf, the milk begins flowing again. Cloistering the cow—isolating her from everything but the feed trough and the milking machines—assures that she will go dry.[30]

To see what can go wrong, consider Cabot Corporation.

> Cabot Corporation supplies carbon black for the rubber, electronics, and plastics industries. Following the BCG matrix, Cabot moved away from its "cash cow," carbon black, and diversified into "stars" such as ceramics and semiconductors in a seemingly overaggressive effort to create more revenue growth for the corporation. Predictably, Cabot's return on assets declined as the firm shifted away from its core competence to unrelated areas. The portfolio model failed by pointing the company in the wrong direction in an effort to spur growth—away from their core

business. Recognizing its mistake, Cabot Corporation returned to its mainstay carbon black manufacturing and divested unrelated businesses. Today the company is a leader in its field with $1.8 billion in 2003 revenues.[31]

Caveat: Is Risk Reduction a Viable Goal of Diversification?

Analysts and academics have suggested that one of the purposes of diversification is to reduce the risk that is inherent in a firm's variability in revenues and profits over time. In essence, the argument is that if a firm enters new products or markets that are affected differently by seasonal or economic cycles, its performance over time will be more stable. For example, a firm manufacturing lawn mowers may diversify into snow blowers to even out its annual sales. Or a firm manufacturing a luxury line of household furniture may introduce a lower-priced line since affluent and lower-income customers are affected differently by economic cycles.

At first glance the above reasoning may make sense, but there are some problems with it. First, a firm's stockholders can diversify their portfolios at a much lower cost than a corporation. As we have noted in this chapter, individuals can purchase their shares with almost no premium (e.g., only a small commission is paid to a discount broker), and they don't have to worry about integrating the acquisition into their portfolio. Second, economic cycles as well as their impact on a given industry (or firm) are difficult to predict with any degree of accuracy.

Notwithstanding the above, some firms have benefited from diversification by lowering the variability (or risk) in their performance over time. Consider Emerson Electronic.

Emerson Electronic is a $16 billion manufacturer that has enjoyed an incredible run—43 consecutive years of earnings growth![32] It produces a wide variety of products, including measurement devices for heavy industry, temperature controls for heating and ventilation systems, and power tools sold at Home Depot. Recently, many analysts questioned Emerson's purchase of companies that sell power systems to the volatile telecommunications industry. Why? This industry is expected to experience, at best, minimal growth. However, CEO David Farr maintained that such assets could be acquired inexpensively because of the aggregate decline in demand in this industry. Additionally, he argued that the other business units, such as the sales of valves and regulators to the now-booming oil and natural gas companies, were able to pick up the slack. Therefore, while net profits in the electrical equipment sector (Emerson's core business) sharply decreased, Emerson's overall corporate profits increased 1.7 percent.

In summary, risk reduction in and of itself is rarely viable as a means to create shareholder value. It must be undertaken with a view of a firm's overall diversification strategy.

The Means to Achieve Diversification

In the prior three sections, we have addressed the types of diversification (e.g., related and unrelated) that a firm may undertake to achieve synergies and create value for its shareholders. In this section, we address the means by which a firm can go about achieving these desired benefits.

We will address three basic means. First, through acquisitions or mergers, corporations can directly acquire the assets and competencies of other firms. Second, corporations may agree to pool the resources of other companies with their resource base. This approach is commonly known as a joint venture or strategic alliance. Although these two forms of partnerships are similar in many ways, there is an important difference. Joint ventures involve the formation of a third-party legal entity where the two (or more) firms each contribute equity, whereas strategic alliances do not. Third, corporations may diversify into new products, markets, and technologies through internal development. This approach, sometimes called corporate entrepreneurship, involves the leveraging and combining of a firm's own resources and competencies to create synergies and enhance shareholder value.

Mergers and Acquisitions

Recently, several of the mergers of huge corporations have approached or exceeded $100 billion in combined market value. Exhibit 6.5 contains the 10 largest mergers and acquisitions in recent business history and the overall dismal results in terms of the erosion of shareholder value.

Growth through mergers and acquisitions has played a critical role in the success of many corporations in a wide variety of high-technology and knowledge-intensive industries. Here, market and technology changes can occur very quickly and unpredictably. Speed—speed to market, speed to positioning, and speed to becoming a viable company— is critical in such industries. For example, Alex Mandl, then AT&T's president, was responsible for the acquisition of McCaw Cellular. Although many industry experts felt the price was too steep, he believed that cellular technology was a critical asset for the telecommunications business and that it would have been extremely difficult to build that business from the ground up. Mandl claimed, "The plain fact is that acquiring is much faster than building."[33]

As we discussed earlier in the chapter, mergers and acquisitions can also be a means of obtaining valuable resources that can help an organization expand its product offerings and services. For example, Cisco Systems, a dominant player in networking equipment, acquired more than 70 companies from 1993 to early 2000.[34] This provides Cisco with access to the latest in networking equipment. Then it uses its excellent sales force to market the new technology to its corporate customers and telephone companies. Cisco also provides strong incentives to the staff of acquired companies to stay on. In order to realize the greatest value from its acquisitions, Cisco also has learned to integrate acquired companies efficiently and effectively.[35]

Merger and acquisition activity also can lead to consolidation within an industry and force other players to merge. In the pharmaceutical industry, the patents for many top-selling drugs are expiring and M&A activity is expected to heat up.[36] For example, SG Cowen Securities predicts that between 2000 and 2005, U.S. patents will expire on pharmaceutical products with annual domestic sales of approximately $34.6 billion. Clearly, this is an example of how the political-legal segment of the general environment (discussed in Chapter 2) can

**Exhibit 6.5
Ten Biggest
Mergers and
Acquisitions of All
Time and Their
Effect on
Shareholder
Wealth***

Deal	Year	Value Created Since Combination	Value Destroyed Since Combination
AOL/Time Warner	2001	——	$148 billion
Vodafone/Mannesmann	2000	——	$299 billion
Pfizer/Warner-Lambert	2000	——	$ 78 billion
Glaxo/SmithKline	2000	——	$ 40 billion
Chase/J. P. Morgan	2000	——	$ 26 billion
Exxon/Mobil	1999	$ 8 billion	——
SBC/Ameritech	1999	——	$ 68 billion
WorldCom/MCI	1998	——	$ 94 billion
Travelers/Citicorp	1998	$109 billion	——
Daimler/Chrysler	1998	——	$ 36 billion

*As of July 1, 2002.

Source: K. H. Hammonds, "The Numbers Don't Lie," *Fast Company,* September 2002, p. 80.

affect a corporation's strategy and performance. Although health care providers and patients are happy about the lower-cost generics that will arrive, drug firms are being pressed to make up for lost revenues. Combining top firms such as Pfizer Inc. and Warner-Lambert Co. as well as Glaxo Wellcome and SmithKline Beecham has many potential long-term benefits. They not only promise significant postmerger cost savings, but also the increased size of the combined companies brings greater research and development possibilities.

Corporations can also enter new market segments by way of acquisitions. Although Charles Schwab & Co. is best known for providing discount trading services for middle America, it clearly is interested in other target markets.[37] In late 2000 Schwab surprised its rivals by paying $2.7 billion to acquire U.S. Trust Corporation, a 147-year-old-financial services institution that is a top estate planner for the wealthy, as noted in the chapter's opening case. However, Schwab is in no way ignoring its core market. The firm also purchased Cybercorp Inc., a Texas brokerage company, for $488 million. That firm offers active online traders sophisticated quotes and stock-screening tools.

Clearly, mergers and acquisitions provide a firm with many potential benefits. They enable a firm to quickly enter new product markets and acquire new skills and competencies, as well as a wide variety of value-creating activities such as sales forces, distribution channels, and manufacturing operations. However, as we have seen earlier in the chapter—particularly in Strategy Spotlight 6.1—there are many potential downsides associated with mergers and acquisitions. Among these are the expensive premiums that are frequently paid to acquire a business, difficulties in integrating the activities and resources of the acquired firm into the corporation's operations, and "synergies" that may be quickly imitated by the competition. Additionally, there are many cultural issues that may doom the intended benefits from M&A endeavors.

Consider, for example, the insights of Joanne Lawrence, who played an important role as vice president and director of communications and investor relations at SmithKline Beecham, in the merger between SmithKline and the Beecham Group, a diversified consumer-oriented group headquartered in the United Kingdom.

> The key to a strategic merger is to create a new culture. This was a mammoth challenge during the SmithKline Beecham merger. We were working at so many different cultural levels, it was dizzying. We had two national cultures to blend—American and British—that compounded the challenge of selling the merger in two different markets with two different shareholder bases. There were also two different business cultures: One was very strong, scientific, and academic; the other was much more commercially oriented. And then we had to consider within both companies the individual businesses, each of which has its own little culture.[38]

Clearly, culture clashes can create major challenges. Strategy Spotlight 6.5 provides an example of many things that can go wrong when two firms merge—despite the best of intentions.

Strategic Alliances and Joint Ventures

Strategic alliances and joint ventures are assuming an increasingly prominent role in the strategy of leading firms, both large and small.[39] Such cooperative relationships have many potential advantages. Among these are entering new markets, reducing manufacturing (or other) costs in the value chain, and developing and diffusing new technologies.[40]

Entering New Markets   Often a company that has a successful product or service wants to introduce it into a new market. However, it may not have the requisite marketing expertise because it does not understand customer needs, know how to promote the product, or have access to the proper distribution channels.

The partnerships formed between Time-Warner, Inc., and three African American–owned cable companies in New York City are examples of joint ventures created to serve a

The Covey and Smith Merger: Ignoring the Seven Habits

Stephen Covey's 13-million-copy best-seller publication *The Seven Habits of Highly Effective People* offers advice that might be good for the soul, but is difficult to implement in corporate acquisitions. When Covey's organization joined forces with Hyrum Smith's firm—founder of the famed *Franklin Day Planner*—Covey's seven habits proved less than effective. *BusinessWeek* referred to Franklin's $137 million acquisition of Covey's company as a "highly ineffective organization."

With high hopes, Franklin acquired the Covey organization, expecting scale economies and a complementary vision. Instead, it experienced a loss in net earnings and hostility among employees. With a 94 percent drop in 1999 operating earnings, the new firm was forced to lay off 600 of its combined 4,200 employees. Robert A. Whitman was hired as chairman and CEO with a 20 percent stake in the company, while Covey and Smith were relegated to nonexecutive vice-chair status.

What went wrong? When the Covey Leadership Center and the Franklin Quest Company merged, they envisioned a combined consulting powerhouse. But they failed to effectively integrate the two enterprises. With division between the customer service and sales forces, the two companies failed to achieve an integrative whole. Rather, they found two distinct organizations were operating under the same corporate umbrella. The win–win strategy for which Covey had become known in writing and speaking endeavors became an us-versus-them situation.

The two firms maintained separate headquarters. The Covey sales force was paid more than the Franklin sales force. Medical coverage was different depending on which company an employee was previously affiliated with. Corporate offices were kept in Salt Lake City, far removed from the firm's customers. Seems that habits effective for people are hard for corporations to actually apply . . .

Exhibit 6.6 contrasts the seven habits of highly effective people that Stephen Covey has advocated with how the merger actually evolved. As a *BusinessWeek* writer noted, "Stephen Covey's best seller details seven ways to be more effective. Too bad his own managers ignored the advice."

(continued)

domestic market. Time-Warner built a 185,000-home cable system in the city and asked the three cable companies to operate it. Time-Warner supplied the product, and the cable companies supplied the knowledge of the community and the know-how to market the cable system. Joining with the local companies enabled Time-Warner to win the acceptance of the cable customers and to benefit from an improved image in the black community.

Reducing Manufacturing (or Other) Costs in the Value Chain Strategic alliances (or joint ventures) often enable firms to pool capital, value-creating activities, or facilities in order to reduce costs. For example, Molson Companies and Carling O'Keefe Breweries in Canada formed a joint venture to merge their brewing operations. Although Molson had a modern and efficient brewery in Montreal, Carling's was outdated. However, Carling had the better facilities in Toronto. In addition, Molson's Toronto brewery was located on the waterfront and had substantial real estate value. Overall, the synergies gained by using their combined facilities more efficiently added $150 million of pre-tax earnings during the initial year of the venture. Economies of scale were realized and facilities were better utilized.

Developing and Diffusing New Technologies Strategic alliances may also be used to build jointly on the technological expertise of two or more companies in order to develop products technologically beyond the capability of the companies acting independently. STMicroelectronics (ST) is a high-tech company based in Geneva, Switzerland, that has thrived—largely due to the success of its strategic alliances.[41] The firm develops

Exhibit 6.6 **The Seven Habits of a Less Than Effective Merger**

Habit #1 Be proactive: "Act or be acted upon."
Reality Company was slow to see the potential of electronic planning devices which initially cut into product sales.

Habit #2 Begin with the end in mind: "You carefully think through the product or the service that you want to provide in terms of your market target, then you organize all the elements . . . to meet that objective."
Reality The company delayed selling off noncore assets, such as a commercial printing business, which occupied management time and cut into profit margins. Now it's being sold off.

Habit #3 Put first things first: "Organize and execute around priorities."
Reality After the 1997 merger between Covey's company and Franklin Resources, management didn't trim overlapping jobs, thus increasing overhead and hurting margins.

Habit #4 Think win–win: "There's plenty for everybody . . . One person's success is not achieved at the expense or the exclusion of the success of others."
Reality The two sales staffs were combined, but initially the compensation systems were not. That caused resentment among those who earned less.

Habit #5 Seek first to understand, then to be understood: "An effective salesperson first seeks to understand the needs, the concerns, the situation of the customer."
Reality Most sales staff were kept at the Utah headquarters, so the company was unable to assess changing client needs in the field.

Habit #6 Synergize: "We create new alternatives—something that wasn't there before."
Reality The combined company maintained two headquarters, limiting opportunities to build on each other's strengths.

Habit #7 Sharpen the saw: "Preserv[e] and enhanc[e] the greatest asset that you have—you . . . Renew the four dimensions of your nature—physical, spiritual, mental, and social/emotional."
Reality Company was true to this principle by giving workers Sundays off. But that meant closing its 127 stores on a busy shopping day.

Source: R. Grover, "Gurus Who Failed Their Own Course," *BusinessWeek*, November 8, 1999, pp. 125–26.

and manufactures computer chips for a variety of applications: mobile phones, set-top boxes, smart cards, and flash memories. In 1995 it teamed up with Hewlett-Packard to develop powerful new processors for various digital applications that are now nearing completion. Another example was its strategic alliance with Nokia to develop a chip that would give Nokia's phones a longer battery life. Here, ST produced a chip that tripled standby time to 60 hours—a breakthough that gave Nokia a huge advantage in the marketplace.

The firm's CEO, Pasquale Pistorio, was among the first in the industry to form R&D alliances with other companies. Now ST's top 12 customers, including HP, Nokia, and Nortel, account for 45 percent of revenues. According to Pistorio, "Alliances are in our DNA." Such relationships help ST keep better-than-average growth rates, even in difficult times. That's because close partners are less likely to defect to other suppliers. ST's financial results are most impressive. During 2000 its revenues grew 55 percent, nearly double the industry average.

Wal-Mart's Strategic Alliance to Sell Used Cars

Wal-Mart recently formed a strategic alliance with the Asbury Automotive Group to sell used cars. Until Asbury went public in March 2002, it was the largest privately owned car retailer in the United States. Wal-Mart and Asbury set up four used-car dealerships in the Houston area and began marketing them under a brand called Price I Auto Stores. Since Wal-Mart is experimenting with the concept, Asbury can't use the Wal-Mart name in any of its promotional materials and, of course, there are no radio or TV ads, nor print media that tell everybody that they can now buy a used car at Wal-Mart. However, the dealerships' cinder-block facade, painted in Wal-Mart blue and gray with that well-known red stripe would be recognized by anybody who frequents Wal-Mart's stores.

Price I's strategy? Salesmen don't get commissions, but they can receive a bonus if they sell a car and the customer provides positive feedback on a follow-up call. All of the cars are relatively new: under five years old and less than 75,000 miles. There is a soft sell, competitive, "no haggle" pricing policy, a five-day money-back guarantee (no questions asked), and a 3,300-mile warranty. And surprisingly, all cars come with 12 months of roadside assistance—a feature unheard of in the used-car business.

There have been other retail giants that have tried to consolidate this industry, such as Circuit City's initiative with auto retailer CarMax. However, none have been very successful. Still, it is quite clear why Wal-Mart would give this market a try: Used cars are a multibillion-dollar market and no single player has a large market share. Wal-Mart can offer a strong brand name with a reputation for low price and reliability in a market where price is uncertain and reliability is highly problematic. Further, Wal-Mart sees it as an opportunity to apply its super efficient distribution system to a highly inefficient, fragmented retailing industry. It will be interesting to see how this alliance plays out.

Source: B. Breen, "First You Get High On It, Then You Buy It," *Fast Company*, January 2003, pp. 86–92; and J. Useem, "One Nation under Wal-Mart," *Fortune*, March 3, 2003, pp. 65–78.

Despite their promise, many alliances and joint ventures fail to meet their expectations for a variety of reasons. First, without the proper partner, a firm should never consider undertaking an alliance, even for the best of reasons. Each partner should bring the desired complementary strengths to the partnership. Ideally, the strengths contributed by the partners are unique—thus synergies created can be more easily sustained and defended over the longer term. The goal must be to develop synergies between the contributions of the partners, resulting in a win–win situation for both. Moreover, the partners must be compatible and willing to trust each other. Unfortunately, often little attention is given to nurturing the close working relationships and interpersonal connections that bring together the partnering organizations. The human or people factors are not carefully considered or, at worst, dismissed as an unimportant consideration.

Strategy Spotlight 6.6 discusses a recent (and somewhat surprising) strategic alliance by Wal-Mart to sell used cars.

Internal Development

Firms can also diversify by means of corporate entrepreneurship and new venture development. In today's economy, internal development is such an important means by which companies expand their businesses that we have devoted a whole chapter to it (see Chapter 12). Sony and the Minnesota Mining & Manufacturing Co. (3M), for example, are known for their dedication to innovation, R&D, and cutting-edge technologies. For example, 3M has developed its entire corporate culture to support its ongoing policy of generating at least 25 percent of total sales from products created within the most recent four-year period. During the 1990s, 3M exceeded this goal by achieving about 30 percent of sales per year from new internally developed products.

Many companies use some form of internal development to extend their product lines or add to their service offerings. This approach to internal development is used by many large publicly held corporations as well as small firms. An example of the latter is Rosa Verde, a small but growing business serving the health care needs of San Antonio, Texas.

> This small company began with one person who moved from Mexico to San Antonio, Texas, to serve the health care needs of inner-city residents.[42] Beginning as a sole proprietor, Dr. Lourdes Pizana started Rosa Verde Family Health Care Group in 1995 with only $10,000 obtained from credit card debt. She has used a strategy of internal development to propel the company to where it is today—six clinics, 30 doctors, and a team of other health care professionals.
>
> How was Dr. Pizana able to accomplish this in such a short time? She emphasizes the company's role in the community, forging links with community leaders. In addition, she hires nearly all her professional staff as independent contractors to control costs. These professionals are paid based on the volume of work they do rather than a set salary; Pizana splits her revenue with them, thus motivating them to work efficiently. Her strategy is to grow the company from the inside out through high levels of service, commitment to the community she serves, and savvy leadership. By committing to a solid plan, Pizana has proven that internal growth and development can be a successful strategy.

Compared to mergers and acquisitions, firms that engage in internal development are able to capture the value created by their own innovative activities without having to "share the wealth" with alliance partners or face the difficulties associated with combining activities across the value chains of several companies or merging corporate cultures. Another advantage is that firms can often develop new products or services at a relatively lower cost and thus rely on their own resources rather than turning to external funding. There are also potential disadvantages. Internal development may be time consuming; thus, firms may forfeit the benefits of speed that growth through mergers or acquisitions can provide. This may be especially important among high-tech or knowledge-based organizations in fast-paced environments where being an early mover is critical. Thus, firms that choose to diversify through internal development must develop capabilities that allow them to move quickly from initial opportunity recognition to market introduction.

Real Options Analysis: A Useful Tool

Real options analysis (ROA) is an investment analysis tool from the field of finance. It has been slowly, but increasingly, adopted by consultants and executives to support strategic decision making in firms. What does real options analysis consist of and how can it be appropriately applied to the investments required to initiate strategic decisions? To understand *real* options it is first necessary to have a basic understanding of what *options* are.

Options exist when the owner of the option has the right but not the obligation to engage in certain types of transactions. The most common are stock options. A stock option grants the holder the right to buy (call option) or sell (put option) shares of the stock at a fixed price (strike price) at some time in the future.[43] Another aspect of stock options important to note is that the investment to be made immediately is small, whereas the investment to be made in the future is generally larger. For example, an option to buy a rapidly rising stock currently priced at $50 might cost as little as $.50.[44] An important point to note is that owners of such a stock option have limited their losses to $.50 per share, while the upside potential is unlimited. This aspect of options is attractive because options offer the prospect of high gains with relatively small up-front investments that represent limited losses.

The phrase "real options" applies to situations where options theory and valuation techniques are applied to real assets or physical things, in contrast to financial assets. Some of the most common applications of real options are with property and insurance. A real estate option grants the holder the right to buy or sell a piece of property at an established price some time in the future. The actual market price of the property may rise above the established (or strike) price—or the market value may sink below the strike price. If the price of the property goes up, the owner of the option is likely to buy it. If the market value of the property drops below the strike price, the option holder is unlikely to execute the purchase. In the latter circumstance, the option holder has limited his or her loss to the cost of the option, but during the life of the option retains the right to participate in whatever the upside potential might be. Casualty insurance is another variation of real options. With casualty insurance, the owner of the property has limited the loss to the cost of the insurance, while the upside potential is the actual loss, ranging, of course, up to the limit of the insurance.[45]

The concept of options can also be applied to strategic decisions where management has flexibility, that is, the situation will permit management to decide whether to invest additional funds to grow or accelerate the activity, perhaps delay in order to learn more, shrink the scale of the activity, or even abandon it. Decisions to invest in business activities such as R&D, motion pictures, exploration and production of oil wells, and the opening and closing of copper mines often have this flexibility.[46] Important issues to note are the following:

◆ Real options analysis is appropriate to use when investments can be staged; in other words, a smaller investment up front can be followed by subsequent investments. In short, real options can be applied to an investment decision that gives the company the right, but not the obligation, to make follow-on investments.

◆ The strategic decision makers have "tollgates" or key points at which they can decide whether to continue, delay, or abandon the project. In short, the executives have the flexibility. There are opportunities to make other go or no–go decisions associated with each phase.

◆ It is expected that there will be increased knowledge about outcomes at the time of the next investment and that additional knowledge will help inform the decision makers about whether to make additional investments (i.e., whether the option is in the money or out of the money).

Many strategic decisions have the characteristic of containing a series of options. The phenomenon is called "embedded options," a series of investments in which at each stage of the investment there is a go/no–go decision. For example, pharmaceutical companies have successfully used real options analysis in evaluating decisions about investments in pharmaceutical R&D projects since the early 1990s.[47] Pharmaceuticals have at least four stages of investments: basic research yielding compounds and the three FDA-mandated phases of clinical trials. Generally, each phase is more expensive to undertake than the previous phase. However, as each phase unfolds management knows more about the underlying drug and the many sources of uncertainty, including the technical difficulties with the drugs themselves as well as external market conditions, such as the results of competitors' research. Management can make the decision to invest more with the intent of speeding up the process, delay the start of the next phase, reduce investment, or even abandon the R&D.[48]

Strategy Spotlight 6.7 provides two examples of companies using ROA to guide their decision-making process.

How Managerial Motives Can Erode Value Creation

Thus far in the chapter we have implicitly assumed that CEOs and top executives are "rational beings"—that is, they act in the best interests of shareholders to maximize long-term shareholder value. In the real world, however, this is not the case. Frequently, they may act in their own self-interest. Following, we address some managerial motives that can serve to erode, rather than enhance, value creation. These include "growth for growth's sake," excessive egotism, and the creation of a wide variety of antitakeover tactics.

strategy spotlight

Applications of Real Options Analysis

The following two examples illustrate how real options analysis (ROA) is enjoying increasing popularity among strategists facing the task of allocating resources in an era of great uncertainty. The first example, a privately held biotechnology firm, is using ROA to analyze an internal development decision. The second example, pharmaceutical giant Merck, uses this tool to decide whether to enter into a strategic alliance. In each of these cases, ROA led to a different decision outcome than that of more traditional net present value (NPV) analysis. NPV is the sum of costs and revenues for the life of the project, discounted typically by current interest rates to reflect the time value of money.

- A privately held biotechnology firm had developed a unique technology for introducing the coat protein of a particular virus into animal feedstock. Ingesting the coat protein generated an immune response, thus protecting the animal from the virus. The firm was at the beginning of the preclinical trials stage, the first of a series of tests required by FDA regulation and conducted through the FDA subagency called the Center for Veterinary Medicine. The company expected the stage to take 18 months and cost $2 million. Long-standing experience indicated that 95 percent of new drug investigations are abandoned during this phase. Subsequent stages would decrease somewhat in terms of the possibility of rejection, but costs would rise, with a total outflow from 2002 through anticipated launch in 2007 of at least $18.5 million. The company's best estimate of the market from 2007 through 2017 was about $85 million per year, with the possibility of taking as much as a 50 percent market share. In short, there was huge potential, but in the interim there was tremendous

chance of failure (i.e., high risk), significant early outflows, and delayed inflows. Analysis using a traditional NPV analysis yielded a negative $2 million with an 11 percent risk-adjusted discount rate. Viewing the investment as a multistage option, however, and incorporating management's flexibility to change its decision at a minimum of four points between 2002 and 2007, changes the valuation markedly. A real options analysis approach to the analysis demonstrated a present value of about $22 million. The question was not whether to risk $18.5 million, but whether to invest $2 million today for the opportunity to earn $22 million.

- Merck has applied real options analysis to a number of its strategic decisions. One was the agreement it signed with Biogen, which in the late 1990s had developed an asthma drug. Instead of purchasing Biogen outright, Merck created a real options arrangement. Merck paid Biogen $15 million up front and retained the right to invest up to an additional $130 million at various points as the biotechnology company reached specified milestones. In essence, Merck purchased a stream of options: the right to scale up and scale down, even abandon, the option. Merck's potential in the deal was unlimited, while its downside risk was limited to the extent of the milestone payments. Analysis suggested that the present value of the deal was about $275 million, considerably more than the present value of the up-front and milestone payments. Using traditional NPV methods would have killed this deal. However, real options analysis encouraged Merck to undertake the arrangement, in part, because Merck was in the process of learning about the underlying technology. Biogen, on the other hand, gained the advantage of committed cash flow to continue development—provided that developments from the various phases continued to be favorable.

Sources: R. L. Stockley, Jr., S. Curtis, J. Jafari, and K. Tibbs, "The Option Value of an Early-Stage Biotechnology Investment," *Journal of Applied Finance* 15, no. 2 (2003), pp. 44–55; and M. H. Mauboussin, "Get Real: Using Real Options in Security Analysis," Equity Research Series by Credit Suite/First Boston, vol. 10, June 23, 1999: 18.

Growth for Growth's Sake

There are huge incentives for executives to increase the size of their firm, and many of these are hardly consistent with increasing shareholder wealth. Top managers, including the CEO, of larger firms typically enjoy more prestige, higher rankings for their companies on the Fortune 500 list (which is based on revenues, not profits), greater incomes, more job security, and so on. There is also the excitement and associated recognition of making a major acquisition. As noted by Harvard's Michael Porter: "There's a tremendous allure to mergers and acquisitions. It's the big play, the dramatic gesture. With one stroke of the pen you can add billions to size, get a front-page story, and create excitement in markets."[49]

In recent years many high-tech firms have suffered from the negative impact of their uncontrolled growth. Consider, for example, Priceline.com's ill-fated venture into an online service to offer groceries and gasoline.[50] A myriad of problems—perhaps most importantly, a lack of participation by manufacturers—caused the firm to lose more than $5 million a *week* prior to abandoning these ventures. Similarly, many have questioned the profit potential of Amazon.com's recent ventures into a variety of products such as tools and hardware, cell phones, and service. Such initiatives are often little more than desperate moves by top managers to satisfy investor demands for accelerating revenues. Unfortunately, the increased revenues often fail to materialize into a corresponding hike in earnings.

At times, executives' overemphasis on growth can result in a plethora of ethical lapses, which can have disastrous outcomes for their companies. A good example (of bad practice) is Joseph Bernardino's leadership at Andersen Worldwide. Bernardino had a chance early on to take a hard line on ethics and quality in the wake of earlier scandals at clients such as Waste Management and Sunbeam. Instead, according to former executives, he put too much emphasis on revenue growth. Consequently, the firm's reputation quickly eroded when it audited and signed off on the highly flawed financial statements of such infamous firms as Enron, Global Crossing, and WorldCom. WorldCom, in fact, is recognized as the biggest financial fraud of all time. Bernardino ultimately resigned in disgrace in March 2002, and his firm was dissolved later that year.[51]

Egotism

Most would agree that there is nothing wrong with ego, per se. After all, a healthy ego helps make a leader confident, clearheaded, and able to cope with change. CEOs, by their very nature, are typically fiercely competitive people in the office as well as on the tennis court or golf course. However, sometimes when pride is at stake, individuals will go to great lengths to win—or at least not to back down. Consider the following anecdote:

> When Warner Bros. CEO Robert Daly walked into the first postmerger gathering of senior Time Warner management in the Bahamas, he felt a hand on his shoulder. It was a Time Inc. executive whom he had never met. The magazine man asked the studio executive if he ever considered that General Motors purchased $30 million worth of advertising in Time Inc. publications before Daly acquired *Roger and Me,* a scathing cinematic indictment of the carmaker.
>
> Daly replied: "No. Did you consider that Warner Bros. spent over $50 million on *Batman* before *Time* ran its lousy review of the movie?" The Time executive smiled, patted his new colleague's shoulder and suggested that they continue their jobs in their own way!

Might one suggest that egos can get in the way of a "synergistic" corporate marriage?

Few executives (or lower-level managers) are exempt from the potential downside of excessive egos. Consider, for example, the reflections of General Electric's former CEO Jack Welch, considered by many to be the world's most admired executive. He admitted to his regrettable decision for GE to acquire Kidder Peabody.[52] According to Welch, "My hubris got in the way in the Kidder Peabody deal. [He was referring to GE's buyout of the soon-to-be-troubled Wall Street firm.] I got wise advice from Walter Wriston and other directors who said, 'Jack, don't do this.' But I was bully enough and on a run to do it. And I got whacked right in the head." In addition to poor financial results, Kidder Peabody was wracked by a widely publicized trading scandal that tarnished the reputations of both GE and Kidder Peabody. Welch ended up selling Kidder in 1994.

The business press has included many stories of how egotism and greed have infiltrated organizations. Some incidents are considered rather astonishing, such as Tyco's

strategy spotlight

Poison Pills: How Antitakeover Strategies Can Raise Ethical Issues

Poison pills are almost always good for managers but not always so good for shareholders. They present managers with an ethical dilemma: How can they balance their own interests with their fiduciary responsibility to shareholders?

Here's how poison pills work. In the event of a takeover bid, existing shareholders have the option to buy additional shares of stock at a discount to the current market price. This action is typically triggered when a new shareholder rapidly accumulates more than a set percentage of ownership, usually 20 percent, through stock purchases. When this happens, managers fear that the voting rights and increased proportional ownership of the new shareholder might be a ploy to make a takeover play.

To protect existing shareholders, stock is offered at a discount, but only to existing shareholders. As the existing owners buy the discounted stock, the stock is diluted (i.e., there are now more shares, each with a lower value). If there has been a takeover offer at a set price per share, the overall price for the company immediately goes up

Sources: J. P. Vicente, "Toxic Treatment: Poison Pills Proliferate as Internet Firms Worry They've Become Easy Marks," *Red Herring,* May 1 and 15, 2001, p. 195; A. Chakraborty and C. F. Baum, "Poison Pills, Optimal Contracting and the Market for Corporate Control: Evidence from Fortune 500 Firms," *International Journal of Finance* 10, no. 3 (1998), pp. 1120–38; C. Sundaramurthy, "Corporate Governance within the Context of Antitakeover Provisions," *Strategic Management Journal* 17 (1996), pp. 377–94.

since there are now more shares. This assures stockholders of receiving a fair price for the company.

Sounds good, but here's the problem. Executives on the company's board of directors retain the right to allow the stock discount. The discounted stock price for existing shareholders may or may not be activated when a takeover is imminent. This brings in the issue of motive: Why did the board enact the poison pill provision in the first place? At times, it may have been simply to protect the existing shareholders. At other times, it may have been to protect the interests of those on the board of directors. In other words, the board may have enacted the rule not to protect shareholders, but to protect their own jobs.

When the board receives a takeover offer, the offering company will be aware of the poison pill provision. This gives negotiating power to board members of the takeover target. They may include as part of the negotiation that the new company keep them as members of the board. In exchange, the board members would not enact the discounted share price; existing stockholders would lose, but the jobs of the board members would be protected.

When a company offers poison pill provisions to shareholders, the shareholders should keep in mind that things are not always as they seem. The motives may reflect concern for shareholders. But on the other hand . . .

former (and now indicted) CEO Dennis Kozlowski's well-chronicled purchase of a $6,000 shower curtain and vodka-spewing, full-size replica of Michaelangelo's David.[53] Other well-known examples of power grabs and extraordinary consumption of compensation and perks include executives at Enron, the Rigas family who were convicted of defrauding Adelphia of roughly $1 billion, former CEO Bernie Ebbers's $408 million loan from WorldCom, and so on. However, executives in the United States clearly don't have a monopoly on such deeds. Consider, for example, Jean-Marie Messier, former CEO of Vivendi Universal.[54]

> In striving to convert a French utility into a global media conglomerate, Messier seldom passed up a chance for self-promotion. Although most French executives have a preference for discreet personal lives, Messier hung out with rock stars and moved his family into a $17.5 million Park Avenue spread paid for by Vivendi. He pushed the company to the brink of collapse by running up $19 billion in debt from an acquisition spree and confusing investors with inconsistent financial transactions which are now under investigation by authorities in both the United States and France. Not one to accept full responsibility, less than five months after his forced resignation, he published a book, *My True Diary,* that blames a group of French business leaders for plotting against him. And his ego is clearly intact: At a recent Paris press conference, he described his firing as a setback for French capitalism.

Antitakeover Tactics

Unfriendly or hostile takeovers can occur when a company's stock becomes undervalued. A competing organization can buy the outstanding stock of a takeover candidate in sufficient quantity to become a large shareholder. Then it makes a tender offer to gain full control of the company. If the shareholders accept the offer, the hostile firm buys the target company and either fires the target firm's management team or strips them of their power. For this reason, antitakeover tactics are common. Three of these will be discussed: greenmail, golden parachutes, and poison pills.[55]

The first, *greenmail,* is an effort by the target firm to prevent an impending takeover. When a hostile firm buys a large block of outstanding target company stock and the target firm's management feels that a tender offer is impending, they offer to buy the stock back from the hostile company at a higher price than the unfriendly company paid for it. The positive side is that this often prevents a hostile takeover. On the downside, the same price is not offered to preexisting shareholders. However, it protects the jobs of the target firm's management.

The second strategy is a *golden parachute.* A golden parachute is a prearranged contract with managers specifying that, in the event of a hostile takeover, the target firm's managers will be paid a significant severance package. Although top managers lose their jobs, the golden parachute provisions protect their income.

Strategy Spotlight 6.8 illustrates how poison pills are used to prevent takeovers. *Poison pills* are means by which a company can give shareholders certain rights in the event of a takeover by another firm. In addition to "poison pills," they are also known as shareholder rights plans.

As you can see, antitakeover tactics can often raise some interesting ethical issues.

summary

A key challenge of today's managers is to create "synergy" when engaging in diversification activities. As we discussed in this chapter, corporate managers do not, in general, have a very good track record in creating value in such endeavors when it comes to mergers and acquisitions. Among the factors that serve to erode shareholder values are paying an excessive premium for the target firm, failing to integrate the activities of the newly acquired businesses into the corporate family, and undertaking diversification initiatives that are too easily imitated by the competition.

We addressed two major types of corporate-level strategy: related and unrelated diversification. With *related diversification* the corporation strives to enter into areas in which key resources and capabilities of the corporation can be shared or leveraged. Synergies come from horizontal relationships between business units. Cost savings and enhanced revenues can be derived from two major sources. First, economies of scope can be achieved from the leveraging of core competencies and the sharing of activities. Second, market power can be attained from greater, or pooled, negotiating power and from vertical integration.

When firms undergo *unrelated diversification* they enter product markets that are dissimilar to their present businesses. Thus, there is generally little opportunity to either leverage core competencies or share activities across business units. Here, synergies are created from vertical relationships between the corporate office and the individual business units. With unrelated diversification, the primary ways to create value are corporate restructuring and parenting, as well as the use of portfolio analysis techniques.

Corporations have three primary means of diversifying their product markets. These are mergers and acquisitions, joint ventures/strategic alliances, and internal development. There are key trade-offs associated with each of these. For example, mergers and acquisitions are typically the quickest means to enter new markets and provide the corporation with a high level of control over the acquired business. However, with the expensive premiums that often need to be paid to the shareholders of the target firm and the challenges associated with integrating acquisitions, they can also be quite expensive. Strategic alliances between two or more firms, on the other hand, may be a means of reducing risk since they involve the sharing and combining of resources. But such joint initiatives also provide a firm with less control (than it would have with an acquisition) since governance is shared between two independent entities. Also, there is a limit to the potential "upside" for each partner because returns must be shared as well. Finally, with internal development, a firm is able to capture all of the value from its initiatives (as opposed to sharing it with a merger or alliance partner). However, diversification by means of internal development can be very time-consuming—a disadvantage that becomes even more important in fast-paced competitive environments.

Traditional tools such as net present value (NPV) analysis are not always very helpful in making resource allocation decisions under uncertainty. Real options analysis (ROA) is increasingly used to make better quality decisions in such situations.

Finally, some managerial behaviors may serve to erode shareholder returns. Among these are "growth for growth's sake," egotism, and antitakeover tactics. As we discussed, some of these issues—particularly antitakeover tactics—raise ethical considerations because the managers of the firm are not acting in the best interests of the shareholders.

summary review questions

1. Discuss how managers can create value for their firm through diversification efforts.

2. What are some of the reasons that many diversification efforts fail to achieve desired outcomes?

3. How can companies benefit from related diversification? Unrelated diversification? What are some of the key concepts that can explain such success?

4. What are some of the important ways in which a firm can restructure a business?

5. Discuss some of the various means that firms can use to diversify. What are the pros and cons associated with each of these?

6. Discuss some of the actions that managers may engage in to erode shareholder value.

Time Warner (formerly AOL Time Warner) is a firm that follows a strategy of related diversification. Evaluate its success (or lack thereof) with regard to how well it has: (1) built on core competencies, (2) shared infrastructures, and (3) increased market power.

experiential exercise

Rationale for Related Diversification	Successful/Unsuccessful?	Why?
1. Build on core competencies		
2. Share infrastructures		
3. Increase market power		

application questions & exercises

1. What were some of the largest mergers and acquisitions over the last two years? What was the rationale for these actions? Do you think they will be successful? Explain.
2. Discuss some examples from business practice in which an executive's actions appear to be in his or her self-interest rather than the corporation's well-being.
3. Discuss some of the challenges that managers must overcome in making strategic alliances successful. What are some strategic alliances with which you are familiar? Were they successful or not? Explain.
4. Use the Internet and select a company that has recently undertaken diversification into new product markets. What do you feel were some of the reasons for this diversification (e.g., leveraging core competencies, sharing infrastructures)?

ethics questions

1. In recent years there has been a rash of corporate downsizing and layoffs. Do you feel that such actions raise ethical considerations? Why or why not?
2. What are some of the ethical issues that arise when managers act in a manner that is counter to their firm's best interests? What are the long-term implications for both the firms and the managers themselves?

references

1. Lee, L., 2002, Closed eyes, open wallet, *BusinessWeek*, November 4, pp. 116–17; Shilling, A. G., 2003, Wall Street's fat, *Forbes*, April 14, p. 242; and Schwab acquires U.S. Trust, 2000, *CNN Money* (online), January 13.
2. Pare, T. P., 1994, The new merger boom, *Fortune*, November 28: 96.
3. Our framework draws upon a variety of sources, including Goold, M., & Campbell, A., 1998, Desperately seeking synergy, *Harvard Business Review* 76 (5): 131–43; Porter, M. E., 1987, From advantage to corporate strategy, *Harvard Business Review* 65 (3): 43–59; and Hitt, M. A., Ireland, R. D., & Hoskisson, R. E., 2001, *Strategic Management: Competitiveness and Globalization*, 4th ed. (Cincinnati, OH: South-Western).
4. Collis, D. J., & Montgomery, C. A., 1987, *Corporate Strategy: Resources and the Scope of the Firm* (New York: McGraw-Hill).
5. This imagery of the corporation as a tree and related discussion draws on Prahalad, C. K., & Hamel, G., 1990, The core competence of the corporation, *Harvard Business Review* 68 (3): 79–91. Parts of this section also draw on Picken, J. C., & Dess, G. G., 1997, *Mission Critical* (Burr Ridge, IL: Irwin Professional Publishing), chap. 5.
6. This section draws on Prahalad & Hamel, op. cit.; and Porter, op. cit.
7. Harley-Davidson, 1993, annual report.
8. Collis & Montgomery, *Corporate Strategy: Resources and the Scope of the Firm.*
9. Henricks, M., 1994, VF seeks global brand dominance, *Apparel Industry Magazine*, August: 21–40; VF Corporation, 1993, 1st quarter, corporate summary report, *1993 VF Annual Report.*
10. Hill, A., & Hargreaves, D., 2001, Turbulent times for GE-Honeywell deal, *Financial Times*, February 28: 26.
11. Lowry, T., 2001, Media, *BusinessWeek*, January 8: 100–1.
12. The Tribune Company, 1999, annual report.
13. This section draws on Hrebiniak, L. G., & Joyce, W. F., 1984, *Implementing Strategy* (New York: MacMillan); and Oster, S. M., 1994, *Modern Competitive Analysis* (New York: Oxford University Press).
14. The discussion of the benefits and costs of vertical integration draws on Hax, A. C., & Majluf, N. S., 1991, *The Strategy Concept and Process: A Pragmatic Approach* (Englewood Cliffs, NJ: Prentice Hall), 139.
15. This discussion draws on Oster, op. cit.; and Harrigan, K., 1986, Matching vertical integration strategies to competitive conditions, *Strategic Management Journal* 7 (6): 535–56.
16. For a scholarly explanation on how transaction costs determine the boundaries of a firm, see Oliver E. Williamson's pioneering books *Markets and Hierarchies: Analysis and Antitrust Implications* (New York: Free Press, 1975) and *The Economic Institutions of Capitalism* (New York: Free Press, 1985).
17. Campbell, A., Goold, M., & Alexander, M., 1995, Corporate strategy: The quest for parenting advantage, *Harvard Business Review* 73 (2): 120–32; and Picken & Dess, op. cit.
18. Anslinger, P. A., & Copeland, T. E., 1996, Growth through acquisition: A fresh look, *Harvard Business Review* 74 (1): 126–35.

19. Campbell et al., op. cit.

20. This section draws on Porter, op. cit.; and Hambrick, D. C., 1985, Turnaround strategies, in Guth, W. D., ed., *Handbook of Business Strategy* (Boston: Warren, Gorham & Lamont), 10-1–10-32.

21. There is an important delineation between companies that are operated for a long-term profit and those that are bought and sold for short-term gains. The latter are sometimes referred to as "holding companies" and are generally more concerned about financial issues than strategic issues.

22. Casico, W. F., 2002, Strategies for responsible restructuring, *Academy of Management Executive* 16 (3): 80–91; and Singh, H., 1993, Challenges in researching corporate restructuring, *Journal of Management Studies* 30 (1): 147–72.

23. Cusack, M., 1987, *Hanson Trust: A Review of the Company and Its Prospects* (London: Hoare Govett).

24. Hax & Majluf, op. cit. By 1979, 45 percent of Fortune 500 companies employed some form of portfolio analysis, according to Haspelagh, P., 1982, Portfolio planning: Uses and limits, *Harvard Busines Review* 60: 58–73. A later study conducted in 1993 found that over 40 percent of the respondents used portfolio analysis techniques, but the level of usage was expected to increase to more than 60 percent in the near future: Rigby, D. K., 1994, Managing the management tools, *Planning Review,* September–October: 20–24.

25. Goold, M., & Luchs, K., 1993, Why diversify? Four decades of management thinking, *Academy of Management Executive* 7 (3): 7–25.

26. Other approaches include the industry attractiveness–business strength matrix developed jointly by General Electric and McKinsey and Company, the life-cycle matrix developed by Arthur D. Little, and the profitability matrix proposed by Marakon. For an extensive review, refer to Hax & Majluf, op. cit., pp. 182–94.

27. Porter, op. cit., pp. 49–52.

28. Collis, D. J., 1995, Portfolio planning at Ciba-Geigy and the Newport investment proposal, Harvard Business School Case No. 9-795-040. Novartis AG was created in 1996 by the merger of Ciba-Geigy and Sandoz.

29. Buzzell, R. D., & Gale, B. T., 1987, *The PIMS Principles: Linking Strategy to Performance* (New York: Free Press); and Miller, A., & Dess, G. G., 1996, *Strategic Management,* 2nd ed. (New York: McGraw-Hill).

30. Seeger, J., 1984, Reversing the images of BCG's growth share matrix, *Strategic Management Journal* 5 (1): 93–97.

31. Picken & Dess, op. cit.; Cabot Corporation, 2001, 10-Q filing, Securities and Exchange Commission, May 14.

32. Koudsi, S., 2001, Remedies for an economic hangover, *Fortune,* June 25: 130–39.

33. Carey, D., moderator, 2000, A CEO roundtable on making mergers succeed, *Harvard Business Review* 78 (3): 146.

34. Shinal, J., 2001, Can Mike Volpi make Cisco sizzle again? *BusinessWeek,* February 26: 102–4; Kambil, A., Eselius, E. D., & Monteiro, K. A., 2000, Fast venturing: The quick way to start web businesses, *Sloan Management Review* 41 (4): 55–67; and Elstrom, P., 2001, Sorry, Cisco: The old answers won't work, *BusinessWeek,* April 30: 39.

35. Like many high-tech firms during the economic slump that began in mid-2000, Cisco Systems has experienced declining performance. On April 16, 2001, it announced that its revenues for the quarter closing April 30 would drop 5 percent from a year earlier—and a stunning 30 percent from the previous three months—to about $4.7 billion. Furthermore, Cisco announced that it would lay off 8,500 employees and take an enormous $2.5 billion charge to write down inventory. By late October 2002, its stock was trading at around $10, down significantly from its 52-week high of $70. Elstrom, op. cit., p. 39.

36. Barrett, A., 2001, Drugs, *BusinessWeek,* January 8: 112–13.

37. Whalen, C. J., Pascual, A. M., Lowery, T., & Muller, J., 2001, The top 25 managers, *BusinessWeek,* January 8: 63.

38. Muoio, A., ed., 1998, Unit of one, *Fast Company,* September: 82.

39. For scholarly perspectives on the role of learning in creating value in strategic alliances, refer to Anard, B. N., & Khanna, T., 2000, Do firms learn to create value? *Strategic Management Journal* 12 (3): 295–317; and Vermeulen, F., & Barkema, H. P., 2001, Learning through acquisitions, *Academy of Management Journal* 44 (3): 457–76.

40. This section draws on Hutt, M. D., Stafford, E. R., Walker, B. A., & Reingen, P. H., 2000, Case study: Defining the strategic alliance, *Sloan Management Review* 41 (2): 51–62; and Walters, B. A., Peters, S., & Dess, G. G., 1994, Strategic alliances and joint ventures: Making them work, *Business Horizons,* 4: 5–10.

41. Edmondson, G., & Reinhardt, A., 2001, From niche player to Goliath, *BusinessWeek,* March 12: 94–96.

42. Clayton, V., 2000, Lourdes Pizana's passions: Confessions and lessons of an accidental business owner, *E-Merging Business,* Fall–Winter: 73–75.

43. Hoskin, R. E., 1994, *Financial Accounting* (New York: Wiley).

44. We know stock options as derivative assets, that is, "an asset whose value depends on or is derived from the value of another, the underlying asset" (Amram, M., & Kulatilaka, N., 1999, *Real Options: Managing Strategic Investment in an Uncertain World* [Boston: Harvard Business School Press], 34).

45. Neufville, R. de, 2001, Real options: Dealing with

uncertainty in systems planning and design, paper presented to the Fifth International Conference on Technology Policy and Innovation at the Technical University of Delft, Delft, Netherlands, June 29.

46. For an interesting discussion on why it is difficult to "kill options," refer to Royer, I., 2003, Why bad projects are so hard to kill, *Harvard Business Review* 81 (2): 48–57.

47. Triantis, A., et al., 2003, University of Maryland roundtable on real options and corporate practice, *Journal of Applied Corporate Finance* 15 (2): 8–23.

48. For a more in-depth discussion of ROA, refer to Copeland, T. E., & Keenan, P. T., 1998, Making real options real, *McKinsey Quarterly,* no. 3; and Luehrman, T. A., 1998, Strategy as a portfolio of real options, *Harvard Business Review*, September–October.

49. Porter, op. cit., pp. 43–59.

50. Angwin, J. S., & Wingfield, N., 2000, How Jay Walker built WebHouse on a theory that he couldn't prove, *Wall Street Journal,* October 16: A1, A8.

51. *BusinessWeek,* 2003, The fallen, January 13: 80–82.

52. The Jack Welch example draws upon Sellers, P., 2001, Get over yourself, *Fortune,* April 30: 76–88.

53. Polek, D., 2002, The rise and fall of Dennis Kozlowski, *BusinessWeek,* December 23: 64–77.

54. *BusinessWeek,* 2003, op. cit., p. 80.

55. This section draws on Weston, J. F., Besley, S., & Brigham, E. F., 1996, *Essentials of Managerial Finance,* 11th ed. (Fort Worth, TX: Dryden Press, Harcourt Brace), 18–20.

chapter 7

International Strategy:

Creating Value in Global Markets

*After
reading this
chapter, you should
have a good understanding of:*

- ◆ The importance of international expansion as a viable diversification strategy.

- ◆ The sources of national advantage, that is, why an industry in a given country is more (or less) successful than the same industry in another country.

- ◆ The motivations (or benefits) and the risks associated with international expansion.

- ◆ The two opposing forces—cost reduction and adaptation to local markets—that firms face when entering international markets.

- ◆ The advantages and disadvantages associated with each of the four basic strategies: international, global, multidomestic, and transnational.

- ◆ The four basic types of entry strategies and the relative benefits and risks associated with each of them.

*t*he global marketplace provides many opportunities for firms to increase their revenue base and their profitability. Furthermore, in today's knowledge-intensive economy, there is the potential to create advantages by leveraging firm knowledge when crossing national boundaries to do business. At the same time, however, there are pitfalls and risks that firms must avoid in order to be successful. In this chapter we will provide insights on how to be successful and create value when diversifying into global markets.

After some introductory comments on the global economy, we address the question: What explains the level of success of a given industry in a given country? To provide a framework for analysis, we draw on Michael Porter's "diamond of national advantage," in which he identified four factors that help to explain performance differences.

In the second section of the chapter, we shift our focus to the level of the firm and discuss some of the major motivations and risks associated with international expansion. Recognizing such potential benefits and risks enables managers to better assess the growth and profit potential in a given country.

Next, in the third section—the largest in this chapter—we address how firms can attain competitive advantages in the global marketplace. We discuss two opposing forces firms face when entering foreign markets: cost reduction and local adaptation. Depending on the intensity of each of these forces, they should select among four basic strategies: international, global, multidomestic, and transnational. We discuss both the strengths and limitations of each of these strategies.

The final section addresses the four categories of entry strategies that firms may choose in entering foreign markets. These strategies vary along a continuum from low investment, low control (exporting) to high investment, high control (wholly owned subsidiaries and greenfield ventures). We discuss the pros and cons associated with each.

Volkswagen has experienced problems with some of the new, high-priced models that it has introduced into the United States automobile market. This illustrates that, regardless of a firm's size or resource base, all companies face new opportunities and threats when they venture beyond the boundaries of their home nation.

A number of carmakers worldwide want to get into the luxury vehicle segment. But competition is very tough in this segment, and a high price does not any longer guarantee a high profit.[1] Volkswagen (VW), the European car manufacturer, also has recently joined this bandwagon, and is currently in the process of transforming itself into a luxury-vehicle company. Ferdinand Piesch, VW's previous chief executive, spent hundreds of millions of dollars to acquire luxury brand names such as Lamborghini, Rolls-Royce/Bentley, and Bugatti. He also started work on VW's own line of luxury models. New production facilities had to be created for manufacturing the luxury models. VW is one of the most successful European car manufacturers in the United States, and it decided to introduce its luxury models in the United States too.

VW has already introduced three of its luxury models in the United States. The Passat W-8 costs around $40,000 and is already on sale. The Touareg, launched in January 2003, is a sports utility vehicle (SUV) and costs around $35,000 to $40,000. The Phaeton, launched during the summer in 2003 costs even more—well over $60,000.

However, the results so far have not been encouraging. The Passat W-8 did not generate the excitement that was expected, and VW sold only 2,000 vehicles of this model in the United States by December 2002, much below the expected 5,000. The Phaeton is a question mark because Americans may hesitate to pay such a high price for a Volkswagen, even if the model is a credible competitor to the Mercedes S class. The Touareg's future is also not clear.

Positioned as "the contemporary interpretation of a luxury off-road vehicle," the Touareg is the first SUV launched by Volkswagen. Volkswagen wants to sell 35,000 Touaregs a year in the United States—not many when compared to the 400,000 Ford Explorers sold every year. However, there are two issues that might make things difficult for Volkswagen. First, and most important, VW has no reputation in the SUV market, and its loyal customers are not accustomed to spending amounts as high as $35,000 to $40,000. Therefore, VW cannot rely on its loyal customer base for selling this product.

Second, there is the problem with the brand name. "The name may sound strange, but we wanted to differentiate the vehicle from everything else," says Jens Neumann, VW's board member responsible for U.S. operations. The name "Touareg" refers to a nomadic tribe in the Sahara who are known for their blue-dyed bodies and their talent for torture. This foreign name is odd and is something that Americans cannot spell or pronounce easily. It is unclear how well this name would be received by U.S. customers. But company officials seem confident. According to Volkswagen spokesman Tony Fouladpour: "Touareg is the name of a resilient, athletic African tribe known for surviving in very hostile environments, including the Sahara desert. So it's a good name for a tough, resilient sport-utility that's athletic on roads and can compete with the best off road." He adds, "Don't forget that Volkswagen is a German company, and the Touareg tribe is well known in Germany, where it's highly regarded. We will sell the Touareg sport-ute internationally and see no reason to give it a different name for America. We knew many Americans wouldn't accept that name at first, but find that many have become accustomed to it now. After all, Volkswagen has used other seemingly obscure names for our cars, such as Passat (the name of a prevailing Atlantic ocean wind), which now are widely accepted."

Will Volkswagen succeed in the U.S. luxury car segment? We'll have to wait and see. Some are pessimistic. Stephen Cheetham, an analyst at Sanford C. Bernstein and Co. in London, believes that Volkswagen "is facing the mother of all marketing problems."

The Global Economy: A Brief Overview

In this chapter we will discuss how firms can create value and achieve competitive advantage—as well as how to avoid pitfalls—in the global marketplace. We will discuss not only the factors that can influence a nation's success in a particular industry but also how firms can become successful when they diversify by expanding the scope of their business to include international operations. But first, let's talk about some of the broader issues in the global economy.

Today's managers face many opportunities and risks when they diversify abroad. As we know, the trade among nations has increased dramatically in recent years. It is estimated that by 2015, the trade *across* nations will exceed the trade within nations. And in a variety of industries such as semiconductors, automobiles, commercial aircraft, telecommunications, computers, and consumer electronics, it is virtually impossible to survive unless firms scan the world for competitors, customers, human resources, suppliers, and technology.[2]

The rise of globalization—meaning the rise of market capitalism around the world—has undeniably contributed to the economic boom in America's New Economy, where knowledge is the key source of competitive advantage and value creation. It is estimated that it has brought phone service to about 300 million households in developing nations and a transfer of nearly $2 trillion from rich countries to poor countries through equity, bond investments, and commercial loans.[3]

At the same time, there have been extremes in the effect of global capitalism on national economies and poverty levels around the world. Clearly, the economies of East Asia have attained rapid growth, but there has been comparatively little progress in the rest of the world. For example, income in Latin America grew by only 6 percent in the past two decades when the continent was opening up to global capitalism. Average incomes in sub-Saharan Africa and the old Eastern European bloc have actually declined. Indeed, the World Bank estimates that the number of people living on $1 per day has *increased* to 1.3 billion over the past decade.

Such disparities in wealth among nations raise an important question: Why do some countries—and their citizens—enjoy the fruits of global capitalism while others are mired in poverty? Stated differently, why do some governments make the best use of inflows of foreign investment and know-how and others do not? There are many explanations. Among these are the need of governments to have track records of business-friendly policies to attract multinationals as well as local entrepreneurs to train workers, invest in modern technology, and nurture local suppliers and managers. Also, it means carefully managing the broader economic factors in an economy, such as interest rates, inflation, unemployment, and so on, as well as a good legal system that protects property rights, strong educational systems, and a society where prosperity is widely shared.

The above policies are the type that East Asia—in locations such as Hong Kong, Taiwan, South Korea, and Singapore—has employed to evolve from the sweatshop economies of the 1960s and 1970s to industrial powers today. On the other hand, many countries have moved in the other direction. Let's look at the example of a country in Central America—Guatemala—in Strategy Spotlight 7.1. Here is a country where, among other unfavorable indicators, only 52.0 percent of males complete fifth grade and an astonishing 39.8 percent of the population subsists on less than $1 per day.[4] (By comparison, the corresponding numbers for South Korea are 98 percent and less than 2 percent, respectively.)

In the next section, we will address in more detail the question as to why some nations and their industries are more competitive. This discussion establishes an important context or setting for the remainder of the chapter; that is, after we discuss why some *nations and their industries* outperform others, we will be better able to address the various strategies that *firms* can take to create competitive advantage when they expand internationally.

Factors Affecting a Nation's Competitiveness

Michael Porter of Harvard University conducted a four-year study in which he and a team of 30 researchers looked at the patterns of competitive success in 10 leading trading nations. He concluded that there are four broad attributes of nations that individually, and as a system, constitute what is termed "the diamond of national advantage." In effect, these

Poverty in Guatemala

Not all countries have shared in the beneficial economic effects of globalization. The world's 20 richest nations have 74 times more income than the world's poorest nations. Guatemala is an example of those on the less fortunate end of the continuum. The country has been left behind as many other nations have emerged into developed economies. A 36-year civil war between Spanish-speaking natives and indigenous Indians has recently ended, but poverty for these individuals continues. Part of the problem is that the Guatemalan government spends only 7.3 percent of its gross domestic product on social services.

Guatemala is basically a two-class economy: the haves and the have-nots. Indeed, 70 percent of land ownership is in the hands of only 2 percent of the population, providing the business class with little incentive to change. Attempts at tax reform to redistribute economic resources among the working class have met strong resistance from business owners.

Decades of ill-designed economic policies have kept the country's masses in poverty—many still work in sweatshops. One worker, Sandra Gonzalez, echoes the sentiment of many Guatemalans: "We do want to work, but we want to work with dignity."

Sources: E. Malkin, "Guatemala's Gap," *BusinessWeek,* November 6, 2000, p. 80; P. Engardio and C. Belton, "Global Trade: Can All Nations Benefit?" *BusinessWeek,* November 6, 2000, pp. 78–100.

attributes jointly determine the playing field that each nation establishes and operates for its industries. These factors are:

- ◆ *Factor conditions.* The nation's position in factors of production, such as skilled labor or infrastructure, necessary to compete in a given industry.
- ◆ *Demand conditions.* The nature of home-market demand for the industry's product or service.
- ◆ *Related and supporting industries.* The presence or absence in the nation of supplier industries and other related industries that are internationally competitive.
- ◆ *Firm strategy, structure, and rivalry.* The conditions in the nation governing how companies are created, organized, and managed, as well as the nature of domestic rivalry.

We will now briefly discuss each of these factors.[5] Then we will provide an integrative example—the Indian software industry—to demonstrate how these attributes interact to explain India's high level of competitiveness in this industry.

Factor Conditions[6]

Classical economics suggests that factors of production such as land, labor, and capital are the building blocks that create usable consumer goods and services.[7] But this tells only part of the story when we consider the global aspects of economic growth. Companies in advanced nations seeking competitive advantage over firms in other nations *create* many of the factors of production. For example, a country or industry dependent on scientific innovation must have a skilled human resource pool to draw upon. This resource pool is not inherited; it is created through investment in industry-specific knowledge and talent. The supporting infrastructure of a country—that is, its transportation and communication systems as well as its banking system—are also critical.

To achieve competitive advantage, factors of production must be developed that are industry and firm specific. In addition, the pool of resources a firm or a country has at its disposal is less important than the speed and efficiency with which these resources are deployed. Thus, firm-specific knowledge and skills created within a country that are rare, valuable, and difficult to imitate and rapidly and efficiently deployed are the factors of production that ultimately lead to a nation's competitive advantage.

For example, the island nation of Japan has little land mass, making the warehouse space needed to store inventory prohibitively expensive. But by pioneering just-in-time inventory management, Japanese companies managed to create a resource from which they gained advantage over companies in other nations that spent large sums to warehouse inventory.

Demand Conditions

Demand conditions refer to the demands that consumers place on an industry for goods and services. Consumers who demand highly specific, sophisticated products and services force firms to create innovative, advanced products and services to meet the demand. This consumer pressure presents challenges to a country's industries. But in response to these challenges, improvements to existing goods and services often result, creating conditions necessary for competitive advantage over firms in other countries.

Demanding consumers push firms to move ahead of companies in other countries where consumers are less demanding and more complacent. Countries with demanding consumers drive firms in that country to meet high standards, upgrade existing products and services, and create innovative products and services. Thus, the conditions of consumer demand influence how firms view a market, with more demanding consumers stimulating advances in products and services. This in turn helps a nation's industries to better anticipate future global demand conditions and proactively respond to product and service requirements before competing nations are even aware of the need for such products and services.

Denmark, for instance, is known for its environmental awareness. Demand from consumers for environmentally safe products has spurred Danish manufacturers to become leaders in water pollution control equipment—products it successfully exports to other nations.

Related and Supporting Industries

Related and supporting industries enable firms to manage inputs more effectively. For example, countries with a strong supplier base benefit by adding efficiency to downstream activities. A competitive supplier base helps a firm obtain inputs using cost-effective, timely methods, thus reducing manufacturing costs. Also, close working relationships with suppliers provide the potential to develop competitive advantages through joint research and development and the ongoing exchange of knowledge, helping both suppliers and manufacturers.

Related industries offer similar opportunities through joint efforts among firms. In addition, related industries create the probability that new entrants will enter the market, increasing competition and forcing existing firms to become more competitive through efforts such as cost control, product innovation, and novel approaches to distribution. Combined, these give the home country's industries a source of competitive advantage over less competitive nations.

The supporting industries in the Italian footwear industry show how such industries can lead to national competitive advantage. In Italy, shoe manufacturers are geographically located near their suppliers. The manufacturers have ongoing interactions with leather suppliers and learn about new textures, colors, and manufacturing techniques while a shoe is still in the prototype stage. The manufacturers are able to project future demand and gear their factories for new products long before companies in other nations become aware of the new styles. Similarly, geographic proximity of industries related to the pharmaceutical industry (e.g., the dye industry) in Switzerland has given that nation a leadership position in this market, with firms such as Ciba-Geigy, Hoffman LaRoche, and Sandoz using dyes from local manufacturers in many pharmaceutical products.

India and the Diamond of National Advantage

Consider the following facts:

- SAP, the German software company, has developed new applications for notebook PCs at its 500-engineer Bangladore facility.

- General Electric plans to invest $100 million and hire 2,600 scientists to create the world's largest research and development lab in Bangalore, India.

- Microsoft plans to invest $400 million in new research partnerships in India.

- Over one-fifth of Fortune 1000 companies outsource their software requirements to firms in India.

- McKinsey & Co. projects that the Indian software and services industry will be an $87 billion business by 2008; $50 billion of this will be exported.

- For the past decade, the Indian software industry has grown at a 50 percent annual rate.

- More than 800 firms in India are involved in software services as their primary activity.

- Software and information technology firms in India are projected to employ 2.2 million people by 2008.

What is causing such global interest in India's software services industry? Porter's diamond of national advantage helps clarify this question. See Exhibit 7.1.

First, *factor conditions* are conducive to the rise of India's software industry. Through investment in human resource development with a focus on industry-specific knowledge, India's universities and software firms have literally created this essential factor of production. For example, India produces the second largest annual output of scientists and engineers in the world, behind only the United States. In a knowledge-intensive industry such as software, development of human resources is fundamental to both domestic and global success.

Second, *demand conditions* require that software firms stay on the cutting edge of technological innovation. India has already moved toward globalization of its software industry; consumer demand conditions in developed nations such as Germany, Denmark, parts of Southeast Asia, and the United States created the consumer demand necessary to propel India's software makers toward sophisticated software solutions.*

Third, India has the *supplier base as well as the related industries* needed to drive competitive rivalry and enhance competitiveness. In particular, information technology (IT) hardware prices have declined rapidly in the 1990s. Furthermore, rapid technological change in IT hardware meant that latecomers like India were not locked into older-generation technologies. Thus, both the IT hardware and software industries could "leapfrog" older technologies. In addition, relationships among *(continued)*

Sources: M. Kripalani, "Calling Bangalore: Multinationals Are Making It a Hub for High-Tech Research," *BusinessWeek,* November 25, 2002, pp. 52–54; D. Kapur and R. Ramamurti, "India's Emerging Competitive Advantage in Services," *Academy of Management Executive* 15, no. 2 (2001), pp. 20–33; World Bank, *World Development Report* (New York: Oxford University Press, 2001), p. 6; Reuters. "Oracle in India Push, Taps Software Talent," *Washington Post Online,* July 3, 2001.

* Although India's success cannot be explained in terms of its home market demand (according to Porter's model), the nature of the industry enables software to be transferred among different locations simultaneously by way of communications links. Thus, competitiveness of markets outside India can be enhanced without a physical presence in those markets.

Firm Strategy, Structure, and Rivalry

Rivalry is particularly intense in nations with conditions of strong consumer demand, strong supplier bases, and high new entrant potential from related industries. This competitive rivalry in turn increases the efficiency with which firms develop, market, and distribute products and services within the home country. Domestic rivalry thus provides a strong impetus for firms to innovate and find new sources of competitive advantage.

Interestingly, this intense rivalry forces firms to look outside their national boundaries for new markets, setting up the conditions necessary for global competitiveness. Among all the points on Porter's diamond of national advantage, domestic rivalry is perhaps the

(continued) knowledge workers in these IT hardware and software industries offer the social structure for ongoing knowledge exchange, promoting further enhancement of existing products. Further infrastructure improvements are occurring rapidly.

Fourth, with over 800 firms in the software services industry in India, *intense rivalry forces firms to develop competitive strategies and structures.* Although firms like TCS, Infosys, and Wipro have become large, they were quite small only five years ago. And dozens of small and midsized companies are aspiring to catch up. This intense rivalry is one of the primary factors driving Indian software firms to develop overseas distribution channels, as predicted by Porter's diamond of national advantage.

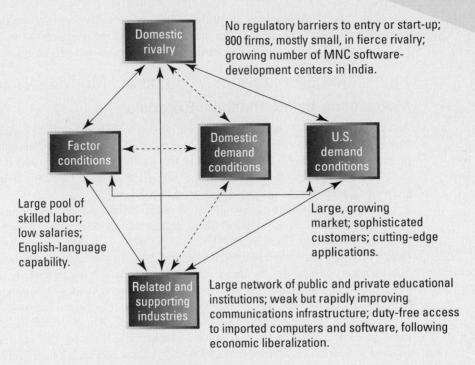

No regulatory barriers to entry or start-up; 800 firms, mostly small, in fierce rivalry; growing number of MNC software-development centers in India.

Large pool of skilled labor; low salaries; English-language capability.

Large, growing market; sophisticated customers; cutting-edge applications.

Large network of public and private educational institutions; weak but rapidly improving communications infrastructure; duty-free access to imported computers and software, following economic liberalization.

Note: Dashed lines represent weaker interactions.

Exhibit 7.1 India's Virtual Diamond in Software

Source: From *Academy of Management Executive: The Thinking Manager's Source* by D. Kampur and R. Ramamurti. Copyright © 2001 by Academy of Management. Reproduced with permission of Academy of Management via Copyright Clearance Center.

strongest indicator of global competitive success. Firms that have experienced intense domestic competition are more likely to have designed strategies and structures that allow them to successfully compete in world markets.

In the United States, for example, intense rivalry has spurred companies such as Dell Computer to find innovative ways to produce and distribute its products. This is largely a result of competition from IBM and Hewlett-Packard.

Strategy Spotlight 7.2 discusses India's software industry. It provides an integrative example of how Porter's "diamond" can help to explain the relative degree of success of an industry in a given country.

Concluding Comment on Factors Affecting a Nation's Competitiveness

Porter drew his conclusions based on case histories of firms in more than 100 industries. Despite the differences in strategies employed by successful global competitors, a common theme did emerge: Firms that succeeded in global markets had first succeeded in intense competition in their home markets. One can conclude that competitive advantage for global firms typically grows out of relentless, continuing improvement, innovation, and change.

Now that we have talked about the important role that nations play in international strategy, let's turn to the level of the individual firm. In the next section, we will discuss a company's motivations and risks associated with international expansion.

International Expansion: A Company's Motivations and Risks

Motivations for International Expansion

As one would expect, there are many motivations for a company to pursue international expansion. The most obvious one is to *increase the size of potential markets* for a firm's products and services.[8] By the end of 2004, the world's population exceeded 6 billion, with the United States representing less than 5 percent. Exhibit 7.2 lists the population of the United States compared to other major markets abroad.

Many multinational firms are intensifying their efforts to market their products and services to countries such as India and China as the ranks of their middle class have increased over the past decade. These include Procter & Gamble's success in achieving a 50 percent share in China's shampoo market as well as PepsiCo's impressive inroads in the Indian soft-drink market.[9] Sometimes the foreign environment in which multinationals compete offers temptations for profits that may lead to unethical conduct. Strategy Spotlight 7.3 discusses some unethical practices taking place in the Indian pharmaceutical industry.

Expanding a firm's global presence also automatically increases its scale of operations, providing it with a larger revenue and asset base. As we noted in Chapter 5 in discussing overall cost leadership strategies, such an increase in revenues and asset base potentially enables a firm to *attain economies of scale*. This provides multiple benefits. One advantage is the spreading of fixed costs such as research and development over a larger volume of production. Examples would include the sale of Boeing's commercial aircraft and Microsoft's operating systems in many foreign countries. Another advantage would be reducing the costs of research and development as well as operating costs. Recall, for example, the establishment of software development operations by Microsoft and other firms in talent-rich India (see Strategy Spotlight 7.2). A final advantage would be the attainment

**Exhibit 7.2
Populations of
Selected Nations**

Country	2004 (estimated)
China	1,294,630,000
India	1,064,071,000
United States	293,028,000
Japan	127,333,000
Germany	82,425,000

Source: www.census.gov/cgi-bin/ipc.

strategy spotlight

Ethical Dilemmas in the Indian Pharmaceutical Industry

Consider how tempting it would be if companies could find a way to effectively introduce new brands, move inventory that has been difficult to sell, enhance quarterly earnings figures through high sales at the end of each quarter, and trounce competitors—all at low cost and a minimum of effort. Although this sounds almost too good to be true, it is reality in India. Pharmaceutical companies have found a way to do the impossible. But there's just one problem: They have to venture across ethical boundaries to achieve these objectives.

The regulatory environment as well as the distribution system for pharmaceuticals in India is much different than in most Western nations. In developed Western countries, pharmaceutical sales representatives educate physicians on new products and encourage them to write prescriptions for effective medications. But in India, it's the pharmacists who have the power to dole out medications. Because there is no requirement that a patient have a prescription to obtain medications, patients often bypass visits to a doctor, going instead directly to pharmacists for advice on which medicines to buy.

This sets up potentially lucrative temptations for pharmaceutical manufacturers, and these firms have readily crossed this ethical boundary. Pharmaceutical companies offer incentives such as prizes, trips, bonus schemes, and high profit margins for pushing certain medications.

Source: D. Pearl and S. Stecklow, "Drug Firms' Incentives to Pharmacists in India Fuel Widespread Abuse," *Wall Street Journal*, August 16, 2001, pp. A1, A5.

Rather than recommending the most effective drugs, pharmacists are encouraged to sell the drug with the biggest incentive attached. One deal offers pharmacists a 250 percent markup and a chance to win a motorcycle for selling a generic version of the antibiotic ciprofloxacin. Another example is GlaxoSmithKline and Schering which, through the independent distributor German Remedies, provide drawings for trips to Nepal, Germany, and several popular tourist destinations in India in exchange for selling the hormone Primolut-N. Unfortunately, Primolut-N can increase the risk of birth defects when used improperly. And the odds are good that it will be used improperly—many pharmacies use untrained counter salespersons to recommend which drugs patients should take.

The drug companies are not the only ones to blame. The All India Organization of Chemists and Druggists is the trade association representing the interests of pharmacists throughout India. By banding pharmacists together, the association has pressured pharmaceutical firms to offer cash bonuses, higher profit margins, and incentive schemes.

But that's the price of success—the Primolut-N incentives cost the drug companies about $100,000, but have generated over $1,000,000 in sales. And a lot of pharmacists won great vacations. Some even started riding to work on new motorcycles. But when firms must cross ethical lines, the price of "success" can become much too high.

of greater purchasing power by pooling purchases. For example, as McDonald's increases the number of outlets it has all over the world, it is able to place larger orders for equipment and supplies, thus increasing its bargaining power with suppliers.

International expansion can also *extend the life cycle of a product* that is in its maturity stage in a firm's home country but that has greater demand potential elsewhere. As we noted in Chapter 5, products (and industries) generally go through a four-stage life cycle of introduction, growth, maturity, and decline. In recent decades, U.S. soft-drink producers such as Coca-Cola and PepsiCo have aggressively pursued international markets to attain levels of growth that simply would not be available in the United States. Similarly, personal computer manufacturers such as Dell and Hewlett-Packard have sought out foreign markets to offset the growing saturation in the U.S. market. The worldwide automobile industry is also intensely competitive. Firms such as General Motors and Ford have invested billions of dollars in Latin America in an effort to capture market share in that growing market.

Finally, international expansion can enable a firm to *optimize the physical location for every activity in its value chain*. Recall from our discussions in Chapters 3 and 5 that the value chain represents the various activities in which all firms must engage to produce products and services. They include primary activities, such as inbound logistics, operations, and marketing, as well as support activities, such as procurement, research and development, and human resource management. All firms have to make critical decisions as to where each activity will take place.[10] Optimizing the location for every activity in the value chain can yield one or more of three strategic advantages: performance enhancement, cost reduction, and risk reduction. We will now discuss each of these in turn.

Performance Enhancement   Microsoft's decision to establish a corporate research laboratory in Cambridge, England, is an example of a location decision that was guided mainly by the goal of building and sustaining world-class excellence in selected value-creating activities.[11] This strategic decision provided Microsoft with access to outstanding technical and professional talent. Location decisions can affect the quality with which any activity is performed in terms of the availability of needed talent, speed of learning, and the quality of external and internal coordination.

Cost Reduction   Two location decisions founded largely on cost-reduction considerations are (1) Nike's decision to source the manufacture of athletic shoes from Asian countries such as China, Vietnam, and Indonesia, and (2) the decision of many multinational companies to set up production operations just south of the United States–Mexico border to access lower-cost labor. These operations are called *maquiladoras.* Such location decisions can affect the cost structure in terms of local manpower and other resources, transportation and logistics, and government incentives and the local tax structure.

Performance enhancement and cost-reduction benefits parallel the business-level strategies (discussed in Chapter 5) of differentiation and overall cost leadership. They can at times be attained simultaneously. Consider our example in the previous section on the Indian software industry. When Oracle set up a development operation in that country, the company benefited both from lower labor costs and operational expenses as well as from performance enhancements realized through the hiring of superbly talented professionals.

Risk Reduction   Given the erratic swings in the exchange ratios between the U.S. dollar and the Japanese yen (in relation to each other as well as other major currencies), an important basis for cost competition between Ford and Toyota has been their relative ingenuity at managing currency risks. One of the ways for such competitors to manage currency risks has been to spread the high-cost elements of their manufacturing operations across a few select and carefully chosen locations around the world. Location decisions such as these can affect the overall risk profile of the firm with respect to currency, economic, and political risks.[12]

Potential Risks of International Expansion

When a company expands its international operations, it does so to increase its profits or revenues. As with any other investment, however, there are potential risks to accompany the anticipated returns.[13] To help companies assess the risk of entering foreign markets, rating systems have been developed to evaluate political, economic, and financial and credit risks. *Euromoney* magazine publishes a semiannual "Country Risk Rating" that evaluates political, economic, and other risks that entrants potentially face. Exhibit 7.3 depicts a sample of country risk ratings, published by the World Bank, from the 178 countries that *Euromoney* evaluates. In the exhibit, note that the lower the score, the higher the country's expected level of risk.

On the next page, we will discuss the four main types of risk: political risk, economic risk, currency risk, and management risk.

Exhibit 7.3
A Sample of
International
Country Risk
Rankings

Rank	Country	Total Risk Assessment	Economic Performance	Political Risk	Total of Debt Indicators	Total of Credit and Access to Finance Indicators
1	Luxembourg	99.51	25.00	24.51	20.00	30.00
2	Switzerland	98.84	23.84	25.00	20.00	30.00
3	United States	98.37	23.96	24.41	20.00	30.00
40	China	71.27	18.93	16.87	19.73	15.74
55	Poland	57.12	18.56	13.97	9.36	15.23
63	Vietnam	52.04	14.80	11.91	18.51	6.82
86	Russia	42.62	11.47	8.33	17.99	4.83
114	Albania	34.23	8.48	5.04	19.62	1.09
161	Mozambique	21.71	3.28	2.75	13.85	1.83
178	Afghanistan	3.92	0.00	3.04	0.00	0.88

Source: Adapted from worldbank.org/html/prddr/trans/so96/art7.htm.

Political and Economic Risk   Generally speaking, the business climate in the United States is very favorable. However, some countries around the globe may be hazardous to the health of corporate initiatives because of political risk. Forces such as social unrest, military turmoil, demonstrations, and even violent conflict and terrorism can pose serious threats.[14] Consider, for example, the ongoing tension and violence in the Middle East between Israelis and Palestinians, and the social and political unrest in Indonesia and Iraq.[15] Because such conditions increase the likelihood of destruction of property and disruption of operations as well as nonpayment for goods and services, countries that are viewed as high risk are less attractive for most types of business. Typical exceptions include providers of munitions and counterintelligence services.

The laws, as well as the enforcement of laws, associated with the protection of intellectual property rights can be a significant potential risk in entering new countries. Microsoft, for example, has lost billions of dollars in potential revenue through piracy of its software products in many countries, including China. Other areas of the globe, such as the former Soviet Union and some eastern European nations, have piracy problems as well. Firms rich in intellectual property have encountered financial losses as imitations of their products have grown through a lack of law enforcement of intellectual property rights.[16]

Strategy Spotlight 7.4 discusses the problems faced by Western companies, especially U.S. firms, in the Middle East because of boycotts organized by political groups. Their complaint is against U.S. foreign policy, but U.S. firms are paying the price.

Currency Risks   Currency fluctuations can pose substantial risks. A company with operations in several countries must constantly monitor the exchange rate between its own currency and that of the host country. Even a small change in the exchange rate can result in a significant difference in the cost of production or net profit when doing business overseas. When the U.S. dollar appreciates against other currencies, for example, U.S. goods can be more expensive to consumers in foreign countries. At the same time, however, appreciation of the U.S. dollar can have negative implications for American companies that have branch operations overseas. The reason for this is that profits from abroad must be exchanged for

Political Risk in the Middle East

Western companies, especially those from the United States, are facing a new form of political risk in the Middle East. Although governments of most of the Arab countries from Egypt to Jordan are friendly to the United States, a grassroots-level boycott of the products of American companies is gathering momentum in many Arab countries. The reason: U.S. support for Israel in the decades-old Palestinian-Israeli conflict.

Most seriously affected is Procter & Gamble's Ariel detergent powder. The Egyptian Committee for Boycott, a self-appointed organization promoting the boycott, is upset with P&G and accused that the product is named after Ariel Sharon, the hard-line Israeli Prime Minister! They even suggest that Ariel's logo resembles a Star of David. P&G, whose sales have been badly hit, responds, "It's ridiculous. Ariel was around long before the Israeli leader. Our logo represents an atom's path, not a religion."

Other American brands targeted include Pampers diapers, Heinz ketchup, and Pepsi soft drinks. Their sales have plummeted by almost 25 percent in the last year. Even worse is the situation with U.S. fast-food companies, which are often perceived as representative of the American way of life. Sales have dropped by as much as 40 percent in many Arab countries! McDonald's is closing two of their six restaurants in Amman, Jordan. Many supermarkets in the Middle East are pulling U.S brands from their shelves. Some have refused to stock Nike shoes.

Sources: "Regime Change," *Economist,* November 2, 2002, p. 65; and "Cairene Shopper's Intifada," *Economist,* November 4, 2000, p. 50.

American firms are not alone in suffering the ire of Arab customers. Sales of European brands like Nestlé, L'Oreal, and Mercedes have also been negatively impacted.

How are Western companies responding to the growing anger against their governments? There is little that they can do to affect American foreign policy. However, they are actively fighting the perception that they are either representative of American government or anti-Islam. Sainsbury, the British retailer that took Egypt by storm in 2002, has posted advertisements signed by "4,800 Egyptian employees" in their stores. They highlight that they have invested $145 million already in Egypt. Further, they state in their advertisements that they do not support Israel and have even started playing Koranic verses in their stores! Procter & Gamble is spending millions of dollars on community projects in Egypt—building schools, financing health education, and even picking up the expenses of the devout making their pilgrimage to Mecca. In Palestine, Coke and its local bottler, National Beverage Company, ferry workers past military check points, offer loans, and provide training and health plans.

Surprisingly, Western companies are among the biggest employers and investors in many Arab countries. Coca-Cola employs 20,000 people directly and another 200,000 indirectly. Western companies also pay wages well above local levels. Locals run and supply all McDonald's franchises. It looks like it is going to be a lose–lose situation for the Western companies and the Arab economies. It may take considerable time, effort, and money for Western multinationals to regain their lost positions.

dollars at a more expensive rate of exchange, reducing the amount of profit when measured in dollars. For example, consider an American firm doing business in Italy. If this firm had a 20 percent profit in euros at its Italian center of operations, this profit would be totally wiped out when converted into U.S. dollars if the euro had depreciated 20 percent against the U.S. dollar. (U.S. multinationals typically engage in sophisticated "hedging strategies" to minimize currency risk, the discussion of which is beyond the scope of this section.)

It is important to note that even when government intervention is well intended, the macroeconomic effects of such action can be very negative for multinational corporations. Such was the case in 1997 when Thailand suddenly chose to devalue its currency, the baht, after months of trying to support it at an artificially high level. This, in effect, made the baht worthless compared to other currencies. And in 1998 Russia not only devalued its ruble, but also elected not to honor its foreign debt obligations.

Management Risks Management risks may be considered the challenges and risks that managers face when they must respond to the inevitable differences that they encounter in foreign markets (as was the case in our opening example of Volkswagen). These take a variety of forms: culture, customs, language, income levels, customer preferences,

**Exhibit 7.4
How Culture
Varies across
Nations:
Implications for
Business**

Ecuador:

◆ Dinners at Ecuadorian homes last for many hours. Expect drinks and appetizers around 8:00 p.m., with dinner not served until 11:00 p.m. or midnight. You will dismay your hosts if you leave as early as 1:00 a.m. A party at an Ecuadorian home will begin late and end around 4:00 a.m. or 5:00 a.m. Late guests may sometimes be served breakfast before they leave.

France:

◆ Most English-speaking French have studied British-style English, which can lead to communication breakdowns with speakers of American-style English. For example, in the United States a presentation that "bombs" has failed, but in England it has succeeded.

◆ Words in French and English may have the same roots but different meanings or connotations. For example, a French person might "demand" something because *demander* in French means "to ask."

Hong Kong:

◆ Negotiations occur over cups of tea. Always accept an offer of tea whether you want it or not. When you are served, wait for the host to drink first.

◆ Chinese negotiators commonly use teacups as visual aids. One cup may be used to represent your company, another cup to represent the Hong Kong company, and the position of the cups will be changed to indicate how far apart the companies are on the terms of an agreement.

Singapore:

◆ Singaporeans associate all of the following with funerals—do not give them as gifts:

a) Straw sandals

b) Clocks

c) A stork or crane

d) Handkerchiefs (they symbolize sadness or weeping)

e) Gifts or wrapping paper where the predominant color is white, black, or blue.

◆ Also avoid any gifts of knives, scissors, or cutting tools; to the Chinese they suggest the severing of a friendship. If you're giving flowers, give an even number of flowers—an odd number would be very unlucky.

Source: T. Morrison, W. Conaway, and G. Borden, *Kiss, Bow, or Shake Hands* (Avon, MA: Adams Media, 1994); and www.executiveplanet.com/business-culture/112565157281.html.

distribution systems, and so on.[17] As we will note later in the chapter, even in the case of apparently standard products, some degree of local adaptation will become necessary.

Differences in cultures across countries can also pose unique challenges for managers. Cultural symbols can evoke deep feelings.[18] For example, in a series of advertisements aimed at Italian vacationers, Coca-Cola executives turned the Eiffel Tower, Empire State Building, and the Tower of Pisa into the familiar Coke bottle. So far, so good. However, when the white marble columns of the Parthenon that crowns the Acropolis in Athens were turned into Coke bottles, the Greeks became outraged. Why? Greeks refer to the Acropolis as the "holy rock," and a government official said the Parthenon is an "international symbol of excellence" and that "whoever insults the Parthenon insults international culture." Coca-Cola apologized for the ad. Exhibit 7.4 demonstrates how cultures vary across countries and some of the implications for the conduct of business across national boundaries.

Let's now look at how firms can attain competitive advantages when they move beyond the boundaries of their home nation.

Achieving Competitive Advantage in Global Markets

We will begin this section by discussing the two opposing forces that firms face when they expand into global markets: cost reduction and adaptation to local markets. Then we will address the four basic types of international strategies that they may pursue: international, global, multidomestic, and transnational. The selection of one of these four types of strategies is largely dependent on a firm's relative pressure to address each of the two forces.

Two Opposing Pressures: Reducing Costs and Adapting to Local Markets

Many years ago, the famed marketing strategist Theodore Levitt advocated strategies that favored global products and brands. That is, he suggested that firms should standardize all of their products and services for all of their worldwide markets. Such an approach would help a firm lower its overall costs by spreading its investments over as large a market as possible. Levitt's approach rested on three key assumptions:

1. Customer needs and interests are becoming increasingly homogeneous worldwide.
2. People around the world are willing to sacrifice preferences in product features, functions, design, and the like for lower prices at high quality.
3. Substantial economies of scale in production and marketing can be achieved through supplying global markets.[19]

However, one can find ample evidence to refute each of these assumptions.[20] With regard to the first assumption, the increasing worldwide homogeneity of customer needs and interests, consider the number of product markets, ranging from watches and handbags to soft drinks and fast foods. Here companies have successfully identified global customer segments and developed global products and brands targeted to those segments. In addition, many other companies adapt lines to idiosyncratic country preferences and develop local brands targeted to local market segments. For example, Nestlé's line of pizzas marketed in the United Kingdom includes cheese with ham and pineapple topping on a French bread crust. Similarly, Coca-Cola in Japan markets Georgia (a tonic drink) as well as Classic Coke and Hi-C.

Consider the second assumption, that is, the sacrifice of product attributes for lower prices. While there is invariably a price-sensitive segment in many product markets, there is no indication that this is on the increase. On the contrary, in many product and service markets—ranging from watches, personal computers, and household appliances, to banking and insurance—there appears to be a growing interest in multiple product features, product quality, and service.

Finally, the third assumption is that significant economies of scale in production and marketing could be achieved for global products and services. Although standardization may lower manufacturing costs, such a perspective neglects to consider three critical and interrelated points. First, as we discussed in Chapter 5, technological developments in flexible factory automation enable economies of scale to be attained at lower levels of output and do not require production of a single standardized product. Second, the cost of production is only one component, and often not the critical one, in determining the total cost of a product. Third, a firm's strategy should not be product-driven. It should also consider other activities in the firm's value chain, such as marketing, sales, and distribution.

Based on the above, one would have a hard time arguing that it is wise to develop the same product or service for all markets throughout the world. While there are some exceptions, such as Harley-Davidson motorcycles and some of Coca-Cola's soft-drink products, managers must also strive to tailor their products to the culture of the country in which they are attempting to do business. Few would argue that "one size fits all" generally applies. But let's look at what happened when Ford took this approach with the launch of its Escort automobile in Europe in the 1980s. According to the company's then CEO, Jacques Nasser:

> The Escort, which was intended to be our first global product, was engineered on two continents—North America and Europe. Obviously, that made it impossible for us to capitalize on global sourcing for components. And it was launched individually in every country. Not only did every country come up with its own positioning for the car, but each devised its own advertising message and hired its own advertising agency to get that message across. So you had one car and a substantial number of value propositions. One market was saying, "Yeah, this car's a limousine." And another market was saying it was a sports vehicle. That made it impossible for us to get customers' input into the product after it was out there.[21]

What we have briefly discussed so far are two opposing pressures that managers face when they compete in markets beyond their national boundaries. These forces place conflicting demands on firms as they strive to be competitive.[22] On the one hand, competitive pressures require that firms do what they can to lower unit costs so that consumers will not perceive their product and service offerings as too expensive. This may lead them to consider locating manufacturing facilities where labor costs are low as well as developing products that are highly standardized across multiple countries.

In addition to responding to pressures to lower costs, managers also must strive to be responsive to local pressures in order to tailor their products to the demand of the local market in which they do business. This requires differentiating their offerings and strategies from country to country to reflect consumer tastes and preferences, as well as making changes to reflect differences in distribution channels, human resource practices, and governmental regulations. However, since the strategies and tactics to differentiate products and services to local markets can involve additional expenses, a firm's costs will tend to rise.

The two opposing pressures result in four different basic strategies that companies can use to compete in the global marketplace: international, global, multidomestic, and transnational. The strategy that a firm selects depends on the degree of pressure that it is facing for cost reductions and the importance of adapting to local markets. Exhibit 7.5 shows the

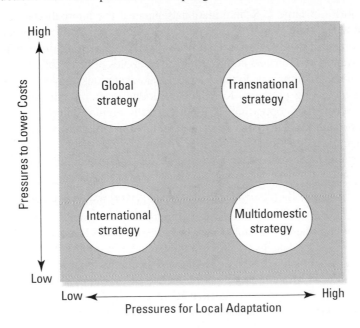

Exhibit 7.5 Opposing Pressures and Four Strategies

conditions under which each of these strategies would be most appropriate. As one would expect, there are advantages and disadvantages associated with each of these strategies. In the following sections we will summarize each strategy, discuss where each is most appropriate, and identify relative advantages and disadvantages.

It is important to note that we consider these strategies to be "basic" or "pure"; that is, in practice, all firms will tend to have some elements of international, global, multidomestic, and transnational strategies.

International Strategy

There are a small number of industries in which pressures for both local adaptation and lowering costs are rather low. An extreme example of such an industry is the "orphan" drug industry. These are medicines for diseases that are severe but affect only a small number of people. Diseases such as the Gaucher disease and Fabry disease fit into this category. Companies such as Genzyme and Oxford GlycoSciences are active in this segment of the drug industry. There is virtually no need to adapt their products to the local markets. And the pressures to reduce costs are low; even though only a few thousand patients are affected, the revenues and margins are significant because patients are charged up to $100,000 per year.

An international strategy is based on diffusion and adaptation of the parent company's knowledge and expertise to foreign markets. Country units are allowed to make some minor adaptations to products and ideas coming from the head office, but they have far less independence and autonomy compared to multidomestic companies. The primary goal of the strategy is worldwide exploitation of the parent firm's knowledge and capabilities. All sources of core competencies are centralized.

For most of its history, Ericsson, a Swedish telecommunications firm, has followed this strategy. Because its home market (Sweden) was too small to support the R&D effort necessary in the industry, Ericsson built its strategy on its ability to transfer and adapt its innovative products and process technologies to international markets. This strategy of sequential diffusion of innovation developed at home helped it to compete successfully against NEC, which followed a global strategy, and ITT, which followed a multidomestic strategy.[23]

The majority of large U.S. multinationals pursued the international strategy in the decades following World War II. These companies centralized R&D and product development but established manufacturing facilities as well as marketing organizations abroad. Companies such as McDonald's and Kellogg are examples of firms following such a strategy. Although these companies do make some local adaptations, they are of a very limited nature. With increasing pressures to reduce costs due to global competition, especially from low-cost countries, opportunities to successfully employ international strategy are becoming more limited. This strategy is most suitable in situations where a firm has distinctive competencies that local companies in foreign markets lack.

Below, we address some of the risks and challenges associated with an international strategy.

- Different activities in the value chain typically have different optimal locations. That is, R&D may be optimally located in a country with an abundant supply of scientists and engineers, whereas assembly may be better conducted in a low-cost location. Nike, for example, designs its shoes in the United States, but all the manufacturing is done in countries like China or Thailand. The international strategy, with its tendency to concentrate most of its activities in one location, fails to take advantage of the benefits of an optimally distributed value chain.
- The international strategy is susceptible to higher levels of currency risk and

political risk. The company is too closely identified with a single country. An increase in the value of the currency may suddenly make the product unattractive abroad.

Global Strategy

As indicated in Exhibit 7.5, a firm whose emphasis is on lowering costs tends to follow a global strategy. Competitive strategy is centralized and controlled to a large extent by the corporate office. Since the primary emphasis is on controlling costs, the corporate office strives to achieve a strong level of coordination and integration across the various businesses.[24] Firms following a global strategy strive to offer standardized products and services as well as to locate manufacturing, R&D, and marketing activities in only a few locations.[25]

A global strategy emphasizes economies of scale due to the standardization of products and services, and the centralization of operations in a few locations. As such, one advantage may be that innovations that come about through efforts of either a business unit or the corporate office can be transferred more easily to other locations. Although costs may be lower, the firm following a global strategy may, in general, have to forgo opportunities for revenue growth since it does not invest extensive resources in adapting product offerings from one market to another.

Consistent with Exhibit 7.5, a global strategy is most appropriate when there are strong pressures for reducing costs and comparatively weak pressures for adaptation to local markets. Identifying potential economies of scale becomes an important consideration.[26] Advantages to increased volume may come not only from larger production plants or runs but also from more efficient logistics and distribution networks. Worldwide volume is also especially important in supporting high levels of investment in research and development. As we would expect, many industries requiring high levels of R&D, such as pharmaceuticals, semiconductors, and jet aircraft, follow global strategies.

Another advantage of a global strategy is that it can enable a firm to create a standard level of quality throughout the world. Let's look at what Tom Siebel, chairman of Siebel Systems, the $2 billion developer of e-business application software, has to say about global standardization.

> Our customers—global companies like IBM, Zurich Financial Services, and Citicorp—expect the same high level of service and quality, and the same licensing policies, no matter where we do business with them around the world. Our human resources and legal departments help us create policies that respect local cultures and requirements worldwide, while at the same time maintaining the highest standards. We have one brand, one image, one set of corporate colors, and one set of messages, across every place on the planet. An organization needs central quality control to avoid surprises.[27]

There are, of course, some risks associated with a global strategy.[28]

- A firm can enjoy scale economies only by concentrating scale-sensitive resources and activities in one or few locations. Such concentration, however, becomes a "double-edged sword." For example, if a firm has only one manufacturing facility, it must export its output (e.g., components, subsystems, or finished products) to other markets, some of which may be a great distance from the operation. Thus, decisions about locating facilities must weigh the potential benefits from concentrating operations in a single location against the higher transportation and tariff costs that result from such concentration.

- The geographic concentration of any activity may also tend to isolate that activity from the targeted markets. Such isolation may be risky since it may hamper the facility's ability to quickly respond to changes in market conditions and needs.

♦   Concentrating an activity in a single location also makes the rest of the firm dependent on that location. Such dependency on a sole source implies that, unless the location has world-class competencies, the firm's competitive position can be eroded if problems arise. A European executive of Ford Motor Co., reflecting on the firm's concentration of activities during a global integration program in the mid-1990s, lamented: "Now if you misjudge the market, you are wrong in 15 countries rather than only one."

Multidomestic Strategy

According to Exhibit 7.5, a firm whose emphasis is on differentiating its product and service offerings to adapt to local markets follows a multidomestic strategy. In contrast to a global strategy in which decision-making authority tends to be highly centralized in the corporate office, decisions evolving from a multidomestic strategy tend to be more decentralized to permit the firm to tailor its products and respond rapidly to changes in demand. This enables a firm to expand its market and to charge different prices in different markets. For firms following this strategy, differences in language, culture, income levels, customer preferences, and distribution systems are only a few of the many factors that must be considered. Even in the case of relatively standardized products, at least some level of local adaptation is often necessary. Consider, for example, Honda motorcycles.

> Although one could argue that a good product knows no national boundaries, there are subtle differences in ways that a product is used and what customers expect of it. Thus, while Honda uses a common basic technology, it must develop different types of motorcycles for different regions of the world. For example, North Americans primarily use motorcycles for leisure and sports; thus aggressive looks and high horsepower are key. Southeast Asians provide a counterpoint. Here, motorcycles are a basic means of transportation. Thus, they require low cost and ease of maintenance. And, in Australia and New Zealand, shepherds use motorcycles to herd sheep. Therefore, they demand low-speed torque, rather than high speed and maintenance.[29]

In addition to the products themselves, how they are packaged must sometimes be adapted to local market conditions. Some consumers in developing countries are likely to have packaging preferences very different from consumers in the West. For example, single-serve packets, or sachets, are very popular in India.[30] They permit consumers to purchase only what they need, experiment with new products, and conserve cash at the same time. Products as varied as detergents, shampoos, pickles, and cough syrup are sold in sachets in India. It is estimated that they make up 20 to 30 percent of the total sold in their categories. In China, sachets are also spreading as a marketing device for such items as shampoos. This reminds us of the importance of considering all activities in a firm's value chain (discussed in Chapters 3 and 5) in determining where local adaptations may be advisable.

Cultural differences may also require a firm to adapt its personnel practices when it expands internationally.[31] For example, some facets of Wal-Mart stores have been easily "exported" to foreign operations, while others have required some modifications.[32] When the retailer entered the German market in 1997, it took along the company "cheer"—Give me a W! Give me an A! Give me an L! Who's Number One? The Customer!—which suited German employees as much as their U.S. counterparts. However, Wal-Mart's 10-Foot Rule, which requires employees to greet any customer within a 10-foot radius, was not so well received in Germany, where employees and shoppers alike weren't comfortable with the custom.

Strategy Spotlight 7.5 describes how U.S. multinationals have adapted to the problem of bribery in various countries while adhering to strict federal laws on corrupt practices abroad.

As one might expect, there are some risks associated with a multidomestic strategy. Among these are the following:

strategy spotlight

Dealing with Bribery Abroad

Most multinational firms experience difficult dilemmas when it comes to the question of adapting rules and guidelines, both formal and informal, while operating in foreign countries. A case in point is the Foreign Corrupt Practices Act of 1977, which makes it illegal for U.S. companies to bribe foreign officials to gain business or facilitate approvals and permissions. Unfortunately, in many parts of the world, bribery is a way of life, with large payoffs to government officials and politicians the norm to win government contracts. At a lower level, goods won't clear customs unless routine illegal, but well-accepted, payments, are made to officials. What is an American company to do in such situations?

Intel follows a strict rule-based definition of bribery as "a thing of value given to someone with the intent of obtaining favorable treatment from the recipient." The company strictly prohibits payments to expedite a shipment through customs if the payment did not "follow applicable rules and regulations, and if the agent gives money or payment in kind to a government official for personal benefit." Texas Instruments, on the other hand, follows a middle approach. They require employees to "exercise good judgment" in questionable circumstances "by avoiding activities that could create even the appearance that our decisions could be compromised." And Analog Devices has set up a policy manager as a consultant to overseas operations. The policy manager does not make decisions for country managers. Instead, the policy manager helps country managers think through the issues and provides information on how the corporate office has handled similar situations in the past.

Source: T. M. Begley and D. P. Boyd, "The Need for a Corporate Global Mindset," *MIT Sloan Management Review,* Winter 2003, pp. 25–32.

- Typically, local adaptation of products and services will increase a company's cost structure. In many industries, competition is so intense that most firms can ill afford any competitive disadvantages on the dimension of cost. A key challenge of managers is to determine the trade-off between local adaptation and its cost structure. For example, cost considerations led Procter & Gamble to standardize its diaper design across all European markets. This was done despite research data indicating that Italian mothers, unlike those in other countries, preferred diapers that covered the baby's navel. Later, however, P&G recognized that this feature was critical to these mothers, so the company decided to incorporate this feature for the Italian market despite its adverse cost implications.

- At times local adaptations, even when well intentioned, may backfire. When the American restaurant chain TGI Fridays entered the South Korean market, it purposely incorporated many local dishes, such as kimchi (hot, spicy cabbage), in its menu. This responsiveness, however, was not well received. Company analysis of the weak market acceptance indicated that Korean customers anticipated a visit to TGI Fridays as a visit to America. Thus, finding Korean dishes was inconsistent with their expectations.

- Consistent with other aspects of global marketing, the optimal degree of local adaptation evolves over time. In many industry segments, a variety of factors, such as the influence of global media, greater international travel, and declining income disparities across countries, may lead to increasing global standardization. On the other hand, in other industry segments, especially where the product or service can be delivered over the Internet (such as music), the need for even greater customization and local adaptation may increase over time. Firms must recalibrate the need for local adaptation on an ongoing basis; excessive adaptation extracts a price as surely as underadaptation.

Transnational Strategy

Let's briefly review global and multidomestic strategies before we discuss how a transnational strategy can be a vehicle for overcoming the limitations of each of these strategies and, in effect, "getting the best of both worlds."[33]

With a *global strategy,* resources and capabilities are concentrated at the center of the organization. Authority is highly centralized. Thus, a global company achieves efficiency primarily by exploiting potential scale economies in all of its value-chain activities. Since innovation is highly centralized in the corporate office, there is often a lack of understanding of the changing market needs and production requirements outside the local market, and there are few incentives to adapt.

The *multidomestic strategy* can be considered the exact opposite of the global strategy. Resources are dispersed throughout many countries in which a firm does business, and a subsidiary of the multinational company can more effectively respond to local needs. However, such fragmentation inevitably carries efficiency penalties. Learning also suffers because knowledge is not consolidated in a centralized location and does not flow among the various parts of the company.

A multinational firm following a *transnational strategy* strives to optimize the trade-offs associated with efficiency, local adaptation, and learning.[34] It seeks efficiency not for its own sake, but as a means to achieve global competitiveness. It recognizes the importance of local responsiveness, but as a tool for flexibility in international operations.[35] Innovations are regarded as an outcome of a larger process of organizational learning that includes the contributions of everyone in the firm.[36] Additionally, a core tenet of the transnational model is that a firm's assets and capabilities are dispersed according to the most beneficial location for a specific activity. Thus, managers avoid the tendency to either concentrate activities in a central location (as with a global strategy) or disperse them across many locations to enhance adaptation (as with a multidomestic strategy). Peter Brabeck, CEO of Nestlé, the giant food company, provides such a perspective.

> We believe strongly that there isn't a so-called global consumer, at least not when it comes to food and beverages. People have local tastes based on their unique cultures and traditions—a good candy bar in Brazil is not the same as a good candy bar in China. Therefore, decision making needs to be pushed down as low as possible in the organization, out close to the markets. Otherwise, how can you make good brand decisions? That said, decentralization has its limits. If you are too decentralized, you can become too complicated—you get too much complexity in your production system. The closer we come to the consumer, in branding, pricing, communication, and product adaptation, the more we decentralize. The more we are dealing with production, logistics, and supply-chain management, the more centralized decision making becomes. After all, we want to leverage Nestlé's size, not be hampered by it.[37]

The Nestlé example illustrates a common approach in determining whether or not to centralize or decentralize a value-chain activity. Typically, primary activities that are "downstream" (e.g., marketing, sales, and service) or closer to the customer tend to require more decentralization in order to adapt to local market conditions. On the other hand, primary activities that are "upstream" (e.g., logistics and operations) or further away from the customer tend to be centralized. This is because there is less need for adapting these activities to local markets and the firm can benefit from economies of scale. Additionally, many support activities, such as information systems and procurement, tend to be centralized in order to increase the potential for economies of scale.

A central philosophy of the transnational organization is enhanced adaptation to all competitive situations as well as flexibility by capitalizing on communication and knowledge flows throughout the organization.[38] A principal characteristic is the integration of unique contributions of all units into worldwide operations. Thus, a joint innovation by headquarters and by one of the overseas units can lead potentially to the development of relatively standardized and yet flexible products and services that are suitable for multiple markets.

Asea Brown Boveri (ABB) is a firm that successfully follows a transnational strategy. ABB, with its home bases in Sweden and Switzerland, illustrates the trend toward cross-national mergers that lead firms to consider multiple headquarters in the future. It is managed as a flexible network of units, and one of management's main functions is the facilitation of information and knowledge flows between units. ABB's subsidiaries have complete responsibility for product categories on a worldwide basis. Such a transnational strategy enables ABB to benefit from access to new markets and the opportunity to utilize and develop resources wherever they may be located.

As with the other strategies, there are some unique risks and challenges associated with a transnational strategy.

- The choice of a seemingly optimal location cannot guarantee that the quality and cost of factor inputs (i.e., labor, materials) will be optimal. Managers must ensure that the relative advantage of a location is actually realized, not squandered because of weaknesses in productivity and the quality of internal operations. Ford Motor Co., for example, has benefited from having some of its manufacturing operations in Mexico. While some have argued that the benefits of lower wage rates will be partly offset by lower productivity, this does not always have to be the case. Since unemployment in Mexico is higher than in the United States, Ford can be more selective in its hiring practices for its Mexican operations. And, given the lower turnover among its Mexican employees, Ford can justify a high level of investment in training and development. Thus, the net result can be not only lower wage rates, but also higher productivity than in the United States.

- Although knowledge transfer can be a key source of competitive advantages, it does not take place "automatically." For knowledge transfer to take place from one subsidiary to another, it is important for the source of the knowledge, the target units, and the corporate headquarters to recognize the potential value of such unique know-how. Given that there can be significant geographic, linguistic, and cultural distances that typically separate subsidiaries, the potential for knowledge transfer can become very difficult to realize. Firms must create mechanisms to systematically and routinely uncover the opportunities for knowledge transfer.

Exhibit 7.6 summarizes the relative advantages and disadvantages of international, global, multidomestic, and transnational strategies.

We've discussed the types of strategies that firms pursue in international markets and their relative advantages and disadvantages. Let's now turn to the types of entry modes that companies may use to enter international markets.

Entry Modes of International Expansion

A firm has many options available to it when it decides to expand into international markets. Given the challenges associated with such entry, many firms first start on a small scale and then increase their level of investment and risk as they gain greater experience with the overseas market in question.[39]

Exhibit 7.7 illustrates a wide variety of modes of foreign entry, including exporting, licensing, franchising, joint ventures, strategic alliances, and wholly owned subsidiaries.[40] As the exhibit indicates, the various types of entry form a continuum that ranges from exporting (low investment and risk, low control) to a wholly owned subsidiary (high investment and risk, high control).[41]

**Exhibit 7.6
Strengths and
Limitations of
Various Strategies**

Strategy	Strengths	Limitations
International	◆ Leverage and diffusion of parent's knowledge and core competencies. ◆ Lower costs because of less need to tailor products and services. ◆ Greater level of worldwide coordination.	◆ Limited ability to adapt to local markets. ◆ Inability to take advantage of new ideas and innovations occurring in local markets.
Global	◆ Strong integration across various businesses. ◆ Standardization leads to higher economies of scale, which lowers costs. ◆ Helps to create uniform standards of quality throughout the world.	◆ Limited ability to adapt to local markets. ◆ Concentration of activities may increase dependence on a single facility. ◆ Single locations may lead to higher tariffs and transportation costs.
Multidomestic	◆ Ability to adapt products and services to local market conditions. ◆ Ability to detect potential opportunities for attractive niches in a given market, enhancing revenue.	◆ Less ability to realize cost savings through scale economies. ◆ Greater difficulty in transferring knowledge across countries. ◆ May lead to "overadaptation" as conditions change.
Transnational	◆ Ability to attain economies of scale. ◆ Ability to adapt to local markets. ◆ Ability to locate activities in optimal locations. ◆ Ability to increase knowledge flows and learning.	◆ Unique challenges in determining optimal locations of activities to ensure cost and quality. ◆ Unique managerial challenges in fostering knowledge transfer.

Admittedly, there can at times be frustrations and setbacks as a firm evolves its international entry strategy from exporting to more expensive types, including wholly owned subsidiaries. For example, according to the CEO of a large U.S. specialty chemical company:

> In the end, we always do a better job with our own subsidiaries; sales improve, and we have greater control over the business. But we still need local distributors for entry, and we are still searching for strategies to get us through the transitions without battles over control and performance.[42]

Let's discuss each of these international entry modes in turn.[43]

Exporting

Exporting consists of producing goods in one country to sell in another. This entry strategy enables a firm to invest the least amount of resources in terms of its product, its or-

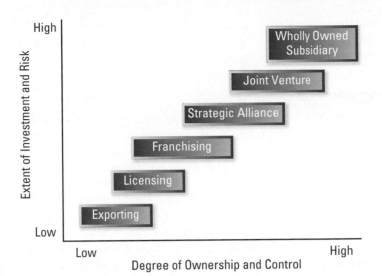

**Exhibit 7.7
Entry Modes for
International
Expansion**

ganization, and its overall corporate strategy. Not surprisingly, many host countries dislike this entry strategy because it provides less local employment than other modes of entry.[44]

Multinationals often stumble onto a stepwise strategy for penetrating markets, beginning with the exporting of products. This often results in a series of unplanned actions to increase sales revenues. As the pattern recurs with entries into subsequent markets, this approach, named a "beachhead strategy," becomes official policy in many organizations.

Such an approach definitely has its advantages. After all, firms start from scratch in sales and distribution when they enter new markets. Because many foreign markets are nationally regulated and dominated by networks of local intermediaries, firms need to partner with local distributors to benefit from their valuable expertise and knowledge of their own markets. Multinationals, after all, recognize that they cannot master local business practices, meet regulatory requirements, hire and manage local personnel, or gain access to potential customers without some form of local partnership.

In addition to the need to partner with local firms, multinationals also want to minimize their own risk. They do this by hiring local distributors and investing very little in the undertaking. In essence, the firm gives up control of strategic marketing decisions to the local partners—much more control than they would be willing to give up in their home market.

As one might expect, exporting is a relatively inexpensive way to enter foreign markets. However, it can still have significant downsides. In a study of 250 instances in which multinational firms used local distributors to implement their exporting entry strategy, the results were dismal. In the vast majority of the cases, the distributors were bought (to increase control) by the multinational firm or fired. By contrast, successful distributors shared two common characteristics:

- They carried product lines that complemented, rather than competed with, the multinational's products.
- They behaved as if they were business partners with the multinationals. They shared market information with the corporations, they initiated projects with distributors in neighboring countries, and they suggested initiatives in their own or nearby markets. Additionally, these distributors took on risk themselves by investing in areas such as training, information systems, and advertising and promotion in order to increase the business of their multinational partners.

The key point is the importance of developing collaborative, win–win relationships.

To ensure more control over operations without incurring significant risks, many firms have used licensing and franchising as a mode of entry. Let's now discuss these and their relative advantages and disadvantages.

Licensing and Franchising

Licensing as an entry mode enables a company to receive a royalty or fee in exchange for the right to use its trademark, patent, trade secret, or other valuable item of intellectual property.[45] In international markets, the advantage is that the firm granting the license incurs little risk, since it does not have to invest any significant resources into the country itself. In turn, the licensee (the firm receiving the license) gains access to the trademark, patent, and so on, and is able to potentially create competitive advantages. In many cases, the country also benefits from the product being manufactured locally. For example, Yoplait yogurt is licensed by General Mills from Sodima, a French cooperative, for sale in the United States. The logos of college and professional athletic teams in the United States are another source of trademarks that generate significant royalty income domestically and internationally.

There are, of course, some important disadvantages with this type of entry. For example, the licensor gives up control of its product and forgoes potential revenues and profits. Furthermore, the licensee may eventually become so familiar with the patent and trade secrets that it may become a competitor; that is, the licensee may make some modifications to the product and manufacture and sell it independently of the licensor without having to pay a royalty fee. This potential situation is aggravated in countries that have relatively weak laws to protect intellectual property. Additionally, if the licensee selected by the multinational firm turns out to be a poor choice, the brand name and reputation of the product may be tarnished.[46]

Although licensing and franchising are both forms of contractual arrangements, franchise contracts generally include a broader range of factors in an operation and have a longer time period during which the agreement is in effect. Franchising has the advantage of limiting the risk exposure that a firm has in overseas markets while expanding the revenue base of the parent company. The other side of the coin is that the multinational firm receives only a portion of the revenues, in the form of franchise fees, instead of the entire revenue—as would be the case if the firm set up the operation itself (e.g., a restaurant) through direct investment.

Franchising remains an overwhelmingly American form of business. According to a recent survey, more than 400 U.S. franchisers have international exposure.[47] This is greater than the combined totals of the next four largest franchiser home countries—France, the United Kingdom, Mexico, and Austria.

Companies often desire a closer collaboration with other firms in order to increase revenue, reduce costs, and enhance their learning—often through the diffusion of technology. To achieve such objectives, they enter into strategic alliances or joint ventures, two entry modes we will discuss next.

Strategic Alliances and Joint Ventures

Joint ventures and strategic alliances have become in recent years an increasingly popular way for firms to enter and succeed in foreign markets. These two forms of partnership differ in that joint ventures entail the creation of a third-party legal entity, whereas strategic alliances do not. In addition, strategic alliances generally focus on initiatives that are smaller in scope than joint ventures.

strategy spotlight

Microsoft's Partnerships in East Asia

Microsoft is forming strategic alliances and joint ventures with companies in East Asia. Rather than competing with existing firms, Microsoft has entered several countries by cooperating with these firms. It has entered the Japanese and Taiwanese markets by joining efforts with mobile phone operator NTT DoCoMo, which has already established itself as a successful provider of cellular phone service through its Mobimagic service. By teaming with Microsoft, both companies stand to profit by integrating Microsoft's software applications, such as e-mail, into the existing service of cell-phone subscribers. Akio Fujii, head of new product development for Microsoft Japan, envisions adding a Web browser to these cell-phone services.

GigaMedia has 100,000 broadband subscribers offering sports, music, news, video-on-demand, as well as on-line karaoke. By hooking up with Microsoft, GigaMedia is now able to move its services from personal computers (PCs) to televisions, with the television serving as the monitor and a set-top box similar to a cable television box functioning as the PC. In exchange for its contribution, Microsoft gleans 2 percent of GigaMedia's broadband

Source: N. Chowdhury, "Gates & Co. Attack Asia," *Fortune.com,* April 17, 2000; G. Mariano, "Palm to Groove with Liquid Audio Music," *New York Times Online,* April 11, 2001.

subscriber fees and significant revenue from GigaMedia's e-commerce sales. In a similar move, the Koos Group, owner of KG Telecom, the second largest cell-phone operator in Taiwan, has joined ranks with Microsoft to integrate Internet capabilities on the televisions and cell phones of subscribers.

Microsoft has taken strategic moves to blunt competition from Palm by joining forces in an alliance with Psion in London, one of Palm's chief rivals. Microsoft has also reduced Palm's competitive threat in the cell-phone market by partnering with Stockholm's Ericsson, a leading manufacturer of mobile phones.

Microsoft has utilized forward-thinking vision to achieve win–win relationships through several joint ventures and strategic alliances throughout the globe. By doing so, it is successfully exporting its influence from an entrenched position in the United States to a global presence. This is good not only for Microsoft and its shareholders; stockholders of other firms around the world stand to prosper from the cooperative agreements Microsoft has forged with their firms. In addition, the added competition from a powerhouse like Microsoft forces other international firms to compete for efficiencies, thus benefiting overall economic prosperity.

As we discussed in Chapter 6, these strategies have been effective in helping firms to increase revenues and reduce costs as well as to enhance learning and diffuse technologies. These partnerships enable firms to share the risks as well as the potential revenues and profits. Also, by gaining exposure to new sources of knowledge and technologies, such partnerships can help firms develop core competencies that can lead to competitive advantages in the marketplace.[48] Finally, entering into partnerships with host country firms can provide very useful information on local market tastes, competitive conditions, legal matters, and cultural nuances.[49] Strategy Spotlight 7.6 discusses how Microsoft has used a variety of partnerships to strengthen its position in East Asia.

Despite the potential benefits, managers must be aware of the risks associated with strategic alliances and joint ventures and how they can be minimized.[50] First, there needs to be a clearly defined strategy that is strongly supported by the organizations that are party to the partnership. Otherwise, the firms may work at cross-purposes and not achieve any of their goals. Second, and closely allied to the first issue, there must be a clear understanding of capabilities and resources that will be central to the partnership. Without such clarification, there will be fewer opportunities for learning and developing competences that could lead to competitive advantages. Third, trust is a vital element. Phasing in the relationship between alliance partners permits them to get to know each other better and develop trust. According to Philip Benton, Jr., former president of Ford Motor Co. (which has been involved in multiple international partnerships over the years): "The first time two companies work together, the chances of succeeding are very slight. But once you find ways to work together, all sorts of opportunities arise." Without trust, one party may take advantage of the other by, for example, withholding its fair share of resources and gaining access to privileged information through unethical (or illegal means). Fourth, cultural issues that can potentially lead to conflict and dysfunctional behaviors need to be addressed. An organization's culture is the set of values, beliefs, and attitudes that influence the behavior and goals of its employees. Thus, recognizing cultural differences as well as striving to develop elements of a "common culture" for the partnership is vital. Without a unifying culture, it will become difficult to combine and leverage resources that are increasingly important in knowledge-intensive organizations (discussed in Chapter 4).[51]

As we know, not all partnerships are successful, for a variety of reasons. One of the most famous in recent business history was the joint venture formed by General Motors and Daewoo Motor Co.

In the mid-1980s General Motors sought cheap labor in Korea while Daewoo (of Korea) wanted to export automobiles. Thus, the two companies joined forces in 1986 to manufacture the ill-fated Pontiac LeMans. Things did not work out as planned. The LeMans experienced a sales decline of 39 percent from 1988 to 1990 and further declines in 1990 until the partnership was dissolved shortly thereafter.

What went wrong? The first cars had quality problems: GM sent engineers to Korea to correct them. Korea's cheap labor didn't materialize because of economic improvement, devaluation of the dollar, and increasingly strong demands from the newly formed labor unions for higher wages. However, the biggest problem was the differing goals of the two firms. While Daewoo wanted to upgrade the models to gain a larger share of the domestic market, GM wanted to keep costs down.

In effect, the alliance failed from the start, due to minimal understanding of each other's objectives and a lack of effort to reevaluate plans when problems appeared.[52]

Finally, the success of a firm's alliance should not be left to chance.[53] To improve their odds of success, many companies have carefully documented alliance-management knowledge by creating guidelines and manuals to help them manage specific aspects of the entire alliance life cycle (e.g., partner selection and alliance negotiation and contracting). For example, Lotus Corp. (part of IBM) created what it calls its "35 rules of thumb" to manage each phase of an alliance from formation to termination. Hewlett-Packard developed 60 different tools and templates, which it placed in a 300-page manual for guiding decision making in specific alliance situations. The manual included such tools as a template for making the business case for an alliance, a partner evaluation form, a negotiations template outlining the roles and responsibilities of different departments, a list of the ways to measure alliance performance, and an alliance termination checklist.

When a firm desires the highest level of control over its international operations, it develops wholly owned subsidiaries. Although wholly owned subsidiaries can generate the greatest returns, they also come with the highest levels of investment and risk. We will now discuss them.

Wholly Owned Subsidiaries

A wholly owned subsidiary is a business in which a multinational company owns 100 percent of the stock. There are two means by which a firm can establish a wholly owned subsidiary. It can either acquire an existing company in the home country or it can develop a totally new operation. The latter is often referred to as a "greenfield venture." Establishing a wholly owned subsidiary is the most expensive and risky of the various entry modes.

Häagen-Dazs's Unique Entry Strategy

The ice-cream and frozen yogurt company Häagen-Dazs has taken a unique route for cross-border entry. Rather than follow traditional entry modes, the Bronx, New York–based company has an unconventional way of moving beyond the boundaries of the United States.

The company uses a three-step process. First, it uses high-end retailers to introduce the brand. Next, it finds high-traffic areas to build company-owned stores. The last step is to sell Häagen-Dazs products in convenience stores and supermarkets.

Häagen-Dazs is quick to adapt to local needs. For instance, freezers in some European stores are notorious for their unreliability. Clearly, a freezer malfunction would ruin a store's stock of Häagen-Dazs products. So Häagen-Dazs buys high-quality freezers for stores willing to carry its brand. Small sacrifices such as this have grown the company from a small ice-cream manufacturer in the Bronx to a worldwide franchiser with 650 stores in 55 countries, including Belgium, France, Japan, and the United Kingdom.

Sources: M. Meremenot, "Screaming for Häagen-Dazs," *BusinessWeek*, October 14, 1991, p. 121; Häagen-Dazs, "Information for Franchisees," Häagen-Dazs company document, 2001, pp. 1–24.

However, as expected, it can also yield the highest returns. In addition, it provides the multinational company with the greatest degree of control of all activities, including manufacturing, marketing, distribution, and technology development.[54]

Wholly owned subsidiaries as well as direct investment in greenfield ventures are most appropriate where a firm already has the appropriate knowledge and capabilities that it can leverage rather easily through multiple locations in many countries. Examples range from restaurants to semiconductor manufacturers. To lower costs, for example, Intel Corporation builds semiconductor plants throughout the world—all of which use virtually the same blueprint. In establishing wholly owned subsidiaries, knowledge can be further leveraged by the hiring of managers and professionals from the firm's home country, often through hiring talent from competitors.

As noted, wholly owned subsidiaries are typically the most expensive and risky of the various modes for entering international markets. With franchising, joint ventures, or strategic alliances, the risk is shared with the firm's partners. With wholly owned subsidiaries, the entire risk is assumed by the parent company. The risks associated with doing business in a new country (e.g., political, cultural, and legal nuances) can be lessened by hiring local talent.

Wal-Mart's expansion into South Korea points out some of the challenges and risks of creating greenfield ventures.

Prior to Wal-Mart entering South Korea, local competitors were fearful that the giant retailer would "devour the local fish" with its extensive financial resources and global buying power. However, after its initial foray, many are now talking about what went wrong with Wal-Mart's initial efforts. For one thing, Wal-Mart used a membership approach similar to the one used by its Sam's warehouse stores. According to Song Kye-Hyon, a financial analyst, "It turned out to be a strategic flaw of Wal-Mart when it first adopted the Western policy of the membership where customers were required to pay a membership fee for shopping privileges and no food (only merchandise)." In South Korea, fresh, quality food is a key ingredient of success. It generates half of a store's revenues. To make matters worse, one of Wal-Mart's competitors, E-Mart, has several thousand local food suppliers with which it has nurtured long-term relationships. E-Mart even owns its own farm that supplies its stores.

The local competitors have also developed mechanisms to create greater customer loyalty. They employ green-capped young men who help bring the shopping carts to the customers' cars in the parking lot. And they operate shuttle buses to go through neighborhoods to pick up customers and drop them off at their homes after they have completed their shopping.

Wal-Mart remains undaunted. It has changed course to adopt the supercenter Wal-Mart concept in which it scrapped the memberships and introduced food. Wal-Mart and its competitors have vowed to further expand their operations in an effort to grab a larger piece of the discount retail market which is expected to reach $25 billion by 2004.[55]

In this closing section, we have addressed entry strategies as a progression from exporting through the creation of wholly owned subsidiaries. However, we must point out that many firms do not follow such an evolutionary approach. Instead, such firms follow rather unique entry strategies; see the discussion of Häagen-Dazs in Strategy Spotlight 7.7.

summary

We live in a highly interconnected global community where many of the best opportunities for growth and profitability lie beyond the boundaries of a company's home country. Along with the opportunities, of course, there are many risks associated with diversification into global markets.

The first section of the chapter addressed the factors that determine a nation's competitiveness in a particular industry. The framework was developed by Professor Michael Porter of Harvard University and was based on a four-year study that explored the competitive success of 10 leading trading nations. The four factors, collectively termed the "diamond of national advantage," were factor conditions, demand characteristics, related and supporting industries, and firm strategy, structure, and rivalry.

The discussion of Porter's "diamond" helped, in essence, to set the broader context for exploring competitive advantage at the firm level. In the second section, we discussed the primary motivations and the potential risks associated with international expansion. The primary motivations included increasing the size of the potential market for the firm's products and services, achieving economies of scale, extending the life cycle of the firm's products, and optimizing the location for every activity in the value chain. On the other hand, the key risks included political and economic risks, currency risks, and management risks. Management risks are the challenges associated with responding to the inevitable differences that exist across countries such as customs, culture, language, customer preferences, and distribution systems.

Next, we addressed how firms can go about attaining competitive advantage in global markets. We began by discussing the two opposing forces—cost reduction and adaptation to local markets—which managers must contend with when entering global markets. The relative importance of these two factors plays a major part in determining which of the four basic types of strategies to select: international, global, multidomestic, or transnational. The chapter covered the benefits and risks associated with each type of strategy.

The final section discussed the four types of entry strategies that managers may undertake when entering international markets. The key trade-off in each of these strategies is the level of investment or risk versus the level of control. In order of their progressively greater investment/risk and control, the strategies range from exporting to licensing and franchising, to strategic alliances and joint ventures, to wholly owned subsidiaries. The relative benefits and risks associated with each of these strategies were addressed.

summary review questions

1. What are some of the advantages and disadvantages associated with a firm's expansion into international markets?

2. What are the four factors described in Porter's diamond of national advantage? How do the four factors explain why some industries in a given country are more successful than others?

3. Explain the two opposing forces—cost reduction and adaptation to local markets—that firms must deal with when they go global.

4. There are four basic strategies—international, global, multidomestic, and transnational. What are the advantages and disadvantages associated with each?

5. Describe the basic entry strategies that firms have available when they enter international markets. What are the relative advantages and disadvantages of each?

The United States is considered a world leader in the motion picture industry. Using Porter's diamond framework for national competitiveness, explain the success of this industry.

experiential exercise

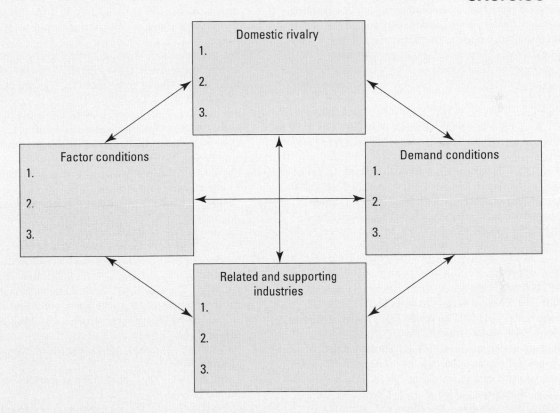

1. Data on the "competitiveness of nations" can be found on www.imd.ch/wcy/ranking/. This website provides a ranking on a variety of criteria for 49 countries. How might Porter's diamond of national advantage help to explain the rankings for some of these countries for certain industries that interest you?

2. The Internet has lowered the entry barriers for smaller firms that wish to diversify into international markets. Why is this so? Provide an example.

3. Many firms fail when they enter into strategic alliances with firms that link up with companies based in other countries. What are some reasons for this failure? Provide an example.

4. Many large U.S.-based management consulting companies such as McKinsey and Company and the BCG Group have been very successful in the international marketplace. How can Porter's diamond explain their success?

application questions & exercises

ethics
questions

1. Over the past few decades, many American firms have relocated most or all of their operations from the United States to countries such as Mexico and China that pay lower wages. What are some of the ethical issues that such actions may raise?
2. Business practices and customs vary throughout the world. What are some of the ethical issues concerning payments that must be made in a foreign country to obtain business opportunities?

references

1. Edmondson, G., 2003, Volkswagen needs a jump, *BusinessWeek,* May 12: 48–49; Flint, J., 2002, Luxury: The cure du jour, *Forbes,* December 9: 88; Snarkhunting. com, 2003, www.snarkhunting.com/2003_01_01_ archive.html, January; The name game Touareg? Murano? Where do they get those new car names? 2003, *Chicago Sun-Times,* January 30, www.automobilemag. com/news/news_30_5/; and www.vw.com/autoshow/ pdf/touareg.pdf.
2. Our discussion of globalization draws upon Engardio, P., & Belton, C., 2000, Global capitalism: Can it be made to work better? *BusinessWeek,* November 6: 72–98.
3. Ibid.
4. The above discussion draws on Clifford, M. L., Engardio, P., Malkin, E., Roberts, D., & Echikson, W., 2000, Up the ladder, *BusinessWeek,* November 6: 78–84.
5. For another interesting discussion on a country perspective, refer to Makino, S., 1999, MITI Minister Kaora Yosano on reviving Japan's competitive advantages, *Academy of Management Executive* 13 (4): 8–28.
6. The following discussion draws heavily upon Porter, M. E., 1990, The competitive advantage of nations, *Harvard Business Review,* March–April: 73–93.
7. Landes, D. S., 1998, *The Wealth and Poverty of Nations* (New York: W. W. Norton).
8. Part of our discussion of the motivations and risks of international expansion draws upon Gregg, F. M., 1999, International strategy, in Helms, M. M., ed., *Encyclopedia of Management* (Detroit: Gale Group), 434–38.
9. These two examples are discussed, respectively, in Dawar, N., & Frost, T., 1999, Competing with giants: Survival strategies for local companies in emerging markets, *Harvard Business Review* 77 (2): 119–29; and Prahalad, C. K., & Lieberthal, K., 1998, The end of corporate imperialism, *Harvard Business Review* 76 (4): 68–79.
10. This discussion draws upon Gupta, A. K., & Govindarajan, V., 2001, Converting global presence into global competitive advantage, *Academy of Management Executive* 15 (2): 45–56.
11. Stross, R. E., 1997, Mr. Gates builds his brain trust, *Fortune,* December 8: 84–98.
12. For a good summary of the benefits and risks of international expansion, refer to Bartlett, C. A., & Ghoshal, S., 1987, Managing across borders: New strategic responses, *Sloan Management Review* 28 (5): 45–53; and Brown, R. H., 1994, *Competing to Win in a Global Economy* (Washington, DC: U.S. Department of Commerce).
13. For an interesting insight into rivalry in global markets, refer to MacMillan, I. C., van Putten, A. B., & McGrath, R. G., 2003, Global gamesmanship, *Harvard Business Review* 81 (5): 62–73.
14. For a discussion of the political risks in China for United States companies, refer to Garten, J. E., 1998, Opening the doors for business in China, *Harvard Business Review* 76 (3): 167–75.
15. Shari, M., 2001, Is a holy war brewing in Indonesia? *BusinessWeek,* October 15: 62.
16. Gikkas, N. S., 1996, International licensing of intellectual property: The promise and the peril, *Journal of Technology Law & Policy* 1 (1): 1–26.
17. For an excellent theoretical discussion of how cultural factors can affect knowledge transfer across national boundaries, refer to Bhagat, R. S., Kedia, B. L., Harveston, P. D., Triandis, H. C., 2002, Cultural variations in the cross-border transfer of organizational knowledge: An integrative framework, *Academy of Management Review* 27 (2): 204–21.
18. Berkowitz, E. N., 2000, *Marketing,* 6th ed. (New York: McGraw-Hill).
19. Levitt, T., 1983, The globalization of markets, *Harvard Business Review* 61 (3): 92–102.
20. Our discussion of these assumptions draws upon Douglas, S. P., & Wind, Y., 1987, The myth of globalization, *Columbia Journal of World Business,* Winter: 19–29.
21. Wetlaufer, S., 1999, Driving change: An interview with Ford Motor Company's Jacques Nasser, *Harvard Business Review* 77 (2): 76–81.
22. Ghoshal, S., 1987, Global strategy: An organizing framework, *Strategic Management Journal* 8: 425–40.
23. Bartlett, C. A., & Ghoshal, S., 1989, *Managing across Borders: The Transnational Solution* (Boston: Harvard Business School Press).
24. For insights on global branding, refer to Aaker, D. A., & Joachimsthaler, E., 1999, The lure of global branding, *Harvard Business Review* 77 (6): 137–46.
25. For an interesting perspective on how small firms can

compete in their home markets, refer to Dawar & Frost, op. cit., pp. 119–29.

26. Hout, T., Porter, M. E., & Rudden, E., 1982, How global companies win out, *Harvard Business Review* 60 (5): 98–107.

27. Fryer, B., 2001, Tom Siebel of Siebel Systems: High tech the old-fashioned way, *Harvard Business Review* 79 (3): 118–30.

28. The risks that are discussed for the global, multidomestic, and transnational strategies draw upon Gupta & Govindarajan, op. cit.

29. Sigiura, H., 1990, How Honda localizes its global strategy, *Sloan Management Review* 31: 77–82.

30. Prahalad & Lieberthal, op. cit., pp. 68–79. Their article also discusses how firms may have to reconsider their brand management, costs of market building, product design, and approaches to capital efficiency when entering foreign markets.

31. Hofstede, G., 1980, *Culture's Consequences: International Differences in Work-Related Values* (Beverly Hills, CA: Sage); Hofstede, G., 1993, Cultural constraints in management theories, *Academy of Management Executive* 7 (1): 81–94; Kogut, B., & Singh, H., 1988, The effect of national culture on the choice of entry mode, *Journal of International Business Studies* 19: 411–32; and Usinier, J. C., 1996, *Marketing across Cultures* (London: Prentice Hall).

32. McCune, J. C., 1999, Exporting corporate culture, *Management Review,* December: 53–56.

33. This discussion draws upon Bartlett and Ghoshal, op. cit.; and Raisinghani, M., 2000, Transnational organization, in Helms, M. M., ed., *Encyclopedia of Management,* 4th ed. (Detroit: Gale Group), 968–69.

34. Prahalad, C. K., & Doz, Y. L., 1987, *The Multinational Mission: Balancing Local Demands and Global Vision* (New York: Free Press).

35. Kidd, J. B., & Teramoto, Y., 1995, The learning organization: The case of Japanese RHQs in Europe, *Management International Review* 35 (Special Issue): 39–56.

36. Gupta, A. K., & Govindarajan, V., 2000, Knowledge flows within multinational corporations, *Strategic Management Journal* 21 (4): 473–96.

37. Wetlaufer, S., 2001, The business case against revolution: An interview with Nestlé's Peter Brabeck, *Harvard Business Review* 79 (2): 112–21.

38. Nobel, R., & Birkinshaw, J., 1998, Innovation in multinational corporations: Control and communication patterns in international R&D operations, *Strategic Management Journal* 19 (5): 461–78.

39. For a rigorous analysis of performance implications of entry strategies, refer to Zahra, S. A., Ireland, R. D., & Hitt, M. A., 2000, International expansion by new venture firms: International diversity, modes of entry, technological learning, and performance, *Academy of Management Journal* 43 (6): 925–50.

40. Li, J. T., 1995, Foreign entry and survival: The effects of strategic choices on performance in international markets, *Strategic Management Journal* 16: 333–51.

41. For a discussion of how home-country environments can affect diversification strategies, refer to Wan, W. P., & Hoskisson, R. E., 2003, Home country environments, corporate diversification strategies, and firm performance, *Academy of Management Journal* 46 (1): 27–45.

42. Arnold, D., 2000, Seven rules of international distribution, *Harvard Business Review* 78 (6): 131–37.

43. Sharma, A., 1998, Mode of entry and ex-post performance, *Strategic Management Journal* 19 (9): 879–900.

44. This section draws upon Arnold, op. cit., pp. 131–37; and Berkowitz, op. cit.

45. Kline, D., 2003, Strategic licensing, *MIT Sloan Management Review* 44 (3): 89–93.

46. Arnold, op. cit.; and Berkowitz, op. cit.

47. Martin, J., 1999, Franchising in the Middle East, *Management Review,* June: 38–42.

48. Manufacturer-supplier relationships can be very effective in global industries, such as automobile manufacturing. Refer to Kotabe, M., Martin, X., & Domoto, H., 2003, Gaining from vertical partnerships: Knowledge transfer, relationship duration, and supplier performance improvement in the U.S. and Japanese automotive industries, *Strategic Management Journal* 24 (4): 293–316.

49. For a good discussion, refer to Merchant, H., & Schendel, D., 2000, How do international joint ventures create shareholder value? *Strategic Management Journal* 21 (7): 723–38.

50. This discussion draws upon Walters, B. A., Peters, S., & Dess, G. G., 1994, Strategic alliances and joint ventures: Making them work, *Business Horizons* 37 (4): 5–11.

51. For a rigorous discussion of the importance of information access in international joint ventures, refer to Reuer, J. J., & Koza, M. P., 2000, Asymmetric information and joint venture performance: Theory and evidence for domestic and international joint ventures, *Strategic Management Journal* 21 (1): 81–88.

52. Treece, J., 1991, Why Daewoo wound up on the road to nowhere, *BusinessWeek,* September 23: 55.

53. Dyer, J. H., Kale, P., & Singh, H., 2001, How to make strategic alliances work, *MIT Sloan Management Review* 42 (4): 37–43.

54. For a discussion of some of the challenges in managing subsidiaries, refer to O'Donnell, S. W., 2000, Managing foreign subsidiaries: Agents of headquarters, or an independent network? *Strategic Management Journal* 21 (5): 525–48.

55. Mi-Young, A., 2000, Wal-Mart has to adapt to the South Korean consumer, *Deutsche-Presse-agentur,* November 8: 1–3.

chapter 8

Digital Business Strategy:

Leveraging Internet and E-Business Capabilities

chapter objectives

*After
reading this
chapter, you should
have a good understanding of:*

- Why use of Internet technologies is more important to achieving competitive advantage than the technologies themselves.

- How Internet technologies are affecting the five competitive forces.

- How e-business capabilities are affecting industry profitability.

- How firms are using Internet technologies to add value and achieve unique advantages.

- How Internet-enabled business models are being used to improve strategic positioning.

- How firms can improve their competitive position by effectively deploying e-business strategies.

- The pitfalls in each competitive strategy that may endanger a firm's attempts to deploy Internet technologies or implement e-business strategies.

*t*he technological advances that have swept in the new digital economy and created many Internet- and Web-based business have enormous strategic implications. Some of the changes will require that business be conducted in entirely new ways. Others will make it more important to pursue traditional business strategies more effectively. This chapter helps sort out the ramifications of the Internet and e-business for strategic management practices.

We begin by revisiting Porter's five-forces approach to industry analysis. We outline how industry and competitive practices are being affected by the capabilities provided by Internet technologies. On the one hand, the Internet and e-business practices can make some of the five forces stronger, thus potentially suppressing profitability in a given industry. On the other hand, new opportunities created by Internet-based technologies are providing firms with new ways to adapt to and overcome the five forces to achieve a competitive advantage. For each of the five forces, we provide examples that illustrate how the Internet is shifting the nature of competition in several critical ways.

The second section explores how Internet-based businesses and incumbent firms are using digital technologies to add value. We consider four activities—search, evaluation, problem solving, and transaction—as well as three types of content—customer feedback, expertise, and entertainment programming. These technology-enhanced capabilities are providing new means with which firms can achieve competitive advantages.

The third section addresses how competitive strategies should be revised and redeployed in light of the shifts in industry and competitive forces caused by the Internet. Examples show new ways firms are providing low-cost leadership, differentiating, and focusing. Some firms are using cutting-edge technology but seem to ignore tried-and-true strategic practices. Others seem slow to respond to e-business but have built a solid strategy by integrating new capabilities with sound strategic principles.

Consider the fate of Agillion, Inc., a software company created to capitalize on digital technologies and the Internet.[1] Agillion was founded in Austin, Texas, in 1999 during the height of the dot-com boom. During that time, techniques for making the best use of the Web were rapidly evolving. Most companies that had implemented e-business systems just a few years earlier had hired Internet-savvy programmers who built websites and systems to manage them from the ground up. But it was soon realized that carrying Web-specific personnel and managing systems internally was impractical for many companies, especially small businesses that needed to outsource solutions. A new type of company called application service providers (ASPs) was emerging to perform those Web tasks for companies that did not want to install a whole division to manage their e-business activities. ASPs were viewed as the next best thing to hit the Internet, because they would drive costs down by providing expert services for a fraction of the cost of developing and maintaining those services internally. One such company was Agillion.

> Agillion was considered a smart young company that would help take the Internet to the next level with its systems for managing customer relationships. It had a product called Customer-Pages that could connect users to hundreds of customers using personalized Web pages for each client. The cost was only $29.95 per user per month. Companies such as Earthcars.com, a Burlington, Vermont, Web developer for auto dealers, loved the product. "The key advantage of the Agillion service," said Earthcars COO Mark Bonfigli, "is being in sync 24 hours a day with customers and staff. . . . We're in a period of hypergrowth, so this is valuable."
>
> Other companies signed on as well. By early 2001, Agillion had strategic alliances with Cisco, Office Depot, and IBM. These partners served as a channel to deliver Agillion's service to small and midsize businesses. Cisco was also one of its venture partners: along with Morgan Stanley and Goldman Sachs, Cisco helped Agillion raise $40 million in 1999.
>
> But by July 2001, with only $100 in the bank and $20 million in debt, Agillion declared bankruptcy. It had burned through more than $60 million in less than three years. According to a suit filed against six of Agillion's former top executives, the company never had more than a handful of customers: "Their revenue was so inconsequential that management never recorded a single dollar in revenue in their internal bookkeeping," according to the suit.

What Went Wrong at Agillion?   For one thing, it did not provide a clear and unique value proposition and offered a product that could easily be imitated. It also had a weak business model, which failed to use Internet technologies to solve small business's most difficult problems, such as inventory control and sales force management. Third, Agillion had a poorly conceived marketing and sales strategy. Rather than develop its own customer relations more expertly, Agillion overestimated the willingness of small businesses to buy business solutions online and underestimated the bandwidth problems that small business were facing. Finally, Agillion was plagued by a problem that seemed rampant among the digital businesses that collapsed when the Internet bubble burst—it did not have a grip on reality when it came to spending money. The company spent lavishly, including $3 million for a 30-second Super Bowl ad, $13 million for a 10-year lease in Austin's upscale Stonecreek Park, and hundreds of thousands of dollars on company parties and all-expenses-paid trips for its employees. Thus, even though it created a technically advanced new product aimed at a fast-growing market, it ultimately collapsed for failure to manage strategically and conduct itself professionally.

As the Agillion case indicates, entry into the fast-moving Internet economy does not guarantee success. Nevertheless, the business world is embracing the Internet and other digital technologies. Alan Greenspan, chairman of the U.S. Federal Reserve System, stated, "the revolution in information technology has altered the structure of the way the American economy works."[2] The information technology (IT) revolution is having a broad impact on industries and this has important strategic implications. Despite the economic slump that accompanied the crash of hundreds of dot-com start-ups in 2000 and 2001, both consumers and businesses remain optimistic that the Internet will have a positive economic impact in the long term.[3]

The impact of the information technology revolution, however, goes beyond the Internet. At a more basic level, it is the shift from analog to digital technologies that is responsible for so many new IT capabilities. Analog was once the primary technology for conveying information such as music recordings, voice communications, and television signals. It represents a type of physical information that requires large amounts of storage and often works only with hard wired equipment. By contrast, digital technologies use information in the form of bits, that is, electronic signals expressed as either on or off, one or zero. These bits can be stored in tiny chips, easily reproduced and transferred rapidly and wirelessly.[4] Many technologies have made the switch from analog to digital—phones, photographs, television signals, and even books—and the trend suggests digitization is here to stay. As a result, digital technology capabilities, which, in essence, make the Internet possible, are a major driver in today's economy. Strategy Spotlight 8.1 describes types of commerce, beyond e-commerce, that have been enabled by digital technology.

These technology-driven initiatives—the Internet, wireless communications, and other digital technologies—are having a significant impact on the economy. They have done so by changing the ways businesses interact with each other and with consumers. This has not only created an environment in which businesses must perform at a higher level—faster, smarter, cheaper—but also it has created many new business opportunities. Consider how one company, British Petroleum (BP), has used the Internet and digital technologies to transform its business:

> British Petroleum (BP) is one company that believes the Internet is here to stay.[5] Not only has it achieved a number of strategic advantages with its Internet initiatives, it recently had $300 million in savings in a single year to show for it. Led by John Leggate, BP's group vice president for digital business, the company has pursued an aggressive policy of implementing Internet-based capabilities. The effort has paid off in several key areas:
>
> ♦ *Finding Crude.* Instead of sending teams to far-off exploration targets, BP scientists now gather in any of 15 data centers around the globe to view digital 3-D images of drilling sites sent over the Web. *Payoff:* Up to $250 million in annual savings.
> ♦ *Buying Gear.* BP's divisions used to bid separately for everything from hard hats to drill bits. In a recent year, BP bought 4 percent of its $25 billion in purchases online. *Payoff:* $100 million in savings by identifying low-cost suppliers.
> ♦ *Getting Smarter.* All employees have personalized Web pages listing their areas of expertise. This helps managers tap into BP's reservoir of knowledge. *Payoff:* In one case, engineers in the Caribbean saved $600,000 by adopting a drilling process developed in Norway just days earlier.
> ♦ *Selling Stuff.* BP is spending $200 million to link service stations to the Net. Web-linked gas pumps and in-store e-kiosks let customers check traffic and weather or get free driving directions. *Payoff:* BP hopes this will help generate half of its service station retail sales from goods other than fuel within five years, up from 20 percent of their $2.6 billion in total sales in a recent year.

BP's experience is rare. Unfortunately, far more companies have had experiences like Agillion's—failed attempts to capitalize on a new technology in a rapidly expanding market. Many firms got caught up in the Internet "gold rush." At the height of the Internet boom, some writers claimed that familiar business terms such as "competitive advantage," "industry analysis," and "long-term customer relations" were relics of a bygone era, icons of the "Old Economy."[6] Others, however, contended that the Internet has created a new climate for business in which sound principles of strategic management are *more*, not less

Beyond E-Commerce: The Wireless, Digital Economy

The Internet has been a leading and highly visible component of a broader technological phenomenon—the emergence of digital technology. These technologies are altering the way business is conducted. According to digital economy visionary Don Tapscott:

> The Net is much more than just another technology development; the Net represents something qualitatively new—an unprecedented, powerful, universal communications medium. Far surpassing radio and television, this medium is digital, infinitely richer, and interactive. . . . Mobile computing devices, broadband access, wireless networks, and computing power embedded in everything from refrigerators to automobiles are converging into a global network that will enable people to use the Net just about anywhere and anytime.

Thus, the Internet provides a staging area for numerous digital technologies. And now with the development of wireless communications, new types of Internet-based commerce have begun to appear. Here are a few examples:

- **T-Commerce.** Television commerce. Wireless keyboards combined with Internet applications that attach to televisions make it possible to interact with the Internet while viewing your living room TV set.

- **M-Commerce.** Mobile commerce. Handheld devices such as cell phones or personal digital

assistants (PDAs) can serve as "wireless wallets" that allow users to purchase products and services from vending machines or businesses without having to use a checkbook, credit card, or cash.

- **U-Commerce.** Universal or ubiquitous commerce. Mobile devices that connect to the Internet through wireless networks make it possible to conduct business anywhere, anytime. These "always-on" technologies, in effect, make the customer the point of sale.

All these forms of commerce rely on wireless communications, a rapidly growing phenomenon. Starbucks, for example, is installing a wireless network (known as "Wi-Fi" for wireless fidelity) in more than 2,100 of its coffee shops. Wireless technologies are being used by businesses for everything from mission-critical communications to attracting singles to nightclubs with text messages that offer free drinks.

But the future is uncertain. The reach and reliability of wireless communications is limited by current technology—Wi-Fi may be replaced by more powerful networks before it ever generates a return on investment for Starbucks and others. And, unlike analog technologies, electronic bits of digital data zooming through space can be more easily lost, stolen, or manipulated.

Not so long ago, the future of the Internet seemed cloudy. Now, the Internet is commonplace across nearly every sector of the economy. Wireless is the next big technological wave that faces an uncertain future. But according to a recent study by the consulting firm Accenture, "Wireless will be bigger and more important than anyone imagines." Stay tuned . . .

Sources: H. Green, "Wi-Fi Means Business," *BusinessWeek,* April 28, 2003, pp. 86–92; L. Ward, "Is M-Commerce Dead and Buried?" *E-Commerce Times,* May 9, 2003, www.ecommercetimes.com; "T-Commerce acceptance already high," *allNetDevices,* April 13, 2001, www.allnetdevices.com; N. Macaluso, "Report: E-tail Needs to Be Ready for 'U-Commerce,' " *E-Commerce Times,* October 2, 2001, www.ecommercetimes.com; and D. Tapscott, "Rethinking Strategy in a Networked World," *Strategy and Business,* 3rd quarter, 2001, 34–41.

important.[7] Indeed, the changes caused by the Internet and digital economy have made strategizing more challenging. Rapid improvements in technology, globalization, shifting patterns of demand, and uncertainty about costs and revenues are highlighting the importance of strategy formulation. Successful implementation, which seemed to be ignored by firms such as Agillion that were poorly focused on building a sustainable e-business, may be even more difficult in the Internet era because of the uncertainty surrounding the new technology. Even so, the Internet phenomenon is steadily expanding. Strategy Spotlight 8.2 describes how the Internet is growing and recent trends in the use of digital technologies.

Clearly, the Internet phenomenon has heightened the need for effective strategic management. However, the keys to success involve more than just putting up a website or creating a dot-com enterprise. Digital business success requires a new strategic perspective

strategy spotlight

The Impact of the Internet on Business and the Economy

According to Jack Welch, former chairman of General Electric, the Internet is "the single most important event in the U.S. economy since the Industrial Revolution." The Internet phenomenon promises to change dramatically the way business is conducted in every corner of the globe.

The growth in Internet use has been especially rapid compared with the adoption rate of other technologies. It took decades for radio, television, and other popular 20th-century technologies to be adopted, but the Internet reached 50 million users in less than five years. Exhibit 8.1 illustrates two of the rapid growth trends that are associated with the Internet.

So what happened in the era of the "Tech Wreck" when so many dot-coms failed and the technology sector of the U.S. economy slumped so dramatically? In the mid-1990s, the economy was propelled by a strong mix of information technology and available venture capital that led to rapid growth, plentiful jobs, and glorious—or so it seemed—investment opportunities. This combination of radically new, vaguely understood, yet unproven forces seemed to defy the laws of economics. It led U.S. Federal Reserve chairman Alan Greenspan to warn that "irrational exuberance" might lead to unwise investments and economic trouble.

Then, in 2000 and 2001 the Internet bubble burst. Investors suddenly realized that dot-coms were overcapitalized and that some might never show profits. Venture capital dried up and stock values plummeted, leading to the demise of many start-ups. The pendulum swung to the opposite extreme, creating an irrational aversion to anything "dot-com." The downturn that followed dragged consumer confidence down as well and corporate capital spending fell to 10-year lows.

Even after such a strong downturn, however, there is solid evidence of growth in Internet business. On the retail side, revenues from business-to-consumer (B2C) e-commerce have been steadily growing. According to a study by Shop.org and Forrester Research, online retail sales reached $76 billion in 2002 and will top the $100 billion mark in 2004, which represents 4.5 percent of total retail sales.

The real future for Internet business, many analysts agree, is in business-to-business (B2B) e-commerce, which is expected to grow worldwide to $4.3 trillion by 2005, according to International Data Corp (IDC). But e-commerce is just one aspect of e-business uses of the Internet. For example, business process outsourcing (BPO), consisting of services ranging from online order management to online payroll and benefits administration, is expected to grow worldwide to $248 billion by 2005. Perhaps even more important from a strategic standpoint are the savings: Giga Information Group Inc. reported that the cost savings globally from business use of e-commerce will grow to $1.25 trillion by the mid-decade.

These factors have led many to conclude that the era of the Internet was not a fluke, but the beginning of a new economic cycle in which technology will drive increases in productivity and entrepreneurial energies will stimulate innovative uses of the Internet's new capabilities. Futurist Alvin Toffler claimed, "Anyone who thinks the New Economy is over because of the dot-com crash is either defining it too narrowly or being naive. That's like saying the Industrial Revolution was over because some London textile plants shut down in the 1830s."

However, it appears that the transformative power of the Internet is being felt unevenly; some sectors of the economy will benefit more than others. Information-intensive industries such as financial services, entertainment, health care, and education could be radically transformed. And e-commerce spending continues to grow in several major categories, including travel services, clothing, computer hardware and software, and electronics.

Even in those industries where the Internet can play a central role, however, the big changes are not going to come overnight, because the industries have huge institutional and regulatory barriers and strong vested interests. As a result, in health care and education, where the benefits from widespread use of the Web are potentially enormous, progress is likely to occur in baby steps over time. In banking, the use of widely anticipated capabilities such as online bill paying has been slowed because banks and the billing organizations can't seem to agree upon the way bills should actually appear online.

One encouraging trend that promises to accelerate the use and effectiveness of the Internet is the improvements in Internet connectivity and speed. In particular, the use of broadband Internet connections (which include both cable TV and DSL) had climbed to 48 million U.S. households by early 2004, a 60 percent increase in a single year. Millions more have access at their place of work. Since broadband connections are always on, people can get online much faster, and usually do. Broadband users spend two-thirds more time online—about 2 hours more per day—after signing up for high-speed *(continued)*

Sources: E. C. Baig, "Internet Surfers Dumping Dial-up for High Speed," *USA Today,* April 18, 2004, www.usatoday.com; L. Walczak, "The Mood Now," *BusinessWeek,* August 27, 2001, pp. 74–78; G. Anders, "Buying Frenzy," *Wall Street Journal,* July 12, 1999, pp. R6–R10; M. J. Mandel and R. D. Hof, "Rethinking the Internet," *BusinessWeek,* March 26, 2001, pp. 117–122; S. Hamm, "E-Biz: Down but Hardly Out," *BusinessWeek,* March 26, 2001, pp. 126–30; "BPO Market to Reach $122B in 2003," *CyberAtlas,* June 11, 2003, www.cyberatlas.com; "B2B E-Commerce Headed for Trillions," *CyberAtlas,* March 6, 2002; www.shop.org; T. J. Mullaney, "At Last, the Web Hits 100 MPH," *BusinessWeek,* June 23, 2003, pp. 80–81.

service. Once there, they also spend more—around $523 annually, which represents an increase of 29 percent.

Clearly, the Internet has already changed the world irrevocably and will continue to have a major impact on business.

(a)

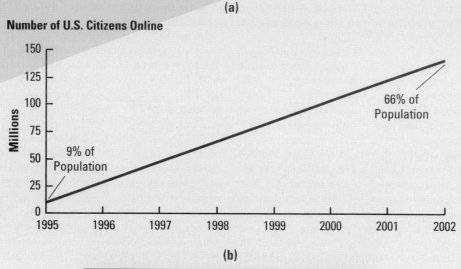

Number of U.S. Citizens Online

(b)

Internet Use Worldwide		
	Internet Users (in millions)	
Geographic Region	**2002**	**2007 (estimated)**
North America	178,530	254,350
Western Europe	151,999	290,999
Eastern Europe/Russia	34,155	98,151
Asia-Pacific	237,922	615,571
South/Central America	39,146	110,893
Middle East/Africa	23,922	96,287
Total Internet Users	665,674	1,466,251

Exhibit 8.1 Growth in Internet Activity

Sources: *CyberAtlas,* Harris Interactive; *Computer Industry Almanac.*

that builds on the possibilities provided by information technologies and permits Internet connectivity to transform the way business is conducted. The dot-com crash provides an important lesson about the strategic implications of the Internet: It is the actual use of the Internet for profitable transactions, not the technology itself, that matters to a company's bottom line. Yet it is the technology that is making it possible to conduct new types of transactions and enhance interactions with nearly every important stakeholder—customers, suppliers, employees, stockholders, competitors, government regulators, and others.

Thus, the Internet presents a new strategic challenge: how to make the best use of the new technology without losing sight of important business fundamentals.

As we have seen, strategy can play a key role in the success of Internet enterprises. Next, we will evaluate Michael Porter's five-forces model in terms of the actual use of the Internet and the new technological capabilities that it makes possible.

How the Internet Is Affecting the Five Competitive Forces
The Threat of New Entrants

In most industries, new entrants will be a bigger threat now because Internet-based technologies lower barriers to entry. For example, it is relatively inexpensive for a new firm to create a Web presence that is even more impressive than the website of a larger or more established competitor. Unlike the traditional "Main Street" business, where customers could assess the firm's size and quality by walking in the door, businesses that exist in cyberspace can create an appearance that makes them seem like strong competitors, regardless of their actual size or the quality of their operations. Thus, scale economies may be less important in this context and new entrants can go to market with lower capital costs. Consider the example of Florist.com.

> When Aron Benon founded Florist.com in 1997, his strategy couldn't have been more different than most of the dot-coms that were exploding onto the Web scene. Instead of raising millions in venture capital, he converted his tiny Beverly Hills, California, flower shop, Floral & Hardy, into an even tinier online operation. He hired just four employees, including his wife, and during the week before Valentine's Day, he told his Web employees to bring their cell phones to work so they wouldn't tie up his company's bare-bones phone system. "I'm going to keep it grassroots," Benon said. "Only when the business proves itself to us will we spend the money to get bigger." The strategy seems to be working: In 2000 Florist.com turned a $1 million profit on $3 million in sales. Today, Florist.com is the fourth largest floral retailer online.[8]

Beyond mere appearances, businesses launched on the Internet may enjoy savings on other traditional expenses such as office rent, sales force salaries, printing, and postage. This may encourage more entrants who, because of the lower start-up expenses, see an opportunity to capture market share by offering a product or performing a service more efficiently than existing competitors. Thus, a new cyberentrant can use the savings provided by the Internet to charge lower prices and compete on price despite the incumbent's scale advantages. Alternatively, because Internet technologies make it possible for young firms to provide services that are equivalent or superior to an incumbent, a new entrant may be able to serve a market more effectively, with more personalized services and greater attention to product details. A new firm may be able to build a reputation in its niche and charge premium prices. By so doing, it can capture small pieces of an incumbent's business and erode profitability.

Another potential benefit of Web-based business is access to distribution channels. Manufacturers or distributors that can reach potential outlets for their products more efficiently by means of the Internet may be encouraged to enter markets that were previously closed to them. Such access is not guaranteed, however, because of the strong barriers to entry that may exist in certain industries.[9] The failure of eToys.com, which did an effective job of building brand recognition over the two or three years that it flourished, was caused by many factors. Perhaps the most damaging blow, however, came just prior to the critical Christmas 2000 season, when it could not obtain the top-selling toys from distributors who had close relationships with established retailers such as Toys "Я" Us, and Wal-Mart. As a result, sales lagged behind projections, and consumers who had once thought that eToys deserved a chance turned elsewhere.[10]

The Bargaining Power of Buyers

The Internet and wireless technologies may increase buyer power by providing consumers with more information to make buying decisions and lowering switching costs. But these technologies may also suppress the power of traditional buyer channels that have concentrated buying power in the hands of a few, giving buyers new ways to access sellers. In industries such as book publishing, where the flow of products to market has traditionally been determined by strong intermediaries such as wholesalers and distributors, buyer power is shifting because of the Internet. To sort out these differences, let's first distinguish between two types of buyers: end users and buyer channel intermediaries.

End users, as the name implies, are the final customers in a distribution channel. They are the consumers who actually buy a product and put it to use. Internet sales activity that is labeled "B2C"—that is, business-to-consumer—is concerned with end users. The Internet is likely to increase the power of these buyers for several reasons. First, a large amount of consumer information is available on the Internet. This gives end users the information they need to shop for quality merchandise and bargain for price concessions. The automobile industry provides an excellent example of this phenomenon. For a small fee, agencies such as Consumers Union (publishers of *Consumer Reports*) will provide customers with detailed information about actual automobile manufacturer costs.[11] This information, available online, can be used to bid down dealers' profits.

Second, an end user's switching costs are also potentially much lower because of the Internet. Setting aside the psychological cost of switching due to an unwillingness by consumers to switch brands, the physical cost of switching may involve only a few clicks of the mouse to find and view a competing product or service online. As a result, according to Web strategist David Siegel, businesses that are serious about selling online will need to become increasingly customer-led. That is, they must be willing to listen to customers more often and respond to them more quickly. "E-customers aren't loyal to a brand," says Siegel. "They may be attracted to a specific business proposition, but their memories are very short. Solve one problem for them, and they have another. Companies must earn their networked customers' loyalty with *every* new deal."[12] In this environment, buyers are likely to have much more bargaining power.[13]

The bargaining power of distribution channel buyers may decrease because of the Internet. *Buyer channel* intermediaries are the wholesalers, distributors, and retailers who serve as intermediaries between manufacturers and end users. In some industries, they are dominated by powerful players that control who gains access to the latest goods or the best merchandise. The Internet and wireless communications, however, make it much easier and less expensive for businesses to reach customers directly. This is especially valuable for specialized companies that can focus their promotional efforts on marketplace segments that are more easily identified via the Internet. Thus, the Internet may increase the power of incumbent firms relative to that of traditional buyer channels.

It is important to note that this new capability to reach customers directly may not always be good for business. Indeed, the Internet has worsened *channel conflict,* the problem that arises when end users can access the same products through several different outlets. The more outlets from which a product can be purchased, the lower the potential profitability for any single outlet. Consider the case of Levi Strauss.

The problem of channel conflict arose for Levi's when it first launched an e-commerce website. Levi Strauss & Co., a San Francisco–based corporation, made a bold move in announcing that its website would be the only place consumers could buy Levi's and Dockers online. But it ran into numerous difficulties in profitably maintaining its online presence. One of the biggest problems concerned the retail outlets for Levi's products. Shoppers were turning to the Internet to buy their jeans, taking business away from Levi's key retail partners. After less than a year, Levi's announced it was pulling the plug on its online store and revamping its strategy: It would direct customers to its top retailers Macy's and JC Penney to handle the task of selling its products.[14]

Even though the Internet provides a valuable new channel for many companies, manufacturers such as Levi's still rely on traditional bricks-and-mortar outlets to sell their products.

The Bargaining Power of Suppliers

Use of the Internet and digital technologies to speed up and streamline the process of acquiring supplies is already benefiting many sectors of the economy. But the net effect of the Internet on supplier power will depend on the nature of competition in a given industry. As with buyer power, the extent to which the Internet is a benefit or a detriment may also hinge on the supplier's position along the supply chain.

The role of suppliers typically involves providing products or services to other businesses. Thus, the term "B2B"—that is, business-to-business—is often used to refer to businesses that supply or sell to other businesses. The effect of the Internet on the bargaining power of suppliers is a double-edged sword. On the one hand, Internet technologies make it possible for suppliers to access more of their business customers at a relatively lower cost per customer. Recall from Chapter 2 how online auction company FreeMarkets saves money by using the Internet to organize auctions that allow its industrial buyers to efficiently contact many suppliers. On the other hand, suppliers may not be able to hold onto these customers, because buyers can do comparative shopping and price negotiations so much faster on the Internet and can turn to other suppliers with a few clicks of the mouse. This is especially damaging to supply-chain intermediaries, such as product distributors, who may not be able to stop suppliers from directly accessing other potential business customers.

In general, one of the greatest threats to supplier power is that the Internet inhibits the ability of suppliers to offer highly differentiated products or unique services. Most procurement technologies can be imitated by competing suppliers, and the technologies that make it possible to design and customize new products rapidly are being used by all competitors. For example, Moen, the faucet manufacturer, sends digital designs of new faucets by way of e-mail to its suppliers worldwide to review. Suggestions for improvement are consolidated and final adjustments are made simultaneously. In a recent period, these practices cut design time from 24 to 16 months and boosted sales by 17 percent.[15] However, Delta and other competitors have implemented similar techniques to improve their own cycle time and boost sales.

Other factors may also contribute to stronger supplier power. First, the growth of new Web-based business in general may create more downstream outlets for suppliers to sell to. Second, suppliers may be able to create Web-based purchasing arrangements that make purchasing easier and discourage their customers from switching. Ariba, a leading vendor of B2B software, develops online procurement systems that suppliers can install on the computer systems of their customers, thus creating a direct link that reduces transactions costs and paperwork.[16] Third, the use of proprietary software that links buyers to a supplier's website may create a rapid, low-cost ordering capability that discourages the buyer from seeking other sources of supply. Amazon.com, for example, created and patented One-Click purchasing technology that speeds up the ordering process for customers who enroll in the service.[17]

Finally, suppliers will have greater power to the extent that they can reach end users directly without intermediaries. Previously, suppliers often had to work through intermediaries who brought their products or services to market for a fee. But a process known as *disintermediation* is removing the organizations or business process layers responsible for

Despite the many benefits of doing business online, there is one feature the Internet cannot replace—human interaction. Sometimes a customer just wants to a talk to a real person. That's why online broker E-Trade launched its Club eTrade service. Aimed at high net worth customers, it is designed to offer a level of personal attention that is otherwise absent from the Internet. In the first four months of operation, it generated $460 million in new assets by directing 2,200 of its existing customers to new financial products.

E-Trade is not the only company to recognize the importance of supplementing its Internet services with the personal touch. According to Marten Hoekstra, executive vice president and director of the client relationship team at UBS PaineWebber, "Traditional financial advisers have not and will not be disintermediated by the Internet." As a result, Hoekstra and other online brokers are following E-Trade's lead.

The personal touch has proven effective for online retailing as well. Lands' End, which implemented a real-time online chat feature at its website, reports that new customers are 70 percent more likely to buy if they "talk" to a sales rep first using online chat. As NetBank President and CEO Michael Fitzgerald put it, "We do need to personalize this impersonal medium."

Sources: T. J. Mullaney, "At Last, the Web Hits 100 MPH," *BusinessWeek*, June 23, 2003, pp. 80–81; A. Collins, "Personal Touch Pays Off," *Business 2.0*, March 2001, www.business2.com.

intermediary steps in the value chain of many industries.[18] This is a major new business reality that the Internet has made possible, and it has significant strategic implications. As Larry Downes and Chunka Mui state in their book, *Unleashing the Killer App:*

> If buyers and sellers can find each other cheaply over the Internet, who needs agents (for instance, insurance) and distributors (for instance, home computers)? Complex transactions are becoming disaggregated, and middlemen who are not adding sufficient value relative to the open market are being disintermediated.[19]

Just as the Internet is eliminating some business functions, it is creating an opening for new functions. These new activities are entering the value chain by a process known as *reintermediation,* the introduction of new types of intermediaries. Many of these new functions are affecting traditional supply chains. In consumer markets, for example, delivery services are enjoying a boom because of the Internet. Many more consumers are choosing to have products delivered to their door rather than going out to pick them up. Electronic delivery is also becoming common. For example, California-based EncrypTix is using bar-code printing technology to let customers print out their own tickets to movies, concerts, and sporting events.[20] In business markets, e-commerce has created the need for new types of financial intermediaries that can perform clearing functions for purchases made online. New products (e.g., online credit cards) and new services (e.g., online escrow services) have been introduced as use of the Internet has grown. Strategy Spotlight 8.3 shows how online stock broker E-Trade refused to be disintermediated. It improved customer service and boosted performance by reintroducing the human factor into the online financial services business. Exhibit 8.2 demonstrates how the processes of disintermediation and reintermediation are altering the traditional channels by which manufacturers reach consumers.

The Threat of Substitutes

Along with traditional marketplaces, the Internet has created a new marketplace; along with traditional channels, it has become a new channel. In general, therefore, the threat of substitutes is heightened because the Internet introduces new ways to accomplish the same tasks.

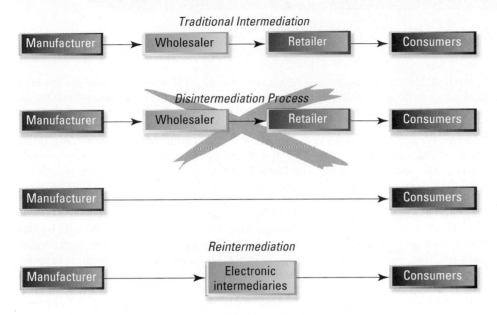

Exhibit 8.2 Disintermediation and Reintermediation

The primary factor that leads to substitution is economic. Consumers will generally choose to use a product or service until a substitute that meets the same need becomes available at a lower cost. The economies created by Internet technologies have led to the development of numerous substitutes for traditional ways of doing business. For example, a company called Conferenza is offering an alternative way to participate in conferences for people who don't want to spend the time and money to attend. The website provides summaries of many conference events, quality ratings using an "event intelligence" score, and schedules of upcoming events.[21]

Another example of substitution is in the realm of electronic storage. With expanded use of desktop computing capabilities during the last 20 years, the need to store information electronically has increased dramatically. Until recently, the trend has been to create increasingly larger desktop storage capabilities and techniques for compressing information using compacting and "zipping" methods that create storage efficiencies. But a viable substitute has recently emerged: storing information on the Web. Companies such as My Docs Online Inc. are providing Web-based storage that firms can access simply by going online. Rather than purchasing more megabytes of storage space, firms can now lease cyberspace. Since these storage places are virtual, they can be accessed anywhere the Web can be accessed. This makes it possible for a traveler to access important documents and files without transporting them physically from place to place. Cyberstorage is not free, but it is still cheaper and more convenient than purchasing and carrying additional disk storage.[22]

Another substitute is in market research, which was traditionally conducted through mailed questionnaires and test marketing. These can be expensive to plan and administer. Questionnaires must be designed, printed, and mailed—all activities that have a hard cost. New products were often rolled out one city at a time to test the responses of a typical group of a few shoppers before a major launch. But Web technologies have reduced the time and cost of marketing. Insight Express is an online market research firm that can survey 300 people for around $1,000. Initially launched to conduct test marketing for mom-and-pop operations, the company is now test-marketing new names, logos, product ideas, and even business concepts for major online players such as E-Trade and Yahoo![23]

Internet Privacy and Ethics

Internet technologies have created new and far-reaching ways to invade consumer privacy. Consider, for example, cookies: Whenever you visit a website for the first time, a record of that visit is generated and stored on your hard drive. These data packets, known as cookies, are used for several purposes. For example, if you return to a website where you have left products in an electronic shopping cart, the cookie on your hard drive is passed back to the Web server to identify you and restore the contents of your shopping cart. This generally occurs without your knowledge or consent.

If this were the only way cookies were used, most Web surfers probably would not care. But cookies can also gather name and address information, phone numbers, the physical location of a computer, and a history of a Web user's browsing habits. These tracking technologies have generated new ways to invade the privacy of consumers. Would you feel invaded if your personal buying habits were linked to your Internet surfing history and this information was sold to businesses that wanted to target you with their direct marketing ads?

Consumer groups have called for legislation to control the extent to which Web-generated information can be used by businesses. Concerns about such practices were

heightened in early 2000, when the Electronic Privacy Information Center (EPIC) filed a complaint with the U.S. Federal Trade Commission concerning the information collection practices of DoubleClick, Inc., a major Internet advertising company. EPIC was alarmed because DoubleClick had merged with Abacus Direct, a large catalog database firm. One of the aims of the newly merged company was to combine DoubleClick's Internet surfing records with the detailed personal profiles contained in the Abacus database. DoubleClick temporarily halted these practices because of the pressure brought by EPIC. Then, in 2002, as part of a settlement with attorneys general in 10 U.S. states who had also filed complaints, DoubleClick agreed to create a "cookie viewer" feature that allowed Internet users to view some of the data it was tracking. Evan Hendricks, publisher of *Privacy Times*, noted that DoubleClick used a rationale similar to that found in the U.S. Fair Credit Report Act, which ensures that people can inspect their personal credit histories. Some privacy advocates, however, feel the company did not go far enough in providing consumer access to individual profiles. And, at the time of the settlement, DoubleClick was unwilling to state when the cookie viewer feature would be available. Clearly, the issue of Internet privacy will continue to be watched closely as the ethical dilemmas created by these new technologies are debated by both consumers and businesses.

Sources: J. Glasner, "DoubleClick to Open Cookie Jar," *Wired News,* August 27, 2002, www.wired.com; S. Caswell, "DoubleClick Caves in to Save Its Cookies," *E-Commerce Times,* March 3, 2000; and www.epic.org.

Products can be tested more quickly in cyberspace. This is driven in part by the Internet's ability to capture detailed information using electronic "cookies," records stored on the user's own hard drive that indicate which websites the user has visited. Other information can also be captured: how long a visitor views a Web page, whether he or she clicks through a banner ad, and whether a purchase is made.[24] Such detailed information is invaluable to marketers trying to determine how to target their advertising. It also has enormous ethical implications for consumer privacy. Strategy Spotlight 8.4 describes some of the ethical issues surrounding this powerful new Internet capability.

The Intensity of Competitive Rivalry

Because the Internet creates more tools and means for competing, rivalry among competitors is likely to be more intense. Only those competitors that can use the Web to give themselves a distinct image, create unique product offerings, or provide "faster, smarter, cheaper" services are likely to capture greater profitability with the new technology. Such gains are hard to sustain, however, because in most cases the new technology can be imitated quickly. Thus, the Internet tends to increase rivalry by making it difficult for firms to differentiate themselves and by shifting customer attention to issues of price.

As we saw in Chapter 2, rivalry is more intense when switching costs are low and product or service differentiation is minimized. Because the Internet makes it possible to shop around with a few clicks of the mouse, it has "commoditized" products that might previously have been regarded as rare or unique. Since the Internet eliminates the importance of location, products that previously had to be sought out in geographically distant outlets are now readily available online. This makes competitors in cyberspace seem more equally balanced, thus intensifying rivalry.

The problem is made worse for marketers by the presence of shopping "bots" and infomediaries that search the Web for the best possible prices. Consumer websites like mySimon and PriceSCAN seek out all the Web locations that sell similar products and provide price comparisons.[25] Obviously, this hinders a firm's ability to establish unique characteristics and focuses the consumer exclusively on price. Some shopping infomediaries, such as BizRate and CNET, not only search for the lowest prices on many different products but also rank the customer service quality of different sites that sell similarly priced items.[26] This is important because research indicates that customer service is three times more important than price to repeat online sales.[27] Such infomediary services are good for consumers because they give them the chance to compare services as well as price. For businesses, however, they increase rivalry by consolidating the marketing message that consumers use to make a purchase decision to a few key pieces of information over which the selling company has little control.

Recognizing that this phenomenon is part of the new Internet reality, many companies willingly participate in such services.[28] For example, BestBookBuys.com is a site that searches for the best prices among the websites of 24 different booksellers, including major ones such as Amazon and Barnes & Noble.[29] The booksellers featured on the site are member participants. They have agreed to have their prices included because it provides another kind of access to consumers. If they refused to be included, book buyers might never consider doing business with them. At least this way, there is a possibility that a new buyer will be attracted to a bookseller's site and make a return visit.

Exhibit 8.3 summarizes many of the ways the Internet is affecting industry structure. These influences will also change how companies develop and deploy strategies to generate above-average profits and sustainable competitive advantage. We turn to these topics next.

How the Internet Adds Value

Using a five-forces framework, we have identified how the Internet and other digital technologies are influencing the competitive landscape. Next we turn to how companies can use these technologies to add value and create competitive advantages. As we noted earlier, the technology itself, whether it is digital or Internet, becomes strategically significant only when its practical application creates new value.

Clearly, the Internet has changed the way business is conducted. By conducting business online and using digital technologies to streamline operations, the Internet is helping companies create new value propositions. Let's take a look at several ways these changes have added new value. Exhibit 8.4 illustrates four related activities that are being revolutionized by the Internet—search, evaluation, problem solving, and transaction.[30]

Search Activities

Search refers to the process of gathering information and identifying purchase options. The Internet has enhanced both the speed of information gathering and the breadth of information that can be accessed. This enhanced search capability is one of the key reasons the Internet has lowered switching costs—by decreasing the cost of search. These efficiency

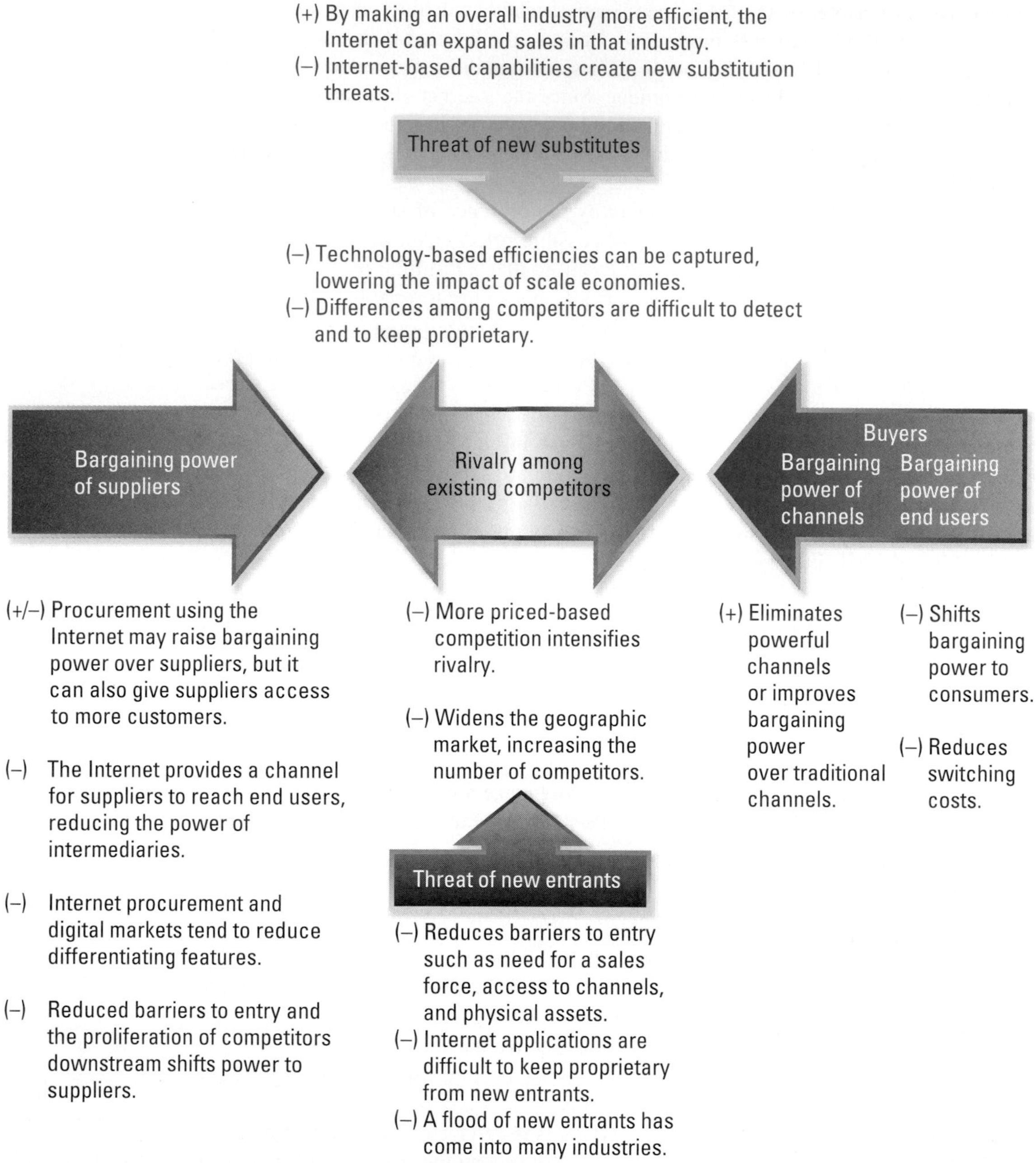

(+) By making an overall industry more efficient, the
Internet can expand sales in that industry.
(−) Internet-based capabilities create new substitution
threats.

Threat of new substitutes

(−) Technology-based efficiencies can be captured,
lowering the impact of scale economies.
(−) Differences among competitors are difficult to detect
and to keep proprietary.

Bargaining power
of suppliers

Rivalry among
existing competitors

Buyers
Bargaining   Bargaining
power of   power of
channels   end users

(+/−) Procurement using the
Internet may raise bargaining
power over suppliers, but it
can also give suppliers access
to more customers.

(−) The Internet provides a channel
for suppliers to reach end users,
reducing the power of
intermediaries.

(−) Internet procurement and
digital markets tend to reduce
differentiating features.

(−) Reduced barriers to entry and
the proliferation of competitors
downstream shifts power to
suppliers.

(−) More priced-based
competition intensifies
rivalry.

(−) Widens the geographic
market, increasing the
number of competitors.

Threat of new entrants

(−) Reduces barriers to entry
such as need for a sales
force, access to channels,
and physical assets.
(−) Internet applications are
difficult to keep proprietary
from new entrants.
(−) A flood of new entrants has
come into many industries.

(+) Eliminates
powerful
channels
or improves
bargaining
power
over traditional
channels.

(−) Shifts
bargaining
power to
consumers.

(−) Reduces
switching
costs.

Exhibit 8.3 How the Internet Influences Industry Structure

Source: Adapted and reprinted by permission of *Harvard Business Review*, exhibit from "Strategy and the Internet," by M. E. Porter,
March 2001. Copyright © 2001 by the Harvard Business School Publishing Corporation; all rights reserved.

gains have greatly benefited buyers. Suppliers also have benefited. Small suppliers that had
difficulty getting noticed can more easily be found, and large suppliers can publish thousands of pages of information for a fraction of the cost that hard-copy catalogs once required. Additionally, online search engines have accelerated the search process to incredible speeds. Consider the example of Google:

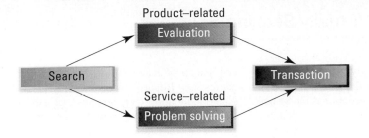

Exhibit 8.4 Internet Activities That Add Value

Sources: Adapted from M. Zeng and W. Reinartz, "Beyond Online Search: The Road to Profitability," *California Management Review,* Winter 2003, pp. 107–30; and C. B. Stabell and O. D. Fjeldstad, "Configuring Value for Competitive Advantage: On Chains, Shops, and Networks," *Strategic Management Journal* 19 (1998), pp. 413–37.

Google, a search engine developed as a project by two graduate students, has become the number one search service in just four years. Why? Because it is capable of incredible things: Using 10,000 networked computers, it searches 3 billion Web pages in an average of 500 milliseconds. To do the same search manually, by thumbing through 3 billion pages at the rate of one minute per page, would take 5,707 years. This ability has made Google an essential tool for many businesses. As a result, Google has built a powerful advertising business. Mark Kini, who runs a small limousine service in Boston, spends 80 percent of his advertising budget on Google and other search engines. "It's how we survive the recession," says Kini.[31]

Evaluation Activities

Evaluation refers to the process of considering alternatives and comparing the costs and benefits of various options. Online services that facilitate comparative shopping, provide product reviews, and catalog customer evaluations of performance have made the Internet a valuable resources. For example, BizRate.com offers extensive product ratings that can help evaluate products. Sites such as CNET that provide comparative pricing have helped lower prices even for quality products that have traditionally maintained premium prices. Opinion-based sites such as ePinions.com and PlanetFeedback.com provide reports of consumer experiences with various vendors.

Many Internet businesses, according to digital business experts Ming Zeng and Werner Reinartz, could improve their performance by making a stronger effort to help buyers evaluate purchases.[32] Even so, only certain types of products can be evaluated online. Products such as CDs that appeal primarily to the sense of sound sell well on the Internet. But products that appeal to multiple senses are harder to evaluate online. This explains why products such as furniture and fashion have never been strong online sellers. It's one thing to look at a leather sofa, but to be able to sit in it as well as touch and smell the leather online is impossible.

Problem-Solving Activities

Problem solving refers to the process of identifying problems or needs and generating ideas and action plans to address those needs. Whereas evaluation is primarily product-related, problem solving is typically used in the context of services. Customers usually have unique problems and therefore are handled one at a time. For example, online travel services such as Travelocity help customers select from many options to form a unique travel package. Furthermore, problem solving often involves providing answers immediately (compared to

Eli Lilly: Virtually Seeking Solutions—Worldwide

In 2001 pharmaceutical giant Eli Lilly was anticipating a big drop in sales. That was the year the patent expired on its blockbuster drug Prozac, which accounted for 34 percent of Lilly's annual sales. But rather than launch a new drug, Lilly launched an Internet business—InnoCentive, LLC.

InnoCentive, as the name implies, provides incentives for innovation. It does so by providing a platform for scientists from around the world to work in virtual communities to solve complex problems. The effort does not just benefit Lilly but provides a virtual, open source R&D organization that any member company can use.

Here's how it works: Drug companies, called "Seek-

ers," put up "Wanted" posters describing problems that need addressing. Bounty-hunting scientists, labeled "Solvers," sign confidentiality agreements that gain them admission to a secure project room where they can access data and product specifications related to the problem. If they solve the problem, they get a reward—around $25,000–$30,000 depending on the problem.

According to InnoCentive president and CEO Darren J. Carroll, what Lilly has done is unusual for two reasons. First, by creating a global community of scientists, "We're punching a hole in the side of the laboratory and exposing mission-critical problems to the outside world," says Carroll, "It's using the Net to communicate, collaborate, and innovate." Second, it makes it possible for scientists to essentially become freelancers. According to Carroll, "Free agency has never been an option in the hard sciences—until now."

Sources: B. Breen, "Lilly's R&D Prescription." *Fast Company,* no. 57 (2002), p. 44; M. Sawhney, "What Lies Ahead: Rethinking the Global Corporation," *Digital Frontier Conference 2002,* www.mohansawhney.com; and www.innocentive.com.

the creation of a new product). Firms in industries such as medicine, law, and engineering are using the Internet and digital technologies to deliver many new solutions. Some of these are quite remarkable. Strategy Spotlight 8.5 describes how Eli Lilly has used the Internet to form a virtual platform where top scientists help drug companies solve complex problems.

Many products involve both a service and a product component; therefore, both problem solving and evaluation may be needed. Dell Computer's website is an example of a site that has combined the benefits of both. By creating a website that allows for customization of individual computers, they address the unique concerns of customers "one computer at a time." But the site also features a strong evaluative component because it allows users to compare the costs and features of various options. Shoppers can even compare their customized selection to refurbished Dell computers that are available at a substantially lower cost.

Transaction Activities

Transaction refers to the process of completing the sale, including negotiating and agreeing contractually, making payments, and taking delivery. Numerous types of Internet-enabled activities have contributed to lowering this aspect of overall transaction costs. Auctions of various sorts, from raw materials used in manufacturing to collectibles sold on eBay, facilitate the process of arriving at mutually agreed-on prices. Services such as PayPal provide a third-party intermediary that facilitates transactions between parties who never have (and probably never will!) meet. Amazon.com's One-Click technology allows for very rapid purchases, and Amazon's overall superiority in managing order fulfillment has made its transactions process rapid and reliable. Amazon's success today can be attributed to a large extent to its having sold this transaction capability to other companies such as Target, Toys "Я" Us and even Borders (another bookstore!).[33]

strategy spotlight

Adding Value in the Auto Industry

The auto industry jumped on the Internet bandwagon in a big way. One of the early successes was Autobytel, and many online auto sales websites quickly followed. The majority of them have now fizzled away. The big automakers also made huge investments in the Internet. Ford was especially aggressive and launched several websites—Trilogy.com, CarOrder.com, FordDirect.com—most of which never amounted to anything. But that was in the late 1990s, when it was still unclear how best to use the Internet. Now the automakers—and the auto-buying public—have found ways to use the Internet profitably. Here are a few examples:

Search

EBay, the online auction giant that makes searching for products of all sorts fast and simple, has become a player in the used car business. Beginning with a few private individuals, the auto auction business took off unexpectedly, so the company formed eBay Motors, which contributed about $100 million to eBay's total revenue of $1.2 billion in a recent year. EBay's technology speeds the process of online search, and buyers that may have been reluctant to shop for cars online are comforted by eBay's reputation. EBay and other online auto sales sites make searching for insurance and auto financing easier as well.

Problem Solving

To help its dealers manage inventories more effectively, General Motors developed SmartAuction. For vehicles

Sources: V. Postrell, "How Much Is That Civic Online?" *New York Times,* April 24, 2003, www.nytimes.com; M. Stepanek, "New Routes in the Internet Car Business," *CIO Insight,* January 23, 2003, www.cioinsight.com; and, N. Wingfield & K. Lundegaard, "EBay Is Emerging As Unlikely Giant in Used-Car Sales," *Wall Street Journal,* February 7, 2003.

that are coming off lease, SmartAuction notifies customers to bring in cars for an inspection before the lease expires. The condition of the car is logged into the system and sent to GM dealers, who use it to purchase cars electronically. The system helps dealers find cars that fit their target audience, manages the auto titling process, and shortens the time cars are carried in inventory.

Evaluation

In the early days of the Internet, most thought that cars would never sell online, because customers like to kick the tires and take a test drive. This is often still true. But customers who go for a test drive and have also already researched the car online usually save money when they buy. Economists researching this phenomenon have labeled it the "information effect"—auto shoppers who first gather information online are better able to evaluate their purchase.

Transaction

Auto referral services such as CarsDirect have streamlined the transaction process by brokering purchases between dealers and consumers. Through these companies, both new and used cars can be purchased online, sight unseen. One shopper, who bought a used car online, flew to Fort Worth, Texas, to pick it up, and drove it 18 hours back home to Ohio, said, "in retrospect, I had more information about this vehicle than if I had gone onto a dealer's lot and started haggling over price." Online auto shoppers typically save money due to the "contract effect," which occurs because third-party auto referral services monitor the information provided by dealers and facilitate the transaction.

These four factors are primary ways that organizations go about adding value. Strategy Spotlight 8.6 describes several examples of how the automobile industry and car buyers have used each of these activities to benefit their own value-adding efforts.

Other Sources of Competitive Advantage

There are other factors that can be important sources of competitive advantage. One of the most important of these is content. The Internet makes it possible to capture vast amounts of content at a very low cost. REI.com, for example, a provider of recreational equipment and apparel, has over 78,000 items described on its 45,000 page website.[34] But firms have not always managed content in ways that add value. Garden.com, a site that started strongly in 1999 and raised enormous venture capital, spent millions on creating detailed and attractive content. But the expense did not generate sales. Content adds value only if it contributes to the overall value proposition. As a result, Garden.com failed in early 2001 (but the name is still being used by the Burpee Company, a 125-year-old supplier of garden products, who bought rights to the name).[35]

Three types of content can improve the value proposition of a website—customer feedback, expertise, and entertainment programming:

- **_Customer feedback._** Buyers often trust what other buyers say more than a company's promises. One type of content that can enhance a website is customer testimonials. Remember the leather sofa in the example above? Even though individuals can't feel and smell a sofa online, the testimonials of other buyers can build confidence and add to the chances that the purchaser will buy online "sight unseen." This is one way that content can be a source of competitive advantage. Being able to interact with like-minded customers by reading their experiences or hearing how they have responded to a new product offering builds a sense of belonging that is otherwise hard to create.

- **_Expertise._** The Internet has emerged as a tremendously important learning tool. Fifty-one percent of users compare the Internet to a library.[36] The prime reason many users go to the Web is to gain expertise. Websites that provide new knowledge or unbiased information are highly valuable. Additionally the problem-solving function often involves educating consumers regarding options and implications of various choices. For example, LendingTree.com, the online loan company, provides a help center that includes extensive information and resources about obtaining loans, maintaining good credit, and so forth. Further, the expertise function is not limited to consumer sites. In the case of B2B businesses, websites that facilitate sharing expert knowledge help build a sense of community in industry or professional groups.

- **_Entertainment Programming._** The Internet is being used by more and more people as an entertainment medium. With technologies such as streaming media, which allows the Internet to send television-like images and sound, computers can provide everything from breaking news to video games to online movies. A study by the Pew Internet and American Life Project indicates that among people using high-speed broadband service, TV viewing is down and online activity has increased. One reason is that the technology is interactive, which means that viewers don't just passively watch, but use the Web to create art or play online games. Businesses have noticed this trend, of course, and are creating Web content that is not just informative but entertaining. Strategy Spotlight 8.7 tells how online game developer Skyworks Technologies is using games to increase product sales.

These three types of content—customer feedback, expertise, and entertainment programming—are potential sources of competitive advantage. That is, they create advantages by making the value creation process even stronger. Or, if they are handled poorly, they diminish performance.

Next we turn to the topic of Internet business models. How the Internet creates value depends to a great extent on how a value proposition is enacted. Business models provide a guide to the effectiveness of the value-adding process.

Business Models

The Internet provides a unique platform or staging area for business activity, which has become, in some ways, like a new marketplace. How do firms conduct business in this new arena? One way of addressing this question is by describing various Internet business mod-

strategy spotlight

"Advergaming": Making Advertisements Interactive and Fun

Video games were popular well before the Web came along. But new digital technologies have made it possible to feature some of the best games online. Combine this with advertisers' need to use the Net's interactivity to make online ads more interesting and what do you get? Advergaming—online games that weave advertisements into the experience. Here are some examples:

- A game designed for Pepsi involves an auto race in which the goal is to recover a stolen shipment of Mountain Dew Code Red. The top 100 gamers received a free case of the soft drink.

- Some games make you buy something to play. To play the Pebbles Big Barney Chase game, players

must answer a question; to learn the answer, you have to purchase a box of Post Cereal.

- Candystand.com, a website developed by Skyworks Technologies to promote Life Savers for Kraft Foods, features dozens of card, racing, and arcade games and ranks as the sixth most popular gaming destination on the Web.

According to Skyworks founder Garry Kitchen, advergaming can leave a deeper and more positive impression than television commercials. The idea is catching on—in a recent year, Skyworks made $4.3 million in revenues, and industry analyst Kent Allen of the Aberdeen Group expects the trend to continue, especially among consumer packaged-goods marketers. "The consumer guys are starting to understand advergaming," says Allen. "They're realizing it's a great way to connect with people."

Sources: M. Athitakis, "The Entertainer," *Business 2.0*, May 2003, p. 88; P. Suciu, "Mobility Takes the Forum," *GameSpy*, May 2, 2003, www.gamespy.com; www.candystand.com; and www.skyworkstech.com.

els. A business model is a method and a set of assumptions that explain how a business creates value and earns profits in a competitive environment. Some of these models are quite simple and traditional even when applied in an Internet context. Others have features that are unique to the digitally networked, online environment. In this section, we discuss seven Internet business models that account for the vast majority of business conducted online.[37]

- *Commission-based* models are used by businesses that provide services for a fee. The business is usually a third-party intermediary, and the commission charged is often based on the size of the transaction. The most common type is a brokerage service, such as a stockbroker (e.g., Schwab.com or Ameritrade.com) or real estate broker (e.g., Remax.com or Century21.com). This category also includes auction companies such as eBay. In exchange for putting buyers and sellers together, eBay earns a commission.

- *Advertising-based* models are used by companies that provide content and/or services to visitors and sell advertising to businesses that want to reach those visitors. It is similar to the broadcast television model, in which viewers watch shows produced with advertising dollars. A key difference is that online visitors can interact with both the ads and the content. Large portals such as Yahoo.com are in this category as well as specialty portals such as iNest.com, a portal that provides services for buyers of newly constructed homes. EPinions.com, a recommender system, is just one example of the many types of content that are often available.

- *Markup-based* models are used by businesses that add value in marketing and sales (rather than production) by acquiring products, marking up the price, and reselling them at a profit. Also known as the merchant model, it applies to both wholesalers and retailers. Amazon.com is the best-known example in this category. It also includes bricks-and-mortar companies such as Wal-Mart, which has a very successful online operation, and vendors whose products are purely digital such as Fonts.com, which sells downloadable fonts and photographs.

♦ ***Production-based*** models are used by companies that add value in the production process by converting raw materials into value-added products. Thus, it is also referred to as the manufacturing model. The Internet adds value to this model in two key ways: First, it lowers marketing costs by enabling direct contact with end users. Second, such direct contact facilitates customization and problem solving. Dell's online ordering system is supported by a state-of-the-art customized manufacturing process. Travelocity uses its rich database of travel options and customer profiles to identify, produce, and deliver unique solutions.

♦ ***Referral-based*** models are used by firms that steer customers to another company for a fee. One type is the affiliate model, in which a vendor pays an affiliate a fee each time a visitor clicks through the affiliate's website and makes a purchase from the vendor. Many name-brand companies use affiliate programs. For example, WeddingChannel.com, which provides a bridal registry where wedding guests can buy gifts from companies such as Tiffany's, Macy's, or Crate & Barrel, receives a fee each time a sale is made through its website. Another referral-based example is Yesmail.com, which generates leads using e-mail marketing.

♦ ***Subscription-based*** models are used by businesses that charge a flat fee for providing either a service or proprietary content. Internet service providers are one example of this model. Companies such as America Online and Earthlink supply Internet connections for fees that are charged whether buyers use the service or not. Subscription-based models are also used by content creators such as the *Economist* or *New York Times.* Although these recognizable brands often provide free content, only a small portion is available free. The *Economist,* for example, advertises that 70 percent of its content is available only to subscribers.

♦ ***Fee-for-service-based*** models are used by companies that provide ongoing services similar to a utility company. Unlike the commission-based model, the fee-for-service model involves a pay-as-you-go system. That is, activities are metered and companies pay only for the amount of service used. Application service providers fall in this category. For example, eProject.com provides virtual work space where people in different physical locations can collaborate online. Users essentially rent Internet space, and a host of tools that make it easy to interact, for a fee based on their usage.

Exhibit 8.5 summarizes the key feature of each Internet business model, suggests what role content may play in the model, and addresses how the four value-adding activities—search, evaluation, problem solving, and transaction—can be sources of competitive advantage.

It's important to keep in mind that many companies combine these models to achieve competitive advantages. For example, a company such as LendingTree not only sells advertising but also earns a commission as a third-party intermediary and earns fees by referring viewers to other sites through its affiliate programs.

Next, we turn to the topic of how the Internet is influencing the three competitive strategies—overall low cost, differentiation, and focus—and discuss further the role of combination strategies in creating competitive advantages for Internet companies.

How the Internet Is Affecting the Competitive Strategies

As we have seen, the Internet is sweeping across the economy and affecting in many ways how business is conducted. It is a resource that companies around the world can access. Thus, to stay competitive, firms must update their strategies to reflect the new possibilities

Exhibit 8.5
Internet Business Models

Type	Features and Content	Sources of Competitive Advantage
Commission-based	Commissions charged for brokerage or intermediary services. Adds value by providing expertise and/or access to a wide network of alternatives.	Search Evaluation Problem solving Transaction
Advertising-based	Web content paid for by advertisers. Adds value by providing free or low-cost content—including customer feedback, expertise, and entertainment programming—to audiences that range from very broad (general content) to highly targeted (specialized content).	Search Evaluation
Markup-based	Reselling marked-up merchandise. Adds value through selection, through distribution efficiencies, and by leveraging brand image and reputation. May use entertainment programming to enhance sales.	Search Transaction
Production-based	Selling manufactured goods and custom services. Adds value by increasing production efficiencies, capturing customer preferences, and improving customer service.	Search Problem solving
Referral-based	Fees charged for referring customers. Adds value by enhancing a company's product or service offering, tracking referrals electronically, and generating demographic data. Expertise and customer feedback often included with referral information.	Search Problem solving Transaction
Subscription-based	Fees charged for unlimited use of service or content. Adds value by leveraging strong brand name, providing high-quality information to specialized markets, or providing access to essential services. May consist entirely of entertainment programming.	Evaluation Problem solving
Fee-for-service-based	Fees charged for metered services. Adds value by providing service efficiencies, expertise, and practical outsourcing solutions.	Problem solving Transaction

Sources: A. Afuah, and C. L. Tucci, *Internet Business Models and Strategies,* 2nd ed. (New York: McGraw-Hill, 2003); M. Rappa, "Business Models on the Web," digitalenterprise.org/models/models.html; and P. Timmers, *Electronic Commerce* (New York: Wiley, 1999).

and constraints that this phenomenon represents. In this section we will revisit the three competitive strategies introduced in Chapter 5—overall cost leadership, differentiation, and focus—and address how the Internet and digital technologies can be used to enhance firm performance. We will also consider two major impacts that the Internet is having on business: lowering transaction costs and enabling mass customization. Finally, we will briefly discuss the pitfalls associated with using the new technologies and address the role of combination strategies in achieving competitive advantages.

Overall Cost Leadership

An overall low-cost leadership strategy involves managing costs in every activity of a firm's value chain and offering no-frills products that are an exceptional value at the best possible price. We have seen how companies such as Wal-Mart and Southwest Airlines achieved this position through vigilant attention to cost control. Internet and digital technologies now provide even more opportunities to manage costs and achieve greater efficiencies. But these capabilities are available to many competing firms, and even specialized capabilities (i.e., those that firms might realize by using proprietary software) often provide only short-lived advantage.

Nevertheless, managing costs, and even changing the cost structures of certain industries, is a key feature of the new Internet economy. Most analysts agree that the Internet's ability to lower transaction costs will transform business. Broadly speaking, *transaction costs* refer to all the various expenses associated with conducting business. It applies not just to buy/sell transactions but to the costs of interacting with every part of a firm's value chain, within and outside the firm. Think about it. Hiring new employees, meeting with customers, ordering supplies, addressing government regulations—all of these exchanges have some costs associated with them. Because business can be conducted differently on the Net, new ways of saving money are changing the competitive landscape.

Earlier in the chapter, we saw how British Petroleum used the Internet to manage costs by lowering procurement costs and creating efficient methods for petroleum engineers to collaborate. Another major corporation to take advantage of such cost savings was General Electric. The first division to try this was GE Lighting. A website was developed called the Trading Process Network to serve as the primary source for all requests for quotes (RFQs) issued by GE. In many ways, it resembled the traditional way of doing business: Potential suppliers would obtain specifications and prepare bids. But it was all done via the Web. Specs were downloaded and bids had to be submitted to GE electronically. After only one year, GE reported that it had saved over $500,000, which included cutting labor costs by 30 percent. It had also cut the cycle time of the bidding process in half and reduced the paperwork requirements of key employees by 60 percent. The process also benefited suppliers by lowering their costs of sales, streamlining the bidding process, and shortening the selling cycle.[38]

Other factors also help to lower transaction costs. The process of disintermediation, described earlier in this chapter, has a similar effect. Each time intermediaries are used in a transaction, additional costs are added. Removing those intermediaries lowers transaction costs. The Internet reduces the costs of traveling to a location to search for a product or service, whether it is a retail outlet (as in the case of consumers) or a trade show (as in the case of business-to-business shoppers). Not only is the need for travel eliminated, but also the need to maintain a physical address, whether it's a permanent retail location or a temporary presence at a trade show.

In terms of strategizing, therefore, the Internet is creating new opportunities for firms to achieve low-cost advantages.[39] Of course, the same potential benefits are available to all companies relatively equally, but some companies have adopted these capabilities more rapidly or implemented them more efficiently. These cost savings are available throughout a firm's value chain, in both primary and support activities:

- Direct access to progress reports and the ability for customers to periodically check work in progress is minimizing rework.
- Online bidding and order processing are eliminating the need for sales calls and minimizing sales force expenses.
- Online purchase orders are making many transactions paperless, reducing the costs of procurement and paper.
- Collaborative design efforts using Internet technologies that link designers, materials suppliers, and manufacturers are reducing the costs and speeding the process of new-product development.
- Human resources departments are using online testing and evaluation techniques in the hiring process and online training after they hire.

Potential Internet-Related Pitfalls for Low-Cost Leaders As Internet technologies become more widespread, the cost advantages that early movers enjoyed may be available to many firms. One of the biggest threats to low-cost leaders is imitation. This problem is intensified for business done by way of the Internet. Most of the advantages associated with contacting customers directly, even capabilities that are software driven (e.g., customized ordering systems or real-time access to the status of work in progress that lowers the cost of rework) can be duplicated quickly and without threat of infringement on proprietary information.

Another major pitfall for low-cost providers is the availability of information online that allows consumers to comparison shop much more easily. Also, companies that become overly enamored with the Internet and its ability to cut costs may suffer if they place too much attention on one business activity and ignore others. They may jeopardize customer relations, as in the case of channel conflict, or neglect other cost centers, such as providing services or controlling turnover and recruiting expenses, which then dig into their cost advantages. In the early days of Internet mania, a strategy aimed at building market share by offering free products and services seemed like a viable low-cost strategy. In fact, it was very costly and led to the demise of numerous start-ups. Consider the example of Juno, an online service provider that is barely surviving its ambitious low-cost approach.

> Juno, one of the first companies to launch a free e-mail service, quietly grew into the third largest Internet service provider (ISP) in the United States in just five years, behind only America Online and Earthlink. Because the service was free, it had to pay for this impressive growth primarily with advertising revenue. By late 2000, however, Juno had dangerously low cash reserves and its stock had lost 85 percent of its value. Upon examining its subscriber base, it found that just 5 percent of its users accounted for more than half of its online costs. So Juno launched a plan to deliberately curb service to the heaviest users and make them look at more advertisements in order to prod them into becoming paying customers. (In contrast, paying subscribers do not receive the persistent ads and maintain a consistent Net connection.) Fewer than 1 million of its 4 million active users made the switch. It was not enough. By mid-2001, Juno announced plans to merge with rival NetZero, the only other major free ISP, and announced a 10-hour cap per month usage for free subscribers. It survives today as part of United Online, the merged company, which thrives by offering low-cost Internet access.[40]

Differentiation

A differentiation strategy involves providing unique, high-quality products and services that promote a favorable reputation and strong brand identity and usually command a premium price. Throughout this text we have seen examples of strong differentiators—

Disney, Nokia, BMW, and others. Internet technologies have created new ways for firms to achieve a competitive advantage. Some of these capabilities are being used to threaten the position of companies that have traditionally maintained the best reputations or strong leadership positions. Other technologies are being employed by industry leaders to make their position even stronger.

Among the most striking trends that the new technologies foster are new ways to interact with consumers. In particular, the Internet is creating new ways of differentiating by enabling *mass customization,* which improves the response of companies to customer wishes. Mass customization is not a new phenomenon; it has been growing for years as flexible manufacturing systems have made manufacturing more adaptable and electronic data interchange has made communications more direct. But the Internet has generated a giant leap forward in the amount of control customers can have in influencing the process. Such capabilities are changing the way companies develop unique product and service offerings, make their reputation, and preserve their brand image. The new technology may affect the structure of entire industries. In the old days, manufacturers built products and waited for customers to respond. Now they are taking directions from customers before manufacturing any products. Consider the following examples.

- ◆ Dell Computer has strengthened its leadership position by creating an online ordering system that allows customers to configure their own computers before they are built.[41]
- ◆ Seven-Eleven, a convenience store operator, has created a finely tuned feedback system that monitors subtle shifts in customer demand and recommends revisions to its product offerings on a daily basis.[42]
- ◆ Footwear giant Nike lets customers choose the color of their shoes and add a personal name or nickname through its NIKEiD program. Customers can view their selection at the Nike.com website before finalizing the order.[43]

Methods like mass customization, which are changing the way companies go to market, are challenging some of the tried-and-true techniques of differentiation. Traditionally, companies reached customers in various ways—the high-end catalog, the showroom floor, the personal sales call—and used numerous means to make products more inviting—prestige packaging, celebrity endorsements, charity sponsorships. All of these avenues are still available and may still be effective, depending on a firm's competitive environment. But many consumers now judge the quality and uniqueness of a product or service by their ability to be involved in planning and design, combined with speed of delivery and reliability of results. Internet capabilities are thus changing the way differentiators make exceptional products and achieve superior service. And these improvements are being made at a reasonable cost, allowing firms to achieve parity on the basis of overall cost leadership relative to competitors (see Chapter 5).

Here again, opportunities to differentiate using Internet technologies are available in all parts of a company's value chain. Some of the techniques firms are using to achieve competitive advantage are fast becoming industry norms; successful differentiators will need to remain attentive to the evolving capabilities of the new technologies. These capabilities are evident in both primary and support activities.

- ◆ Internet-based knowledge management systems that link all parts of the organization are shortening response times and accelerating organization learning.
- ◆ Personalized online access provides customers with their own "site within a site" in which their prior orders, status of current orders, and requests for future orders are processed directly on the supplier's web site.

◆ Quick online responses to service requests and rapid feedback to customer surveys and product promotions are enhancing marketing efforts.

◆ Online access to real-time sales and service information is being used to empower the sales force and continually update R&D and technology development efforts.

◆ Automated procurement and payment systems provide both suppliers and customers with access to detailed status reports and purchasing histories.

Potential Internet-Related Pitfalls for Differentiators   As applications of these technologies become part of the mainstream, it will become harder to use the Web to differentiate. The sustainability of Internet-based gains from differentiation will deteriorate if companies offer differentiating features that customers don't want or create a sense of uniqueness that customers don't value. This has been the case with some of the personalization and customization software that early dot-com companies added to their sites at great expense. Users did not care about these features and that led to a failed value proposition—the value companies thought they were offering did not translate into sales.

Other problems can result from overpricing products and services or developing brand extensions that dilute a company's image or reputation. For example, Dow Jones & Co. has struggled to develop an online version of the *Wall Street Journal,* its highly respected publication.

> The *Wall Street Journal* had already been criticized for adding new color sections—some readers thought this detracted from the high-quality, reliable image that the traditional black-and-white editions portrayed. With the online version of the paper, it has a new problem: Internet users had grown accustomed to getting their online information for free. Companies such as Financial Times and TheStreet.com, both of which tried to sell online subscriptions to the latest financial news were not able to build a large enough base of paying subscribers and had to scramble to redefine their businesses. Even the *Wall Street Journal* is having trouble developing a subscriber base for the online version. Print subscribers typically pay over $100 a year, but the *Journal* has had trouble getting online subscribers to pay $79 for a service that is arguably more customizable, more up to date, and more complete. By 2003, WSJ.com had about 664,000 paid subscribers but still was not profitable and is a long way from repaying the $140 million its parent company, Dow Jones, has plowed into it since 1995.[44]

Now consider the efforts of one firm that has drawn on the Internet's technological capabilities to attempt a new approach to strategizing. Strategy Spotlight 8.8 profiles Buy.com, an Internet company with an unusual approach. Is it a differentiator or an overall cost leader? Whether the answer is "neither" or "both," Buy.com appears so far to have defied traditional strategic thinking.

Focus

A focus strategy involves targeting a narrow market segment with customized products and/or specialized services. For companies that pursue focus strategies, the Internet offers new avenues in which to compete because they can access markets less expensively (low cost) and provide more services and features (differentiation). Some claim that the Internet has opened up a new world of opportunities for niche players who seek to access small markets in a highly specialized fashion.[45] Niche businesses are among the most active users of digital technologies and e-business solutions. According to the ClickZ.com division of Jupitermedia Corporation, 77 percent of small businesses agree that a website is essential for small business success. Small businesses also report that the Internet has helped them grow (58 percent), made them more profitable (51 percent), and helped reduce business costs (49 percent).[46] Clearly, niche players and small businesses are using the Internet to create more viable focus strategies.

Buy.Com's Risky Strategy

In terms of Michael Porter's competitive strategies, Buy.com tried something very risky. It tried to build brand with an overall cost leadership strategy. Developing a brand image that customers will turn to and rely on is traditionally associated with a differentiation strategy. Heavy investments in advertising to create brand recognition are generally considered ineffective for low-cost providers because customers seeking the lowest price tend to be less loyal. They follow the low price, not the brand.

This didn't stop Buy.com, an online retailer of electronics, books, video games, and more. From the beginning it sought to build a reputation as the lowest-cost provider with the advertising slogan "lowest prices on earth." It purchased hundreds of domain names that started with the term "buy": BuyNokia.com, BuySony.com, and so forth. Then it offered incredibly low prices, well below market value. In the case of hot, new high-demand products, it sold loss leaders at negative gross margins to attract buyers. The hope was to make up the difference in advertising revenues. As a self-proclaimed "superstore" offering 30,000 different products, Buy.com sought to build a reputation as the best place to shop for low prices and thus an ideal venue for the ads of other vendors.

Has this strategy worked? It's still too early to tell. Buy.com did achieve $100 million in sales faster than any

other company in history, but it also chalked up significant losses. In addition to negative profitability, Buy.com has had numerous problems with order fulfillment and developed a reputation for advertising products that were back-ordered for weeks. Its hopes for advertising revenue were not fulfilled either, as the luster of banner ads faded and the dot-com downturn caused everyone to have second thoughts about online advertising.

In late 2001, Buy.com founder Scott Blum reacquired the company for $23.6 million and took it private. This purchase price was equivalent to 17 cents per share even though at one time the company's stock sold for $35 per share. Blum, who earlier in 2001 had provided Buy.com with $9 million in interim financing, said he would return the company to its "Internet Superstore" roots and relaunch its "Lowest Prices on Earth" marketing campaign. More recently, Buy.com has launched a glossy magazine and boasted it will outperform Amazon.com by offering free shipping on everything.

Such features are costly and make Buy.com appear to be differentiating. However, it continues to position itself as an overall low-cost leader in terms of pricing. "I do not believe that Buy.com's pricing assault on Amazon.com is sustainable," said Ken Cassar, senior analyst at Jupiter Media Metrix. "It is very likely . . . that Buy.com will steal market share from Amazon in the short term. Whether that is sustainable will depend upon whether customers will come back to Buy.com when there is no promotion." Clearly, the company's long-terms prospects are still uncertain as it continues to invest in a potentially risky strategy.

Sources: "Playing I-Ball," *Economist,* November 6, 1999, p. 65; M. E. Porter, "Strategy and the Internet," *Harvard Business Review,* March 2001, pp. 63–78; B. Cox, "E-Commerce Price War Escalates, Amazon Expands." *InternetNews,* June 25, 2002, www.internetnews.com; B. Cox, "And Now, Buy.com the Magazine," *InternetNews,* February 27, 2002; M. Singer, "Scott Blum Re-acquires Buy.com," *InternetNews,* November 28, 2001; and B. Cox, "Buy.com Returns to Its Roots," *InternetNews,* September 25, 2001.

Nevertheless, even though the Internet presents some exciting new possibilities, the same problems that low-cost leaders and differentiators face in an e-business environment will affect focusers as well. Achieving competitive advantage will depend on how effectively firms use Internet technologies and deploy focus strategies. Let's look at SalvageSale, Inc., an online broker of salvage goods.

SalvageSale, Inc., has become the top choice of insurance and transportation companies that need to quickly liquidate commercial salvage goods. The Houston-based company has been successful by carefully watching costs, relying on word-of-mouth advertising, and staying focused on the narrow salvage goods market. Traditionally, when salvage goods become available, insurance adjusters and transportation agents seek bids from local brokers using faxes and telephone calls. But SalvageSale posts such information online, where many brokers can bid using an eBay-style auction. Because of the time saved by this method and the larger number of bidders reached, companies are getting higher prices for the salvaged goods. This, in turn, raises the total earnings of SalvageSale even though it charges considerably lower commissions than traditional brokers. The result: SalvageSale has become a leader in the $50 billion salvage goods industry.[47]

To create focus strategies that work, firms must consider how best to deploy their resources throughout every value-creating activity. Both primary and support activities can be enhanced using the kind of singlemindedness that is characteristic of a focus strategy. Companies that have adapted their strategies to serve specialized markets, however, may enjoy only a temporary advantage unless they seize the capabilities that the Internet provides for focusers:

- Permission marketing techniques are focusing sales efforts on specific customers who opt to receive advertising notices.
- Chat rooms, discussion boards, and member functions that create community for customers with common interests are increasing website usage.
- Niche portals that target specific groups are providing advertisers with access to viewers with specialized interests.
- Virtual organizing and online "officing" are being used to minimize firm infrastructure requirements.
- Procurement technologies that use Internet software to match buyers and sellers are highlighting specialized buyers and drawing attention to smaller suppliers.

Potential Internet-Related Pitfalls for Focusers   Many aspects of the Internet economy seem to favor focus strategies because niche players and small firms can often implement Internet capabilities as effectively as their larger competitors. However, the same technologies—and the same cost savings—that are creating new opportunities for focusers are also available to major players. Thus, focusers must use the new technology to provide the kinds of advantages that have been the hallmark of a focus strategy in the past: specialized knowledge, rapid response, and strong customer service.

These advantages may be challenged if focusers misread the scope and interests of their target markets. This can cause them to focus on segments that are too narrow to be profitable, or lose their uniqueness by going after overly broad niches, making them vulnerable to imitators or new entrants. Consider the case of Pets.com.

> Pets.com failed by attempting to "do it all" with its online pet store. It spent millions on advertising, including pricey Super Bowl ads featuring its now defunct sock puppet. All its efforts to build brand recognition went for nothing because they were based on a faulty business model that included selling bags of inexpensive pet food with skimpy 10 percent margins. In contrast, Waggin' Tails is an online retailer that specializes in products like high-end dog food and hard-to-find pet vitamins that command 30 percent margins. By remaining small, carefully monitoring market costs, and keeping a laser focus on high-margin niches, some focusers are successfully producing profits online.[48]

What happens when an e-business focuser tries to overextend its niche? Efforts to appeal to a broader audience—by carrying additional inventory, developing additional content, or offering additional services—can cause it to lose the cost advantages associated with a limited product or service offering. Conversely, when focus strategies become too narrow, the e-business may have trouble generating enough activity to justify the expense of operating the website. The wireless technology firm Bluetooth was briefly seen as the leading provider of personal area networks, a wireless means to connect cell phones, laptops, and personal digital assistants (PDAs). Bluetooth's technology worked fine with laptops and PDAs, but it could not complete one of the major functions needed in the anticipated wireless world: providing reliable links to cell phones. As a result, the company lost its lead to technologies such as Wi-Fi (wireless fidelity) with a broader functionality.[49]

Are Internet-Based Advantages Sustainable?

The Internet provides many ways to achieve above-average returns, but it may create even more possibilities for eroding unique advantages. So what's the bottom line? Strategy is about achieving competitive advantage and sustaining it. Does the Internet contribute to or detract from a firm's efforts to attain sustainable competitive advantages?

On the one hand, it appears that the Internet and the achievements in digital technology that it makes possible are creating new opportunities for strategic success. A few business models—those that offer capabilities that are unique to the Internet, such as eBay's auction system—seem to be providing strong, *lasting* opportunities for above-average profitability. Such new applications have also created opportunities for companies that supply equipment to run the Internet, such as Cisco Systems and Sun Microsystems, and companies that provide software applications management and online fulfillment services, such as Jupiter Networks and SAP. Many such companies are thriving because of the e-business revolution launched by the Internet.

On the other hand, the cycle of dot-com failures that burst the Internet bubble suggests that the Internet boom was only temporary and that the rapid growth of new firms and new opportunities for commerce were built on an unsustainable base. Most observers agree that the downturn resulted, to a great extent, from ignoring business fundamentals and overlooking basic economic requirements. Consider, for example, Boo.com, headquartered in Sweden.

> Boo.com attempted to create a global fashion e-tailer that offered services in seven different languages and conducted transactions in 18 different currencies. It anticipated a technology that allowed customers to view products from every angle and use a virtual fitting room that made it possible to "try things on" in cyberspace. Unlike almost every other e-commerce business, it planned to charge full price for everything. But once launched, only one in four attempts to make a purchase worked, Macintosh users could not log on, and the phone lines were crammed with angry customers. Boo.com spiraled downward quickly from there, losing $10 million in investment commitments within a week of its launch. Boo.com burned through $185 million in just 18 months and, in the end, its assets were sold for less than $2 million.[50] Clearly, strategies such as this are unsustainable.

Another major reason why so many start-ups failed was that the service or capability that they offered could easily be imitated. This was especially damaging for the young start-ups and "pure plays" (i.e., firms that exist only in cyberspace and have no other physical outlets). The reason? Larger firms with greater resources could observe what was working over time and bring more resources and talent to bear on an effective imitation strategy.

Thus, Internet technologies can benefit firms that use them effectively in ways that genuinely set them apart from rivals. But the extent to which the Internet can create advantages that are rare and difficult to imitate is highly questionable. Perhaps combination strategies (see Chapter 5) hold the key to successful digital business.

Are Combination Strategies the Key to E-Business Success?

Because of the changing dynamics presented by the Internet and Internet-based technologies, new strategic combinations that make the best use of the competitive strategies just described may hold the greatest promise for future success. Several things are clear in this regard. First, the Internet in general is eroding opportunities for sustainable advantage. Many experts agree that the net effect of the Internet is fewer rather than more opportunities for sustainable advantages.[51] This means strategic thinking is even more important in the Internet age.

More specifically, the Internet has provided all companies with greater tools for managing costs. So it may be that cost management and control will increase in importance as a management tool. In general, this may be good if it leads to an economy that makes more efficient use of its scarce resources. However, for individual companies, it may shave critical percentage points off profit margins and create a climate that makes it impossible to survive, much less achieve sustainable above-average profits.

Many differentiation advantages are also diminished by the Internet. The ability to comparison shop—to check product reviews and inspect different choices with a few clicks of the mouse—is depriving some companies, such as auto dealers, of the unique advantages that were the hallmark of their success in a previous time. Differentiating is still an important strategy, of course. But how firms achieve it may change, and the best approach may be to combine a differentiation strategy with other competitive strategies.

Perhaps the greatest beneficiaries are the focusers, who can use the Internet to capture a niche that previously may have been inaccessible. Even this is not assured, however, because the same factors that make it possible for a small niche player to be a contender may make that same niche attractive to a big company. That is, an incumbent firm that previously thought a niche market was not worth the effort may use Internet technologies to enter that segment for a lower cost than in the past. The larger firm can then bring its market power and resources to bear in a way that a smaller competitor cannot match.

Firms using combination strategies may also fall short if they underestimate the demands of combining strategic approaches and get "stuck in the middle." This can lead to inaccurately assessing the costs and benefits of a strategy that combines differentiating and low-cost features: Firms may believe they can keep prices and costs low but still offer high-end services that are expensive to provide. Many dot-com start-ups, such as Kozmo.com, fell into this trap.

> Kozmo.com sought to develop a rapid-response delivery service using one of the cheapest forms of delivery—bicycles. It believed that urban Internet users would grow accustomed to receiving everything delivered to their door on short notice—from a cup of coffee to a video to show tickets—and that its bicycle delivery "army" could provide it. But the products it focused on tended to be low-price items and there were too few users. Kozmo tried to broaden its service by delivering higher-margin products and forming an alliance with Starbucks, but this failed to produce significant additional revenue. In the end, it was unable to generate enough business to keep its cyclists employed.[52]

Another potential pitfall for companies using combination strategies relates to the difficulty of managing complex strategies. Managers tend to develop a bias in favor of the functional areas with which they are most familiar. Furthermore, companies in general tend to fall into the trap of believing that there is "one best way" to accomplish organizational goals. A combination strategy, by definition, challenges a company to carefully blend alternative strategic approaches and remain mindful of the impact of different decisions on the firm's value-creating processes and its extended value-chain activities. Strong leadership is needed to maintain a bird's-eye perspective on a company's overall approach and coordinate the multiple dimensions of a combination strategy.

Indeed, the key to effectively implementing any e-business strategy is for the leaders of today's firms to recognize that the Internet has forever changed the way business is conducted and to adopt practices that use the advantages it has to offer without ignoring business fundamentals. Companies will increasingly need to adapt to the Internet and implement the capabilities that make e-business possible because, as Intel Chairman Andy Grove expressed it, "The world now runs on Internet time."[53]

Leveraging Internet Capabilities

In this chapter we have emphasized the importance of the Internet and digital technologies in creating e-business capabilities and new strategic initiatives. We have addressed how the Internet is affecting the five competitive forces and how it contributes to a firm's efforts to add value and create competitive advantages. We conclude by discussing how digital technologies and Internet-based capabilities can affect business-level strategy (Chapter 5), corporate-level strategy (Chapter 6), and international-level strategy (Chapter 7).

Leveraging Internet Capabilities and Business-Level Strategy   Chapter 5 addressed attributes and potential pitfalls of business-level strategies. Earlier in this chapter, we presented a rather detailed section on how the Internet and digital technologies are affecting overall low-cost, differentiation, and focus strategies and how combination strategies may be effective in the context of e-business. By providing new ways to add value and shifting the power of the five competitive forces, the Internet and digital technologies have altered the competitive climate in numerous industries. These changes often require modifications in generic strategies, sometimes leading to new strategic combinations. While many strategic imperatives remain the same, in some cases, such as Buy.com, this has led to a complete rethinking of how firms use resources and position themselves in a competitive environment.

Leveraging Internet Capabilities and Corporate-Level Strategy   Chapter 6 addressed how firms strategically diversify and manage portfolios of businesses at the corporate level. In the case of related diversification, the Internet has created new means of generating synergies and enhancing revenue among elements of a diverse firm. For example, by linking sources of supply more efficiently and streamlining distribution, digital technologies can enhance profitability. In the case of unrelated diversification, corporate offices that manage portfolios of businesses can use the Internet to deal with suppliers more efficiently and increase negotiating power. In both cases, when the Internet becomes integrated into a corporation's infrastructure and procurement system, it supports activities that contribute to the bottom line. In terms of internal development and acquisition as avenues of corporate growth, e-business models that have proven successful can be a welcome addition to a firm's portfolio. British Petroleum's investment in Web-linked gas pumps and e-kiosks in service stations is designed to increase sales by offering customer-friendly Internet services.

Leveraging Internet Capabilities and International-Level Strategies
Chapter 7 addressed how and why businesses grow beyond their national boundaries. Expanding into international markets involves special challenges that may be mitigated by using Internet and digital technologies. In terms of controlling costs, the Internet has enhanced the ability to conduct business without the time and expense of physically traveling to various locations. In terms of adapting to local markets, the ability to conduct research and communicate online has increased the level of access to local cultures and market conditions. This combination of capabilities has, in some cases, enhanced the ability of firms to pursue a transnational strategy by addressing both cost reduction and local adaptation issues. The Internet has also allowed firms to leapfrog the usual path of international development with technologies that reach customers and facilitate transactions around the globe. Whereas prior to the Internet, local distributors or licensees were essential international partners for firms expanding into new regions, now an online presence can accomplish the same thing. Additionally, new types of international commerce are possible, as suggested by Eli Lilly's InnoCentive venture, which enables scientists from around the world to address difficult problems. Collaboration at such a scale was virtually impossible prior to the Internet.

summary

The Internet is changing the way business is conducted. This has enormous implications that today's managers need to take into account when formulating and implementing firm strategies. Two factors are especially important: First, Internet-based and digital technologies are creating new capabilities that are altering the rules of competition. These technologies are allowing businesses to interact with each other and customers in faster, smarter, cheaper ways that are forever changing the competitive landscape. As Internet-based capabilities and related information technologies become more widespread in all parts of the globe, strategic managers need to increasingly integrate the Internet into their strategic plans.

In terms of a firm's competitive environment, most of the changes brought about by the Internet can be understood in the context of Porter's five-forces model of industry analysis. The threat of new entrants is expected to increase as Internet technologies reduce many barriers to entry. The process of disintermediation has enhanced the power of some suppliers by simplifying supply chains, but it may also shift bargaining power to customers. Buyer power has increased for many end users due to lower switching costs, but in some industries the Internet has become a new source of channel conflict. The threat of substitutes will generally be higher, because Internet technologies are providing new methods for achieving old tasks. Finally, the Internet heightens the intensity of rivalry among similar competitors, as competition tends to be more price-oriented and technology-based advantages are easily imitated.

The Internet and digital technologies have created new opportunities for firms to add value. Four value-adding activities that have been enhanced by Internet capabilities are search, evaluation, problem solving, and transaction. Search activities include processes for gathering information and identifying purchase options. Evaluation activities refers to the process of considering alternatives and comparing the costs and benefits of various options. Problem-solving activities include identifying problems or needs and generating ideas and action plans to address those needs. Transaction activities involve the process of completing a sale, including negotiating and agreeing contractually, making payments, and taking delivery. These four activities are supported by three different types of content that Internet businesses often use—customer feedback, expertise, and entertainment programming. Strategic use of these attributes can help build competitive advantages and contribute to profitability. Seven business models have been identified that are proving successful for use by Internet firms. These include commission, advertising, markup, production, referral, subscription, and fee-for-service based models. Firms have also found that combinations of these business models can contribute to greater success.

The way companies formulate and deploy strategies is also changing because of the impact of the Internet on many industries. Overall low-cost strategies may be more important as some firms use Internet technologies to lower transaction costs and increase the efficiency of their operations. Differentiation strategies may be harder to achieve for many firms, because the Internet is eroding some of their most unique features. Further, Internet technologies are enabling the mass customization capabilities of greater numbers of competitors. Focus strategies are likely to increase in importance because the Internet provides highly targeted and lower-cost access to narrow or specialized markets. These strategies are not without their pitfalls, however, and firms need to understand the dangers as well as the potential benefits of Internet-based approaches.

Thus, the Internet, while promising to provide new opportunities for creating value and fostering firm growth, may make the competitive landscape more challenging for many incumbent firms. In this chapter we have addressed both the pitfalls and the possibilities provided by the rapidly expanding presence of the Internet in today's economy.

summary review questions

1. How do Porter's five competitive forces affect companies that compete primarily on the Internet? Provide an example.

2. What effects does the Internet have on the three competitive strategies—overall low-cost, differentiation, and focus? How does this relate to a firm's competitive advantage?

3. What effect does e-commerce have on the profitability an industry is able to achieve? How can companies use e-commerce to enhance their own profitability?

4. Explain the difference between the effective use of technology and the technology *itself* in terms of achieving and sustaining competitive advantages.

5. Describe how the three competitive strategies can be combined to create competitive advantages when firms compete primarily by means of e-commerce.

experiential exercise

Using the Internet, identify two firms—one an Internet "pure play" and the second a traditional bricks-and-mortar company—that have a strong Internet presence. Consider how each of these firms is adding value by using the Internet and digital technologies.

1. Bricks-and-mortar firm: _____

Which of the following Internet-based activities is the company using to add value?

Value-Adding Activity	Examples of How the Company Uses the Activity	Is It Creating Value? (Yes/No)
Type:		
Search		
Evaluation		
Problem solving		
Transaction		
Content:		
Customer feedback		
Expertise		
Entertainment programming		

2. Internet pure-play firm: _____

Which of the following Internet-based activities is the company using to add value?

Value-Adding Activity	Examples of How the Company Uses the Activity	Is It Creating Value? (Yes/No)
Type:		
Search		
Evaluation		
Problem solving		
Transaction		
Content:		
Customer feedback		
Expertise		
Entertainment programming		

3. How do the two firms compare? Is one adding more value than the other? What is the pure play doing that might help the bricks-and-mortar firm? What is the bricks-and-mortar firm doing that could benefit the pure play?

application questions exercises

1. Select a company that has implemented an Internet strategy. Look up the company on the Internet and discuss how it has increased (or decreased) its competitive advantage vis-à-vis Porter's five forces.
2. Choose an Internet firm that is competing with a bricks-and-mortar company. What are the relative advantages and disadvantages of the Internet firm? Do you think it will be successful in the long term?
3. Select a small firm that has used the Internet to its advantage in entering international markets. Do you believe such advantages will be sustainable over time? Explain.
4. How can a firm use an Internet strategy to enhance its overall cost leadership or differentiation competitive advantages? Provide examples.

ethics questions

1. Discuss the ethical implications of the use of "cookies" by e-commerce companies to track customer visits to websites.
2. How can Internet companies that provide free access to other users' computers to download copyrighted material (e.g., Morpheus) guard against infringing on the rights of the artists who develop the material?

references

1. Pope, C., 2003, Bankruptcy trustee claims Papermaster, other Agillion execs "squandered" assets, *Austin Business Journal,* April 18; Mears, J., 2001, Update: Agillion going under, *Network World Fusion,* March 16, www.nwfusion.com; McCabe, L., 2001, Just say no: Customers ditch traditional software for Web services, *Summit Strategies, Inc.,* December 26, www.summitstrat.com; Hamblen, M., 2000, Companies turn to low-cost customer management deals, *ComputerWorld,* September 4, www.computerworld.com.

2. Greenspan, A., U.S. Congressional hearing, quoted in Lewis, M., 2000, *The New Thing* (New York: W. W. Norton), 251.

3. Walczak, L., 2001, The mood now, *BusinessWeek,* August 27: 74–78.

4. Evans, P., & Wurster, T. S., 2000, *Blown to Bits* (Cambridge: Harvard Business School Press); Negroponte, N., 1995, *Being Digital* (New York: Alfred A. Knopf).

5. Echikson, W., 2001, When oil gets connected, *BusinessWeek e.biz,* December 3: EB28–EB30; British Petroleum, 2002, BP unveils Chicago's gas station of the future, May 14, www.bp.com.

6. Oliver, R. W., 2000, The seven laws of e-commerce strategy, *Journal of Business Strategy* 21 (5): 8–10.

7. Porter, M. E., 2001, Strategy and the Internet, *Harvard Business Review,* 79: 63–78.

8. Weintraub, A., 2001, The mighty mini-dots, *BusinessWeek e.biz,* March 19: EB45–EB48; www.florist.com.

9. For an interesting perspective on changing features of firm boundaries, refer to Afuah, A., 2003, Redefining firm boundaries in the face of Internet: Are firms really shrinking? *Academy of Management Review* 28 (1): 34–53.

10. Munarriz, R. A., 2001, The ghost of eToys past, *Motley Fool/Fool.com,* March 19.

11. www.consumerreports.org.

12. Siegel, D., 1999, *Futurize Your Enterprise* (New York: Wiley), 5.

13. For an alternative perspective on the role of customers in an Internet environment, refer to Nambisan, S., 2002, Designing virtual customer environments for new product development: Toward a theory, *Academy of Management Review* 27 (3): 392–413.

14. Warner, B., 1999, Levi's sites wear out, October 29, www.thestandard.com.

15. Keenan, F., 2001, Opening the spigot, *BusinessWeek e.biz,* June 4: EB17–EB20.

16. Time to rebuild, 2001, *Economist,* May 19: 55–56.

17. www.amazon.com.

18. For more on the role of the Internet as an electronic intermediary, refer to Carr, N. G., 2000, Hypermediation: Commerce as clickstream, *Harvard Business Review* 78 (1): 46–48.

19. Downes, L., & Mui, C., 1998, *Unleashing the Killer App* (Boston: Harvard Business School Press), 45–46.

20. Poe, R., 2001, Tickets to go, *Business 2.0,* March 20: 60–61.

21. Olofson, C., 2001, The next best thing to being there, *Fast Company,* April: 175.

22. Lelii, S. R., 2001, Free online storage a thing of the past? *eWEEK,* April 22.

23. McKay, N., 2000, Ballpark figures, *Red Herring,* May: 360; www.insightexpress.com.

24. www.privacy.net; and www.epic.org.

25. www.mysimon.com; and www.pricescan.com.

26. www.cnet.com; and www.bizrate.com.

27. Hanrahan, T., 1999, Price isn't everything, *Wall Street Journal,* July 12: R20.

28. For a discussion of strategic implications of partnering and competing, refer to Gulati, R., Nohria, N., and Zaheer, A., 2000, Strategic networks, *Strategic Management Journal* 21: 203–15.

29. www.bestbookbuys.com.

30. The ideas in this section draw on several sources, including Zeng, M., & Reinartz, W., 2003, Beyond online search: The road to profitability, *California Management Review,* Winter: 107–30; and Stabell, C. B., & Fjeldstad, O. D., 1998, Configuring value for competitive advantage: On chains, shops, and networks, *Strategic Management Journal* 19: 413–37.

31. Hardy, Q., 2003, All eyes on Google, *Forbes,* May 26, www.forbes.com.

32. Zeng & Reinartz, op. cit.

33. Bayers, C., 2002, The last laugh, *Business 2.0,* September: 86–93.

34. Yamada, K., 2001. Web trails, *Forbes,* December 3.

35. Weintraub, A., 2001, E-assets for sale—dirt cheap, *BusinessWeek e.biz,* May 14: EB20–EB22.

36. Greenspan, R., 2003, Internet not for everyone, *CyberAtlas,* April 16, www.cyberatlas.com.

37. Afuah, A., & Tucci, C. L., 2003, *Internet Business Models and Strategies,* 2nd ed. (New York: McGraw-Hill); Timmers, P., 1999, *Electronic Commerce* (New York: Wiley).

38. Big, boring, booming, 1998, *The Economist,* July 18: 15–16; Madden, J., & Shein, E., 1998, Web purchasing attracts more pioneers, *PC Week Online,* March 6; see www.tpn.geis.com and www.ge.com/news/welch/index.htm.

39. For an interesting discussion of the cost and pricing implications of Internet technology, refer to Sinha, I., 2000, Cost transparency: The net's real threat to prices and brands, *Harvard Business Review* 78 (2): 43–51.

40. Borland, J., 2001, NetZero, Juno to unite in merger, *CNET News.com,* June 7; Borrus, A., 2001, Someone has to pay the freight, *BusinessWeek,* March 26: 134–36; Hu, J., 2000, Juno attempts to limit heavy Net use, *CNET News.com,* November 21; Hellweg, E., 2003, The low-cost alternative, *Business 2.0,* May: 90.

41. Evans, P., & Wurster, T. S., 2000, *Blown to Bits* (Boston: Harvard Business School Press), 82–83.

42. Over the counter e-commerce, 2001, *Economist,* May 26: 77–78.

43. Collett, S., 1999, Nike offers mass customization on-line, *ComputerWorld,* November 23.

44. McHugh, J., 2000, Will online publishing ever fly? *Business 2.0,* July; Mullaney, T. J., 2001, Sites worth paying for? *BusinessWeek e.biz,* May 14: EB10–EB12; Mount, I., 2003, If they have to pay, will they come? *Business 2.0,* February: 45.

45. Seybold, P., 2000, Niches bring riches, *Business 2.0,* June 13: 135.

46. Greenspan, R., 2004, Net drives profits to small biz, *ClickZ.com,* March 25, www.clickz.com; Greenspan, 2002, Small biz benefits from Internet tools, *ClickZ.com,* March 28, www.clickz.com.

47. Lii, J., 2001, Salvagesale.com gets the goods where they're needed, *Lexington* (KY) *Herald-Leader,* February 25: H2.

48. Green, H., 2001, How to reach John Q. Public, *BusinessWeek,* March 26: 132–33; Weintraub, A., 2001, E-assets for sale—dirt cheap, *BusinessWeek e.biz,* May 14: EB 20–EB22.

49. Miller, M. J., 2001, A tangled, wireless web, *PC Magazine,* February 2.

50. Sorkin, A. R., 2000, From big idea to big bust: The wild ride of Boo.com, *New York Times,* December 13: 3.

51. Porter, op. cit., pp. 63–78.

52. Regan, K., 2001, Kozmo cans Starbucks drop-off plan, *E-Commerce Times,* March 27; Delio, M., 2001, Kozmo kills the messenger, *Wired News,* April 13, www.wired.com/news/print/0,1294,43025,00.html.

53. Downes & Mui, op. cit., p. 13.

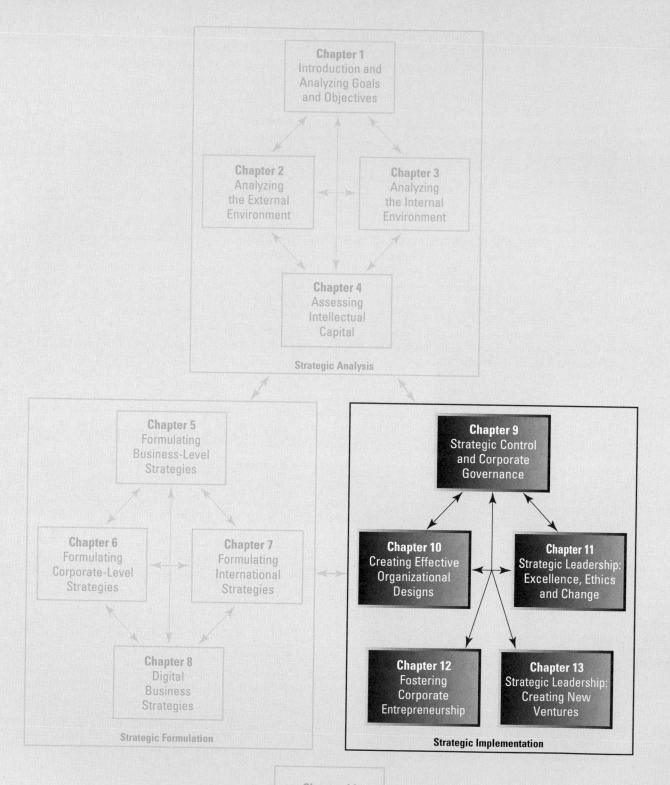

Chapter 1
Introduction and Analyzing Goals and Objectives

Chapter 2
Analyzing the External Environment

Chapter 3
Analyzing the Internal Environment

Chapter 4
Assessing Intellectual Capital

Strategic Analysis

Chapter 5
Formulating Business-Level Strategies

Chapter 6
Formulating Corporate-Level Strategies

Chapter 7
Formulating International Strategies

Chapter 8
Digital Business Strategies

Strategic Formulation

Chapter 9
Strategic Control and Corporate Governance

Chapter 10
Creating Effective Organizational Designs

Chapter 11
Strategic Leadership: Excellence, Ethics and Change

Chapter 12
Fostering Corporate Entrepreneurship

Chapter 13
Strategic Leadership: Creating New Ventures

Strategic Implementation

Chapter 14
Case Analysis

Strategic Implementation

outline

Strategic Control and Corporate Governance

9

Creating Effective Organizational Designs

10

Strategic Leadership: Creating a Learning Organization and an Ethical Organization

11

Managing Innovation and Fostering Corporate Entrepreneurship

12

Recognizing Opportunities and Creating New Ventures

13

chapter 9

Strategic Control
and Corporate Governance

*After
reading this
chapter, you should
have a good understanding of:*

- The value of effective strategic control systems in strategy implementation.

- The key difference between "traditional" and "contemporary" control systems.

- The imperative for "contemporary" control systems in today's complex and rapidly changing competitive and general environments.

- The benefits of having the proper balance among the three levers of behavioral control: culture, rewards and incentives, and boundaries.

- Why there is no "one best way" to design strategic control systems and the important contingent roles of business- and corporate-level strategies.

- The three key participants in corporate governance: shareholders, management (led by the CEO), and the board of directors.

- The role of corporate governance mechanisms in ensuring that the interests of managers are aligned with those of shareholders.

Organizations must have effective strategic controls if they are to successfully implement their strategies. This includes systems that exercise both informational control and behavioral control. In addition, a firm must promote sound corporate governance as well as have controls that are consistent with the strategy that the firm is following.

In the first section, we address the need to have effective informational control, contrasting two approaches to informational control. The first approach, which we call "traditional," is highly sequential. Goals and objectives are set, then implemented, and after a set period of time, performance is compared to the desired standards. In contrast, the second approach, termed "contemporary," is much more interactive. Here the internal and external environment is continually monitored, and managers determine whether the strategy itself needs to be modified. Today, the contemporary approach is required—given the rapidly changing conditions in virtually all industries.

Next we discuss behavioral control. Here the firm must strive to maintain a proper balance between culture, rewards, and boundaries. We also argue that organizations that have strong, positive cultures and reward systems can rely less on boundaries, such as rules, regulations, and procedures. When individuals in the firm internalize goals and strategies, there is less need for monitoring behavior, and efforts are focused more on important organizational goals and objectives.

The third section takes the perspective that there is no "one best way" to design an organization's strategic control system. Here we address two important contingencies: business- and corporate-level strategy. For example, when strategies require a great deal of collaboration, as well as resource and information sharing, there must be incentives and cultures that encourage and reward such initiatives.

The fourth section addresses the role of corporate governance in ensuring that managerial and shareholder interests are aligned. We provide examples of both effective and ineffective corporate governance practices. We discuss three governance mechanisms for aligning managerial and shareholder interests: a committed and involved board of directors, shareholder activism, and effective managerial rewards and incentives. Public companies are also subject to external control. We discuss several external control mechanisms, such as the market for corporate control, auditors, banks and analysts, the media, and public activists.

If a firm has a few greedy and unethical executives but exercises sound strategic control, the problem may (*arguably*) be correctable. If a firm has poor control systems but all employees seemingly strive toward similar goals in an ethical manner, things may not deteriorate too much. However, when there are greedy executives, unethical behavior, *and* poor control throughout the organization, disaster is waiting. Case in point: Tyco International under CEO Dennis Kozlowski:

> As CEO of Tyco International Ltd., Dennis Kozlowski was the most prolific corporate acquirer of all time.[1] At the height of his hyperactivity, he acquired 200 companies in a single year. Under his direction, Tyco grew from $3.1 billion to $36 billion in revenues and enjoyed an astonishing 70-fold increase in its market capitalization over a 10-year period. In 2001 Kozlowski proclaimed his desire to be remembered as the world's greatest business executive, a "combination of what Jack Welch put together at GE . . . and Warren Buffett's very practical ideas on how you go about creating a return for shareholders."
>
> The year 2002 was, to say the least, not a good year for Kozlowski. His claims to legendary status came crashing down when he faced two sets of indictments brought by Manhattan's District Attorney Robert M. Morgenthau. The first was astonishing in the pettiness of the greed that it exposed: A mogul with a net worth of at least $500 million tries to cheat New York City out of $1 million in sales tax due on fine art. However, the second, handed down on September 12, 2002, was shocking in the scale of corruption that was alleged. Prosecutors, in essence, accused Kozlowski and former chief financial officer Mark Swartz of running a criminal enterprise at Tyco. The two were charged with 38 felony counts for stealing $170 million directly from the company and for obtaining another $430 million through tainted sales of stock.
>
> During his tenure as CEO, Kozlowski also engaged in numerous accounting irregularities which later forced Tyco to have about $7 billion in charges, restatements of earnings, and writedowns since his ouster. And since late 2002, Tyco has lost more than $100 billion in market capitalization. (This would represent more than the amount of Enron's market value at its peak!)
>
> While it would be a tremendous understatement to claim that there were ethical lapses at Tyco, there were also very poor controls throughout the organization—from the operating units up to the board of directors. Tyco, following a strategy of unrelated diversification, was organized into six operating groups: fire protection, flow control, disposable medical products, Simplex Technologies, packaging materials, and specialty products. Given that there were few opportunities for synergies across businesses, Tyco operated in a highly decentralized manner, with an extremely small corporate staff and few controls—other than stringent financial targets. According to Kozlowski, "What's special about Tyco are its financial controls, good incentive programs, strong manufacturing, and operating managers who enjoy working without a whole lot of support." Tyco cut staff in acquired companies and tried to make operations as efficient as possible. The unsparing, top-down budgeting process held division managers accountable for financial performance of their individual units—with no incentives for overall corporate performance.
>
> It now appears that Tyco was not run or structured like any other company. Its lean, mean management structure allowed only a relative handful of trusted lieutenants to work with Kozlowski at headquarters. Its tiny corporate staff now appears to be more intended to keep out prying eyes than to save money. Kozlowski wielded immense power: He never appointed a president, and he handpicked his top managers, ensuring that they were cut from his own cloth: "smart, poor, and want to be rich."
>
> Kozlowski also went to great lengths to keep outside directors in the dark. He controlled all information—including internal audits—that should have gone to the board of directors. That should have been a red flag, and an alert board would have insisted on hearing directly from internal auditors—not from Kozlowski. Although the board approved an extremely generous corporate loan program for top executives, it did not closely monitor transactions. Further, *BusinessWeek* claimed that "Kozlowski also used Tyco's extraordinarily generous bonus system to co-opt many key executives at headquarters and in the field . . . cutting at least 50 of them in on his under-the-table largess." The board should have also objected to management's decision to have the finance department, rather than the general counsel, responsible for Tyco's SEC filings.

The board of directors' fiduciary duty is to closely monitor top management to ensure that they act in the shareholders' best interests. Why didn't this happen? A major reason was that the "outside directors" (who are not part of management) were hardly "independent." One director, Joshua Berman, was receiving $360,000 annually for "legal services," according to SEC filings. Another, Frank E. Walsh (who was lead director and chaired the compensation committee), controlled two companies that did substantial business with Tyco. In addition to his usual director fees, he was rewarded with a $20 million fee (which was never disclosed to the full board of directors) for helping to arrange Tyco's 2001 disastrous acquisition of commercial financial company CIT Group. CIT Group was divested a year later, in 2002, with Tyco booking a huge loss of $7.2 billion. Walsh later pleaded guilty to securities fraud, repaying the $20 million plus a $2.5 million fine.

Prior to his own downfall, Kozlowski provided some useful insights on corporate governance: "Most of us make it to the chief executive position because of a particularly high degree of responsibility. . . . We are offended most by the perception that we would waste the resources of a company that is a major part of our life and livelihood, and that we would be happy with directors who would permit that waste. . . . So as a CEO I want a strong, competent board." Sadly, his story would have had a much happier ending had he followed his own advice.

What Went Wrong at Tyco?   An aggressive culture and an emphasis on performance and incentives drove the organization. But, in a sense, the culture and reward system drove it too far, too fast, and nearly off a cliff! To succeed at Tyco, managers had a straightforward mission—make the numbers. Such a focus on ends—growth at all costs—caused executives to overlook several questionable means that were used to assure the desired end.

In this chapter, we will focus on how organizations can develop and use effective strategic control.[2] We first explore two central aspects of strategic control: (1) *informational control,* which is the ability to respond effectively to environmental change, and (2) *behavioral control,* which is the appropriate balance and alignment among a firm's culture, rewards, and boundaries. In the final section of this chapter, we focus on strategic control from a much broader perspective—what is referred to as *corporate governance.* Here, we direct our attention to the need for a firm's shareholders (the owners) and their elected representatives (the board of directors) to ensure that the firm's executives (the management team) strive to fulfill their fiduciary duty: maximizing long-term shareholder value. Many would agree that Tyco International could easily be a poster child for poor corporate governance.

Ensuring Informational Control: Responding Effectively to Environmental Change

In this section we will discuss two broad types of control systems. The first one, which we label "traditional," is based largely on a feedback approach—that is, there is little or no action taken to revise strategies, goals, and objectives until the end of the time period in question, usually a quarter or a month. The second one, which we call "contemporary," emphasizes the importance of continually monitoring the environment (both internal and external) for important trends and events that signal the need to make important modifications to a firm's strategies, goals, and objectives. As both general and competitive environments become more unpredictable and complex, the need for contemporary systems increases.

A Traditional Approach to Strategic Control

The traditional approach to strategic control is sequential: (1) strategies are formulated and top management sets goals, (2) strategies are implemented, and (3) performance is measured against the predetermined goal set, as illustrated in Exhibit 9.1.

Control is based on a feedback loop from performance measurement to strategy formulation. This process typically involves lengthy time lags, often tied to a firm's annual

Exhibit 9.1 Traditional Approach to Strategic Control

planning cycle. Such traditional control systems, termed "single-loop" learning by Chris Argyris of Harvard University, simply compare actual performance to a predetermined goal.[3] They are most appropriate when the environment is stable and relatively simple, goals and objectives can be measured with a high level of certainty, and there is little need for complex measures of performance. Sales quotas, operating budgets, production schedules, and similar quantitative control mechanisms are typical. The appropriateness of the business strategy or standards of performance is seldom questioned.[4]

The idea that well-managed companies should move forward in accordance with detailed and precise plans has come under attack from several directions.[5] James Brian Quinn of Dartmouth College has argued that grand designs with precise and carefully integrated plans seldom work. Rather, most strategic change proceeds incrementally—one step at a time. Leaders can best serve their organizations by introducing some sense of direction, some logic in incremental steps.[6]

Similarly, McGill University's Henry Mintzberg has written about leaders "crafting" a strategy.[7] Drawing on the parallel between the potter at her wheel and the strategist, Mintzberg pointed out that the potter begins work with some general idea of the artifact she wishes to create, but the details of design—even possibilities for a different design— emerge as the work progresses. For businesses facing complex and turbulent business environments, the craftsperson's method seems more appropriate than that provided by the traditional, more rational, planner. The former helps us deal with the uncertainty about how a design will work out in practice and allows for a creative element.

Mintzberg's argument, like Quinn's, casts doubt on the value of rigid planning and goal-setting processes. Fixed strategic goals also become dysfunctional for firms competing in highly unpredictable competitive environments where strategies need to change frequently and opportunistically. An inflexible commitment to predetermined goals and milestones can prevent the very adaptability that is often required of a good strategy.

Even organizations that have been extremely successful in the past can become complacent. Often they may fail to anticipate important changes in the competitive environment and adapt their goals and strategies to the new conditions. An example of such a firm is Cisco Systems, whose market value at one time approached an astonishing $600 billion, but as of late 2004 was about $150 billion. Cisco has minimized the potential for such problems in the future by improving its informational control systems. Other firms such as Siebel Systems have been more successful in anticipating change and have made proper corrections to their strategies. We discuss these firms in Strategy Spotlight 9.1.

Without doubt, the traditional "feedback" approach to strategic control has some important limitations. Is there another, better, way?

A Contemporary Approach to Strategic Control

Adapting to and anticipating both internal and external environmental change is an integral part of strategic control. The relationships between strategy formulation, implementation, and control are highly interactive, as suggested by Exhibit 9.2. It also illustrates two different types of strategic control: informational control and behavioral control. Informational control is primarily concerned with whether or not the organization is "doing the

strategy spotlight

When the Tech Bubble Burst

We can learn some lessons from fallen stars. Cisco Systems, Inc., once the invincible momentum stock adored by Wall Street, came crashing down just as we were beginning the 21st century. What went wrong?

Problems started when Cisco announced a $2.2 billion inventory write-off—Wall Street severely punished the stock as a result. With all of its experience, why didn't Cisco see the problems coming? Cisco made a common mistake: It projected the past into the future.

Past demand had been vigorous, but customers were requiring less and less of the firm's products. And financing was cheap—it was no problem for a company like Cisco to find capital to finance ongoing operations even when things didn't look so bright on the horizon. Overtaken by its own success, Cisco failed to see the slowdown

Sources: J. Weber, "Management Lessons from the Bust," *BusinessWeek,* August 27, 2001, pp. 104–12; S. Morrison, "Positive Sales News Takes the Sting out of Cisco Revamp," *Financial Times Online,* August 26, 2001; "Siebel Sees Economic Rebound Late 2002," Reuters, August 20, 2001.

in customer demand. John Sterman at MIT sums up the situation: "If you were in the pasta business, you want to know how much pasta people are cooking and eating, not how much they're buying, and certainly not how much supermarkets and distributors are ordering from the factory." Consumers ultimately determine demand; Cisco missed this important point and inaccurately forecast new sales orders. When the orders didn't materialize, a stockpile of inventory sat on the shelves while Wall Street annulled the short-lived marriage between investors and their beloved Cisco.

In contrast, Siebel Systems, Inc., kept its eye on the future. The company rewarded its sales force for providing accurate information concerning future demand. Salespeople receive commissions not only for sales, but also for forecast information. Haim Mendelson at Stanford University remarked that this provides the company "with a deep understanding of what customers are going to do."

right things." Behavioral control, on the other hand, asks if the organization is "doing things right" in the implementation of its strategy. Both the informational and behavioral components of strategic control are necessary, but not sufficient, conditions for success. That is, what good is a well-conceived strategy that cannot be implemented? Or, alternatively, what use is an energetic and committed workforce if it is focused on the wrong strategic target?

John Weston is the former CEO of ADP Corporation, the largest payroll and tax-filing processor in the world. He captures the essence of contemporary control systems.

> At ADP, 39 plus 1 adds up to more than 40 plus 0. The 40-plus-0 employee is the harried worker who at 40 hours a week just tries to keep up with what's in the "in" basket. He tries to do whatever he thinks he's supposed to do. Because he works with his head down, he takes zero hours to think about what he's doing, why he's doing it, and how he's doing it. Does he need to do it

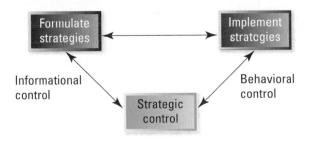

Exhibit 9.2 Contemporary Approach to Strategic Control

in the first place? On the other hand, the 39-plus-1 employee takes at least 1 of those 40 hours to think about what he's doing and why he's doing it. That's why the other 39 hours are far more productive.[8]

Informational control deals with the internal environment as well as the external strategic context. It addresses the assumptions and premises that provide the foundation for an organization's strategy. The key question addressed by information control is: Do the organization's goals and strategies still "fit" within the context of the current strategic environment?

This involves two key issues. First, managers must scan and monitor the external environment. This includes the general environment and the industry (or competitive) environment, as we discussed in Chapter 2. Recall, for example, the failure of Motorola to properly revise its strategic objectives once the demand for digital cell phones increased. Also, conditions can change in the internal environment of the firm, requiring continuous monitoring and, perhaps, changes in the strategic direction of the firm. These may include, for example, the resignation of key executives, delays in the completion of major production facilities, and unexpected wildcat strikes. As we discussed in Chapter 3, the internal environment may be viewed in terms of the primary and support activities (as well as relationships among them) in the value chain that create value for the firm.

The important difference is this: In the traditional approach, the understanding of the assumption base is an initial step in the process of strategy formulation. In the contemporary approach, information control is part of an ongoing process of organizational learning that continuously updates and challenges the assumptions that underlie the organization's strategy. In such "double-loop" learning, the organization's assumptions, premises, goals, and strategies are continuously monitored, tested, and reviewed. The benefits of continuous monitoring are evident—time lags are dramatically shortened, changes in the competitive environment are detected earlier, and the organization's ability to respond with speed and flexibility is enhanced.

A key question becomes: OK, but how is this done? Contemporary control systems must have four characteristics to be effective.[9]

1. They must focus on constantly changing information that top managers identify as having potential strategic importance.
2. The information is important enough to demand frequent and regular attention from operating managers at all levels of the organization.
3. The data and information generated by the control system are best interpreted and discussed in face-to-face meetings of superiors, subordinates, and peers.
4. The contemporary control system is a key catalyst for an ongoing debate about underlying data, assumptions, and action plans.

Contemporary control systems track the strategic uncertainties that may keep senior managers awake at night. Depending on the type of business, such uncertainties may relate to changes in technology, customer tastes, government regulation, and industry competition. Since control systems must be designed to gather information that might challenge the strategic visions of the future, they are, by definition, hot buttons for senior managers.

An executive's decision to use the control system interactively—in other words, to invest the time and attention to review and evaluate new information—sends a clear signal to the organization about what is important. The dialogue and debate that emerges from such an interactive process can often lead to new strategies and innovations. Strategy Spotlight 9.2 discusses how executives at *USA Today*, Gannett Co.'s daily newspaper, review information delivered each Friday.

Let's now turn our attention to behavioral control.

strategy spotlight

USA Today's Interactive Control System

Top managers at Gannett-owned *USA Today* meet each Friday to discuss ongoing strategy. Every week, they review information ranging from day-to-day operations information to year-to-date data. This information enables top management to check the pulse of the industry on a frequent basis. This minimizes the surprises that frequently beset other companies that don't keep close tabs on available information. Senior managers frequently meet with operations-level managers for intensive discussion to analyze the weekly information. The results of these high-level meetings on information control allow managers from the operating core of the newspaper to respond to industry trends and events on nearly a real-time basis.

By controlling information, *USA Today* managers:

♦ Compare projected advertising volume with actual volume.

Sources: R. Simons, "Control in an Age of Empowerment," *Harvard Business Review* 73, no. 2 (1995), pp. 80–88; D. Caney, "Gannett, Knight Ridder Walloped by Ad Slump," Reuters, July 17, 2001.

♦ Assess new advertising revenues by client type to better target client markets.

♦ Quickly discover revenue shortfalls before major problems arise.

♦ Become aware of unexpected successes that have often led to innovations.

These weekly meetings have returned significant rewards for *USA Today*. Innovations that have been implemented as a result of high information control include:

♦ A new market survey service targeted at the automobile industry (a potential source of high-volume advertising).

♦ The addition of fractional page color advertising (increasing the number of advertisers that use color, thereby increasing advertising revenue).

♦ Expanding the job function of circulation employees to include regional sales of advertising space.

♦ Developing a program of advertising inserts targeted toward specific customers and products.

Attaining Behavioral Control: Balancing Culture, Rewards, and Boundaries

Behavioral control is focused on implementation—doing things right. Effectively implementing strategy requires manipulating three key control "levers": culture, rewards, and boundaries. These three levers are illustrated in Exhibit 9.3. Furthermore, there are two compelling reasons for an increased emphasis on culture and rewards in implementing a system of behavioral controls.

First, the competitive environment is increasingly complex and unpredictable, demanding both flexibility and quick response to its challenges. As firms simultaneously downsize and face the need for increased coordination across organizational boundaries, a control system based primarily on rigid strategies and rules and regulations is dysfunctional. Thus, the use of rewards and culture to align individual and organizational goals becomes increasingly important.

Second, the implicit long-term contract between the organization and its key employees has been eroded.[10] Today's younger managers have been conditioned to see themselves as "free agents" and view a career as a series of opportunistic challenges. As managers are advised to "specialize, market yourself, and have work, if not a job," the importance of culture and rewards in building organizational loyalty claim greater importance. (We addressed this issue at length in Chapter 4.)

Each of the three levers—culture, rewards, and boundaries—must work in a balanced and consistent manner. Let's consider the role of each.

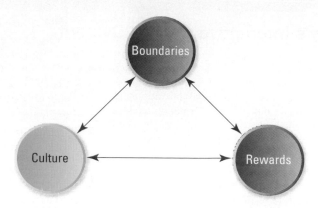

Exhibit 9.3 Essential Elements of Behavioral Control

Building a Strong and Effective Culture

What is culture? Consistent with our discussion in Chapter 4, organizational culture is a system of shared values (what is important) and beliefs (how things work) that shape a company's people, organizational structures, and control systems to produce behavioral norms (the way we do things around here). How important is culture? Very. Over the years, numerous best sellers—*Theory Z, Corporate Cultures, In Search of Excellence,* and *Good to Great*[11]—have emphasized the powerful influence of culture on what goes on within organizations and how they perform.

Collins and Porras argued in *Built to Last* that the key factor in sustained exceptional performance is a cultlike culture.[12] You can't touch it—you can't write it down—but it's there, in every organization, and its influence is pervasive. It can work for you or against you.[13] Effective leaders understand its importance and strive to shape and use it as one of their important levers of strategic control.[14]

The Role of Culture   Culture wears many different hats, each woven from the fabric of those values that sustain the organization's primary source of competitive advantage. Some examples are:

♦   Federal Express and Southwest Airlines focus on customer service.
♦   Lexus (a division of Toyota) and Hewlett-Packard emphasize product quality.
♦   Newell Rubbermaid and 3M place a high value on innovation.
♦   Nucor (steel) and Emerson Electric are concerned, above all, with operational efficiency.

Culture sets implicit boundaries—that is, unwritten standards of acceptable behavior—in dress, ethical matters, and the way an organization conducts its business.[15] By creating a framework of shared values, culture encourages individual identification with the organization and its objectives. Thus, culture acts as a means of reducing monitoring costs.[16]

Sustaining an Effective Culture   Powerful organizational cultures just don't happen overnight, and they don't remain in place without a strong commitment—both in terms of words and deeds—by leaders throughout the organization. A discussion of the content of an organization's culture is beyond the scope of our present discussion. Rather, our focus will be on the process, that is, how a viable and productive organizational culture can be strengthened and sustained. It cannot be "built" or "assembled"; instead, it must be cultivated, encouraged, and "fertilized."

Storytelling is one way effective cultures are maintained. Many are familiar with the story of how Art Fry's failure to develop a strong adhesive led to 3M's enormously successful Post-it Notes. Perhaps less familiar is the story of Francis G. Okie.[17] In 1922 Okie came up with the idea of selling sandpaper to men as a replacement for razor blades. The idea obviously didn't pan out, but Okie was allowed to remain at 3M. Interestingly, the technology developed by Okie led 3M to develop its first blockbuster product: a waterproof sandpaper that became a staple of the automobile industry. Such stories foster the importance of risk taking, experimentation, freedom to fail, and of course innovation—all vital elements of 3M's culture.

Rallies or "pep talks" by top executives also serve to reinforce a firm's culture. The late Sam Walton was well known for his pep rallies at local Wal-Mart stores. Four times a year, the founders of Home Depot—CEO Bernard Marcus and Arthur Blank—used to don orange aprons and stage Breakfast with Bernie and Arthur, a 6:30 a.m. pep rally, broadcast live over the firm's closed-circuit TV network to most of its 45,000 employees.[18]

Southwest Airlines's "Culture Committee" is a unique vehicle designed to perpetuate the company's highly successful culture. The following excerpt from an internal company publication describes its objectives:

> The goal of the Committee is simple—to ensure that our unique Corporate Culture stays alive. . . . Culture Committee members represent all regions and departments across our system and they are selected based upon their exemplary display of the "Positively Outrageous Service" that won us the first-ever Triple Crown; their continual exhibition of the "Southwest Spirit" to our Customers and to their fellow workers; and their high energy level, boundless enthusiasm, unique creativity, and constant demonstration of teamwork and love for their fellow workers.[19]

Motivating with Rewards and Incentives

Reward and incentive systems represent a powerful means of influencing an organization's culture, focusing efforts on high-priority tasks, and motivating individual and collective task performance.[20] Since much of culture deals with influencing beliefs, behaviors, and attitudes of people within an organization, the reward system—by specifying who gets rewarded and why—is an effective motivator and control mechanism.[21] Strategy Spotlight 9.3 discusses how the China-based Legend Group varies its incentives based upon the different hierarchical levels in its organization.

The Potential Downside   Generally speaking, people in organizations act rationally, each motivated by his or her personal best interest.[22] However, the collective sum of individual behaviors of an organization's employees does not always necessarily result in what is best for the organization—that is, individual rationality does not always guarantee organizational rationality.

As corporations grow and evolve, they often develop different business units with multiple reward systems. They may differ based on industry contexts, business situations, stage of product life cycles, and so on. Thus, subcultures within organizations may reflect differences among an organization's functional areas, products, services, and divisions.

Problems arise when countercultures emerge that have shared values in direct opposition to the patterns of the dominant culture. To the extent that reward systems reinforce such behavioral norms, attitudes, and belief systems, organizational cohesiveness is reduced; important information is hoarded rather than shared, individuals begin working at cross-purposes, and they lose sight of overarching goals and objectives.

Such conflicts are commonplace in many organizations. For example, sales and marketing personnel promise unrealistically quick delivery times to bring in business, much to the dismay of operations and logistics; overengineering by R&D creates headaches for

Legend Group: Providing Incentives at All Levels

One of the key tasks of management is to keep the employees motivated. Designing the right kind of incentives that meet the expectations of employee groups at different levels in the hierarchy is a big challenge. Here is how Liu Chuanzhi, chairman of Legend Group, dealt with this issue. Legend is a global personal computer manufacturer based in Beijing, China.

Our executive team needs a sense of ownership in the company. Many state-owned enterprises in China face a special challenge: They cannot give their senior executives stock. But we took an untraditional approach; we reformed our ownership structure to make Legend a joint stock company, enabling us to give all our executive team members stock. In addition, senior executives need recognition, so we provide them with opportunities

to speak to the media. To date, we've lost no senior executives to other companies.

Midlevel managers want to become senior managers, so they respond best to challenges—to opportunities to display and hone their talents. We set very high performance standards for our middle managers, and we let them participate in strategic processes, in designing their own work, and in making and executing their own decisions. If they get good results, they are handsomely rewarded.

Line employees need a sense of stability. If they take responsibility and are conscientious, they earn a predictable bonus. We also tie team performance to company or unit performance, and individual performance to team performance. For example, we might let the team decide how to allocate a percentage of their team bonus to individuals, with some general guidelines from the corporate level.

Source: L. Chuanzhi, "Set Different Incentive Levels," *Harvard Business Review* 81, no. 1 (2003), p. 47.

manufacturing; and so on. Conflicts also arise across divisions when divisional profits become a key compensation criterion. As ill will and anger escalate, personal relationships and performance may suffer.

Creating Effective Reward and Incentive Programs   To be effective, incentive and reward systems need to reinforce basic core values and enhance cohesion and commitment to goals and objectives. They also must not be at odds with the organization's overall mission and purpose.[23]

Consider how incentives are used at General Mills. To ensure a manager's interest in the overall performance of his or her unit, half of a manager's annual bonus is linked to business-unit results and half to individual performance.[24] For example, if a manager simply matches a rival manufacturer's performance, his or her salary is roughly 5 percent lower. However, if a manager's product ranks in the industry's top 10 percent in earnings growth and return on capital, the manager's total compensation can rise to nearly 30 percent beyond the industry norm.

Effective reward and incentive systems share a number of common characteristics.

- Objectives are clear, well understood, and broadly accepted.
- Rewards are clearly linked to performance and desired behaviors.
- Performance measures are clear and highly visible.
- Feedback is prompt, clear, and unambiguous.
- The compensation "system" is perceived as fair and equitable.
- The structure is flexible; it can adapt to changing circumstances.[25]

The perception that a plan is "fair and equitable" is critically important. Similarly, the firm must have the flexibility to respond to changing requirements as its direction and objectives change. In recent years many companies have begun to place more emphasis on growth. Emerson Electric is one company that has shifted its emphasis from cost cutting to growth. To ensure that changes take hold, the management compensation formula has been changed from a largely bottom-line focus to one that emphasizes growth, new products, acquisitions, and international expansion. Discussions about profits are handled separately, and a culture of risk taking is encouraged.[26]

Setting Boundaries and Constraints

In an ideal world, a strong culture and effective rewards should be sufficient to ensure that all individuals and subunits work toward the common goals and objectives of the whole organization.[27] In the real world, however, this is not usually the case. Counterproductive behavior can arise because of motivated self-interest, lack of a clear understanding of goals and objectives, or outright malfeasance. Boundaries and constraints, when used properly, can serve many useful purposes for organizations, including:

- Focusing individual efforts on strategic priorities.
- Providing short-term objectives and action plans to channel efforts.
- Improving efficiency and effectiveness.
- Minimizing improper and unethical conduct.

Focusing Efforts on Strategic Priorities   Boundaries and constraints play a valuable role in focusing a company's strategic priorities. A well-known strategic boundary in U.S. industry is Jack Welch's (former CEO of General Electric) demand that any business in the corporate portfolio be ranked first or second in its industry. In a similar vein, Eli Lilly has reduced its research efforts to five broad areas of disease, down from eight or nine a decade ago.[28] This concentration of effort and resources provides the firm with greater strategic focus and the potential for stronger competitive advantages in the remaining areas.

Norman Augustine, Lockheed Martin's former chairman, provided four criteria for selecting candidates for diversification into "closely related" businesses.[29] They must (1) be high tech, (2) be systems oriented, (3) deal with large customers (either corporations or government) as opposed to consumers, and (4) be in growth businesses. Augustine said, "We have found that if we can meet most of those standards, then we can move into adjacent markets and grow."

Boundaries also have a place in the nonprofit sector. For example, a British relief organization uses a system to monitor strategic boundaries by maintaining a list of companies whose contributions it will neither solicit nor accept. Such boundaries clearly go beyond simply taking the moral high road. Rather, they are essential for maintaining legitimacy with existing and potential benefactors.

Providing Short-Term Objectives and Action Plans   In Chapter 1 we discussed the importance of a firm having a vision, mission, and strategic objectives that are internally consistent and provide strategic direction. In addition, short-term objectives and action plans provide similar benefits. That is, they represent boundaries that help to allocate resources in an optimal manner and to channel the efforts of employees at all levels throughout the organization.[30] To be effective, short-term objectives must have several attributes. They should:

- Be specific and measurable.
- Include a specific time horizon for their attainment.
- Be achievable, yet challenging enough to motivate managers who must strive to accomplish them.

Developing Meaningful Action Plans: Aircraft Interior Products, Inc.

MSA Aircraft Interior Products, Inc., is a manufacturing firm based in San Antonio, Texas, that was founded in 1983 by Mike Spraggins and Robert Plenge. The firm fulfills a small but highly profitable niche in the aviation industry with two key products. The Accordia line consists of patented, lightweight, self-contained window-shade assemblies. MSA's interior cabin shells are state-of-the-art assemblies that include window panels, side panels, headliners, and suspension system structures. MSA's products have been installed on a variety of aircraft, such as the Gulfstream series, the Cessna Citation, and Boeing's 727, 737, 757, and 707.

Much of MSA's success can be attributed to carefully articulated action plans consistent with the firm's mission and objectives. During the past five years, MSA has increased its sales at an annual rate of 15 to 18 percent. It has also succeeded in adding many prestigious companies to its customer base. Below are excerpts from MSA's mission statement and objectives as well as the action plans to achieve a 20 percent annual increase in sales.

Source: For purposes of confidentiality, some of the information presented in this spotlight has been disguised. We would like to thank company management and Joseph Picken, consultant, for providing us with the information used in this application.

Mission Statement

- Be recognized as an innovative and reliable supplier of quality interior products for the high-end, personalized transportation segments of the aviation, marine, and automotive industries.

- Design, develop, and manufacture interior fixtures and components that provide exceptional value to the customer through the development of innovative designs in a manner that permits decorative design flexibility while retaining the superior functionality, reliability, and maintainability of well-engineered, factory-produced products.

- Grow, be profitable, and provide a fair return, commensurate with the degree of risk, for owners and stockholders.

Objectives

1. Achieve sustained and profitable growth over the next three years:

   - 20 percent annual growth in revenues
   - 12 percent pretax profit margins
   - 18 percent return on shareholder's equity

2. Expand the company's revenues through the development and introduction of two or more *(continued)*

Research has found that performance is enhanced when individuals are encouraged to attain specific, difficult, yet achievable, goals (as opposed to vague "do your best" goals).[31]

Short-term objectives must provide proper direction while at the same time providing enough flexibility for the firm to keep pace with and anticipate changes in the external environment. Such changes might include new government regulations, a competitor introducing a substitute product, or changes in consumer taste. Additionally, unexpected events within a firm may require a firm to make important adjustments in both strategic and short-term objectives. For example, the emergence of new industries can have a drastic effect on the demand for products and services in more "traditional" industries.

Along with short-term objectives, action plans are critical to the implementation of chosen strategies. Unless action plans are specific, there may be little assurance that managers have thought through all of the resource requirements for implementing their strategies. In addition, unless plans are specific, managers may not understand what needs to be implemented nor have a clear time frame for completion. This is essential for the scheduling of key activities that must be implemented. Finally, individual managers must be held accountable for the implementation of action plans. This helps to provide the necessary motivation and "sense of ownership" to implement action plans on a timely basis. Strategy

(continued) new products capable of generating revenues in excess of $8 million a year by 2007.

3. Continue to aggressively expand market opportunities and applications for the Accordia line of window-shade assemblies, with the objective of sustaining or exceeding a 20 percent annual growth rate for at least the next three years.

Exhibit 9.4 details an "Action Plan" for Objective 3.

MSA's action plans are supported by detailed month-by-month budgets and strong financial incentives for its executives. Budgets are prepared by each individual department and include all revenue and cost items. Managers are motivated by their participation in a profit-sharing program, and the firm's two founders each receive a bonus equal to 3 percent of total sales.

Exhibit 9.4   Action Plan for Objective 3

Description	Primary Responsibility	Target Date
1. Develop and implement 2005 marketing plan, including specific plans for addressing Falcon 20 retrofit programs and expanded sales of cabin shells.	R. H. Plenge (V.P. Marketing)	December 15, 2004
2. Negotiate new supplier agreement with Gulfstream Aerospace.	M. Spraggins (President)	March 1, 2005
3. Continue and complete the development of the UltraSlim window and have a fully tested and documented design ready for production at a manufacturing cost of less than $900 per unit.	D. R. Pearson (V.P. Operations)	June 15, 2005
4. Develop a window design suitable for L-1011 and similar wide-body aircraft and have a fully tested and documented design ready for production at a manufacturing cost comparable to the current Boeing window.	D. R. Pearson (V.P. Operations)	September 15, 2005

Spotlight 9.4 illustrates how action plans fit into the mission statement and objectives of a small manufacturer of aircraft interior components.

Improving Operational Efficiency and Effectiveness   Rule-based controls are most appropriate in organizations with the following characteristics:

- Environments are stable and predictable.
- Employees are largely unskilled and interchangeable.
- Consistency in product and service is critical.
- The risk of malfeasance is extremely high (e.g., in banking or casino operations), and controls must be implemented to guard against improper conduct.[32]

For example, McDonald's Corp. has extensive rules and regulations that regulate the operation of its franchises.[33] Its policy manual states, "Cooks must turn, never flip, hamburgers. If they haven't been purchased, Big Macs must be discarded in 10 minutes after being cooked and French fries in 7 minutes. Cashiers must make eye contact with and smile at every customer."

Guidelines can also be effective in setting spending limits and the range of discretion for employees and managers, such as the $2,500 limit that hotelier Ritz-Carlton uses to empower employees to placate dissatisfied customers. Regulations also can be initiated to improve the use of an employee's time at work.[34] Computer Associates restricts the use of e-mail during the hours of 10 a.m. to noon and 2 p.m. to 4 p.m. each day.[35]

Minimizing Improper and Unethical Conduct   Guidelines can be useful in specifying proper relationships with a company's customers and suppliers.[36] For example, many companies have explicit rules regarding commercial practices, including the prohibition of any form of payment, bribe, or kickback. Cadbury Schweppes has followed a rather simple but effective step in controlling the use of bribes by specifying that all payments, no matter how unusual, are recorded on the company's books. Its chairman, Sir Adrian Cadbury, contended that such a practice causes managers to pause and consider whether a payment is a necessary and standard cost of doing business or simply a bribe.[37] Consulting companies, too, typically have strong rules and regulations directed at protecting client confidentiality and conflicts of interest.

Chemical Bank (now part of J.P. Morgan Chase Bank), to ensure fair and equitable treatment of its suppliers, forbids any review that determines whether suppliers are Chemical customers before the bank awards contracts. Regulations backed up with strong sanctions can also help an organization to avoid conducting business in an unethical manner. In the wake of the corporate scandals of the early 21st century and the passing of the Sarbanes-Oxley Act (which, among other things, provides for stiffer penalties for financial reporting misdeeds), many chief financial officers (CFOs) have taken steps to ensure ethical behavior in the preparation of financial statements. For example, Home Depot's CFO, Carol B. Tome, strengthened the firm's code of ethics and developed stricter guidelines. Now all 25 of her subordinates must sign personal statements that all of their financial statements are correct—just as she and her boss, CEO Robert Nardelli, have to do now according to the congressional legislation.[38]

Behavioral Control in Organizations: Situational Factors

We have discussed the behavioral dimension of control. Here, the focus is on ensuring that the behavior of individuals at all levels of an organization is directed toward achieving organizational goals and objectives. The three fundamental types of control are culture, rewards and incentives, and boundaries and constraints. An organization may pursue one or a combination of them on the basis of a variety of internal and external factors.

Not all organizations place the same emphasis on each type of control.[39] For example, in professional organizations, such as high-technology firms engaged in basic research, members may work under high levels of autonomy. Here, an individual's performance is generally quite difficult to measure accurately because of the long lead times involved in research and development activities. Thus, internalized norms and values become very important.

In organizations where the measurement of an individual's output or performance is quite straightforward, control depends primarily on granting or withholding rewards. Frequently, a sales manager's compensation is in the form of a commission and bonus tied directly to his or her sales volume, which is relatively easy to determine. Here, behavior is influenced more strongly by the attractiveness of the compensation than by the norms and values implicit in the organization's culture. Furthermore, the measurability of output precludes the need for an elaborate system of rules to control behavior.

Control in bureaucratic organizations has long been recognized as dependent on members following a highly formalized set of rules and regulations. In such situations, most activities are routine and the desired behavior can be specified in a detailed manner because there is generally little need for innovative or creative activity. In business organizations, for example, managing an assembly plant requires strict adherence to many rules as well

Exhibit 9.5
Organizational
Control:
Alternative
Approaches

Approach	Some Situational Factors
Culture: A system of unwritten rules that forms an internalized influence over behavior.	◆ Often found in professional organizations. ◆ Associated with high autonomy. ◆ Norms are the basis for behavior.
Rules: Written and explicit guidelines that provide external constraints on behavior.	◆ Associated with standardized output. ◆ Tasks are generally repetitive and routine. ◆ Little need for innovation or creative activity.
Rewards: The use of performance-based incentive systems to motivate.	◆ Measurement of output and performance is rather straightforward. ◆ Most appropriate in organizations pursuing unrelated diversification strategies. ◆ Rewards may be used to reinforce other means of control.

as exacting sequences of assembly operations. In the public sector, the Department of Motor Vehicles in most states must follow clearly prescribed procedures when issuing or renewing driver licenses.

Exhibit 9.5 provides alternate approaches to behavioral control and some of the situational factors associated with them.

Evolving from Boundaries to Rewards and Culture

In most environments, organizations should strive to provide a system of rewards and incentives, coupled with a culture strong enough that boundaries become internalized. This reduces the need for external controls such as rules and regulations. We suggest several ways to move in this direction.

First, hire the right people—individuals who already identify with the organization's dominant values and have attributes consistent with them. We addressed this issue in detail in Chapter 4; recall the "Bozo Filter" that was developed by Cooper Software of Palo Alto, California. Microsoft's David Pritchard is well aware of the consequences of failing to hire properly.

> If I hire a bunch of bozos, it will hurt us, because it takes time to get rid of them. They start infiltrating the organization and then they themselves start hiring people of lower quality. At Microsoft, we are always looking for people who are better than we are.

Second, training plays a key role. For example, in elite military units such as the Green Berets and Navy SEALs, the training regimen so thoroughly internalizes the culture that individuals, in effect, lose their identity. The group becomes the overriding concern and focal point of their energies. At firms such as FedEx, training not only builds skills, but also plays a significant role in building a strong culture on the foundation of each organization's dominant values.

Third, managerial role models are vital. Andy Grove at Intel doesn't need (or want) a large number of bureaucratic rules to determine who is responsible for what, who is

Culture and Rewards: The Success Story at Semco

Rules and regulations can often substitute for individual judgment. In other words, when a company has sufficient rules to address a situation, there is no need for employees to exercise reasoning and judgment. But in the absence of rules, a company can have either pandemonium or a smoothly running, innovative operation. What separates chaos from order in firms with few rules to govern employee behavior? Semco provides an excellent example.

Semco, Inc., is a Brazil-based firm that began as a small pump machinery manufacturer but has grown into a large diversified corporation. When new employees join the firm, among the first things they notice are the lack of titles and the absence of numerous rules. Semco's CEO, Ricardo Semler, disdains highly bureaucratic hierarchies. He believes that employees will perform well and work for the goals of the company because they are motivated

to do so without him having to regulate their actions with a long list of regulations.

Semco's culture is one of trust. Semler commented, "Another way of looking at Semco is to say we treat our employees as responsible adults. We never assume that they will take advantage of us, our rules, or lack of them." Doesn't Semler worry that employees will take advantage of the company's trust? No, he doesn't worry about it—he simply deals swiftly with those employees who on rare occasions abuse the trust. Semler suggested that adding rules to control the few who abuse the situation is pandering to the "lowest common denominator."

In addition to the strong culture, the reward system is unique as well. Employees bid for their own salaries. Semco provides data to employees regarding internal wage rates and prevailing external wage rates for similar jobs in the industry. Armed with this information, employees negotiate their salary. Divisions within the firm "hire" employees from other divisions as needed. What if an employee sets his or her salary at an unreasonably high level? No problem—it won't be long until that employee will no longer be hired by any division. Employees who set their wages too high will simply price themselves out of work.

Sources: J. Fierman, "Winning Ideas from Maverick Managers," *Fortune,* February 6, 1995, pp. 70, 73; R. Semler, "Managing without Managers," *Harvard Business Review* 67, no. 5 (1989), pp. 76–84; Institute of Personnel and Development, "Empowering Employees—Maverick Style," M2 Presswire, May 15, 1997; K. Killian, F. Perez, and C. Siehl, "Ricardo Semler and Semco S.A.," *American Graduate School of International Management,* August 2001, pp. 1–12; L. D. T. Mann, *Maverick: The Success behind the World's Most Unusual Workplace* (New York: Warner Books, 2001).

supposed to talk to whom, and who gets to fly first class (no one does). He encourages openness by not having many of the trappings of success—he works in a cubicle like all the other professionals. Can you imagine any new manager asking whether or not he can fly first class? Grove's personal example eliminates such a need.

Fourth, reward systems must be clearly aligned with the organizational goals and objectives. Where do you think rules and regulations are more important in controlling behavior—Home Depot with its generous bonus and stock option plan, or Kmart, which does not provide the same level of rewards and incentives?

We will close this section by discussing Brazil-based Semco in Strategy Spotlight 9.5. This success story shows how a strong culture and an effective reward system reduced the need for rules and regulations.

Linking Strategic Control to Business-Level and Corporate-Level Strategies

As we will see in this section, there is no "one best way" to design strategic control systems for an organization. Instead, it is contingent on many factors. Two of the most important factors in relation to strategic control are business-level strategy (from Chapter 5) and corporate-level strategy (from Chapter 6).

Business-Level Strategy and Strategic Control

In Chapter 5 we discussed two different approaches that firms may take to secure competitive advantages in the marketplace: overall cost leadership and differentiation.[40] As one might expect, implementing these strategies requires fundamentally different organizational arrangements, approaches to control, and reward and incentive systems.

Overall Cost Leadership   This strategy requires that product lines remain rather stable and that innovations deal mostly with production processes. Given the emphasis on efficiency, costly changes even in production processes will tend to be rare. Since products are quite standardized and change rather infrequently, procedures can be developed to allow the division of work into its basic components—those that are routine, standardized, and ideal for semiskilled and unskilled employees. As such, firms competing on the basis of cost must implement tight cost controls, frequent and comprehensive reports to monitor the costs associated with outputs, and highly structured tasks and responsibilities. As one might expect, incentives tend to be based on explicit financial targets since innovation and creativity are expensive and might tend to erode competitive advantages. Let's take another look at Nucor, which we discussed earlier in the chapter.

Nucor competes primarily on the basis of cost and, as one might expect, has a reward and incentive system that is largely based on financial outputs and financial measures.[41] Nucor uses four incentive compensation systems that correspond to the levels of management.

1. *Production incentive program.* Groups of 20 to 40 people are paid a weekly bonus based on either anticipated product time or tonnage produced. Each shift and production line is in a separate bonus group.
2. *Department managers.* Bonuses are based on divisional performance, primarily measured by return on assets.
3. *Employees not directly involved in production.* These include engineers, accountants, secretaries, receptionists, and others. Bonuses are based on two factors: divisional and corporate return on assets.
4. *Senior incentive programs.* Salaries are lower than comparable companies, but a significant portion of total compensation is based on return on stockholder equity. A portion of pretax earnings is placed in a pool and divided among officers as bonuses that are part cash and part stock.

As one might expect, the culture at Nucor reflects its reward and incentive system. Since incentive compensation can account for more than half of their paycheck, employees become nearly obsessed with productivity and apply a lot of pressure on each other. Ken Iverson, a former CEO, recalled an instance in which one employee arrived at work in sunglasses instead of safety glasses, preventing the team from doing any work. Furious, the other workers chased him around the plant with a piece of angle iron!

Differentiation   This strategy typically involves the development of innovative products and services that require the employment of experts who can identify the crucial elements of intricate, creative designs and marketing decisions. As such, highly trained professionals such as scientists and engineers are essential for devising, assessing, implementing, and continually changing complex product designs. New product design also requires the collaboration and cooperation among specialists and functional managers from different areas within a firm. Such individuals must, for example, evaluate and implement a new design, constantly bearing in mind marketing, financial, production, and engineering considerations.

As one might expect, given the need for cooperation and coordination among professionals in many functional areas, it becomes quite difficult to evaluate individuals using hard-and-fast quantitative criteria. It is much more difficult to measure specific outcomes of such efforts as well as attribute outcomes to specific individuals. Thus, more behavioral measures (such as how effectively employees collaborate and share information) and intangible incentives and rewards become necessary to support a strong culture and motivate employees. Consider 3M, a company we discussed earlier in this chapter, whose core value is innovation.

> At 3M, rewards are tied closely to risk-taking and innovation-oriented behavior. Managers are not penalized for product failures; instead, those same people are encouraged to work on another project that borrows from their shared experience and insight. A culture of creativity and "thinking out of the box" is reinforced by their well-known "15 percent rule," which permits employees to set aside 15 percent of their work time to pursue personal research interests. And a familiar 3M homily, "Thou shall not kill new ideas for products," is known as the 11th commandment. It is the source of countless stories, including one that tells how L. D. DeSimone (3M's former CEO) tried five times (and failed) to kill the project that yielded the 3M blockbuster product, Thinsulate.[42]

Corporate-Level Strategy and Strategic Control

In Chapter 6 we discussed two broad types of diversification strategies: related and unrelated. The type of diversification strategy that a firm follows has important implications for the type of controls that it should use.

Sharp Corporation, a $17 billion Japanese consumer electronics giant, follows a *related* diversification strategy.[43] Its most successful technology has been liquid crystal displays (LCDs) that are critical components in nearly all of the firm's products. With their expertise in this area, they are moving into high-end displays for cellular telephones, handheld computers, and digital computers.[44]

Given the need to leverage such technologies across multiple product lines, Sharp must have control systems that foster coordination and sharing. It must focus more on individuals' behavior rather than on short-term financial outcomes. For example, promotion is the most powerful incentive, and it is generally based on seniority and subtle skills exhibited over time, such as teamwork and communication. It is critical to ensure that the company's reward system will not reward short-term self-interested orientations.

Like many Japanese companies, Sharp's culture reinforces the view that the firm is a family or community whose members should cooperate for the greater good. In accordance with the policy of lifetime employment, turnover is low. This encourages employees to pursue what is best for the entire company. Such an outlook lessens the inevitable conflict over sharing important resources such as R&D knowledge.

In contrast to Sharp, firms such as Hanson plc (a British conglomerate) followed a strategy of unrelated diversification for most of its history, at one time owning as many as 150 operating companies in areas such as tobacco, footwear, building products, brewing, and food. There were limited product similarities across businesses and therefore little need for sharing of resources and knowledge across divisional boundaries. James Hanson and Gordon White, founders of the company, actually did not permit any sharing of resources between operating companies even if it was feasible!

Their control system placed such heavy emphasis on individual accountability that they viewed resource sharing, with its potential for mutual blaming, unacceptable. The operating managers had more than 60 percent of their compensation tied to annual financial performance of their subsidiaries. All decision making was decentralized, so that subsidiary managers could be held responsible for the return on capital they employed. However, there was one area in which they had to obtain approval from the corporate office. No subsidiary manager was allowed to incur a capital expenditure greater than $3,000 with-

Level of Strategy	Types of Strategy	Need for Interdependence	Primary Type of Rewards and Controls
Business-level	Overall cost leadership	Low	Financial
Business-level	Differentiation	High	Behavioral
Corporate-level	Related diversification	High	Behavioral
Corporate-level	Unrelated diversification	Low	Financial

Exhibit 9.6
Summary of Relationships between Control and Business-Level and Corporate-Level Strategies

out permission from the corporate office. Hanson managed to be successful with a very small corporate office because of its decentralized structure, tight financial controls, and an incentive system that motivated managers to meet financial goals. Gordon White was proud of claiming that he had never visited any of the operating companies that were part of the Hanson empire![45]

To summarize our discussion of the contingent relationship between levels of strategy and evaluation and control systems, the key issue becomes the need for *in*dependence versus *inter*dependence. In the cases of cost leadership strategies and unrelated diversification, there tends to be less need for interdependence. Thus, the reward and control systems focus more on the use of financial indicators because unit costs, profits, and revenues can be rather easily attributed to a given business unit or division.

By contrast, firms that follow differentiation or related diversification strategies have intense needs for tight interdependencies among the functional areas and business units within the corporation. In these firms, sharing of resources, including raw materials, R&D knowledge, marketing information, and so on, is critical to organizational success. That is, synergies are more important to achieve across value-creating activities and business units than with cost leadership or unrelated strategies. To facilitate sharing and collaboration, reward and control systems tend to incorporate more behavioral indicators. Exhibit 9.6 summarizes our discussion of the relationship between strategies and control systems.

Finally, we must apply an important caveat. Exhibit 9.6 suggests guidelines on how an organization should match its strategies to its evaluation and reward systems. In actual practice, there is clearly a need for all organizations to have combinations of both financial and behavioral reward and control systems. In fact, in both overall cost leadership and unrelated diversification strategies there is clearly a need for collaboration and the sharing of best practices across both value-creating activities and business units. General Electric, for example, has developed many integrating mechanisms to enhance sharing "best practices" across what would appear to be rather unrelated businesses such as jet engines, appliances, and network television. And, for both differentiation and related diversification strategies, financial indicators such as revenue growth and profitability should not be overlooked at both the business-unit and corporate level.

The Role of Corporate Governance

In the first two sections of this chapter we addressed how management can exercise strategic control over the firm's overall operations through the use of informational and behavioral controls. Now we address the issue of strategic control in a broader perspective, typically referred to as "corporate governance." Here we focus on the need for both shareholders (the owners of the corporation) and their elected representatives, the board of directors, to actively ensure that management fulfills its overriding purpose: increasing long-term shareholder value.

Robert Monks and Nell Minow, two leading scholars in corporate governance, define it as "the relationship among various participants in determining the direction and performance of corporations. The primary participants are (1) the shareholders, (2) the management (led by the chief executive officer), and (3) the board of directors."* Consistent with Monks and Minow's definition, our discussion will center on how corporations can succeed (or fail) in aligning managerial motives with the interests of the shareholders and their elected representatives, the board of directors. As you will recall from Chapter 1, we discussed the important role of boards of directors and provided some examples of effective and ineffective boards.[46]

There is little doubt that effective corporate governance can affect a firm's bottom line. Good corporate governance plays an important role in the investment decisions of major institutions, and a premium is often reflected in the price of securities of companies that practice it. The corporate governance premium is larger for firms in countries with sound corporate governance practices compared to countries with weaker corporate governance standards.[47] In addition, there is a strong correlation between strong corporate governance and superior financial performance. Strategy Spotlight 9.6 briefly summarizes three studies that provide support for this contention.

As indicated in our discussion above and in Strategy Spotlight 9.6, there is solid evidence linking good corporate governance with higher performance. At the same time, few topics in the business press are generating as much interest (and disdain!) as corporate governance. Quoting from an article in *BusinessWeek,* we find that:

> Faith in Corporate America hasn't been so strained since the early 1900s, when the public's furor over the monopoly powers of big business led to years of trust busting by Theodore Roosevelt. The latest wave of skepticism may have started with Enron Corp.'s ugly demise, but with each revelation of corporate excess or wrongdoing, the goodwill built up during the boom of the past decade has eroded a little more, giving way to a widespread suspicion and mistrust. An unrelenting barrage of headlines that tell of Securities & Exchange Commission investigations, indictments, guilty pleas, government settlements, financial restatements, and fines has only lent greater credence to the belief that the system is inherently unfair.[48]

A few recent notable examples of flawed corporate governance include:[49]

- AOL buys Time Warner in a deal worth $183 billion—which later results in a $54 billion write-off, the largest ever. (April 25, 2002)
- Oracle CEO Larry Ellison exercises 23 million stock options for a record gain of more than $706 million—weeks before lowering earnings forecasts. (January 2001)
- Arthur Andersen, the accounting firm, agrees to pay $110 million to settle a shareholders suit for alleged fraud in its audit of Sunbeam. (May 2001)
- Former company CEO Al Dunlap agrees to pay $15 million to settle a lawsuit from Sunbeam shareholders and bondholders alleging that he cooked the books of the maker of small appliances. (January 11, 2002)
- Global Crossing, once a high-flying telecom service provider, files for Chapter 11. In the preceding three years, the company's insiders had cashed in $1.3 billion in stock. (January 28, 2002)

---

*Management, of course, cannot ignore the demands of other important firm stakeholders such as creditors, suppliers, customers, employees, and government regulators. At times of financial duress, powerful creditors can exert strong and legitimate pressures on managerial decisions. In general, however, the attention to stakeholders other than the owners of the corporation must be addressed in a manner that is still consistent with maximizing long-term shareholder returns. For a seminal discussion on stakeholder management, refer to R. E. Freeman, *Strategic Management: A Stakeholder Approach* (Boston: Pitman, 1984).

strategy spotlight

Good Corporate Governance and Performance: Research Evidence

Three studies found a positive relationship between the extent to which a firm practices good corporate governance and its performance outcomes. The results of these studies are summarized below.

1. *A strong correlation between corporate governance and price performance of large companies.* Over a recent three-year period, the average return of large capitalized firms with the best governance practices was more than five times higher than the performance of firms in the bottom corporate governance quartile.

2. *Across emerging markets.* In 10 of the 11 Asian and Latin American markets, companies in the top corporate governance quartile for their respective regions had a significantly higher (averaging 10 percentage points) return on capital employed (ROCE) than their market sample. In 12 of the emerging markets analyzed, companies in the lowest corporate governance quartile had a lower ROCE than the market average.

Sources: McKinsey & Company, *Investor Opinion Survey on Corporate Governance,* June 2000; Gill, Amar, Credit Lyonnais Securities (Asia), *Corporate Governance in Emerging Markets: Saints and Sinners,* April 2001; and C. K. Low, *Corporate Governance: An Asia-Pacific Critique* (Hong Kong: Sweet & Maxwell Asia, 2002).

3. *Attitudes toward investing.* McKinsey & Company conducted three surveys from September 1999 to April 2000, which studied attitudes toward investing in Asia, Europe, the United States, and Latin America. Over three-quarters of the more than 200 investors surveyed agreed that "board practices were at least as important as financial performance." Over 80 percent of investors agreed that they "would pay a premium for the shares of a better-governed company than for those of a poorly governed company with comparable financial performance." Interestingly, the study demonstrated that the value of good corporate governance—that is, the premium that investors are willing to pay—varied across regions. Good corporate governance in the United States and the United Kingdom brought the lowest premium, at 18 percent. However, for investments in Asian and Latin American countries, the premium rose to between 20 and 28 percent. The difference in the premium reflected the lack of good corporate governance standards in Asia and Latin America compared to the standards of companies in the United States and the United Kingdom.

- Tyco International discloses that it paid a director $10 million in cash and gave an additional $10 million to his favorite charity in exchange for his help in closing an acquisition deal. (January 29, 2002)
- The New York State Attorney General charges that Merrill Lynch analysts were privately referring to certain stocks as "crap" and "junk" while publicly recommending them to investors. (April 8, 2002)

Clearly, because of the many lapses in corporate governance, one can see the benefits associated with effective practices. However, corporate managers may behave in their own self-interest, often to the detriment of shareholders. Next we address the implications of the separation of ownership and management in the modern corporation, and some mechanisms that can be used to ensure consistency (or alignment) between the interests of shareholders and those of the managers to minimize potential conflicts.

The Modern Corporation: The Separation of Owners (Shareholders) and Management

Some of the proposed definitions for a *corporation* include:

- "The business corporation is an instrument through which capital is assembled for the activities of producing and distributing goods and services and making investments. Accordingly, a basic premise of corporation law is that a business corporation should have as its objective the conduct of such activities with a view to enhancing the corporation's profit and the gains of the corporation's owners, that is, the shareholders." (Melvin Aron Eisenberg, *The Structure of Corporation Law*)

- "A body of persons granted a charter legally recognizing them as a separate entity having its own rights, privileges, and liabilities distinct from those of its members." (*American Heritage Dictionary*)
- An ingenious device for obtaining individual profit without individual responsibility." (Ambrose Bierce, *The Devil's Dictionary*)[50]

All of these definitions have some validity and each one, including that from *The Devil's Dictionary*, reflects a key feature of the corporate form of business organization—its ability to draw resources from a variety of groups and establish and maintain its own persona that is separate from all of them. As Henry Ford once said, "A great business is really too big to be human."

Simply put, a corporation is a mechanism created to allow different parties to contribute capital, expertise, and labor for the maximum benefit of each party. The shareholders (investors) are able to participate in the profits of the enterprise without taking direct responsibility for the operations. The management can run the company without the responsibility of personally providing the funds. And, in order to make both of these possible, the shareholders have limited liability as well as rather limited involvement in the company's affairs. However, they reserve the right to elect directors who have the fiduciary obligation to protect their interests.

Over 70 years ago, Columbia University professors Adolf Berle and Gardiner C. Means addressed the divergence of the interests of the owners of the corporation from the professional managers who are hired to run it. They warned that widely dispersed ownership "released management from the overriding requirement that it serve stockholders." The separation of ownership from management has given rise to a set of ideas called "agency theory." Central to agency theory is the relationship between two primary players—the *principals* who are the owners of the firm (stockholders) and *agents*, who are the people paid by principals to perform a job on their behalf (management). The stockholders elect and are represented by a board of directors that has a fiduciary responsibility to ensure that management acts in the best interests of stockholders to ensure long-term financial returns for the firm.

Agency theory is concerned with resolving two problems that can occur in agency relationships.[51] The first is the agency problem that arises (1) when the goals of the principals and agents conflict, and (2) when it is difficult or expensive for the principal to verify what the agent is actually doing. In a corporation, this means that the board of directors would be unable to confirm that the managers were actually acting in the shareholders' interests because, in most cases, managers are "insiders" with regard to the businesses they operate and thus are better informed than the principals. Thus, managers may act "opportunistically" in pursuing their own interests—to the detriment of the corporation.[52] Managers may, for example, spend corporate funds on expensive perquisites (e.g., company jets and expensive art), devote time and resources to pet projects (initiatives in which they have a personal interest but which have limited market potential), engage in power struggles (where they may fight over resources for their own betterment, to the detriment of what is best for the firm), and negate (or sabotage) attractive merger offers because they may result in increased employment risk.[53]

The second issue is the problem of risk sharing. This arises when the principal and the agent have different attitudes and preferences toward risk. For example, the executives in a firm may favor additional diversification initiatives because—by their very nature—they

strategy spotlight

Crises in International Corporate Governance

Everywhere around the world there seems to be an increased awareness about the need for transparency in corporate accounting and greater controls on management and boards of directors. Europe and Asia seem to have their own crop of homegrown disasters, as does the United States (the names Enron, Arthur Andersen, and Tyco come to mind).

- In Europe the Swiss-Swedish engineering giant ABB was found to have secretly given its outgoing chairman and CEO Percy Barnevik severance pay of $89 million.

- In Japan, the Justice Ministry is pushing legislation that will allow the appointment of independent members to boards of directors—an immense improvement over current Japanese boards that are solely composed of senior executives.

- South Korea's reform was instigated by the unearthing of Daewoo's founder and former chairman's creative accounting practices. He is now in hiding to avoid prosecution for having falsely inflated the company's net worth by $30 billion.

- Even Russia, one of the world's murkiest corporate swamps, is taking some action. Russia's largest energy company, Gazprom, is undertaking a series of reforms, including the establishment of a board-level audit committee by holding an unusual tender to choose an auditor by competitive bid.

While it is clear that none of the new legislation can stop those determined to defraud, countries are hoping these rules will inspire better behavior from corporations and those running them.

Sources: S. Rowland, "The Corporate Cleanup Goes Global," *BusinessWeek,* January 15, 2003, pp. 24–27; www.lib.uchicago.edu/~llou/corpgov.html; J. Citrin, "Recruiting CEOs from Outside: In Defense of Corporate Boards," *Business 2.0,* August 14, 2002, pp. 14–16.

increase the size of the firm and thus the level of executive compensation. At the same time, such diversification initiatives may erode shareholder value because they fail to achieve some of the synergies that we discussed in Chapter 6 (e.g., building on core competencies, sharing activities, or enhancing market power). In effect, agents (executives) may have a stronger preference toward diversification than shareholders because it reduces their personal level of risk from potential loss of employment. In contrast, research has shown that executives who have large holdings of stock in their firms were more likely to have diversification strategies that were more consistent with shareholder interests, that is, increasing long-term returns.[54]

Examples of self-interest behaviors are not limited to U.S. corporations. Strategy Spotlight 9.7 provides examples from other countries.

Governance Mechanisms: Aligning the Interests of Owners and Managers

As noted above, a key characteristic of the modern corporation is the separation of ownership from control. To minimize the potential for managers to act in their own self-interest, or "opportunistically," the owners can implement some governance mechanisms.[55] We address three of these in the next sections. First, there are two primary means of monitoring the behavior of managers. These include (1) a committed and involved *board of directors* that acts in the best interests of the shareholders to create long-term value for shareholders and (2) *shareholder activism,* wherein the owners of the corporation view themselves as share*owners* instead of share*holders* and become actively engaged in the governance of the corporation. As we will see later in this section, shareholder activism has increased dramatically in recent years. Finally, there are managerial incentives, sometimes called "contract-based outcomes," which consist of *reward and compensation agreements.* Here the goal is to carefully craft managerial incentive packages to align the interests of management with those of the stockholders.

A Committed and Involved Board of Directors

The board of directors acts as a fulcrum between the owners and controllers of a corporation. In effect, they are the "middlemen" or "middlewomen" who provide a balance between a small group of key managers in the firm based at the corporate headquarters and a sometimes vast group of shareholders typically spread out over the world. In the United States, the law imposes on the board a strict and absolute fiduciary duty to ensure that a company is run consistent with the long-term interests of the owners, the shareholders. The reality, as we have seen, is somewhat more ambiguous.[56]

The Business Roundtable, representing the largest U.S. corporations, describes the duties of the board as follows:

1. Select, regularly evaluate, and, if necessary, replace the chief executive officer. Determine management compensation. Review succession planning.
2. Review and, where appropriate, approve the financial objectives, major strategies, and plans of the corporation.
3. Provide advice and counsel to top management.
4. Select and recommend to shareholders for election an appropriate slate of candidates for the board of directors; evaluate board processes and performance.
5. Review the adequacy of the systems to comply with all applicable laws/regulations.[57]

Given these principles, what makes for a good board of directors? According to the Business Roundtable, the most important quality is a board of directors who are active, critical participants in determining a company's strategies.[58] That does not mean board members should micromanage or circumvent the CEO. Rather, they should provide strong oversight that goes beyond simply approving the chief executive's plans. Today, a board's primary responsibilities are to ensure that strategic plans undergo rigorous scrutiny, evaluate managers against high performance standards, and take control of the succession process.

Although boards in the past were often dismissed as CEO's rubber stamps, increasingly they are playing a more active role by forcing out CEOs who cannot deliver on performance. According to a recent study by the consulting firm Booz Allen Hamilton, the rate of CEO departures for performance reasons has more than tripled, from 1.3 percent to 4.2 percent, between 1995 and 2002.[59] Well-known CEOs like Gerald M. Levin of AOL Time Warner and Jack M. Greenberg of McDonald's paid the price for poor financial performance by being forced to leave. Others, such as Bernard Ebbers of WorldCom, Inc., and Dennis Kozlowski of Tyco International, lost their jobs due to scandals. In 2003 the board of American Airlines forced Don Carty to resign for failure to disclose executive compensation plans during negotiations with unions. "Deliver or depart" is clearly the new message from the boards.

Another key component of top-ranked boards is director independence. Governance experts believe that a majority of directors should be free of all ties to either the CEO or the company. That means a minimum of "insiders" (past or present members of the management team) should serve on the board, and that directors and their firms should be barred from doing consulting, legal, or other work for the company.[60] Interlocking directorships—in which CEOs and other top managers serve on each other's boards—are not desirable. But perhaps the best guarantee that directors act in the best interests of shareholders is the simplest: Most good companies now insist that directors own significant stock in the company they oversee.[61]

Such guidelines are not always followed. At times, it would appear that the practices of the boards of directors of some companies are the antithesis of such guidelines. Consider the Walt Disney Co. Over a recent five-year period, Michael Eisner pocketed an astonishing $531 million. Although, over a 10-year period, Eisner had led Disney to provide shareholder returns of over 20 percent, he likely had very little resistance from his board of directors.

> Many investors view the Disney board as an anachronism. Among Disney's 16 directors is Eisner's personal attorney—who for several years was chairman of the company's compensation committee! There was also the architect who designed Eisner's Aspen home and his parents' apartment. Joining them are the principal of an elementary school once attended by his children and the president of a university to which Eisner donated $1 million. The board also includes the actor Sidney Poitier, seven current and former Disney executives, and an attorney who does business with Disney. Moreover, most of the outside directors own little or no Disney stock. "It is an egregiously bad board—a train wreck waiting to happen," warns Michael L. Useem, a management professor at the University of Pennsylvania's Wharton School.[62]

This example also demonstrates that "outside directors" are only beneficial to strong corporate governance if they are engaged and vigilant in carrying out their responsibilities.[63] As humorously suggested by Warren Buffett, founder and chairman of Berkshire Hathaway: "The ratcheting up of compensation has been obscene. . . . There is a tendency to put cocker spaniels on compensation committees, not Doberman pinschers."[64]

Many firms have exemplary board practices. Exhibit 9.7 addresses some of the excellent practices at Intel Corp., the world's largest semiconductor chip manufacturer, with $30 billion in revenues in 2003.

Shareholder Activism As a practical matter, there are so many owners of the largest American corporations that it makes little sense to refer to them as "owners" in the sense of individuals becoming informed and involved in corporate affairs. However, even as an individual shareholder, one does have several rights. These include (1) the right to sell the stock, (2) the right to vote the proxy (which includes the election of board members), (3) the right to bring suit for damages if the corporation's directors or managers fail to meet their obligations, (4) the right to certain information from the company, and (5) certain residual rights following the company's liquidation (or its filing for reorganization under bankruptcy laws), once creditors and other claimants are paid off.[65]

Collectively, shareholders have the power to direct the course of corporations.[66] This may involve acts such as being party to shareholder action suits and demanding that key issues be brought up for proxy votes at annual board meetings. In addition, the power of shareholders has intensified in recent years because of the increasing influence of large institutional investors such as mutual funds (e.g., T. Rowe Price and Fidelity Investments) and retirement systems such as TIAA-CREF (for university faculty members and school administrative staff).[67] Institutional investors hold approximately 50 percent of all listed corporate stock in the United States.

Many institutional investors are aggressive in protecting and enhancing their investments. In effect, they are shifting from traders to owners. They are assuming the role of permanent shareholders and rigorously analyze issues of corporate governance. In the process they are reinventing systems of corporate monitoring and accountability.[68]

Consider the proactive behavior of CalPERS, the California Public Employees' Retirement System, which manages approximately $150 billion in assets and is the third largest pension fund in the world. Every year CalPERS reviews the performance of U.S. companies in its stock portfolio and identifies those that are among the lowest long-term relative performers and have governance structures that do not ensure full accountability

**Exhibit 9.7
Intel Corporation's
Exemplary
Governance
Practices**

One of the best examples of governance guidelines are those of Intel Corp. The company's practices address some of the most important current issues in governance, such as director independence, meetings of outside directors, evaluation, and succession planning. The guidelines are on the Intel website for everyone to see. How many other companies would be that proud of their governance Magna Carta? Below are a few highlights:

Board Composition

1. **Mix of inside and outside directors.**

   The Board believes that there should be a majority of independent directors on the Board. However, the Board is willing to have members of management, in addition to the chief executive officer, as directors.

Board Meetings

1. **Board presentations and access to employees.**

   The Board has complete access to any Intel employee.

   The Board encourages management to schedule managers to be present at meetings who: (a) can provide additional insight into the items being discussed because of personal involvement in these areas, or (b) have future potential that management believes should be given exposure to the Board.

Management Review and Responsibility

1. **Formal evaluation of officers.**

   The Compensation Committee conducts, and reviews with the outside directors, an evaluation annually in connection with the determination of the salary and executive bonus of all officers (including the chief executive officer).

Sources: R. D. Ward, *Improving Corporate Boards* (New York: Wiley, 2000); and www.intel.com/intel/finance/corp_gov.htm.

to company owners. This generates a long list of companies, each of which may potentially be publicly identified as a CalPERS "Focus Company"—corporations to which CalPERS directs specific suggested governance reforms. CalPERS meets with the directors of each of these companies to discuss performance and governance issues. The CalPERS Focus List contains those companies that continue to merit public and market attention at the end of the process. Exhibit 9.8 identifies two companies on the CalPERS Focus List for 2003.

While appearing punitive to company management, such aggressive activism has paid significant returns for CalPERS (and other stockholders of the "Focused" companies). For example, a Wilshire Associates study of the "CalPERS Effect" of corporate governance examined the performance of 62 targets over a five-year period. The results indicated that, while the stock of these companies trailed the Standard & Poors Index by 89 percent in the five-year period before CalPERS acted, the same stocks outperformed the index by 23 percent in the following five years, adding approximately $150 million annually in additional returns to the Fund.

Managerial Rewards and Incentives   As we discussed earlier in the chapter, incentive systems must be designed to help a company achieve its goals. Similarly, from the perspective of governance, one of the most critical roles of the board of directors is to

Exhibit 9.8
The CalPERS 2003
Focus List

CalPERS, the California Public Employees' Retirement System, is actively engaged in monitoring the stocks in its portfolio. Below are two of the corporations on the CalPERS Focus List for the year 2003, with information about the firms' corporate headquarters, the extent of CalPERS's holdings, and the governance changes that CalPERS is trying to institute.

Corporation (CalPERS holdings)	CalPERS Proposed Governance Changes
JDS Uniphase Corp. San Jose, California (5.1 million shares)	◆ Conduct a formal governance review using an independent external consultant. ◆ Make a formal commitment to maintain a majority of independent directors. ◆ Conduct Board needs assessment and add members with appropriate skill sets. ◆ Adopt CalPERS's definition of an independent director. ◆ Develop and seek shareholder approval for a formal executive compensation policy. ◆ Seek shareholder approval to maintain the company's poison pill. ◆ Eliminate the co-chairman structure and commit to maintain separate roles of chairman and CEO.
Xerox Corp. Stanford, Connecticut (3 million shares)	◆ Add three new independent directors. ◆ Consider eliminating the executive committee. ◆ Adopt CalPERS definition of an independent director. ◆ Maintain 100 percent independent directors on the audit, compensation, and nominating committees. ◆ Split chairman and CEO roles. ◆ Adopt a board evaluation process. ◆ Develop and seek shareholder approval for executive compensation policy.

Source: Reprinted with permission of California Public Employees' Retirement System (CalPERS).

create incentives that align the interests of the CEO and top executives with the interests of owners of the corporation—long-term shareholder returns.[69] After all, shareholders rely on CEOs to adopt policies and strategies that maximize the value of their shares. A combination of three basic policies may create the right monetary incentives for CEOs to maximize the value of their companies:

1. Boards can require that the CEOs become substantial owners of company stock.
2. Salaries, bonuses, and stock options can be structured so as to provide rewards for superior performance and penalties for poor performance.
3. Threat of dismissal for poor performance can be a realistic outcome.

In recent years the granting of stock options has enabled top executives of publicly held corporations to earn enormous levels of compensation. In 2001 the CEOs of large corporations in the United States averaged $11 million, or 411 times as much as the average factory worker. Over the past decade, the wages of rank-and-file workers increased only 36 percent while the pay of CEOs climbed 340 percent. Stock options can be a valuable governance mechanism to align the CEO's interests with those of the shareholders. The extraordinarily high level of compensation can often be grounded in sound governance principles.[70] For example, Howard Solomon, CEO of Forest Laboratories, received a total compensation of $148.5 million in 2001.[71] This represented $823,000 in salary, $400,000 in bonus, and $147.3 million in stock options that were exercised. However, shareholders also did well—receiving gains of 40 percent. The firm has enjoyed spectacular growth over the past five years and Solomon has been CEO since 1977. Thus, huge income is attributed largely to gains that have built up over many years. As stated by compensation committee member Dan Goldwasser: "If a CEO is delivering substantial increases in shareholder value . . . it's only appropriate that he be rewarded for it."

However, the "pay for performance" principle doesn't always hold. Consider Oracle, for example.

> By 2001, with the tech bubble bursting, Oracle stock was in a free fall. Rather than sit tight in a show of confidence, CEO Laurence Ellison sold 29 million shares in a single week in January, flooding the market when investors already were jittery. He exercised 23 million options the same week for a gain of more than $706 million. Within a month, Oracle stock had lost a third of its value and the company was announcing that it would miss third-quarter forecasts. That triggered further price declines and a rash of shareholder lawsuits alleging that Ellison engaged in "what appears to be the largest insider trading in the history of the U.S. financial market," according to one suit. Ellison's stock sales were a factor in the sell-off that followed, says Henry Asher, president of Northstar Group, Inc., which owns 48,000 Oracle shares. "Was that a ringing endorsement for the company's short-term prospects?" asks Asher. "I don't think so."[72]

There is a fundamental difference between investors, who risk their own money, and executives with stock options, who do not.[73] Good governance endeavors to balance the interests of executives with those of the corporation. On the one hand, this suggests that the board of directors' compensation committee should provide appropriate incentives for outstanding performance. On the other hand, corporate boards must use incentives to protect shareholder interests. However, boards of directors often have not upheld the interests of shareholders when they, in effect, shield top executives from a falling market and erosion of their firms' market values. Many boards have awarded huge option grants despite poor executive performance, and others have made performance goals easier to reach. In 2002 nearly 200 companies swapped or repriced options—all to enrich wealthy executives who are already among the country's richest people.

In addition to the granting of stock options, boards of directors are often failing to fulfill their fiduciary responsibilities to shareholders when they lower the performance targets that executives need to meet in order to receive millions of dollars. At General Motors, for example, CEO G. Richard Wagoner, Jr., and other top executives were entitled to a special performance bonus if the company's net profit margin reached 5 percent by the end of 2003. However, the 5 percent target was later lowered. And Coca-Cola's CEO, Douglas Daft, was scheduled to receive one million performance-based shares if the firm achieved 20 percent annual earnings growth over a five-year period. In 2001 this target was lowered to 16 percent. So much for sound corporate governance.

TIAA-CREF has provided several principles of corporate governance with regard to executive compensation.[74] These include the importance of aligning the rewards of all employees—rank and file as well as executives—to the long-term performance of the corporation; general guidelines on the role of cash compensation, stock, and "fringe benefits"; and the mission of a corporation's compensation committee. Exhibit 9.9 addresses TIAA-CREF's principles on the role of stock in managerial compensation.

Stock-based compensation plans are a critical element of most compensation programs and can provide opportunities for managers whose efforts contribute to the creation of shareholder wealth. In evaluating the suitability of these plans, considerations of reasonableness, scale, linkage to performance, and fairness to shareholders and all employees also apply. TIAA-CREF, the largest pension system in the world, has set forth the following guidelines for stock-based compensation. Proper stock-based plans should:	**Exhibit 9.9 TIAA-CREF's Principles on the Role of Stock in Executive Compensation**

- Allow for creation of executive wealth that is reasonable in view of the creation of shareholder wealth. Management should not prosper through stock while shareholders suffer.
- Have measurable and predictable outcomes that are directly linked to the company's performance.
- Be market oriented, within levels of comparability for similar positions in companies of similar size and business focus.
- Be straightforward and clearly described so that investors and employees can understand them.
- Be fully disclosed to the investing public and be approved by shareholders.

Source: www.tiaa-cref.org/pubs.

External Governance Control Mechanisms

Our discussion so far has been on internal governance mechanisms. Internal controls, however, are not always enough to ensure good governance. The separation of ownership and control that we discussed earlier requires multiple control mechanisms, some internal and some external, to ensure that managerial actions lead to shareholder value maximization. Further, society-at-large wants some assurance that this goal is met without harming other stakeholder groups. In this section, we discuss several external control mechanisms that have developed in most modern economies. These include the market for corporate control, auditors, governmental regulatory bodies, banks and analysts, media, and public activists.

The Market for Corporate Control   Let us for a moment assume that internal control mechanisms in a company are failing. This means that the board is ineffective in monitoring managers and is not exercising the oversight required of them and that shareholders are passive and are not taking any actions to monitor or discipline managers. Theoretically, under these circumstances managers may behave opportunistically.[75] Opportunistic behavior can take many forms. First, they can *shirk* their responsibilities. Shirking means that managers fail to exert themselves fully, as is required of them. Second, they can engage in *on the job consumption.* Examples of on the job consumption include private jets, club memberships, expensive art work in the offices, and so on. Each of these represents consumption by managers that does not in any way increase shareholder value. Instead, they actually diminish shareholder value. Third, managers may engage in *excessive product-market diversification.*[76] As we discussed in Chapter 6, such diversification serves to reduce only the employment risk of the managers rather than the financial risk of the shareholders, who can more cheaply diversify their risk by owning a portfolio of investments. Is there any external mechanism to stop managers from shirking, consumption on the job, and excessive diversification?

The market for corporate control is one such external mechanism that provides at least some partial solution to the problems described above. If internal control mechanisms fail and the management is behaving opportunistically, the likely response of most shareholders will be to sell their stock rather than engage in activism.[77] As more and more stockholders vote with their feet, the value of the stock begins to decline. As the decline continues, at some point the market value of the firm becomes less than the book value. That is, a corporate raider can take over the company for a price less than the book value of the assets of the company. The first thing that the raider may do on assuming control over the company will be to fire the underperforming management. The risk of being acquired by a hostile raider is often referred to as the *takeover constraint*. The takeover constraint deters management from engaging in opportunistic behavior.[78]

Although in theory the takeover constraint is supposed to limit managerial opportunism, in recent years its effectiveness has become diluted as a result of a number of defense tactics adopted by incumbent management (see Chapter 6). Foremost among them are poison pills, greenmail, and golden parachutes. Poison pills are provisions adopted by the company to reduce its worth to the acquirer. An example would be payment of a huge one-time dividend, typically financed by debt. Greenmail involves buying back the stock from the acquirer, usually at an attractive premium. Golden parachutes are employment contracts that cause the company to pay lucrative severance packages to top managers fired as a result of a takeover, often running to several million dollars.

Auditors   Even when there are stringent disclosure requirements, there is no guarantee that the information disclosed will be accurate. Managers may deliberately disclose false information or withhold negative financial information. It is also possible that they may use accounting methods that distort results based on highly subjective interpretations. Therefore, all accounting statements are required to be audited and certified to be accurate by external auditors. These auditing firms are independent organizations staffed by certified professionals who verify the books of accounts of the company. Audits can unearth financial irregularities and ensure that financial reporting by the firm conforms to standard accounting practices.

Recent developments leading to the bankruptcy of firms such as Enron and WorldCom and a spate of earnings restatements raise questions about the failure of the auditing firms to act as effective external control mechanisms. Why did an auditing firm like Arthur Andersen, with decades of reputation in the auditing profession at stake, fail to raise red flags about accounting irregularities? First, auditors are appointed by the firm being audited. The desire to continue that business relationship sometimes makes them overlook financial irregularities. Second, most auditing firms also do consulting work and often have lucrative consulting contracts with the firms that they audit. Understandably, some of them tend not to ask too many difficult questions, because they fear jeopardizing the consulting business, which is often more profitable than the auditing work. The recent restatement of earnings by Xerox is an example of the lack of independence of auditing firms. The Securities and Exchange Commission filed a lawsuit against KPMG, the world's third largest accounting firm in January 2003 for allowing Xerox to inflate its revenues by $3 billion between 1997 and 2000. Of the $82 million that Xerox paid KPMG during these four years, only $26 million was for auditing. The rest was for consulting services. When one of the auditors objected to Xerox's practice of booking revenues for equipment leases earlier than it should have, Xerox asked KPMG to replace him, which it did.[79]

Banks and Analysts   Two external groups that monitor publicly held firms are financial institutions and stock analysts. Commercial and investment banks do so because they have lent money to corporations and therefore have to ensure that the borrowing firm's finances are in order and that the loan covenants are being followed. Stock analysts conduct ongoing in-depth studies of the firms that they follow and make recommendations to their clients to buy, hold, or sell. Their rewards and reputation depend on the quality of these recommendations. Their access to information, knowledge of the industry and the firm, and insights they gain from interactions with the management of the company enable them to alert the investing community of both positive and negative developments relating to a company.

In reality, it is generally observed that analyst recommendations are often more optimistic than warranted by facts. "Sell" recommendations tend to be exceptions rather than the norm. Many analysts seem to have failed to grasp the gravity of the problems surrounding failed companies such as Enron and Global Crossing till the very end. Part of the explanation may lie in the fact that most analysts work for firms that also have investment banking relationships with the companies they follow. Negative recommendations by analysts can displease the management, who may decide to take their investment banking business to a rival firm. Thus, otherwise independent and competent analysts may be pressured to overlook negative information or tone down their criticism. A recent settlement between the Securities and Exchange Commission and the New York State Attorney General with 10 banks requires them to pay $1.4 billion in penalties and to fund independent research for investors.[80]

Regulatory Bodies   All corporations are subject to some regulation by the government. The extent of regulation is often a function of the type of industry. Banks, utilities, and pharmaceuticals, for example, are subject to more regulatory oversight because of their importance to society. Public corporations are subject to more regulatory requirements than private corporations. All public corporations are required to disclose a substantial amount of financial information by bodies such as the Securities and Exchange Commission. These include quarterly and annual filings of financial performance, stock trading by insiders, and details of executive compensation packages. There are two primary reasons behind such requirements. First, markets can operate efficiently only when the investing public has faith in the market system. In the absence of disclosure requirements, the average investor suffers from a lack of reliable information and therefore may completely stay away from the capital market. This will negatively impact an economy's ability to grow. Second, disclosure of information such as insider trading protects the small investor to some extent from the negative consequences of information asymmetry. That is, the insiders and large investors typically have more information than the small investor and can therefore use that information to buy or sell before the information becomes public knowledge.

The failure of a variety of external control mechanisms led the U.S. Congress to pass the Sarbanes-Oxley Act in 2002. This act calls for many stringent measures that would ensure better governance of U.S. corporations. Some of these measures include:[81]

- *Auditors* are barred from certain types of nonaudit work. They are not allowed to destroy records for five years. Lead partners auditing a client should be changed at least every five years.
- *CEOs* and *CFOs* must fully reveal off-balance-sheet finances and vouch for the accuracy of the information revealed.
- *Executives* must promptly reveal the sale of shares in firms they manage and are not allowed to sell when other employees cannot.
- *Corporate lawyers* must report to senior managers any violations of securities law lower down.

Will International Companies Abide by American Rules?

In a bid to improve corporate governance and accounting, the Sarbanes-Oxley Act was made a law in the United States on July 30, 2002. However, some of the provisions of the act conflict with the laws of other countries, and this caused a furor in Europe and Asia. The law can pose problems to foreign companies listed on the New York Stock Exchange (NYSE) and other U.S. markets. Under the Sarbanes-Oxley Act, CEOs are required to vouch for financial statements, companies must have audit boards drawn from independent directors, and company loans can no longer be extended to corporate directors. Many of these are in conflict with the rules and customs in some countries, and that is causing serious problems. For example, in the United Kingdom the practice is to have a majority of independent directors on the audit committee as opposed to entirely independent directors. In Germany, employee directors (deemed nonindependent by the U.S.

legislation) serve on the supervisory board that oversees audit matters.

If no compromise is found, there is a lot at risk. Foreign companies trading on U.S. markets could delist, and those considering listing in the United States might delay doing so. There are 470 non-U.S. companies listed on the NYSE, with a combined global market capitalization of $3.8 *trillion,* about 30 percent of the total exchange. Even if a fraction of these companies delist, the impact could be severe. Porsche in Germany and Daiwa Securities Group in Japan have delayed listing on the NYSE already. Many companies listed in the United States are considering leaving the U.S. exchanges, according to Jim Sylph, a technical director at the International Federation of Accountants. Christoph Hutten, SAP finance director, warns, "If the SEC doesn't give an exemption to German companies, we would all have a problem." If foreign companies delist or reconsider their plans to list in U.S. exchanges, U.S. investors will find it difficult to invest in foreign companies, while the companies that delist will lose easy access to American capital. According to most foreign executives, the likelihood of such an exodus occurring is low. But it is not out of the question.

Sources: L. Lavelle and M. McNamee, "Will Overseas Boards Play by American Rules?" *BusinessWeek,* December 16, 2002, p. 35; S. Kemp, "U.S. Laws to Hinder SA Companies," *CFOweb,* November 2002; *PR Newswire,* November 2002, www.prnewswire.co.uk/disclose2/news_nov2002.shtml.

Strategy Spotlight 9.8 describes some of the complex issues and implications associated with the Sarbanes-Oxley Act for foreign companies listed on U.S. stock exchanges.

Media and Public Activists   The press is not usually recognized as an external control mechanism in the literature on corporate governance. There is, however, no denying that in all developed capitalist economies, the financial press and media play an important indirect role in monitoring the management of public corporations. In the United States, business magazines such as *BusinessWeek* and *Fortune,* financial newspapers such as the *Wall Street Journal* and *Investors Business Daily,* as well as television networks like Financial News Network and CNBC are constantly reporting on companies. Public perceptions about a company's financial prospects and the quality of its management are greatly influenced by the media. As we discussed in Chapter 5, Food Lion's reputation was sullied when ABC's *Prime Time Live* in 1992 charged the company with employee exploitation, false package dating, and unsanitary meat handling practices. Bethany McLean of *Fortune* magazine is often credited as the first to raise questions about Enron's long-term financial viability.[82]

Similarly, consumer groups and activist individuals often take a crusading role in exposing corporate malfeasance. Well-known examples include Ralph Nader and Erin

Exhibit 9.10 Watchdogs for Corporate America

Ralph Nader, an activist politician in the United States, established more than 30 public interest groups to act as "watchdogs" for corporate America. Together, the loose federation of independent groups constitutes, in effect, an anticorporate conglomerate. Here are a few examples.

- **Aviation Consumer Action Project:** Works to propose new rules to prevent flight delays, impose penalties for deceiving passengers about problems, and push for higher compensation for lost luggage.

- **Center for Auto Safety:** Helps consumers find plaintiff lawyers and agitates for vehicle recalls, increased highway safety standards, and lemon laws.

- **Center for Study of Responsive Law:** This is Nader's headquarters. Home of a consumer project on technology, this group sponsored seminars on Microsoft remedies and pushed for tougher Internet privacy rules. It also took on the drug industry over costs.

- **Commercial Alert:** This group fights excessive commercialism. Its targets include Primedia for delivering ads in educational programming and Coke and Pepsi for aggressive sales tactics in schools.

- **Pension Rights Center:** Employees of IBM, General Electric, and other companies were helped by this center in organizing themselves against cash-balance pension plans.

- **Public Citizen:** This is the umbrella organization that sponsors Global Trade Watch, Congress Watch, the Critical Mass Energy & Environment program, Health Research Group, and Public Citizen Litigation Group. Issues taken up include tort reform, oil mergers, and reform of campaign finance.

Source: A. Bernstein, "Too Much Corporate Power?" *BusinessWeek*, September 11, 2000, p. 153.

Brockovich, who played important roles in bringing to light the safety issues related to GM's Corvair and environmental pollution issues concerning Pacific Gas and Electric Company, respectively. Exhibit 9.10 summarizes the many watchdog groups founded by Ralph Nader to monitor and change the behavior and strategies of major corporations.

summary

For firms to be successful, they must practice effective strategic control and corporate governance. Without such controls, the firm will not be able to achieve competitive advantages and outperform rivals in the marketplace.

We began the chapter with the key role of informational control. We contrasted two types of control systems: what we termed "traditional" and "contemporary" information control systems. Whereas traditional control systems may have their place in placid, simple competitive environments, there are fewer of those in today's economy. Instead, we advocated the contemporary approach wherein the internal and external environment are constantly monitored so that when surprises emerge, the firm can modify its strategies, goals, and objectives.

Behavioral controls are also a vital part of effective control systems. We argued that firms must develop the proper balance between culture, rewards and incentives, and boundaries and constraints. Where there are strong and positive cultures and rewards, employees tend to internalize the organization's strategies and objectives. This permits a firm to spend fewer resources on monitoring behavior, and the firm is assured that the efforts and initiatives of employees are more consistent with the overall objectives of the organization.

We took a contingency approach to the subject of control systems. That is, we argued that there is no one best way to design a strategic control system; rather, it is dependent on a variety of factors. The two that we discussed were the firm's business- and corporate-level strategies. We argued that with overall cost leadership strategies and unrelated diversification, it is appropriate to rely on cultures and reward systems that emphasize the production outcomes of the organization, because it is rather easy to quantify such indicators. On the other hand, with differentiation strategies and related diversification, there must be culture and incentive systems that encourage and reward creativity initiatives as well as cooperation among professionals in many different functional areas. Here it becomes more difficult to measure accurately each individual's contribution, and more subjective indicators become necessary.

In the final section of this chapter, we addressed corporate governance, which can be defined as the relationship between various participants in determining the direction and performance of the corporation. The primary participants include shareholders, management (led by the chief executive officer), and the board of directors. We reviewed studies that indicated a consistent relationship between effective corporate governance and financial performance. There are also several internal and external control mechanisms that can serve to align managerial interests and shareholder interests. The internal mechanisms include a committed and involved board of directors, shareholder activism, and effective managerial incentives and rewards. The external mechanisms include the market for corporate control, banks and analysts, regulators, the media, and public activists.

summary review questions

1. Why are effective strategic control systems so important in today's economy?

2. What are the main advantages of "contemporary" control systems over "traditional" control systems? What are the main differences between these two systems?

3. Why is it important to have a balance between the three elements of behavioral control—culture, rewards and incentives, and boundaries?

4. Discuss the relationship between types of organizations and their primary means of behavioral control.

5. Boundaries become less important as a firm develops a strong culture and reward system. Explain.

6. Why is it important to avoid a "one best way" mentality concerning control systems? What are the consequences of applying the same type of control system to all types of environments?

7. What is the role of effective corporate governance in improving a firm's performance? What are some of the key governance mechanisms that are used to ensure that managerial and shareholder interests are aligned?

experiential exercise

McDonald's Corporation, the world's largest fast-food restaurant chain, with 2003 revenues of $17.1 billion, has encountered declining shareholder value in the early 2000s. Using the Internet or library sources, evaluate the quality of the corporation in terms of management, the board of directors, and shareholder activism. Are the issues you list favorable or unfavorable for sound corporate governance?

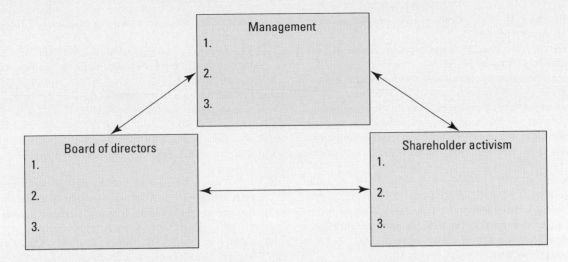

application questions exercises

1. Most of Tyco's problems may be attributed to a "traditional" control system that failed to continuously monitor the environment and make necessary changes in its strategy and objectives. What companies are you familiar with that responded appropriately (or inappropriately) to environmental change?

2. How can a strong, positive culture enhance a firm's competitive advantage? How can a weak, negative culture erode competitive advantages? Explain and provide examples.

3. Use the Internet to research a firm that has an excellent culture and/or reward and incentive system. What are this firm's main financial and nonfinancial benefits?

4. Using the Internet, go to the website of a large, publicly held corporation in which you are interested. What evidence do you see of effective (or ineffective) corporate governance?

ethics questions

1. Strong cultures can have powerful effects on employee behavior. How does this create inadvertent control mechanisms? That is, are strong cultures an ethical way to control behavior?

2. Rules and regulations can help reduce unethical behavior in organizations. To be effective, however, what other systems, mechanisms, and processes are necessary?

references

1. Foust, D., Symonds, W. C., & Grover, R., 2003, Just how independent are these "lead directors"? *BusinessWeek,* May 12: 56; Bianco, A., Symonds, W., & Byrnes, N., 2002, The rise and fall of Dennis Kozlowski, *BusinessWeek,* December 23: 64–77; www.thecorporate library.com/spotlight/scandals/scandal-quicksheet.html; Lavelle, M., 2002, Rogue of the year, *Time,* December 30: 32–45; and Symonds, W. C., 2002, Tyco: How did they miss a scam so big? *BusinessWeek,* September 30: 40–42.

2. This chapter draws upon Picken, J. C., & Dess, G. G.,

1997, *Mission Critical* (Burr Ridge, IL: Irwin Professional Publishing).

3. Argyris, C., 1977, Double loop learning in organizations, *Harvard Business Review* 55: 115–25.

4. Simons, R., 1995, Control in an age of empowerment, *Harvard Business Review* 73: 80–88. This chapter draws on this source in the discussion of informational control.

5. Goold, M., & Quinn, J. B., 1990, The paradox of strategic controls, *Strategic Management Journal* 11: 43–57.

6. Quinn, J. B., 1980, *Strategies for Change* (Homewood, IL: Richard D. Irwin).

7. Mintzberg, H., 1987, Crafting strategy, *Harvard Business Review* 65: 66–75.

8. Weston, J. S., 1992, Soft stuff matters, *Financial Executive,* July–August: 52–53.

9. This discussion of control systems draws upon Simons, op. cit.

10. For an interesting perspective on this issue and how a downturn in the economy can reduce the tendency toward "free agency" by managers and professionals, refer to Morris, B., 2001, White collar blues, *Fortune,* July 23: 98–110.

11. Ouchi, W., 1981, *Theory Z* (Reading, MA: Addison-Wesley); Deal, T. E., & Kennedy, A. A., 1982, *Corporate Cultures* (Reading, MA: Addison-Wesley); Peters, T. J., & Waterman, R. H., 1982, *In Search of Excellence* (New York: Random House); Collins, J., 2001, *Good to Great* (New York: HarperCollins).

12. Collins, J. C., & Porras, J. I., 1994, *Built to Last: Successful Habits of Visionary Companies* (New York: HarperBusiness).

13. Lee, J., & Miller, D., 1999, People matter: Commitment to employees, strategy, and performance in Korean firms, *Strategic Management Journal* 6: 579–94.

14. For an insightful discussion of IKEA's unique culture, see Kling, K., & Goteman, I., 2003, IKEA CEO Anders Dahlvig on international growth and IKEA's unique corporate culture and brand identity, *Academy of Management Executive* 17 (1): 31–37.

15. For a discussion of how professionals inculcate values, refer to Uhl-Bien, M., & Graen, G. B., 1998, Individual self-management: Analysis of professionals' self-managing activities in functional and cross-functional work teams, *Academy of Management Journal* 41 (3): 340–50.

16. A perspective on how antisocial behavior can erode a firm's culture can be found in Robinson, S. L., & O'Leary-Kelly, A. M., 1998, Monkey see, monkey do: The influence of work groups on the antisocial behavior of employees, *Academy of Management Journal* 41 (6): 658–72.

17. Mitchell, R., 1989, Masters of innovation, *BusinessWeek,* April 10: 58–63.

18. Sellers, P., 1993, Companies that serve you best, *Fortune,* May 31: 88.

19. Southwest Airlines Culture Committee, 1993, *Luv Lines* (company publication), March–April: 17–18; for an interesting perspective on the "downside" of strong "cult-like" organizational cultures, refer to Arnott, D. A., 2000, *Corporate Cults* (New York: AMACOM).

20. Kerr, J., & Slocum, J. W., Jr., 1987, Managing corporate culture through reward systems, *Academy of Management Executive* 1 (2): 99–107.

21. For a unique perspective on leader challenges in managing wealthy professionals, refer to Wetlaufer, S., 2000, Who wants to manage a millionaire, *Harvard Business Review* 78 (4): 53–60.

22. These next two subsections draw upon Dess, G. G., & Picken, J. C., 1997, *Beyond Productivity* (New York: AMACOM).

23. For a discussion of the benefits of stock options as executive compensation, refer to Hall, B. J., 2000, What you need to know about stock options, *Harvard Business Review* 78 (2): 121–29.

24. Tully, S., 1993, Your paycheck gets exciting, *Fortune,* November 13: 89.

25. For a recent discussion linking pay to performance, refer to Rappaport, A., 1999, New thinking on how to link pay to performance, *Harvard Business Review* 77 (2): 91–105.

26. Zellner, W., Hof, R. D., Brandt, R., Baker, S., & Greising, D., 1995, Go-go goliaths, *BusinessWeek,* February 13: 64–70.

27. This section draws on Dess & Picken, op. cit., chap. 5.

28. Simons, op. cit.

29. Davis, E., 1997, Interview: Norman Augustine, *Management Review,* November: 11.

30. This section draws upon Dess, G. G., & Miller, A., 1993, *Strategic Management* (New York: McGraw-Hill).

31. For a good review of the goal-setting literature, refer to Locke, E. A., & Latham, G. P., 1990, *A Theory of Goal Setting and Task Performance* (Englewood Cliffs, NJ: Prentice Hall).

32. For an interesting perspective on the use of rules and regulations that is counter to this industry's (software) norms, refer to Fryer, B., 2001, Tom Siebel of Siebel Systems: High tech the old fashioned way, *Harvard Business Review* 79 (3): 118–30.

33. Thompson, A. A., Jr., & Strickland, A. J., III., 1998, *Strategic Management: Concepts and Cases,* 10th ed. (New York: McGraw-Hill), 313.

34. Ibid.

35. Teitelbaum, R., 1997, Tough guys finish first, *Fortune,* July 21: 82–84.

36. Weaver, G. R., Trevino, L. K., & Cochran, P. L., 1999, Corporate ethics programs as control systems: Influences of executive commitment and environmental factors, *Academy of Management Journal* 42 (1): 41–57.

37. Cadbury, S. A., 1987, Ethical managers make their own rules, *Harvard Business Review* 65: 3, 69–73.

38. Weber, J., 2003, CFOs on the hot seat, *BusinessWeek,* March 17: 66–70.

39. William Ouchi has written extensively about the use of clan control (which is viewed as an alternate to bureaucratic or market control). Here, a powerful culture results in people aligning their individual interests with those of the firm. Refer to Ouchi, op. cit. This section also draws on Hall, R. H., 2002, *Organizations: Struc-*

tures, Processes, and Outcomes, 8th ed. (Upper Saddle River, NJ: Prentice Hall).

40. This discussion of generic strategies and their relationship to organizational control draws upon Porter, M. E., 1980, *Competitive Strategy* (New York: Free Press); and Miller, D., 1988, Relating Porter's business strategies to environment and structure: Analysis and performance implications, *Academy of Management Journal* 31 (2): 280–308.

41. Rodengen, J. L., 1997, *The Legend of Nucor Corporation* (Fort Lauderdale, FL: Write Stuff Enterprises).

42. The 3M example draws upon *Blueprints for Service Quality,* 1994 (New York: American Management Association); personal communication with Katerine Hagmeier, program manager, external communications, 3M Corporation, March 26, 1998; Lei, D., Slocum, J. W., & Pitts, R. A., 1999, Designing organizations for competitive advantage: The power of unlearning and learning, *Organizational Dynamics* 27 (3): 24–38; and Graham, A. B., & Pizzo, V. G., 1996, A question of balance: Case studies in strategic knowledge management, *European Management Journal* 14 (4): 338–46.

43. The Sharp Corporation and Hanson plc examples are based on Collis, D. J., & Montgomery, C. A., 1998, Creating corporate advantage, *Harvard Business Review* 76 (3): 70–83.

44. Kunii, I., 2002, Japanese companies' survival skills, *BusinessWeek,* November 18: 18.

45. White, G., 1988, How I turned $3,000 into $10 billion, *Fortune,* November 7: 80–89. After the death of the founders, the Hanson plc conglomerate was found to be too unwieldy and was broken up into several separate, publicly traded corporations. For more on its more limited current scope of operations, see www.hansonplc.com.

46. Monks, R., & Minow, N., 2001, *Corporate Governance,* 2nd ed. (Malden, MA: Blackwell).

47. Pound, J., 1995, The promise of the governed corporation, *Harvard Business Review* 73 (2): 89–98.

48. Byrne, J. A., Lavelle, L., Byrnes, N., Vickers, M., & Borrus, A., 2002, How to fix corporate governance, *BusinessWeek:* May 6: 44–52.

49. Ibid.

50. This discussion draws upon Monks & Minow, op. cit.

51. Eisenhardt, K. M., 1989, Agency theory: An assessment and review, *Academy of Management Review* 14 (1): 57–74. Some of the seminal contributions to agency theory include Jensen, M., & Meckling, W., 1976, Theory of the firm: Managerial behavior, agency costs, and ownership structure, *Journal of Financial Economics* 3: 305–60; Fama, E., & Jensen, M., 1983, Separation of ownership and control, *Journal of Law and Economics* 26: 301, 325; and Fama, E., 1980, Agency problems and the theory of the firm, *Journal of Political Economy* 88: 288–307.

52. Managers may also engage in "shirking," that is, reducing or withholding their efforts. See, for example, Kidwell, R. E., Jr., & Bennett, N., 1993, Employee propensity to withhold effort: A conceptual model to intersect three avenues of research, *Academy of Management Review* 18 (3): 429–56.

53. For an interesting perspective on agency and clarification of many related concepts and terms, visit the following website: www.encycogov.com.

54. Argawal, A., & Mandelker, G., 1987, Managerial incentives and corporate investment and financing decisions, *Journal of Finance* 42: 823–37.

55. For an insightful, recent discussion of the academic research on corporate governance, in particular the role of boards of directors, refer to Chatterjee, S., & Harrison, J. S., 2001, Corporate governance, in Hitt, M. A., Freeman, R. E., & Harrison, J. S., eds., *Handbook of Strategic Management* (Malden, MA: Blackwell), 543–63.

56. This opening discussion draws on Monks & Minow, op. cit, pp. 164, 169; see also Pound, op. cit.

57. Business Roundtable, 1990, *Corporate Governance and American Competitiveness,* March, p. 7.

58. Byrne, J. A., Grover, R., & Melcher, R. A., 1997, The best and worst boards, *BusinessWeek,* November 26: 35–47. The three key roles of boards of directors are monitoring the actions of executives, providing advice, and providing links to the external environment to provide resources. See Johnson, J. L., Daily, C. M., & Ellstrand, A. E., 1996, Boards of directors: A review and research agenda, *Academy of Management Review* 37: 409–38.

59. McGeehan, P., 2003, More chief executives shown the door, study says, *New York Times,* May 12: C2.

60. There are benefits, of course, to having some insiders on the board of directors. Inside directors would be more aware of the firm's strategies. Additionally, outsiders may rely too often on financial performance indicators because of information asymmetries. For an interesting discussion, see Baysinger, B. D., & Hoskisson, R. E., 1990, The composition of boards of directors and strategic control: Effects on corporate strategy, *Academy of Management Review* 15: 72–87.

61. Hambrick, D. C., & Jackson, E. M., 2000, Outside directors with a stake: The linchpin in improving governance, *California Management Review* 42 (4): 108–27.

62. Ibid.

63. Disney has begun to make many changes to improve its corporate governance, such as assigning only independent directors to important board committees, restricting directors from serving on more than three boards, and appointing a lead director who can convene the board without approval by the CEO. In recent years, the Disney Co. has shown up on some "best" board lists. In addition Eisner has recently relinquished the chairman position.

64. Talk show, 2002, *BusinessWeek,* September 30: 14.

65. Monks and Minow, op. cit., p. 93.

66. A discussion of the factors that lead to shareholder activism is found in Ryan, L. V., & Schneider, M., 2002, The antecedents of institutional investor activism, *Academy of Management Review* 27 (4): 554–73.

67. There is strong research support for the idea that the presence of large block shareholders is associated with value-maximizing decisions. For example, refer to Johnson, R. A., Hoskisson, R. E., & Hitt, M. A., 1993, Board of director involvement in restructuring: The effects of board versus managerial controls and characteristics, *Strategic Management Journal,* 14:33–50.

68. For an interesting perspective on the impact of institutional ownership on a firm's innovation strategies, see Hoskisson, R. E., Hitt, M. A., Johnson, R. A., & Grossman, W., 2002, *Academy of Management Journal* 45 (4): 697–716.

69. Jensen, M. C., & Murphy, K. J., 1990, CEO incentives—It's not how much you pay, but how, *Harvard Business Review* 68 (3): 138–49.

70. Research has found that executive compensation is more closely aligned with firm performance in companies with compensation committees and boards dominated by outside directors. See, for example, Conyon, M. J., & Peck, S. I., 1998, Board control, remuneration committees, and top management compensation, *Academy of Management Journal* 41: 146–57.

71. Lavelle, L., Jespersen, F. F., & Arndt, M., 2002, Executive pay, *BusinessWeek,* April 15: 66–72.

72. Ibid.

73. Byrne, Lavelle et al., op. cit.

74. www.tiaa-cref.org/pubs.

75. Such opportunistic behavior is common in all principal-agent relationships. For a description of agency problems, especially in the context of the relationship between shareholders and managers, see Jensen, M. C., & Meckling, W. H., 1976, Theory of the firm: Managerial behavior, agency costs, and ownership structure, *Journal of Financial Economics* 3: 305–60.

76. Hoskisson, R. E., & Turk, T. A., 1990, Corporate restructuring: Governance and control limits of the internal market, *Academy of Management Review* 15: 459–77.

77. For an insightful perspective on the market for corporate control and how it is influenced by knowledge intensity, see Coff, R., 2003, Bidding wars over R&D-intensive firms: Knowledge, opportunism, and the market for corporate control, *Academy of Management Journal* 46 (1): 74–85.

78. Walsh, J. P., & Kosnik, R. D., 1993, Corporate raiders and their disciplinary role in the market for corporate control, *Academy of Management Journal* 36: 671–700.

79. Gunning for KPMG, 2003, *Economist,* February 1: 63.

80. Timmons, H., 2003, Investment banks: Who will foot their bill? *BusinessWeek,* March 3: 116.

81. Wishy-washy: The SEC pulls its punches on corporate-governance rules, 2003, *Economist,* February 1: 60.

82. McLean, B., 2001, Is Enron overpriced? *Fortune,* March 5: 122–25.

chapter 10

Creating Effective
Organizational Designs

*After
reading this
chapter, you should
have a good understanding of:*

- The importance of organizational structure and the concept of the "boundaryless" organization in implementing strategies.

- The growth patterns of major corporations and the relationship between a firm's strategy and its structure.

- Each of the traditional types of organizational structure: simple, functional, divisional, and matrix.

- The relative advantages and disadvantages of traditional organizational structures.

- The implications of a firm's international operations for organizational structure.

- The different types of boundaryless organizations—barrier-free, modular, and virtual—and their relative advantages and disadvantages.

*t*o implement strategies successfully, firms must have appropriate organizational structures. These include the processes and integrating mechanisms necessary to ensure that boundaries among internal activities and external parties, such as suppliers, customers, and alliance partners, are flexible and permeable. A firm's performance will suffer if its managers don't carefully consider both of these organizational design attributes.

In the first section, we begin by discussing the growth patterns of large corporations to address the important relationships between the strategy that a firm follows and its corresponding structure. For example, as firms diversify into related product-market areas, they change their structure from functional to divisional. We then address the different types of traditional structures—simple, functional, divisional, and matrix—and their relative advantages and disadvantages. We then close with a discussion of the implications of a firm's international operations for the structure of their organization. The primary factors that are taken into account are (1) the type of international strategy (e.g., global or multidomestic), (2) the level of product diversity, and (3) the extent to which a firm depends on foreign sales.

The second section discusses the concept of the "boundaryless" organization. We do *not* argue that organizations should have no internal and external boundaries. Instead, we suggest that in rapidly changing and unpredictable environments, organizations must strive to make their internal and external boundaries both flexible and permeable. We suggest three different types of boundaryless organizations: barrier-free, modular, and virtual. Whereas the barrier-free type focuses on creating flexible and permeable internal and external boundaries, the modular type addresses the strategic role of outsourcing, and the virtual type centers on the viability of strategic alliances and network organizations in today's global economy.

In early 2002, Ford Motor Company shocked Wall Street with a $1 billion write-off of the value of its stockpile of precious metals, primarily palladium. Why had the number two car company made a massive bet on a commodity notorious for its price volatility?[1]

All of the big carmakers buy precious metals used in their exhaust systems to make emissions cleaner. Ford had accumulated an unusually large supply in recent years, anticipating growing need and fearing unpredictable supplies from Russia. But, according to Martin Inglis, Ford's chief financial officer, the company left the job of acquiring palladium to the same purchasing department employees who buy its steel and copper. He says the purchasing staff did not take the sort of precautions sophisticated buyers routinely use to hedge risk in dicey markets. Ford's treasury department regularly used such tools to buffer risks related to interest rates and currency exchange. But the more financially savvy treasury department employees did not work closely with the purchasing staff.

What's more, Ford's own engineering innovations were shrinking its need for palladium, even as the purchasing department was loading up on it at near-record prices. Procurement also appears not to have consulted closely enough about Ford's palladium needs with Haren Gandhi, a 35-year Ford veteran and technical fellow (the highest rank for a technical professional). Gandhi and the research team succeeded in finding ways to cut palladium use in catalytic converters in half in recent years as a result of a research project that started in 1996.

Not only was the company now overstocked with an exotic commodity it had less need for, but demand generally began to fall, while supplies stabilized. In these circumstances, the value of the stockpile of palladium took a nosedive. Demand fell, in part, because other automakers had also succeeded in capping or reducing their use of palladium. Demand from the electronics industry, which also consumes a lot of palladium for use in capacitors, had diminished with the overall weakening of the world economy. On the supply side, high prices had spurred mine operators in South Africa to increase palladium production. And the unpredictable Russian supply began to stabilize. All these factors led to a drop in the price of palladium, and Ford had to write off its costly stockpile.

What Went Wrong at Ford?   The strategy of accumulating palladium would have paid off handsomely if the technology did not change. Surprisingly, the purchasing department was completely unaware that engineering was developing technologies to reduce the use of the very item it was buying. Additionally, the purchasing staff did not seek the treasury department's expertise in trading precious metals. Such a lack of coordination led to a billion dollar loss for the company.

One of the central concepts in this chapter is the importance of boundaryless organizations. That is, successful organizations create permeable boundaries—among the internal activities as well as between the organization and its external customers, suppliers, and alliance partners. We introduced this idea in Chapter 3 in our discussion of the value-chain concept, which consisted of several primary (e.g., inbound logistics, marketing and sales) and support activities (e.g., procurement, human resource management). Clearly, the underlying cause of Ford's problem was its inability to establish close and effective working relationships between its internal activities: purchasing, treasury, and engineering.

The most important implication of this chapter is that today's managers are faced with two ongoing and vital activities in structuring and designing their organizations. First, they must decide on the most appropriate type of organization structure. Second, they need to assess what mechanisms, processes, and techniques are most helpful in enhancing the permeability of the internal and external boundaries of their organization.

Traditional Forms of Organizational Structure

Organizational structure refers to the formalized patterns of interactions that link the tasks, technologies, and people of a firm.[2] Structures are designed to ensure that resources are used most effectively toward accomplishing an organization's mission. Structure provides managers with a means of balancing two conflicting forces: a need for the division of tasks into meaningful groupings and the need to integrate such groupings in order to ensure organizational efficiency and effectiveness. Structure identifies the executive, managerial, and administrative organization of a firm as well as indicating responsibilities and hierarchical relationships. It also influences the flow of information as well as the context and nature of human interactions.

Most organizations begin very small and either die or remain small. Those few that survive and prosper embark on strategies designed to increase the overall scope of operations and enable them to enter new product-market domains. Such growth places additional pressure on executives to control and coordinate the firm's increasing size and diversity. The most appropriate type of structure depends on the nature and magnitude of growth in a firm. In this section, we address various types of structural forms, their advantages and disadvantages, as well as their relationships to the strategies that organizations undertake.

Patterns of Growth of Large Corporations

A firm's strategy and structure change as it increases in size, diversifies into new product-markets, and expands its geographic scope.[3] Exhibit 10.1 illustrates some of the common growth patterns that firms may follow.

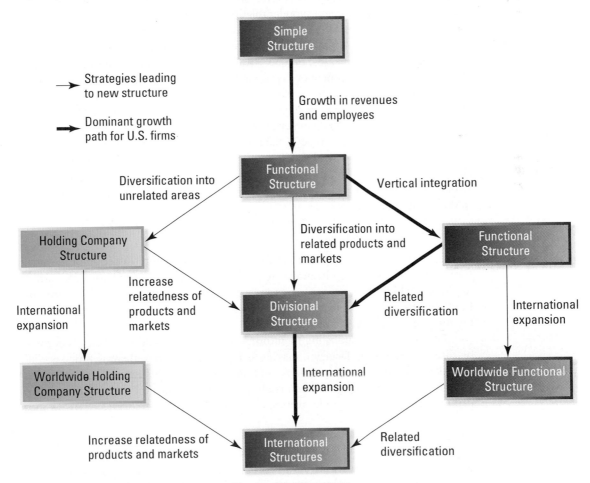

Exhibit 10.1 Dominant Growth Patterns of Large Corporations

Source: From *Strategy Implementation: The Role of Structure and Process,* 2nd edition by J. R. Galbraith and R. K. Kazanjian. Copyright © 1986. Reprinted with permission of South-Western, a division of Thomson Learning: www.thomsonrights.com. Fax: 800-730-2215.

A new firm with a *simple structure* typically increases its sales revenue and volume of outputs over time. It may also engage in some vertical integration to secure sources of supply (backward integration) as well as channels of distribution (forward integration). After a time, the simple-structure firm implements a *functional structure* to concentrate efforts on both increasing efficiency and enhancing its operations and products. This structure enables the firm to group its operations into either functions, departments, or geographic areas. As its initial markets mature, a firm looks beyond its present products and markets for possible expansion. Such a strategy of related diversification requires a need to reorganize around product lines or geographic markets. This leads to a *divisional structure.* As the business expands in terms of sales revenues, and domestic growth opportunities become somewhat limited, a firm may seek opportunities in international markets. At this time, a firm has a wide variety of structures to choose from. These include *international division, geographic area, worldwide product division, worldwide functional,* and *worldwide matrix.* As we will see later in this section, deciding upon the most appropriate structure when a firm has international operations depends on three primary factors: the extent of international expansion, type of strategy (global, multidomestic, or transnational), and the degree of product diversity.[4]

There are some other common growth patterns. For example, some firms may find it advantageous to diversify into several product lines rather than focus their efforts on strengthening distributor and supplier relationships through vertical integration. Thus, they would organize themselves according to product lines by implementing a divisional structure. Also, some firms may choose to move into unrelated product areas, typically by acquiring existing businesses. Frequently, their rationale is that acquiring assets and competencies is more economical or expedient than developing them internally. Such an unrelated, or conglomerate, strategy requires relatively little integration across businesses and sharing of resources. Thus, a *holding company structure* becomes appropriate. As one would expect, there are many other growth patterns, but these are the most common.*

Now we will discuss some of the most common types of organizational structures—simple, functional, divisional (including two variants: *strategic business unit* and *holding company*), and *matrix* and their advantages and disadvantages. We will close the section with a discussion of the structural implications of a firm's expansion of its operations into international markets.

Simple Structure

As one might expect, the simple structure is the oldest, and most common, organizational form. After all, most organizations are very small and have a single or very narrow product line in which the owner-manager (or top executive) makes almost all of the decisions. In effect, the owner-manager controls all activities, and the staff serves as an extension of the top executive's personality.

The simple structure is highly informal and the coordination of tasks is accomplished by direct supervision. Decision making is highly centralized, there is little specialization of tasks, few rules and regulations, and an informal evaluation and reward system. Although the owner-manager is intimately involved in almost all phases of the business, a manager is often employed to oversee day-to-day operations.

---

*The lowering of transaction costs and globalization have led to some changes in the common historical patterns that we have discussed. Some firms are, in effect, bypassing the vertical integration stage. Instead, they focus on core competencies and outsource other value-creation activities. Also, even relatively young firms are going global early in their history because of lower communication and transportation costs. For an interesting perspective on global start-ups, see P. P. McDougall and B. M. Oviatt, "New Venture Internationalization, Strategic Change and Performance: A Follow-up Study," *Journal of Business Venturing* 11 (1996): 23–40; and P. P. McDougall and B. M. Oviatt, eds., "The Special Research Forum on International Entrepreneurship," *Academy of Management Journal,* October 2000: 902–1003.

A small firm with a simple structure may often foster creativity and individualism since there are generally few rules and regulations. However, such "informality" may lead to problems. Employees may not clearly understand their responsibilities, which can lead to conflict and confusion. Employees also may take advantage of the lack of regulations and act in their own self-interest. Such actions can erode motivation and satisfaction as well as lead to the possible misuse of organizational resources. Further, small organizations have flat structures (i.e., few vertical, hierarchical levels) that limit opportunities for upward mobility. Without the potential for future advancement, recruiting and retaining talent may become very difficult.

Functional Structure

When an organization is small (15 employees or less), it is not necessary to have a variety of formal arrangements and grouping of activities. However, as firms grow, excessive demands may be placed on the owner-manager in order to obtain and process all of the information necessary to run the business. Chances are the owner will not be skilled in all specialties (e.g., accounting, engineering, production, marketing) at a level necessary to run a growing business. Thus, he or she will need to hire specialists in the various functional areas. Such growth in the overall scope and complexity of the business necessitates a functional structure wherein the major functions of the firm are grouped internally and led by a specialist. The coordination and integration of the functional areas becomes one of the most important responsibilities of the chief executive of the firm. Exhibit 10.2 presents a diagram of a functional structure.

Functional structures are generally found in organizations in which there is a single or closely related product or service, high production volume, and some vertical integration. Initially, firms tend to expand the overall scope of their operations by penetrating existing markets, introducing similar products in additional markets, or increasing the level of vertical integration. Such expansion activities clearly increase the scope and complexity of the operations. Fortunately, the functional structure provides for a high level of centralization that helps to ensure integration and control over the related product-market activities or multiple primary activities (from inbound logistics to operations to marketing, sales, and service) in the value chain (addressed in Chapters 3 and 4).

Many firms use a functional structure successfully. One example is Sharp, the $17 billion consumer electronics giant.

> Sharp Corporation is a heavy hitter in the consumer electronics industry, with approximately $17 billion in annual sales. The firm is organized into functional units, allowing coordination of tasks involving research and development, production, marketing, and management. Key components such as LCDs (liquid crystal displays) are developed and produced in single functional

Exhibit 10.2 Functional Organizational Structure

units using the talents of each of these specialties. By using a centralized, functional structure, Sharp is able to achieve economies of scale with its applied research and manufacturing skills. It would be much more expensive if such skills and resources were distributed over many different, relatively autonomous business units. To make sure that these units are not completely sealed off from the other business units in the firm, product managers have the responsibility of coordinating similar products in multiple functional areas throughout the organization.[5]

As with any type of organizational structure, there are some relative advantages and disadvantages associated with the functional structure. By bringing together specialists into functional departments, a firm is able to enhance its coordination and control within each of the functional areas. The structure also ensures that decision making in the firm will be centralized at the top of the organization. This enhances the organizational-level (as opposed to functional area) perspective across the various functions in the organization. In addition, the functional structure provides for a more efficient use of managerial and technical talent since functional area expertise is pooled in a single department (e.g., marketing) instead of being spread across a variety of product-market areas. Finally, career paths and professional development in specialized areas are facilitated.

There are also some significant disadvantages associated with the functional structure. First, the differences in values and orientations among functional areas may impede communication and coordination. Edgar Schein of MIT has argued that shared assumptions, often based on similar backgrounds and experiences of members, form around functional units in an organization. This leads to what are often called "stove pipes" or "silos," in which departments view themselves as isolated, self-contained units with little need for interaction and coordination with other departments. This erodes communication because functional groups may have not only different goals but also differing meanings of words and concepts. According to Schein:

> The word "marketing" will mean product development to the engineer, studying customers through market research to the product manager, merchandising to the salesperson, and constant change in design to the manufacturing manager. When they try to work together, they will often attribute disagreements to personalities and fail to notice the deeper, shared assumptions that color how each function thinks.[6]

Such narrow functional orientations also may lead to short-term thinking—based largely upon what is best for the functional area, not the organization as a whole. For example, in a manufacturing firm, sales may want to offer a wide range of customized products to appeal to the firm's customers; research and development may overdesign products and components to achieve technical elegance; and manufacturing may favor no-frills products that can be produced at low cost by means of long production runs. In addition, functional structures may overburden the top executives in the firm because conflicts have a tendency to be "pushed up" to the top of the organization since there are no managers who are responsible for the specific product lines. Finally, functional structures make it difficult to establish uniform performance standards across the whole organization. Whereas it may be relatively easy to evaluate production managers on the basis of production volume and cost control, establishing performance measures for engineering, research and development, and accounting become more problematic.

Divisional Structure

The divisional structure (sometimes called the multidivisional structure or M-Form) is organized around products, projects, or markets. Each of the divisions, in turn, includes its own functional specialists who are typically organized into departments. A divisional structure encompasses a set of relatively autonomous units governed by a central corpo-

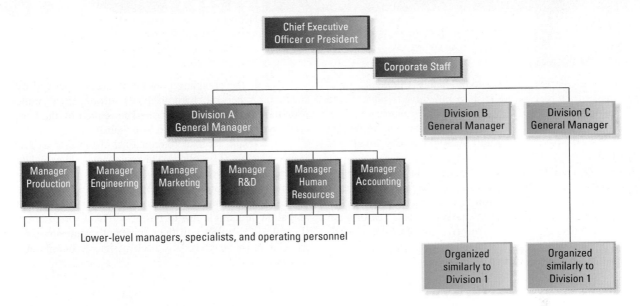

Exhibit 10.3 Divisional Organizational Structure

rate office. The operating divisions are relatively independent and consist of products and services that are different from those of the other divisions. Divisional executives play a key role. In conjunction with corporate-level executives, they help to determine the product-market and financial objectives for the division as well as their division's contribution to overall corporate performance.[7] The rewards are based largely on measures of financial performance such as net income and revenue. Exhibit 10.3 illustrates a divisional structure.

General Motors was among the earliest firms to adopt the divisional organization structure.[8] In the 1920s the company formed five major product divisions (Cadillac, Buick, Oldsmobile, Pontiac, and Chevrolet) as well as several industrial divisions. Since then, many firms have discovered that as they diversified into new product-market activities, functional structures—with their emphasis on single functional departments—were unable to manage the increased complexity of the entire business. Operational decision making in a large business places excessive demands on the firm's top management. In order to attend to broader, longer-term organizational issues, top-level managers must delegate decision making to lower-level managers. Between the middle and end of the 20th century, the percentage of Fortune 500 firms that became diversified and the number of firms that adopted the divisional structure rapidly increased.[9]

There are many advantages associated with the divisional structure. By creating separate divisions to manage individual product markets, there is a separation of strategic and operating control. That is, divisional managers can focus their efforts on improving operations in the product markets for which they are responsible, and corporate officers can devote their time to overall strategic issues for the entire corporation. The focus on a division's products and markets—by the divisional executives—provides the corporation with an enhanced ability to respond quickly to important changes in the external environment. Since there are functional departments within each division of the corporation, the problems associated with sharing resources across functional departments are minimized. Finally, because there are multiple levels of general managers (that is, executives responsible for integrating and coordinating all functional areas), the development of general

Although Brinker International had a traditional functional structure, changes in its competitive outlook forced management to take a closer look at the organizational design of the firm. The firm controls a variety of restaurant chains and bakeries, including Wildfire, Big Bowl, and Chili's.

With all these interests under one corporate roof, management of these disparate entities became difficult. The fragmented $330 billion restaurant and bakery industry caters to highly focused market niches. The original functional design of the Brinker chain had some disad-

vantages as the company grew. With areas separated by function, it became hard to focus efforts on a single restaurant chain. The diverse markets served by the bakeries and restaurants began to lose their focus.

As a result, Brinker International changed to a divisional structure. This allowed the company to consolidate individuals who worked with a single restaurant or bakery chain into a separate division. Brinker referred to these as concept teams, with each concept team responsible for the operation of a single line of business. This focused effort streamlined the ability of the company to concentrate on the market niche served by each of its restaurants and bakeries.

Source: "CEO Interview: Ronald A. McDougall, Brinker International," *Wall Street Transcript,* January 20, 1999, pp. 1–4.

management talent is enhanced. Strategy Spotlight 10.1 discusses the rationale behind Brinker Corporation's change in structure from functional to divisional.

As one would expect, a divisional structure also has potential disadvantages. First, it can be very expensive; that is, there can be increased costs due to the duplication of personnel, operations, and investment since each division must staff multiple functional departments. There can also be dysfunctional competition among divisions since each division tends to become concerned solely about its own operations. Furthermore, divisional managers are often evaluated on common measures such as return on assets and sales growth. Thus, if goals are conflicting, there can be a sense of a "zero-sum" game that would discourage sharing ideas and resources among the divisions for the common good of the corporation. As noted by Ghoshal and Bartlett, two leading scholars in strategic management:

> As their label clearly warns, divisions divide. The divisional model fragmented companies' resources; it created vertical communication channels that insulated business units and prevented them from sharing their strengths with one another. Consequently, the whole of the corporation was often less than the sum of its parts.[10]

Another potential disadvantage is that with many divisions providing different products and services, there is the chance that differences in image and quality may occur across divisions. For example, one division may offer no-frills products of lower quality that may erode the brand reputation of another division that has top quality, highly differentiated offerings. Finally, since each division is evaluated in terms of financial measures such as return on investment and revenue growth, there is often an urge to focus on short-term performance. For example, if corporate management uses quarterly profits as the key performance indicator, divisional management may tend to put significant emphasis on "making the numbers" and minimizing activities, such as advertising, maintenance, and capital investments, which would detract from short-term performance measures.

Before moving on, we'll discuss two variations of the divisional form of organizational structure: the strategic business unit (SBU) and holding company structures.

Strategic Business Unit (SBU) Structure   Corporations that are highly diversified such as ConAgra, a $20 billion food producer, may consist of dozens of different divisions.[11] If ConAgra were to use a purely divisional structure, it would be nearly impossible for the corporate office to plan and coordinate activities because the span of control would be too large. Instead, to attain synergies, ConAgra has put its diverse businesses into three primary SBUs: food service (restaurants), retail (grocery stores), and agricultural products.

With an SBU structure, divisions with similar products, markets, and/or technologies are grouped into homogenous groups in order to achieve some synergies. These include those discussed in Chapter 6 for related diversification, such as leveraging core competencies, sharing infrastructures, and market power. Generally speaking, the more related businesses are within a corporation, the fewer SBUs will be required. Each of the SBUs in the corporation operates as a profit center.

The major advantage of the SBU structure is that it makes the task of planning and control by the corporate office more manageable. Also, since the structure provides greater decentralization of authority, individual businesses can react more quickly to important changes in the environment than if all divisions had to report directly to the corporate office.

There are also some disadvantages to the SBU structure. Since the divisions are grouped into SBUs, it may become difficult to achieve synergies across SBUs. That is, if divisions that are included in different SBUs have potential sources of synergy, it may become difficult for them to be realized. The additional level of management increases the number of personnel and overhead expenses, while the additional hierarchical level removes the corporate office further from the individual divisions. Thus, the corporate office may become unaware of key developments that could have a major impact on the corporation.

Holding Company Structure   The holding company structure (sometimes referred to as a *conglomerate*) is also a variation of the divisional structure. Whereas the SBU structure is often used when similarities exist between the individual businesses (or divisions), the holding company structure is appropriate when the businesses in a corporation's portfolio do not have much in common. Thus, the potential for synergies is limited.

Holding company structures are most appropriate for firms that follow a strategy of unrelated diversification. Companies such as Hanson Trust, ITT, and the CP group of Thailand have relied on the holding company structure to implement their unrelated diversification strategies. Since there are few similarities across the businesses, the corporate offices in these companies provide a great deal of autonomy to operating divisions and rely on financial controls and incentive programs to obtain high levels of performance from the individual businesses. As one would expect, corporate staffs at these firms tend to be small because their involvement in the overall operation of their various businesses is limited.[12]

An important advantage of the holding company structure is the savings of expenses associated with fewer personnel and the lower overhead resulting from a small corporate office and fewer levels in the corporate hierarchy. In addition, the autonomy of the holding company structure increases the motivational level of divisional executives and enables them to respond quickly to market opportunities and threats.

The primary disadvantage of the holding company structure is the inherent lack of control and dependence that corporate-level executives have on divisional executives. Major problems could arise if key divisional executives leave the firm, because the corporate office has very little "bench strength," that is, additional managerial talent ready to fill key positions on short notice. And, if problems arise in a division, it may become very difficult to turn around individual businesses because of limited staff support in the corporate office.

Matrix Structure

At times, managers may find that none of the structures that we have described above fully meet their needs. One approach that tries to overcome the inadequacies inherent in the other structures is the matrix structure. It is, in effect, a combination of the functional and divisional structures. Most commonly, functional departments are combined with product groups on a project basis. For example, a product group may want to develop a new addition to its line; for this project, it obtains personnel from functional departments such as marketing, production, and engineering. These personnel work under the manager of the product group for the duration of the project, which can vary from a few weeks to an open-ended period of time. The individuals who work in a matrix organization become responsible to two managers: the project manager and the manager of their functional area. Exhibit 10.4 illustrates a matrix structure.

In addition to the product-function matrix, other bases may be related in a matrix. Some large multinational corporations rely on a matrix structure to combine product groups and geographical units. Product managers have global responsibility for the development, manufacturing, and distribution of their own line, while managers of geographical regions have responsibility for the profitability of the businesses in their regions. In the mid-1990s, Caterpillar, Inc., implemented this type of structure.

Michael Eisner, CEO of Disney, relies on the matrix concept—with its dual-reporting responsibility—to enhance synergy. Consider the perspective that he shared in a recent interview.[13]

> We're also trying to increase the amount of synergy in our global operations country by country. We've just reorganized our international organization into a hybrid type of structure, so the person running movies in Italy, for instance, not only reports to an executive in the movie division, as he or she did before, but also reports to a country head. That country head is responsible for synergy. Hopefully, this will duplicate what we do in Burbank [Disney's headquarters] every week.

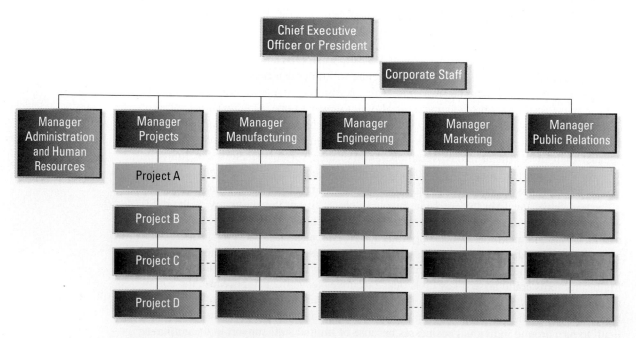

Exhibit 10.4 Matrix Organizational Structure

A primary advantage of the matrix structure is that it facilitates the use of specialized personnel, equipment, and facilities. Rather than duplicating functions, as would be the case in a divisional structure based on products, the resources are shared as needed. Individuals with high expertise can divide their time among multiple projects at one time. Such resource sharing and collaboration enable a firm to use resources more efficiently and to respond more quickly and effectively to changes in the competitive environment. In addition, the flexibility inherent in a matrix structure provides professionals with a broader range of responsibility and the experience enables them to develop their skills and competencies.

There are also many potential disadvantages associated with matrix structures. The dual-reporting structures can result in uncertainty and lead to intense power struggles and conflict over the allocation of professional personnel and other resources. Additionally, working relationships become more complicated. This may result in excessive reliance on group processes and teamwork, along with a diffusion of responsibility, which in turn may erode timely decision making. Exhibit 10.5 briefly summarizes the advantages and disadvantages of the functional, divisional, and matrix organizational structures.

International Operations: Implications for Organizational Structure

Today's managers must maintain an international outlook on their firm's businesses and competitive strategies. To be successful in the global marketplace, managers must ensure consistency between their strategies (at the business, corporate, and international levels) and the structure of their organization. As firms expand into foreign markets, they generally follow a pattern of change in structure that parallels the changes in their strategies. Three major contingencies that seem to influence the structure adopted by firms with international operations are (1) the type of strategy that is driving a firm's foreign operations, (2) product diversity, and (3) the extent to which a firm is dependent on foreign sales.[14]

As international operations become an important part of a firm's overall operations, managers must make changes that are consistent with their firm's structure. The primary types of structures used to manage a firm's international operations are:[15]

- International division
- Geographic-area division
- Worldwide functional
- Worldwide product division
- Worldwide matrix

As we discussed in Chapter 7, multidomestic strategies are driven by political and cultural imperatives that require managers within each country to respond to local conditions. The structures that would be consistent with such a strategic orientation are the *international division* and *geographic-area division* structures. Here local managers are provided with a high level of autonomy to manage their operations within the constraints and demands of their geographic market. As a firm's foreign sales increase as a percentage of its total sales, it will likely change from an international division structure to a geographic-area division structure. And, as a firm's product and/or market diversity becomes large, it is more likely to benefit from a *worldwide matrix structure.*

Global strategies, on the other hand, are driven by economic pressures that require managers to view operations in different geographic areas as only a component of an overall operation that must be managed for overall efficiency. The structures consistent with the efficiency perspective are the *worldwide functional* and *worldwide product division* structures. Here, division managers view the marketplace as homogeneous and devote relatively

Exhibit 10.5
Functional, Divisional, and Matrix Organizational Structures

Functional Structure	
Advantages	**Disadvantages**
◆ Pooling of specialists enhances coordination and control.	◆ Differences in functional area orientation impede communication and coordination.
◆ Centralized decision making enhances an organizational perspective across functions.	◆ Tendency for specialists to develop short-term perspective and narrow functional orientation.
◆ Efficient use of managerial and technical talent.	◆ Functional area conflicts may overburden top-level decision makers.
◆ Career paths and professional development in specialized areas are facilitated.	◆ Difficult to establish uniform performance standards.

Divisional Structure	
Advantages	**Disadvantages**
◆ Increases strategic and operational control, permitting corporate-level executives to address strategic issues.	◆ Increased costs incurred through duplication of personnel, operations, and investment.
◆ Quick response to environmental changes.	◆ Dysfunctional competition among divisions may detract from overall corporate performance.
◆ Increased focus on products and markets.	◆ Difficulty in maintaining uniform corporate image.
◆ Minimizes problems associated with sharing resources across functional areas.	◆ Overemphasis on short-term performance.
◆ Facilitates development of general managers.	

Matrix Structure	
Advantages	**Disadvantages**
◆ Increases market responsiveness through collaboration and synergies among professional colleagues.	◆ Dual-reporting relationships can result in uncertainty regarding accountability.
◆ Allows more efficient utilization of resources.	◆ Intense power struggles may lead to increased levels of conflict.
◆ Improves flexibility, coordination, and communication.	◆ Working relationships may be more complicated and human resources duplicated.
◆ Increases professional development through a broader range of responsibility.	◆ Excessive reliance on group processes and teamwork may impede timely decision making.

little attention to local market, political, and economic factors. The choice between these two types of structures is guided largely by the extent of product diversity. Firms with relatively low levels of product diversity may opt for a worldwide product division structure. However, when a firm has significant product-market diversity resulting from a series of highly unrelated international acquisitions, a worldwide holding company structure is likely to be implemented. Such firms are characterized by very little commonality among products, markets, or technologies, and have little need for integration.

How an Organization's Structure Can Influence Strategy Formulation

Generally speaking, discussions of the relationship between strategy and structure strongly imply that structure follows strategy. That is, the strategy that a firm chooses (e.g., related diversification) dictates such structural elements as the division of tasks, the appropriate patterns of information flow, the need for integration of activities, and authority relationships within the organization. However, we must also recognize the role that an existing structure can play in strategy formulation. For example, once a firm's structure is in place, it is very difficult and expensive to change.[16] Executives may not be able to modify their duties and responsibilities greatly, or may not welcome the disruption associated with a transfer to a new location. Further, there may be costs associated with hiring, training, and replacing executive, managerial, and operating personnel. Thus, strategy cannot be formulated without considering structural elements.

The type of organization structure can also strongly influence a firm's strategy, day-to-day operations and performance.[17] For example, as we discussed earlier, the functional structure of Sharp Corp., the consumer electronics giant, enables the company to achieve economies of scale with its applied research and manufacturing skills. Also, managers have the responsibility to coordinate similar products in multiple functional areas throughout the organization. Such structural arrangements should help increase operating performance because of lower costs as well as enable Sharp to enter new product markets through its applied research. These opportunities would likely not be realized if Sharp had extensive redundant manufacturing resources throughout its divisions and did not effectively coordinate functional area operations across its divisions. The history of success of Sharp's functional structure also suggests that the company is unlikely to consider diversification—a strategy that would require them to move away from the functional structure. Similarly, we discussed Brinker International's move to a divisional structure in order to organize its restaurant groups into different units to focus on market niches. This new structure should enable the firm to adapt to change more rapidly and innovate more effectively with the various restaurant brands. Brinker's management did not feel that they were as effective with their previous functional organization structure.

Today, most organizations compete in environments that may be characterized as rapidly changing and unpredictable. To succeed, they must make their boundaries more flexible and permeable. In the next section we will discuss three types of what we term "boundaryless" organizations: barrier-free, modular, and virtual. We do not suggest that boundaryless structures replace the more traditional forms of organizational structure. Rather, they should complement them to make an organization more flexible and responsive to change.

Boundaryless Organizational Designs

The term *boundaryless* may bring to mind a chaotic organizational reality in which "anything goes." This is not the case. As Jack Welch, GE's former CEO, has suggested, boundaryless does not imply that all internal and external boundaries vanish completely. Although boundaries may continue to exist in some form, they become more open and permeable.[18] Strategy Spotlight 10.2 discusses four types of boundaries and provides examples of how organizations have made them more permeable.

As we have noted, we are not suggesting that boundaryless structures replace the traditional forms of organizational structure. Rather, they should complement them. For example, Sharp Corp. has implemented a functional structure to attain economies of scale

Boundary Types

There are primarily four types of boundaries that place limits on organizations. In today's dynamic business environment, different types of boundaries are needed to foster high degrees of interaction with outside influences and varying levels of permeability.

1. *Vertical boundaries between levels in the organization's hierarchy.* SmithKline Beecham asks employees at different hierarchical levels to brainstorm ideas for managing clinical trial data. The ideas are incorporated into action plans that significantly cut the new product approval time of its breakthrough pharmaceuticals. This would not have been possible if the barriers between levels of individuals in the organization had been too high.

2. *Horizontal boundaries between functional areas.* Fidelity Investments makes the functional barriers more porous and flexible among divisions, such as marketing, operations, and customer service, in order to offer customers a more integrated experience when conducting business with the company. Customers can take their questions to one person, reducing the chance that customers will "get the runaround" from employees who feel customer service is not their responsibility. At Fidelity, customer service is everyone's business, regardless of functional area.

3. *External boundaries between the firm and its customers, suppliers, and regulators.* GE Lighting, by working closely with retailers, functions throughout the value chain as a single operation. This allows GE to track point-of-sale purchases, giving it better control over inventory management.

4. *Geographic boundaries between locations, cultures, and markets.* The global nature of today's business environment spurred PricewaterhouseCoopers to use a global groupware system. This allows the company to instantly connect to its 26 worldwide offices.

Source: R. Ashkenas, "The Organization's New Clothes," in F. Hesselbein, M. Goldsmith, and R. Beckhard, eds., *The Organization of the Future* (San Francisco: Jossey Bass, 1997), pp. 104–6.

with its applied research and manufacturing skills. However, to bring about this key objective, Sharp has relied on several integrating mechanisms and processes—key attributes of the boundaryless concept.

> To prevent functional groups from becoming vertical chimneys that obstruct product development, Sharp's product managers have responsibility—but not authority—for coordinating the entire set of value-chain activities. And the company convenes enormous numbers of cross-unit and corporate committees to ensure that shared activities, including the corporate R&D unit and sales forces, are optimally configured and allocated among the different product lines. Sharp invests in such time-intensive coordination to minimize the inevitable conflicts that arise when units share important activities.[19]

We discuss three approaches to making boundaries more permeable. In the process, these approaches help to facilitate the widespread sharing of knowledge and information across both the internal and external boundaries of the organization. We'll begin with the *barrier-free* type, which involves making all organizational boundaries—internal and external—more permeable. We'll place particular emphasis on team concepts, because we view teams as a central building block for implementing the boundaryless organization. In the next two sections, we will address the *modular* and *virtual* types of organizations. These forms focus on the need to create seamless relationships with external organizations such as customers or suppliers. While the modular type emphasizes the outsourcing of noncore activities, the virtual (or network) organization focuses on alliances among independent entities formed to exploit specific market opportunities.

strategy spotlight

Teamwork at Toyota

When Takeshi Yoshida was given the job of the chief engineer for the 2003 Toyota Corolla and its all-new five-door version, the Matrix, he knew the small-car design would have big stakes. The Corolla carried all of the Toyota DNA—of quality, reliability, and affordability. So keeping the price of the new Corolla under $15,000 while reinvigorating the design to appeal to young drivers was a challenging task. Yoshida responded with a technique called *oobeya:* Japanese for "big, open office." If he was going to change the way he created a product, he figured he would need all the help he could get. And *oobeya* means bringing people together. People from all parts of the company—from design, engineering, manufacturing, logistics, and sales—came together every month for two years before the car went into production. The meetings took place everywhere—from Toyota City, Japan, to Erlanger, Kentucky—and everything, from cost-cutting techniques to reducing bottlenecks, was open for discussion.

At the outset the *oobeyas* were all about cost cutting. Virtually every penny spent on the Corolla was argued and fought over. As the players looked beyond their departmental budgets, all kinds of smart savings came into view. A revision in the assembly process canceled out a $300 per car charge that was currently being incurred. Toyota's four-color brochures were expensive to produce. Instead, they enhanced the company website to include the full-color brochures that dealers or customers could print out. That in itself saved the company another $2 million. By the time the new Corolla and the Matrix came to the market in March 2002, Yoshida was pleased with what *oobeya* had helped him accomplish. He had managed to keep the price tag under $15,000 and not give up anything in quality. Yoshida's insight was to see that *oobeya* was all about the power of open minds and creating a barrier-free organization.

Sources: www.business2.com/articles/mag/0,1640,8828,FF.html; F. Warner "In a Word, Toyota Drives for Innovation," *Fast Company,* August 2002, p. 36; and www.autofieldguide.com/columns/gary/0102oncar.html.

The Barrier-Free Organization

The "boundary" mind-set is ingrained deeply into bureaucracies. It is evidenced by such clichés as "That's not my job," "I'm here from corporate to help," or endless battles over transfer pricing. In the traditional company, boundaries are clearly delineated in the design of an organization's structure. These boundaries are rigid. Their basic advantage is that the roles of managers and employees are simple, clear, well-defined, and long-lived. A major shortcoming was pointed out to the authors during an interview with a high-tech executive: "Structure tends to be divisive; it leads to territorial fights."

Today such structures are being replaced by fluid, ambiguous, and deliberately ill-defined tasks and roles. Just because work roles are no longer defined by traditional structures, however, does not mean that differences in skills, authority, and talent disappear.

A barrier-free organization enables a firm to bridge real differences in culture, function, and goals to find common ground that facilitates information sharing and other forms of cooperative behavior. Eliminating the multiple boundaries that stifle productivity and innovation can enhance the potential of the entire organization.

Creating Permeable Internal Boundaries   For barrier-free organizations to work effectively, the level of trust and shared interests among all parts of the organization must be raised. Similarly, the organization needs to develop among its employees the skill level needed to work in a more democratic organization. Barrier-free organizations also require a shift in the organization's philosophy from executive development to organizational development, and from investments in high-potential individuals to investments in leveraging the talents of all individuals. Strategy Spotlight 10.3 demonstrates how Toyota effectively uses teamwork.

Teams can be an important aspect of barrier-free structures. Jeffrey Pfeffer, author of several insightful books, including *The Human Equation,* suggests that teams have three primary advantages.[20] First, teams substitute peer-based control for hierarchical control of work activities. In essence, employees control themselves, reducing the time and energy management needs to devote to control.

Second, teams frequently develop more creative solutions to problems because they encourage the sharing of the tacit knowledge held by individual team members.[21] Brainstorming, or group problem solving, involves the pooling of ideas and expertise to enhance the chances that at least one group member will think of a way to solve the problems at hand.

Third, by substituting peer control for hierarchical control, teams permit the removal of layers of hierarchy and absorption of administrative tasks previously performed by specialists. This avoids the cumbersome costs of having people whose sole job is to watch the people who watch other people do the work. To carry the argument one step further, Norman Augustine humorously pointed out in *Augustine's Laws* that "If a sufficient number of management layers are superimposed on top of each other, it can be assured that disaster is not left to chance!"[22]

Effective barrier-free organizations must go beyond achieving close integration and coordination within divisions in a corporation. Past research on the multidivisional type of organization has pointed to the importance of interdivisional coordination and resource sharing.[23] Means to this end include interdivisional task forces and committees, reward and incentive systems that emphasize interdivisional cooperation, and common training programs.

A study of professional service firms provides some additional insights.[24] The most important assets of these firms were not the individual technical expertise of their members. That was merely a precondition at these firms. Rather, the collective wisdom of multidisciplinary teams was what set them apart. Further, the researchers found that the average performers excel at using the combined knowledge of boundary-crossing teams to solve especially complex problems with the speed and efficiency that competitors could not match. The competitor of a top-performing investment bank lamented:

> They are the team to beat. Why? They don't slow themselves down with the clutter of bureaucracy. They overwhelm the problem. That *could* yield inefficiency, but it doesn't. They are smart and quick and work seamlessly together.

The capacity to work together rested on an individual willingness to learn and a belief that no single person had all the answers.[25] A partner in a law firm made the following observation:

> One thing that I look at in a prospective partner is the ability to recognize when you don't know the answer. None of us are expected to be experts across the board. Our practice is highly sophisticated, so that we have to bring to bear front-line and top-level expertise in different categories. I need to be smart enough to recognize that there's an issue and go to my partners for assistance.
>
> Work is so interdisciplinary that I just can't imagine doing my work without substantial help from others. Right at the top of the firm, everybody's convinced that we are stronger than we are as individuals.

Given the importance of collaboration and collective efforts, what makes a good team becomes of critical importance. Frank Carruba (former head of Hewlett-Packard's labs) provides some interesting insights.[26] He discovered over time that the difference between mediocre teams and good teams was generally varying levels of motivation and talent. But what explained the difference between good teams and truly superior teams? Carruba found that the key difference—and this explained a 40 percent overall difference in performance—was the way members treated each other, that is, the degree to which they be-

strategy spotlight

Why Some Teams Fail and Others Excel

Why do some teams fail, while others succeed? What are the differences that lead to success? The following four points summarize 20 years of research by Harold J. Leavitt and Jean Lipman-Blumen:

- *Work matters.* Job satisfaction doesn't necessarily translate into successful teams. Employees can be quite happy and very unproductive. What's more important is what individuals find in their work. This creates intrinsic motivation that results in both satisfaction and productivity.

- *Titles don't matter.* Great teams ignore hierarchies. They focus on getting the work done, not who has the most prestigious title. Titles create expectations rather than teamwork.

- *People bond in the heat of battle.* There's a mistaken notion that building relationships through social interaction makes great teams. But working together through crisis and challenge is what brings people together.

- *Teams take care of their own.* Teamwork doesn't exclude individualism; teams make it safe to be an individualist. Individual contributions are brought together in a synergistic fashion. "Groupthink" only hinders creativity.

Source: H. J. Leavitt and J. Lipman-Blumen. "Extreme Teams," *Fast Company,* November 1999, pp. 309–26.

lieved in one another and created an atmosphere of encouragement rather than competition. In other words, vision, talent, and motivation could carry a team only so far. What clearly stood out in the "super" teams were higher levels of authenticity and caring, which allowed the full synergy of their individual talents, motivation, and vision to be expressed without barriers.

Harold Leavitt and Jean Lipman-Blumen, coauthors of the book *Hot Groups,* spent 20 years exploring why some teams excel, others do fairly well, and still others fail. Their work provides many interesting insights. Strategy Spotlight 10.4 summarizes some of their key findings.

Developing Effective Relationships with External Constituencies In barrier-free organizations, managers must also create flexible, porous organizational boundaries and establish communication flows and mutually beneficial relationships with internal (e.g., employees) and external (e.g., customers) constituencies. Michael Dell, founder and CEO of Dell Computer, is a strong believer in fostering close relationships with his customers. In an interview, he explained:

> We're not going to be just your PC vendor anymore. We're going to be your IT department for PCs. Boeing, for example, has 100,000 Dell PCs, and we have 30 people that live at Boeing, and if you look at the things we're doing for them or for other customers, we don't look like a supplier, we look more like Boeing's PC department. We become intimately involved in planning their PC needs and the configuration of their network.
>
> It's not that we make these decisions by ourselves. They're certainly using their own people to get the best answer for the company. But the people working on PCs together, from both Dell and Boeing, understand the needs in a very intimate way. They're right there living it and breathing it, as opposed to the typical vendor who says, "Here are your computers. See you later."[27]

Thus far, we have argued that barrier-free organizations create successful relationships between both internal and external constituencies. However, there is one additional constituency—competitors—with whom some organizations have benefited as they developed cooperative relationships.

For example, after years of seeing its empty trucks return from warehouses back to production facilities after deliveries, General Mills teamed up with 16 of its competitors.[28] The network of competitors formed an e-commerce business, allowing the companies to find carriers with empty cargo trailers to piggyback freight loads to distributors near the production facilities. This increases revenue for all network members and reduces wasted carrier miles.

Risks, Challenges, and Potential Downsides   In spite of its potential bene-fits, many firms are discovering that creating and managing a barrier-free organization is a frustrating experience.[29] For example, Puritan-Bennett Corporation, a Lenexa, Kansas, manufacturer of respiratory equipment, found that its product development time more than doubled after it adopted team management. Roger J. Dolida, director of R&D, attributed this failure to a lack of top management commitment, high turnover among team members, and infrequent meetings. Similarly, efforts at Jerome Goods, a turkey producer in Baron, Wisconsin, to switch to entrepreneurial teams have largely stalled due to a failure to link executive compensation to team performance. Very often, managers trained in rigid hier-archies find it difficult to make the transition to the more democratic, participative style that teamwork requires.

Christopher Barnes, now a consultant with PricewaterhouseCoopers in Atlanta, previ-ously worked as an industrial engineer for Challenger Electrical Distribution (a subsidiary of Westinghouse, now part of CBS) at a plant in Jackson, Mississippi, which produced circuit-breaker boxes. His assignment was to lead a team of workers from the plant's trou-bled final-assembly operation with the mission: "Make things better." Not surprisingly, that vague notion set the team up for failure.

After a year of futility, the team was disbanded. In retrospect, and after several suc-cesses with teams, Barnes identified several reasons for the debacle in Jackson: (1) limited personal credibility—he was viewed as an "outsider"; (2) a lack of commitment to the team—everyone involved was forced to be on the team; (3) poor communications—no-body was told why the team was important; (4) limited autonomy—line managers refused to give up control over team members; and (5) misaligned incentives—the culture re-warded individual performance over team performance. Barnes's experience has important implications for all types of teams, whether composed of managerial, professional, cleri-cal, or production personnel.[30] The pros and cons of barrier-free structures are summarized in Exhibit 10.6.

**Exhibit 10.6
Pros and Cons
of Barrier-Free
Structures**

Pros	Cons
◆ Leverages the talents of all employees.	◆ Difficult to overcome political and authority boundaries inside and outside the organization.
◆ Enhances cooperation, coordination, and information sharing among functions, divisions, SBUs, and external constituencies.	◆ Lacks strong leadership and common vision, which can lead to coordination problems.
◆ Enables a quicker response to market changes through a single-goal focus.	◆ Time-consuming and difficult-to-manage democratic processes.
◆ Can lead to coordinated win-win initiatives with key suppliers, customers, and alliance partners.	◆ Lacks high levels of trust, which can impede performance.

The Modular Organization

As Charles Handy, author of *The Age of Unreason,* has noted:

> Organizations have realized that, while it may be convenient to have everyone around all the time, having all of your workforce's time at your command is an extravagant way of marshaling the necessary resources. It is cheaper to keep them outside the organization, employed by themselves or by specialist contractors, and to buy their services when you need them.[31]

To capture Handy's vision, the modular organization type outsources nonvital functions, tapping into the knowledge and expertise of "best in class" suppliers of goods and services, but retains strategic control. Outsiders may be used to manufacture parts, handle logistics, or perform accounting activities. As we discussed in Chapters 3 and 5, the value chain can be used as a framework to identify the key primary and support activities performed by a firm to create value. The key question becomes: Which activities do we keep "in-house" and which activities do we outsource to suppliers? In effect, the organization becomes a central hub surrounded by networks of outside suppliers and specialists and, much like Lego blocks, parts can be added or taken away. Both manufacturing and service units may be modular.[32]

In the personal computer industry, the shift to the modular structure has been pioneered by relative newcomers like Dell and Gateway, as well as by workstation innovators like Sun Microsystems. These companies either buy their products ready-made or purchase all the parts from suppliers and perform only the final assembly. Their larger, more established competitors—IBM and Hewlett-Packard—produce most of their parts in-house. As a result, the smaller modular companies are often ahead of their older rivals in profitability.[33]

Apparel is another industry in which the modular type has been widely adopted. Nike and Reebok, for example, have succeeded by concentrating on their strengths: designing and marketing high-tech, fashionable footwear. Nike has very limited production facilities and Reebok owns no plants. These two companies contract virtually all their footwear production to suppliers in Taiwan, South Korea, and other countries with low-cost labor. Avoiding large investments in fixed assets helps them derive large profits on minor sales increases. By being modular, Nike and Reebok can keep pace with changing tastes in the marketplace because their suppliers have become expert at rapidly retooling for the manufacture of new products.

In a modular company, outsourcing the noncore functions offers three advantages.

1. A firm can decrease overall costs, stimulate new product development by hiring suppliers whose talent may be superior to that of in-house personnel, avoid idle capacity, realize inventory savings, and avoid becoming locked into a particular technology.
2. Outsourcing enables a company to focus scarce resources on the areas where it holds a competitive advantage. These benefits can translate into more funding for research and development, hiring the best engineers, and providing continuous training for sales and service staff.
3. By enabling an organization to tap into the knowledge and expertise of its specialized supply-chain partners, it adds critical skills and accelerates organizational learning.[34]

The modular type enables a company to leverage relatively small amounts of capital and a small management team to achieve seemingly unattainable strategic objectives. Freed from the need to make big investments in fixed assets, the modular company can achieve rapid growth. Certain preconditions must exist or be created, however, before the modular approach can be successful. First, the company must work closely with suppliers to ensure that the interests of each party are being fulfilled. Companies need to find loyal, reliable vendors who can be trusted with trade secrets. They also need assurances that suppliers will dedicate their financial, physical, and human resources to satisfy strategic objectives such as lowering costs or being first to market. Second, the modular company must make sure that it selects the proper competencies to keep in-house. An organization must be wary of outsourcing critical components of its business that may compromise long-term competitive advantages.

Firms applying the modular concept must identify core competencies and areas that are important for future development, and then attempt to outsource noncritical functions. For Nike and Reebok, the core competencies are design and marketing, not shoe manufacturing; for Honda, the core competence is engine technology. These firms are unlikely to outsource any activity that involves their core competence.

Strategic Risks of Outsourcing   While adopting the modular form clearly has some advantages, managers must also weigh associated risks. The main strategic concerns are (1) loss of critical skills or developing the wrong skills, (2) loss of cross-functional skills, and (3) loss of control over a supplier.[35]

Too much outsourcing can result in a firm "giving away" too much skill and control. Outsourcing relieves companies of the requirement to maintain skill levels needed to manufacture essential components. Over time, these skills that were once part of the knowledge base of the company disappear. At one time, semiconductor chips seemed like a simple technology to outsource. But now, they have become a critical component of a wide variety of products. Companies that have outsourced the manufacture of these chips run the risk of losing the ability to manufacture them as the technology has rapidly escalated. Thus, they may become increasingly dependent upon their suppliers.

Cross-functional skills refer to the skills acquired through the interaction of individuals in various departments within a company. Often, such interaction assists a department in solving problems as employees interface with others across functional units. However, if a firm outsources key functional responsibilities, such as manufacturing, communication across departments can become more difficult. This is because a firm and its employees must now integrate their activities with a new, outside supplier. This typically brings about new challenges in the coordination of joint efforts.

Another serious drawback can occur when the outsourced products give suppliers too much power over the manufacturer. This can happen when the manufacturer is dependent on a single supplier, or just a few suppliers, for critical components. Suppliers that are key to a manufacturer's success can, in essence, hold the manufacturer "hostage." Nike manages this potential problem by sending full-time "product expatriates" to work at the plants of its suppliers. Also, the company often brings top members of supplier management and technical teams to Nike headquarters. This way, Nike keeps close tabs on the pulse of new developments, builds rapport and trust with suppliers, and develops long-term relationships with suppliers to prevent hostage situations.

Strategy Spotlight 10.5 discusses outsourcing initiatives by a governmental agency, the U.S. Army. Exhibit 10.7 summarizes the pros and cons of modular structures.[36]

The Virtual Organization

One of the lessons America's mythological cowboys learned well in the rough-and-tumble days on the frontier was that paranoia was smart psychology: "Don't trust anyone—they're all out to get you. They'll all steal from you (or worse yet, shoot you!) once your back is turned." Staking an ownership claim to a territory or to a herd was necessary (but not sufficient) to guarantee you a piece of the action. Similarly, "self-reliance" was the best-known phrase associated with the influential 19th-century New Englander, Ralph Waldo Emerson. A century later Robert Frost observed, "Good fences make good neighbors."[37]

strategy spotlight

The Pentagon: Outsourcing Noncore Functions

Focusing on the core competencies and outsourcing the noncore functions seems to be the order of the day. Keeping in line with practices in the private sector, now it seems to be the Pentagon's turn to outsource. The U.S. Army is considering contracting out 214,000 military and civilian employee positions, the largest transfer of jobs to the private sector by a government agency.

According to former Army Secretary Thomas White, the army needs to direct as many resources as it can to antiterrorism efforts and let support jobs go to the private sector, where they can be done at a lesser cost. On the line are the jobs of 58,727 military personnel and 154,910 civilian employees in areas such as accounting, legal counsel, maintenance, and communications. The army is also considering trimming the public payroll jobs that are not considered to be central to its mission of national de-

fense. The methods for outsourcing considered include allowing defense contractors to compete with army employees to see who could do a particular job best and at the lowest cost, creating public-private partnerships and quasi-governmental corporations, moving jobs to the private sector, and simply wiping out some job categories altogether. But some of these moves might require new legislation from Congress. Those military personnel whose jobs are affected will be reassigned, and, while layoffs are possible, civilian employees will be helped to move out with their jobs to contractors or to other government jobs.

Federal unions, however, denounced the army plan as an attempt to do away with their jobs and benefit contractors. Also, whether the Defense Department will be able to manage such a large workforce of contract personnel is another concern. In all, if the outsourcing initiative is successful, it could affect more than one in six army jobs around the world and will mean a drastic change in the structure of the U.S. Army.

Sources: "Army Considers Contracting out Jobs," *Dallas Morning News,* November 3, 2002; J. Peckenpaugh, "Army Plan to Outsource Jobs Will Increase Costs," *GovExec.com,* October 24, 2002, www.govexec.com/dailyfed/1002/102402p1.htm; and www.fas.org/MHonArc/MSWG_archive/msg00080.html.

Traditional management assumptions echo these themes: Good fences make good corporations. After all, if you don't own it, if it hasn't been branded with your mark, you don't control it, and it might hurt you. What you own is "inside" the fence; everything else is "outside" and must be treated as a potential enemy or adversary unless brought under your domination.

Pros	Cons
◆ Directs a firm's managerial and technical talent to the most critical activities.	◆ Inhibits common vision through reliance on outsiders.
◆ Maintains full strategic control over most critical activities—core competencies.	◆ Diminishes future competitive advantages if critical technologies or other competences are outsourced.
◆ Achieves "best in class" performance at each link in the value chain.	◆ Increases the difficulty of bringing back into the firm activities that now add value due to market shifts.
◆ Leverages core competencies by outsourcing with smaller capital commitment.	◆ May lead to an erosion of cross-functional skills.
◆ Encourages information sharing and accelerates organizational learning.	◆ Decreases operational control and potential loss of control over a supplier.

Exhibit 10.7
Pros and Cons of Modular Structures

Times have certainly changed. Now the strategic challenge becomes doing more with less and looking outside the firm for opportunities and solutions to problems. The virtual type of organization provides a new means of leveraging resources and exploiting opportunities.[38]

The virtual type can be viewed as a continually evolving network of independent companies—suppliers, customers, even competitors—linked together to share skills, costs, and access to one another's markets.[39] The members of a virtual organization, by pooling and sharing the knowledge and expertise of each of the component organizations, simultaneously "know" more and can "do" more than any one member of the group could do alone. By working closely together in a cooperative effort, each gains in the long run from the resulting individual and organizational learning that takes place.[40] The term *virtual,* meaning "being in effect but not actually so," is commonly used in the computer industry. A computer's ability to appear to have more storage capacity than it really possesses is called virtual memory. Similarly, by assembling resources from a variety of entities, a virtual organization may seem to have more capabilities than it really possesses.[41]

The virtual organization consists of a grouping of units of different organizations that have joined in an alliance to exploit complementary skills in pursuing common strategic objectives. A case in point is Lockheed Martin's use of specialized coalitions between and among three entities—the company, academia, and government—to enhance competitiveness. According to former CEO Norman Augustine:

> The underlying beauty of this approach is that it forces us to reach outward. No matter what your size, you have to look broadly for new ideas, new approaches, new products. Lockheed Martin used this approach in a surprising manner when it set out during the height of the Cold War to make stealth aircraft and missiles. The technical idea came from research done at the Institute of Radio Engineering in Moscow in the 1960s that was published, and publicized, quite openly in the academic media.
>
> Despite the great contrasts among government, academia and private business, we have found ways to work together that have produced very positive results, not the least of which is our ability to compete on a global scale.[42]

Virtual organizations need not be permanent. Participating firms may be involved in multiple alliances at any one time. Virtual organizations may involve different firms performing complementary value activities, or different firms involved jointly in the same value activities, such as production, R&D, advertising, and distribution. The percentage of activities that are jointly performed with alliance partners may vary significantly from alliance to alliance.[43]

How does the virtual type of structure differ from the modular type? Unlike the modular type, in which the focal firm maintains full strategic control, the virtual organization is characterized by participating firms that give up part of their control and accept interdependent destinies. Participating firms pursue a collective strategy that enables them to cope with uncertainty in the environment through cooperative efforts. The benefit is that, just as virtual memory increases storage capacity, the virtual organizations enhance the capacity or competitive advantage of participating firms. Strategy Spotlight 10.6 addresses the variety of collaborative relationships in the biotechnology industry.

Each company (as Strategy Spotlight 10.6 illustrates) that links up with others to create a virtual organization contributes only what it considers its core competencies. It will mix and match what it does best with the best of other firms by identifying its critical capabilities and the necessary links to other capabilities.[44]

Challenges and Risks   Despite their many advantages, alliances often fail to meet expectations. For example, the alliance between IBM and Microsoft soured in early 1991 when Microsoft began shipping Windows in direct competition to OS/2, which was jointly

Collaborative Relationships in Biotechnology

Collaboration in biotechnology has benefited a variety of firms. Amgen collaborates with a number of smaller firms including ARRIS, Environgen, Glycomex, and Interneuron, among others. The companies work on joint marketing projects as well as bring R&D scientists together to explore opportunities for new pharmaceutical product development. In exchange for the expertise of the scientists and marketers at the smaller companies, Amgen provides financial clout and technical assistance when new-product opportunities are identified.

Another biotech company that utilizes collaborative relationships with competitors is Biogen. This large pharmaceutical firm once outsourced clinical testing of its new drugs. But now, the company brings experts from other firms to Biogen laboratories to work with Biogen scientists.

Chiron, one of the largest pharmaceutical firms, with over 7,500 employees, makes extensive use of collaborative efforts with its competitors. The company currently collaborates with over 1,400 companies, tapping into the knowledge base of R&D experts with a wide variety of skill and expertise in the field. Chiron considers this network one of its core competencies.

Source: W. W. Powell, "Learning from Collaboration: Knowledge and Networks in the Biotechnology and Pharmaceutical Industries," *California Management Review* 40, no. 3 (1998), pp. 228–40; E. Williams and R. Langreth, "A Biotech Wonder Grows Up," *Forbes,* September 3, 2001, p. 118.

developed by the two firms. The runaway success of Windows frustrated IBM's ability to set an industry standard. In retaliation, IBM entered into an alliance with Microsoft's archrival, Novell, to develop network software to compete with Microsoft's LAN Manager.

The virtual organization demands a unique set of managerial skills. Managers must build relationships with other companies, negotiate win–win deals for all parties involved, find the right partners with compatible goals and values, and provide the temporary organization with the right balance of freedom and control. In addition, information systems must be designed and integrated to facilitate communication with current and potential partners.

An ever-changing pattern of alliances that is constantly being formed and dissolved does not necessarily imply mutually exploitative arrangements or lack of long-term relationships. The key is for managers to be clear about the strategic objectives while forming alliances. Some objectives are time bound and those alliances need to be dissolved once the objective is fulfilled. Some alliances may have relatively long-term objectives and will need to be clearly monitored and nurtured to produce mutual commitment and avoid bitter fights for control. The highly dynamic personal computer industry, for example, is characterized by multiple temporary alliances among hardware, operating systems, and software producers.[45] But alliances in the more stable automobile industry, such as those involving Nissan and Volkswagen as well as Mazda and Ford, have long-term objectives and tend to be relatively stable.

The virtual organization is a logical culmination of joint-venture strategies of the past. Shared risks, shared costs, and shared rewards are the facts of life in a virtual organization.[46] When virtual organizations are formed, they involve tremendous challenges for strategic planning. As with the modular corporation, it is essential to identify core competencies. However, for virtual structures to be successful, a strategic plan is also needed to determine the effectiveness of combining core competencies.

The strategic plan must address the diminished operational control and overwhelming need for trust and common vision between the partners. This new structure may be appropriate for firms whose strategies require merging technologies (e.g., computing and communication) or for firms exploiting shrinking product life cycles that require simultaneous

**Exhibit 10.8
Pros and Cons of
Virtual Structures**

Pros	Cons
◆ Enables the sharing of costs and skills.	◆ Harder to determine where one company ends and another begins, due to close interdependencies among players.
◆ Enhances access to global markets.	
◆ Increases market responsiveness.	
◆ Creates a "best of everything" organization since each partner brings core competencies to the alliance.	◆ Leads to potential loss of operational control among partners.
	◆ Results in loss of strategic control over emerging technology.
◆ Encourages both individual and organizational knowledge sharing and accelerates organizational learning.	◆ Requires new and difficult-to-acquire managerial skills.

Source: R. E. Miles and C. C. Snow, "Organizations: New Concepts for New Forms," *California Management Review,* Spring 1986, pp. 62–73; Miles and Snow, "Causes of Failure in Network Organizations," *California Management Review,* Summer 1999, pp. 53–72; and H. Bahrami, "The Emerging Flexible Organization: Perspectives from Silicon Valley," *California Management Review,* Summer 1991, pp. 33–52.

entry into multiple geographical markets. Further, it may be effective for firms that desire to be quick to the market with a new product or service; an example is the recent profusion of alliances among airlines, primarily motivated by the need to provide seamless travel demanded by the full-fare paying business traveler. Exhibit 10.8 summarizes the advantages and disadvantages of the virtual form.

Boundaryless Organizations: Making Them Work

Designing an organization that simultaneously supports the requirements of an organization's strategy, is consistent with the demands of the environment, and can be effectively implemented by the people around the manager, is a tall order for any manager.[47] Many times, the most effective solution is a combination of organizational types. That is, a firm may outsource many parts of its value chain to reduce costs and increase quality, engage simultaneously in multiple alliances to take advantage of technological developments or penetrate new markets, and break down barriers within the organization to enhance flexibility. In Strategy Spotlight 10.7, we look at how an innovative firm, Technical Computer Graphics, effectively combines both barrier-free and virtual forms of organization.

When an organization faces external pressures, resource scarcity, and declining performance, it tends to become more internally focused, rather than directing its efforts toward managing and enhancing relationships with existing and potential external stakeholders. We believe that this may be the most opportune time for managers to carefully analyze their value-chain activities and evaluate the potential for adopting elements of modular, virtual, and barrier-free organizational types. The benefits of such endeavors may help an organization to enhance or establish multiple forms of competitive advantage—differentiation, overall low cost, and combination differentiation and overall low cost leadership—when they are most needed to compete effectively.

Regardless of the form of organization ultimately chosen, achieving the coordination and integration necessary to maximize the potential of an organization's human capital involves much more than just creating a new structure. Techniques and processes designed and implemented to ensure the necessary coordination and integration of an organization's key value-chain activities are critical. Teams are key building blocks of the new organi-

strategy spotlight

Technical Computer Graphics' Boundaryless Organization

The Technical Computer Graphics (TCG) group manufactures items such as handheld bar code readers and scanning software. The company uses 13 "alliances," small project teams employing a total of 200 employees. Each team is responsible for either specific customers or specific products. Alliance teams share a common infrastructure, but they can develop new business opportunities without approval from upper management. Projects often emerge from listening to what customers need.

TCG uses a "triangulation approach"—alliances that include customers, suppliers, and other alliances. Suppliers and customers who provide funding are involved at the outset of the project. The alliances recognize that attaining the initial customer funding is crucial; it stimulates them to focus on what customers have to say. With an emphasis on speed, new products come to market quickly, providing the firm and its partners with tangible benefits.

Source: C. Snow, "Twenty-first Century Organizations: Implications for a New Marketing Paradigm," *Journal of the Academy of Marketing Science,* Winter 1997, pp. 72–74; B. Allred, C. Snow, and R. Miles, "Characteristics of Managerial Careers of the 21st Century," *Academy of Management Executive,* November 1996, pp. 17–27; V. L. Herzog, "Trust Building on Corporate Collaborative Teams," *Project Management Journal,* March 2001, pp. 28–41.

Sometimes another alliance acts as either the customer or the supplier and provides funding.

While each alliance is independent, it shares financial concern for other alliance teams. When a new business opportunity is discovered, an alliance draws on technical expertise from the other alliances. The purpose is not only to acquire additional knowledge, but also to share accumulated learning. There's no benefit to hoarding information: Learning gained from one software project might prove especially valuable to one under way in another alliance. This technological diffusion of information produces products that quickly reach the market.

TCG's formal structure is designed to ensure that such knowledge diffusion occurs. The company's culture is structured to encourage this as well. The TCG culture attracts both the entrepreneur and the team-oriented person at the same time. Working with multiple stakeholders through TCG's triangulation model forces employees to listen to the customers and respond quickly. Because the customer matters more than the functional title, teams lend expertise to each other in return for sharing the gains realized from supplying value to the customer.

zational forms, and teamwork requires new and flexible approaches to coordination and integration.

Often managers trained in rigid hierarchies find it difficult to make the transition to the more democratic, participative style that teamwork requires. As Douglas K. Smith, co-author of *The Wisdom of Teams,* pointed out, "A completely diverse group must agree on a goal, put the notion of individual accountability aside and figure out how to work with each other. Most of all, they must learn that if the team fails, it's everyone's fault."[48] Within the framework of an appropriate organizational design, managers must select a mix and balance of tools and techniques to facilitate the effective coordination and integration of key activities. Some of the factors that must be considered include:

◆   Common culture and shared values.
◆   Horizontal organization structures.
◆   Horizontal systems and processes.
◆   Communications and information technologies.
◆   Human resource practices.

Common Culture and Shared Values   Shared goals, mutual objectives, and a high degree of trust are essential to the success of boundaryless organizations. It is neither feasible nor desirable to attempt to "control" suppliers, customers, or alliance partners in the traditional sense. In the fluid and flexible environments of the new organizational architectures, common cultures, shared values, and carefully aligned incentives are often less expensive to implement and are often a more effective means of strategic control than rules, boundaries, and formal procedures.

Horizontal Organizational Structures   Horizontal organizational structures, which group similar or related business units under common management control, facilitate sharing resources and infrastructures to exploit synergies among operating units, and help to create a sense of common purpose. Consistency in training and the development of similar structures across business units facilitates job rotation and cross training, and enhances understanding of common problems and opportunities. Cross-functional teams and interdivisional committees and task groups represent important opportunities to improve understanding and foster cooperation among operating units.

Horizontal Systems and Processes   Organizational systems, policies, and procedures are the traditional mechanisms for achieving integration among functional units. Too often, however, existing policies and procedures do little more than institutionalize the barriers that exist from years of managing within the framework of the traditional model. The concept of business reengineering focuses primarily on these internal processes and procedures. Beginning with an understanding of basic business processes in the context of "a collection of activities that takes one or more kinds of input and creates an output that is of value to the customer," Michael Hammer and James Champy's 1993 best-selling *Reengineering the Corporation* outlined a methodology for redesigning internal systems and procedures that has been embraced, in its various forms, by many organizations.[49] Proponents claim that successful reengineering lowers costs, reduces inventories and cycle times, improves quality, speeds response times, and enhances organizational flexibility. Others advocate similar benefits through the reduction of cycle times, total quality management, and the like. General Electric and others have used benchmarking and adopted "best practices" from leading companies around the world in an effort to streamline their internal systems and procedures.

Communications and Information Technologies   Improved communications through the effective use of information technologies can play an important role in bridging gaps and breaking down barriers between organizations. Electronic mail and videoconferencing can improve lateral communications across long distances and multiple time zones and, by short-circuiting vertical structures, tend to circumvent many of the barriers of the traditional model. Information technology can be a powerful ally in the redesign and streamlining of internal business processes and in improving coordination and integration between suppliers and customers. Internet technologies have eliminated the paperwork of purchase order and invoice documentation in many buyer-supplier relationships, enabling cooperating organizations to reduce inventories, shorten delivery cycles, and reduce operating costs. Some have argued that information technology must be viewed more as a prime component of an organization's overall strategy than simply in terms of its more traditional role as administrative support. The close relationships that must exist between technology and other value-creating activities were addressed in Chapters 3 and 4.

Human Resource Practices   Change, whether in structure, process, or procedure, always involves and impacts the human dimension of organizations. As we noted in Chapter 4, the attraction, development, and retention of human capital are vital to value creation. As boundaryless structures are implemented, processes are reengineered, and organizations become increasingly dependent on sophisticated information technologies, the skills of workers and managers alike must be upgraded to realize the full benefits.

Successful organizations must ensure that they have the proper type of organizational structure. Furthermore, they must ensure that their firms incorporate the necessary integration and processes so that the internal and external boundaries of their firms are flexible and permeable. Such a need is increasingly important as the environments of firms become more complex, rapidly changing, and unpredictable.

In the first section of the chapter, we discussed the growth patterns of large corporations. Although most organizations remain small or die, some firms continue to grow in terms of revenues, vertical integration, and diversity of products and services. In addition, their geographical scope may increase to include international operations. We traced the dominant pattern of growth, which evolves from a simple structure to a functional structure as a firm grows in terms of size and increases its level of vertical integration. After a firm expands into related products and services, its structure changes from a functional to a divisional form of organization. Finally, when the firm enters international markets, its structure again changes to accommodate the change in strategy.

We also addressed the different types of organizational structure—simple, functional, divisional (including two variations, strategic business unit and holding company), and matrix as well as their relative advantages and disadvantages. We closed the section with a discussion of the implications for structure when a firm enters international markets. The three primary factors to take into account when determining the appropriate structure are type of international strategy, product diversity, and the extent to which a firm is dependent on foreign sales.

The second, and final, section of the chapter introduced the concept of the boundaryless organization. We did not suggest that the concept of the boundaryless organization replaces the traditional forms of organizational structure. Rather, it should complement them. This is necessary to cope with the increasing complexity and change in the competitive environment. We addressed three types of boundaryless organizations. The barrier-free type focuses on the need for the internal and external boundaries of a firm to be more flexible and permeable. The modular type emphasizes the strategic outsourcing of noncore activities. The virtual type centers on the strategic benefits of alliances and the forming of network organizations. We discussed both the advantages and disadvantages of each type of boundaryless organization as well as suggested some techniques and processes that are necessary to successfully implement them. These are common culture and values, horizontal organizational structures, horizontal systems and processes, communications and information technologies, and human resource practices.

summary

summary review questions

1. Why is it important for managers to carefully consider the type of organizational structure that they use to implement their strategies?

2. Briefly trace the dominant growth pattern of major corporations from simple structure to functional structure to divisional structure. Discuss the relationship between a firm's strategy and its structure.

3. What are the relative advantages and disadvantages of the types of organizational structure—simple, functional, divisional, matrix—discussed in the chapter?

4. When a firm expands its operations into foreign markets, what are the three most important factors to take into account in deciding what type of structure is most appropriate? What are the types of international structures discussed in the text and what are the relationships between strategy and structure?

5. Briefly describe the three different types of boundaryless organizations: barrier-free, modular, and virtual.

6. What are some of the key attributes of effective groups? Ineffective groups?

7. What are the advantages and disadvantages of the three types of boundaryless organizations: barrier-free, modular, and virtual?

experiential exercise

Many firms have recently moved toward a modular structure. For example, they have increasingly outsourced many of their information technology (IT) activities. Identify three such organizations. Using secondary sources, evaluate (1) the firm's rationale for IT outsourcing and (2) the implications for performance.

Firm	Rationale	Implication(s) for Performance
1.		
2.		
3.		

application questions exercises

1. Select an organization that competes in an industry in which you are particularly interested. Go on the Internet and determine what type of organizational structure this organization has. In your view, is it consistent with the strategy that it has chosen to implement? Why? Why not?

2. Choose an article from *BusinessWeek, Fortune, Forbes, Fast Company,* or any other well-known publication that deals with a corporation that has undergone a significant change in its strategic direction. What are the implications for the structure of this organization?

3. Go on the Internet and look up some of the public statements or speeches of an executive in a major corporation about a significant initiative such as entering into a joint venture or launching a new product line. What do you feel are the implications for making the internal and external barriers of the firm more flexible and permeable? Does the executive discuss processes, procedures, integrating mechanisms, or cultural issues that should serve this purpose? Or are other issues discussed that enable a firm to become more boundaryless?

4. Look up a recent article in the publications listed in question 2 above that addresses a firm's involvement in outsourcing (modular organization) or in strategic alliance or network organizations (virtual organization). Was the firm successful or unsuccessful in this endeavor? Why? Why not?

1. If a firm has a divisional structure and places extreme pressures on its divisional executives to meet short-term profitability goals (e.g., quarterly income), could this raise some ethical considerations? Why? Why not?
2. If a firm enters into a strategic alliance but does not exercise appropriate behavioral control of its employees (in terms of culture, rewards and incentives, boundaries—as discussed in Chapter 9) that are involved in the alliance, what ethical issues could arise? What could be the potential long-term and short-term downside for the firm?

ethics questions

references

1. White, G. L., 2002, A mismanaged palladium stockpile was catalyst for Ford's write-off, *Wall Street Journal Online,* February 6; Briton, B., 2002, When an elephant rolls over: Living with the Ford Motor Company, *Guardian,* February 13, www.cpa.org.au/garchve5/1079 ford.html; and Losses persist at Ford, 2002, *BBC News,* April 17, news.bbc.co.uk/1/hi/business/1935070.stm.
2. This introductory discussion draws upon Hall, R. H., 2002, *Organizations: Structures, Processes, and Outcomes,* 8th ed. (Upper Saddle River, NJ: Prentice-Hall); and Duncan, R. E., 1979, What is the right organization structure? Decision-tree analysis provides the right answer, *Organizational Dynamics* 7 (3): 59–80. For an insightful discussion of strategy-structure relationships in the organization theory and strategic management literatures, refer to Keats, B., & O'Neill, H. M., 2001, Organization structure: Looking through a strategy lens, in Hitt, M. A., Freeman, R. E., & Harrison, J. S., 2001, *The Blackwell Handbook of Strategic Management* (Malden, MA: Blackwell), 520–42.
3. This discussion draws upon Chandler, A. D., 1962, *Strategy and Structure* (Cambridge, MA: MIT Press); Galbraith J. R., & Kazanjian, R. K., 1986, *Strategy Implementation: The Role of Structure and Process* (St. Paul, MN: West Publishing); and Scott, B. R., 1971, Stages of corporate development, Intercollegiate Case Clearinghouse, 9-371-294, BP 998, Harvard Business School.
4. Our discussion of the different types of organizational structures draws on a variety of sources, including Galbraith & Kazanjian, op. cit.; Hrebiniak, L. G., & Joyce, W. F., 1984, *Implementing Strategy* (New York: Macmillan); Distelzweig, H., 2000, Organizational structure, in Helms, M. M., ed., *Encyclopedia of Management* (Farmington Hills, MI: Gale), 692–99; and Dess, G. G., & Miller, A., 1993, *Strategic Management* (New York: McGraw-Hill).
5. Collis, D. J., & Montgomery, C. A., 1998, Creating corporate advantage, *Harvard Business Review* 76 (3): 70–83.
6. Schein, E. H., 1996, Three cultures of management: The key to organizational learning, *Sloan Management Review* 38 (1): 9–20.
7. For a discussion of performance implications, refer to Hoskisson, R. E., 1987, Multidivisional structure and performance: The contingency of diversification strategy, *Academy of Management Journal* 29: 625–44.
8. For a thorough and seminal discussion of the evolution toward the divisional form of organizational structure in the United States, refer to Chandler, op. cit. A rigorous empirical study of the strategy and structure relationship is found in Rumelt, R. P., 1974, *Strategy, Structure, and Economic Performance* (Cambridge: Harvard Business School Press).
9. See, for example, Hill, C. W. L., Hitt, M. A., & Hoskisson, R. E., 1988, Declining U.S. competitiveness: Reflections on a crisis, *Academy of Management Executive* 2 (1): 51–60.
10. Ghoshal, S., & Bartlett, C. A., 1995, Changing the role of management: Beyond structure to processes. *Harvard Business Review* 73 (1): 88.
11. Koppel, B., 2000, Synergy in ketchup? *Forbes,* February 7: 68–69; and Hitt, M. A., Ireland, R. D., & Hoskisson, R. E., 2001, *Strategic Management: Competitiveness and Globalization,* 4th ed. (Cincinnati, OH: Southwestern Publishing).
12. Pitts, R. A., 1977, Strategies and structures for diversification, *Academy of Management Journal* 20 (2): 197–208.
13. Wetlaufer, S., 2000, Common sense and conflict: An interview with Disney's Michael Eisner, *Harvard Business Review* 78 (1): 121.
14. Daniels, J. D., Pitts, R. A., & Tretter, M. J., 1984, Strategy and structure of U.S. multinationals: An exploratory study, *Academy of Management Journal* 27 (2): 292–307.
15. Habib, M. M., & Victor, B., 1991, Strategy, structure, and performance of U.S. manufacturing and service MNCs: A comparative analysis, *Strategic Management Journal* 12 (8): 589–606.
16. See, for example, Miller, D., & Friesen, P. H., 1980, Momentum and revolution in organizational structure, *Administrative Science Quarterly* 13:65–91.
17. Many authors have argued that a firm's structure can influence a firm's strategy and performance. These

include Amburgey, T. L., & Dacin, T., 1995, As the left foot follows the right? The dynamics of strategic and structural change, *Academy of Management Journal* 37: 1427–52; Dawn, K., & Amburgey, T. L., 1991, Organizational inertia and momentum: A dynamic model of strategic change, *Academy of Management Journal* 34: 591–612; Fredrickson, J. W., 1986, The strategic decision process and organization structure, *Academy of Management Review* 11: 280–97; Hall, D. J., & Saias, M. A., 1980, Strategy follows structure! *Strategic Management Journal* 1: 149–164; and Burgelman, R. A., 1983, A model of the interaction of strategic behavior, corporate context, and the concept of strategy, *Academy of Management Review* 8: 61–70.

18. An interesting discussion on how the Internet has affected the boundaries of firms can be found in Afuah, A., 2003, Redefining firm boundaries in the face of the Internet: Are firms really shrinking? *Academy of Management Review* 28 (1): 34–53.

19. Collis & Montgomery, op. cit.

20. Pfeffer, J., 1998, *The Human Equation: Building Profits by Putting People First* (Cambridge: Harvard Business School Press).

21. For a discussion on how functional area diversity affects performance, see Bunderson, J. S., & Sutcliffe, K. M., 2002, *Academy of Management Journal* 45 (5): 875–93.

22. Augustine, N. R., 1983, *Augustine's Laws* (New York: Viking Press).

23. See, for example, Hoskisson, R. E., Hill, C. W. L., & Kim, H., 1993, The multidivisional structure: Organizational fossil or source of value? *Journal of Management* 19 (2): 269–98.

24. Kuedtjam, H., Haskins, M. E., Rosenblum, J. W., & Weber, J., 1997, The generative cycle: Linking knowledge and relationships, *Sloan Management Review* 39 (1): 47–58.

25. Thompson, L., 2003, Improving the creativity of organizational work groups, *Academy of Management Executive* 17 (1): 96–111.

26. Pottruck, D. A., 1997, speech delivered by the co-CEO of Charles Schwab Co., Inc., to the Retail Leadership Meeting, San Francisco, CA, January 30; and Miller, W., 1999, Building the ultimate resource, *Management Review,* January: 42–45.

27. Magretta, J., 1998, The power of virtual integration: An interview with Dell Computer's Michael Dell, *Harvard Business Review* 76 (2): 75.

28. Forster, J., 2001, Networking for cash, *BusinessWeek,* January 8: 129.

29. Dess, G. G., Rasheed, A. M. A., McLaughlin, K. J., & Priem, R., 1995, The new corporate architecture, *Academy of Management Executive* 9 (3): 7–20.

30. Barnes, C., 1998, A fatal case, *Fast Company,* February–March: 173.

31. Handy, C., 1989, *The Age of Unreason* (Boston: Harvard Business School Press); Ramstead, E., 1997, APC maker's low-tech formula: Start with the box, *Wall Street Journal,* December 29: B1; Mussberg, W., 1997, Thin screen PCs are looking good but still fall flat, *Wall Street Journal,* January 2: 9; Brown, E., 1997, Monorail: Low cost PCs, *Fortune,* July 7: 106–8; and Young, M., 1996, Ex-Compaq executives start new company, *Computer Reseller News,* November 11: 181.

32. Tully, S., 1993, The modular corporation, *Fortune,* February 8: 196.

33. For a recent review of the relationship between outsourcing and firm performance, see Gilley, K. M., & Rasheed, A., 2000, Making more by doing less: An analysis of outsourcing and its effects on firm performance, *Journal of Management* 26 (4): 763–90.

34. Quinn, J. B., 1992, *Intelligent Enterprise: A Knowledge and Service Based Paradigm for Industry* (New York: Free Press).

35. This discussion draws upon Quinn, J. B., & Hilmer, F. C., 1994, Strategic outsourcing, *Sloan Management Review* 35 (4): 43–55.

36. See also Stuckey, J., & White, D., 1993, When and when not to vertically integrate, *Sloan Management Review,* Spring: 71–81; Harrar, G., 1993, Outsource tales, *Forbes ASAP,* June 7: 37–39, 42; and Davis, E. W., 1992, Global outsourcing: Have U.S. managers thrown the baby out with the bath water? *Business Horizons,* July–August: 58–64.

37. The opening three paragraphs draw on Kanter, R. M., 1989, Becoming PALS: Pooling, allying, and linking companies, *Academy of Management Executive,* August: 183. Some authors have used a similar term, *constellational structures,* to refer to organizations that are strongly tied to highly supportive collectives. For an illuminating perspective on how such structures can lead to higher growth and flexibility and lower costs in the Italian textile industry, refer to Lorenzoni, G., & Ornati, O., 1988, Constellations of firms and new ventures, *Journal of Business Venturing* 3: 41–57.

38. For a discussion of knowledge creation through alliances, refer to Inkpen, A. C., 1996, Creating knowledge through collaboration, *California Management Review* 39 (1): 123–40; and Mowery, D. C., Oxley, J. E., & Silverman, B. S., 1996, Strategic alliances and interfirm knowledge transfer, *Strategic Management Journal* 17, Special Issue, Winter: 77–92.

39. Doz, Y., & Hamel, G., 1998, *Alliance Advantage: The Art of Creating Value through Partnering* (Boston: Harvard Business School Press).

40. DeSanctis, G., Glass, J. T., & Ensing, I. M., 2002, Organizational designs for R&D, *Academy of Management Executive* 16 (3): 55–66.

41. Barringer, B. R., & Harrison, J. S., 2000, Walking a

tightrope: Creating value through interorganizational alliances, *Journal of Management* 26: 367–403.

42. Davis, E., 1997, Interview: Norman Augustine. *Management Review,* November: 14.

43. One contemporary example of virtual organizations is R&D consortia. For an insightful discussion, refer to Sakaibara, M., 2002, Formation of R&D consortia: Industry and company effects, *Strategic Management Journal* 23 (11): 1033–50.

44. Bartness, A., & Cerny, K., 1993, Building competitive advantage through a global network of capabilities, *California Management Review,* Winter: 78–103. For an insightful historical discussion of the usefulness of alliances in the computer industry, see Moore, J. F., 1993, Predators and prey: A new ecology of competition, *Harvard Business Review* 71 (3): 75–86.

45. See Lorange, P., & Roos, J., 1991, Why some strategic alliances succeed and others fail, *Journal of Business Strategy,* January–February: 25–30; and Slowinski, G.,

1992, The human touch in strategic alliances, *Mergers and Acquisitions,* July–August: 44–47. A compelling argument for strategic alliances is provided by Ohmae, K., 1989, The global logic of strategic alliances, *Harvard Business Review* 67 (2): 143–54.

46. Some of the downsides of alliances are discussed in Das, T. K., & Teng, B. S., 2000, Instabilities of strategic alliances: An internal tensions perspective, *Organization Science* 11: 77–106.

47. This section draws upon Dess, G. G., & Picken, J. C., 1997, *Mission Critical* (Burr Ridge, IL: Irwin Professional Publishing).

48. Katzenbach, J. R., & Smith, D. K., 1994, *The Wisdom of Teams: Creating the High Performance Organization* (New York: HarperBusiness).

49. Hammer, M., & Champy, J., 1993, *Reengineering the Corporation: A Manifesto for Business Revolution* (New York: HarperCollins).

chapter 11

Strategic Leadership:

Creating a Learning Organization and an Ethical Organization

*After
reading this
chapter, you should
have a good understanding of:*

- The three key activities in which all successful leaders must be continually engaged.

- The importance of recognizing the interdependence of the three key leadership activities, and the salience of power in overcoming resistance to change.

- The crucial role of emotional intelligence (EI) in successful leadership.

- The value of creating and maintaining a "learning organization" in today's global marketplace.

- The five central elements of a "learning organization."

- The leader's role in establishing an ethical organization.

- The benefits of developing an ethical organization.

- The high financial and nonfinancial costs associated with ethical crises.

*t*o compete in the global marketplace, organizations need to have strong and effective leadership. This involves the active process of both creating and implementing proper strategies. In this chapter we address key activities in which leaders throughout the organization must be involved to be successful in creating competitive advantages.

In the first section we provide a brief overview of the three key leadership activities. These are setting a direction, designing the organization, and nurturing a culture committed to excellence and ethical behavior. Each of these activities is "necessary but not sufficient"; that is, to be effective, leaders must give proper attention to each of them. We also address the importance of a leader's effective use of power to overcome resistance to change.

The second section discusses the vital role of emotional intelligence (EI) in effective strategic leadership. EI refers to an individual's capacity for recognizing one's emotions and those of others. It consists of five components: self-awareness, self-regulation, motivation, empathy, and social skills.

Next we address the important role of a leader in creating a "learning organization." Here leaders must strive to harness the individual and collective talents of individuals throughout the entire organization. Creating a learning organization becomes particularly important in today's competitive environment, which is increasingly unpredictable, dynamic, and interdependent. Clearly, everyone must be involved in learning. It can't be only a few people at the top of the organization. The key elements of a learning organization are inspiring and motivating people with a mission or purpose, empowering employees at all levels, accumulating and sharing internal and external information, and challenging the status quo to enable creativity.

The final section discusses a leader's challenge in creating and maintaining an ethical organization. The benefits of having an ethical organization are many. In addition to financial benefits, it can enhance human capital and help to ensure positive relationships with suppliers, customers, society at large, and governmental agencies. On the other hand, the costs of ethical crises can be very expensive for many reasons. We address four key elements of an ethical organization: role models, corporate credos and codes of conduct, reward and evaluation systems, and policies and procedures.

Morrison Knudsen (MK) is in the large-scale construction business.[1] In years past, it was an impressive company, gaining contracts for projects such as the Hoover Dam, the Trans-Alaska Pipeline, and the San Francisco–Oakland Bay Bridge. Then the company decided to start building railroad cars. The firm's investors wanted to know why this decision had been made, as they saw a very successful industry leader sink to the bottom of the heap. Here's the unfortunate story of a good company gone bad from ineffective leadership.

When MK began looking for a new CEO in 1987, it found Bill Agee. Agee had all the right credentials: a Harvard MBA, prior experience as chief financial officer with Boise Cascade, and CEO of auto parts manufacturer Bendix. And Agee was familiar with Morrison Knudsen, having served on the firm's board for the past six years. He seemed the natural candidate for the job. That's too bad—in only a few years, Agee nearly drove the company to ruin.

The company had run upon a spell of bad fortune prior to Agee's appointment as CEO. Land development ventures and shipbuilding went sour as real estate values declined and the price of oil increased during the 1970s and early 1980s. Just before Agee was appointed CEO, Morrison Knudsen reported losses of $60 million from $1.9 billion in revenues. It was Agee's job to turn things around.

In the first annual financial report, he promised to return the company to its core strengths. That might have worked had Agee followed through on his promise. But instead of developing the firm's core competencies, he steered it in another direction. He began pursuing large contracts for infrastructure and transportation development—areas in which the company had little expertise. And, of course, there were the railroad cars. It's odd how a company can go from successfully building dams, pipelines, and bridges to building railroad cars. Turns out, it can't. The first railcars were rejected by the company that ordered them.

Agee continued to venture into unknown territory, increasingly moving the company into areas it knew nothing about. With the company in a downward financial spiral, Agee began taking greater and greater risks. The results were dismal. He would bid projects below cost to try to develop the expertise to gain future contracts. It didn't work. Losses mounted. Agee began dealing in securities and unrelated assets with the firm's cash. His successes were reported on Morrison Knudsen's financial statements as operating income rather than investment income. He also capitalized operating expenses to increase profits in the short term. These schemes disguised the firm's problems from investors and bought some more time for Agee.

Agee also had extravagant tastes, especially when Morrison Knudsen paid the bill. Agee traveled frequently on the company's $4 million corporate jet to his Pebble Beach, California, mansion. The jet cost the company 13 percent of its general and administrative budget. He also developed a bit of an ego to go along with his extravagance; for example, he spent $7,000 of the firm's money on a portrait of himself. Of course, one couldn't go without professional landscaping services; in a single month Agee paid $10,000—of Morrison Knudsen funds—to have his lawn professionally maintained.

Agee had a penchant for hiring top executives with relatively little experience. This kept dissension down—the young executives were afraid to speak up, instead allowing Agee to continue with risky strategies and accounting trickery. While the company was plunging into debt, the company's 1993 annual report claimed a "banner year" with "milestone events, new projects of grand proportions, and strong financial results." You have to wonder if the grand proportions referred to Agee's ego rather the firm's financial performance.

Two years later, the annual financial report finally told the truth about the firm's condition: The company expected a large loss for the previous year, was in default on its debt, and was eliminating its annual dividend.

In the end, Agee's tactics caught up with him. The board of directors finally had enough and fired him in 1995. At this point Morrison Knudsen was in deep financial water. *Fortune* ranked the firm as one of the "least admired companies" in America.

After Agee was fired, the company recovered and things looked better for stockholders. Earnings have increased, revenue is stable and on the rise, and the firm has returned to its core business. In 2000 the company had rebuilt itself to the point that it became a lucrative acquisition target and was purchased by Washington Group International, a company in the engineering, construction, and project management business.

What Went Wrong at Morrison Knudsen?   When the board hired Agee, he intended to "refocus on MK's basic strengths." But this was only the first in a long line of broken promises. Agee's focus was not on the firm's strengths, but on his own image and power. But does all the responsibility lie with Agee or was the board at fault for failing to exercise control of its CEO? The things that went wrong at Morrison Knudsen make up a long list. Some of these are:

- Agee's vision was seriously flawed. His diversification strategy led the company away from, rather than back to, its core competencies.
- Agee took full credit for the large contracts, but by bidding them under cost, how could the company make a profit? Many of the contracts ended up being big money losers—something that Morrison Knudsen could hardly afford.
- Agee was not the type to empower others. Indeed, he put together a management team that he was certain would support his decisions, regardless of the financial soundness of those decisions.
- Clear communication was out of the question. Creative accounting temporarily increased earnings but disguised the true status of the firm from the board, shareholders, and financial markets. Board meetings were held away from the company's headquarters, limiting information access to other members of the management team.
- Agee insulated himself from the company, managing (or mismanaging) the firm from Pebble Beach while living a luxurious lifestyle at Morrison Knudsen's expense. This raises important ethical considerations.

Looking back, Morrison Knudsen's board should not have hired Agee as CEO. Agee failed to successfully lead the organization and, by most accounts, he left the firm in worse condition than it was when he took over. In contrast to Morrison Knudsen's Bill Agee, effective leaders play an important and often pivotal role in the development and implementation of strategies.

This chapter provides insights into how organizations can more effectively manage change and cope with increased environmental complexity and uncertainty. Below we will define leadership and introduce what are considered to be the three most important leadership activities as well as the important role of power. The second section focuses on a key trait, emotional intelligence, that has become increasingly recognized as critical to successful leadership. Then, the third major section, "Developing a Learning Organization" provides a useful framework for how leaders can help their firms learn and proactively adapt in the face of accelerating change. Central to this contemporary idea is the concept of empowerment, wherein employees and managers throughout the organization truly come to have a sense of self-determination, meaning, competence, and impact. The fourth section addresses the leader's role in building an ethical organization. Here, we address both the value of an ethical culture for a firm as well as the key elements that it encompasses.

Leadership: Three Interdependent Activities

In today's chaotic world, few would argue against the need for leadership—but how does one go about encouraging it? Let's focus on business organizations. Is it enough to merely keep the organization afloat, or is it essential to make steady progress toward some well-defined objective? We believe custodial management is not leadership. Rather, leadership is proactive, goal-oriented, and focused on the creation and implementation of a creative vision. *Leadership is the process of transforming organizations from what they are to what the leader would have them become.* This definition implies a lot: *dissatisfaction* with the status quo, a *vision* of what should be, and a *process* for bringing about change. An insurance company executive recently shared the following insight on leadership: "I lead by the Noah Principle: It's all right to know when it's going to rain, but, by God, you had better build the ark."

Doing the right thing is becoming increasingly important in today's competitive environment. After all, many industries are declining; the global village is becoming increasingly complex, interconnected, and unpredictable; and product and market life cycles are becoming increasingly compressed. Recently, when asked to describe the life cycle of his company's products, the CEO of a supplier of computer components replied: "Seven months from cradle to grave—and that includes three months to design the product and get it into production!" Richard D'Aveni, author of *Hypercompetition,* went even further. He argued that in a world where all dimensions of competition appear to be compressed in time and heightened in complexity, *sustainable* competitive advantages are no longer possible.

Despite the importance of doing the "right thing," leaders must also be concerned about doing "things right." Charan and Colvin argued strongly that implementation (or execution) is also essential to success.

> Any way that you look at it, mastering execution turns out to be the odds-on best way for a CEO to keep his job. So what's the right way to think about that sexier obsession, strategy? It's vitally important—obviously. The problem is that our age's fascination feeds the mistaken belief that developing exactly the right strategy will enable a company to rocket past competitors. In reality, that's less than half the battle.[2]

Thus, leaders are change agents whose success is measured by how effectively they implement a strategic vision and mission.

Accordingly, many authors contend that successful leaders must recognize three interdependent activities that must be continually reassessed for organizations to succeed. As shown in Exhibit 11.1, these are: (1) determining a direction, (2) designing the organization, and (3) nurturing a culture dedicated to excellence and ethical behavior.[3]

The interdependent nature of these three activities is self-evident. Consider an organization with a great mission and a superb organizational structure and design, but a culture that implicitly encourages shirking and unethical behavior. Or a strong culture and organizational design but little direction and vision—in caricature, a highly ethical and efficient

Exhibit 11.1 Three Interdependent Activities of Leadership

buggy whip manufacturer. Or one with a sound direction and strong culture, but counter-productive teams and a "zero-sum" reward system, which leads to the dysfunctional situation in which one party's gain is viewed as another party's loss, and collaboration and sharing are severely hampered. Obviously, the examples could go on and on. We contend that much of the failure of today's organizations can be attributed to a lack of equal consideration of these three activities. The imagery of a three-legged stool is instructive: It will collapse if one leg is missing or broken. Let's briefly look at each of these activities. We'll also address the important role of a leader's power in overcoming resistance to change.

Setting a Direction

Leaders need a holistic understanding of an organization's stakeholders. This requires an ability to scan the environment to develop a knowledge of all of the company's stakeholders (e.g., customers, suppliers, shareholders) and other salient environmental trends and events and integrate this knowledge into a vision of what the organization could become. It necessitates the capacity to solve increasingly complex problems, become proactive in approach, and develop viable strategic options. Developing a strategic vision provides many benefits: a clear future direction, a framework for the organization's mission and goals, and enhanced employee communication, participation, and commitment.

At times the creative process involves what the CEO of Yokogawa, GE's Japanese partner in the Medical Systems business, called "bullet train" thinking.[4] That is, if you want to increase the speed by 10 miles per hour, you look for incremental advances. However, if you want to double the speed, you've got to think "out of the box" (e.g., widen the track, change the overall suspension system). In today's challenging times, leaders typically need more than just keeping the same train with a few minor tweaks. Instead, they must come up with more revolutionary visions.

Consider how Robert Tillman, CEO of Lowe's, dramatically revitalized his firm by setting a clear and compelling direction. He made it into a formidable competitor to Home Depot, Inc., the Goliath of the home-improvement and hardware retailing industry.[5] In his six years as CEO, Tillman has transformed the $26.5 billion chain, based in Wilkesboro, North Carolina. Its shares have climbed more than 80 percent over a recent two-year period, while Home Depot's have fallen 40 percent.

Tillman has redirected Lowe's strategy by responding effectively to research showing that women initiate 80 percent of home projects. While Home Depot has focused on the professionals and male customers, Tillman has redesigned Lowe's stores to give them a brighter appearance, stocked them with more appliances, and focused on higher-margin goods (including everything from Laura Ashley paints to high-end bathroom fixtures). And, like Wal-Mart, Lowe's has one of the best inventory systems in retailing. As a result, Lowe's profits are expected to continue to rise faster than Home Depot's.

Let's now turn to another key leadership activity: the design of the organization's structure, processes, and evaluation and control systems.

Designing the Organization

At times, almost all leaders have difficulty implementing their vision and strategies. Such problems—many of which we discussed in Chapter 10—may stem from a variety of sources, including:

- Lack of understanding of responsibility and accountability among managers.
- Reward systems that do not motivate individuals (or collectives such as groups and divisions) toward desired organizational goals.
- Inadequate or inappropriate budgeting and control systems.
- Insufficient mechanisms to coordinate and integrate activities across the organization.

Marshall Industries: Problems with Incentives

Marshall Industries is a large Los Angeles distributor of 170,000 different electronic components. The company has 30,000 customers and receives supplies from more than 150 suppliers. CEO Rod Rodin became concerned about some irregularities in the company. He saw that an average of 20 percent of monthly sales were being shipped in the last three days of the month. He discovered that divisions within the company were hiding customer returns and opening bad credit accounts to beef up monthly numbers. Employees in divisions with scarce supplies were hiding the supplies from other divisions. Sales representatives, working on commission, were constantly fighting with one another over how commissions should be split on joint sales efforts.

Rodin came to the conclusion that his employees were doing exactly what they were being paid to do. The commission structure encouraged employees to hide returns, put in nonexistent orders the last few days of a month to make their monthly sales goals, and hide resources from one another. The key objective, of course, was sales, but the compensation structure failed to motivate employees in that direction. "Creative accounting" could easily make sure representatives made their sales goals each month whether or not the sales actually occurred. Until Rodin noticed the irregularities, there were few control mechanisms in place to integrate sales activities between divisions.

Rodin's solution? Scrap the commission system. From now on, all salespeople would receive a salary plus a bonus based on company profitability. *Electronic Buyers News* published an editorial criticizing the decision. Most people thought it was a crazy idea. But sometimes crazy ideas work pretty well. Four years after the change, sales had grown from $582 million to $1.2 billion and the stock price of Marshall Industries had nearly quadrupled. Aligning the goals of employees with the objectives of the company seemed to be just the thing needed to bring control, integration, and coordination out of chaos.

Sources: G. G. Dess and J. C. Picken, *Beyond Productivity* (New York: AMACOM, 1999); A. Muoio, "The Truth Is, the Truth Hurts," *Fast Company*, April–May 1998, pp. 93–102; T. Wilson, "Marshall Industries: Wholesale Shift to the Web," *InternetWeek*, July 20, 1998, pp. 14–15.

Successful leaders are actively involved in building structures, teams, systems, and organizational processes that facilitate the implementation of their vision and strategies. For example, we have discussed the necessity for consistency between business-level and corporate-level strategies and organizational control in Chapter 9. Clearly, a firm would generally be unable to attain an overall low-cost advantage without closely monitoring its costs through detailed and formalized cost and financial control procedures. In a similar vein, achieving a differentiation advantage would necessitate encouraging innovation, creativity, and sensitivity to market conditions. Such efforts would be typically impeded by the use of a huge set of cumbersome rules and regulations, as well as highly centralized decision making. With regard to corporate-level strategy, we addressed in Chapter 9 how a related diversification strategy would necessitate reward systems that emphasize behavioral measures to promote sharing across divisions within a firm, whereas an unrelated strategy should rely more on financial (or objective) indicators of performance, such as revenue gains and profitability, since there is less need for collaboration across business units because they would have little in common.

Strategy Spotlight 11.1 focuses on how the reward and evaluation system at Marshall Industries had unintended consequences, making budgeting and control very difficult. However, Ron Rodin, Marshall's CEO, recognized the problem and took decisive and bold action. This example shows how leaders must, at times, make decisions that appear to be counter to "conventional wisdom."

Nurturing a Culture Dedicated to Excellence and Ethical Behavior

In Chapter 9 we discussed how organizational culture can be an effective and positive means of organizational control. Leaders play a key role in developing and sustaining—as well as changing, when necessary—an organization's culture. For example, Ray Gilmartin has transformed Merck's "turf-conscious culture" since becoming CEO on June 9, 1994.[6]

> As an outsider to both Merck and the pharmaceutical industry, Gilmartin initially met with Merck's top 40 or so executives and humbly admitted he had a lot to learn. He posed questions such as, "What do you think are the major issues we need to resolve?" and "If you had my job, what would you focus on?" During the interviews, he demonstrated a key element of his leadership style: He likes to air problems and debate without regard for hierarchy. He said, "Where you want the contest is not among people but among ideas. It's very important for people to be able to challenge, to be very open."
>
> Gilmartin makes symbolic gestures to strengthen Merck's culture. For example, he disdains many of the trappings of his office. It is not only for symbolic reasons that he has unlocked the doors to the executive suite at the company's Whitehouse Station, New Jersey, headquarters. He has regular breakfast meetings with staffers.
>
> He has also won the loyalty of his top executives by granting high levels of autonomy. For example, the highly respected CFO, Judy Lewent, is pleased that Gilmartin has asked her to oversee Merck's joint ventures with DuPont, Johnson & Johnson, and Astra. And research chief Dr. Edward M. Scolnick—earlier a rival for the CEO post—says he doesn't regret being passed over. "The company is far better off having him as CEO and me as head of research." Part of the reason for Scolnick's magnanimity is that nonscientist Gilmartin, unlike former CEO Roy Vagelos, is "completely dependent" on Scolnick's judgment on lab matters. Scolnick claims, "He's delegated to me . . . and my responsibility is to make sure that I come through for him."
>
> The financial results have also been impressive. Sales and profits are way up. After Gilmartin became CEO in 1994, Merck's stock zoomed from 30¾ to nearly 130 within four years of his becoming CEO—an impressive gain even for the soaring drug stocks.

Clearly, Gilmartin not only was able to help Merck post impressive financial results, but also strengthened the firm's valuable human capital.

Managers and top executives must also accept personal responsibility for developing and strengthening ethical behavior throughout the organization. They must consistently demonstrate that such behavior is central to the vision and mission of the organization. Several elements must be present and reinforced for a firm to become a highly ethical organization: role models, corporate credos and codes of conduct, reward and evaluation systems, and policies and procedures. Given the importance of these issues, we address them in detail in the last major section of this chapter.

Strategy Spotlight 11.2 discusses how Kerry Killinger, Washington Mutual's CEO, effectively performs all three leadership activities that we have addressed in this section.

Overcoming Barriers to Change and the Effective Use of Power

Now that we have discussed the three interdependent activities that leaders perform, we must address a key question: What are the barriers to change that leaders often encounter and how can they use power to bring about meaningful change in their organizations? After all, people generally have some level of choice about how strongly they support a leader's change initiatives (or resist them, for that matter). Why is there often so much resistance? There are many reasons as to why organizations and managers at all levels are prone to inertia and slow to learn, adapt, and change.

1. Many people have *vested interests in the status quo.* There is a broad stream of organizational literature on the subject of "escalation," wherein certain individuals

strategy spotlight

Strategic Leadership at Washington Mutual, Inc.

11.2

Effective leadership includes making the right moves when times are hard. One of the smartest things that Kerry Killinger, the chairman, president, and CEO of Washington Mutual, Inc. (WAMU), did was to stay focused on the long-term strategic plan of becoming America's leading consumer bank. This meant growing the company when many others became conservative. Under Killinger's leadership, three major steps were taken toward this goal in recent years. First, an entry has been made into the New York–New Jersey market through an acquisition. This market is critical for any company aspiring to be America's leading consumer bank. The emphasis is on establishing the brand in that market and also getting the new employees to learn Washington Mutual's business culture. Second, the company has completed a major exercise in integrating all the companies that were bought in recent years. WAMU is America's leading home lender today. Third, Killinger personally visited more than 20,000 employees to communicate the strategies in place, the core values of the company, and what the brand stands for. This was a necessary step, especially in the aftermath of September 11, 2001, to reinforce the unity of direction, thought, and action in the company. With such effective strategic leadership, WAMU is no doubt poised to make giant strides in the future.

Source: A. Overholt, "Fast Talk: One Shrewd Move," *Fast Company,* December 2002, p. 72.

(in both controlled laboratory settings and actual management practice) continue to throw "good money at bad decisions" despite negative performance feedback.[7]

2. There are *systemic barriers.* Here, the design of the organization's structure, information processing, reporting relationships, and so forth impede the proper flow and evaluation of information. A bureaucratic structure with multiple layers, onerous requirements for documentation, and rigid rules and procedures will often "inoculate" the organization against change.

3. *Behavioral barriers* are associated with the tendency of managers to look at issues from a biased or limited perspective. This can be attributed to their education, training, work experiences, and so forth. For example, consider an incident shared by David Lieberman, marketing director at GVO, an innovation consulting firm based in Palo Alto, California.

> A company's creative type had come up with a great idea for a new product. Nearly everybody loved it. However, it was shot down by a high-ranking manufacturing representative who exploded: "A new color? Do you have any idea of the spare-parts problem that it will create?" This was not a dimwit exasperated at having to build a few storage racks at the warehouse. He'd been hearing for years about cost cutting, lean inventories, and "focus." Lieberman's comment: "Good concepts, but not always good for innovation."

4. *Political barriers* refer to conflicts arising from power relationships. This can be the outcome of a myriad of symptoms such as vested interests (e.g., the aforementioned escalation problems), refusal to share information, conflicts over resources, conflicts between departments and divisions, and petty interpersonal differences.

5. *Personal time constraints* bring to mind the old saying about "not having enough time to drain the swamp when you are up to your neck in alligators." In effect, Gresham's law of planning states that operational decisions will drive out the time necessary for strategic thinking and reflection. This tendency is accentuated in organizations experiencing severe price competition or retrenchment wherein managers and employees are spread rather thin.

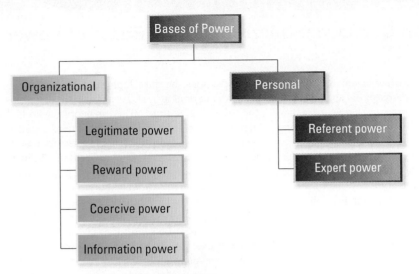

Exhibit 11.2 A Leader's Bases of Power

Successful leadership requires effective use of power in overcoming barriers to change.[8] Power refers to a leader's ability to get things done in a way he or she wants them to be done. It is the ability to influence other people's behavior, to persuade them to do things that they otherwise would not have done, and to overcome resistance and opposition to changing direction. Effective exercise of power is essential for successful leadership.

A leader derives his or her power from several sources or bases. Numerous classifications of such sources or bases abound in the literature on power. However, the simplest way to understand the bases of power is by classifying them as organizational and personal bases of power, as shown in Exhibit 11.2.

Organizational bases of power refer to the power that a person wields because of holding a formal management position. These include legitimate power, reward power, coercive power, and information power. *Legitimate power* is derived from organizationally conferred decision-making authority and is exercised by virtue of a manager's position in the organization. *Reward power* depends on the ability of the leader or manager to confer rewards for positive behaviors or outcomes. *Coercive power* is the power exercised by use of fear of punishment for errors of omission or commission on the part of the employees. *Information power* arises from a manager's access, control, and distribution of information that is not freely available to everyone in an organization.

Apart from the organizationally derived power, a leader might be able to influence subordinates because of the leader's personality characteristics and behavior. These would be considered the "personal" bases of power. The personal bases of power are referent power and expert power. The source of *referent power* is a subordinate's identification with the leader. A leader's personal attributes or charisma might influence subordinates and make them devoted to that leader. On the other hand, the source of *expert power* is the leader's expertise and knowledge in a particular field. The leader is the expert on whom subordinates depend for information that they need to do their job successfully.

Successful leaders use the different bases of power, often a combination of them, as appropriate to meet the demands of a situation, such as the nature of the task, the personality characteristics of the subordinates, the urgency of the issue, and other factors. They also recognize that virtually everybody has a need for power, and leaders endeavor to

William C. Weldon: Utilizing Multiple Bases of Power

William C. Weldon, the CEO of Johnson & Johnson (J&J), is well known in the company for his charisma and powers of persuasion. He can convince, cajole, or sometimes even just sweet-talk his colleagues into seeing things his way. A few years ago, the chief of pharmaceutical research and development of J&J, Dr. Per A. Peterson, was so disappointed with the personnel problems that he was contemplating leaving the company and told Weldon about it. The next morning, Weldon made a call to Dr. Peterson as early as 5:30 a.m. and invited him for breakfast. The two men were talking well into the afternoon about Peterson's concerns. Eventually, Peterson agreed to remain in the company. And within a week Weldon made the changes that Peterson was asking for. Weldon used his charisma to get Peterson to agree with him.

Weldon has worked his way up from being a drug salesman to the top executive position in the company. He was head of Ethicon Endo Surgery, Inc., a J&J company that was supposed to establish itself in the emerging field of endoscopic surgery in the early 1990s. While there, he often set higher goals for his region than were set by the headquarters. He was always hungry for more. This, however, did not mean that Weldon did not understand the power of rewards or positive reinforcement. On at least

two occasions, he gave higher bonuses to his managers than was normal at J&J. At another time, he closed shop for a day to give time off to his people, who had worked hard for a particularly difficult couple of months. Neither he nor his people ever told this to executives at the corporate headquarters. According to Weldon, "Sometimes it is better to beg forgiveness than to ask permission."

For executives who fell short of expectations, Weldon made it clear that he did not like to be disappointed. When Centocor, Inc., a new J&J drug business, did not meet the aggressive sales goals it set for the year 2000, Weldon was at the offices before the week was out. David Holveck, a former company group chairman of Centocor who now runs J&J's venture-capital arm, says, "He is a man of few words. But his body language was very clear: In the game there are two strikes. In 2001, we were expected to get it right." And they did it. Weldon effectively leveraged his coercive power in driving his teams toward excellence. However, not everybody appreciated Weldon's demands. Several former executives at Ethicon Endo say that Weldon alienated those he felt were not a part of the team. "He is an intimidator and a dominator," says one former executive who feels that Weldon turned against him after he opposed an acquisition. Such pitfalls are likely in the use of coercive power, even for successful managers. Therefore, it must be exercised with caution.

Source: A. Barret. "Staying on Top," *BusinessWeek*, May 5, 2003, pp. 60–68.

satisfy that need in the process of exercising their power effectively. An example of how Johnson & Johnson's new CEO, William C. Weldon, exercised these different bases of power is addressed in Strategy Spotlight 11.3.

Emotional Intelligence: A Key Leadership Trait

In the previous section, we discussed three of the salient activities of strategic leadership. In a sense, the focus was on "what leaders *do*." In this section, the issue becomes "who leaders *are*," that is, what are the most important traits (or capabilities) of leaders. Clearly, these two issues are related, because successful leaders possess the valuable traits that, at the end of the day, enable them to engage in the activities that they must perform effectively in order to create value for their organization.

There has been, as one would expect, a huge literature on the successful traits of leaders—including business leaders at the highest level.[9] These include integrity, maturity, energy, judgment, motivation, intelligence, expertise, and so on. However, for simplicity, these traits may be grouped into three broad sets of capabilities:

- Purely technical skills (like accounting or operations research).
- Cognitive abilities (like analytical reasoning or quantitative analysis).
- Emotional intelligence (such as the ability to work with others and a passion for work).

One attribute of successful leaders that has become popular in both the literature and management practice in recent years is "emotional intelligence."[10] Some evidence of this popularity is that *Harvard Business Review* articles published in 1998 and 2000 by psychologist/journalist Daniel Goleman, who is most closely associated with the concept, have become this widely read management journal's most highly requested reprint articles. And two of Goleman's recent books, *Emotional Intelligence* and *Working with Emotional Intelligence,* were both on the *New York Times*'s best-seller lists. Goleman defines emotional intelligence (EI) as the capacity for recognizing one's own emotions and those of others.[11]

Recent studies of successful managers have found that effective leaders consistently have a high level of emotional intelligence.[12] Findings indicate, for example, that EI is a better predictor of life success (economic well-being, satisfaction with life, friendship, family life), including occupational attainments, than IQ. Such evidence has been extrapolated to the catchy phrase: "IQ gets you hired, but EQ gets you promoted." And surveys show that human resource managers believe this statement to be true, and perhaps even for highly technical jobs such as those of scientists and engineers.

This is not to say that IQ and technical skills are irrelevant. Obviously, they do matter, but they should be viewed as "threshold capabilities." That is, they are the necessary requirements for attaining higher level managerial positions. EI, on the other hand, is essential for leadership success. Without it, Goleman has argued, a manager can have excellent training, an incisive analytical mind, and many smart ideas, but will still not be a great leader.

There are five components of EI: self-awareness, self-regulation, motivation, empathy, and social skill. They are included in Exhibit 11.3. Next, we will briefly discuss each of them.

Self-Awareness Self-awareness is the first component of EI and brings to mind that Delphic oracle who gave the advice "know thyself" thousands of years ago. Self-awareness involves having a deep understanding of one's emotions, strengths, weaknesses, and drives. People with strong self-awareness are neither overly critical nor unrealistically optimistic. Instead, they are honest—with themselves and others.

People generally admire and respect candor. Further, leaders are constantly required to make judgment calls that require a candid assessment of capabilities—their own and those of others. People who assess themselves honestly (i.e., self-aware people), are well suited to do the same for the organizations they run.

Self-Regulation Biological impulses drive our emotions. Although we cannot do away with them, we can strive to manage them. Self-regulation, which is akin to an ongoing inner conversation, frees us from being prisoners of our feelings. People engaged in such conversation feel bad moods and emotional impulses just as everyone else does. However, they find ways to control them and even channel them in useful ways.

People who are in control of their feelings and impulses are able to create an environment of trust and fairness. In such an environment, political behavior and infighting are sharply reduced and productivity tends to be high. Further, people who have mastered their emotions are better able to bring about and implement change in an organization. When a new initiative is announced, they are less likely to panic; rather, they are able to suspend judgment, seek out information, and listen to executives explain the new program.

Motivation Successful executives are driven to achieve beyond expectations—their own and everyone else's. They are driven to achieve. Although many people are driven by external factors, such as money and prestige, those with leadership potential are driven by a deeply embedded desire to achieve for the sake of achievement.

EXHIBIT 11.3
The Five Components of Emotional Intelligence at Work

	Definition	Hallmarks
Self-management skills:		
Self-awareness	• The ability to recognize and understand your moods, emotions, and drives, as well as their effect on others.	• Self-confidence • Realistic self-assessment • Self-deprecating sense of humor
Self-regulation	• The ability to control or redirect disruptive impulses and moods. • The propensity to suspend judgment—to think before acting.	• Trustworthiness and integrity • Comfort with ambiguity • Openness to change
Motivation	• A passion to work for reasons that go beyond money or status. • A propensity to pursue goals with energy and persistence.	• Strong drive to achieve • Optimism, even in the face of failure • Organizational commitment
Managing relationships:		
Empathy	• The ability to understand the emotional makeup of other people. • Skill in treating people according to their emotional reactions.	• Expertise in building and retaining talent • Cross-cultural sensitivity • Service to clients and customers
Social skill	• Proficiency in managing relationships and building networks. • An ability to find common ground and build rapport.	• Effectiveness in leading change • Persuasiveness • Expertise in building and leading teams

Source: Adapted and reprinted by permission of *Harvard Business Review*, exhibit from "What Makes a Leader," by D. Goleman, January 2004. Copyright © 2004 by the Harvard Business School Publishing Corporation; all rights reserved.

How can one tell if one is motivated by a drive for achievement instead of external rewards? Look for a sign of passion for the work itself, such as seeking out creative challenges, a love of learning, and taking pride in a job well done. Also, motivated people have a high level of energy to do things better as well as a restlessness with the status quo. They are eager to explore new approaches to their work.

Empathy   Empathy is probably the component of EI that is most easily recognized. In a business setting, empathy means thoughtfully considering an employee's feelings—along with other factors—in the process of making intelligent decisions. Empathy is particularly important in today's business environment for at least three reasons: the increasing use of teams, the rapid pace of globalization, and the growing need to retain talent.

When leading a team, one is often charged with arriving at a consensus—often in the face of a high level of emotions. Empathy enables one to sense and understand the viewpoints of everyone around the table.

Globalization typically involves cross-cultural dialogue that can easily lead to miscues. Empathetic people are attuned to the subtleties of body language; they can hear the message beneath the words being spoken. In a more general sense, they have a deep understanding of the existence and importance of cultural and ethnic differences.

strategy spotlight

Emotional Intelligence: Pat Croce

Every businessperson knows the story of a highly qualified, well-trained executive who was promoted to a leadership position, only to fail at the job. This is not because the executive didn't have a high IQ or sound technical fundamentals. It is about the presence or lack of *emotional intelligence*. When Pat Croce took over as the new president of the Philadelphia 76ers in May 1996, people were skeptical of his cornball style and unabashed attitude. At his national debut as the president of the 76ers, he erupted with glee as the team wound up with the number one pick at the nationally televised broadcast of the NBA's draft lottery. He leaped to his feet, pumped his fists and slapped the palms of the other team representatives. But that was not all. He then hugged David Stern, the gray-haired, tight-laced NBA commissioner, kissing him on the cheek and patting him on the sleeve of his suit jacket.

People who meet Croce on the street or at work salute him with either a high-five or a hey-dude. Those who know him say his high-energy and full red-bloodedness are infectious and his vivacious style is how he exhibits the virtues of a can-do attitude and never-say-die perseverance. A self-made man, Croce founded a fitness center called the Sports Physical Therapists (SPT), successfully turned it into an 11-state chain, and eventually sold it off for $40 million in 1993.

His record as the basketball baron is no less impressive. His team was the Cinderella story of the NBA. Before he took over, the team's dismal business management and apathetic player attitudes had led to a very unimpressive record. Croce is widely credited with reinvigorating the business with his hurricane-force personality and leading the born-again team to its first chance to compete in the NBA finals in more than a decade. And for all this, Croce has but his emotional intelligence to thank. His self-awareness, motivation, empathy, and social skills make him detail-oriented and competitive—the stereotypical qualities of a successful entrepreneur.

Sources: J. Rosenbloom, "Why It's Pat Croce's World," *Inc.*, April 2002, pp. 77–83; www.patcroce.com/NonMember/pages/index.html; and L. Brokaw, "Pat Croce's Bottom Line," *Fast Company*, January 1, 2002, pp. 45–47.

Empathy also plays a key role in retaining talent. As we discussed in Chapter 4, human capital is particularly important to a firm in the knowledge economy when it comes to creating advantages that are sustainable. Leaders need empathy to develop and keep top talent. Today, that's even more important, because when high performers leave, they take their tacit knowledge with them.

Social Skill   While the first three components of emotional intelligence are all self-management skills, the last two—empathy and social skill—concern a person's ability to manage relationships with others. Social skill may be viewed as friendliness with a purpose: moving people in the direction you desire, whether that's agreement on a new marketing strategy or enthusiasm about a new product.

Socially skilled people tend to have a wide circle of acquaintances as well as a knack for finding common ground and building rapport. They recognize that nothing gets done alone. Rather, one needs to have a network in place when the time for action comes.

Social skill can be viewed as the culmination of the other dimensions of EI. People will be effective at managing relationships when they can understand and control their own emotions and can empathize with the feelings of others. Motivation also contributes to social skill. People who are driven to achieve tend to be optimistic, even when confronted with setbacks or failure. And when people are upbeat, their "glow" is cast upon conversations and other social encounters. They are popular, and for good reason.

Strategy Spotlight 11.4 discusses Pat Croce's approach to leadership. He is president of the National Basketball Association's Philadelphia 76ers. It illustrates some of the components of emotional intelligence.

We'll close with some summary comments from Dan Goleman:

It would be foolish to assert that good old-fashioned IQ and technical ability are not important ingredients to strong leadership. But the recipe would not be complete without emotional intelligence. It was once thought that the components of emotional intelligence were "nice to have" in business leaders. But now we know that, for the sake of performance, these are ingredients that leaders "need to have."

It is fortunate, then, that emotional intelligence can be learned. The process is not easy. It takes time and, most of all, commitment. But the benefits that come from having a well-developed emotional intelligence, both for the individual and for the organization, make it worth the effort.[13]

In the next section, we will discuss some guidelines for developing a "learning organization." In today's competitive environment, the old saying about "a chain is only as strong as the weakest link" applies more than ever before. People throughout organizations must become involved in leadership processes and play greater roles in the formulation and implementation of an organization's strategies and tactics. Put another way, to learn and adapt proactively, firms need "eyes, ears, and brains" throughout all parts of the organization. One person—or a small group of individuals—can no longer think and learn for the entire entity.

Developing a Learning Organization

An amusing story was shared by Charles Handy, author of *The Age of Unreason* and *The Age of Paradox* and one of today's most respected business visionaries.

The other day, a courier could not find my family's remote cottage. He called his base on his radio, and the base called us to ask directions. He was just around the corner, but his base managed to omit a vital part of the directions. So he called them again, and they called us again. Then the courier repeated the cycle a third time to ask whether we had a dangerous dog. When he eventually arrived, we asked whether it would not have been simpler and less aggravating to everyone if he had called us directly from the roadside telephone booth where he had been parked. "I can't do that," he said, "because they won't refund any money I spend." "But it's only pennies!" I exclaimed. "I know," he said, "but that only shows how little they trust us!"[14]

At first glance, it would appear that the story simply epitomizes the lack of empowerment, and trust, granted to the hapless courier: Don't ask questions, Do as you're told![15] However, implicit in this scenario is also the message that learning, information sharing, adaptation, decision making, and so on are *not* shared throughout the organization. In contrast to this admittedly rather extreme case, leading-edge organizations recognize the importance of having everyone involved in the process of actively learning and adapting. As noted by today's leading expert on learning organizations, MIT's Peter Senge, the days when Henry Ford, Alfred Sloan, and Tom Watson *"learned for the organization"* are gone.

In an increasingly dynamic, interdependent, and unpredictable world, it is simply no longer possible for anyone to "figure it all out at the top." The old model, "the top thinks and the local acts," must now give way to integrating thinking and acting at all levels. While the challenge is great, so is the potential payoff. "The person who figures out how to harness the collective genius of the people in his or her organization," according to former Citibank CEO Walter Wriston, "is going to blow the competition away."[16]

Learning and change typically involve the ongoing questioning of an organization's status quo or method of procedure. This inevitably involves the necessity of individuals throughout the organization—not just those at the top—to reflect. Although this seems simple enough, it is easy to ignore. After all, organizations, especially successful ones, are so caught up in carrying out their day-to-day work that they rarely, if ever, stop to think objectively about themselves and their businesses. They often fail to ask the probing questions that might lead them to call into question their basic assumptions, to refresh their strategies, or to reengineer their work processes. According to Michael Hammer and Steven Stanton, the pioneer consultants who touched off the reengineering movement:

> Reflection entails awareness of self, of competitors, of customers. It means thinking without preconception. It means questioning cherished assumptions and replacing them with new approaches. It is the only way in which a winning company can maintain its leadership position, by which a company with great assets can ensure that they continue to be well deployed.[17]

Successful learning organizations create a proactive, creative approach to the unknown, actively solicit the involvement of employees at all levels, and enable all employees to use their intelligence and apply their imagination. Higher-level skills are required of everyone, not just those at the top. A learning environment involves organizationwide commitment to change, an action orientation, and applicable tools and methods. It must be viewed by everyone as a guiding philosophy and not simply as another change program that is often derisively labeled the new "flavor of the month."

A critical requirement of all learning organizations is that everyone feels and supports a compelling purpose. In the words of William O'Brien, CEO of Hanover Insurance, "Before there can be meaningful participation, people must share certain values and pictures about where we are trying to go. We discovered that people have a real need to feel that they're part of an enabling mission."[18]

Inspiring and motivating people with a mission or purpose is a necessary but not a sufficient condition for developing an organization that can learn and adapt to a rapidly changing, complex, and interconnected environment. In the next four sections, we'll address four other critical ongoing processes of learning organizations.

- ◆ Empowering employees at all levels.
- ◆ Accumulating and sharing internal knowledge.
- ◆ Gathering and integrating external information.
- ◆ Challenging the status quo and enabling creativity.

Empowering Employees at All Levels

"The great leader is a great servant," asserted Ken Melrose, CEO of Toro Company and author of *Making the Grass Greener on Your Side*.[19] A manager's role becomes one of creating an environment where employees can achieve their potential as they help move the organization toward its goals. Instead of viewing themselves as resource controllers and power brokers, leaders must truly envision themselves as flexible resources willing to assume numerous (and perhaps unaccustomed) roles—coaches, information providers, teachers, decision makers, facilitators, supporters, or listeners—depending on the needs of their employees.

The central key to empowerment is effective leadership. Empowerment can't occur in a leadership vacuum. According to Melrose, "I came to understand that you best lead by serving the needs of your people. You don't do their jobs for them; you enable them to learn and progress on the job." In their article in *Organizational Dynamics*, Robert Quinn and Gretchen Spreitzer made an interesting point regarding what may be viewed as two diametrically opposite perspectives on empowerment.[20] In the top-down perspective, empowerment is about delegation and accountability—senior management has developed a clear vision and has communicated specific plans to the rest of the organization. This strategy for empowerment encompasses the following:

- Start at the top.
- Clarify the organization's mission, vision, and values.
- Clearly specify the tasks, roles, and rewards for employees.
- Delegate responsibility.
- Hold people accountable for results.

By contrast, the bottom-up view looks at empowerment as concerned with risk taking, growth, and change. It involves trusting people to "do the right thing" and having a tolerance for failure. They would act with a sense of ownership and typically "ask for forgiveness rather than permission." Here the salient elements of empowerment are:

- Start at the bottom by understanding the needs of employees.
- Teach employees skills of self-management and model desired behavior.
- Build teams to encourage cooperative behavior.
- Encourage intelligent risk taking.
- Trust people to perform.

Clearly, these two perspectives draw a sharp contrast in assumptions that people make about trust and control. Interestingly, Quinn and Spreitzer recently shared these contrasting views of empowerment with a senior management team. After an initial heavy silence, someone from the first group voiced a concern about the second group's perspective, "We can't afford loose cannons around here." A person in the second group retorted, "When was the last time you saw a cannon of any kind around here?"

Many leading-edge organizations are moving in the direction of the second perspective—recognizing the need for trust, cultural control, and expertise (at all levels) instead of the extensive and cumbersome rules and regulations inherent in hierarchical control.[21] Some have argued that too often organizations fall prey to the "heroes-and-drones syndrome," wherein the value of those in powerful positions is exalted and the value of those who fail to achieve top rank is diminished. Such an attitude is implicit in phrases such as "Lead, follow, or get out of the way" or, even less appealing, "Unless you're the lead horse, the view never changes." Of course, few will ever reach the top hierarchical positions in organizations, but in the information economy, the strongest organizations are those that use effectively the talents of all the players on the team. Strategy Spotlight 11.5 illustrates how one company, Chaparral Steel, empowers its employees.

Accumulating and Sharing Internal Knowledge

Effective organizations must also *redistribute information, knowledge* (i.e., skills to act on the information), and *rewards.*[22] For example, a company might give frontline employees the power to act as "customer advocates," doing whatever is necessary to please the customers. Employees, however, also need to have the appropriate training to act as businesspeople. The company needs to disseminate information by sharing customer expectations and feedback as well as financial information. The employees need to know about the goals and objectives of the business as well as how key value-creating activities in the organization are related to each other. Finally, organizations should allocate rewards on the basis of how effectively employees use information, knowledge, and power to improve customer service quality and the company's financial performance.

Jack Stack is the president and CEO of Springfield ReManufacturing Corporation (SRC) in Springfield, Missouri, and author of *The Great Game of Business.* He is generally considered the pioneer of "open book" management—an innovative way to gather and disseminate internal information. Implementing this system involved three core activities.[23] First, numbers were generated daily for each of the company's employees, reflect-

Employee Empowerment at Chaparral Steel

Managers at Chaparral Steel, a steel minimill in Midlothian, Texas, are convinced that employee ownership empowers workers to act in the best interests of the company. They believe that ownership is not composed solely of the firm's equity, but also of its knowledge. By sharing financial and knowledge resources with employees, Chaparral Steel is a model of employee empowerment—90 percent of its employees own company stock and everyone is salaried, wears the same white hard hats, drinks the same free coffee, and has access to the knowledge that goes into the innovative processes at the firm's manufacturing plants.

Rather than using managers as buffers between customers and line workers, Chaparral directly involves employees with customers. Customer concerns are routed directly to the line workers responsible for manufacturing a customer's specific products. "Everyone here is part of the sales department," president and CEO Gordon Forward said. "They carry their own business cards. If they visit a customer, we want them to come back and look at their own process differently. This helps employees from all levels to view operations from the customer's perspective." Forward believes that "if a melt shop crew understands why a customer needs a particular grade of steel, it will make sure the customer gets that exact grade."

This encourages employees to think beyond traditional functional boundaries and find ways to improve the organization's processes. By integrating the customer's perspective into their efforts, employees at Chaparral Steel become more than just salaried workers; they feel responsible to the firm as if each production process was their own creation and responsibility.

Sources: D. Johnson, "Catching the Third Wave: How to Succeed in Business When It's Changing at the Speed of Light," *Futurist,* March 1998, pp. 32–38; C. Petry, "Chaparral Poised on the Brink of Breakthrough: Chaparral Steel Developing Integrated Automobile Shredder-Separation Facility," *American Metal Market,* September 10, 1997, p. 18; D. Leonard-Barton, "The Factory as a Learning Laboratory," *Sloan Management Review* 34 (1992), pp. 23–38; and "TXI Chaparral Steel Midlothian Registered to ISO 2002," Chaparral Steel press release, July 8, 2001.

ing his or her work performance and production costs. Second, it involved sharing this information, aggregated once a week, with all of the company's people from secretaries to top management. Third, it involved extensive training in how to use and interpret the numbers—how to understand balance sheets as well as cash flows and income statements.

In explaining why SRC embraces open book management, Stack provided an insightful counterperspective to the old adage "Information is power."

> We are building a company in which everyone tells the truth every day—not because everyone is honest but because everyone has access to the same information: operating metrics, financial data, valuation estimates. The more people understand what's really going on in their company, the more eager they are to help solve its problems. Information isn't power. It's a burden. Share information, and you share the burdens of leadership as well.

These perspectives help to point out both the motivational and utilitarian uses of sharing company information. It can apply to organizations of all sizes. Let's look at a very small company—Leonhardt Plating Company, a $1.5 million company that makes steel plating.

> Its CEO, Daniel Leonhardt, became an accidental progressive, so to speak. Recently, instead of trying to replace his polishing foreman, he resorted to a desperate, if cutting-edge, strategy. He decided to let the polishing department rule itself by committee.
>
> The results? Revenues have risen 25 percent in the past year. After employees had access to company information such as material prices, their decisions began paying off for the whole firm. Says Leonhardt: "The workers are showing more interest in the company as a whole." Not surprisingly, he plans to introduce committee rule to other departments.[24]

Additional benefits of management's sharing of company information can be gleaned from a look at Whole Foods Market, Inc., the largest natural foods grocer in the United

States.[25] An important benefit of the sharing of internal information at Whole Foods becomes the active process of *internal benchmarking*. Competition is intense at Whole Foods. Teams compete against their own goals for sales, growth, and productivity; they compete against different teams in their stores; and they compete against similar teams at different stores and regions. Similarly, there is an elaborate system of peer reviews through which teams benchmark each other. The "Store Tour" is the most intense. On a periodic schedule, each Whole Foods store is toured by a group of as many as 40 visitors from another region. The tour is a mix of social interaction, reviews, performance audits, and structured feedback sessions. Lateral learning—discovering what your colleagues are doing right and carrying those practices into your organization—has become a driving force at Whole Foods.

In addition to enhancing the sharing of company information, both up and down as well as across the organization, leaders also have to develop means to tap into some of the more informal sources of internal information. In a recent survey of presidents, CEOs, board members, and top executives in a variety of nonprofit organizations, respondents were asked what differentiated the successful candidates for promotion. The consensus: The executive was seen as a person who listens. According to Peter Meyer, the author of the study, "The value of listening is clear: You cannot succeed in running a company if you do not hear what your people, customers, and suppliers are telling you. Poor listeners do not survive. Listening and understanding well are key to making good decisions."[26]

John Chambers, president and CEO of Cisco Systems, the networking giant, also uses an effective vehicle for getting candid feedback from employees and for discovering potential problems.[27] Every year during their birthday month, employees at Cisco's corporate headquarters in San Jose, California, receive an e-mail invitation to a "birthday breakfast" with Chambers. Each month, several dozen of the employees fire some pretty tough questions, including bruising queries about partnering strategy and stark assessments of perceived management failings. Any question is fair game, and directors and vice presidents are strongly discouraged from attending.

Although not always pleasant, Chambers believes it is an indispensable hour of unmediated interaction. At times, he finds there is inconsistency between what his executives say they are doing and what is actually happening. For example, at one quarterly meeting with 500 managers, Chambers asked how many managers required potential hires to have five interviews. When all raised their hands, he retorted, "I have a problem, because at the past three birthday breakfasts, I asked the new hires how many had interviewed that way, and only half raised their hands. You've got to fix it." His take on the birthday breakfasts: "I'm not there for the cake."

Strategy Spotlight 11.6 discusses how Intel Corporation effectively shares information through a unique mentoring program.

Gathering and Integrating External Information

Recognizing opportunity—as well as threats—in the external environment is vital to a firm's success. Focusing exclusively on the efficiency of internal operations may result in a firm becoming, in effect, the world's most efficient producer of manual typewriters or leisure suits—hardly an enviable position! As organizations *and* environments become more complex and evolve rapidly, it is far more critical for employees and managers to become more aware of environmental trends and events—both general and industry-specific—as well as knowledgeable about their firm's competitors and customers. Next, we will discuss some ideas on how to do it.

First, the Internet has dramatically accelerated the speed with which anyone can track down useful information or locate people who might have useful information. Prior to the Net, locating someone who used to work at a company—always a good source of

strategy spotlight

Information Sharing through Mentoring Relationships at Intel

Intel veteran Ann Otero seems to be an unlikely mentor. She is neither a star engineer nor a fast-track sales executive. She has, however, been with the company for the past 12 years and is currently a senior administrative assistant. Ann is part of Intel's new wedge—an innovative new mentoring movement that matches people not by job title or years of service but by specific skills that are in demand. The program uses an intranet-based questionnaire to match partners with the right mentor, creating relationships that stretch across state lines and national boundaries. The system works by having potential mentors list their top skills at Circuit, Intel's internal employee site. Partners click on topics they want to master, then an algo-rithm computes all of the variables and the database hashes out a list of possible matches. Once a match is made, an automatic e-mail goes to the mentor asking her to set up a time to meet and talk. The mentor and partner learn and follow some simple guidelines:

1. The partner controls the relationship.
2. A mentoring contract is drawn up about what needs to be accomplished by the end of the mentoring.
3. Both the partner and the mentor decide what to talk about.

Unlike many corporations, Intel does not use its mentoring for career advancement. Its style is all about learning and sharing the knowledge pool of someone whom you have probably never met.

Sources: www.intel.com/jobs/news/news.htm; F. Warner, "Inside Intel's Mentoring Movement," *Fast Company,* April 2002, pp. 67–69.

---

information—was quite a challenge. However, today people post their résumés on the Web; they participate in discussion groups and talk openly about where they work. It is pretty straightforward.

An example of the effective use of the Internet is provided by Marc Friedman, manager of market research at Andrew Corporation, a fast-growing manufacturer of wireless communications products with annual revenues of nearly $1 billion.[28] One of Friedman's preferred sites to visit is Corptech's website, which provides information on 45,000 high-tech companies and more than 170,000 executives. One of his firm's product lines consisted of antennae for air-traffic control systems. He got a request to provide a country-by-country breakdown of upgrade plans for various airports. Although he knew nothing about air-traffic control at the time, he found a site on the Internet for the International Civil Aviation Organization. Fortunately, it had a great deal of useful data, including several research companies working in his area of interest.

Second, in addition to the Internet, company employees at all levels can use "garden variety" traditional sources for the acquisition of external information. Much can be gleaned by reading trade and professional journals, books, and popular business magazines such as *BusinessWeek, Forbes, Fortune,* and *Fast Company.* (Some professional journals might have an extremely narrow focus and, while they could prove to be very useful, are not fireside reading for the general public.) Other venues for gathering external information include membership in professional or trade organizations and attendance at meetings and conventions. Networking among colleagues inside and outside of one's industry is also a very useful means. Intel's Andy Grove, for example, gathers information from people like DreamWorks SKG's Steven Spielberg and Tele-Communications Inc.'s John Malone.[29] He believes that such interaction provides insights into how to make personal computers more entertaining and better at communicating. Internally, Grove spends time with the young "propeller-heads" who run Intel Architecture labs, an Oregon-based facility that Grove hopes will become the de facto R&D lab for the entire PC industry.

Third, benchmarking can be a useful means of employing external information. Here managers seek out the best examples of a particular practice as part of an ongoing effort to improve the corresponding practice in their own organization.[30] There are two primary types of benchmarking. *Competitive benchmarking* restricts the search for best practices to competitors, while *functional benchmarking* endeavors to determine best practices regardless of industry. Industry-specific standards (e.g., response times required to repair power outages in the electric utility industry) are typically best handled through competitive benchmarking, whereas more generic processes (e.g., answering 1-800 calls) lend themselves to functional benchmarking because the function is essentially the same in any industry.

Ford Motor Company benefited from benchmarking by studying Mazda's accounts payable operations.[31] Its initial goal of a 20 percent cut in its 500-employee accounts payable staff was ratcheted up to 75 percent—and met. Ford's benchmarkers found that staff spent most of their time trying to match often conflicting data in a mass of paper, including purchase orders, invoices, and receipts. Following Mazda's example, Ford created an "invoiceless system" in which invoices no longer trigger payments to suppliers. The receipt does the job.

Fourth, focus directly on customers for information. For example, William McKnight, head of 3M's Chicago sales office, required that salesmen of abrasives products talk directly to the workers in the shop to find out what they needed, instead of calling only on front-office executives.[32] This was very innovative at the time: 1909! But it illustrates the need to get to the end user of a product or service. (McKnight went on to become 3M's president from 1929 to 1949 and chairman from 1949 to 1969.) More recently, James Taylor, senior vice president for global marketing at Gateway 2000, discussed the value of customer input in reducing response time, a critical success factor in the PC industry.

> We talk to 100,000 people a day—people calling to order a computer, shopping around, looking for tech support. Our website gets 1.1 million hits per day. The time it takes for an idea to enter this organization, get processed, and then go to customers for feedback is down to minutes. We've designed the company around speed and feedback.[33]

Challenging the Status Quo and Enabling Creativity

Earlier in this chapter we discussed some of the barriers that leaders face when trying to bring about change in an organization. These were: vested interests in the status quo, systemic barriers, behavioral barriers, political barriers, and personal time constraints. For a firm to become a "learning organization," it must overcome such barriers in order to foster creativity and enable it to permeate the firm. This becomes quite a challenge, of course, if the firm is entrenched in a status quo mentality.

Perhaps the primary means to directly challenge the status quo is for the leader to forcefully create a sense of urgency. For example, Tom Kasten, vice president of Levi Strauss, has a direct approach to initiating change. He is charged with leading the campaign to transform the company for the 21st century.

> You create a compelling picture of the risks of *not* changing. We let our people hear directly from customers. We videotaped interviews with customers and played excerpts. One big customer said, "We trust many of your competitors implicitly. We sample their deliveries. We open *all* Levi's deliveries." Another said, "Your lead times are the worst. If you weren't Levi's, you'd be gone." It was powerful. I wish we had done more of it.[34]

Such initiative—if sincere and credible—establishes a sharing of mission and need for major transformations. If effective, it can channel energies to bring about both change and creative endeavors.

Establishing a "culture of dissent" can be another effective means of questioning the status quo and serving as a spur toward creativity. Here norms are established whereby dissenters can openly question a superior's perspective without fear of retaliation or retribution. Consider the perspective of Steven Balmer, Microsoft's CEO.

> Bill [Gates] brings to the company the idea that conflict can be a good thing. . . . Bill knows it's important to avoid that gentle civility that keeps you from getting to the heart of an issue quickly. He likes it when anyone, even a junior employee, challenges him, and you know he respects you when he starts shouting back.[35]

Motorola has, in effect, gone a step further and institutionalized its culture of dissent.[36] By filing a "minority report," an employee can go above his or her immediate supervisor's head and officially lodge a different point of view on a business decision. According to former CEO George Fisher, "I'd call it a healthy spirit of discontent and a freedom by and large to express your discontent around here or to disagree with whoever it is in the company, me or anybody else."

Closely related to the culture of dissent is the fostering of a culture that encourages risk taking. "If you're not making mistakes, you're not taking risks, and that means you're not going anywhere," claimed John Holt, coauthor of *Celebrate Your Mistakes*.[37] "The key is to make errors faster than the competition, so you have more chances to learn and win."

Companies that cultivate cultures of experimentation and curiosity make sure that *failure* is not, in essence, an obscene word. People who stretch the envelope and ruffle feathers are protected. More importantly, they encourage mistakes as a key part of their competitive advantage. Wood Dickinson, CEO of the Kansas City–based Dickinson movie theater chain, told his property managers that he wanted to see them committing "intelligent failures in the pursuit of service excellence."[38] This philosophy was shared by Stan Shih, CEO of Acer, a Taiwan-based computer company. If a manager at Acer took an intelligent risk and made a mistake—even a costly one—Shih wrote off the loss as tuition payment for the manager's education. Such a culture must permeate the entire organization. As a high-tech executive told us during an interview: "Every person has a freedom to fail."

Strategy Spotlight 11.7 discusses how BMW enhances its creativity through developing a diversity of perspectives on its new automobile models.

Creating an Ethical Organization

What is ethics?[39] Ethics may be defined as a system of right and wrong. Ethics assists individuals in deciding when an act is moral or immoral, socially desirable or not. There are many sources for an individual's ethics. These include religious beliefs, national and ethnic heritage, family practices, community standards and expectations, educational experiences, friends, and neighbors. Business ethics is the application of ethical standards to commercial enterprise.

Individual Ethics versus Organizational Ethics

Many leaders may think of ethics as a question of personal scruples, a confidential matter between employees and their consciences. Such leaders are quick to describe any wrongdoing as an isolated incident, the work of a rogue employee. They assume the company should not bear any responsibility for an individual's misdeeds—it may not ever even enter their minds. After all, in their view, ethics has nothing to do with leadership.

In fact, ethics has everything to do with leadership. Seldom does the character flaw of a lone actor completely explain corporate misconduct. Instead, unethical business practices typically involve the tacit, if not explicit, cooperation of others and reflect the values,

Diversity of Perspectives: The Core of Creativity at BMW

Designers at BMW not only compete against Mercedes-Benz and Audi, but also with each other. Competition creates the winning car at BMW, not just collaboration. Chris Bangle, the chief of design at BMW, is an ardent believer in diversity. He typically assigns six teams that compete with each other to develop concepts for a single new BMW. Experience has shown him that the front-runner does not always turn out to be a winning design. He therefore prepares for such an outcome by instructing another team to come up with a diametrically opposite concept compared to the front-runner. Such was the competition to design the new 7 series, in which an unconventional model emerged as the final winner.

Source: B. Breen, "BMW: Driven by Design," *Fast Company*, September 2002, p. 135.

BMW encourages designers to work out their visions for the new models of cars. Ideas generated through this process are seldom discarded even if they do not find their way into the model for which they were developed. "The key here is diversity. If our people all thought the same way, we wouldn't have a design culture; we'd just have mass opinion," explains Bangle. "That's why internal competition is a fundamental premise of this organization: It gives us this dynamic exchange of viewpoints. The outcome is far more powerful than what a single person could produce," he adds. To keep the design teams fresh over the three- to four-year process of developing a new car is a difficult and complex challenge. Bangle says that BMW is willing to live with this high-risk strategy in the short term, to reap the larger benefits in the long run.

attitudes, and behavior patterns that define an organization's operating culture. Clearly, ethics is as much an organizational as a personal issue. Leaders who fail to provide proper leadership to institute proper systems and controls that facilitate ethical conduct share responsibility with those who conceive, execute, and knowingly benefit from corporate misdeeds.

The ethical orientation of a leader is generally considered to be a key factor in promoting ethical behavior among employees. Ethical leaders must take personal, ethical responsibility for their actions and decision making. Leaders who exhibit high ethical standards become role models for others in the organization and raise its overall level of ethical behavior. In essence, ethical behavior must start with the leader before the employees can be expected to perform accordingly.

Over the last few decades, there has been a growing interest in corporate ethical performance. Perhaps some reasons for this trend may be the increasing lack of confidence regarding corporate activities, the growing emphasis on quality of life issues, and a spate of recent corporate scandals at such firms as Enron and Tyco. Clearly, concerns about protecting the environment, fair employment practices, and the distribution of unsafe products have served to create powerful regulatory agencies such as the Environmental Protection Agency, the Equal Opportunity Commission, and the Federal Drug Administration. Recently, however, other concerns are becoming salient such as: problems associated with fetal tissue for research, disproportionate executive pay levels, corporate crises such as the Firestone/Ford Explorer tire fiasco, race debacles at Texaco and at Denny's Restaurants, the *Exxon Valdez* oil spill, and the practices of major financial services institutions in the wake of the dot-com crash. Merely adhering to the minimum regulatory standards may not be enough to remain competitive in a world that is becoming more socially conscious.

Without a strong ethical culture, the chance of ethical crises occurring is enhanced. They can be very expensive—both in terms of financial costs and in the erosion of human capital and overall firm reputation. Consider, for example, Texaco's class-action discrimination lawsuit.

In 1994 a senior financial analyst, Bari-Ellen Roberts, and one of her co-workers, Sil Chambers, filed a class-action discrimination suit against Texaco after enduring racial slurs and being passed over for promotion on several occasions. The discrimination suit charged Texaco with using an "old boys network" to systematically discriminate against African Americans.

Roberts remembers, "The hardest part of the suit was deciding to do it. I'd worked so hard to get where I was, and I had to risk all of that. Then I had to deal with loneliness and isolation. Even some of the other African Americans viewed me as a troublemaker. When you're standing up and calling for change, it makes people fear for their own security."

Two years later, in 1996, Texaco settled the suit, paying $141 million to its African-American workers. This was followed with an additional $35 million to remove discriminatory practices.[40]

Please note that the financial cost alone of $176 million was certainly not the proverbial "drop in the bucket." This amount represented nearly 10 percent of Texaco Inc.'s entire net income for 1996.

As we are all aware, the past several years have been characterized by numerous examples of unethical and illegal behavior by many top-level corporate executives. For example, in Strategy Spotlight 1.2 (p. 18), we explained how Sprint Corporation's top two executives were fired because of questionable tax shelters created for them by the firm's accountants—Ernst & Young. And we led off Chapter 9 with a discussion of the greedy, unethical, and illegal activities of Tyco's CEO, Dennis Kozlowski. Exhibit 11.4 briefly summarizes the unethical and illegal activities of other well-known corporate leaders.

The ethical organization is characterized by a conception of ethical values and integrity as a driving force of an enterprise.[41] Ethical values shape the search for opportunities, the design of organizational systems, and the decision-making process used by individuals and groups. They provide a common frame of reference that serves as a unifying force across different functions, lines of business, and employee groups. Organizational ethics helps define what a company is and what it stands for.

The potential benefits of an ethical organization are many but often indirect. The research literature in organizational behavior has found somewhat inconsistent results concerning the overall relationship between ethical performance and measures of financial performance.[42] However, positive relationships have generally been found between ethical performance and strong organizational culture, increased employee efforts, lower turnover, higher organizational commitment, and enhanced social responsibility.

Clearly, the advantages of a strong ethical orientation can have a positive effect on employee commitment and motivation to excel. This is particularly important in today's knowledge-intensive organizations, where human capital is critical in creating value and competitive advantages. As we discussed in Chapter 4, positive, constructive relationships among individuals (i.e., social capital) are vital in leveraging human capital and other resources in an organization. However, there are many other potential benefits as well. Drawing on the concept of stakeholder management that we discussed in Chapter 1, an ethically sound organization can also strengthen its bonds among its suppliers, customers, and governmental agencies. John E. Pepper, former chairman of Procter & Gamble, addresses such a perspective in Strategy Spotlight 11.8.

Integrity-Based versus Compliance-Based Approaches to Organizational Ethics

Before discussing the key elements for building an ethical organization, it is important to understand the essential links between organizational integrity and the personal integrity of an organization's members.[43] There cannot be high-integrity organizations without high-integrity individuals. At the same time, individual integrity is rarely self-sustaining. Even

EXHIBIT 11.4
Unethical and Illegal Behavior by Top-Level Corporate Executives

Name/Company	Summary
Bernard J. Ebbers, CEO *WorldCom, Inc.*	Ebbers built WorldCom, Inc., by acquiring companies during the 1990s boom. Now he's under scrutiny by members of the Justice Department, who wonder whether he had any inkling of the massive accounting fraud that WorldCom undertook to boost its results. The Securities and Exchange Commission estimates the magnitude of the deceit at over $9 billion. Investigators may also be looking at a $408 million loan that WorldCom made to Ebbers. WorldCom became the largest bankruptcy in history—losing $140 billion in market value, along with 170,000 layoffs.
John J. Rigas, CEO *Adelphia*	Patriarch of a Coudersport, Pennsylvania, family cable empire, Rigas and his two sons have been convicted for looting the nation's fifth largest cable company. Adelphia is now operating in bankruptcy, and its stock, trading at pennies a share, has lost $4.4 billion in value. John Rigas was taken in handcuffs from his Manhattan residence in July 2002.
Kenneth Lay, CEO Jeffrey Skilling, President Andrew Fastow, CFO *Enron*	These men led Enron as it fell into the first megascandal—resulting in a loss in investor wealth of $67 billion. Once the nation's seventh-largest company—a "new economy" archetype—Enron allegedly cooked its books in order to pump up profits and hide billions of dollars in debt. In October 2002, Fastow was charged with 78 counts of fraud, money laundering, and conspiracy. In January 2004, Fastow agreed to serve a ten-year sentence, pay a $23 million fine, and cooperate with the U.S. government's continuing investigation. Skilling, who combatively appeared before a congressional panel, and Lay were indicted on criminal charges in February 2004 and July 2004, respectively.
Richard M. Scrushy, CEO *Healthsouth Corp.*	In mid-March 2003, the Securities and Exchange Commission (SEC) filed a lawsuit that accused Scrushy of engaging in a $1.4 billion accounting fraud. The SEC alleges that since 1999, at the insistence of Scrushy, the firm overstated its earnings by at least $1.4 billion in order to meet or exceed Wall Street expectations. Days after the suit was made public, Scrushy and CFO William T. Owens were placed on leave for certifying the company's financials to the SEC in August. Owens later pleaded guilty to federal securities fraud and conspiracy charges and was fired. On March 31, the Healthsouth board declared the employment agreement with Richard Scrushy "null and void" and fired him as chairman and chief executive officer.

Sources: M. Lavelle, "Rogue of the Year," *Time*, December 30, 2002, pp. 32–45; "The Best (and Worst) Managers of the Year," *BusinessWeek*, January 13, 2003, pp. 58–92; and www.thecorporatelibrary.com/spotlight/scandals/scandal-quicksheet.html.

Note: Some of the additional titles of these executives have been omitted to conserve space.

good people can lose their bearings when faced with pressures, temptations, and heightened performance expectations in the absence of organizational support systems and ethical boundaries. Organizational integrity, on the other hand, is beyond personal integrity. It rests on a concept of purpose, responsibility, and ideals for an organization as a whole. An important responsibility of leadership in building organizational integrity is to create this ethical framework and develop the organizational capabilities to make it operational.

Procter & Gamble: Using Ethics to "Build the Spirit of the Place"

John Pepper, former CEO and chairman of Procter & Gamble Company, shares his perspective on ethics.

Let me start by saying that while ethics may seem like a soft concept—not as hard, say, as strategy or budgeting or operations—it is, in fact, a very hard concept. It is tangible. It is crucial . . . it is good for business.

There are several reasons for this. First, a company's values have a tremendous impact on who is attracted to your company and who will stay with it. We only have one life to live. All of us want to live it as part of an institution committed to high goals and high-sighted means of reaching these goals. This is true everywhere I've been. In our most mature countries and our newest.

Strong corporate values greatly simplify decision making. It is important to know the things you won't even think about doing. Diluting a product. Paying a bribe. Not being fair to a customer or an employee.

Strong values earn the respect of customers and suppliers and governments and other companies, too. This is absolutely crucial over the long term.

A company which pays bribes in a foreign market becomes an open target for more bribes when the word gets out. It never stops.

A company which is seen to be offering different trade terms to different customers based on how big they are or how hard they push will forever be beset by requests for special terms.

A company which is seen by a government as having weak or varying standards will not be respected by that government.

And more positively, governments and other companies really do want to deal with companies they feel are pursuing sound values because, in many, if not most cases, they believe it will be good for them.

One final but very fundamental reason for operating ethically is that strong values create trust and pride among employees. Simply put, they build the spirit of the place.

Source: J. E. Pepper, "The Boa Principle: Operating Ethically in Today's Business Environment," speech presented at Florida A&M University, Tallahassee, January 30, 1997.

It is also important to know the approaches or strategies organizations take in dealing with ethics. Lynn Paine, a researcher at Harvard, identifies two such approaches: the compliance-based approach and the integrity-based approach. (See Exhibit 11.5 for a comparison of compliance-based and integrity-based strategies.) Faced with the prospect of litigation, several organizations reactively implement compliance-based ethics programs. Such programs are typically designed by a corporate counsel with the goal of preventing, detecting, and punishing legal violations. But being ethical is much more than being legal, and an integrity-based approach addresses the issue of ethics in a more comprehensive manner.

An integrity-based approach to ethics management combines a concern for law with an emphasis on managerial responsibility for ethical behavior. This approach is broader, deeper, and more demanding than a legal compliance initiative. It is broader in that it seeks to enable responsible conduct. It is deeper in that it cuts to the ethos and operating systems of an organization and its members, their core guiding values, thoughts, and actions. And it is more demanding because it requires an active effort to define the responsibilities and aspirations that constitute an organization's ethical compass. Most importantly, in this approach, organizational ethics is seen as the work of management. A corporate counsel may play a role in designing and implementing integrity strategies, but it is managers at all levels and across all functions that are involved in the process. Once integrated into the day-to-day operations of an organization, such strategies can help prevent damaging ethical lapses, while tapping into powerful human impulses for moral thought and action. Ethics then become the governing ethos of an organization and not burdensome constraints to be

Exhibit 11.5
Approaches or Strategies for Ethics Management

Characteristics	Compliance-Based Approach	Integrity-Based Approach
Ethos	Conformity with externally imposed standards	Self-governance according to chosen standards
Objective	Prevent criminal misconduct	Enable responsible conduct
Leadership	Lawyer-driven	Management-driven with aid of lawyers, HR, and others
Methods	Education, reduced discretion, auditing and controls, penalties	Education, leadership, accountability, organizational systems and decision processes, auditing and controls, penalties
Behavioral assumptions	Autonomous beings guided by material self-interest	Social beings guided by material self-interest, values, ideals, peers

Source: L. S. Paine, "Managing for Organizational Integrity," *Harvard Business Review* 72, no. 2 (1994), p. 113 (with permission).

adhered to. Here is an example of an organization that goes beyond mere compliance to laws in building an ethical organization.

In teaching ethics to its employees, Texas Instruments, the $8 billion chip and electronics manufacturer, asks them to run an issue through the following steps: Is it legal? Is it consistent with the company's stated values? Will one feel bad doing it? What will the public think if the action is reported in the press? Does one think it is wrong? Further, if the employees are not sure of the ethicality of the issue, they are encouraged to ask someone until they are clear about it. In the process, employees can approach high-level personnel and even the company's lawyers. As can be clearly noted, at Texas Instruments, the question of ethics goes much beyond merely being legal. It is no surprise, therefore, that this company is a benchmark for corporate ethics and has been a recipient of three ethics awards: the David C. Lincoln Award for Ethics and Excellence in Business, American Business Ethics Award, and Bentley College Center for Business Ethics Award.[44]

To sum up, compliance-based approaches are externally motivated, that is, based on the fear of punishment for doing something unlawful. On the other hand, integrity-based approaches are driven by a personal and organizational commitment to ethical behavior.

A firm must have several key elements before it can become a highly ethical organization. These elements must be both present and constantly reinforced in order for the firm to be successful:

◆ Role models.
◆ Corporate credos and codes of conduct.
◆ Reward and evaluation systems.
◆ Policies and procedures.

These elements are highly interrelated. For example, reward structures and policies will be useless if leaders throughout the organization are not sound role models. That is, leaders who implicitly say, "Do as I say, not as I do," will quickly have their credibility eroded and such actions will, in effect, sabotage other elements that are essential to building an ethical organization.

Role Models

For good or for bad, leaders are role models in their organizations. As we noted in Chapter 9, leaders must "walk the talk"; that is, they must be consistent in their words and deeds. The values as well as the character of leaders become transparent to an organization's employees through their behaviors. In addition, when leaders do not believe in the ethical standards that they are trying to inspire, they will not be effective as good role models. Being an effective leader often includes taking responsibility for ethical lapses within the organization—even though the executives themselves are not directly involved. Consider, for example, the perspective of Dennis Bakke, CEO of AES, the $8 billion global electricity company based in Arlington, Virginia.

> There was a major breach (in 1992) of the AES values. Nine members of the water treatment team in Oklahoma lied to the EPA about water quality at the plant. There was no environmental damage, but they lied about the test results. A new, young chemist at the plant discovered it, and she told a team leader, and, of course, we then were notified. Now, you could argue that the people who lied were responsible and were accountable, but the senior management team also took responsibility by taking pay cuts. My reduction was about 30 percent.[45]

Such action enhances the loyalty and commitment of employees throughout the organization. Many would believe that it would have been much easier (and personally less expensive!) for Bakke and his management team to merely take strong punitive action against the nine individuals who were acting contrary to the behavior expected in AES's ethical culture. However, by taking responsibility for the misdeeds, the top executives—through their highly visible action—made it very clear that responsibility and penalties for ethical lapses goes well beyond the "guilty" parties. Such courageous behavior by leaders helps to strengthen an organization's ethical environment.

Corporate Credos and Codes of Conduct

Corporate credos or codes of conduct are another important element of an ethical organization. Such mechanisms provide a statement and guidelines for norms and beliefs as well as guidelines for decision making. They provide employees with a clear understanding of the organization's position regarding employee behavior. Such guidelines also provide the basis for employees to refuse to commit unethical acts and help to make them aware of issues before they are faced with the situation. For such codes to be truly effective, organization members must be aware of them and what behavioral guidelines they contain.

Large corporations are not the only ones to develop and use codes of conduct. Consider the example of Wetherill Associates (WAI), a small, privately held supplier of electrical parts to the automotive market.

> Rather than a conventional code of conduct, WAI has a Quality Assurance Manual—a combination of philosophy text, conduct guide, technical manual, and company profile—that describes the company's commitment to honesty, ethical action, and integrity.
>
> Interestingly, WAI doesn't have a corporate ethics officer, because the company's corporate ethics officer is top management. Marie Bothe, WAI's chief executive officer, sees her main function as keeping the 350-employee company on the path of ethical behavior and looking for opportunities to help the community. She delegates the "technical" aspects of the business—marketing, finance, personnel, and operations—to other members of the organization.[46]

Perhaps the best-known credo, a statement describing a firm's commitment to certain standards, is that of Johnson & Johnson (J&J). It is reprinted in Exhibit 11.6. The credo stresses honesty, integrity, superior products, and putting people before profits. What distinguishes the J&J credo from those of other firms is the amount of energy the company's top managers devote to ensuring that employees live by its precepts.

**Exhibit 11.6
Johnson &
Johnson's Credo**

We believe our first responsibility is to the doctors, nurses and patients, to mothers and fathers and all others who use our products and services. In meeting their needs everything we do must be of high quality. We must constantly strive to reduce our costs in order to maintain reasonable prices. Customers' orders must be serviced promptly and accurately. Our suppliers and distributors must have an opportunity to make a fair profit.

We are responsible to our employees, the men and women who work with us throughout the world. Everyone must be considered as an individual. We must respect their dignity and recognize their merit. They must have a sense of security in their jobs. Compensation must be fair and adequate, and working conditions clean, orderly, and safe. We must be mindful of ways to help our employees fulfill their family responsibilities. Employees must feel free to make suggestions and complaints. There must be equal opportunity for employment, development, and advancement for those qualified. We must provide competent management, and their actions must be just and ethical.

We are responsible to the communities in which we live and work and to the world community as well. We must be good citizens—support good works and charities and bear our fair share of taxes. We must encourage civic improvements and better health and education. We must maintain in good order the property we are privileged to use, protecting the environment and natural resources.

Our final responsibility is to our stockholders. Business must make a sound profit. We must experiment with new ideas. Research must be carried on, innovative programs developed, and mistakes paid for. New equipment must be purchased, new facilities provided, and new products launched. Reserves must be created to provide for adverse times. When we operate according to these principles, the stockholders should realize a fair return.

Source: Johnson & Johnson Co.

Over a three-year period, Johnson & Johnson undertook a massive effort to assure that its original credo, already decades old, was still valid. More than 1,200 managers attended two-day seminars in groups of 25, with explicit instructions to challenge the credo. The president or CEO of the firm personally presided over each session. In the end, the company came out of the process believing that its original document was still valid. However, the questioning process continues. Such "challenge meetings" are still replicated every other year for all new managers. These efforts force J&J to question, internalize, and then implement its credo. Such investments paid off handsomely many times—most notably in 1982, when eight people died from swallowing capsules of Tylenol, one of its flagship products, that someone had laced with cyanide. Leaders such as James Burke, who without hesitation made an across-the-board recall of the product even though it affected only a limited number of untraceable units, send a strong message throughout their organization.

Reward and Evaluation Systems

It is entirely possible for a highly ethical leader to preside over an organization that commits several unethical acts. How? It may reflect a flaw in the organization's reward structure. A reward and evaluation system may inadvertently cause individuals to act in an inappropriate manner if rewards are seen as being distributed on the basis of outcomes instead of the means by which goals and objectives are achieved. Such was the situation with Tyco International, discussed in Chapter 9. Recall that much of the illegal and uneth-

strategy spotlight

No More Whistleblowing Woes!

The landmark Sarbanes-Oxley Act of 2002 gives those who expose corporate misconduct strong legal protection. Henceforth, an executive who retaliates against the corporate whistleblower can be held criminally liable and imprisoned for up to 10 years. That's the same sentence a mafia don gets for threatening a witness. The Labor Department can order a company to rehire an employee without going to court. If the fired workers feel their case is moving too slowly, they can request a federal jury after six months.

Companies need to revisit their current policies, including nondisclosure pacts. They may no longer be able to enforce rules requiring employees to get permission to speak to the media or lawyers. Even layoffs should be planned in advance, lest they seem retaliatory.

Sources: www.sarbanes-oxley.com/pcaob.php/level=2&pub_id=Sarbanes-Oxley&chap_id=PCAOB11; P. Dwyer, D. Carney, A. Borrus, L. Woellert, and C. Palmeri, "Year of the WhistleBlower," *BusinessWeek*, December 16, 2002, pp. 107–9; and www.buchalter.com/FSL5CS/articles/articles204.asp.

Employees of publicly traded companies are now the most protected whistleblowers. Provisions coauthored by Senator Grassley in the Sarbanes-Oxley corporate-reform law:

- Make it unlawful to "discharge, demote, suspend or threaten, harass, or in any manner discriminate against" a whistleblower.

- Establish criminal penalties of up to 10 years in jail for executives who retaliate against whistleblowers.

- Require board audit committees to establish procedures for hearing whistleblower complaints.

- Allow the secretary of labor to order a company to rehire a terminated whistleblower with no court hearings whatsoever.

- Give a whistleblower a right to jury trial, bypassing months or years of cumbersome administrative hearings.

ical behavior could probably be traced to the absence of rules and regulations to guide behavior. Instead, the message was, in effect: "Do whatever it takes to make the numbers." Clearly, both the firm's reputation and its market valuation suffered.

Consider the example of Sears, Roebuck & Co.'s automotive operations. Here, unethical behavior, rooted in a faulty reward system, took place primarily at the operations level: its automobile repair facilities.[47]

> In 1992 Sears was flooded with complaints about its automotive service business. Consumers and attorneys general in more than 40 states accused the firm of misleading customers and selling them unnecessary parts and services, from brake jobs to front-end alignments. What were the causes?
>
> In the face of declining revenues and eroding market share, Sears's management attempted to spur the performance of its auto centers by introducing new goals and incentives for mechanics. Automotive service advisers were given product-specific quotas for a variety of parts and repairs. Failure to meet the quotas could lead to transfers and reduced hours. Many employees spoke of "pressure, pressure, pressure" to bring in sales.
>
> Not too surprisingly, the judgment of many employees suffered. In essence, employees were left to chart their own course, given the lack of management guidance and customer ignorance. The bottom line: In settling the spate of lawsuits, Sears offered coupons to customers who had purchased certain auto services over the most recent two-year period. The total cost of the settlement, including potential customer refunds, was estimated to be $60 million. The cost in terms of damaged reputation? Difficult to assess, but certainly not trivial.

The Sears automotive example makes two important points. First, inappropriate reward systems may cause individuals at all levels throughout an organization to commit unethical acts that they might not otherwise do. Second, the penalties in terms of damage to reputations, human capital erosion, and financial loss—in the short run and long run—are typically much higher than any gains that could be obtained through such unethical behavior.

Policies and Procedures

Many situations that a firm faces have regular, identifiable patterns. Typically, leaders tend to handle such routine by establishing a policy or procedure to be followed that can be applied rather uniformly to each occurrence. As we noted in Chapter 9, such guidelines can be useful in specifying the proper relationships with a firm's customers and suppliers. For example, Levi Strauss has developed stringent global sourcing guidelines and Chemical Bank (now part of J. P. Morgan Chase Bank) has a policy of forbidding any review that would determine whether or not suppliers are Chemical customers when the bank awards contracts.

Clearly, it is important to carefully develop policies and procedures to guide behavior so that all employees will be encouraged to behave in an ethical manner. However, it is not enough merely to have policies and procedures "on the books." Rather, they must be reinforced with effective communication, enforcement, and monitoring, as well as sound corporate governance practices. Strategy Spotlight 11.9 describes how the recently enacted Sarbanes-Oxley Act provides considerable legal protection to employees of publicly traded companies who report unethical or illegal practices.

summary

Strategic leadership is vital in ensuring that strategies are formulated and implemented in an effective manner. Leaders must play a central role in performing three critical and interdependent activities: setting the direction, designing the organization, and nurturing a culture committed to excellence and ethical behavior. In the chapter we provided the imagery of these three activities as a "three-legged stool." If leaders ignore or are ineffective in performing any one of the three, the organization will not be very successful. Leaders must also use power effectively to overcome barriers to change.

For leaders to effectively fulfill their activities, emotional intelligence (EI) is very important. Five elements that contribute to EI are self-awareness, self-regulation, motivation, empathy, and social skills. The first three elements pertain to self-management skills, whereas the last two are associated with a person's ability to manage relationships with others.

Leaders must also play a central role in creating a learning organization. Gone are the days when the top-level managers "think" and everyone else in the organization "does." With the rapidly changing, unpredictable, and complex competitive environments that characterize most industries, leaders must engage everyone in the ideas and energies of people throughout the organization. Great ideas can come from anywhere in the organization—from the executive suite to the factory floor. The five elements that we discussed as central to a learning organization are inspiring and motivating people with a mission or purpose, empowering people at all levels throughout the organization, accumulating and sharing internal knowledge, gathering external information, and challenging the status quo to stimulate creativity.

In the final section of the chapter, we addressed a leader's central role in instilling ethical behavior in the organization. We discussed the enormous costs that firms face when ethical crises arise—costs in terms of financial and reputational loss as well as the erosion of human capital and relationships with suppliers, customers, society at large, and governmental agencies. And, as one would expect, the benefits of having a strong ethical organization are also numerous. We contrasted compliance-based and integrity-based approaches to organizational ethics. Compliance-based approaches are largely externally motivated, that is, motivated by the fear of punishment for doing something that is unlawful. Integrity-based approaches, on the other hand, are driven by a personal and organizational commitment to ethical behavior. We also addressed the four key elements of an ethical organization: role models, corporate credos and codes of conduct, reward and evaluation systems, and policies and procedures.

summary review questions

1. Three key activities—setting a direction, designing the organization, and nurturing a culture and ethics—are all part of what effective leaders do on a regular basis. Explain how these three activities are interrelated.

2. Define emotional intelligence (EI). What arc the key elements of EI? Why is EI so important to successful strategic leadership?

3. The knowledge a firm possesses can be a source of competitive advantage. Describe ways that a firm can continuously learn to maintain its competitive position.

4. How can the five central elements of "learning organizations" be incorporated into global companies?

5. What are the benefits to firms and their shareholders of conducting business in an ethical manner?

6. Firms that fail to behave in an ethical manner can incur high costs. What are these costs and what is their source?

7. What are the most important differences between an "integrity organization" and a "compliance organization" in a firm's approach to organizational ethics?

8. What are some of the important mechanisms for promoting ethics in a firm?

Select two well-known business leaders—one you admire and one you do not. Evaluate each of them on the five characteristics of emotional intelligence.

experiential exercise

Emotional Intelligence Characteristics	Admired Leader	Leader Not Admired
Self-awareness		
Self-regulation		
Motivation		
Empathy		
Social skills		

application questions & exercises

1. Identify two CEOs whose leadership you admire. What is it about their skills, attributes, and effective use of power that causes you to admire them?
2. Founders have an important role in developing their organization's culture and values. At times, their influence persists for many years. Identify and describe two organizations in which the cultures and values established by the founder(s) continue to flourish. You may find research on the Internet helpful in answering these questions.
3. Some leaders place a great emphasis on developing superior human capital. In what ways does this help a firm to develop and sustain competitive advantages?
4. In this chapter we discussed the five elements of a "learning organization." Select a firm with which you are familiar and discuss whether or not it epitomizes some (or all) of these elements.

ethics questions

1. Sometimes organizations must go outside the firm to hire talent, thus bypassing employees already working for the firm. Are there conditions under which this might raise ethical considerations?
2. Ethical crises can occur in virtually any organization. Describe some of the systems, procedures, and processes that can help to prevent such crises.

references

1. The sources for the Morrison Knudsen example include Johnson, S. S., 1995, Dithering, *Forbes,* May 22: 45; O'Reilly, B., 1995, Agee in exile, *Fortune,* May 29: 51–74; Rigdon, J. E., 1995, Morrison Knudsen's loss estimates are widened: Acting chairman resigns, *Wall Street Journal,* March 21: A4; Rigdon, J. E., 1995, William Agee will leave Morrison Knudsen, *Wall Street Journal,* February 2: B1, B11; and Stern, R. L., & Abelson, R., 1992, The imperial Agees, *Forbes,* June 8: 88–92. We would like to thank Connie Bookholt for her input and assistance in the preparation of this example. The Morrison Knudsen example draws upon Picken, J. C., & Dess, G. G., 1997, *Mission Critical* (Burr Ridge, IL: Irwin Professional Publishing).
2. Charan, R., & Colvin, G., 1999, Why CEOs fail, *Fortune,* June 21: 68–78.
3. These three activities and our discussion draw from Kotter, J. P., 1990, What leaders really do, *Harvard Business Review* 68 (3): 103–11; Pearson, A. E., 1990, Six basics for general managers, *Harvard Business Review* 67 (4): 94–101; and Covey, S. R., 1996, Three roles of the leader in the new paradigm, in *The Leader of the Future,* Hesselbein, F., Goldsmith, M., & Beckhard, R., eds. (San Francisco: Jossey-Bass), 149–60. Some of the discussion of each of the three leadership activity concepts draws on Dess, G. G., & Miller, A., 1993, *Strategic Management* (New York: McGraw-Hill), 320–25.
4. Day, C., Jr., & LaBarre, P., 1994, GE: Just your average everyday $60 billion family grocery store, *Industry Week,* May 2: 13–18.
5. The best (& worst) managers of the year, 2003, *BusinessWeek,* January 13: 63.
6. The Merck example is drawn from Weber, J., 1996, Mr.

Nice Guy with a mission, *BusinessWeek,* November 25: 132–42.
7. For insightful perspectives on escalation, refer to Brockner, J., 1992, The escalation of commitment to a failing course of action, *Academy of Management Review* 17 (1): 39–61; and Staw, B. M., 1976, Knee-deep in the big muddy: A study of commitment to a chosen course of action, *Organizational Behavior and Human Decision Processes* 16: 27–44. The discussion of systemic, behavioral, and political barriers draws on Lorange, P., & Murphy, D., 1984, Considerations in implementing strategic control, *Journal of Business Strategy* 5: 27–35. In a similar vein, Noel M. Tichy has addressed three types of resistance to change in the context of General Electric: technical resistance, political resistance, and cultural resistance. See Tichy, N. M., 1993, Revolutionize your company, *Fortune,* December 13: 114–18. Examples draw from O'Reilly, B., 1997, The secrets of America's most admired corporations: New ideas and new products, *Fortune,* March 3: 60–64.
8. This section draws on Champoux, J. E., 2000, *Organizational Behavior: Essential Tenets for a New Millennium* (London: South-Western); and, The mature use of power in organizations, 2003, *RHR International-Executive Insights,* May 29, 12.19.168.197/execinsights/8-3.htm.
9. For a review of this literature, see Daft, R., 1999, *Leadership: Theory and Practice* (Fort Worth, TX: Dryden Press).
10. This section draws on Luthans, F., 2002, Positive organizational behavior: Developing and managing psychological strengths, *Academy of Management Executive* 16 (1): 57–72; and Goleman, D., 1998, What makes a leader? *Harvard Business Review* 76 (6): 92–105.
11. EI has its roots in the concept of "social intelligence" that

was first identified by E. L. Thorndike in 1920 (Intelligence and its uses, *Harper's Magazine* 140: 227–35). Psychologists have been uncovering other intelligences for some time now and have grouped them into such clusters as abstract intelligence (the ability to understand and manipulate with verbal and mathematical symbols), concrete intelligence (the ability to understand and manipulate with objects), and social intelligence (the ability to understand and relate to people). See Ruisel, I., 1992, Social intelligence: Conception and methodological problems, *Studia Psychologica* 34 (4–5): 281–96. Refer to trochim.human.cornell.edu/gallery.

12. See, for example, Luthans, op. cit.; Mayer, J. D., Salvoney, P., & Caruso, D., 2000, Models of emotional intelligence, in Sternberg, R. J., ed., *Handbook of Intelligence* (Cambridge, UK: Cambridge University Press); and Cameron, K., 1999, Developing emotional intelligence at the Weatherhead School of Management, *Strategy: The Magazine of the Weatherhead School of Management,* Winter: 2–3.

13. Goleman, op. cit, p. 102.

14. Handy, C., 1995, Trust and the virtual organization, *Harvard Business Review* 73 (3): 40–50.

15. This section draws upon Dess, G. G., & Picken, J. C., 1999, *Beyond Productivity* (New York: AMACOM). The elements of the learning organization in this section are consistent with the work of Dorothy Leonard-Barton. See, for example, Leonard-Barton, D., 1992, The factory as a learning laboratory, *Sloan Management Review* 11: 23–38.

16. Senge, P. M., 1990, The leader's new work: Building learning organizations, *Sloan Management Review* 32 (1): 7–23.

17. Hammer, M., & Stanton, S. A., 1997, The power of reflection, *Fortune,* November 24: 291–96.

18. Covey, S. R., 1989, *The Seven Habits of Highly Effective People: Powerful Lessons in Personal Change* (New York: Simon & Schuster).

19. Melrose, K., 1995, *Making the Grass Greener on Your Side: A CEO's Journey to Leading by Servicing* (San Francisco: Barrett-Koehler).

20. Quinn, R. C., & Spreitzer, G. M., 1997, The road to empowerment: Seven questions every leader should consider, *Organizational Dynamics* 25: 37–49.

21. Helgesen, S., 1996, Leading from the grass roots, in *Leader of the Future,* Hesselbein et al., 19–24.

22. Bowen, D. E., & Lawler, E. E., III, 1995, Empowering service employees, *Sloan Management Review* 37: 73–84.

23. Stack, J., 1992, *The Great Game of Business* (New York: Doubleday/Currency).

24. Lubove, S., 1998, New age capitalist, *Forbes,* April 6: 42–43.

25. Schafer, S., 1997, Battling a labor shortage? It's all in your imagination, *Inc.,* August: 24.

26. Meyer, P., 1998, So you want the president's job . . . *Business Horizons,* January–February: 2–8.

27. Goldberg, M., 1998, Cisco's most important meal of the day, *Fast Company,* February–March: 56.

28. Imperato, G., 1998, Competitive intelligence: Get smart! *Fast Company,* May: 268–79.

29. Novicki, C., 1998, The best brains in business, *Fast Company,* April: 125.

30. The introductory discussion of benchmarking draws on Miller, A., 1998, *Strategic Management* (New York: McGraw-Hill), 142–43.

31. Port, O., & Smith, G., 1992, Beg, borrow—and benchmark, *BusinessWeek,* November 30: 74–75.

32. Main, J., 1992, How to steal the best ideas around, *Fortune,* October 19: 102–6.

33. Taylor, J. T., 1997, What happens after what comes next? *Fast Company,* December–January: 84–85.

34. Sheff, D., 1996, Levi's changes everything, *Fast Company,* June–July: 65–74.

35. Isaacson, W., 1997, In search of the real Bill Gates, *Time,* January 13: 44–57.

36. Baatz, E. B., 1993, Motorola's secret weapon, *Electronic Business,* April: 51–53.

37. Holt, J. W., 1996, *Celebrate Your Mistakes* (New York: McGraw-Hill).

38. Harari, O., 1997, Flood your organization with knowledge, *Management Review,* November: 33–37.

39. This opening discussion draws upon Conley, J. H., 2000, Ethics in business, in Helms, M. M., ed., *Encyclopedia of Management,* 4th ed. (Farmington Hills, MI: Gale Group), 281–85; Paine, L. S., 1994, Managing for organizational integrity, *Harvard Business Review* 72 (2): 106–17; and Carlson, D. S., & Perrewe, P. L., 1995, Institutionalization of organizational ethics through transformational leadership, *Journal of Business Ethics* 14: 829–38.

40. Kiger, P. J., 2001, Truth and consequences, *Working Woman,* May: 57–61.

41. Soule, E., 2002, Managerial moral strategies—in search of a few good principles, *Academy of Management Review* 27 (1): 114–24.

42. Carlson & Perrewe, op cit.

43. This discussion is based upon Paine, Managing for organizational integrity; Paine, L. S., 1997, *Cases in Leadership, Ethics, and Organizational Integrity: A Strategic Approach* (Burr Ridge, IL: Irwin); and Fontrodone, J., Business ethics across the Atlantic, Business Ethics Direct, www.ethicsa.org/BED_art_fontrodone.html.

44. www.ti.com/corp/docs/company/citizen/ethics/benchmark .shtml; and www.ti.com/corp/docs/company/citizen/ ethics/quicktest.shtml.

45. Wetalufer, S., 1999, Organizing for empowerment: An interview with AES's Roger Sant and Dennis Bakke, *Harvard Business Review* 77 (1): 110–26.

46. Paine, Managing for organizational integrity.

47. Ibid.

chapter 12

Managing Innovation and Fostering Corporate Entrepreneurship

After reading this chapter, you should have a good understanding of:

chapter objectives

- The importance of implementing strategies and practices that foster innovation.

- The challenges and pitfalls of managing corporate innovation processes.

- The role of product champions and exit champions in internal corporate venturing.

- How independent venture teams and business incubators are used to develop corporate ventures.

- How corporations create an internal environment and culture that promotes entrepreneurial development.

- How an entrepreneurial orientation can enhance a firm's efforts to develop promising corporate venture initiatives.

*t*o remain competitive, established firms must continually seek out opportunities for growth and new methods for strategically renewing their performance. Changes in customer needs, new technologies, and shifts in the competitive landscape require that companies continually innovate and initiate corporate ventures in order to compete effectively. This chapter addresses how entrepreneurial activities can be an avenue for achieving competitive advantages.

In the first section, we address the importance of innovation in identifying venture opportunities and strategic renewal. Innovations can take many forms, including radical breakthrough innovations as well as incremental innovative improvements, and be used either to update products or renew organizational processes. We discuss how firms can successfully manage the innovation process. Impediments and challenges to effective innovation are discussed and examples of good innovation practices are presented.

We discuss the unique role of corporate entrepreneurship in the strategic management process in the second section. Here we highlight two types of activities corporations use to remain competitive—focused and dispersed. New venture groups and business incubators are often used to focus a firm's entrepreneurial activities. In other corporations, the entrepreneurial spirit is dispersed throughout the organization and gives rise to product champions and other autonomous strategic behaviors that organizational members engage in to foster internal corporate venturing.

In the final section we describe how a firm's entrepreneurial orientation can contribute to its growth and renewal as well as enhance the methods and processes strategic managers use to recognize opportunities and develop initiatives for internal growth and development. The chapter also evaluates the pitfalls that firms may encounter when implementing entrepreneurial strategies.

Companies often grow by commercializing new technologies. This is one of the most important paths to corporate entrepreneurship. But technologies change and yesterday's exciting innovation eventually becomes today's old news. Consider the case of Polaroid, a company that captivated the marketplace with its instant photography technology and grew to become a multibillion dollar enterprise on the strength of that innovation.[1]

Polaroid Corporation's founder, Edward Land, was a Harvard dropout. He was also a genius in optics, chemistry, and engineering who started his Cambridge, Massachusetts, company in 1937 to focus on sunglasses and other technologies that polarize light. During World War II, the company built infrared filters for gunsights and dark-adaptation goggles. It was after the war, however, that one of Land's innovations struck gold. In 1947 he introduced a single-step photographic process that would develop film in 60 seconds and launched the Land Camera. Over the next 30 years, the camera and its film evolved into the Polaroid One-Step, and sales surged to $1.4 billion by 1978.

In the process, Polaroid became one of the most admired companies and a best bet among stock pickers. It was a member of the "Nifty Fifty," a group of companies known for their innovative ideas whose stocks regularly traded at 40 or more times earnings. In 1991 it won a huge patent infringement lawsuit against rival Eastman Kodak, which had to pay Polaroid $925 million. The company also continued to launch new products using its instant film technology in a variety of different cameras with updated features.

On the surface, Polaroid seemed to be the picture of success. Land had been hailed as a new breed of corporate leader—both technically savvy and entrepreneurial. But by 1991, the year Land died, the company he built was unraveling. Instead of using the cash from the Kodak lawsuit to pay down its heavy debt, Polaroid spent the money to develop a new camera—the Captiva—which flopped in the marketplace. A few years later the I-Zone Pocket Camera, a product targeted at adolescents, had weak sales because the image quality was inconsistent and replacement film was considered too expensive for teens. Meanwhile, internally, Polaroid was spending 37 percent of its sales on administrative costs, compared to Kodak's 21 percent. Even though the company continued to sell millions of cameras each year—a record 13.1 million in 2000—its strength was deteriorating.

Polaroid's most serious problems began when it failed to get on the digital photography bandwagon. Rather than make the move into digital, Polaroid decided to stick with its proprietary technology. Once Polaroid realized the extent of the digital photography trend, it was too late. It eventually introduced digital cameras but they were often ranked low in consumer ratings. Polaroid even developed digital printing technologies, called Opal and Onyx, designed to deliver high resolution digital images. But because of its weakened financial state, it could not get the funding from investors to advertise and develop them. By 2001, it was in real trouble. Its debt was $950 million, it laid off 2,950 employees—35 percent of its workforce—and began missing interest payments to bondholders. In October 2001, it filed for Chapter 11 bankruptcy protection. Sale of its stock, which had traded as high as $60 in July 1997, was halted at 28 cents per share on the New York Stock Exchange.

What Went Wrong at Polaroid?   Considered by many to be one of the first great research-based companies, Polaroid failed largely because it lost its ability to effectively innovate and launch new products. Many factors contributed to its downfall. Clearly, its failure to respond quickly to the digital photography phenomenon caused a serious setback. But the roots of the problem were deeper. As one writer put it, "They overestimated the value of their core business." That is, Polaroid's overconfidence in its early success prevented it from envisioning a purpose beyond its instant imaging capability. This phenomenon is sometimes referred to as "the innovator's dilemma"—firms become so preoccupied with meeting current needs that they fail to take steps to meet future needs.[2] This dilemma inhibited Polaroid's ability to change and affected every aspect of its business:

◆   Even though sales of its core products were strong, it lost touch with its customers. As a result, several of its innovations failed in the marketplace.

◆   It did not have a long-term strategy for financing growth. Because it relied heavily on investors to finance new product initiatives, when one failed, it created cash flow problems. To regain profitability, Polaroid would offer more shares and bonds to investors, which, in turn, devalued the stock and created even more indebtedness. Eventually, investors turned away.

◆   Buoyed by revenues that grew annually for over 30 years, it failed to control personnel costs and was weighed down by too many employees. Eventually these expenses overtook its sales.

In short, Polaroid stopped thinking and acting like an entrepreneurial firm. The Polaroid brand is still loved by many, and its products can still be found in the marketplace. (In 2002, Polaroid's assets were purchased by OEP Imaging Operating Corporation and, as part of the agreement, OEPI changed its name to Polaroid Corporation). But the company that had once changed the world of photography was itself unable to make the changes necessary to remain viable. As a result of its lack of vision and failure to change, what had once been a leading innovator and top financial performer slowly fizzled out.[3]

Managing change, as we suggested in Chapter 11, is one of the most important functions performed by strategic leaders. The transformative activity of bringing organizations "from what they are to what the leader would have them become" requires fresh ideas and a vision of the future. Most organizations want to grow. To do so, they must expand their product offering, reach into new markets, and obtain new customers. Sometimes profitability can be increased by streamlining processes and operating more efficiently. These activities inevitably involve change, and a firm's leaders must be effective change agents.

What options are available to organizations that want to change and grow? This chapter addresses two major avenues through which companies can expand or improve their business—innovation and corporate entrepreneurship. These two activities go hand-in-hand because they both have similar aims. The first is strategic renewal. Innovations help an organization stay fresh and reinvent itself as conditions in the business environment change. This is why managing innovation is such an important strategic implementation issue. The second is the pursuit of venture opportunities. Innovative breakthroughs, as well as new product concepts, evolving technologies, and shifting demand, create opportunities for corporate venturing. In this chapter we will explore these topics—how change and innovation can stimulate strategic renewal and foster corporate entrepreneurship. First we turn to the challenge of managing innovation.

Managing Innovation

One of the most important sources of growth opportunities is innovation. Innovation involves using new knowledge to transform organizational processes or create commercially viable products and services. The sources of new knowledge may include the latest technology, the results of experiments, creative insights, or competitive information. However it comes about, innovation occurs when new combinations of ideas and information bring about positive change.

The emphasis on newness is a key point. For example, for a patent application to have any chance of success, one of the most important attributes it must possess is novelty. You can't patent an idea that has been copied. This is a central idea. In fact, the root of the word *innovation* is the Latin *novus,* which means new. Innovation involves introducing or changing to something new.[4]

Among the most important sources of new ideas is new technology. Technology creates new possibilities. Technology provides the raw material that firms use to make innovative new products and services. But it should not be thought that technology is the only source of innovations. There can be innovations in human resources, firm infrastructure,

strategy spotlight

12.1

Rubbermaid: Building Advantages through Marketing Innovations

Rubbermaid is a consistent winner of innovation kudos, including the 2002 *Chicago Sun-Times* Innovation Awards and *Retail Merchandiser*'s 2002 Marketing Innovation award winner in two categories. Yet Rubbermaid's innovations would rarely be considered "high-tech." Although the company (which consolidated in 1999 to form Newell Rubbermaid, Inc.) is known for its synthetic rubber materials, it is the application of those materials to develop innovative products that is responsible for its winning strategies. Here are some examples:

Tool Tower—Consumers have been crying out for help in organizing their garages, according to Adrian Fernandez, director of product management for Rubbermaid's Home Products unit. In fact, storing tools efficiently is the number one complaint by homeowners about garages. The Tool Tower, a simple and efficient plastic rack designed to hold long- and short-handle tools in one place, was a welcome solution. It is easily assembled, takes up little space, and is much safer than hanging tools on nails or racks.

Sources: H. Wolinsky, "2002 Chicago Innovation Award Winners," *Chicago Sun-Times,* October 7, 2002, www.suntimes.com; W. Schmitt, "Rubbermaid Inc.," in R. M. Kanter, J. Kao, and F. Wiersma, eds., *Innovation: Breakthrough Thinking at 3M, DuPont, GE, Pfizer, and Rubbermaid* (New York: HarperCollins, 1997), pp. 168–70; www.retail-merchandiser.com; and www.rubbermaid.com.

High-Heat Scraper—While on site at one of its restaurant customers, a Rubbermaid business team noticed that chefs preferred synthetic rubber scrapers instead of metal spatulas when using nonstick cookware. But the scrapers quickly warped from the heat and lost their shape. Based on this experience, a new scraper of pliable synthetic rubber was developed with chefs in mind. It still did not scratch but could sustain temperatures as high as 500 degrees Fahrenheit.

Hardware Blue—Many products are tested in the company's "Everything Rubbermaid" experimental lab stores. Rubbermaid noticed that more and more women were buying tool boxes and workshop organizers. They wondered how women shoppers liked their traditional colors—yellow, black, and gray. Through focus groups, they identified a new color," Hardware Blue," that outsold all other colors and appealed to both men and women.

Clearly, the high-heat scraper required technological know-how to develop. But the impetus for it came from proactive customer contact, and the product itself was simple. As can be seen from these examples, Rubbermaid is concerned not only with technologically based innovations but also with marketing innovations.

marketing, service, or in many other value-adding areas that have little to do with anything "high-tech." Strategy Spotlight 12.1 highlights three innovations by the Rubbermaid Corporation that met customer needs and generated sales but were relatively low-tech.

As the Rubbermaid example suggests, innovation can take many forms. Next we will consider two frameworks that are often used to distinguish types of innovation.

Types of Innovation

Although innovations are not always high-tech, changes in technology can be an important source of change and growth. When an innovation is based on a sweeping new technology, it often has a more far-reaching impact. However, sometimes even a small innovation can add value and create competitive advantages. Innovation can and should occur throughout an organization—in every department and all aspects of the value chain.

One way to view the impact of an innovation is in terms of its degree of innovativeness, which falls somewhere on a continuum that extends from incremental to radical.[5]

- *Radical innovations* produce fundamental changes by evoking major departures from existing practices. These breakthrough innovations usually occur because of technological change. They tend to be highly disruptive and can transform a company or even revolutionize a whole industry. They may lead to products or processes that can be patented, giving a firm a strong competitive advantage. Examples include electricity, the telephone, the transistor, desktop computers, fiber optics, artificial intelligence, and genetically engineered drugs.

♦ *Incremental innovations* enhance existing practices or make small improvements in products and processes. They may represent evolutionary applications within existing paradigms of earlier, more radical innovations. Because they often sustain a company by extending or expanding its product line or manufacturing skills, incremental innovations can be a source of competitive advantage. They increase revenues by creating a new marketplace offering or reduce costs by providing new capabilities that minimize expenses or speed productivity. Examples include frozen food, sports drinks, steel-belted radial tires, electronic bookkeeping, shatterproof glass, and digital telephones.

Some innovations are highly radical; others are only slightly incremental. But most innovations fall somewhere between these two extremes. Exhibit 12.1 shows where several innovations fall along the radical–incremental continuum.

Another distinction that is often used when discussing innovation is between process innovation and product innovation.[6] *Product innovation* refers to efforts to create product designs and applications of technology to develop new products for end users. Recall from Chapter 5 how generic strategies were typically different depending on the stage of the industry life cycle. Product innovations tend to be more radical and are more common during the earlier stages of an industry's life cycle. As an industry matures, there are fewer opportunities for newness, so the innovations tend to be more incremental. Product innovations are also commonly associated with a differentiation strategy. Firms that differentiate by providing customers new products or services that offer unique features or quality enhancements often engage in product innovation.

Process innovation, by contrast, is typically associated with improving the efficiency of an organizational process, especially manufacturing systems and operations. By drawing on new technologies and an organization's accumulated experience (Chapter 5), firms can often improve materials utilization, shorten cycle time, and increase quality. Process innovations are more likely to occur in the later stages of an industry's life cycle as companies seek ways to remain viable in markets where demand has flattened out and competition

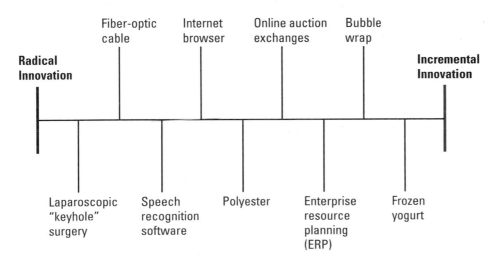

Exhibit 12.1 Continuum of Radical and Incremental Innovations

is more intense. As a result, process innovations are often associated with overall cost leader strategies, because the aim of many process improvements is to lower the costs of operations.

As you can see from this discussion of different types of innovation, the innovation process itself has numerous strategic implications. Innovation is a force in both the external environment (technology, competition) and also a factor affecting a firm's internal choices (generic strategy, value-adding activities). Nevertheless, innovation can be quite difficult for some firms to manage, especially those that have become comfortable with the status quo. Next, we turn to the challenges associated with successful innovation.

Challenges of Innovation

Innovation is essential to sustaining competitive advantages. Recall from Chapter 3 that one of the four elements of the Balanced Scorecard is the innovation and learning perspective. The extent and success of a company's innovation efforts are indicators of its overall performance. As management guru Peter Drucker warned, "An established company which, in an age demanding innovation, is not capable of innovation is doomed to decline and extinction."[7] To put it simply, in today's competitive environment, most firms have only one choice: "Innovate or die."

As with change, however, firms are often resistant to innovation. Only those companies that actively pursue innovation, even though it is often difficult and uncertain, will get a payoff from their innovation efforts. But managing innovation is challenging. As former Pfizer chairman and CEO William Steere puts it: "In some ways, managing innovation is analogous to breaking in a spirited horse. You are never sure of success until you achieve your goal. In the meantime, everyone takes a few lumps."[8]

What is it that makes innovation so difficult? Clearly the uncertainty about outcomes is one factor. Companies that keep an eye on their bottom line (and most of them do!) are often reluctant to invest time and resources into activities with an unknown future. Another factor is that the innovation process involves so many choices. These choices present five dilemmas that companies must wrestle with when pursuing innovation.[9]

- ◆ **Seeds versus Weeds.** Most companies have an abundance of innovative ideas. They must decide which of these is most likely to bear fruit—the "Seeds"—and which should be cast aside—the "Weeds." This is an ongoing dilemma that is often complicated by the fact that some innovation projects require a considerable level of investment before a firm can fully evaluate whether they are worth pursuing. As a result, firms need a mechanism with which they can choose among various innovation projects.
- ◆ **Experience versus Initiative.** Companies must decide who will lead an innovation project. Senior managers may have experience and credibility but tend to be more risk averse. Midlevel employees, who may be the innovators themselves, may have more enthusiasm because they can see firsthand how an innovation would address specific problems. As a result, firms need to support and reward organizational members who bring new ideas to light.
- ◆ **Internal versus External Staffing.** Innovation projects need competent staffs to succeed. People drawn from inside the company may have greater social capital and know the organization's culture and routines. But this knowledge may actually inhibit them from thinking outside the box. Staffing innovation projects with external personnel requires that project managers justify the hiring and spend time recruiting, training, and relationship building. As a result, firms need to streamline and support the process of staffing innovation efforts.

◆ ***Building Capabilities versus Collaborating.*** Innovation projects often require new sets of skills. Firms can seek help from other departments and/or partner with other companies that bring resources and experience as well as share costs of development. However, such arrangements can create dependencies and inhibit internal skills development. Further, struggles over who contributed the most or how the benefits of the project are to be allocated may arise. As a result, firms need a mechanism for forging links with outside parties to the innovation process.

◆ ***Incremental versus Preemptive Launch.*** Companies must manage the timing and scale of new innovation projects. An incremental launch is less risky because it requires fewer resources and serves as a market test. But a launch that is too tentative can undermine the project's credibility. It also opens the door for a competitive response. A large-scale launch requires more resources, but it can effectively preempt a competitive response. As a result, firms need to make funding and management arrangements that allow for projects to hit the ground running and be responsive to market feedback.

These dilemmas highlight why the innovation process can be daunting even for highly successful firms. How can companies successfully address these problems? Next, we consider three steps that firms can take to address the innovation challenge.[10]

Defining the Scope of Innovation

Firms must have a means to focus their innovation efforts. By defining the "strategic envelope," that is, the scope of a firm's innovation efforts, firms ensure that their innovation efforts are not wasted on projects that are highly uncertain or outside the firm's domain of interest. Strategic enveloping defines the range of acceptable projects. As Alistair Corbett, an innovation expert who directs the Toronto office of the global consulting firm Bain & Company, recently said, "One man's radical innovation is another man's incremental innovation."[11] Thus, a strategic envelope creates a firm-specific view of innovation that defines how a firm can create new knowledge and learn from an innovation initiative even if the project fails. Although such limitations might seem overly constraining, they also give direction to a firm's innovation efforts, which helps separate seeds from weeds and build internal capabilities.

One way to determine which projects to work on is to focus on a common technology. Then, innovation efforts across the firm can aim at developing skills and expertise in a given technical area. Another potential focus is on a market theme. Consider how DuPont responded to a growing concern for environmentally sensitive products:

> In the early 1990s, DuPont sought to use its knowledge of plastics to identify products to meet a growing market demand for biodegradable products. Over the next decade, it conducted numerous experiments with a biodegradable polyester resin it named Biomax. By trying different applications and formulations demanded by potential customers, the company was finally able to create a product that could be produced economically and had market appeal. Recently, Biomax was certified biodegradable and compostable by the Biodegradable Products Institute, an endorsement that should further boost sales.[12]

In defining a strategic envelope, companies must be clear not only about the kinds of innovation they are looking for but also the expected results. Therefore, each company needs to develop a set of questions to ask itself about its innovation efforts:

◆ How much will the innovation initiative cost?

◆ How likely is it to actually become commercially viable?

◆ How much value will it add; that is, what will it be worth if it works?

◆ What will be learned if it does not pan out?

In other words, however a firm envisions its innovation goals, it needs to develop a systematic approach to evaluating its results and learning from its innovation initiatives. Viewing innovation from this perspective helps firms manage the process.

Managing the Pace of Innovation

Along with clarifying the scope of an innovation by defining a strategic envelope, firms also need to regulate the pace of innovation. An advantage of assessing the extent to which an innovation is radical or incremental is that it helps determine how long it will take for an innovation initiative to realistically come to fruition. The project time line of an incremental innovation may be six months to two years, whereas a more radical innovation is typically long term—10 years or more.[13] Thus, radical innovations often begin with a long period of exploration in which experimentation makes strict timelines unrealistic. In contrast, firms that are innovating incrementally in order to exploit a window of opportunity may use a milestone approach that is more stringently driven by goals and deadlines. As suggested in Chapter 9, this kind of sensitivity to realistic time frames helps companies separate dilemmas temporally so they are easier to manage.

The idea of time pacing can also be a source of competitive advantage, because it helps a company manage transitions and develop an internal rhythm.[14] In their book *Competing on the Edge,* Shona Brown and Kathleen Eisenhardt contrasted time pacing with event pacing. They argue that, by controlling the pace of the innovation process (time pacing), a company can more effectively learn from it and grow internally. In contrast, when outside events, such as shifts in technology or the actions of competitors, determine the pace of innovation (event pacing), then firms lose their ability to manage the change process. Time pacing does not mean the company ignores the demands of market timing. Instead, it means that companies have a sense of their own internal clock in a way that allows them to thwart competitors by controlling the innovation process.

Not all innovation lends itself to speedy development, however. Radical innovation often involves open-ended experimentation and time-consuming mistakes. Further, the creative aspects of innovation are often difficult to time. When software maker Intuit's new CEO, Steve Bennett, began to turn around that troubled business, he required every department to implement Six Sigma, a quality control management technique that focuses on being responsive to customer needs. Everybody, that is, but the techies.

> "We're not GE, we're not a company where Jack says 'Do it,' and everyone salutes," says Bill Hensler, Intuit's vice president for process excellence. That's because software development, according to many, is more of an art than a science. At the Six Sigma Academy, president of operations Phil Samuel says even companies that have embraced Six Sigma across every other aspect of their organization usually maintain a hands-off policy when it comes to software developers. Techies, it turns out, like to go at their own pace.[15]

The example of software developers makes an important point about strategic pacing: some projects can't be rushed. Companies that hurry up their research efforts or go to market before they are ready can damage their ability to innovate—and their reputation. Thus, managing the pace of innovation can be an important factor in long-term success.

Collaborating with Innovation Partners

Innovation involves gathering new knowledge and learning from one's mistakes. It is rare for any one work group or department to have all the information it needs to carry an innovation from concept to commercialization. Even a company that is highly competent with its current operations usually needs new capabilities to achieve new results. Innovation partners can provide the skills and insights that are often needed to make innovation projects succeed.

Partners can come from several sources:

◆   Other personnel within the department.
◆   Personnel within the firm but from another department.
◆   Partners outside the firm.

Innovation partners may also come from nonbusiness sources, including research universities and the federal government. Each year the federal government issues requests for proposals (RFPs) asking private companies for assistance in improving services or finding solutions to public problems. Universities are another type of innovation partner. Chipmaker Intel, for example, has benefited from underwriting substantial amounts of university research. Rather than hand universities a blank check, Intel bargains for rights to patents that emerge from Intel-sponsored research. The university retains ownership of the patent, but Intel gets royalty-free use of it.[16]

Strategic partnering has other benefits as well. It requires firms to identify their strengths and weaknesses and make choices about which capabilities to leverage, which need further development, and which are outside the firm's current or projected scope of operations. Such knowledge can bring a level of realism to the process. It also helps managers get clear about what they need partners to do.

Consider the example of Nextel in its decision to partner with RadioFrame Networks, a Seattle-based start-up.

> RadioFrame had developed an innovative radio transmitter that could be used inside buildings to make cell-phone signals clearer. Nextel, which did not have as much network capacity as some of its larger competitors, saw this as a way to increase bandwidth and add value to its existing set of services. Not only did the two firms form a partnership, but Nextel also became involved in the development process by providing senior engineers and funding to help build the system. "We really worked hand-in-hand with Nextel," says RadioFrame CEO Jeff Brown, "from user requirements to how to physically get the finished product into their distribution systems."[17]

Firms need a mechanism to help decide whom to partner with. Several factors will enter into the decision, including the issues mentioned above regarding the pace and scope of innovation initiatives. To choose partners, firms need to ask what competencies they are looking for and what the innovation partner will contribute. These contributions might include knowledge of markets, technology expertise, or contacts with key players in an industry. Innovation partnerships also typically need to specify how the rewards of the innovation will be shared and who will own the intellectual property that is developed.

Innovation efforts that involve multiple partners and the speed and ease with which partners can network and collaborate are changing the way innovation is conducted. These changes have prompted one Harvard University professor to claim that the innovation process itself has experienced a paradigm shift. Strategy Spotlight 12.2 emphasizes the role of collaboration and partnerships in a new approach to innovation labeled "open innovation."

As this section indicates, managing innovation is an important and challenging organizational activity. For it to be successful, the innovation process has to stay focused on its ultimate purpose—to introduce new products and/or deploy new processes that build competitive advantages and make the company profitable. Innovation involves a company-wide commitment because the results of innovation affect every part of the organization. Innovation also requires an entrepreneurial spirit and skill set to be effective. One of the most important ways that companies improve and grow is when innovation is put to the task of creating new corporate ventures. It is that topic that we turn to next.

Open Innovation: A Better Way to Build Value?

Recall from Chapter 8 the example of InnoCentive, the Internet-based collaboration platform launched by Eli Lilly to provide an open source, virtual R&D community to solve complex scientific problems. Not only is InnoCentive a savvy application of digital technology, it is also an example of what Harvard business professor Henry Chesbrough calls "open innovation." The concept of open innovation builds on two other concepts seen in previous chapters—the importance of intellectual assets in today's economy (Chapter 4) and the use of boundaryless organizational arrangements to achieve strategic ends (Chapter 10).

Chesbrough claims that the open innovation model will become increasingly important in the future. His argument is as follows: innovation teams and R&D departments have acted with a fairly traditional mind-set for years about how to profit from innovation initiatives. The old mind-set, however, has created a paradox—in an era when ideas and knowledge abound, innovation and industrial research seem less effective. The old way of innovating no longer seems to be bearing fruit, because new technologies and the speed of innovation are creating new demands on companies to look beyond their traditional boundaries and share their intellectual property (IP). The innovation process itself, according to Chesbrough, needs innovating.

The old approach to innovation, labeled "closed innovation," operates on several key assumptions:

1. The smart people in our field work for us.
2. We should control the IP developed by our smart people so that competitors don't profit from our ideas.
3. To profit from R&D and innovation, we have to discover it, develop it, and ship it ourselves.

Source: H. Chesbrough. *Open Innovation: The New Imperative for Creating and Profiting from Technology* (Boston: Harvard Business School Press, 2003).

4. If we discover it first, we will get it to market first.
5. If we get it to market first, we win.

In contrast, Chesbrough argues, the open way to successfully innovate involves collaborating and drawing on the knowledge and resources of competitors and other strategic partners. In other words, disclose your intellectual property, cross organizational boundaries to achieve innovation goals, and let others share in the wealth. Here are the contrasting assumptions that are central to open innovation:

1. Not all the smart people work for us. Some of the smart people that we need to work with work somewhere else.
2. We should profit when others use our IP and be willing to buy their IP if it advances our innovation business model.
3. Internal R&D is not the only way to add value; external R&D can also benefit us.
4. We don't have to originate the research to profit from it.
5. Building a smarter innovation business model is better than getting to market first.

In his book, Chesbrough describes how innovation leader IBM, once an exemplar of the closed innovation approach, has transformed itself by being willing to cross boundaries and share its IP with others. He also describes how companies such as Cisco and Intel have succeeded by using an open approach while their rivals Lucent and Xerox have struggled. It remains to be seen whether other companies will adopt open innovation, but Chesbrough is convinced that the ones that are willing to seize this new approach will be the long-term winners.

Corporate Entrepreneurship

Corporate entrepreneurship (CE) has two primary aims: the pursuit of new venture opportunities and strategic renewal.[18] The innovation process keeps firms alert by exposing them to new technologies, making them aware of marketplace trends, and helping them evaluate new possibilities. Corporate entrepreneurship uses the fruits of the innovation process to help firms build new sources of competitive advantage and renew their value propositions. Just as the innovation process helps firms to make positive improvements, corporate entrepreneurship helps firms identify opportunities and launch new ventures. In Chapter 6 we addressed corporate growth through mergers and acquisitions as well as through joint ventures and strategic alliances. Here the focus is on internal venture development and growth.

Corporate new venture creation was labeled "intrapreneuring" by Gifford Pinchot because it refers to building entrepreneurial businesses within existing corporations.[19] However, to engage in corporate entrepreneurship that yields above-average returns and contributes to sustainable advantages, it must be done effectively. In this section we will examine the sources of entrepreneurial activity within established firms and the methods large corporations use to stimulate entrepreneurial behavior.

In a typical corporation, what determines how entrepreneurial projects will be pursued? That depends on many factors, including:

- Corporate culture.
- Leadership.
- Structural features that guide and constrain action.
- Organizational systems that foster learning and manage rewards.

In other words, all of the factors that influence the strategy implementation process will also shape how corporations engage in internal venturing.

Other factors will also affect how entrepreneurial ventures will be pursued.

- The use of teams in strategic decision making.
- Whether the company is product or service oriented.
- Whether its innovation efforts are aimed at product or process improvements.
- The extent to which it is high-tech or low-tech.

Because these factors are different in every organization, some companies may be more involved than others in identifying and developing new venture opportunities. These factors will also influence the nature of the CE process. Two distinct approaches to corporate venturing are found among firms that pursue entrepreneurial aims. The first is *focused* corporate venturing, in which CE activities are isolated from a firm's existing operations and worked on by independent work units. The second approach to CE is *dispersed*, in which all parts of the organization and every organization member are engaged in intrapreneurial activities. In the next two sections, we will address these approaches and provide examples of each.

Focused Approaches to Corporate Entrepreneurship

Firms using a focused approach typically separate the corporate venturing activity from the other ongoing operations of the firm. That is, corporate entrepreneurship is usually the domain of autonomous work groups that pursue entrepreneurial aims independent of the rest of the firm. The advantage of this approach is that it frees entrepreneurial team members to think and act without the constraints imposed by existing organizational norms and routines. This independence is often necessary for the kind of open-minded creativity that leads to strategic breakthroughs. The disadvantage is that, because of their isolation from the corporate mainstream, the work groups that concentrate on internal ventures may fail to obtain the resources or support needed to carry an entrepreneurial project through to completion. Two forms—new venture groups (NVGs) and business incubators—are among the most common types of focused approaches.

New Venture Groups (NVGs)   Corporations often form new venture groups whose goal is to identify, evaluate, and cultivate venture opportunities. These groups typically function as semi-autonomous units with little formal structure. The new venture group may simply be a committee that reports to the president on potential new ventures.

Or it may be organized as a corporate division with its own staff and budget. The aims of the new venture group may be open-ended in terms of what ventures it may consider. Alternatively, some corporations use them to promote concentrated effort on a specific problem. In both cases, they usually have a substantial amount of freedom to take risks and a supply of resources to do it with.[20]

New venture groups usually have a larger mandate than a typical R&D department. That is, their involvement extends beyond innovation and experimentation to coordinating with other corporate divisions, identifying potential venture partners, gathering resources, and, in some cases, actually launching the venture.

Nortel Networks, a global producer of telecom equipment, provides an example of how the NVG of a major corporation successfully launches new ventures.[21] Responsibility for its venturing activities lies with a senior vice president who oversees corporate strategy, alliances, and venturing—including the company's NVG. Company employees submit ideas through a company intranet. Once the NVG decides to pursue an opportunity, two teams are set up—an opportunity team, which investigates the marketability of the venture concept, and a commercialization team, which manages venture investments and value development. Nortel's NVG is only interested in ventures that are likely to become stand-alone businesses, not extensions of current product lines. As a result, governance of new ventures usually includes outside board members and external investors who can be involved in managing the venture once it is spun off. Recently, Nortel used this process to create a spin-off called NetActive, which offers digital rights management (DRM) technology used to protect Internet-based content.

Firms that want to expand by way of new venture start-ups usually acquire existing ventures, as discussed in Chapter 6, or develop ventures internally. Strategy Spotlight 12.3 describes a third alternative for firms that want to be entrepreneurial but still maintain their autonomy: corporate venture funding.

Business Incubators   The term *incubator* was originally used to describe a device in which eggs are hatched. Business incubators are designed to "hatch" new businesses. They are a type of corporate new venture group with a somewhat more specialized purpose—to support and nurture fledgling entrepreneurial ventures until they can thrive on their own as stand-alone businesses. Corporations often use incubators as a way to grow businesses identified by the new venture group. Although they often receive support from many parts of the corporation, they still operate independently until they are strong enough to go it alone. Then, depending on the type of business, they are either integrated into an existing corporate division or continue to operate as a subsidiary of the parent firm. Additionally, the type of corporate venturing support reported in Strategy Spotlight 12.3 that external new ventures receive may also include allowing a young venture into the corporation's incubator.

Incubators are sometimes found outside the domain of corporate entrepreneurship (see Chapter 13). However, a company-sponsored incubator often has advantages because of the experience and resources that the parent corporation can provide. Incubators typically provide some or all of the following five functions.[22]

♦   ***Funding.*** Usually includes capital investments but may also include in-kind investments and loans.

♦   ***Physical space.*** A common problem for new ventures; incubators in which several start-ups share space often provide fertile ground for new ideas and collaboration.

♦   ***Business services.*** Along with office space, young ventures need basic services and infrastructure; may include anything from phone systems and computer networks to public relations and personnel management.

strategy spotlight

Corporate Venture Capital

What does a company do when it wants to enjoy the benefits of an entrepreneurial start-up but does not want to acquire a venture or take time to develop one internally? It finances one by providing venture capital.

Since the 1970s, major U.S. corporations such as Exxon Mobil have invested in externally generated business ideas in order to strengthen their innovation profile. Some firms invest in technologies that are similar to their core business or provide potential future synergies. Intel, for example, has invested in several e-business start-ups that are in a position to increase demand for Intel processors. With the high growth potential of industries such as information technology and biotechnology, the level of corporate venture capital is increasing. Between 1998 and 1999, corporate venture unit investments jumped by a factor of five, from $1.4 billion to $7.8 billion. In 2000 alone, corporations worldwide invested nearly $17 billion in venture capital.

Several major corporations have launched venture financing efforts. In Germany alone there are over 20 corporate venture funds, including global players Siemens, Bertelsmann, and Deutsche Telekom. Even utilities are investing in emerging companies. AEP, a major U.S. electric power company, recently invested in PHPK, a cryogenics firm based in Columbus, Ohio. PHPK is poised to provide support of superconductivity applications, a rapidly growing energy niche that is seeking innovations. AEP prefers expansion-stage firms that need capital and guidance rather than earlier-stage firms. And AEP invests only in energy-related companies. PHPK has nearly doubled its business since AEP made its investment, which served as an immediate endorsement of PHPK's technology and capabilities.

The result? Intel, for one, has enjoyed tremendous returns. It has a portfolio of businesses worth $8 billion. But Intel's goal is not just to make money—it is looking for ways to cement ties early with promising start-ups. "Companies have discovered that it's a good way to do market development," according to Les Vadasz, head of Intel's venture program. "I do see it as a competitive weapon."

Even so, corporate funding for external ventures dried up rapidly after the technology bubble burst in the early 2000s. In the first half of 2002, only $1.1 billion was invested, compared to $17 billion in 2000. Not only have new investments by corporations dropped dramatically, but also corporations such as Hewlett-Packard and Accenture have sold off large portions of their portfolios. Nevertheless, as a long-term strategy, corporate venture funding can benefit both new ventures and corporations and remains a viable alternative to internal corporate venturing.

Sources: T. Stein, "Rip Cord," *Red Herring,* November 28, 2002, www .redherring.com; E. Franzke, "Four Keys to Corporate Venturing Success," *European Venture Capital Journal,* June 1, 2001, pp. 36–37; J. Letzelter, "The New Venture Capitalists: Utilities Go Shopping for Deals," *Public Utilities Fortnightly,* December 2000, pp. 34–38; and J. Rabinovitz, "Venture Capital, Inc.," *Industry Standard,* April 17, 2000, pp. 88–90.

- ◆ *Mentoring.* Senior executives and skilled technical personnel often provide coaching and experience-based advice.
- ◆ *Networking.* Contact with other parts of the firm and external resources such as suppliers, industry experts, and potential customers facilitates problem solving and knowledge sharing.

As the above list suggests, business incubators provide a safe and supportive environment for corporate ventures. Nevertheless, the risk associated with launching ventures should not be overlooked. Companies have at times spent millions incubating new ideas with very little to show for it. Major corporations such as Lucent, British Airways, and Hewlett-Packard inactivated their incubators and scaled back new venture portfolios after experiencing major declines in value after the Internet bubble burst in the early 2000s.[23]

Thus, to encourage entrepreneurship, corporations sometimes need to do more than create independent work groups or venture incubators to generate new enterprises. In some firms, the entrepreneurial spirit is spread throughout the organization. It is this dispersed approach to corporate entrepreneurship that we turn to next.

Dispersed Approaches to Corporate Entrepreneurship

The second type of corporate entrepreneurship is dispersed. For some companies, a dedication to the principles and practices of entrepreneurship is spread throughout the organization. One advantage of this approach is that organizational members don't have to be reminded to think entrepreneurially or be willing to change. The ability to change is considered to be a core capability. Such corporations often have a reputation for being entrepreneurial. This leads to a second advantage: Because of this entrepreneurial reputation, stakeholders such as vendors, customers, or alliance partners can bring new ideas or venture opportunities to anyone in the organization and expect them to be well-received. Such opportunities make it possible for the firm to stay ahead of the competition. However, there are disadvantages as well. Firms that are overzealous about corporate entrepreneurship sometimes feel they must change for the sake of change, causing them to lose vital competencies or spend heavily on R&D and innovation to the detriment of the bottom line. Two related aspects of dispersed entrepreneurship include entrepreneurial cultures that have an overarching commitment to CE activities and the use of product champions in promoting entrepreneurial behaviors.

Entrepreneurial Culture   In some large corporations, the corporate culture embodies the spirit of entrepreneurship. A culture of entrepreneurship is one in which the search for venture opportunities permeates every part of the organization. Recall from Chapter 3 that the key to creating value successfully is viewing every value-chain activity as a source of competitive advantage. In a similar way, the effect of corporate entrepreneurship on a firm's strategic success is strongest when it animates all parts of an organization. It is found in companies where the strategic leaders and the culture together generate a strong impetus to innovate, take risks, and seek out new venture opportunities.

In companies with an entrepreneurial culture, everyone in the organization is attuned to opportunities to leverage the assets and capabilities of the corporation to help create new businesses. Many such firms use a top-down approach to stimulate entrepreneurial activity. That is, the top leaders of the organization support programs and incentives that foster a climate of entrepreneurship. Many of the best ideas for new corporate ventures, however, come from the bottom up. Here's what Martin Sorrell, CEO of the WPP Group, a London-based global communication services group, says about drawing on the talents of lower-level employees:

> The people at the so-called bottom of an organization know more about what's going on than the people at the top. The people in the trenches are the ones in the best position to make critical decisions. It's up to the leaders to give those people the freedom and the resources they need.[24]

Thus, an entrepreneurial culture is one in which change and renewal are on everybody's mind. Sony, 3M, Intel, and Cisco are among the corporations best known for their corporate venturing activities. Many fast-growing young corporations also attribute much of their success to an entrepreneurial culture. Virgin Group, the British conglomerate that began as Virgin Airlines under the leadership of Richard Branson, has spawned nearly 200 new businesses in its short history. Strategy Spotlight 12.4 describes a few of Virgin's start-up successes.

Product Champions   CE does not always involve making large investments in start-ups or establishing incubators to spawn new divisions. Often, innovative ideas emerge in the normal course of business and are brought forth and become part of the way of doing business. In many firms, especially small, informally run ones, this may happen organically through the energetic efforts of individuals with good ideas. Larger firms often have more

strategy spotlight

Growing New Ventures at Virgin Group

While most large companies have to work hard to stoke the fires of entrepreneurship, they burn with ferocious intensity at the Virgin Group. As a US$4.25 billion company that has created nearly 200 businesses, it stands as clear evidence that ideas, capital, and talent can flow as freely in big, far-flung organizations as they can among the start-ups of Silicon Valley.

The mix of businesses that Virgin has spawned is indicative of the fun-loving, eclectic culture that its chairman, Richard Branson, has developed. Branson and his deputies have worked hard to create a culture where employees speak up and share their ideas. There are no gleaming corporate headquarters or executive privileges, just a large house in London where meetings are held in a small room. "Rules and regulations are not our forte," Branson said. "Analyzing things to death is not our kind of thing."

There aren't even any job descriptions at Virgin, because they are thought to place too many limits on what people can do. Instead, senior executives work shoulder to shoulder with first-line employees. Branson believes that employees should be given top priority, and he has created a friendly, nonhierarchical, family-like environment in which people have fun and enjoy themselves. His advice to his employees reflects his personal philosophy: "Do things that you like. If your work and your hobby are the same, you will work long hours because you are motivated."

The result is that Virgin's businesses include entertainment megastores, cinemas, a fun-to-fly airline, an all-in-one consumer banking system, a hip radio station, and a passenger train service. Smaller ventures have also been launched by persistent employees with good ideas. A woman who believed the company's airline should offer passengers onboard massages camped on Branson's doorstep until she was allowed to give him a neck and shoulder rub. Now an in-flight massage is a valued perk in Virgin Atlantic's Upper Class. On another occasion, a soon-to-be-married flight attendant came up with the idea of offering an integrated bridal-planning service, everything from wedding apparel and catering to limousines and honeymoon reservations. She became the first CEO of Virgin Bride.

Sources: G. Hamel, "Bringing Silicon Valley Inside," *Harvard Business Review* 77, no. 5 (1999), pp. 71–84; M. F. R. Kets de Vries, "The Transformational Abilities of Virgin's Richard Branson and ABB's Percy Barnevik," *Organizational Dynamics* 26, no. 3 (1998), pp. 7–21.

formal efforts to encourage innovation among their employees. In both cases, it is often product champions who are needed to take charge of internally generated ventures. Product (or project) champions are those individuals working within a corporation who bring entrepreneurial ideas forward, identify what kind of market exists for the product or service, find resources to support the venture, and promote the venture concept to upper management.[25]

When lower-level employees identify a product idea or novel solution, they will take it to their supervisor or someone in authority. Similarly, a new idea that is generated in a technology lab may be introduced to others by its inventor. If the idea has merit, it gains support and builds momentum across the organization.[26] Thus, even though the corporation may not be looking for new ideas or have a program for cultivating internal ventures, the independent behaviors of a few organizational members can have important strategic consequences.

No matter how an entrepreneurial idea comes to light, however, a new venture concept must pass through two critical stages or it may never get off the ground: project definition and project impetus:

1. ***Project definition.*** A promising opportunity has to be justified in terms of its attractiveness in the marketplace and how well it fits with the corporation's other strategic objectives.
2. ***Project impetus.*** For a project to gain impetus, its strategic and economic impact must be supported by senior managers who have experience with similar projects. The project then becomes an embryonic business with its own organization and budget.

For a project to advance through these stages of definition and impetus, a product champion is often needed to generate support and encouragement. Champions are especially important during the time after a new project has been defined but before it gains momentum. They form a link between the definition and impetus stages of internal development, which they do by procuring resources and stimulating interest for the product among potential customers.[27] Often, they must work quietly and alone. Consider the example of Ken Kutaragi, the Sony engineer who championed the PlayStation.

> Even though Sony had made the processor that powered the first Nintendo video games, no one at Sony in the mid-1980s saw any future in such products. "It was a kind of snobbery," Kutaragi recalled. "For Sony people, the Nintendo product would have been very embarrassing to make because it was only a toy." But Kutaragi was convinced he could make a better product. He began working secretly on a video game. Kutaragi said, "I realized that if it was visible, it would be killed." He quietly began enlisting the support of senior executives, such as the head of R&D. He made a case that Sony could use his project to develop capabilities in digital technologies that would be important in the future. It was not until 1994, after years of "underground" development and quiet building of support, that Sony introduced the PlayStation. By the year 2000, Sony had sold 55 million of them, and Kutaragi became CEO of Sony Computer Entertainment.[28]

Thus, product champions play an important entrepreneurial role in a corporate setting by encouraging others to take a chance on promising new ideas.[29]

In some firms, the entrepreneurial spirit is so strong that they simultaneous pursue both focused and dispersed approaches to corporate entrepreneurship. Some of the most familiar CE firms are leading companies that create products nearly all consumers have used: Sony, Panasonic, Intel, and Microsoft. One of the most successful of these firms is Nokia. Strategy Spotlight 12.5 describes how both focused and dispersed practices at Nokia have led it to become one of the most admired and successful firms in the world.

Measuring the Success of Corporate Entrepreneurship Activities

At this point in the discussion it is reasonable to ask, Is corporate entrepreneurship successful? Corporate venturing, like the innovation process, usually requires a tremendous effort. Is it worth it? In this section we consider factors that corporations need to take into consideration when evaluating the success of CE programs. We also examine techniques that companies can use to limit the expense of venturing or to cut their losses when CE initiatives appear doomed.

Comparing Strategic and Financial CE Goals   Not all corporate venturing efforts are financially rewarding. Recall the example of NetActive, the Nortel Networks venture. The company was greeted with great enthusiasm once Nortel spun it off, and it attracted over $20 million in capital investment from the venture community. It also provided a technology that was highly demanded. But NetActive became . . . inactive. The company's website went dark, and it is reported to be for sale, a victim of the dot-com crash.[30] By most accounts, Nortel Networks did all the right things in developing NetActive in terms of establishing it as a stand-alone business and endowing it with assets and funding. But the business was a flop financially.

In terms of financial performance, slightly more than 50 percent of corporate venturing efforts reach profitability (measured by ROI) within six years of their launch.[31] If this were the only criterion for measuring success, it would seem to be a rather poor return. On the one hand, these results should be expected, because CE is more risky than other investments such as expanding ongoing operations. On the other hand, corporations expect a higher return from corporate venturing projects than from normal operations. Thus, in terms of the risk-return trade-off, it seems that CE often falls short of expectations.[32]

strategy spotlight

Nokia's Spirit of Corporate Entrepreneurship

When it comes to corporate entrepreneurship, Nokia is a company that does it all. It is totally committed to innovation, and that dedication can be seen across the entire organization as well as in each of its independent work teams. Nokia's entrepreneurial energies are both focused and dispersed.

It's Focused

Nokia's organizational structure is designed to foster entrepreneurship. It is organized into autonomous work units at 69 sites in 15 countries. Business units are flexible and small—no more than about 50 members each. Team members are encouraged to be creative and voice their opinion. And there are only three decision-making layers between the most junior engineers and the president of the company. "That's why freaky ideas from junior engineers can end up in a product rather quickly," says Lauri Rosendahl, Nokia's analyst at Deutsche Bank.

Nokia supports the various team efforts by providing cost-effective central services. Yet each unit operates as a profit center and has the authority to create its own business model and conduct its own R&D and marketing. "By allowing teams the space they need to dig deeper into their area of interest, we've enabled them to create a big business," says Matti Alahuhta, president of Nokia Mobile Phones (NMP). "People feel they can make a difference. And they need to have the power to make their ideas happen. We've created a small-company soul inside a big-company body."

In addition to independent work teams, Nokia also has a venture group, Innovent, that identifies and invests in early-stage entrepreneurs as well as an incubator, New Growth Businesses, that spawns new ventures that are aligned with Nokia's core business activities.

Sources: I. Wylie, "Calling for a Renewable Future," *Fast Company,* May 2003: 46–48; and P. Kaihla, "Nokia's Hit Factory," *Business 2.0,* August 2002, pp. 66–70; www.hoovers.com.

It's Dispersed

From the lunchroom to the boardroom, everyone is involved in the entrepreneurial process. It's built into the company culture. Nokia's employees have a reputation for being risk-taking rule-breakers, and the culture is one that welcomes mistakes. Yrjö Neuvo, who heads research and development at Nokia, encourages his staff to confront rather than shrink from making mistakes. "If you're not making them," says Nuevo, "you're not pushing the envelope hard enough." Nuevo is one of the executives who has created the entrepreneurial culture at Nokia: "We operate the way a great jazz band plays. There is a leader and each member is playing the same piece, but they can improvise on the theme. . . . This is how you get art. Our artists aren't just closing their eyes and waiting until the innovation comes. We are innovating all the time."

To get an idea of how thoroughly engaged Nokia is in the entrepreneurial process, consider the following. Nokia spends a whopping $3 billion a year on R&D and 40 percent of its 52,000 employees are involved in R&D. That means that just about anyone could champion a product improvement. And many do. Without consulting her boss, 24-year-old Lone Sørenson made a last-minute change to the Nokia 3310 phone when she added a program that allows users to send text messages in a chat room. Industry-changing innovations like hers and others, such as the internal antenna and user-changeable handset covers, are a big part of Nokia's success.

And what a success it has been. Nokia's record has been impressive in recent years. In 2003 it had more than $37 billion in annual sales across 130 countries. Its share of the mobile phone market is 38 percent worldwide, including a 50 percent share in Western Europe. It admits that some of its mistakes have been costly, and it knows that its run of good fortune may not last. But it has not dampened the entrepreneurial spirit that is alive and well at Nokia.

There are several other important criteria, however, for judging the success of a corporate venture initiative. In addition to financial goals, most CE programs have strategic goals. The strategic reasons for undertaking a corporate venture include strengthening competitive position, entering into new markets, expanding capabilities by learning and acquiring new knowledge, and building the corporation's base of resources and experience. Different corporations may emphasize some of these goals more than others, but in general three questions should be used to assess the effectiveness of a corporation's venturing initiatives:[33]

1. ***Are the products or services offered by the venture accepted in the marketplace?*** That is, is the venture considered to be a market success? If so, the financial returns are likely to be satisfactory. In addition, the venture may open doors into other markets and suggest avenues for other venture projects.

2. ***Are the contributions of the venture to the corporation's internal competencies and experience valuable?*** That is, does the venture add to the worth of the firm internally? If so, strategic goals such as leveraging existing assets, building new knowledge, and enhancing firm capabilities are likely to be met.

3. ***Is the venture able to sustain its basis of competitive advantage?*** That is, does the value proposition offered by the venture insulate it from competitive attack? If so, it is likely to place the corporation in a stronger position relative to competitors and provide a base from which to build other advantages.

As you can see these criteria include both strategic and financial goals of CE. Another way to evaluate a corporate venture is in terms of the four criteria from the Balanced Scorecard (Chapter 3). In a successful venture, not only are financial and market acceptance (customer) goals met, but also internal business and innovation and learning goals. Thus, when assessing the success of corporate venturing, it is important to look beyond simple financial returns and consider a well-rounded set of criteria.

Next, we revisit the concept of real options as a way to evaluate the progress of a venture development program and consider the role of "exit champions" in helping corporations to limit their exposure to venture projects that are unlikely to succeed.

Exit Champions   Although a culture of championing venture projects is advantageous for stimulating an ongoing stream of entrepreneurial initiatives, many—in fact, most—of the ideas will not work out. At some point in the process, a majority of initiatives will be abandoned. Sometimes, however, companies wait too long to terminate a new venture and do so only after large sums of resources are used up or, worse, result in a marketplace failure. Motorola's costly global satellite telecom project known as Iridium provides a useful illustration. Even though problems with the project were known during the lengthy development process, Motorola refused to pull the plug. Only after investing $5 billion and years of effort was the project abandoned.[34]

How can companies avoid these costly and discouraging defeats? One way is to support a key role in the CE process: "exit champions." In contrast to product champions and other entrepreneurial enthusiasts within the corporation, exit champions are willing to question the viability of a venture project.[35] By demanding hard evidence and challenging the belief system that is carrying an idea forward, exit champions hold the line on ventures that appear shaky.

Both product champions and exit champions must be willing to energetically stand up for what they believe. Both put their reputations on the line. But they also differ in important ways. Product champions deal in uncertainty and ambiguity. Exit champions reduce ambiguity by gathering hard data and developing a strong case for why a project should be killed. Product champions are often thought to be willing to violate procedures and operate outside normal channels. Exit champions, by contrast, often have to reinstate procedures and reassert the decision-making criteria that are supposed to guide venture decisions. Whereas product champions often emerge as heroes, exit champions run the risk of losing status by opposing popular projects.

Thus, the role of exit champion may seem unappealing. But it is one that could save a corporation both financially and in terms of its reputation in the marketplace. It is especially important because one measure of the success of a firm's CE efforts is the extent to which it knows when to cut its losses and move on.

Johnson Controls's Real Options Approach to Innovation

Wisconsin-based Johnson Controls has grown from a low-cost provider of automobile seats into a high-end manufacturer of instrument panels and cockpits. How has it done it?—by fostering a grassroots innovation campaign that taps the intellectual assets and market savvy of its skilled workforce. What makes Johnson's approach unique is its implicit use of a real options style of decision making to advance the innovation development process. Johnson options each new innovative idea by making a small investment in it. To decide whether to exercise an option, the idea must continue to prove itself at each stage of development. Here's how Jim Geschke, vice president and general manager of electronics integration at Johnson, describes the process:

> Think of Johnson as an innovation machine. The front end has a robust series of gates that each idea must pass through. Early on, we'll have many ideas and spend a lit-

tle money on each of them. As they get more fleshed out, the ideas go through a gate where a go or no–go decision is made. A lot of ideas get filtered out, so there are far fewer items, and the spending on each goes up. . . . Several months later each idea will face another gate. If it passes, that means it's a serious idea that we are going to develop. Then the spending goes way up, and the number of ideas goes way down.

> By the time you reach the final gate, you need to have a credible business case in order to be accepted. At a certain point in the development process, we take our idea to customers and ask them what they think. Sometimes they say, "That's a terrible idea. Forget it." Other times they say, "That's fabulous. I want a million of them."

The process of evaluating innovation ideas at each stage in the process allows Johnson to evaluate its options and reduce uncertainty. Winning ideas are separated from losers in a way that keeps investments low. This approach, using a real options type of logic, has helped Johnson increase revenues at a double-digit rate to $12 billion a year.

Sources: A. Slywotzky and R. Wise, "Double-Digit Growth in No-Growth Times," *Fast Company*, April 2003, pp. 66–72; www.hoovers.com; and www.johnsoncontrols.com.

Real Options Another way firms can minimize failure and avoid losses from pursuing faulty ideas is to apply the logic of real options (Chapter 6). Applied to entrepreneurship, real options suggest a path that corporations can use to manage the uncertainty associated with launching new ventures.

Options are created whenever a company begins to explore a new venture concept. That is, initial investments, such as conducting market tests, building prototypes, and forming venture teams, bestow an option to invest further. Retail giant Wal-Mart provides an interesting example of this limited approach. It's safe to say Wal-Mart could enter just about any market it wanted to in a big way. But its recent decision to enter the used-car business began with an experiment. Four dealerships were set up in the Houston, Texas, area under a brand called Price 1 Auto Stores. According to Ira Kalish, chief economist for Retail Forward, Inc., a consulting group that specializes in retailing, "Wal-Mart will seek to test the outer boundaries of what consumers are willing to let Wal-Mart be."[36]

With its four-store experiment, Wal-Mart is obtaining an option to invest more at a later date. The results of Wal-Mart's market test will be factored into the next round of decisions. This is consistent with the logic of real options—based on feedback at each stage of development, firms decide whether to exercise their options by making further investments. Alternatively, they may decide that the idea is not worth further consideration. In so doing, that is, by making smaller and more incremental investments, firms keep their total investment low and minimize downside risk. Often it's the job of an exit champion or some other practically minded organization member to decide that a project does not warrant further investment. Strategy Spotlight 12.6 describes the real options logic that Johnson Controls, a maker of car seats, instrument panels, and interior control systems, uses to advance or eliminate entrepreneurial ideas.

The types of venture projects and entrepreneurial initiatives that corporations pursue are more likely to succeed if their organizational members behave entrepreneurially. In the next section, we look at the practices and characteristics that are associated with an entrepreneurial orientation.

Entrepreneurial Orientation

Firms that want to engage in successful corporate entrepreneurship need to have an entrepreneurial orientation (EO). EO refers to the strategy-making practices that businesses use in identifying and launching corporate ventures. It represents a frame of mind and a perspective toward entrepreneurship that is reflected in a firm's ongoing processes and corporate culture.[37]

An entrepreneurial orientation has five dimensions that permeate the decision-making styles and practices of the firm's members. These are autonomy, innovativeness, proactiveness, competitive aggressiveness, and risk taking. These factors can work together to enhance a firm's entrepreneurial performance. But even those firms that are strong in only a few aspects of EO can be very successful.[38] Exhibit 12.2 summarizes the dimensions of an entrepreneurial orientation. Below we discuss the five dimensions of entrepreneurial orientation and how they have been used to enhance internal venture development.

Autonomy

Autonomy refers to a willingness to act independently in order to carry forward an entrepreneurial vision or opportunity. It applies to both individuals and teams that operate outside an organization's existing norms and strategies. In the context of corporate entrepre-

**Exhibit 12.2
Dimensions of
Entrepreneurial
Orientation**

Dimension	Definition
Autonomy	Independent action by an individual or team aimed at bringing forth a business concept or vision and carrying it through to completion.
Innovativeness	A willingness to introduce novelty through experimentation and creative processes aimed at developing new products and services as well as new processes.
Proactiveness	A forward-looking perspective characteristic of a marketplace leader that has the foresight to seize opportunities in anticipation of future demand.
Competitive aggressiveness	An intense effort to outperform industry rivals. It is characterized by a combative posture or an aggressive response aimed at improving position or overcoming a threat in a competitive marketplace.
Risk taking	Making decisions and taking action without certain knowledge of probable outcomes; some undertakings may also involve making substantial resource commitments in the process of venturing forward.

Source: J. G. Covin and D. P. Slevin, "A Conceptual Model of Entrepreneurship as Firm Behavior," *Entrepreneurship Theory & Practice,* Fall 1991, pp. 7–25; G. T. Lumpkin and G. G. Dess, "Clarifying the Entrepreneurial Orientation Construct and Linking It to Performance," *Academy of Management Review* 21, (1996), pp. 135–72; D. Miller, "The Correlates of Entrepreneurship in Three Types of Firms," *Management Science* 29 (1983), pp. 770–91.

neurship, autonomous work units are often used to leverage existing strengths in new arenas, identify opportunities that are beyond the organization's current capabilities, and encourage development of new ventures or improved business practices.[39]

The need for autonomy may apply to either dispersed or focused entrepreneurial efforts. Clearly, because of the emphasis on venture projects that are being developed outside of the normal flow of business, a focused approach suggests a working environment that is relatively autonomous. But autonomy may also be important in an organization where entrepreneurship is part of the corporate culture. Everything from the methods of group interaction to the firm's reward system must make organizational members feel as if they can think freely about venture opportunities, take time to investigate them, and act without fear of condemnation. This implies a respect for the autonomy of each individual and an openness to the independent thinking that goes into championing a corporate venture idea. Thus, autonomy represents a type of empowerment (see Chapter 11) that is directed at identifying and leveraging entrepreneurial opportunities.

Two techniques that organizations often use to promote autonomy include:

1. ***Using skunkworks to foster entrepreneurial thinking.*** To help managers and other employees set aside their usual routines and practices, companies often develop independent work units called "skunkworks" to encourage creative thinking and brainstorming about new venture ideas. The term is used to represent a work environment that is often physically separate from corporate headquarters and free of the normal job requirements and pressures. Nearly every major corporation that grows by means of entrepreneurship uses some form of skunkworks.[40] Consider, for example, Corning, Inc.

   In 1997 Corning, Inc., sold off the kitchenware division that had made Corning a household word. To revive Corning, CEO Roger Ackerman used several skunkworks-type meetings. He challenged his top technologists to "dive deep" and find a way to reposition Corning. They had evidence from the lab that they could increase the efficiency of their optical fibers. To do the work, they rented space away from Corning's headquarters, where the team would not be distracted. As a result, new products were developed in record time, and by 2000, 84 percent of the products Corning sold had been introduced in the last four years.[41]

2. ***Designing organization structures that support independent action.*** Sometimes corporations need to do more than create independent think tanks to help stimulate new ideas. Changes in organizational structure may also be necessary. Established firms with traditional structures often have to break out of such molds in order to remain competitive. This was the conclusion of Deloitte Consulting, a division of Deloitte Touche Tohmatsu, one of the world's largest accounting consultancies. After losing millions in e-business consulting jobs to young Internet consultancies, Deloitte decided to reorganize. The first step was to break the firm into small, autonomous groups called "chip-aways" that could operate with the speed and flexibility of a start-up. "This allows them to react more like a Navy SEAL team rather than an Army division," according to Tom Rodenhauser, author of *Inside Consulting*. One of Deloitte's first chip-aways was Roundarch, a Web technology and marketing venture that projected first-year revenues of $40 million and beat its own projections by 10 percent.[42] Other organization structures may also help promote autonomy, such as virtual organizations that allow people to work independently and communicate via the Web.

Creating autonomous work units and encouraging independent action may have pitfalls that can jeopardize their effectiveness. Autonomous teams, for example, often lack coordination. Excessive decentralization has a strong potential to create inefficiencies, such as duplication of effort and wasting of resources on projects with questionable feasibility.

For example, Chris Galvin, former CEO of Motorola, scrapped the skunkworks approach the company had been using to develop new wireless phones. Fifteen teams had created 128 different phones, which led to spiraling costs and overly complex operations.[43]

Thus, for autonomous work units and independent projects to be effective, such efforts have to be measured and monitored. This requires a delicate balance for corporations—having the patience and budget to tolerate the explorations of autonomous groups, and having the strength to cut back efforts that are not bearing fruit. It must be undertaken with a clear sense of purpose—namely, to generate new sources of competitive advantage.

Innovativeness

Innovativeness refers to a firm's efforts to find new opportunities and novel solutions. In the beginning of this chapter we discussed innovation; here the focus is on innovativeness, that is, a firm's attitude toward innovation and willingness to innovate. It involves creativity and experimentation that result in new products, new services, or improved technological processes. Innovativeness is one of the major components of an entrepreneurial strategy. As indicated at the beginning of the chapter, however, the job of managing innovativeness can be very challenging.

Innovativeness requires that firms depart from existing technologies and practices and venture beyond the current state of the art. Inventions and new ideas need to be nurtured even when their benefits are unclear. However, in today's climate of rapid change, effectively producing, assimilating, and exploiting innovations can be an important avenue for achieving competitive advantages.

As our earlier discussion of CE indicated, many corporations owe their success to an active program of innovation-based corporate venturing. Few, however, have a more exemplary reputation for effective entrepreneurship than 3M Co. (formerly Minnesota Mining & Manufacturing Co.). With its overarching philosophy of entrepreneurship, 3M is a strong example of how a corporate strategy can induce internal venture development. Every aspect of 3M's management approach is aimed at entrepreneurial development. Exhibit 12.3 describes the policies that create a climate of innovativeness at 3M.

Two of the methods companies can use to enhance their competitive position through innovativeness are:

1. *Fostering creativity and experimentation.* To innovate successfully, firms must break out of the molds that have shaped their thinking. They must also create avenues for employees to express themselves. Tim Warren, director of research and technical services at the oil giant Royal Dutch/Shell, was sure that Shell's employees had vast reserves of innovative talent that had not been tapped. He also felt that more radical innovations were needed for Shell to achieve its performance goals. So Warren allocated $20 million to be used for breakthrough ideas that would change the playing field. He also asked his people to devote up to 10 percent of their time to nonlinear thinking. The initiative became known as the "GameChanger." With the help of Strategos Consulting, the GameChanger review panel developed an Innovation Lab to help employees develop game-changing ideas. The first lab attracted 72 would-be entrepreneurs who learned how to uncover new opportunities and challenge industry conventions. By the end of the three-day lab, a portfolio of 240 ideas had been generated. The GameChanger process, which now provides funding of $100,000 to $600,000 within 10 days after approval, has now found a permanent home within Shell and has become a critical part of its internal entrepreneurial process.[44]

2. *Investing in new technology, R&D, and continuous improvement.* For successful innovation, companies must seek advantages from the latest technologies. This often

Exhibit 12.3
3M's Rules
for Fostering
Innovativeness

Rule	Implications
Don't kill a project.	Managers exhibit patience in nurturing projects. Ideas can be kept alive by individual staffers who believe in a project, even if it can't find a home in one of 3M's divisions.
Tolerate failure.	If at first you don't succeed, 3M believes that you should be able to try and try again. Thus, it encourages experimentation and risk taking on projects, even when the outcome is unclear. This strategy has helped 3M achieve one of its key objectives: obtain 25–30 percent of sales from products introduced in the past five years.
Keep divisions small.	Divisions are split up if they get too big, say, over $250 million in sales. 3M believes its divisions should be granted autonomy and that division managers should know staffers by their first names.
Motivate the champions.	Product champions are challenged to be innovative. When successful, they are rewarded with salaries and promotions. If a product takes off, a champion forms an action team and may get to run his or her own product group.
Stay close to customers.	Product development is not conducted in isolation. Customers are often invited to join 3M researchers and marketers to brainstorm about uses for a technology and new product concepts.
Share the wealth.	Divisions and product groups do not have an exclusive claim on the technologies they develop. An atmosphere of open communication helps everyone benefit from the technological insights and breakthroughs that others at 3M discover.

Sources: P. Lukas, "3M: The Magic of Mistakes," *Fortune,* April 18, 2003, www.fortune.com; J. C. Collins and J. I. Porras, *Built to Last* (New York: HarperBusiness, 1997); and R. Mitchell, "Masters of Innovation," *BusinessWeek,* April 10, 1989, pp. 58–63.

requires a substantial investment. Consider, for example, Dell Computer Corp.'s new production capability. With its new OptiPlex manufacturing system, Dell is attempting to revolutionize the way computers are made. Of course, it is still necessary to connect part A to part B, that is, to conduct the basic assembly process. But how those parts are received, handled, and turned into finished product is changing radically because of Dell's state-of-the-art automation techniques. The OptiPlex factory is managed by a network of computers that take in orders, communicate with suppliers, draw in components, organize the assembly process, and arrange shipping. The result: Hundreds of computers can be custom-built in an eight-hour shift, productivity per person is up 160 percent, and most parts are kept on hand for a mere two hours. Dell was already leading other major PC manufacturers by maintaining product inventories for only 5 or 6 days compared with the industry average of 50 to 90 days. With its latest innovation, Dell now expects to cut inventory turnover down to two-and-a-half days.[45]

Innovativeness can be a source of great progress and strong corporate growth, but there are also major pitfalls for firms that invest in innovation. Expenditures on R&D

aimed at identifying new products or processes can be a waste of resources if the effort does not yield results. Another danger is related to the competitive climate. Even if a company innovates a new capability or successfully applies a technological breakthrough, another company may develop a similar innovation or find a use for it that is more profitable. Finally, in many firms, R&D and other innovation efforts are among the first to be cut back during an economic downturn.

Therefore, even though innovativeness is an important means of internal corporate venturing, it also involves major risks because investments in innovations may not pay off. For strategic managers of entrepreneurial firms, however, successfully developing and adopting innovations can generate competitive advantages and provide a major source of growth for the firm.

Proactiveness

Proactiveness refers to a firm's efforts to seize new opportunities. Proactive organizations monitor trends, identify the future needs of existing customers, and anticipate changes in demand or emerging problems that can lead to new venture opportunities. Proactiveness involves not only recognizing changes but being willing to act on those insights ahead of the competition. Strategic managers who practice proactiveness have their eye on the future in a search for new possibilities for growth and development.

Such a forward-looking perspective is important for companies that seek to be industry leaders. Many proactive firms seek out ways not only to be future oriented but also to change the very nature of competition in their industry. From its beginning, Dell sold personal computers directly to consumers, diminishing the role of retail stores as a way to reach customers. Its success changed the way PCs were sold.[46]

Proactiveness is especially effective at creating competitive advantages, because it puts competitors in the position of having to respond to successful initiatives. The benefit gained by firms that are the first to enter new markets, establish brand identity, implement administrative techniques, or adopt new operating technologies in an industry is called first mover advantage.[47]

First movers usually have several advantages. First, industry pioneers, especially in new industries, often capture unusually high profits because there are no competitors to drive prices down. Second, first movers that establish brand recognition are usually able to retain their image and hold on to the market share gains they earned by being first. Sometimes these benefits also accrue to other early movers in an industry, but, generally speaking, first movers have an advantage that can be sustained until firms enter the maturity phase of an industry's life cycle.[48]

First movers are not always successful. For one thing, the customers of companies that introduce novel products or embrace breakthrough technologies may be reluctant to commit to a new way of doing things. In his book *Crossing the Chasm,* Geoffrey A. Moore noted that most firms seek evolution, not revolution, in their operations. This makes it difficult for a first mover to sell promising new technologies.[49] Second, some companies try to be a first mover before they are ready. Consider Apple Computer's Newton.

Newton, the first personal digital assistant (PDA), was released in 1993. Because it was revolutionary, it generated a great deal of media attention and initial sales success. But the Newton was troubled from the beginning because it was launched before it was ready. For too many customers, it could not do what it claimed: recognize handwriting. But Apple was desperate to launch ahead of Microsoft. "We cut corners and ignored problems . . . to gain an edge in a reckless public relations battle," said Larry Tesler, who headed the Newton group until a few months before its release. In 1998, after five years of trying to recover from its initial failure, the Newton project was killed.[50]

Even with these caveats, however, companies that are first movers can enhance their competitive position. Firms can use two other methods to act proactively.

1. ***Introducing new products or technological capabilities ahead of the competition.*** Maintaining a high level of proactiveness is central to the corporate culture of some major corporations. Sony's mission statement asserts, for example, "We should always be the pioneers with our products—out front leading the market. We believe in leading the public with new products rather than asking them what kind of products they want."[51] Sony has launched numerous new products that have not only succeeded financially but have changed the competitive landscape. Walkman, PlayStation, Betacam, and Vaio laptop computers are just a few of the many leading products that Sony has introduced.

2. ***Continuously seeking out new product or service offerings.*** Firms that provide new resources or sources of supply can benefit from a proactive stance. Aerie Networks is a Denver company that aspires to expand the U.S. fiber-optic network extensively. Two factors make its efforts especially proactive. First, it is laying cable that contains 432 fibers (compared with the 96 strands that established companies like AT&T typically install). This approach fits Aerie's goal of being the low-cost wholesaler of bandwidth to long-distance carriers and other fiber users. Second, it worked for over a year to form an alliance with gas pipeline rivals that made it possible to use up to 25,000 miles of pipeline rights-of-way across 26 states. The partnering was more difficult than the technology—Aerie had to give a 30 percent stake to the gas pipeline companies—but the potential payoff is enormous.[52]

Being an industry leader does not always lead to competitive advantages. Some firms that have launched pioneering new products or staked their reputation on new brands have failed to get the hoped-for payoff. Two major entertainment companies—NBC and Disney—that made large investments in promising Internet ventures had to pull back after suffering millions of dollars in losses. Disney spent an estimated $2.5 billion to create a major portal called the Go Network (Go.com) but abandoned its portal plans when it started losing $250 million per quarter. NBC Internet (NBCi), with the support of its parent company, General Electric, was an early mover in acquiring assets and leading other media companies into the Internet age. But its venture never got off the ground and it was postponed indefinitely.[53]

Thus, careful monitoring and scanning of the environment, as well as extensive feasibility research, are needed for a proactive strategy to lead to competitive advantages. Firms that do it well usually have substantial growth and internal development to show for it. Many of them have been able to sustain the advantages of proactiveness for years.

Competitive Aggressiveness

Competitive aggressiveness refers to a firm's efforts to outperform its industry rivals. Companies with an aggressive orientation are willing to "do battle" with competitors. They might slash prices and sacrifice profitability to gain market share, or spend aggressively to obtain manufacturing capacity. As an avenue of firm development and growth, competitive aggressiveness may involve being very assertive in leveraging the results of other entrepreneurial activities such as innovativeness or proactiveness.

Unlike innovativeness and proactiveness, however, which tend to focus on market opportunities, competitive aggressiveness is directed toward competitors. The SWOT (strengths, weaknesses, opportunities, threats) analysis discussed in Chapters 2 and 3 provides a useful way to distinguish between these different approaches to corporate entrepreneurship. Proactiveness, as we saw in the last section, is a response to opportunities—

the O in SWOT. Competitive aggressiveness, by contrast, is a response to threats—the T in SWOT. A competitively aggressive posture is important for firms that seek to enter new markets in the face of intense rivalry.

Strategic managers can use competitive aggressiveness to combat industry trends that threaten their survival or market position. Sometimes firms need to be forceful in defending the competitive position that has made them an industry leader. Firms often need to be aggressive to ensure their advantage by capitalizing on new technologies or serving new market needs.

Two of the ways competitively aggressive firms enhance their entrepreneurial position are:

1. ***Entering markets with drastically lower prices.*** Smaller firms often fear the entry of resource-rich large firms into their marketplace. Because the larger firms usually have deep pockets, they can afford to cut prices without being seriously damaged by an extended period of narrow margins. In the mid-1990s, the retail record store business was nearly wiped out when larger new entrants launched a price war. It started when Best Buy, a "big box" electronics retailer with hundreds of stores, was looking for a way to increase traffic in its large suburban stores. It decided to sell compact disks (CDs). Most record stores were paying about $10 at wholesale for CDs and selling them for $14 or more. Best Buy priced new releases at $9.98. Soon, archrival Circuit City also started retailing CDs and a major price war followed. Within two years, seven record stores declared bankruptcy. The Best Buy executive who championed the CD policy said, "The whole goal of getting into business is taking market share and building your business. That's what it's about."[54]

2. ***Copying the business practices or techniques of successful competitors.*** We've all heard that imitation is the highest form of flattery. But imitation may also be used to take business from competitors; as long as the idea or practice is not protected by intellectual property laws, it's not illegal. This was the conclusion of Chris Bogan, CEO of Best Practices, LLC, a North Carolina consulting group with $8 million in revenues. Best Practices seeks out best practices in order to repackage and resell them or use them internally. Its mission is to find superstar performers in the business world and then sell their secrets to others. Best Practices's revenues come from one-time consulting projects and products like databases and benchmarking reports on subjects such as managing call centers and launching new products. Bogan's philosophy is that companies don't have to invent solutions to their problems; they can "steal" them from successful companies.[55]

Another practice companies use to overcome the competition is to make preannouncements of new products or technologies. This type of signaling is aimed not only at potential customers but at competitors, to see how they will react or to discourage them from launching similar initiatives. Sometimes the preannouncements are made just to scare off competitors, an action that has potential ethical implications. Strategy Spotlight 12.7 describes how the problem has affected the software industry.

Competitive aggressiveness may not always lead to competitive advantages. Some companies (or their CEOs) have severely damaged their reputations by being overly aggressive. Microsoft is a good example. Although it continues to be a dominant player, its highly aggressive profile makes it the subject of scorn by some businesses and individuals. Microsoft's image also contributed to the huge antitrust suit brought against it by the U.S. government and several states. Efforts to find viable replacements for the Microsoft products upon which users have become overly dependent may eventually erode Microsoft's leading role as a software provider.

strategy spotlight

Vaporware: Unethical or Just Good Business?

In the fast-moving, competitive world of software development, timing is nearly everything. New products are launched continually and, because some products represent original design concepts, first releases nearly always enjoy a sales spike. This is especially true for productivity software, operating system enhancements, and games. Because release dates are so important, some firms often preannounce the arrival of a new product, hoping that customers will wait until their version is ready. The problem is that sometimes all these companies have to offer is "vaporware."

Vaporware is defined as software announced long before its delivery. According to a survey of 100 information systems (IS) professionals conducted by *Computerworld*, a large majority believe that preannouncements of new software releases are useful for planning and decision making, but only if the announcements are made less than a year before the actual release. Some firms, however, preannounce products well before they are ready. For many, vaporware refers to products that are not available until long after the promised release date—if ever.

Sources: J. Schwarz, "The Dangers of Inhaling Vaporware," *New York Times*, July 6, 2003, www.nytimes.com; M. Berger, "Smooth Sailing for Microsoft's .Net?" *PCWorld.com*, May 4, 2000; www.pcworld.com; S. J. Johnston, "Vaporware Tactics Elicit Mixed Reviews," *Computerworld*, May 1, 1995; www.computerworld.com; and S. Rosenberg, "Microsoft's .Net: Visionary or Vaporware?" *Salon.com*, June 30, 2000, www.salon.com.

One of the biggest purveyors of vaporware is Microsoft. Of those surveyed, 74 percent agreed that Microsoft is the most aggressive preannouncer; 70 percent said they especially need this kind of information from Microsoft. Because Microsoft systems are in such widespread use, IS managers need advance notice for planning and development purposes.

More than two-thirds (68 percent) of the IS professionals also agreed that preannouncements by major vendors such as Microsoft can have a market-freezing effect on smaller competitors. For that reason, one of the issues facing Microsoft when it first went to court in 1995 was the extent to which it used vaporware to thwart the sales of competitors. U.S. District Judge Stanley Sporkin ruled that Microsoft had engaged in unfair practices. Microsoft claimed it was just good business.

Recently, Microsoft has been accused again of pushing vaporware with the introduction of its ".Net" initiative. The software giant appears to be trying to get the many parts of its company—platforms, infrastructure, operating systems, and services—to work together in a system that also integrates with the Internet. But the Gartner Group, an Internet business research firm, warned that .Net may be the latest in a series of Microsoft vaporware—promises of capabilities that are hoped for and envisioned but not yet practically available.

Therefore, competitive aggressiveness is a strategy that is best used in moderation. Companies that aggressively establish their competitive position and vigorously exploit opportunities to achieve profitability may, over the long run, be better able to sustain their competitive advantages if their goal is to defeat, rather than decimate, their competitors.

Risk Taking

Risk taking refers to a firm's willingness to seize a venture opportunity even though it does not know whether the venture will be successful—to act boldly without knowing the consequences. To be successful through corporate entrepreneurship, firms usually have to take on riskier alternatives, even if it means forgoing the methods or products that have worked in the past. To obtain high financial returns, firms take such risks as assuming high levels of debt, committing large amounts of firm resources, introducing new products into new markets, and investing in unexplored technologies.

In some ways, all of the approaches to internal development that we have discussed are potentially risky. Whether they are being aggressive, proactive, or innovative, firms on the path of corporate entrepreneurship must act without knowing how their actions will turn out. Before launching their strategies, corporate entrepreneurs must know their firm's appetite for risk. How far is it willing to go without knowing what the outcome will be?

Three types of risk that organizations and their executives face are business risk, financial risk, and personal risk:

- *Business risk taking* involves venturing into the unknown without knowing the probability of success. This is the risk associated with entering untested markets or committing to unproven technologies.
- *Financial risk taking* requires that a company borrow heavily or commit a large portion of its resources in order to grow. In this context, risk is used to refer to the risk/return trade-off that is familiar in financial analysis.
- *Personal risk taking* refers to the risks that an executive assumes in taking a stand in favor of a strategic course of action. Executives who take such risks stand to influence the course of their whole company, and their decisions can also have significant implications for their careers.

In many business situations, all three types of risk taking are present. Taking bold new actions rarely affects just one part of the organization. Consider the example of David D'Alessandro of John Hancock Financial Services, Inc.

David D'Alessandro joined insurance giant John Hancock in 1984 as its vice president of corporate communications. At the time, Hancock's image was weak due in part to a series of forgettable TV ads that failed to distinguish it from other insurance carriers. D'Alessandro championed a new advertising campaign that featured "real life" images, such as a husband and wife arguing, and a lesbian couple adopting a Vietnamese baby. Although it was costly to produce and risky for the image of the traditional insurance carrier, sales surged 17 percent in the first year of the ad campaign. The risk also paid off for D'Alessandro personally: In May 2000 he was named John Hancock's chairman.[56]

Even though risk taking involves taking chances, it is not gambling. The best-run companies investigate the consequences of various opportunities and create scenarios of likely outcomes. Their goal is to reduce the riskiness of business decision making. As we saw in the section on product champions, a key to managing entrepreneurial risks is to evaluate new venture opportunities thoroughly enough to reduce the uncertainty surrounding them.

Companies can use the following two methods to strengthen their competitive position through risk taking.

1. ***Researching and assessing risk factors to minimize uncertainty.*** Although all new business endeavors are inherently risky, firms that do their homework can usually reduce their risk. For example, Graybar Electric Co., a privately held 136-year-old provider of data and telecom equipment, had to revamp its warehouse and distribution system. The Internet was creating booming demand. But with 231 local distribution centers, each run independently, Graybar could not get its products to customers fast enough. After careful analysis, the company hatched a plan that consolidated 16 supply warehouses without displacing any local managers, thus preserving the quality of service for both customers and employees. The changeover was expensive: $144 million over four years. But the plan called for a payback after five years, and even with telecom sector sales slipping, Graybar's prudent risk taking led to a 21 percent surge in sales in 2000.[57]
2. ***Using techniques that have worked in other domains.*** Risky methods that other companies have applied successfully may be used to advance corporate ventures. Consider the actions of Autobytel.com, one of the first companies to sell cars online. Although it had enjoyed early success by being a first mover, it wanted to jump-start its sales. It decided to make a risky move. In a year when Autobytel.com earned only $6 million in revenues, it committed $1.2 million to a 30-second TV advertisement.

But that ad was run during the Super Bowl and Autobytel was the first dot-com ever to use that venue. The free publicity and favorable business press it received extended far beyond the 30 seconds that Autobytel's $1.2 million had bought it.[58]

Risk taking, by its nature, involves potential dangers and pitfalls. Only carefully managed risk is likely to lead to competitive advantages. Actions that are taken without sufficient forethought, research, and planning may prove to be very costly. The era of dot-com start-ups and subsequent failures proved that businesses are often launched—at great expense—without a clear sense of the long-term or even, in some cases, short-term consequences. When the Internet bubble burst, more than $3 trillion of investment wealth was wiped out of the U.S. stock markets, due in large part to the collapse of the dot-com surge.[59] Along with the financial losses, the business and personal losses were enormous.

Strategic managers must always remain mindful of potential risks. In his book *Innovation and Entrepreneurship,* Peter Drucker argued that successful entrepreneurs are typically not risk takers. Instead, they take steps to minimize risks by carefully understanding them. That is how they avoid focusing on risk and remain focused on opportunity.[60] Thus, risk taking is a good place to close this chapter on corporate entrepreneurship. Companies that choose to grow through internal corporate venturing must remember that entrepreneurship always involves embracing what is new and uncertain.

summary

To remain competitive in today's economy, established firms must find new avenues for development and growth. This chapter has addressed how innovation and corporate entrepreneurship can be a means of internal venture creation and strategic renewal, and how an entrepreneurial orientation can help corporations enhance their competitive position.

Innovation is one of the primary means by which corporations grow and strengthen their strategic position. Innovations can take several forms, ranging from radical breakthrough innovations to incremental improvement innovations. Innovations are often used to update products and services or for improving organization processes. Managing the innovation process is often challenging, because it involves a great deal of uncertainty and there are many choices to be made about the extent and type of innovations to pursue. By defining the scope of innovation, managing the pace of innovation, and collaborating with innovation partners, firms can more effectively manage the innovation process.

We also discussed the role of corporate entrepreneurship in venture development and strategic renewal. Corporations usually take either a focused or dispersed approach to corporate venturing. Firms with a focused approach usually separate the corporate venturing activity from the ongoing operations of the firm in order to foster independent thinking and encourage entrepreneurial team members to think and act without the constraints imposed by the corporation. In corporations where venturing activities are dispersed, a culture of entrepreneurship permeates all parts the company in order to induce strategic behaviors by all organizational members. In measuring the success of corporate venturing activities, both financial and strategic objectives should be considered.

Most entrepreneurial firms need to have an entrepreneurial orientation: the methods, practices, and decision-making styles that strategic managers use to act entrepreneurially. Five dimensions of entrepreneurial orientation are found in firms that pursue corporate venture strategies. Autonomy, innovativeness, proactiveness, competitive aggressiveness, and risk taking each make a unique contribution to the pursuit of new opportunities. When deployed effectively, the methods and practices of an entrepreneurial orientation can be used to engage successfully in corporate entrepreneurship and new venture creation. However, strategic managers must remain mindful of the pitfalls associated with each of these approaches.

summary review questions

1. What is meant by the concept of a continuum of radical and incremental innovations?

2. What are the dilemmas that organizations face when deciding what innovation projects to pursue? What steps can organizations take to effectively manage the innovation process?

3. What is the difference between focused and dispersed approaches to corporate entrepreneurship?

4. How are business incubators used to foster internal corporate venturing?

5. What is the role of the product champion in bringing a new product or service into existence in a corporation? How can companies use product champions to enhance their venture development efforts?

6. Explain the difference between proactiveness and competitive aggressiveness in terms of achieving and sustaining competitive advantage.

7. Describe how the entrepreneurial orientation (EO) dimensions of innovativeness, proactiveness, and risk taking can be combined to create competitive advantages for entrepreneurial firms.

experiential exercise

Select two different major corporations from two different industries (you might use Fortune 500 companies to make your selection). Compare and contrast these organizations in terms of their entrepreneurial orientation.

Entrepreneurial Orientation	Company A	Company B
Autonomy		
Innovativeness		
Proactiveness		
Competitive Aggressiveness		
Risk Taking		

Based on your comparison:

1. How is the corporation's entrepreneurial orientation reflected in its strategy?
2. Which corporation would you say has the stronger entrepreneurial orientation?
3. Is the corporation with the stronger entrepreneurial orientation also stronger in terms of financial performance?

application questions exercises

1. Select a firm known for its corporate entrepreneurship activities. Research the company and discuss how it has positioned itself relative to its close competitors. Does it have a unique strategic advantage? Disadvantage? Explain.
2. Explain the difference between product innovations and process innovations. Provide examples of firms that have recently introduced each type of innovation. What are the types of innovations related to the strategies of each firm?
3. Using the Internet, select a company that is listed on the Nasdaq or New York Stock Exchange. Research the extent to which the company has an entrepreneurial culture. Does the company use product champions? Does it have a corporate venture capital fund? Do you believe its entrepreneurial efforts are sufficient to generate sustainable advantages?
4. How can an established firm use an entrepreneurial orientation to enhance its overall strategic position? Provide examples.

ethics questions

1. Innovation activities are often aimed at making a discovery or commercializing a technology ahead of the competition. What are some of the unethical practices that companies could engage in during the innovation process? What are the potential long-term consequences of such actions?
2. Discuss the ethical implications of using "vaporware" to signal competitors and potential customers about software products that have not yet been released.

references

1. Sources for the Polaroid example include Charan, R., & Useem, J., 2002, Why companies fail, *Fortune,* May 15; Knox, N., 2001, Rivals push Polaroid toward Chapter 11, *USA Today,* October 11; McLaughlin, T., 2001, Harvard dropout made Polaroid an icon, *Toronto Star,* October 15; Pope, J., 2001, Polaroid's fortunes rose with Land, but fell under the burden of debt, *Daily Kent Stater* (OH), October 15; and www.polaroid.com.
2. Christensen, C. M., 1997, *The Innovator's Dilemma: When New Technologies Cause Great Firms to Fail* (Cambridge, MA: Harvard Business School Press).
3. For a discussion about Polaroid, see Gavetti, G., & Levinthal, D., 2000, Looking forward and looking backward: Cognitive and experiential search, *Administrative Science Quarterly* 45: 113–37.
4. For an interesting discussion, see Johannessen, J.-A., Olsen, B., & Lumpkin, G. T., 2001, Innovation

as newness: What is new, how new, and new to whom? *European Journal of Innovation Management* 4 (1): 20–31.
5. The discussion of radical and incremental innovations draws from Leifer, R., McDermott, C. M., Colarelli, G., O'Connor, G. C., Peters, L. S., Rice, M. P., & Veryzer, R. W., 2000, *Radical Innovation: How Mature Companies Can Outsmart Upstarts* (Boston: Harvard Business School Press); Damanpour, F., 1996, Organizational complexity and innovation: Developing and testing multiple contingency models, *Management Science* 42 (5): 693–716; and Hage, J., 1980, *Theories of Organizations* (New York: Wiley).
6. The discussion of product and process innovation is based on Roberts, E. B., ed., 2002, *Innovation: Driving Product, Process, and Market Change* (San Francisco: Jossey-Bass); Hayes, R., & Wheelwright, S., 1985, Competing through manufacturing, *Harvard Business*

Review 63 (1): 99–109; and Hayes & Wheelwright, 1979, Dynamics of product-process life cycles, *Harvard Business Review* 57 (2): 127–36.

7. Drucker, P. F., 1985, *Innovation and Entrepreneurship* (New York: Harper & Row, 200).

8. Steere, W. C., Jr., & Niblack, J., 1997, Pfizer, Inc., in Kanter, R. M., Kao, J., & Wiersema, F., eds., *Innovation: Breakthrough Thinking at 3M, DuPont, GE, Pfizer, and Rubbermaid* (New York: HarperCollins), 123–45.

9. Morrissey, C. A., 2000, Managing innovation through corporate venturing, *Graziadio Business Report,* Spring, gbr.pepperdine.edu; and Sharma, A., 1999, Central dilemmas of managing innovation in large firms, *California Management Review* 41 (3): 147–64.

10. Sharma, op. cit.

11. Canabou, C., 2003, Fast ideas for slow times, *Fast Company,* May: 52.

12. Biodegradable Products Institute, 2003, "Compostable Logo" of the Biodegradable Products Institute gains momentum with approval of DuPont™ Biomax® resin, www.bpiworld.org, June 12; Leifer et al., op. cit.

13. Leifer et al., op. cit.

14. Bhide, A.V., 2000, *The Origin and Evolution of New Businesses* (New York: Oxford University Press); Brown, S. L., & Eisenhardt, K. M., 1998, *Competing on the Edge: Strategy as Structured Chaos* (Cambridge: Harvard Business School Press).

15. Caulfield, B., 2003, Why techies don't get Six Sigma, *Business 2.0,* June: 90.

16. Chesbrough, H., 2003, *Open Innovation: The New Imperative for Creating and Profiting from Technology* (Boston: Harvard Business School Press).

17. Bick, J., 2003, Gold bond, *Entrepreneur,* March: 54–57.

18. Guth, W. D., & Ginsberg, A., 1990, Guest editor's introduction: Corporate entrepreneurship, *Strategic Management Journal* 11: 5–15.

19. Pinchot, G., 1985, *Intrapreneuring* (New York: Harper & Row).

20. Birkinshaw, J., 1997, Entrepreneurship in multinational corporations: The characteristics of subsidiary initiatives, *Strategic Management Journal* 18 (3): 207–29; and Kanter, R. M., 1985, *The Change Masters* (New York: Simon & Schuster).

21. The information in this example is from Leifer et al., op. cit.; Vance, A., 2000, NetActive looks to role as download police, *IDG News Service,* November 14, www.idg.net; and www.hoovers.com.

22. Hansen, M. T., Chesbrough, H. W., Nohria, N., & Sull, D., 2000, Networked incubators: Hothouses of the new economy, *Harvard Business Review* 78 (5): 74–84.

23. Stein, T., 2002, Corporate venture investors are bailing out, *Red Herring,* December: 74–75.

24. Is your company up to speed? 2003, *Fast Company,* June: 86.

25. For an interesting discussion, see Davenport, T. H.,

Prusak, L., & Wilson, H. J., 2003, Who's bringing you hot ideas and how are you responding? *Harvard Business Review* 80 (1): 58–64.

26. Greene, P., Brush, C., & Hart, M., 1999, The corporate venture champion: A resource-based approach to role and process, *Entrepreneurship Theory & Practice* 23 (3): 103–22; and Markham, S. K., & Aiman-Smith, L., 2001, Product champions: Truths, myths and management, *Research Technology Management,* May–June: 44–50.

27. Burgelman, R. A., 1983, A process model of internal corporate venturing in the diversified major firm, *Administrative Science Quarterly* 28: 223–44.

28. Hamel, G., 2000, *Leading the Revolution* (Boston: Harvard Business School Press).

29. Greene, Brush, & Hart, op. cit.; and Shane, S., 1994, Are champions different from non-champions? *Journal of Business Venturing* 9 (5): 397–421.

30. Vance, op. cit.; and www.info-mech.com/netactive .html.

31. Block, Z., & MacMillan, I. C., 1993, *Corporate Venturing—Creating New Businesses with the Firm* (Cambridge: Harvard Business School Press).

32. For an interesting discussion of these trade-offs, see Stringer, R., 2000, How to manage radical innovation, *California Management Review* 42 (4): 70–88; and Gompers, P. A., & Lerner, J., 1999, *The Venture Capital Cycle* (Cambridge, MA: MIT Press).

33. Albrinck, J., Hornery, J., Kletter, D., & Neilson, G., 2001, Adventures in corporate venturing. *Strategy + Business* 22: 119–29; and McGrath, R. G., & MacMillan, I. C., 2000, *The Entrepreneurial Mind Set* (Cambridge, MA: Harvard Business School Press).

34. Crockett, R. O., 2001, Motorola, *BusinessWeek,* July 15: 72–78.

35. The ideas in this section are drawn from Royer, I., 2003, Why bad projects are so hard to kill, *Harvard Business Review* 80 (1): 48–56.

36. Breen, B. 2003, How does a 900-pound gorilla get to be an 1,800-pound gorilla? *Fast Company,* January: 87–89.

37. Covin, J. G., & Slevin, D. P., 1991, A conceptual model of entrepreneurship as firm behavior, *Entrepreneurship Theory and Practice* 16 (1): 7–24; Lumpkin, G. T., & Dess, G. G., 1996, Clarifying the entrepreneurial orientation construct and linking it to performance, *Academy of Management Review* 21 (1): 135–72; and McGrath, R. G., & MacMillan, I. C., 2000, *The Entrepreneurial Mind Set* (Cambridge, MA: Harvard Business School Press).

38. Lumpkin, G. T., & Dess, G. G., 2001, Linking two dimensions of entrepreneurial orientation to firm performance: The moderating role of environment and life cycle, *Journal of Business Venturing* 16: 429–51.

39. For an interesting discussion, see Day, J. D., Mang, P. Y., Richter, A., & Roberts, J., 2001, The innovative organi-

zation: Why new ventures need more than a room of their own, *McKinsey Quarterly* 2: 21–31.

40. Quinn, J. B., 1992, *Intelligent Enterprise* (New York: Free Press).

41. Holstein, W. J., 2000, Dump the cookware, *Business 2.0,* May 11: 68–73.

42. Cross, K., 2001, Bang the drum quickly, *Business 2.0,* May 1: 28–30.

43. Crockett, R. O., 2001, Chris Galvin shakes things up—again, *BusinessWeek,* May 28: 38–39.

44. Hamel, G., 1999, Bringing Silicon Valley inside, *Harvard Business Review* 77 (5): 71–84.

45. Perman, S., 2001, Automate or die, www.business2.com, July; and Dell, M., 1999, *Direct from Dell* (New York: HarperBusiness).

46. Evans, P., & Wurster, T. S., 2000, *Blown to Bits* (Boston: Harvard Business School Press).

47. Lieberman, M. B., & Montgomery, D. B., 1988, First mover advantages, *Strategic Management Journal* 9 (Special Issue): 41–58.

48. The discussion of first mover advantages is based on several articles, including Lambkin, M., 1988, Order of entry and performance in new markets, *Strategic Management Journal* 9: 127–40; Lieberman & Montgomery, op. cit., pp. 41–58; and Miller, A., & Camp, B., 1985, Exploring determinants of success in corporate ventures, *Journal of Business Venturing* 1 (2): 87–105.

49. Moore, G. A., 1999, *Crossing the Chasm,* 2nd ed. (New York: HarperBusiness).

50. Tesler, L., 2001, Why the Apple Newton failed, www.techtv.com/print/story/0,23102,3013675,00.html; Veitch, M., 1998, Apple kills off Newton PDA, news.zdnet.co.uk/story/printer/0,,s2067739,00.html.

51. Collins, J. C. & Porras, J. I., 1997, *Built to Last* (New York: HarperBusiness); see also www.sony.com.

52. Hardy, Q., & Godwin, J., 2000, Other people's money, *Forbes,* August 7: 116–18.

53. The failure of new media, 2000, *Economist,* August 9: 53–55.

54. Carvell, T., 1997, The crazy record business: These prices are really insane, *Fortune,* August 4: 109–16.

55. Bogan, C. E., & English, M. J., 1994, *Benchmarking for Best Practices* (New York: McGraw-Hill); Mochari, I., 2001, Steal this strategy, *Inc.,* July: 62–67.

56. Helman, C., 2001, Stand-up brand, *Forbes,* July 9: 27.

57. Keenan, F., & Mullaney, T. J., 2001, Clicking at Graybar, *BusinessWeek,* June 18: 132–34.

58. Weintraub, A., 2001, Make or break for Autobytel, *BusinessWeek e.biz,* July 9: EB30–EB32; see also www.autobytel.com.

59. Coy, P., & Vickers, M., 2001, How bad will it get? *BusinessWeek,* March 12: 36–42.

60. Drucker, op. cit., pp. 109–10.

chapter 13

Recognizing Opportunities and Creating New Ventures

*After
reading this
chapter, you should
have a good understanding of:*

- The role of new ventures and small businesses in the U.S. economy.

- The importance of opportunity recognition, as well as the role of opportunities, resources, and entrepreneurs, in successfully pursuing new ventures.

- The role of vision, dedication, and commitment to excellence in determining the quality of entrepreneurial leadership.

- The different types of financing that are available to new ventures depending on their stage of development.

- The importance of human capital and social capital as well as government resources in supporting new ventures and small businesses.

- The three types of entry strategies—pioneering, imitative, and adaptive—that are commonly used to launch a new venture.

- How the generic strategies of overall cost leadership, differentiation, and focus are used by new ventures and small businesses.

*n*ew technologies, shifting social and demographic trends, and sudden changes in the business environment create opportunities for entrepreneurship. New ventures, which often emerge under such conditions, face unique strategic challenges if they are going to survive and grow. Small businesses, which are a major engine of growth in the U.S. economy because of their role in job creation and innovation, must rely on sound strategic principles to be successful.

This chapter addresses how new ventures and small businesses can achieve competitive advantages. In the first section we review various perspectives of entrepreneurship and how the size, age, and growth goals of a firm help distinguish between small businesses and entrepreneurial firms. We also examine the contribution of small businesses to the U.S economy.

In the second section we address the role of opportunity recognition in the process of new venture creation. We highlight the importance of three factors in determining whether a potential venture opportunity should be pursued—the nature of the opportunity itself, the resources available to undertake it, and the characteristics of the entrepreneur(s) pursuing it.

In section three we expand on the topic of entrepreneurial resources. We discuss various types of financing that may be available during early and later stages of the new venture creation process. We also address how other resources including human capital, social capital, and government programs aimed at supporting entrepreneurial firms provide important resources for the small business owner.

In the fourth section we focus on the qualities of entrepreneurial leadership. Business founders need vision in order to conceive of realities that do not yet exist. Dedication and drive are essential to maintain the level of motivation and persistence needed to succeed. A commitment to excellence as seen in the quality of products and services, the talent and skill level of employees, and superior customer service is another element of effective entrepreneurial leadership.

In section five we show how many of the strategic concepts discussed in this text apply to new ventures and small businesses. Three different types of new entry strategies are discussed—pioneering, imitative, and adaptive. Then, the generic strategies (Chapter 5) as well as combination strategies are addressed in terms of how they apply to new ventures and entrepreneurial firms. Additionally, some of the pitfalls associated with each of these strategic approaches are presented.

The success of an entrepreneurial venture—whether it is undertaken by a major corporation or a small start-up—depends on many factors. The right combination of resources, know-how, and strategic action can lead to above-average profitability and new advantages. However, many things can go wrong. To see how a firm's entrepreneurial efforts, even in the face of technological progress, can turn to failure, consider the example of Rosen Motors.[1]

> By the early 1990s the auto emission requirements of the Clean Air Act and concern about oil prices and supply had many people thinking about alternatives to the internal combustion engine. One of them was Harold Rosen, a Hughes Electronics engineer. Around 1992 Rosen learned about a low-polluting turbogenerator that might be used as a substitute to the internal combustion engine in a new type of automobile drivetrain. He took the idea to the Hughes automotive group, but they were not interested. Hughes is owned by General Motors, which was already developing battery-powered cars. When Hughes turned him down, he called his brother Ben, a venture capitalist who had made his fortune launching technology companies, including Compaq Computer Corp.
>
> Soon, Rosen Motors was launched by the two brothers. With just 60 employees and no government grants, the Rosens began working on their innovative new automobile drivetrain. The task was daunting for several reasons. First, there were major technical obstacles to overcome. Internal combustion engines are popular because they can do both of the tasks that an auto engine must do: accelerate and cruise. Most alternative engines, such as all-electric motors, can accomplish only one of these tasks efficiently.
>
> The Rosen brothers focused on a hybrid system that combines a carbon-fiber flywheel for acceleration with the gas-fed turbogenerator for cruising. The flywheel stores energy that is dissipated during braking and releases it for sudden bursts of acceleration—acceleration that the small turbine can't handle alone. But the Rosens wanted more than just a new engine. They envisioned a system that would go from zero to 60 in six seconds and emit virtually no pollutants. "It's all potentially doable," admitted University of Michigan auto industry expert David Cole, "It is a long shot, it is a really long shot."
>
> Even more challenging to the Rosen brothers was the task of selling their hybrid drivetrain to the big automakers. This was where their troubles began. When they thought the drivetrain was ready, the Rosens rented a race track in the Mojave Desert to showcase their breakthrough. But the test was a dismal failure. For 14 hours, as the press and auto executives looked on, the car would not move. Humbled, they went back to work on their project and eventually had a successful trial. But it was too late. Even though they had worked out most of the problems, the product development process was about to enter a costly crash-test phase. With no sales and few prospects, the Rosens laid off their employees and closed up shop.

What Went Wrong with Rosen Motors?   They had successfully created a breakthrough product with the potential to save customers millions in fuel costs. However, they couldn't get it off the ground. Despite their technological success, the Rosens ignored two key factors in the competitive environment. First, their failed test allowed time for other technologies to move ahead. By the time the Rosens had a working prototype, the big automakers had made advances in other hybrid solutions and were not willing to scrap their investment and adopt the Rosens' approach.

Second, the Rosens misread the market for their product. By focusing on developing a drivetrain, they put themselves at the mercy of powerful buyers—the giant automakers. Although auto manufacturers purchase many parts, they are reluctant to contract out this central component. "The drivetrain is just so critical for the big manufacturers," said J. P. MacDuffie of the University of Pennsylvania. "It was a gamble to try to break into the industry that way."[2] If the Rosens had taken steps to develop a whole car, their customer would have been the average car buyer, some of whom might have accepted their innovation and provided them with a sustainable niche. Instead, even though the Rosens had developed a cutting-edge capability, the auto industry's control of the dominant technology and power over the supply chain created an environment that led to a strategic failure.

The Rosen Motors case illustrates the importance of thinking and acting strategically in the entrepreneurial process. Even though the Rosens had a bright idea and invested $24 million in their innovation, they were not able to convert their investment into a profitable business. Even when market conditions are creating new opportunities (e.g., a growing interest in alternative vehicles), industry and competitive forces may prevent a new technology from reaching the marketplace. Thus, to be successful, new ventures need to apply the lessons of strategic management to evaluate business conditions, assess their internal capabilities, formulate effective strategies, and implement sound business practices. New ventures and small businesses are often vulnerable because they lack experience and/or resources, and because established firms may be relatively more powerful. In this chapter we address how new ventures and small businesses, by applying the principles and practices of strategic management, can improve their chances of success. To begin our discussion, we address some of the differences and similarities found among the many types of entrepreneurial firms and address the importance of entrepreneurship to the economy.

New Ventures and Small Businesses

The majority of new business creation is the result of entrepreneurial efforts by new ventures and small businesses. The strategic concepts introduced in this text can be applied to the effective management of entrepreneurial firms. Because there are several types of entrepreneurial firms, the application of these principles may differ somewhat depending on factors such as the size, age, or growth goals of the firm. Generally speaking, however, entrepreneurial activities will be more successful if strategic thinking guides decision making.

In this section we will investigate several types of entrepreneurial ventures and how the unique circumstances surrounding each type affect the strategies they pursue. First, let's consider the important role that small business and entrepreneurship play in the U.S. economy. Strategy Spotlight 13.1 addresses some of the reasons why small business and entrepreneurship are viewed favorably in the United States.

Categories of Entrepreneurial Ventures

There are many ways to categorize entrepreneurial ventures. The term *entrepreneurship* itself has come to represent a wide array of meanings.[3] For example:

- Working for oneself rather than for someone else for a salary.
- Entering into a new or established market with new or existing products or services.
- Operating a firm in which there is no separation between ownership and management.
- Discovering, evaluating, and exploiting opportunities.
- Creating new organizations.

All of these definitions have been used to characterize entrepreneurial firms and/or small businesses. For purposes of strategic analysis, it is useful to note three differences among entrepreneurial firms, because these distinctions have strategic implications. The first of these is size. Small businesses, of course, are small. However, some ventures are small because they are new. This leads to the second criterion, age. Start-ups and new ventures are often considered to be entrepreneurial simply because they are young. That is, size is often correlated with age. New ventures usually begin small and grow over time as their business activity increases. Thus, as the age of a firm increases, so does its size. There is a third factor, however, that may limit an entrepreneurial firm's size—its growth goals.

The Contribution of Small Business and Entrepreneurship to the U.S. Economy

In the late 1970s, MIT professor David Birch launched a study to explore the sources of business growth. "I wasn't really looking for anything in particular," says Birch. But the findings surprised him: Small businesses create the most jobs. Since then, Birch and others have shown that it's not just big companies that power the economy. The actual number of businesses, as measured by tax returns, has been growing faster than the civilian labor force for the past three decades. There is no sign of a reversal in that trend. Small business and entrepreneurship have become a major component of the economy.

Here are the facts:

◆ In the United States, there are approximately 5.7 million companies with fewer than 100 employees. Another 100,000 companies have 100–500 employees. In addition, 17.2 million individuals are nonemployer sole proprietors.

◆ Small businesses create the majority of new jobs. According to recent data, small business created three-quarters of U.S. net new jobs in 1999–2000 (2.5 million of the 3.4 million total). A small percentage of the fastest growing entrepreneurial firms (5–15 percent) account for a majority of the new jobs created.

◆ Small businesses (fewer than 500 employees) employ more than half of the private sector workforce (57.1 million in 2000) and account for more than 50 percent of nonfarm private gross domestic product (GDP).

◆ Small firms produce 13 to 14 times more patents per employee than large patenting firms and employ 39 percent of high-tech workers (such as scientists, engineers, and computer workers). In addition, smaller entrepreneurial firms account for 55 percent of all innovations.

◆ Small businesses make up 97 percent of all U.S. exporters and accounted for 29 percent of known U.S. export value in 2001.

Exhibit 13.1 shows the number of small businesses in the United States and how they are distributed through different sectors of the economy.

Even though thousands of small businesses are formed each year, thousands also close. In a recent year, between 600,000 and 800,000 businesses with employees were formed. This translates into an annual birth rate of 14 to 16 percent. But in the same year, 12 to 14 percent of existing businesses were terminated, resulting in a net annual increase of about 2 percent. Among those that close each year, about one-fourth are sold or transferred (e.g., through inheritance). Another half simply "fade away," (i.e., the owners allow them to become inactive). Some of the deactivated firms are terminated not because they were unprofitable, but because the owner found a better business opportunity elsewhere. Thus, even though some businesses fail or turn out to be less lucrative than expected, the overall trend is positive. Small business and entrepreneurship will continue to be a major force in the economy for years to come.

Sources: Small Business Administration, "Small Business by the Numbers," *SBA Office of Advocacy,* May 2003, www.sba.gov/advo/; "Small Business 2001: Where We Are Now," *Inc.,* May 29, 2001, pp. 18–19; W. J. Dennis, Jr., *Business Starts and Stops* (Washington, DC: National Federation of Independent Business, 1997); A. L. Zacharakis, W. D. Bygrave, and D. A. Shepherd, *Global Entrepreneurship Monitor—National Entrepreneurship Assessment: United States of America 2000, Executive Report* (Kansas City, MO: Kauffman Center for Entrepreneurial Leadership, 2000); and "The Heroes: A Portfolio," *Fortune,* October 4, 2001, p. 74.

Firms that do not aspire to grow large usually don't. Therefore, a young firm's growth goals often determine whether it will remain small as it ages or grow large. In fact, growth goals are one of the key factors used to distinguish between entrepreneurial firms and small businesses. Small businesses are generally thought to have low or modest growth goals. Because small business owners prefer to maintain control of their business, they are often unwilling to take steps that are considered necessary to grow, even though they may have growth potential. These steps include, most notably, borrowing heavily or going public to obtain the funding needed to finance growth. As a result, they remain small businesses.

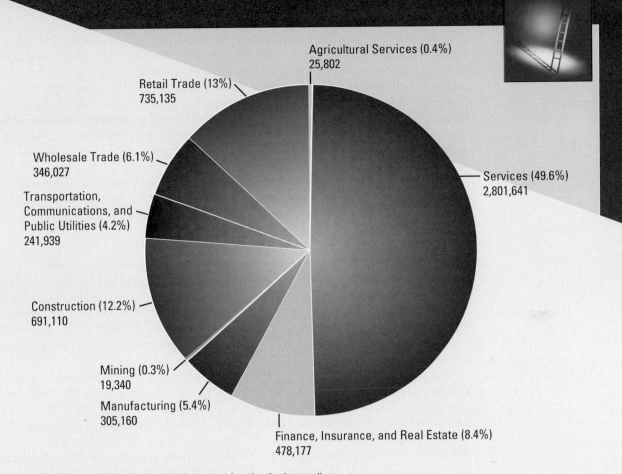

Agricultural Services (0.4%)
25,802

Retail Trade (13%)
735,135

Wholesale Trade (6.1%)
346,027

Transportation,
Communications, and
Public Utilities (4.2%)
241,939

Construction (12.2%)
691,110

Mining (0.3%)
19,340

Manufacturing (5.4%)
305,160

Services (49.6%)
2,801,641

Finance, Insurance, and Real Estate (8.4%)
478,177

Exhibit 13.1 All U.S. Small Companies by Industry*

* Businesses with 500 or fewer employees in 2001.

Source: SBA's Office of Advocacy, based on data provided by the U.S. Census Bureau, statistics of U.S. businesses. (Percentages don't add to 100% because of rounding.)

By contrast, entrepreneurial firms generally favor growth. Because growth is a priority, founders with high growth goals will often sell a share of the business (thus giving up some control) in order to finance growth. As a result, successful businesses founded by high-growth entrepreneurs develop a life of their own. In contrast, small businesses are often associated so closely with their founders that when the founder is gone, the business ceases to operate. Of course, there may be intervening factors that affect growth outcomes unexpectedly—some entrepreneurs may want to grow large businesses but cannot; others may become bigger than they ever expected because market forces propel them onto a growth curve they did not anticipate. But in general, the difference between entrepreneurial firms and small businesses is related to their path of growth.

These three factors—size, age, and growth goals—are captured in a model of entrepreneurial firms that was developed by David Birch, the famed small-business researcher whose findings are presented in Spotlight 13.1 Birch identified three categories of firms—elephants, mice, and gazelles. Let's look briefly at each of these.

Elephants   As the name suggests, these are large firms. They also tend to be older and are the types of firms that appear in the Fortune 500. They have some disadvantages relative to entrepreneurial firms. For one thing, they cannot change direction quickly, and it is sometimes difficult to get them to move forward at all. As a group, these large firms have laid off more people than they have hired in the last 25 years.[4] On the other hand, they have obvious advantages. They can be hard chargers and move quite rapidly because of their overall power in the marketplace. Like elephants, these large firms usually command respect and can influence marketplace conditions (competition, technology) as well as business conditions (political/legal) in their industry.

As you might imagine from the image of the lumbering elephant, it is often difficult for such firms to be entrepreneurial. That's why some of the large firms introduced in Chapter 12 that have been strong innovators and generated an entrepreneurial spirit—3M, Sony, Virgin Group—have been so highly successful.

Mice   This term refers to the many small firms that power the U.S. economy. Over 80 percent of all firms in the United States have fewer than 20 employees.[5] The mice represent the many types of locally run businesses, including small retailers, small manufacturers, and all kinds of local service firms from auto repair shops and heating and air conditioning contractors to restaurants and banks. Mice typically do not have as much market power as large firms, but they can change direction more quickly in response to changes in business conditions.

As suggested earlier, many of these firms do not aspire to grow large as long as they remain profitable and competitive. Even so, since 1980, small businesses have added more jobs than large firms.[6] Even small firms that are committed to remaining small often add jobs or become the target of corporate takeovers. Consider the example of Kiehl's, a New York City natural cosmetics company founded in 1851 and co-owned by Jami Morse, a third-generation family business owner. Despite offers to sell her product line abroad from distributors in Asia and Europe, Morse prefers the advantages that come from being small.

> "My goal was never to be the biggest. I want to be small, not get overextended, and keep things manageable," she said. Rather than growth, Kiehl's emphasizes outstanding customer service. Visitors who stop at Kiehl's cosmetic counters (at upscale department stores in New York) get a 45-minute consultation and many free samples. As a result, Kiehl's has developed a chic underground mystique that has spread by word-of-mouth all the way to fashion magazines in Japan, France, and Brazil and made its East Village store a tourist stop for international travelers. After 150 years, Kiehl's finally decided to open a second freestanding store as well as offer its products in upscale department stores. It now has shops in Boston, San Francisco, and a few other carefully selected locations. "We're not trying to be difficult," said assistant vice president Cammie Cannella when asked why Kiehl's products are not widely available. "We've just focused on quality, not quantity, and we wanted to take our time to do this right."[7]

Small businesses represent a bedrock of economic strength in the U.S. economy. Although many have chosen to remain small, many others aspire to grow into major corporations. It is these growth-oriented firms that we turn to next.

Gazelles   An important third category identified by Birch is known as gazelles. These are the firms that seek rapid growth and above average profitability. They are likely to be listed in the *Inc.* 500 or the *Entrepreneur* Hot 100, both of which highlight the fastest-growing small companies. To be a gazelle, a firm must grow at least 20 percent a year for four years, from a base of at least $100,000 in revenues.[8] A firm that meets these criteria doubles in size during the four-year period.

Gazelles are important to the economy for several reasons. For one thing, their value proposition often includes a radical innovation or the implementation of a new technology. Thus, they are an important engine for innovation in the U.S. economy. For example, Sur-Modics, Inc., is a Minnesota-based manufacturer of coatings for medical devices such as stents—metal coils that help hold blood vessels open after heart surgery. SurModics's coatings help make stents more slippery and less likely to carry infections, thus improving their effectiveness. By partnering with companies such as Johnson & Johnson, which pays SurModics to conduct innovative research and then pays again to license the technology, SurModics has created a winning business model that recently earned it a place on the Fortune FSB 100 list of fast-growing small businesses. In 2003, with fewer than 200 employees, it had revenues of $43.2 million and posted sales growth of 31 percent and net income growth of 47 percent.[9]

Although technology is often a hot growth area, the majority of gazelles are not in high-tech fields. Approximately 30 percent are in retail and wholesale trades (primarily low-tech) and another 30 percent are in services (including both high- and low-tech). Gazelles are not necessarily young either. Although some young firms take off rapidly from birth, many firms have growth spurts only after a long period of gradual development. Around one-fifth of gazelles have been in operation 30 years or more.[10]

Occasionally a small firm will, after operating locally for years, make decisions that turn it into a growth company and set it on a path that takes it well beyond its local roots. Strategy Spotlight 13.2 describes one such company, Krispy Kreme, that, after a long, slow start, has emerged as a rising star. The once small company enjoyed a 400 percent increase in the value of its stock between 1998 and 2003.[11]

Perhaps the most important contribution gazelles make is in job growth. Because gazelles are highly entrepreneurial, they seek growth rather than control. As they grow, their need for additional employees also increases rapidly. As a result, the Small Business Administration (SBA) has estimated that gazelles, of which there were approximately 386,000 in 2002, have created as many jobs during the last 25 years as have the mice, which numbered around 17 million in 2002.[12] Thus, it is no surprise that local and state governments often seek out gazelles because of their role in boosting economic development in a region.

There are many other ways to categorize new ventures and small businesses. For example, according to the IRS, over 17.9 million self employment tax returns (Schedule C) were filed in 2000, indicating that a large proportion of the adult population is engaged in money-making enterprises. Exhibit 13.2 identifies three other major business categories that are generally considered to be entrepreneurial in nature—franchises, family businesses, and home-based businesses.

All entrepreneurial firms that wish to launch a new venture must first identify a strong business opportunity. Thus, next we address the strategic issues and techniques that firms use to recognize and develop new venture opportunities.

Opportunity Recognition: Identifying and Developing Market Opportunities

The starting point for any new venture is the presence of an entrepreneurial opportunity. Where do opportunities come from? For new business start-ups, opportunities come from many sources: current or past work experiences, hobbies that grow into businesses or lead to inventions, suggestions by friends or family, or a chance event that makes an entrepreneur aware of an unmet need. For established firms, new business opportunities come from

Krispy Kreme: The Mouse That Became a Gazelle

Krispy Kreme Doughnut Corp. (KKD), the maker of tasty and hot-selling doughnuts whose revenues have reached about $1 billion annually, was started in Winston-Salem, North Carolina, in 1937. Founder Vernon Rudolph began as a wholesaler, but when folks in the neighborhood smelled the doughnuts baking, they started banging on the doors and asking to buy them. Rudolph cut a hole in the factory wall to install a store, and a retail legend was born. Locals loved the specialty doughnuts and its reputation spread, but slowly. Rudolph added a store here and there and even sold a few franchises. But for over 30 years, Krispy Kreme was little more than a regional business quietly capitalizing on a secret southern recipe.

Rudolph died in 1973, and his family had to sell the business to settle his estate. Chicago-based Beatrice Foods finally bought it in 1976 but did little to boost sales. "They didn't want to invest in stores or grow the company, they just wanted cash," says Scott Livengood, KKD's current CEO, who had just started working there when Beatrice bought it. Poor marketing and changes to the doughnut recipe caused sales to slip, and soon Beatrice was looking for a buyer.

At that point, a group of franchisees who were upset with Beatrice anyway banded together to buy back the company. The group paid $24 million in 1982. Step-by-step the company, led by Livengood and Mack McAller, began re-creating the Krispy Kreme brand. They reinstated its retro logo, changed back to the original doughnut formula, put the doughnut-making equipment behind glass windows where customers could watch them cook, and increased the size of the doughnuts by 40 percent to make them more appealing to retailers. By 1990, they had grown to a total of 66 stores.

Since then, Krispy Kreme has achieved remarkable success as a result of some very smart marketing. However, it does not do any traditional media advertising. Instead, it just sends doughnuts. When it opened its New York City store in 1996, it sent dozens of boxes to the *Today Show* and garnered huge national exposure. When it went public in April 2000, it sent the doughnuts to Wall Street. Krispy Kreme doughnuts have appeared in numerous movies and TV shows including *Bruce Almighty* and *The Sopranos.* And the company provides millions of doughnuts at a discount to charitable organizations, which sell them for fundraising. The result: KKD enjoys operating margins of 16 percent, its stock is up four times since its IPO, and its net income per share has compounded more than 45 percent since 1998.

In late 2002 financial pundits were still questioning whether the business could grow. But by the end of 2003, its performance was stronger than Starbucks or Panera Bread, it had rolled out its own brand of coffee, and it was making plans to grow to 1,000 U.S. stores. Who knew a mouse could grow into a gazelle on a diet of doughnuts!

Sources: A. Serwer, "The Hole Story: How Krispy Kreme Became the Hottest Brand in America," *Fortune,* June 23, 2003, www.fortune.com; and K. Kazanjian, *Making Dough: The 12 Secret Ingredients of Krispy Kreme's Sweet Success* (New York: Wiley, 2003).

the needs of existing customers, suggestions by suppliers, or technological developments that lead to new advances.[13] For all types of firms, there is a major, overarching factor that is behind all viable opportunities that emerge in the business landscape: change. Change creates opportunities. Consider the following examples of entrepreneurial activity that are related to some of the changes and trends described in earlier chapters:

♦ **Free agent employees.** In Chapter 4 we discussed the changing role of human capital and the importance of knowledge workers in the new economy. Skilled professionals who value freedom and flexibility over security and regular pay are changing human resource management practices. Online start-up eLance is helping them do it. By providing a platform where freelancers offer services and corporations post projects, it is creating a virtual marketplace for independently minded workers to contract out for temporary assignments.[14]

Type	Characteristics
Family businesses	• *Definition:* A family business, broadly defined, is a privately held firm in which family members have some degree of effective control over the strategic direction of the firm and intend for the business to remain within the family.
	• *Scope:* According to the Family Firm Institute (FFI), family-owned businesses that meet the broad definition above comprise 80 to 90 percent of all business enterprises in North America, 30 to 35 percent of the Fortune 500 companies, and the majority of enterprises internationally. Further, 50 percent of the U.S. Gross Domestic Product (GDP), over $3.3 trillion, is generated by family-owned businesses.
Franchises	• *Definition:* A franchise exists when a firm that already has a successful product or service (franchisor) contracts with another business to be a dealer (franchisee) by using the franchisor's name, trademark, and business system in exchange for a fee. There are several types, but the most common is the business format franchise, in which the franchisor provides a complete plan, or format, for managing the business.
	• *Scope:* According to the International Franchise Association (IFA), franchising accounted for $1 trillion in annual retail sales in the United States in 2000. There are about 320,000 franchise businesses, employing more than 8 million people in 75 different industries.
Home-based businesses	• *Definition:* A home-based business, also commonly referred to as SOHO (Small Office/Home Office), consists of a company with 20 or fewer employees, including the self-employed, free agents, e-lancers, telecommuters, or other independent professionals working from a home-based setting.
	• *Scope:* According to the National Association of Home-Based Businesses (NAHBB), approximately 20 million businesses are home-based. The U.S. Commerce Department estimates that more than half of all small businesses are home-based.

**Exhibit 13.2
Types of
Entrepreneurial
Ventures**

♦ **Recycling profits.** In Chapter 1 we saw how some companies have changed their corporate missions to include socially responsible goals like protecting the environment. Carpet maker Interface, Inc., has found a way to profit by being environmentally friendly. By leasing rather than selling carpets, Interface is able to take back worn carpets and "remanufacture" them. As a result, it has cut its raw materials input costs by nearly 100 percent and customers get to deduct the cost of leasing. According to Interface, 27 percent of its operating profit now comes from eliminated waste. In a recent period, this added $143 million to its bottom line.[15]

◆ **Global reach.** In Chapter 7 we discussed the rapid pace of globalization. In Chapter 8 we saw how the Internet is changing the way new products enter the market. One company, Nova Cruz Products LLC, is capitalizing on both of these trends. Nova Cruz manufactures a highly engineered, upmarket scooter that sells for $269 to $489 each. Sales grew quickly in the United States through retailers such as Sharper Image and FAO Schwartz. But once its simple and appealing website went online, sales soared to $10 million annually and it was able to build distribution links in Europe, Asia, and Australia.[16]

Each of these examples demonstrates how entrepreneurial firms are making the most of changes brought about by new technology, sociocultural trends, and shifts in consumer demand. Even tragedy stimulates business development. Since September 11, 2001, initiatives related to strengthening homeland security and building military capabilities have stimulated billions of dollars of demand for new products and services such as night vision systems and unmanned aerial vehicles.[17]

The Opportunity Recognition Process

How do such changes in the external environment lead to new business creation? They spark innovative new ideas. Businesspeople often have ideas for entrepreneurial ventures. However, not all such ideas are good ideas, that is, viable business opportunities. To determine which ideas are strong enough to become new ventures, entrepreneurs must go through a process of identifying, selecting, and developing potential opportunities. This is the process of opportunity recognition.

Opportunity recognition refers to more than just the "Eureka!" feeling that people sometimes experience at the moment they identify a new idea. Although such insights are often very important, the opportunity recognition process involves two phases of activity—discovery and formation—that lead to viable new venture opportunities.[18]

The discovery phase refers to the period when you first become aware of a new business concept. Many entrepreneurs report that their idea for a new venture occurred to them in an instant, as a sort of "Aha!" experience—that is, they had some insight or epiphany, often based on their prior knowledge, that gave them an idea for a new business. This may occur unintentionally, because the discovery of new opportunities is often spontaneous and unexpected. For example, Howard Schultz, CEO of Starbucks, was in Milan, Italy, when he suddenly realized that the coffee-and-conversation café model that was common in Europe would work in the United States as well. According to Schultz, he didn't need to do research to find out if Americans would pay $3 for a cup of coffee—he just *knew.* Starbucks was just a small business at the time but Schultz began literally shaking with excitement about growing it into a bigger business.[19]

Opportunity discovery may also occur as the result of a deliberate search for new venture opportunities or creative solutions to business problems. New venture ideas often emerge only after a concerted effort to identify good opportunities or realistic solutions. It is very similar to a creative process, which may be unstructured and "chaotic" at first but eventually leads to a practical solution or business innovation. To stimulate the discovery of new opportunities, companies often encourage creativity, out-of-the-box thinking, and brainstorming. Consider the example of Oakshire Mushroom Farm, Inc.

While trying to figure out how to recover from its 40 percent decline in market share for shiitake mushrooms, Oakshire came up with an idea that at first seemed ridiculous—selling a product to competitors. "We kicked around a lot of ideas—franchising, expanding geographically to be more local" to supermarkets and restaurants, explained Gary Schroeder, CEO of the Kennett

Square, Pennsylvania, grower. "But these other competitors were already there." Finally, they decided to sell rival farms their most unique innovation: a sawdust log for growing shiitakes that reduces the harvest time from four years to four months. The solution worked: Sales increased 45 percent to $5 million in the first year and nearly doubled the next. Now the logs account for about 10 percent of its revenues, and Oakshire has become a vendor within other segments of its industry.[20]

New ventures are often launched because founding entrepreneurs find innovative ways to apply new technologies. This is supported by the statistics in Strategy Spotlight 13.1, which indicates that a majority of patents and innovations come from small firms. Why is this so? Research indicates that entrepreneurial firms are often more successful at discovering radically different technology-based venture opportunities than large firms. Strategy Spotlight 13.3 explains why young firms often have a competitive edge when it comes to technological innovation.

Opportunity formation, which occurs after an opportunity has been identified, involves evaluating an opportunity to determine whether it is viable and strong enough to be developed into a full-fledged new venture. Ideas that have been developed by new-product groups or in brainstorming sessions are tested by various methods, including talking to potential target customers and discussing operational requirements with production or logistics managers. A technique known as feasibility analysis is used to evaluate these and other critical success factors. This type of analysis often leads to the decision that a new venture project should be discontinued. If the venture concept continues to seem viable, a more formal business plan may be developed.

Among the most important factors to evaluate is the market potential for the product or service. Established firms tend to operate in established markets. They have to adjust to market trends and to shifts in consumer demand, of course, but they usually have a customer base for which they are already filling a marketplace need. New ventures, in contrast, must first determine whether a market exists for the product or service they are contemplating. Thus, a critical element of opportunity recognition is assessing to what extent the opportunity is viable *in the marketplace.* Most definitions of entrepreneurial opportunity suggest that, for it to be an opportunity, it must be viable in terms of its potential to earn a profit.

Several of the techniques suggested in Chapters 2 and 3 can be used to assess the market potential of a business concept. Questions that might emerge in a test of the market for a new product or service include:

- Do market forces support the introduction of it? For example, is market demand growing because of shifting demographics or sociocultural trends?
- How is the need that it addresses currently being met?
- What firms would be the closest competitors?
- How are competitive products priced?
- What is its value proposition, that is, in what ways does it add value relative to products or services already being sold?
- Can its value be enhanced by combining it with other value-adding activities?

For a more complete assessment of how well a new business concept would be received, marketing techniques such as product concept testing, focus groups, and/or extended trial runs with end users are often necessary. In some respects, assessing marketability is as much an art as it is a science. Nevertheless, it is essential to create a model of how the product or service will perform in the marketplace in order to develop a plan for launching it. Thus, the aim of the opportunity recognition process is to explore and test a new venture concept in order to determine whether it is a viable opportunity.

Technological Innovation: Why Entrepreneurial Firms Have a Competitive Advantage

Young firms have a knack for seeing things differently. As a result, they tend to be net winners in the game of technological innovation. This was the finding of Harvard Professor Clayton M. Christensen as well, author of *The Innovator's Dilemma*. In his study of disruptive technologies (technologies that change the rules of an industry, similar to radical innovations) in the computer disk drive industry, Christensen found that new entrants outperformed incumbent firms—"from the simplest to the most radical, the firms that led the industry in every instance of developing and adopting disruptive technologies were entrants to the industry, not its incumbent leaders."

What makes entrepreneurial firms better innovators? For one thing, they are able to recognize possibilities and approach problems with a fresh perspective. They are not burdened by old ways of thinking or beliefs about how things have always been. Here are three examples of what entrepreneurial firms do to excel at innovation:

1. ***Painting pictures, not assembling puzzles.*** Innovative thinking requires a broad perspective, just as a painter needs to draw on a full palate of colors when creating an image that is wholly new. Entrepreneurial firms often have the freedom to see the big picture as well as its component parts. Large companies, be-

cause of the constraints under which they operate, are often required to approach innovation as they would assembling a puzzle—piecing together a set number of predetermined shapes (in the form of personnel, budgets, existing technologies, and so forth) that someone else has devised.

Consider the example of Carol Latham, a staff chemist at British Petroleum (BP), who discovered how plastic parts could be used to keep computers cool. When she approached the top brass with her idea at BP's Ohio research lab where she worked, they weren't interested. It turns out that BP, generally considered to be entrepreneurially minded, was having a bad year—oil stock values were down—and the company did not want to fund any initiatives that detracted from its core business. Perhaps more importantly, most of Latham's colleagues were researching ceramics, and her plastics idea seemed threatening to their efforts. BP just couldn't see what she could see. But Latham was sure she was on to something. She quit her job, labored for months in her basement with mixing bowls and a blender, and formed Thermagon, Inc. Once she had an actual product—superthin polymer sheets cut to fit between computer components, they sold themselves. Named to the *Inc.* 500 list of fastest growing companies three years in a row, Thermagon now has 120 employees, 1,300 customers, and annual revenues of $19 million.

Sources: L. Buchanan, "The Innovation Factor: A Field Guide to Innovation." *Forbes,* April 21, 2003, www.forbes.com; S. Hansen, "You Had Your Chance!" *Inc.,* November 2001, www.inc.com; C. M. Christensen, *The Innovator's Dilemma* (Boston: Harvard Business School Press, 1997); and www.foster-miller.com.

Characteristics of Good Opportunities

The opportunity recognition process involves discovering and forming business concepts into realistic business opportunities. For an opportunity to be viable, it needs to have four qualities.[21]

- ◆ ***Attractive.*** The opportunity must be attractive in the marketplace; that is, there must be market demand for the new product or service. Motorola spent $2.5 billion on Iridium, a global satellite phone system. However, customers didn't like the heavy and bulky phones that could only be used outdoors and cost $1,500 each, so the project was abandoned.[22]
- ◆ ***Achievable.*** The opportunity must be practical and physically possible. Round-trip vacations to the moon might sell really well, but they remain unrealistic. (Orbiting the earth by tourists, however, may be closer than we think. A company called Space Adventures is promising to provide joyrides into space for around $90,000 a trip. It's a service the company cannot even provide yet, but it already has 144 reservations!)[23]

2. ***Solving the big guy's little problems.*** Small firms often succeed by forming alliances with larger firms. And quite often, the big firms need the help. As an incumbent firm grows, the task of management becomes more complicated. Some large firms find it difficult to manage internal processes because their problem-solving capability does not match the complexity of their problems. The innovation process is loaded with choices and uncertainties, making it one of the areas where large firms often lose their edge. One of the ways large firms deal with such problems is by turning to small firms for help.

> Foster-Miller is an engineering and technology development firm that specializes in innovative solutions. With its staff of 200 engineers and scientists, Foster-Miller tackles problems the big firms can't seem to solve. For example, Nabisco, the largest cookie maker in the world, was having trouble making a low-fat version of its Fig Newton because the fat-free batter kept sticking to the cutting equipment. Unable to solve the problem, Nabisco called in Foster-Miller, which designed a noncontact cookie cutter that solved the problem.

3. ***Setting up a big tent.*** Recall from Strategy Spotlight 12.2 the closed model of innovation. According to that perspective, many large firms believe they should "go it alone and do it ourselves" when it comes to innovation. The problem with that approach, according to *Open Innovation* author Henry Chesbrough, is that firms miss out on talent and resources that could make the innovation process more efficient and cost effective. Additionally, other firms that might benefit from an innovation are left out or left to discover it on their own.

> MicroUnity, Inc., a designer of microprocessor software for communications, approaches innovation differently. For one thing, it accepts the fact that it is small. As a result, the private software company welcomes the support and collaboration of others. MicroUnity CEO John Moussouris calls it his "big tent" theory and claims, "If you have a new technology that can make money for a lot of related companies, then you can get other companies to help fund the deployment." When MicroUnity recently worked on a technology to improve computers' high-speed communications, it involved chip vendors, network operators, content providers, and others. All of these companies stood to profit from MicroUnity's innovation. "The ideal situation for a small company," said Moussouris, "is to have the booth near the entrance of the big tent but to allow lots of other folks to come in."

Clearly, large firms have several strengths that small firms do not have. They can bring substantial resources to bear on a problem, and they are often in a position to gain market acceptance of an innovation because of their market power. But the ability to see things with a fresh perspective and not labor under the constraints that often impede large firms may provide small and entrepreneurial firms with a competitive advantage that is often overlooked.

- ◆ ***Durable.*** The opportunity must be attractive long enough for the development and deployment to be successful; that is, the window of opportunity must be open long enough for it to be worthwhile. Toy maker Playing Mantis figured out that retro toys have an enduring appeal. After buying the rights to Johnny Lightning die-cast cars (a Hot Wheels knock-off from the 1960s), founder Tom Lowe generated millions in sales to baby boomers who still loved the toy cars they had as kids.[24]
- ◆ ***Value creating.*** The opportunity must be potentially profitable; that is, the benefits must surpass the cost of development by a significant margin. Kingsley Management LLC thinks it has found a profitable niche in the crowded car wash business. Using state-of-the-art equipment that adjusts to the dimensions of each car, its "Swash" car washes are cheaper than full service, but more convenient than self-wash. Kingsley is building stand-alone units in high-traffic areas, and gas stations are buying in because they need the high-margin car washes to improve profitability.[25]

If a new business concept meets these criteria, two other factors must be considered before the opportunity is launched as a business. First, the readiness and skills of the entrepreneurial founder or team must be evaluated. Do the founders have the necessary

Exhibit 13.3 Opportunity Analysis Framework

Sources: Based on J. A. Timmons and S. Spinelli, *New Venture Creation,* 6th ed. (New York: McGraw-Hill/Irwin, 2004); and W. D. Bygrave, "The Entrepreneurial Process," in W. D. Bygrave, ed., *The Portable MBA in Entrepreneurship,* 2nd ed. (New York: Wiley, 1997).

knowledge and experience to make the venture successful? Second, the availability and access to resources needed for the launch must be considered. Given an analysis of the start-up costs and operational expenses, can the venture obtain the necessary funding? These three factors—the nature of the opportunity itself, the resources available to undertake it, and the characteristics of the entrepreneur(s) pursuing it—are essential for the successful launch of a new venture.[26] In the next section, we address the issue of entrepreneurial resources; following that, we address the importance of entrepreneurial leadership. Exhibit 13.3 identifies the three factors that are needed to successfully proceed—opportunity, resources, and entrepreneur(s).

Both established firms and new ventures must do a good job of opportunity recognition in order to be successful. For the entrepreneurial start-up, however, the issue of available resources and a qualified and motivated founding team are especially critical. Larger firms are more likely to have access to resources and may already have key personnel on board. But for new business founders, starting a new venture is an uphill climb. In the next section, we turn to the challenge of identifying and obtaining resources for small business and entrepreneurial start-ups.

Entrepreneurial Resources

As Exhibit 13.3 indicates, resources are an essential component of a successful entrepreneurial launch. One of the major challenges that entrepreneurial firms face is a lack of resources. For start-ups, the most important resource is usually money. A new firm typically has to expend large sums just to open the door for business. However, financial resources are not the only kind of resource a young firm needs. Human capital and social capital are also important during the early days of a new venture and throughout the life of a small business. Some small firms also rely on government resources to help them thrive.

Young and small firms have many of the same needs as larger firms—financial resources, skilled and experienced workers, and the ability to operate in a network of beneficial relationships. But they also have unique needs that stem from being young or small. Nearly all young firms face the liability of newness.[27] This phrase refers to the vulnerability that most new firms feel because they lack experience, are unknown in their industry, and are unfamiliar to customers. Until they have proven themselves, young firms lack credibility: Banks often will not lend them money, and suppliers may not extend them credit. Tim Demello, chairman and CEO of Internet start-up Streamline, summed it up this way:

> Here I am, the budding entrepreneur. I have next to nothing. No money, no credibility. I also have a big challenge: I have to get people to understand who I am, what my company does, what we have to offer. I not only have to sell my product or service, I also have to sell my company to the people I want to work for me—people who will have to give up really good careers for this unknown start-up. I also have to sell my company to people who will invest capital in it. I have to sell my company to vendors, to get them to extend me credit. The point is that in the early stages of my start-up, I have absolutely no credibility. So my challenge becomes, How do I use somebody else's credibility?[28]

Demello, like so many dot-com entrepreneurs, was unable to leverage the credibility of others, and Streamline ultimately failed. (The name "streamline," however, is now being used by another Internet company). To overcome the liability of newness and build credibility, therefore, founders must find practical ways to obtain resources. These include financial as well as other resources. In this section we will address some of the resource requirements of entrepreneurial firms and how they can meet their needs.

New-Venture Financing

Hand-in-hand with the importance of markets (and marketing) to new-venture creation, start-up firms must also have financing. In fact, the level of available financing is often a strong determinant of how the business is launched and its eventual success. Cash finances are, of course, highly important. But access to capital, such as a line of credit or favorable payment terms with a supplier, can also help a start-up to succeed.

A new firm's financing requirements and sources of funds typically change as it grows. In the next two sections, we address sources of financing in the earlier and later stages of launching a new venture.

Early-Stage Financing The vast majority of new firms are low-budget start-ups launched with personal savings and the contributions of family and friends.[29] Even among firms included in the 2003 *Entrepreneur* list of the 100 fastest-growing new businesses, 61 percent reported that their start-up funds came from personal savings.[30] Although bank financing, public financing, and venture capital are important sources of small business finance, these types of financial support are typically available only after a company has started to conduct business and generate sales. Therefore, the founders usually carry the initial burden of financing most new firms.

The burdens are many: renting space, buying inventory, installing phones and equipment, obtaining insurance, and paying salaries. How does a cash-strapped entrepreneur make ends meet? One way is by *bootstrapping*. The term is used to describe persons who rely on their personal resources—and resourcefulness—to succeed. Applied to entrepreneurs, it refers to techniques used to minimize borrowing and avoid selling parts of a business to investors or venture capitalists. For the young start-up, this involves getting the most out of every dollar and doing without anything but the bare necessities. It may mean buying used equipment, operating out of a basement, or forgoing a new car purchase in order to reinvest in the business.

The typical new business owner has just $4,000 invested the day the business opens.[31] Therefore, bootstrapping to make ends meet is a common practice among start-up entrepreneurs. For example, Brad and Gia Boyle of Moab, Utah, got their start running Walkabout Travel Gear out of a 37-foot recreational vehicle. Using a motor home as an office not only helped them save money on rent, it also kept them in touch with their industry—travel. Their bootstrapping philosophy is expressed by a quote on their website: "A tight budget is the mother of adventure." In a recent year, the business brought in about $250,000.[32]

Bootstrapping may shift a start-up's priorities. To successfully bootstrap, a new firm may have to get cash-generating products or services to market quickly in order to jump-start cash flow. As a result, the new firm may postpone development activities or investments in technology. Consider the example of Stacy's Pita Chip Co.:

> In 1996 founders Mark and Stacy Andrus were operating a successful pita-wrap sandwich business that was ready to grow. But customers kept asking for the baked chips they made every night from leftover pita bread and handed out free to customers waiting in line. "We thought we could get bigger faster with the chips," said Stacy. The couple, who were still paying off six-figure student loans, decided to take their chips nationwide. The business they created is a model of bootstrapping efficiency. The paper sign on the door, folding tables, and used dining room chairs are the first signs of their spartan approach to business. They also saved over $250,000 buying used equipment. "Everything goes into the business," said Stacy, who takes home a scavenger-level salary. But it has paid off. Their baked pita chips' annual revenues recently hit $1.3 million, with sales in 37 states.[33]

If personal savings and bootstrapping efforts are insufficient to finance the business, entrepreneurs must turn to other sources of funds. One of the most common mistakes business founders often make is trying to launch a business with insufficient capital. Thus, seeking external sources of financing is often essential for start-up success.

Funding that comes from others, unless it is a gift, will take one of two forms—debt or equity. There are important differences between the two types of financing:

♦   *Debt.* This refers to borrowed funds, such as an interest-bearing loan, that must be repaid regardless of firm performance. To obtain it usually requires that some business or personal assets be used as collateral.

♦   *Equity.* This refers to invested funds, such as in shares of stock, that increase or decrease in value depending on the performance of the business. To obtain it usually requires that business founders give up some ownership and control of the business.

There are many possible sources of external funding. One of the most important sources is family and friends. This can be an especially helpful resource during the very early stages of a new venture. Among the 2003 *Entrepreneur* 100 fastest-growing firms, 18 percent received start-up financing from family and friends.[34] This type of financing may be in the form of either debt or equity. Doing business with family and friends, however, can be a delicate matter, because personal relationships are very different from business dealings. To avoid creating hard feelings, it is best to treat money loaned or invested by an acquaintance or family member in a businesslike way. Have a clear understanding whether the money is a loan (debt) or an investment (equity). If it is a loan, put the terms of repayment in writing. Be as realistic as possible about what the prospects for the business are and suggest some alternative ways to pay back the money in the event of failure. If the funds represent an equity investment, describe how the investor will obtain a return and make it clear that if the business fails, the money will be lost. Specifying loan repayment terms and methods of cashing-out investments are common requirements for firms that receive funding from banks or venture investors. Applying the same practices to interactions with family and friends is a good way to get experience as well as avoid hard feelings.

To preserve cash, another technique start-up businesses use involves relying on unconventional or creative financing sources. Exhibit 13.4 describes five financing alternatives often used by young and small firms.

Method	Description
Leasing	Allows a start-up to hold on to its cash and minimize commitments to equipment or real estate that might need updating as the company grows (or shrinks). Leasing costs are deductible as a business expense.
Barter	A traditional noncash means of exchanging products or services. Bartering has enjoyed a resurgence in popularity because exchange services now available on the Internet are facilitating more barter transactions.
Credit cards	One of the fastest-growing techniques for financing start-ups and number one among female entrepreneurs. It's like a bank loan without the lengthy approval process. But the high interest rates that some cards charge could make it risky.
Supplier financing	Suppliers that let you pay for goods or services in 60 or 90 days rather than after only 10 to 30 days are, in effect, financing your purchase. Some suppliers will agree to this because they need your business as badly as you need their credit.
Factoring	Factoring is a method of raising cash by selling accounts receivables to a third party or financing against the value of receivables. It's generally used only for short-term cash needs and often comes with a hefty interest charge.

**Exhibit 13.4
Alternatives to
Traditional
Financing**

Sources: J. A. Fraser, "Plans for Growth," *Inc.,* March 2001, pp. 56–57; J. A. Fraser, "A Hitchhiker's Guide to Capital Resources," *Inc.,* February 1998, pp. 74–82; and T. Owens, "Getting Financing in 1990," *Small Business Reports,* June 1990, pp. 61–72.

Later-Stage Financing   Once an entrepreneur has a going concern, certain types of financing become more readily available. Young firms that have contracted with a first customer or can demonstrate several months of sales are considered a better risk by investors and creditors. Even "angel" investors—private individuals who provide seed capital during the early stages of a new venture—favor companies that already have a winning business model and dominance in a market niche.[35] This is especially true in the post–dot-com era, because financing has become harder to obtain. According to Cal Simmons, coauthor of *Every Business Needs an Angel,* "I would much rather talk to an entrepreneur who has already put his money and his effort into proving the concept. And I think most angels I know feel the same way right now."[36]

Angel investors are an important source of equity investment for many entrepreneurial firms. They often invest modest amounts—under $1 million—and help firms that are trying to grow beyond their initial start-up success. Angels also provide mentoring and contacts for young firms that are trying to become established.

Start-ups that involve large capital investments or extensive development costs—such as manufacturing or engineering firms that are trying to commercialize an innovative product—may have high cash requirements soon after they are founded. Others need financing only when they are on the brink of rapid growth. To obtain such funding, entrepreneurial firms often seek venture capital. Venture capital is a form of private equity financing through which entrepreneurs raise money by selling shares in the new venture. In contrast to angel investors, who are actively engaged in investing their own money, venture capital

Aptus Financial: Experience and Commitment Win Venture Capital Support

Aptus Financial, LLC, is the name of a Portland, Oregon, start-up that develops and markets wireless banking technology. One of its first products was a technology that allows consumers who use prepaid phone cards to buy additional minutes at an ATM machine. Customers can either use funds from their bank account or other electronic sources to "refuel" their calling cards. Aptus is also developing technology that automates how banks cash checks made payable to nonbank customers. Its approach uses iris scanning or fingerprinting technology for identification and is designed to eliminate the use of tellers for such transactions.

To grow their business, Aptus founders Rick Holt and David Grano went looking for $1.5 million in venture

Sources: N. L. Torres, "The Thrill of the Chase: Building Trust and Credibility," *Entrepreneur,* July 2003, pp. 62–63; R. Goldfield, "Grano Wants ATMs to Do More than Give Cash," *Business Journal of Portland,* June 6, 2002, www.bizjournals.com/portland/; and www.aptusfinancial.com.

capital in 2002. Both had extensive experience—Holt as the vice president of sales at E*Trade and Grano as president and CEO of Card Capture Services, a distributor of ATMs. But neither had sought venture capital before. Even so, they got the money they were seeking. They attribute their success to two factors—experience and their personal investment in and commitment to the business.

According to Grano, "We had a successful track record in a like industry segment, so we weren't trying something that none of us had been involved in before, where we were initiating new relationships." Aptus's 2002 sales were $4.2 million, so the business clearly had a going concern by the time it sought additional investment capital. This helped them to not only obtain funding, but also to get favorable terms. "One of the reasons we got the terms we wanted," says Holt, "was that we had so much skin in the game to start—not only with experience but with our own capital already at play. That lent a lot of credibility."

companies are organized to place the funds of private investors into lucrative business opportunities.

Venture capital is an important source of funding for certain types of entrepreneurial firms.[37] Entrepreneurs who seek large infusions of capital usually turn to some form of private capital financing. Venture capital was a primary driver of the rapid growth in Internet start-ups. Although loans by venture capitalists have declined sharply since their rapid expansion during the Internet boom of 1999–2000, venture capital investing in 2002 totaled over $21 billion.[38]

Equity financing, however, often comes with strings attached. On the one hand, venture capitalists often have high performance expectations and demand a regular accounting. On the other hand, sometimes these "strings" can enhance a firm's chances for success. Venture capital groups often provide important managerial advice, links to key contacts in an industry, and the peace of mind of knowing that financial backers support your project. But founders who use venture capital forfeit part of the payoff if the venture succeeds. Further, they must agree to let the venture capitalists influence management decisions. For Phil Trubey, founder of Netpartners Internet Solutions, it meant losing his job. The Morgan Stanley venture partners who agreed to back his start-up became powerful members of his board of directors. Four months after putting up $6 million in equity, they informed Trubey that his company had outgrown him.[39]

One of the problems with Internet start-ups was that they were often launched by founders who had little experience. Strategy Spotlight 13.4 highlights Aptus Financial and describes how the founders' industry experience and commitment helped them obtain venture capital from investors who are happy to let the professionals run the show.

Venture capital groups also help start-ups by sponsoring independent business incubators. Recall from Chapter 12 the use of in-house incubators by large corporations to launch new ventures. Incubators are also used by or in conjunction with venture capital groups to help facilitate the growth of both start-up and later-stage companies. The venture capital groups provide management assistance; the incubators provide office space, technology infrastructure, and business support services. An example is TechSpace, an international network of incubators with offices in New York, California, and several other global locations. Besides providing the usual incubator services, TechSpace and its venture capital partners often invest in the young firms that reside in its office communities.[40]

Angels and venture capitalists provide equity investments for entrepreneurial firms. Another important source of funding is from debt. The primary provider of debt financing for new ventures is commercial banks. Although credit cards often provide an important source of funding for very young firms (see Exhibit 13.4), banks provide an important source of ongoing funding. Because banks make their money by receiving interest on the loans as well as a return of principal, they are keenly interested in the firm's ability to repay the loan. That is why businesses with a track record of generating revenues are more likely to get bank loans. Besides cash flow, banks are also interested in collateral—assets that an entrepreneurial firm could sell to repay its loan in the event of a default. As a result, one of the ways that young firms often get start-up capital is through a home equity loan. Why? Because the house provides collateral which, in the event that the entrepreneur fails to make payments, the bank could force the homeowner to sell to satisfy its debt.

Clearly, financial resources are essential for new ventures and small businesses. But other types of resources are also vitally important. In the next section, we will address the role of human capital, social capital, and government resources in the entrepreneurial start-up process.

Other Entrepreneurial Resources

Whether an entrepreneur starts by bootstrapping or brings a large sum of assets to a new venture, founders often turn to three other types of resources that were discussed in Chapter 4: human capital, social capital, and government resources. Young and small firms have many of the same needs as larger firms—skilled and experienced workers and the ability to operate in a network of beneficial relationships. But they also have unique needs that stem from being young or small. By relying on the talents of other people, their network of contacts, and support services provided by government programs, entrepreneurial firms can often strengthen their ability to survive and succeed.

Human Capital   The most important human capital may be in the founding team. Bankers, venture capitalists, and angel investors who invest in start-up firms and small businesses agree that the most important asset an entrepreneurial firm can have is strong and skilled management. According to Stephen Gaal, founding member of Walnut Venture Associates, venture investors do not invest in businesses, "We invest in people . . . very smart people with very high integrity." Managers need to have a strong base of experience and extensive domain knowledge, as well as an ability to make rapid decisions and change direction as shifting circumstances may require. Additionally, among start ups, more is better. New ventures that are started by teams of three, four, or five entrepreneurs are more likely to succeed in the long run than ventures launched by "lone wolf" entrepreneurs.[41]

Social Capital   New ventures founded by entrepreneurs who have extensive social contacts are more likely to succeed than ventures started without the support of a social network.[42] This is one of the major avenues for overcoming the problem of the liability of newness. Even though a firm may be new, if the founders have contacts who will vouch for them, they gain exposure and build legitimacy faster. This support can come from several sources: prior jobs, industry organizations, and local business groups such as the chamber

strategy spotlight 13.5

How Nancy Michaels's Networking Paid Off

Nancy Michaels had a service she wanted to sell—a small-business seminar entitled "Creative Marketing Strategies." She noticed that Office Depot, the office supply chain, was making an effort to distinguish itself by offering services to small businesses. "Just look at the Office Depot website," Michaels observed, "you can see they want to add value to their small-business customers. They want to provide knowledge and expertise." She reasoned that offering her class at Office Depot retail sites would make the store a regular destination for small-business owners and give the stores a chance to offer coupons and other incentives to attendees. It seemed like a win–win situation. Now she just had to sell the idea.

As the founder of a small marketing company, Impression Impact, and the former publicist for Matt Lauer, currently cohost of the *Today Show,* Michaels knew a thing or two about networking. She also knew the importance of going to the top when you want to do business

with an organization. So Michaels began reaching out to her network to find a way to contact Office Depot's chairman and CEO, Bruce Nelson.

She learned that Nelson was to be a speaker at an Office Depot–sponsored event for the Women's Business Enterprise Council (WBENC) in Boca Raton, Florida. At the event's silent auction fund-raiser, Michaels bid $1,050 to have lunch with Nelson. She recalls that the colleagues sitting with her thought she was crazy to bid so high. But she won the auction, and at lunch two months later she pitched her idea. After a market test, Office Depot gave Michaels the in-store seminars assignment. She is also OfficeDepot.com's lead consultant for its Web Café Series for Successful Business Women.

Michaels's networking paid off. Not only did she form a successful alliance with Office Depot, but also she has landed many more speaking engagements and made alliances with other major corporations, including Merrill Lynch, Fleet Bank (now Bank of America), and Staples. Thomas G. Stemberg, chairman and CEO of Staples, said of Michaels's appearances at his stores, "retail sales increase 200 to 300 percent on the days of these events."

Sources: J. Bick, "Gold Bond," *Entrepreneur,* March 2003, pp. 54–57; E. Segal, "Schmoozing Your Way to Business Success," *Startup Journal,* August 27, 2002, www.startupjournal.com; and www.impressionimpact.com.

of commerce. These contacts can all contribute to a growing network that provides support for the young or small firm. Janina Pawlowski, cofounder of the online lending company E-Loan, attributes part of her success to the strong advisors she persuaded to serve on her board of directors, including Tim Koogle, CEO of Yahoo![43]

Strategy Spotlight 13.5 describes how marketing consultant Nancy Michaels used her social contacts and networking skills to get a lunch date with the CEO of Office Depot. Over lunch, she pitched an idea and eventually won a big contract.

Government Resources In the United States, the federal government is an important resource for many young and small businesses. It provides support for entrepreneurial firms in two key arenas—financing and government contracting. The Small Business Administration (SBA) has several loan guarantee programs designed to support the growth and development of entrepreneurial firms. The government itself does not lend money but underwrites loans made by banks to small businesses, thus reducing the risk associated with lending to firms that have unproven records. The SBA also offers training, counseling, and other support services through its local offices and Small Business Development Centers.[44]

Another key area of support is in government contracting. Programs sponsored by the SBA and other government agencies ensure that small businesses have the opportunity to bid on contracts to provide goods and services to the government. Strategy Spotlight 13.6 describes how several small firms have benefited from government contracts.

State and local governments also have hundreds of programs to provide funding, contracts, and other support for new ventures and small businesses. Local economic develop-

strategy spotlight

Government Work: It's Good Enough for Many Small Businesses

Homeland security, the war in Afghanistan, the rebuilding of Iraq—these projects and more have been keeping the U.S. government busy since the September 11 tragedies. To meet the needs created by these initiatives, more and more private companies are being called on to serve as contractors. Federal spending on information technology (IT) alone increased 18 percent from 2002 to 2003 to $59 billion, and it is expected to grow. This has allowed companies such as Cyveillance, a northern Virginia start-up that specializes in Internet espionage software, to grow its business by providing online monitoring services for the government.

To encourage businesses to bid on contracts, government agencies are proactively seeking bidders. This has created numerous opportunities for small businesses, because federal law requires that prime contracts use subcontractors on any job that is larger than $500,000. Although the big contracts go to major contractors like Boeing, Unisys, and Lockheed Martin, there are many subcontracting opportunities. This is how Gryphon Technologies, an IT logistics company, got its start. Its first contract was a small job for Northrop Grumman. Although at the time it seemed to founder Pam Braden like a low-level opportunity, she did not hesitate to take it. This led to bigger contracts, and now Gryphon is a prime contractor for the Department of Defense. "If you want to be a large business, which I want to be," says Braden, "you need to network the big companies and the government itself."

Sources: C. Y. Chen, "Getting a Piece of the D.C. Pie," *Fortune,* May 12, 2003, p. 34; R. Kurtz, "What Your Country Can Do for You," *Inc.,* July 2003, pp. 33–34; www.cyveillance.com; and www.sba.gov/sbir/.

Not all of the government work is IT related. Thousands of projects, ranging from high-end engineering to maintenance and supply projects, are available to small business subcontractors. There are many peacetime opportunities available as well. The Small Business Administration (SBA) in cooperation with the National Science Foundation (NSF) runs a program known as Small Business Innovation Research (SBIR). The program funded $1.5 billion of research in 2001. Here is a description of SBIR's goals from its website:

> SBIR targets the entrepreneurial sector because that is where most innovation and innovators thrive. However, the risk and expense of conducting serious R&D efforts are often beyond the means of many small businesses. By reserving a specific percentage of federal R&D funds for small business, SBIR protects the small business and enables it to compete on the same level as larger businesses. SBIR funds the critical start-up and development stages, and it encourages the commercialization of the technology, product, or service, which, in turn, stimulates the U.S. economy.

As these various programs suggest, the federal government is potentially a rich resource for small firms, which supports innovation and the successful commercialization of new venture opportunities. Dealing with the government, however, can be time consuming and involve lots of "red tape," that is, reporting requirements and regulations that are quite demanding. Even so, many small companies owe their success to the support they have gotten from government-sponsored programs.

ment initiatives such as the Southwest Minnesota Initiative Fund (SWMIF) are often designed specifically to stimulate small business activity. State-sponsored microenterprise funds such as the Utah Microenterprise Loan Fund (UMLF) provide funding as well as training for companies with fewer than five employees that are seeking less than $25,000.[45] Consider the example of Lissa D'Aquanni, who launched a gourmet chocolate business in her basement in 1998. As the business grew, she needed more space. To get it, she combined creative financing with government support.

> D'Aquanni had her eye on an abandoned building close to her home, but it cost $95,000 and needed $260,000 of renovation, more than her business could afford. So she turned to the local community. First, she asked for the support of local residents who were attracted to her plans to revitalize an empty building in the neighborhood and helped raised $25,000. Then the Albany Local Development Corporation, an economic development group, loaned her $95,000 to buy the building. A local credit union provided her with a government guaranteed loan to begin the

renovations. A community development group helped her apply to a state program that funds energy-efficient upgrades such as windows, siding, and light fixtures. A matching grant program to encourage commercial development provided funds to upgrade the buildings facade. Eventually, she got the whole job done. "There are pockets of money out there, whether it be municipalities, counties, chambers of commerce," says Bill Brigham, director of the Albany Small Business Development Center. "Those are the loan programs that no one seems to have information about. A lot of these programs will not require the collateral and cash that is typical of traditional [loans]."[46]

As you can see, the government provides numerous funding opportunities for small business and new ventures. Although working with the government sometimes has its drawbacks in terms of issues of regulation and time-consuming decision making, programs to support young and small firms constitute an important resource for firms to use during the start-up and growth process.

Clearly, the resource needs of new ventures are enormous. Unlike established firms, which often have a stockpile of resources—both human and physical—to draw upon, entrepreneurial firms are usually starting from scratch. Meeting the resource requirements of a new venture can be critically important to its success in the short run and over the long term. In the next section we will consider another type of capability that is especially important for the success of small or young firms: entrepreneurial leadership.

Entrepreneurial Leadership

Whether a venture is launched by an individual entrepreneur or an entrepreneurial team, effective leadership is needed. Launching a new venture requires a special kind of leadership. It involves courage, belief in one's convictions, and the energy to work hard even in difficult circumstances. Entrepreneurs and small business owners work for themselves. They don't have bosses to inspire them or tell them what to do. Their next paycheck will arrive only as a result of their own efforts. They must oversee all aspects of a company's operations as well as monitor quality and performance. Yet these are the very challenges that motivate most business owners. Entrepreneurs put themselves to the test and get their satisfaction from acting independently, overcoming obstacles, and thriving financially. To do so, they must embody three characteristics of leadership—vision, dedication and drive, and commitment to excellence—and pass these on to all those who work with them.

Vision

Vision may be an entrepreneur's most important asset. The entrepreneur has to envision realities that do not yet exist. This may consist of a new product or a unique service. It may include a competitive goal, such as besting a close competitor. For many entrepreneurs, the vision may be personal: building something from scratch, being one's own boss, making a difference, achieving financial security. In every case, entrepreneurs must exercise a kind of transformational leadership that aims to create something new and, in some way, change their world. Not all founders of new ventures succeed. Indeed, the majority fail. But without a vision, most entrepreneurs would never even get a new business off the ground.

The idea of creating something new is captured in the vision of Paul Robbins, founder of Caribbean Shipping & Cold Storage.

In a run-down part of Jacksonville, Florida, Paul Robbins envisioned opportunity. Where others saw a stretch of ramshackle houses, a lot strewn with rubble, and an abandoned warehouse, Robbins saw promise and profits. Caribbean Shipping & Cold Storage handles food products that need cold storage on their way to Puerto Rico and other Caribbean islands. In the past, shipments from far-flung U.S. locations might be transferred from truck to train to ship as many as six times. Instead of making arrangements with all those carriers, customers such as Outback Steakhouse and the Ritz-Carlton have Robbins handle the entire shipment. So why the run-down lot in Jacksonville? Because it's one block from Interstate 95 and only half a mile from Interstate 10. CSX train lines are so close that train whistles interrupt meetings. And the lot is adjacent to Jacksonville's shipping port. In other words, it's a crossroads—one that has paid off. Caribbean Shipping's revenues rose from $3.5 million to $20 million in just four years.[47]

By itself, however, just having a vision is not enough. The new venture idea must be effectively articulated as well. To develop support, get financial backing, and attract employees, entrepreneurial leaders must share their vision with others. The following leadership skills are needed to enact an entrepreneurial vision:[48]

♦ *Be able to communicate with a wide audience.* Entrepreneurial founders must reach a diverse collection of stakeholders. Understanding how these constituencies differ and fitting the vision message to their concerns is an important element of good leadership.

♦ *Be willing to make unpopular decisions.* As the new venture concept is developed, tough decisions will have to be made that define and shape the boundaries of the vision. Good leaders realize their decisions will not please everyone, but they still have to make them and move on.

♦ *Be determined to make sure your message gets through.* Employees of a venture start-up must have a clear sense of the leader's vision. It's not enough to just make a vision statement. Good leaders must demonstrate how it is defining the direction of the company so the employees internalize it.

♦ *Create and implement quality systems and methods that will survive.* For a vision to be meaningful on a daily basis, leaders need to think of it as a tool. As such, it can be used to identify benchmarks that are needed to maintain quality, control outcomes, and measure success.

Creating and articulating a vision provide an essential starting point for an entrepreneurial venture. But the vision itself is not enough. Without enthusiasm and perseverance, many ventures never get off the ground. Next, we turn to the important qualities of dedication and drive.

Dedication and Drive

Dedication and drive are key success factors for the start-up entrepreneur. Dedication and drive are reflected in hard work. They require patience, stamina, and a willingness to work long hours. One of the key reasons that start-up businesses fail is that the founders lack commitment and neglect the business. Thus, drive involves internal motivation, while dedication calls for an intellectual commitment to the enterprise that keeps the entrepreneur going even in the face of bad news or poor luck. Entrepreneurs typically have a strong enthusiasm, not just for their venture but for life in general. As a result, their dedication and drive are like a magnet that draws people to the business and builds confidence in what the entrepreneurs are doing. Consider the example of Bill Nguyen.

Bill Nguyen is the founder and CEO of Seven Networks, a wireless software development start-up. Nguyen, who is only 30 years old and sleeps just three hours a night, has already been a part of six high-tech start-ups. One month after selling his previous start-up, Onebox.com, to Openwave Systems for $850 million, Nguyen launched Seven Networks and started raising venture capital. Initially, the venture capital firm Ignition and Greylock told him, "Bill, we love you, but it's not going to work." This didn't stop Nguyen. He went home and worked on the technical problems for three days straight with no sleep. When he showed up at Ignition's offices with a

The model of the charismatic leader is wrong for entrepreneurs, according to veteran *Inc.* magazine editor Michael Hopkins. Why? Because it requires the entrepreneur to be a larger-than-life figure who is supposed to inspire dedication, solve all problems, and work long hours. But that leadership style is not only a formula for personal burnout, it can also ultimately sabotage the business by placing too much responsibility on the shoulders of one person. In fact, it's hardly leading at all in the sense of delegating or supervising the work of others. "It demands of leaders far more than it gives back," says Hopkins. "For entrepreneurs, it's toxic."

Instead, entrepreneurs need to adopt a style of leadership that enables them to be nurtured by the business rather than drained by it. It is a style that Hopkins calls the "antihero" because it refers to an approach that is the opposite of the tireless, workaholic leader. Here are four rules for the antihero leader:

♦ **Rule #1**—*Ask why you're here. Know what you want. Don't apologize.* Business founders must be clear about why they have started the business and what they hope it will do for them. Rather than wishing for a typical financial goal such as "grow 10 percent per year," leaders must go deeper to understand what the business means to them and what meaning they want to give it. Only then can they be honest with themselves about how best to run it.

♦ **Rule #2**—*Don't ask "How?" Ask "Who?" Assume you're not the answer.* Too often, leaders envision a new opportunity but dismiss it because they

conclude they don't have enough time or know-how to get it done. Leaders need to turn their attention instead to who can execute the vision for them or help them accomplish it. Such an approach gets the best qualified people working on the vision and lets the leader lead.

♦ **Rule #3**—*Embrace the difference between "I am my company" and "I have a company."* Antihero leaders must make room for other people to shine. If the leader overidentifies with the company and becomes its only face and voice, there is no room for other organization members to make contributions or share responsibilities. When the company, rather than the leader, is the focus, employees can be more engaged and find meaningful ways to have impact.

♦ **Rule #4**—*Forget Superman. Be a part of something.* Leaders who give up on the charismatic approach lose their chance to be heroes. But they also lose the sense of isolation that comes from feeling that they must supply all the emotion and momentum and that if they stop performing, the business will grind to a halt. There is also much to be gained. Instead of feeling separated, the antihero leader becomes part of a community dedicated to a cause greater than themselves.

An approach such as this is utterly practical. It converts employees from being bearers of bad news to responsible problem solvers. It takes the entrepreneur/founder out of the limelight and shifts the emphasis to the company itself. In an era when businesses have to be run well to survive, the leader as antihero embodies the kind of down-to-earth approach that may be necessary for long-term success.

Source: M. S. Hopkins. "Why Leadership Is the Most Dangerous Idea in American Business," *Inc.*, June 2003, pp. 87–94.

revised plan, he had solved the problem. Soon thereafter, the venture capitalists pledged $34 million to Nguyen's Seven Networks venture. According to Brad Silverberg, CEO at Ignition, "He's a rocket; you just strap in and try to hold on."[49]

Clearly, Nguyen is an example of a driven entrepreneur who has used his personal experience and sheer stamina to make his businesses succeed. Such dedication may be more important for some entrepreneurial firms. However, a business built on the heroic efforts of one person may suffer in the long run—especially if something happens to that person. Strategy Spotlight 13.7 describes an alternative perspective—the entrepreneurial leader as "antihero."

Dedication and drive are important to success. But even hard-charging entrepreneurs can fail if they don't make an effort to do quality work or lack the competencies to achieve their aims. It is this commitment to excellence that we turn to next.

Commitment to Excellence

Successfully managing the many elements of an entrepreneurial start-up requires a commitment to excellence. Entrepreneurs sometimes launch businesses without understanding what it will take to succeed. One of the major causes of business failure is managerial incompetence; too many business owners don't have a serious appreciation for the strategic implications of their behavior. Another source of problems is insensitivity to the needs of customers and other stakeholders, To achieve excellence, therefore, venture founders and small business owners must:

- Understand the customer.
- Provide quality products and services.
- Manage the business knowledgeably and expertly.
- Pay attention to details.
- Continuously learn.

As we learned above, new firms are often vulnerable because they lack credibility and experience. To improve the chances of survival, entrepreneurial founders must devote themselves to surpassing the performance of other competitors. To do so, they need to develop a sensitivity to how the elements of their value chain fit together and contribute to overall success. Having this type of "whole organization" perspective can help a venture founder manage the synergies that might exist between different value-adding functions in a firm's value chain. For the firm to survive and become successful, the entrepreneurial leader must manage a firm's value proposition and set high standards for quality and customer service. Consider the example of Sue Bhatia and Rose International:

> Rose International is a fast-growing information technology firm located in St. Louis, Missouri. Its CEO is Sue Bhatia, whose commitment to excellence helped her firm grow to 250 employees in just seven years despite its being a minority, female-owned firm in a male-dominated industry. Bhatia said, "I think it's important to remember that the customer is looking for good service. They don't care what your gender or race is. They want to see you deliver your service better than anyone, every time. If you can do that, you have a chance." According to Joe Hartmann, president of Digital Dimensions, Inc., who hired Bhatia's company to provide database architecture and network management solutions, Rose is a model of excellence. "Rose International has delivered more than promised since day one," Hartmann said. "They listen, and have an ability to draw upon their nationwide resources to provide the best solution possible."[50]

Another indicator of an entrepreneur's commitment to excellence is what kind of people they surround themselves with. Founders who think they can "do it all" and fail to recognize the importance of drawing on the talents and experience of others often fail. Successful entrepreneurs often report that they owe their success to hiring people smarter than themselves to make things happen.

In his book *Good to Great,* Jim Collins makes an important point: Great companies are typically not led by lone-wolf leaders. Building a start-up on the vision or charisma of a single person can hinder a young firm, because when that person leaves, it creates a vacuum that may be hard to fill. In fact, the reason some companies never go from good to great is because they never fill the void left by the founder. Instead, business leaders with a commitment to excellence recognize that skilled and experienced people are needed to make the business successful. Such people are themselves leaders who attract other top-quality people to the organization.[51]

Another important practice is to let people go who don't fit with the company's culture. Even skilled persons can create problems for a firm if they do not embrace the company's goals and work ethic. Poor performers or laggards must also be proactively dismissed. Success requires focused and disciplined action. In the case of employees, that means leaders must have a willingness to get rid of people who are not working out. In an excellent company, says Collins, "Those people who do not share the company's core values find themselves surrounded by corporate antibodies and ejected like a virus."[52]

Although entrepreneurs must also exhibit other qualities of strong leadership, as we have suggested in earlier chapters, the combined elements of vision, dedication, drive, and commitment to excellence are especially important to the start-up entrepreneur. In the previous sections, we have examined three factors involved in effectively pursuing a venture opportunity—the opportunity itself, the available resources, and the qualities of entrepreneurial leadership. Next, we will turn to the elements of entrepreneurial strategy that are commonly associated with successful new venture creation.

Entrepreneurial Strategy

Successfully creating new ventures requires several ingredients. As indicated in Exhibit 13.3, three factors are necessary—a viable opportunity, sufficient resources, and a skilled and dedicated entrepreneur or entrepreneurial team. The previous three sections have addressed these requirements. Once these elements are in place, the new venture needs a strategy. For any given venture, the best strategy for the enterprise will be determined to some extent by the unique features of the opportunity, resources, and entrepreneur(s) in combination with other conditions in the business environment. But there are still numerous strategic choices to be made. The tools and techniques introduced in this text, such as five-forces and value-chain analyses, can also be used to guide decision making among new ventures and small businesses. In this section, we consider several different strategic factors that are unique to new ventures and also how the generic strategies introduced in Chapter 5 can be applied to entrepreneurial firms. We also indicate how combination strategies might benefit young and small firms and address the potential pitfalls associated with launching new venture strategies.

As noted earlier, identifying strong opportunities is an important first step for any company that wants to launch an entrepreneurial venture. In addition to opportunity recognition, young and small businesses can benefit from strategically analyzing the situation surrounding a venture. To be successful, small and new ventures must evaluate industry conditions, the competitive environment, and market opportunities in order to position themselves strategically.

However, a traditional strategic analysis may have to be altered somewhat to fit the entrepreneurial situation. For example, five-forces analysis (as discussed in Chapter 2) is typically used by established firms. It can also be applied to the analysis of new ventures to assess the impact of industry and competitive forces. But you may ask, How does a new entrant evaluate the threat of new entrants?

First, the new entrant needs to examine barriers to entry. If the barriers are too high, the potential entrant may decide not to enter or to gather more resources before attempting to do so. Compared to an older firm with an established reputation and available resources, the barriers to entry may be insurmountable for an entrepreneurial start-up. Therefore, understanding the force of these barriers is critical in making a decision to launch.

A second factor that may be especially important to a young or small firm is the threat of retaliation by incumbents. In many cases, entrepreneurial ventures *are* the new entrants that pose a threat to incumbent firms. Therefore, in applying the five-forces model to young firms, the threat of retaliation by established firms needs to be considered. This threat can be deadly for a young start-up.

New ventures often face challenges that threaten their survival. They tend to have less power than large firms, which can put them at a disadvantage. To overcome this problem, small firms and start-ups must look for a strategic opportunity to offer a unique value proposition to potential customers. Part of any decision about what opportunity to pursue is a consideration of how a new entrant will actually enter a new market. The concept of entry strategies provides a useful means of addressing the types of choices that new ventures have, and that is the subject we turn to next.

Entry Strategies

As suggested earlier, one of the most challenging aspects of launching a new venture is finding a way to begin doing business that generates cash flow, builds credibility, attracts good employees, and overcomes the liability of newness. One aspect of that effort is the initial decision about how to get a foothold in the market. The idea of an entry strategy or "entry wedge" describes several approaches that firms may take.[53] Several factors discussed earlier will affect this decision.

♦ Does the entrepreneur prefer control or growth?
♦ Is the product/service high-tech or low-tech?
♦ What resources are available for the initial launch?
♦ What are the industry and competitive conditions?
♦ What is the overall market potential?

In some respects, any type of entry into a market for the first time may be considered entrepreneurial. But the entry strategy will vary depending on how risky and innovative the new business concept is. New-entry strategies typically fall into one of three categories—pioneering new entry, imitative new entry, or adaptive new entry.

Pioneering New Entry A young firm with a radical new product or highly innovative service may change the way business is conducted in an industry. This kind of pioneering—creating new ways to solve old problems or meeting customer's needs in a unique new way—is referred to as a pioneering new entry. If the product or service is unique enough, a pioneering new entrant may actually have little direct competition. The first personal computer was a pioneering product—there had never been anything quite like it and it revolutionized computing. The first Internet browser provided a type of pioneering service. These breakthroughs created whole new industries and changed the competitive landscape. But breakthrough innovations continue to inspire pioneering entrepreneurial efforts. Consider the example of SkyTower Telecommunications, a year 2000 start-up that is hoping to take wireless communications to new heights:

> Wireless communications systems have only three ways to get to your cell phone or computer—radio towers that are often not tall enough, satellites that cost $50 million to $400 million to launch, and short-range Wi-Fi transmitters (see Chapter 8). SkyTower proposes a fourth alternative: unmanned, solar-powered airplanes that look like flying wings and send out Internet, mobile phone, and high-definition TV signals. The planes have already been successfully tested over Hawaii. They are able to fly at an altitude of 12 miles in a tight 2,000-foot-wide circle for six months at a time without landing. Designed as private communication systems for both businesses and consumers, they are able to deliver Internet service for about a third of the cost of DSL or cable. SkyTower has already received the backing of NASA and $80 million in investment capital. Its target customers are major Internet Service Providers (ISPs). The plan is not without problems, however. For one thing, the Federal Aviation Administration (FAA) currently prohibits the

launch of unpiloted planes. Even so, SkyTower's flying wing satellite is a breakthrough technology that addresses the increasing demand for cost-effective wireless communications.[54]

The pitfalls associated with a pioneering new entry are numerous. For one thing, there is a strong risk that the product or service will not be accepted by consumers. The history of entrepreneurship is littered with new ideas that never got off the launching pad. Take, for example, Smell-O-Vision, an invention designed to pump odors into movie theatres from the projection room at preestablished moments in a film. It was tried only once (for the film *Scent of a Mystery*) before it was declared a major flop. Innovative? Sure. But hardly a good idea at the time.[55]

A pioneering new entry is disruptive to the status quo of an industry. It is similar to a radical innovation and may actually be based on a technological breakthrough such as the one proposed by SkyTower. If it is successful, other competitors will rush in to copy it. This can create issues of sustainability for an entrepreneurial firm, especially if a larger company with greater resources introduces a similar product. For a new entrant to sustain its pioneering advantage, therefore, it may be necessary to protect its intellectual property, advertise heavily to build brand recognition, form alliances with businesses that will adopt its products or services, and offer exceptional customer service.

Imitative New Entry   In many respects, an imitative new-entry strategy is the opposite of entering by way of pioneering. Entrepreneurs who start imitative businesses have a very different perspective: Whereas pioneers are often inventors or tinkerers with new technology, imitators usually have a strong marketing orientation. They look for opportunities to capitalize on proven market successes. An imitation strategy is used by entrepreneurs who see products or business concepts that have been successful in one market niche or physical locale and introduce the same basic product or service in another segment of the market.

Sometimes the key to success with an imitative strategy is to fill a market space where the need had previously been filled inadequately. This was the approach used by Fixx Services, Inc., a restaurant and retail store maintenance service.

> Maintenance and repairs is hardly a new business concept. But Mark Bucher found that restaurants and retail stores were poorly served. He provides a facility management service designed to alleviate the headaches associated with keeping everything running. "Customers want one number to call if their oven breaks or if someone throws a brick through their front window," says Bucher. Founded in 1999, home-based and self-funded for the first three years, Fixx Services now has 12 employees and annual sales of nearly $10 million.[56]

Entrepreneurs are also prompted to be imitators when they realize that they have the resources or skills to do a job better than an existing competitor. This can actually be a serious problem for entrepreneurial start-ups if the imitator is an established company. Consider the example of Hugger Mugger Yoga Products, a Salt Lake City producer of yoga apparel and equipment such as yoga mats for practitioners of the ancient exercise art, with sales of $7.5 million annually.

> When founder Sara Chambers started the business in the mid-1980s, there was little competition. But once yoga went mainstream and became the subject of celebrity cover stories, other competitors saw an opportunity to imitate. Then Nike and Reebok jumped into the business with their own mats, clothes, and props. Hugger Mugger was a leading provider and had enjoyed 50 percent annual growth. But even after introducing a mass market line for stores such as Linens 'n' Things and hiring 50 independent sales reps, its growth rate has leveled off.[57]

Recall from Chapter 3 that the quality "difficult to imitate" was viewed as one of the keys to building sustainable advantages. A strategy that can be imitated, therefore, seems

strategy spotlight

Franchising: A Tried-and-True Imitative Strategy

Franchising, by any measure, is a success story. One of every 12 retail businesses is a franchise—just over 8 percent of all retailers. Yet these businesses account for 40 percent of all retail sales in the United States. Franchising as an opportunity to own a business and work independently continues to expand. Industry experts estimate that a new franchise outlet opens somewhere in the United States every eight minutes, and franchising is rapidly becoming a global phenomenon.

Many people are familiar with major franchises. The first names that come to mind when most people think of franchises are the fast-food chains—McDonald's, Wendy's, Subway. But there are hundreds of other franchise businesses in industries such as accounting, printing and copying, advertising services, home repair and remodeling, environmental services, education services, and automotive repairs to name a few. These businesses provide entrepreneurial opportunities for business owners and employment for hundreds of thousands of workers.

The most common type of franchise is known as the business format franchise, in which the franchisor provides the franchisee with a step-by-step guide for managing all major aspects of the business. With this approach, everything from the operational systems to the name, logo, and color scheme are prescribed by the franchisor. Regulations have been introduced during the last 10 years to provide franchisees with the essential information they need to choose a franchisor. This has taken away some of the mystery in the deals being offered by franchisors and made franchisees more confident about buying in. At the same time, the procedures for operating the business sys-

tems have also improved. "It's easier for a new franchisee to enter the system now," says Paul Sweeney, a McDonald's franchisee in Cranberry Township, Pennsylvania. "They give you handbooks that tell you how to run your business so you don't have to come up with the context for construction and development on your own."

Clearly, franchising is built on the idea of imitating what another business has already done. If a business format is so easy to imitate, can it possibly have any competitive advantages? In the minds of many consumers of franchise products and services, the advantage is *because of* imitation. That is, consumers have confidence in franchises because they are familiar with them. "As time has gone by, the public has come to embrace franchising because they're familiar with the successful franchises and brand," claims Tony DeSio, founder of Mail Boxes Etc. "They know that, from one location to another, they can rely on product consistency." Thus, imitation is one of the central reasons why franchises are successful.

Even though consistency and sameness are highly valued in a franchise system, most franchisors are also open to suggestions for how to improve. Franchisees who think of a better way to market a service or showcase products are usually welcome to do so. For example, Navin Bhatia, owner of nine Valvoline Instant Oil Changes in San Antonio, Texas, masterminded the "good, better, best" marketing strategy for differentiating between the type of oil and level of service that is recommended to customers. Thus, through the efforts of independent franchisees, many franchises are able to continually improve their systems and hone their product and service offerings. Of course, when that happens, what do most of the other franchisees in the system do? They imitate it.

Sources: G. Williams, "Keep Thinking," *Entrepreneur,* September 2002, pp. 100–103; D. Smith, "Want Franchises with That?" *Entrepreneur,* May 2002, pp. 102–6; and www.franchise.org.

like a poor way to build a business. In essence, this is true. But then consider the example of a franchise. Strategy Spotlight 13.8 addresses the question of how and why the franchise approach to imitation has worked well for many entrepreneurs.

Adaptive New Entry   Most new entrants use a strategy somewhere between "pure" imitation and "pure" pioneering. That is, they offer a product or service that is somewhat new and sufficiently different to create new value for customers and capture market share. Such firms are adaptive in the sense that they are aware of marketplace conditions and conceive entry strategies to capitalize on current trends.

According to business creativity coach Tom Monahan, "Every new idea is merely a spin of an old idea. [Knowing that] takes the pressure off from thinking [you] have to be totally creative. You don't. Sometimes it's one slight twist to an old idea that makes all the

AltiTunes: Success through Adaptation

"Darwin said it is not the strongest or fastest that survive but those that can adapt quickly," says Thomas Barry, chief investment officer at Bjurman, Barry & Associates. That's what Amy Nye Wolf learned when she launched her AltiTunes Partners LP business. She had been listening to the same music over and over during a six-week backpacking trip through Europe. At the end of the trip, she was elated to find a store selling music at London's Heathrow Airport. "I was so sick of the music I had, and I was just happy to see it."

About five years later, after finishing college and working as an investment banker, Wolf remembered her experience in the airport. She realized that selling CDs

was not an original idea but she thought there might be a need anyway. "I stole the idea," says Wolf, "and then did some serious adapting." Airports, she figured, constituted a unique market niche. She estimated that if she could sell just 30 CDs per day, she could keep the business afloat. Naming her business AltiTunes, Wolf took the plunge.

Today, AltiTunes sells 3,000 to 4,000 CDs per day at stores in 26 airports and one train station. Sales of CDs and products such as portable stereos and computer games are expected to reach $15 million in 2003. And Wolf is still adapting. Her latest innovation is a gadget that lets shoppers roam around the store and sample any CD on the racks. It's a PDA-sized device developed by a company name MusiKube, LLC, that shoppers use by scanning a CD bar code to hear selections of music. It's just the latest improvement in Wolf's plan to stay cutting edge by continually adapting what she calls her "small format, extraordinary-location," music retailing business.

Sources: A. Barrett and D. Foust, "Hot Growth Companies," *BusinessWeek*, June 9, 2003, pp. 74–77; G. Goldsmith, "Retailers Try New Devices to Make CD Purchasing More Enjoyable," *Wall Street Journal*, June 12, 2003, www.wsj.com; G. Williams, "Looks Like Rain," *Entrepreneur*, September 2002, pp. 104–11; and www.altitunes.com.

difference."[58] Thus, an adaptive approach does not involve "reinventing the wheel," nor is it merely imitative either. It involves taking an existing idea and adapting it to a particular situation. Let's look at the example of Citipost:

> Richard Trayford was working temporarily while he waited for his new job in music promotion to begin. But he noticed that the bicycle-messenger company he was working for charged just one dollar for overnight delivery as a gimmick to get customers to use its more expensive same-day delivery service. Trayford realized that some customers would pay much more as long as it was less expensive than UPS and FedEx. So he borrowed $19,500 and launched Citipost. His strategy was to adapt an overnight delivery service to high-volume customers in New York's central business district. Citipost's first customer was Random House, a publisher that sends hundreds of overnight packages to agents, reviewers, and others within Manhattan every day. The service saved Random House 50 percent on delivery costs, and within four months Citipost was handling all of its deliveries. Twice named to the *Inc.* 500 list of the fastest-growing companies, Citipost now operates low-cost central city overnight delivery services in a dozen cities around the globe and earns revenues of $30 million annually.[59]

There are several pitfalls that might limit the success of an adaptive new entrant. First, the value proposition set forth by the new entrant firm must be perceived as unique. Unless potential customers believe a new product or service does a superior job of meeting their needs, they will have little motivation to try them out. Second, there is nothing to prevent a close competitor from mimicking the new firm's adaptation as a way to hold on to its customers. Third, once an adaptive entrant achieves initial success, the challenge is to keep the idea fresh. If the attractive features of the new business wear off or are copied, the entrepreneurial firm must find ways to adapt and improve the product or service offering. Strategy Spotlight 13.9 describes how adaptive new entrant Amy Nye Wolf has continually improved her entrepreneurial venture in order to hold her customer's interest and grow her business.

A new entrant must decide not only the best way to enter into business for the first time, but also what type of strategic positioning will work best as the business goes forward. Those strategic choices can be informed by the guidelines suggested for the generic strategies. We turn to that subject next.

Generic Strategies

Typically, an entrepreneurial firm begins with a single business model that is equivalent in scope to a business-level strategy (Chapter 5). Thus, most small businesses and new ventures can benefit from applying the generic strategies. There is rarely any reason for a new venture to consider a corporate-level strategy (Chapter 6) except in a case when an entrepreneur decides to diversify into related or unrelated businesses or to purchase an existing business. Then, some of the guidelines that make the acquisition process more successful may be helpful to new entrants. In general, however, new ventures are single-business firms using business-level strategies. In this section we address how overall low cost, differentiation, and focus strategies can be used by new ventures to achieve competitive advantages.

Overall Cost Leadership   One of the ways entrepreneurial firms achieve success is by doing more with less. That is, by holding down costs or making more efficient use of resources than larger competitors, new ventures are often able to offer lower prices and still be profitable. Thus, under the right circumstances, a low-cost leader strategy is a viable alternative for some new ventures. The way new ventures achieve low-cost leadership, however, is typically different for young or small firms. Let's look first at why a cost-leadership strategy might be difficult for a new venture.

Recall from Chapter 5 that three of the features of a low-cost approach included operating at a large enough scale to spread costs over many units of production (i.e., economies of scale), making substantial capital investments in order to increase scale economies, and using knowledge gained from experience to make cost-saving improvements. These elements of a cost-leadership strategy may be unavailable to new ventures. Because new ventures are typically small, they usually don't have high economies of scale relative to competitors. Because they are usually cash strapped, they can't make large capital investments to increase their scale advantages. And because they are young, they often don't have a wealth of accumulated experience to draw on to achieve cost reductions.

Given these constraints, how can new ventures successfully deploy cost-leader strategies? Compared to large firms, new ventures often have simple organizational structures that make decision making both easier and faster. The smaller size also helps young firms change more quickly when upgrades in technology or feedback from the marketplace indicate that improvements are needed. New ventures are also able to make decisions at the time they are founded that help them deal with the issue of controlling costs. For example, they may source materials from a supplier that provides them more cheaply or set up manufacturing facilities in another country where labor costs are especially low. The Internet offers other potential cost-saving alternatives. Firms may choose to manage supplier relations through a website or sell products online that competitors sell by using a sales force. Thus, new firms have several avenues for achieving low cost leadership.

Consider the example of UTStarcom, a fast-growing wireless phone service being marketed in mainland China:

> Taiwan-born founder Hong Liang Lu was an executive at Japan's Kyocera Corp. when he made his first visit to China in 1990. He found a population that badly needed decent phone service. "Before that trip, I hadn't really thought about doing business in China. Afterward, I felt it made

no sense to do business anywhere else." Using Personal Access System (PAS), a technology that had never caught on in Japan, he created a low-cost service that uses existing copper networks as its backbone. The service costs only $100 per subscriber to deploy, about half the price of cellular-based systems. Customers pay nothing for incoming calls and outgoing ones are 25 percent of the cellular rate. Competing against the big telecom providers was difficult at first, but once they marketed the "Little Smart" as a low cost alternative to cellular, sales took off. Average annual revenues have grown 73 percent since 1999, and 2003 sales reached $1.96 billion. Says CEO Lu, "Our biggest problem is keeping up with demand."[60]

Whatever methods young firms use to achieve a low-cost advantage, this has always been a way that entrepreneurial firms take business away from incumbents—by offering a comparable product or service at a lower price.

Differentiation   Both pioneering and adaptive entry strategies involve some degree of differentiation. That is, the new entry is based on being able to offer a differentiated value proposition. Clearly, in the case of pioneers, the new venture is attempting to do something strikingly different, either by using a new technology or deploying resources in a way that radically alters the way business is conducted. Often, entrepreneurs do both. A classic example is FedEx founder Fred Smith, who combined delivery, air transportation, and some innovative tracking technology to revolutionize the overnight delivery business. He literally created demand with his suggestive ad campaign that asked customers what they must do "When it absolutely, positively has to be there overnight."

More recently, Jeff Bezos set out to use Internet technology to revolutionize the way books are sold. He garnered the ire of other booksellers and the attention of the public by making bold claims about being the world's largest bookseller. As a bookseller, Bezos was not doing anything that had not been done before. But two key differentiating features— doing it on the Internet and offering extraordinary customer service—have made Amazon a differentiated success.

Even though the Internet and new technologies have provided many opportunities for entrepreneurs, differentiators don't have to be highly sophisticated to succeed. Consider the example of Spry Learning Co., a Portland, Oregon, start-up begun in 2000.

> Founders Sarah Chapman and Devin Williams believed that older people would benefit from using computers and surfing the Internet—if they only knew how. Working with gerontologists and instructional designers, they designed a computer-skills curriculum aimed at seniors. After piloting the program at two retirement communities, they successfully launched the differentiated service and, after just a few years, projected annual revenues over $4 million.[61]

There are several factors that make it more difficult for young firms to be successful as differentiators. For one thing, the strategy is generally thought to be expensive to enact. For example, differentiation is often associated with strong brand identity, and establishing a brand is usually considered to be expensive because of the cost of advertising and promotion, paid endorsements, exceptional customer service, aggressive warranties and return guarantees, as well as other expenses typically associated with building brand. Differentiation successes are sometimes built on superior innovation or use of technology. These are also factors where it may be challenging for young firms to excel relative to established competitors.

On the other hand, all of these areas—innovation, technology, customer service, distinctive branding—are also arenas where new ventures have sometimes made a name for themselves even though they must operate with limited resources and experience. To be successful, according to Garry Ridge, CEO of the WD-40 Company, "You need to have a great product, make the end user aware of it, and make it easy to buy."[62] It sounds simple, but it is a difficult challenge for entrepreneurs with differentiation strategies.

Focus   Because of the competitive environment facing most ventures, focus or "niche" strategies provide one of the most effective strategies for any new firm. A niche represents a small segment within a market. A young or small firm can play an important role in such a market space if there is an opportunity to thrive in that environment. Typically, a focus strategy is used to pursue a niche. Focus strategies are associated with small businesses because there is a natural fit between the narrow scope of the strategy and the small size of the firm. As we learned earlier, a focus strategy may include elements of differentiation and overall cost leadership, as well as combinations of these approaches. But to be successful within a market niche, the key strategic requirement is to stay focused. Here's why:

Despite all the attention given to fast-growing new industries, most start-ups enter industries that are mature.[63] In mature industries, growth in demand tends to be slow and there are often many competitors. Therefore, if a start-up wants to get a piece of the action, it often has to take business away from an existing competitor. If a start-up enters a market with a broad or aggressive strategy, it is likely to evoke retaliation from a more powerful competitor. Therefore, young firms can often succeed best by finding a market niche where they can get a foothold and make small advances that erode the position of existing competitors.[64] From this position, they can build a name for themselves and grow. Consider the example of Corporate Interns, Inc.:

> When Jason Engen was an undergraduate student at the University of St. Thomas in St. Paul, Minnesota, he learned the value of internships in which students worked for local companies. He wrote a business plan for one of his classes about forming an internship placement service in which he would screen students and match them with local companies. It's a "win–win situation," said Engen. "The student gets the experience, and the company gets eager talent." The interest in his idea was high, and a week after graduation he started Corporate Interns, Inc. It was difficult at first, however, because companies handle internships differently than other placement activities. But as Engen learned more, he realized this difference was an advantage: By positioning himself only in the college intern market, he avoided competing directly with large staffing companies. "Specialization is important," says Engen. "You have to stay focused on that niche." For Engen, that niche now generates $2 million in annual revenues.[65]

As the Corporate Interns example indicates, many small businesses are very successful even though their share of the market is quite small. Giant companies such as Procter & Gamble, Johnson & Johnson, and Ford are often described in terms of their market share—that is, their share of sales in a whole market. But many of the industries that small firms participate in have thousands of participants that are not direct competitors. For example, small restaurants and auto repair shops in California don't compete with those in Michigan or Georgia. These industries are considered "fragmented" because no single company is strong enough to have power over other competitors. Therefore, small firms need to focus on the market share only in their trade area. This may be defined as a geographical area or a small segment of a larger product group.

Consider, for example, the "Miniature Editions" line of books launched by Running Press, a small Philadelphia publisher. The books are palm-sized minibooks positioned at bookstore cash registers as point-of-sale impulse items costing about $4.95. Beginning with just 10 titles in 1993, Running Press grew rapidly and within ten years had sold over 20 million copies. Even though these books represent just a tiny fraction of total sales in the $23 billion publishing industry, they have been a mainstay for Running Press, which eventually had to sue other publishers to protect its two-and-a-half by three-inch "trade dress" format.[66]

LeapFrog Enterprises: Winning through Combination Strategies

LeapFrog Enterprises is living up to its name. In 2001 its LeapPad toy brought in more revenue than any other toy in the United States, helping the company to jump over toy-making giants such as Hasbro, Fisher-Price, and Mattel. Its breakthrough product looks like a book and is geared to kindergartners learning to read. The goal from the start was to make paper come alive with sound and music. By combining impressive technology with clever design, the company seems to have succeeded. In fact, one of LeapFrog's most distinguishing characteristics is its combination of technology and expertise in early childhood education and play. Along with these skills, it has developed a combination strategy that touches on all three generic strategies.

Low Cost Leadership

From its beginning in 1995, LeapFrog has had a policy of keeping all production and development in-house, everything from coding software and developing chips to writing and illustrating content. Nothing is done by outside contractors. This has not only kept costs low, but also built a knowledge base that will save it money in the future. "There's a lot of institutional wisdom that gets passed around when all of us are working in the same space," says Mike Wood, LeapFrog's president and CEO.

Sources: B. Breen, "LeapFrog's Great Leap Forward," *Fast Company,* June 2003, pp. 88–96; and S. Lawrence, "LeapFrog Looks Like a Prince," *Red Herring,* November 2002, p. 28.

Differentiation

The product is a success because of a technology that allows kids to touch words and images with a wand and hear words, phonetic sounds, and music. The quality of the design and the sounds it utters are among its distinguishing features. Surprisingly, however, the company realizes that the technology itself is of little value. "We need technology to deliver a spectacular experience, but the experience itself comes out of the content. Ultimately, the technology is irrelevant," says Wood.

Focus

The niche that LeapFrog entered is the preschool electronic learning market. With its LeapPad product, it claims to have a product that is "a toy in its shape, but an educational product in its soul." Appealing to parents who want the preschool years to be well-spent, the product also appeals to children. "Our worst nightmare was that kids would pick the thing up, play with it for a few minutes, and forget about it," says Jim Marggraff, Executive Vice President for Content who directs all creative design. Clearly that didn't happen—so far the company has sold more than 8.6 million LeapPads.

LeapFrog is a model of entrepreneurial savvy. The company has made the most of technology while keeping an eye on its end user. This combination of strengths and insight has made LeapFrog a huge success.

Although each of the three strategies hold promise—and pitfalls—for new ventures and small businesses, firms that can make unique combinations of the generic approaches may have the greatest chances of success. It is that subject we turn to next.

Combination Strategies

Strategic positioning has different implications for small firms and entrepreneurial start-ups. For small firms, the issues they face in terms of their marketplace are often confined to a geographical locale or a small class of products. For start-ups, a key issue is the scope of their strategic efforts relative to those of their competitors. In determining a strategic position, both types of firms must address fundamental issues of how to achieve a distinct competitive advantage that will earn above-average profits as well as how to create value for their customers in the marketplace.

One of the best ways for new ventures and small businesses to achieve success is by pursuing combination strategies. By combining the best features of low-cost, differentiation, and focus strategies, young and small firms can often achieve something that is truly distinctive.

Entrepreneurial firms are often in a strong position to offer a combination strategy, because they have the flexibility to approach situations uniquely. For example, holding down expenses can be difficult for big firms because each layer of bureaucracy adds to the cost of communicating and doing business. To get a part made, for example—or to outsource it—may be complicated and expensive for many large firms. By contrast, the Nartron Corporation, a small engineering firm whose innovations include the first keyless automobile entry system, solves that problem by building everything itself. By engineering its own products from its own designs, it not only saves money but also creates better parts. "Our parts look different from other people's because we keep adding functionality," says Nartron CEO Norman Rautiola. According to Rautiola, this capability allows the company to "run rings" around its competitors, which include Texas Instruments and Motorola.[67]

A similar argument could be made about entrepreneurial firms that differentiate. Large firms often find it difficult to offer highly specialized products or superior customer services. Entrepreneurial firms, by contrast, can often create high-value products and services through their unique differentiating efforts. Strategy Spotlight 13.10 examines LeapFrog Enterprises, a company that has outperformed industry giants by combining strategies.

For nearly all small firms, one of the major dangers is that a large firm with more resources will copy what they are doing. That is, well-established larger competitors that observe the success of a new entrant's product or service will copy it and use their market power to overwhelm the smaller firm. Although this happens often, the threat may be lessened for firms that use combination strategies. Because of the flexibility and quick decision-making ability of entrepreneurial firms, they can often enact their combination strategies in ways that the large firms cannot copy. This makes the strategies much more sustainable.

Perhaps more threatening than large competitors for many entrepreneurial firms are other small firms that are close competitors. Because they have similar structural features that help them adjust quickly and be flexible in decision making, close competitors are often a danger to young and small firms. Here again, a carefully crafted and executed combination strategy may be the best way for an entrepreneurial firm to thrive in a competitive environment.

summary

New ventures and small businesses that capitalize on marketplace opportunities make an important contribution to the U.S. economy. They are leaders in terms of implementing new technologies and introducing innovative products and services. Entrepreneurial firms face unique challenges if they are going to survive and grow. The size, age, and growth goals of small firms affect how they achieve competitive advantages.

To successfully launch new ventures or implement new technologies, firms must develop a strong ability to recognize viable opportunities. Opportunity recognition is a process of determining which venture ideas are, in fact, promising business opportunities. It consists of two phases. First is the discovery phase, in which new ideas are identified by alert individuals or generated by means of deliberate search processes. Second is the formation phase, in which the feasibility of opportunities is evaluated and plans are made to support and fund the new venture. In addition to strong opportunities, entrepreneurial firms need sufficient resources and entrepreneurial leadership to thrive.

The resources that start-ups need include financial resources as well as human capital and social capital. Many small firms also benefit from government programs that support their development and growth. Various avenues for obtaining resources are available to start-ups, depending on whether the new venture is in early or later stages of development.

In early stages, personal savings and financial support from family and friends are the most common types of initial funding. Most start-ups can also benefit from bootstrapping, that is, operating economically and relying on as few outside resources as possible. Bank financing and venture capital are often used by entrepreneurial firms in later stages of development.

Young and small firms thrive best when they are led by founders or owners who have vision, drive and dedication, and a commitment to excellence. Vision provides entrepreneurial leaders with an ability to conceive of realities that do not yet exist. Dedication and drive are needed in order to persist in the face of difficulties and keep up the level of motivation necessary to succeed. Commitment to excellence is reflected in an entrepreneurial leader's focus on quality and customer service as well as a desire to be surrounded by talented and skilled employees.

New ventures and small businesses face numerous strategic challenges. However, many of the tools of strategic management can be applied to these firms. Decisions about the strategic positioning of young and small firms can benefit from applying five-forces analysis and evaluating the requirements of niche markets. Entry strategies used by new ventures take several forms, including pioneering new entry, imitative new entry, and adaptive new entry. Entrepreneurial firms can benefit from using overall low-cost, differentiation, and focus strategies, although each of these approaches has pitfalls that are unique to young and small firms. Entrepreneurial firms are also in a strong position to benefit from combination strategies.

summary review questions

1. Explain how an entrepreneurial firm's size, age, and growth goals help determine its character and strategic direction.

2. What is the difference between discovery and formation in the process of opportunity recognition? Give an example of each.

3. What types of financing are typically available to entrepreneurs in early stages and later stages of a new venture start-up?

4. How can bootstrapping help a young start-up or small business minimize its resource requirements? How might bootstrapping efforts affect decisions about strategic positioning?

5. Describe the three characteristics of entrepreneurial leadership: vision, dedication and drive, and commitment to excellence.

6. Briefly describe the three types of entrepreneurial entry strategies: pioneering, imitative, and adaptive.

7. Explain why entrepreneurial firms are often in a strong position to use combination strategies.

experiential exercise

E-Loan is a young firm that offers lending services over the Internet. Evaluate the qualities of the opportunity E-Loan identified in terms of the four characteristics of an opportunity. In each category:

1. Evaluate the extent to which they met the criteria (using high, medium, or low).
2. Explain your rationale. That is, what features of the opportunity account for the score you gave them?

Characteristics	High/Medium/Low?	Rationale
1. Attractive		
2. Achievable		
3. Durable		
4. Value Creating		

application questions & exercises

1. Using the Internet, research the website of the Small Business Administration (www.sba.gov). What different types of financing are available to small firms? Besides financing, what other programs are available to support the growth and development of small businesses?
2. Think of an entrepreneurial firm that has been successfully launched in the last 10 years. What are the characteristics of the entrepreneur(s) who launched the firm?
3. Select a small business that you are familiar with in your local community. Research the company and discuss how it has positioned itself relative to its close competitors. Does it have a unique strategic advantage? Disadvantage? Explain.
4. Using the Internet, find an example of a young entrepreneurial firm (founded within the last five years). What kind of entry strategy did it use—pioneering, imitative, or adaptive? Since the firm's initial entry, how has it used or combined overall low-cost, differentiation, and/or focus strategies?

ethics questions

1. Imitation strategies are based on the idea of copying another firm's idea and using it for your own purposes. Is this unethical or simply a smart business practice? Discuss the ethical implications of this practice (if any).
2. The prices of some foreign products that enter the United States are regulated to keep prices high, and "dumping" laws have been established to prevent some foreign companies from selling below wholesale prices. Should price wars that drive small businesses or new entrants out of business be illegal? What ethical considerations are raised (if any)?

references

1. Gentlemen, start your engine, 1996, *Fortune,* September 30, www.fortune.com; Useem, J., 1998, Exotic auto venture is $24-million nonstarter, *Inc.,* June 29, www.inc.com; and Wouk, V., 1997, Hybrid electric vehicles, *Scientific American,* October: 17, www.sciam.com.

2. Useem, op. cit., p. 29.

3. Shane, S., & Venkataraman, S., 2000, The promise of entrepreneurship as a field of research, *Academy of Management Review* 25 (1): 217–26; Lumpkin, G. T., & Dess, G. G., 1996, Clarifying the entrepreneurial orientation construct and linking it to performance, *Academy of Management Review* 21 (1): 135–72; and Gartner, W. B., 1988, Who is an entrepreneur? is the wrong question, *American Journal of Small Business* 12 (4): 11–32.

4. Martin, J., & Birch, D., 2002, Slump? What slump? *Fortune,* December 1, www.fortune.com.

5. Dennis, W. J., Jr., 2000, *NFIB Small Business Policy Guide* (Washington, DC: National Federation of Independent Business); and www.nfib.com.

6. Small Business Administration, 2002, A report from Advocacy's 25th anniversary symposium, *SBA Office of Advocacy,* February 22, www.sba.gov/advo/.

7. Stout, H. J., 2003, Kiehl's opens personal care products shop in NW Portland, *Business Journal of Portland,* July 22, www.bizjournals.com/portland/; and Morse, J., 2000, *Working Woman,* June: 68.

8. Case, J., 2001, The gazelle theory, *Inc.,* May 15, www.inc.com; and Birch, D., 1979, *The Job Generation Process,* MIT Program on Neighborhood and Regional Change (Cambridge, MA: MIT Press).

9. Sloane, J., 2003, Hearts and minds, *Fortune,* July 11, www.fortune.com; www.surmodics.com; and www.hoovers.com.

10. Case, J., op. cit.

11. Serwer, A., 2003, The hole story, *Fortune,* June 23, www.fortune.com.

12. Small Business Administration, op. cit.

13. Fromartz, S., 1998, How to get your first great idea, *Inc.,* April 1: 91–94; and Vesper, K. H., 1990, *New Venture Strategies,* 2nd ed. (Englewood Cliffs, NJ: Prentice Hall).

14. Hof, R. D., 2000, E-marketplace: eLance, *BusinessWeek E.Biz,* June 5: 68–72; and www.elance.com.

15. Fishman, C., 1998, Sustainable growth—Interface, Inc., *Fast Company,* April 1998: 136; Hawken, P., Lovins, A., & Lovins, H., 2000, *Natural Capitalism* (Boston: Back Bay Books); see also www.ifsia.com.

16. Judge, P. C., 2000, Professor Ulrich's excellent adventure, *Fast Company,* August: 248–57.

17. Carey, J., & Yang, C., 2001, From smart to brilliant weapons, *BusinessWeek,* October 8: 62–63.

18. Gaglio, C. M., 1997, Opportunity identification: Review, critique and suggested research directions, in J. A. Katz, ed., *Advances in Entrepreneurship, Firm Emergence and Growth,* vol. 3 (Greenwich, CT: JAI Press), 139–202; Hills, G. E., Shrader, R. C., & Lumpkin, G. T., 1999, Opportunity recognition as a creative process, in *Frontiers of Entrepreneurship Research, 1999* (Wellesley, MA: Babson College), 216–27; and Long, W., & McMullan, W. E., 1984, Mapping the new venture opportunity identification process, in *Frontiers of Entrepreneurship Research, 1984* (Wellesley, MA: Babson College), 567–90.

19. Stewart, T. A., 2002, How to think with your gut, *Business 2.0,* November: 99–104.

20. Bennet, E., 2000, Fungus fanatic, *Philadelphia Business Journal,* February 18, www.bizjournals.com/philadelphia/; and Greco, S., 1998, Where great ideas come from, *Inc.,* April: 76–86.

21. Timmons, J. A., 1997, Opportunity recognition, in Bygrave, W. D., ed., *The Portable MBA in Entrepreneurship,* 2nd ed. (New York: Wiley), 26–54.

22. Finkelstein, S., & Sanford, S. H., 2000, Learning from corporate mistakes: The rise and fall of Iridium, *Organizational Dynamics* 29 (2): 138–48.

23. Schonfeld, E., 2000, Going long, *Fortune,* March 20: 172–92.

24. Warshaw, M., 2000, The thing that would not die, *Inc. Tech* 1:89–100.

25. Welles, E. O., 2001, Hell-bent for lather, *Inc.,* September: 50–52.

26. Timmons, J. A., & Spinelli, S., 2004, *New Venture Creation,* 6th ed. (New York: McGraw-Hill/Irwin); and Bygrave, W. D., 1997, The entrepreneurial process, in Bygrave, ed., *The Portable MBA,* 1–26.

27. Stinchcombe, A. L., 1965, Social structure in organizations, in March, J. G., ed., *Handbook of Organizations* (Chicago: Rand McNally), 142–93.

28. Fast Pack 1999, 1999, *Fast Company,* February–March: 139.

29. Small business 2001: Where are we now? 2001, *Inc.,* May 29: 18–19; and Zacharakis, A. L., Bygrave, W. D., & Shepherd, D. A., 2000, *Global Entrepreneurship Monitor—National Entrepreneurship Assessment: United States of America 2000 Executive Report* (Kansas City, MO: Kauffman Center for Entrepreneurial Leadership).

30. Cooper, S., 2003, Cash cows, *Entrepreneur,* June: 36.

31. Small business 2001: Where are we now? op. cit.; and Dennis, W. J., Jr., 1997, *Business Starts and Stops* (Washington, DC: National Federation of Independent Business).

32. www.keepwalking.com; and www.walkabouttravelgear.com.

33. Stuart, A., 2001, The pita principle, *Inc.,* August: 58–64.

34. Cooper, op. cit.
35. Seglin, J. L., 1998, What angels want, *Inc.,* May: 43–44.
36. Torres, N. L., 2002, Playing an angel, *Entrepreneur,* May: 130–38.
37. Fraser, J. A., 2001, The money hunt, *Inc.,* March: 49–63.
38. Lefteroff, T. T., 2003, The thrill of the chase, *Entrepreneur,* July: 56.
39. Osborne, D. M., 2001, Dear John, *Inc.,* May: 45–48.
40. Hatching a new plan, 2000, *Economist,* August 12: 53–54; www.techspace.com; and www.nbia.org.
41. Eisenhardt, K. M., & Schoonhoven, C. B., 1990, Organizational growth: Linking founding team, strategy, environment, and growth among U.S. semiconductor ventures, 1978–1988, *Administrative Science Quarterly* 35: 504–29.
42. Dubini, P., & Aldrich, H., 1991, Personal and extended networks are central to the entrepreneurship process, *Journal of Business Venturing* 6 (5): 305–33.
43. Vogel, C., 2000, Janina Pawlowski, *Working Woman,* June: 70.
44. For more information, go to the Small Business Administration website at www.sba.gov.
45. Torres, N. L., 2002, Under the microscope, *Entrepreneur,* August: 106–9.
46. Detamore-Rodman, C., 2003, Out on a limb, *Entrepreneur,* March: 78–83.
47. Tanner, J., 2000, Meals on wheels (and rails and water), *Inc.,* May: 124–26.
48. Based on Kurlantzick, J., 2003, Got what it takes? *Entrepreneur,* March: 52.
49. Briody, D., 2001, Top ten entrepreneurs: Bill Nguyen, *Red Herring,* August 1: 58–60.
50. Himanshu "Sue" Bhatia, 2000, *Working Woman,* June: 91; see also roseint.com.
51. Collins, J., 2001, *Good to Great* (New York: HarperBusiness).
52. Collins, *Good to Great;* and Collins, 2003, Bigger, better, faster, *Fast Company,* June: 74–78.
53. The idea of entry wedges was discussed by Vesper, K., 1990, *New Venture Strategies,* 2nd ed. (Englewood Cliffs, NJ: Prentice Hall); and Drucker, P. F., 1985, *Innovation and Entrepreneurship* (New York: HarperBusiness).
54. Frauenfelder, M., 2002, Look! Up in the sky! It's a flying cell phone tower! *Business 2.0,* November: 108–12.
55. Maiello, M., 2002, They almost changed the world, *Forbes,* December 22: 217–20.
56. Pedroza, G. M., 2003, Blanket statement, *Entrepreneur,* March: 92.
57. Gull, N., 2003, Just say om, *Inc.,* July: 42–44.
58. Williams, G., 2002, Looks like rain, *Entrepreneur,* September: 104–11.
59. Fromartz, op. cit.; and Grossman, J., 1999, Courier's foreign niche, *Inc.,* October 15: 57.
60. Burrows, P., 2003, Ringing off the hook in China, *BusinessWeek,* June 9: 80–82; www.hoovers.com.
61. Pedroza, G. M., 2002, Tech tutors, *Entrepreneur,* September: 120.
62. Barrett, A., 2003, Hot growth companies, *BusinessWeek,* June 9: 74–77.
63. Dennis, W. J., Jr., 1992, *The State of Small Business: A Report of the President, 1992* (Washington, DC: U.S. Government Printing Office), 65–90.
64. Romanelli, E., 1989, Environments and strategies of organization start-up: Effects on early survival, *Administrative Science Quarterly* 34 (3): 369–87.
65. Torres, N. L., 2003, A perfect match, *Entrepreneur,* July: 112–14.
66. Wallace, B., 2000. Brothers, *Philadelphia Magazine,* April: 66–75.
67. Buchanan, L., 2003, The innovation factor: A field guide to innovation, *Forbes,* April 21, www.forbes.com.

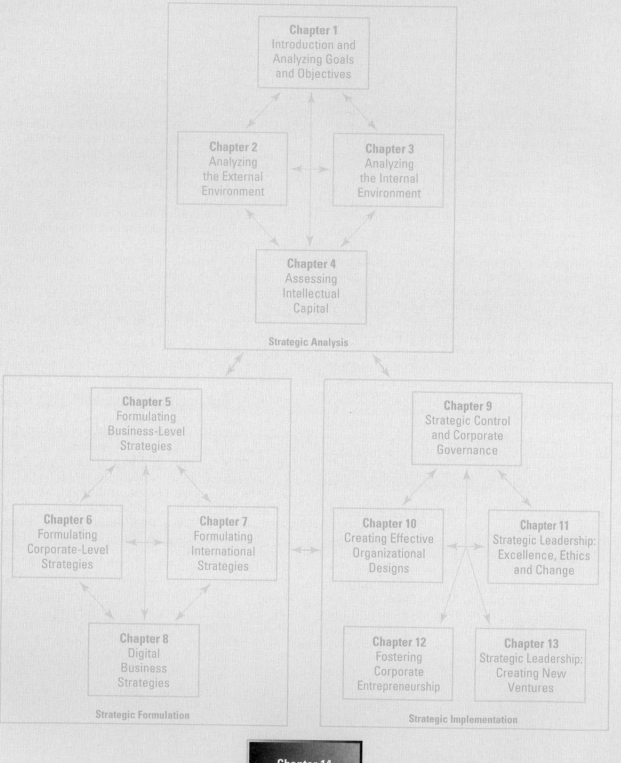

Chapter 1
Introduction and
Analyzing Goals
and Objectives

Chapter 2
Analyzing
the External
Environment

Chapter 3
Analyzing
the Internal
Environment

Chapter 4
Assessing
Intellectual
Capital

Strategic Analysis

Chapter 5
Formulating
Business-Level
Strategies

Chapter 6
Formulating
Corporate-Level
Strategies

Chapter 7
Formulating
International
Strategies

Chapter 8
Digital
Business
Strategies

Strategic Formulation

Chapter 9
Strategic Control
and Corporate
Governance

Chapter 10
Creating Effective
Organizational
Designs

Chapter 11
Strategic Leadership:
Excellence, Ethics
and Change

Chapter 12
Fostering
Corporate
Entrepreneurship

Chapter 13
Strategic Leadership:
Creating New
Ventures

Strategic Implementation

Chapter 14
Case
Analysis

Case Analysis

outline

Analyzing Strategic Management Cases

14

Analyzing Strategic Management Cases

*After
reading this
chapter, you should
have a good understanding of:*

- How strategic case analysis is used to simulate real-world experiences.

- How analyzing strategic management cases can help develop the ability to differentiate, speculate, and integrate when evaluating complex business problems.

- The steps involved in conducting a strategic management case analysis.

- How conflict-inducing discussion techniques can lead to better decisions.

- How to get the most out of case analysis.

- How to use the strategic insights and material from each of the 13 previous chapters in the text to analyze issues posed by strategic management cases.

Case analysis is one of the most effective ways to learn strategic management. It provides a complement to other methods of instruction by asking you to use the tools and techniques of strategic management to deal with an actual business situation. Strategy cases include detailed descriptions of management challenges faced by executives and business owners. By studying the background and analyzing the strategic predicaments posed by a case, you first see that the circumstances businesses confront are often difficult and complex. Then you are asked what decisions you would make to address the situation in the case and how the actions you recommend will affect the company. Thus, the processes of analysis, formulation, and implementation that have been addressed by this textbook can be applied in a real-life situation.

In this chapter we will discuss the role of case analysis as a learning tool in both the classroom and the real world. One of the benefits of strategic case analysis is to develop the ability to differentiate, speculate, and integrate. We will also describe how to conduct a case analysis and address techniques for deriving the greatest benefit from the process including the effective use of conflict-inducing decision techniques. Finally, we will discuss how case analysis in a classroom setting can enhance the process of analyzing, making decisions, and taking action in real-world strategic situations.

Why Analyze Strategic Management Cases?

It is often said that the key to finding good answers is to ask good questions. Strategic managers and business leaders are required to evaluate options, make choices, and find solutions to the challenges they face every day. To do so, they must learn to ask the right questions. The study of strategic management poses the same challenge. The process of analyzing, decision making, and implementing strategic actions raises many good questions.

- Why do some firms succeed and others fail?
- Why are some companies higher performers than others?
- What information is needed in the strategic planning process?
- How do competing values and beliefs affect strategic decision making?
- What skills and capabilities are needed to implement a strategy effectively?

How does a student of strategic management answer those questions? By strategic case analysis. Case analysis simulates the real-world experience that strategic managers and company leaders face as they try to determine how best to run their companies. It places students in the middle of an actual situation and challenges them to figure out what to do.[1]

Asking the right questions is just the beginning of case analysis. In the previous chapters we have discussed issues and challenges that managers face and provided analytical frameworks for understanding the situation. But once the analysis is complete, decisions have to be made. Case analysis forces you to choose among different options and set forth a plan of action based on your choices. But even then the job is not done. Strategic case analysis also requires that you address how you will implement the plan and the implications of choosing one course of action over another.

A strategic management case is a detailed description of a challenging situation faced by an organization.[2] It usually includes a chronology of events and extensive support materials, such as financial statements, product lists, and transcripts of interviews with employees. Although names or locations are sometimes changed to provide anonymity, cases usually report the facts of a situation as authentically as possible.

One of the main reasons to analyze strategic management cases is to develop an ability to evaluate business situations critically. In case analysis, memorizing key terms and conceptual frameworks is not enough. To analyze a case, it is important that you go beyond textbook prescriptions and quick answers. It requires you to look deeply into the information that is provided and root out the essential issues and causes of a company's problems.

The types of skills that are required to prepare an effective strategic case analysis can benefit you in actual business situations. Case analysis adds to the overall learning experience by helping you acquire or improve skills that may not be taught in a typical lecture course. Three capabilities that can be learned by conducting case analysis are especially useful to strategic managers—the ability to differentiate, speculate, and integrate.[3] Here's how case analysis can enhance those skills.

1. **Differentiate.** Effective strategic management requires that many different elements of a situation be evaluated at once. This is also true in case analysis. When analyzing cases, it is important to isolate critical facts, evaluate whether assumptions are useful or faulty, and distinguish between good and bad information. Differentiating between the factors that are influencing the situation presented by a case is necessary for making a good analysis. Strategic management also involves understanding that problems are often complex and multilayered. This applies to case analysis as well. Ask whether the case deals with operational, business-level, or corporate issues. Do the problems stem from weaknesses in the internal value chain or threats in the

external environment? Dig deep. Being too quick to accept the easiest or least controversial answer will usually fail to get to the heart of the problem.

2. ***Speculate.*** Strategic managers need to be able to use their imagination to envision an explanation or solution that might not readily be apparent. The same is true with case analysis. Being able to imagine different scenarios or contemplate the outcome of a decision can aid the analysis. Managers also have to deal with uncertainty since most decisions are made without complete knowledge of the circumstances. This is also true in case analysis. Case materials often seem to be missing data or the information provided is contradictory. The ability to speculate about details that are unknown or the consequences of an action can be helpful.

3. ***Integrate.*** Strategy involves looking at the big picture and having an organizationwide perspective. Strategic case analysis is no different. Even though the chapters in this textbook divide the material into various topics that may apply to different parts of an organization, all of this information must be integrated into one set of recommendations that will affect the whole company. A strategic manager needs to comprehend how all the factors that influence the organization will interact. This also applies to case analysis. Changes made in one part of the organization affect other parts. Thus, a holistic perspective that integrates the impact of various decisions and environmental influences on all parts of the organization is needed.

In business, these three activities sometimes "compete" with each other for your attention. For example, some decision makers may have a natural ability to differentiate among elements of a problem but are not able to integrate them very well. Others have enough innate creativity to imagine solutions or fill in the blanks when information is missing. But they may have a difficult time when faced with hard numbers or cold facts. Even so, each of these skills is important. The mark of a good strategic manager is the ability to simultaneously make distinctions and envision the whole, and to imagine a future scenario while staying focused on the present. Thus, another reason to conduct case analysis is to help you develop and exercise your ability to differentiate, speculate, and integrate.

Case analysis takes the student through the whole cycle of activity that a manager would face. Beyond the textbook descriptions of concepts and examples, case analysis asks you to "walk a mile in the shoes" of the strategic decision maker and learn to evaluate situations critically. Executives and owners must make decisions every day with limited information and a swirl of business activity going on around them. Consider the example of Sapient Health Networks, an Internet start-up that had to undergo some analysis and problem solving just to survive. Strategy Spotlight 14.1 describes how this company transformed itself after a serious self-examination during a time of crisis.

As you can see from the experience of Sapient Health Networks, businesses are often faced with immediate challenges that threaten their life. The Sapient case illustrates how the strategic management process helped it survive. First, the company realistically assessed the environment, evaluated the marketplace, and analyzed its resources. Then it made tough decisions, which included shifting its market focus, hiring and firing, and redeploying its assets. Finally, it took action. The result was not only firm survival, but also a quick turnaround leading to rapid success.

How to Conduct a Case Analysis

The process of analyzing strategic management cases involves several steps. In this section we will review the mechanics of preparing a case analysis. Before beginning, there are two things to keep in mind that will help make your understanding of the process more clear and the results of the process more meaningful.

Analysis, Decision Making, and Change at Sapient Health Network

Sapient Health Network (SHN) had gotten off to a good start. CEO Jim Kean and his two cofounders had raised $5 million in investor capital to launch their vision: an Internet based health care information subscription service. The idea was to create an Internet community for people suffering from chronic diseases. It would provide members with expert information, resources, a message board, and chat rooms so that people suffering from the same ailments could provide each other with information and support. "Who would be more voracious consumers of information than people who are faced with life-changing, life-threatening illnesses?" thought Bill Kelly, one of SHN's cofounders. Initial market research and beta tests had supported that view.

During the beta tests, however, the service had been offered for free. The troubles began when SHN tried to convert its trial subscribers into paying ones. Fewer than 5 percent signed on, far less than the 15 percent the company had projected. Sapient hired a vice president of marketing who launched an aggressive promotion, but after three months of campaigning SHN still had only 500 members. SHN was now burning through $400,000 per month, with little revenue to show for it.

At that point, according to SHN board member Susan Clymer, "there was a lot of scrambling around trying to figure out how we could wring value out of what we'd already accomplished." One thing SHN had created was an expert software system which had two compo-

nents: an "intelligent profile engine" (IPE) and an "intelligent query engine" (IQE). SHN used this system to collect detailed information from its subscribers.

SHN was sure that the expert system was its biggest selling point. But how to use it? Then the founders remembered that the original business plan had suggested there might be a market for aggregate data about patient populations gathered from the website. Could they turn the business around by selling patient data? To analyze the possibility, Kean tried out the idea on the market research arm of a huge East Coast health care conglomerate. The officials were intrigued. SHN realized that its expert system could become a market research tool.

Once the analysis was completed, the founders made the decision: They would still create Internet communities for chronically ill patients, but the service would be free. And they would transform SHN from a company that processed subscriptions to one that sold market research.

Finally, they enacted the changes. Some of it was painful, including laying off 18 employees. Instead, SHN needed more health care industry expertise. It even hired an interim CEO, Craig Davenport, a 25-year veteran of the industry, to steer the company in its new direction. Finally, SHN had to communicate a new message to its members. It began by reimbursing the $10,000 of subscription fees they had paid.

All of this paid off dramatically in a matter of just two years. Revenues jumped to $1.9 million in 1998. Early in 1999 SHN was purchased by WebMD and less than a year later, WebMD merged with Healtheon. The combined company still operates a thriving office out of SHN's original location in Portland, Oregon.

Sources: K. Brenneman, "Healtheon/WebMD's Local Office Is Thriving," *Business Journal of Portland,* June 2, 2000; D. Raths, "Reversal of Fortune," *Inc. Technology,* 2 (1998), pp. 52–62.

First, unless you prepare for a case discussion, there is little you can gain from the discussion and even less that you can offer. Effective strategic managers don't enter into problem-solving situations without doing some homework—investigating the situation, analyzing and researching possible solutions, and sometimes gathering the advice of others. Good problem solving often requires that decision makers be immersed in the facts, options, and implications surrounding the problem. In case analysis, this means reading and thoroughly comprehending the case materials before trying to make an analysis.

The second point is related to the first. To get the most out of a case analysis you must place yourself "inside" the case—that is, think like an actual participant in the case situation. However, there are several positions you can take. These are discussed in the following paragraphs:

◆ ***Strategic decision maker.*** This is the position of the senior executive responsible for resolving the situation described in the case. It may be the CEO, the business owner, or a strategic manager in a key executive position.

◆ ***Board of directors.*** Since the board of directors represents the owners of a corporation, it has a responsibility to step in when a management crisis threatens the company. As a board member, you may be in a unique position to solve problems.

◆ ***Outside consultant.*** Either the board or top management may decide to bring in outsiders. Consultants often have an advantage because they can look at a situation objectively. But they may also be at a disadvantage since they have no power to enforce changes.

Before beginning the analysis, it may be helpful to envision yourself assuming one of these roles. Then, as you study and analyze the case materials, you can make a diagnosis and recommend solutions in a way that is consistent with your position. Try different perspectives. You may find that your view of the situation changes depending on the role you play. As an outside consultant, for example, it may be easy for you to conclude that certain individuals should be replaced in order to solve a problem presented in the case. However, if you take the role of the CEO who knows the individuals and the challenges they have been facing, you may be reluctant to fire them and will seek another solution instead.

The idea of assuming a particular role is similar to the real world in various ways. In your career, you may work in an organization where outside accountants, bankers, lawyers, or other professionals are advising you about how to resolve business situations or improve your practices. Their perspective will be different from yours but it is useful to understand things from their point of view. Conversely, you may work as a member of the audit team of an accounting firm or the loan committee of a bank. In those situations, it would be helpful if you understood the situation from the perspective of the business leader who must weigh your views against all the other advice that he or she receives. Case analysis can help develop an ability to appreciate such multiple perspectives.

One of the most challenging roles to play in business is as a business founder or owner. For small businesses or entrepreneurial start-ups, the founder may wear all hats at once—key decision maker, primary stockholder, and CEO. Hiring an outside consultant may not be an option. However, the issues faced by young firms and established firms are often not that different, especially when it comes to formulating a plan of action. Business plans that entrepreneurial firms use to raise money or propose a business expansion typically revolve around a few key issues that must be addressed no matter what the size or age of the business. Strategy Spotlight 14.2 reviews business planning issues that are most important to consider when evaluating any case, especially from the perspective of the business founder or owner.

Next we will review five steps to follow when conducting a strategic management case analysis: becoming familiar with the material, identifying the problems, analyzing the strategic issues using the tools and insights of strategic management, proposing alternative solutions, and making recommendations.[4]

Become Familiar with the Material

Written cases often include a lot of material. They may be complex and include detailed financials or long passages. Even so, to understand a case and its implications, you must become familiar with its content. Sometimes key information is not immediately apparent. It may be contained in the footnotes to an exhibit or an interview with a lower-level employee. In other cases the important points may be difficult to grasp because the subject

Using a Business Plan Framework to Analyze Strategic Cases

Established businesses often have to change what they are doing in order to improve their competitive position or sometimes simply to survive. To make the changes effectively, businesses usually need a plan. Business plans are no longer just for entrepreneurs. The kind of market analysis, decision making, and action planning that is considered standard practice among new ventures can also benefit going concerns that want to make changes, seize an opportunity, or head in a new direction.

The best business plans, however, are not those loaded with decades of month-by-month financial projections or that depend on rigid adherence to a schedule of events that is impossible to predict. The good ones are focused on four factors that are critical to new-venture success. These same factors are important in case analysis as well because they get to the heart of many of the problems found in strategic cases.

1. *The People.* "When I receive a business plan, I always read the résumé section first," says Harvard Professor William Sahlman. The people questions that are critically important to investors include: What are their skills? How much experience do they have? What is their reputation? Have they worked together as a team? These same questions may also be used in case analysis to evaluate the role of individuals in the strategic case.

2. *The Opportunity.* Business opportunities come in many forms. They are not limited to new ventures. The chance to enter new markets, introduce new products, or merge with a competitor provide many of the challenges that are found in strategic management cases. What are the consequences of such actions? Will the proposed changes affect the firm's business concept? What factors might stand in the way of success? The same issues are also present in most strategic cases.

3. *The Context.* Things happen in contexts that cannot be controlled by a firm's managers. This is particularly true of the general environment where social trends, economic changes, or events such as the September 11, 2001, terrorist attacks can change business overnight. When evaluating strategic cases, ask: Is the company aware of the impact of context on the business? What will it do if the context changes? Can it influence the context in a way that favors the company?

4. *Risk and Reward.* With a new venture, the entrepreneurs and investors take the risks and get the rewards. In strategic cases, the risks and rewards often extend to many other stakeholders—employees, customers, suppliers, and so on. When analyzing a case, ask: Are the managers making choices that will pay off in the future? Are the rewards evenly distributed? Will some stakeholders be put at risk if the situation in the case changes? What if the situation remains the same—could that be even more risky?

Whether a business is growing or shrinking, large or small, industrial or service oriented, the issues of people, opportunities, context, and risks and rewards will have a large impact on its performance. Therefore, you should always consider these four factors when evaluating strategic management cases.

Sources: E. Wasserman, "A Simple Plan," *MBA Jungle,* February 2003, pp. 50–55; C. A. DeKluyver, *Strategic Thinking: An Executive Perspective* (Upper Saddle River, NJ: Prentice Hall, 2000); W. A. Sahlman, "How to Write a Great Business Plan," *Harvard Business Review* 75, no. 4 (1997), pp. 98–108.

matter is so unfamiliar. When you approach a strategic case try the following technique to enhance comprehension:

♦ Read quickly through the case one time to get an overall sense of the material.
♦ Use the initial read-through to assess possible links to strategic concepts.
♦ Read through the case again, in depth. Make written notes as you read.
♦ Evaluate how strategic concepts might inform key decisions or suggest alternative solutions.
♦ After formulating an initial recommendation, thumb through the case again quickly to help assess the consequences of the actions you propose.

Identify Problems

When conducting case analysis, one of your most important tasks is to identify the problem. Earlier we noted that one of the main reasons to conduct case analysis was to find solutions. But you cannot find a solution unless you know the problem. Another saying you may have heard is, "A good diagnosis is half the cure." In other words, once you have determined what the problem is, you are well on your way to identifying a reasonable solution.

Some cases have more than one problem. But the problems are usually related. For a hypothetical example, consider the following: Company A was losing customers to a new competitor. Upon analysis, it was determined that the competitor had a 50 percent faster delivery time even though its product was of lower quality. The managers of company A could not understand why customers would settle for an inferior product. It turns out that no one was marketing to company A's customers that its product was superior. A second problem was that falling sales resulted in cuts in company A's sales force. Thus, there were two related problems: inferior delivery technology and insufficient sales effort.

When trying to determine the problem, avoid getting hung up on symptoms. Zero in on the problem. For example, in the company A example above, the symptom was losing customers. But the problems were an underfunded, understaffed sales force combined with an outdated delivery technology. Try to see beyond the immediate symptoms to the more fundamental problems.

Another tip when preparing a case analysis is to articulate the problem.[5] Writing down a problem statement gives you a reference point to turn to as you proceed through the case analysis. This is important because the process of formulating strategies or evaluating implementation methods may lead you away from the initial problem. Make sure your recommendation actually addresses the problems you have identified.

One more thing about identifying problems: Sometimes problems are not apparent until *after* you do the analysis. In some cases the problem will be presented plainly, perhaps in the opening paragraph or on the last page of the case. But in other cases the problem does not emerge until after the issues in the case have been analyzed. We turn next to the subject of strategic case analysis.

Conduct Strategic Analyses

This textbook has presented numerous analytical tools (e.g., five-forces analysis and value-chain analysis), contingency frameworks (e.g., when to use related rather than unrelated diversification strategies), and other techniques that can be used to evaluate strategic situations. The previous 13 chapters have addressed practices that are common in strategic management, but only so much can be learned by studying the practices and concepts. The best way to understand these methods is to apply them by conducting analyses of specific cases.

The first step is to determine which strategic issues are involved. Is there a problem in the company's competitive environment? Or is it an internal problem? If it is internal, does it have to do with organizational structure? strategic controls? uses of technology? Or perhaps the company has overworked its employees or underutilized its intellectual capital. Has the company mishandled a merger? Chosen the wrong diversification strategy? Botched a new product introduction? Each of these issues is linked to one or more of the concepts discussed earlier in the text. Determine what strategic issues are associated with the problems you have identified. Remember also that most real-life case situations involve issues that are highly interrelated. Even in cases where there is only one major problem, the strategic processes required to solve it may involve several parts of the organization.

Once you have identified the issues that apply to the case, conduct the analysis. For example, you may need to conduct a five-forces analysis or dissect the company's competitive strategy. Perhaps you need to evaluate whether its resources are rare, valuable, difficult to imitate, or difficult to substitute. Financial analysis may be needed to assess the company's economic prospects. Perhaps the international entry mode needs to be reevaluated because of changing conditions in the host country. Employee empowerment techniques may need to be improved to enhance organizational learning. Whatever the case, all the strategic concepts introduced in the text include insights for assessing their effectiveness. Determining how well a company is doing these things is central to the case analysis process.

Financial analysis is one of the primary tools used to conduct case analysis. The Appendix to Chapter 3 includes a discussion and examples of the financial ratios that are often used to evaluate a company's performance and financial well-being. Exhibit 14.1 provides a summary of the financial ratios presented in the Appendix to Chapter 3.

In this part of the overall strategic analysis process, it is also important to test your own assumptions about the case.[6] First, what assumptions are you making about the case materials? It may be that you have interpreted the case content differently than your team members or classmates. Being clear about these assumptions will be important in determining how to analyze the case. Second, what assumptions have you made about the best way to resolve the problems? Ask yourself why you have chosen one type of analysis over another. This process of assumption checking can also help determine if you have gotten to the heart of the problem or are still just dealing with symptoms.

As mentioned earlier, sometimes the critical diagnosis in a case can only be made after the analysis is conducted. However, by the end of this stage in the process, you should know the problems and have completed a thorough analysis of them. You can now move to the next step: finding solutions.

Propose Alternative Solutions

It is important to remember that in strategic management case analysis, there is rarely one right answer or one best way. Even when members of a class or a team agree on what the problem is, you may not agree upon how to solve the problem. Therefore, it is helpful to consider several different solutions.

After conducting strategic analysis and identifying the problem, develop a list of options. What are the possible solutions? What are the alternatives? Generate a list first, listing all of the options you can think of without prejudging any one of them. Remember that not all cases call for dramatic decisions or sweeping changes. Some companies just need to make small adjustments. In fact, "Do nothing" may be a reasonable alternative in some cases. Although that is rare, it might be useful to consider what will happen if the company does nothing. This point illustrates the purpose of developing alternatives: to evaluate what will happen if a company chooses one solution over another.

Thus, during this step of a case analysis, you will evaluate choices and the implications of those choices. One aspect of any business that is likely to be highlighted in this part of the analysis is strategy implementation. Ask how the choices made will be implemented. It may be that what seems like an obvious choice for solving a problem creates an even bigger problem when implemented. But remember also that no strategy or strategic "fix" is going to work if it cannot be implemented. Once a list of alternatives is generated, ask:

- Can the company afford it? How will it affect the bottom line?
- Is the solution likely to evoke a competitive response?

Exhibit 14.1
Summary of Financial Ratio Analysis Techniques

Ratio	What It Measures
Short-term solvency, or liquidity, ratios:	
Current ratio	Ability to use assets to pay off liabilities.
Quick ratio	Ability to use liquid assets to pay off liabilities quickly.
Cash ratio	Ability to pay off liabilities with cash on hand.
Long-term solvency, or financial leverage, ratios:	
Total debt ratio	How much of a company's total assets are financed by debt.
Debt-equity ratio	Compares how much a company is financed by debt with how much it is financed by equity.
Equity multiplier	How much debt is being used to finance assets.
Times interest earned ratio	How well a company has its interest obligations covered.
Cash coverage ratio	A company's ability to generate cash from operations.
Asset utilization, or turnover, ratios:	
Inventory turnover	How many times each year a company sells its entire inventory.
Days' sales in inventory	How many days on average inventory is on hand before it is sold.
Receivables turnover	How frequently each year a company collects on its credit sales.
Days' sales in receivables	How many days on average it takes to collect on credit sales (average collection period).
Total asset turnover	How much of sales is generated for every dollar in assets.
Capital intensity	The dollar investment in assets needed to generate $1 in sales.
Profitability ratios:	
Profit margin	How much profit is generated by every dollar of sales.
Return on assets (ROA)	How effectively assets are being used to generate a return.
Return on equity (ROE)	How effectively amounts invested in the business by its owners are being used to generate a return.
Market value ratios:	
Price-earnings ratio	How much investors are willing to pay per dollar of current earnings.
Market-to-book ratio	Compares market value of the company's investments to the cost of those investments.

- Will employees throughout the company accept the changes? What impact will the solution have on morale?
- How will the decision affect other stakeholders? Will customers, suppliers, and others buy into it?
- How does this solution fit with the company's vison, mission, and objectives?
- Will the culture or values of the company be changed by the solution? Is it a positive change?

The point of this step in the case analysis process is to find a solution that both solves the problem and is realistic. A consideration of the implications of various alternative solutions will generally lead you to a final recommendation that is more thoughtful and complete.

Make Recommendations

The basic aim of case analysis is to find solutions. Your analysis is not complete until you have recommended a course of action. In this step the task is to make a set of recommendations that your analysis supports. Describe exactly what needs to be done. Explain why this course of action will solve the problem. The recommendation should also include suggestions for how best to implement the proposed solution because the recommended actions and their implications for the performance and future of the firm are interrelated.

Recall that the solution you propose must solve the problem you identified. This point cannot be overemphasized; too often students make recommendations that treat only symptoms or fail to tackle the central problems in the case. Make a logical argument that shows how the problem led to the analysis and the analysis led to the recommendations you are proposing. Remember, an analysis is not an end in itself; it is useful only if it leads to a solution.

The actions you propose should describe the very next steps that the company needs to take. Don't say, for example, "If the company does more market research, then I would recommend the following course of action . . ." Instead, make conducting the research part of your recommendation. Taking the example a step further, if you also want to suggest subsequent actions that may be different *depending* on the outcome of the market research, that's OK. But don't make your initial recommendation conditional on actions the company may or may not take.

In summary, case analysis can be a very rewarding process but, as you might imagine, it can also be frustrating and challenging. If you will follow the steps described above, you will address the different elements of a thorough analysis. This approach can give your analysis a solid footing. Then, even if there are differences of opinion about how to interpret the facts, analyze the situation, or solve the problems, you can feel confident that you have not missed any important steps in finding the best course of action.

Students are often asked to prepare oral presentations of the information in a case and their analysis of the best remedies. This is frequently assigned as a group project. Or you may be called upon in class to present your ideas about the circumstances or solutions for a case the class is discussing. Exhibit 14.2 provides some tips for preparing an oral case presentation.

How to Get the Most from Case Analysis

One of the reasons case analysis is so enriching as a learning tool is that it draws on many resources and skills besides just what is in the textbook. This is especially true in the study of strategy. Why? Because strategic management itself is a highly integrative task that draws on many areas of specialization at several levels, from the individual to the whole of society. Therefore, to get the most out of case analysis, expand your horizons beyond the concepts in this text and seek insights from your own reservoir of knowledge. Here are some tips for how to do that.[7]

♦   ***Keep an open mind.*** Like any good discussion, a case analysis discussion often evokes strong opinions and high emotions. But it's the variety of perspectives that makes case analysis so valuable: Many viewpoints usually lead to a more complete analysis. Therefore, avoid letting an emotional response to another person's style or

Exhibit 14.2
Preparing an Oral Case Presentation

Rule	Description
Organize your thoughts.	Begin by becoming familiar with the material. If you are working with a team, compare notes about the key points of the case and share insights that other team members may have gleaned from tables and exhibits. Then make an outline. This is one of the best ways to organize the flow and content of the presentation.
Emphasize strategic analysis.	The purpose of case analysis is to diagnose problems and find solutions. In the process, you may need to unravel the case material as presented and reconfigure it in a fashion that can be more effectively analyzed. Present the material in a way that lends itself to analysis—don't simply restate what is in the case. This involves three major categories with the following emphasis: Background/Problem Statement 10–20% Strategic Analysis/Options 60–75% Recommendations/Action Plan 10–20% As you can see, the emphasis of your presentation should be on analysis. This will probably require you to reorganize the material so that the tools of strategic analysis can be applied.
Be logical and consistent.	A presentation that is rambling and hard to follow may confuse the listener and fail to evoke a good discussion. Present your arguments and explanations in a logical sequence. Support your claims with facts. Include financial analysis where appropriate. Be sure that the solutions you recommend address the problems you have identified.
Defend your position.	Usually an oral presentation is followed by a class discussion. Anticipate what others might disagree with and be prepared to defend your views. This means being aware of the choices you made and the implications of your recommendations. Be clear about your assumptions. Be able to expand on your analysis.
Share presentation responsibilities.	Strategic management case analyses are often conducted by teams. Each member of the team should have a clear role in the oral presentation, preferably a speaking role. It's also important to coordinate the different parts of the presentation into a logical, smooth-flowing whole. How well a team works together is usually very apparent during an oral presentation.

opinion keep you from hearing what he or she has to say. Once you evaluate what is said, you may disagree with it or dismiss it as faulty. But unless you keep an open mind in the first place, you may miss the importance of the other person's contribution. Also, people often place a higher value on the opinions of those they consider to be good listeners.

◆ *Take a stand for what you believe.* Although it is vital to keep an open mind, it is also important to state your views proactively. Don't try to figure out what your friends or the instructor wants to hear. Analyze the case from the perspective of your own background and belief system. For example, perhaps you feel that a decision is unethical or that the managers in a case have misinterpreted the facts. Don't be afraid to assert that in the discussion. For one thing, when a person takes a strong stand, it often encourages others to evaluate the issues more closely. This can lead to a more thorough investigation and a more meaningful class discussion.

♦ *Draw on your personal experience.* You may have experiences from work or as a customer that shed light on some of the issues in a case. Even though one of the purposes of case analysis is to apply the analytical tools from this text, you may be able to add to the discussion by drawing on your outside experiences and background. Of course, you need to guard against carrying that to extremes. In other words, don't think that your perspective is the only viewpoint that matters! Simply recognize that firsthand experience usually represents a welcome contribution to the overall quality of case discussions.

♦ *Participate and persuade.* Have you heard the phrase, "Vote early . . . and often"? Among loyal members of certain political parties, it has become rather a joke. Why? Because a democratic system is built on the concept of one person, one vote. Even though some voters may want to vote often enough to get their candidate elected, it is against the law. Not so in a case discussion. People who are persuasive and speak their mind can often influence the views of others. But to do so, you have to be prepared and convincing. Being persuasive is more than being loud or long-winded. It involves understanding all sides of an argument and being able to overcome objections to your own point of view. These efforts can make a case discussion more lively. And they parallel what happens in the real world; in business, people frequently share their opinions and attempt to persuade others to see things their way.

♦ *Be concise and to the point.* In the previous point, we encouraged you to speak up and "sell" your ideas to others in a case discussion. But you must be clear about what you are selling. Make your arguments in a way that is explicit and direct. Zero in on the most important points. Be brief. Don't try to make a lot of points at once by jumping around between topics. Avoid trying to explain the whole case situation at once. Remember, other students usually resent classmates who go on and on, take up a lot of "airtime," or repeat themselves unnecessarily. The best way to avoid this is to stay focused and be specific.

♦ *Think out of the box.* It's OK to be a little provocative; sometimes that is the consequence of taking a stand on issues. But it may be equally important to be imaginative and creative when making a recommendation or determining how to implement a solution. Albert Einstein once stated, "Imagination is more important than knowledge." The reason is that managing strategically requires more than memorizing concepts. Strategic management insights must be applied to each case differently—just knowing the principles is not enough. Imagination and out-of-the-box thinking help to apply strategic knowledge in novel and unique ways.

♦ *Learn from the insights of others.* Before you make up your mind about a case, hear what other students have to say. Get a second opinion, and a third, and so forth. Of course, in a situation where you have to put your analysis in writing, you may not be able to learn from others ahead of time. But in a case discussion, observe how various students attack the issues and engage in problem solving. Such observation skills may also be a key to finding answers within the case. For example, people tend to believe authority figures, so they would place a higher value on what a company president says. In some cases, however, the statements of middle managers may represent a point of view that is even more helpful for finding a solution to the problems presented by the case.

◆ ***Apply insights from other case analyses.*** Throughout the text, we have used examples of actual businesses to illustrate strategy concepts. The aim has been to show you how firms think about and deal with business problems. During the course, you may be asked to conduct several case analyses as part of the learning experience. Once you have performed a few case analyses, you will see how the concepts from the text apply in real-life business situations. Incorporate the insights learned from the text examples and your own previous case discussions into each new case that you analyze.

◆ ***Critically analyze your own performance.*** Performance appraisals are a standard part of many workplace situations. They are used to determine promotions, raises, and work assignments. In some organizations, everyone from the top executive down is subject to such reviews. Even in situations where the owner or CEO is not evaluated by others, they often find it useful to ask themselves regularly, Am I being effective? The same can be applied to your performance in a case analysis situation. Ask yourself, Were my comments insightful? Did I make a good contribution? How might I improve next time? Use the same criteria on yourself that you use to evaluate others. What grade would you give yourself? This technique will not only make you more fair in your assessment of others, but also indicate how your own performance can improve.

◆ ***Conduct outside research.*** Many times, you can enhance your understanding of a case situation by investigating sources outside the case materials. For example, you may want to study an industry more closely or research a company's close competitors. Recent moves such as mergers and acquisitions or product introductions may be reported in the business press. The company itself may provide useful information on its website or in its annual reports. Such information can usually spur additional discussion and enrich the case analysis. (*Caution:* It is best to check with your instructor in advance to be sure this kind of additional research is encouraged. Bringing in outside research may conflict with the instructor's learning objectives.)

Several of the points suggested above for how to get the most out of case analysis apply only to an open discussion of a case, like that in a classroom setting. Exhibit 14.3 provides some additional guidelines for preparing a written case analysis.

Using Conflict-Inducing Decision-Making Techniques in Case Analysis

Next we address some techniques often used to improve case analyses that involve the constructive use of conflict. In the classroom—as well as in the business world—you will frequently be analyzing cases or solving problems in groups. While the word *conflict* often has a negative connotation (e.g., rude behavior, personal affronts) it can be very helpful in arriving at better solutions to cases. It can provide an effective means for new insights as well as for rigorously questioning and analyzing assumptions and strategic alternatives. In fact, if you don't have constructive conflict, you may only get consensus. When this happens, decisions tend to be based on compromise rather than collaboration.

In your organizational behavior classes, you probably learned the concept of "groupthink."[8] Groupthink, a term coined by Irving Janis after he conducted numerous studies on executive decision making, is a condition in which group members strive to reach agreement or consensus without realistically considering other viable alternatives. In effect, group norms bolster morale at the expense of critical thinking and decision making is impaired.[9]

Exhibit 14.3
Preparing a Written Case Analysis

Rule	Descripton
Be thorough.	Many of the ideas presented in Exhibit 14.2 about oral presentations also apply to written case analysis. However, a written analysis typically has to be more complete. This means writing out the problem statement and articulating assumptions. It is also important to provide support for your arguments and reference case materials or other facts more specifically.
Coordinate team efforts.	Written cases are often prepared by small groups. Within a group, just as in a class discussion, you may disagree about the diagnosis or the recommended plan of action. This can be healthy if it leads to a richer understanding of the case material. But before committing your ideas to writing, make sure you have coordinated your responses. Don't prepare a written analysis that appears contradictory or looks like a patchwork of disconnected thoughts.
Avoid restating the obvious.	There is no reason to restate material that everyone is familiar with already, namely, the case content. It is too easy for students to use up space in a written analysis with a recapitulation of the details of the case—this accomplishes very little. Stay focused on the key points. Only restate the information that is most central to your analysis.
Present information graphically.	Tables, graphs, and other exhibits are usually one of the best ways to present factual material that supports your arguments. For example, financial calculations such as break-even analysis, sensitivity analysis, or return on investment are best presented graphically. Even qualitative information such as product lists or rosters of employees can be summarized effectively and viewed quickly by using a table or graph.
Exercise quality control.	When presenting a case analysis in writing, it is especially important to use good grammar, avoid misspelling words, and eliminate typos and other visual distractions. Mistakes that can be glossed over in an oral presentation or class discussion are often highlighted when they appear in writing. Make your written presentation appear as professional as possible. Don't let the appearance of your written case keep the reader from recognizing the importance and quality of your analysis.

Many of us have probably been "victims" of groupthink at one time or another in our life. We may be confronted with situations when social pressure, politics, or "not wanting to stand out" may prevent us from voicing our concerns about a chosen course of action. We saw an example of groupthink in the opening case in the text. Here, EDS executives were unwilling to address their concerns when their CEO, Richard Brown, set unrealistic revenue goals. Brown told them there was "gold in the hills and go look for it." Executives were afraid that if they spoke out they would be publicly humiliated. They did not want to appear to be "quitters," according to one senior executive.

Let's first look at some of the symptoms of groupthink and suggest ways of preventing it. Then, we will suggest some conflict-inducing decision-making techniques—devil's advocacy and dialectical inquiry—that can help to prevent groupthink and lead to better decisions.

Symptoms of Groupthink and How to Prevent It

Irving Janis identified several symptoms of groupthink. These include:

- *An illusion of invulnerability.* This reassures people about possible dangers and leads to overoptimism and failure to heed warnings of danger.
- *A belief in the inherent morality of the group.* Because individuals think that what they are doing is right, they tend to ignore ethical or moral consequences of their decisions.
- *Stereotyped views of members of opposing groups.* Members of other groups are viewed as weak or not intelligent.
- *The application of pressure to members who express doubts about the group's shared allusions or question the validity of arguments proposed.*
- *The practice of self-censorship.* Members keep silent about their opposing views and downplay to themselves the value of their perspectives.
- *An illusion of unanimity.* People assume that judgments expressed by members are shared by all.
- *The appointment of mindguards.* People sometimes appoint themselves as mindguards to protect the group from adverse information that might break the climate of consensus (or agreement).

Clearly, groupthink is an undesirable and negative phenomenon which can lead to poor decisions. Irving Janis considers it to be a key contributor to such faulty decisions as the failure to prepare for the attack on Pearl Harbor, the escalation of the Vietnam conflict, and the failure to prepare for the consequences of the Iraqi invasion. Many of the same sorts of flawed decision making occur in business organizations—as we discussed above with the EDS example. Janis has provided several suggestions for preventing groupthink that can be used as valuable guides in decision making and problem solving:

- Leaders must encourage group members to address their concerns and objectives.
- When higher-level managers assign a problem for a group to solve, they should adopt an impartial stance—not mention their preferences.
- Before a group reaches its final decision, the leader should encourage members to discuss their deliberations with trusted associates and then report the perspectives back to the group.
- The group should invite outside experts and encourage them to challenge the group's viewpoints and positions.
- The group should divide into subgroups, meet at various times under different chairpersons, and then get together to resolve differences.
- After reaching a preliminary agreement, the group should hold a "second chance" meeting which provides members a forum to express any remaining concerns and rethink the issue prior to making a final decision.

Using Conflict to Improve Decision Making

In addition to the above suggestions, the effective use of conflict can be a means of improving decision making. Although conflict can have negative outcomes, such as ill will, anger, tension, and lowered motivation, both leaders and group members must strive to assure that it is managed properly and used in a constructive manner.

Two conflict-inducing decision-making approaches that have become quite popular are *devil's advocacy* and *dialectical inquiry.* Both approaches incorporate conflict into the decision-making process through formalized debate. A group charged with making a decision or solving a problem is divided into two subgroups and each will be involved in the analysis and solution.

Devil's Advocacy   With the devil's advocate approach, one of the groups (or individuals) acts as a critic to the plan. The devil's advocate tries to come up with problems with the proposed alternative and suggest reasons as to why it should not be adopted. The role of the devil's advocate is to create dissonance. This ensures that the group will take a hard look at its original proposal or alternative. By having a group (or individual) assigned the role of devil's advocate, it becomes clear that such an adversarial stance is legitimized. It brings out criticisms that might otherwise not be made.

Some authors have suggested that the use of a devil's advocate can be very helpful in helping boards of directors to ensure that decisions are addressed comprehensively and avoid groupthink.[10] And Charles Elson, a director of Sunbeam Corporation, has argued that:

> Devil's advocates are terrific in any situation because they help you to figure a decision's numerous implications. . . . The better you think out the implications prior to making the decision, the better the decision ultimately turns out to be. That's why a devil's advocate is always a great person, irritating sometimes, but a great person.

As one might expect, there can be some potential problems with using the devil's advocate approach. If one's views are constantly criticized, one may become demoralized. Thus, that person may come up with "safe solutions" in order to minimize embarrassment or personal risk and become less subject to criticism. Additionally, even if the devil's advocate is successful with finding problems with the proposed course of action, there may be no new ideas or counterproposals to take its place. Thus, the approach sometimes may simply focus on what is wrong without suggesting other ideas.

Dialectical Inquiry   Dialectical inquiry attempts to accomplish the goals of the devil's advocate in a more constructive manner. It is a technique whereby a problem is approached from two alternative points of view. The idea is that out of a critique of the opposing perspectives—a thesis and an antithesis—a creative synthesis will occur. Dialectical inquiry involves the following steps:

1. Identify a proposal and the information that was used to derive it.
2. State the underlying assumptions of the proposal.
3. Identify a counter plan (antithesis) that is believed to be feasible, politically viable, and generally credible. However, it rests on assumptions that are opposite to the original proposal.
4. Engage in a debate in which individuals favoring each plan provide their arguments and support.
5. Identify a synthesis which, hopefully, includes the best components of each alternative.

There are some potential downsides associated with dialectical inquiry. It can be quite time consuming and involve a good deal of training. Further, it may result in a series of compromises between the initial proposal and the counter plan. In cases where the original proposal was the best approach, this would be unfortunate.

Despite some possible limitations associated with these conflict-inducing decision-making techniques, they have many benefits. Both techniques force debate about underlying assumptions, data, and recommendations between subgroups. Such debate tends to prevent the uncritical acceptance of a plan that may seem to be satisfactory after a cursory analysis. The approach serves to tap the knowledge and perspectives of group members

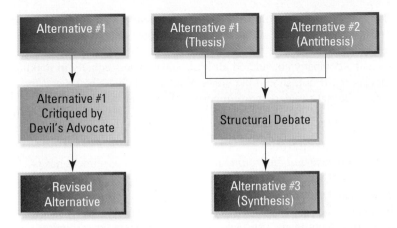

Exhibit 14.4 Two Conflict-Inducing Decision-Making Processes

and continues until group members agree on both assumptions and recommended actions. Given that both approaches serve to use, rather than minimize or suppress, conflict, higher quality decisions should result. Exhibit 14.4 briefly summarizes these techniques.

Following the Analysis-Decision-Action Cycle in Case Analysis

In Chapter 1 we defined strategic management as the analysis, decisions, and actions that organizations undertake to create and sustain competitive advantages. It is no accident that we chose that sequence of words because it corresponds to the sequence of events that typically occurs in the strategic management process. In case analysis, as in the real world, this cycle of events can provide a useful framework. First, an analysis of the case in terms of the business environment and current events is needed. To make such an analysis, the case background must be considered. Next, based on that analysis, decisions must be made. This may involve formulating a strategy, choosing between difficult options, moving forward aggressively, or retreating from a bad situation. There are many possible decisions, depending on the case situation. Finally, action is required. Once decisions are made and plans are set, the action begins. The recommended action steps and the consequences of implementing these actions are the final stage.

Each of the previous 13 chapters of this book includes techniques and information that may be useful in a case analysis. However, not all of the issues presented will be important in every case. As noted earlier, one of the challenges of case analysis is to identify the most critical points and sort through material that may be ambiguous or unimportant.

In this section we draw on the material presented in each of the 13 chapters to show how it informs the case analysis process. The ideas are linked sequentially and in terms of an overarching strategic perspective. One of your jobs when conducting case analysis is to see how the parts of a case fit together and how the insights from the study of strategy can help you understand the case situation.

1. *Analyzing organizational goals and objectives.* A company's vision, mission, and objectives keep organization members focused on a common purpose. They also influence how an organization deploys its resources, relates to its stakeholders, and matches its short-term objectives with its long-term goals. The goals may even impact how a company formulates and implements strategies. When exploring issues of goals and objectives, you might ask:

- ◆ Has the company developed short-term objectives that are inconsistent with its long-term mission? If so, how can management realign its vision, mission, and objectives?
- ◆ Has the company considered all of its stakeholders equally in making critical decisions? If not, should the views of all stakeholders be treated the same or are some stakeholders more important than others?
- ◆ Is the company being faced with an issue that conflicts with one of its long-standing policies? If so, how should it compare its existing policies to the potential new situation?

2. *Analyzing the external environment.* The business environment has two components. The general environment consists of demographic, sociocultural, political/legal, technological, economic, and global conditions. The competitive environment includes rivals, suppliers, customers, and other factors that may directly affect a company's success. Strategic managers must monitor the environment to identify opportunities and threats that may have an impact on performance. When investigating a firm's external environment, you might ask:

- ◆ Does the company follow trends and events in the general environment? If not, how can these influences be made part of the company's strategic analysis process?
- ◆ Is the company effectively scanning and monitoring the competitive environment? If so, how is it using the competitive intelligence it is gathering to enhance its competitive advantage?
- ◆ Has the company correctly analyzed the impact of the competitive forces in its industry on profitability? If so, how can it improve its competitive position relative to these forces?

3. *Analyzing the internal environment.* A firm's internal environment consists of its resources and other value-adding capabilities. Value-chain analysis and a resource-based approach to analysis can be used to identify a company's strengths and weaknesses and determine how they are contributing to its competitive advantages. Evaluating firm performance can also help make meaningful comparisons with competitors. When researching a company's internal analysis, you might ask:

- ◆ Does the company know how the various components of its value chain are adding value to the firm? If not, what internal analysis is needed to determine its strengths and weakness?
- ◆ Has the company accurately analyzed the source and vitality of its resources? If so, is it deploying its resources in a way that contributes to competitive advantages?
- ◆ Is the company's financial performance as good as or better than that of its close competitors? If so, has it balanced its financial success with the performance criteria of other stakeholders such as customers and employees?

4. *Assessing a firm's intellectual assets.* Human capital is a major resource in today's knowledge economy. As a result, attracting, developing, and retaining talented workers is a key strategic challenge. Other assets such as patents and trademarks are also critical. How companies leverage their intellectual assets through social networks and strategic alliances, and how technology is used to manage knowledge may be a major influence on a firm's competitive advantage. When analyzing a firm's intellectual assets, you might ask:

- ◆ Does the company have underutilized human capital? If so, what steps are needed to develop and leverage its intellectual assets?

◆ Is the company missing opportunities to forge strategic alliances? If so, how can it use its social capital to network more effectively?

◆ Has the company developed knowledge-management systems that capture what it learns? If not, what technologies can it employ to retain new knowledge?

5. ***Formulating business-level strategies.*** Firms use the competitive strategies of differentiation, focus, and overall cost leadership as a basis for overcoming the five competitive forces and developing sustainable competitive advantages. Combinations of these strategies may work best in some competitive environments. Additionally, an industry's life cycle is an important contingency that may affect a company's choice of business-level strategies. When assessing business-level strategies, you might ask:

◆ Has the company chosen the correct competitive strategy given its industry environment and competitive situation? If not, how should it use its strengths and resources to improve its performance?

◆ Does the company use combination strategies effectively? If so, what capabilities can it cultivate to further enhance profitability?

◆ Is the company using a strategy that is appropriate for the industry life cycle in which it is competing? If not, how can it realign itself to match its efforts to the current stage of industry growth?

6. ***Formulating corporate-level strategies.*** Large firms often own and manage portfolios of businesses. Corporate strategies address methods for achieving synergies among these businesses. Related and unrelated diversification techniques are alternative approaches to deciding which business should be added to or removed from a portfolio. Companies can diversify by means of mergers, acquisitions, joint ventures, strategic alliances, and internal development. When analyzing corporate-level strategies, you might ask:

◆ Is the company competing in the right businesses given the opportunities and threats that are present in the environment? If not, how can it realign its diversification strategy to achieve competitive advantages?

◆ Is the corporation managing its portfolio of businesses in a way that creates synergies among the businesses? If so, what additional business should it consider adding to its portfolio?

◆ Are the motives of the top corporate executives who are pushing diversification strategies appropriate? If not, what action can be taken to curb their activities or align them with the best interests of all stakeholders?

7. ***Formulating international-level strategies.*** Foreign markets provide both opportunities and potential dangers for companies that want to expand globally. To decide which entry strategy is most appropriate, companies have to evaluate the trade-offs between two factors that firms face when entering foreign markets: cost reduction and local adaptation. To achieve competitive advantages, firms will typically choose one of three strategies: global, multidomestic, or transnational. When evaluating international-level strategies, you might ask:

◆ Is the company's entry into an international marketplace threatened by the actions of local competitors? If so, how can cultural differences be minimized to give the firm a better chance of succeeding?

◆ Has the company made the appropriate choices between cost reduction and local adaptation to foreign markets? If not, how can it adjust its strategy to achieve competitive advantages?

♦ Can the company improve its effectiveness by embracing one international strategy over another? If so, how should it choose between a global, multidomestic, or transnational strategy?

8. *Formulating Internet strategies.* The Internet and digital technologies have created a new arena for strategic analysis, decisions, and action. The technologies and applications that the Internet makes possible are having an impact on competitive forces in many industries. Internet business models and value-adding strategies that combine elements of low cost, differentiation, and focus are creating new wealth in this new economy. When conducting an analysis that involves Internet strategies, you might ask:

♦ Has the company correctly assessed shifts in the five competitive forces that have been brought about by the Internet? If so, what new strategies should it formulate to take advantage of—or defend itself—in the new Internet economy?

♦ Does the company have an opportunity to lower its transaction costs by using digital technologies or doing business over the Internet? If so, what supply-chain or distribution channel relationships might be disrupted?

♦ Is the company using the right mix of competitive strategies to make the most of Internet-based technologies? If not, how might it deploy its resources and capabilities differently?

9. *Achieving effective strategic control.* Strategic controls enable a firm to implement strategies effectively. Informational controls involve comparing performance to stated goals and scanning, monitoring, and being responsive to the environment. Behavioral controls emerge from a company's culture, reward systems, and organizational boundaries. When assessing the impact of strategic controls on implementation, you might ask:

♦ Is the company employing the appropriate informational control systems? If not, how can it implement a more interactive approach to enhance learning and minimize response times?

♦ Does the company have a strong and effective culture? If not, what steps can it take to align its values and rewards system with its goals and objectives?

♦ Has the company implemented control systems that match its strategies? If so, what additional steps can be taken to improve performance?

10. *Creating effective organizational designs.* Organizational designs that align with competitive strategies can enhance performance. As companies grow and change, their structures must also evolve to meet new demands. In today's economy, firm boundaries must be flexible and permeable to facilitate smoother interactions with external parties such as customers, suppliers, and alliance partners. New forms of organizing are becoming more common. When evaluating the role of organizational structure on strategy implementation, you might ask:

♦ Has the company implemented organizational structures that are suited to the type of business it is in? If not, how can it alter the design in ways that enhance its competitiveness?

♦ Is the company employing boundaryless organizational designs where appropriate? If so, how are senior managers maintaining control of lower-level employees?

♦ Does the company use outsourcing to achieve the best possible results? If not, what criteria should it use to decide which functions can be outsourced?

11. *Creating a learning organization and an ethical organization.* Strong leadership is essential for achieving competitive advantages. Two leadership roles are

especially important. The first is creating a learning organization by harnessing talent and encouraging the development of new knowledge. Second, leaders play a vital role in motivating employees to excellence and inspiring ethical behavior. When exploring the impact of effective strategic leadership, you might ask:

- Do company leaders promote excellence as part of the overall culture? If so, how has this influenced the performance of the firm and the individuals in it?
- Is the company committed to being a learning organization? If not, what can it do to capitalize on the individual and collective talents of organizational members?
- Have company leaders exhibited an ethical attitude in their own behavior? If not, how has their behavior influenced the actions of other employees?

12. ***Fostering corporate entrepreneurship.*** Many firms continually seek new growth opportunities and avenues for strategic renewal. In some corporations, autonomous work units such as business incubators and new-venture groups are used to focus corporate venturing activities. In other corporate settings, product champions and other firm members provide companies with the impetus to expand into new areas. When investigating the impact of entrepreneurship on strategic effectiveness, you might ask:

- Has the company resolved the dilemmas associated with managing innovation? If so, is it effectively defining and pacing its innovation efforts?
- Has the company developed autonomous work units that have the freedom to bring forth new product ideas? If so, has it used product champions to implement new venture initiatives?
- Does the company have an entrepreneurial orientation? If not, what can it do to encourage entrepreneurial attitudes in the strategic behavior of its organizational members?

13. ***Creating new ventures.*** Young and small firms launch ventures that add jobs and create new wealth. In order to do so, they must identify opportunities that will be viable in the marketplace. The strategic management concepts introduced in this text can guide new ventures and small businesses in their efforts to identify markets, obtain resources, and create effective strategies. When examining the role of strategic thinking on the success of small business management and new venture creation, you might ask:

- Is the company engaged in an ongoing process of opportunity recognition? If not, how can it enhance its ability to recognize opportunities?
- Do the entrepreneurs who are launching new ventures have vision, dedication and drive, and a commitment to excellence? If so, how have these affected the performance and dedication of other employees involved in the venture?
- Have strategic principles been used in the process of obtaining valuable resources and crafting effective entrepreneurial strategies? If not, how can the venture apply the tools of five-forces and value-chain analyses to improve its strategy making and performance?

summary

Strategic management case analysis provides an effective method of learning how companies analyze problems, make decisions, and resolve challenges. Strategic cases include detailed accounts of actual business situations. The purpose of analyzing such cases is to gain exposure to a wide variety of organizational and managerial situations. By putting yourself in the place of a strategic decision maker, you can gain an appreciation for the difficulty and complexity of many strategic situations. In the process you can learn how to ask good strategic questions and enhance your analytical skills. Presenting case analyses can also help develop oral and written communication skills.

In this chapter we have discussed the importance of strategic case analysis and described the five steps involved in conducting a case analysis: becoming familiar with the material, identifying problems, analyzing strategic issues, proposing alternative solutions, and making recommendations. We have also discussed how to get the most from case analysis. Finally, we have described how the case analysis process follows the analysis-decision-action cycle of strategic management and outlined issues and questions that are associated with each of the previous 13 chapters of the text.

references

1. The material in this chapter is based on several sources, including Barnes, L. A., Nelson, A. J., & Christensen, C. R., 1994, *Teaching and the Case Method: Text, Cases and Readings* (Boston: Harvard Business School Press); Guth, W. D., 1985, Central concepts of business unit and corporate strategy, in W. D. Guth, ed., *Handbook of Business Strategy* (Boston: Warren, Gorham & Lamont), 1–9; Lundberg, C. C., & Enz, C., 1993, A framework for student case preparation, *Case Research Journal* 13 (Summer): 129–40; and Ronstadt, R., 1980, *The Art of Case Analysis: A Guide to the Diagnosis of Business Situations* (Dover, MA: Lord Publishing).

2. Edge, A. G., & Coleman, D. R., 1986, *The Guide to Case Analysis and Reporting,* 3rd ed. (Honolulu, HI: System Logistics).

3. Morris, E., 1987, Vision and strategy: A focus for the future, *Journal of Business Strategy* 8: 51–58.

4. This section is based on Lundberg & Enz, op. cit.; and Ronstadt, op. cit.

5. The importance of problem definition was emphasized in Mintzberg, H., Raisinghani, D., & Theoret, A., 1976, The structure of "unstructured" decision processes, *Administrative Science Quarterly* 21 (2): 246–75.

6. Drucker, P. F., 1994, The theory of the business, *Harvard Business Review* 72 (5): 95–104.

7. This section draws on Edge & Coleman, op. cit.

8. Irving Janis is credited with coining the term *groupthink,* and he applied it primarily to fiascos in government (such as the Bay of Pigs incident in 1961). Refer to Janis, I. L., 1982, *Victims of Groupthink,* 2nd ed. (Boston: Houghton Mifflin).

9. Much of our discussion is based upon Finkelstein, S., & Mooney, A. C., 2003, Not the usual suspects: How to use board process to make boards better, *Academy of Management Executive* 17 (2): 101–13; Schweiger, D. M., Sandberg, W. R., & Rechner, P. L., 1989, Experiential effects of dialectical inquiry, devil's advocacy, and consensus approaches to strategic decision making, *Academy of Management Journal* 32 (4): 745–72; and Aldag, R. J., & Stearns, T. M., 1987, *Management* (Cincinnati: South-Western Publishing).

10. Finkelstein and Mooney, op. cit.

Appendix to Chapter 14

Sources of Company and Industry Information*

In order for business executives to make the best decisions when developing strategy, it is critical for them to be knowledgeable about their competitors and about the industries in which they compete. This appendix provides an overview of important sources of information that may be useful in conducting company and industry analysis. Much information of this nature is available in libraries in article databases, business reference books, and on websites. This list will recommend a variety of them. Ask a librarian for assistance because library collections and resources vary.

The information sources are organized into 10 categories: Competitive Intelligence; Public or Private, Subsidiary or Division, U.S. or Foreign?; Annual Report Collections—Public Companies; Guides and Tutorials; SEC Filings/EDGAR—Company Disclosure Reports; Company Rankings; Business Metasites and Portals; Strategic and Competitive Analysis—Information Sources; Sources for Industry Research and Analysis; and Search Engines.

Competitive Intelligence

Students and other researchers who want to learn more about the value and process of competitive intelligence should see four recent books on this subject.

Craig S. Fleisher. *Strategic and Competitive Analysis: Methods and Techniques for Analyzing Business Competition.* Upper Saddle River, NJ: Prentice Hall, 2003.

John J. McGonagle and Carolyn M. Vella. *Bottom Line Competitive Intelligence.* Westport, CT: Quorum Books, 2002.

Craig S. Fleisher and David L. Blenkhorn, eds. *Managing Frontiers in Competitive Intelligence.* Westport, CT: Quorum Books, 2001.

Jerry Miller and the Business Intelligence Braintrust. *Millennium Intelligence: Understanding and Conducting Competitive Intelligence in the Digital Age.* Medford, NJ: Information Today/CyberAge Books, 2000.

Public or Private, Subsidiary or Division, U.S. or Foreign?

Companies traded on stock exchanges in the United States are required to file a variety of reports that disclose information about the company. This begins the process that produces a wealth of data on public companies and at the same time distinguishes them from private companies that often lack available data. Similarly, financial data of subsidiaries and divisions are typically filed in a consolidated financial statement by the parent company, rather than treated independently, thus limiting the kind of data available on them. On the other hand, foreign companies that trade on U.S. stock exchanges are required to file 20F reports, similar to the 10-K for U.S. companies, the most comprehensive of the required reports, although the number of foreign companies doing so is relatively small.

Corporate Directory of U.S. Public Companies. San Mateo, CA: Walker's Research, 2003. The Corporate Directory provides company profiles of more than 10,000 publicly traded companies in the United States, including 1,200 foreign companies trading on U.S. exchanges (American depositary receipts, or ADRs).

*This information was compiled by Ruthie Brock and Carol Byrne, Business Librarians at the University of Texas at Arlington. We greatly appreciate their valuable contribution.

Corporate Affiliations. New Providence, NJ: National Register Publishing, A Lexis-Nexis Group Company, 2003 edition. This directory features brief profiles identifying major U.S. and foreign corporations, both public and private, as well as their subsidiaries, divisions, and affiliates. The directory also indicates hierarchies of corporate affiliation for each firm.

Ward's Directory of Public and Private Companies. Detroit, MI: Gale Group, 2003. 8 vols. This directory lists brief profiles on more than 110,000 public and private companies and indicates whether they are public or private, a subsidiary or a division. Two volumes of the set are arranged using the Standard Industrial Classifications (SIC) and the North American Industry Classification System (NAICS) and feature company rankings within industries.

Annual Report Collections—Public Companies

A growing number of companies have their annual report to shareholders and other financial reports available on corporate websites. A few "aggregators" have cumulated links to many of these websites for both U.S. and international corporations.

Annual Report Gallery. This website contains over 2,200 annual reports (in HTML or PDF format) with additional links to company websites. www.reportgallery.com.

Company Annual Reports Online (CAROL). This website is based in the United Kingdom; therefore, many reports are European. Links are also provided for companies in Asia and the United States. A pull-down menu allows users to select companies within an industry. www.carol.co.uk/.

Public Register's Online Annual Report Service. Visitors to this website may choose from more than 2,000 company annual reports to view online or order a paper copy. www.annualreportservice.com/.

Mergent Online. New York: Mergent, Inc. Mergent Online provides company financial data for public companies headquartered in the United States, as well as those headquartered in other countries, including a large collection of corporate annual reports in portable document format (PDF). Library subscriptions to Mergent Online may vary. www.mergentonline.com.

Guides and Tutorials

Guide to Corporate Filings and Forms. This part of the Securities Exchange Commission's website explains and defines a 10-K and other SEC-required reports that corporations must file. www.sec.gov/edaux/forms.htm.

Guide to Understanding Financials. This guide gives basic information on how to read the financial statements in a company's annual report. www.ibm.com/investor/financialguide/.

Researching Companies Online. This site provides a step-by-step process for finding free company and industry information on the Web. home.sprintmail.com/~debflanagan/index.html.

SEC Filings/EDGAR—Company Disclosure Reports

SEC Filings are the various reports that publicly traded companies must file with the Securities Exchange Commission to disclose information about themselves. These are often referred to as "EDGAR" filings, the acronym for the Electronic Data Gathering, Analysis and Retrieval System. Some websites and commercial databases improve access to these reports by offering additional retrieval features not available on the official (www.sec.gov) website.

Academic Universe—SEC Filings and Reports. Lexis-Nexis. EDGAR filings and reports are available through the "Business" option of Academic Universe. These reports and filings can be retrieved by company name, industry code (Standard Industrial Classification, or SIC) or ticker symbol for a particular time period or by a specific report. Proxy, prospectus, and registration filings are also available.

EDGAR Database—Securities Exchange Commission. The 10-K reports and other corporate documents are made available in the EDGAR database within 24 hours after being filed. Annual Reports, on the other hand, are sent to shareholders and are not required as part of EDGAR by the SEC although some companies voluntarily provide them. Both 10-Ks and shareholders' annual reports are considered basic sources of company research. www.sec.gov/edgar.shtml.

EdgarScan—an Intelligent Interface to the SEC EDGAR Database. PricewaterhouseCoopers. Using filings from the SEC's servers, EdgarScan's intelligent interface parses the data automatically to a common format that is comparable across companies. A small Java applet called the "Benchmarking Assistant" performs graphical financial benchmarking interactively. Extracted financial data from the 10-K includes ratios with links to indicate where the data was derived and how it was computed. Tables showing company comparisons can be downloaded as Excel charts. www.edgarscan.pwcglobal.com/servlets/edgarscan.

Mergent Online—EDGAR. Mergent, Inc. (formerly Moody's). From the "EDGAR Search" tab within *Mergent Online,* EDGAR SEC filings and reports can be searched by company name or ticker symbol, filing date range and file type (e.g., 10-K, 8-K, ARS). The reports are available in HTML or MS word format. Using the "Find in Page" option from the browser provides the capability of jumping to specific sections of an SEC report.

FreeEDGAR. Norwalk, CT: EDGAR Online, Inc. This website offers free access to basic SEC filings with a table of contents for easy access. Premium features such as Watchlist Alerting, Rich Text Format (RTF), Excel Downloading, and Full Text Search are now available only to subscribers of EDGAR Online, the parent company of FreeEDGAR. www.FreeEDGAR.com/.

Company Rankings

Fortune 500. New York: Time Warner. The Fortune 500 list and other company rankings are available at the *Fortune* magazine website. www.fortune.com/fortune/fortune500/.

Global 500. New York: Time Warner. The Global 500 list and other company rankings are available at the *Fortune* magazine website. www.fortune.com/fortune/global500/.

Ward's Directory of Public and Private Companies. Detroit, MI: Gale Group, 2003. 8 vols. *Ward's Business Directory* is one of the few directories to rank both public and private companies together by sales within an industry, using both the Standard Industrial Classification (SIC) system (in volume 5 only) and the North American Industry Classification system (in volume 8 only). With this information, it is easy to spot who the big "players" are in a particular product or industry category.

Market share within an industry group can be calculated by determining a company's percentage of sales from the total given by Ward's for that industry group.

Business Metasites and Portals

@Brint.com, The Biz Tech Network. Syracuse, NY: Brint Institute. Brint's business metasite has a concentration of Web links related to e-business, knowledge management, and technology. www.brint.com/.

CI—CorporateInformation. Milford, CT: Winthrop Corporation. CorporateInformation's website includes information on public and private companies, both in the United States and worldwide. It also provides access to company profiles and research reports alphabetically, geographically by specific countries or U.S. states, and by industry sector. Each interactive research report analyzes sales, dividends, earnings, profit ratios, research and development, and inventory, and allows up to three companies to be compared to the company selected. www.corporateinformation.com/.

Hoover's Online. Hoover's Inc., Short Hills, NJ: D&B (formerly Dun & Bradstreet Corporation). Hoover's Online includes capsules of over 50,000 companies with links to corporate websites. Some information is free and some is available only to member subscribers. (The lock symbol indicates members only.) www.hoovers.com/free.

Strategic and Competitive Analysis—Information Sources

Analyzing a company can take the form of examining its internal and external environment. In the process, it is useful to identify the company's strengths, weaknesses, opportunities, and threats (SWOT). Sources for this kind of analysis are varied, but perhaps the best would be to locate articles from the *Wall Street Journal,* business magazines, and industry trade publications. Publications such as these can be found in the following databases available at many public and academic libraries. When using a database that is structured to allow it, try searching the company name combined with one or more key words, such as "IBM and competition" or "Microsoft and courts" or "AMR and acquisition" to retrieve articles relating to the external environment.

ABI/ Inform. ProQuest Information & Learning. Ann Arbor, MI. ABI/Inform provides abstracts and full-text articles covering management, law, taxation, human resources, and company and industry information from more than 1,000 business and management journals. ABI/Inform includes market condition reports, case studies, and executive profiles.

Business & Company Resource Center. Detroit, MI: Gale Group. Business & Company Resource Center provides company and industry intelligence for a selection of public and private companies. Company profiles include parent-sibling relationships, industry rankings, products and brands, current investment ratings, and financial ratios. Use the geographic search to locate company contact information.

Business Source Premier. Ispswich, MA: EBSCO Publishing. Business Source Premier is a full-text database with over 2,800 scholarly business journals covering management, economics, finance, accounting, international business, and more. Contact information is available from an expansive company directory. *Business Source Premier* contains over 900 peer-reviewed business journals.

Investext. Detroit, MI: Gale Group. Investext offers full-text analytical reports on more than 11,000 public and private companies and 53 industries. Developed by a global roster of brokerage, investment banking, and research firms, these full-text investment reports include a wealth of hard-to-find private company data. *Investext* is also a component of the Gale Group's *Business & Company Resource Center.*

International Directory of Company Histories. Detroit, MI: St. James Press, 1988– present. 57 volumes to date. This directory covers more than 4,500 multinational companies. Each company history is approximately three to four pages in length and provides a summary of the company's mission, goals, and ideals, followed by company milestones, principal subsidiaries, and competitors. Strategic decisions made during the company's period of existence are usually noted. This series covers public and private companies and nonprofit entities. Entry information includes a company's legal name, headquarters information, URL, incorporation date, ticker symbol, stock exchange prices, sales figures, and the primary North American Industry Classification System (NAICS) code. Further reading selections complete the entry information.

LexisNexis Academic. Bethesda, MD: LexisNexis. The "business" category in LexisNexis Academic provides access to a wide range of business information. Timely business articles can be retrieved from newspapers, magazines, journals, wires, and broadcast transcripts. Other information available in this section includes detailed company financials, company comparisons, and industry and market information for over 25 industries.

LexisNexis Statistical. Bethesda, MD: LexisNexis. LexisNexis Statistical provides access to a variety of statistical publications indexed in the American Statistics Index (ASI), Statistical Reference Index (SRI), and the Index to International Statistics (IIS). Use the PowerTables search to locate historical trends, future projections, industry, or demographic information. LexisNexis Statistical provides links to originating government websites when available.

Notable Corporate Chronologies. Julie A. Mitchell, ed. Detroit, MI: Gale Group, 2002. This two-volume set provides chronologies for over 1,800 corporations that operate in the United States and abroad. Each company entry includes the company address, phone and fax numbers, a timeline, and a further reading selection. The timeline explains the major events that affected the company's history. Dates of mergers and acquisitions, product introductions, financial milestones, and major stock offerings are also included in the chronologies. The Chronology Highlights in volume 2 provide a historical snapshot of major events for the companies listed.

CorpTech EXPLORE Database. Concord, MA: OneSource Information Services. The CorpTech CD-ROM database covers over 50,000 U.S. technology-related companies, both public and private, headquartered in the United States or affiliated with a foreign parent company. Narrative descriptions of each company, along with sales, number of employees, and other details are provided by the database. CorpTech can be searched by industry, product, geographic location, sales category, employee size, and so forth to create lists of companies that meet certain criteria. Percentage of employment growth compared with the prior year is stated. Website addresses, 800 numbers, or fax numbers are frequently provided. CorpTech is one of the best sources for information on private companies, as long as the company is in some way related to technology.

Wall Street Journal. Dow Jones Reuters Business Interactive. This respected business newspaper is available in searchable full text from 1984 to the present in the *Factiva* database. The "News Pages" link provides access to current articles and issues of the *Wall Street Journal.*

Sources for Industry Research and Analysis

CI—Corporate Information. This is a meta website covering over 65 industry sectors, and company and country information. www.corporateinformation.com.

Factiva. New York: Dow Jones Reuters Business Interactive. The *Factiva* database has several options for researching an industry. One would be to search the database for articles in the business magazines and industry trade publications. A second option in *Factiva* would be to search in the "Companies/Markets" category for company/industry comparison reports.

F & S Index, United States. Detroit, MI: Gale Group, 2003. *F & S Index* provides a compilation of company, product, and industry information from more than 750 financial publications, business-oriented newspapers, special reports, and trade magazines. Volume 1, *Industries & Products,* uses a modified seven-digit SIC product code to organize, by industry, articles on new products, market data, plant capacities, equipment expenditure, and technologies. Volume 2 provides articles accessed by company name. Companies are arranged alphabetically and topics include mergers and acquisitions, corporate announcements, profits, and sales information. *F&S Index Europe and F&S Index International* are companion services.

Mergent Online. New York: Mergent, Inc. In *Mergent Online,* the "advanced" search option has a feature for searching by industry codes (either SIC or NAICS). Once the search is executed, a list of companies in that industry should be listed. A custom or standard peer group analysis can be created to compare companies in the same industry on various criteria.

Industry Norms and Key Business Ratios. New York: D&B (Dun & Bradstreet), 2002. *Industry Norms and Key Business Ratios* provides key financial measures and business ratios, based on efficiency, profitability, and solvency, that are used as a benchmark to compare the performance of a company with the industry average. Industries are presented by the four-digit Standard Industrial Classification (SIC) code, and cover agriculture, mining, construction, transportation, communication, utilities, manufacturing, wholesaling, retailing, financial, real estate, and services.

Standard & Poor's Industry Surveys. New York: Standard & Poor's, 2003. 3 vols. *S&P's Industry Surveys* provides an overview of 52 U.S. industries. Each industry report includes a table of contents, narrative description, history, trends, financial and company information, glossary of terms, and a section on how to perform an analysis of the industry. Industry References (associations, periodicals, and websites), Composite Industry Data (industry norms and ratios), and Comparative Company Analysis (comparison of 50 major companies, their operating ratios, P/E, revenue, and so forth) complete the industry report section.

Search Engines

Google. Mountain View, CA: Google, Inc. Recognized for its advanced technology, quality of results, and simplicity, the search engine Google is highly recommended by librarians and other expert Web "surfers." www.google.com.

Vivisimo. Pittsburgh, PA: Vivisimo, Inc. One of the newer search engines that not only finds relevant results, but organizes them in logical subcategories. www.vivisimo.com.

Case 1 Adolph Coors in the Brewing Industry

"Rarely in Adolph Coors Company's 113-year history has there been a year with as many success stories as 1985." Coors's annual report for 1985 went on to cite records set by the company's Brewing Division. In a year when domestic beer consumption was flat, Coors's beer volume had jumped by 13% to a new high of 14.7 million barrels. And its revenues from beer had topped $1 billion for the first time in the company's history.

The Brewing Division accounted for 84% of Coors's revenues in 1985, and over 100% of its operating income. Although Coors had diversified into several businesses, including porcelain, food products, biotechnology, oil and gas, and health systems, Chairman Bill Coors acknowledged that for the foreseeable future, the company's fortunes were tied to brewing.

The strategy of the Brewing Division had changed drastically over the 1975–1985 period. The changes continued: in a decision that the company billed as "the most significant event of 1985 and perhaps our history," Coors announced plans to build its second brewery in Virginia's Shenandoah Valley.

The first section of this case describes competition in the U.S. brewing industry and its structural consequences. The next two sections describe Coors's position within the industry, and the plans that it had announced for its second brewery.

Competition in the U.S. Brewing Industry

In 1985, Americans spent $38 billion to buy 183 million barrels of beer.[1] Of their expenditure, 12% was applied to taxes, 42% to retailers' margins, 12% to wholesalers' margins, and the remainder to beer at (net) wholesale prices. Domestic producers supplied 96% of the market at an average wholesale price of $67 per barrel. The rest of this section describes the ways in which the major U.S. brewers made and sold beer, and the industry structure that had resulted.

Procurement   Raw materials cost major brewers over half their net revenues. Agricultural inputs accounted for a quarter or a fifth of total raw material costs, and packaging inputs for the remainder. The key agricultural inputs were malt (germinated and dried barley), a starchy cereal such as rice or corn, hops, and yeast. Large, relatively ef-

Professor Pankaj Ghemawat prepared this case as the basis for class discussion rather than to illustrate either effective or ineffective handling of an administrative situation.

Reprinted by permission of Harvard Business School Publishing. Copyright © 1988 by the Harvard Business School Publishing Corporation; all rights reserved. Harvard Business School Case 5-388-018.

[1]One barrel contains enough beer to fill 331 12-ounce bottles or cans.

ficient markets existed for all these commodities. A brewer with a single, efficiently sized plant—about 3% of the U.S. market in 1985—could buy them on the best terms available.

Packaging inputs included cans, bottles, kegs. In 1945, 3% of the beer produced in the United States had been canned, 61% bottled, and 36% kegged; by 1985, these proportions had shifted to 57%, 30% and 13%, respectively. Cans had been promoted by steel and aluminum manufacturers, bottles had proved relatively overweight, and sales of kegs had dwindled as Americans drank more and more of their beer at home.

Since World War II, beer prices had declined in real terms, and input costs had come to account for a thicker slice of them: up from 35% in 1945 to the 50–60% range by 1985. In response, major brewers had integrated backward. The most recent, and perhaps most costly, bout of integration had focused on cans, whose prices had risen sharply in the mid-1970s after the removal of price controls. In 1985, major brewers made some—but not all—of the cans they required. An efficient canmaking facility cost $40–$50 million and produced one billion cans per year. Independent canmakers had experienced significant excess capacity throughout the 1980s.

Production   Production costs, split more or less equally between direct labor and other cost components, accounted for about a quarter of major brewers' net revenues. Production involved two steps, brewing and packaging. In brewing, the agricultural inputs were mixed with water, fermented, and aged. Beer that was meant to be bottled or canned was also usually pasteurized so that it could last unrefrigerated for up to six months. Smaller brewers had traditionally pasteurized less of their beer; they sold more of it as draft, packaged in kegs. The major postwar innovation in brewing had been a fermentation process that cut the aging time of beer from 30 days to just 20. Since aging cellars were often production bottlenecks, this "stretched" brewing capacity by 20%–30%, beginning in the late 1960s.

In packaging, containers were filled with beer, labelled, and (in the case of cans and bottles) packed together. Scale economies in packaging had increased since World War II, for two reasons. First, newer vintages of filling lines—especially lines for canning and bottling—were faster and more efficient. Second, package sizes had proliferated; because of changeover costs, this increased the importance of run length.

As a result, the minimal efficient production scale for an integrated brewery (a brewing and packaging facility) had increased from 100,000 barrels per year in 1950 to

1 million barrels by 1960, 2 million barrels by 1970, and had approximated 4–5 million barrels since the mid-1970s. In 1985, a 5-million-barrel brewery cost $250–$300 million. Capital costs underlay much of the effect of increasing or decreasing production scale; according to one source, they displayed a 75% scale slope. In other words, doubling brewery scale would cut unit capital costs by 25%; halving it would increase unit capital costs by 33%. Breweries could be expanded if they had been built with that possibility in mind.

The brewing industry's capacity utilization had hovered in the 60% range in the 1950s because of stagnant demand. It increased in the 1960s and early 1970s as demand rose rapidly: the large brewers, particularly Anheuser-Busch and Schlitz, added relatively large breweries and sold them out quickly; many smaller breweries were closed. The industry's capacity utilization peaked in the mid-1970s at close to 90%. In the late 1970s, capacity surged despite stagnant demand. Miller's expansions were the most aggressive, but the other national brewers also moved to tap economies of scale. For instance, only four out of Anheuser-Busch's ten breweries exceeded four million barrels apiece in 1977; by 1985, all eleven of its breweries cleared that hurdle. Capacity utilization dropped toward 80% and stayed at that level throughout the 1980s. In 1984, excess capacity in the East forced Miller to take a $280 million pretax write-off on a nearly completed 10-million-barrel brewery in Ohio that it had intended to open in 1982.

Exhibit 1 depicts changes in breweries' actual capacities since the late 1950s, and Exhibit 2 summarizes the production configurations of the major U.S. brewers in 1985. By that time, all of them except Coors operated several breweries apiece. Multiplant configurations reduced the risk of catastrophic shutdowns due to strikes, fires, or explosions, permitted centralized production of low-volume packages (which increased run lengths), and let brewers absorb the output repercussions of a large new brewery over several existing ones.

Distribution   Beer made its way from producers to consumers via wholesalers and retailers. There were two broad categories of retail outlets for beer: on-premise and off-premise. On-premise outlets such as bars or restaurants carried a limited number of brands of beer, and averaged margins of 190% in 1985. Bars, in particular, sold more than their share of dark, local draft beers. State and federal laws prevented brewers from operating on-premise outlets except at their breweries. Off-premise outlets included supermarkets, and grocery, convenience, and liquor stores. They carried a much broader selection of brands and averaged margins of 21% in 1985. Since 1945, off-premise outlets' share of beer volume had increased from 42% to 67%.

Smaller brewers had traditionally distributed their beer directly in their local markets, with a particular emphasis on selling kegged draft beer to on-premise outlets. But less than 5% of major U.S. brewers' volume went direct. They tended to rely, instead, on independent wholesalers who purchased the beer, stored it at their warehouses, and sold and delivered it to retail accounts. Wholesalers also worked with brewers to open large accounts, secure prime shelf-space, and fund local promotions. In 1985, wholesalers averaged a 28% margin on their "laid-in" or landed cost.

There were 4,500 independent wholesalers in the United States in 1985. Each wholesaler had exclusive rights to sell a specific brand within a market usually no larger than a metropolitan area. Wholesalers often carried more than one brand, and might represent more than one brewer. In 1985, a market usually had at least two large wholesalers (one for Anheuser-Busch and one for Miller), one or two other large ones that might carry another major as their lead brewer, and several smaller ones who carried brands or retail outlets that the larger ones didn't. Anheuser-Busch's network was the strongest: its 970 wholesalers usually did not carry other brewers' beer, simplifying inventory management and delivery. Miller's wholesalers were about as large, but often carried 5–12 brands besides Miller's. The

Exhibit 1   Surviving Breweries by Capacity: 1959–1983 (thousands of barrels)

Capacity	1959	1963	1967	1971	1975	1979	1983
0–100	68	54	36	21	11	10	21
100–1000	121	105	79	65	32	21	14
1000–2000	18	17	18	21	13	11	13
2000–3000	5	6	5	9	9	6	4
3000–4000	3	4	5	3	3	7	5
4000+	2	3	4	7	15	20	23

Source: Kenneth G. Elzinga, "The Beer Industry," in *The Structure of American Industry,* edited by Walter Adams. New York: Macmillan, 1986.

Exhibit 2   Configurations of Major U.S. Brewers in 1985ª (million barrels)

Company	Number of Breweries	Total Capacity	Capacity in Efficiently Scaled Breweries (%)ª	Capacity Utilization (%)
Anheuser-Busch	11	74.0	100	85
Miller	6	44.0	100	84
Stroh	7	24.5	70	96
Heileman	10	26.0	42	62
Coors	1	16.0	100	92
Pabst	4	11.0	60	81

ªEfficient scale is defined as 4.5 million barrels of annual capacity. The figures for Stroh and Pabst are rough estimates.

Source: Gregory Pieschala, "G. Heileman Brewing Company," Harvard Business School, 1985.

other competitors had had increasing difficulty finding large wholesalers to carry them as lead brewers. The average pretax return on sales for wholesalers had fallen from 3.0% in 1981 to 2.1% by 1984.

In 1985, five of the six majors—Coors was the exception—distributed their beer in all 50 states. The five national brewers shipped beer a median distance of 300–400 miles to wholesalers' warehouses, at an average cost of $1.50–$2.00 per barrel. Wholesalers picked up this cost in name only; brewers absorbed it, in effect, by ad-justing their F.O.B. prices. Median shipping distances had stayed the same over the past three decades because the national brewers, who had displaced regional and local competitors, had all moved to multiplant configurations.

Marketing   Exhibit 3 tracks U.S. beer consumption over the 1945–1985 period. Demand grew at less than a 1% rate over 1945–1960 and 1980–1985; that was also the rate of growth predicted for the 1985–2000 period. Virtually all the volume gains in the postwar period had

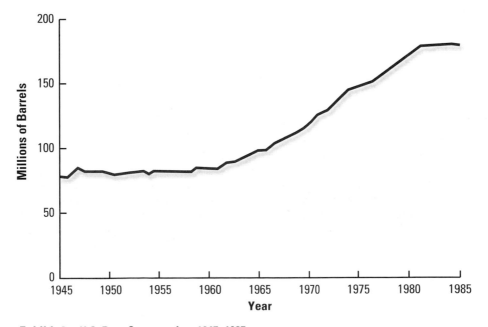

Exhibit 3   U.S. Beer Consumption: 1945–1985

Source: David J. Collis, "The Value Added Structure and Competition within Industries," unpublished Ph.D. dissertation, Harvard University, 1986.

Exhibit 4   Advertising by Major U.S. Brewers in 1985

Company	Total Advertising ($ millions)	Advertising/ Barrel ($)	Advertising/ Sales (%)
Anheuser-Busch	471	6.92	8.9
Miller[a]	300	8.09	11.6
Stroh[a]	150	6.41	9.4
Heileman	103	6.36	12.0
Coors	165	11.20	15.3
Pabst	15	1.70	3.1

[a]Rough estimates.

Sources: Annual reports and casewriter's estimates.

been registered between 1960 and 1980. The major reason for the gains was demographic: as baby boomers reached the legal drinking age, they swelled the number of beer drinkers; volume went up even more because younger drinkers consumed more beer than older ones. The second important reason was related to the marketing variables brewers worked with: price and differentiation.

Without controlling for changes in mix, beer prices fell by 30% between 1960 and 1980; this must have stimulated volume even though the price-elasticity of demand for beer seemed to be relatively low (between −0.7 and −0.9). Most observers thought that prices fell because of cost reductions and pressures to fill excess capacity rather than because of conscious predation. Anheuser-Busch and, to a lesser extent, Miller continued to charge higher-than-average prices. Brewers used low prices to enter new markets or promote new products but, if they kept them low, could impair the images of all but downscale "popular" brands. Pabst and Schlitz were often cited as cautionary examples of companies that had weakened their premium brands by discounting them.

Brewers differentiated their beers through advertising, segmentation, and packaging. Advertising increased after the war because of the emergence of TV, rising consumer incomes, the shift to off-premise consumption, and brewers' moves to broaden distribution: total advertising expenditures jumped from $50 million (2.6% of the industry's gross sales) in 1945 to $255 million (7.1% of sales) by 1965. Partly because the 1965 expenditures were "overkill," and partly because the national rollouts of the major brands had been completed, advertising expenditures drifted down to $200 million (3.3% of sales) by 1973. But then they skyrocketed again because of a steep increase by Miller (which had been acquired by Philip Morris in 1969), a delayed but even steeper response by Anheuser-Busch, and attempts by the next-largest brewers to keep up. In 1980, advertising expenditures reached

$641 million (4.5% of sales); by 1985, they approximated $1,200 million (about 10% of sales; see Exhibit 4). Statistical studies suggested that 90% of the effect of advertising dissipated within a year.

Intensified advertising helped national brewers in several ways: they could buy space or time in larger quantities, use media such as network TV and national magazines, achieve critical thresholds of exposure, and spread the fixed costs of advertising campaigns over more volume. Nevertheless, a large regional brewer still had a wide choice of effective media: for instance, spot TV, even though it cost 15%–30% more than network TV, could be tailored to local market conditions. According to a careful study conducted in the early 1970s, "The cost savings attributable to advertising on a nationwide scale [rather than regionally] could hardly amount to more than one percent of . . . revenues, other things held equal."[2]

Segmentation was the second tool used to differentiate beer. Before 1970, there were just two categories of beer: popular beers which were sold primarily on the basis of price, and premium beers which didn't cost more to produce, but were sold primarily on the basis of their images. The premium segment had gotten off the ground when brewers going national had added price premiums to their products to offset extra transportation costs. The construction of regionally dispersed breweries had since eliminated national brewers' extra transportation costs, but the price premia remained: they were used, among other things, to fund advertising. Because of increased advertising by brewers and trading up by customers, popular beers' share of volume had declined from 86% in 1947 to 58% by 1970.

Over the 1970–1985 period, the major U.S. brewers introduced even higher-priced brands and also differentiated beers according to their alcohol content (see Exhibit 5).

[2]F.M. Scherer et al., *The Economics of Multi-Plant Operation,* Harvard University Press, 1975, p. 248.

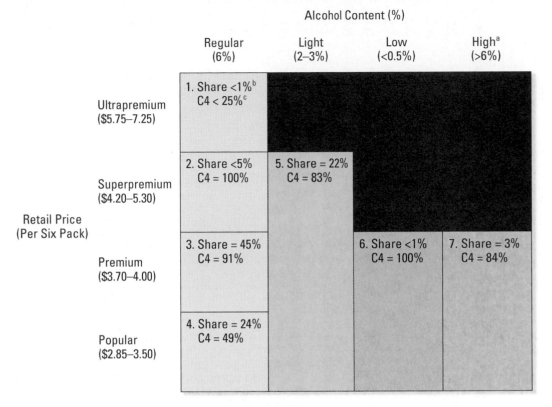

Alcohol Content (%)

	Regular (6%)	Light (2–3%)	Low (<0.5%)	High[a] (>6%)

Exhibit 5   **The Segmentation of Domestic Beers in 1985**

[a]Malt liquors.

[b]Share denotes the proportion of domestic production accounted for by a particular segment (all brands).

[c]C4 denotes the proportion of a particular segment's volume accounted for by the top four brands within it.

Sources: Coors Corporate Communications Department, *Beer Marketer's INSIGHT.*

Over the 1970–1975 period, popular beers yielded 16 points of share, mainly to premium beers. Between 1975 and 1980, popular beers gave up another 22 points, but this time, light beers, paced by the premium-priced Lite brand Miller had introduced in 1975, absorbed most of the increase. And over 1980–1985, premium beers yielded eight share points; light beers registered an equivalent gain. Superpremium beers, led by Anheuser-Busch's Michelob brand, had increased their share from 1% in 1970 to 6% by 1980, but had since receded to 4%.

Major brewers' brands proliferated as segments multiplied: between 1977 and 1981 alone, their number increased from 30 to 60. Larger brewers had several advantages in introducing new brands: their existing brand names provided leverage, they could afford launch costs ($20–$35 million per brand) and maintenance advertising (about $10 million annually per brand), and their production and distribution capabilities let them quickly ramp up sales. By 1985, a major brewer typically had a popular, a premium, and a superpremium brand in the regular category, and at least one brand in the light category. Exhibit

6 tracks the market shares of the six largest brewers' major brands over the 1977–1985 period.

Packaging was the third way in which beer was differentiated. Brewers had traditionally bottled or canned their output in 12-ounce containers. That changed in 1972 with Miller's introduction of the seven-ounce "pony" bottle, which attracted consumers who drank beer in small amounts or slowly. As states eased their regulation of package sizes in the 1970s, beer was made available in 7, 8, 10, 12, 14, 16, 24, and 32 ounce containers packed in units of 6, 8, 12, or 24.

Structural Impact   By 1934, a year after the repeal of Prohibition, 700 breweries had reopened in the United States. A third went out of business before World War II broke out. After the war, consolidation continued. Six major brewers had since come to account for virtually all domestic shipments: Exhibits 7–9 supply information on their market shares and operating performance. Only the uppermost end of the market had resisted consolidation. Several hundred imported brands, which wholesaled at twice the

Exhibit 6 Major U.S. Brands' Market Shares: 1977–1985 (% of total domestic volume)

Company	Beer Brand	Segment	1977	1978	1979	1980	1981	1982	1983	1984	1985
Anheuser-Busch	Michelob	Superpremium	4.0	4.5	4.6	4.8	4.7	4.7	4.0	3.8	3.2
	Budweiser	Premium	15.7	16.4	17.4	19.0	20.8	21.7	22.8	24.0	25.8
	Busch	Popular	2.0	2.0	1.6	1.7	1.6	1.9	2.4	2.9	3.3
	Michelob Light	Light	—	0.6	1.0	1.2	1.3	1.4	1.4	1.5	1.5
	Bud Light	Light	—	—	—	—	—	1.8	2.1	2.3	3.1
	Natural Light	Light	1.0	1.4	1.4	1.3	1.1	1.1	NA	NA	NA
Miller	Lowenbrau	Superpremium	0.3	0.7	0.5	0.7	0.6	0.9	0.9	0.8	0.8
	High Life	Premium	10.6	12.6	13.7	12.8	12.3	11.2	9.6	7.8	7.0
	Lite	Light	4.3	5.7	6.1	7.4	9.0	9.6	9.7	10.0	10.5
Schlitz[a]	Schlitz	Premium	9.1	7.5	5.4	4.0	3.1	2.3	NA	NA	NA
	Old Milwaukee	Popular	2.7	2.2	1.8	2.9	3.3	3.3	3.7	2.8	4.1
Stroh	Stroh's	Premium	3.6	3.2	3.2	3.0	3.0	3.1	3.1	3.2	2.6
Heileman	Old Style	Premium	1.9	2.3	2.7	3.0	3.1	3.0	3.0	2.9	2.0
Coors	Coors Banquet	Premium	8.2	7.4	6.7	6.5	5.7	4.8	5.5	4.8	4.9
	Coors Light	Light	—	0.3	1.0	1.4	1.8	1.8	2.1	2.6	3.4
Pabst	Blue Ribbon	Popular	9.4	8.5	7.5	6.3	5.3	4.8	4.3	3.4	2.8

[a]Schlitz was acquired by Stroh in 1982.

Source: Research Corporation of America.

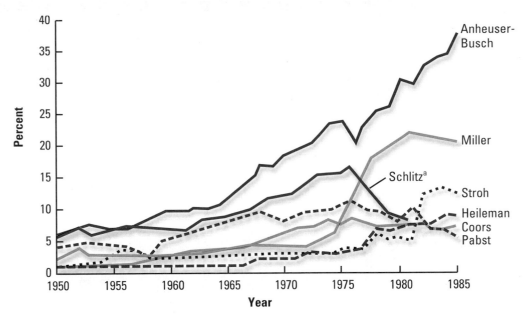

Exhibit 7   Major U.S. Brewers' National Market Shares: 1950–1985

[a]Stroh acquired Schlitz in 1982.

Source: David J. Collis, "The Value Added Structure and Competition within Industries," unpublished Ph.D. dissertation, Harvard University, 1986.

average price of domestic brands, accounted for 4% of domestic consumption. And the ultrapremium "boutique" beers offered by domestic microbrewers added up to less than 1% of domestic consumption. In the words of one analyst, imports and boutique beers might eventually account for "two or three drops in the bucket, rather than just one."

Most other large industrialized countries had highly concentrated brewing industries as well. West Germany, the second largest market for beer after the United States, was a striking exception to this rule.[3] The West German market was characterized by long-term contracts between brewers and retail outlets that guaranteed brewers exclusive supply rights, and by restrictions on the television advertising of beer. Although industry concentration had increased significantly in West Germany since the 1960s, mainly because of mergers, the three largest brewers still accounted for less than 30% of total ouput and approximately 1,300 breweries continued to operate there. Medium-to-large German brewers dominated the low-price category; many of the small local brewers, in contrast, operated in the mid-price segment.

The Brewing Division of Adolph Coors

Background   Adolph Coors, Sr., opened the doors of his brewery in Golden, Colorado, in 1873. His beer company got through Prohibition by making near beer, malted milk, cement, and porcelain. Adolph Coors, Jr., took over

[3]John Sutton, *Sunk Costs and Market Structure*, MIT Press, pp. 300–301.

in 1929 when his father died. Four years later, Prohibition was repealed; that year, Coors sold 90,000 barrels of beer. It also appointed its first independent wholesalers and began selling outside Colorado by adding Arizona to its distribution territory.

During the 1930s, Coors began to sell beer in eight other western states: California, Idaho, Kansas, Nevada, New Mexico, Oklahoma, Utah, and Wyoming. In 1941, it introduced its premium "Banquet" label. And in 1948, it started rolling into Texas. It confined itself to those 11 states through 1975.

Sales of Coors's beer had jumped from 137,000 barrels in 1940 to 666,000 barrels by 1950. Between 1951 and 1974, Coors posted uninterrupted year-to-year volume gains: volume reached 1.9 million barrels by 1960, 7.3 million barrels by 1970, and 12.3 million barrels by 1974. One analyst, commenting on the 16% ROS that Coors had posted in 1972, said, "It's the best private company in America. I'd pay any multiple for that stock." A mystique had developed around the company's only brand, premium Coors Banquet (usually referred to as just Coors). Paul Newman and Clint Eastwood insisted on having it on location; Gerald Ford and Henry Kissinger flew cases back east; college students outside Coors's 11-state distribution territory paid premia of several hundred percent for bootlegged supplies. Concerned about maintaining quality (i.e., consistent refrigeration), Coors even placed an unusual advertisement in the Washington Post: "Please do not buy our beer."

Exhibit 8 Major U.S. Brewers' Sales by Region (millions of barrels)

1977

Region	AB	Miller	Schlitz	Stroh	Heileman	Coors	Pabst	Others	Total
New England	2.0	1.8	1.6	—	NA	—	0.3	1.7	7.4
Southeast	6.4	4.4	4.1	NA	NA	—	1.6	1.8	18.2
East North Central	3.6	3.3	1.4	3.2	1.8	—	5.9	3.6	22.9
West North Central	2.7	1.4	1.7	NA	NA	0.9	2.2	3.3	12.2
West South Central	3.0	2.7	5.1	—	NA	3.7	0.3	2.5	17.3
Mountain	2.2	0.6	0.9	—	NA	3.1	0.2	1.5	8.4
Pacific	6.0	1.8	1.7	—	NA	5.1	0.5	6.3	21.4
Nonreporting States and Exports	10.9	8.1	5.7	NA	NA	—	5.0	24.1	53.8
Total	36.6	24.2	22.1	6.1	6.2	12.6	16.0	37.8	161.7

1981

Region	AB	Miller	Schlitz	Stroh	Heileman	Coors	Pabst	Others	Total
New England	2.9	2.8	0.6	NA	0.1	—	0.2	1.4	8.0
Southeast	8.6	6.4	2.8	0.7	0.8	0.3	1.1	1.2	21.9
East North Central	3.8	6.3	1.0	2.5	3.6	—	4.1	3.2	24.4
West North Central	3.5	2.6	1.2	NA	1.9	1.5	1.8	1.3	13.7
West South Central	5.7	6.1	3.2	—	0.2	4.5	0.3	2.0	22.0
Mountain	3.5	1.9	0.8	—	0.4	2.9	0.2	1.1	10.7
Pacific	10.4	3.1	1.3	—	1.8	4.1	1.1	3.6	25.5
Nonreporting States and Exports	16.1	11.2	3.5	NA	5.1	—	4.6	18.0	58.5
Total	54.5	40.3	14.3	9.1	14.0	13.3	13.5	25.7	184.6

1983

Region	AB	Miller	Schlitz/Stroh	Heileman	Coors	Pabst	Others	Total
New England	3.4	2.4	0.7	0.2	—	0.1	1.2	8.0
Southeast	9.1	5.3	4.4	1.4	2.2	0.8	1.1	24.2
East North Central	4.3	6.7	4.0	4.1	—	3.2	2.1	24.3
West North Central	4.1	2.3	1.5	2.2	1.2	1.7	0.5	13.5
West South Central	6.6	5.9	3.2	1.0	3.8	0.3	1.2	22.0
Mountain	3.9	1.7	0.8	0.7	2.4	0.8	0.3	10.6
Pacific	11.2	3.0	1.2	2.6	3.4	2.1	1.8	25.2
Nonreporting States and Exports	18.0	10.3	8.5	5.7	0.8	4.2	11.4	58.9
Total	60.5	37.5	24.3	17.9	13.7	13.2	19.5	186.6

1985

Region	AB	Miller	Schlitz/Stroh	Heileman	Coors	Pabst	Others	Total
New England	3.5	1.8	0.4	0.1	0.9	0.1	0.9	7.8
Southeast	11.4	5.3	4.0	1.3	1.7	0.7	1.1	25.5
East North Central	5.8	6.5	3.5	3.5	0.5	2.1	2.1	24.0
West North Central	4.4	2.2	2.0	1.9	1.1	1.0	0.3	13.0
West South Central	7.5	6.4	2.9	0.9	3.2	0.2	1.1	22.1
Mountain	4.4	1.7	1.0	0.7	2.1	0.5	0.3	10.7
Pacific	11.5	3.2	1.5	2.4	3.2	0.1	3.3	25.3
Nonreporting States and Exports	19.5	9.9	8.0	5.3	2.0	2.9	10.4	58.0
Total	68.0	37.1	23.4	16.2	14.7	8.9	18.0	186.4

Regions. New England: Maine, Massachusetts, New Hampshire, Rhode Island, and Vermont. **Southeast:** Alabama, Florida, Georgia, Mississippi, South Carolina, Tennessee, and West Virginia. **East North Central:** Indiana, Michigan, Ohio, and Wisconsin. **West North Central:** Iowa, Kansas, Minnesota, Missouri, Nebraska, North Dakota, and South Dakota. **West South Central:** Arkansas, Louisiana, Oklahoma, and Texas. **Mountain:** Arizona, Colorado, Idaho, Montana, Nevada, New Mexico, Utah, and Wyoming. **Pacific:** California, Oregon, and Washington. **Nonreporting:** Connecticut, Virginia, North Carolina, Kentucky, Maryland, Alaska, Hawaii, Illinois, New York, New Jersey, Delaware, and Pennsylvania; Washington, D.C.; Exports.

Sources: *Beer Marketer's INSIGHT;* Beer Statistics News.

Exhibit 9   **Major U.S. Brewers' Operating Statements (in millions of units)**

	Anheuser-Busch	Miller[a]	Schlitz[b]	Stroh[a]	Heileman	Coors	Pabst[a]
1977							
Barrels Sold	36.6	24.2	22.1	5.8	6.2	12.8	16.0
Net Revenue	$1,684	$1,110	$ 900	$ 223	$ 216	$ 532	$583
Cost of Goods Sold	1,340	NA	698	180	152	371	486
Advertising	73	60	54	11	13	14	27
Other SG&A	102	NA	90	19	27	38	32
Operating Income	$ 169	$ 106	$ 58	$ 13	$ 25	$ 109	$ 38
1985							
Barrels Sold	68.0	37.1	23.4		16.2	14.7	8.9
Net Revenue	$5,260	$2,591	$1,592		$ 860	$1,079	$490
Cost of Goods Sold	3,524	NA	NA		617	727	NA
Advertising	471	300	150		103	165	<15
Other SG&A	491	NA	NA		74	94	NA
Operating Income	$ 774	$ 136	NA		$ 67	$ 93	NA

[a]Figures for 1985 have been estimated.

[b]Schlitz was acquired by Stroh in 1982.

Sources: Annual reports and casewriter's estimates.

In 1975, Coors's volume dropped for the first time in two decades: by 4% to 11.9 million barrels. At roughly the same time, it began adding new states to its distribution territory: its official position became, "We do want to go national if it makes sense financially."[4] Since then, its growth and profitability had come under pressure, as had its market valuation. The Coors family had first offered stock—all of it nonvoting—to the public in June 1975 in order to settle a $50 million inheritance tax bill. The stock sold for $25.50 at the end of 1975, had paid dividends of $2.79 per share through 1985, and sold for $21.25 in 1985. In 1985, the Coors family continued to hold all of the voting stock (4% of the total), as well as 16% of the nonvoting stock. The book value of all shareholder equity was $936 million at the end of the year, corresponding to $26.46 per share, and the company had set itself the target of a 10% after-tax return on equity.

In May 1985, the company's operations were officially handed over to the fourth generation of the Coors family.

[4] *Beverage World,* November 1977, p. 134.

Bill Coors, 68, relinquished his title of CEO but retained his position as chairman; Joe Coors, 67, stepped down as president but remained the company's vice chairman. Joe's sons, Jeff, 40, and Peter, 38, took over as presidents of the holding company and the Brewing Division, respectively. All four members of the Coors family remained on the board; the other five directors were also insiders.

The younger members of the Coors family believed that the company's traditional strengths in production had to be supplemented with attention to and expertise at marketing skills. Peter Coors had, in fact, cast the first dissenting board vote in the company's history back in 1976, against the retention of a hard-to-open press tab on its beer cans. Peter and Jeff were also expected to steer clear of the controversies that the older members of the family had periodically ignited. One example dated from March 1984: the *Rocky Mountain News* alleged that Bill Coors had told an audience of more than 100 minority businessmen that blacks "lack the intellectual capacity to succeed"; Bill Coors insisted that he had been grossly misquoted. Under the new generation, Coors had committed itself to spending $650 million over five years working with minority vendors and distributors, hiring minority employees, and supporting local communities.

The rest of this section describes Coors's traditional strategy in brewing, and the changes that had been made to it between 1975 and 1985. Exhibit 10 summarizes the vital statistics of the Brewing Division over the 1975–1985 period.

Procurement   In procuring inputs, Coors had always stressed quality and self-reliance. The "pure Rocky Mountain spring water" Coors had emphasized on its label for half a century came from 60 springs on company-owned land in Golden, Colorado, the site of its brewery; it continued to acquire water rights and to add reservoir capacity as a hedge against a prolonged drought.

Of the various agricultural inputs to brewing, Coors made its own malt out of proprietary strains of Moravian barley grown for it by 2,000 farmers under long-term contract. Its brewing process could use either rice or refined cereal starch; Coors had long operated its own rice-processing facilities to protect itself from fluctuations in the price of broken "brewing" rice and, in 1983, had acquired a grain processing facility that supplied a third of its refined cereal starch requirements during 1985. Premium hops were purchased from both domestic and European suppliers. According to a Coors legal brief, "From a raw [agricultural] materials standpoint, Coors is . . . the most expensive beer made in America."

Although bottles cost slightly less than cans, Coors canned more of its beer than did other U.S. brewers: 69% versus an average of 57% for the industry as a whole in 1985. Coors had pioneered the first two-piece, all-aluminum can for beverages in 1959 and, since then, had sourced all its cans from a captive canmaking facility that had grown to be the largest in the world. It was the first brewer to start a can recycling program and in 1984, using technology developed with Alusuisse, had opened its own can recycling facility. The new facility was still experiencing start-up problems. It had, however, supplied 14% of the company's aluminum requirements in 1985; long-range plans called for it to supply a third of the company's aluminum needs.

Coors also made most of its labels and secondary packaging and, after the 1976 acquisition of its principal glass bottle supplier, virtually all the bottles that it required (unlike any other major brewer). This pattern of above-average vertical integration extended into areas other than packaging. In an industry where even the biggest brewer bought machinery from outside suppliers, Coors built all of its malting equipment, 90% of its brewing equipment, and 75% of its packaging equipment. Since the mid-1970s, it had also invested heavily to become self-sufficient in energy, mainly by developing its own coalfield.

Production   In the area of production, Coors had emphasized quality and scale. The company's claims of superior quality hinged not only on the ingredients that it used, but also on two unique aspects of its brewing process. First, Coors aged its beer for 70 days, compared to an average of 20–30 days for other brewers; part of the reason was the company's "natural" fermentation process, which minimized the use of additives. The longer brewing cycle tied up more capital: in 1984, assets per barrel of capacity amounted to $57 for Coors, $45 for Anheuser-Busch, $43 for Miller, and $16 for Heileman, which had bought capacity cheaply from failing regional brewers.

Second, Coors, unlike other major brewers, did not pasteurize the beer that it bottled or canned; it claimed that intense heat harmed the taste of beer. (As a result, all Coors beer was draft, irrespective of whether it had been canned, bottled, or kegged). To check bacterial contamination, Coors brewed its beer aseptically, used a sterile-fill process to package it, and stored it in refrigerated warehouses. The extra costs of refrigeration roughly equalled the energy saved in skipping pasteurization.

Coors had traditionally controlled its production costs by brewing a single kind of beer, running the fastest packaging lines in the industry, and operating the largest brewery in the world. Coors had expanded its single brewery in Golden, Colorado, from 3 million barrels in 1963 to 7 million barrels by 1970, and 13 million barrels by 1975. Although plans had originally called for expanding the Golden brewery to 20 million barrels by the mid-1980s, they had to be deferred because of stagnant demand: in 1985, the capacity at Golden was 16 million barrels.

Through 1975, Coors's capacity additions had lagged its sales growth, leading to shortages during peak consumption periods. One analyst described Coors's capacity expansion strategy as follows: "We make a little beer, if we sell it, we make a little more." Capacity utilization had traditionally hovered in the 90%–95% range. Since 1977, however, average capacity utilization had fallen to 84%, only slightly above the level for the industry as a whole.

One factor that had helped Coors's capacity utilization in the sixties and early seventies was the capacity shortfall in the ten states west of Colorado (including New Mexico but excluding Alaska and Hawaii): in 1975, for instance, 24 million barrels of beer were consumed in these states, but only 17 million barrels of capacity were located within the region. Coors was well-positioned to make up this deficit because its brewery in Colorado was closer to most of these markets than were competitors' breweries in Texas, Missouri, and Wisconsin. But in the late seventies and early eighties, Anheuser-Busch and Miller reacted to the vacuum by adding 11 and 3 million barrels of capacity, respectively, in California. By 1985, 31 million barrels of capacity were available from breweries within the region to meet 34 million barrels of demand.

Exhibit 10 Summary Data on Coors' Brewing Division

	1975	1976	1977	1978	1979	1980	1981	1982	1983	1984	1985
A. Volumes											
Distribution Territory											
# of States	11	13	14	16	16	17	20	20	28	37	44
% of U.S. Market	25%	27%	28%	32%	32%	34%	40%	40%	54%	67%	79%
Wholesalers	NA	212	223	254	254	260	266	374	368	521	574
Capacity (millions of barrels)	13.2	14.2	15.1	15.6	15.6	15.9	15.9	15.9	16.0	16.0	16.0
Sales (millions of barrels)											
Coors Banquet	11.9	13.5	12.8	12.1	11.3	11.3	10.0	8.5	9.7	8.4	8.5
Coors Light	—	—	—	0.5	1.6	2.5	3.1	3.2	3.8	4.6	6.0
Other	—	—	—	—	—	—	0.1	0.2	0.2	0.2	0.2
Total	11.9	13.5	12.8	12.6	12.9	13.8	13.2	11.9	13.7	13.2	14.7
Capacity Utilization (%)	90%	95%	85%	81%	83%	87%	83%	75%	86%	83%	92%
B. Financials[a]											
Sales	NA	545	532	549	639	759	788	766	948	938	1,079
Cost of Goods Sold	NA	NA	371	396	447	538	559		614	666	727
Advertising	7	10	14	29	40	57	73	88	119	139	165
Other SG&A	NA	NA	38	46	54	77	92		66	80	94
Operating Income	118	139	109	79	98	87	64	46	149	53	93
Depreciation	NA	31	37	40	42	45	50	54	57	65	72
Additions to Properties	NA	69	72	72	64	92	130	84	120	92	60
Total Assets	NA	518	562	605	650	704	754	772	850	905	893
Consumer Price Index	161	171	182	195	217	247	272	289	298	311	322

[a]All financials are in current millions of dollars except for the consumer price index.

Sources: Annual reports, 10-K reports, and *Beer Marketer's INSIGHT.*

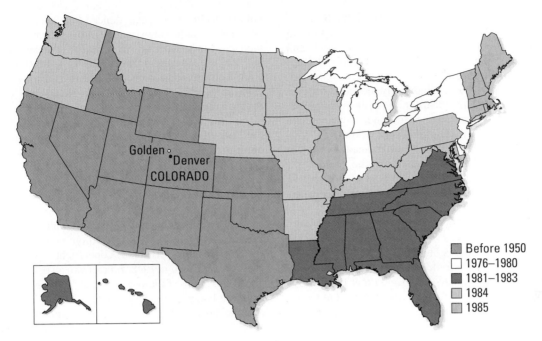

Exhibit 11 Coors's National Rollout

Source: Annual Reports.

Coors's operating practices had led to numerous strikes over the years by workers, and occasional suits by federal agencies. The grounds included alleged racial and sexual discrimination, mandatory lie-detector tests and loyalty oaths, and dismissals for reasons such as denigration of the Coors family and refusal to be searched at work. To quote a 1978 article in *Forbes,* "Coors ranks with J.P. Stevens on union hate lists." The most recent strike was the one called in April 1977 by the Brewery Workers Union, which represented 1,500 of the company's 8,200 employees. Coors said that workers who crossed the picket line, employees transferred from other departments, and new hires had returned the brewery to normal production levels in three weeks. The strike officially ended in December 1978 when workers voted to oust the Brewery Workers Union as their bargaining agent. Since then, the AFL-CIO and other groups had organized a boycott of Coors, which had finally retaliated with lawsuits that were still in process. According to Bill Coors, "This is the kind of war we want to get into, not shy away from."[5] The boycott continued in 1985, although independent analysts thought that it had proved ineffective. And Coors continued to be the only major brewer that was not unionized.

Distribution Coors's distribution was governed by the fact that its unpasteurized beer tended to spoil rather quickly. The company shipped its beer in refrigerated rail

[5]*Wall Street Journal,* October 6, 1982, p. 27.

cars and trucks to wholesalers' warehouses. Wholesalers had to keep it chilled and to abide by a strict "freshness policy": any Coors beer that had been on the shelves longer than 60 days was destroyed at the wholesaler's expense. By its own account, "Adolph Coors Company has one of the industry's most extensive distributor monitoring programs."

The company's tough policies towards its channels had been challenged in 1971 by the FTC, which attacked Coors for restricting the geographic distribution of its beer, and also charged that Coors had refused to sell its draft beer to bars unless they carried it exclusively, that it did not allow its wholesalers to cut prices, and that its provisions for terminating wholesalers were high-handed. By January 1975, the courts had conclusively found for the FTC on the first three counts, and for Coors on the fourth.

Citing economic advantages, Coors began to widen its 11-state distribution territory in 1976, initially by moving into two or three new states each year. In 1981, it began to sell beer east of the Mississippi River for the first time. In 1983, it stepped up the pace: over the 1983–1985 period, it added an average of eight states each year. Exhibit 11 summarizes the pattern of the rollout into 44 states through 1985. The company planned to enter Michigan in 1986, New York and New Jersey in 1987, and the three remaining states—Pennsylvania, Delaware, and Indiana by the end of the decade.

The national rollout had two important consequences. First, the median distance Coors shipped its beer increased from 800 miles in 1977 to 1,500 miles by 1985. Coors responded by establishing distribution centers in outlying markets (Sacramento, Baltimore, Memphis, and Greenville (S.C.)) in 1983; it absorbed the cost of shipping beer from its brewery to these centers directly and, in line with industry practice, indirectly picked up the cost of getting beer from the distribution centers to wholesalers. Second, Coors quickly had to find new wholesalers in new states. It typically chose weaker wholesalers willing to carry Coors as their lead brand instead of stronger Anheuser-Busch or Miller wholesalers who would have carried it as a secondary brand. Each new wholesaler had to spend about $500,000–$2 million on market development, depending on the size of its territory.

The circumstances of Coors's existing wholesalers had also changed. In the 1970s, they were so profitable that dozens and sometimes hundreds of applicants clamored for each new Coors franchise; over two-thirds of the company's wholesalers then carried no other brands. But in the 1980s, wholesalers who carried nothing but Coors dwindled to a minority, and one-fifth of the company's franchises changed hands over the 1980–1982 period alone. (In some of the states penetrated after 1975, that proportion was as high as one-third). In response, Coors had begun to place more importance on applicants' previous experience in the beer business; its wholesalers also agreed that it had become more responsive to their concerns and suggestions.

In 1985, Coors's distribution network comprised 569 independent wholesalers and 5 company-owned ones. The company shipped 74% of its beer in refrigerated rail cars, and the remainder in refrigerated trucks. The company's trucking subsidiary, Coors Transportation Company, hauled nearly half of the truck shipments—a higher proportion than at other major brewers. Even though Coors Transportation Company had gained common carrier status in 1982, it hadn't managed to tap as many sources of traffic or secure as much backhaulage as independent carriers; this probably elevated its costs by 10%–15%.

Marketing   Coors had traditionally relied on its beer to market itself by virtue of its "drinkability." Coors's beer was supposed to derive its superior drinkability from Rocky Mountain spring water and other choice ingredients, as well as the company's unique brewing process. In blind taste tests, however, consumers that managed to distinguish Coors from other premium brands did so mainly on the basis of its relatively light body—not a characteristic with universal appeal. Bill Coors had once admitted, "You could make Coors from swamp water and it would be exactly the same."[6]

Whatever their reasons, consumers drank as much Coors beer as they could get through in 1975. Despite the

volume decline Coors experienced that year, it sold more beer than any other brewer in 10 of the 11 states that it had targeted. Since then, however, its volume had been flat and had spread across an increasing number of states. Even though it had achieved double-digit market shares in entering several new states, those shares had typically dropped off in subsequent years.

In the late seventies, the slump persuaded Bill and Joe Coors that the company needed to spend more money on marketing. Coors began to hire marketeers from other companies and to target niches in which its penetration had been limited, such as black and Hispanic consumers. It also launched new brands and sharply increased its advertising expenditures.

The launches caused much debate within the company because since 1958, it had offered only one brand, Coors Banquet. The first new brand, Coors Light, a premium light beer, was launched in 1978. Entries into all but the popular-priced segments followed. Herman Joseph's, a super-premium brand under development since 1977, went into test markets in 1980, and was finally introduced to seven states in 1984. George Killian's Irish Red ale, another superpremium brand for which Coors had secured U.S. brewing rights, was test marketed in 1981 and introduced more quickly; by 1985, Coors sold Killian's in 34 states. Golden Lager, a darker and more robust premium brand than Coors Banquet, was test marketed in 1983 and then withdrawn; Coors repositioned the brand as Coors Extra Gold and recommenced test marketing in 1985. In 1985, Coors also joined Molson of Canada and Kaltenberg Castle of West Germany in forming the Masters Brewing Company to brew ultrapremium Masters III and test market it in four cities. That same year, Coors granted Molson a license to brew Coors in Canada. These new products had contributed to the proliferation of packages: in 1984, for instance, Coors ran 320 different packages on its lines.

Coors experienced its first success at advertising with the "Silver Bullet" theme for Coors Light. (Coors Light's label was silver; Coors Banquet's label was golden.) Each Coors Light commercial presented a vignette of men and women who worked or imbibed at the Silver Bullet bar. The characters did not endorse Coors Light; the beer was, instead, background to the story. That differentiated it from the two other leading light beers, Miller Lite and Bud Light: Miller Lite's commercials featured male athletes endorsing the beer, and Bud Light's commercials victimized male characters who ordered light beer generically in bars. By 1985, Coors Light had become the second best selling light beer; it also accounted for more than 40% of Coors's total volume. Although the introduction of Coors Light had created early technical and operational problems, it had come to contribute more to Coors's profitability than Coors Banquet. Part of the reason was that light beers used less of everything (except water) than premium beers, reducing total manufacturing costs by $2–$3 per barrel.

It took Coors longer to advertise its premium-regular Banquet brand successfully; in a 1984 survey, its wholesalers had given it a C+ in this regard.[7] After years of thematic churn, a breakthrough came in 1985 with Coors's first national advertising campaign, "Coors is the One." The advertisements were quiet—settings included mountain lakes and barley fields—and featured Mark Harmon, a quarterback-turned-actor with considerable sex appeal (according to *People* magazine) expounding on why Coors was a fresher and better beer. Other premium beers, in contrast, used life-style commercials packed with people (usually a group of men), action, and music that did not discuss product quality. According to a survey by *Advertising Age,* the new Coors commercials were the most recalled beer advertisements in 1985.

As Coors beefed up its advertising, it also increased its prices, particularly in new distribution territories. Coors Banquet had traditionally been priced well below Budweiser in the west; in eastern markets, it was priced much closer to Budweiser. Most of the added revenue per barrel was negated, however, by the additional cost of shipping beer greater distances.

Coors's Plans for Multisite Expansion

As Coors began its national rollout, concern about the 25–30 million barrel ceiling on capacity at the Golden site and about the increase in shipping distances prompted it to study a second site. By 1979, it had identified two possible locations: one in Rockingham County, Virginia, on the Shenandoah River and the other in Anson County, North Carolina, on the Pee Dee River. In 1981, it completed the acquisition of 2,100 acres of land in Rockingham County. And in August 1985, it announced plans to construct a 10 million barrel brewery there.

The construction was to proceed in two phases. In the first phase, for which ground had been broken in November 1985, Coors would add a 2.4-million-barrel packaging facility that would bottle and can beer shipped in refrigerated rail cars from Golden. The packaging facility was expected to cost $95 million and to start up in spring 1987. Coors estimated that it would reduce the cost of shipping beer to the East Coast by $2.50 per barrel, helping the company complete its national rollout.

In the second phase, which had not yet been committed to, the facility would be expanded into an integrated 10-million-barrel-per-year brewery. Analysts thought that the second phase might cost $500–$600 million and reduce transportation costs by another $2.50 per barrel. They also noted that to construct the brewery, Coors would probably have to resort to external financing for only the second time in its history. The idea of issuing debt, however, continued to be resisted by Jeff and Peter Coors.

The International Brotherhood of Teamsters quickly announced its intention to organize the 225–250 workers that the new facility would employ in its first phase. The Teamsters, and other unions, were relatively strong in the markets that the Rockingham plant was meant to serve.

[7]*Beverage World,* October 1984, p. 43.

Case 2   American Red Cross in 2002 (A)*

As Marsha "Marty" Johnson Evans took the helm of the American Red Cross on August 5, 2002, she was faced with the challenge of restoring the public's faith in the organization. During the past 24 months, there had been a barrage of negative publicity regarding the American Red Cross. In June 2000 Red Cross workers went on strike. The organization was hit by a lawsuit filed by HemaCare Corporation and Coral Blood Services in January 2001. The plaintiffs alleged that the American Red Cross engaged in unfair trade practices in the pricing of blood. The Better Business Bureau made false public statements about the ability of the American Red Cross to meet their standards for charitable solicitations. Then on September 11, 2001, Americans watched in horror as terrorists flew two planes into the World Trade Center buildings and a third into the Pentagon in Washington. In the aftermath of this tragedy, donations poured into the American Red Cross, and a special fund—the Liberty Disaster Relief Fund—was established by the then-president of the Red Cross, Dr. Bernadine Healy. When it was announced that not all donations would be used for victims of the 9/11 disaster, there was a huge public outcry from donors. Healy was forced to retire, and interim president and CEO Harold Decker announced that all donations to the Liberty Disaster Relief Fund would be used in the organization's 9/11 relief efforts. Finally, on March 10, 2002, *60 Minutes,* a CBS news show, ran a misleading and inaccurate story about the American Red Cross.

On June 27, 2002, Marsha Johnson Evans was named new CEO and president of the American Red Cross. At the time of this announcement, Evans stated:

> This is a time of great challenge for many charitable organizations including the American Red Cross. On the one hand, we need to motivate Americans to donate their time and their treasure, which is never easy, but always comes down to whether they trust an organization and believe in their work. On the other hand, we face a host of challenges including the need to better prepare this nation for disasters both natural and man-made; as well as the rigors of furnishing a safe and available blood supply with all the costs and complexity this involves.[1]

History and Operations of the American Red Cross

Henry Dunant set forth the idea of the Red Cross in 1859 when he saw wounded and dying soldiers on the battlefield in Solferino, Italy. He organized local people to bind the soldiers' wounds and to feed and care for them. Henry Dunant called for the creation of a national relief society and this pointed the way to the future Geneva Convention. Four years later, in 1863, the International Red Cross was created in Geneva, Switzerland, with the purpose of providing nonpartisan care in time of war. The Red Cross emblem was adopted as a symbol of neutrality although today the Red Crescent is also a recognized symbol. Today the Red Cross incorporates the International Committee of the Red Cross and the International Federation of Red Cross and Red Crescent Societies as well as national societies in 175 countries. The fundamental principles of the International Red Cross are listed in Exhibit 1. Clara Barton successfully organized the first lasting Red Cross Society in America in Washington, D.C., on May 21, 1881. The American Red Cross provided services beyond those of the International Red Cross by providing disaster relief in addition to battlefield assistance. Clara Barton served as the organization's president through 1904.[2]

As stated in its 2000–2001 Annual Report, "the American Red Cross is a humanitarian organization, led by volunteers, whose mission is to provide relief to victims of disasters and help people prevent, prepare for, and respond to emergencies." The vision of the American Red Cross is "the American Red Cross . . . always there . . . touching more lives, in new ways . . . under the same trusted symbol." Since its founding, the American Red Cross has symbolized the nobility of the human spirit by representing service and goodwill across America. Its purpose, or intent, is to "prevent and relieve human suffering." Each year March is proclaimed as American Red Cross month. To support the fundamental principles of the International Red Cross, the American Red Cross has adopted a set of values (see Exhibit 2).

The American Red Cross is governed by a Board of Governors that formulates policy and delegates authority to the volunteer boards of its 1,000 local chapters. Decentralization allows the Red Cross to provide immediate, effective, and efficient assistance to those in need.[3] Annually, the American Red Cross helps victims of more than 63,000 natural and man-made disasters. The worst disaster ever dealt with by the American Red Cross was the hurricane that killed an estimated 6,000 people in Galveston, Texas, in 1900.

The American Red Cross helps victims through a wide range of services:[4]

♦ Armed Forces Emergency Services. Provides military families with emergency communication services, financial assistance, counseling, and so forth.

*This case was prepared by Professors Debora J. Gilliard and Rajendra Khandekar of Metropolitan State College—Denver as a basis for class discussion rather than to illustrate either effective or ineffective handling of an administrative situation. Copyright © 2004 Debora J. Gilliard and Rajendra Khandekar. All rights reserved.

Exhibit 1   Principles of International Red Cross

- **Humanity:** The International Red Cross and Red Crescent Movement, born of a desire to bring assistance without discrimination to the wounded on the battlefield, endeavors, in its international and national capacity, to prevent and alleviate human suffering where it may be found. Its purpose is to protect life and health and to ensure respect for the human being. It promotes mutual understanding, friendship, cooperation, and lasting peace amongst all peoples.
- **Impartiality:** It makes no discrimination as to nationality, race, religious beliefs, class, or political opinions. It endeavors to relieve the suffering of individuals, being guided solely by their needs, and to give priority to the most urgent cases of distress.
- **Neutrality:** In order to continue to enjoy the confidence of all, the Movement may not take sides in hostilities or engage at any time in controversies of a political, racial, religious, or ideological nature.
- **Independence:** The Movement is independent. The National Societies, while auxiliaries in the humanitarian services of their governments and subject to the laws of their respective countries, must always maintain their autonomy so that they may be able at all times to act in accordance with the principles of the Movement.
- **Voluntary Service:** It is a voluntary relief movement not prompted in any manner by desire for gain.
- **Unity:** There can be only one Red Cross or one Red Crescent Society in any one country. It must be open to all. It must carry on its humanitarian work throughout its territory.
- **Universality:** The International Red Cross and Red Crescent Movement, in which all Societies have equal status and share equal responsibilities and duties in helping each other, is worldwide.

Source: American Red Cross, www.redcross.org.

Exhibit 2   Values of the American Red Cross

- **Humanitarianism:** We exist to serve others in need, independently, and without discrimination, providing relief for victims of disasters and helping people prevent, prepare for, and respond to emergencies.
- **Stewardship:** We act responsibly, effectively, and efficiently with resources entrusted to us, always seeking to improve.
- **Helping Others:** We are attentive and responsive to those we serve, always listening to their needs and looking for ways to serve through existing or new initiatives.
- **Respect:** We acknowledge, respect, and support the rights and diversity of each person in our organization and in the communities we serve.
- **Voluntary Spirit:** As a family of donors, volunteers, and staff we search for ways to provide hope to those we serve while demonstrating compassion, generosity, and appreciation.
- **Continuous Learning:** We seek, collectively and individually, to identify, obtain, and maintain competencies and the awareness required for exceptional service.
- **Integrity:** We act with honesty, demonstrate courage and accountability under pressure, and openly share ideas and information with each other.

Source: www.redcross.org.

- Biomedical Services. Blood, tissue, and plasma services; research; and national testing labs. In fiscal year 2001 more than 3.8 million volunteers donated in excess of 6 million pints of blood. The American Red Cross supplies 3,000 hospitals with about half of the blood used in the United States.

◆ Community Services. Help for the homeless, seniors, and youth; food and nutrition information; transportation; and so forth.

◆ Disaster Services. Educational services to prepare for disasters. Each year 83,000 volunteers help disaster victims by providing food, shelter, financial assistance, mental health counseling, and so on.

◆ Health and Safety Services. Swimming and lifeguard classes, HIV/AIDS education, living well programs, and so forth. Each year more than 12 million Americans take advantage of lifesaving courses offered by the Red Cross.

◆ International Services. Emergency disaster response, feeding programs, primary health care programs, Geneva Conventions, and so on. The Red Cross is able to provide long-term aid and education to those in need. Also, Red Cross delegates help local citizens rebuild infrastructure, strengthen public health, and improve response time to local disasters.

◆ Nursing. Student nurses, Jane Delano Society, and so forth.

◆ Youth Involvement. Helping kids, teens, and young adults.

◆ Volunteering. Recruiting and organizing volunteers.

Financial Overview

In fiscal year 2001–2002 the American Red Cross had operating revenues of $4.117 billion. Total operating revenues for fiscal year 2000–2001 were $2.743 billion. Three main funding sources for the American Red Cross were:[5]

◆ Contributions: Fund-raising efforts by the United Way & Combined Federal Campaign, legacies, grants, other monetary and in-kind contributions.

◆ Products and services: Fees for products, materials, and courses; fees from collecting, testing, and distributing blood and tissue.

◆ Investment income and other income: Investment income from endowments and reserve funds and income from contracts to provide various programs.

Total operating expenses for the 2000–2001 fiscal year were $2.712 billion, and major expenses included:[6]

◆ Disaster costs: Assistance to victims.

◆ Funding disaster services: Expenses to solicit donations, administer funds; staff expenses at disaster sites; and so on.

◆ Biomedical services: Facility maintenance; expenses in blood, plasma, and tissue services.

Total operating expenses for the fiscal year 2001–2002 were $3.570 billion (see Exhibits 3, 4, and 5).[7]

Technology and Operations

Technology has helped the American Red Cross better coordinate its efforts among its 1,400 chapters and to expand its reach across America. In 2000 it launched "iGiveLife," a service that enables blood drive sponsors to use their intranets to recruit donors and allows hospital customers to order blood products online.[8]

The Internet provides information about nonprofit organizations and can provide "click-to-donate" sites for those individuals who are willing to help out with contributions while they are online. These "click" sites appeal to a newer and often younger audience for the nonprofits. For Cindee Archer, online media manager for the American Red Cross in Washington, D.C., the Internet serves as a vital source of information to the American public and as a new way to collect donations. Archer stated, "The Internet has definitely changed how the whole organization thinks. You feel this sense of urgency whenever there's a disaster—you want that information up as quickly as you can get it."[9] Archer worked on developing a Web site where visitors could enter a zip code and quickly find information. The Web site helps visitors locate local Red Cross shelters, find relatives in a disaster area, keep up with breaking news, and obtain information about donating and volunteering. Cindy Archer also believed that "more and more people are coming online—this isn't going to go away, it's only going to get more pervasive."[10] However, there were costs associated with a Web site that many nonprofit groups did not realize. Russ Finkelstein, director of outreach at Action Without Borders has stated, "Some of them think this is going to be a kind of panacea for doing fund-raising, and it's not necessarily that."[11]

About 12 million Americans enroll in Red Cross courses each year. It is now possible to make these courses available online. The Red Cross has routinely published the latest public health information, and the use of new technology will make this information available online. Wireless communication allows the American Red Cross to make faster damage assessment at the scene. Communication network allows it to locate family members during crises more efficiently. In the near future, it may be possible for the American Red Cross to offer an online shopping network to generate additional resources.[12]

Strategic Alliances

The American Red Cross has established a number of alliances with other organizations. It works with the World Health Organization to alleviate malnutrition, lack of pure water, and diarrhea in poor countries and to support primary health care. A donation to the World Hemophilia Foundation of plasma product is used to treat hemophilia. In 1999 the American Red Cross joined the Federal Emergency Management Agency for "TOPOFF," a nationwide disaster simulation to help prepare for acts of terrorism. As a result of recent research and development, Massachusetts General Hospital and the American Red Cross jointly own a patent for a protein associated with the underlying cause of Alzheimer's disease. In addition, the American Red Cross supplies over 3,000 hospitals with blood donations.[13]

In February 2001 the American Red Cross teamed up with Coinstar, Inc., to collect Red Cross donations for disaster relief efforts. Consumers could drop loose change

Exhibit 3 Consolidated Statement of Financial Position, June 30, 2002 (with summarized information as of June 30, 2001) (in thousands)

Assets	Unrestricted	Temporarily Restricted	Permanently Restricted	Totals 2002	2001
Current assets:					
Cash and cash equivalents	$ 146,247	$439,569	$ 1,386	$ 587,202	$ 177,492
Investments	309,913	11,050	12,514	333,477	355,090
Receivables, net of allowance for doubtful accounts of $19,604 in 2002 and $19,301 in 2001:					
Trade	304,543	15,258	—	319,801	317,767
Contributions, current portion	16,411	110,103	56	126,570	133,183
Other	—	—	15,825	15,825	9,302
Inventories, net of allowance for obsolescence of $7,750 in 2002 and $6,784 in 2001	197,252	6,402	—	203,654	190,272
Other assets	12,547	3,162	183	15,892	23,289
Total current assets	986,913	585,544	29,964	1,602,421	1,206,395
Investments	548,633	155,674	325,238	1,029,545	1,120,773
Contributions receivable	4,209	28,374	2,243	34,826	39,339
Prepaid pension costs	—	—	—	—	11,858
Land, buildings, and other property, net	823,541	—	—	823,541	733,177
Other assets	11,089	1,500	22,704	35,293	26,171
Total assets	2,374,385	771,092	380,149	3,525,626	3,137,713
Liabilities and Net Assets					
Current liabilities:					
Accounts payable and accrued expenses	287,209	9,453	—	296,662	293,476
Current portion of debt and capital leases	39,894	—	—	39,894	89,372
Postretirement benefits	18,924	—	—	18,924	16,807
Other current liabilities	20,653	2,840	63	23,556	18,068
Total current liabilities	366,680	12,293	63	379,036	417,723
Debt and capital leases	357,453	—	—	357,453	360,870
Pension and postretirement benefits	120,042	—	—	120,042	108,339
Other liabilities	92,623	1,180	20	93,823	86,644
Total liabilities	936,798	13,473	83	950,354	973,576
Net assets	1,437,587	757,619	380,066	2,575,272	2,164,137
Commitments and contingencies					
Total liabilities and net assets	$2,374,385	$771,092	$380,149	$3,525,626	$3,137,713

Source: American Red Cross, Annual Report, 2002.

Exhibit 4 Consolidated Statement of Activities, Year ended June 30, 2002 (with summarized information for the year ended June 30, 2001) (in thousands)

	Unrestricted	Temporarily Restricted	Permanently Restricted	Totals 2002	Totals 2001
Operating revenues and gains					
Public Support:					
United Way and other federated	$ 65,616	$ 122,452	$ —	$ 188,068	$ 205,549
Disaster relief	—	133,376	—	133,376	84,601
Liberty disaster relief—Sept. 11 response	—	989,060	—	989,060	—
Legacies and bequests	67,118	6,745	22,022	95,885	115,594
Services and materials	22,034	96,222	—	118,256	49,728
Grants	21,236	67,175	—	88,411	76,351
Other contributions	213,289	36,915	705	250,909	230,845
Products and services:					
Biomedical	1,924,077	—	—	1,924,077	1,686,090
Program materials	136,582	906	—	137,488	121,724
Contracts	58,171	—	—	58,171	50,175
Investment income	81,394	1,069	—	82,463	81,405
Other revenues	49,089	2,008	—	51,097	40,844
Net assets released from restrictions	1,035,410	(1,035,410)	—	—	—
Total operating revenues and gains	3,674,016	420,518	22,727	4,117,261	2,742,906
Operating expenses					
Program services:					
Armed Forces Emergency Services	61,513	—	—	61,513	65,756
Disaster services	308,156	—	—	308,156	284,822
Liberty disaster relief—Sept. 11 response	617,960	—	—	617,960	—
Biomedical services	1,872,967	—	—	1,872,967	1,699,978
Health and safety services	213,614	—	—	213,614	203,058
Community services	152,902	—	—	152,902	150,108
International services	32,736	—	—	32,736	45,238
Total program services	3,259,848	—	—	3,259,848	2,448,960
Supporting services:					
Fund raising	136,901	—	—	136,901	108,616
Management and general	174,182	—	—	174,182	154,726
Total supporting services	311,083	—	—	311,083	263,342
Total operating expenses	3,570,931	—	—	3,570,931	2,712,302
Change in net assets from operations	103,085	420,518	22,727	546,330	30,604
Nonoperating gains (losses)	(131,900)	(548)	(2,747)	(135,195)	(63,876)
Cumulative effect of accounting change	—	—	—	—	2,201
Change in net assets	(28,815)	419,970	19,980	411,135	(31,071)
Net assets, beginning of year	1,466,402	337,649	360,086	2,164,137	2,195,208
Net assets, end of year	$1,437,587	$ 757,619	$380,066	$2,575,272	$2,164,137

Source: American Red Cross, Annual Report, 2002.

into the Coinstar machines located in local supermarkets. Coinstar machines were located within two miles of 130 million Americans. John Clizbe, vice president of Disaster Services at the American Red Cross, indicated that "If every American near a Coinstar machine would donate a handful of change on their next supermarket visit, the Red Cross would be that much better prepared to respond to disaster immediately." Rich Stillman, COO of Coinstar, said, "You no longer need a credit card or checkbook to provide financial support to those in need. If all Americans donate the change in their wallet or pocket, those handfuls will make a huge difference in our capacity to help others this year."[14]

Masterfoods USA, a Mars Incorporated Company, created a special package of red, white, and blue M&Ms specifically to benefit the Red Cross. The national campaign theme used for this promotion was "Taking Care of America Everyday." "Through appearances on television, radio and newspapers, and creative displays in stores across the country, the new 'M&Ms' captured the heart of America," stated Skip Seitz, senior vice president, American Red Cross Growth and Integrated Development.[15] One hundred percent of all profits from the sales of these M&Ms were donated to the American Red Cross Disaster Relief Fund. In January 2002 Masterfoods USA presented a check to the Red Cross in the amount of $3.5 million.

In August 2001 the American Red Cross and the American Society of Association Executives (ASAE) signed an agreement under which the two organizations will share data regarding disasters, declarations, and changes in legislation, and will explore efforts in joint training exercises. The ASAE provides the Red Cross with demographic information about associations and assistance with identifying organizations they wish to contact during times of need.[16]

Recent Problems

Events between 2000 and 2002 provided the American Red Cross with a number of challenges.

Worker Strike   In June 2000 Red Cross workers who collected blood donations and delivered them to hospitals went on strike after rejecting a contract offer by the American Red Cross. The workers were unhappy about long hours, frequent schedule changes, and increasing health benefit costs.[17]

Unfair Trade Practices Lawsuit   The Red Cross derived 60 percent of its revenues from the sale of blood. In providing more than half the nation's blood, the Red Cross had annual sales of more than $1.3 billion.[18] In January 2001 a California blood supplier filed an antitrust suit against the American Red Cross claiming the organization used its clout to eliminate competitors. HemaCare Corp. and Coral Blood Services alleged the Red Cross had cost them more than $25 million in lost business.

They further alleged that the American Red Cross priced some blood products (e.g., platelets) below production costs to drive out competitors while it charged higher prices for the same products in markets where there is no competition. In the lawsuit, the plaintiffs alleged the Red Cross violated Section 2 of the Sherman Antitrust Act, which prohibits monopolization. The lawsuit also charged tortuous interference, unfair trade practices, and unfair competition under the California Business and Professional Code. William Nicely, HemaCare's chief executive officer, stated, "We believe that's unfair and illegal. The Red Cross is a fine organization. We just want them to play by the rules that are reasonable and fair and compete on a level playing field."[19] Blythe Kubina, a Red Cross spokeswoman, said in a written statement, "We believe the American Red Cross has done nothing inappropriate regarding HemaCare's claims to unfair business practices and we were surprised by this lawsuit. We have been in full compliance with the law, and we will vigorously defend this lawsuit."[20]

Liberty Disaster Relief Fund   After the terrorist attacks on September 11, the American Red Cross rose to the challenge of providing the most extensive relief operation in its 120-year history. In response to the tragedy, the Red Cross set up family assistance centers to provide counseling, child care, food, financial assistance, and other services to victims' families and others affected. Respite centers were set up in New York City, Somerset County, Pennsylvania, and at the Pentagon to provide meals, sleeping quarters, and other items to relief workers and volunteers. Funds were used for travel, lodging, and meals for volunteers and staff working on-site. Financial assistance, counseling, and transportation were provided to families of missing foreign nationals.

Millions of dollars, thousands of blood donations, and help from a myriad of volunteers contributed to Red Cross efforts to provide aid to survivors, victims' families, and relief workers. Because of the large dollar amount of donations from the American people, the Red Cross created the Liberty Disaster Relief Fund to be used exclusively to meet the needs of people directly affected by the September 11 tragedy.

Within 15 days of the September 11, 2001, attack, the Red Cross had collected $202 million in donations. Deborah Goldburg, a Red Cross spokesperson, stated, "Everything is happening at such a fast pace. Right now we are just trying to keep up with responses."[21] Goldburg stated that the entire amount raised by the Red Cross since the disaster would go into the newly created Liberty Fund. She indicated that organization officials earmarked $100 million from the fund to provide short-term financial assistance to families of victims. Bernadine Healy, MD, the president and chief executive officer of the Red Cross, said in a written statement, "What has taken place is extraordinary, and

Exhibit 5 Consolidated Statement of Functional Expenses, Year ended June 30, 2002 (with summarized information for the year ended June 30, 2001) (in thousands)

	Armed Forces Emergency Services	Disaster Services	Liberty Disaster Relief—Sept. 11 Response	Biomedical Services	Health and Safety Services	Community Services	International Services	Total Program Services
			Program Services					
Salaries and wages	$35,329	$ 76,450	$ 4,966	$ 749,046	$100,866	$ 66,654	$ 8,340	$1,041,651
Employee benefits	6,701	16,758	773	165,697	19,894	13,698	1,706	225,227
Subtotal	42,030	93,208	5,739	914,743	120,760	80,352	10,046	1,266,878
Travel and maintenance	1,673	20,479	32,601	35,515	5,068	4,111	1,826	101,273
Equipment maintenance and rental	1,173	11,105	11,387	62,322	5,005	5,950	515	97,457
Supplies and materials	3,394	25,095	10,416	417,349	44,001	21,937	849	523,041
Contractual services	8,252	42,887	61,479	379,081	27,643	20,859	1,788	541,989
Financial and material assistance	2,803	106,406	496,338	14,132	3,528	13,811	17,236	654,254
Depreciation and amortization	2,188	8,976	—	49,825	7,609	5,882	476	74,956
Total expenses	$61,513	$308,156	$617,960	$1,872,967	$213,614	$152,902	$32,736	$3,259,848

| | **Supporting Services** | | | **Total Operating Expenses** | |
	Fund Raising	Management and General	Total Supporting Services	2002	2001
Salaries and wages	$ 42,260	$ 81,174	$123,434	$1,165,085	$1,046,171
Employee benefits	8,436	16,145	24,581	249,808	199,204
Subtotal	50,696	97,319	148,015	1,414,893	1,245,375
Travel and maintenance	3,708	6,466	10,174	111,447	78,208
Equipment maintenance and rental	1,902	5,260	7,162	104,619	84,227
Supplies and materials	35,167	6,494	41,661	564,702	477,547
Contractual services	41,147	44,991	86,138	628,127	563,436
Financial and material assistance	1,713	4,285	5,998	660,252	175,994
Depreciation and amortization	2,568	9,367	11,935	86,891	87,515
Total expenses	$136,901	$174,182	$311,083	$3,570,931	$2,712,302

Source: American Red Cross, Annual Report, 2002.

we must respond in an extraordinary way. The American Red Cross has a heavy burden—to live up to the inspiration and memory of those lost. It is with great humility and pride that we carry out this noble obligation."[22]

On October 12, 2001, the American Red Cross released a spending plan for the first $300 million in the Liberty Fund. Less than 50 percent of the money raised was targeted for victims, their families, or rescue workers. The remainder was earmarked to help the Red Cross improve its own organization and expand into new aid programs that might be needed in the event of future terrorist attacks.[23] This planned distribution of funds, based on Healy's policy of using donations for a "long period of uncertainty and recovery," caused a huge uproar.[24] The donors blasted Healy because they expected their donations to be helping September 11 disaster victims now. The attorney general of New York State threatened legal action.[25] Healy finally responded with her announcement of retirement. "I had no choice," she said, claiming that the organization's board had pushed her out.[26]

On November 14, 2001, interim CEO and president of the Red Cross, Harold Decker, announced changes adopted by the American Red Cross Board of Governors to meet the immediate and long-term needs of people affected by the September 11 terrorist attacks. The Red Cross would provide increased financial support to families, participate in a database to be shared among relief agencies, hire an additional 200 caseworkers, and extend the use of toll-free telephone lines. David T. McLaughlin, chairman of the American Red Cross Board of Governors, stated, "The people of this country have given the Red Cross their hard-earned dollars, their trust, and very clear direction for our September 11 relief effort. Regrettably, it took us too long to hear their message."[27] In an article in *U.S. News & World Report*, David McLaughlin stated, "If we don't subject ourselves to public scrutiny, we will never have public trust."[28]

In addition to donating money, the American public donated blood for the disaster victims. These donations were given in response to Healy's "Together, we can save a life" public service announcement. Experts questioned the wisdom of calling for blood donations when there were very few blood recipients. By November 2001 about 10 percent of the red blood cells collected on September 11 and 12 had expired.[29] In a congressional hearing, Healy was confronted with allegations of "panicking the public into wasteful donations of blood." *The Lancet* reported, "Donors charged the organization with abuse of their good intentions."[30]

On March 7, 2002, the American Red Cross saluted the 54,000 staff and volunteers who provided assistance to the more than 54,500 families affected by the attacks. David McLaughlin stated, "Today we are recognizing the work of our staff, volunteers, and donors who responded

to September 11th." Harold Decker, interim president, announced that the American Red Cross received $930 million in contributions and this money was used to provide the following:[31]

	$ millions
Direct assistance to 3,266 families of deceased and seriously injured	$169
Assistance to 51,000 families of displaced workers and disaster workers	270
Provision for 14 million meals, mental health services for 232,000 people, and health services for 129,000 people	94

BBB Wise Giving Alliance On February 16, 2002, the Better Business Bureau Wise Giving Alliance removed the American Red Cross from its "give.org" Web site, allegedly because the American Red Cross did not provide a timely report to the alliance. In addition, H. Art Taylor, president of the alliance, made some unsupported public statements regarding the Red Cross that were reported in the *Philadelphia Inquirer.* A letter from Harold Decker to the Wise Giving Alliance explained that a request by the alliance for an updated report from the Red Cross was received in January 2002. Given the recent activities of the American Red Cross, it was determined that such a report could not be provided by the due date. Jack Campbell, CFO of the Red Cross, and Bennett Weiner, COO of the alliance, agreed to a March 30 deadline for the updated report. In his letter Decker requested a public retraction of Taylor's statements and that the Better Business Bureau's current report on the Red Cross be restored to the give.org Web site.[32]

***60 Minutes* Program** Another onslaught of negative publicity for the American Red Cross occurred March 10, 2002, on the CBS news show *60 Minutes.* It appears to have contained some inaccuracies concerning floods, fires, and the financial accountability of Red Cross chapters. Deborah Daley, a spokesperson for the Red Cross, sent a letter to CBS News indicating the errors and an explanation:[33]

1. In a comment about advertising practices, Mike Wallace reported, "They also decided to put a disclaimer in their ads saying that donations will be used for this and other disasters. The trouble is, it's in small print."

   In response, Deborah Daley reported, "In the West Virginia flood ad, the "this and other disasters" language appears in the same font and size as the rest of the body copy appealing for support.

2. Wallace reported, "Outside audits of local Red Cross chapters are rare. In fact, there is so little accountability that local chapters—and there are more than one thousand of them—aren't even required to submit financial reports to Red Cross headquarters in Washington."

Deborah Daley responded that chapters are accountable in a number of ways. All chapters must have an independent annual review. Chapters that have over $100,000 in annual expenses must have an external audit conducted by an independent CPA. The largest 126 chapters must send quarterly financial reports to the national Red Cross. The Red Cross does regular audits of chapters. Chapters must meet specific national guidelines to maintain their charters. She stated that Wallace's claim that chapters "are not even required to submit financial reports" is completely false.

3. As for the Alpine fire in Southern California, Wallace reported, "As of last week, 14 months after the fire, San Diego was still waiting for a full accounting of how the money donated for the fire victims has been and will be spent."

Deborah Daley responded that the chapter has provided up-to-date financial information on its response to the Alpine fire three times since November.

Looking to the Future

After a five-month search, Marsha Johnson Evans was named president and CEO of the American Red Cross on June 27, 2002. Evans has served as national executive director of the Girl Scouts of the USA for the past four years, prior to which she had a 29-year career in the U.S. Navy, where she earned the rank of rear admiral. In his announcement, David McLaughlin, chairman of the Board of Governors of the American Red Cross, said, "Marty's unique style of leadership along with her experience as established administrator will bring new vigor to the American Red Cross. With great insight into our mission, she is well poised to guide our organization as we continue to provide vital services in a world faced by new challenges."[34] Evans remarked that:

> In the midst of responding to the extraordinary demands of 9/11 and a lot of criticism about these efforts, my observation is that the Red Cross never lost sight of its responsibility to every community and every victim of the other disasters that occurred, some 45,000 in the months since last September. The timely and capable response day-in and day-out to these disasters speaks volumes about the character of the volunteers and staff, their talent, and most especially their dedication.[35]

As she begins to guide the organization, Marsha Johnson Evans must confront the many issues faced by the American Red Cross. How should she proceed?

Endnotes

1. American Red Cross, 2002, Press release, June 27.
2. American Red Cross, www.redcross.org.
3. American Red Cross, 2002, Press release, February 1.
4. American Red Cross, 2000–2001, Annual Reports.
5. American Red Cross, 2001–2002, Annual Reports.
6. Ibid.
7. Ibid.
8. American Red Cross, 2000, Annual Report.
9. Sanborn, Stephanie, 2000, Nonprofits reap rewards of the Web—Internet proves to be a great fund-raising tool for charities, but there are costs, *Infoworld*, 22 (25): 37.
10. Ibid.
11. Ibid.
12. American Red Cross, 2000, Annual Report.
13. Ibid.
14. American Red Cross and Coinstar to launch new fundraising technology to prepare for disasters, 2001, *US Newswire*, February 12.
15. American Red Cross, 2002, Press release, February 1.
16. ASAE and American Red Cross formalize partnership agreement, 2001, *Association Management* 53 (8): 12.
17. Red Cross workers on strike, 2000, *Fund Raising Management* 31 (4): 33.
18. Greenberg, Daniel S., 2001, Blood, politics, and the American Red Cross, *Lancet*, November 24: 1789; Taylor, Mark, 2001, Red Cross faces antitrust lawsuit, *Modern Healthcare* 31, January 1: 20.
19. Taylor, Red Cross faces antitrust lawsuit.
20. Ibid.
21. Becker, Cinda, 2001, A torrent of donations; charities wrestle with how best to spend money pouring in since attacks, *Modern Healthcare* 31, October 1: 8.
22. Ibid.
23. Tyrangiel, Josh, 2001, The charity olympics: After weeks of record giving, Americans want to know: Is that money helping? *Time*, November 5: 75.
24. Newsweek: Former Red Cross head says her fundraising message was clear . . . , 2001, *PR Newswire*, December 9.
25. Greenberg, Blood, politics, and the American Red Cross.
26. Tyrangiel, Charity olympics.
27. Red Cross announces major changes in Liberty

Fund: Fund solely used for people affected by September 11 tragedy, 2001, *US Newswire,* November 14.

28. Levine, Samantha, Red Crossroads, 2001, *U.S. News & World Report,* November 19.

29. Tyrangiel, Charity olympics.

30. Greenberg, Blood, politics, and the American Red Cross.

31. American Red Cross, 2002, Press release, March 7.

32. American Red Cross letter to Better Business Bureau's Wise Giving Alliance, 2002, *PR Newswire,* February 16.

33. Red Cross announces major changes in Liberty Fund.

34. American Red Cross, 2002, Press release, June 27.

35. Ibid.

Case 3   American Red Cross, 2002–2004 (B)*

By mid-2004 the American Red Cross continued to experience internal problems and adverse publicity, but had few successes. The Red Cross participated in the "TOPOFF 2" national training exercise in May 2003. This event was to test the country's ability to respond to and handle terrorist attacks. The organization has long helped the many victims of disasters such as fires and hurricanes. The Red Cross has improved its response times so that victims can receive aid more quickly. However, the American Red Cross has also seen a slowdown in donations which has depleted its Disaster Relief Fund (see Exhibits 1, 2, and 3 for financial data).

Problems Facing the Red Cross

The American Red Cross has faced a number of other problems since 2002.

Donor DIRECT and Disaster Relief Fund

On June 5, 2002, the American Red Cross announced a series of changes in its fund-raising practices. It planned to begin a national initiative to help donors understand the American Red Cross Disaster Relief Fund, and how their wishes regarding the use of donations would be positively confirmed and acknowledged to ensure compliance with their wishes. The program is named Donor DIRECT, an acronym that stands for *Donor Intent REcognition, Confirmation, and Trust.* Donor DIRECT was the result of a six-month-long process to examine existing practices and consult with experts in charitable giving and with existing and potential donors. Donor DIRECT was praised by people like H. Art Taylor, president of the Better Business Bureau Wise Giving Alliance, an organization that had at one time delisted the American Red Cross from its Web site.

Despite good words from people about Donor DIRECT, there was a decrease in charitable contributions to the American Red Cross Disaster Relief Fund. The fund, which boasted a balance of $65.8 million in July 2002, was empty by September 2003. On September 17, 2003, the Red Cross launched a Disaster Relief Fund Cabinet comprising 14 entrepreneurs and innovative leaders.[1]

Blood Safety

On October 22, 2002, CBS news correspondent Sharyl Attkisson reported the case of a patient who had received a blood transfusion four years earlier and as a result had contracted hepatitis C. The contaminated blood had come from the Red Cross. The CBS story was troublesome because it reported that the Red Cross

insisted the "blood supply is as safe as it has ever been," that the organization was "working cooperatively with the FDA," and that only a tiny fraction of blood recipients will ever get a disease. "Yet it's impossible to pinpoint the numbers because it turns out nobody's counting." What was worse was that the Food and Drug Administration (FDA) accused the American Red Cross of:

> the long-standing practice of the American Red Cross not to correct and prevent recurrence of *known* violations until after FDA becomes aware of them through inspections . . . and insists that they be fixed . . . Even when the Red Cross gets around to addressing the FDA's observations, it construes them as discrete deviations, without fixing the systemic problems . . . Nor does the Red Cross even investigate all the causes of problems, ensure the effectiveness of the limited corrective actions it takes belatedly, or prevent violations in the first place.[2]

On January 2, 2003, CBS News reported that FDA inspectors had found more than 200 safety violations at the American Red Cross, some of which the Red Cross had repeatedly been ordered to fix. "The Red Cross shipped infected blood, failed to screen out risky donors, even some who admitted having HIV, and lost track of more than a thousand units, including small amounts infected with HIV or hepatitis C."[3]

On April 11, 2003, the FDA announced that the American Red Cross had agreed to substantial revisions in its consent decree with the FDA. The consent decree allowed the FDA to assess financial penalties if the Red Cross failed in the future to comply with the laws and regulations that ensure the safety of the nation's blood supply.

On February 6, 2004, the FDA notified the Red Cross that the Problem Management Standard Operating Procedures (SOPs) submitted on October 28, 2003, did not meet the terms of the amended consent decree. The Problem Management SOPs, which are similar to the ISO 9001 standards, are used within an organization's operating system to detect, investigate, and correct problems. The FDA intended to assess fines.

Reducing Sponsored Research and Development

On November 12, 2003, the Red Cross announced that the Biomedical Services had reevaluated its activities and had decided to narrow R&D to those activities that directly support blood products. It was therefore going to stop supporting externally funded research grants and programs or cellular therapies. The Red Cross would, however, continue supporting research related to blood banking, an action that would allow it to refocus on its core mission: to provide a safe and available blood supply.[4]

*This case was prepared by Professors Debora J. Gilliard and Rajendra Khandekar of Metropolitan State College—Denver as a basis for class discussion rather than to illustrate either effective or ineffective handling of an administrative situation. Copyright © 2004 Debora J. Gilliard and Rajendra Khandekar. All rights reserved.

Tissue Processing   After an inspection of the Costa Mesa Tissue Processing Center in the fall of 2003, the FDA issued a warning letter indicating it had observed problems with the quality systems design for heart valves and procedures related to allograft skin. On April 1, 2004, the Red Cross suspended the distribution of allograft skin and cardiovascular tissues while corrective actions were implemented.[5]

Changes in Leadership at Biomedical Services

On March 19, 2004, the Red Cross announced that John F. "Jack" McGuire would join the organization as executive vice president for Biomedical Services. McGuire had more than 22 years of experience in the field of biomedical technology, most recently as president of Whatman, PLC North America, a U.K.-based manufacturer of filtration and separation materials and devices for laboratory and industrial customers. He would report directly to the president and CEO of the American Red Cross, Marsha Evans, and serve as the liaison to the FDA to ensure that the biomedical services of the American Red Cross continued to meet FDA requirements.

The Red Cross also hired C. William Cherry as the senior vice president for Quality Assurance and Regulatory Affairs. Cherry brought strong credentials to the job. Earlier he had been vice president for Quality and Compliance at Aventis Bio Services, Inc. In this capacity, he was responsible for improving quality assurance and compliance support and oversight, and worked closely with the FDA to resolve issues.

"With the addition of these stellar candidates to our team, I believe we will be able to make significant head-way in solidifying our position as the nation's foremost blood banking organization," said Evans. "We are at the brink of an entirely new era for American Red Cross Biomedical Services, and I am excited about the future."[6]

What Next?

Marsha Evans had promised a great deal when she was hired in 2002 by the American Red Cross. However, the organization continues to be plagued by problems. What should Evans do?

Endnotes

1. American Red Cross, American Red Cross announces Disaster Relief Fund Cabinet Leadership, Press release, www.redcross.org/pressrelease/0,1077,0_314_1628,00.html.
2. CBS News.com, Red Cross failing blood test, www.cbsnews.com/stories/2002/08/22/eveningnews/printable519527.shtml.
3. CBS News.com, Red Cross under fire, www.cbsnews.com/stories/2002/12/30/health/main534783.shtml.
4. American Red Cross, Statement regarding changes at Holland lab, Press release, www.redcross.org/pressrelease/printer/ 0,1080,0_314_1951,00.html.
5. American Red Cross, Statement regarding Costa Mesa tissue processing facility, Press release, www.redcross.org/pressrelease/printer/ 0,1080,0_314_2445,00.html.
6. American Red Cross, American Red Cross taps new executives to lead Biomedical Services, Press release, www.redcross.org/pressrelease/ 0,1077,0_314_2402,00.html.

Exhibit 1 The American Red Cross

Consolidated Statement of Financial Position, June 30, 2003 (in thousands)

Assets	Unrestricted	Temporarily Restricted	Permanently Restricted	Totals 2003	2002
Current assets:					
Cash and cash equivalents	$ 184,108	$262,042	$ 742	$ 446,892	$ 609,973
Investments	265,809	12,825	10,726	289,360	310,706
Receivables, net of allowance for doubtful accounts of $17,022 in 2003 and $19,604 in 2002:					
Trade	223,977	15,241	—	239,218	319,801
Contributions, current portion	15,697	97,370	162	113,229	126,570
Other	—	—	23,448	23,448	15,825
Inventories, net of allowance for obsolescence of $6,925 in 2003 and $7,750 in 2002	167,940	2,981	—	170,921	203,654
Other assets	11,022	4,177	203	15,402	15,892
Total current assets	868,553	394,636	35,281	1,298,470	1,602,421
Investments	599,994	79,751	346,715	1,026,460	1,029,545
Contributions receivable	3,151	23,644	637	27,432	34,826
Pension intangible asset	15,632	—	—	15,632	—
Land, buildings, and other property, net	930,110	—	—	930,110	823,541
Other assets	11,153	2,880	21,052	35,085	35,293
Total assets	2,428,593	500,911	403,685	3,333,189	3,525,626
Liabilities and Net Assets					
Current liabilities:					
Accounts payable and accrued expenses	344,857	26,936	—	371,793	296,662
Current portion of debt and capital leases	75,505	—	—	75,505	39,894
Postretirement benefits	12,828	—	—	12,828	18,924
Other current liabilities	30,997	2,589	44	33,630	23,556
Total current liabilities	464,187	29,525	44	493,756	379,036
Debt and capital leases	344,912	—	—	344,912	357,453
Pension and postretirement benefits	237,741	—	—	237,741	120,042
Other liabilities	88,816	1,113	35	89,964	93,823
Total liabilities	1,135,656	30,638	79	1,166,373	950,354
Net assets	1,292,937	470,273	403,606	2,166,816	2,575,272
Commitments and contingencies					
Total liabilities and net assets	$2,428,593	$500,911	$403,685	$3,333,189	$3,525,626

Source: American Red Cross, Annual Report, 2003.

Exhibit 2   **The American Red Cross**
Consolidated Statement of Activities, Year Ended June 30, 2003 (in thousands)

	Unrestricted	Temporarily Restricted	Permanently Restricted	Totals 2003	Totals 2002
Operating revenues and gains:					
Public Support:					
United Way and other federated	$ 68,620	$107,873	$ —	$ 176,493	$ 188,068
Disaster relief	—	57,575	—	57,575	133,376
Liberty disaster relief—Sept. 11 response	—	12,121	—	12,121	989,060
Legacies and bequests	60,600	8,909	24,272	93,781	95,885
Services and materials	21,257	39,814	—	61,071	118,256
Grants	16,877	58,314	—	75,191	88,411
Other contributions	172,798	43,387	—	216,185	250,909
Products and services:					
Biomedical	2,016,768	—	—	2,016,768	1,924,077
Program materials	147,634	1,058	—	148,692	137,488
Contracts	59,970	—	—	59,970	58,171
Investment income	67,918	1,567	—	69,485	82,463
Other revenues	45,462	981	—	46,443	51,097
Net assets released from restrictions	618,317	(618,317)	—	—	—
Total operating revenues and gains	3,296,221	(286,718)	24,272	3,033,775	4,117,261
Operating expenses:					
Program services:					
Armed Forces Emergency Services	67,743	—	—	67,743	61,513
Disaster services	367,435	—	—	367,435	308,156
Liberty disaster relief—Sept. 11 response	209,117	—	—	209,117	617,960
Biomedical services	2,033,915	—	—	2,033,915	1,872,967
Health and safety services	221,619	—	—	221,619	213,614
Community services	153,180	—	—	153,180	152,902
International services	17,618	—	—	17,618	32,736
Total program services	3,070,627	—	—	3,070,627	3,259,848
Supporting services:					
Fund raising	122,946	—	—	122,946	136,901
Management and general	176,080	—	—	176,080	174,182
Total supporting services	299,026	—	—	299,026	311,083
Total operating expenses	3,369,653	—	—	3,369,653	3,570,931
Change in net assets from operations	(73,432)	(286,718)	24,272	(335,878)	546,330
Nonoperating gains (losses)	(17,115)	(628)	(732)	(18,475)	(135,195)
Additional minimum pension liability	(54,103)	—	—	(54,103)	—
Change in net assets	(144,650)	(287,346)	23,540	(408,456)	411,135
Net assets, beginning of year	1,437,587	757,619	380,066	2,575,272	2,164,137
Net assets, end of year	$1,292,937	$470,273	$403,606	$2,166,816	$2,575,272

Source: American Red Cross, Annual Report, 2003.

Exhibit 3   The American Red Cross
Statement of Functional Expenses, Year Ended June 30, 2003 (in thousands)

	Program Services								Supporting Services			Total Expenses	
	Armed Forces Emergency Services	Disaster Services	Liberty Disaster Relief—Sept. 11 Response	Biomedical Services	Health and Safety Services	Community Services	International Services	Total Program Services	Fund Raising	Management and General	Total Supporting Services	2003	2002
Salaries and wages	$36,754	$84,873	$7,971	$798,330	$102,571	$65,728	$7,127	$1,103,354	$46,154	$84,612	$130,766	$1,234,120	$1,165,085
Employee benefits	8,621	19,859	1,417	193,728	23,270	15,433	1,709	264,037	10,541	20,484	31,025	295,062	249,808
Subtotal	45,375	104,732	9,388	992,058	125,841	81,161	8,836	1,367,391	56,695	105,096	161,791	1,529,182	1,414,893
Travel and maintenance	1,549	29,078	1,200	36,329	4,681	3,917	759	77,513	3,338	5,582	8,920	86,433	111,447
Equipment maintenance and rental	1,182	14,226	647	58,332	4,385	5,837	236	84,845	1,470	4,833	6,303	91,148	104,619
Supplies and materials	4,191	21,407	583	443,959	46,955	20,401	505	538,001	20,837	6,770	27,607	565,608	564,702
Contractual services	9,270	51,679	8,715	430,242	29,198	22,370	2,491	553,965	36,970	39,419	76,389	630,354	628,127
Financial and material assistance	3,993	136,319	188,584	24,649	2,744	13,809	4,414	374,512	1,233	2,689	3,922	378,434	660,252
Depreciation and amortization	2,183	9,994	—	48,346	7,815	5,685	377	74,400	2,403	11,691	14,094	88,494	86,891
Total expenses	$67,743	$367,435	$209,117	$2,033,915	$221,619	$153,180	$17,618	$3,070,627	$122,946	$176,080	$299,026	$3,369,653	$3,570,931

Source: American Red Cross, Annual Report, 2003.

Case 4   Atari and InfoGrames Entertainment SA*

Bruno Bonnell, CEO of Infogrames Entertainment SA (IESA), announced officially in May 2003 that it had renamed all of its U.S. operations from "Infogrames Inc." to "Atari Inc." This achievement was over three years in the making. During the summer of 2000, Bonnell worked on ways to prevent his company from falling victim to an acquisition or becoming prey to a larger company seeking to consolidate and gobble up smaller software gaming publishers. Later that year, Bonnell and IESA announced plans to purchase Hasbro Interactive, Inc., and along with it the rights to the name of Atari. The deal was concluded in January 2001, by which time the video gaming industry was on the cusp of surpassing Hollywood in total annual revenues. It was obvious to Bonnell that IESA required a significant move if the company was to remain a major player in the gaming industry.

In 2000 Bonnell and most software gaming publishers recognized the incredible growth and potential of the industry, which was then defining itself as the most lucrative of entertainment industries.

> Our business has grown from a niche market for young boys and teenagers to a much broader audience, with many more adults playing. People will play games as simply as they watch TV.[1]

Perhaps the connection between Atari and IESA was evident: taking classic game company and resurrecting it in the new millennium as a way to market games to adults who were once the quarter-feeding teenagers from the 1980s. Atari was an eighties icon for computer nerds and video game geeks, who eventually became the parents of the interactive entertainment, multimedia, AI, CGI special effects generation.

The gaming industry went from $1 billion annually in video-console sales in 1982 to $10 billion almost 20 years later. It was clear to Bonnell that video games were fast becoming the central source for interactive home entertainment and would soon supplant digital video disks (DVDs), videocassette recorders (VCRs), cable, and satellite TV programming. IESA bought the Atari brand name in hopes of leapfrogging other industry stalwarts Activision and Take 2, and ultimately knocking off Electronic Arts (EA) from the top perch of the gaming industry.

Background

To understand the full story of Atari, it is necessary to realize that the Atari name has a two-part history. The first part of Atari's history covered the "Atari classic"—the company that created old-school video games such as Asteroids; the second part commenced with IESA's acquisition of the Atari name in 2001.

Atari Classic   Atari classic's life began in the early 1970s when a computer programmer named Nolan Bushnell created *Pong*. As one may recall, *Pong* was an early, two-dimensional video game that involved two players volleying a dot back and forth on-screen between parallel rectangular paddles. Pong debuted in 1972 as an arcade machine in a tavern in Sunnyvale, California, and included a simple instruction: "Avoid missing ball for high score." With this simple format and objective, imaginations were ignited and the gaming industry was officially born. Bushnell progressed from *Pong* by making a $500 investment as the cofounder of a new computer game company named Atari (the origin of *atari* derives from the term for "check" in the Japanese game of Go).[2] Only a few years later, in 1976, Warner Communications purchased Atari from Bushnell for $28 million. A year later, the Atari company took its first step toward pop culture fame when it launched the 2600 Video Computer System (also known as 2600). The system realized only fair success until three years later when Midway's *Space Invaders* game arrived and propelled the 2600 into the mainstream household market in the United States. The 2600 realized incredible success in the early 1980s, despite stiff competition from Mattel's Intellivision and Colleco's CollecoVision systems. During this period Atari also broadened their product selection by creating cartridge versions for smash hit arcade games like Centipede, Asteroids, and Missile Command.

Atari classic enjoyed a fairly rapid rise to the top, but beginning around 1982 entered a period of downturn. Bushnell left the company because of a feud with Warner Communications over the continuing development philosophy of the 2600. At that time, the hot project for Atari programmers was the conversion of the arcade game *Pac-Man* into a cartridge version. Atari gambled and decided to manufacture the game with a cheaper 4k chip instead of 8k as suggested by the project manager. It launched prematurely and proved a failure because of the gross simplification of its graphics and technology. *Pac-Man* never took off with the 2600 and fell flat. Atari grossly miscal-

---

*This case was prepared by graduate student Carlito Cabelin and Professor Alan B. Eisner of Pace University as a basis for class discussion rather than to illustrate either effective or ineffective handling of an administrative situation. Copyright © 2004 Alan B. Eisner.

[1]Europe's no. 1 video-game player, 2000, *BusinessWeek,* June 12.

[2]B.I.K.: How Pong invented geekdom, 1999, *US News & World Report,* December 27: 67.

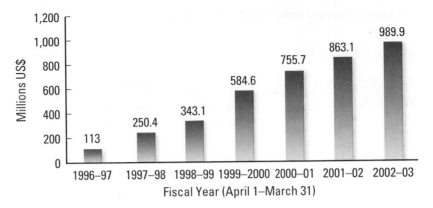

Exhibit 1   **Atari/Infogrames Gross Revenues**

culated and overforecasted the *Pac-Man* project and suffered as a result: the number of company employees fell from 10,000 in December 1982 to only 200 by July 1984.[3]

This marked the beginning of the end for Atari classic. Japanese-based companies Nintendo and Sega soon became the pioneers that took over the gaming industry from the 1980s to the 1990s. Atari classic petered out and slowly withered away in 1996 when it posted a $13.5 million third-quarter loss due to its fledgling 64-bit Jaguar game system. Layoffs at Atari ensued and the resignation of the president of North American operations, Ted Hoff, signaled the end of Atari classic. That same year Atari merged with JTS, a disk drive company, which eventually folded too. In 1998 Hasbro bought the rights to Atari's home titles.

Atari's disintegration was not a reflection of the game industry's health. While Atari was suffocating, Sony's PlayStation and Nintendo's 64 were catching on fire. Those within the industry knew there was still plenty of consumer pie to be consumed; they just needed the right strategy to claim a significant piece.

Atari, Inc.—Infogrames Entertainment SA Infogrames Entertainment SA was founded in 1983 by Bruno Bonnell and Christopher Sapet as a software game company based in Lyon, France. Both Bonnell and Sapet were in their twenties and invested only $10,000 to start their new company. In 1987 the average age of the company's employees was only 27—an obvious reflection of the youthful vigor of the founders. The company grossed $113 million in revenues in 1996 and by 2002 it grossed $863.1 million to become Europe's largest video game maker. See Exhibit 1.

Infogrames started out offering a wide range of entertainment and educational games, and developing artificial intelligence and online service software.[4] The company made a string of key acquisitions from the mid-1990s through 2000 (see Exhibit 2). Of particular importance was the purchase in 2002 of Shiny Entertainment studios, which held the rights to develop a game based on the movie *The Matrix Reloaded* and *Matrix Revolutions*. (Details of this strategy will be examined later in this case.) Infogrames eventually produced several quality hit games like *Dragon Ball Z, Unreal Championship, Monopoly,* and *Backyard Sports,* to name a few; it also distributed franchise labels in movie games such as *Mission Impossible, Men in Black, Stuart Little,* and of course *The Matrix.*

The acquisition of key interest here is Atari by way of Hasbro Interactive, Inc., in 2000. This marked the end of the first part of Atari's history, and the beginning of a new history as part of the IESA family.

The series of acquisitions that cost about $300 million from 1999 through 2000, combined with the development of high-stakes projects such as the *Enter the Matrix* game, all weighed heavily on the future profitability of Infogrames. The issue at hand in the early 2000s was whether IESA, the parent company, could maximize the biggest bang for every dollar spent on the Atari brand. "It can't hurt them," said Michael Pachter, who covered Atari for Wedbush Morgan Securities. According to Goldman, Sachs & Co., Infogrames was on track to book a net loss for the fiscal year ending June 30, 2003, on revenues of $1 billion while carrying a debt of more than $550 million.[5] Could the *Atari* name help bail IESA out of debt and launch it into its next growth phase? And equally unknown was how long it would take for IESA to become profitable again after the costly purchase of the *Matrix* movie sequels.

[3]Driscoll, Edward B., Jr., 2002, The Atari 2600: The cartridge family rides again, *Poptronics*, August.

[4]Gross, Daniel, 1987, Infogrames: A French connection, *Information Today*, December.

[5]Reinhardt, Andy, & Grover, Ronald, 2003, Will Enter the Matrix save Infogrames' skin? Europe's top video-game maker badly needs a blockbuster, *BusinessWeek*, May 26.

Exhibit 2   **Acquisition History of Infogrames Entertainment SA**

Year	Company Acquired	Country	Activity
1996	Ocean Software	U.K.	Publishing
1997	Philips Media	Netherlands	Distribution
1998	ABS Multimedia	Portugal	Distribution
1998	Arcadia	Spain	Distribution
1998	Gremlin	U.K.	Development and publishing
1998	Game City	Switzerland	Distribution
1998	Psygnosis	France	Development
1999	Accolade	U.S.	Development and publishing
1999	Beam Software	Australia	Development
1999	Ozisoft	Australia	Distribution
1999	GT Interactive	U.S.	Development/publishing/distribution
1999	Den-O-Tech	Canada	Development
2000	Hasbro Interactive	U.S.	Publishing
2000	Paradigm Entertainment	U.S.	Development
2002	Shiny Entertainment	U.S.	Development
2002	Eden Studios	France	Development

The Video Gaming Industry

In 1982 *Time* magazine ran a cover story on video games titled, "Games that Play People."[6] The article reported how the arcade game frenzy took the nation by storm as video games found their way into a variety of public domains besides the local arcade parlor: pizza shops, doctors' offices, airports, restaurants, and even beauty salons.

Market Demographics   In the 1980s the ideal arcade game addict was simply a teenager with a pocket full of quarters. Back then, record high scorers of games like *Defender* needed only a quarter to play 16 hours worth of entertainment. Now fast-forward 20 years to the article "The (R)evolution of Video Games" in the November 2002 issue of *Siliconindia,* which describes an industry still made up of those teenagers from the 1980s who, now in their thirties, were still buying video games for home entertainment.

> Its market no longer consists only of kids and teenagers, though they still comprise a large part of sales, but now the same youngsters from twenty years ago are adults with careers and money of their own.[7]

The consumer demographics for video games had changed quite a bit from 1980 to 2003. Primarily, the market had expanded in its consumer age bracket. "The kids who fell in love with Mario when they were 6, they're now 26," said marketing director Perrin Kaplan of Nintendo.[8] According to the Interactive Digital Software Association, the average American gamer in 2000 was 28 years old, 58 percent of the consumers were over 18, and 21 percent were 35 or older.[9] The older the gamer became, the more likely the gamer was to spend some disposable income on entertainment. Teenagers, preteens, and kids in general didn't have as much luxury nor were they normally allowed such luxury from their parents.

The breadth of ages in video game consumers required companies in the gaming industry to broaden their appeal to a larger demographic profile. Gaming companies had always been challenged with providing the proper age-appropriate content in the games they produced. How to make the games age-appropriate became a tug-of-war battle between management and designers. Ratings such as "M" for mature, "T" for teens, and "E" for everyone was the game industry's equivalent of motion picture ratings "R," "PG-13," and "G." In the early

[6]Skow, John, 1982, Games that play people, *Time,* January 18.

[7]Ridlen, Richard, 2002, The (r)evolution of video games, *Siliconindia,* November.

[8]Ibid.

[9]Croal, N'Gai, 2000, The art of darkness, *Newsweek,* June 12.

2000s the hottest-selling title games were rated M. For instance, Take 2's *Grand Theft Auto: Vice City* was all about being a mobster, shooting cops, killing drug dealers, and consorting with prostitutes. Although the game went on to become the fastest-selling video game in history, it also carried a huge risk of receiving backlash from consumer advocacy groups such as the National Institute on Media and the Family, which campaigned against excessive sex and violence in entertainment. Even family-friendly Nintendo, with the *Donkey Kong* and *Mario Bros.* mascots, received negative feedback when it developed, under a separate label called Rare, an M-rated game titled *Perfect Dark.* According to Bruno Bonnell of Atari, "Nintendo is the light balancing the darkness of teenage games."[10] Gaming companies were forced to respond to the threat of outside consumer advocacy groups tarnishing their brand image.

Gaming Relationship with Motion Pictures

The video game industry built a structure that was very similar to the motion picture industry. When a blockbuster video game was on the drawing board, large production teams were assembled with fat and costly budgets, and the teams worked separately to create an entirely new and profitable product. This Hollywood-like trend of video game production helped make this a large-scale industry—$10.5 billion in 2002. For example, *Enter the Matrix* cost a whopping $80 million, which included all of its marketing expenses and the $50 million needed to acquire Shiny Entertainment. In comparison, the average video game cost $2.5 million to $4 million to produce in 2002.[11] In the early 2000s the sale of 1 million units became the industry benchmark for game title success. Through May 2003, *Enter the Matrix* surpassed 1 million units sold and through June it passed 2.5 million. In comparison, Activision's *Spiderman* sold 2 million units in 2002.

During the early years of the 21st century, mergers and acquisitions activity was commonplace whenever software developers needed to secure franchise rights to blockbuster movies. They would spend millions to purchase smaller entertainment studios with the philosophy that if a movie was a blockbuster the success would carry over to the planned release of its video game. The same was also true with DVDs, and gaming companies started packaging multimedia product launches. For example, the trailer for the movie would run on the DVD and vice versa. In the case of *Enter the Matrix,* scenes were shot specifically for the game and not the movie, so that the consumer could play through the game while using it as a continuum for the movie. In essence, the movie just continued to live on in the game even after the end credits rolled. Examples of this cross-pollination were Take 2's purchase of Rock-star games and Atari's acquisition of Shiny Entertainment. The gaming industry had strong, established relationships between independent software publishers and hardware platform companies, especially among the top market leaders (e.g., licensing arrangements between Electronic Arts and Microsoft or between Atari and Sony). Under the terms of agreement between the software company and the hardware company, the gaming company was authorized to develop and distribute software-compatible games for the respective hardware platform.

Hardware Platform

After Atari classic paved the way for hardware gaming companies, Atari, Nintendo, and Sega were the only companies remaining from the 1980s that still continued in production during the 1990s. In 1996 two significant events occurred: Atari went out of business and Sony launched its PlayStation console game. Through 2002 Sony was the leading hardware console gaming company with its PlayStation and PlayStation 2 systems. Sony's video game division contributed 53 percent to the company's bottom line in 2001. Microsoft entered the console market in 2001 with the launch of its Xbox system, but the software giant remained a remote second.

Nintendo was more diversified in its product offerings with the Nintendo 64, Gamecube's 128-bit system, and the handheld gaming devices Game Boy Advance and Game Boy Advance SP. Despite diversification, the company still ranked a distant third in overall sales in the early years of the 21st century.

Hardware companies realized that to be the market leader and gain market share they also had to participate in the software publishing segment. Besides licensing their hardware to software developers and collecting fees, they also needed to develop in-house software titles. All three top hardware companies did so in the early 2000s, but to successfully continue to develop in-house software, a company needed a supply of high quality in-house talent. Recognizing this need, Sony and Microsoft continually tried to recruit top talent away from independent software developers.

Software engineers were often recruited from smaller firms to the ranks of industry leaders. And while keeping the talent in-house was a real trick, managing the team of programmers was even more challenging. Getting the right mix of talent, personality, and team chemistry was vital for the development of a title game. If the chemistry or the personalities of the software developers conflicted, then a project could be compromised.[12] Atari went overseas to Vietnam to hire subcontractors to assist in providing additional components to some of its games. The cost savings from outsourcing were enormous; a programmer's average annual salary in Vietnam was $4,000 versus $70,000 to $100,000 in the United States.

[10]Ibid.

[11]Delaney, Kevin, A game maker's big gamble, 2003, *Wall Street Journal,* May 14: B1.

[12]Judd, James, 2000, Add more quarters, *Upside,* October.

Industry Ebb and Flow   The video gaming industry was cyclical but nonetheless independent of the overall performance of the economy; if the economy was in a recession, the video gaming industry would not necessarily decline too. The gaming industry cycle was driven first by the launches of the hardware platform. Whenever a next-generation system came to market, the industry began a three- to five-year cycle. Many software companies immediately went into production to meet demand quotas forecasted for the new hardware platform. The initial two years following the launch of next-generation hardware saw software company sales at their highest and inventory flying off the shelves. As the third year approached, the industry reached optimal output where profits were maximized and diminishing returns began to kick in. When a newer, more advanced hardware platform was rolled out, the cycle would begin again.

As suggested above, the video gaming sector was an intensely competitive industry. Through 2002, Electronic Arts (EA) was still the industry top dog with annual sales of $1.7 billion for fiscal 2002. Of the top five software publishers, two were hardware platform companies— Nintendo and Sony—who recognized they had to increasingly position gaming software as a top core strategy (see Exhibit 3). Notice how Microsoft didn't even penetrate the top 10, but understood clearly that developing its own software for its console was industrywide.

However, other gaming software vendors like EA and Activision rivaled Atari in very similar strategies: planning, developing, publishing, and distributing software game titles. During 2003, Atari maintained a top-ten position for all video game titles (see Exhibit 4).

Historically, game titles went up and down the ranks and were very unpredictable after the initial sales launch. Atari's *Enter the Matrix* was expected to be the top seller for the month after it was released simultaneously with its movie counterpart. Game titles performed similarly to major motion pictures during the summer season: A blockbuster might go from the top-grossing film during the Memorial Day weekend to number five within a month. For example, Take 2's *Grand Theft Auto: Vice City* dropped from number 5 in March 2003 to number 20 just three months later. During the April to June 2003 period EA's *NBA Street Vol. 2* remained at number five and Atari's *Dragon Ball Z* held the number nine spot; this perhaps reflected the fanfare for the NBA's playoff season for the former, and a strong franchise label for the latter. In any event, chart busters could go up and down the ranks within months, always vulnerable to the next hot title.

Gaming History Summary   The 1970s could be seen as the video gaming industry's infancy stage with the invention of *Pong,* Atari's 2600, and, closing out the decade, *Space Invaders.* At that point the industry went through growing pains, which continued through the 1980s. Com-

Exhibit 3   Top 10 Video Game Software Publishers (Includes Console & Portable Software) Ranked on Dollars Annual 2003

Rank	Publisher
1	Electronic Arts
2	Nintendo of America
3	THQ
4	Sony
5	Activision
6	Take 2 Interactive
7	Atari
8	Konami of America
9	Vivendi Universal
10	NAMCO

© 2003 NPD Group, Inc. All rights reserved.

panies like Atari, Colleco, Mattel, and Magnavox all experienced some failures with their respective hardware systems. During the '80s arcade games raked in billions annually and reached critical mass; throughout the '90s hardware console companies Nintendo and Sony began to take root as the industry goliaths; and at the beginning of the new millennium, the gaming industry mimicked Hollywood with blockbuster movie tie-ins and projects with gigantic budgets. One could speculate that the future of the gaming industry might be in online entertainment.

Atari's Growth Strategy

After concluding a one-year survey of brand recognition around the world (Asia, Europe, South America), Bonnell announced in May 2003 that the U.S. subsidiary of IESA would be rebranded Atari Inc. In September 2003 shareholders were scheduled to vote to approve a name change for the parent company IESA. Going forward, management expected Atari Inc. to contribute 60–70 percent of the bottom-line profits for IESA

According to Bonnell, the name-change strategy shouldn't have been a surprise; a survey found that people over 30 tended to remember Atari and many under 15 had their own associations with the venerable brand. "Even if they have never played on an Atari machine, they know what *Pong* is about . . . older people still associate the brand with innovation," said Bonnell.[13] For Bonnell, a recreational marathon runner, the Atari acquisition was the equivalent of the moment in a race when a runner

[13]Digits, *Wall Street Journal,* 2003, May 8.

Exhibit 4   Top 20 Video Game Titles Ranked by Total U.S. Units Annual 2003

Rank	Title	Platform	Publisher	Release Date	Average Retail Price $
1	Madden NFL 2004	PS2	Electronic Arts	Aug '03	$49
2	Pokemon Ruby	GBA	Nintendo of America	Mar '03	31
3	Pokemon Sapphire	GBA	Nintendo of America	Mar '03	31
4	Need Speed: Underground	PS2	Electronic Arts	Nov '03	49
5	Zelda: The Wind Waker	GCN	Nintendo of America	Mar '03	47
6	Grand Theft Auto: Vice City	PS2	Rockstar Games	Oct '02	41
7	Mario Kart: Double Dash	GCN	Nintendo of America	Nov '03	49
8	Tony Hawk Underground	PS2	Activision	Oct '03	47
9	Enter the Matrix	PS2	Atari	May '03	46
10	Medal Honor Rising	PS2	Electronic Arts	Nov '03	49
11	NCAA Football 2004	PS2	Electronic Arts	Jul '03	49
12	Halo	XBX	Microsoft	Nov '01	38
13	True Crime: Streets LA	PS2	Activision	Nov '03	48
14	Final Fantasy X-2	PS2	Square ENIX USA	Nov '03	50
15	NBA Live 2004	PS2	Electronic Arts	Oct '03	49
16	SOCOM II: Navy Seals	PS2	Sony Computer Ent.	Nov '03	49
17	Grand Theft Auto 3	PS2	Rockstar Games	Oct '01	21
18	NBA Street Vol. 2	PS2	Electronic Arts	Apr '03	48
19	The Getaway	PS2	Sony Computer Ent. (Sony)	Jan '03	40
20	Mario Bros 3: Mario 4	GBA	Nintendo of America	Oct '03	29

Source: The NPD Group/NPD Funworld ®/Point-of-Sale. David Riley 516-625-2277.

Copyright 2004. The NPD Group, Inc. All rights reserved. Proprietary and Confidential.

would "break away" from the competition in order to separate from the rest of the pack. In the fall of 2001 Atari Inc. was inaugurated under new management with three games: *Splashdown and MXRider* for PlayStation 2, and *Transworld Surf* for the Xbox.

Mission   Atari's mission was to lead mass-market demand for interactive entertainment (see Exhibit 5). This mission was not at all contrary to Bonnell's original founding goal for IESA in 1983: to bring interactive entertainment to consumers around the world across every available distribution platform.

Atari's vision and overall mission was clearly stated in its corporate Web site in contrast to the lack of clarity among the competing top five software game publishers (see Exhibit 3). In order not to divulge any trade secrets, Sony deferred to silence when probed about what strategy

it would take with its next-generation PlayStation 3.[14] Only Activision had an equally thorough and detailed explanation of its corporate objectives and goals as Atari's.

Products   Atari's core offerings included kids/family games, action/adventure games, and sports/racing games. From its founding in 1983, Bonnell and his partner Sapet built Infogrames on an educational software game—*Le Cube Informatique.* It sold 60,000 copies, setting the standard for educational titles.

By the beginning of the new century Atari was consistently a top 10 software gaming company worldwide and the leading software company in Europe. Although the company described itself as "one of the top 5 third-party publishers of interactive entertainment software in

[14]Brown, Eryn, 2002, Sony's big bazooka, *Fortune,* December 30.

Exhibit 5   Atari's Corporate Philosophy

> "Atari will lead mass-market demand for interactive entertainment."
>
> —**Bruno Bonnell,** Chairman and CEO, Atari.
>
> Atari's vision is to be the premier global source of digital interactive entertainment, transporting people of all ages and interest levels to a world of wonder and imagination by drawing from next-generation technologies.
>
> While entertainment is at the heart of Atari's products, the company also believes that games must reward players by allowing them to follow their imagination and become immersed in new worlds and fantasies. By adapting next-generation technologies, and cultivating the imagination, innovation, and energy of its people, Atari designs products that facilitate growth in the person who is playing, whether that growth is hand-eye coordination, logic skills, or simply a sense of wonder and inspiration.
>
> Source: www.atari.com.

the world," the description was a modest one indeed, considering industry analysts considered Atari the top software publisher in Europe, and according to NPD, it had the following rankings in the United States.

- No. 1 publisher of Children's Entertainment games for the PC.
- No. 1 publisher of Arcade and Fighting games for the PC.
- No. 2 publisher of Role Playing Games for the PC.
- No. 2 publisher of Family Entertainment games for the PC.[15]

Atari offered the masses a wide variety of titles, franchises, and brand labels covering three major categories: movie tie-in hits, television version games, and general strategy games. In movie tie-ins, Atari had licenses to Warner Brothers' *Looney Tunes, Mission Impossible* and *MI2, Men in Black, Stuart Little 2, The Matrix* sequels, and *Terminator 3.* For its television franchise games, Atari had developed software for the hit series *Survivor* and for the Japanese animation series *Dragon Ball Z,* which was rated the number one animation program in many countries. In the general strategy category, Atari offered such strong brand name titles as *Monopoly,* and *Unreal Tournament,* which in 1992 won the "game of the year" award and in the fall of 2002 was ranked as the number one game for the personal computer. For the sports genre, Atari got high marks for its *Backyard Sports* franchise. *Backyard Sports* received positive remarks and numerous awards from parenting magazines and parenting organizations. The games, which offered customized products for children, allowed a child to play sports—baseball, hockey, or football—with the kid versions of the games played by professional athletes.

IESA used the brand name "Atari" in rolling out some vintage Atari games to connect the adult consumer

[15]Atari, Corporate profile, www.atari.com.

to the company that started the whole video game craze in the 1980s. Atari had a "10-in-1" TV games product that provided the consumer with a single joystick modeled after the classic 2600 joystick; built into the hardware were 10 classic games such as Centipede, Asteroids, Missile Command, and Battlezone—essentially, a turnkey lightweight plug-in and play system.

Top Management   There was no doubt that Atari had assembled some of the brightest and most talented senior management teams in the industry. Much of the assembly came by way of the series of acquisitions in the late 1990s (see Exhibit 2). Exhibit 6 lists the executives and senior management at Atari in 2002 and their prior accomplishments.

Atari had indeed created a formidable management team by gathering executives from the "best in class" of companies that were leaders in the interactive entertainment world: Disney, Viacom, EA, Virgin Games, and NBC. Bonnell founded his computer games industry start-up on the energy and youth of wiz kids of the eighties, but he built IESA into an industry titan on the solid foundation of experience provided by a collection of executives with impressive résumés from the greatest and most successful U.S. entertainment businesses.

However, the foundation of experience was not without its cracks. Bonnell was successful in surrounding himself with top-level talent, but over time some of his top management was sneaking out the back door and walking across the street to the competitors. Dawn Paine, senior executive in charge of marketing, left in 2002 to join Nintendo; Matt Woodley joined Sega in 2003 as European marketing director; and Larry Sparks, vice president of European marketing, left just two week after Woodley.

Additional Information   Atari's global distribution in 2002 was in excess of 50,000 retail outlets. In Europe alone it had a network of 30,000 retail outlets and in

Exhibit 6   Atari's Senior Management

- *Bruno Bonnell, chief executive officer.* Prior to founding Infogrames, Bonnell was involved in the launch of the Thomson TO7, one of the first computers designed for domestic use.
- *Harry Ruin, senior vice president.* From 1988 to 1993, Rubin worked at NBC, where he served as vice president and general manager of its domestic and international Home Video Divisions.
- *Thomas Heymann, director of Digital Cost Partners.* Heymann was formerly president of The Disney Stores, Inc.
- *Nancy Bushkin, vice president, corporate communications.* Bushkin was vice president, corporate communications, for Spelling Entertainment in Los Angeles from 1997 through 1999. Prior to Spelling, she spent eight years in corporate relations at Viacom Inc. as an integral member of the communications team handling the company's acquisitions of Paramount Communications and Blockbuster.
- *Jason Bell, senior vice president, creative development, Atari Inc.* Bell spent a year at Electronic Arts as producer and senior producer on various multiplayer and online games with responsibility for product design, service quality, and development planning.
- *David Perry, president and founder, Shiny Entertainment.* At age 17, Perry spent four years working for key publishers like Virgin Games. He developed such hits as Teenage Mutant Ninja Turtles and The Terminator for Orion Pictures.

North America it encompassed more than 22,000. Atari also distributed for its affiliate labels such as Strategy First, Xicat, and Codemasters. These affiliates outsourced their outbound logistics to Atari, which ultimately gave Atari a firmer hold on the overall worldwide distribution of the video gaming industry. Atari then set itself up to compete for the same distribution network used by EA: mass merchants and superstores such as Wal-Mart, electronics specialty stores like Best Buy, and software specialty stores such as Electronics Boutique.

In a manner similar to the way motion picture firms outsourced advertising for films, Atari chose to outsource all of its advertising. This practice had become increasingly common among the leading gaming companies. Advertising budgets for Atari were estimated in the $20 million range for 2002.[16]

Selected Competitor Information

Consider the licensing arrangements and brand name titles among the competitors in the early 2000s: Activision had Marvel's *Spiderman,* Disney's *Toy Story 2,* and *Star Trek* from television; Eidos had *Lara Croft Tomb Raider;* and EA owned the Harry Potter franchise and endless titles of sports games, including the cash cow *Madden NFL.*

EA Sports had an "It's in the Game" motto. This helped its young athletic-minded audience to identify with catchphrases such as Nike's "Just Do It" signature. EA's products, like *Madden NFL,* had become annuities, with the company re-releasing the titles every year with updated versions of the players, teams, and stadiums. Fans bought

it year in and year out, as if the older versions were annual trends that went out of style. Thus, every year these products produced a consistent stream of revenue for EA.

Take 2's *Grand Theft Auto* series was also a smash hit. Take 2 did not have as much product diversification in its offerings as Atari or EA and it received a great deal of adverse feedback from the parent population.

> Take 2 made two strategic bets that paid off big . . . decided in 1999 to focus its development dollars on harder-edged, mature-content games . . . All is not rosy, to be sure. Game marketers have come under attack from groups like the National Institute on Media and the Family.[17]

Despite the negative feedback from parents for its sex, drugs, and rock-and-roll image, Take 2 stock continued to perform positively. In 2002 Take 2 generated gross revenues second only to EA (see Exhibit 7). But while Take 2's stock rose, stock in EA, Activision, and Atari all fell.[18] Analysts claimed this was due in part to the expanding consumer age group.

The Future of Atari

Could IESA take the Atari brand name and use it to leapfrog industry stalwarts Activision and Take 2, and ultimately knock off Electronic Arts from its top perch? Could the Atari name help bail IESA out of debt and launch the company into its next growth phase? How long would it take for IESA to become profitable again after the costly purchase of *The Matrix* movie sequels?

---

[16]Flass, Rebecca, & van der Pool, Lisa, 2002, Infogrames in play, *Adweek,* March 25.

[17]Brull, Steven, 2003, Gamers II—magazine platinum, *Institutional Investor,* February.

[18]Ibid.

Exhibit 7   Selected Five-Year Net Revenues
(in thousands)

	2003	2002	2001	2000	1999	1998
EA[1]	$2,482,244	$1,724,675	$1,322,273	$1,420,011	$1,211,863	
Take 2	N/A	$ 793,976	$ 448,801	$ 364,001	$ 304,714	$194,052
Activision	$ 864,116	$ 786,434	$ 620,183	$ 572,205	$ 436,526	$312,906
Atari[2]	$ 989,900	$ 863,100	$ 755,700	$ 584,600	$ 343,100	$250,400

[1]EA fiscal year ends March 31.

[2]USD at exchange rate as of March 31, 2004.

Source: Various company annual reports.

Exhibit 8   Atari, Inc., and Subsidiaries Consolidated Statements of Operations
(in thousands, except per share data)

	Nine Months Ending Dec 31	
	2002 (unaudited)	2003 (unaudited)
Net revenues	$ 449,564	$ 402,540
Cost of goods sold	218,062	202,712
Gross profit	**231,502**	**199,828**
Selling and distribution expenses	81,122	71,270
General and administrative expenses	30,904	25,157
In-process research and development	7,400	—
Research and development	60,461	72,734
Gain on sale of development project to a related party	—	3,744
Depreciation and amortization	5,850	6,757
Operating income	**45,765**	**27,654**
Interest expense, net	10,678	7,215
Other (expense) income	(2,844)	(2,297)
Income before provision for income taxes	32,243	18,142
Provision for income taxes	2,167	63
Net (loss) income	**30,076**	**18,079**
Dividend to parent	—	(39,351)
Net (loss) income attributable to common shareholders	**30,076**	**(21,272)**
Basic and diluted net (loss) income per share	0.43	(0.24)
Basic weighted average shares outstanding	69,847	88,891
Diluted weighted average shares outstanding	80,078	88,891
Net Income	**$ 30,076**	**$ 18,079**

Source: Atari annual reports.

Atari was more recognized as a brand name worldwide than IESA. Family-friendly products were one of Atari's core strategies; Atari offered customized sports games for children such as *Backyard Sports.* However, if Atari wanted to gain market share from EA's sports division, licensing some big household names in sports may have been a wise strategic move.

Atari's diverse portfolio ranging from family-friendly products to blockbuster movie games similarly reflect EA's model. Bonnell took a large gamble in 2002 and spent an enormous amount on the Shiny Entertainment acquisition to gain *Enter the Matrix,* but the short-run results showed the gamble was a good one. Within months of its May 15, 2003, release the game sold more than 3 million units worldwide (see Exhibit 8 for financials).

The future of Atari depended on many things, including whether Atari could retain its in-house talent by keeping its existing design team, or if it would be forced to compete with industry rivals who insisted on luring them away with higher compensation packages. Also in question was whether Atari could continue to afford the trend in huge blockbuster movie games that ran short-term budgetary deficits. But the biggest question that created uncertainty around IESA's acquisition of the Atari name was whether Bonnell would succeed long term in his rebranding efforts of adopting Atari as the new company name for Infogrames. Could the '80s legacy carry IESA to an iconoclastic position in the new millennium?

In early 1995, Robert Holland, the recently appointed CEO of Ben & Jerry's Homemade, Inc., was considering what he should do to return the troubled company to its former status as a fast-growth company which prided itself on its socially responsible approach to business. Holland's statements in several interviews provided some insights into his goals for the company.

> The challenge is to move to the next phase of growth. It's not so much the issues as the opportunities. The biggest opportunity is how to preserve all the terrific things and to add to that some things for the next level. You certainly want to preserve the commitment to the social mission. (*Boston Globe,* 2/2/95)

For the longer term, Holland exhibited a commitment to substantial growth.

> His goal for Ben & Jerry's is to go from $150 million to a half-billion or more in revenues, he said . . . (*New York Times,* 2/2/95)

Holland had been selected by the directors of the socially conscious Ben & Jerry's company because he seemed to possess the range of leadership, managerial, and personal characteristics they sought in the new CEO. Ben & Jerry's wanted a person who could lead the company out of its problems, and set a course for the last half-decade of the century. And they sought someone who subscribed to their socially conscious values which had been the foundation of the company's culture since its inception. They believed they had found this person in Robert Holland, who in accepting the job as Ben & Jerry's CEO, gained national prominence. As one journal stated:

> Holland today presides over one of America's best-known consumer brands. His leadership of a company famous for its down-home culture, off-the-wall marketing and social activism has catapulted him into the ranks of the nation's most visible black executives. (*Boston Globe,* 3/1/95)

Robert Holland's Background

Robert Holland's road to Ben & Jerry's began in Albion, Michigan, as the eldest of five children in a family he described as "financially poor and psychologically rich, be-

cause we had each other" (*Boston Globe,* 3/1/95). His mother labored in a cafeteria while his father worked in a steel foundry until hospitalized for years, at which time young Robert became "the man of the house." And although neither parent had gotten beyond the eighth grade, Holland completed his degree in mechanical engineering at Union College in New York State where he served for three years as president of his class. After completing an MBA degree at night at City College of New York, he was hired by the famous consulting firm of McKinsey & Company in 1968, a very rare event since McKinsey normally hired candidates only from the nation's most prestigious MBA programs. He rose to become the first African-American partner of that firm after seven years, before leaving to go out on his own in 1981. While at McKinsey, he gained a reputation as a strategist and turnaround specialist, and also spent two years working in Amsterdam, as well as time in England, Mexico, and Brazil.

From 1981 until 1994, Holland was involved in a series of entrepreneurial activities ranging from a beer distributorship, to a plastic injection molding company, to his latest endeavor, a closely held consulting business specializing in the turnaround of troubled companies.

But it was not only his business talents that attracted the attention of Ben & Jerry's board and executives.

> Bob's key talents and abilities aren't related to making ice cream, but more to leadership, management, and strategic planning (says Mr. Cohen). Just as important, Mr. Holland has a good track record in the social arena as well. (*Wall Street Journal,* 2/2/95)

Holland had strong views on personal social responsibility. He insisted, "Doing good works is an obligation for being alive" (*Boston Globe,* 3/1/95).

His particular interest has been in the education of minority youths. Holland served as the Chairman of the Trustees of Spelman College, a black women's college in Atlanta, Georgia. During the 1980s, he funded and created a dropout prevention program in a Detroit inner-city school, and he also served as a board member of the Harlem Junior Tennis Program.

Holland realized he was in a position to influence hiring and promotion decisions in the business world, but understood the difficulties as well.

> There are a lot of women and minorities who on paper, on facts, on accomplishments, are outstanding talents. But somehow things didn't work out that way. It's the subjective component in the process, he says. I'm just looking forward to dispelling whatever concerns people have. (*Boston Globe,* 3/1/95)

* This case was prepared from published materials by Professor Daniel J. McCarthy to provide a basis for class discussion. The author appreciates the assistance of many Northeastern University students whose help in class or as research assistants contributed to the development of the case.

Copyright © 1997 by the Business Case Journal and Professor Daniel J. McCarthy. Reprinted with permission of Daniel J. McCarthy, Northeastern University.

The Situation Entering 1995

Early in 1995, Ben & Jerry's reported the first annual loss in the company's history, $1.87 million on 1994 sales of $149 million. The loss followed years of double-digit growth in sales and profits which culminated in 1992 sales of nearly $132 million, before a relatively flat year in 1993 which saw a sales increase of only 6 percent. The company's common stock price reflected its poor financial performance and dropped below $10 in early January 1995 from its high of $28 two years earlier. See Exhibit 1 for the company's financial data, and Exhibit 2 for industry profitability data.

In a company quarterly report during 1994, President Chuck Lacy explained:

Exhibit 1   Ben & Jerry's Homemade, Inc.—Financial Statements

Consolidated Statements of Income (Dollar figures in thousands)					
	1994	**1993**	**1992**	**1991**	**1990**
Net Sales	$148,802	$140,328	$131,969	$96,997	$77,024
Cost of Sales	109,760	100,210	94,389	68,500	54,202
Gross Profit	39,041	40,118	37,580	28,497	22,822
Other Expenses	43,032	28,270	36,243	21,264	17,639
Operating Income	(3,990)	11,848	11,337	7,233	5,183
Other Income (Expense)	229	198	(23)	(729)	(709)
Income before taxes	(3,762)	12,046	11,314	6,504	4,474
Income taxes	(1,893)	4,845	4,639	2,765	1,864
Net income	$ (1,869)	$ 7,201	$ 6,675	$ 3,739	$ 2,610

Consolidated Balance Sheet (Dollar figures in thousands)					
	1994	**1993**	**1992**	**1991**	**1990**
Assets					
Current Assets					
Cash and Equivalents	$ 20,778	$ 14,705	$ 7,356	$ 6,704	$ 796
Accounts Receivable (net)	11,905	11,679	8,649	6,940	5,044
Inventories	13,463	13,452	17,090	9,000	10,083
Other	5,778	2,537	2,246	1,091	519
Total Current Assets	51,923	42,373	35,541	23,735	16,442
Total Noncurrent Assets	68,372	63,988	52,666	19,321	17,857
Total Assets	$120,295	$106,361	$ 88,207	$43,056	$34,299
Liabilities and Stockholder's Equity					
Total Current Liabilities	$ 14,468	$ 13,082	$ 17,487	$12,700	$ 8,240
Total Noncurrent Liabilities	33,326	19,017	3,960	4,087	9,958
Total Liabilities	47,793	32,099	21,447	16,787	18,198
Total Stockholder's Equity	$ 72,502	$ 74,262	$ 66,760	$26,269	$16,101
Total Liabilities and Stockholder's Equity	$120,295	$106,361	$ 88,207	$43,056	$34,299

Source: Ben & Jerry's Annual Reports.

Exhibit 2   Industry Profitability and Key Operating Ratios 1989–1994 (percentages)

	1989	1990	1991	1992	1993	1994
Profitability						
Return on Sales	3	3	4	4	5	3
Return on Assets	5	6	8	9	7	5
Return on Net Worth	12	11	11	14	15	11
Efficiency						
Asset to Sales	37	40	41	36	47	39
Sales to Net Working Capital	10	10	9	13	10	8

Source: Dun & Bradstreet, Industry Norms and Key Business Ratios, 1989, 1990, 1991, 1992, 1993, and 1994. Data reported based on the medium for establishments included in the surveys. These data are not necessarily representative of the entire industry and the ratios may not be directly comparable over time due to the potential change in the sample from year to year. These data are, however, based on the most extensive annual survey conducted for individual breakouts.

Lower earnings in the quarter reflect planned marketing and selling expenses supporting the introductions of our "Smooth, No Chunks!" line, and lower gross margins . . . In the last two years we have more than doubled the number of pints we offer, and this has increased the complexity of our business which has highlighted inefficiencies in our production, planning, purchasing, and inventory management . . .

Disappointing financial results, strategic business problems, and questionable leadership decisions were seen by some company observers to be results of management's disagreement about company goals which was seen to be one reason for the resignation of Ben Cohen as CEO in mid-1994. *The Boston Globe* quoted Ben on July 3, 1994,

We need someone who's been down the pike before . . . I don't have the skills to lead and manage a company this size. I'm really stretched right now.

Cohen also added that he intended to stay on as chairman of the company's board of directors, focusing on flavor and product development, and marketing, as well as directing the company's social agenda and corporate image. Having heard this, some industry analysts wondered how readily Cohen would turn over daily operations of his company to a new chief executive officer. Ben, together with Jerry, still owned 42 percent of the company's voting stock. When asked if Cohen was ready to let go, Ben & Jerry's co-founder, Jerry Greenfield said: "It's definitely a question. I happen to think he is, but I've been wrong about Ben before."

In spite of its problems, however, Ben & Jerry's in 1994 had nearly succeeded in achieving its long-term goal of becoming the leader in the superpremium segment of the ice-cream industry. After years of being second, the company had actually drawn even with Häagen-Dazs with each attracting equal market shares of 42 percent, thereby dominating the segment.

Company Background

Ben & Jerry's Homemade, Inc., based in Vermont, produced Ben & Jerry's superpremium ice cream, ice-cream novelties, and frozen yogurt, all products considered to be within the frozen dessert industry. These products were distributed through supermarkets, grocery stores, convenience stores, restaurants, and franchised and licensed ice-cream scoop shops. Ben Cohen and Jerry Greenfield, founders of Ben & Jerry's Homemade, began their successful ice-cream careers on May 5, 1978, in Burlington, Vermont. With combined savings of $8,000, and a $5 ice-cream–making correspondence course from Penn State, the two opened an ice-cream shop in an abandoned gas station. For 1994, while employing 537 people, the company reported a net loss of $1.87 million on sales of $148.8 million. The total value of the superpremium segment of the ice-cream market at that time was $415 million, or 13 percent of the total ice-cream market (see Exhibit 3).

The company had pursued geographic growth by gaining market share in specific target markets. Its product line expanded during the company's 17 years, by offering exotic ice-cream flavors such as Chocolate Chip Cookie Dough, Cherry Garcia, and Rain Forest Crunch, as well as frozen yogurt and ice-cream novelties. In early 1994, Ben & Jerry's had introduced a new product called "Smooth, No Chunks," which was developed to offer people a more traditional ice-cream product, without the large pieces of candy or nuts found in most Ben & Jerry's products.

Cohen and Greenfield developed Ben & Jerry's corporate culture around the value of social responsibility. The company's philosophy, principles, and practices were

Exhibit 3   Packaged Ice Cream, Ice Milk, and Frozen Yogurt Quality Segments, 1994

	% of Packaged Ice Cream Dollar Sales	% of Packaged Ice Milk Dollar Sales	% of Packaged Frozen Yogurt Dollar Sales
Superpremium	13.0	0.9	22.4
Premium	42.3	58.7	56.9
Regular	34.8	29.5	19.0
Economy	10.0	11.0	1.7

Source: Information Resource, Inc., data from IICA's Ice Cream Market Research Project.

dictated by its mission statement. The ideologies supporting this document were unusual in traditional corporate America, and constantly challenged Ben & Jerry's in implementation of policies such as salary limits. Over time, Ben & Jerry's had been extremely successful balancing stockholders' desires with social responsibility due partly to a young, motivated, and dedicated workforce. But success was often attributed to the guidance the company received from its nontraditional, "funky" founders, Ben Cohen and Jerry Greenfield.

At times, the two questioned and feared rapid growth because they were unsure how it would affect the company's culture and values. Yet, Cohen felt the more the company grew, the more it could do to further social causes, and always sought to maintain the young spirit of the company in spite of double-digit growth. Cohen directed the company during the mid-1980s without the help of his good friend, Jerry Greenfield, who had retired from management to assume responsibility for operating the Ben & Jerry's Foundation, Inc., the vehicle the company used to foster its social values beyond the company's walls.

Ben & Jerry's Mission Statement

Ben & Jerry's was dedicated to producing ice cream and related products in a manner that linked the product with their socially responsible corporate perspective. The corporate mission, as stated in its 1994 Annual Report, was divided into three interrelated parts.

Social Mission:
To operate the company in a way that actively recognizes the central role that business plays in the structure of society by initiating innovative ways to improve the quality of a broad community: local, national, and international.

Product Mission:
To make, distribute, and sell the finest quality all-natural ice cream and related products in a wide variety of innovative flavors made from Vermont dairy products.

Economic Mission:
To operate the company on a sound financial basis of profitable growth, increasing value for our shareholders, and creating opportunities and financial rewards for our employees.

While Ben & Jerry's held a deep respect for individuals both inside and outside the company and for the community at large, the company always sought to make a profit as well. However, their success was not measured by profit alone. Most company ventures were evaluated on the quality of the product, and by the contribution made to local, national, and global communities, as well as return on investment. Ben & Jerry's constantly tried to find unique and creative ways to integrate all three parts of their mission into business decisions.

The introduction of the Peace Pop, a frozen novelty item, was an example of Ben & Jerry's attempt to balance social, economic, and market requirements. The Peace Pop addressed the product mission because it contained popular superpremium ice-cream flavors. The sales of the product met the financial mission since it provided a high margin. Finally, the social mission was realized through the use of packaging as a vehicle to communicate the goals of the 1 Percent for Peace Organization. This organization received 1 percent of supporting companies' designated product sales to help promote peace in all geographic areas of the world.

Culture

Social responsibility was central to Ben & Jerry's corporate purpose. The company image has been built, in a large part, by the public's awareness of its social actions. Social responsibility had directly affected the company's culture in its efforts to enhance the quality of life in Vermont communities. For example, establishing manufacturing plants in small Vermont towns presented Ben & Jerry's with the opportunity to play a vital part in the lives of the individuals in these communities. In late 1994, Ben & Jerry's opened its third production plant in that state. To comply with the company's philosophy, the plant was located in an area of northern Vermont that had been extremely depressed economically. By bringing over 30 jobs to this small community, Ben & Jerry's expected to improve the quality of life for residents of the area.

The company regularly donated second quality ice-cream products to the homeless, handicapped, and community groups, at times donating truckloads of ice cream to food banks nationwide. Such practices were commonplace for the company. This community commitment trickled down to employees. Ben & Jerry's employees had continuously participated in fund-raising activities for causes as diverse as disaster relief to providing holiday gifts for disadvantaged citizens. In 1989, the company instituted a policy allowing its workers to perform community service work on company time. Another example of the level of Ben & Jerry's employee commitment to the company's social values was the garden located on company-owned land which was used to contribute vegetables to a local community food bank.

To support communities beyond the direct reach of the company and its employees, Ben and Jerry's established The Ben & Jerry's Foundation, Inc., a nonprofit foundation which received 7.5 percent of the company's pretax profits. The foundation issued over 100 grants a year to help people and groups improve the environment, promote the needs of minorities and women, combat racism, support children's rights groups, and fight anti-immigrant activities. Recipients of these grants included the Children's Defense Fund, Massachusetts Coalition for the Homeless, Center for Immigrant Rights, and the Brattleboro, Vermont, Area AIDS Project.

Ben & Jerry's not only encouraged employees to help those outside the company, but was sensitive to its employees' needs as well. The company respected the skills and needs of its workforce and viewed these men and women as a key investment in the company's future. A company saying stated, "If you give the company 110 percent, you should get it back—maybe not in cash but certainly in joy." The management worked to improve its organizational structure, working conditions, wages, and benefits in order to increase the quality of the workplace and to strengthen the company. Ben & Jerry's also felt that it was important for all employees, no matter what their position, to have the ability to air their concerns and grievances without fear of retribution. Production was stopped once a month for a companywide meeting to help accomplish this.

The mission statement was at the heart of the company's human resources policies as well. The basic benefits package covered all areas of employee needs including medical coverage, disability and life insurance, vacations, holiday, and sick pay. Workers were also allowed three free pints of ice cream per day. To adjust for changes in the company's workforce and attack bias toward women in the workplace, the company, in 1991, added 12 weeks unpaid maternity leave, child care centers, and health insurance benefits for domestic partners.

To foster a sense of ownership and to share prosperity with employees, Ben & Jerry's offered a 401(k) thrift plan, stock purchase plans, and a profit-sharing plan based on length of service, not wages. To address the health and well-being of employees, the company offered health club memberships, blood pressure and cholesterol screening, courses on weight loss and smoking cessation, and anonymous alcohol and drug counseling. The "Gang of Joy," established to plan companywide events and celebrations designed to ease workplace stress and build a spirit of fun at work, was another means by which Ben & Jerry's promoted employee well-being. Companywide outings to baseball and hockey games as well as free and subsidized food in the break rooms were other examples. A culture developed that emphasized fun, charity, and goodwill toward fellow workers.

Frozen Dessert Industry

According to *Restaurant Business,* Americans consumed more ice cream per capita than people in any other country. Per capita consumption of ice-cream products in 1994 reached a record high of 48 pints per year. In the same year, $10.5 billion was spent at retail on ice cream and related products such as frozen novelties and yogurts with sales virtually equal between at-home and away-from-home consumption (see Exhibit 4). The industry experienced a 3.3 percent increase in growth in 1994, but this had been achieved by the popularity of lower-fat, frozen desserts such as water ices and sherbet. Ice cream grew only 1.2 percent over its 1993 level, while frozen yogurt sales leveled off as did sales of superpremium ice cream (see Exhibit 5).

Retail shops experienced some seasonality in sales which generally increased in the summer months and decreased during the winter. In supermarkets, however, there was no more than a 5 percent fluctuation in the total ice-cream business in any one quarter.

The ice-cream industry was divided into four major categories—economy, regular, premium, and superpremium—of which the premium totaled 13 percent of packaged ice cream dollar sales in 1994, while the superpremium category totaled over 22 percent of frozen yogurt sales. The superpremium segment offered retailers hefty margins, roughly 30 percent, compared to the typical 10–15 percent found in the other categories. Most gourmet ice cream marketers used in-store tasting and price competition to increase brand recognition and product demand. In the other market segments, advertising was the traditional tool used by the marketing departments.

Superpremium ice-cream products were characterized by a greater richness and density than other ice creams. They had less air content and contained a butterfat level of 14 percent to 20 percent. This rich, indulgent

Exhibit 4   **Retail Value of the Ice Cream Industry by Product and Outlet, 1994***
(In billions of dollars)

Product	At Home	Away from Home	Total
Ice Cream	2.3	1.1	3.4
Ice Milk	0.3	1.1	1.4
Frozen Yogurt	0.7	1.0	1.7
Nonfat/Lowfat	0.2	—	0.2
Frozen Novelties	1.5	1.9	3.4
Other**	0.3	0.1	0.4
Total	5.3	5.2	10.5

*Estimated by the International Ice Cream Association.

**Includes sherbet, sorbet, tofu-based products, mellorine, and miscellaneous frozen dairy products.

Source: *The Latest Scoop,* International Dairy Food Association, 1995 edition.

Exhibit 5   **Ice Cream and Related Frozen Desserts Total and Per Capita Production**
(Thousands of gallons)

	1993	1994	% Change from 1993
Total, Ice Cream and Related Frozen Desserts	1,516,432	1,565,940	3.3
Per Capita Production (Quarts)	23.53	24.06	2.30
Ice Cream (Hard and Soft)	866,248	876,434	1.2
Per Capita Production (Quarts)	13.44	13.47	0.2
Ice Milk (Hard and Soft)*	325,346	359,895	10.6
Per Capita Production (Quarts)	5.05	5.53	9.5
Frozen Yogurt (Hard and Soft)	149,933	150,795	0.6
Per Capita Production (Quarts)	2.33	2.32	−4.3
Sherbet (Hard and Soft)	50,813	54,771	7.8
Per Capita Production (Quarts)	0.79	0.84	6.3
Water Ices**	58,129	63,873	9.9
Per Capita Production (Quarts)	0.90	0.98	8.8
Other Frozen Dairy Products***	65,963	60,172	−8.8
Per Capita Production (Quarts)	1.02	0.92	−9.7

*Includes freezer-made milkshakes.

**Also contains sorbet, frozen juice bars, and gelatin pops.

***Includes nonfat dairy desserts, pudding pops, tofu-based products, and other miscellaneous frozen dairy products.

Source: *The Latest Scoop,* International Dairy Food Association, 1995 edition.

ice cream usually retailed for $2.75 to $3.00 per pint. So-called economy and regular brands were priced at $2.00 and $3.00 per half gallon, respectively. Superpremium ice milk and frozen yogurt were also far richer in fat content than other categories.

Growth of the superpremium market segment had increased steadily at around 5 percent per year, until 1992, when the segment growth shot up to 15 percent before leveling off in 1994. In comparison, sales of regular ice cream grew at an average annual rate of only about 1 percent.

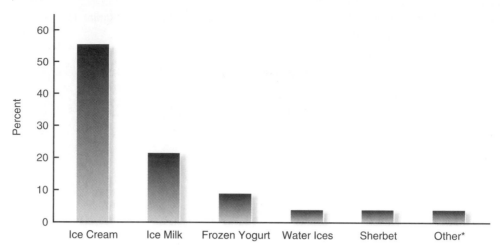

Exhibit 6   1994 Share of the Frozen Dessert Market by Product Types

*Includes nonfat dairy desserts.

Source: *The Latest Scoop,* International Dairy Food Association, 1995 Edition.

The increased growth rate of the superpremium segment before 1994, according to industry experts, was spurred by a growing market of younger, more affluent consumers. Growth occurred primarily in supermarket sales, creating intense competition for freezer space. Market shares for different product categories in 1994 are shown in Exhibit 6.

The adult ice cream novelty segment was also grouped into several categories: premium, gourmet, low-calorie, and confectionery. Adult frozen novelties ranged from ordinary chocolate-covered ice-cream bars to deluxe ice-cream sandwiches and sundaes. The frozen novelty segment was the boom category of the 1980s, supported by aggressive advertising and promotion. The segment offered supermarkets profit margins similar to the superpremium segment, making it one of the most profitable items in the freezer case. Because of attractive margins, supermarket demand increased, but subsequently, a glut of new frozen novelty products appeared, often replacing proven products. After experiencing nine years of more than 15 percent average annual sales growth, frozen novelty sales fell for the first time in 1991, and subsequently made up less and less of the total market for ice-cream products.

The downturn in the superpremium segment was said by industry analysts to be due to its fat and cholesterol levels which were two to three times that of regular ice cream. It was not uncommon for a 4-ounce serving of superpremium ice cream (½ cup) to contain 20 grams of fat and 120 milligrams of cholesterol. Such information was available to consumers by early 1994, when a federal food-labeling regulation took effect requiring ice-cream products to display nutritional information such as fat and cholesterol contents. A trend toward nonfat or low-fat

products resulted in impressive 1994 gains for water ices, sherbet, and sorbets.

A short-lived fad in the 1970s, frozen yogurt had evolved in the early 1990s to become the fastest-growing area of the frozen dessert industry. This growth was seen as a result of an increase in healthier eating habits, and the link of cholesterol and saturated fats to heart disease. In the 1990s yogurt could be produced with less live yogurt cultures, and could be made to taste more like traditional ice cream with very little of the tartness of earlier products. By 1993, frozen yogurt products were offered in all market segments of traditional ice cream, including superpremium. Franchising was also a major reason for the sales growth of frozen yogurt, which increased 400 percent annually in the early 1990s. The superpremium segment of frozen yogurt was estimated at $50 million in 1993. Overall, the frozen yogurt business grew approximately 20 percent per year through the 1980s and early 1990s, although the growth rate slowed as the market had begun to mature, resulting in the flat sales of 1994.

Ice milk had also gained popularity as processing improved, making it a richer and creamier product, more comparable to ice cream, unlike the product's previously dense, gummy, and coarse texture. The refinement was due in large part to the addition of more butterfat. Although comparatively low, ice milk still contained 2 percent to 7 percent butterfat, which was the major source of cholesterol in ice cream.

Since retailers had limited freezer space, it was allocated to items with high turnover. Retailers also used a product's uniqueness, manufacturer's advertising support, and estimated direct product profit in deciding whether to add a new product. Obtaining and maintaining good distribution was a critical factor for the ice-cream marketer. Without good distribution, penetration through supermarkets was difficult to attain. Small volume manufacturers did not have much power with distributors, unlike major, high-volume manufacturers such as Häagen-Dazs and Sealtest, and in some regions, Ben & Jerry's.

Competition

Ben and Jerry's had many different competitors with the most consistent nemesis being Häagen-Dazs. Other important players throughout the company's history were Frusen Gladje and Steve's, with many other regional companies having limited distribution. The ownership of Häagen-Dazs changed in 1992 from Pillsbury Corporation to Grand Metropolitan PLC, a giant British conglomerate.

Häagen-Dazs began in New York's Bronx, and until 1994 had the largest market share in the superpremium segment. For the 52-week period ended April 4, 1994, however, Häagen-Dazs sales had slipped by 6.7 percent to an annual level of $151.5 million, even though its line included all products of the superpremium segment, including frozen yogurt. By then, Häagen-Dazs shared 84 percent of the superpremium segment equally with Ben & Jerry's. New products tested by the company in recent years included ice-cream bars, a fruit and yogurt platter, baked goods, and soft serve ice cream. In 1991, Häagen-Dazs had 260 franchised retail stores, for which the initial franchise fee was approximately $25,000. Royalties varied with volume, while an additional 4 percent of sales was paid by franchisees for regional advertising. These stores accounted for 10 percent of 1991 sales. International sales made up approximately 30 percent of sales in that same year, but the company expected this figure to grow to 50 percent by 1996. Häagen-Dazs had been advertising continuously since 1986. Its main strength, broad distribution in supermarkets, was due to its relationships with Pillsbury and Grand Metropolitan, each of which had tremendous supermarket penetration.

Frusen Gladje, a domestic brand, with less than half the sales volume of Ben & Jerry's in 1991, was traditionally a weak number three in the superpremium segment and competed only in supermarket sales. By early 1994, the brand had all but disappeared from supermarket freezers bringing in only $3 million in sales, 62 percent less than the previous year. Kraft, which bought the rights to Frusen Gladje in 1985, had merged with Philip Morris. That company planned to use the brand's previous visibility to capitalize on lower fat gourmet frozen desserts like yogurt and reduced fat superpremium ice cream to recapture market share.

Steve's Ice Cream, which started in Somerville, Massachusetts, had been the fourth competitor in the superpremium ice cream and novelties segment, but was only a minor regional player by 1994. Steve's franchises numbered around 100 in the late 1980s but had since dwindled. A Steve's franchise cost around $25,000 with approximately 6 percent of sales going to royalties and 1 percent to advertising. Steve's ice cream was also distributed in supermarkets, but at least one chain store buyer stated that the company was weak in this area.

In 1994, there were four other competitors of note. Columbo from Bonogram SA of Italy had total 1994 sales of $10.3 million, 24 percent less than its previous year's total. Another was Elan whose sales dropped 33 percent to $5.1 million, and the newest entrant into the market, Dannon, which attained an 0.8 percent market share or around $3 million in its first year. Mattus competed with a nonfat superpremium ice cream product, not yogurt. The company founder, Reuben Mattus, was also the inventor of Häagen-Dazs. In 1994, however, the product was only available in the New York Metro area, but had begun to establish brand recognition.

Other competitors were also prominent in the ice-cream industry, but did not compete in the superpremium segment. International Dairy Queen, with over $2 billion in annual sales, had over 5,000 stores, and Baskin-Robbins, the leader in dipped ice cream sales, with over $500 million in revenues, had both introduced product offerings in the reduced fat and yogurt categories. By the early 1990s, new competition and flavors continued to enter the ice-cream novelty market each year. Dove Bar International introduced Dove Light Bars as well as light versions of its popular Bon Bon. In addition, Healthy Choice, Weight Watchers, Klondike, Kraft, Dole, General Foods, and Hood entered the frozen dessert market with either frozen fruit, ice cream or low-calorie bars.

TCBY (The Country's Best Yogurt) became Ben & Jerry's most affordable competitor in the superpremium retail market. The brand offered numerous flavors of soft serve yogurts with blend-ins and toppings, as well as cakes and novelties. In 1988, with the introduction of one of the first noncholesterol frozen dessert products, the company began a meteoric rise, similar to the growth of Ben & Jerry's earlier in the decade. By the early 1990s the company had around $500 million in sales, and nearly 2,000 stores. In 1993, the company distributed its products only through company-owned or franchised stores, but had begun to look into the possibility of expanding its distribution network. Early in the company's growth period, the initial franchise fee was around $20,000, with approximately 4 percent of sales going to royalties and an additional 3 percent to advertising.

Products, Markets, and Marketing

Ben & Jerry's produced several different product lines. Its superpremium ice cream, which contained up to 15 percent butterfat, gave it a distinctive rich and creamy taste. The company also produced ice-cream novelties, including the Peace Pop and Brownie Bar, as well as many flavors of frozen yogurt, with some offered in low-fat versions. The products were all made from natural ingredients with no preservatives. In 1988, Ben & Jerry's had introduced a "light" ice cream which was quickly taken off the shelves due to the consumer's preference for frozen yogurt as a lower fat alternative dessert product.

The majority of Ben & Jerry's revenue came from supermarket and convenience store sales serviced by distributors, and from franchise stores. Only 3 percent of 1994 sales were from company-owned stores which made up a small percentage of the retail "scoop shops." Packaged pints of ice cream and yogurts accounted for 85 percent of 1994 sales, and although the majority of these sales were ice cream, an increasing proportion was yogurt which had grown by 35 percent between 1993 and 1994. Two and one-half gallon containers accounted for 7 percent, and novelties 5 percent of company sales.

Exhibit 7 shows U.S. ice-cream production by regional areas during the early 1990s.

Ben & Jerry's products were available in all 50 states by 1990, but in some regions, Ben & Jerry's realized a more favorable market share position than in others. It ranged from 20 percent in Los Angeles to 53 percent in Boston, the first market in which Ben & Jerry's market share surpassed Häagen-Dazs. The Company had begun to expand its markets internationally in the late 1980s, and in 1987 granted to an exclusive licensee the right to manufacture and sell Ben & Jerry's ice cream in Canada. The company also offered a nonexclusive license to manufacture and market its ice cream in Israel. By 1993, licensees operated 10 stores in Israel, 3 Russian outlets, and 4 Canadian scoop shops. Exhibit 8 shows the total dollar value of U.S. exports of frozen dessert production for 1994.

Exhibit 7   Ice Cream and Related Products per Capita Production by Region 1991–1994 (In quarts)

Product and Year	North Atlantic	South Atlantic	E.N. Central	W.N. Central	South Central	West	United States
Ice Cream							
1991	15.66	9.66	14.69	24.69	10.95	12.87	13.68
1992	15.05	9.57	14.99	24.5	10.65	13.14	13.58
1993	15.64	9.39	15.98	23.4	9.34	12.74	13.43
1994	15.06	10.07	15.30	24.41	9.38	13.08	13.47
Ice Milk							
1991	5.20	3.74	6.73	9.11	4.74	5.29	5.42
1992	4.59	3.58	6.55	8.92	4.46	5.15	5.15
1993	4.49	3.69	6.19	9.46	4.31	4.94	5.05
1994	4.60	3.70	7.65	11.13	4.44	5.30	5.53
Frozen Yogurt							
1991	1.68	1.69	2.00	4.72	3.29	2.20	2.33
1992	2.62	1.33	1.44	3.40	2.60	1.95	2.10
1993	2.02	1.94	2.09	4.81	3.08	1.71	2.33
1994	2.03	1.92	2.10	4.77	3.05	1.71	2.32
Total Frozen Products*							
1991	24.72	17.35	25.99	44.44	20.46	21.64	23.65
1992	24.29	17.05	25.61	41.64	19.26	22.63	23.25
1993	24.71	17.44	27.61	43.19	18.23	22.03	23.52
1994	23.76	18.22	28.03	46.78	18.52	23.13	24.06

*Includes ice cream, ice milk, frozen yogurt, sherbet, water ices, and other frozen dairy products. Prepared by the International Ice Cream Association from production data released by the U.S. Department of Agriculture and population estimates from Bureau of the Census, U.S. Department of Commerce.

Source: *The Latest Scoop,* International Dairy Food Association, 1995 edition.

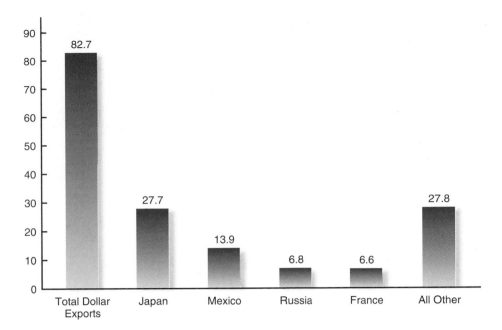

Exhibit 8   **Total Dollar Value of U.S. Frozen Dessert Exports, 1994**
(In millions of dollars)

Source: *The Latest Scoop*, International Dairy Food Association, 1995 edition.

The company traditionally employed a grassroots approach to sales promotion. For example, free ice-cream samples were always available at the plant for visitors who toured the facility. The company had depended almost exclusively on word of mouth to generate sales, and although direct advertising was done by competitors, Ben and Jerry's had done very little by 1995. Its public relations activities took on a lighthearted, down-home, made-in-Vermont theme, and some activities included sponsoring community events both in Vermont and in franchise areas, sponsoring "fun" activities such as Scoopathons.

Ben & Jerry's distribution capabilities also continued to grow and the company distributed 2.5 gallon containers of Ben & Jerry's products in 45 different flavors and varieties to scoop shops. They also sold a variety of novelty products and souvenir T-shirts through franchise shops, company-owned stores, and restaurants. Pints and quarts were distributed to supermarkets, grocery and convenience stores, and retail food outlets. Of the 28 superpremium flavors, 14 were traditional Ben & Jerry's flavors like Cherry Garcia, Chocolate Chip Cookie Dough, and Heath Bar Crunch. Eight flavors were frozen yogurts, of which five were low fat, and the company planned on offering 3 no-fat yogurts in 1995. The remaining six flavors were in the new category called "Smooth, no Chunks!" like White Russian, Double Chocolate Fudge Swirl, and Vanilla Caramel Fudge. Four of the traditional flavors were also available in quart size containers for customers

with a larger appetite. Exhibit 9 displays the company's product offerings in 1994.

The distribution network was comprised of several independent regional ice-cream distributors located primarily in New England, Florida, and Texas. Sut's Premium Ice Cream, for instance, distributed Ben & Jerry's products throughout New England. In 1987, a distribution agreement was reached with Dreyer's Grand Ice Cream, Inc., opening the Midwestern states and the West Coast to Ben & Jerry's, and by the end of 1994, Dreyer's distribution handled 52 percent of the company's net sales.

By 1994, there were 110 Ben & Jerry's scoop shops, mostly franchised with a small number company-owned. The company had imposed a moratorium on new franchises in the late 1980s, but this had been lifted in 1993. Most franchise agreements were for a ten-year term with an option to the franchisee to renew for a second ten years. The franchise fees were relatively low at $17,600 per store. No royalties were required, but franchises were required to pay 4 percent of gross annual sales to Ben & Jerry's for local and regional marketing, usually in the form of promotional activities. The company frequently used franchises to test new products and flavors, like Bluesberry. The franchise agreement granted the franchisee an exclusive area, and required the franchisee to purchase all its ice cream and certain other products, principally baked goods and hot fudge sauce, exclusively from Ben & Jerry's.

Exhibit 9   Ben & Jerry's Family of Products

Original	Smooth, no Chunks!	Frozen Yogurt	Scoop Shop Flavor	Fruit Ices	Peace Pops	Quarts
Chocolate Chip Cookie Fudge	Vanilla	Apple Pie	*Original Ice Creams:*	Lemon Daiquiri	Chocolate Chip Cookie Dough	Chocolate Chip Cookie Dough
Chocolate Fudge Brownie	Vanilla Bean	Chocolate Raspberry Swirl	Chocolate	Frozen Yogurt	New York Super Fudge Chunk	Cherry Garcia
Cherry Garcia	Double Chocolate Fudge Swirl	English Toffee Crunch	Sweet Cream with Cookies	Banana Strawberry	English Toffee Crunch	Vanilla
Coconut Almond Fudge Chip	Aztec Harvests Coffee	Bluesberry	Aztec Harvests Coffee	Chocolate Fudge Brownie	Cherry Garcia Yogurt	Chocolate Fudge Brownie
Coffee Toffee Crunch	Vanilla Caramel Fudge	Coffee Almond Fudge	Coconut Almond Fudge Chip	Chocolate Raspberry Swirl	Vanilla	
Rainforest Crunch	Deep Dark Chocolate	Chocolate Fudge Brownie	Double Chocolate Fudge Swirl	Mandarin		
English Toffee Crunch	White Russian	Banana Strawberry	Cappuccino Chocolate Chunk	Bluesberry		
Mint Chocolate Cookie		Cherry Garcia	Deep Dark Chocolate	Raspberry		
Butter Pecan			Vanilla	Apple Pie		
New York Upper Fudge Crunch			Chocolate Orange Fudge	English Toffee Crunch		
Chunky Monkey			Mint Chocolate Chunk	Cherry Garcia		
Chocolate Peanut Butter Cookie Dough			Apple Pie	Coffee Almond Fudge		
Peanut Butter Cup			Cherry Garcia			
Wavy Gravy			Strawberry			
			Vanilla Bean			
			Coffee			
			Reverse Chocolate Chunk			
			Butter Pecan			
			Chocolate Fudge Brownie			
			Swiss Chocolate Almond			
			Coffee Toffee Crunch			
			Maple Walnut			
			Peanut Butter			
			Vanilla Chocolate Chunk			
			Praline Pecan			
			Chocolate Peanut Butter Cookie Dough			

Source: Ben & Jerry's 1993 Annual Report.

Ice Cream Making

The company's first two manufacturing facilities were located in Vermont, and a third Vermont plant, located in St. Albans, which opened in late 1994, would eventually increase total capacity of packaged pints from 9 million to 22 million gallons per year. The new plant, however, incurred serious start-up problems resulting in large cost overruns, product shortages, and delays in production. The computer-controlled production equipment and related software were still causing problems as 1994 came to a close, and it was the $6.8 million write-down of this equipment that accounted for most of the company's 1994 loss.

The Waterbury, Vermont, plant had begun operations in June 1985 with its 27,000 square feet dedicated to producing superpremium ice cream, only in pints. Production was automated and included a mix batching facility and a quality control lab to assure consistent quality production. Two production lines operated five to six days each week in two 8½ hour shifts that produced a maximum capacity of 15,300 gallons per day.

The 24,000-square-foot Springfield, Vermont, plant began production in September 1988 and produced bulk ice cream, in 2½ gallon containers used by franchises and restaurants, as well as ice-cream novelties. The company designed and modified the plant's equipment resulting in the capability to insert larger chunks of cookies and candies into the ice cream. It was a highly mechanized ice-cream production facility, but Ben & Jerry's flavors did not conform completely to traditional ice-cream production norms. For example, Heath Bars were made into bite-size chunks by having shop workers lift boxes of bars over their heads and slam them down on the floor. The pieces were then mixed into the ice cream, and this unusual process had required the company to alter its machinery.

Ben & Jerry's, at times, had used subcontractors to augment production in order to meet demand. Through 1985, in fact, their ice-cream mix was made by regional dairies. Production was brought in-house after that, however, when the Waterbury facility was completed. But again in 1989, because demand had been significantly underestimated, Ben & Jerry's was forced to subcontract ice-cream manufacturing to one of its distributors, Dreyer's Ice Cream. This manufacturing agreement was due to expire in late 1995, when the St. Albans plant was expected to be running at capacity.

Ben & Jerry's dairy suppliers were all Vermont-based farmers and there was tremendous pride in being a Ben & Jerry's supplier. Since there were numerous dairy farms in Vermont, and a limited number of customers for dairy products, Ben & Jerry's provided one of the few major markets for dairy products in the state. The company also tried to use as many other products as possible that were either manufactured or sold by Vermont-based firms. In fact, the company often received its supply of brownies from a community of recovering substance abusers. The company's materials cost was always relatively high due to the premium quality and expensive ingredients used in its products, such as unpreserved extracts, fresh fruits and dairy products, premium candy flavors, and the exotic nuts for which Ben & Jerry's ice cream was so well known.

Regulation was an important part of the business environment, and Ben & Jerry's was subject to regulation by the Federal Department of Agriculture as well as the Vermont Department. They also had to obtain licenses from the states in which Ben & Jerry's ice cream was sold. The franchise program was subject to regulation by the Federal Trade Commission with regard to required information disclosure to investors prior to their investing in franchises. Finally, operation of plants had to comply with Vermont law and regulations relating to land use and waste discharge.

Company environmental projects over time included the construction of a dairy waste pre-treatment plant. Industrial waste was particularly important to Ben & Jerry's since the company had committed itself to socially responsible behavior. At one point, in its attempt to handle wasted ice cream, the company arranged for a local pig farmer to feed this by-product to his animals. This turned troublesome waste into "Vermont's Swinest" pork. The waste treatment plant was required because of the physical properties of dairy waste. Since fat is not water soluble, it is difficult to dispose of properly, and the plant helped in the breakdown of fat for environmentally friendly disposal.

Financing Growth

Ben & Jerry's Homemade, Inc., had $213,000 in net income for the year 1984, and until that year, the company had always been able to satisfy its financial requirements through its cash flow from operations and bank borrowings. In 1984, however, the company had outgrown its plant in South Burlington, Vermont, and planned additional capacity at a proposed plant in Waterbury, Vermont. To finance the plant, it undertook an intrastate common stock offering in Vermont for approximately $770,000. Both Cohen and Greenfield felt they owed it to their fellow Vermonters to offer them exclusive rights to participate in the growth of the company. The product had a strong identification with the state of Vermont and many Vermonters, such as cooperative dairy farmers, had enabled the company to succeed. By the end of 1985, one in every ten Vermont families owned a portion of the company, further reinforcing its "grassroots image." Announcements on cartons of ice cream and newspapers read "scoop up our stock," and interested state residents were encouraged to call a toll-free number for a prospectus.

After this effort, the company went to Wall Street with an initial public offering. In order to emphasize the unique values of the firm to those who might be unfamiliar with Ben & Jerry's, Cohen and Greenfield stood on Wall Street in blue jeans and T-shirts, handing out free ice-cream cones to young stockbrokers. This offbeat way of selling stock typified their anti-corporate approach to business.

The November 1985 IPO of class A common stock raised over $5 million which provided the funds needed to finance an expanded storage freezer, supplemented working capital needed to support increased sales, and financed the expansion of the Waterbury plant. This expansion added a third production line, upgraded the plant's sprinkler supply system, and allowed the construction of an additional dry storage area and dairy waste pre-treatment facility. A unique use of the proceeds saw $500,000 set aside for the establishment of the company's charitable vehicle, Ben & Jerry's Foundation, Inc. To solidify its relationship with the company, the foundation then purchased 900 shares of preferred stock which entitled it to special voting rights.

Proceeds from the $6.3 million raised in the 1987 public offering of a 9½ percent convertible subordinated debenture were also applied to expanding the Waterbury plant, as well as to the purchase of a 12-acre site and 24,000-square-foot building in Springfield, Vermont, which expanded the company's distribution capacity.

On October 20, 1993, the company successfully completed the issue of $20 million of notes at 5.9 percent and $10 million of notes at 5.73 percent, both due in 2003. These funds, along with company profits, were used to finance the construction of the St. Albans plant, and to improve distribution and marketing. The marketing effort was intended to introduce the "Smooth, no Chunks!" line of products which was to be produced at the St. Albans plant.

Management Issues and Decisions

The company's management problems were recounted in a *Wall Street Journal* article in February 1995.

> As Ben & Jerry's has attempted to make the transition out of its youth, it has said its main challenge is finding managers who can help it reach midsize maturity.

For most of the company's history, a strict pay policy stated that the salary for the highest paying position would not be greater than five times the lowest company salary. In 1990 this was changed to a seven-to-one relationship to attract and keep high-quality management, and in 1994, Ben & Jerry's made an even more difficult decision. With the downturn in the business's growth rate, and reportedly inconsistent leadership, the company decided to abandon its salary policy. With over $140 million in sales, the company seemed to be in need of strong and experienced management, starting with the CEO. Ben Cohen had come to realize he no longer possessed the skills needed to run the large and growing company which had evolved from its humble garage start-up. Since the average salary for a CEO of a company of Ben & Jerry's size was around $300,000, the salary ratio presented a serious problem in filling the position left vacant by Ben's relin-

quishing the CEO post. The policy change, however, was met with resistance from Ben & Jerry's employees.

The company's various problems which culminated in 1994 with its first loss, however, had actually begun some years earlier, although strong growth in the super-premium ice-cream segment allowed the company to operate very successfully through 1992. One incident is indicative of the questions and issues that confronted Ben personally, as well as the company as it continued its successful growth.

During 1988, the company had faced the question of whether or not management wanted to continue growing the company at its rapid pace, since Ben feared that it was becoming too corporate-like. Friends, however, had convinced him not to sell the company, but instead to rally the managers to the company mission during its annual retreat.

> After this retreat, which Ben & Jerry did not attend, the management team met with the various departments and began to hammer out goals and strategic plans. It was the most concentrated planning the company had ever done and was very business-like and attuned to the bottom line. The plan was presented to the then Board of Directors (Ben Cohen, Jeff Furman, Fred Lager, and Jerry Greenfield) who felt that the management team had not fully bought into the company's social agenda. The managers, it seemed, felt that the company had become less creative, less ready to move to new ideas. Ben felt the management team was saying to him, "You've brought the company to where it is, and all of a sudden were saying, 'OK, you've done your job, now we'll do ours. We don't need you anymore.'" (*Inc.*, July 1988)

At that time, the President and COO, Fred "Chico" Lager, developed departmental strategies aimed at providing more specific direction and structure to the company, but faced some opposition from the board of directors. Ben & Jerry's seemed to be at a crossroads. By the end of 1990, Lager was CEO and continued as a member of the board, while Chuck Lacy, who had been COO and general manager, became president and COO. In 1994, Lacey remained as president, and Ben Cohen was chairman of the board of directors, as well as the acting chief executive officer, having taken over for Chico Lager who left the company in 1991. Jerry Greenfield was the director of the Ben & Jerry's Foundation and vice chairman of the Board. These managers, advised by a mainstream Manhattan consulting group, set out to shape the future of the company. The decision to begin a search for a new chief executive officer in mid-1994 was one outcome of their deliberations.

The Search Process

In typical Ben & Jerry's fashion, the search process was an offbeat, one-of-a-kind event. Candidates were to write a 100-word essay titled "Yo, I'm Your CEO," sending it to the search firm, including a label from his or her favorite Ben & Jerry's ice-cream flavor. The contest drew over 20,000 responses ranging from a three-year-old "finalist" to serious business types. Many observers saw the whole process as another Ben & Jerry's marketing gimmick.

A parallel formal search was also conducted, however, which produced among others, the eventual choice for CEO, Robert Holland. Melanie Kusin, who managed the search, described the task.

> Ben & Jerry's has a strong social commitment, yet it needed a leader with proven skills in running businesses and taking them through the transition to the next level. (*New York Times*, 2/2/95)

Holland, in fact, had not written an essay before his selection, but after that was asked to do so by Cohen and the board of directors. He chose, however, to submit a poem "Time, Values and Ice Cream" which, although exceeding the word limit, was explained by the author with notable humor, to be within limits, before translation (see Exhibit 10). His unanimous selection from the 20,000 essayists and 500 candidates occurred only after extensive interviews with the board committee and Ben and Jerry's, in what were described as a series of "bonding sessions."

> The double-barreled process (essay and formal search) produced two finalists who did extensive bonding time over dinners and ice cream with Cohen, Greenfield, and Board members, Kusin said. That's something Ben likes to do, hang out. We wanted to be sure someone could hang with him. (*Boston Globe*, 2/2/95)

Some industry observers felt Holland was an excellent choice, while others questioned his experience for the job. One analyst who followed the industry and company stated,

> Holland's experience in working with other companies as a McKinsey consultant will be very helpful because they (B&J's) need a broader perspective . . . Bringing in someone from the outside made a lot of sense. (*New York Times*, 2/2/95)

Exhibit 10   Time, Values and Ice Cream*
by Robert Holland, Jr.

Born before the baby boom
as war's drums raged across distant waters—
way beyond my family's lore since our 1600's coming to this far off land called America.

'Twas a simple time, as I grew tall.
Shucks! Uncle Sam really wanted you (so the poster said)—pride in work, parades and proms, company picnics 'tween eve'ns spent with "Suspense," "The Shadow," and everybody's "Our Miss Brooks." Good ole days in the summertime, indeed! . . . in America.
Yet, some nostalgia stayed 'yond one's grasp, like Sullivan's, the ice cream place on Main—swivelstools, cozy booths, and sweet smells pleasure.

Sometimes, dear 'Merica of thee I simply hum.
Much, so much has changed in twenty springs. Sputnik no longer beeps so loud; Bay of pigs, Vietnam, and contentions in Chicago . . . come and gone . . . All that noise almost drowning out "One small step for a man . . ." and . . . "Willie, time to say goodbye to baseball."

Confusing place, this melodious mix called America.
Now I sit by eyeing distant twilight, Engineer and MBA, smiling wide on having not forgotten the forbidden seats of Sullivan's, with miles to go before we sleep . . . and time left yet to get there.
Only in America!

*Only 100 words before translation from the language of Chunky Mandarin Orange with natural wild Brazil nuts.

And a *Boston Globe* quote was even stronger in its praise:

> Holland's many supporters say he possesses the strategic thinking of a management consultant, the hands-on savvy of an entrepreneur and the conscience of a social activist—all of which should serve him well at Ben & Jerry's. (*Boston Globe,* 3/1/95)

But another analyst who followed the company had a different view.

> His résumé doesn't come across to me as that of a marketing genius with a lot of experience with consumer products . . . How do you transfer experience from plastic injection molding to Ben & Jerry's? (*New York Times,* 2/2/95)

Time for Action

Robert Holland knew that his decisions and actions would be the subjects of much attention and scrutiny. Industry analysts and journalists were ready to assess and publicize them. Shareholders watched anxiously. Employees, as well as Ben, Jerry, and the board of directors watched to see if the choice was a good one. Finally, there were the legions of ice-cream "aficionados," many of whom valued social responsibility in the company they supported. What would these groups think of Ben & Jerry's as the 1990s came to a close? The answer would depend largely on the decisions and actions of the new CEO, something Robert Holland fully realized.

References

Collins, Glenn. 1995. Ben & Jerry's talent hunt ends. *New York Times,* February 2.

Larger, Fred. 1994. Ben & Jerry's: The inside scoop. New York: Crown Trade Paperbacks.

Larson, Erik. 1988. Forever Young. *Inc.,* July.

Pereira, Joseph, and Lublin, Joann S. 1995. A new CEO for Cherry Garcia's creator. *Wall Street Journal,* February 2.

Shao, Maria. 1994. Ben & Jerry's grows up: Has caring capitalism become a casualty of big company reality? *Boston Globe,* July 3.

———. 1995. "The new emperor of ice cream. *Boston Globe,* February 2.

———. 1995. A scoopful of credentials: CEO Holland brings an activist's blend to Ben & Jerry's. *Boston Globe,* March 1.

Case 6 The Best-Laid Incentive Plans*

Hiram Phillips finished tying his bow tie and glanced in the mirror. Frowning, he tugged on the left side, then caught sight of his watch in the mirror. Time to get going. Moments later, he was down the stairs, whistling cheerfully and heading toward the coffeemaker.

"You're in a good mood," his wife said, looking up from the newspaper and smiling. "What's that tune? 'Accentuate the Positive'?"

"Well done!" Hiram called out. "You know, I do believe you're picking up some pop culture in spite of yourself." It was a running joke with them. She was a classically trained cellist and on the board of the local symphony. He was the one with the Sinatra and Bing Crosby albums and the taste for standards. "You're getting better at naming that tune."

"Or else you're getting better at whistling." She looked over her reading glasses and met his eye. They let a beat pass before they said in unison: "Naaah." Then, with a wink, Hiram shrugged on his trench coat, grabbed his travel mug, and went out the door.

Fat and Happy

It was true. Hiram Phillips, CFO and chief administrative officer of Rainbarrel Products, a diversified consumer-durables manufacturer, was in a particularly good mood. He was heading into a breakfast meeting that would bring nothing but good news. Sally Hamilton and Frank Ormondy from Felding & Company would no doubt already be at the office when he arrived and would have with them the all-important numbers—the statistics that would demonstrate the positive results of the performance management system he'd put in place a year ago. Hiram had already seen many of the figures in bits and pieces. He'd retained the consultants to establish baselines on the metrics he wanted to watch and had seen various interim reports from them since. But today's meeting would be the impressive summation capping off a year's worth of effort. Merging into the congestion of Route 45, he thought about the upbeat presentation he would spend the rest of the morning preparing for tomorrow's meeting of the corporate executive council.

It was obvious enough what his introduction should be. He would start at the beginning—or, anyway, his own beginning at Rainbarrel Products a year ago. At the time, the company had just come off a couple of awful quarters.

Harvard Business Review's cases, which are fictional, present common managerial dilemmas and offer concrete solutions from experts.

*Steve Kerr is the chief learning officer at Goldman Sachs in New York. Prior to joining Goldman Sachs in 2001, he spent seven years as the chief learning officer and head of leadership development at General Electric. He was responsible for GE's leadership development center at Crotonville.

Reprinted by permission of Harvard Business Review. "The Best Laid Incentive Plans" by Steve Kerr, January 2003. Copyright © 2003 by the Harvard Business School Publishing Corporation; all rights reserved.

It wasn't alone. The sudden slowdown in consumer spending, after a decade-long boom, had taken the whole industry by surprise. But what had quickly become clear was that Rainbarrel was adjusting to the new reality far less rapidly than its biggest competitors.

Keith Randall, CEO of Rainbarrel, was known for being an inspiring leader who focused on innovation. Even outside the industry, he had a name as a marketing visionary. But over the course of the ten-year economic boom, he had allowed his organization to become a little lax.

Take corporate budgeting. Hiram still smiled when he recalled his first day of interviews with Rainbarrel's executives. It immediately became obvious that the place had no budget integrity whatsoever. One unit head had said outright, "Look, none of us fights very hard at budget time, because after three or four months, nobody looks at the budget anyway." Barely concealing his shock, Hiram asked how that could be; what did they look at, then? The answer was that they operated according to one simple rule: "If it's a good idea, we say yes to it. If it's a bad idea, we say no."

"And what happens," Hiram had pressed, "when you run out of money halfway through the year?" The fellow rubbed his chin and took a moment to think before answering. "I guess we've always run out of good ideas before we've run out of money." Unbelievable!

"Fat and happy" was how Hiram characterized Rainbarrel in a conversation with the headhunter who had recruited him. Of course, he wouldn't use those words in the CEC meeting. That would sound too disparaging. In fact, he'd quickly fallen in love with Rainbarrel and the opportunities it presented. Here was a company that had the potential for greatness but that was held back by a lack of discipline. It was like a racehorse that had the potential to be a Secretariat but lacked a structured training regimen. Or a Ferrari engine that needed the touch of an expert mechanic to get it back in trim. In other words, the only thing Rainbarrel was missing was what someone like Hiram Phillips could bring to the table. The allure was irresistible; this was the assignment that would define his career. And now, a year later, he was ready to declare a turnaround.

Lean and Mean

Sure enough, as Hiram steered toward the entrance to the parking garage, he saw Sally and Frank in a visitor parking space, pulling their bulky file bags out of the trunk of Sally's sedan. He caught up to them at the security checkpoint in the lobby and took a heavy satchel from Sally's hand.

Moments later, they were at a conference table, each of them poring over a copy of the consultants' spiral-bound report. "This is great," Hiram said. "I can hand this out just as it is. But what I want to do while you're here is to really nail down what the highlights are. I have the floor

555

for 40 minutes, but I guess I'd better leave ten for questions. There's no way I can plow through all of this."

"If I were you," Sally advised, "I would lead off with the best numbers. I mean, none of them are bad. You hit practically every target. But some of these, where you even exceeded the stretch goal . . ."

Hiram glanced at the line Sally was underscoring with her fingernail. It was an impressive achievement: a reduction in labor costs. This had been one of the first moves he'd made, and he'd tried to do it gently. He'd come up with the idea of identifying the bottom quartile of performers throughout the company and offering them fairly generous buyout packages. But when that hadn't attracted enough takers, he'd gone the surer route. He'd imposed an across-the-board headcount reduction of 10% on all the units. In that round, the affected people were given no financial assistance beyond the normal severance.

"It made a big difference," he nodded. "But it wasn't exactly the world's most popular move." Hiram was well aware that a certain segment of the Rainbarrel workforce currently referred to him as "Fire 'em." He pointed to another number on the spreadsheet. "Now, that one tells a happier story: lower costs as a result of higher productivity."

"And better customer service to boot," Frank chimed in. They were talking about the transformation of Rainbarrel's call center—where phone representatives took orders and handled questions and complaints from both trade and retail customers. The spreadsheet indicated a dramatic uptick in productivity: The number of calls each service rep was handling per day had gone up 50%. A year earlier, reps were spending up to six minutes per call, whereas now the average was less than four minutes. "I guess you decided to go for that new automated switching system?" Frank asked.

"No!" Hiram answered. "That's the beauty of it. We got that improvement without any capital investment. You know what we did? We just announced the new targets, let everyone know we were going to monitor them, and put the names of the worst offenders on a great big 'wall of shame' right outside the cafeteria. Never underestimate the power of peer pressure!"

Sally, meanwhile, was already circling another banner achievement: an increase in on-time shipments. "You should talk about this, given that it's something that wasn't even being watched before you came."

It was true. As much as Rainbarrel liked to emphasize customer service in its values and mission statement, no reliable metric had been in place to track it. And getting a metric in place hadn't been as straightforward as it might've seemed—people had haggled about what constituted "on time" and even what constituted "shipped." Finally, Hiram had put his foot down and insisted on the most objective of measures. On time meant when the goods were promised to ship. And nothing was counted as shipped till it left company property. Period. "And once again," Hiram

announced, "not a dollar of capital expenditure. I simply let people know that, from now on, if they made commitments and didn't keep them, we'd have their number."

"Seems to have done the trick," Sally observed. "The percentage of goods shipped by promise date has gone up steadily for the last six months. It's now at 92%."

Scanning the report, Hiram noticed another huge percentage gain, but he couldn't recall what the acronym stood for. "What's this? Looks like a good one: a 50% cost reduction?"

Sally studied the item. "Oh, that. It's pretty small change, actually. Remember we separated out the commissions on sales to employees?" It came back to Hiram immediately. Rainbarrel had a policy that allowed current and retired employees to buy products at a substantial discount. But the salespeople who served them earned commissions based on the full retail value, not the actual price paid. So, in effect, employee purchases were jacking up the commission expenses. Hiram had created a new policy in which the commission reflected the actual purchase price. On its own, the change didn't amount to a lot, but it reminded Hiram of a larger point he wanted to make in his presentation: the importance of straightforward rules—and rewards—in driving superior performance.

"I know you guys don't have impact data for me, but I'm definitely going to talk about the changes to commission structure and sales incentives. There's no question they must be making a difference."

"Right," Sally nodded. "A classic case of 'keep it simple,' isn't it?" She turned to Frank to explain. "The old way they calculated commissions was by using this really complicated formula that factored in, I can't remember, at least five different things."

"Including sales, I hope?" Frank smirked.

"I'm still not sure!" Hiram answered. "No, seriously, sales were the most important single variable, but they also mixed in all kinds of targets around mentoring, prospecting new clients, even keeping the account information current. It was all way too subjective, and salespeople were getting very mixed signals. I just clarified the message so they don't have to wonder what they're getting paid for. Same with the sales contests. It's simple now: If you sell the most product in a given quarter, you win."

With Sally and Frank nodding enthusiastically, Hiram again looked down at the report. Row after row of numbers attested to Rainbarrel's improved performance. It wouldn't be easy to choose the rest of the highlights, but what a problem to have! He invited the consultants to weigh in again and leaned back to bask in the superlatives. And his smile grew wider.

Cause for Concern

The next morning, a well-rested Hiram Phillips strode into the building, flashed his ID badge at Charlie, the guard, and joined the throng in the lobby. In the crowd waiting for the elevator, he recognized two young women from Rainbarrel, lattes in hand and headphones around their necks. One was grimacing melodramatically as she turned to her friend. "I'm so dreading getting to my desk," she said. "Right when I was leaving last night, an e-mail showed up from the buyer at Sullivan. I just know it's going to be some big, hairy problem to sort out. I couldn't bring myself to open it, with the day I'd had. But I'm going to be sweating it today trying to respond by five o'clock. I can't rack up any more late responses, or my bonus is seriously history."

Her friend had slung her backpack onto the floor and was rooting through it, barely listening. But she glanced up to set her friend straight in the most casual way. "No, see, all they check is whether you responded to an e-mail within 24 hours of opening it. So that's the key. Just don't open it. You know, till you've got time to deal with it."

Then a belltone announced the arrival of the elevator, and they were gone.

More Cause for Concern

An hour later, Keith Randall was calling to order the quarterly meeting of the corporate executive council. First, he said, the group would hear the results of the annual employee survey, courtesy of human resources VP Lew Hart. Next would come a demonstration by the chief marketing officer of a practice the CEO hoped to incorporate into all future meetings. It was a "quick market intelligence," or QMI, scan, engaging a few of Rainbarrel's valued customers in a prearranged—but not predigested—conference call, to collect raw data on customer service concerns and ideas. "And finally," Keith concluded, "Hiram's going to give us some very good news about cost reductions and operating efficiencies, all due to the changes he's designed and implemented this past year."

Hiram nodded to acknowledge the compliment. He heard little of the next ten minutes' proceedings, thinking instead about how he should phrase certain points for maximum effect. Lew Hart had lost him in the first moments of his presentation on the "people survey" by beginning with an overview of "purpose, methodology, and historical trends." Deadly.

It was the phrase "mindlessly counting patents" that finally turned Hiram's attention back to his colleague. Lew, it seemed, was now into the "findings" section of his remarks. Hiram pieced together that he was reporting on an unprecedented level of negativity in the responses from Rainbarrel's R&D department and was quoting the complaints people had scribbled on their surveys. "Another one put it this way," Lew said. "We're now highly focused on who's getting the most patents, who's getting the most copyrights, who's submitting the most grant proposals, etc. But are we more creative? It's not that simple."

"You know," Rainbarrel's chief counsel noted, "I have thought lately that we're filing for a lot of patents for products that will never be commercially viable."

"But the thing that's really got these guys frustrated seems to be their 'Innovation X' project," Lew continued. "They're all saying it's the best thing since sliced bread, a generational leap on the product line, but they're getting no uptake."

Eyes in the room turned to the products division president, who promptly threw up his hands. "What can I say, gang? We never expected that breakthrough to happen in this fiscal year. It's not in the budget to bring it to market."

Lew Hart silenced the rising voices, reminding the group he had more findings to share. Unfortunately, it didn't get much better. Both current and retired employees were complaining about being treated poorly by sales personnel when they sought to place orders or obtain information about company products. There was a lot of residual unhappiness about the layoffs, and not simply because those who remained had more work to do. Some people had noted that, because the reduction was based on headcount, not costs, managers had tended to fire low-level people, crippling the company without saving much money. And because the reduction was across the board, the highest performing departments had been forced to lay off some of the company's best employees. Others had heard about inequities in the severance deals: "As far as I can tell, we gave our lowest performers a better package than our good ones," he quoted one employee as saying.

And then there was a chorus of complaints from the sales organization. "No role models." "No mentoring." "No chance to pick the veterans' brains." "No knowledge sharing about accounts." More than ever, salespeople were dissatisfied with their territories and clamoring for the more affluent, high-volume districts. "It didn't help that all the sales-contest winners this year were from places like Scarsdale, Shaker Heights, and Beverly Hills," a salesperson was quoted as saying. Lew concluded with a promise to look further into the apparent decline in morale to determine whether it was an aberration.

The Ugly Truth

But if the group thought the mood would improve in the meeting's next segment—the QMI chat with the folks at longtime customer Brenton Brothers—they soon found out otherwise. Booming out of the speakerphone in the middle of the table came the Southern-tinged voices of Billy Brenton and three of his employees representing various parts of his organization.

"What's up with your shipping department?" Billy called out. "My people are telling me it's taking forever to get the stock replenished."

Hiram sat up straight, then leaned toward the speakerphone. "Excuse me, Mr. Brenton. This is Hiram Phillips—I don't believe we've met. But are you saying we are not shipping by our promise date?"

A cough—or was it a guffaw?—came back across the wire. "Well, son. Let me tell you about that. First of all, what y'all promise is not always what we are saying we require—and what we believe we deserve. Annie, isn't that right?"

"Yes, Mr. Brenton," said the buyer. "In some cases, I've been told to take a late date or otherwise forgo the purchase. That becomes the promise date, I guess, but it's not the date I asked for."

"And second," Billy continued, "I can't figure out how you fellas define 'shipped.' We were told last Tuesday an order had been shipped, and come to find out, the stuff was sitting on a railroad siding across the street from your plant."

"That's an important order for us," another Brenton voice piped up. "I sent an e-mail to try to sort it out, but I haven't heard back about it." Hiram winced, recalling the conversation in the lobby that morning. The voice persisted: "I thought that might be the better way to contact your service people these days? They always seem in such an all-fired hurry to get off the phone when I call. Sometimes it takes two or three calls to get something squared away."

The call didn't end there—a few more shortcomings were discussed. Then Keith Randall, to his credit, pulled the conversation onto more positive ground by reaffirming the great regard Rainbarrel had for Brenton Brothers and the mutual value of that enduring relationship. Promises were made and hearty thanks extended for the frank feed-back. Meanwhile, Hiram felt the eyes of his colleagues on him. Finally, the call ended and the CEO announced that he, for one, needed a break before the last agenda item.

Dazed and Confused

Hiram considered following his boss out of the room and asking him to table the whole discussion of the new metrics and incentives. The climate was suddenly bad for the news he had looked forward to sharing. But he knew that delaying the discussion would be weak and wrong. After all, he had plenty of evidence to show he was on the right track. The problems the group had just been hearing about were side effects, but surely they didn't outweigh the cure.

He moved to the side table and poured a glass of ice water, then leaned against the wall to collect his thoughts. Perhaps he should reframe his opening comments in light of the employee and customer feedback. As he considered how he might do so, Keith Randall appeared at his side.

"Looks like we have our work cut out for us, eh, Hiram?" he said quietly—and charitably enough. "Some of those metrics taking hold, um, a little too strongly?" Hiram started to object but saw the seriousness in his boss's eyes.

He lifted the stack of reports Felding & Company had prepared for him and turned to the conference table. "Well, I guess that's something for the group to talk about."

Should Rainbarrel revisit its approach to performance management?

Case 7   Carly Fiorina: The Reinvention of Hewlett-Packard*

[W]e owe you . . . three things. We owe you a clear vision and a sense of direction, how we are going to help you be successful in the next millennium. We owe you enough focus and leverage to execute well, each and every time. And we owe you an understanding of the total experience that we provide and an understanding on our part of how to make that experience a competitive advantage for you as well as for us.

Carleton (Carly) Fiorina, CEO and President of HP, San Francisco, August 17, 1999.[1]

It was July 19, 1999, and Carleton (Carly) Fiorina, spoke with exuberance and confidence as she thanked Lewis (Lew) Platt, a 33-year company veteran for his leadership as the former president and CEO of Hewlett-Packard (HP) from 1992 through July 1999. Fiorina was the first female CEO of one of America's largest companies, the only female heading the ranks at a Dow 30 company. She did not believe in a glass ceiling, rather that competence would prevail. It certainly seemed she was right; two of the four finalists for the job were women, and Fiorina was the only one without significant computer industry experience. How did she move into the coveted position with the magnum computer company? She convinced the board of directors that computer experience was not what HP lacked; rather, it was the ability to pick up quickly and help the struggling HP develop a stronger strategic vision. She shrewdly convinced the board their skills were complementary, turning what some thought to be a negative into a positive. Fiorina was confident and poised at the helm; however, she realized that as a newcomer to HP, she needed to work diligently to maintain alignment of internal forces while at the same time move the company forward in a new direction. The former president of Lucent Technologies's Global Service Provider business, Fiorina led the Lucent spin-off from AT&T and ran the largest initial public offering (IPO) at that time, totaling more than $3 billion. Fiorina saw a unique opportunity in Hewlett-Packard; she saw an opportunity to rethink HP's approach to the market, structure, and resources the company needed to achieve its objectives.[2]

Hewlett-Packard designs and manufacturers computing and imaging solutions and services for both business and home use. There are three major businesses within HP. The first is Imaging and Printing Systems, which provides laser and inkjet printers, scanners, all-in-one devices, personal color copiers and faxes, digital senders, large format and wide printers, printer servers, network management software, networking solutions, digital photography, imaging and printing supplies and software, and other professional and consulting services. The second arm of HP is Computing Systems, which provides computing systems for both commercial and consumer use. The third arm is Information Technology services, which provides consulting, education, design and installation services, ongoing support and maintenance, outsourcing, and utility computing capabilities.[3] She knew she needed to transform HP into a fast, customer-focused maker of computers and printers and place heavy emphasis on the company's commitment to e-services.

In recent years, price competition in printers, servers, workstations, and personal computers caused growth rates to slow. On March 2, 1999, then president and CEO Lew Platt made two critical announcements: first that Hewlett-Packard would spin off their Test and Measurement division later that year, and second that he would retire after a new CEO was recruited. When Carly joined HP, Platt agreed to stay on as chairman until December 31, 1999, to assist in the spin-off of the Test and Measurement division (soon to be known as Agilent Technologies) and to assist Fiorina with her transition.

Hewlett-Packard was in need of reinvention; Carly Fiorina was the person hired to lead the charge. The company was at a pivotal point; poised to take full advantage of the Internet age, yet steadfast in its traditional core values.

> Reinvention to me is about four things. It's about culture, it's about strategy, it's about what you measure and how you reward those measurements, and it's about business process. All of those levers need to be pulled. (*Carly Fiorina, President and CEO, HP*)[4]

Hewlett-Packard had become too slow to react and position itself in the global economy of the 21st century. Platt worked hard to maintain a consensus spirit. Fiorina needed to preserve the core values that had made the company successful.

History of Hewlett-Packard

Hewlett-Packard became the foundation for the entrepreneurial fountain of American innovation now known as Silicon Valley.[5] Two Stanford electrical engineering graduates, Dave Packard and Bill Hewlett, set out on a small business venture upon the advice of their professor, Fred Terman. Professor Terman told them to "make a run for it." After a two-week camping trip to the Colorado mountains, Packard and Hewlett decided to join forces to form the seedling of what was to become known to the world

*This case was prepared by Patricia A. Ryan of Colorado State University. It was previously published in the *Business Case Journal* (2001/2002, Volume 9, Issue 2: 75–97). We wish to express our appreciation to *BCJ* for granting permission for us to use this case.

as Hewlett-Packard. They soon found there was a demand for a lower-priced audio oscillator similar to the type they had developed while at Stanford. Interestingly, the ordering of their names was determined by a coin toss in a small Palo Alto, California, garage. In 1940, total revenues were $34,000 and Dave and Bill had three employees. Business was boosted significantly by the war effort and high defense spending; HP was able to internally finance all its growth through World War II. Its expertise in microwave technology developed through the war years, and HP had little difficulty expanding its product line to meet the burgeoning electronics industry in the postwar boom. It was not until 1957 that the company went public with 10 percent of its shares. At that time, four divisions were created, divisions that remained up to the spin-off of the Test and Measurement division in 1999. In 1962, Hewlett-Packard joined the Standard & Poor's 500 where the company remains today. In 1999, revenue topped $47.1 billion, and HP employed over 124,000 workers throughout the world. (See Exhibit 1 for historical milestones.)

Walt Disney was one of its first customers with the purchase of eight audio oscillators to test the sound equipment in the movie *Fantasia*. In the 1950s, Hewlett-Packard developed its corporate objectives and began globalization of HP. The philosophy that was to become known as the "HP Way," depictive of the innovative and generous relationships with employees, was formally developed in this decade of change and growth. The company went public on November 6, 1957, with 373 products, $30 million in net revenue, and 1,778 employees. In the late 1950s, marketing emphasis was placed on European markets in Switzerland and West Germany. In the 1960s, the computing division bloomed and the Test and Measurement division became known for its progressive position in the market. Hewlett-Packard was respected as a well-managed company. The 1960s brought joint ventures in Japan and Germany. John Young was named CEO in 1978 and served in that capacity until 1992. Young succeeded in growing the company into a major computer giant. By the 1980s, the increasing global presence of HP was partially due to the onslaught of personal computers and peripherals. Hewlett-Packard strove to provide high performance at reasonable cost. In the early 1990s, Young's efforts to corral the company's independent units led to bureaucracy that bogged the company down. In 1992, the popular engineer Lew Platt was named president and CEO of the computing and measurement giant. That same year, Hewlett-Packard introduced a new atomic clock that became the world's most precise timekeeper. The remainder of the 1990s brought accelerated Web-based information and increased focus on the computing side of the company. In the very fast growth period of that decade, Hewlett-Packard struggled to keep up with all the new technological breakthroughs while operating in multiple industries. It became clear that some action would now have to be taken to streamline the company. Platt succeeded in managing HP's growth in the nineties, but missed the Internet revolution in the late 1990s.

Corporate Culture: The HP Way

Hewlett-Packard, from its early beginnings, was a company that emphasized invention, innovation, and work-life balance. However, along the road, work-life balance appeared to take a stronger position in the triad, leaving innovation and invention to suffer in a rapidly changing technological environment.

> The most important thing about HP's culture is the assumption it is built upon, namely, that people want to do a good job, a creative job, and will do so if given the right environment. (*Bill Hewlett, referenced by Lew Platt*)[6]

Hewlett's statement was central to the culture at Hewlett-Packard. This culture operated with five basic values:

- We have trust and respect for individuals.
- We focus on a high level of achievement and contribution.
- We focus on a high level of business with uncompromising integrity.
- We achieve our common objectives through teamwork.
- We encourage flexibility and innovation.[7]

Lew Platt was proud of HP's position as one of America's favorite employers and spoke frequently about work-life balance, the need for a company to assist employees to maintain the appropriate balance between their work life and home life. He felt strongly that work-life balance was important to maintain happy, creative employees and believed the employees were the most significant assets HP had.

The HP Way, as defined by top management, included six key elements. They are:

1. *Profit:* To achieve sufficient profit to finance our company growth and to provide the resources we need to achieve our other corporate objectives.
2. *Customers:* To provide products and services of the highest quality and the greatest possible value to our customers, thereby gaining and holding their respect and loyalty.
3. *Fields of Interest:* To participate in those fields of interest that build upon our technologies, competencies, and customer interests, that offer opportunities for continuing growth, and that enable us to make a needed and profitable contribution.
4. *Growth:* To let our growth be limited only by our profits and our ability to develop and produce innovative products that satisfy real customer needs.

Exhibit 1   Historical Milestones in the History of Hewlett-Packard

Date	Event
1938	Bill Hewlett and Dave Packard began working part time in a garage at 367 Addison Avenue, Palo Alto, California, with an initial investment of $538.
1940	Sales: $34,000, employees: 3, products: 8.
August 18, 1947	Incorporated, annual sales were $679,000 with 111 employees.
1951	Sales were $5.5 million with 215 employees.
November 6, 1957	First public offering, wrote first corporate objectives. Company began manufacturing in new facilities in Palo Alto, California.
1958	Sales topped $30 million with 1,778 employees and 373 products.
1959	Established first presence overseas in Switzerland and West Germany.
1960	Established first U.S. manufacturing facility outside Palo Alto, in Loveland, Colorado.
1961	Listed on the New York and the Pacific Stock Exchanges.
1962	First HP listing on *Fortune*'s list of largest U.S. industrial companies at #460.
1963	First joint venture in Japan.
1964	Dave Packard elected chairman, Bill Hewlett elected president.
1965	HP entered analytical-instrumentation field with acquisition of F&M Scientific Corporation, located in Avondale, Pennsylvania. HP sales totaled $165 million with 9,000 employees.
1966	HP Laboratories formed as the company's central research facility. It went on to become one of the world's leading electronics industry research centers.
1969	Dave Packard was appointed U.S. deputy secretary of defense (1969–71).
1970	Sales reached $365 million with 16,000 employees.
1977	John Young named president (appointed CEO in 1978).
1980	Sales reached $3 billion with 57,000 employees. Introduced first personal computer, HP-85.
1985	HP Laboratories opened research facility in Bristol, England. HP sales reached $6.5 billion with 85,000 employees.
1987	Bill Hewlett retired as vice chairman of the board of directors. His son, Walter Hewlett, along with Dave Packard's son, David Woodley Packard, were elected to the board.
1988	Company sales reached $10 billion, were listed on the Tokyo Stock Exchange, and were ranked #49 on the Fortune 500.
1989	Listed on 4 European stock exchanges: London, Zurich, Paris, and Frankfurt. Acquired Apollo Computer, workstation manufacturer. Original HP garage was designated a California State Historical Landmark in this 50th anniversary year.
1990	Opened research lab in Tokyo. Company sales were $13.2 billion with 91,500 employees.
1992	CEO John Young retires, Lew Platt named president and CEO.
1993	Dave Packard retired as chairman. Lew Platt named chairman, president, and CEO. Shipped 10 millionth LaserJet printer. Company sales were $20.3 billion with 96,200 employees.
1994	Sales topped $25 billion with 98,400 employees. Introduced HP Color LaserJet printer and HP OfficeJet printer/fax machine/copier.
1995	Introduced HP Pavilion PC for the home computing market.
1996	Co-Founder David Packard dies of pneumonia.
1997	Acquired Verifone, the industry leader in electronic-payments systems, through a stock-for-stock merger valued at $1.29 billion.
1998	Sales reach $47.1 billion with 124,600 employees. The company's Pavilion PC reached its peak in the U.S. market.
March 2, 1999	Hewlett-Packard announces strategic realignment into 2 companies.
July 17, 1999	Carly Fiorina joined HP as the new president and CEO; Platt would remain on board 6 months.
Mid-2000	Agilent's independence is achieved when Hewlett-Packard distributes its remaining Agilent stock holdings to Hewlett-Packard shareholders.

5. *Our People:* To help HP people share in the company's success which they make possible; to provide them employment security based on performance; to create with them an injury-free, pleasant, and inclusive work environment that values their diversity and recognizes individual contributions; and to help them gain a sense of satisfaction and accomplishment from their work.

6. *Management:* To foster initiative and creativity by allowing the individual great freedom of action in attaining well-defined objectives.[8]

These corporate objectives form the basis of the "HP Way," an ideology that sought to create a work environment designed to allow well-trained, innovative, enthusiastic, and competent people to give their all for the company.

With new leadership comes change, and Carly would do just that. Carly Fiorina saw that the HP culture needed to be reshaped more along the revolutionary and radical lines developed by Hewlett and Packard in 1939. In order to see revolution, the culture had to accept radical and not always popular decisions. For example, HP created the first handheld calculator, a revolutionary change; HP also created flexible work hours on the factory floor, a revolutionary change. Fiorina saw her challenge to reignite the spirit of HP and focus on the inventive nature of the original core business.

In a speech on November 15, 1999, Fiorina emphasized the need to maintain balance while focusing on innovation, invention, and change. "In many ways we are truly returning to our roots." She emphasized the changes were necessary to maintain a competitive position in the marketplace.

Top Management

The main executive offices in Palo Alto, California, serve as corporate headquarters. (See Exhibit 2 for Executive Officers and Board of Directors and Exhibit 3 for Selected Executive Compensation and Stock Options.)

Carleton (Carly) S. Fiorina, 45, President and CEO of Hewlett-Packard. She assumed that position on July 17, 1999, and on July 23, 1999, was elected to the board of directors. Prior to joining HP, Fiorina spent nearly 20 years with AT&T and Lucent, most recently as the president of the Global Services Provider business of Lucent Technologies after having worked her way up the executive ranks. Perhaps her most successful accomplishment at Lucent was spearheading Lucent's initial public offering and subsequent spin-off from AT&T. In addition to leading HP into the new millennium, Fiorina served as a member of the board of directors of the Kellogg Company and Merck and Company and was recently appointed to the U.S. China Board of Trade.

Ann M. Livermore, 41, President of the Enterprise and Commercial Business Division. One of the frontrunners to succeed Lew Platt as president and CEO, Fiorina worked quickly to maintain Livermore as an ally, naming her to her current position in October 1999. This highly visible division would be responsible for many of the e-business initiatives HP would like to take on in the immediate future. Livermore also served on the board of directors for the United Parcel Service and on the Board of Visitors of the Kenan-Flagler Business School at the University of North Carolina in Chapel Hill.

Antonio M. Perez, 54, President of Consumer Business. Appointed by Fiorina in November 1999, Perez had previously served HP in the capacity of general manager and later president of Inkjet Imaging Solutions.

Carolyn M. Ticknor, 52, President of Imaging and Printing Systems. Ticknor was known as a take-no-prisoners operations whiz. Her goal is to pioneer e-publishing, the ability to manipulate images in cyberspace.[9]

Duane E. Zitzer, 52, President of the Computer Products division. Zitzer served HP as general manager of the Personal Information Products Group since 1996. The most recent promotion came one month after Platt announced the spin-off of the Test and Measurement business into what became known as Agilent Technologies.

Robert P. Wayman, 54, Executive Vice President of Finance and Administration and Chief Financial Officer (CFO). Additionally, Wayman has served on HP's board of directors since 1993. He has held the position as CFO since 1984. Wayman was an outside member of the board of directors of Sybase, Inc., and CNF Transportation. Finally, he is active in academia, serving as a member of the Kellogg Advisory Board to Northwestern University School of Business.

Raymond W. Cookingham, 56, Controller and Vice President. Cookingham has served as controller since 1986 and was elected a vice president in 1993.

Susan D. Bowick, 51, Vice President of Human Resources. Bowick was elected a vice president in November 1999. She previously served as business personnel manager for the Computer Organization and personnel manager for the San Diego site.

Debra L. Dunn, 43, Vice President and General Manager, Strategy and Corporate Operations. Dunn was elected vice president in November 1999. Prior to that, she served as general manager of HP's Executive Staff and manager of the Video Communications Division. She joined HP in 1994.

William V. Russell, 47, Vice President of Enterprise Systems and Software. Russell was appointed to his current

Exhibit 2   **Executive Officers and Board of Directors**

Executive Officers		
Name	**Title, Background**	**Executive Since**
Stephen L. Squires	Vice President, Chief Science Officer	2000
Carleton S. Fiorina, 45	President and Chief Executive Officer	1999
Ann M. Livermore, 41	President, Enterprise and Commercial Business	1995
Antonio M. Perez, 54	President, Consumer Business	1995
Carolyn M. Ticknor, 52	President, Imaging and Printing Systems	1995
Duane E. Zitzner, 52	President, Computing Systems	1996
Robert P. Wayman, 54	Executive Vice President, Finance, and CFO	1984
Raymond W. Cookingham, 56	Vice President and Controller	1986
Susan D. Bowick, 51	Vice President, Human Resources	1993
Debra L. Dunn, 43	Vice President and General Manager, Strategy and Corporate Operations	1999
William V. Russell, 47	Vice President, Enterprise Systems and Software	1998
Joshi Vyomesh	President of Imaging and Printing Systems Business	1980

Board of Directors		
Name	**Inside or Outside Director**	**Affiliation**
Carleton S. Fiorina, 45	Inside	President and CEO, HP
Robert P. Wayman, 54	Inside	Executive Vice President, Finance, HP
Philip M. Condit, 57	Outside	Chairman and CEO, The Boeing Company
Patricia C. Dunn, 46	Outside	Chairman and co-CEO, Barclays Global Investors
Sam Ginn, 62	Outside	Vodafone AirTouch
Richard A. Hackborn, 62	Outside	Designated Chairman, HP, effective January 2000
Walter B. Hewlett, 55	Outside	Chairman, Vermont Telephone
George A. Keyworth II, 60	Outside	Chairman and Senior Fellow, The Progress & Freedom Foundation
Susan Packard Orr, 53	Outside	President, Technology Resource Assistance Center
Lewis E. Platt, 58	Inside	Retiring Chairman as of December 31, 1999
Thomas E. Everhart, 67	Outside	President Emeritus, California Institute of Technology, retired September 1999
David M. Lawrence, MD	Outside	Chairman and CEO, Kaiser Foundation Health Plans, Inc., Kaiser Foundation Hospitals
John B. Fcry, 70	Outside	Retired Chairman and CEO, Boise Cascade Corporation, retiring from the Board February 2000
Jean-Paul G. Gimon	Outside	Retired General Representative in North America, Credit Lyonnais SA, retiring February 2000

Source: 1999 10-K, pages 55–56, and 1999 Annual Report.

Exhibit 3 Hewlett-Packard's Executive Compensation and Stock Options for the Fiscal Year Ending October 31, 1999

Name	Year	Annual Compensation		Long Term & Other Compensation	
		Salary	Bonus	Restricted Stock Award	Other Compensation[5]
Carleton S. Fiorina, President, CEO, Director[1]	1999	$ 287,933	$ 366,438	$65,557,400[4]	$3,223,867
Lewis E. Platt, Former Chairman, President, and CEO[2]	1999	$1,000,000	$3,114,721	$ 1,298,501	$ 600,089
	1998	$1,000,000	$ 910,700	$ 2,265,258	$ 6,491
	1997	$1,700,000	$ 111,435	$ 2,712,071	$ 6,427
Robert P. Wayman, Executive Vice President, CFO, Director	1999	$ 930,000	$ 471,590	$ 4,208,840	$ 264,384
	1998	$ 997,625	$ 147,804	$ 1,289,516	$ 6,491
	1997	$ 968,750	$ 63,550	$ 1,360,426	$ 6,427
Antonio M. Perez, President, Consumer Business	1999	$ 530,875	$ 431,066	$ 1,301,374	$ 6,485
	1998	$ 600,875	$ 33,055	$ 926,250	$ 6,491
	1997	$ 517,500	$ 33,964	$ 679,936	$ 6,427
Carolyn M. Ticknor, President, Imaging and Printing Systems	1999	$ 603,125	$ 310,773	$ 1,897,088	$ 9,303
	1998	$ 629,250	$ 34,612	$ 1,185,025	$ 6,283
	1997	$ 538,750	$ 35,364	$ 654,834	$ 6,427
Edward W. Barnholt, Former Executive Vice President[3]	1999	$ 920,635	$ 474,684	$ 416,589	$ 313,892
	1998	$ 759,488	$ 115,754	$ 967,581	$ 6,491
	1997	$ 702,500	$ 46,092	$ 1,083,627	$ 6,427

[1]Ms. Fiorina was elected President and CEO effective July 17, 1999, and a director effective July 23, 1999.

[2]Mr. Platt resigned as President and CEO effective July 31, 1999, and as Chairman effective December 31, 1999.

[3]Mr. Barnholt resigned as Executive Vice President effective October 31, 1999, and was appointed CEO of Agilent Technologies effective May 4, 1999.

[4]Ms. Fiorina received 290,000 shares of restricted stock and 290,000 shares of unrestricted stock units, which vest annually over a 3-year period with an aggregate value of $65,557,400 at the time of the grant. These shares were provided in order to partially compensate her for stock and options she forfeited upon her departure from Lucent Technologies.

[5]These amounts include a $3 million signing bonus for Ms. Fiorina, mortgage assistance of $36,343, relocation allowance of $187,500, and $24,000 for term life insurance for Ms. Fiorina. Other executives received compensation in 401(k) retirement plans, term life insurance, and accrued sick leave payments.

Source: 1999 Notice of Annual Meeting and Proxy Statement, pp. 27–31.

position in October 1999. Prior to that, he was the general manager of Europe, Asia, and the Middle East for the Computer Systems organization and later the general manager for the Enterprise Systems Group.

Stephen L. Squires, Vice President, Chief Science Officer, 2000. Squires is well known as an architect of the Strategic Computing and High Performance Computing programs that work with the Internet, maximizing performance and speed. He has also worked on long-term strategic issues that involve joint issues in biology, information technology, and the physical sciences. An accomplished scientist, Squires has also worked to provide technical leadership in information security.

Joshi Vyomesh, President of Imaging and Printing Systems Business. Vyomesh joined HP in 1980 as Research and Development scientist and has worked his way up the ranks mainly through the Inkjet business. He led the team that developed the first HP color inkjet cartridge and, in 1995, led HP's entry into the digital imaging business. More recently, Vyomesh led the company's Inkjet Systems business as well as the latest efforts in digital imaging including the development of the digital camera, photo scanner, and photo printer offerings.

Board of Directors

Hewlett-Packard's Board of Directors consisted of 14 members with the majority of them outside directors. Inside directors include President and CEO Fiorina and CFO Wayman. Other board members are listed in Exhibit 2. The board of directors represents a widely diverse group of industries including aircraft manufacturing, financial services, technology, medical, and education. Family members Walter Hewlett, son of co-founder Bill Hewlett, and Susan Packard Orr, daughter of Bill Packard, sit on the board.

The Tightening Computer Hardware Industry

The computer hardware industry was very competitive throughout the 1990s. The main PC players in 1999 were Dell, Compaq, Gateway, IBM, and HP. In 1999, Dell enjoyed the largest market share of PC shipments of 17.1 percent, up from 13.4 percent in 1998. Compaq was second with a 15.3 percent market share in 1999 compared with 15 percent in 1998. Gateway came in third, accruing a market share of 9.3 percent in 1999, up from 8.2 percent in 1998. Hewlett-Packard came in fourth with 8.2 percent market share in 1999, down from 8.4 percent in 1998. Finally, IBM dropped market share from 8.9 percent in 1998 to 7.6 percent in 1999. In sum, both Hewlett-Packard and IBM lost market share, while Dell, Compaq, and Gateway gained. All five companies saw unit sales increase in 1999 over 1998 with Dell enjoying a 56.5 percent increase, Gateway a 40.1 percent increase, Compaq a 24.9 percent increase, Hewlett-Packard a 19.4 percent increase, and IBM a 5.3 percent increase.[10] These numbers show that significant increases in unit sales translate to small changes in market share; for example, Compaq saw a 24.9 percent increase in unit sales, but only a 0.3 percent increase in market share. Hewlett-Packard and IBM both saw unit sale increases, but market share losses. These numbers reflect a growing industry and indicate that it is difficult to increase market share via increased sales. There are more smaller competitors entering the market each year, making market share points harder and harder to come by; however, Hewlett-Packard has good name recognition as do the other leaders in the market. Therefore, they have the opportunity to leverage their brand name into increased revenue and market share if they operate efficiently and strategically in this ever-tightening market.

Lew Platt's Era

Lew Platt was not HP's first choice to replace John Young as CEO in 1992. Their first choice was Dick Hackborn, who had built their industry-leading printer business from scratch. Hackborn declined the position and HP then chose Platt, a competent yet low-key manager and conservative dresser who some believed lacked the innovation of Hackborn. Platt was a competent leader, but did not catch onto the Internet revolution until too late, which left HP in a secondary position in 1999.[11] Platt was wise to see the need to split HP into two divisions, divesting the company of the Test and Measurement division that they started years earlier. Platt was able to make this decision with the clarity and foresight that few top CEOs would recognize, shrinking the size of his empire down to allow a new CEO to come in and reinvigorate the company.

After two years of spotty growth, Platt's move to separate the two companies and leave HP was seen as a bold move, one that placed HP ahead of personal goals. Clearly a successful CEO, he would have other opportunities, and at 58, he appeared interested in moving toward a slightly lower profile company with fewer internal pressures. At HP, there was a lot of money and market share at risk. Demand was booming in the United States and wireless communications were expanding rapidly through Latin America and Asia. During Platt's first six years as CEO, HP succeeded in tripling revenues and increasing profits fivefold.

Platt was a strong advocate of work-life balance, recognizing the difficulties many of today's working families had in maintaining the proper balance between work and home life. He attributed part of his consideration to the passing of his first wife and the realization of how difficult it was to maintain a career and be a good parent to his children. He recognized this challenge was greater in Silicon Valley than in many other areas because of the sheer speed of business development and the demand on employees to commit more than full time to their job. Along these lines, Platt expanded HP's leave of absence policies to allow for greater flexibility, developed an HP financed insurance program for elder care to assist employees caring for aging parents, provided assistance with dependent care, implemented alternative work schedules including telecommuting for employees—all with the thought of assisting the employees to better balance their work and home life. Platt clearly saw that a happy employee was an empowered employee and worked more effectively.

From an analyst's perspective, Platt agreed HP was hard to analyze since the company was involved in so many diverse areas. Known worldwide for computers and printers, HP started as a test and measurement company and kept that division until 1999. Platt was not a media personality, but rather a relatively quiet man who spoke when he had something to say. He recognized HP was now in a position in which it needed someone with more flash, a more outgoing personality, and most likely an outsider to the company. HP needed a fearless leader, one without bias, without inside allegiances, commitments, or relationships.

> In retrospect, I wish I was more rebellious. We live in a world where visibility and what you say have become more important. Leaders in the industry—Michael Dell, Scott McNealy [of Sun Microsystems]—generate a lot of interest. There's a positive aura that surrounds their companies because they're upfront. I was brought up in a world that said, "Do great things and the world will notice." *(Lew Platt, former CEO, Hewlett-Packard)*[12]

Under Platt, the vision for developing HP's presence on the Internet was developed. He believed HP's future was tied to the tremendous growth of the Internet. In a speech at the Edison Electric Institute Annual Convention in Long Beach, California, on June 13, 1999, he spoke about this exponential growth. In the past five years, approximately $70 billion of business was conducted on the Internet. Platt estimated that $2.7 trillion of business would be done via the Internet between 1999 and 2004. Platt emphasized that by 2003, 10 percent of all U.S. business would be conducted over the Internet.

The Current Situation and Industry Trends

Hewlett-Packard's main geographic offices are located in Cupertino, California; Geneva, Switzerland; and Hong Kong, with suboffices and manufacturing facilities in Colorado, Delaware, Oregon, Texas, Washington, Idaho, and Utah. International facilities include Canada, France, Germany, India, China, Japan, Malaysia, Ireland, Netherlands, the United Kingdom, Korea, Taiwan, and Israel.[13]

Hewlett-Packard's computer business, which constituted 84 percent of revenues, included personal computers, servers, workstations, and printers. Additionally, they provided service and support in each area. Their servers and workstations run both HP's version of the Unix operating system and Windows NT. Unix sales have lagged in recent years, but printer sales remained a strong point. HP was especially well known for its position in the printer market with the popular HP LaserJet and DeskJet family of printers. Hewlett-Packard dominates the printer market despite very aggressive pricing from competitors such as Lexmark. Printers were one area where the HP brand name appeared to dominate.

While enjoying annual revenue growth in the 20 percent range in the mid-1990s, growth slowed significantly in 1998 and 1999. Really facing a somewhat uncertain future, HP suffered through months of sluggish growth after the burgeoning mid-1990s, all of which placed tremendous pressure on Lew Platt. After all, the country was still in one of the largest bull markets in American history, yet HP was stagnating. Faced with inconsistent financial performance, HP needed a jump start and a strong sense of direction.

Hewlett-Packard's industry is one that demands constant change and innovation. Market share and customer base may be easily lost if the company cannot keep up with ever-changing demand. Furthermore, product life cycles are short and investment commitments are generally long term. Often management will have to accept the risk and move forward on a particular path while still uncertain about the outcome. Such decisions involve large capital investments. Transition from one product to another must be smooth and with 36,000 products in the business, HP faces enormous challenges to maintain the competitive edge in the marketplace. Inventory management is complex and requires constant updating to maintain accurate database control.

Hewlett-Packard uses third-party distributors to market and sell its products, especially personal computers and printers. The reliance on these third-party vendors is significant and HP is reliant on the financial strength of each distributor to maximize market access. While the company has maintained third-party distributorship to accommodate changing customer preferences, Fiorina realizes there are risks inherent in this decision.

Hewlett-Packard relies heavily on patent, copyright, and trade secret laws in the United States and around the world as well as agreements with employees, partners, and customers to establish and maintain proprietary intellectual property rights for technology and products. Since intellectual property provides companies such as HP with significant competitive advantage, it is critical these rights not be violated. Clearly, management faces substantial costs if such a violation would occur and must protect intangible and intellectual property as much as possible.

Over half of Hewlett-Packard's revenues are generated outside of the United States. Additionally, significant manufacturing occurs abroad. In this light, Hewlett-Packard must carefully watch international issues such as other countries' political and economic conditions, trade protection measures, import or export licensing requirements, multinational tax structures, regulatory requirements, different technology standards, foreign currency exchange rate risk, as well as unavoidable natural disasters.

Gordon Moore, founder of Intel, was the first to quantify the speed of improvement and the microprocessor. In what became known as Moore's law, he has shown how the functionality and performance of a microprocessor and similar technology doubles roughly every 18 months. While the speed of change may present its own problems, there are significant business opportunities for Hewlett-Packard because of the new challenges in the computer and peripheral market, not to mention electronic commerce. In this environment, invention must remain a top priority and HP must fund their research labs. It is common for businesses to decrease the funds allocated to research and development during economic downturns since much of these expenditures are intangible. HP cannot afford to do this; rather it must do the opposite. Research funding must remain a top priority for management because of the sheer speed of product improvement.

The Repositioning of Hewlett-Packard

In her October 1, 1999, presentation to security analysts, Fiorina outlined what was working well for HP and what areas needed improvement. She first mentioned printers and imaging products, noting that color LaserJets had done especially well over the past year. Increased market share in this area was an important focus point. Also faring well was the PC business, both home and business.

Market share was improved in Europe and in the Asia-Pacific region. Previously weak, the Unix server line was doing much better in Europe and Asia. Finally, Fiorina noted increased strength in e-services.

When discussing areas of concern, Fiorina first spoke of North American sales of the Unix server product line. To improve sales in this area, HP recently changed its compensation system for the North American sales staff and planned to implement an incentive-based compensation system in November 1999. She felt this system would work better than the salary structure many were used to and would reward and provide direction for top performers.

Second, Fiorina discussed the earthquake in Taiwan in mid-1999. While this was not an event HP could control, it had a significant impact on revenue since many of the semiconductor products were manufactured in the now destroyed facilities. This problem created a backlog problem for HP and their competitors alike. Fiorina noted the disruption was temporary, albeit significant for 1999.[14]

> Hewlett-Packard was started over 60 years ago as a company of inventors. Today, they are reinventing themselves again. They also believe the future knows no limits and guiding this vision is a CEO who perfectly represents the bold and groundbreaking spirit. If her new positions make headlines, and yes, even history, it's the history she's about to make that is the most exciting thing of all. *(Eric Chappt, Chairman and CEO, Ziff Davis, introducing Carly Fiorina as a speaker at COMDEX, November 15, 1999)*

Hewlett-Packard faces aggressive competition in all areas of business. Competitors range from the large, multinational firms like Compaq and Dell to small, high-technology specialized start-ups that sought a competitive edge in one or two product lines. Product life cycles are short, which forces constant innovation at HP. Furthermore, the consumer base is price sensitive, which can easily cut into profit margins.

> In the last quarter, HP did a good job increasing unit shipment of its Unix servers—they were up 16%. But because of price pressures, revenue increased only 5%. *(Kelly Sprang, Industry Analyst, Technology Business Group)[15]*

Fiorina faced a challenge unlike what she had faced earlier with Lucent. She successfully took Lucent public for over $3 billion, now she needed to define Hewlett-Packard in the Internet age. Unlike previous technological advances, the Internet age promised to be different. Successfully taming this animal meant reaching out to consumers with products that use the Internet. The future of information technology was to bring information technology to the masses, not the select.

The Financial Situation

Fiorina saw HP's respect and service to customers and the community as the shining soul of the company, so much so that she believed it was this that provided HP with its competitive edge.[16] Analysts have had concern about HP's asset intensity compared to many of its competitors. CFO Wayman noted that one benefit from spinning off Agilent would be to gain two distinct business models. Capital expenditures dropped in 1999 when Agilent was taken out of the equation. (See Balance Sheet, Income Statement, Statement of Cash Flows, and Selected Industry Ratios in Exhibits 4, 5, 6, and 7, respectively. See Exhibit 8a for stock price history from January 1998 through the spin-off in November 1999, Exhibit 8b for stock prices from November 1999 through December 2000.) Wall Street rewarded HP with an appreciating stock price through October 1999, when the price dropped because management stated they might not make analysts' earnings estimates for the year ending October 31. Additionally, Agilent Technologies was receiving much media attention as the largest Silicon Valley initial public offering in history, scheduled the next month. After the spin-off, HP's employee base dropped from 123,000 to 85,000.

Immediate goals for HP included aggressive profitable growth and increased consistency of financial results. Fiorina also planned to work hard to improve the total customer experience, which, if done successfully, should transfer to the bottom line. HP will also have to aggressively seek to improve U.S. sales of its Unix server line. In his address to security analysts, CFO Robert Wayman commented that the "New" HP would be more focused on growth by:

- Defending and growing our key printing and server businesses.
- Investing in carefully chosen growth opportunities.
- Continuing to demand and reward superior performance.
- Accelerating key operational initiatives.
- Eliminating redundant activities.[17]

Finally, Wayman commented that the initial ratios would likely reflect the diseconomies caused by developing two separate infrastructures, but HP planned to offset some of these expenses with reduced infrastructure costs in information technology, operations procurement, and human resources, as well as real estate and site services. Financial management must also manage risk by carefully hedging with derivatives, covering exposed positions, and holding a diversified portfolio.

Marketing

Hewlett-Packard was not known for its marketing expertise. Rather than be vocal about its products and services, HP tended to be modest and unassuming, a strategy that

Exhibit 4 Hewlett-Packard Balance Sheets, 1989–1999
(Dollars are in millions)

	1999	1998	1997	1996	1995	1994	1993	1992	1991	1990	1989
Assets											
Cash & Equivalents	$ 5,590	$ 4,067	$ 4,569	$ 3,327	$ 2,616	$ 2,478	$ 1,644	$ 1,035	$ 1,120	$ 1,077	$ 926
Net Receivables	7,847	7,752	8,173	7,126	6,735	5,028	4,208	3,497	2,976	2,883	2,494
Inventories	4,863	6,184	6,763	6,401	6,013	4,273	3,691	2,605	2,273	2,092	1,947
Other Current Assets	3,342	3,581	1,442	1,137	875	730	693	542	347	458	364
Total Current Assets	$21,642	$21,584	$20,947	$17,991	$16,239	$12,509	$10,236	$ 7,679	$ 6,716	$ 6,510	$ 5,731
Gross Plant, Property & Equipment	8,920	12,570	11,776	10,198	8,747	7,938	7,527	6,592	5,961	5,565	4,982
Accumulated Depreciation	4,587	6,212	5,464	4,662	4,036	3,610	3,347	2,943	2,616	2,364	2,089
Net Plant, Property & Equipment	$ 4,333	$ 6,358	$ 6,312	$ 5,536	$ 4,711	$ 4,328	$ 4,180	$ 3,649	$ 3,345	$ 3,201	$ 2,883
Intangibles	189	174	165	288	398	528	623	620	0	0	403
Other Assets	9,133	5,557	4,325	3,884	3,079	2,202	1,697	1,752	1,912	1,684	1,048
Total Assets	$35,297	$33,673	$31,749	$27,699	$24,427	$19,567	$16,736	$13,700	$11,973	$11,395	$10,075
Liabilities											
Long Term Debt Due in One Year	$ 468	$ 1,007	$ 254	$ 85	$ 0	$ 0	$ 20	$ 36	$ 24	$ 387	$ 51
Notes Payable	2,637	238	972	2,040	3,214	2,469	2,170	1,348	1,177	1,509	1,290
Accounts Payable	3,517	3,203	3,185	2,375	2,422	1,466	1,223	925	686	660	642
Taxes Payable	2,152	2,796	1,515	1,514	1,494	1,245	922	490	381	257	309
Accrued Expenses	2,823	4,776	4,141	3,658	3,032	2,452	2,026	1,846	1,420	1,283	1,195
Other Current Liabilities	2,724	1,453	1,152	951	782	598	507	449	375	347	256
Total Current Liabilities	$14,321	$13,473	$11,219	$10,623	$10,944	$ 8,230	$ 6,868	$ 5,094	$ 4,063	$ 4,443	$ 3,743
Long Term Debt	$ 1,764	$ 2,063	$ 3,158	$ 2,579	$ 663	$ 547	$ 667	$ 425	$ 188	$ 139	$ 474
Deferred Taxes	NA	NA	NA	NA	NA	NA	31	49	243	261	248
Other Liabilities	917	1,218	1,217	1,059	981	864	659	633	210	189	164
Total Liabilities	$17,002	$16,754	$15,594	$14,261	$12,588	$ 9,641	$ 8,225	$ 6,201	$ 4,704	$ 5,032	$ 4,629
Equity											
Common Stock	$ 10	$ 10	$ 1,041	$ 1,014	$ 510	$ 255	$ 253	$ 251	$ 252	$ 244	$ 238
Capital Surplus	0	0	146	0	361	778	684	623	758	495	221
Retained Earnings	18,285	16,909	14,968	12,424	10,968	8,893	7,574	6,625	6,259	5,624	4,987
Total Equity	$18,295	$16,919	$16,155	$13,438	$11,839	$ 9,926	$ 8,511	$ 7,499	$ 7,269	$ 6,363	$ 5,446
Total Liabilities and Equity	$35,297	$33,673	$31,749	$27,699	$24,427	$19,567	$16,736	$13,700	$11,973	$11,395	$10,075
Number of Shares Outstanding (millions)	1,005	1,015	1,041	1,014	1,020	1,019	1,011	1,003	1,006	976	951

Source: Standard & Poor's Compustat database.

Exhibit 5 Hewlett-Packard Income Statement, 1989–99
($ millions, except per share data)

	1999	1998	1997	1996	1995	1994	1993	1992	1991	1990	1989
Sales	$42,370	$47,061	$42,895	$38,420	$31,519	$24,991	$20,317	$16,410	$14,494	$13,233	$11,899
Cost of Goods Sold	28,404	29,943	26,763	24,202	18,875	14,484	11,380	8,519	7,253	6,505	5,673
Gross Profit	$13,966	$17,118	$16,132	$14,218	$12,644	$10,507	$ 8,937	$ 7,891	$ 7,241	$ 6,728	$ 6,226
SG&A Expense	8,962	11,148	10,237	9,195	7,937	6,952	6,315	5,785	5,351	5,078	4,596
Operating Income before Depreciation	$ 5,004	$ 5,970	$ 5,895	$ 5,023	$ 4,707	$ 3,555	$ 2,622	$ 2,106	$ 1,890	$ 1,650	$ 1,630
Depreciation and Amortization	1,316	1,869	1,556	1,297	1,139	1,006	743	596	555	488	435
Operating Profit	$ 3,688	$ 4,101	$ 4,339	$ 3,726	$ 3,568	$ 2,549	$ 1,879	$ 1,510	$ 1,335	$ 1,162	$ 1,195
Interest Expense	202	235	215	327	206	155	121	96	130	172	126
Non-Operating Income/Expense	708	485	331	295	270	29	25	48	72	66	91
Special Items	0	(260)	0	0	0	0	0	(137)	(150)	0	(9)
Pretax Income	$ 4,194	$ 4,091	$ 4,455	$ 3,694	$ 3,632	$ 2,423	$ 1,783	$ 1,325	$ 1,127	$ 1,056	$ 1,151
Total Income Taxes	1,090	1,146	1,336	1,108	1,199	824	606	444	372	317	322
Income before Extraordinary Items and Discontinued Operations	$ 3,104	$ 2,945	$ 3,119	$ 2,586	$ 2,433	$ 1,599	$ 1,177	$ 881	$ 755	$ 739	$ 829
Extraordinary Items	0	0	0	0	0	0	0	(332)	0	0	0
Discontinued Operations	387	0	0	0	0	0	0	0	0	0	0
Net Income	$ 3,491	$ 2,945	$ 3,119	$ 2,586	$ 2,433	$ 1,599	$ 1,177	$ 549	$ 755	$ 739	$ 829
Common Shares for Basic EPS	1,009	1,034	1,057	1,052	1,052	1,042	1,013	1,010	1,001	967	942
Common Shares for Diluted EPS	1,052	1,072	NA	NA	NA	NA	NA	NA	NA	NA	NA
Closing Stock Price, October 31	$ 74.19	$ 60.25	$ 61.63	$ 44.13	$ 92.63	$ 97.88	$ 73.63	$ 56.88	$ 50.38	$ 26.00	$ 47.75

Source: Standard & Poor's Compustat database.

Exhibit 6 Hewlett-Packard Statement of Cash Flows, 1989–1999 (Dollars are in millions)

	1999	1998	1997	1996	1995	1994	1993	1992	1991	1990	1989
INDIRECT OPERATING ACTIVITIES											
Income before Extraordinary Items	$ 3,104	$ 2,945	$ 3,119	$ 2,586	$ 2,433	$ 1,599	$ 1,177	$ 881	$ 755	$ 739	$ 829
Depreciation and Amortization	1,316	1,869	1,556	1,297	1,139	1,006	846	673	624	566	462
Extraordinary Items and Discontinued Operations	0	0	0	0	0	0	0	0	0	0	0
Deferred Taxes	(62)	(1,263)	(232)	(284)	(102)	(156)	(137)	(35)	(41)	78	(6)
Funds from Operations—Other	(171)	0	(249)	(94)	(220)	57	86	(69)	48	(43)	(181)
Receivables—Decrease (Increase)	(1,637)	(1,019)	(752)	(293)	(1,696)	(848)	(709)	(480)	(117)	(409)	(385)
Inventory—Decrease (Increase)	(171)	563	(279)	(356)	(1,740)	(582)	(1,056)	(267)	(181)	(145)	(324)
Accounts Payable & Accrued Liabilities—Increase (Decrease)	751	1	775	(55)	956	243	283	226	26	18	134
Income Taxes—Accrued—Increase (Decrease)	(639)	1,216	(63)	102	180	320	452	31	124	(52)	(130)
Other Assets and Liabilities—Net Change	543	1,130	446	553	663	585	200	328	314	47	97
Operating Activities—Net Cash Flow	**3,034**	**5,442**	**4,321**	**3,456**	**1,613**	**2,224**	**1,142**	**1,288**	**1,552**	**799**	**496**
INVESTING ACTIVITIES											
− Investments—Increase	$ 8	$ 762	$ 0	$ 734	$ 308	$ 332	$ 22	$ 53	$ 394	$ 157	$ 0
+ Sale of Investments	0	0	0	0	0	47	22	4	145	6	0
+ Short-Term Investments—Change	41	1,476	(1,055)	422	478	(366)	(351)	101	(466)	11	116
− Capital Expenditures	1,134	1,997	2,338	2,201	1,601	1,257	1,405	1,032	862	955	857
+ Sale of Property, Plant, and Equipment	542	413	333	316	294	291	215	183	163	159	120
− Acquisitions	0	0	0	0	0	62	86	411	0	0	486
+ Investing Activities—Other	(69)	75	48	22	(38)	69	23	(58)	0	(30)	(45)
= Investing Activities—Net Cash Flow	**(628)**	**(795)**	**(3,012)**	**(2,175)**	**(1,175)**	**(1,610)**	**(1,604)**	**(1,266)**	**(1,414)**	**(966)**	**(1,152)**
FINANCING ACTIVITIES											
+ Sale of Common and Preferred Stock	$ 660	$ 467	$ 419	$ 363	$ 361	$ 300	$ 308	$ 293	$ 251	$ 220	$ 223
− Purchase of Common and Preferred Stock	2,643	2,424	724	1,089	686	325	314	530	79	0	140
− Cash Dividends	650	625	532	450	358	280	228	183	120	102	85
+ Long-Term Debt—Issuance	240	223	1,182	1,989	434	64	387	309	131	90	31
− Long-Term Debt—Reduction	1,047	580	273	0	0	0	0	0	0	0	0
+ Current Debt—Changes	2,399	(734)	(1,194)	(1,178)	423	91	579	107	(778)	111	704
+ Financing Activities—Other	0	0	0	(4)	4	4	(22)	(2)	5	19	15
= Financing Activities—Net Cash Flow	**(1,041)**	**(3,673)**	**(1,122)**	**(369)**	**178**	**(146)**	**710**	**(6)**	**(590)**	**338**	**748**
Cash and Equivalents—Change	1,365	974	187	912	616	468	248	16	(452)	171	92
DIRECT OPERATING ACTIVITIES											
Interest Paid—Net	$ 1,866	$ 205	$ 325	$ 267	$ 187	$ 143	$ 109	$ 84	$ 137	$ 162	$ 108
Income Taxes Paid	224	1,039	1,488	1,159	1,058	626	293	459	335	283	484

Source: Standard and Poor's Compustat database.

Exhibit 7   **Selected Industry Financial Ratios**

Ratio	Formula	Industry
Liquidity		
Current	$\dfrac{\text{Current assets}}{\text{Current liabilities}}$	1.24
Quick	$\dfrac{\text{Current assets} - \text{Inventory}}{\text{Current liabilities}}$	0.75
Asset Management		
Inventory Turnover	Sales/Inventory	4.65
Days Sales Outstanding	Receivables/(Annual sales/360)	77
Fixed Asset Turnover	Sales/Net fixed assets	4.79
Total Asset Turnover	Sales/Total assets	1.32
Debt Management		
Total Debt to Assets	Total liabilities/Total assets	37.74%
Times Interest Charged	Operating profit/Interest changes	4.68
Profitability		
Profit Margin on Sales	Net income/Sales	2.27%
Return on Assets	Net income/Total assets	3.30%
Return on Equity	Net income/Total equity	5.55%
Market Value		
Price to Earnings	Price per share/Earnings per share	18.5

Source: Industry data from Standard and Poor's Compustat database, 1999 edition.

caused the company to slip in world markets. The company was reactive, rather than proactive, defensive rather than offensive. Recently, the company had begun to consolidate its sales and challenge management to focus on emerging markets and better capitalize on their growth. For example, in electronic commerce, HP merged with Verifone in a $1.3 billion stock-for-stock transfer. The intent of this agreement was to leverage the power of the Internet to offer new products and services.[18] Fiorina referred to the early marketing programs as modest and unassuming, and indicated the need to become more vocal about the company's abilities.[19]

Fiorina planned to institute a $200 million brand campaign in December 1999 to promote the spirit of HP. Since many of its competitors appeared to do a much better job of tooting their horns, Fiorina set out to improve HP's marketing program. The goal was to reinvigorate and relaunch the HP brand name in the marketplace as a symbol of a new, energized company moving forward into the new millennium, rather than stagnating. The essence of the campaign went back to the "Rules of the Garage" where Bill Hewlett and Dave Packard started in 1939. The campaign was designed to be a reminder of the inventive capability of the employees. Fiorina set out to not only build an organization where roles and responsibilities were clear, but where there was also a strong demand for interdependence and collaboration. The spirit she intended to present was that the company and its people were unbeatable by leveraging the company's human resource capabilities.

Carly Fiorina: Reinventing the HP Way

One of Fiorina's first decisions was to change the salary structure for HP salespeople. She instituted pay for performance rather than set salary, a move that pleased analysts such as Michael Kwatinetz of Credit Suisse First Boston Advisory Partner. "Let's face it: If you're an aggressive salesperson and you think you can blow out your numbers, you want to work in a place where you'll be rewarded for that."[20] A new logo was adopted in November 1999 consisting of a single lower case word, "invent" by the lowercase graphic of the initials "hp." The intent of this logo was partially to remind employees, customers, and investors of the company's creative roots and frugal beginnings.

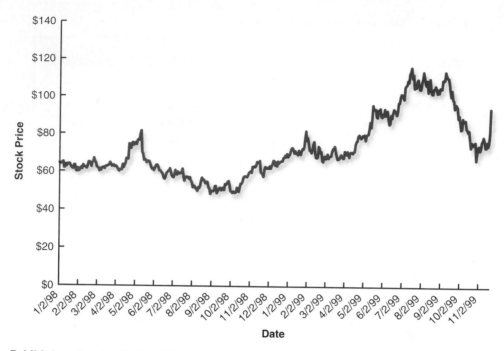

Exhibit 8a   Hewlett-Packard Closing Stock Prices: January 1, 1998–November 18, 1999

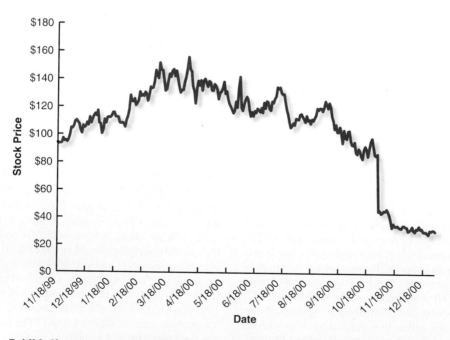

Exhibit 8b   Hewlett-Packard Closing Stock Prices: November 18, 1999–December 31,

Fiorina promoted Duane Zitzner to President and CEO of HP's Computer Products, leading the company's Unix and NT server products, enterprise storage, and software initiatives. She kept Ann Livermore as a strong ally by leaving her in charge of all e-service initiatives as well as HP's services, financing, and consulting businesses.

Ann Livermore, chief executive and president of HP's Enterprise Computing Solution, commented, "Quality of service will be one key factor in whether a company wins or loses on the Internet. The companies that win have technical innovation and business model innovation. We're creating loyalty to HP when we help businesses create their wealth."[21]

Fiorina made aggressive revenue and earnings growth goals of 12 to 15 percent for fiscal year 2000. She made it clear that she wanted to reopen Hewlett and Packard's garage philosophy and reminded staffers that the founders "didn't operate a democracy and they made very fast decisions."

Separation for Hewlett-Packard and Formation of Agilent Technologies

Hewlett-Packard wanted to revitalize its stifled business. On March 2, 1999, the company announced a strategic realignment that would essentially spin-off the Test and Measurement division of the business while maintaining the computing divisions. Test and Measurement, with an estimated $7.6 billion in annual sales, or 16 percent of revenues, consisted of several business lines including Chemical Analysis, Healthcare Solutions, and Semiconductors and would go public in November 1999 as Agilent Technologies. The new company went unnamed for four months as Hewlett-Packard attempted to realign with a new "HP Way," one that would and could keep up with the lightning fast speed of change. At the same time, Lew Platt announced that he would retire after the spin-off, allowing a new chief executive to start with the revitalized Hewlett-Packard. Hewlett-Packard would continue to focus on computing, imaging, and peripherals. The new company would take the other business units and operate independently of Hewlett-Packard. Hewlett-Packard believed this transition would allow better focus on the remaining businesses since growth rates had slowed significantly since the mid-1990s. The stock market reacted cautiously to this news with HP earning a modest gain of $0.19 on the day of the announcement to close at $68.81.

In 1966, when HP entered the computer business, few would have believed the company would one day split and the HP name would go with the computer business rather than Test and Measurement. It was 25 years after the introductions of the HP 3000 series that HP would formally reorganize and acknowledge the computer division to be its core business.[22] Times change; technology changes even faster. Hewlett-Packard opted to spin off the

Test and Measurement division to enable the remaining HP businesses to place greater strategic focus on core computing, imaging, and printing businesses. As with any major change, however, it remained uncertain as to whether or not HP would retain all the benefits the company perceived. In other words, would they regret the decision to realign, or would they gain from the decision? The key to that issue was only to become available as the future unraveled. When asked about the spin-off, Fiorina spoke in favor of it.

> Focus is crucial for a company, especially a large one. I believe it was a wise decision to spin off Agilent—making up HP's former test and measurement, medical products, chemical analysis, and semiconductor businesses. What continues under the HP name—computers, printing and imaging products, information technology services and software—has a rich history in innovation, outstanding people and technologies, and world-class partnerships. We're confident both companies will be able to innovate better and faster as separate entities. And there's no reason we can't partner on certain things. *(Carly Fiorina, President and CEO, HP)*[23]

Historically, Hewlett-Packard tended to have slowdowns every six to seven years, usually matching the business cycle. However, the Internet revolution presents a much more radical shift in the way HP will need to operate. It is about speed, agility, and the ability to change direction. The Internet economy provides a lot of uncertainty, which makes 5- to 10-year business plans difficult and of limited value. While the core of HP did not need significant change, the HP Way could hamper progress. While the HP Way made the company successful, it also could hamper growth, especially as HP moves into the new millennium. The HP Way does not promote the change that would be necessary in the Internet revolution. HP was reluctant to take risks, and carefully calculated risks were exactly what HP would need to undertake to succeed. HP would need to grow faster, sell more, and do so more profitably. Not an easy task for managers used to the HP Way.

> Ten years may sound like a lot in "Internet time," but it's not in reality—not when you're talking about something as fundamental as replacing a technology, like silicon, that will finally reach its physical and financial limits. You've got to start now or risk being left behind or missing out altogether. Basically high-tech companies have to do both: continue their efforts to extend current technologies, and to work on "disruptive" technologies that show great promise for the future. There are very few companies in the world that have the resources to do both successfully. HP is one of them. *(Carly Fiorina, President and CEO, HP)*[24]

The Future of Hewlett-Packard: To Keep the Best . . . and the Rest?

With a bachelor's degree in medieval history and philosophy from Stanford, an MBA from the University of Maryland, and an MS degree from MIT, 20 years of experience in the communications industry, two years heading *Fortune* magazine's list of the most powerful women in America, Fiorina accepted the challenge to reinvent Hewlett-Packard. She moved quickly to institute changes immediately upon her arrival. She utilized HP talent and expected her people to work as hard as she did. After four months on the job, HP announced it had narrowly beat analysts' earnings estimates for the fourth quarter of 1999 which ended on October 31, 1999. On November 18, 1999, HP announced that net income for the last quarter rose 7 percent to $760 million or $0.73 per diluted share from the $710 million or $0.68 per diluted share from the same quarter in 1998. The financial results excluded those of the spun-off Test and Measurement division, Agilent Technologies, and were a pleasant boost to Fiorina's fifth month on the job. Y2K problems remained a concern, as did the uncertainty about the success of Fiorina's changes yet to be fully implemented. However, she appeared to be off to a cautiously optimistic start. "Pieces are in place, there are no holes in the solution, but mindshare counts for a lot," commented Tony Iams, Senior Analyst, D. H. Brown Associates.[25]

The spin-off of the Test and Measurement Division, to be known as Agilent Technologies, posed certain risks for HP shareholders. The spin-off allowed HP shareholders to retain 84 percent ownership in Agilent Technologies. Agilent was scheduled to go public in November 1999 and distribute the 84 percent ownership to HP shareholders in June 2000. Since stock prices can fluctuate wildly, especially around an initial public offering (IPO), there was considerable uncertainty as to the value HP shareholders would receive in June 2000.

> Exponential growth is based on the principle that the state of change is proportional to the level of effort expended. The level of effort will be far greater in the twenty-first century than it has been in the twentieth century. (*Bill Hewlett, Co-founder, Hewlett-Packard*)[26]

Where does the future lie for HP? Hewlett-Packard must work hard to capitalize in e-services and digital imaging while continuing to aggressively defend and develop its core business. The company needs to maintain and grow its position as a global provider of computing and imaging solutions, but must focus heavily on the opportunities the Internet provides with the proliferation of e-business and e-services. The Asia-Pacific region remained a concern as did the struggling Unix server lines. Marketing would be revamped. E-services would be rev-olutionized. If it can do that and earn more, faster, and more efficiently, it will succeed. Otherwise, Fiorina may find it difficult to justify her $65 million in stock options to an employee base from many of whom she demands work on a pay-for-performance basis.

> [S]ee your life as a journey, pause at moments like this to see life's markers and the patterns that emerge, know yourself, be true to yourself, engage your whole self in everything you do. Remember that leadership is not in fact about you, but about the people you are trying to inspire by unleashing their talents, their hopes, their aspirations. Remember that leadership comes in small acts as well as bold strokes. And last, if technology is your passion, then make sure people are at the heart of your endeavors. And finally, remember that throughout this journey, the only limits that really matter are the ones that you place on yourself, and that those crucial moments of your life, when you know what you need to, but others advise against what they perceive to be a detour from your path, know yourself, trust your whole self, and don't blink. (*Carly Fiorina*)[27]

Blinking would not allow Hewlett-Packard to regain its power, grow to its potential, maximize e-service, or grow at 12 to 15 percent in 2000. Blinking was not an option for Carly in November 1999.

Endnotes

1. *HP World,* 1999, Carly Fiorina's incoming speech as President and CEO of Hewlett-Packard, San Francisco, August 17.
2. Presentation to security analysts, 1999, July 19.
3. Marketguide at http://yahoo.marketguide.com.
4. Wake-up call for HP, 2000, *Technology Review,* 103 (3): 94–100.
5. Best practices at Hewlett-Packard, 2000, *Dealerscope,* 42 (3): 57.
6. Platt, L., 1997, Managing innovation: An oxymoron? Speech at Yale University Sheffield School, February 28.
7. Ibid.
8. Hewlett-Packard corporate objectives, 1996, *Corporate Literature.*
9. Burrows, P., and Elstrom, P., 1999, The boss, *Business Week,* August 2: 76–84.
10. Hamilton, D. P., 1999, Dell beat Compaq in 3rd-period U.S. PC sales, *Wall Street Journal,* October 25: A3, A10.
11. Nee, E., and Platt, L., 2000, Why I dismembered HP, *Fortune,* March 29: 167–70.
12. Lancaster, H., 1999, Managing your career: An ex-CEO reflects: HP's Platt regrets he wasn't a rebel, *Wall Street Journal,* November 16: B1.

13. *Moody's Industrial Manual,* 1999, Vol. 1: 3579–80.
14. Fiorina, C., 1999, Presentation to security analysts, October 1.
15. Korzenowski, P., 1999, Hewlett-Packard's makeover starts turning heads, *Informationweek,* November 15: 189–92.
16. Wake-up call for HP, 94–100.
17. Wayman, R., Executive Vice President and CFO, 1999, Presentation to security analysts, September 21.
18. Standard and Poor's Compustat database, 1999.
19. Torode, C., 1999, CRN business close-up: An interview with Carly Fiorina—Hewlett-Packard," *Computer Reseller,* October 11: 176.
20. Ibid.
21. Ibid.
22. Goff, L., 1999, HP's radical move, *Computerworld,* May 3: 80.
23. Wake-up call for HP, 94–100.
24. Ibid.
25. Ibid.
26. Gouldson, T., 1999, Realignment: The HP way, *Canadian Electronics,* 14 (3): 60.
27. Fiorina, C., 2000, Commencement address, Massachusetts Institute of Technology, June 2.

On a cool and cloudy day in September 1998, Kyle Craig, the new CEO of Breckenridge Holding Company, the parent organization of Breckenridge Brewery and principal owner of its brewpubs (see Exhibit 1 for brewpub ownership details), was looking down at the article that lay on his desk. He had been reviewing recent industry data on the craft beer industry to help him determine the direction that Breckenridge should pursue. The *Denver Post* article (6/24/98), titled "Growth Bubble Burst for Craft-Brewing Industry," stared up at him. It reported that the annual growth of the microbrew industry had fallen from over 50 percent in 1995 to just 3.3 percent in 1997. "This business sure is changing," Kyle thought to himself, "and changing fast." While he recognized that no industry could maintain such explosive rates of growth forever, the reality of the precipitous decline in industry growth would have an impact on the way Breckenridge would move forward in its business.

Kyle had been hired in February 1998 by founder Richard Squire, who had been at the helm of the microbrewery and brewpub company since its inception in 1990, and Richard's longtime partner Ed Cerkovnik. From its start in 1990 in a converted gas station across the street from the base of the world famous Breckenridge Ski Area in the mountain resort town of Breckenridge, Colorado, the company had grown rapidly. Riding the tidal wave of growth in the craft brewing industry, Breckenridge had expanded its operations across the continental United States, from Colorado to Buffalo, New York, to Tucson, Arizona. Between 1995 and 1997 the company had opened six new brewpubs and grown its wholesale beer distribution to over 30 states to complement its two original brewpubs in Colorado. Driven primarily by opportunistic real estate deals and executed without a comprehensive plan, however, the brewpubs suffered from a lack of consistency, poor communication, and inefficiency. By the fall of 1998, Breckenridge had reached an annualized sales rate in excess of $15 million but was losing significant sums of cash on the brewpub side of the business. Kyle wondered whether it would soon feel the effects of the slowdown in annual growth on the beer side of the business as well.

Kyle turned to his computer and skimmed the memo he had begun to his key management staff. Most of these people had been with the company for over two years, and a few had been with Richard almost from the beginning. Several of them had extensive experience in the beer or restaurant industries. Each one recognized the variety of challenges the company faced as it moved forward within an increasingly competitive craft beer industry. Through his memo, Kyle hoped to initiate discussion among his

team about the future of Breckenridge Brewery. "I sure was optimistic when I wrote that March memo to the shareholders" (Exhibit 2), Kyle thought. "I wonder how much of that, if any, is still achievable." In his memo, Kyle asked for his staff's input regarding market conditions, opportunities, and a realistic view of Breckenridge's position in the current market. He also asked them to consider whether and how the company's strategy should change in light of the company's capabilities and resources and the current market and industry conditions. He valued their experience and insight and knew they would be affected by and would be charged with carrying out any change in the company's strategy. If the company's strategy needed to change, he wanted such a change to be a team decision.

The Craft Beer Industry

The craft beer industry[1] was highly fragmented without a dominant player, thus spurring competition among breweries and promoting quality, freshness, and variety. Because microbrewed beers were marketed for their freshness, production practices revolved around small batches and hands-on craft brewing processes under the supervision of an experienced brewmaster. Most industry brewpubs did not distribute their beers outside of the restaurants because capacity was insufficient or the cost was prohibitive, although the Breckenridge Brewpub in Buffalo did until 1997. While some observers felt the industry would most likely remain fragmented, others felt that the breakneck pace of growth was bound to slow, and that some consolidation of the industry was inevitable. Richard had anticipated this: "A shakeout is inevitable in this industry, but Breckenridge makes quality beer and has good market position. We will survive and be one of the few to remain on top."

The craft beer industry had been the shining star in an otherwise lackluster beer industry, in which overall beer sales had been flat for many years. The 51 percent growth in craft beer sales from 1994 to 1995 had dropped to 26 percent for 1995 to 1996, and by 1997 the honeymoon period had ended when the growth curve flattened to a mere 3.3 percent (see Exhibit 3). By the end of 1997, microbrews had a 3 percent market share, imports controlled 7 percent, and the large mass-production breweries (like Anheuser-Busch, Miller, and Coors) dominated the

*Reprinted by permission from The Case Research Journal. Copyright by John Mullins and The North American Case Research Association. All rights reserved.

[1] According to the *North American Brewer's Resource Directory 1997–98* (Boulder, CO: Institute for Brewing Studies, Association of Brewers, 1997) the craft beer industry included several categories: *microbreweries* produced less than 15,000 barrels of beer per year; *regional specialty breweries* like the Breckenridge facility on Kalamath Street in Denver produced between 15,000 and one million barrels per year; *contract brewers* like the Boston Beer Company hired other breweries to produce their beer; *brewpubs* were combination restaurants-breweries that sold more than half their production for on-site consumption.

Exhibit 1   Consolidated Income Statements for Breckenridge Brewpubs

Consolidated Statement of Income ($000)
Breckenridge Brewpub Business
For the Year Ended December 31, 1997

	Buffalo, NY[1]	Birmingham, AL[2]	Tucson, AZ[3]	Memphis, TN[4]	Breckenridge, CO[5]	Blake Street, CO[6]	Omaha, NE[7]	Total
Revenues	$ 1,492.1	$ 1,647.1	$ 1,646.1	$ 1,505.4	$ 1,287.0	$ 446.4	$ 328.2	$ 8,352.3
Cost of Goods Sold	508.3	463.4	461.2	442.3	349.1	143.8	113.5	2,481.6
Gross Profit	983.8	1,183.7	1,184.9	1,063.1	937.9	302.6	214.7	5,870.7
Payroll	579.2	777.1	728.8	631.7	503.2	195.7	193.3	3,609.0
Sales/Marketing	90.4	50.2	101.9	58.7	75.5	47.9	12.3	436.9
Operating Expenses	273.1	401.7	290.2	297.5	168.8	73.5	60.4	1,565.2
Rent and Occupancy	123.8	150.9	187.7	157.6	121.5	40.2	21.1	802.8
Store Level General and Administrative	36.9	42.9	45.7	47.7	13.7	9.9	17.7	214.5
EBITDA	−119.6	−239.1	−169.4	−130.1	55.2	−64.6	−90.1	−757.7
Depreciation and Amortization	129.9	290.6	297.4	150.6	59.7	20.5	38.7	987.4
Income from Operations	−249.5	−529.7	−466.8	−280.7	−4.5	−85.1	−128.8	−1,745.1
Interest and Other	91.3	83.5	48.7	30.6	54.5	10.8	2.6	322.0
Net Income before Taxes (Net Loss)	$ (340.8)	$ (613.2)	$ (515.5)	$ (311.3)	$ (59.0)	$ (95.9)	$ (131.4)	$ (2,067.1)

Consolidated Statement of Income ($000)
Breckenridge Brewpub Business
For the Half-Year Ended June 30, 1998

	Buffalo	Birmingham	Tucson	Memphis	Breckenridge	Blake Street	Omaha	Total
Revenues	$ 688.3	$ 630.4	$ 713.2	$ 824.6	$ 1,661.3	$ 576.0	$ 508.8	$ 5,602.5
Cost of Goods Sold	187.9	181.3	185.5	230.6	403.5	173.7	147.1	1,509.7
Gross Profit	500.3	449.2	527.6	594.0	1,257.7	402.3	361.7	4,092.9
Payroll	284.2	275.5	277.2	335.7	503.0	220.3	243.3	2,139.2
Sales/Marketing	62.5	46.3	48.0	81.8	97.5	52.0	45.2	433.3
Operating Expenses	182.9	176.3	156.1	196.3	217.3	106.5	124.7	1,160.0
Rent and Occupancy	66.2	59.7	104.4	126.2	110.9	42.8	51.5	561.7
Store Level General and Administrative	20.1	24.9	21.2	26.7	54.8	15.4	19.2	182.3
EBITDA	−115.7	−133.4	−79.1	−172.8	274.3	−34.7	−122.3	−383.6
Depreciation and Amortization	61.7	44.2	43.5	90.2	51.3	52.2	77.5	420.7
Income from Operations	−177.4	−177.6	−122.6	−263.0	223.0	−86.9	−199.8	−804.3
Interest and Other	8.8	41.6	33.3	19.3	47.9	11.2	−1.6	160.5
Net Income before Taxes (Net Loss)	$ (186.2)	$ (219.3)	$ (155.9)	$ (282.2)	$ 175.1	$ (98.1)	$ (198.2)	$ (964.8)

[1]Opened December 1995. 1997 figures represent total revenue for twelve months' operation. BHC owns 50% stake.
[2]Opened December 1996. 1997 figures represent total revenue for twelve months' operation. BHC owns 100% at September 1998.
[3]Opened January 1997. 1997 figures represent total revenue for twelve months' operation. BHC owns 100% at September 1998.
[4]Opened May 1997. 1997 figures represent total revenue for eight months' operation. BHC owns 100% at September 1998.
[5]Accrued June 1997. 1997 figures represent total revenue for seven months' operation. BHC owns 100% at September 1998.
[6]Acquired August 1997. 1997 figures represent total revenue for five months' operation. BHC owns 50%. Due to baseball, expected to earn $50,000 on sales of $1.6 million in 1998.
[7]Opened September 1997. 1997 figures represent total revenue for four months' operation. BHC owns 50%.

Exhibit 2   **Excerpts from Letter to Shareholders, March 1998**

Breckenridge Holding Company
471 Kalamath Street
Denver, CO 80204
303-623-BREW
Fax 303-573-4877

March 13, 1998

Dear Shareholder:

As I hit my "one month" mark as the new CEO of Breckenridge Brewery, I thought it would be an appropriate time to write to you about the future direction of the Company. Specifically, I'll try to address my early observations and our plans for the balance of the year.

As far as the current business assessment, I see an extremely strong "brand" in the Breckenridge Beer name. We are on a track for record sales of our branded beer products and through the first 10 weeks of the year our sales are up approximately 35 percent over last year. This is coming primarily in our 6- and 12-packs, and is occurring across all of our primary beers (Avalanche, Mountain Wheat, India Pale Ale, and Oatmeal Stout). Our seasonal beers, which change every two months, are also "selling out" at a record pace and we're getting ready to produce Avalanche and Mountain Wheat in a lower 3.2 percent alcohol version that will sell through supermarkets in Colorado. Our current strategy is to focus on expanding our line and adding distribution in our current states—and we're finding that this is more profitable growth than trying to add new geography. We will continue to focus on providing superior quality in our beers—and we get ongoing feedback that people are adding our products due to the strong consumer preference for our beers.

On the restaurant side, our key challenge is to drive top-line sales and bottom-line profitability in our current eight brewpubs. As you know, we've added six new brewpubs in the last 18 months, and going from a base of two to eight in 18 months has put a strain on our system. Our focus for 1998 will be to optimize sales and profitability in these existing units. We will not add any new units this year, and we plan to begin renewed expansion again in 1999 at a slightly slower pace of approximately two units per year. Several of our brewpubs outside of Colorado (most notably Birmingham and Tucson) have not met our expectations from a top-line sales standpoint. The good news is that units have had very little marketing—and in fact have low awareness in many of our markets. This is good news because I'm convinced that we can actively market our brewpubs to drive sales to significantly higher levels. We have done a lot of shopper surveys over the last six months, and we've found that consumers have an excellent food and beer experience in our brewpubs when they visit. However, if they don't know about us, it is hard to get them to visit. Thus, we will focus on aggressive marketing this year to drive our top-line sales. We have recently brought our food and labor costs in line to the point that we're convinced that when we drive incremental sales into the restaurants, we should be able to flow through almost 40 percent of the new sales to the net profit line.

We plan to drive this marketing through several activities; the principal ones are as follows:

1. **Menu Changes/Upgrades**—We will be adding new items in several of our restaurants in order to meet consumer demand and stimulate consumer news. Current products under consideration include a line of pizzas and quesadillas, new pasta dishes, barbecue, and new desserts. We will probably add two new menu changes per year.

2. **Seasonal Beers**—We will feature seasonal beers which complement our menu additions. We stand for great beer—and we have to aggressively market this competitive advantage.

3. **Facility Upgrades**—We know that our brewpubs need to be more inviting, and reflect a warmer and more distinctive ambiance. We will also be looking for ways to create a more unique atmosphere with greater emphasis on the wonderful features of Breckenridge (skiing, mountain biking, hiking, etc.). We believe we can bring a "slice of Colorado" to each of our brewpubs.

Once we drive new traffic into our brewpubs, it is then critical that we provide great food and service. Our food appears to be receiving consumer acceptance. However, our service, while good, is not distinctive—so we will embark on additional training to achieve "knock-your-socks-off" service. This combination of aggressive marketing, an exciting menu of quality foods, the industry's best beers, improved ambiance, and great service has been the formula for success in the restaurant business for many years.

In order to help us drive the business as we've described above, the Company needs to raise working capital. *Edited as proprietary information by the Company.*

One final note. We are planning on having our annual shareholders' meeting on April 20. Also indicate on the enclosed form whether or not you plan on attending the annual shareholders' meeting.

I look forward to meeting you, and if you have any additional questions, please give me a call.

Best Regards,

Kyle Craig

Exhibit 3   Craft Beer Industry Growth

	Craft Beer Market Share	Annual Growth of Craft Beer Segment
1995	2.30%	51%
1996	2.80%	26%
1997	3.00%	3.3%

Source: *North American Brewers Resource Directory, 1997–1998.*

other 90 percent of the $50 billion American beer market. Industry leaders anticipated craft breweries would continue to grow and predicted ultimate market penetration of up to 10 percent, but the annual growth rate for 1997 and excess capacity being reported by many microbreweries painted another picture. A craft-brewing industry veteran, Jim Koch of the Boston Beer Company, brewer of Samuel Adams beers, remarked that, "This [decline in annual growth] is just the beginning. I don't know if the growth rate will continue to slow, but there will be ongoing consolidation and retrenchment." Why growth had slowed was a question to which no one had an answer.

Malt Beverage Consumption and the Target Market

Like all consumer products, malt beverage consumption varied across the states, and per capita consumption figures could be used to identify regions of the United States where demand was strongest. In 1995, the West South Central region and the Mountain region had the highest annual per capita consumption rates at 22.7 case equivalents and 22.0 case equivalents, respectively. The lowest consumption rates were in the Middle Atlantic region where consumption was 17.3 case equivalents annually per capita (see Exhibit 4).

Distinct demographic trends had also developed for growth within the beer industry. According to *American Demographics* magazine, education and income were the two most significant factors affecting the consumer preference for craft beers over mass-produced beers. A 1996

Exhibit 4   Malt Beverage Consumption Figures by Region, 1995

Region	Population Total (000)	Malt Beverage Consumption	
		Total Case Equivalents (000)	Per Capita Case Equivalents
New England (CT, ME, MA, NH, RI, VT)	13,313	249,751	18.8
Middle Atlantic (NJ, NY, PA)	38,153	659,868	17.3
East North Central (IL, IN, MI, OH, WI)	43,456	883,707	20.3
West North Central (IA, KS, MN, MO, NE, ND, SD)	18,348	366,506	20.0
South Atlantic (DE, DC, FL, GA, MD, NC, SC, VA, WV)	46,994	939,683	20.0
East South Central (AL, KY, MS, TN)	16,066	299,828	18.7
West South Central (AR, LA, OK, TX)	28,828	654,467	22.7
Mountain (AZ, CO, ID, MT, NV, NM, UT, WY)	15,644	344,461	22.0
Pacific (CA, OR, WA)	40,161	713,577	17.8
National Totals	260,963	5,111,846	19.6

Source: *North American Brewers Resource Directory, 1997–1998.*

NRA survey reported that 18.9 percent of consumers with incomes of more than $50,000 reported ordering more microbrewery beer than in 1994. The same survey indicated that Generation Xers (those born between 1964 and 1978) were more loyal to craft beers, with 70 percent of those under the age of 34 preferring to purchase local handcrafted or microbrewed beers, while only 40 percent of those over the age of 55 exhibited similar buying patterns. This young and relatively affluent population spurred the rapid growth of the microbrew industry, and surveys indicated that these same individuals would continue to support fresh, flavorful microbrews.

Breckenridge Brewery's Wholesale Beer Business

Sales and Marketing   Based on surveys such as the one described above and other industry data, Breckenridge Brewery identified its target market as affluent 24- to 45-

year-olds who were well educated, interested in outdoor recreation, and relatively health conscious.

The image projected by Breckenridge Brewery emphasized an outdoor culture reminiscent of the ski town of Breckenridge, Colorado (where the business had been founded), and the Rocky Mountains. The slogan "Beer at its Peak" and labels picturing the mountain town of Breckenridge also sought to identify the microbrewery with an outdoor/ski culture and, thus, a certain market segment of beer drinkers.

Breckenridge beer was distributed in about 30 states, but the sales price per case to the distributors and shipping expense and excise taxes for each state varied considerably (Exhibit 5). Out of those states, five of them, Colorado, Arizona, Florida, Virginia, and New York, accounted for more than three-quarters of Breckenridge's total beer business (Exhibit 6). The local Colorado market generated over 50 percent of total sales and shipping costs were

Exhibit 5   Wholesale Pricing and Costs by State

State	Selling Price: $ Per Case FOB Denver*	State Excise Taxes Per Case	Shipping Costs Per Case Full Truck	Total Distributor's Cost
Arkansas	$14.25	$0.56	$2.50	$17.31
Arizona	14.25	0.36	1.30	15.91
Colorado	15.00	0.18	Negligible	15.18
Florida	13.25	1.44	2.00	16.69
Georgia	13.25	2.44	2.00	17.69
Indiana	14.25	0.26	1.50	16.01
Illinois	14.25	0.16	1.50	15.91
Iowa	14.25	0.43	1.33	16.01
Kansas	14.50	0.41	1.21	16.12
Kentucky	14.50	0.56	1.57	16.63
Michigan	14.50	0.46	1.94	16.90
Missouri	14.25	0.13	1.37	15.75
Montana	14.25	0.31	1.67	16.23
Nebraska	14.25	0.52	1.09	15.86
New Mexico	14.25	0.92	1.15	16.32
North Carolina	13.50	1.20	2.19	16.89
New York	14.25	0.47	2.50	17.22
Ohio	14.50	0.41	1.94	16.85
South Carolina	13.50	1.73	2.41	17.64
Tennessee	13.50	3.44	1.68	18.62
Texas	13.10	0.81	1.22	15.13
Virginia	14.25	0.65	2.18	17.08
Utah	14.25	0.80	1.30	16.35
Wyoming	14.25	0.05	1.30	15.60

* FOB Denver means freight costs from Denver are additional, to be paid by the distributor.

Source: Breckenridge Brewery.

Exhibit 6   Breckenridge Total Beer Sales (Brewery and Brewpub) by State

State	1997 Sales Case equivalents	$	1998 Sales (January–July) Case equivalents	$
Alaska[1]	912	11,810	—	—
Arkansas	711	8,973	984	11,866
Arizona	13,680	173,785	3,627	49,800
California	240	3,600	—	—
Colorado[2]	220,782	2,961,760	154,507	2,124,884
Connecticut	2,035	30,866	—	—
Florida	15,134	190,093	6,804	83,094
Georgia	1,435	19,377	400	5,300
Idaho	2,299	28,863	—	—
Indiana[3]	—	—	460	5,400
Illinois	6,184	84,948	2,841	40,238
Iowa	645	8,280	2,849	35,697
Kansas	5,865	75,473	3,297	44,087
Kentucky	926	12,179	1,264	17,377
Louisiana	1,535	19,785	644	8,542
Maine	147	2,132	—	—
Maryland	496	7,192	—	—
Massachusetts	2,304	28,910	—	—
Michigan	1,535	25,032	842	13,086
Missouri	9,177	111,987	2,548	34,215
Montana	2,939	42,383	1,392	19,183
Nebraska	5,766	78,010	3,511	46,359
New Hampshire	1,090	15,805	—	—
New Jersey	2,152	28,493	1,236	15,546
New Mexico	6,223	82,514	4,950	60,792
North Carolina[4]	1,680	23,580	1,250	16,494
New York[5]	17,190	239,313	2,419	25,889
Oklahoma[6]	2,400	34,935	4,793	64,749
Ohio	7,862	108,828	2,744	37,816
Rhode Island	906	12,804	—	—
South Carolina[7]	1,470	20,106	660	8,910
South Dakota[8]	1,211	15,140	1,866	24,446
Tennessee[9]	4,384	54,950	5,166	63,130
Texas[10]	10,276	121,214	7,189	88,968
Utah[11]	—	—	560	7,476
Virginia	9,899	135,291	2,017	29,960
Wisconsin	995	13,794	—	—
Wyoming	3,437	48,583	2,128	28,364
Totals	365,922	4,880,788	222,948	3,011,668

[1] Sales in Alaska started in March 1997.
[2] Includes sales from Colorado brewpubs.
[3] Sales in Indiana started in March 1998.
[4] Sales in North Carolina started in June 1997.
[5] Includes sales from Buffalo brewpub.
[6] Sales in Oklahoma started in October 1997.
[7] Sales in South Carolina started in April 1997.
[8] Sales in South Dakota started in April 1997.
[9] Includes 1997 sales from Memphis brewpub.
[10] Sales in Texas started in March 1997.
[11] Sales in Utah started in April 1998.

Source: Breckenridge Brewery.

negligible. Kyle wondered about the wisdom of distributing to so many states. "Are we spread too thin, reaping little reward from our geographic expansion? Or have Richard and Ed shrewdly set the stage to take advantage of a possible consolidation of the industry, by leveraging our distribution channels to gain market share as smaller firms withdraw from the now more competitive market?" Kyle knew this was an important question to address with his management team.

Production   Capacity had always been an issue for microbreweries. When Richard Squire had opened his first Breckenridge Brewpub, it had a capacity of only 3,000 barrels per year. Demand quickly outstripped the ability of Richard and his staff of friends. By 1992, they were selling kegs and bombers (22-ounce bottles) off-premises, but could not produce beer fast enough to meet the ever-increasing demand. They needed to expand.

Fortuitously, Richard bought an old warehouse in a run-down neighborhood of Denver, and opened a second brewpub with larger brewing capacity. Shortly after Richard's purchase of the building, Colorado won a Major League Baseball franchise, and the soon-to-be Colorado Rockies announced they would build their ballpark across the street from the new Breckenridge facility! By 1998, the no longer run-down neighborhood was a part of the rejuvenated LoDo (for lower downtown), a hotspot in Denver for nightlife. In 1996, a much larger brewery was opened on Kalamath Street, an industrial area in Denver, to further increase overall production and to permit packaging Breckenridge beers in six-packs of 12-ounce bottles. This state-of-the-art facility had room to more than double its current 36,000-barrel output, was highly effi-

cient, and had a high-speed packaging line the equivalent of that at any large-scale brewery. Exhibit 7 shows the seasonal and growth patterns in Breckenridge's wholesale operations. Breckenridge's fresh, microbrewed beers were in ever-increasing demand.

Beer production at Breckenridge was overseen by brewmaster Todd Usry, who had grown into his job as the company had grown. Having learned his craft at the renowned Siebel Institute in Chicago, Todd, with Richard Squire's help, had developed a knack for creating successful beer recipes. Breckenridge Avalanche, the company's signature beer, had won several industry awards, and was its best seller. Three other beers rounded out the year-round product line, and were supplemented by a series of seasonal beers that quickly sold out during the short periods they were available. Richard relied on Todd to ensure that all Breckenridge beers were distinctive and consistent in their taste and quality.

Logistics   The nature of a microbrewery was to focus on freshness. Breckenridge Brewery used only pure ingredients, no adjuncts (like corn or rice), and no pasteurization. While this freshness and combination of natural ingredients set it apart from mass-brewed beers, the microbrew process sacrificed a long shelf life and required constant, costly refrigeration.

These requirements forced Breckenridge Brewery to transport its beer in refrigerated trucks, and to educate its retailers on the importance of keeping the beer cold. Costs for transportation skyrocketed when the company hit the East Coast, ranging from $2.00 per case in Florida to $2.50 in New York, when shipped in full-truckload quantities of 1,560 cases (Exhibit 5 contains average rates for

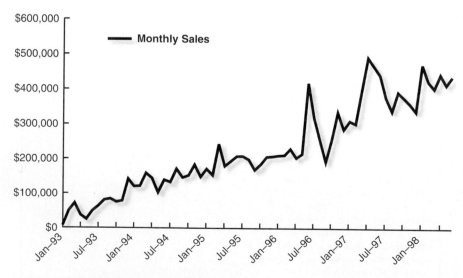

Exhibit 7   **Monthly Brewery Sales, 1993–1998**
Source: Breckenridge Brewery.

individual states). Distribution costs almost doubled when only half a truck was shipped.

In addition, the beer's life span had to be monitored and rotated so that it didn't sit on the shelf past its 100-day life, which meant shipping no less than every 45 days. This had to be monitored by sales representatives (nationwide there were eight at an average cost of $50,000 per year), distributors, retailers, and customers. The readable date label on all Breckenridge beers enabled the customer to support this process. Key product risks—freshness and distributor control—increased with the distance from Colorado. These logistical issues forced Breckenridge to constantly consider ways to lower its transportation costs and effectively manage the shelf life of its freshly brewed beer.

In spite of all these challenges, the steady growth in wholesale beer sales had put the brewery portion of the business solidly into the black, with EBITDA (on the beer side) in the first half of 1998 of nearly $400,000 and income before tax approaching half a million dollars on an annual basis (Exhibit 8).

Breckenridge Brewpubs

California, Colorado, Florida, New York, Oregon, Texas, and Washington were the most popular states for brewpubs, yet at the same time, more brewpubs had closed in California than in any other state in 1996. Industry trends seemed to show that demand was leveling off and competition was becoming more intense.

By 1998, Breckenridge Brewery was operating seven brewpubs across the country, in Buffalo, Omaha, Memphis, Tucson, and Birmingham, as well as the original units in Breckenridge and Denver (plus a small eighth one in a corner of the Kalamath Street brewery). All the locations were leased, in most cases from unrelated parties, though some landlords were either joint ventures between Breckenridge and local partners or shareholders in Breckenridge Brewery. To secure the leases, Richard and Ed had signed personal guarantees. The plan was to fulfill Richard's concept of a two-tiered marketing synergy by dovetailing its craft beers with a solid chain of restaurants. Unfortunately, the more remote units suffered from a variety of operating problems, including low or inconsistent sales and poor profit margins (Exhibit 1). Kyle believed that the profitability problems with the out-of-state brewpubs stemmed largely from low revenues: "Sales in several units simply aren't where they need to be. We appear to have a serious awareness problem."

As Kyle knew from his previous experience in the restaurant business, most customers were only willing to drive about 15 minutes to a restaurant, so brewpubs needed to be located close to customers and in areas where the target market was plentiful. As Kyle liked to say, "In the end, there are three critical success factors in the restaurant business: location, location, and location." Thus, to be successful, brewpubs had to be well located, though

they also needed to have good food, good service, attractive ambiance, and reasonable prices.

In order to gain a better understanding of the brewpubs' performance problems, Kyle reviewed the notes he had made in his earlier visits to all the locations:

- *Breckenridge:* A home-run location, across the street from the ski area. Richard lived there, knew the market well.
- *Blake Street:* Good location by accident, with the arrival of Coors Field and the Colorado Rockies. Gave Richard the idea that downtown redevelopment could be a winning formula. Traffic is down, however, when the Rockies are not playing. Three blocks from the heart of LoDo.
- *Buffalo:* In a downtown redevelopment area, but way premature. Downtown may develop some day, but has not happened yet. Dead in the evening; must do the business at lunch.
- *Birmingham:* An older neighborhood near the University of Alabama–Birmingham, one half block from the main intersection. Opened very strong, so strong that local management could not handle the business. Gained a reputation for poor service the first six weeks, from which we have not recovered.
- *Memphis:* In a downtown redevelopment, premature. Off the beaten path—three blocks from main Beale Street music corridor. Other businesses have failed in this slow-to-redevelop area.
- *Omaha:* Successful downtown redevelopment, but we are three or four blocks away. Will customers walk that far?
- *Tucson:* Adjacent to a suburban mall about two miles from the University of Arizona. Nearby resorts and condos serve an older clientele.

Kyle also thought about his own habits as a consumer. "How far am I willing to walk from one location to another when I'm out for a night on the town?"

Kyle also noted that the Breckenridge Brewery and Brewpub concept, embracing the Rocky Mountains and alpine skiing themes, was not always well identified. "Some of our units just don't communicate the Colorado image, and some lack character and ambiance." He observed that the brewpubs had developed with a "design schizophrenia" without a common theme and needed significant upgrades in order to "make the units come alive." He also noted that the menus varied widely across the seven stores. In part, this was due to differences in regional food tastes (people in Tucson, Arizona, did eat differently than their counterparts in Birmingham, Alabama, for example), but it also reflected the lack of consistency in the company's brewpub strategy.

As Kyle pondered the future of his company's brewpubs, he wondered where Breckenridge Brewery should

Exhibit 8   Consolidated Income Statements for Breckenridge Beer Business

Consolidated Statement of Income ($000) Breckenridge Wholesale Beer Business For the Year Ended December 31, 1997			
	Kalamath Street Brewery[1]	**Blake Street Wholesale[2]**	**Total**
Revenues	$2,833.2	$498.1	$3,331.3
Cost of Goods Sold	1,153.8	100.2	1,254.0
Gross Profit	1,679.4	397.9	2,077.3
Payroll	282.7	77.4	360.1
Sales/Marketing	559.1	79.9	639.0
Operating Expenses	390.4	96.0	486.4
Rent and Occupancy	153.9	41.0	194.9
Brewery General and Administrative	95.2	6.6	101.8
EBITDA	198.1	97.0	295.1
Depreciation and Amortization	141.2	62.6	203.8
Income from Operations	56.9	34.4	91.3
Interest and Other	109.4	6.7	116.1
Net Income before Taxes (Net Loss)	$ (52.5)	$ 27.7	$ (24.8)

Consolidated Statement of Income ($000) Breckenridge Wholesale Beer Business For the Half-Year Ended June 30, 1998			
	Kalamath Street Brewery[3]	**Blake Street Wholesale[4]**	**Total[5]**
Revenues	$1,792.5	$642.9	$2,435.4
Cost of Goods Sold	695.7	109.3	805.0
Gross Profit	1,096.7	533.6	1,630.4
Payroll	151.6	123.2	274.8
Sales/Marketing	285.0	119.2	404.2
Operating Expenses	241.3	113.4	354.7
Rent and Occupancy	86.0	50.7	136.8
Brewery General and Administrative	61.9	−0.5	61.4
EBITDA	270.9	127.5	398.4
Depreciation and Amortization	68.6	62.7	131.3
Income from Operations	202.3	64.8	267.1
Interest and Other	50.4	6.0	56.3
Net Income before Taxes	$ 151.9	$ 58.8	$ 210.8

[1]Figures represent twelve months' operation.

[2]Blake Street Brewpub was partially (50%) acquired by Breckenridge Holding Company in August 1997. 1997 figures represent five months' operation.

[3]Revenue up 49% over same period 1997.

[4]Wholesale revenue down 29% over same period 1997, due to shift of production to the more efficient Kalamath Street facility.

[5]Total revenue up 16% over same period 1997.

Source: Breckenridge Brewery.

focus its brewpub effort. "The two Colorado units are doing well, and clearly outperforming the others, but other regions, too, are good markets for restaurants. Are they where we need to be in the future?"

In determining future locations for expansion, Kyle also wondered where the Colorado ski mystique and the Rocky Mountain attraction provided marketing leverage. One thing Kyle—as a person born and raised in Kansas—was certain of and had said more than once, "Colorado is a vacation land for the Midwest," but that knowledge alone did not answer all of his questions. "Who are the destination skiers who come to Colorado? Where do they come from?" Stuart Close, director of brewpub marketing, had gathered some data on the origins of Colorado skiers (Exhibit 9).

Finally, the laws that existed pertaining to microbreweries and brewpubs were ambiguous and complex, and they varied from state to state. For Breckenridge Brewery, that meant that for any state in which it wanted to do business, it was necessary to contact the proper state agency and verify its current laws, production ceilings, distribution and labeling requirements, and fee schedules. While time consuming, the consequences for not contacting the proper agency meant that business could be shut down and revenues lost. According to the records kept by the National Brewers Institute, brewpubs were legal in every state except Montana and Mississippi, but several states did not allow brewpubs to distribute their microbrew to retailers or permit off-premise sales. In fact, the company had opened a brewpub in Dallas a couple of years earlier, only to later discover that doing so would prevent it from selling beer retail in Texas. The Dallas brewpub was subsequently closed.

Management Team

Breckenridge Brewery's founder, Richard Squire, had served as the company's president until February 1998, at which time he had hired Kyle Craig to replace him. Richard's creativity, vision, and energy had been key factors in the company's growth. As Caty Hayes, plant coordinator at the brewery and the company's longest-term employee other than Richard, put it, "What Richard does best is sell. He is charismatic and charming, brazen and somewhat intimidating. He motivates people to believe in Breckenridge Brewery and to work together for a common goal." With his long curly black hair and flamboyant dress, Richard was a figure not easily forgotten.

Richard's visionary nature was complemented by Ed Cerkovnik, the company's legal counsel in its early days and, since 1994, Richard's partner. In Richard's words, Ed was "the voice of sanity and reason in our company." Ed's business and legal background had been instrumental in putting together the joint ventures that owned most of the company's brewpubs, and he was the architect of the new holding company structure that hoped to consolidate the fragmented ownership of the various parts of the Breckenridge family into a coherent and cohesive operating entity.

Exhibit 9   Geographic Origin of Colorado Skiers/Snowboarders, 1997–98*

Colorado	33.19%
Texas	8.35%
International	7.95%
Florida	4.56%
California	4.10%
Illinois	3.96%
New York	3.25%
Georgia	2.14%
Kansas	2.10%
Missouri	2.07%
New Jersey	1.79%
Michigan	1.72%
Ohio	1.68%
Pennsylvania	1.63%
Minnesota	1.45%
Oklahoma	1.39%
Virginia	1.39%
Louisiana	1.24%
North Carolina	1.22%
Massachusetts	1.10%
Maryland	1.07%
Nebraska	1.05%
Wisconsin	1.04%
Iowa	0.93%
Arizona	0.92%
Indiana	0.91%
Tennessee	0.84%
Connecticut	0.78%
Arkansas	0.67%
Other states combined	5.48%

* Based on total of 12 million skier days. The average stay for out-of-state skiers is 5 days.

Source: *Colorado Ski Country USA,* 1998.

Unfortunately, however, Richard and Ed had found themselves unable to resolve the company's recent performance problems and had decided they needed help. Kyle Craig, the new CEO, was their answer. Years ago, as a freshly minted MBA graduate, Kyle had learned the necessity of making hard decisions while employed at an orange juice company. It seems the parent company had been siphoning money from Kyle's subsidiary while failing to pay the subsidiary's income taxes, and had therefore attracted the attention of the IRS. Kyle then found the cash to pay the IRS bill and promptly tendered his resignation. His subsequent work experiences were much more positive. He worked for PepsiCo's Kentucky Fried Chicken division as a general manager at a time when business was soft and the tired concept needed rejuvenation, which he helped lead. Later, at a Pillsbury subsidiary, Steak and Ale, red meat and liquor consumption were down industrywide, but Kyle's leadership helped the business remain profitable. Kyle's now 20-some years of experience had prepared him for a position like CEO of Breckenridge where opportunities were plentiful but hard decisions needed to be made and the company needed to turn around its financial performance. As partners in a cash-strapped business with several straight years of operating losses mounting, Richard and Ed had attracted Kyle by offering him stock options and a chance to build a

major brand in the still fragmented craft brewing industry. Kyle signaled his commitment to Breckenridge by buying additional stock in the company.

A next level of management that included a mix of experienced industry veterans and young up-and-comers supported the top management team. Cathy O'Hollearn, formerly a sales manager at the country's leading brewer, Anheuser Busch, was National Sales Manager. Dave Runberg, a CPA with Big Six experience, was CFO. Ron Piscitelli, director of Restaurant Operations, brought 25 years of restaurant industry experience. Brewmaster Todd Usry, who had grown into his job as the company had grown, ran the brewery. Up-and-comers Stuart Close (brewpubs) and Krisahn Gren (brewery) served as directors of marketing.

Recent Company Performance

In 1997, the company had experienced a tough year (Exhibits 10 and 11). The good news, though, was that the beer side of the business was contributing positively to

Exhibit 10   BHC Consolidated Statement of Operations (Unaudited)

	Six Months Ended June 28, 1998	Year Ended December 28, 1997
Revenues:		
Brewery	$ 642,907	$ 498,114
Restaurants	4,364,213	3,337,851
Total revenues	5,007,120	3,835,965
Operating costs and expenses:		
Cost of sales	1,474,444	1,169,256
Restaurant salaries and benefits	1,675,130	1,480,737
Operating expenses	1,378,963	1,043,855
Sales, general and administrative	754,257	673,839
Depreciation and amortization	393,248	400,434
Total operating costs and expenses	5,676,042	4,768,121
Loss from operations	(668,922)	(932,156)
Other income (expense):		
Interest income	16,345	25,361
Interest expense	(244,754)	(231,019)
Equity in losses of joint ventures*	(44,037)	(670,433)
Other	27,779	104,981
Loss before income taxes	(913,589)	(1,703,266)
Income tax benefit	—	—
Net income	$ (913,589)	$(1,703,266)

* Represents BHC share of net losses at Kalamath Street Brewery, Blake Street, Buffalo, and Omaha brewpubs, all of which are 50% owned by BHC.

Note: Brewery and restaurant revenues do not tie to the figures in Exhibit 1 due to the varied timing with which some joint venture partners' interests were acquired by BHC.

Exhibit 11   BHC Consolidated Balance Sheets
(Unaudited)

	June 28, 1998	December 28, 1997
Assets		
Current Assets:		
Cash and cash equivalents	$ 231,120	$ 467,056
Short-term investments, restricted	100,000	400,000
Accounts receivable	120,397	271,681
Inventories	348,580	302,915
Receivables from affiliates*	804,782	629,485
Other current assets	19,235	30,945
Total current assets	1,624,114	2,102,082
Property and equipment, net	4,325,967	4,149,468
Investment in joint ventures	59,931	103,968
Investment in future breweries	—	32,187
Goodwill and other assets*	4,446,900	4,885,033
Deferred charges and other assets	94,272	85,551
Total assets	$10,551,184	$11,358,289
Liabilities and Stockholders' Equity		
Current liabilities:		
Accounts payable and accrued liabilities	$ 1,417,017	$ 1,228,405
Payable to shareholders of acquired company	38,018	77,193
Accounts payable to affiliates	—	
Long-term debt due within one year	1,407,063	1,481,363
Total current liabilities	2,862,098	2,786,961
Long-term debt	3,109,767	3,230,114
Stockholders' equity:		
Common stock, $.001 par value, 20,000,000 shares authorized, 2,408,762 and 1,821,177 shares issued and outstanding as of December 28, 1997, and December 29, 1996, respectively	2,426	2,409
Preferred stock, $.10 par value, 5,000,000 shares authorized, no shares issued and outstanding	—	—
Additional paid-in capital	9,639,868	9,488,191
Accumulated deficit	(5,062,975)	(4,149,386)
Total stockholders' equity	4,579,319	5,341,214
Total liabilities and stockholders' equity	$10,551,184	$11,358,289

* Includes amounts loaned to joint ventures operating Buffalo and Omaha brewpubs.

overhead and profit (Exhibit 1), and volume had continued to grow, in spite of the slowdown in craft beer industry growth. Good performance on the beer side of the business seemed to be continuing into the last half of 1998. The brewpubs, however, were another story. In spite of strong sales in the two Colorado units, the brewpub side of the business had collectively lost more than $2 million in 1997. The result was a balance sheet that was stretched precariously thin (Exhibit 11). Key vendors and the employees were being paid on time, but some suppliers and several landlords were being asked to accept payments far beyond their terms. As Dave Runberg had said just a few days ago, "Kyle, I'm concerned about our cash position. The $231,000 we had in the bank at the end of June has dwindled further. And we know cash doesn't grow on trees."

During Kyle's first six months on the job, he and Ron Piscitelli, Director of Restaurant Operations, had made progress with the brewpubs. Menus had been reviewed and updated, and the barbecue for which the Colorado units were known had been brought to the other units. While these and other changes had improved performance somewhat since the beginning of the year, the brewpub operation remained a significant cash drain on the business. When the restaurants were short and needed cash to make payroll or buy supplies, the holding company loaned the money to the restaurants (three of which it owned only partially, in 50–50 partnerships with other entities, see Exhibit 11) in the form of intercompany payables. At mid-1998, the intercompany payables totaled more than $3 million and the total debt of the restaurants stood at $4.5 million. The company had, in the past, been able to raise additional cash when cash was needed. Kyle knew that simply was not possible now, in light of the di-minished luster of the craft beer industry and the poor performance of the company's brewpubs, and because most of the company's assets were already encumbered by bank debt. While the company still had some cash on its balance sheet, unless performance improved that cash would soon run out.

Potential Directions for Breckenridge Brewery

Kyle initialed his memo and sent it out for distribution to his staff. There were several issues he asked them to consider. The questions he posed in his memo were these:

♦ "Should Breckenridge Brewery seek to be America's brewpub, as Richard envisioned, or should we reevaluate the market, the company's strengths and resources, and the increasingly competitive industry and develop a new vision?

♦ Should we continue our strategy of dovetailing the beer and brewpub sides of business? Should one or the other be the primary engine for growth, or should both proceed side by side?

♦ What competencies and resources can we depend on to survive and grow in our increasingly competitive environment?

♦ Finally, what should be the company's geographic focus? Should we continue to aggressively expand our geographical coverage for our beers and brewpubs, or should we be more selective about where our beer is sold and our brewpubs are built?"

"These are tough decisions," Kyle thought to himself. "It's a good thing we have a strong and experienced team to make them."

Case 9   Chiquita's Global Turnaround*

On January 12, 2004, Chiquita Brands International named Fernando Aguirre as the company's new president and CEO, replacing Cyrus Freidhem who had held the position since the company's emergence from bankruptcy in March 2002. In his 23 years with Cincinnati-based Procter & Gamble (P&G), Aguirre served in a variety of positions, including president of P&G Brazil and president of P&G Mexico. In his first remarks to Chiquita employees and investors, Aguirre reiterated the importance of corporate responsibility:

> In terms of managing businesses and people, while I am profit-conscious, I make decisions first and foremost based on values and principles. In that respect, I'm proud to be joining a company with core values that guide day-to-day operations and one where corporate responsibility is an important part of our company culture. (*Chiquita press release*)

Over the past three years, social responsibility has become the moniker for this traditional company with Midwestern roots but a checkered history. Chiquita in 2004 scarcely resembled the company that once held a reputation as cold, uncaring, and indifferent, frustrated with mediocre returns, a lack of innovation, and a demoralized workforce. Throughout the 20th century, hostile relationships with its labor unions and employees and an immoral reputation solidified by the actions of its predecessor company, United Fruit, helped to slow Chiquita's growth. In addition, consumption of bananas had declined in major markets by the late 1990s, and Chiquita's position in Europe had been compromised by the European Union's (EU) preferential import relationships with its former developing country colonies. These factors helped push Chiquita to seek Chapter 11 bankruptcy protection in November 2001.

Through a serious and dedicated internal analysis, a thorough reevaluation of its core mission and business principles, and a concerted effort to reach out to some of its primary stakeholders—such as employees—who had become disenchanted and alienated, by early 2003 Chiquita had engineered the beginnings of a turnaround. One of the most impressive aspects of this recovery was Chiquita's success in redirecting and redefining its reputation through a more open and transparent approach to its global operations and the range of stakeholders with which it interacted. In addition, Chiquita had substantially reformed its labor practices and relations, and initiated a set of projects in sustainable development and community action in its various locations around the world. These steps were lauded both by labor unions and nongovernmental organizations (NGOs).

Yet, despite Chiquita's apparent turnaround, lingering problems remained with financial performance, organizational efficiency, and a strategy for the future. In short, how could Chiquita sustain the positive momentum from its turnaround in reputation and employee relations to deliver improved and sustainable business performance in a global industry environment plagued by low margins and intense competition?

Chiquita's Background

Chiquita Brands International, Inc., is a multinational producer, distributor, and marketer of bananas and other fresh produce. The company also distributes and markets fresh-cut fruit and other branded, value-added fruit products. Approximately 60 percent of its 2003 revenues of $2.6 billion are from bananas.[1] The banana division consists of 19,000 employees, who work mainly on more than 100 banana farms in five Latin American countries: Guatemala, Honduras, Costa Rica, Panama, and Colombia. Approximately 45 percent of all bananas sold by Chiquita are from owned farms; independent suppliers in Latin America produce the remainder. Chiquita is one of the global market leaders in banana supply and production (see Exhibit 1). Since Chiquita's exports are often a substantial part of the foreign trade of the Latin American countries in which it operates, relationships with suppliers, workers' unions, and communities are critical elements for success.

Chiquita sources bananas from many developing countries in Latin America, countries that historically have struggled with poverty, literacy, access to affordable health care, and limited infrastructure. The image of the banana

*© McGraw-Hill/Irwin. This case was prepared by Professor Jonathan Doh and research associate Erik Holt, both of Villanova University, as the basis for class discussion. All rights reserved. It is not intended to illustrate either effective or ineffective managerial capability or administrative responsibility. We appreciate assistance from Sherrie Terry and Michael Mitchell of Chiquita International; any errors remain those of the authors.

Exhibit 1   Banana World Market Share Leaders, 1999 and 2002 (%)

	2002	1999
Chiquita	23%	25%
Dole	25	25
Del Monte	16	15
Fyfess	8	8
Noboa	11	11

Source: Banana Link.

industry has long been tarnished by its historical support of the failed U.S. invasion of Cuba in 1961, child labor, unsafe working conditions, sexual discrimination, low wages, and accusations of serious brutality against unionizing workers.[2] Chiquita's reputation had been damaged by past events, notably those associated with its predecessor company, United Fruit. These included allegations of the company's participation in the suppression of labor rights in Colombia in the 1920s, the use of company ships in the U.S.-backed overthrow of the Guatemalan government in 1954, and involvement in a bribery scandal in Honduras in 1975.[3] In the 1980s and 1990s Chiquita clearly projected a defensive and protective culture, conveying a closed-door impression regarding its policies and practices. See Exhibit 2 for key developments in Chiquita's history.

Since bananas are produced all year long, local communities are closely tied to the performance of farms. Many employees live in company-owned houses, most of which are located on the farms themselves. In many of these areas, Chiquita provides electricity, potable water, medical facilities, and other basic services.[4] However, labor relations remained strained throughout the 1980s and 1990s.

Chiquita's Downward Spiral

Although Chiquita improved its environmental procedures throughout the 1990s, many human rights groups, including Banana Link and the US/Labor Education in the

Exhibit 2   Key Developments in Chiquita's History

1899	The United Fruit Company is created through a merger of fruit companies.
1903	Company listed on the New York Stock Exchange; it builds refrigerated ships.
1918	Thirteen banana ships are lost in World War I, after being commissioned by Allied forces in the war effort.
1941	Allied forces commission company ships for the World War II effort, and the banana industry virtually shuts down.
1945	Twenty-seven ships and 275 men lost on company ships serving the Allied forces in World War II.
1950	The company starts massive postwar banana planting projects.
1961	Company ships provide support for failed U.S.-backed invasion of Cuba.
1964	The company begins a large-scale branding program for produce and starts using banana stickers bearing the Chiquita name.
1970	United Fruit merges with AMK Corp., which had earlier acquired the John Morrell & Co. meatpacking firm, and becomes the United Brands Company.
1975	United Brands is involved in a Honduran bribery scandal, which leads to enactment of U.S. Foreign Corrupt Practices Act. Company stocks plunge and CEO Eli Black commits suicide.
1990	Name changed to Chiquita Brands International.
1992	European Union (EU) banana regulations cut Chiquita's market share by more than 50%. Company begins working with Rainforest Alliance and Better Banana project.
1994	Start of the "banana wars" between the EU and the World Trade Organization. Follows complaints by Chiquita that EU favors Caribbean banana suppliers over Latin American importers.
1998	Becomes largest U.S. private-label fruit canner. Also becomes first large company to meet with COLSIBA, an affiliation of Latin America banana unions.
1999	Faces possible auction proposed by large shareholder American Financial Group.
2000	Adopts expanded code of conduct. All 115 Chiquita-owned farms achieve Better Banana certification.
2001	Restructuring of debt after stopping payments on $862 million loan; Chiquita cites prejudiced trade pacts by EU.
2001	Files for Chapter 11 bankruptcy protection.
2001	Issues first corporate responsibility (CR) report for the year 2000.
2002	Chiquita shareholders and bondholders support reorganization plan.
2002	Issues CR report for the year 2001.
2003	Chiquita reports positive net income under reorganized company.
2003	SustainableBusiness.com names Chiquita as one of top 20 sustainable stock picks for the second year in a row.

Americas, organized an outspoken campaign against all banana companies to improve social conditions on their plantations. One morning in early 1998, executives at Chiquita were devastated to see their company splashed all over the newspapers after an undercover investigation into "dangerous and illegal business practices" throughout its Latin American operations. This was a watershed moment for Chiquita.

The *Cincinnati Enquirer,* a newspaper based in the same town as Chiquita's corporate headquarters, printed an exposé contending that Chiquita was guilty of "labor, human rights, environmental, and political violations in Central America."[5] Although the newspaper was later forced to retract the series after it was discovered that a reporter had illegally penetrated Chiquita's voice-mail system, the damage was done. The corporate image was further damaged when the firm emphasized the violation of its privacy, rather than addressing the possible validity of the claims made. According to Jeff Zalla, current corporate responsibility officer at Chiquita, it backfired. "It left some people with an unsavory impression of our company," he said.[6]

Damaging media coverage as well as a renewed desire to evaluate its own ethics performance, and gain support for a common set of values and standards for environmental and social performance served as a catalyst for the institution of corporate social responsibility policies at Chiquita. After recognizing the need for a complete corporate makeover, Steve Warshaw, then Chiquita's CEO, declared his commitment to leading in the area of corporate responsibility and pledged that the company would do much more than just repair previous damage. Four years later, and despite changes in the executive management group, Chiquita's corporate social responsibility programs are a positive example of leading change for responsibility in today's multinational business environment.

In January 2001 Chiquita announced that it could no longer pay the interest on its $862 million debt. The fiercely competitive banana industry, downward trends in prices owing to excess supply, restrictive trade quotas in the European Union, poor relations with labor unions, and the market view of bananas as a low-margin commodity all contributed to Chiquita's bankruptcy filing. Chiquita attributed much of the blame to the European Union. In 1993 the EU imposed quotas that gave a preference to banana imports from African, Caribbean, and Pacific countries that had been European colonies, ostensibly to assist the former colonies in bolstering international trade and commerce. Before the 1993 act, 70 percent of the bananas sold in Europe came from Latin America, giving Chiquita a 22 percent share of the world's banana market.[7] After the quotas were imposed, Chiquita claimed that its European market share was cut in half, costing $200 million a year in lost earnings.

Although many of its difficulties were exacerbated by the EU policy, Chiquita's problems began to develop before the 1993 decision. Most importantly, miscalculations on increases in European demand in the 1990s resulted in an oversuppy of stock which led to depressed banana prices worldwide. Although prices have recently recovered somewhat (see Exhibit 3), CEO Keith Linder blamed the $284 million in losses during the previous year on a "decline in product quality resulting from an extraordinary outbreak of disease and unusual weather patterns."[8]

Exhibit 3   Banana Prices, 2002–2003
Regional Year-to-Year Change (%)

Region	Q1 2003	Q2 2003	Q3 2003	Q4 2003	Year
North America	3%	–4%	1%	–2%	–1%
European Core Markets—US$	11	12	5	18	12
European Core Markets— Local currency	–9	–10	–9	0	–7
Central & E. Europe/Mediterranean—US$	4	–3	4	2	–2
Central & E. Europe/Mediterranean— Local currency	–15	–22	–10	14	19
Asia—US$	–7	0	3	12	0
Asia—Local currency	–18	–7	3	6	–5

Source: Chiquita Brands, company reports.

Dispute over Access to European Banana Markets

Chiquita has long claimed its recent struggles are a direct result of the European Union decision in 1993 to put restrictive quotas on imports from Latin American suppliers. Immediately after the EU's decision to extend preferential quotas to its former Caribbean and African colonies, Chiquita took the issue to the U.S. Trade Representative suggesting violations of free trade. In 1994 a General Agreement on Tariffs and Trade (GATT) panel ruled that the new restrictive quotas violated GATT obligations, but the EU blocked adoption of the ruling by the full GATT. In 1996, the United States, along with Ecuador, Guatemala, Honduras, and Mexico, challenged the new quotas under the new World Trade Organization (WTO) dispute-settlement mechanism which came into force after the Uruguay Round of GATT negotiations.

In May 1997 a WTO panel ruled that the EU bananas import tariff violated WTO obligations under the General Agreement on Trade in Services and the Agreement on Import Licensing Procedures. In September 1997 the WTO appellate body upheld the panel ruling, granting the EU 15 months, until January 1, 1999, to comply with the ruling. In January 1999, the deadline for EU compliance expired and the United States sought WTO authorization to impose retaliatory tariffs. In April 1999, the WTO Dispute Settlement Body authorized U.S. retaliatory tariffs amounting to $191.4 million a year, the level of damage to U.S. companies calculated by arbitrators. The United States immediately took steps to withhold European imports, the first step in the imposition of the tariffs.[9]

In April 2001 the United States and the European Commission announced that they had reached agreement on resolving their dispute. The agreement took effect on July 1, 2001, at which time the United States suspended the retaliatory sanctions it had imposed on EU imports in 1999. Import volumes of bananas were returned to levels comparable to those prior to 1993, and the EU has committed to moving to a tariff-only system in 2006 as part of its overall WTO obligations.

The dispute has taken its toll on the banana trade by creating uncertainty for smaller producers relying on EU markets under the quota system, and for large producers such as Chiquita who were forced to expend considerable financial and other resources in the course of the dispute.

Corporate Responsibility

Chiquita had already begun to initiate corporate responsibility projects in 1992 when it adopted the Better Banana Project standards designed to improve environmental and worker conditions on its farms. After the 1998 exposé in the *Cincinnati Enquirer,* however, Chiquita management carried out a series of broader companywide reviews of its conduct, policies, and internal and external operations and relationships, all designed to integrate corporate responsibility (CR) throughout the company's operations.

In 1998 Chiquita initiated several projects aimed at implementing its corporate responsibility efforts worldwide. Two internal groups were formed: the Senior Management Group and the Corporate Responsibility Steering Committee. The former consisted of eight top managers of Chiquita's global businesses including the president/chief executive officer and chief operating officer of banana operations. The Senior Management Group was ultimately responsible for providing strategic vision and leadership for CR. The task of the steering committee, also consisting of eight members, was to help streamline corporate social responsibility policies throughout each operational area of the firm.

In August 1999, after a year of discussions, interviews, and debates on the merits of an internal CR policy, Chiquita developed the following four core values to guide all strategic business decision making worldwide.

- *Integrity.* We live by our core values. We communicate in an open, honest, and straightforward manner. We conduct our business ethically and lawfully.
- *Respect.* We treat people fairly and respectfully. We recognize the importance of family in the lives of our employees. We value and benefit from individual and cultural differences. We foster individual expression, open dialogue, and a sense of belonging.
- *Opportunity.* We believe the continuous growth and development of our employees is key to our success. We encourage teamwork. We recognize employees for their contributions to the company's success.
- *Responsibility.* We take pride in our work, in our products, and in satisfying our customers. We act responsibly in the communities and environments in which we live and work. We are accountable for the careful use of all resources entrusted to us and for providing appropriate returns to our shareholders.[10]

In support of the four key values, Chiquita undertook reforms to link its corporate governance and corporate responsibility policies. These included expanding the role of the board of directors' Audit Committee to oversee the firm's corporate responsibility mission, and to evaluate whether it had the right people, policies, and programs in place to properly advance the CR agenda.[11] In addition, in May 2000 Chiquita appointed a full-time vice president and CR officer responsible for all aspects of corporate social responsibility. According to Chiquita, the four core values, supported by the Senior Management Group and CR committee, have helped drive the change toward responsibility throughout the entire organization.

In turn, each business decision must be evaluated through the lens of CR policies.

Chiquita also began to realize that a corporate social responsibility platform could mean a competitive advantage in the banana market. Dennis Christou, vice president of marketing in Europe, explained, "Bananas are, by definition, a commodity and U.K. consumers do not generally see fruit as branded. Chiquita is trying to change this. We have a brand because we own certain values and a relationship with consumers. And we communicate with them. They have expectations about Chiquita."[12] In particular, environmental and social performance is of keen interest to some leading European customers. In 2002, 56 percent of Chiquita's sales in northern European markets were to customers who had either inspected Chiquita's farms or formally asked questions about environmental and social performance. This is a 5 percent increase, or about 13,000 40 lb. boxes a week, over the prior year.

Chiquita also strengthened its commitment to the Better Bananas Project. Under this program, external auditors examine all Chiquita farms annually. The Rainforest Alliance has annually accredited every Chiquita farm since 2000. Chiquita also encourages its independent producers, which supply Chiquita with about 50 percent of its bananas, to achieve Rainforest Alliance certification. In 2002 the volume of purchased bananas from certified farms rose from 33 to 46 percent, and farms certified through June 2003 have brought the total to 65 percent. Exhibit 4 presents the nine principles of the Better Banana Project. According to insiders, the adoption of third-party standards

has helped Chiquita drive a stronger internal commitment to achieving excellence and to cut costs.[13] In 2003 the Rainforest Alliance estimated that Chiquita reduced production spending by $100 million as a result of a $20 million investment to cut the use of agrochemicals.[14]

And Chiquita is receiving increasing recognition for its efforts. In July 2003 SustainableBusiness.com, publisher of the *Progressive Investor* newsletter, named Chiquita to its list of the world's top 20 sustainable stock picks, known as the SB20, for the second year in a row. Sustainable-Business.com selects its picks by asking leading investment advisors to recommend companies that stand out as world leaders in terms of sustainability and financial strength. In April 2004, the Trust for the Americas, a division of the Organization of American States, selected Chiquita Brands as the winner of the 2004 Corporate Citizen of the Americas Award for Chiquita's Nuevo San Juan Home-Ownership Project in Honduras.[15]

Global Codes of Conduct, Standards, and Labor Practices

In late 2001 Ron Oswald, general secretary of the International Union of Food Workers (IUF), was asked if he had seen improvements in Chiquita's internal and external corporate policies. He responded, "Yes. It is a company that is totally unrecognizable from five years ago."[16] Clearly Chiquita had come a long way.

Traditionally, relations between Chiquita and labor unions in Latin America have been mired in conflict and mistrust. In 1998, after recognizing the need for change in

Exhibit 4   Principles of the Better Banana Project

1. **Ecosystem Conservation**—Protect existing ecosystems, recovery of damaged ecosystems in plantation area.
2. **Wildlife Conservation**—Protect biodiversity, especially endangered species.
3. **Fair Treatment and Good Conditions for Workers**—Comply with local and international labor laws/norms; maintain policy of nondiscrimination; support freedom of association.
4. **Community Relations**—Be a "good neighbor," contributing to the social and economic development of local communities.
5. **Integrated Pest Management**—Reduce use of pesticides; training for workers in pesticide use/management/risks.
6. **Integrated Waste Management**—Reduce the production of wastes that contaminate the environment and harm human health; institute recycling.
7. **Conservation of Water Resources**   Reduce and reuse the water used in production; establish buffer zones of vegetation around waterways; protect water from contamination.
8. **Soil Conservation**—Control erosion; promote soil conservation and replenishment.
9. **Planning and Monitoring**—Plan and monitor banana cultivation activities according to environmental, social, and economic measures.

Source: Adapted from Rainforest Alliance, *Normas Generales para la Certificación del Cultivo de Banano*, May 2002, www. rainforest-alliance.org/programs/cap/socios/banana-s.pdf.

the way it deals with its production workers line, Chiquita began striving to adhere to SA8000, the widely accepted international labor rights standard. Management struggled with the decision to adopt an outside standard or to develop an internal measurement gauge for CR. After much deliberation, management believed that adopting the SA8000 standard would yield the most credibility with external stakeholders, especially since it contains detailed requirements concerning the adequacy of management systems for implementation of the standards. Clearly, having an external standard forces Chiquita to push CR change down through each organizational level so it is able to meet third-party requirements.

In May 2000 Chiquita expanded its code of conduct to include SA8000. Standards now included areas such as food safety, labor standards, employee health and safety, environmental protection, and legal compliance.[17] Recognizing the importance of labor support and its resounding effect on corporate image, Chiquita began an open dialogue with the IUF and the Coalition of Latin American Banana Workers' Unions (COLSIBA). By June 2001 the firm had reached an agreement with both organizations, leading the way for continuous improvement in labor standards. Management credits this agreement as helping

to build a positive image and to improve relations with both internal and external stakeholders. In mid-2001 Chiquita published its first corporate responsibility report detailing the firm's future CR strategies and goals. Both stakeholders and media outlets have been impressed with the complete turnaround in the transparency of Chiquita's corporate agenda, leading to a much more favorable impression of the company.

In order to adhere to the core values and SA8000 labor standard, Chiquita routinely performs internal audits in all of its Latin American operations. External audits are also conduct by NGOs. After the audits are completed, each local management team must make a plan of corrective action, using the firm's code of conduct and core values as decision-making guides. Each year since 2000 the Rainforest Alliance has certified 100 percent of Chiquita-owned farms. In addition, 65 percent of the bananas Chiquita purchased from independent producers in 2003 were certified by the Rainforest Alliance, up from 33 percent in 2001. At year-end 2003 independent auditors certified Chiquita's operations in Costa Rica, Colombia, and Panama to the SA8000 standard. Chiquita's operations are the first ever to earn SA8000 certification in each of these countries.

Exhibit 5   Chiquita Brands International Balance Sheet, 2000–2003

	As of December 31			
	2003	**2002**	**2001**	**2000**
	(In thousands)			
Assets				
Cash and equivalents	$ —	$ —	$ —	$ 26,715
Other current assets	951	810	732	42,375
Total current assets	951	810	732	69,090
Investments in and accounts with subsidiaries	1,035,915	908,404	1,424,961	1,399,708
Other assets	5,607	5,429	15,328	29,872
Total assets	$1,042,473	$ 914,643	$ 1,441,021	$1,498,625
Liabilities and Shareholder Equity				
Accounts payable and accrued liabilities	$ 17,182	$ 16,541	$ 10,735	$ 86,930
Total current liabilities	17,182	16,451	10,735	125,833
Long-term debt	250,000	250,000	—	772,380
Total liabilities	285,127	285,354	992,427	916,082
Shareholders equity	757,346	629,289	448,594	582,543
Total liabilities and shareholders equity	$1,042,473	$ 914,643	$ 1,441,021	$1,498,625

Source: Chiquita Brands, company reports.

Exhibit 6   Chiquita Brands International Income Statement, 2001–2003

	Reorganized Company		Predecessor Company	
	Year Ended December 31, 2003	9 Months Ended December 31, 2002	Three Months Ended March 31, 2002	Year Ended December 31, 2001
	(In thousands)			
Net sales	$2,613,548	$1,443,049	$ 546,990	$2,242,261
Cost of sales	2,224,658	1,211,312	434,168	1,890,050
SG&A	(38,500)	(30,443)	(6,545)	(31,188)
Equity in earnings of subsidiaries (loss)	170,398	68,822	(368,899)	32,674
Operating income (loss)	131,898	38,379	(375,444)	1,486
Interest income	—	—	—	783
Interest expense	(27,392)	(20,384)	(1,250)	(81,633)
Financial restructuring items	—	—	124,394	(33,604)
Income before income taxes and accounting change	104,506	17,995	(252,300)	(112,968)
Income taxes	(5,300)	(4,800)	(1,000)	(5,800)
Income (loss) before accounting change	99,206	13,195	(253,300)	(118,768)
Cumulative effect of accounting change	—	—	(144,523)	—
Net income (loss)	$ 99,206	$ 13,195	$(397,823)	$ (118,768)

Source: Chiquita Brands, company reports.

Marketing the Message

While it would seem advantageous for Chiquita to communicate and leverage the great strides it has made through its CR effort, company management seems reluctant to promote these achievements through typical mass communication vehicles. Instead the firm has opted for a longer-term marketing strategy based on educating leading opinion makers and critics alike. Dennis Christou contends there is a natural suspicion among consumers about commercially driven messages; customers feel more trust in the message if it is delivered by an external body rather than by the company or a paid advocate of the business.[18]

That is a main reason why the firm is relying on viral marketing tactics and third-party testimonials as the means of spreading its message. Retailers are treated differently; they must be exposed to improvements at Chiquita since they determine which exclusive brand to carry on an annual basis. However, Christou believes creating brand recognition with consumers will ultimately resonate through nonobtrusive, reputable means.

Defining and conveying a brand's differences in a commodities marketplace is difficult. Nevertheless, Chiquita believes it can carve out its own niche by distinguishing itself as a leader in CR. Instead of positioning itself solely on the basis of price, Chiquita is hoping that its distinctive competency in CR will help it stand out from the pack. In this regard, Chiquita, along with Ben and Jerry's, received in April 2003 the first-ever Award for Outstanding Sustainability Reporting presented by the Coalition for Environmentally Responsible Economies (CERES) and the Association of Chartered Certified Accountants.[19]

Recent Performance and Future Path

Chiquita has drastically shifted its strategic decision-making models and broader corporate operating principles. During its reorganization, debt repayments and other reorganization costs resulted in significant losses. Chiquita has made great strides in improving its financial performance by cutting costs and streamlining its local and global operations. Net sales for 2003 were $2.6 billion, up from

$1.6 billion the year before (see Exhibits 5 and 6). Since its emergence from bankruptcy in early 2002, Chiquita has been profitable.

Chiquita's future financial stability depends, in part, on external market factors such as steady or rising international banana prices and consumer demand. Internally, the company's performance will result from the effectiveness of financial controls on the cost side, and successful marketing, emphasizing differentiation and value-added production, on the revenue side. While Chiquita has gone to impressive lengths to turn its reputation and performance around, it continues to face a challenging and competitive international business environment and must make continuous progress in its management and operations in order to achieve a healthy and sustainable financial future.

References

1. Murray, Shanon, 2002, Chiquita's exit plan jumps big hurdle, *Daily Deal,* March 5: C3.
2. Were, Marco, 2003, Implementing corporate responsibility—The Chiquita case, *Journal of Business Ethics* 44 (2/3): 247.
3. Trade feud on bananas not as clear as it looks, 2001, *New York Times,* February 7: A5.
4. Sherwood, Sonja, 2002, Chiquita's top executive, *Chief Executive Magazine,* June: 18.
5. De Lombaerde, Geert, 2001, Chiquita outlook improves following EU deal, *Business Courier,* April 20.
6. Stein, Nicholas, 2001, Yes, we have no profits, *Fortune,* November 26: 182–196.
7. Mortimer, Ruth, 2003, A strategy that's bearing fruit: When is a banana not a banana? When it's a brand, *Brand Strategy,* May 26: 40.
8. Stein, Yes, we have no profits, 182–196.
9. Goldstein, Jerome, 2003, Greasing the wheels of sustainable business, *Business Magazine,* March–April: 21.
10. Corporate social responsibility, www.Chiquita.com.
11. Sherwood, Chiquita's top executive, 18.
12. Were, Implementing corporate responsibility, 247.
13. Trade feud on bananas, B12.
14. Mortimer, A strategy that's bearing fruit, 40.
15. Chiquita earns 2004 Corporate Citizen of the Americas Award, 2004, *PR Newswire,* April 15.
16. Stein, Yes, we have no profits, 182–196.
17. Were, Implementing corporate responsibility, 247.
18. Lucas, Kintto, 2001, Chiquita brand suffers in banana wars, *Interpress Service: Global Information Network,* November 30.
19. CERES (Coalition for Environmentally Responsible Economies) Sustainability Awards 2004, www.ceres.org/newsroom/press/rep_award_slist.htm.

Case 10   Crown Cork & Seal in 1989

John F. Connelly, Crown Cork & Seal's ailing octogenarian chairman, stepped down and appointed his long-time disciple, William J. Avery, chief executive officer of the Philadelphia can manufacturer in May 1989. Avery had been president of Crown Cork & Seal since 1981, but had spent the duration of his career in Connelly's shadow. As Crown's new CEO, Avery planned to review Connelly's long-followed strategy in light of the changing industry outlook.

The metal container industry had changed considerably since Connelly took over Crown's reins in 1957. American National had just been acquired by France's state-owned Pechiney International, making it the world's largest beverage can producer. Continental Can, another long-standing rival, was now owned by Peter Kiewit Sons, a privately held construction firm. In 1989, all, or part of Continental's can-making operations, appeared to be for sale. Reynolds Metals, a traditional supplier of aluminum to can makers, was now also a formidable competitor in cans. The moves by both suppliers and customers of can makers to integrate into can manufacturing themselves had profoundly redefined the metal can industry since John Connelly's arrival.

Reflecting on these dramatic changes, Avery wondered whether Crown, with $1.8 billion in sales, should consider bidding for all or part of Continental Can. Avery also wondered whether Crown should break with tradition and expand its product line beyond the manufacture of metal cans and closures. For 30 years Crown had stuck to its core business, metal can making, but analysts saw little growth potential for metal cans in the 1990s. Industry observers forecast plastics as the growth segment for containers. As Avery mulled over his options, he asked: Was it finally time for a change?

The Metal Container Industry

The metal container industry, representing 61% of all packaged products in the United States in 1989, produced metal cans, crowns (bottle caps), and closures (screw caps, bottle lids) to hold or seal an almost endless variety of consumer and industrial goods. Glass and plastic containers split the balance of the container market with shares of 21% and 18%, respectively. Metal cans served the beverage, food, and general packaging industries.

Metal cans were made of aluminum, steel, or a combination of both. Three-piece cans were formed by rolling a sheet of metal, soldering it, cutting it to size, and attaching two ends, thereby creating a three-piece, seamed can. Steel was the primary raw material of three-piece cans, which were most popular in the food and general packaging industries. Two-piece cans, developed in the 1960s, were formed by pushing a flat blank of metal into a deep cup, eliminating a separate bottom, a molding process termed "drawn and ironed." While aluminum companies developed the original technology for the two-piece can, steel companies ultimately followed suit with a thin-walled steel version. By 1983, two-piece cans dominated the beverage industry where they were the can of choice for beer and soft drink makers. Of the 120 billion cans produced in 1989, 80% were two-piece cans.

Throughout the decade of the 1980s, the number of metal cans shipped grew by an annual average of 3.7%. Aluminum can growth averaged 8% annually, while steel can shipments fell by an average of 3.1% per year. The number of aluminum cans produced increased by almost 200% during the period 1980-1989, reaching a high of 85 billion, while steel can production dropped by 22% to 35 billion for the same period (see Exhibit 1).

Industry Structure
Five firms dominated the $12.2 billion U.S. metal can industry in 1989, with an aggregate 61% market share. The country's largest manufacturer—American National Can—held a 25% market share. The four firms trailing American National in sales were Continental Can (18% market share), Reynolds Metals (7%), Crown Cork & Seal (7%), and Ball Corporation (4%). Approximately 100 firms served the balance of the market.

Pricing
Pricing in the can industry was very competitive. To lower costs, managers sought long runs of standard items, which increased capacity utilization and reduced the need for costly changeovers. As a result, most companies offered volume discounts to encourage large orders. Despite persistent metal can demand, industry operating margins fell approximately 7% to roughly 4% between 1986 and 1989. Industry analysts attributed the drop in operating margins to (1) a 15% increase in aluminum can sheet prices at a time when most can makers had guaranteed volume prices that did not incorporate substantial cost increases; (2) a 7% increase in beverage can production capacity between 1987 and 1989; (3) an increasing number of the nation's major brewers producing containers in house; and (4) the consolidation of soft

Professor Stephen P. Bradley and Research Associate Sheila M. Cavanaugh prepared this case. Harvard Business School cases are developed solely as the basis for class discussion. Cases are not intended to serve as endorsements, sources of primary data, or illustrations of effective or ineffective management.

Harvard Business School Case 5-395-224. Reprinted by permission of Harvard Business School Publishing. Copyright © 2003 by The Harvard Business School Publishing Corporation; all rights reserved. To order copies or request permission to reproduce materials, call 1-800-545-7685, write Harvard Business School Publishing, Boston, MA 02163, or go to http://www.hbsp.harvard.edu. No part of this publication may be reproduced, stored in a retrieval system, used in a spreadsheet, or transmitted in any form or by any means—electronic, mechanical, photocopying, recording, or otherwise—without the permission of Harvard Business School.

Exhibit 1   Metal Can Shipments by Market and Product, 1981–1989 (millions of cans)

	1981	%	1983	%	1985	%	1987	%	(Est.) 1989	%
Total Metal Cans Shipped	88,810		92,394		101,899		109,214		120,795	
By Market										
For sale:	59,433	67	61,907	67	69,810	69	81,204	74	91,305	76
Beverage	42,192		45,167		52,017		62,002		69,218	
Food	13,094		12,914		13,974		15,214		18,162	
General packaging	4,147		3,826		3,819		3,988		3,925	
For own use:	29,377	33	31,039	33	32,089	31	28,010	26	29,490	24
Beverage	14,134		16,289		18,160		14,771		17,477	
Food	15,054		14,579		13,870		13,167		11,944	
General packaging	189		171		59		72		69	
By Product										
Beverage:	56,326	63	61,456	67	70,177	69	76,773	70	86,695	72
Beer	30,901		33,135		35,614		36,480		37,276	
Soft drinks	25,425		28,321		34,563		40,293		49,419	
Food:	28,148	32	26,941	29	27,844	27	28,381	26	30,106	25
Dairy products	854		927		1,246		1,188		1,304	
Juices	13,494		11,954		11,385		11,565		12,557	
Meat, poultry, seafood	2,804		3,019		3,373		3,530		3,456	
Pet food	3,663		3,571		4,069		4,543		5,130	
Other	7,333		7,470		7,771		7,555		7,659	
General packaging:	4,336	5	3,997	4	3,878	4	4,060	4	3,994	3
Aerosol	2,059		2,144		2,277		2,508		2,716	
Paint: varnish	813		817		830		842		710	
Automotive products	601		229		168		128		65	
Other nonfoods	863		807		603		582		503	
By Materials Used										
Steel	45,386	52	40,116	45	34,316	37	34,559	34	35,318	29
Aluminum	42,561	48	48,694	55	58,078	63	67,340	66	85,477	71

Source: Can Shipment Report, Can Manufacturers Institute, 1981–1989.

drink bottlers throughout the decade. Forced to economize following costly battles for market share, soft drink bottlers used their leverage to obtain packaging price discounts.[1] Over capacity and a shrinking customer base contributed to an unprecedented squeeze on manufacturers' margins, and the can manufacturers themselves contributed to the margin deterioration by aggressively discounting to protect market share. As one manufacturer confessed, "When you look at the beverage can industry, it's no secret that we are selling at a lower price today than we were 10 years ago."

Customers   Among the industry's largest users were the Coca-Cola Company, Anheuser-Busch Companies, Inc., Pepsico Inc., and Coca-Cola Enterprises Inc. (see Exhibit 2). Consolidation within the soft drink segment of

the bottling industry reduced the number of bottlers from approximately 8,000 in 1980 to about 800 in 1989 and placed a significant amount of beverage volume in the hands of a few large companies.[2] Since the can constituted about 45% of the total cost of a packaged beverage, soft drink bottlers and brewers usually maintained relationships with more than one can supplier. Poor service and uncompetitive prices could be punished by cuts in order size.

Distribution   Due to the bulky nature of cans, manufacturers located their plants close to customers to minimize transportation costs. The primary cost components of the metal can included (1) raw materials at 65%; (2) direct labor at 12%; and (3) transportation at roughly 7.5%. Various estimates placed the radius of economical distri-

[1]Salomon Brothers, *Beverage Cans Industry Report,* March 1, 1990.

[2]T. Davis, "Can Do: A Metal Container Update," *Beverage World* (June 1990): 34.

Exhibit 2   Top U.S. Users of Containers, 1989

Rank	Company	Soft Drink/ Beverage Sales ($000)	Principal Product Categories
1	The Coca-Cola Company[a] (Atlanta, GA)	$8,965,800	Soft drinks, citrus juices, fruit drinks
2	Anheuser-Busch Companies, Inc.[b] (St. Louis, MO)	7,550,000	Beer, beer imports
3	PepsiCo Inc. (Purchase, NY)	5,777,000	Soft drinks, bottled water
4	The Seagram Company, Ltd. (Montreal, Quebec, Canada)	5,581,779	Distilled spirits, wine coolers, mixers, juices
5	Coca-Cola Enterprises, Inc.[a] (Atlanta, GA)	3,881,947	Soft drinks
6	Philip Morris Companies, Inc. (New York, NY)	3,435,000	Beer
7	The Molson Companies, Ltd. (Toronto, Ontario, Canada)	1,871,394	Beer, coolers, beer imports
8	John Labatt, Ltd. (London, Ontario, Canada)	1,818,100	Beer, wine
9	The Stroh Brewery Company[c] (Detroit, MI)	1,500,000	Beer, coolers, soft drinks
10	Adolph Coors Company[d] (Golden, CO)	1,366,108	Beer, bottled water

Source: Beverage World, 1990–1991 Databank.

[a]The Coca-Cola Company and Coca-Cola Enterprises purchased (versus in-house manufacture) all of its cans in 1989. Coca-Cola owned 49% of Coca-Cola Enterprises—the largest Coca-Cola bottler in the United States.

[b]In addition to in-house manufacturing at its wholly owned subsidiary (Metal Container Corporation), Anheuser-Busch Companies purchased its cans from four manufacturers. The percentage of cans manufactured by Anheuser-Busch was not publicly disclosed.

[c]Of the 4 to 5 billion cans used by The Stroh Brewery in 1989, 39% were purchased and 61% were manufactured in-house.

[d]Adolph Coors Company manufactured all of its cans, producing approximately 10 to 12 million cans per day, five days per week.

bution for a plant at between 150 and 300 miles. Beverage can producers preferred aluminum to steel because of aluminum's lighter weight and lower shipping costs. In 1988, steel cans weighed more than twice as much as aluminum.[3] The costs incurred in transporting cans to overseas markets made international trade uneconomical. Foreign markets were served by joint ventures, foreign subsidiaries, affiliates of U.S. can manufacturers, and local overseas firms.

Manufacturing   Two-piece can lines cost approximately $16 million, and the investment in peripheral equipment raised the per-line cost to $20–$25 million.

[3]J. J. Sheehan, "Nothing Succeeds Like Success," *Beverage World* (November 1988): 82.

The minimum efficient plant size was one line and installations ranged from one to five lines. While two-piece can lines achieved quick and persistent popularity, they did not completely replace their antecedents—the three-piece can lines. The food and general packaging segment—representing 28% of the metal container industry in 1989—continued using three-piece cans throughout the 1980s. The beverage segment, however, had made a complete switch from three-piece to two-piece cans by 1983.

A typical three-piece can production line cost between $1.5 and $2 million and required expensive seaming, end-making, and finishing equipment. Since each finishing line could handle the output of three or four can-forming lines, the minimum efficient plant required at least $7 million in basic equipment. Most plants had 12 to 15 lines for the increased flexibility of handling more than one type of can at once. However, any more than 15 lines became unwieldy because of the need for duplication of set-up crews, maintenance, and supervision. The beverage industry's switch from three- to two-piece lines prompted many manufacturers to sell complete, fully operational three-piece lines "as is" for $175,000 to $200,000. Some firms shipped their old lines overseas to their foreign operations where growth potential was great, there were few entrenched firms, and canning technology was not well understood.

Suppliers   Since the invention of the aluminum can in 1958, steel had fought a losing battle against aluminum. In 1970, steel accounted for 88% of metal cans, but by 1989 had dropped to 29%. In addition to being lighter, of higher, more consistent quality, and more economical to recycle, aluminum was also friendlier to the taste and offered superior lithography qualities. By 1989, aluminum accounted for 99% of the beer and 94% of the soft drink metal container businesses, respectively.

The country's three largest aluminum producers supplied the metal can industry. Alcoa, the world's largest aluminum producer with 1988 sales of $9.8 billion, and Alcan, the world's largest marketer of primary aluminum, with 1988 sales of $8.5 billion, supplied over 65% of the domestic can sheet requirements. Reynolds Metals, the second-largest aluminum producer in the United States, with 1988 sales of $5.6 billion, supplied aluminum sheet to the industry and also produced about 11 billion cans itself.[4] Reynolds Metals was the only aluminum company in the United States that produced cans (see Exhibit 3).

Steel's consistent advantage over aluminum was price. According to The American Iron and Steel Institute in 1988, steel represented a savings of from $5 to $7 for every thousand cans produced, or an estimated savings of $500 million a year for can manufacturers. In 1988, aluminum prices increased an estimated 15%, while the lower steel prices increased by only 5% to 7%. According to a representative of Alcoa, the decision on behalf of the firm to limit aluminum price increases was attributed to the threat of possible inroads by steel.[5]

Industry Trends   The major trends characterizing the metal container industry during the 1980s included (1) the continuing threat of in-house manufacture; (2) the emergence of plastics as a viable packaging material; (3) steady competition from glass as a substitute for aluminum in the beer market; (4) the emergence of the soft drink industry as the largest end-user of packaging, with aluminum as the primary beneficiary; and (5) the diversification of, and consolidation among, packaging producers.

In-House Manufacture   Production of cans at "captive" plants—those producing cans for their own company use—accounted for approximately 25% of the total can output in 1989. Much of the expansion in in-house manufactured cans, which persisted throughout the 1980s, occurred at plants owned by the nation's major food producers and brewers. Many large brewers moved to hold can costs down by developing their own manufacturing capability. Brewers found it advantageous to invest in captive manufacture because of high-volume, single-label production runs. Adolph Coors took this to the extreme by producing all their cans in-house and supplying almost all of their own aluminum requirements from their 130-million-pound sheet rolling mill in San Antonio, Texas.[6] By the end of the 1980s, the beer industry had the capacity to supply about 55% of its beverage can needs.[7]

Captive manufacturing was not widespread in the soft drink industry, where many small bottlers and franchise operations were generally more dispersed geographically compared with the brewing industry. Soft drink bottlers were also geared to low-volume, multilabel output, which was not as economically suitable for the in-house can manufacturing process.

Plastics   Throughout the 1980s, plastics was the growth leader in the container industry with its share growing from 9% in 1980 to 18% in 1989. Plastic bottle sales in the United States were estimated to reach $3.5 billion in 1989, with food and beverage—buoyed by soft drinks sales—accounting for 50% of the total. Plastic bottles accounted for 11% of domestic soft drink sales, with most of its penetration coming at the expense of glass. Plastic's light weight and convenient handling contributed to widespread consumer acceptance. The greatest challenge facing plastics, however, was the need to produce a material that simultaneously retained carbonation and prevented infiltration of oxygen. The plastic bottle often allowed carbonation to escape in less than 4 months, while aluminum cans held carbonation for more than 16 months. Anheuser-Busch claimed that U.S. brewers expected beer containers to have at least a 90-day shelf-life, a requirement that had not been met by any plastic can or bottle.[8] Additionally, standard production lines that filled 2,400

---

[4]Until 1985, aluminum cans were restricted to carbonated beverages because it was the carbonation that prevented the can from collapsing. Reynolds discovered that by adding liquid nitrogen to the can's contents, aluminum containers could hold noncarbonated beverages and still retain their shape. The liquid nitrogen made it possible for Reynolds to make cans for liquor, chocolate drinks, and fruit juices.

[5]L. Sly, "A 'Can-Do Crusade' By Steel Industry," *Chicago Tribune* (July 3, 1988): 1.

[6]Merrill Lynch Capital Markets, *Containers and Packaging Industry Report,* March 21, 1991.

[7]Salomon Brothers Inc., *Containers/Packaging: Beverage Cans Industry Report,* April 3, 1991.

[8]A. Agoos, "Aluminum Girds For The Plastic Can Bid," *Chemical Week,* January 16, 1985: 18.

Exhibit 3   Comparative Performance of Major Aluminum Suppliers, 1988 (dollars in millions)

	Sales	Net Income	Net Profit Margin %	Long-Term Debt	Net Worth	Earnings Per Share
Alcan Aluminum						
1988	$8,529.0	$931.0	10.9%	$1,199.0	$4,320.0	$3.85
1987	6,797.0	445.0	6.5	1,336.0	3,970.0	1.73
1986	5,956.0	177.0	3.0	1,366.0	3,116.0	.79
1985	5,718.0	25.8	0.5	1,600.0	2,746.0	.12
1984	5,467.0	221.0	4.0	1,350.0	2,916.0	1.00
ALCOA						
1988	9,795.3	861.4	8.8	1,524.7	4,635.5	9.74
1987	7,767.0	365.8	4.7	2,457.6	3,910.7	4.14
1986	4,667.2	125.0	2.7	1,325.6	3,721.6	1.45
1985	5,162.7	107.4	2.1	1,553.5	3,307.9	1.32
1984	5,750.8	278.7	4.8	1,586.5	3,343.6	3.41
Reynolds Metals[a]						
1988	5,567.1	482.0	8.7	1,280.0	2,040.1	9.01
1987	4,283.8	200.7	4.7	1,567.7	1,599.6	3.95
1986	3,638.9	50.3	1.4	1,190.8	1,342.0	.86
1985	3,415.6	24.5	0.7	1,215.0	1,151.7	.46
1984	3,728.3	133.3	3.6	1,146.1	1,341.1	3.09

Source: *Value Line.*

[a]Reynolds Metals Company was the second-largest aluminum producer in the United States. The company was also the third-largest manufacturer of metal cans with a 7% market share.

beer cans per minute required containers with perfectly flat bottoms, a feature difficult to achieve using plastic.[9] Since 1987, the growth of plastics slowed somewhat apparently due to the impact on the environment of plastic packaging. Unlike glass and aluminum, plastics recycling was not a "closed loop" system.[10]

There were many small players producing plastic containers in 1988, often specializing by end-use or geographic region. However, only seven companies had sales of over $100 million. Owens-Illinois, the largest producer

[9]B. Oman, "A Clear Choice?" *Beverage World,* June 1990: 78.

[10]In response to public concern, the container industry developed highly efficient "closed loop" recycling systems. Containers flowed from the manufacturer, through the wholesaler/distributor, to the retailer, to the consumer, and back to the manufacturer or material supplier for recycling. Aluminum's high recycling value permitted can manufacturers to sell cans at a lower cost to beverage producers. The reclamation of steel cans lagged that of aluminum because collection and recycling did not result in significant energy or material cost advantages.

of plastic containers, specialized in custom-made bottles and closures for food, health and beauty, and pharmaceutical products. It was the leading supplier of prescription containers, sold primarily to drug wholesalers, major drug chains, and the government. Constar, the second-largest domestic producer of plastic containers, acquired its plastic bottle operation from Owens-Illinois, and relied on plastic soft drink bottles for about two-thirds of its sales. Johnson Controls produced bottles for the soft drink industry from 17 U.S. plants and six non-U.S. plants, and was the largest producer of plastic bottles for water and liquor. American National and Continental Can both produced plastic bottles for food, beverages, and other products such as tennis balls (see Exhibit 4 for information on competitors).

Glass   Glass bottles accounted for only 14% of domestic soft drink sales, trailing metal cans at 75%. The cost advantage that glass once had relative to plastic in the popular 16-ounce bottle size disappeared by the mid-1980s

Exhibit 4   Major U.S. Producers of Blow-Molded Plastic Bottles, 1989 (dollars in millions)

Company	Total Sales	Net Income	Plastic Sales	Product Code	Major Market
Owens-Illinois	$3,280	$ (57)	$754	1,3,4,6	Food, health and beauty, pharmaceutical
American National	4,336	52	566	1,2,3,6	Beverage, household, personal care, pharmaceutical
Constar	544	12	544	1,2,3,4,6	Soft drink, milk, food
Johnson Controls	3,100	104	465	2	Soft drink, beverages
Continental Can	3,332	18	353	1,2,3,4,5,6	Food, beverage, household, industrial
Silgan Plastics	415	96	100	1,2,3,4,6	Food, beverage, household, pharmaceutical, personal care
Sonoco Products Co.	1,600	96	N/A	1,3,4,6	Motor oil, industrial

Source: *The Rauch Guide to the U.S. Plastics Industry,* 1991; company annual reports.

Product code: (1) HDPE; (2) PET; (3) PP; (4) PVC; (5) PC; (6) multilayer.

because of consistently declining resin prices. Moreover, soft drink bottlers preferred the metal can to glass because of a variety of logistical and economic benefits: faster filling speeds, lighter weight, compactness for inventory, and transportation efficiency. In 1989, the delivered cost (including closure and label) of a 12-ounce can (the most popular size) was about 15% less than that of glass or plastic 16-ounce bottles (the most popular size).[11] The area in which glass continued to outperform metal, however, was the beer category where consumers seemed to have a love affair with the "long neck" bottle that would work to its advantage in the coming years.[12]

Soft Drinks and Aluminum Cans Throughout the 1980s, the soft drink industry emerged as the largest end-user of packaging. In 1989, soft drinks captured more than 50% of the total beverage market. The soft drink industry accounted for 42% of metal cans shipped in 1989—up from 29% in 1980. The major beneficiary of this trend was the aluminum can. In addition to the industry's continued commitment to advanced technology and innovation, aluminum's penetration could be traced to several factors: (1) aluminum's weight advantage over glass and steel; (2) aluminum's ease of handling; (3) a wider variety of graphics options provided by multipack can containers; and (4) consumer preference.[13] Aluminum's growth was also supported by the vending machine market, which was built around cans and dispensed approximately 20% of all soft drinks in 1989. An estimated 60% of Coca Cola's and 50% of Pepsi's beverages were packaged in metal cans. Coca Cola Enterprises and Pepsi Cola Bottling Group together accounted for 22% of all soft drink cans shipped in 1989.[14] In 1980, the industry shipped 15.9 billion aluminum soft drink cans. By 1989, that figure had increased to 49.2 billion cans. This increase, representing a 12% average annual growth rate, was achieved during a decade that experienced a 3.6% average annual increase in total gallons of soft drinks consumed.

Diversification and Consolidation Low profit margins, excess capacity, and rising material and labor costs prompted a number of corporate diversifications and subsequent consolidations throughout the 1970s and 1980s. While many can manufacturers diversified across the spectrum of rigid containers to supply all major end-use markets (food, beverages, and general packaging), others diversified into nonpackaging businesses such as energy (oil and gas) and financial services.

Over a 20-year period, for example, American Can reduced its dependence on domestic can manufacturing, moving into totally unrelated fields, such as insurance. Between 1981 and 1986 the company invested $940 million to acquire all or part of six insurance companies. Ultimately, the packaging businesses of American Can were

[11]N. Lang, "A Touch of Glass," *Beverage World,* June 1990: 36.

[12]Lang, "A Touch of Glass."

[13]U.S. Industrial Outlook, 1984–1990.

[14]The First Boston Corporation, *Packaging Industry Report,* April 4, 1990.

acquired by Triangle Industries in 1986, while the financial services businesses re-emerged as Primerica. Similarly, Continental Can broadly diversified its holdings, changing its name to Continental Group in 1976 when can sales dropped to 38% of total sales. In the 1980s, Continental Group invested heavily in energy exploration, research, and transportation, but profits were weak and they were ultimately taken over by Peter Kiewit Sons in 1984.

While National Can stuck broadly to containers, it diversified through acquisition into glass containers, food canning, pet foods, bottle closures, and plastic containers. However, instead of generating future growth opportunities, the expansion into food products proved a drag on company earnings.

Under the leadership of John W. Fisher, Ball Corporation, a leading glass bottle and can maker, expanded into the high-technology market and by 1987 had procured $180 million in defense contracts. Fisher directed Ball into such fields as petroleum engineering equipment, and photo-engraving and plastics, and established the company as a leading manufacturer of computer components.

Major Competitors in 1989

For over 30 years, three of the current five top competitors in can manufacturing dominated the metal can industry. Since the early 1950s, American Can, Continental Can, Crown Cork & Seal, and National Can held the top four rankings in can manufacturing. A series of dramatic mergers and acquisitions among several of the country's leading manufacturers throughout the 1980s served to shift as well as consolidate power at the top. Management at fourth-ranked Crown Cork & Seal viewed the following four firms as constituting its primary competition in 1989: American National Can, Continental Can, Reynolds Metals, and Ball Corporation. Two smaller companies—Van Dorn Company and Heekin Can—were strong competitors regionally (see Exhibit 5).

American National Can   Representing the merger of two former, long-established competitors, American National—a wholly-owned subsidiary of the Pechiney International Group—generated sales revenues of $4.4 billion in 1988. In 1985, Triangle Industries, a New Jersey–based maker of video games, vending machines, and jukeboxes, bought National Can for $421 million. In 1986, Triangle bought the U.S. packaging businesses of American Can for $550 million. In 1988, Triangle sold American National Can (ANC) to Pechiney, SA, the French state-owned industrial concern, for $3.5 billion. Pechiney was the world's third-largest producer of aluminum and, through its Cebal Group, a major European manufacturer of packaging. A member of the Pechiney International Group, ANC was the largest beverage can maker in the world—producing more than 30 billion cans annually. With more than 100 facilities in 12 countries, ANC's product line of aluminum and steel cans, glass containers, and caps and closures served the major beverage, food, pharmaceuticals, and cosmetics markets.

Continental Can   Continental Can had long been a financially stable container company; its revenues increased every year without interruption from 1923 through the mid-1980s. By the 1970s, Continental had surpassed American Can as the largest container company in the United States. The year 1984, however, represented a turning point in Continental's history when the company became an attractive takeover target. Peter Kiewit Sons Inc., a private construction firm in Omaha, Nebraska, purchased Continental Group for $2.75 billion in 1984. Under the direction of Vice Chairman Donald Strum, Kiewit dismantled Continental Group in an effort to make the operation more profitable. Within a year, Strum had sold $1.6 billion worth of insurance, gas pipelines, and oil and gas reserves. Staff at Continental's Connecticut headquarters was reduced from 500 to 40. Continental Can generated sales revenues of $3.3 billion in 1988, ranking it second behind American National. By the late 1980s, management at Kiewit considered divesting—in whole or in part—Continental Can's packaging operations, which included Continental Can USA, Europe, and Canada, as well as metal packaging operations in Latin America, Asia, and the Middle East.

Reynolds Metals   Based in Richmond, Virginia, Reynolds Metals was the only domestic company integrated from aluminum ingot through aluminum cans. With 1988 sales revenues of $5.6 billion and net income of $482 million, Reynolds served the following principal markets: packaging and containers; distributors and fabricators; building and construction; aircraft and automotive; and electrical. Reynolds' packaging and container revenue amounted to $2.4 billion in 1988. As one of the industry's leading can makers, Reynolds was instrumental in establishing new uses for the aluminum can and was a world leader in can-making technology. Reynolds' developments included high-speed can-forming machinery with capabilities in excess of 400 cans per minute, faster inspection equipment (operating at speeds of up to 2,000 cans per minute), and spun aluminum tops which contained less material. The company's next generation of can end-making technology was scheduled for installation in the early 1990s.

Ball Corporation   Founded in 1880 in Muncie, Indiana, Ball Corporation generated operating income of $113 million on sales revenues of $1 billion in 1988. Considered one of the industry's low-cost producers, Ball was the fifth-largest manufacturer of metal containers as well as the third-largest glass container manufacturer in the United States. Ball's packaging businesses accounted for 82.5% of total sales and 77.6% of consolidated operating earnings in 1988. Ball's can-making technology and manufacturing

Exhibit 5 Comparative Performance of Major Metal Can Manufacturers (dollars in millions)

Company[a]	Net Sales	SG&A as a % of Sales	Gross Margin	Operating Income	Net Profit	Return on Sales	Return on Average Assets	Return on Average Equity
Ball Corporation								
1988	$1,073.0	8.1%	$161.7	$113.0	$47.7	4.4%	5.7%	11.6%
1987	1,054.1	8.5	195.4	147.6	59.8	5.7	7.8	15.7
1986	1,060.1	8.2	168.0	150.5	52.8	5.0	7.6	15.2
1985	1,106.2	7.5	140.7	140.5	51.2	4.6	8.1	16.4
1984	1,050.7	7.9	174.1	123.9	46.3	4.4	7.8	16.6
1983	909.5	8.2	158.2	114.6	39.0	4.3	7.3	15.6
1982	889.1	8.4	147.4	100.5	34.5	3.9	6.9	15.8
Crown Cork & Seal								
1988	1,834.1	2.8	264.6	212.7	93.4	5.1	8.6	14.5
1987	1,717.9	2.9	261.3	223.3	88.3	5.1	8.7	14.5
1986	1,618.9	2.9	235.3	202.4	79.4	4.9	8.8	14.3
1985	1,487.1	2.9	216.4	184.4	71.7	4.8	8.6	13.9
1984	1,370.0	3.1	186.6	154.8	59.5	4.4	7.3	11.4
1983	1,298.0	3.3	182.0	138.9	51.5	4.0	6.2	9.3
1982	1,351.8	3.3	176.2	132.5	44.7	3.3	5.2	7.9
Heekin Can, Inc.								
1988	275.8	3.7	38.9	36.4	9.6	3.5	4.8	22.6
1987	230.4	4.0	33.6	30.2	8.8	3.8	5.8	26.3
1986	207.6	4.1	31.1	28.0	7.0	3.4	5.4	27.5
1985	221.8	3.2	31.8	29.0	6.8	3.1	5.2	42.5
1984	215.4	2.7	28.4	26.5	5.5	2.6	4.3	79.7
1983	181.6	3.2	24.4	22.8	3.8	2.1	3.3	102.7
1982[b]	—							

Van Dom Company

Year								
1988	333.5	16.5	75.3	26.7	11.7	3.5	6.6	12.2
1987	330.0	15.7	73.6	28.4	12.3	3.7	7.7	12.7
1986	305.1	16.3	70.4	26.5	11.7	3.8	7.7	12.9
1985	314.3	15.1	75.6	33.6	15.4	4.9	10.6	19.0
1984	296.4	14.7	74.9	36.5	16.8	5.7	12.9	24.9
1983	225.9	14.8	48.5	20.1	7.4	3.3	6.8	12.8
1982	184.3	16.1	37.7	12.7	3.6	2.0	3.5	6.6

American Can Company[c]

Year								
1985	2,854.9	22.6	813.4	1670.0	149.1	5.2	5.2	10.9
1984	3,177.9	18.0	740.8	168.3	132.4	4.2	4.9	11.2
1983	3,346.4	15.0	625.4	123.6	94.9	2.8	3.5	9.7
1982	4,063.4	16.1	766.3	113.4	23.0	0.6	0.8	2.4
1981	4,836.4	15.0	949.6	223.0	76.7	1.2	2.7	7.2
1980	4,812.2	15.8	919.5	128.1	85.7	1.8	3.1	8.0

National Can Company[d]

Year								
1983	1,647.5	5.1	215.3	93.5	22.1	1.3	2.7	6.3
1982	1,541.5	4.6	206.3	100.7	34.1	2.2	4.4	10.0
1981	1,533.9	4.6	191.7	86.3	24.7	1.6	3.1	7.5
1980	1,550.9	5.4	233.7	55.0	50.6	3.3	6.4	16.7

The Continental Group, Inc.[e]

Year								
1983	4,942.0	6.3	568.0	157.0	173.5	3.5	4.4	9.4
1982	5,089.0	6.4	662.0	217.0	180.2	3.5	4.3	9.6
1981	5,291.0	7.2	747.0	261.0	242.2	4.6	5.9	13.6
1980	5,171.0	7.2	700.0	201.0	224.8	4.3	5.5	13.7
1979	4,544.0	6.5	573.0	171.0	189.2	4.2	5.3	13.1

Source: *Value Line* and company annual reports (for SGA, COGS, and Asset figures).

[a]Refer to Exhibit 3 for Reynolds Metals Company. [b]Figures not disclosed for 1982. [c]In 1985, packaging made up 60% of total sales at American Can, with the remainder in specialty retailing. In 1986 Triangle Industries purchased the U.S. packaging business of American Can. In 1987, American National Can was formed through the merger of American Can Packaging and National Can Corporation. In 1989, Triangle sold American National Can to Pechiney, SA. [d]In 1985, Triangle Industries bought National Can. [e]In 1984, Peter Kiewit Sons purchased The Continental Group. SG&A as a percentage of sales for Continental Can hovered around 6.5% through the late 1980s.

605

flexibility allowed the company to make shorter runs in the production of customized, higher-margin products designed to meet customers' specifications and needs. In 1988, beverage can sales accounted for 62% of total sales. Anheuser-Busch, Ball's largest customer, accounted for 14% of sales that year. In 1989, Ball was rumored to be planning to purchase the balance of its 50%-owned joint venture, Ball Packaging Products Canada, Inc. The acquisition would make Ball the number two producer of metal beverage and food containers in the Canadian market.

Van Dorn Company   The industry's next two largest competitors, with a combined market share of 3%, were Van Dorn Company and Heekin Can, Inc. Founded in 1872 in Cleveland, Ohio, Van Dorn manufactured two product lines: containers and plastic injection molding equipment. Van Dorn was one of the world's largest producers of drawn aluminum containers for processed foods, and a major manufacturer of metal, plastic, and composite containers for the paint, petroleum, chemical, automotive, food, and pharmaceutical industries. Van Dorn was also a leading manufacturer of injection molding equipment for the plastics industry. The company's Davies Can Division, founded in 1922, was a regional manufacturer of metal and plastic containers. In 1988, Davies planned to build two new can manufacturing plants at a cost of about $20 million each. These facilities would each produce about 40 million cans annually. Van Dorn's consolidated can sales of $334 million in 1988 ranked it sixth overall among the country's leading can manufacturers.

Heekin Can   James Heekin, a Cincinnati coffee merchant, founded Heekin Can in 1901 as a way to package his own products. The company experienced rapid growth and soon contained one of the country's largest metal lithography plants under one roof. Three generations of the Heekin family built Heekin into a strong regional force in the packaging industry. The family sold the business to Diamond International Corporation, a large, diversified publicly held company, in 1965. Diamond operated Heekin as a subsidiary until 1982 when it was sold to its operating management and a group of private investors. Heekin went public in 1985. With 1988 sales revenues of $275.8 million, seventh-ranked Heekin primarily manufactured steel cans for processors, packagers, and distributors of food and pet food. Heekin represented the country's largest regional can maker.

Crown Cork & Seal Company

Company History   In August 1891, a foreman in a Baltimore machine shop hit upon an idea for a better bottle cap—a piece of tin-coated steel with a flanged edge and an insert of natural cork. Soon this crown-cork cap became the hit product of a new venture, Crown Cork & Seal Company. When the patents ran out, however, com-

petition became severe and nearly bankrupted the company in the 1920s. The faltering Crown was bought in 1927 by a competitor, Charles McManus.[15]

Under the paternalistic leadership of McManus, Crown prospered in the 1930s, selling more than half of the United States and world supply of bottle caps. He then correctly anticipated the success of the beer can and diversified into can making, building one of the world's largest plants in Philadelphia. However, at one million square feet and containing as many as 52 lines, it was a nightmare of inefficiency and experienced substantial losses. Although McManus was an energetic leader, he engaged in nepotism and never developed an organization that could run without him. Following his death in 1946, the company ran on momentum, maintaining dividends at the expense of investment in new plants. Following a disastrous attempt to expand into plastics and a ludicrous diversification into metal bird cages, Crown reorganized along the lines of the much larger Continental Can, incurring additional personnel and expense that again brought the company near to bankruptcy.

At the time, John Connelly was just a fellow on the outside, looking to Crown as a prospective customer and getting nowhere. The son of a Philadelphia blacksmith, Connelly had begun in a paperbox factory at 15 and worked his way up to become eastern sales manager of the Container Corporation of America. When he founded his own company, Connelly Containers, Inc., in 1946, Crown promised him some business. That promise was forgotten by the post-McManus regime, which loftily refused to "take a chance" on a small supplier like Connelly. By 1955, when Crown's distress became evident, Connelly began buying stock and in November 1956 was asked to be an outside director—a desperate move by the ailing company.[16]

In April 1957, Crown Cork & Seal teetered on the verge of bankruptcy. Bankers Trust Company withdrew Crown's line of credit; it seemed that all that was left was to write the company's obituary when John Connelly took over the presidency. His rescue plan was simple—as he called it, "just common sense." Connelly's first move was to pare down the organization. Paternalism ended in a blizzard of pink slips. Connelly moved quickly to cut headquarters staff by half to reach a lean force of 80. The company returned to a simple functional organization. In 20 months Crown had eliminated 1,647 jobs or 24% of the payroll. As part of the company's reorganization, Connelly discarded divisional accounting practices; at the same time he eliminated the divisional line and staff concept. Except for one accountant maintained at each plant

[15]R.J. Whalen, "The Unoriginal Ideas That Rebuilt Crown Cork," *Fortune*, October 1962.

[16]Whalen, "The Unoriginal Ideas That Rebuilt Crown Cork": 156.

location, all accounting and cost control was performed at the corporate level; the corporate accounting staff occupied one-half the space used by the headquarters group. In addition, Connelly disbanded Crown's central research and development facility.

The second step was to institute the concept of accountability. Connelly aimed to instill a deep-rooted pride of workmanship throughout the company by establishing Crown managers as "owner-operators" of their individual businesses. Connelly gave each plant manager responsibility for plant profitability, including any allocated costs. (All company overhead, estimated at 5% of sales, was allocated to the plant level.) Previously, plant managers had been responsible only for controllable expenses at the plant level. Although the plant managers' compensation was not tied to profit performance, one senior executive pointed out that the managers were "certainly rewarded on the basis of that figure." Connelly also held plant managers responsible for quality and customer service.

The next step was to slow production to a halt and liquidate $7 million in inventory. By mid-July Crown paid off the banks. Connelly introduced sales forecasting dovetailed with new production and inventory controls. This move put pressure on the plant managers, who were no longer able to avoid layoffs by dumping excess products into inventory.

By the end of 1957, Crown had, in one observer's words, "climbed out of the coffin and was sprinting." Between 1956 and 1961, sales increased from $115 million to $176 million and profits soared. Throughout the 1960s, the company averaged an annual 15.5% increase in sales and 14% in profits. Connelly, not satisfied simply with short-term reorganizations of the existing company, developed a strategy that would become its hallmark for the next three decades.

Connelly's Strategy

According to William Avery, "From his first day on the job, Mr. Connelly structured the company to be successful. He took control of costs and did a wonderful job taking us in the direction of becoming owner-operators." But what truly separated Connelly from his counterparts, Avery explained, was that while he was continually looking for new ways of controlling costs, he was equally hellbent on improving quality. Connelly, described by *Forbes* as an individual with a "scrooge-like aversion to fanfare and overhead," emphasized cost efficiency, quality, and customer service as the essential ingredients for Crown's strategy in the decades ahead.

Products and Markets Recognizing Crown's position as a small producer in an industry dominated by American Can and Continental Can, Connelly sought to develop a product line built around Crown's traditional strengths in metal forming and fabrication. He chose to emphasize the areas Crown knew best—tin-plated cans and crowns—and to concentrate on specialized uses and international markets.

A dramatic illustration of Connelly's commitment to this strategy occurred in the early 1960s. In 1960, Crown held over 50% of the market for motor oil cans. In 1962, R. C. Can and Anaconda Aluminum jointly developed fiber-foil cans for motor oil, which were approximately 20% lighter and 15% cheaper than the metal cans then in use. Despite the loss of sales, management decided that it had other more profitable opportunities and that new materials, such as fiber-foil, provided too great a threat in the motor oil can business. Crown's management decided to exit from the oil can market.

In the early 1960s Connelly singled out two specific applications in the domestic market: beverage cans and the growing aerosol market. These applications were called "hard to hold" because cans required special characteristics to either contain the product under pressure or to avoid affecting taste. Connelly led Crown directly from a soldered can into the manufacture of two-piece steel cans in the 1960s. Recognizing the enormous potential of the soft drink business, Crown began designing its equipment specifically to meet the needs of soft drink producers, with innovations such as two printers in one line and conversion printers that allowed for rapid design changeover to accommodate just-in-time delivery.[17] After producing exclusively steel cans through the late 1970s, Connelly spearheaded Crown's conversion from steel to aluminum cans in the early 1980s.

In addition to the specialized product line, Connelly's strategy was based on two geographic thrusts: expand to national distribution in the United States and invest heavily abroad. Connelly linked domestic expansion to Crown's manufacturing reorganization; plants were spread out across the country to reduce transportation costs and to be nearer customers. Crown was unusual in that it did not set up plants to service a single customer. Instead, Crown concentrated on providing products for a number of customers near their plants. In international markets, Crown invested heavily in developing nations, first with crowns and then with cans as packaged foods became more widely accepted. Metal containers generated 65% of Crown's $1.8 billion 1988 sales, while closures generated 30% and packaging equipment 5%.

Manufacturing When Connelly took over in 1957, Crown had perhaps the most outmoded and inefficient production facilities in the industry. Dividends had taken precedence over new investment, and old machinery combined with the cumbersome Philadelphia plant had generated very high production and transportation costs. Soon after he gained control, Connelly took drastic action, closing

---

[17]In the mid-1960s, growth in demand for soft drink and beer cans was more than triple that for traditional food cans.

down the Philadelphia facility and investing heavily in new and geographically dispersed plants. From 1958 to 1963, the company spent almost $82 million on relocation and new facilities. From 1976 through 1989, Crown had 26 domestic plant locations versus 9 in 1955. The plants were small (usually 2 to 3 lines for two-piece cans) and were located close to the customer rather than the raw material source. Crown operated its plants 24 hours a day with unique 12-hour shifts. Employees had two days on followed by two days off and then three days on followed by three days off.

Crown emphasized quality, flexibility, and quick response to customer needs. One officer claimed that the key to the can industry was "the fact that nobody stores cans" and when customers need them "they want them in a hurry and on time. . . . Fast answers get customers." To accommodate customer demands, some of Crown's plants kept more than a month's inventory on hand. Crown also instituted a total quality improvement process to refine its manufacturing processes and gain greater control. According to a Crown spokesperson, "The objective of this quality improvement process is to make the best possible can at the lowest possible cost. You lower the cost of doing business not by the wholesale elimination of people, but by reducing mistakes in order to improve efficiency. And you do that by making everybody in the company accountable."

Recycling   In 1970, Crown formed Nationwide Recyclers, Inc., as a wholly owned subsidiary. By 1989, Crown believed Nationwide was one of the top four or five aluminum can recyclers in the country. While Nationwide was only marginally profitable, Crown had invested in the neighborhood of $10 million in its recycling arm.

Research and Development (R&D)   Crown's technology strategy focused on enhancing the existing product line. As one executive noted, "We are not truly pioneers. Our philosophy is not to spend a great deal of money for basic research. However, we do have tremendous skills in die forming and metal fabrication, and we can move to adapt to the customer's needs faster than anyone else in the industry."[18] For instance, Crown worked closely with large breweries in the development of the two-piece drawn-and-ironed cans for the beverage industry. Crown also made an explicit decision to stay away from basic research. According to one executive, Crown was not interested in "all the frills of an R&D section of high-class, ivory-towered scientists. . . . There is a tremendous asset inherent in being second, especially in the face of the ever-changing state of flux you find in this industry. You try to let others take the risks and make the mistakes. . . ."

This philosophy did not mean that Crown never innovated. For instance, Crown was able to beat its com-

petitors into two-piece can production. Approximately $120 million in new equipment was installed from 1972 through 1975, and by 1976 Crown had 22 two-piece lines in production—more than any other competitor.[19] Crown's research teams also worked closely with customers on specific customer requests. For example, a study of the most efficient plant layout for a food packer or the redesign of a dust cap for the aerosol packager were not unusual projects.

Marketing and Customer Service   The cornerstone of Crown's marketing strategy was, in John Connelly's words, the philosophy that "you can't just increase efficiency to succeed; you must at the same time improve quality." In conjunction with its R&D strategy, the company's sales force maintained close ties with customers and emphasized Crown's ability to provide technical assistance and specific problem solving at the customer's plant. Crown's manufacturing emphasis on flexibility and quick response to customer's needs supported its marketing emphasis on putting the customer first. Michael J. McKenna, president of Crown's North American Division, insisted, "We have always been and always will be extremely customer driven."[20]

Competing cans were made of identical materials to identical specifications on practically identical machinery, and sold at almost identical prices in a given market. At Crown, all customers' gripes went to John Connelly, who was the company's best salesman. A visitor recalled being in his office when a complaint came through from the manager of a Florida citrus-packing plant. Connelly assured him the problem would be taken care of immediately, then casually remarked that he would be in Florida the next day. Would the plant manager join him for dinner? He would indeed. As Crown's president put the telephone down, his visitor said that he hadn't realized Connelly was planning to go to Florida. "Neither did I," confessed Connelly, "until I began talking."[21]

Financing   After he took over in 1957, Connelly applied the first receipts from the sale of inventory to get out from under Crown's short-term bank obligations. He then steadily reduced the debt/equity ratio from 42% in 1956 to 18.2% in 1976 and 5% in 1986. By the end of 1988, Crown's debt represented less than 2% of total capital. Connelly discontinued cash dividends in 1956, and in 1970 repurchased the last of the preferred stock, eliminating preferred dividends as a cash drain. From 1970 forward, management applied excess cash to the repurchase of stock. Connelly set ambitious earnings goals and most years he achieved them. In the 1976 annual report he

[18]R.G. Hamermesh, M.J. Anderson, Jr., and J.E. Harris, "Strategies for Low Market Share Business," *Harvard Business Review,* May–June 1978: 99.

[19]In 1976, there were 47 two-piece tinplate and 130 two-piece aluminum lines in the United States.

[20]*One Hundred Years,* Crown Cork & Seal Company, Inc.

[21]Whalen, "The Unoriginal Ideas That Rebuilt Crown Cork."

wrote, "A long time ago we made a prediction that some day our sales would exceed $1 billion and profits of $60.00 per share. Since then, the stock has been split 20-for-1 so this means $3.00 per share." Crown Cork & Seal's revenues reached $1 billion in 1977 and earnings per share reached $3.46. Earnings per share reached $10.11 in 1988 adjusted for a 3-for-1 stock split in September 1988.

International   A significant dimension of Connelly's strategy focused on international growth, particularly in developing countries. Between 1955 and 1960, Crown received what were called "pioneer rights" from many foreign governments aiming to build up the industrial sectors of their countries. These "rights" gave Crown first chance at any new can or closure business introduced into these developing countries. Mark W. Hartman, president of Crown's International Division, described Connelly as "a Johnny Appleseed with respect to the international marketplace. When the new countries of Africa were emerging, for example, John was there offering crown-making capabilities to help them in their industrialization, while at the same time getting a foothold for Crown. John's true love was international business."[22] By 1988, Crown's 62 foreign plants generated 44% of sales and 54% of operating profits. John Connelly visited each of Crown's overseas plants. (See Exhibit 6 for map of plant locations.)

Crown emphasized national management wherever possible. Local people, Crown asserted, understood the local marketplace: the suppliers, the customers, and the unique conditions that drove supply and demand. Crown's overseas investment also offered opportunities to recycle equipment that was, by U.S. standards, less sophisticated. Because can manufacturing was new to many regions of the world, Crown's older equipment met the needs of what was still a developing industry overseas.

Performance   Connelly's strategy met with substantial success throughout his tenure at Crown. With stock splits and price appreciation, $100 invested in Crown stock in 1957 would be worth approximately $30,000 in 1989. After restructuring the company in his first three years, revenues grew at 12.2% per year while income grew at 14.0% over the next two decades (see Exhibit 7). Return on equity averaged 15.8% for much of the 1970s, while Continental Can and American Can lagged far behind at 10.3% and 7.1%, respectively. Over the period 1968-1978 Crown's total return to shareholders ranked 114 out of the Fortune 500, well ahead of IBM (183) and Xerox (374).

In the early 1980s, flat industry sales, combined with an increasingly strong dollar overseas, unrelenting penetration by plastics, and overcapacity in can manufacturing at home, led to declining sales revenues at Crown. Crown's sales dropped from $1.46 billion in 1980 to $1.37 billion

by 1984. However, by 1985 Crown had rebounded and annual sales growth averaged 7.6% from 1984 through 1988 while profit growth averaged 12% (see Exhibits 8 and 9). Over the period 1978–1988 Crown's total return to shareholders was 18.6% per year, ranking 146 out of the Fortune 500. In 1988, *BusinessWeek* noted that Connelly—earning a total of only $663,000 in the three years ending in 1987—garnered shareholders the best returns for the least executive pay in the United States. As an industry analyst observed, "Crown's strategy is a no-nonsense, back-to-basics strategy—except they never left the basics."[23]

John Connelly's Contribution to Success   Customers, employees, competitors, and Wall Street analysts attributed Crown's sustained success to the unique leadership of John Connelly. He arrived at Crown as it headed into bankruptcy in 1957, achieved a 1,646% increase in profits on a relatively insignificant sales increase by 1961, and proceeded to outperform the industry's giants throughout the next three decades. A young employee expressed the loyalty created by Connelly: "If John told me to jump out the window, I'd jump—and be sure he'd catch me at the bottom with a stock option in his hand."

Yet Connelly was not an easy man to please. Crown's employees had to get used to Connelly's tough, straight-line management. *Fortune* credited Crown's success to Connelly, "whose genial Irish grin masks a sober salesman executive who believes in the eighty-hour week and in traveling while competitors sleep." He went to meetings uninvited, and expected the same devotion to Crown of his employees as he demanded of himself. As one observer remembered:

> The Saturday morning meeting is standard operating procedure. Crown's executives travel and confer only at night and on weekends. William D. Wallace, vice president for operations, travels 100,000 miles a year, often in the company plane. But Connelly sets the pace. An associate recalls driving to his home in the predawn blackness to pick him up for a flight to a distant plant. The Connelly house was dark, but he spotted a figure sitting on the curb under a street light, engrossed in a loose-leaf book. Connelly's greeting, as he jumped into the car: "I want to talk to you about last month's variances."[24]

Avery's Challenge in 1989   Avery thought long and hard about the options available to him in 1989. He considered the growing opportunities in plastic closures and containers, as well as glass containers. With growth slowing in metal containers, plastics was the only container segment that held much promise. However, the possibility

---

[22]*One Hundred Years,* Crown Cork & Seal Company, Inc.

[23]"These Penny-Pinchers Deliver A Big Bang For Their Bucks," *BusinessWeek,* May 4, 1987.

[24]Whalen, "The Unoriginal Ideas That Rebuilt Crown Cork."

of diversifying beyond the manufacture of containers altogether had some appeal, although the appropriate opportunity was not at hand. While Crown's competitors had aggressively expanded in a variety of directions, Connelly had been cautious, and had prospered. Avery wondered if now was the time for a change at Crown.

Within the traditional metal can business, Avery had to decide whether or not to get involved in the bidding for Continental Can. The acquisition of Continental Can Canada (CCC)—with sales of roughly $400 million—would make Canada Crown's largest single presence outside of the United States. Continental's USA business—with estimated revenues of $1.3 billion in 1989—would double the size of Crown's domestic operations. Continental's Latin American, Asian, and Middle Eastern operations were rumored to be priced in the range of $100 million to $150 million. Continental's European operations generated estimated sales of $1.5 billion in 1989 and included a work force of 10,000 at 30 production sites. Potential bidders for all, or part of Continental's operations,

included many of Crown's U.S. rivals in addition to European competition: Pechiney International of France, Metal Box of Great Britain (which had recently acquired Carnaud SA), and VIAG AG, a German trading group, among others.

Avery knew that most mergers in this industry had not worked out well. He also thought about the challenge of taking two companies that come from completely different cultures and bringing them together. There would be inevitable emotional and attitudinal changes, particularly for Continental's salaried managers and Crown's "owner-operators." Avery also knew that the merger of American Can and National Can had its difficulties. That consolidation was taking longer than expected and, according to one observer, "American Can would be literally wiped out in the end."

Avery found himself challenging Crown's traditional strategies and thought seriously of drafting a new blueprint for the future.

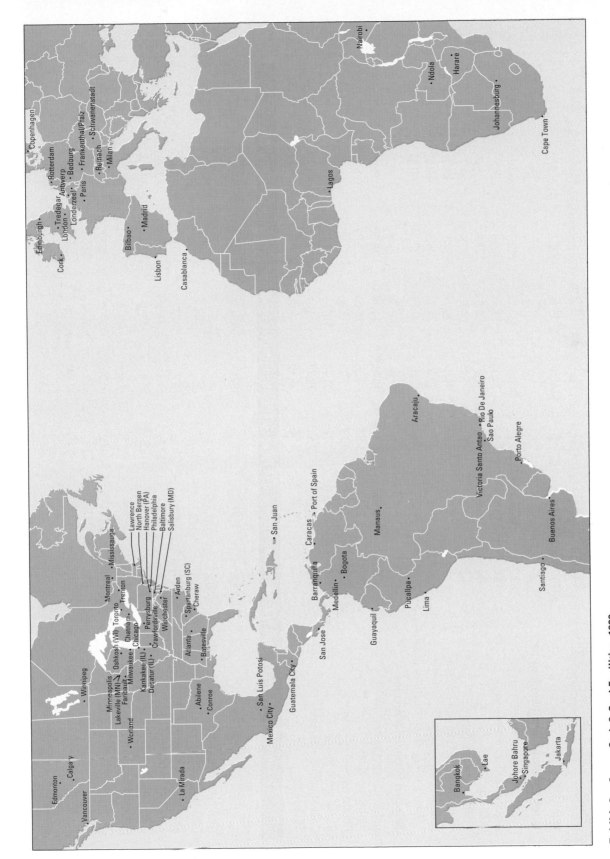

Exhibit 6   Crown Cork & Seal Facilities, 1989

611

Exhibit 7 Crown Cork & Seal Company Consolidated Statement of Income (dollars in millions, year-end December 31)

	1956	1961	1966	1971	1973	1975	1977	1979
Net Sales	$115.1	$177.0	$279.8	$448.4	$571.8	$825.0	$1,049.1	$1,402.4
Costs, Expenses and Other Income:								
Cost of products sold	95.8	139.1	217.2	350.9	459.2	683.7	874.1	1,179.3
Sales and administration	13.5	15.8	18.4	21.1	23.4	30.1	34.8	43.9
Depreciation	2.6	4.6	9.4	17.0	20.9	25.4	5.6	16.4
Net interest expense	1.2	1.3	4.6	5.1	4.4	7.4	31.7	40.1
Provision for taxes on income	.1	7.6	12.7	24.6	26.7	34.9	48.7	51.8
Net income	.3	6.7	16.7	28.5	34.3	41.6	53.8	70.2
Earnings per common share (actual)	(6.01)	.28	.80	1.41	1.81	2.24	3.46	4.65
Selected Financial Statistics								
Return on average equity	0.55%	9.66%	16.44%	14.05%	14.46%	15.20%	15.88%	15.57%
Return on sales	0.24	3.76	5.99	6.35	6.00	5.04	5.13	5.00
Return on average assets	0.32	6.00	6.76	7.25	8.00	7.69	9.13	8.93
Gross profit margin	16.76	21.43	22.37	21.76	19.69	17.13	16.68	15.90
Cost of goods sold/sales	83.24	78.57	77.63	78.24	80.31	82.87	83.32	84.29
SGA/sales	11.73	8.65	6.56	4.70	4.09	3.65	3.32	3.13

Crown Cork & Seal Company Consolidated Statement of Financial Position (dollars in millions, year-end December 31)

	1956	1961	1966	1971	1973	1975	1977	1979
Total current assets	$50.2	$ 66.3	$109.4	$172.3	$223.4	$265.0	$340.7	$463.3
Total assets	86.5	129.2	269.5	398.1	457.5	539.0	631.1	828.2
Total current liabilities	15.8	24.8	75.3	110.2	139.6	170.0	210.8	287.1
Total long-term debt	20.2	17.7	57.9	41.7	37.9	29.7	12.8	12.2
Shareholders' equity	50.3	77.5	110.8	211.8	243.9	292.7	361.8	481.0
Selected Financial Statistics								
Debt/equity	0.40	0.23	0.52	0.20	0.16	0.10	0.04	0.03
Capital expenditures	1.9	11.8	32.7	33.1	40.4	49.0	58.9	55.9
Book value per share of common	1.57	2.74	5.19	10.62	13.13	16.64	23.54	31.84

Source: Adapted from Annual Reports.

Exhibit 8   Crown Cork & Seal Company Consolidated Statement of Income (dollars in millions except earnings per share, year-end December 31)

	1981	1982	1983	1984	1985	1986	1987	1988
Net Sales	**$1,373.9**	**$1,351.9**	**$1,298.0**	**$1,369.6**	**$1,487.1**	**$1,618.9**	**$1,717.9**	**$1,834.1**
Costs, Expenses, and Other Income:								
Cost of products sold	1,170.4	1,175.6	1,116.0	1,172.5	1,260.3	1,370.2	1,456.6	1,569.5
Sales and administrative	45.3	44.2	42.9	42.1	43.0	46.7	49.6	50.9
Depreciation	38.0	39.9	38.4	40.2	43.7	47.2	56.9	57.2
Interest expense	12.3	9.0	9.0	8.9	12.2	6.2	8.9	10.0
Interest income	—	—	—				(15.2)	(14.8)
Total Expenses	1,266.1	1,268.6	1,206.2	1,263.6	1,359.2	1,470.3	1,556.8	1,672.9
Income before taxes	107.8	83.2	91.8	105.9	127.9	148.6	161.1	161.2
Provision for taxes on income	43.0	38.5	40.2	46.4	56.2	69.2	72.7	67.8
Net income	64.8	44.7	51.5	59.5	71.7	79.4	88.3	93.4
Earnings per common share	1.48	1.05	1.27	1.59	2.17	2.48	2.86	3.37

Note: Earnings per common share have been restated to reflect a 3-for-1 stock split on September 12, 1988.

Selected Financial Statistics

	1981	1982	1983	1984	1985	1986	1987	1988
Return on Average Equity (%):	11.72%	7.94%	9.34%	11.42%	13.94%	14.34%	14.46%	14.45%
Return on sales	4.72	3.31	3.97	4.35	4.82	4.91	5.14	5.09
Return on average assets	7.38	5.19	6.20	7.31	8.58	8.80	8.67	8.61
Gross profit margin	14.81	13.04	14.03	14.39	15.25	15.36	15.21	14.42
Cost of goods sold/sales	85.19	86.96	85.97	85.61	84.75	84.64	84.79	85.58
SGA/sales	3.30	3.27	3.30	3.07	2.89	2.88	2.89	2.78
Net Sales ($):								
United States	775.0	781.0	749.9	844.5	945.3	1,010.3	985.5	1,062.5
Europe	324.0	304.4	298.7	283.0	282.8	365.6	415.6	444.2
All others	283.6	273.1	259.1	261.3	269.3	269.0	342.5	368.6
Operating Profit ($):								
United States	62.8	58.9	55.0	67.1	88.9	92.8	95.4	70.6
Europe	20.6	19.0	24.0	17.2	17.0	21.9	22.4	33.4
All others	40.0	37.3	33.1	38.3	40.6	39.6	64.9	66.1
Operating Ratio (%):								
United States	8.1	7.5	7.3	7.9	9.4	9.7	9.6	6.6
Europe	6.3	6.2	8.0	6.0	6.0	5.9	5.4	7.5
All others	14.1	13.6	12.7	14.6	15.0	14.7	18.9	17.9

Source: Adapted from Annual Reports.
Note: The above sales figures are before the deduction of intracompany sales.

Exhibit 9 Crown Cork & Seal Company Consolidated Statement of Financial Position (dollars in millions, year-end December 31)

	1981	1982	1983	1984	1985	1986	1987	1988
Current Assets:								
Cash	$ 21.5	$ 15.8	$ 21.0	$ 7.0	$ 14.8	$ 16.5	$ 27.6	$ 18.0
Accounts receivables	262.8	257.1	240.6	237.6	279.0	270.4	280.7	248.1
Inventory	206.2	184.4	170.2	174.6	171.9	190.1	228.1	237.6
Total Current Assets	490.6	457.3	431.7	419.2	465.6	477.0	536.4	503.8
Investments	12.4	14.6	26.7	28.8	41.5	43.7	NA	NA
Goodwill	11.2	10.8	9.6	10.3	11.8	14.1	16.7	16.5
Property, plant and equipment	368.4	357.8	353.7	348.0	346.9	404.0	465.7	495.9
Other noncurrent assets	NA	NA	NA	NA	NA	NA	79.1	57.0
Total Assets	882.6	840.6	821.7	806.4	865.8	938.8	1,097.9	1,073.2
Current Liabilities:								
Short-term debt	22.7	21.6	24.4	42.0	16.3	17.2	44.0	20.2
Accounts payable	193.0	165.6	163.1	177.9	197.1	220.1	265.9	277.6
U.S. and foreign taxes	17.3	4.7	11.4	6.0	11.4	11.3	28.4	23.3
Total Current Liabilities	233.0	191.9	198.8	225.8	224.8	248.5	338.2	321.2
Long-term debt	5.8	5.6	2.8	2.7	2.2	1.4	19.7	9.4
Other	14.5	18.5	12.8	15.8	31.2	29.3	0.0	0.0
Total Long-term Debt	20.3	24.1	15.6	18.5	33.5	30.7	19.7	9.4
Deferred income taxes	55.5	57.7	57.8	60.7	71.3	79.2	89.4	93.7
Minority equity in subsidiaries	7.2	7.2	5.2	3.7	4.7	3.8	5.0	0.9
Shareholders' equity	566.7	559.8	544.3	497.8	531.5	576.6	645.6	648.0
Liability and owners' equity	882.6	840.6	821.7	806.4	865.8	938.8	1,097.9	1,073.2

Selected Financial Statistics

	1981	1982	1983	1984	1985	1986	1987	1988
Debt/equity	1.02%	0.99%	0.51%	0.54%	0.42%	0.24%	3.06%	1.45%
Debt/(debt + equity)	3.5%	4.1%	2.7%	3.5%	6.0%	5.0%	3.0%	1.4%
Shares outstanding at year end (M)	14.5	14.0	13.2	11.5	10.5	10.0	9.5	27.0
Capital expenditures ($M)	$63.8	$ 50.3	$ 55.5	$ 53.8	$ 50.9	$ 94.0	$ 99.5	$ 102.6
Shares repurchased (000)	75.4	528.3	863.1	1,694.5	1,006.0	677.1	638.7	2,242.9
Stock price: High[a]	$12.00	$ 10.00	$ 13.00	$ 15.75	$ 29.62	$ 38.25	$ 46.87	$ 46.72
Stock price: Low[a]	$ 8.00	$ 7.00	$ 10.00	$ 11.75	$ 15.12	$ 25.25	$ 28.00	$ 30.00

Source: Adapted from Annual Reports.

[a]Restated for 9/1988 stock split.

Case 11   Dippin' Dots Ice Cream*

In 2004 Dippin' Dots was a 16-year-old-company with over $36 million in annual sales, 160 employees, and headquartered in Paducah, Kentucky.[1] The company's chief operation is the sale of Dippin' Dots ice cream to franchisees and national accounts throughout the world. Curt Jones is the founder and CEO of Dippin' Dots.[2] So who is Curt Jones and what is Dippin' Dots?

Dippin' Dots is the marriage between old-fashioned handmade ice cream and space-age technology. Dippin' Dots are tiny round beads of ice cream that are made at supercold temperatures, served at subzero temperatures in a soufflé cup, and eaten with a spoon. The supercold freezing of Dippin' Dots ice cream done by liquid nitrogen cryogenically locks in both flavor and freshness in a way that no other manufactured ice cream can offer. Not only had Curt discovered a new way of making ice cream, but many feel his product proved to be much more flavorful and richer than regular ice cream. According to Curt, "I created a way . . . [to] get a quicker freeze so the ice cream wouldn't get large ice crystals . . . About six months later, I decided to quit my job and go into business."

Jones is a microbiologist by trade with one area of expertise in cryogenics. Curt's first job was researching and engineering as a microbiologist for ALLtech Inc., a bioengineering company based in Lexington, Kentucky. During his days at ALLtech, Curt worked with different types of bacteria to find new ways of preserving them so they could be transported throughout the world. He applied a method of freezing using supercold temperatures with substances like liquid CO_2 and liquid nitrogen—the same method used to create Dippin' Dots.

One method Curt developed was to "microencapsulate" the bacteria by freezing their medium with liquid nitrogen. Other scientists thought he was crazy because nothing like this had ever been done before. Curt, however, was convinced his idea would work. He spent months trying to perfect this method, and continued to make progress in making his idea materialize.

While Curt was working over 80 hours a week in ALLtech's labs to perfect the microencapsulating process, he made the most influential decision of his life when he took a weekend off and attended a family barbeque at his parents' house. It just so happened that his mother was making ice cream the day of the barbeque. Curt began to reminisce about homemade ice cream prepared the slow, old-fashioned way. Then Curt began to wonder if it was possible to flash-freeze ice cream? Instead of using a bacteria medium, was it possible to microencapsulate ice cream?

The answer was yes to both questions he posed to himself. After virtually reinventing a frozen dessert that had been around since the second century BC,[3] Curt patented his idea to flash-freeze liquid cream and eventually opened the first Dippin' Dots store. Today, the "Ice Cream of the Future" can be found at thousands of shopping malls, amusement parks, water parks, fairs, and festivals worldwide.

Dippin' Dots are transported coast-to-coast and around the world by truck, train, plane, and ship. In addition to specially designed cryogenic transport containers, Dippin' Dots are transported in refrigerated boxes known as Pallet Reefers. Both types of containers ensure the fastest and most efficient method of delivery of these premium products to dealers around the globe. The product is served in 4-, 5-, and 8-ounce cups, and 5-ounce vending prepacks.

Product Specifics

Dippin' Dots are flash-frozen beads of ice cream typically served in a cup or vending package. The ice cream averages 190 calories per serving, depending upon the flavor, and has 9 grams of fat. The ice cream is produced by a patented process that introduces flavored liquid cream into a vat with liquid nitrogen. The liquid cream is flash-frozen in the $-325°$ vat to produce the bead or dot shape. Once frozen, the dots are collected and either mixed with other flavors or packaged separately for delivery to retail locations. The product must be stored in subzero temperatures to maintain the consistency of the dots. Subzero storage temperatures are achieved by utilizing special equipment and freezers, and supplemented with dry ice. To maintain product integrity and consistency, the ice cream must be served at 10 to 20 degrees below zero. A retail location must have special storage and serving freezers. Because the product must be stored and served at such low temperatures, it is unavailable in regular frozen food cases and cannot be stored in a typical household freezer. Therefore, it can only be consumed at or near

---

*This case was prepared by graduate student Brian R. Callahan and Professor Alan B. Eisner of Pace University as a basis for class discussion rather than to illustrate either effective or ineffective handling of an administrative situation. Copyright © 2004 Alan B. Eisner.

[1]Figures provided by Dippin' Dots, Inc.

[2]Information unless otherwise stated is derived from the Dippin' Dots Web site. www.DippinDots.com; the Dippin' Dots 10-year anniversary video; or from the self-published Dippin' Dots Corporate Profile.

[3]Ice cream's origins are known to reach back as far as the second century BC, although no specific date of origin or inventor has been indisputably credited with its discovery. We know that Alexander the Great enjoyed snow and ice flavored with honey and nectar. Biblical references also show that King Solomon was fond of iced drinks during harvesting. During the Roman Empire, Nero (AD 54–86) frequently sent runners into the mountains for snow, which was then flavored with fruits and juices. Information from Ice Cream Media Kit, International Dairy Foods Association.

a retail location, unless stored with dry ice to maintain the necessary storage temperature.

Industry Overview

According to the market research firm Datamonitor, the U.S. ice-cream market experienced a stable growth rate of 0.93 percent from 1999 to 2003, increasing in value by 3.8 percent over the period. The size of the U.S. ice-cream market was $8.8 billion in 2003. According to data from ACNielsen, ice cream and related frozen desserts are consumed by more than 90 percent of households in the United States.[4]

Only a short while ago, the frozen dairy industry was occupied by family-owned businesses like Dippin' Dots, full-line dairies, and a couple of large international companies that focused on only a single sales region. The past year has been marked by a slight increase in the production and sale of ice cream, as volume in traditional varieties remained flat and new types of ice-cream forms emerged. Despite higher ingredient costs, manufacturers are continually churning out new products ranging from super-premium selections to good-for-you varieties to co-branded packages and novelties. Most novelty ice creams can be found together in a supermarket freezer case, small freezers in convenience stores, and in carts, kiosks, or trucks at popular summertime events. Ice-cream makers have been touched by consolidation trends affecting the overall food and beverage industry that extend beyond their products, as even the big names are folded into global conglomerates.

In 2003 the ice-cream segment became a battleground for two huge international consumer products companies seeking to corner the ice-cream market. Those two industry giants are Nestlé SA of Switzerland, the world's largest food company with more than $46 billion in annual sales, and Unilever PLC, of London and Rotterdam, with over $26 billion in annual revenues. Both have been buying into U.S. firms for quite awhile, but Nestlé, which already owns the Häagen-Dazs product line, upped the ante with its June 2003 merger with Dreyer's Grand/Edy's Ice Cream Inc., of Oakland, California.

The reason behind the fierce competition in the frozen dairy industry is the market's potential. A look at the most recent product and sales trends of ice cream shows a category with opportunities for innovation (see Exhibit 1). According to Jay Brigham, executive vice president of a candy and inclusions company in Dallas, "Ice cream has a lot of potential . . . if you look at what milk has done with single serve in the convenience store

[4]Ice cream consists of a mixture of dairy ingredients such as milk and nonfat milk, and ingredients for sweetening and flavoring, such as fruits, nuts, and chocolate chips. Functional ingredients, such as stabilizers and emulsifiers, are often included in the product to promote proper texture and enhance the eating experience. By federal law, ice cream must contain at least 10 percent butterfat, before the addition of bulky ingredients, and must weigh a minimum of 4.5 pounds to the gallon.

Exhibit 1   Top 10 Ice Cream Brands, 2004 (excludes Wal-Mart)

Brand	Sales ($ millions)	Percent Change from 2003
Private label	$1,001.9	−4.20%
Breyers	659.0	2.60%
Dreyer's/Edy's Grand	474.3	1.40%
Blue Bell	241.6	1.40%
Häagen-Dazs	214.6	0.54%
Ben & Jerry's	199.7	0.89%
Wells Blue Bunny	108.4	−.40%
Turkey Hill	107.0	−5.30%
Dreyer's/Edy's Grand Light	100.0	6.90%
Healthy Choice	94.0	−12.60%
Total category	$4,930.2	−1.90%

Source: Information Resources Inc.

market, ice cream still has the potential to do something like that. It's a very innovative category, and there's a lot of opportunity to do things like color-changing ingredients, or to try pop-rocks or to develop sugar-free products for instance," Brigham says. Ice cream by its very nature is a source of imaginative flavors and forms.

The estimated total value of the frozen dessert industry grew 3 percent in 2002 to $20.7 billion, attributable in part to higher prices which did not prevent consumers from spending more for ice cream (see Exhibit 2). The International Dairy Foods Association reported that, of that total, $7.7 billion was spent on products for at-home consumption while almost twice that, $13 billion, went toward away-from-home purchases.

The relatively cool summer of 2003 in the United States translated into flat overall sales and unit volume figures. Information Resources Inc. (IRI) of Chicago tallied total 2003 ice-cream sales in supermarkets, drugstores, and mass merchandisers (excluding Wal-Mart) at $4.51 billion. Ice-cream sales were down 1.2 percent in terms of dollars over 2002, yet unit sales were up 0.3 percent. According to IRI, frozen novelties sales were $2.5 billion during 2003. Novelty sales were up 5 percent over 2002 and unit sales increased by 0.9 percent.

In October 2002, it was announced that Good Humor–Breyers Ice Cream of Green Bay, Wisconsin, and Ben & Jerry's of Vermont had formed a unified retail sales division named Unilever Ice Cream. The new organization

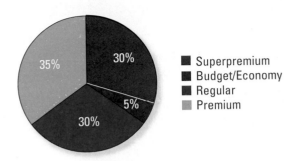

Exhibit 2   Ice-Cream Volume by Price, 2002

brought together both companies and represented the five Unilever North American ice-cream brands, which include Ben & Jerry's, Breyers, Good Humor, Popsicle, and Klondike. Good Humor–Breyers has created several new co-branded novelties specifically for convenience store and vending locations. The company also set out to expand the availability of single-serve novelties by placing freezers of its products in Blockbuster video stores and Breyers-branded kiosks in 30 Chicago-area Loew's theaters. In addition to prepackaged products, freshly scooped ice cream is served at the kiosks. The new sales team will focus exclusively on the out-of-home ice cream business and, therefore, exclude grocery channels (see Exhibit 3 for the top 10 novelty brands).

Exhibit 3   Top 10 Novelties Brands, 2004 (excludes Wal-Mart)

Brand	Sales (millions)	Market Share (%)
Private label	$ 367.1	14.5%
Klondike	175.8	7.0%
Silhouette	129.2	5.1%
Nestlé Drumstick	118.2	4.7%
Popsicle	108.1	4.3%
Weight Watchers	106.3	4.2%
Carvel	75.9	3.0%
Häagen-Dazs	50.2	2.0%
Dreyer's/Edy's	48.9	1.9%
Fudgsicle	45.4	1.8%
Other Brands	1301.1	51.5%
Total category	$2,526.2	100.0%

Source: Information Resources Inc.

Industry Segmentation Frozen desserts come in many forms. Each of the following foods has its own definition, and many are standardized by federal regulations:[5]

Ice Cream consists of a mixture of dairy ingredients, such as milk and nonfat milk, and ingredients for sweetening and flavoring, such as fruits, nuts, and chocolate chips. Functional ingredients, such as stabilizers and emulsifiers, are often included in the product to promote proper texture and enhance the eating experience. By federal law, ice cream must contain at least 10 percent butterfat, before the addition of bulky ingredients, and must weigh a minimum of 4.5 pounds to the gallon.

Novelties are separately packaged single servings of a frozen dessert, such as ice-cream sandwiches, fudge sticks, and juice bars, which may or may not contain dairy ingredients.

Frozen Custard or **French Ice Cream** must also contain a minimum of 10 percent butterfat, as well as at least 1.4 percent egg yolk solids.

Sherbets have a butterfat content of between 1 percent and 2 percent, and a slightly higher sweetener content than ice cream. Sherbet weighs a minimum of 6 pounds to the gallon and is flavored either with fruit or other characterizing ingredients.

Gelato is characterized by an intense flavor and is served in a semifrozen state. Gelato contains sweeteners, milk, cream, egg yolks, and flavoring.

Sorbet and **Water Ices** are similar to sherbets, but contain no dairy ingredients.

A **Quiescently Frozen Confection** is a frozen novelty such as a water ice novelty on a stick.

Frozen Yogurt consists of a mixture of dairy ingredients, such as milk and nonfat milk, which have been cultured, as well as ingredients for sweetening and flavoring.

Growth Stages[6]

Initiation The growth of Dippin' Dots Inc. has been recognized in the United States and the world by industry watchdogs such as *Inc.* magazine, which ranked Dippin' Dots as one of the 500 fastest-growing companies two years in a row in 1996 and 1997. Most recently, Dippin' Dots Franchising, Inc., ranked number four on *Entrepreneur* magazine's 2004 list of the top 50 new franchise companies and achieved the 101st spot on *Entrepreneur's*

[5]All definitions taken from the IDFA Web site: www.idfa.org/facts/icmonth/page4.cfm.

[6]Dippin' Dots 10th Anniversary Promotional Video.

Exhibit 4   Franchise Growth

Year	U.S. Franchises	Canadian Franchises	Foreign Franchises	Company Owned
2004	615	1	0	2
2003	580	0	0	2
2002	580	0	0	2
2001	569	0	0	3
2000	525	0	0	1

Source: Entrepreneur.com.

"Franchise 500" for 2004. Exhibit 4 shows the growth of franchises for Dippin' Dots.

However, the success of Curt Jones and Dippin' Dots has not been without obstacles. Once Curt perfected his idea, he needed to start a company for the new process of flash-freezing ice cream. Like many new entrepreneurs, Curt enlisted the help of his family to support his endeavor. It was essential to start selling his product, but he had no protection for his idea from competitors.

The first obstacle confronting Curt was to locate funding to accomplish his goals. He needed money for the patent to protect his intellectual property and seed money to start manufacturing the ice cream once the patent was granted. At the same time Curt was perfecting the flash-freezing process for his ice cream, he was also working on a small business association (SBA) loan to convert the family farm into one that would manufacture ethanol. However, instead of using the farm to produce the alternative fuel, Curt's parents took out a first, and then a second, mortgage to help fund Curt's endeavor. Thus, Curt initiated the entire venture by self-funding his company with personal and family assets.

However, the money from his parents was only enough to pay for the patent and some crude manufacturing facilities (liquid nitrogen tanks in his parent's garage). Curt always believed that his ice cream would sell, but with the patent he felt reassured by the protection it offered from any competitors. He next had to open a store to validate his faith that consumers would buy his product, but opening the store required more money—money that Curt and his family did not have. They were unable to get the SBA loan because, while the product was novel and looked promising, there was no proof that it would sell. So Curt and his newly appointed CFO (his sister) went to an "alternative lender" who lent them cash at an exorbitant interest rate which was tacked onto the principal weekly if unpaid.

With the seed money they needed, Curt Jones and his family opened their first store. Soon after the store opened in the summertime, there was a buzz in the community—and the store was mobbed every night. Dippin' Dots was legitimized by public demand. Through the influx of cash, Curt was able to move his manufacturing operation into a vacant warehouse. There he set up shop and personally made flash-frozen ice cream for 12 hours every day to supply the store.

Development   Once the store had been operating for a few months the Joneses were able to secure small business loans from local banks to cover the expenses of a modest manufacturing plant and office. At the same time, Curt's sister made calls to fairs and events to learn if Dippin' Dots products could be sold there. Luckily for the Joneses, the amusement park at Opryland in Nashville, Tennessee, was willing to have them as a vendor. Unfortunately, the first Dippin' Dots stand was placed in front of a roller coaster and people generally do not want ice cream before they go on a ride. After a few unsuccessful weeks, they moved the stand and business picked up considerably. Eventually, they were able to move to an inline location, which was similar to a store, where Dippin' Dots had its own personnel and sitting area to serve customers.

Just by word of mouth, the speculation about Curt Jones and Dippin' Dots spread. Soon other entrepreneurs contacted Curt to open up stores to sell Dippin' Dots. In 1991 a dealership network was developed to sell ice cream to authorized vendors and provide support with equipment and marketing. Over the course of nine years, Dippin' Dots grew into a multimillion dollar company with authorized dealers operating in all 50 states and internationally (see Exhibit 5). During that time, Curt employed friends to assume corporate jobs.

Plateau Busting By the end of the 1990s Curt was happy with his company, but felt as if Dippin' Dots had hit a plateau and needed to reach the "next level" to continue to prosper. He began working with his friend and now controller and director of franchising, Chad Wilson, to develop the franchise system. By January 2000, all existing

Exhibit 5   Milestones

1988	Dippin' Dots established as a company in Grand Chain, Illinois.
1989	First amusement park account debuts at Opryland USA in Nashville.
1990	Production facility moves to Paducah, Kentucky.
1991	Dealer network established for fair, festival, and commercial retail locations.
1994	First international licensee (Japan).
1995	New 32,000 sq. ft. production facility opens in Paducah.
1997	Production facility expands by 20,000 sq. ft.; earns spot on *Inc.* 500 list of USA's fastest-growing private companies in the United States.
2000	Dippin' Dots Franchising, Inc., established and first franchise offered; initiation of litigation against competitors to protect patent.
2001	Dippin' Dots enlists 30 new franchisees.
	Franchise Times magazine lists Dippin' Dots third nationally behind Baskin Robbins and Dairy Queen in number of franchises.
2002	Dippin' Dots Franchising, Inc., achieves 112th spot on *Entrepreneur* magazine's "Franchise 500" list.
	Dippin' Dots Franchising, Inc., ranked 69th on *Entrepreneur* magazine's list as "Fastest Growing" franchise company.
	Dippin' Dots Franchising, Inc., ranked the number one "New Franchise Company" by *Entrepreneur.*
	Dippin' Dots becomes a regular menu offering on menus at McDonald's restaurants in the San Francisco Bay area.
	Dippin' Dots product and plant featured as one of the world's most unique frozen desserts on the Food Network's new show *Unwrapped.*
	The Paducah plant builds a new freezer to hold 50,000 gallons of product at an average temperature of 55 degrees below zero (Dippin' Dots started with a 19,000-gallon freezer, and added a 45,000-gallon freezer in 1997).
2003	Dippin' Dots Franchising, Inc., achieves 144th spot on *Entrepreneur* magazine's "Franchise 500" list.
	Dippin' Dots Franchising, Inc., ranks number four on *Entrepreneur's* magazine's list of the Top 50 New Franchise Companies.
	Dippin' Dots Franchising, Inc., conducts first nationwide sweepstakes.
	Dippin' Dots Korea Ansong manufacturing plant, a 20,000 sq. ft. facility located 80 miles south of Seoul in South Korea.
2004	Dippin' Dots Franchising, Inc., ranks number four on *Entrepreneur's* list of the Top 50 New Franchise Companies.
	Dippin' Dots Franchising, Inc., achieves 101st spot on *Entrepreneur* magazine's "Franchise 500" list.
	Curt Jones and Dippin' Dots featured on a segment of the *Oprah Winfrey Show* appearing in 110 countries.
	Dippin' Dots featured among the "Top 10 Ice Cream Palaces" on the Travel Channel.
	Curt Jones quoted in Donald Trump's best-selling *The Way to the Top* (p. 131).

Dippin' Dots dealers were required to sign a franchise agreement and pay the associated franchise fees for any location they operated or planned to operate. A franchised location is any mall, fair, "national account," or large family entertainment center. The result was a cash flow for Dippin' Dots franchising.

Future Growth

Dippin' Dots is counting on youthful exuberance to expand growth above the $36 million mark of 2003. "Our core demographic is pretty much 8- to 18-year-olds," said Terry Reeves, corporate communications director. "On

top of that, we're starting to see a generation of parents who grew up on Dippin' Dots and are starting to introduce the products to their kids."

In 2002 McDonald's reportedly spent $1.2 million on advertising to roll out Dippin' Dots in about 250 restaurants in the San Francisco area. Because the response was good, McDonald's expanded into the Reno, Nevada, and Sacramento, California, areas, believing it would do well. Jones called the deal "open-ended" if it works favorably for both firms. "I think both companies are proceeding with the impression that nothing is going to be overcommitted," he said. "We're growing at a 10 to 15 percent annual rate and we're excited about the potential of McDonald's, but it's too early to tell." By mid-2004 Dippin' Dots was available in 800 western region McDonald's stores. McDonald's was a good fit for Dippin' Dots as a unique ice cream available in an exceptional restaurant for kids. McDonald's generous co-op advertising and promotions made dealing with McDonald's exacting standards, regulations, and inspections worthwhile. Expansion eastward for Dippin' Dots has been delayed by McDonald's efforts to refocus internally.

Second, Dippin' Dots ads have been running in issues of *Seventeen* and *Nickelodeon* magazines, marking the first time the company has purchased national consumer advertising. Reeves said the company has been "inundated with e-mails" since the June 2002 issue of *Seventeen* hit the newsstands. Additionally, Dippin' Dots has hired a Hollywood firm to place its ice cream in the background of television and movie scenes, including the 2003 hit *Cheaper by the Dozen.* In 2002 the Food Network's "Summer Foods: Unwrapped" showcased Dippin' Dots as one of the most unique and coolest ice cream treats. 'N Sync member Joey Fatone ordered a Dippin' Dots freezer for his home after seeing a Dots vending machine at a theater the band rented in Orlando. Caterers also sought Dippin' Dots for their star clients. A recent birthday party at the home of NBA star Shaquille O'Neal featured Dippin' Dots ice cream. In 2003 Jones, Reeves, and other company officials personally served their products to the band before an 'N Sync show in Memphis. Franchisees must contribute a half-percent of their gross incomes to an advertising fund, which Jones says has greatly enhanced marketing.

Challenges   Dippin' Dots has been in business for 16 years now and has had great success. However, the company has met increased competition in the once infrequent out-of-home ice-cream market. The major threats to Dippin' Dots are Nestlé and Unilever, the industry giants that are now focusing on the out-of-home ice-cream market. In addition, a very similar type of flash-frozen ice cream called Frosty Bites was introduced in the spring of 2000 by disenfranchised former dealers of Dippin' Dots. In 2002 Curt thought that introducing a formal franchising agreement would unify the company's public image—Dippin' Dots was often unrecognizable under a nonstructured dealership network of locations—and put the company on the map with other franchises like Dunkin' Donuts, Baskin Robbins, Häagen-Daaz, and Good Humor.

Terry Reeves, corporate communication director, said:

[T]he stronger and more unified Dippin' Dots retail offering becomes through franchising, the more [franchisees] were able to be considered for better retail properties (high-end malls, better locations, and so on). This obviously strengthens our system and bolsters overall sales for the company and for our franchisees. While franchise fees and royalties are a new income source, much of the profit is put back into the business to promote future growth.

One dealer commented that Dippin' Dots used that money, along with the incoming franchise fees for royalties on sales, for their own corporate means. On the other hand, most dealers did convert to the new franchise system. Dippin' Dots Franchising, Inc., grandfathered existing dealers' locations by issuing a franchise and waiving the franchise fee for the first contract period of five years. Many dealers had to renew their contracts in 2004; while many were initially apprehensive of converting to a franchised system, less than 2 percent left the system, and the firm has shown substantial franchise growth.

Jones, always the inventor, has been back in the lab and investing in R&D to create a conventional ice-cream product that has superfrozen dots embedded in it. He is developing a new product that could withstand conventional freezers while preserving the superfrozen dots in the ice cream. With this product Dippin' Dots could finally have a take-home ice-cream option. A grocery store product offering might be the ticket to national exposure for Dippin' Dots.

However, the company's experience and resource base are clearly in the ice-cream manufacturing and scoop shop retailing businesses. Dealing with supermarket chains, packaging, and distributors would be a new adventure for this relatively small firm. On the other hand, many opportunities can still be pursued in enlarging the franchise and national accounts businesses for scoop shops. In order to develop the business, Jones will have to choose either a big push with scoop shops or target the grocery store business or some combination of the two. Jones continues to assess his company's situation and then will identify and choose among the best strategic options for Dippin' Dots' growth over the remainder of this decade and beyond.

Case 12   eBay: King of the Online Auction Industry*

As Pierre Omidyar (pronounced oh-*mid*-ee-ar), chairman and founder of eBay, set his morning copy of the *Wall Street Journal* down on the desk, he nervously wondered how long eBay's amazing run of success would continue. He had just read an article detailing the explosion in sales of Amazon.com to $650 million during the fourth quarter of 1999, a number that exceeded the company's entire sales for the year of 1998. Even more disconcerting to Pierre was that online auctions were the fastest-growing part of Amazon's business in 1999. Competition from Amazon.com, Yahoo!, and several other enterprising dot-com companies that had started holding auctions at their Web sites had reduced eBay's dominant market share from 80 percent to 60 percent during 1999. Other outsiders, including Microsoft and Dell, had announced plans to fund new ventures to enter the online auction business.

When Pierre formed eBay in 1995, he had never imagined the company would become so successful. He had continued to work at his old job even after forming eBay. Soon, however, he realized that the online auction industry represented a tremendous market opportunity—eBay gave hobbyists and collectors a convenient way to locate items of interest, a way for sellers to generate income, and a means for bargain hunters to pick up a wanted item at less than they might have paid in a retail store. Still, the rapid growth of eBay had surprised almost everyone (see Exhibit 1).

By 1999, when people thought about online auctions, the first name that popped into their heads was eBay. Going into 2000, eBay had created the world's largest Web-based community of consumer-to-consumer auctions using an entertaining format that allowed people to buy and sell collectibles, automobiles, jewelry, high-end and premium art items, antiques, coins and stamps, dolls and figures, pottery and glass, sports memorabilia, toys, consumer electronics products, and a host of other practical and miscellaneous items. At year-end 1999, eBay had listed over 3 million items in over 3,000 categories; browsers and buyers could search listings by item, category, key word, seller name, or auction dates. The company Web site had approximately 10 million registered users and, on average, attracted 1.8 million unique visitors daily. eBay members listed more than 375,000 items on the site every day.

However, Pierre Omidyar, Margaret Whitman (eBay's president and CEO), and other eBay executives were well aware that eBay needed to address a myriad of emerging market challenges. The complexion of the online auction industry was changing almost daily. While eBay's management team had met past challenges successfully, it wasn't going to be easy to hurdle the competitive and market challenges ahead.

The Growth of e-Commerce and Online Auctions

Although the ideas behind the Internet were first conceived in the 1960s, it wasn't until the 1990s that the Internet garnered widespread use and became a part of everyday life. The real beginning of the Internet economy took place in 1991, when the National Science Foundation (NSF) lifted a restriction on commercial use of the Internet, making electronic commerce, or business conducted over the Internet, a possibility for the first time. By 1996, there were Internet users in almost 150 countries worldwide, and the number of computer hosts was close to 10 million. International Data Corporation (IDC) estimated there would be 320 million Internet users worldwide by 2002 and 500 million by year-end 2003.

The GartnerGroup forecast that business-to-business e-commerce would grow from $145 billion in 1999 to $7.29 trillion in 2004, while business-to-consumer revenues would climb from $31.2 billion in 1999 to over $380 billion in 2003. Within the business-to-consumer segment, where eBay operated, U.S. e-commerce accounted for over 65 percent of all Internet transactions in 1999 but was expected to account for only about 38 percent in 2003, due to rapid expansion in other parts of the world.

Business-to-consumer e-commerce in Europe was projected to grow from $5.4 billion in 1999 (17.3 percent of the world total) to over $115 billion (more than 30 percent of the world total) by 2003. As can be seen from Exhibit 2, online auction sales of collectibles and personal merchandise was expected to represent an $18.7 billion market in 2002.

Key Success Factors in Online Retailing   While it was relatively easy to create a Web site that functioned like a retail store, the big challenge was for an online retailer to generate traffic to the site in the form of both new and returning customers. Most online retailers strived to provide extensive product information, include pictures of the merchandise, make the site easily navigable, and have enough new things happening at the site to keep customers coming back. (A site's ability to generate repeat visitors was known as "stickiness.") Retailers also had to overcome users' nervousness about using the Internet itself to shop for items they generally bought at stores and their wariness about entering their credit card numbers over the Internet. Online retailing had severe limitations in the case of those goods and services people wanted to see in person to verify their quality. From the retailer's

*Case written by Louis Marino, The University of Alabama, and Patrick Kreiser, The University of Alabama. Copyright © 2000 by Lou Marino; all rights reserved.

Exhibit 1   Selected Indicators of eBay's Growth, 1996–99

	1996	1997	1998	1999
Number of registered users	41,000	341,000	2,181,000	10,006,000
Gross merchandise sales	$7 million	$95 million	$745 million	$2.8 billion
Number of auctions listed	289,000	4,394,000	33,668,000	129,560,000

Exhibit 2   Estimated Growth in Global e-Commerce and Online Auction Sales, 1999–2004

	1999	2000	2001	2002	2003	2004
Estimated business-to-business sales	$145 billion	$403 billion	$953 billion	$2.18 trillion	$3.95 trillion	$7.29 trillion

Source: GartnerGroup.

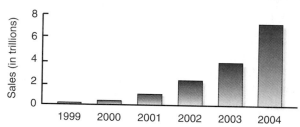

Estimated Growth in Global Business-to-Business e-Commerce

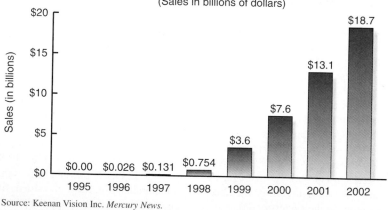

Online Auction Sales of Collectibles and Personal Merchandise
(Sales in billions of dollars)

Source: Keenan Vision Inc. *Mercury News.*

perspective, there was the issue of collecting payment from buyers who wanted to use checks or money orders instead of a credit card.

History of Auctions

An auction is a method of buying and selling goods to the highest bidder. A seller offers a particular product or service for sale, and the buyer who makes the highest offer for it is considered the auction winner. As the demand for a particular good rises among the buyers (typically due to its scarcity or desirability), the price also rises. Competition among bidders for a desirable good drives up the price. Sometimes the highest bid will exceed the generally accepted market value of the good, a phenomenon known as the "winner's curse." In this situation, the buyer becomes so emotionally attached to the good or to placing the highest bid that he or she ends up bidding more than the good would cost in a nonauction setting.

The first known auctions were held in Babylon around 500 BC. In these auctions, women were sold to the highest bidder on the condition that they marry the auction winner. In ancient Rome, soldiers would auction the spoils of their victories and wealthy citizens would auction their expensive belongings and prized possessions. In 193 AD, the entire Roman Empire was put up for auction after the emperor Pertinax was executed. Didius Julianus bid 6,250 drachmas per royal guard and was immediately named emperor of Rome. However, Julianus was executed only two months later, indicating that he may have been the first-ever victim of the winner's curse.

Since that time, auctions have been conducted in every corner of the globe. The possessions of deceased Buddhist monks were auctioned off as early as the seventh century. In the late 16th century, auctions began to be held in taverns and alehouses in Great Britain. Sotheby's was founded in 1744, and Christie's was established in 1766; both have now become world-renowned auction houses for rare and valuable items. Auctions for tobacco, horses, and other domestic animals were commonplace in colonial America.

Auctions have endured throughout history for several reasons. First, they give sellers a convenient way to find a buyer for something they would like to dispose of. Second, auctions are an excellent way for people to collect difficult-to-find items, such as Beanie Babies or historical memorabilia, that have a high value to them personally. Finally, auctions are one of the "purest" markets that exist for goods, in that they bring buyers and sellers into contact to arrive at a mutually agreeable price. Experts estimated that the national market for auctions, garage sales, flea markets, and classified purchases was greater than $100 billion in 1999.

Online Auctions

Online auctions worked in essentially the same way as traditional auctions, the difference being that the auction process occurred over the Internet rather than at a specific geographic location with buyers and sellers physically present. In 2000, there were three categories of online auctions:

1. Business-to-business auctions, which accounted for $2.5 billion in sales in 1998 and involved such items as computers, used equipment, and surplus merchandise.
2. Business-to-consumer auctions, in which businesses sold goods and services to consumers via the Internet. Many such auctions involved companies interested in selling used or discontinued goods, or liquidating unwanted inventory.
3. Person-to-person auctions, which gave interested sellers and buyers the opportunity to engage in competitive bidding.

Since eBay's pioneering of the person-to-person on-line auction process in 1995, the number of online auction sites on the Internet had grown to well over 1,600 by the end of 1999. Forrester Research predicted that 6.5 million customers would use online auctions in 2002. In 1999 an estimated 8.2 percent of Internet users had registered at an auction site; the percentage was expected to be 14.5 percent by 2002.

Online auction operators could generate revenue in four principal ways:

1. Charging sellers for listing their good or service.
2. Charging a commission on all sales.
3. Selling advertising on their Web sites.
4. Selling their own new or used merchandise via the online auction format.

Most sites charged sellers either a fee or a commission and sold advertising to companies interested in promoting their goods or services to users of the auction site.

Auction Software Packages   In 1996, OpenSite Technologies began to offer packaged software applications to firms interested in creating their own online auction Web sites. Moai Technologies and Ariba, Inc., were other sources for auction software. The ready availability of commercial software packages made it easy for firms to create and operate online auction sites. OpenSite had marketed over 600 auction packages to such companies as The Sharper Image, CNET, and John Deere. OpenSite claimed that its purpose was to bring together "buyers and sellers, helping businesses dynamically manage inventory, create sales channels, attract customers, and test-market new products, to create efficient markets for goods and services."

Providers of Site Hosting and Online Auction Services

Auction firms could, if they wished, outsource all the hosting functions associated with online auctions to independent site-hosting enterprises and could even turn the entire auction process over to an independent online auction specialist. FairMarket, the leader in auction outsourcing in 1999, provided companies such as ZDNet, MicroWarehouse, and CollegeBytes.com with a means of selling their goods at online auction at Fair-Market's Web site. The use of site hosts and independent online auction services was a particularly appealing option for companies that wanted to use online auctions as a distribution channel but preferred to devote only minimal time and energy to site construction and upkeep. By paying FairMarket an annual hosting fee between $2,000 and $10,000, as well as a percentage fee on all transactions, firms were able to have an auction site without having to worry about the hassle of site upkeep.

Online Auction Users   Participants in online auctions could be grouped into three categories: (1) bargain hunters, (2) hobbyists/collectors, and (3) sellers.

Bargain Hunters Bargain hunters viewed online auctions primarily as a form of entertainment; their objective usually was to find a great deal. One bargain hunter described the eBay experience as follows:

> A friend and I would spend one day a week going flea marketing and auctioning. Since school has started again, time has become a hot commodity. We've found that we can use eBay to fill that flea marketing, auctioning need. We'll call each other, then get on eBay and hunt and find things together even though we can't be together. EBay has definitely been a great way to spend quality time together!

Bargain hunters were thought to make up only 8 percent of active online users but 52 percent of eBay visitors. To attract repeat visits from bargain hunters, industry observers said, sites must appeal to them on both rational and emotional levels, satisfying their need for competitive pricing, the excitement of the search, and the desire for community.[1]

Hobbyists and Collectors Hobbyists and collectors used auctions to search for specific goods that had a high value to them personally. They were very concerned with both price and quality. Collectors prized eBay for its wide variety of product offerings. One user commented:

> My sister collects Princess House hand-blown ornaments. She needed the first three to complete her series. I posted to the Wanted Board several times, and also put a note on my About Me page. Well, we have now successfully completed her series. We could never have done this without eBay because the first one is so hard to find. Thanks eBay!

Sellers Those in the sellers category could be further differentiated into at least three types: casual sellers, hobbyists/collectors, and power sellers. Casual sellers included individuals who used eBay as a substitute for a classified ad listing or a garage sale to dispose of items they no longer wanted. While many casual sellers listed only a few items, some used eBay to raise money for some new project. One such seller stated:

> Thank you! After just starting to use your site less than a month ago, I have increased my earnings by over $1,000. I have not yet received all the cash, but so far the response has been fantastic. This all started with a Kool-Aid container and four cups I had that were collecting dust in a box in the attic. I was "browsing for bargains" and saw someone else had made $29.00 from those plastic things! I was AMAZED! Needless to say, I listed them. I only made $8.00, but I received my first positive feedback. Since then I am listing daily.

> My wife and I are scrimping to save for an adoption of a baby. The fees are much more than our modest income can afford, and this extra cash will come in handy. My wife and I sincerely thank you and your company for the opportunity to be a part of eBay.

Sellers who were hobbyists or collectors typically dealt in a limited category of goods and looked to eBay as a way to sell selected items in their collections to others who might want them. Power sellers were typically small- to medium-sized businesses that favored eBay as a primary distribution channel for their goods and often sold tens of thousands of dollars' worth of goods every month on the site. One estimate suggested that while these power sellers accounted for only 4 percent of eBay's population, they were responsible for 80 percent of eBay's total business.[2]

Concerns about Buyer Addiction to Online Auctions

Some members of the online auction community reportedly found the experience so intriguing that they became addicted. According to the Center for Online Addiction, symptoms of online auction addiction ranged from "using online auctions as a way of escaping from problems or relieving feelings of helplessness, guilt, anxiety, or depression" to "needing to bid with increasing amounts of money in order to achieve the desired excitement."[3] The center predicted that "online auction houses will be the next frenzy leading to shopping addiction" and had treated online auction addicts who had to take out a second mortgage or file bankruptcy as a result of their excessive online purchases.[4] One online auction addict told of his experience as follows:

> It became critical when my boss confronted me. [My employer] had monitored my Internet use, and it was even more than I was aware of. My boss told me he had no choice but to terminate me. I've been at this job almost five years, have achieved recognition at the national level for the program, and have previously been a very capable employee. How can I [justify] throwing all that away? There is no doubt, though, that my productivity had really begun to suffer.
>
> I was truthful with my boss about how this had become a compulsion I just could not control. I attributed it to some real stresses in my personal life, and kept telling myself that when things settled down, I would get a handle on it. He has put me on [administrative] leave while he thinks things over.[5]

[1]"Internet Consumer Segments Identified for First Time," PR Newswire, April 17, 2000.

[2]Claire Tristram, "'Amazoning' Amazon," www.contextmag.com, November 1999.

[3]www.netaddiction.com, April 16, 2000.

[4]Ibid.

[5]www.auctionwatch.com, April 16, 2000.

Pierre Omidyar and the Founding of eBay

Pierre Omidyar was born in Paris, France, to parents who had left Iran decades earlier. The family emigrated to the United States when Pierre's father began a residency at Johns Hopkins University Medical Center. Pierre grew up in modest circumstances; his parents divorced when he was two but remained near each other so he could be with both of them. Pierre's passion for computers began at an early age; he would sneak out of gym class in high school to play with computers. While still in high school, at age 14 he took his first computer-related job in the school's library, where he was hired for $6.00 an hour to write a program to print catalog cards.[6] After high school Pierre attended Tufts University, where he met his future wife, Pamela Wesley, who came to Tufts from Hawaii to get a degree in biology. Upon graduating in 1988, the couple moved to California, where Pierre, who had earned a BS in computer science, joined Claris, an Apple Computer subsidiary in Silicon Valley, and wrote a widely used graphics application, MacDraw. In 1991, Omidyar left Claris and cofounded Ink Development (later renamed eShop), which became a pioneer in online shopping and was eventually sold to Microsoft in 1996. In 1994 Omidyar joined General Magic as a developer services engineer and remained there until mid-1996, when he left to pursue full-time development of eBay.

Internet folklore has it that eBay was founded solely to allow Pamela to trade Pez dispensers with other collectors. While Pamela was certainly a driving force in launching the initial Web site, Pierre had long been interested in how one could establish a marketplace to bring together a fragmented market. Pierre saw eBay as a way to create a person-to-person trading community based on a democratized, efficient market where everyone could have equal access through the same medium, the Internet. Pierre set out to develop his marketplace and to meet both his and Pamela's goals. In 1995 he launched the first online auction under the name of Auctionwatch at the domain name of www.eBay.com. The name eBay stood for "electronic Bay area," coined because Pierre's initial concept was to attract neighbors and other interested San Francisco Bay area residents to the site to buy and sell items of mutual interest. The first auctions charged no fees to either buyers or sellers and contained mostly computer equipment (and no Pez dispensers). Pierre's fledgling venture generated $1,000 in revenue the first month and an additional $2,000 the second. Traffic grew rapidly, however, as word about the site spread in the Bay area; a community of collectors emerged, using the site to trade and chat—some marriages resulted from exchanges in eBay chat rooms.[7]

By February 1996, the traffic at Pierre Omidyar's site had grown so much that his Internet service provider informed him that he would have to upgrade his service. When Pierre compensated for this by charging a listing fee for the auction, and saw no decrease in the number of items listed, he knew he was on to something. Although he was still working out of his home, Pierre began looking for a partner and in May asked his friend Jeffrey Skoll to join him in the venture. While Jeff had never cared much about money, his Stanford MBA degree provided the firm with the business background that Pierre lacked.[8] With Pierre as the visionary and Jeff as the strategist, the company embarked on a mission to "help people trade practically anything on earth." Their concept for eBay was to "create a place where people could do business just like in the old days—when everyone got to know each other personally, and we all felt we were dealing on a one-to-one basis with individuals we could trust."

In eBay's early days, Pierre and Jeff ran the operation alone, using a single computer to serve all of the pages. Pierre served as CEO, chief financial officer, and president, while Jeff functioned as co-president and director. It was not long until Pierre and Jeff grew the company to a size that forced them to move out of Pierre's living room, due to the objections of Pamela, and into Jeff's living room. Shortly thereafter, the operations moved into the facilities of a Silicon Valley business incubator for a time until the company settled in its current facilities in San Jose, California.

Exhibits 3 and 4 present eBay's recent financial statements.

eBay's Transition to Professional Management

From the beginning Pierre Omidyar intended to hire a professional manager to serve as the president of eBay: "[I would] let him or her run the company so . . . [I could] go play."[9] In 1997 both Omidyar and Skoll agreed that it was time to locate an experienced professional to function as CEO and president. In late 1997 eBay's headhunters came up with a candidate for the job: Margaret Whitman, then general manager for Hasbro Inc.'s preschool division. Whitman had received her BA in economics from Princeton and her MBA from the Harvard Business School; her first job was in brand management at Procter & Gamble. Her experience also included serving as the president and CEO of FTD, the president of Stride Rite Corporation's Stride Rite Division, and as the senior vice president of marketing for the Walt Disney Company's consumer product division.[10]

When first approached by eBay, Whitman was not especially interested in joining a company that had fewer than 40 employees and less than $6 million in revenues the

[6]tbwt.com/interaction/1pomid/1pomid.htm.

[7]Quentin Hardy, "The Radical Philanthropist," *Forbes,* May 1, 2000, p. 118.

[8]Adam Cohen, "The eBay Revolution," www.time.com.

[9]Business 2.0, "Billionaires of the Web," *The Candyman,* June 1999.

[10]www.ebay.com, Company Overview page.

Exhibit 3   eBay's Income Statements, 1996–99 ($000, Except Per Share Figures)

	1996	1997	1998	1999
Net revenues	$32,051	$41,370	$86,129	$224,724
Cost of net revenues	6,803	8,404	16,094	57,588
Gross profit	25,248	32,966	70,035	167,136
Operating expenses				
Sales and marketing	13,139	15,618	35,976	95,956
Product development	28	831	4,640	23,785
General and administrative	5,661	6,534	15,849	43,055
Amortization of acquired intangibles	—	—	805	1,145
Merger related costs	—	—	—	4,359
Total operating expenses	18,828	22,983	57,270	168,300
Income (loss) from operations	6,420	9,983	12,765	(1,164)
Interest and other income (expense), net	(2,607)	(1,951)	(703)	21,377
Income before income taxes	3,813	8,032	12,062	20,213
Provision for income taxes	(475)	(971)	(4,789)	(9,385)
Net income	$ 3,338	$ 7,061	$ 7,273	$ 10,828
Net income per share				
Basic	$0.39	$0.29	$0.14	$0.10
Diluted	.07	0.08	0.06	0.08
Weighted average shares				
Basic	8,490	24,428	52,064	108,235
Diluted	45,060	84,775	116,759	135,910

Source: Company financial documents.

previous year. It was only after repeated pleas that Whitman agreed to meet with Omidyar in Silicon Valley. After a second meeting, Whitman realized the company's enormous growth potential and agreed to give eBay a try. According to Omidyar, Meg Whitman's experience in global marketing with Hasbro's Teletubbies, Playskool, and Mr. Potato Head brands made her "the ideal choice to build upon eBay's leadership position in the one-to-one online trading market without sacrificing the quality and personal touch our users have grown to expect."[11] In addition to convincing Margaret Whitman to head eBay's operations, Omidyar had been instrumental in helping bring in other talented senior executives and in assembling a capable board of directors. Notable members of eBay's board of directors included Scott Cook, the founder of Intuit, a highly successful financial software company, and Howard Schultz, the founder and CEO of Starbucks. (For a profile of eBay's senior management team, check out the Company Overview section at www.ebay.com.)

Whitman ran the operation from the time she came on board. Omidyar, who owned 27.9 percent of eBay's stock (worth approximately $6 billion as of March 2000), spent considerable time in Paris. He and Pamela, still in their mid-30s and concerned about the vast wealth they had accumulated in such a short period of time, were devoting a substantial amount of their energy to exploring philanthropic causes.[12] They had decided to give most of their fortune to charity and were scrutinizing alternative ways to maximize the impact of their philanthropic contributions on the overall well-being of society. Jeffrey Skoll owned 16.7 percent of eBay's shares (worth about $3.6 billion), and Margaret Whitman owned 5.2 percent (worth about $1 billion).

How an eBay Auction Worked

eBay endeavored to make it very simple to buy and sell goods. In order to sell or bid on goods, users first had to register at the site. Once they registered, users selected both a user name and a password. Nonregistered users

[11]eBay press release, May 7, 1998.

[12]Hardy, "The Radical Philanthropist."

Exhibit 4 eBay's Consolidated Balance Sheets, 1997–99 ($000)

	December 31, 1997	December 31, 1998	December 31, 1999
Assets			
Current assets			
Cash and cash equivalents	$3,723	$ 37,285	$219,679
Short-term investments	—	40,401	181,086
Accounts receivable, net	1,024	12,425	36,538
Other current assets	220	7,479	22,531
Total current assets	4,967	97,590	459,834
Property and equipment, net	652	44,062	111,806
Investments	—	—	373,988
Deferred tax asset	—	—	5,639
Intangible and other assets, net	—	7,884	12,675
Total assets	$5,619	$149,536	$963,942
Liabilities and Stockholders' Equity			
Current liabilities			
Accounts payable	$ 252	$ 9,997	$ 31,538
Accrued expenses and other current liabilities	—	6,577	32,550
Deferred revenue and customer advances	128	973	5,997
Debt and leases, current portion	258	4,047	12,285
Income taxes payable	169	1,380	6,455
Deferred tax liabilities	—	1,682	—
Other current liabilities	128	5,981	7,632
Total current liabilities	1,124	24,656	88,825
Debt and leases, long-term portion	305	18,361	15,018
Other liabilities	157		
Total liabilities	1,586	48,998	111,475
Series B mandatorily redeemable convertible preferred stock and Series B warrants	3,018	—	—
Total stockholders' equity	1,015	100,538	852,467
Total liabilities and stockholders' equity	$5,619	$149,536	$963,942

Source: Company financial documents.

were able to browse the Web site but were not permitted to bid on any goods or list any items for auction. On the Web site, search engines helped customers determine what goods were currently available. When registered users found an item they desired, they could choose to enter a single bid or to use automatic bidding. In automatic bidding the customer entered an initial bid sufficient to make him or her the high bidder and then the bid would be automatically increased as others bid for the same object until the auction ended and either the bidder won or another bidder surpassed the original customer's maximum specified bid. Regardless of which bidding method

they chose, users could check bids at any time and either bid again, if they had been outbid, or increase their maximum amount in the automatic bid. Users could choose to receive e-mail notification if they were outbid. Once the auction had ended, the buyer and seller were each notified of the winning bid and were given each other's e-mail address. The parties to the auction would then privately arrange for payment and delivery of the good.

Fees and Procedures for Sellers eBayers were not charged a fee for bidding on items on the site, but sellers were charged an insertion fee and a "final value" fee; they could also elect to pay additional fees to promote their listing. Listing, or insertion, fees ranged from 25 cents for auctions with opening bids between $0.01 and $9.99, to $2.00 for auctions with opening bids of $50.00 and up. Final value fees ranged from 1.25 to 5 percent of the final sale price and were computed based on a graduated fee schedule in which the percentage fell as the final sales price rose. As an example, in a basic auction with no promotion, if the item had brought an opening bid of $100 and eventually sold for $1,500, the total fee paid by the seller would be $33.88—the $2.00 insertion fee plus $31.88. The $31.88 is based on a fee structure of 5 percent of the first $25.00 (or $1.25), 2.5 percent of the additional amount between $25.01 and $1,000.00 (or $24.38), and 1.25 percent of the additional amount between $1,000.01 and $1,500.00 (or $6.25).

A seller who wished to promote an item could choose a bold heading for an additional fee of $2.00. A seller with a favorable feedback rating (discussed below) could have his or her auction listed either as a "Featured Auction" for $99.95, which allowed the seller's item to be rotated on the eBay home page, or as a "Category Featured Auction" for $14.95, which allowed the item to be featured within a particular eBay category. For $1.00, a seller could choose to place a seasonal icon (such as a shamrock in connection with St. Patrick's Day) next to his or her listing. A seller could also include a description of the product with links to the seller's Web site. In addition, a seller could indicate a photograph in the item's description if the seller posted the photograph on a Web site and provided eBay with the appropriate Web address. Items could be showcased in the Gallery section with a catalog of pictures rather than text. A seller who used a photograph in his or her listing could have this photograph included in the Gallery section for 25 cents or featured there for $19.95. A Gallery section was available in all categories of eBay. Certain categories of items—such as real estate, automobiles, and "Great Collections"—had special promotion rates.

New sellers were required to file a credit card number with eBay for automatic monthly billing, while sellers who had opened accounts prior to October 22, 1999, could alternatively choose a pay-as-you-go method. The latter option, however, was relatively unattractive since it allowed eBay to block any account whose balance due reached $25.00. The block was removed once the fee was paid, or once the seller had registered a credit card with eBay.

How Transactions Are Completed When an auction ended, the eBay system validated that the bid fell within the acceptable price range. If the sale was successful, eBay automatically notified the buyer and seller via e-mail; the buyer and seller could then work out the transaction details independent of eBay. At no point during the process did eBay take possession of either the item being sold or the buyer's payment. Rather, the buyer and seller had to independently arrange for the shipment of and payment for the item; buyers typically paid for shipping. A seller could view a buyer's feedback rating (discussed below) and then determine the manner of payment, such as personal check, cashier's check, or credit card, and also whether to ship the item before or after receiving payment. Under the terms of eBay's user agreement, if a seller received one or more bids above the stated minimum, or reserve, price, the seller was obligated to complete the transaction, although eBay had no enforcement power beyond suspending a noncompliant buyer or seller from using eBay's service. In the event the buyer and seller were unable to complete the transaction, the seller notified eBay, which then credited the seller the amount of the final value fee. When items carrying a reserve price sold, sellers were credited the $1.00 reserve fee. Invoices for placement fees, additional listing fees, and final value fees were sent via e-mail to sellers on a monthly basis.

Feedback Forum In early 1996 eBay pioneered a feature called Feedback Forum to build trust among buyers and sellers and to facilitate the establishment of reputations within its community. Feedback Forum encouraged individuals to record comments about their trading partners. At the completion of each auction, both the buyer and seller were allowed to leave positive, negative, or neutral comments about each other. Individuals could dispute feedback left about them by annotating comments in question. By assigning values of +1 for a positive comment, 0 for a neutral comment, and –1 for a negative comment, each trader earned a ranking that was attached to his or her user name. A user who had developed a positive reputation over time had a color-coded star symbol displayed next to his or her user name to indicate the amount of positive feedback. The highest ranking a trader could receive was "over 10,000," indicated by a shooting star. Well-respected high-volume traders could have rankings well into the thousands. Users who received a sufficiently negative net feedback rating (typically a –4) had their registrations suspended and were thus unable to bid on or list items for sale. eBay users could review a person's feedback profile before deciding to bid on an item listed by that person or before choosing payment and delivery methods.

The terms of eBay's user agreement prohibited actions that would undermine the integrity of the Feedback Forum, such as leaving positive feedback about oneself through other accounts or leaving multiple negative comments about someone else through other accounts. eBay's Feedback Forum system had several automated features designed to detect and prevent some forms of abuse. For example, feedback posted from the same account, positive or negative, could not affect a user's net feedback rating by more than one point, no matter how many comments an individual made. Furthermore, a user could only make comments about his or her trading partners in completed transactions. The company believed its Feedback Forum was extremely useful in overcoming users' initial hesitancy about trading over the Internet, since it reduced the uncertainty of dealing with an unknown trading partner.

eBay's Strategy to Sustain Its Market Dominance

Meg Whitman assumed the helm of eBay in February 1998 and began acting as the public face of the company. Pierre Omidyar stepped back to become chairman of eBay's board of directors and focused his time and energy on overseeing eBay's strategic direction and growth, business model and site development, and community advocacy. Jeff Skoll, who became the vice president of strategic planning and analysis, concentrated on competitive analysis, new business planning and incubation, the development of the organization's overall strategic direction, and supervision of customer support operations.

The Move to Go Public   Within months of assuming the presidency of eBay, Whitman took on the challenge of preparing the company to raise capital for expansion through an initial public offering (IPO) of common stock. Through a series of road shows designed to convince investors of the potential of eBay's business model, Whitman and her team generated significant interest in eBay's IPO. When the shares opened for trading on September 24, 1998, eBay's executives had high hopes for the offering, but none of them dreamed that it would close the day at $47, or 160 percent over the initial offering of $18 per share. The IPO generated $66 million in new capital for the company and was so successful that *Bloomberg Personal* magazine designated eBay as the "Hot IPO of 1998"; *Euromoney* magazine named eBay as the best IPO in the U.S. market in January 1999. The success of the September 1998 offering led eBay to issue a follow-up offering in April 1999 that raised an additional $600 million. As a qualification to the IPOs, eBay's board of directors retained the right to issue as many as 5 million additional shares of preferred stock with no further input from the current shareholders in case of a hostile takeover attempt.

With the funds received from the IPOs, eBay launched strategic initiatives aimed at six specific objectives:[13]

1. Growing the eBay community and strengthening our brand, both to attract new members and to maintain the vitality of the eBay community;

2. Broadening the company's trading platform by growing existing product categories, promoting new product categories, and offering services for specific regions;

3. Fostering eBay community affinity and increasing community trust and safety through services such as user verification and insurance;

4. Enhancing Web site features and functionality through the introduction of personalization features such as About Me, which permits users to create their own home page free of charge, and the Gallery, an opportunity for sellers to showcase their items as pictures in a photo catalog;

5. Expanding pre- and post-trade value-added services, such as assistance with scanning and uploading photographs of listed items, third-party escrow services, and arrangements to make shipping of purchased items easier;

6. Developing international markets by actively marketing and promoting our Web site in selected countries.

To pursue these objectives, eBay employed three main competitive tactics. First, it sought to build strategic partnerships in all stages of its value chain, creating an impressive portfolio of over 250 strategic alliances with companies such as America Online (AOL), Yahoo!, Lycos, Compaq, and Warner Brothers. Second, it actively sought customer feedback and made improvements based on this information. Third, it actively monitored the external environment for developing opportunities.

eBay's Business Model   eBay's business model was based on creating and maintaining a person-to-person trading community where buyers and sellers could readily and conveniently exchange information and goods. eBay's role was to function as a value-added facilitator of online buyer-seller transactions by providing a supportive infrastructure that enabled buyers and sellers to come together in an efficient and effective manner. Success depended not only on the quality of eBay's infrastructure but also on the quality and quantity of buyers and sellers attracted to the site; in management's view, this entailed maintaining a compelling trading environment, a number of trust and safety programs, a cost-effective and convenient trading experience, and strong community affinity. By developing the eBay brand name and increasing the customer base, eBay endeavored to attract a sufficient number of high-quality buyers and sellers necessary to meet the organization's goals. The online auction format meant that eBay carried zero inventory and could operate a marketplace without the need for a traditional sales force.

Growing the eBay Community and Strengthening the Brand   In developing the eBay brand name and attracting new users, the company initially relied largely on word-of-mouth advertising, supplemented by public relations initiatives such as executive interviews and speaking engagements, special online events, and astute management of the public press. Then, with funds from the public offerings of common stock, eBay expanded its marketing activities to include advertising online as well as in traditional media, such as national magazines like *Parade, People, Entertainment Weekly, Newsweek,* and

---

[13]eBay company S-1 filing with the Securities and Exchange Commission, March 25, 1999, p. 4.

Sports Illustrated. A cornerstone of the strategy to increase eBay's exposure was the formation of alliances with a variety of partners, including Kinko's, First Auction, and Z Auction as well as Internet portals AOL, Netscape, and GO.com.

The Alliance with First Auction   In January 1998, eBay entered into a marketing agreement with First Auction, the auction division of the Internet Shopping Network. The terms of this agreement allowed both companies to advertise their services on each other's sites. While both organizations offered online auctions, eBay featured person-to-person trading, and First Auction engaged in business-to-consumer transactions, which eBay did not consider direct competition. A similar agreement was formed in February 1998 with Z Auction, another vendor-based auction site.

The Alliance with America Online   eBay's initial alliance with AOL, announced in February 1998, was limited to eBay's providing a person-to-person online auction service in AOL's classifieds section. However, in September 1998 this agreement was expanded. In return for $12 million in payments over three years, AOL made eBay the preferred provider of personal trading services to AOL's 13 million members and the 2 million members of AOL's affiliate CompuServe. In 1998 eBay also became a "distinguished partner" of Netscape's Netcenter. In February 1999 eBay's relationship with Netscape was broadened to include banner ads and bookmarks. In March 1999 eBay's arrangement with AOL was expanded to feature eBay as the preferred provider of personal trading services on all of AOL's proprietary services, including Digital Cities, ICQ, CompuServe (both international and domestic), Netscape, and AOL.com. In return for this four-year arrangement, eBay agreed to pay CompuServe $75 million and to develop a co-branded version of its services for each of AOL's properties involved in the agreement, with AOL receiving all of the advertising revenues from these co-branded sites.[14]

The Alliance with Kinko's   In February 2000 eBay formed strategic marketing agreements with Kinko's, a global retail provider of document copying and business services, and GO.com, the Internet arm of Walt Disney Company. eBay's alliance with Kinko's allowed eBay to place signage in Kinko's stores across the country, and to offer its users 15 minutes of free computing rental at Kinko's locations. In return, eBay featured Web links to Kinko's Web pages in eBay's Computer, Business/Office, and Big Ticket categories, and encouraged users to go to Kinko's for photo scanning, e-mail, document faxing, and teleconferencing services.

The Alliance with GO.com   The long-term intention for the cooperative agreement with GO.com was for eBay to eventually become the exclusive online trading service

across all of Disney's Internet properties. In the initial stages of the agreement, however, eBay was only to market and develop co-branded person-to-person and merchant-to-person sites on behalf of the Walt Disney Company.[15]

Broadening the Trading Platform   Efforts intended to broaden the eBay trading platform concentrated on growing the content within current categories, on broadening the range of products offered according to user preferences, and on developing regionally targeted offerings. Growth in existing product categories was facilitated by deepening the content within the categories through the use of content-specific chat rooms and bulletin boards as well as targeted advertising at trade shows and in industry-specific publications. Further, in April 1998, custom home pages were created for each category so collectors could search for their next treasured acquisition without having to sort through the entirety of eBay's offerings.

In June 1999 eBay formed a collaborative relationship with the Collecting Channel, a portal owned by ChannelSpace Entertainment, Inc. The Collecting Channel was a premier Internet information source for virtually every conceivable category of collectibles. It delivered content in ways ranging from original audio/video programming to live chats to live videoconferencing. EBay's agreement called for The Collecting Channel to provide in-depth content to eBay collectors and for eBay, in return, to provide links to The Collecting Channel's Web site.

Part of eBay's strategy to broaden its user base was to establish regional auctions. In 1999 eBay launched 53 regional auction sites focused on the 50 largest metropolitan areas in the United States. Management believed that having regional auction sites would encourage the sale of items that were prohibitively expensive to ship, items that tended to have only a local appeal, and items that people preferred to view before purchasing. eBay had also done several promotional or feature auctions, partnering with Guernsey to sell home-run balls hit by baseball stars Mark McGwire and Sammy Sosa in their 1998 home-run race and partnering with BMW in 1999 to auction the first BMW X5 sports activity vehicle to be delivered, with the proceeds going to the Susan G. Komen Breast Cancer Foundation.

Additional efforts to broaden the trading platform involved the development of new product categories. Over 2,000 new categories were added between 1998 and 2000, bringing the total to 3,000 categories (greatly expanded from the original 10 categories in 1995). One of the most significant new categories was eBay Great Collections, a showcasing of rare collectibles such as coins, stamps, jewelry, and timepieces as well as fine art and antiques from leading auction houses around the world. This category came from eBay's April 1999 acquisition of Butterfield and Butterfield, one of the world's largest and most prestigious auction houses.

[14]eBay's 1999 10-K report.

[15]eBay press release, www.ebay.com, February 8, 2000.

The growing popularity of automobile trading on the eBay Web site prompted the creation of a special automotive category supported by Kruse International, one of the world's most respected organizations for automobile collectors. The automotive category was further expanded in March 2000 through a partnership with AutoTrader.com, the world's largest used-car marketplace, that established a co-branded auction site for consumers and dealers to buy and sell used cars.

Fostering eBay Community Affinity and Building Trust   Since its founding in 1995, eBay had considered developing a loyal, vivacious trading community to be a cornerstone of its business model. To foster a sense of community among eBay users, the company employed tools and tactics designed to promote both business and personal interactions between consumers, to foster trust between bidders and sellers, and to instill a sense of security among traders.

Interactions between community members were facilitated through the creation of chat rooms based on personal interests. These chat rooms allowed individuals to learn about their chosen collectibles and to exchange information about items they collected. To manage the flow of information in the chat rooms, eBay employees went to trade shows and conventions to seek out individuals who had both knowledge about and a passion for either a specific collectible or a category of goods. These enthusiasts would act as community leaders or ambassadors; they were never referred to as employees but were compensated $1,000 a month to host online discussions with experts.

Although personal communication between members fostered a sense of community, as eBay's community grew from "the size of a small village to a large city"[16] additional measures were necessary to ensure a continued sense of trust and honesty among users. One of eBay's earliest trust-building efforts was the 1996 creation of the Feedback Forum, described earlier.

Unfortunately, the Feedback Forum was not always sufficient to ensure honesty and integrity among traders. While eBay estimated that far less than 1 percent of the millions of auctions completed on the site involved some sort of fraud or illegal activity, some users would agree with Clay Monroe, a Seattle-area trader of computer equipment, who estimated that while "ninety percent of the time everybody is on the up and up . . . ten percent of the time you get some jerk who wants to cheat you."[17] Fraudulent or illegal acts perpetrated by sellers included misrepresentation of goods; trading in counterfeit goods or pirated goods that infringed on others' intellectual property rights; failure to deliver goods paid for by buyers; and shill bidding, whereby sellers would use a false bidder to artificially drive up the price of a good. Buyers could manipulate bids by placing an unrealistically high bid on a good to discourage other bidders and then withdraw their bid at the last moment to allow an ally to win the auction at a bargain price. Buyers could also fail to deliver payment on a completed auction.

Recognizing that fraudulent activities represented a significant danger to eBay's future, management took the Feedback Forum a step further in 1998 by launching the SafeHarbor program to provide guidelines for trade, provide information to help resolve user disputes, and respond to reports of misuse of the eBay service.[18] The SafeHarbor initiative was expanded in 1999 to provide additional safeguards and to actively work with law enforcement agencies and members of the trading community to make eBay more secure. New elements of SafeHarbor included free insurance, with a $25.00 deductible, through Lloyd's of London for transactions under $200.00; enhancements to the Feedback Forum; a new class of verified eBay users with an accompanying icon; easy access to escrow services; tougher policies relating to nonpaying bidders and shill bidders; clarification of which items were not permissible to list for sale; and a strengthened anti-piracy and anti-infringement program. The use of verified buyer and seller accounts was viewed as especially significant because it allowed eBay to ensure that suspended users did not open new eBay accounts under different names. User information was verified through Atlanta-based Equifax Inc.

To implement these new initiatives between 1999 and 2000, eBay increased the number of positions in its SafeHarbor department from 24 to 182, including full-time employees and independent contractors. It also organized the department around the functions of investigations, community watch, and fraud prevention. The investigations group was responsible for examining reported trading violations and possible misuses of eBay. The fraud-prevention group mediated customer disputes over such things as the quality of the goods sold. If a written complaint of fraud was filed against a user, eBay generally suspended the alleged offender's account, pending an investigation. The community watch group worked with over 100 industry-leading companies, ranging from software publishers to toy manufactures to apparel makers, to protect intellectual property rights. To ensure that illegal items were not being sold and sale items listed did not violate intellectual property rights, this SafeHarbor group automated daily keyword searches on auction content. Offending auctions were closed and the seller was notified of the violation. Repeated violations resulted in suspension of the seller's account.

As eBay expanded its categories to include Great Collections and the new automobile categories, new safeguards were introduced to meet the unique needs of these areas. In the eBay Great Collections category, the company partnered with Collector's Universe to offer authentication

[16]Tristram, "'Amazoning' Amazon."

[17]Stephen Buel, "eBay Inc. Feeling Growing Pains," *San Jose Mercury News,* December 26, 1998.

[18]eBay 10-K, filed July 15, 1998.

and grading services for specific products such as trading cards, coins, and autographs. In the automobile area, eBay partnered with carclub.com to provide users with access to carclub.com's inspection and warranty service.

Enhancing Web Site Features and Functionality

In designing its Web site, eBay went to great lengths to make it intuitive, easy to use by both buyers and sellers, and reliable. Efforts to ensure ease of use ranged from narrowly defining categories (to allow users to quickly locate desired products) to introducing services designed to personalize a user's eBay experience. Two specific services developed by eBay to increase personalization were "My eBay" and "About Me."

My eBay was launched in May 1998 to give users centralized access to confidential, current information regarding their trading activities. From his or her My eBay page a user could view information pertaining to his or her current account balances with eBay; feedback rating; the status of any auctions in which he or she was participating, as either a buyer or a seller; and auctions in favorite categories. In October of the same year, eBay introduced the About Me service, which allowed users to create customized home pages that could be viewed by all other eBay members. These pages could include elements from the My eBay page such as user ratings or items the user had listed for auction, as well as personal information and pictures. This service not only increased customer ease of use but also contributed to the sense of community among the traders; one seller stated that the About Me service "made it easier and more rewarding for me to do business with others."[19]

When eBay first initiated service, the only computer resource it had was a single Sun Microsystems setup with no backup capabilities. By 1999 eBay's explosive growth required 200 Windows NT servers and a Sun Microsystems server to manage the flow of users on the site, process new members, accept bids, and manage the huge database containing the list of all items sold on the site. On June 10, 1999, the strain of managing these processes while attempting to integrate new product and service offerings proved too much for the system and the eBay site crashed. It stayed down for 22 hours. The outage not only seriously shook user confidence in eBay's reliability but also cost the company some $4 million in fees; the company's stock price reacted to the outage by falling from $180 to $136.[20]

Unfortunately, the June 10 site crash proved to be the first in a string of outages. While none of them was as significant as the first (most lasted only one to four hours), confidence in eBay continued to decline in both the online community and on Wall Street as eBay's stock fell to 87 11/16 in August 1999. To counter these problems, eBay sought

out Maynard Webb, a premier software engineer and troubleshooter who was working at Gateway Computer.

Webb put a moratorium on new features until system stability was restored. Webb believed that it was virtually impossible to completely eliminate outages, so he set a goal of reducing system downtime and limiting outages to one hour.[21] To achieve this goal Webb believed he would need a backup for the 200 Windows NT servers, another for the Sun Microsystems unit, and a better system for managing communications between the Windows NT and Sun systems. In attacking these challenges, eBay acquired seven new Sun servers, each valued at $1 million, and outsourced its technology and Web site operations to Exodus Communications and Abovenet. These outsourcing agreements were intended to allow Exodus and Abovenet to "manage network capacity and provide a more robust backbone" while eBay focused on its core business.[22] While eBay still experienced minor outages when it changed or expanded services (for example, a system crash coincided with the introduction of the 22 regional Web sites), system downtime decreased. However, the stability of the system under eBay's explosive growth and continuous introduction of new features and services was a major and continuing management concern.

Expanding Value-Added Services

To make it easier for eBay's sellers and buyers to transact business, in 1998 the company announced that it would offer an "'end-to-end' person-to-person trading service . . . [by providing] a variety of pre- and post-trade services to enhance the user experience."[23] Pre-trade services that eBay planned to offer included authentication and appraisal services, while planned post-trade services included third-party escrow services as well as shipping and payment services.

In preparation for Christmas 1998, eBay formed alliances with Parcel Plus, a leading shipping service, and with Tradesafe and I-Escrow, both of which guaranteed that buyers would get what they paid for. According to eBay's agreement with I-Escrow, monies paid to the seller were held in an escrow account until the buyer received and approved the merchandise. eBay's arrangement with Tradesafe called for the seller to register a credit card with Tradesafe to guarantee funds up to $1,200; proceeds of a sale were deposited directly into the seller's bank account. If the buyer was not satisfied with the transaction, all or part of the money was refunded. Both I-Escrow and Tradesafe charged a small percentage of the purchase price for their services.

In April 1999, eBay entered into a five-year partnership with Mail Boxes, Etc. (the world's largest franchiser of retail business, communications, and postal service centers), and iShip.com (the leader in multicarrier Web-based

[19]Ann Pearson, in an eBay press release dated October 15, 1998.

[20]Julie Pita, "Webb Master," *Forbes*, December 13, 1999.

[21]Ibid.

[22]eBay press release, October 8, 1999.

[23]eBay S-1 report filed July 15, 1998, p. 46.

shipping services for e-commerce) to offer person-to-person e-commerce shipping solutions.[24] eBay's agreement with iShip gave eBay users access to accurate zip-code-to-zip-code shipping rates with various shipping services and allowed users to track packages. The agreement with Mail Boxes, Etc. (MBE), required eBay to promote MBE's retail locations as a place where sellers could pack and ship their goods; eBay and MBE were contemplating expanding their agreement to allow buyers to open and inspect their newly purchased goods at MBE retail stores prior to accepting the shipment.

To facilitate person-to-person credit card payments, eBay acquired Billpoint, a company that specialized in transferring money from one cardholder to another. Using the newly acquired capabilities of Billpoint, eBay was able to offer sellers the option of accepting credit card payments from other eBay users; for this service, eBay charged sellers a small percentage of the transaction. eBay's objective was to make credit card payment a "seamless and integrated part of the trading experience."[25] In March 2000 eBay and Wells Fargo, the owner-operator of the largest Internet bank, entered into an arrangement whereby Wells Fargo would purchase a minority stake in Billpoint and Billpoint would use Wells Fargo's extensive customer care and payment processing infrastructure to process credit card payments from eBay buyers to eBay sellers.

In January 2000, eBay entered into an exclusive agreement with E-Stamp that allowed E-Stamp to become the exclusive provider of Internet postage from the U.S. Postal Service on eBay's Web site. In return for being prominently featured on eBay's Web site, E-Stamp gave eBay users easy access to its Web site, offered them reduced fees for its service, and gave them a significant discount on the E-Stamp Internet postage starter kit. According to sources close to the deal, E-Stamp paid eBay close to $10 million a year for gaining such access to eBay's customers.[26]

Developing International Markets   As competition increased in the online auction industry, eBay began to seek growth opportunities in international markets in an effort to create a global trading community. While international buyers and sellers had been trading on eBay for some time, there were no facilities designed especially for the needs of these community members. In entering international markets, eBay considered three options. It could build a new user community from the ground up, acquire a local organization, or form a partnership with a strong local company. In realizing its goals of international growth, eBay employed all three strategies.

In late 1998 eBay's initial efforts at international expansion into Canada and the United Kingdom relied on building new user communities. The first step in establishing these communities was creating customized home pages for users in those countries. These home pages were designed to provide content and categories locally customized to the needs of users in specific countries, while providing them with access to a global trading community. Local customization in the United Kingdom was facilitated through the use of local management, grassroots and online marketing, and participation in local events.[27]

In February 1999 eBay partnered with PBL Online, a leading Internet company in Australia, to offer a customized Australian and New Zealand eBay home page. When the site went live in October 1999, transactions were denominated in Australian dollars and, while buyers could bid on auctions anywhere in the world, they could also search for items located exclusively in Australia. Further, local chat boards were designed to facilitate interaction between Australian users, and country-specific categories, such as Australian coins and stamps as well as cricket and rugby memorabilia, were offered.

To further expand its global reach, eBay acquired Germany's largest online person-to-person trading site, alando.de AG, in June 1999. eBay's management handled the transition of service in a manner calculated to be smooth and painless for alando.de AG's users. While users would have to comply with eBay rules and regulations, the only significant change for alando.de AG's 50,000 registered users was that they would have to go to a new URL to transact their business.

To establish an Asian presence, in February 2000 eBay formed a joint venture with NEC to launch eBay Japan. According to the new CEO of eBay Japan, Merle Okawara, an internationally renowned executive, NEC was pleased to help eBay in leveraging the tried-and-trusted eBay business model to provide Japanese consumers with access to a global community of active online buyers and sellers. In customizing the site to the needs of Japanese users, eBay wrote the content exclusively in Japanese and allowed users to bid in yen. The site had over 800 categories ranging from internationally popular categories (such as computers, electronics, and Asian antiques) to categories with a local flavor (such as Hello Kitty, Pokémon, and pottery). The eBay Japan site also debuted a new merchant-to-person concept known as Supershops, which allowed consumers to bid on items listed by companies.

Honors and Awards   As a result of the relentless implementation of its business model, eBay had met with significant success. Not only was the company financially profitable from its first days (see again Exhibits 3 and 4), but it had won many prestigious honors and awards in 1998 and 1999. Among the most significant were Best Internet Auction Site (*San Francisco Bay Guardian,* July 1998); Electronic Commerce Excellence (CommerceNet,

---

[24]eBay press release, April 8, 1999.

[25]eBay press release, May 18, 1999.

[26]Jane Weaver, "eBay: Can It Keep Customers Loyal?" www.zdnet.com, May 13, 2000.

[27]eBay 10-K report filed March 30, 2000.

October 1998); Top e-Commerce Program/Service (Computer Currents Readers' Choice Awards, February 1999); Editor's Choice Award (*PC* magazine, March 1999), and Top 50 CEOs (*Worth* magazine, May 1999).

How eBay's Auction Site Compared with That of Rivals

Auction sites varied in a number of respects: site design and ease of use, the range of items up for auction, number of simultaneous auctions, duration of the bidding process, and fees. Gomez Advisors, a company designed to help Internet users select which online enterprises to do business with, had developed rankings for the leading online auction sites as a basis for recommending which sites were best for bargain hunters, hobbyists/collectors, and sellers. To be considered in the Gomez ratings, an auction site had to (1) have more than 500 lots of original content; (2) conduct auctions for items in at least three of the following six categories: collectibles, computers/electronics, jewelry, sports, stamps/coins, and toys; (3) have more than five lots in each qualifying category; and (4) have sustained bidding activity in each category. Exhibit 5 shows the winter 1999 Gomez ratings of online auction competitors—the latest ratings can be viewed at www.gomez.com.

eBay's Main Competitors

In the broadest sense, eBay competed with classified advertisements in newspapers, garage sales, flea markets, collectibles shows, and other venues such as local auction houses and liquidators. As eBay's product mix broadened beyond collectibles to include practical household items, office equipment, toys, and so on, the company's competitors broadened to include brick-and-mortar retailers, import/export companies, and catalog and mail order companies. Management saw these traditional competitors as inefficient because their fragmented local and regional nature made it expensive and time-consuming for buyers and sellers to meet, exchange information, and complete transactions. Moreover, they suffered from three other deficiencies: (1) they tended to offer limited variety and breadth of selection as compared to the millions of items available on eBay, (2) they often had high transactions costs, and (3) they were "information inefficient" in the sense that buyers and sellers lacked a reliable and convenient means of setting prices for sales or purchases. Thus, eBay's management saw its online auction format as competitively superior to these rivals because it (1) facilitated buyers and sellers meeting, exchanging information, and conducting transactions; (2) allowed buyers and sellers to bypass traditional intermediaries and trade directly, thus lowering costs; (3) provided global reach, greater selection, and a broader base of participants; (4) permitted trading at all hours and provided continuously updated information; and (5) fostered a sense of community among individuals with mutual interests.

From an e-commerce perspective, Amazon.com and Yahoo! Auctions had emerged as eBay's main competitors going into 2000, but FairMarket, AuctionWatch, GO Network Auctions, and Auctions.com were beginning to make market inroads and contribute to erosion of eBay's share of the online auction business. Moreover, the prospects of attractive profitability and low barriers to entry were stimulating more firms to enter the online auction industry and imitate eBay's business model. eBay management saw competition in the online auction industry as revolving around 9 factors: the volume and selection of goods, the population of buyers and sellers, community interaction, customer service, reliability of delivery and payment by users, brand image, Web site construction, fees and prices, and quality of search tools.

Exhibit 6 provides selected statistics for the leading competitors in the online auction market. Exhibit 7 provides comparative financial data, and Exhibit 8 provides comparative Web site traffic.

Amazon.com   At the end of 1999, Gomez.com ranked Amazon.com as the second best online auction Web site. Amazon.com, created in July 1995 as an online bookseller, had rapidly turned into a full-line, one-stop-shopping retailer with a product offering that included books, music, toys, electronics, tools and hardware, lawn and patio products, video games, software, and a mall of boutiques (called z-shops)—some 18 million items at last count. Amazon.com was the Internet's number one music, video, and book retailer. The company's 1999 revenues of $1.64 billion were up 169 percent over 1998, but despite the company's rapid revenue growth it was incurring huge losses due to the expenses of (1) establishing an infrastructure to support its sales (the company expanded its worldwide distribution capacity from 300,000 square feet to over 5 million square feet in 1999) and (2) attracting customers via advertising and online (See Exhibit 9).

While Amazon's management was under mounting pressure to control expenses and prove to investors that its business model and strategy were capable of generating good bottom-line profitability, it was clear that management's decisions and strategy were focused on the long term and on solidifying Amazon's current position as a market leader. Management believed that its business model was inherently capital efficient, citing the fact that going into 2000 the company had achieved annualized sales of $2 billion with just $220 million in inventory and $318 million in fixed assets. The company's customer base rose from 6.2 million to 16.9 million during 1999. The company invested more than $300 million in infrastructure in 1999 and opened two international sites: Amazon.co.uk and Amazon.de. These two sites, along with Amazon.com, were the three most popular online retail domains in Europe. Amazon also entered into a number of strategic alliances. During the fourth quarter of 1999 and the first

Exhibit 5 Comparative Gomez Advisors' Ratings of Leading Online Auction Sites

A. Ratings Based on Site Characteristics (Rating scale: 0 = lowest; 10 = highest)

Auction Site	Ease of Use[a]	Customer Confidence[b]	On-Site Resources[c]	Relationship Services[d]	Overall Score
1. eBay	9.07	6.99	8.40	8.40	7.97
2. Amazon.com	9.05	8.49	7.03	6.17	7.67
3. Yahoo! Auctions	8.69	6.91	4.18	8.62	7.11
4. GO Network Auctions	9.14	7.44	6.49	5.89	7.00
5. FairMarket Network	7.97	6.89	6.73	5.17	6.42
6. Auctions.com	8.22	6.78	5.50	5.10	6.41
7. utrade	8.87	4.60	2.43	6.57	5.65
8. Boxlot	7.20	7.83	3.19	4.09	5.63
9. Haggle Online	7.62	4.65	4.80	4.72	5.29
10. edeal	8.05	4.04	2.35	5.83	5.17
11. ehammer	7.59	5.35	4.21	3.15	5.09

[a]Based on such factors as screen layout, tightly integrated content, functionality, useful demos, and the extensiveness of online help.

[b]Includes the reliability and security of the online auction site, knowledgeable and accessible customer service, and quality guarantees.

[c]Based on the range of products, services, and information offered, information look-up tools, and transactions data.

[d]Based on personalization options, programs, and perks that build a sense of community and customer loyalty to the site.

B. Ratings Based on Type of Auction Site User (Rating scale: 0 = lowest; 10 = highest)*

Auction Site	Bargain Hunters	Hobbyists/Collectors	Sellers
1. eBay	8.43	7.98	7.94
2. Amazon.com	7.46	7.71	6.87
3. Yahoo! Auctions	7.37	6.67	6.96
4. GO Network Auctions	6.84	6.72	6.54
5. FairMarket Network	6.16	6.44	6.10
6. Auctions.com	5.94	6.31	5.47
7. utrade	5.65	5.01	5.34
8. edeal	5.61	4.83	4.89
9. ehammer	5.05	5.27	4.60
10. Haggle Online	5.00	4.88	5.07
11. Boxlot	4.79	5.57	4.57

* Each of the four criteria in part A above were weighted according to their perceived importance to bargain hunters, hobbyists/collectors, and sellers. These criteria were then averaged together to develop a score for each of the three types of online auction site users.

Source: Gomez Advisors, www.gomez.com, March 2, 2000.

month of 2000, the company announced partnerships with NextCard, Ashford.com, Greenlight.com, Audible, and living.com, as well as an expanded partnership with drugstore.com. It already had e-commerce partnerships with Gear.com; Homegrocer.com; Della.com (an online service for gift registry, gift advice, and personalized gift suggestions); Pets.com; and Sotheby's (a leading auction house for art, antiques, and collectibles).

With its customer base of almost 17 million users in over 150 countries and a very well-known brand name, Amazon.com was considered an imposing competitive threat to eBay. Amazon.com launched its online auction

Exhibit 6   Selected Auction Statistics for eBay, Amazon, and Yahoo!, December 1999

	eBay	Yahoo! Auctions	Amazon.com
Number of items listed for auction	3.8 million	1.3 million	415,000
Percentage of listed auctions closing with a sale	65%	14%	11%
Average number of bids per item	3.03	0.59	0.33
Average selling price for completed auctions	$65.19	$31.09	$25.77

Source: Taken from "Internet: eBay: Crushing the Competition," *Individual Investor*, January 21, 2000.

Exhibit 7   Comparative 1999 Financial Statistics for eBay, Amazon, and Yahoo!*

	eBay	Amazon.com	Yahoo.com
Net revenues	$224,724,000	$1,639,839,000	$588,608,000
Cost of goods sold	57,588,000	1,349,194,000	92,334,000
Net income	10,828,000	(719,968,000)	61,133,000
Net income per share	$0.04	$(2.20)	$0.20

*Includes all business areas for Amazon.com and Yahoo!, not just online auctions.

Source: 1999 company financial statements.

Exhibit 8   Number of Unique Visitors during December 1999

Web Site	Total Number of Unique Visitors
Yahoo! sites	42,361,000
GO Network	21,348,000
Amazon.com	16,631,000
eBay.com	10,388,000

Source: www.mediametrix.com.

Exhibit 9   Amazon.com's Losses

Year	Net Loss
1996	$ 6.2 million
1997	31.0 million
1998	124.5 million
1999	720.0 million

site in March 1999. The site charged sellers for listing their products and also charged a commission on sales. Although Amazon's selection of auctions did not match the one offered by eBay, the company reported that online auctions were the fastest-growing part of its business. The number of auctions on Amazon grew from 140,000 to 415,000 during the second half of 1999. Amazon.com offered three major marketplaces for its users: Auctions, zShops, and sothebys.amazon.com. Its auction site formed partnerships with DreamWorks to promote that company's films *Stuart Little* and *American Beauty* (72 auctions, averaging 27 bids per auction, total gross merchandise sales

of over $25,000, yielding an average of over $400 per item) and with television celebrity Oprah Winfrey (25 auctions, averaging 38 bids per auction, total gross merchandise sales of over $130,000, yielding an average of over $6,000 per item).[28]

Yahoo! Auctions   Yahoo.com, the first online navigational guide to the Web, launched Yahoo! Auctions in 1997. Yahoo.com offered services to nearly 120 million users every month and the Yahoo! Network operated in North America, Europe, Asia, and Latin America. Yahoo! reported net revenues of $588 million in 1999 (up 140 percent from 1998) and net income of $142 million. Yahoo's user base grew from 60 million to 120 million during

[28]Amazon.com press release, February 2, 2000.

1999, and 40 million of these users were outside the United States. In December 1999, Yahoo's traffic increased to an average of 465 million page views per day. Yahoo! had entered into numerous alliances and marketing agreements to generate additional site traffic and was investing in new technology to improve the site's performance and attractiveness.

Its auction services were provided to users free of charge, and the number of auctions listed on Yahoo! increased from 670,000 to 1.3 million during the second half of 1999. Yahoo! Auctions was expanded to include Hong Kong, Taiwan, Korea, Mexico, Brazil, and Denmark at the end of 1999. Localized Yahoo! auctions outside the United States were being conducted in 16 countries in 11 different languages. Yahoo! Japan Auctions was the largest localized online auction service in Japan. At the end of 1999, Yahoo! launched Yahoo! Merchant Auctions and Featured Auctions in order to allow retailers and sellers to promote their auctions. Yahoo! Auctions also offered many extra services to its users. Gomez.com rated Yahoo! Auctions as the number one online auction site in the Relationship Services category.

FairMarket   FairMarket, a new online auction provider that went online in September 1999, had quickly emerged as one of the leading providers of private-label, outsourced, networked auction services for business clients. It offered a number of formats: hosted auctions, fixed-price auctions, declining-price or markdown auctions for merchants wishing to dispose of overstocked merchandise, and shopping-by-request services. The company was formed through an alliance of Microsoft, Dell Computer, Lycos, Excite, CBS Sportsline, CompUSA, and several others. The FairMarket network of auctions included Alta Vista Auctions, CityAuction, Excite Auctions, GO Auction, Lycos Auctions, and MSN Auctions. The company went public in early 2000, raising approximately $75 million to support expansion.

FairMarket managed and maintained online auctions for such customers as JCPenney (which had auctions that allowed customers to purchase new, quality merchandise and auctions that incorporated an automatic markdown format for overstocked merchandise from JCPenney retail store and catalog operations); the Times Digital Company (which conducted local auctions in New York City and other locations); Dell Computer (which held auctions for customers wishing to sell their used computers and for equipment coming off lease); Ritz Camera (which used auctions to sell end-of-life camera equipment); Outpost.com (which auctioned a mix of new and refurbished computer and computer accessory items); and SportingAuction (which used FairMarket's network systems to auction an extensive selection of high-quality sporting goods). FairMarket received a percentage fee of all the items sold on auctions it conducted for its customer-sellers.

AuctionWatch   AuctionWatch.com was formed in July 1998 and incorporated in January 1999 as a privately held company backed by several venture capital firms and private investors. The company, a very small online auction site originally, had raised $10 million in capital in August 1999 to expand both its site and its available features. The AuctionWatch site was designed to model eBay and had many of the same types of offerings. By the end of 1999, AuctionWatch.com was conducting over 25,000 auctions daily, had served over 2 million auction images per day, and received over 20,000 posts each month in its visitor center. AuctionWatch catered to businesses looking to use online auctions as a new distribution channel and to attract new customers. One of the unique features at AuctionWatch was a content service that allowed users to compare and contrast the fee structures of the top consumer-to-consumer, business-to-consumer, and business-to-business auction sites; the information was updated monthly.

As of April 2000, AuctionWatch had over 250,000 registered users and was conducting about 1 million auctions monthly. AuctionWatch attracted 1.7 million unique visitors in March 2000, an increase of over 100 percent from February and over 500 percent from December 1999. In the first quarter of 2000, businesses and auction enthusiasts used AuctionWatch to sell over $120 million worth of merchandise.

GO Network Auctions   GO.com was the result of a November 1999 merger between Walt Disney's online unit, the Buena Vista Internet Group (BVIG), and Infoseek Corporation. The company oversaw ABC.com, ESPN.com, and Disney.com, as well as several other popular Web sites; its chief activity was serving as the Internet business arm of the Walt Disney Company. The GO.com portal focused on entertainment, leisure, and recreation activities. The online auction section of the GO Network, auction.go.com, was experiencing rapid growth. GO Network Auctions offered over 100 product categories and provided users with a guarantee against fraudulent listings; one of its main features was auctioning Disney products, including movie sets, props, and memorabilia from movies produced by Walt Disney Studios and from ABC-produced shows. The Web site was also considered extremely easy to navigate. Gomez.com ranked GO Network Auctions number one in the Ease of Use category among online auctions.

In February 2000 GO.com and eBay announced a four-year agreement to develop and market online trading and auction experiences in a co-branded person-to-person site and new merchant-to-person sites. According to terms of the agreement, eBay would ultimately become the online trading and auction service for all of Disney's Internet properties, including the GO Network portal, and would collaborate on merchant-to-person auctions for authenticated products, props, and memorabilia from throughout the Walt Disney Company.

Auctions.com   Auctions.com was originally launched as Auction Universe in November 1997. After being acquired by Classified Ventures in 1998, the site was relaunched as Auctions.com on December 13, 1999. The company claimed to be "the world's fastest growing online auction network" at the beginning of 2000.[29] Auctions.com had hundreds of categories and several thousand product listings available for users. Not only did the company's Web site offer 24-hour customer service support, but it also had the premier online transaction security program (Bid$afe). The Federal Trade Commission claimed that Bid$afe was one of the "best fraud protection programs on the Web."[30]

Formed in 1997 and headquartered in London, QXL.com was moving rapidly to try to dominate the online auction market in Europe. Rather than create one Web site for Europe, QXL's strategy was to methodically enter one European country after another, launching its own new sites in some countries and acquiring already established players in others. While QXL was thinking globally, it was acting locally, operating in 12 different languages, accommodating 12 different currencies (until use of the euro), and tailoring its merchandise features to the preferences of users in each country. QXL's market reach included Great Britain, Germany, France, Italy, Spain, the Netherlands, Denmark, Finland, Poland, Norway, and Sweden. QXL was developing technology so that it could quickly and economically customize its sites for each country. Currently, however, its sites were slow and antiquated compared to eBay.

In 2000, the online aution market in Europe was much less developed than in the United States; there were not as many Internet users and many European Web surfers were leery of entering bids to purchase an item online. To combat the wariness of online auctions exhibited by actual and prospective visitors to its online auction site, QXL was conducting a number of auctions for goods put up for sale by retail merchants. QXL management reasoned that site visitors who were reluctant to buy items from a stranger would feel comfortable enough to enter bids to buy merchandise from an established retailer.

Niche Auctions

Many new competitors had also begun offering auctions targeted at smaller segments of the online auction industry. These auctions primarily specialized in one product or service type, such as computers/electronics, fine art, industrial products, music-related goods, international auctions, and just about any other product or service imaginable. There were sites offering laptop computers (AuctionLaptops.com), guitars (Guitarauction.com), Ger-

man wines (Koppe and Partner Wine Auctions), and even a site that auctioned nothing but racing pigeons (ipigeon. com). There were several significant companies conducting niche auctions:

- *Outpost.com*—Outpost.com was founded in 1995 to service primarily the small-office/home-office market. By the end of 1999, the company offered over 170,000 products online, primarily in the computer/electronics area. Bizrate.com rated Outpost.com the number one consumer shopping experience on the Web, and Forrester Research awarded the company the 1999 number one PowerRanking for Computing. The company had a half million customers and 4 million monthly visitors. In 2000, the company announced separate partnerships with Golf Galaxy and Computer.com. Outpost claimed to differentiate itself from other online auction sites "by focusing on the needs of the customer and delivering its services with reliability, fully encrypted secure servers, depth of product selection, and building a team of dedicated and knowledgeable professionals that support all efforts of the business."[31]

- *eWanted.com*—eWanted.com pioneered the idea of the "backward auction" in October 1998. A backward auction was the exact opposite of a traditional online auction. Buyers would place ads specifying the item they wanted, as well as the product's primary characteristics. Then sellers would browse these ads and submit offers to the buyers. The theory was that sellers would compete with each other for a particular buyer, thus driving the auction price down. In return, sellers entered a marketplace where they knew that buyers existed for their particular product or service.

- *eRock.com*—eRock.com specialized in offering rock-and-roll memorabilia to "serious die-hard fans, collectors, and dealers."[32] The site had 12 different categories of music auctions available, and also offered a chat room for users to talk about their musical interests and links to the Web pages of several popular rock groups.

The Future

As eBay headed into the second quarter of 2000, it was looking for new avenues to expand its services. According to Brian Swette, eBay's chief operating officer, the company was "at the five yard line with its core business."[33] The next driver of the company's growth was expected to be international expansion, followed by business-to-

[29]Auctions.com, www.auctions.com/backgrounder.asp, April 20, 2000.

[30]Ibid.

[31]www.outpost.com, Investor Relations, April 20, 2000.

[32]www.erock.com, April 20, 2000.

[33]"The One Thing Not for Sale on eBay," www.thestandard.com, April 20, 2000.

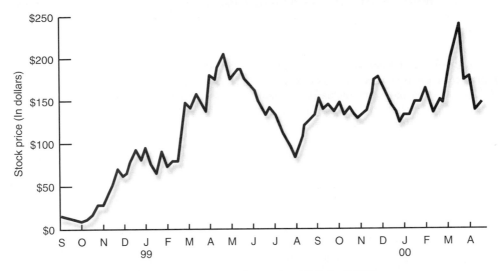

Exhibit 10   eBay's Stock Price Performance, September 1998–April 2000

business and automobile and regional sites.[34] Swette predicted that each of these areas could wind up "as large as the core eBay."[35]

In response to the increasing opportunities in the business-to-business auction segment, and the number of small companies trading on eBay, the company developed the eBay Business Exchange in March 2000. To avoid head-on competition with other auction sites in this market segment, eBay was focusing on businesses with fewer than 100 employees. Swette saw Business Exchange as a natural evolution of eBay's business model and expected that larger companies would eventually participate. Specific categories offered in the new eBay Business Exchange included computer hardware, software, electronics, industrial equipment, office equipment, and professional tools.

eBay had recently announced plans to enter France, Europe's third largest online commerce market. eBay management viewed France as critical in capturing the European market. However, well-established competition existed in the French market in the form of QXL.com, the leading British online auctioneer, and the I-Bazar Group, a French-based corporation that had anticipated eBay's arrival in 1998 and purchased the domain name eBay.fr.

While the number of concurrently active eBay auctions soared from approximately 1 million to 4.5 million between 1998 and year-end 1999, from January 2000 to March 2000 the number of auctions was holding at a relatively constant 4.2 to 4.4 million. eBay spokesperson Kevin Pursglove dismissed the flat trend, stating, "Listings are an interesting thing to look at, but sellers are more interested

in selling their merchandise."[36] Wall Street analysts, however, saw the lack of growth in the number of auctions as signaling a coming slowdown in eBay's revenue and profit growth and an indication of market share erosion.

Pierre Omidyar folded his newspaper to prepare for a meeting with Meg Whitman and Jeff Skoll to discuss two developing situations. The first topic on the list was to review the possibility of a cross-marketing strategic alliance with competitor Yahoo! to gain broader exposure to Yahoo's broad customer base. Partnering with a competitor that also offered auction services seemed to have pluses and minuses. The second item on the agenda involved the potential of launching storefront operations where eBayers could purchase goods at a fixed price, much like Amazon. As he headed down the hall to the meeting, Pierre recalled a statement that Meg Whitman had made in a recent interview: "I have this philosophy that you really need to do things 100 percent. Better to do 5 things at 100 percent than 10 things at 80 percent. Because the devil in so much of this is in the detail and while we have to move very, very fast, I think you are not well served by moving incredibly rapidly and not doing things that well."[37] Given recent developments, Pierre was forced to wonder if they were operating at 100 percent. Also, if Forrester Research was correct in their recent prediction that the majority of online retailers would be out of business by the end of 2000, would 100 percent be enough?[38] The recent drop in the company's stock price had been troubling (see Exhibit 10), and the company needed to launch strategic initiatives that would sustain rapid growth and get it back on the road to market dominance.

[34]Ibid.

[35]Ibid.

[36]"Auction Growth Slows at eBay, Can Earnings Growth Be Far Behind?" *Barron's Online,* April 17, 2000.

[37]"What's Behind the Boom at eBay?" *BusinessWeek Online,* May 21, 1999.

[38]Forrester.com press release, April 11, 2000.

Case 13   Edward Marshall Boehm, Inc.

Edward Marshall Boehm—a farmer, veterinarian, and nature lover living near New York City—was convinced by his wife and friends to translate some of his clay animal sculptures into pieces for possible sale to the gift and art markets. Boehm recognized that porcelain was the best medium for portraying his creations because of its translucent beauty, permanence, and fidelity of color as well as form. But the finest of the porcelains, hard paste porcelain, was largely a secret art about which little technical literature existed. Boehm studied this art relentlessly, absorbing whatever knowledge artbooks, museums, and the few U.S. ceramic factories offered. Then, after months of experimentation in a dingy Trenton, New Jersey, basement, Boehm and some chemist friends developed a porcelain clay equal to the finest in the world.

Next Boehm had to master the complex art of porcelain manufacture. Each piece of porcelain sculpture is a technical as well as artistic challenge. A 52-step process is required to convert a plasticine sculpture into a completed porcelain piece. For example, one major creation took 509 mold sections to make 151 parts, and consumed 8 tons of plaster in the molds. Sculptural detail included 60,000 individually carved feather barbs. Each creation had to be kiln-fired to 2400° where heat could change a graceful detail into a twisted mass. Then it had to be painted, often in successive layers, and perhaps fired repeatedly to anneal delicate colors. No American had excelled in hard paste porcelains. And when Boehm's creations first appeared no one understood the quality of the porcelain or even believed it was hard paste porcelain.

But Boehm began to create in porcelain what he knew and loved best—nature, particularly the more delicate forms of animals, birds, and flowers. In his art Boehm tried "to capture that special moment and setting which conveys the character, charm, and loveliness of a bird or animal in its natural habitat." After selling his early creations for several years during her lunch hours, his talented wife, Helen, left an outstanding opthalmic marketing career to "peddle" Boehm's porcelains full time. Soon Mrs. Boehm's extraordinary merchandising skills, promotional touch, and sense for the art market began to pay off. People liked Boehm's horses and dogs, but bought his birds. And Boehm agreeably complied, striving for ever greater perfection on ever more exotic and natural bird creations.

By 1968 some Boehm porcelains (especially birds) had become recognized as collectors items. An extremely complex piece like "Fondo Marino" might sell for $28,500 at retail, and might command much more upon resale. Edward Marshall Boehm, then 55—though flattered by his products' commercial success—considered his art primarily an expression of his love for nature. He felt the ornithological importance of portraying vanishing species like U.S. prairie chickens with fidelity and traveled to remote areas to bring back live samples of rare tropical birds for study and later rendering into porcelain. A single company, Minton China, was the exclusive distributor of Boehm products to some 175 retail outlets in the United States. Boehm's line included (1) its "Fledgling" series of smaller, somewhat simpler pieces, usually selling for less than $100, (2) its profitable middle series of complex sculptures like the "Snowy Owl" selling from $800 to $5,000, and (3) its special artistic pieces (like "Fondo Marino" or "Ivory Billed Woodpeckers") which might sell initially for over $20,000.

Individual Boehm porcelains were increasingly being recognized as outstanding artistic creations and sought by some sophisticated collectors. Production of such designs might be sold out for years in advance, but it was difficult to anticipate which pieces might achieve this distinction. Many of the company's past policies no longer seemed appropriate. And the Boehms wanted to further position the company for the long run. When asked what they wanted from the company, they would respond, "to make the world aware of Mr. Boehm's artistic talent, to help world wildlife causes by creating appreciation and protection for threatened species, and to build a continuing business that could make them comfortably wealthy, perhaps millionaires." No one goal had great precedence over the others.

Republished with permission from H. Mintzberg and J. B. Quinn, *The Strategy Process,* Prentice Hall, New York, 1996.

Case 14 Ford Motor Company in 2004: Entering Second Century of Existence*

In its centennial year, 2003, Ford Motor Company, the company that revolutionized car production in the world, was facing doubts about its existence. There were rumors about the possibility of Ford filing for Chapter 11. From a company sitting on an overwhelming $23 billion cash reserve in 1998[1] and optimistic about ousting General Motors (GM) from its leadership position, Ford in 2003 was in deep red with its bonds poised on junk status. William Clay Ford Jr., 45 (the great-grandson of Henry Ford who founded Ford Motor Company), appointed chief executive of Ford Motor Company after the ousting of Jacques Nasser in October 2001, was faced with the monumental task of reviving the world famous automaker from the brink of death. William Clay Ford Jr., also called Bill Ford, believed that the company had lost focus in several areas, and launched the "back to basics" campaign throughout the company. He wanted to make the "blue oval" shine again. He was optimistic about the company's turnaround and said, "When people look back on 2003, I want them to remember it as a turning point."[2]

However, reality indicated that the optimism might have been a bit premature. The automaker was losing money on almost every car sale. There was mounting pressure in terms of increased competition, declining market share, a poor cash situation, large unfunded pension and retiree medical liabilities, and, above all, a top management team that was not working together. Quality improvement programs had stalled and product introductions were being delayed. To nail it all, Toyota Motor Company, the Japanese carmaker, unseated Ford from the world's number two automaker position in January 2004.[3] The company slipped from the zenith to a nadir in a span of just four years.

Bill Ford and Ford Motor Company[4]

Bill Ford replaced Nasser as the chief executive officer of Ford Motor Company in October 2001. Bill Ford brought with him a new management team: Nick Scheele, the group vice-president of North America, became the chief operating officer; James Padilla, group vice president for manufacturing and quality, succeeded Nick Scheele as group vice-president North America; and Carl Reichardt, a longtime board member of Ford and retired CEO and chairman of Wells Fargo & Co., became the vice-chairman of the board and was to take an active role overseeing financial operations, including that of Ford Credit. Several other seniors who left Ford on early retirement during Nasser's term were brought back.

In terms of experience in managing a company of Ford's size and complexity, Bill Ford and his team (Scheele and Padilla) did not compare very well with the top management teams of other big automobile companies. Of course some attributes of Bill Ford were promising. Ford was known to have a "nontraditional personality" for a CEO. He was also known for his strong views regarding environment protection which gave him a "tree hugger" label. According to many sources, he had a relatively "pro-employee, even pro-union reputation." He was very popular among the company's blue-collar and white-collar employees who distrusted Nasser. Workers gave him an enthusiastic response on October 30, 2001, when he became the CEO. Bill Ford viewed building relationships as his key job going forward. "You can't build the business if you don't have strong partnerships," Ford said. "Dealers, United Autoworkers Union, white-collar employees, suppliers, Wall Street—we have a lot of relationships that are important to us. A lot of those are broken and not healthy," he said.

According to some sources, Bill Ford was the right person to lead the Ford company at that juncture. The Ford name gave him the credibility and employee support so crucial for the success of any efforts for change. He

*This case study was prepared by Ms. Naga Lakshmi Damaraju of the University of Texas at Dallas, and Professors John C. Byrne and Alan B. Eisner at Pace University. All rights reserved to the authors. The purpose of the case is to stimulate class discussion rather than illustrating effective or ineffective handling of a business situation. The authors thank Dr. Michael Oliff and Mr. Charles Hazzard at the University of Texas at Dallas, for their valuable comments on an earlier version of this case. A special thanks is expressed to Charles Hazzard for the extensive research support he extended.

[1]Muller, J., Kerwin, K., Welch, D., Moore, P. L., & Brady, D., 2001, Ford: Why it's worse than you think? *BusinessWeek Online*, June 25; www.businessweek.com/magazine/content/01_26/b3738001.htm.

[2]Kerwin, K., 2003, Can Ford pull out of its skid? *BusinessWeek Online*, March 31; www.businessweek.com/magazine/content/03_13/b3826055_mz017.htm.

[3]Toyota surpasses Ford as no. 2 carmaker, January 25, 2004; http://biz.yahoo.com/ap/040125/japan_toyota_4.html.

[4]This discussion draws heavily from the following sources: Isidore, C., 2001, Nasser out as Ford CEO, *CNNmoney*, October 30; http://money.cnn.com/2001/10/30/ceos/ford/; Taylor, A., III, 2003, Getting Ford in gear, *Fortune*, April 28; www.fortune.com/fortune/print/0,15935,446373,00.html?; Teather, D., 2002, Ford's losses climb to $5.5 bn for year, *Guardian*, January 18; www.guardian.co.uk/Print/0,3858,4337912,00.html; Kerwin, K., 2002, Where are Ford's hot cars? *BusinessWeek Online*, June 24; www.businessweek.com/magazine/content/02_25/b3788084.htm; Shirouzu, N., White, G. L., & White, J. B., 2002, Ford's retrenchment seeks to cut costs and make its factories more flexible, *Wall Street Journal*, January 14:1; http://interactive.wsj.com/archive/retrieve.cig?id=SB1010758959555716440.djm.

considered bringing back a focus on operations as crucial for success. "We won't hesitate to pull the trigger if something isn't fitting in well," said Ford. "I think we have lost the focus in a couple of areas." Consistent with his beliefs, Ford and his team outlined a back-to-basics approach for the company in which the focus of the company was to be on "designing, building, and selling the industry's best cars and trucks—and restoring the company's profitability." He wanted a "product-led renaissance." As part of this strategy, a sweeping restructuring plan that included closure of three assembly plants in North America, closure of two plants making auto parts, employee layoffs, and sale of noncore assets including the Kwik-Fit retail chain was announced in January 2002. The company also planned to reduce production by more than 1 million cars, keeping in view the chronic overcapacity in the industry. Additionally, he unveiled plans to cut off every bit of wasteful expenditure.

Another area that received attention was Ford Credit. The expansion of Ford Credit, which generated more profit margins than the core auto business, was of questionable benefit in the changing times. With a shrinking market share, expansion of Ford Credit meant lending not only for Ford's own vehicles but also for other brands and sometimes for customers with less than a strong credit history. Even risky borrowers were charged highly competitive interest rates in its ambition to become "global auto-finance superpower." The strategy might not have been wise in a soft economy where default rates increased. The company abandoned this ambition in January 2002 and decided to concentrate on lending for its own vehicles.

In the meantime, in January 2002, Ford shocked Wall Street by writing off $1 billion on its palladium stockpile. Palladium, a precious metal, was used in catalytic converters to make the emissions from automobiles cleaner. Due to the erratic nature of the metal's availability, Ford's purchasing department was building up its palladium inventory while there were concurrent research efforts to reduce the amount of palladium required in its products. With a change in the demand–supply situation, and also because of technological breakthroughs, the massive stockpile had to be written off. While General Motors and other companies successfully hedged their risks on purchases of precious metals, the lack of communication between the purchasing and treasury departments (which routinely engaged in "hedging") led to the huge write-off.[5] The failure of communication between purchasing, research, and the treasury departments reflected the deep-rooted problems at Ford Motor Company. The problem of internal fights for power that led to the palladium stockpile episode continued. Even the new management team

assembled by Bill Ford was mired with problems to the extent that the top executives needed coaching by etiquette trainers to learn how to deal with each other.[6]

As a result of the transformation efforts of Bill Ford, the company announced in January 2004 net earnings of $495 million compared to a net loss of $980 million in 2002 (refer to Exhibit 1 for financial information).[7] The company had cut its cost per vehicle by $240 and trimmed expenses by $3.2 billion and raised $1 billion from the sale of assets.[8] The company was still credited with having 3 or 4 of the top 10 selling vehicles in America in the previous 10 years (see Exhibit 2 for top selling cars in February 2004) and it had a history of great resilience in coming out of crisis situations. However, Wall Street might not yet have been convinced. While stocks traded at $14.10 a share in March 2004 compared to an all-time low of $6.54 in March 2003, its bonds continued to be just above "junk" status.[9] See Exhibit 3 (page 645) for Ford's stock performance compared to the Standard & Poor (S&P) 500.

Automobile Industry in the United States

The automotive industry in the United States was a highly competitive cyclical business. The number of cars and trucks sold to retail buyers or "industry demand" varied substantially from year to year depending on "general economic conditions, the cost of purchasing and operating cars and trucks, the availability of credit and fuel."[10] Because cars and trucks were durable items, consumers could wait to replace them; industry demand reflected this factor. The U.S. automobile industry was characterized by a capability to overproduce as many as 20 million cars.[11] Also, competition in the United States had intensified in the last few decades with Japanese carmakers (e.g., Toyota and Honda) gaining a foothold in the market. To counter the "foreign" problem, Japanese companies had set up production facilities in the United States and gained acceptance from American consumers. Product quality and lean production were judged to be the major weapons that Japanese carmakers used to gain an advantage over American carmakers. In addition, increasing concern for the environment led companies to explore newer hybrid technologies to produce more environment-friendly cars.

[5]White, G. L., 2002, A mismanaged palladium stockpile was catalyst for Ford's write-off, *Wall Street Journal,* February 6; www2.uta.edu/hyland/Derivative%20News%20Stories/ford's%20palladium%20problem.html.

[6]Taylor, 2003, Getting Ford in gear.

[7]Hakim, D., 2004, Ford reports 2003 profit but posts loss in 4th quarter, *New York Times,* January 23.

[8]Associated Press, 2004, Ford's 4Q loss widens to $793 million, *New York Times,* January 23.

[9]2004, *New York Times,* March 6; http://marketwatch.nytimes.com/custom/nyt-com/html-financials.asp?symb=F&sid=205397.

[10]SEC filings, www.sec.gov/Archives/edgar/data/37996/000003799603000013/0000037996-03-000013.txt.

[11]Naughton, K., Miller, K. L., Muller, J., Thornton, E., & Edmondson, G., 1999, Autos: The global six, *BusinessWeek Online,* January 25; www.businessweek.com/1999/99_04/b3613010.htm.

Exhibit 1   Selected Financial Data, 1999–2003 (All amounts in $ millions, except per share amounts)

	Years Ended				
	2003	2002	2001	2000	1999
Total Company					
Sales and revenues	$164,196	$162,256	$160,504	$168,930	$160,053
Income/(loss) before income taxes	1,370	951	(7,419)	8,311	9,856
Provision/(credit) for income taxes	135	301	(2,096)	2,722	3,247
Minority interests in net income of subsidiaries	314	367	24	127	112
Income/(loss) from continuing operations	921	283	(5,347)	5,462	6,497
Income/(loss) from discontinued/held-for-sale operations	(8)	(62)	(106)	257	740
Loss on disposal of discontinued/held-for-sale operations	(154)	(199)	—	(2,252)	—
Cumulative effects of change in accounting principle	(264)	(1,002)	—	—	—
Net income/(loss)	$ 495	$ (980)	$ (5,453)	$ 3,467	$ 7,237
Automotive sector					
Sales	$138,442	$134,273	$130,736	$140,765	$135,022
Operating income/(loss)	(1,531)	(528)	(7,390)	5,298	7,190
Income/(loss) before income taxes	(1,957)	(1,153)	(8,857)	5,333	7,296
Financial Services Sector					
Revenues	$ 25,754	$ 27,983	$ 29,768	$ 28,165	$ 25,031
Income/(loss) before income taxes	3,327	2,104	1,438	2,978	2,560
Total Company Data per Share of Common and Class B Stock[a]					
Basic:					
Income/(loss) from continuing operations	1	0.15	(2.96)	3.69	5.38
Income/(loss) from discontinued/held-for-sale operations	—	(0.04)	(0.06)	0.18	0.61
Loss on disposal of discontinued/held-for-sale operations	(0)	(0.11)	—	(1.53)	—
Cumulative effects of change in accounting principle	(0)	(0.55)	—	—	—
Net income/(loss)	$ 0	$ (0.55)	$ (3.02)	$ 2.34	$ 5.99
Diluted:					
Income/(loss) from continuing operations	1	0.15	(2.96)	3.62	5.26
Income/(loss) from discontinued/held-for-sale operations	—	(0.03)	(0.06)	0.17	0.60
Loss on disposal of discontinued/held-for-sale operations	(0)	(0.11)	—	(1.49)	—
Cumulative effects of change in accounting principle	(0)	(0.55)	—	—	—
Net income/(loss)	$ 0	$ (0.54)	$ (3.02)	$ 2.30	$ 5.86
Cash dividends[b]	0	0.4	1.05	1.8	1.88
Common stock price range (NYSE Composite)					
High	17	18.23	31.42	31.46	37.3
Low	7	6.9	14.7	21.69	25.42
Average number of shares of Common and Class B stock outstanding (in millions)	1,832	1,819	1,820	1,483	1,210
Total Company Balance Sheet Data at Year-End					
Assets					
Automotive sector	$120,641	$107,790	$ 88,319	$ 94,312	$ 99,201
Financial Services sector	195,279	187,432	188,224	189,078	171,048
Total assets	$315,920	$295,222	$276,543	$283,390	$270,249
Long-term Debt					
Automotive	$ 18,987	$ 13,607	$ 13,467	$ 11,769	$ 10,398
Financial Services	100,764	106,525	107,024	86,865	67,170
Total long-term debt	$119,751	$120,132	$120,491	$ 98,634	$ 77,568
Stockholders' Equity	$ 11,651	$ 5,590	$ 7,786	$ 18,610	$ 27,604

[a]Share data have been adjusted to reflect stock dividends and stock splits. Common stock price range (NYSE Composite) has been adjusted to reflect the spin-offs of Visteon and The Associates, and a recapitalization known as the Value Enhancement Plan.

[b]Adjusted for the Value Enhancement Plan effected in August 2000; cash dividends were $1.16 per share in 2000.

Source: SEC filings for 2003; www.sec.gov/Archives/edgar/data/37996/000095012404000885/k83502e10vk.htm#008.

Exhibit 2   Top Selling Vehicles in February 2004

No.	Vehicle Name
1	Ford F-Series pickup
2	Chevy Silverado-C/K pickup
3	Toyota Camry
4	Dodge Ram pickup
5	Ford Explorer
6	Honda Accord
7	Toyota Corolla/Matrix
8	Honda Civic
9	Chevrolet Impala
10	Ford Taurus
11	Chevrolet TrailBlazer
12	Nissan Altima
13	Dodge Caravan
14	Chevrolet Cavalier
15	Jeep Grand Cherokee
16	Ford Focus
17	Jeep Liberty
18	Chevrolet Tahoe
19	Toyota Sienna
20	GMC Sierra pickup

Source: Reports of Detroit carmakers; http://biz.yahoo.com/rf/040302/autos_top20_table_1.html.

Cost pressures, cutthroat pricing, and overcapacity heralded a phase of consolidation in the industry. The 1998 merger between Daimler Benz of Germany and the Chrysler Corporation in the United States sparked the phenomenon. According to industry experts, the 40 players in the automobile industry were expected to shrink to 6 in the span of a decade during which each company needed a sales volume of more than 5 million vehicles just to remain profitable.[12] Yet, in 1999, only two companies—General Motors and Ford—qualified for that mark while other companies worked feverishly to reach that level. Faced with increased competition and fast-changing customer preferences, innovative product designs became more critical then ever in the industry. Highly competitive consumer financing offers, in an attempt to retain or gain market share, squeezed the profit margins of even the ma-

jor players and American companies faced growth without profitability. However, Japanese carmakers, with their better product designs and quality, were capturing better value than American carmakers.[13] The troubles in the automotive industry were accentuated by the attacks on the World Trade Center and Pentagon on September 11, 2001, and the recession in the economy pushed the already stressed automakers to the edge.

While there was a glut in the U.S. market for automobiles, the markets of Asia, Central and South America, and central and eastern Europe all showed increasing promise for automobiles, and the automobile industry entered into an era of "global motorization."[14] To address this opportunity for expansion, companies had to gear up to meet the tastes and preferences of customers around the world if they wished to secure market leadership.

Ford Motor Company—The Background

Ford Motor Company was started by Henry Ford in 1903 to produce and sell the automobiles he designed and engineered. The company was incorporated in Delaware in 1919 and went public in 1956, but the Ford family still retained 40 percent of the voting shares.[15] The company founded the first modern auto assembly line, which allowed its Model T to be produced at a cost within the reach of the masses.[16] However, Ford lost its leadership position to General Motors soon after it produced the Model T because the company was not able to address the market need for vehicles that were other than "black."

The two core businesses of Ford were automotive and financial services. The automotive sector encompassed the design, development, manufacture, sale, and services of cars and trucks. The financial services sector operations were comprised of the Ford Motor Credit Company, a wholly owned subsidiary of Ford, and the Hertz Corporation, an indirect wholly owned subsidiary. Ford Credit provided leasing, insurance, and vehicle-related financing while Hertz rented cars, light trucks, and industrial and construction equipment.[17] Ford was the world's largest producer of trucks and second to GM as the largest producer of cars and trucks in the United States.[18]

[12]Ibid.

[13]Muller, J., Kerwin, K., Welch, D., Moore, P. L., & Brady D., 2001, Ford: Why it's worse than you think? *BusinessWeek Online*, June 25; www.businessweek.com/magazine/content/01_26/b3738001.htm; Hakim, D., 2002, All that easy credit haunts Detroit now, *New York Times*, January 6; Hakim, D., 2003, Long road ahead for Ford, *New York Times*, March 14.

[14]Okuda, H., 2002, Chairman's messages, August; www.toyota.co.jp/IRweb/invest_rel/top_message/chairmans/index2.html.

[15]Ford Motor Company, 2002, SEC filings; www.sec.gov/Archives/edgar/data/37996/000003799603000013/0000037996-03-000013.txt.

[16]www.ford.com/en/heritage/history/default.htm.

[17]Ford Motor Co., company profile, yahoo finance, http://biz.yahoo.com/p/f/f.html.

[18]General Motors, 2000, press release, November 16; http://media.gm.com/news/releases/corp_infrastructure_111600.html.

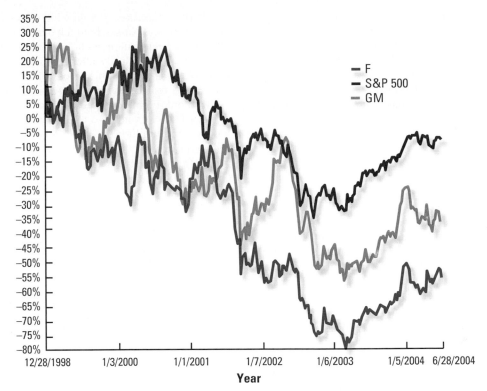

Exhibit 3   Price History—Ford Motor Company (12/28/1998–7/2/2004)

Source: MSN Money, CSI

Ford had production facilities on six continents and sold its products worldwide. The majority of its sales, like that of other major carmakers, came from the U.S. market. Ford had an extremely strong brand recognition and a strong financial and marketing network and was known for its innovative products. Several of its products were particularly well known and enjoyed great demand. About one million of the Mustang models were built in the two years following their introduction. The Ford Escort set a record as the "fastest first million units for a new car" and the original Model T was named as the car of the century in 1999.[19] Ford had nearly $5.9 billion in net income from continuing operations in 1998, making it the world's most profitable automaker. Ford's Taurus, Explorer, and other brands were extremely popular and Ford also managed to gain a strong hold in the markets for sport utility vehicles (SUVs) and pickup trucks, the profitability of which then attracted many other automakers to vie for the segment. Ford had been named among the best-managed compa-

nies in Detroit if not the world.[20] Ford's stock price rose by 130 percent since 1996 and by 1999 it was far ahead of the 71 percent gain of the S&P 500 stock price index and its global auto rivals.[21] With nearly $23 billion in cash reserves, Ford was eager to oust GM from its leadership position in the auto industry, and some predicted it soon would.

Jacques Nasser, who became the chief executive officer of Ford Motor Company in January 1999, pursued an ambitious diversification strategy. It was understood as the cradle-to-grave strategy in which Ford was to deal with all aspects of the car business (e.g., retailing, junkyard recycling, among others), not just making cars. To implement part of this strategy, Ford paid about $1.6 billion to acquire Kwik-Fit, a chain of nearly 20,000 auto service centers in Great Britain.[22] These were high-margin businesses that

[19]Ford Motor Company, www.fordmotorcompany.co.za/corporate/history/ford.asp.

[20]Ford worries overshadow auto show, 2002, Fox Channel News, January 7; www.foxnews.com/story/0,2933,42353,00.html.

[21]Kerwin, K., & Naughton, K., 1999, Remaking Ford, *BusinessWeek,* October 11: 132–36; www.businessweek.com/magazine/content/01_25/b3737047.htm.

[22]Kerwin & Naughton, 1999, Remaking Ford; www.businessweek.com/1999/99_41/b3650001.htm.

were expected to "add value" to Ford's operations. Ford also bought dealerships in selected U.S. markets and sold back a majority stake to the dealers who formerly owned them. The move was expected to protect Ford's distribution network base by not allowing a concentration of dealerships with a few big retail chains such as Auto Nation Inc.[23] Lower-margin operations, such as Visteon automotive systems which made automotive parts, were spun off.

The luxury car business division was substantially increased with the acquisition of the Swedish automaker Volvo for $6.47 billion in 1999 and Land Rover from BMW in 2000. Additional resources were spent on Mazda and Lincoln to restore the ailing units to good health, and the Jaguar line was expanded. Ford created the Premier Automotive Group (PAG) to manage these luxury brands; the luxury brand business was expected to contribute one-third of global profits by 2005.[24] On the personnel front, a new performance review ranking system was introduced to promote internal competition. Under this system, the managers were to be ranked against each other. Those who received poor grades (the bottom 5 percent) for two consecutive evaluation periods were to be fired.[25] Many of these initiatives ended up alienating various stakeholder groups in the organization. The diversification strategy did not pay off as well as expected because of aggressive competition during that period. General Motors' Silverado and Sierra pickups, for instance, overtook the Ford Division's top-selling F-series in 2001. New pickups launched by Toyota and Dodge also cut into F-series sales and profits.[26]

Added to this was the issue with Firestone over the Wilderness AT tires. These Firestone tires installed on SUVs were believed to cause the vehicles to roll over and crash for reasons other than tread separation. The problem was claimed to be higher with Ford Explorer than other vehicles. A formal investigation by the National Highway Traffic and Safety Administration (NHTSA) was launched in May 2000. Both companies blamed each other, leading to bad publicity and loss of customer trust.[27] Firestone issued a massive recall of 6.5 million tires in August 2000. Ford followed in 2001 by issuing a recall of all its vehicles that had these Firestone tires on them. The move cost the company over $3 billion, one of the biggest recalls ever in the automobile industry, and also ended the century-old relationship between Firestone and Ford.[28]

Further, there was the growing divide between Bill Ford and Jacques Nasser. Ford felt that Nasser was cutting off his communication with top executives. With the downturn in the industry after the September 11, 2001, terrorist attacks and with his loss of corporate support, Nasser was replaced as chief executive in October 2001 by Bill Ford. From being the world's most profitable automaker in 1999 with $7.2 billion in net income,[29] Ford posted a $500 million loss in October 2001 for the preceding quarter, the first time that the company was in the red for two successive quarters since the 1992 recession.[30] Overall, the company incurred a loss of $5.5 billion by 2001.[31] Ford's market share and quality ratings dropped, as did its S&P credit rating.[32]

The Challenges for Bill Ford

Despite Bill Ford's efforts, the situation did not change much by March 2004. Ford's problems persisted. Its car market share fell from 20.3 percent in 2002 to 19.5 percent in 2003, according to Autodata Corp, a New Jersey–based research firm.[33] Ford's combined car and truck market share in the United States fell from 21.1 percent in 2002 to 20.5 percent in 2003 (see Exhibit 4).[34] By March 2004 weak sales and rising inventories forced Ford to slash second-quarter production by 5 percent compared with the previous year.[35] Ford was struggling to retain its market share.[36]

The Premier Automotive Group had engineering facilities in Sweden, England, and Michigan though marketing was headquartered in its California offices. While grand plans were being made for each brand, the businesses were shrinking. Lincoln lost $1 billion in 2001, Jaguar lost $500 million in 2002, and Land Rover turned profitable only in 2003. Lincoln's expansion plans have been scaled down.[37] PAG posted a slim operating profit of $164 million for 2003 compared to a loss of $897 million in 2002 largely attributable to the introduction of hot new products: Jaguar's new flagship XJ sedans and Volvo's

[23]Box, T., 2002, Ford sells last of retail network, *Dallas Morning News,* April 5; www.dallasnews.com/cgi-bin/gold_print.cgi.

[24]Kerwin & Naughton, 1999, Remaking Ford.

[25]Labor and Employment Law Update, 2002, The lessons of Ford's forced ranking performance review system, June; www.shpclaw.com/updates/lessonsford.html.

[26]Kerwin, 2002, Where are Ford's hot cars?

[27]Ackman, D., 2001, Ford, Firestone on the hill. *Forbes,* June 19; www.forbes.com/2001/06/19/0619tires.html.

[28]Recalled Tire—Firestone and Ford, www.recalledproduct.com/recalledtire/.

[29]Muller, Kerwin et al., 2001, Ford: Why it's worse than you think?; Jackson, M., 2002, The leaders who run toward crises, *New York Times,* December 22; www.nytimes.com/2002/12.../22EXLI.html?tntemail) =&pagewanted=print&position=to.

[30]Treanor, J., & Gow, D., 2001, Ford ploughs deeper into red, *Guardian,* October 18; www.guardian.co.uk/Print/0,3858,4279588,00.html; Glover, M., 2001, Analysis: Nasser lost clan's confidence as PR disasters kept growing, October 31; http://classic.sacbee.com/ib/news/old/ib_news03_20011031.html.

[31]Teather, 2002, Ford's losses climb to $5.5 bn.

[32]Treanor & Gow, 2001, Ford ploughs deeper into red.

[33]Associated Press, 2004, Ford's 4Q loss widens to $793 million.

[34]Ford Motor Company, 2003, SEC filings.

[35]Bloomberg news, 2004, Ford sales fall, but GM and Chrysler gain, *International Herald Tribune Online,* March 3.

[36]Kerwin, K., 2003, Can Ford pull out of its skid? *BusinessWeek Online,* March 31; www.businessweek.com/magazine/content/03_13/b3826055_mz017.htm.

[37]Taylor, 2003, Getting Ford in gear.

Exhibit 4 Market Share Data in the U.S. Market

U.S. Car Market Shares* %					
	Years Ended December 31				
	2003	**2002**	**2001**	**2000**	**1999**
Company Name					
Ford**	6.9%	7.7%	8.6%	9.5%	9.9%
General Motors	11.5	12.1	13.0	14.2	14.9
DaimlerChrysler	3.8	4.1	4.1	4.5	5.1
Toyota	5.9	5.8	5.5	5.5	5.1
Honda	4.8	4.9	5.1	5.0	4.9
All Other***	12.0	12.7	11.9	11.0	10.0
Total U.S. Car Retail Deliveries	44.9%	47.3%	48.2%	49.7%	49.9%

U.S. Truck Market Shares* %					
	Years Ended December 31				
	2003	**2002**	**2001**	**2000**	**1999**
Company Name					
Ford**	13.6%	13.4%	14.2%	14.2%	14.3%
General Motors	16.4	16.2	15.0	13.6	13.9
DaimlerChrysler	10.0	10.0	10.1	10.8	11.1
Toyota	5.1	4.5	4.5	3.6	3.4
Honda	3.1	2.4	1.8	1.6	1.3
All Other***	6.9	6.2	6.2	6.5	6.1
Total U.S. Truck Retail Deliveries	55.1%	52.7%	51.8%	50.3%	50.1%

U.S. Combined Car and Truck Market Shares* %					
	Years Ended December 31				
	2003	**2002**	**2001**	**2000**	**1999**
Company Name					
Ford**	20.5%	21.1%	22.8%	23.7%	24.2%
General Motors	27.9	28.3	28.0	27.8	28.8
DaimlerChrysler	13.8	14.1	14.2	15.3	16.2
Toyota	11.0	10.3	10.0	9.1	8.5
Honda	7.9	7.3	6.9	6.6	6.2
All Other***	18.9	18.9	18.1	17.5	16.1
Total U.S. Car and Truck Retail Deliveries	100.0%	100.0%	100.0%	100.0%	100.0%

* All U.S. retail sales data are based on publicly available information from the media and trade publications.

** Ford purchased Volvo Car on March 31, 1999, and Land Rover on June 30, 2000. The figures shown here include Volvo Car and Land Rover on a pro forma basis for the periods prior to their acquisition by Ford. In 1999 Land Rover represented less than 0.2 of total market share.

*** "All Other" includes primarily companies based in various European countries, Korea, and other Japanese manufacturers; the U.S. Truck Market Shares table and U.S. Combined Car and Truck Market Shares table include heavy truck manufacturers.

XC90 SUV.[38] PAG shifted its focus away from mass markets where its rivals took the lead. Ford continued to bet on its redesigned F-150 pickup truck to make it big again.

According to industry analysts, Ford's survival depended on concentrating in the major areas of product development, manufacturing systems, and finance.[39] Vehicle development at Ford was hampered by virtually no sharing of designs and technologies among similar vehicles. It was estimated that it took Ford at least 25 percent more time to produce a vehicle design than its competitors; the result was an "overly engineered," costly vehicle for the hypercompetitive U.S. car market. As recently as April 2003, Ford's engineering operations were built around five teams organized by vehicle types each with its own budget and technologies. The teams often created their own unique body frames, suspension, brakes, engines, and transmissions and seldom made any effort to share the technologies.[40] Indicative of this creative approach were at least 126 different types of fuel caps used in Ford vehicles in Europe alone.[41] There were many concerns that the better companies thrived on commonality—the sharing of designs and the use of common platforms of basic architecture—to roll out similar models faster and more efficiently. Ford just embarked on the process.[42]

On the manufacturing front, Ford's Japanese rivals and even GM progressed well with their flexible manufacturing systems. Flexible manufacturing systems allowed the production of two or three different sizes and shapes of cars in one plant without major production halts.[43] It would take Ford at least a decade to catch up. Quality problems persisted. *Consumer Reports* of April 2003 ranked Ford low among the big auto companies in terms of quality and reliability.[44] Ford's older factories were a possible reason because even the new models had defects. According to J. D. Power's 2003 Vehicle Dependability Study, which measured the durability of vehicles three years after their purchase, Toyota was in the number two position while Ford was eighth and below the industry average in terms of long-term quality (see Exhibit 5).[45] Even as late as March 2004, quality issues forced Ford to

Exhibit 5   J. D. Power's Long-Term Quality Survey: Problems per 100 Vehicles

Manufacturer	Score*
Porsche	193
Toyota	196
Honda	215
Nissan	258
BMW	262
General Motors	264
Subaru	266
Average	273
Ford	287
DaimlerChrysler	311
Mitsubishi	339
Hyundai	342
Isuzu	368
Volkswagen	378
Suzuki	403
Kia	509

* A lower score means fewer problems per 100 vehicles.

Source: J. D. Power and Associates, "Car Quality: Japanese Dominate," *CNNMoney,* July 8, 2003; http://money.cnn.com/2003/07/08/pf/autos/bc.autos.durability/?cnn=yes.

recall more than 1.3 million Taurus and Sable cars for its 2000 to 2003 models.[46] The Ford Focus model (after a lot of reworking) was the only Ford vehicle that made it as the top pick in 2 out of 10 categories, according to *Consumer Reports Annual 2004;* all other eight slots were taken up by the Japanese manufacturers Toyota and Honda.[47]

Ford's key focus was more on financing options for its customers than on competing with better models and quality. Even its newest models were being sold only with the help of incentives and discounts.[48] To add to the company's woes, in 2004 Japanese rivals started launching in-

[38]Kerwin, K., 2004, Ford learns the lessons of luxury, *Business Week,* March 1: 116–17.

[39]Shirouzu, White, & White, 2002, Ford's retrenchment seeks to cut costs.

[40]Shirouzu, N., 2003, Ford's new development plan: Stop reinventing its wheels, *Wall Street Journal,* April 16.

[41]Morris, B., 2002, Can Ford save Ford? *Fortune,* November 18; www.fortune.com/fortune/ceo/articles/0,15114,390071,00.html.

[42]Shirouzu, White, & White, 2002, Ford's retrenchment seeks to cut costs.

[43]Ibid.

[44]Kerwin, 2003, Can Ford pull out of its skid?; Smith, B. C., 2003, Back to basics, *Automotive Design and Production,* www.autofieldguide.com/columns/smith/1201ob.html.

[45]Car Quality: Japanese dominate; http://money.cnn.com/2003/07/08/pf/autos/bc.autos.durability/?cnn=yes.

[46]Ford recalls Taurus and Sable sedans, 2004, *Automotive News,* March 10; www.autonews.com/news.cms?newsId=8079.

[47]Consumer Reports: U.S. cars beat Europeans, still trail Asians in reliability, 2004, *Automotive News,* March 9; www.autonews.com/news.cms?newsId=8057.

[48]Shirouzu, White, & White, 2002, Ford's retrenchment seeks to cut costs.

centive schemes more aggressively, thereby intensifying the price-based competition. While the American automakers aimed at attracting consumers with discounts, the foreign automakers were effective in luring the dealers to close the sale (see Exhibit 6).[49] To compete at this level, Ford became concerned that it could run into dangerously low levels of cash, jeopardizing new product launches and factory modernization. Already the balance sheet, with huge retiree obligations and massive debt from Ford Credit, was a serious concern. With credit ratings declining, the cost of its debt was on the rise. Also, the models already in the pipeline and those due in the years to come would cost Ford more than the vehicles they replaced, forcing the company into further cost cutting.[50] While Ford was making gains with respect to cost cutting, its market share and new product launches were still falling behind target. Even the slim profit that Ford posted for 2003 came primarily from its lending to car and truck buyers and other financial operations rather than its core automotive manufacturing business.[51]

Will Bill Ford's optimism prove realistic? Will Ford be able to make a turnaround?

Exhibit 6   **The Percentage Increase in Automaker Incentives, 2003–2004**

Company Name	Consumer/Dealer Incentives (Jan. 2004)	Increase %
General Motors	$4,431	12%
Ford	4,296	23
Toyota	2,891	33
Honda	1,593	65
Nissan	1,631	10

Source: C. Tierney, "Foreign Automakers Turn Up Volume on Incentives," *Detroit News,* March 6, 2004; CNW Marketing Research Inc.

[49]Tierney, C., 2004, Foreign automakers turn up volume on incentives, *Detroit News,* March 6; www.detnews.com/2004/autosinsider/ 0403/02/a01e-79606.htm.

[50]Kim, C. R., & Hyde, J., 2004, Toyota overtakes Ford as world's no. 2 auto maker, Reuters news dispatch, January 25.

[51]Hakim, 2004, Ford reports 2003 profit.

Case 15   FreshDirect*

Company Profile

Operating out of its production center in Long Island City, Queens, FreshDirect offered online grocery shopping and delivery service to Manhattan's East Side and Battery Park City. When it was launched in July 2001 by Joe Fedele and Jason Ackerman, FreshDirect pronounced to the New York area that it was "the new way to shop for food." This was a bold statement given that the previous decade had witnessed the demise of numerous other online grocery ventures. However, the creators of FreshDirect were confident in the success of their business because their entire operation had been designed to deliver one simple promise to grocery shoppers: "higher quality at lower prices."

While this promise was an extremely common tagline used within and outside the grocery business, FreshDirect had integrated numerous components into its system to give real meaning to these words. To offer the highest-quality products to its customers, FreshDirect had created a state-of-the-art production center and staffed it with top-notch personnel. The 300,000-square-foot production facility located in Long Island City was composed of 12 separate temperature zones, ensuring that each piece of food was kept at its optimal temperature for ripening or preservation. Each department of the facility, including the coffee roaster, butcher, and bakery, was staffed by carefully selected experts, enabling FreshDirect to offer premium fresh coffees, pastries, breads, meats, and seafood. Further quality management was achieved by the SAP manufacturing-software system that controlled every detail of the facility's operations. All of the thermometers, scales, and conveyor belts within the facility were connected to a central command center. Each specific setting was programmed into the system by an expert from the corresponding department, including everything from the ideal temperature for ripening a cantaloupe to the amount of flour that went into French bread. The system was also equipped with a monitoring alarm that alerted staff to any skew from the programmed settings.

Another quality control element that had been made an integral part of the FreshDirect facility was an extremely high standard for cleanliness, health, and safety. The facility itself was kept immaculately clean and all food-preparation areas and equipment were bathed in antiseptic foam at the end of each day. Incoming and outgoing food was tested in FreshDirect's in-house laboratory, which was managed by a 32-year veteran U.S. Department of Agriculture inspection supervisor, who ensured the facility adhered to USDA guidelines and the Hazard Analysis and Critical Control Point food safety system, and that all food passing through FreshDirect met the company's high safety standards.

System efficiency had been the key to FreshDirect's ability to offer its high-quality products at such low prices. FreshDirect's biggest operational design component for reducing costs had been the complete elimination of the middleman. Instead of going through an intermediary, both fresh and dry products were ordered from individual growers and producers, and shipped directly to FreshDirect's production center where FreshDirect's expert staff prepared them for selling. In addition, FreshDirect did not accept any slotting allowances. This unique relationship with growers and producers allowed FreshDirect to enjoy reduced purchase prices from its suppliers, enabling them to pass even greater savings on to their customers.

The proximity of FreshDirect's processing facility to its Manhattan customer base was also a critical factor in its cost-effective operational design. The processing center's location in Long Island City put approximately 4 million people within a 10-mile radius of the FreshDirect facility, allowing the firm to deliver a large number of orders in a short amount of time.[1] Further cost controls had been implemented through FreshDirect's order and delivery protocols. Orders had to be a minimum of $40.00 with a delivery charge of $3.95 per order. FreshDirect prohibited tipping the delivery person. Delivery was made by one of FreshDirect's 23 trucks and was available only during a prearranged two-hour window on weekdays after 4:30 p.m. and all day on the weekends, which kept delivery trucks out of the heaviest New York City traffic, thus reducing FreshDirect's delivery-related costs.

Founding Partners

FreshDirect was launched in July 2001. CEO Joe Fedele was able to bring a wealth of experience with New York City's food industry to FreshDirect. In 1993 he cofounded Fairway Uptown, a 35,000-foot supermarket located on West 133rd Street in Harlem. Many critics originally scoffed at the idea of a successful store in that location, but Fairway's low prices and quality selection of produce and meats made it a hit with neighborhood residents, as well as many downtown and suburban commuters.

CFO Jason Ackerman had gained exposure to the grocery industry as an investment banker with Donaldson Lufkin & Jenrette, where he specialized in supermarket mergers and acquisitions.

---

*This case was prepared by Professor Alan B. Eisner and graduate student Keeley Townsend of Pace University as a basis for class discussion rather than to illustrate either effective or ineffective handling of an administrative situation. Copyright © 2004 Alan B. Eisner.

[1]Laseter, Tim, et. al., 2003, What FreshDirect learned from Dell, *Strategy+Business* (30), Spring.

Fedele and Ackerman first explored the idea of starting a large chain of fresh-food stores, but realized maintaining a high degree of quality would be impossible with a large enterprise. As an alternative, they elected to pursue a business that incorporated online shopping with central distribution.

FreshDirect acquired the bulk of its $100 million investment from several private sources, with a small contribution coming from the State of New York. By locating FreshDirect's distribution center within the state border, and promising to create at least 300 new permanent, full-time private sector jobs in the state, FreshDirect became eligible for a $500,000 training grant from the Empire State Development Jobs Now Program. As its name implied, the purpose of the Jobs Now program was to create new, immediate job opportunities for New Yorkers.

Business Plan

While business started out relatively slow, Fedele had hoped to capture around 5 percent of the New York grocery market, with projected revenues of about $100 million in the first year and $225 million by 2004. As of March 2003, FreshDirect had reached the milestone of 2,000 orders a day and was attracting around 3,000 new customers a day, for a total customer base of around 40,000.[2] FreshDirect service was originally slated for availability citywide by the end of 2002. However, in order to maintain its superior service and product quality, FreshDirect had chosen to slowly expand its service area. Services were expected to cover New York City and parts of Suffolk and Nassau counties by the end of 2004, and possibly start up in several other metropolitan regions nationwide by 2005.

The company had employed a relatively low-cost marketing approach, which originally consisted mainly of billboards, public relations, and word of mouth to promote its products and services. In 2003 FreshDirect hired Trumpet, an ad agency that promoted FreshDirect as a better way to shop by emphasizing the problems associated with traditional grocery shopping. For example, one commercial stressed the unsanitary conditions in a supermarket by showing a grocery shopper bending over a barrel of olives as she sneezed, getting an olive stuck in her nose, and then blowing it back into the barrel. The advertisement ended with the question, "Where's your food been?" Another ad showed a checkout clerk morph into an armed robber, demand money from the customer, and then morph back into a friendly checkout clerk once the money was received. The ad urged viewers to "stop getting robbed at the grocery store."[3]

Another innovative marketing approach that had been very successful was the offer of free food. FreshDirect offered $50 worth of free groceries to any first-time service user, believing that once people saw the quality of the food and the convenience of the service they would return as a paying customer.

Operating Strategy

FreshDirect's operating strategy had employed a make-to-order philosophy, eliminating the middleman in order to create an efficient supply chain.[4] By focusing its energy on providing produce, meat, seafood, baked goods, and coffees that were made to the customer's specific order, FreshDirect offered its customers an alternative to the standardized cuts and choices available at most brick-and-mortar grocery stores. This strategy had created a business model that was unique within the grocery business community.

A typical grocery store carried about 25,000 packaged goods, which accounted for around 50 percent of its sales, and about 2,200 perishable products, which accounted for the other 50 percent of sales. In contrast, FreshDirect offered around 5,000 perishable products, accounting for about 75 percent of its sales, but only around 3,000 packaged goods, which comprised the remaining 25 percent of sales.[5] While this stocking pattern enabled a greater array of fresh foods, it severely limited the number of brands and available sizes of packaged goods, such as cereal, crackers, and laundry detergent. However, FreshDirect believed customers would accept a more limited packaged good selection in order to get lower prices, as evidenced in the success of wholesale grocery stores which offered bulk sales of limited items. Jason Ackerman identified the ideal FreshDirect customers as those who bought their bulk staples from Costco on a monthly basis, and bought everything else from FreshDirect on a weekly basis.[6]

FreshDirect's Web Site

FreshDirect's Web site not only offered an abundance of products to choose from, but also provided a broad spectrum of information on the food that was sold and the manner in which it was sold. Web surfers could take a pictorial tour of the FreshDirect facility; get background information on the experts who managed each department; get nutritional information on food items; compare produce or cheese based on taste, price, and usage; specify the thickness of meat orders and opt for one of several marinades or rubs (see Exhibit 1); search for the right kind of coffee based on taste preferences; and read nutritional information for a variety of fully prepared meals.

For example, if you wanted to purchase chicken, you were first asked to choose from Breasts & Cutlets, Cubes

[2]Five months in Manhattan and FreshDirect passes the 2,000-order-a-day mark and has over 40,000 customers, 2003, *Business Wire*, February 12.

[3]Elliot, Stuart, 2003, A "fresh" and "direct" approach, *New York Times*, February 11.

[4]Laseter, What FreshDirect learned from Dell.

[5]Ibid.

[6]Ibid.

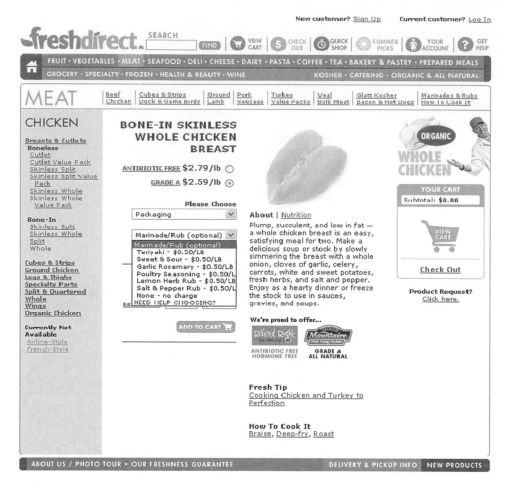

Exhibit 1   Example of FreshDirect Meat Selection Options

& Strips, Ground, Legs & Thighs, Specialty Parts, Split & Quartered, Whole, or Wings. Once your selection was made—let's say you chose Breasts & Cutlets—you were given further options based on your preference for skin, bone, and thickness. The final selection step offered you a choice of rubs and marinades, including Teriyaki, Sweet & Sour, Garlic Rosemary, Poultry Seasoning, Lemon Herb Rub, and Salt & Pepper Rub. All along the way, the pages offered nutritional profiles of each cut of meat as well as tips for preparation and storage.

FreshDirect employed two different delivery models, one for its urban customers and another for those in the suburbs. Customers within the city were attracted to the FreshDirect service because it eliminated the need to carry groceries for possibly a substantial distance from the closest grocery store, or to deal with trying to park a car near their apartment to unload their purchases. Orders made by customers within the city were delivered directly to their homes by a FreshDirect truck during a pre-arranged two-hour delivery window (see Exhibit 2).

Suburban customers were serviced in a slightly different manner. Most suburban residents had the convenience of automobile access and easy parking, but were looking for a time-saving device. The widespread congregation of these residents in train station parking lots or office parks made these areas perfect central delivery stations. FreshDirect would send a refrigerated truck, large enough to hold 500 orders, to these key spots during designated periods of time. Suburbanites could then exit the train or their office building, return to their cars, swing by the FreshDirect truck, pick up their order, and head home.

The Retail Grocery Industry

In 2003 the U.S. retail grocery industry was a $682.3 billion business, according to the U.S. Department of Commerce, with almost $362.4 billion of sales made by supermarket chains.[7] The top 10 supermarket chains in the

[7]Food Market Institute, *Supermarket Facts: Industry Overview 2003,* www.fmi.org/facts_figs/superfact.htm.

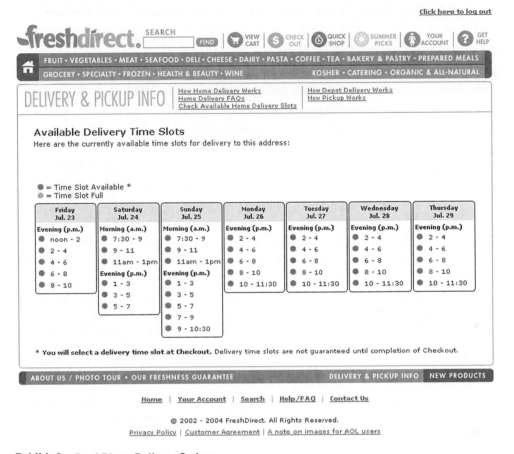

Exhibit 2   FreshDirect Delivery Options

United States commanded more than 44 percent of the market share for the grocery industry (see Exhibit 3).

In 2003 no single supermarket chain had an industry market share above 10 percent. The typical supermarket store carried an average of 32,000 items, averaged 44,000 square feet in size, and averaged $18 million in sales annually.

The supermarket business had traditionally been a low-margin business, with net profits of only 1 to 2 percent of revenues. Store profits depended heavily on creating a high volume of customer traffic and rapid inventory turnover, especially for perishables such as produce and fresh meat. Competitors had to operate efficiently to make money, so tight control of labor costs and product spoilage was essential. Because capital investment costs were modest—involving mainly the construction of distribution centers and stores—it was not unusual for supermarket chains to realize 15 to 20 percent returns on invested capital.

The Online Grocery Segment   The online-grocery shopping business was still in the early stages of development in 2004. Analysts believed that this segment accounted for less than 1 percent of total grocery sales in 2004. Total online sales were about $2.4 billion, but

Exhibit 3   Market Share for Top 10 Supermarket Chains

Supermarket Chain	Market Share (%)
Wal-Mart Super Centers	9.6%
Kroger	7.3
Albertson's	5.6
Safeway	5.0
Royal Ahold	3.4
Supervalu	3.1
Costco Wholesale Corp.	3.0
Sam's Club	2.7
Fleming	2.3
Publix Super Markets	2.2
Total Market Share	44.2

Source: *Advertising Age*.

Exhibit 4   Types of Online Shoppers and Their Propensity to Be Attracted to Online Grocery Shopping

Types of Online Shoppers	Comments
Traditionals	Might be an older technology-avoider, or simply a shopper who likes to sniff-test their own produce and eyeball the meat selection.
Responsibles	Feed off the satisfaction of accomplishing this persistent to-do item.
Time Starved	Find the extra costs associated with delivery fees or other markups a small price to pay for saving them time.
New Technologists	Use the latest technology for any and every activity they can, because they can.
Necessity Users	People with physical or circumstantial challenges that make grocery shopping difficult. Likely to be the most loyal group of shoppers.
Avoiders	Dislike the grocery shopping experience for a variety of reasons.

Source: Anderson Consulting study cited in Sherry Anderson, "Is Online Grocery Shopping for You," *Computer Bits*, 11, April 2001.

were expected to reach $6.5 billion by 2008.[8] Online grocery shopping had been slow to catch on, and industry newcomers had encountered high start-up and operating costs. Sales volumes and profit margins remained too small to cover the high costs. The problem, according to industry analysts, was that consumers had been largely disappointed in the service, selection, and prices they had gotten from industry members.

However, some analysts expected online grocery sales to grow at a rapid pace as companies improved their service and selection, PC penetration of households rose, and consumers became more accustomed to making purchases online.[9] An article in *Computer Bits* examined the customer base for online grocers, looking specifically at the types of consumers that would be likely to shop online and the kinds of home computer systems that were required for online shopping. An Anderson Consulting report, cited in *Computer Bits,* identified six major types of online shoppers (See Exhibit 4) and estimated that by 2007, 15 to 20 million households would order their groceries online.[10] A MARC Group study concluded that "consumers who buy groceries online are likely to be more loyal to their electronic supermarkets, spend more per store 'visit,' and take greater advantage of coupons and premiums than traditional customers."[11]

One of the problems with online grocery shopping was that consumers were extremely price sensitive when it came to buying groceries, and the prices of many online

grocers were above those at supermarkets. Shoppers, in many cases, were unwilling to pay extra to online grocers for the convenience of home delivery. Consumer price sensitivity meant that online grocers had to achieve a cost structure that would allow them to (1) price competitively, (2) cover the cost of selecting items in the store and delivering individual grocery orders, and (3) have sufficient margins to earn attractive returns on their investment. Some analysts estimated that to be successful, online grocers had to do 10 times the volume of a traditional grocer.[12]

Supermarket Chains as Potential Competitors in the Online Grocery Segment   When online grocers started appearing within the industry, many established brick-and-mortar grocers began offering online shopping in an attempt to maintain and expand their customer base. Two basic models had been used for online order fulfillment: (1) to pick items from the shelves of existing stores within the grocer's chain, and (2) to build special warehouses dedicated to online orders. The demand for home delivery of groceries had been increasing, but in many market areas the demand had not yet reached a level that would justify the high cost of warehouses dedicated to the fulfillment of online orders.[13]

Safeway began an ambitious online grocery venture by establishing Grocery Works, an online shopping system that included a series of warehouses dedicated to filling online orders. Unfavorable returns forced Safeway to reevaluate its system, and it eventually chose to form a partnership with Tesco, a U.K.–based grocer. Tesco filled its online orders from the shelves of local stores in close proximity to the customer's home. Safeway and Tesco worked

[8]McTaggart, Jenny, 2004, Fresh direction, *Progressive Grocer* 83 (4), 58–60.

[9]Machlis, Sharon, 1998, Filling up grocery carts online, *Computerworld,* July 27: 4.

[10]Anderson, Sherry, 2001, Is online grocery shopping for you, *Computer Bits,* 11, April.

[11]Woods, Bob, 1998, America Online goes grocery shopping for e-commerce bargains, *Computer News,* August 10: 42.

[12]Fisher, Lawrence M., 1999, On-line grocer is setting up delivery system for $1 billion, *New York Times,* July 10: 1.

[13]Online supermarkets keep it simple, 2002, *Frontline Solutions,* 3 (2): 46–49.

Exhibit 5   Profiles of Selected Online Grocers

Name	Area Covered	Minimum Order	Delivery Charge	Delivery Method	Specialization
FreshDirect	Manhattan's East Side, Battery Park City	$40	$3.95, no tipping	Trucks; avail. weeknights after 4:30 p.m. and all day on weekends	◆ Mostly perishables: fresh produce, meats, baked goods ◆ Low prices because there is no middleman
YourGrocer	Manhattan, Bronx, Westchester, Greenwich	$75	$9.95	Rented vans; avail. on select days and times, depending on location	◆ Bulk orders of packaged goods
Peapod	Chicago, Boston, DC, southern Connecticut, Long Island	$50	$4.95 for order greater than $75; $9.95 for order less than $75; tipping optional	Truck; avail. 7 a.m.–1 p.m. and 4 p.m.–10 p.m. weekdays, 7 a.m.–1 p.m. weekends	◆ Partner with Giant Foods and Stop & Shop; items picked from shelves of local store near customer's home
NetGrocer	Lower 48 states, DC	None	$3.99–$599.99, depends on order size and destination	FedEx; will receive order within 1 to 4 business days	◆ Only nonperishables; no fresh produce

Source: Company Web sites.

Exhibit 6   Comparison of Prices for Selected Online Grocers, February 2003

Grocery Item	FreshDirect's Price	YourGrocer's Price	PeaPod's Price	NetGrocer's Price
Tide laundry detergent	$7.99 / 100 oz.	$21.99 / 300 oz. ($7.33 / 100 oz.)	$8.79 / 100 oz.	$9.99 / 100 oz.
Wish-Bone Italian dressing	$1.49 / 8 oz.	$4.69 / 36 oz. ($1.04 / 8 oz.)	$1.69 / 8 oz.	$1.79 / 8 oz.
Cheerios	$3.69 / 15 oz.	$7.49 / 35 oz. ($3.21 / 15 oz.)	$3.89 / 15 oz.	$4.29 / 15 oz.
Ragu spaghetti sauce	$1.99 / 26 oz.	$7.99 / 135 oz. ($1.54 / 26 oz.)	$1.99 / 26 oz.	$2.49 / 26 oz.
Granny Smith apples	$1.29 / lb.	$5.99 / 5 lb. bag ($1.20 / lb.)	$2.99 / 3 lb. bag ($1.00 / lb.)	Fresh produce not available

Source: Company Web sites.

together on GroceryWorks in Portland, Oregon, where they received a positive initial response from customers.[14]

Online Grocery Industry

YourGrocer.com   FreshDirect's most geographically significant competitor in the online grocery industry was YourGrocer.com. (See Exhibit 5 for profiles of online grocers. Exhibit 6 compares prices of selected items at these same online grocers.) YourGrocer was launched in New

[14]Ibid.

York City in 1998 with the goal of being the leading online grocery service for the New York metropolitan area. By November 2001 the company ran out of money and was forced to shut down. In the spring of 2002 new capital resources were found and the company reopened for business. However, the second time around YourGrocer's approach was a little different.

YourGrocer was created with a bulk-buying strategy, believing that customers would order large, economical quantities of goods from the Web site and the company would make home deliveries in company trucks. During YourGrocer's first life, the ambitious business plan covered a large service area and included the acquisition of another online grocery company, NYCGrocery.com.[15] But the business plan was modified in the second life. The company reduced the size of its staff, got rid of warehouses, decided to rent instead of owning its delivery vans, and scaled down its delivery routes.[16] Queens, Nassau County, and New Jersey were eliminated from the service area, leaving only Manhattan, the Bronx, Westchester County, and Fairfield County (Connecticut).

YourGrocer offered a limited selection of items that could only be purchased in bulk. Deliveries were made in varied time slots, depending on the customer's location in the New York area. There was a $75 minimum order with a $9.95 delivery charge (see Exhibits 7 and 8).

Peapod   Founded in 1989 by brothers Andrew and Thomas Parkinson, Peapod (see Exhibits 9 and 10) was an early pioneer in e-commerce, inventing an online home-shopping service for grocery items years ahead of the commercial emergence of the Internet. With its tagline "Smart Shopping for Busy People," the company began providing consumers with a home-shopping experience in the early 1990s, going so far as to install modems in customer homes to provide an online connection. From its founding in 1989 until 1998, the company's business model involved filling customer orders by forming alliances with traditional grocery retailers. The company chose a retail partner in each geographic area where it operated and used the partner's local network of retail stores to pick and pack orders for delivery to customers. Peapod personnel would cruise the aisles of a partner's stores, selecting the items each customer ordered, pack and load them into Peapod vehicles, and then deliver them to customers at prearranged times. Peapod charged customers a fee for its service and collected fees from its retail supply partners for using their products in its online service. Over the next several years, Peapod built delivery capabilities in eight market areas: Chicago; Columbus, Ohio; Boston; San Francisco/San Jose; Houston, Dallas, and Austin, in Texas; and Long Island, New York.

In 1997, faced with mounting losses despite growing revenues, Peapod management shifted to a new order fulfillment business model utilizing a local company owned and operated central distribution warehouse to store, pick, and pack customer orders for delivery. By mid-1999 the company had opened new distribution centers in three of the eight markets it served—Chicago, Long Island, and

Boston; a fourth distribution center was under construction in San Francisco.

In the late spring of 2000, Peapod created a partnership with Royal Ahold, an international food provider based in the Netherlands. At the time, Ahold operated five supermarket companies in the United States: Stop & Shop, Tops Market, Giant-Landover, Giant-Carlisle, and BI-LO. In September 2000 Peapod acquired Streamline.com, Inc.'s operations in Chicago and the Washington, D.C., markets, and announced that it planned to exit its markets in Columbus, Ohio, and Houston, Dallas, and Austin, Texas. All of these moves were made as a part of Peapod's strategic plan for growth and future profitability.

Under Peapod's initial partnership agreement with Ahold, Peapod was to continue as a stand-alone company, with Ahold supplying Peapod's goods, services, and fast-pick fulfillment centers. However, in July 2001 Ahold acquired all the outstanding shares of Peapod and merged Peapod into one of Ahold's subsidiaries.

In 2003 Peapod provided online shopping and delivery service in five metropolitan areas: Chicago, Boston, southern Connecticut, Long Island, and Washington, D.C. Peapod employed a centralized distribution model in every market: in large markets, orders were picked, packed, loaded, and delivered from a freestanding centralized fulfillment center; in smaller markets, Peapod established fast-pick centralized fulfillment centers adjacent to the facilities of retail partners.[17] Peapod's proprietary transportation routing system ensured on-time delivery and efficient truck and driver utilization.

NetGrocer   NetGrocer.com was founded in 1996 and advertised itself as the first online grocer to sell nonperishable items nationwide (see Exhibits 11 and 12). NetGrocer serviced all 48 continental U.S. states and the District of Columbia. All customer orders were filled in its single, 120,000-square-foot warehouse in North Brunswick, New Jersey. Orders were shipped by Federal Express and were guaranteed to reach any part of NetGrocer's service area within two to four days.

NetGrocer offered its customers a large selection of brand-name and specialty nonperishable items that were difficult to find in a local supermarket. The key customer segment for NetGrocer's services were busy families, urban dwellers, special-needs groups (e.g., dieters, diabetics), and senior citizens. Customers purportedly enjoyed the benefits of convenient online shopping from home 24 hours a day, access to thousands of products, and delivery of their orders directly to their home. Manufacturers also benefited from NetGrocer, as they were able to distribute their products nationwide, rapidly and easily.

In 2002 NetGrocer became a part of a larger grocery enterprise. A new entity named NeXpansion was created

[15]Joyce, Erin, 2002, YourGrocer.com wants to come back, *ECommerce,* May 15; http://ecommerce.internet.com/news/news/article/0,,10375_1122671,00.html.

[16]Fickenscher, Lisa, 2002, Bouncing back from cyber limbo: Resurgence of failed dot-coms after downsizing, *Crain's New York Business,* June 24.

[17]Peapod, Inc., Corporate fact sheet, www.peapod.com/corpinfo/peapodFacts.pdf.

Exhibit 7   YourGrocer.com Web Site

Exhibit 8   YourGrocer's Service Focus

New YourGrocer will focus on providing the three benefits that families in the area most value:

1. Easy ordering over the Internet or on the phone, which saves hours of thankless shopping time.
2. Delivery right to the home or office, which eliminates the burden of lifting and transporting heavy and bulky items each month.
3. Meaningful savings everyday, which reduces the prices paid for stock-up groceries and supplies by 20–30%, on average, below local supermarkets.

Exhibit 9   Peapod Web Site

Exhibit 10   Peapod Product Selection

Exhibit 11   **Netgrocer.com Web Site**

SHIPPING REGION 2	
ORDER BRACKETS	SHIPPING RATE
$0 - 24.99	$8.99
$25 - 49.99	$12.99
$50 - 74.99	$15.99
$75 - 99.99	$19.99
$100 - 124.99	$23.99
$125 - 149.99	$27.99
$150 - 199.99	$41.99
$200 - 299.99	$66.99
$300 - 499.99	$101.99
$500 - 749.99	$201.99
$750 - 999.99	$301.99
$1000 + **	$601.99

SHIPPING REGION 1	
ORDER BRACKETS	SHIPPING RATE
$0 - 24.99	$3.99
$25 - 49.99	$5.99
$50 - 74.99	$7.99
$75 - 99.99	$9.99
$100 - 124.99	$11.99
$125 - 149.99	$13.99
$150 - 199.99	$15.99
$200 - 299.99	$24.99
$300 - 499.99	$39.99
$500 - 749.99	$99.99
$750 - 999.99	$149.99
$1000 + **	$399.99

Exhibit 12   **NetGrocer Shipping Charges**

that included the existing NetGrocer service and also a new service called Endless Aisle. Rather than competing with local grocery stores, Endless Aisle offered local grocers a way to greatly expand their product assortment. The program worked through Endless Aisle kiosks installed in participating brick-and-mortar supermarkets. Shoppers could visit the kiosk to shop online for products that were unavailable in the grocery store, such as specialty products, hard-to-find regional items, and product categories not traditionally carried by grocery stores. The products offered through Endless Aisles were designed to complement, not compete, with the local store's product selection. Consumers enjoyed one-stop shopping for all of their grocery needs while local retailers benefited from the Endless Aisles service because they were able to offer their customers easy access to a much wider range of products, without having to use valuable shelf space for products that had a lower sales velocity.

As General Motors (GM) was preparing to showcase its new car models at the annual Detroit auto show in early 2004, news leaked out that the firm was not planning to sell a hybrid vehicle until 2007, two years later than originally planned. Hybrid vehicles save on gasoline by supplementing internal combustion with electrical power. Japanese automakers such as Toyota and Honda had already been offering hybrids since the late 1990s. Other car producers had not yet introduced any hybrids, although Ford was planning to offer a hybrid version of its Escape sport utility vehicle (SUV) sometime in 1994.

The news that GM would delay its introduction of hybrid vehicles caught many analysts by surprise. The firm was better positioned than either of its U.S.–based rivals to make a push into this new segment. The firm had clearly regained leadership of the Big Three car companies, reflecting real operational improvements that G. Richard Wagoner Jr. had achieved over the past decade, starting when he was chief financial officer (CFO) and later as chief operating officer.

After GM lost a staggering $30 billion during a single three-year stretch in the early '90s, Wagoner had worked with Chairman John F. "Jack" Smith, Jr., to force GM to return to basics. They had slashed costs, cut payroll, and overhauled aging plants. When he took over as CEO in May 2000, Wagoner began to work even harder to bring the firm in line with most of its rivals. As a result of his efforts, GM has been able to come much closer to Japanese firms such as Honda and Toyota through making tremendous increases in productivity and attaining significant improvements in quality.

The results had been quite remarkable. GM had finished 2002 with an operating profit of $3.9 billion, nearly double what it had earned in 2001, on 5 percent higher sales of $186.2 billion. (See Exhibit 1. Exhibit 2 illustrates GM's balance sheet.) Furthermore, the firm had been able to recapture leadership of the truck business from rival Ford Motor Company, a coup that helped it to add billions of dollars to its revenues. During 2003 GM even managed to increase its overall share of the U.S. market to 28.3 percent from 28.1 percent during the previous year (see Exhibit 3 on GM's market share in the United States).

In spite of these achievements, GM was still plagued by weak car brands and huge pension obligations. Wagoner was well aware that mistakes made by the firm's management over the last 30 years would make progress

slow and cumbersome. Former chief executives from Frederic Donner to Roger Smith had built up a bloated bureaucracy that had cranked out boring, low-quality cars for many years. Turf battles at headquarters had sapped resources and diverted attention away from a rising threat posed by competitors from Asia and Europe. Those competitors had already managed to make formidable inroads into the car market and were beginning to attack the market for SUVs and trucks.

Allocating Responsibilities

In many ways, Wagoner may be well qualified for the job of turning GM around. After receiving his MBA from Harvard Business School, he chose to take a job at the automotive firm, turning down more lucrative jobs on Wall Street. Wagoner's knack for crunching numbers propelled him through stints at GM units in Canada, Europe, and Brazil. His big break came in 1992, when the board made some changes to the top management that led to Wagoner's appointment as the firm's CFO.

As a longtime GM insider, Wagoner possessed distinct advantages that he brought to his job as CEO. He knew what brutal facts needed to be confronted, and he was aware of the specific veterans who could handle key jobs. Wagoner also broke with GM tradition by recruiting respected outsiders for key positions. He recruited Robert A. Lutz as head of product development and John Devine as vice-chairman and chief financial officer. Lutz had sparked Chrysler's resurgence during the 1990s with cars such as the Dodge Viper and PT Cruiser.

After Wagoner had assembled his executive team, he delegated responsibilities to each of them. To make sure they were motivated to fulfill these responsibilities, he also gave them extraordinary leeway to fix the company's problems. "Rick acts more like a coach than a boss," said David E. Cole, director of the Center for Automotive Research in Ann Arbor.[1]

Against all odds, Wagoner also made real progress in energizing GM's torpid culture. His low-key style allowed him to tear down the firm's warring fiefdoms. GM used to have different studios for each division working on car designs that would get passed on to marketing, then engineering, then manufacturing. Lutz formed one committee to cover the entire process. Every Thursday, he hashed out what vehicles should look like and which division would build them, along with a small group that included key top managers from design and engineering.

Although Wagoner may have a low-key style, this does not mean that he does not get involved. His executives may be able to make the day-to-day decisions on various matters, but Wagoner reserves final say. During one trip through the design studio last year, he expressed

This case was prepared by Professor Jamal Shamsie of Michigan State University. This case was developed from published sources as a basis for class discussion rather than to illustrate either effective or ineffective handling of an administrative situation. Copyright © 2004 Jamal Shamsie.

Exhibit 1 Income Statement
(All numbers in thousands)

	Period Ending December 31		
	2003	**2002**	**2001**
Total Revenue	$185,524,000	$186,763,000	$177,260,000
Cost of Revenue	152,071,000	153,344,000	143,850,000
Gross Profit	33,453,000	33,419,000	33,410,000
Selling General and Administrative	21,008,000	23,624,000	23,302,000
Operating Income or Loss	12,445,000	9,795,000	10,108,000
Total Other Income/Expenses Net	612,000	—	—
Earnings before Interest and Taxes	12,445,000	9,795,000	10,108,000
Interest Expense	9,464,000	7,715,000	8,590,000
Income before Tax	2,981,000	2,080,000	1,518,000
Income Tax Expense	731,000	533,000	768,000
Minority Interest	—	189,000	(149,000)
Net Income from Continuing Operations	2,862,000	1,736,000	601,000
Discontinued Operations	960,000	—	—
Net Income	3,822,000	1,736,000	601,000
Preferred Stock and Other Adjustments	—	(47,000)	(99,000)
Net Income Applicable to Common Shares	$ 3,822,000	$ 1,689,000	$ 502,000

Source: General Motors annual reports.

his interest in a sexy two-door version of the Cadillac CTS sports sedan. Although he left the job to the designers, Wagoner kept himself well informed of the progress that the design team was making on the new car. "Rick trusts my judgment implicitly," Lutz said, "but if I came up with some wacky product proposals, he'd pull me back."[2]

Wagoner also exerts control by imposing tough performance standards. As he rose through GM's finance division, Wagoner developed a reputation as a legendary number cruncher who holds top managers to strict measures. Although GM, like most big companies, had performance goals, they never went nearly as deep or into as much detail. Says GM North America President Gary L. Cowger: "Everything can be measured."[3] Lutz was judged on 12 criteria last year, from how well he used existing parts to save money in new vehicles to how many engineering hours he cut from the development process.

Speeding Up Product Development

Since Wagoner delegated product development to Lutz, . he has moved to reorganize the design-by-committee system and cut the time it takes to develop a new car to 20 months from nearly four years. In the past, even if a bold design made it off the drawing board, it had little chance of surviving to the showroom. A concept would go from a designer to the marketing staff, which would try to tailor it to consumers. Then it would go to engineers, who would try to figure out how to build it, and so on. Separate teams worked with factories and parts suppliers on their individual slice of the process, with little interaction.

This resulted in a very slow and expensive development process. The SSR concept vehicle, started a few months after Wagoner had taken over, exposed the problems that GM faced in developing new cars. Everyone agreed that this combination of hot rod and pickup, with its distinctive chrome bars splitting the front grille and taillights, would be a great image builder. Because it was announced before engineers had a precise blueprint to build it, the program quickly ran longer than expected and went well over budget. When the $42,000 SSR finally hit the showrooms in the summer of 2003, the costs had risen from the original $300 million to almost $500 million.

Since then, Wagoner and Lutz have smoothed things out a bit. Lutz works with other members of the top

Exhibit 2   Balance Sheet (All numbers in thousands)

	Period Ending December 31		
	2003	**2002**	**2001**
Assets			
Current Assets			
Cash and Cash Equivalents	$ 32,554,000	$ 21,449,000	$ 18,555,000
Short-Term Investments	22,215,000	2,174,000	790,000
Net Receivables	20,532,000	18,223,000	13,283,000
Inventory	10,960,000	15,272,000	14,558,000
Total Current Assets	86,261,000	57,118,000	47,186,000
Long-Term Investments	198,778,000	189,859,000	183,661,000
Property Plant and Equipment	72,594,000	36,152,000	39,724,000
Goodwill	3,790,000	6,992,000	10,006,000
Intangible Assets	970,000	7,619,000	6,921,000
Accumulated Amortization	—	—	—
Other Assets	58,924,000	41,372,000	14,177,000
Deferred Long-Term Asset Charges	27,190,000	32,759,000	22,294,000
Total Assets	448,507,000	371,871,000	323,969,000
Liabilities			
Current Liabilities			
Accounts Payable	99,352,000	69,517,000	53,513,000
Short/Current Long-Term Debt	—	1,516,000	2,402,000
Other Current Liabilities	—	—	8,331,000
Total Current Liabilities	99,352,000	71,033,000	64,246,000
Long-Term Debt	271,756,000	200,424,000	163,912,000
Other Liabilities	44,316,000	92,766,000	71,053,000
Deferred Long-Term Liability Charges	7,508,000	—	4,305,000
Minority Interest	307,000	834,000	746,000
Total Liabilities	423,239,000	365,057,000	304,262,000
Stockholders' Equity			
Common Stock	937,000	1,032,000	1,020,000
Retained Earnings	13,421,000	10,198,000	9,463,000
Capital Surplus	15,185,000	21,583,000	21,519,000
Other Stockholder Equity	(4,275,000)	(25,999,000)	(12,295,000)
Total Stockholder Equity	25,268,000	6,814,000	19,707,000
Net Tangible Assets	$ 20,508,000	$ (7,797,000)	$ 2,780,000

Source: General Motors annual reports.

Exhibit 3   **U.S. Market Share**

	Cars	Trucks	Total
2002	25.4%	31.0%	28.3%
2001	26.9	29.2	28.1
2000	28.6	27.0	27.8
1999	29.8	27.8	28.8
1998	30.2	27.4	28.8

Source: General Motors.

management team to decide which ideas for new car models from the design studios will be considered for funding by GM's Automotive Strategy Board, chaired monthly by Wagoner. Lutz says he and Wagoner have disagreed on some product decisions, but he hasn't been turned down yet. Now the vast majority of the engineering work has already been finished when a program manager sits down to build a car.

Furthermore, GM is trying to improve its product development process by adopting a practice that the Japanese have perfected over many years. In past decades only a small percentage of parts were reused from one generation of cars to the next. Now Lutz is trying to raise that to 40 percent to 60 percent, about on a par with Japanese automakers. As GM develops the next generation Chevy Silverado and GMC Sierra pickups for 2008, it aims to reuse much of the existing platform. That should cut development costs by nearly half.

The firm is trying to imitate the Japanese by developing several models that share a similar chassis or frame parts. The new Chevy Malibu, for instance, uses the same platform and many of the same parts as the Saab 9-3 sedan. GM is now planning to reuse the skeleton beneath the sleek body of its Pontiac Solstice for its upcoming Saturn coupe and possibly for the sporty Chevrolet wagon called the Nomad. "GM is managing its product development more efficiently than ever," Lutz recently declared.[4]

Building Better Cars

GM, along with its other U.S.–based rivals, has been putting a renewed emphasis on sedans, coupes, and station wagons, a category in which they have especially struggled with foreign competition. Many of GM's divisions have struggled to make profits with their offerings. The much-heralded Saturn division that was created to revive the firm's fortunes has been plagued with problems. While the division's sales have rebounded somewhat from the lows of the late 1990s, it is still expected to lose about $1 billion. With only three models, Saturn sales are expected to drop 3 percent in 2004 to about 273,000 vehicles, roughly what was sold a decade ago.

Wagoner is certain that Lutz will push GM to develop cars that will have more appeal for buyers. A few years ago Lutz had derided many of the automobile designs coming out of Detroit, claiming that they lacked the emotional appeal of classic American cars. He had commented: "One critically bad thing at GM has been the subordination of design. People who rent our cars at airports look at them and say 'Isn't this depressing?'"[5] To turn this around, Lutz has managed to get almost two-thirds of GM's annual $7 billion product-development budget for its new cars, shifting its focus away from trucks.

In fact, GM is trying to return to its roots with legendary Chairman Alfred P. Sloan's philosophy of "a car for every purse and purpose." The auto giant is offering a huge array, from the $60,000 Cadillac STS flagship sedan to Chevrolet's $15,000 Cobalt compact and $10,000 Korean-built Aveo subcompact. In between, GM has its newly redesigned Chevy Malibu, a plain vanilla sedan aimed at the popular Toyota Camry and Honda Accord markets. For the sportier crowd, Pontiac is introducing the sexy Solstice and the flashy G6 sedan, already winning praise for its sleek styling.

Like his competitors, Wagoner is also banking on crossover vehicles, which combine SUV-like space and looks with a carlike ride and better fuel economy, as a hedge against a big-truck backlash. Cadillac has introduced a luxury SRX model and Chevrolet is set to launch its Equinox as an all-wheel-drive crossover. Lutz has tentatively approved a highly stylized 2007 replacement for the Chevy Silverado and GMC Sierra pickups, which hold a commanding 40 percent of the pickup market. It will be based on the slick Cheyenne concept truck that was recently unveiled by GM, which has improved driver and passenger room and doors on each side of the pickup bed to provide easier cargo access.

Wagoner has also moved to streamline GM's factories to build better cars at lower cost. GM is now the most productive domestic automaker, having cut the time it takes to assemble a vehicle from an average of 32 hours in 1998 to 26 hours in 2001, according to Harbour & Associates. That compares with 27 hours for Ford, almost 31 at DaimlerChrysler, 22.5 at Toyota, and 17.9 at Nissan (see Exhibit 4). GM's plants are also becoming more flexible. Seven of its full-size pickup and SUV plants can make any of the vehicles designed on that platform.

As a result of this focus on revamping production, the cars rolling off GM's assembly lines today are undeniably better built than they used to be. Once ranked below the industry average, GM now trails only Honda and Toyota in J. D. Power & Associates Inc.'s initial quality survey, which measures problems in the first 90 days of ownership (see Exhibit 5). Some cars, such as the Chevrolet Impala, have even beaten the likes of the Toyota Camry. In 2003, *Consumer Reports* recommended as many as 13 GM vehicles, up from only 5 the year before. GM is hoping that

Exhibit 4   Productivity Gains

Hours Per Vehicle		
	GM	Toyota
2001	26.0	22.5
2000	26.8	21.6
1999	28.5	21.7
1998	32.0	21.6
1997	31.5	21.5

Source: General Motors, Toyota Motor.

Exhibit 5   Quality Rankings of Automobile Companies

Defects per 100 Vehicles during First 90 Days of Ownership		
	2003	1999
Toyota	115	132
Honda	126	137
Industry Average	133	170
General Motors	134	179
Ford	136	172
DaimlerChrysler	139	183
Volkswagen	141	215

Source: J. D. Power & Associates.

these improvements will lead to a shift in the buyer's perceptions of its brands as musty and second-rate.

Dealing with the Benefits Crunch

Wagoner's biggest challenge lies in dealing with the lavish health and retirement benefits that GM accorded to its workers. The firm had agreed to these terms during its more profitable days as a way to buy peace with the United Auto Workers (UAW). GM pays its UAW workers only slightly more per hour than Toyota, Honda, and Nissan pay their American factory workers. But the cost of pension and health care benefits for current workers is huge, running to about $24 per hour at GM. This is almost double the costs incurred by the U.S.–based operations set up by foreign manufacturers.

The pension costs alone should cut 2003 net income from $4.2 billion to $3.8 billion. Providing for retirees saddles each car rolling off a GM assembly line with a $1,350 penalty when compared with a Japanese car built in a new, nonunion U.S. plant, according to analyst Scott Hill of Sanford C. Bernstein & Company. This represents a formidable disadvantage in an industry that struggles to make an average operating profit of $800 per vehicle.

Costs for retirees have escalated as a result of other recent decisions by GM's management. Underestimating the speed of its decline, GM agreed to pay workers for years after a furlough. As losses mounted, GM resorted to early-retirement offers, avoiding billions in unemployment benefits but adding thousands of retirees. Since GM was shrinking faster than Ford, its pension rolls grew more quickly, to 2.5 retirees per worker today, compared to Ford's 1-to-1 ratio.

Those huge legacy costs explain why Wagoner has kept the heat on his competition with the rock-bottom financing deals he rolled out aggressively in the wake of the attacks on September 11, 2001. Closing plants and accepting a smaller chunk of the U.S. market would have given GM fewer vehicles over which to spread those big pension and health care costs. Said Wagoner: "We have a huge fixed-cost base. It's 30 years of downsizing and 30 years of increased health care costs. It puts a premium on us running this business to generate cash. Our goal is to grow. We don't care who we take it from."[6]

All that would make the outlook for GM pretty bleak. But Wagoner estimates that these legacy costs will eventually start to diminish. Starting around 2008, the ranks of GM's elderly retirees will begin to drop, relieving some of the burden. After that, more of the incremental gains Wagoner has been achieving will fall to the bottom line rather than to retirees. The results could be dramatic. Nevertheless, he has to keep up the cash flow to cover those benefit costs until they start to shrink. At the same time, he must continue to rack up improvements in quality, efficiency, design, and brand appeal.

Moving Beyond Past Problems

Clearly, Wagoner has moved swiftly to start dealing with the problems that have been plaguing GM. Competitors concede that they have been impressed by the progress that he has made. GM's operating profit of $3.9 billion during the last year beat the $872 million reported by Ford. And GM's stock, trading around 37, is only down 26 percent from a year ago compared to the 36 percent decline in Ford's stock price.

Wagoner has also used cost cutting to double the margins—to 2.6 percent of sales—for GM's operations in North America last year. Due to efficiency gains, GM has now become one of the leanest car builders, with variable costs amounting to 62 percent of revenues, according to UBS Warburg. That puts it ahead of Ford and Chrysler at

68 percent, and it isn't far behind leaders Toyota and Honda at 60 percent.

But these steps have just given Wagoner some breathing room. He has barely managed to keep a handle on the growing pension and health care issues. These obligations have been reduced for the time being through the sale of the DirecTV business and a successful bond issue. But Wagoner is also betting that the cars that GM launches in the future will be good enough to sell on merit, not price. If he can cut back on the incentives, the firm may be able to generate enough profits to place it back on a sound financial footing.

GM has a long way to go before it can win customers back who will pay higher prices for its cars. Wagoner and his team are still learning to design and manufacture better cars. Under Lutz, the design team is trying to speed up the development process by designing more cars around existing common platforms. Even as GM is building up some momentum on designing new vehicles, however, the firm has been finding that its plants are not yet flexible enough to switch between different models without glitches.

Above all, it is clear that GM will have to turn out a steady stream of consistently competitive, reliable, and stylish cars in order to turn its image around. The image of most of its brands has been damaged by decades of cars that fell apart, lost their value quickly, or were just plain ugly. UBS Warburg analyst Saul Rubin believes that the firm, like its U.S. counterparts, faces an uphill battle in changing the perceptions of consumers about their cars.

But Wagoner clearly realizes that GM has no choice. It has to try to turn things around in order to survive against the growing competition. "This is one major last-ditch effort to save themselves in the car market," said Joseph Phillippi, a former Wall Street analyst who consults for the industry.[7]

Endnotes

1. Welch, David, & Kerwin, Kathleen, 2003, Rick Wagoner's game plan, *BusinessWeek,* February 10: 54.
2. Ibid., 56.
3. Ibid., 54.
4. Welch, David, & Kerwin, Kathleen, 2004, Detroit tries it the Japanese way, *BusinessWeek,* January 26: 76.
5. Taylor, Alex, III, 2002, Finally GM is looking good, *Fortune,* April 1: 51–52.
6. Welch & Kerwin, 2003 Rick Wagoner's game plan, 53.
7. Ibid., pp. 55–56.

Case 17   Go Global—or No?

"Why aren't they biting?" wondered Greg McNally as he laid down another perfectly executed cast. He was fly-fishing in the most beautiful spot he had ever seen, on the Alta in Norway—reputedly the home of Scandinavia's worthiest salmon. And he had plenty of opportunity to admire the view. No fish were getting in the way.

What a difference from the luck he'd had a couple of weeks earlier trout fishing at Nelson's Spring Creek in Montana. It seemed like so much more time had passed since the two-day off-site he had called there, designed to be part celebration of the past, part planning for the future.

Some celebration had definitely been in order. The company, DataClear, was really taking off, fueled by the success of its first software product, ClearCloud. In 1999, its first full year of operation, DataClear's sales reached $2.2 million. Now, the following September, it was looking like 2000 sales could easily reach $5.3 million. At the all-staff meeting on the Friday before the off-site, Greg had announced the company's success in recruiting two more great executives, bringing the staff to 38. "I'm more confident than ever that we'll hit our goals: $20 million in 2001 and then $60 million in 2002!"

Clouds on the Horizon

A New Jersey native, Greg held an MSc from Rutgers and then went West to get his PhD in computer science from UC Berkeley. He spent the next 15 years at Borland and Oracle, first as a software developer and then as a senior product manager. He started DataClear in Palo Alto, California, in the spring of 1998.

At that time, Greg realized that companies were collecting information faster than they could analyze it and that data analysis was an underexploited segment of the software business. It was at a seminar at Northwestern University that he saw his opportunity. Two researchers had developed a set of algorithms that enabled analysts to sift through large amounts of raw data in powerful ways without programmers' help. Greg cashed in his Oracle options and, in partnership with the two researchers, created Data-Clear to develop applications based on the algorithms.

His partners took responsibility for product development and an initial stake of 20% each; Greg provided $500,000 in financing in return for 60% of the shares and the job of CEO. A year later, Greg offered David Lester, founder of DL Ventures and a former Oracle executive, 30% of the company in return for $5 million in additional funding.

Reprinted by permission of Harvard Business Review. "Go Global—Or No?" by Walter Kuemmerle, June 2001. Copyright © 2001 by the Harvard Business School Publishing Corporation; all rights reserved.

In his previous positions, Greg had shown a knack for leading "fizzy" technical teams, and under his leadership, the two researchers came up with a state-of-the-art data analysis package they dubbed ClearCloud (from the clarity the software brought to large data clouds). Two versions, one for the telecommunications industry and the other for financial services providers, were officially launched in September 1998. ClearCloud had a number of immediate and profitable applications. For instance, it could be used to help credit card companies detect fraud patterns more quickly in the millions of transactions that occurred every day. Greg conservatively estimated the annual demand from the U.S. telecommunications and financial services sectors to be around $600 million. The challenge was to make potential users aware of the product.

ClearCloud was an instant hit, and within just a month of its launch, Greg had needed to recruit a dozen sales and service staffers. One of the first was Susan Moskowski, a former sales rep at Banking Data Systems, who had worked successfully with Greg on several major joint pitches to financial institutions. She had spent two years at BDS's Singapore subsidiary, where she had laid the groundwork for a number of important contracts. She had left BDS to do an MBA at Stanford and joined Data-Clear immediately on graduating as the new company's head of sales. She was an immediate success, landing DataClear's first major contract, with a large West Coast banking group.

Greg realized that ClearCloud had huge potential outside the telecommunications and financial services industries. In fact, with relatively little product development, Greg and his partners believed, ClearCloud could be adapted for the chemical, petrochemical, and pharmaceutical industries. Annual demand from customers in those sectors could reach as high as $900 million.

But accessing and serving clients in those fields would involve building specialized sales and service infrastructures. Just two months ago, to spearhead that initiative, Greg recruited a new business-development manager who had 20 years' experience in the chemical industry. A former senior R&D manager at DuPont, Tom Birmingham was excited by ClearCloud's blockbuster potential in the U.S. market. "The databases can only get bigger," he told Greg and Susan. Greg had asked Tom to put together a presentation for the off-site in Montana on the prospects for expanding into these new sectors.

Just two weeks before the outing, however, Susan burst into Greg's office and handed him an article from one of the leading trade journals. It highlighted a British start-up, VisiDat, which was beta testing a data analysis package that was only weeks away from launch. "We're not going to have the market to ourselves much longer," she told Greg. "We need to agree on a strategy for dealing with this kind of competition. If they start out as a global player, and we stay hunkered down in the U.S., they'll kill us. I've seen this before."

The news did not take Greg altogether by surprise. "I agree we've got to put together a strategy," he said. "Why don't we table the domestic-expansion discussion and talk about this at our off-site meeting, where we can get everyone's ideas? Unlike the rest of us, you've had some experience overseas, so perhaps you should lead the discussion. I'll square things with Tom."

Go Fish

In Montana, Susan kicked off the first session with the story of GulfSoft, a thinly disguised case study of her former employer. The company had developed a software package for the oil and gas exploration business, which it had introduced only in the United States. But at almost the same time, a French company had launched a comparable product, which it marketed aggressively on a global basis. A year later, the competitor had a much larger installed base worldwide than GulfSoft and was making inroads into GulfSoft's U.S. sales. When she reached the end of the story, Susan paused, adding ominously, "Today, we have only 20 installations of ClearCloud outside the U.S.—15 in the U.K. and five in Japan—and those are only U.S. customers purchasing for their overseas subsidiaries."

At Susan's signal, the room went dark. Much of what followed, in a blizzard of overhead projections, was market research showing a lot of latent demand for ClearCloud outside the United States. The foreign markets in telecommunications and financial services were shown to be about as large as those in the U.S.—that is, another $600 million. The potential in pharmaceuticals, petrochemicals, and chemicals looked to be about $660 million. Taken together, that meant a potential market of $1.5 billion domestically and $1.26 billion abroad.

In ending, Susan drew the obvious moral. "It seems pretty clear to me that the only defense for this kind of threat is to attack. We don't have any international sales strategy. We're here because we need one—and fast."

She glanced at Greg for any hint of objection, didn't see it, and plunged ahead: "We know we can sell a lot of software in the U.S., but if we want DataClear to succeed in the long run, we need to preempt the competition and go worldwide. We need a large installed base ASAP.

"I propose that for the afternoon we split into two groups and focus on our two options for going forward. Group A can consider building our own organization to serve Europe. Group B can think about forming alliances with players already established there. Based on what you come back with tomorrow, we'll make the call."

As the lights came back on, Greg blinked. He was dazzled. But he sensed that he needed to do some thinking, and he did his best thinking knee-deep in the river. After lunch, as the two groups got to work, Greg waded into Nelson's Spring Creek. The fish seemed to leap to his hook, but his thoughts were more elusive and ambivalent.

Money, Money, Money

Greg decided he needed a reality check, and that night he called David Lester to review the day's discussion. Not too surprisingly, Lester didn't have a lot of advice to give on the spot. In fact, he had questions of his own. "Instead of focusing on foreign markets in our core industries, what if we focus on developing ClearCloud for the domestic pharmaceutical, chemical, and petrochemical industries and capitalize on that $900 million U.S. market?" he asked. "How much would that cost?" Greg offered a best guess of $2 million for the additional software-development costs but hadn't yet come up with a number for marketing and sales; the industries were so different from the ones DataClear currently focused on. "Whatever the cost turns out to be, we're going to need another round of financing," Greg allowed. "Right now we're on track to generate a positive cash flow without raising any additional capital, but it won't be enough to fund a move beyond our core industries."

"That's not where I was headed," Lester replied. "What if we went out and raised *a lot* more money and expanded the product offering and our geographic reach at the same time?"

Greg swallowed hard; he was usually game for a challenge, but a double expansion was daunting. He couldn't help thinking of the sticky note he'd posted on the frame of his computer screen a few days after he started DataClear. It clung there still, and it had just one word on it: "Focus."

Lester sensed Greg's hesitation: "Look. We're not going to decide this tonight. And really, at the end of the day it's up to you, Greg. You've done the right things so far. Keep doing them." Hanging up, Greg was reminded of how pleased he was with Lester's hands-off approach. For the first time, he wondered what things would be like if he had a more hands-on venture capitalist as an investor—maybe one with some experience in international expansion.

Greg was also reminded of his own lack of international management experience. Eight years earlier, he had politely turned down an opportunity to lead a team of 50 Oracle development engineers in Japan, primarily because he had been unwilling to relocate to Tokyo for two years. His boss at the time had told him: "Greg, software is a global business, and what you don't learn early about cross-border management will come back to haunt you later."

Options on the Table

At ten o'clock the next morning, Group A took the floor and made their recommendation right off the bat: DataClear should immediately establish an office in the U.K.

and staff it with four to six salespeople. Britain would be a beachhead into all of Europe, but eventually there would also be a sales office somewhere on the Continent, maybe in Brussels. They had even drafted a job description for a head of European sales.

Greg was impressed, if a little overwhelmed. "Any idea how much this would cost us in terms of salaries and expenses over the first year?" he asked.

"Conservatively, about $500,000 a year; probably more," the group leader replied. "But cost is not so much the point here. If we don't make this move, we'll get killed by VisiDat—or some other competitor we don't even know about yet. Imagine if SAP introduced a similar product. With their marketing machine, they would just crush us."

Tom Birmingham started to object. "Where are we going to find local staff to install and support the product?" he wanted to know. "I mean, this is not just about setting up an office to sell: ClearCloud is a complex product, and it needs a service infrastructure. We'd have to translate the interface software, or at least the manuals, into local languages. We'd need additional resources in business development and product support to manage all this. Selling ClearCloud in Europe is going to cost a lot more than $500,000 a year—"

Susan was quick to jump in. "Good point, Tom, and that isn't all we'll need. We also have to have somebody in Asia. Either Singapore or Tokyo would be an ideal base. Probably Tokyo works better because more potential clients are headquartered there than in the rest of Asia. We need at least four people in Asia, for the time being." Tom frowned but, feeling that Susan had the momentum, decided to hold his fire.

After lunch, it was Group B's turn. They suggested using autonomous software distributors in each country. That would help DataClear keep a tight grip on expenses. Greg spoke up then. "What about teaming up with some local firm in Europe that offers a complementary product? Couldn't we get what we need through a joint venture?"

"Funny you should mention that, Greg," said the presenter from Group B. "We came up with the idea of Benro but didn't have time to pursue it. They might be willing to talk about reciprocal distribution." Benro was a small software shop in Norway. Greg knew it had made about $5 million in sales last year from its data-mining package for financial services companies. Benro was very familiar with European customers in the financial services sector but had no experience with other industries. "Working with Benro might be cheaper than doing this all on our own, at least for now," the presenter said.

Susan chose that moment to speak up again. "I have to admit I'm skeptical about joint ventures. I think it will probably take too long to negotiate and sign the contracts, which won't even cover all the eventualities. At some point we will have to learn how to succeed in each region on our own."

That's when Greg noticed Tom studying Susan, his eyes narrowing. So he wasn't surprised—in fact he was a little relieved—when Tom put the brakes on: "I guess I don't see how we can make that decision until we gather a little more input, Susan," Tom said. "At the very least, we need to have a conversation with Benro and any other potential partners. And I know I'd want to meet some candidates to lead a foreign sales office before I'd be comfortable going that route. But my real concern is more fundamental. Are we up to doing all this at the same time we're building our market presence in the U.S.? Remember, we don't yet have the capability to serve the chemical and pharmaceutical industries here. There are still only 38 of us, and I estimate that building the support infrastructure we need just for domestic expansion could cost as much $2 million—on top of product development."

Before Susan could object, Greg struck the compromise. "Tell you what. Let's commit to making this decision in no more than three weeks. I'll clear my calendar and connect with Benro myself. At the same time, Susan, you can flush out some good candidates for a foreign sales office and schedule them to meet with Tom and me."

Casting About

And that's how Greg McNally found himself up a creek in Norway that Sunday morning. Benro's CEO had been interested; Greg was confident that the meeting with him on Monday would yield some attractive options. And once the trip was booked, it didn't take Greg long to realize that he'd be near some fabled fishing spots.

He also realized it would be a great chance to pick the brain of his old Berkeley classmate, Sarah Pappas. A hardware engineer, Sarah had started her own company, Desix, in Mountain View, California, in 1993. The company designed specialty chips for the mobile communications industry. Within seven years, Desix had grown into one of the most successful specialized design shops around the world, with about 400 employees. Like Greg, Sarah had received funding from a venture capitalist. Since a lot of demand for Desix's services was in Scandinavia and to a lesser degree in Japan as well, Sarah had opened subsidiaries in both places and even decided to split her time between Mountain View and Oslo.

Greg arrived in Oslo on Thursday morning and met Sarah that evening at a waterfront restaurant. They spent the first half-hour swapping news about mutual friends. Sarah hadn't changed much, thought Greg. But when the conversation turned to potential geographic expansion and he asked about her experience, Greg saw her smile grow a little tense. "Ah, well," she began. "How much time do you have?"

"That bad?"

"Actually, to be honest, some things were easier than we thought," she allowed. "Recruiting, for example. We never expected to get any great engineers to leave Nokia or Hitachi to join us, but we ended up hiring our Oslo and Tokyo core teams without much trouble. Still, some things turned out to be so hard—like coordinating the three sites across borders. There were so many misunderstandings between Oslo and Mountain View that at first our productivity went down by 40%."

The story got worse. Sarah explained how, in 1998, her venture capitalist sought to exit its investment. Since an IPO seemed inadvisable for various reasons, the parties agreed to sell the company to Pelmer, a large equipment manufacturer. Sarah agreed to stay on for three years but couldn't do much to keep the engineers in her Oslo and Tokyo subsidiaries from leaving. No one had fully anticipated the clash between Pelmer's strong U.S. culture and Desix's local cultures in Oslo and Tokyo. By this point, Sarah felt, the merger had destroyed much that had gone into making Desix a small multinational company.

"I can tell I've been a real buzz killer," she laughed apologetically, as Greg picked up the check. "But if I were you, given what I've been through, I'd stay focused on the U.S. for as long as possible. You might not build the next Oracle or Siebel that way, but you'll live a happier life."

"So you think you made the wrong choice in expanding internationally?"

"Well, no," said Sarah, "because I don't think we had a choice. You, on the other hand, can sell much more product in the U.S. than we could have."

Up to His Waist

The next day brought its own worries, as Greg met with Pierre Lambert, a candidate for head of European sales, whom Susan had identified through a headhunter. Lambert had graduated from the École des Mines in Paris and then worked for four years at Alcatel and five years at Lucent. As they talked, it occurred to Greg that he had no experience in reading résumés from outside the States. Was École des Mines a good school? He noted that Lambert had worked only in France and the U.S. How successful would he be in the U.K. or Germany? As he wrapped up the interview, Greg figured he would need to see at least five candidates to form an opinion about the European labor market. And Asia would be even harder.

That evening, he compared notes with Tom, who had interviewed Lambert by phone the previous day. Tom expressed some doubts: he suspected that Lambert wasn't mature enough to deal with the level of executives—CIOs and chief scientists—that DataClear would be targeting. That call only just ended when the cell phone rang again, with Susan on the line. "Greg—I thought you would want to know. VisiDat just made its first significant sale—to Shell. The deal is worth at least $500,000. This is huge for them."

And now, two days later, here he stood in the glorious, frustrating Alta. He could see the salmon hanging just under the surface. He cast his line again, an elegant, silvery arc across the river and maneuvered the fly deftly through the water. Nothing.

Greg slogged back to shore and peered into the box housing his extensive collection of hand-tied salmon flies. Was it just that he was so preoccupied? Or were the conditions really so different here that none of his flies would work? One thing was for sure: it was a lot chillier than he'd expected. Despite the liner socks, his feet were getting cold.

Case 18   Green Mountain Coffee Roasters*

In comparing the growing strength of Starbucks, Bob Britt, Green Mountain Coffee's former vice president and CFO, questioned whether Green Mountain Coffee Roasters (GMCR) was missing the window of opportunity by not moving faster to expand. Growth was imminent for Green Mountain but competition was growing increasingly fierce. As Britt sipped his cup of Rain Forest Nut coffee, his thoughts turned to distribution.

To accelerate distribution of its coffee brand in the grocery channel, Starbucks had selected a long-term licensing agreement with Kraft. In contrast, GMCR relied on its own distribution and sales force to expand the Green Mountain brand in the grocery channel. According to Britt, the Starbucks-Kraft venture was believed to generate, on average, sales of 20–40 pounds of coffee per store per week. In comparison, GMCR averaged 100 pounds of coffee per store per week in the grocery channel. Primarily generated through the retail and office channels, consumer demand pulled specialty coffee through the grocery channel.

Background

In 1981 Green Mountain Coffee Roasters hung its shingle on the front of a small cafe in Waitsfield, Vermont. The company roasted and served premium coffee on the premises. The demand for high-quality, freshly roasted coffee soon grew beyond the cafe's walls. Restaurants and inns in the area asked for coffee and equipment. Green Mountain Coffee Roasters was soon in the wholesale business. Before long, skiers asked if the cafe could send Green Mountain Coffee to their homes in New York, Connecticut, Pennsylvania, and Florida. This demand was filled by the birth of the company's mail-order business. Today, Green Mountain is one of the leading specialty coffee companies in its established markets. See Exhibit 1 for established markets.

Green Mountain Coffee roasts over 25 high-quality Arabica beans to produce over 100 varieties of finished coffee products, which it sells through a coordinated multichannel distribution network in its wholesale and direct mail operations.

The majority of Green Mountain's revenue is derived from more than 7,000 wholesale customer accounts located primarily in the northeastern United States. The wholesale operation serves supermarkets, specialty food stores, convenience stores, food service, hotels, restaurants, universities, and travel and office coffee services. Wholesale customers resell the coffee in whole bean or

*This case was prepared by graduate student Keith F. Moody and Professor Alan B. Eisner of Pace University as a basis for class discussion rather than to illustrate either effective or ineffective handling of an administrative situation. Copyright © 2004 Keith F. Moody and Alan B. Eisner.

ground form for home consumption and/or brew and sell coffee beverages at their places of business. Green Mountain offers single-origin, estate, certified organic, Fair Trade, flavored, and proprietary blends of coffee. The company roasts its coffee in small batches to ensure consistency. Green Mountain utilizes state-of-the-art roasting software that enables it to duplicate specific roasts more exactly, ensuring Green Mountain's ability to offer consistent taste profiles.

Green Mountain uses convection air roasters, offering a higher degree of flexibility than other commercially available roasters. In addition, the company has developed specific roasting programs for each bean type to establish a Green Mountain "signature" for that type, which the company calls its "appropriate roast." Green Mountain believes that this process distinguishes it from other specialty coffee companies and has resulted in strong customer brand loyalty.

Green Mountain flushes nitrogen into its packaged coffee and employs one-way valve bag packaging technology that provides a minimum shelf life of six months for the company's coffees. This technology enables Green Mountain to expand its distribution while maintaining its high standards for quality and freshness. For 2003 Forbes magazine ranked Green Mountain Coffee 70 overall, 20 by five-year average return on equity, and 10 by five-year earnings per share growth. The criterion used to screen the Forbes list of the "200 Best Small Companies in America" was rigorous. Companies had to have sales of between $5 million and $600 million for the latest 12-month period, a five-year average return on equity of 5 percent or more, a stock price of $5 or more, and a net profit margin of 5 percent or more, excluding extraordinary and nonrecurring items.

Retail Operations

In fiscal 1997 Green Mountain Coffee Roasters was operating 12 company-owned stores in Vermont, Connecticut, Illinois, Maine, Massachusetts, New Hampshire, and New York, which made up approximately 10 percent of total revenues. However, by April 1998, sales had fallen to 6 percent of total net sales. Reasons for the decrease included the elimination of the Plattsburgh, New York, store (for which the lease had expired), the temporary closing of two stores due to relocation, and overall flat sales in other company-owned retail stores. Furthermore, the stores did not generate positive cash flows, nor did they contribute positively to the company's net income. Management at Green Mountain Coffee Roasters made the strategic decision to close the company-owned and -operated retail stores. Since 1981 the company-owned stores

Exhibit 1   Wholesale Coffee Pounds by Geographic Region
(As a % of total wholesale coffee lbs. sold)

Region	52 Weeks Ended		Full Year to Year Increase	
	September 27, 2003 (%)	September 28, 2002 (%)	(lbs.)	(%)
Northern New England (ME, NH, VT)	29.7%	31.6%	358,000	8.4%
Southern New England (MA, CT, RI)	19.3	21.0	162,000	5.7
Mid-Atlantic (NY, NJ, PA)	28.4	27.9	652,000	17.3
South Atlantic	9.3	8.6	283,000	24.3
South Central	4.0	3.7	124,000	24.6
Midwest	3.5	3.4	95,000	20.9
West	5.0	3.1	370,000	89.4
International	0.8	0.6	22,000	25.3
Pounds sold	**15,569,000**	**13,503,000**	**2,066,000**	**15.3%**

Source: Green Mountain Coffee Roasters, Inc., 2003 Annual Report.

had been an important part of Green Mountain's strategy of getting consumers to sample its own brand of coffee by the cup (see Exhibit 2 for financial data).

Socially Responsible Business Practices

Green Mountain is committed to conducting its business in a socially responsible manner. The company believes that doing well financially can go hand in hand with giving back to the community and protecting the environment. In fiscal 2003 the company contributed over 5 percent of its pretax income to various coffee farms, cooperatives, and nonprofit organizations in the United States and in coffee-producing countries. Domestic organizations benefiting from cash or coffee product donations in 2003 included Heifer International, Grounds for Health, Coffee Kids, and the National Wildlife Federation.

Exhibit 2   Green Mountain Financial Data

Fiscal Year Ended	Sept. 27, 2003	Sept. 28, 2002	Sept. 29, 2001	Sept. 30, 2000	Sept. 25, 1999
	(In thousands, except per share data)				
Coffee pounds sold	15,570	13,504	12,408	10,871	9,004
Net sales from continuing operations[1]	$116,727	$100,000	$95,576	$84,001	$64,881
Income from continuing operations[1]	$ 6,266	$ 5,970	$ 5,782	$ 4,153	$ 2,247
Income per share from continuing operations—diluted	$ .86	$ 0.82	$ 0.80	$ 0.59	$ 0.32
Total assets	$ 59,990	$ 54,687	$34,496	$27,244	$23,878

Source: Green Mountain Coffee Roasters, Inc., 2003 Annual Report.

[1]Excludes results from the company's discontinued company-owned retail store operations.

The company is committed to improving the quality of life in coffee-producing countries, and therefore supports projects that foster self-sufficiency which, it believes, yield the best results. In fiscal year 2003, GMCR donated over $180,000 to social and environmental partners in Mexico, Guatemala, Peru, Indonesia, and other coffee-growing countries. Examples of projects include environmental improvements on farms in Mexico and Guatemala with the Rainforest Alliance, improvements in coffee-milling operations in the war-torn Indonesian region of Aceh, and a new customer-based initiative with Wild Oats Markets, Inc., to construct organic vegetable gardens for coffee-growers in rural Mexico. In an effort to enhance its impact in coffee-growing countries, GMCR partnered with the U.S. Agency for International Development (USAID) and Ecological Enterprise Ventures, Inc. (EEV), a nonprofit organization, to develop a new preharvest financing mechanism for sustainable coffee producers. The $1 million award from USAID to EEV will help coffee producers address cash flow needs throughout the year. GMCR also expanded partnerships with Heifer International, Inc., and Newman's Own Organics, and started a new effort with the National Wildlife Federation to use proceeds from the sale of Green Mountain coffee to support social and environmental causes. GMCR was ranked number eight on *Business Ethics'* list of "100 Best Corporate Citizens" and *Global Finance* included Green Mountain Coffee Roasters on its list of "The World's Most Socially Responsible Companies" in October 2003.

The Coffee Industry

Today the U.S. coffee market is flat, even with the success of the specialty sector. The dynamism it once displayed has moved on to Europe and Asia, particularly Japan. The United States, responsible for up to 80 percent of world coffee consumption during World War II, now accounts for only 20 percent. While part of this decline results from a stagnant U.S. market, much of it has been due to growth in coffee drinking elsewhere. Consumption has grown in traditional and new coffee-drinking countries in Europe and Asia, and also in coffee-producing countries to the extent that Brazil is now the second-largest consumer after the United States. According to the National Coffee Association, more than 108 million people in the United States are daily coffee drinkers, and more than 166 million have consumed coffee in the past. Americans consumed more than 6.2 billion gallons of coffee in 2002, a 1.8 percent increase over consumption in 2001.[1] The annual U.S. per capita consumption of coffee is estimated to be 424 servings, which includes in-home and out-of-home roast and ground, instant, and ready-to-drink (bottled or canned) coffee.[2] The total coffee market in 2003 is estimated to be 1.8 billion pounds, or $19.3 billion.[3] According to the National Coffee Association's 2003 Trend Report, the average American coffee drinker now consumes over three cups a day. More daily coffee drinkers consume regular coffee (41 percent) than any other type; 12 percent drink specialty coffee, 8 percent drink decaf, and 7 percent drink instant coffee.[4]

According to marketing consultants Adrian Slywotzky and Kevin Mundt:

> What occurred was value migration . . . The majors' business designs—their customer selection, resource allocation, and growth strategies—were marred by an overly categorical definition of products and benefits, a limited field of competitive vision, and an obsolete view of the customer. New innovators implemented business designs that anticipated shifts in customer priorities ahead of the established three.

Value migration occurred rapidly. The three majors held nearly 90 percent of the multibillion-dollar retail market in 1987. Within six years, the gourmet, whole bean roasters, Starbucks, and other regional cafes had collectively created nearly $1 billion in shareholder value, and together obtained 22 percent of the coffee market share. By the end of 1993, the approximate market value of the majors was $4 billion, down $1 billion from 1988. The majors failed to create a new design for their coffee business to respond to the trend. Instead, they reverted to price-cutting and coupons.[5]

During the 1980s and 1990s, the large corporations paid scant attention to the new specialty roasters. Industry executives spent millions on advertising to maintain their firms' share in the shrinking market. Discounting and millions of coupons did nothing to raise brand prestige. Despite constant price promotion, coffee was a supermarket loss leader.

The Big Three—Procter & Gamble (P&G), Altria Group (formerly Philip Morris/Kraft), Nestlé—did not feel threatened by the growing host of regional whole bean roasters who were marketing their premium brands in supermarkets and specialty stores (see Exhibit 3). Although these start-ups were experiencing double-digit growth rates, their total sales seemed miniscule to the majors. It was difficult for the majors to measure or even imagine the momentum of such tiny numbers relative to a $5 billion industry. Having made several failed attempts at marketing gourmet coffee, the brand leaders falsely assumed that gourmet coffee was a fad.[6]

In the United States, and increasingly abroad, the specialty coffee industry continues to grow. By the year 2005, sales of specialty coffee at Starbucks alone will exceed $5.0 billion, up from total specialty coffee sales of $1.5 billion in 1990. According to the Specialty Coffee Association of America (SCAA), sales of brewed, whole bean, and ground specialty coffee totaled approximately $8.4 billion in the United States alone. This new U.S. industry now consumes 5 percent of the world's coffee out-

Exhibit 3   Market Share, Revenues, and Brands of Major Coffee Companies

Company	Share of U.S. Coffee Market %	Revenue from U.S. Coffee Sales		Brands
		%	1996 $ billions	
Procter & Gamble	35%	4%	$1.5	Folgers High Point Millstone
Altria Group (formerly Philip Morris/Kraft)	30	2	1.2	Maxim Maxwell House Brim Gevalia Sanka General Foods International Coffee Chase & Sanborn
Nestlé SA	10	0.9	0.4	Hills Bros. MJB Nescafe Taster's Choice

put—diverting some fine coffees from European markets that were accustomed to high-quality beans.

An important aspect of the specialty coffee industry is that it does not consider coffee purely as a commodity. Where the conglomerates had been concerned only with coffee's price and consistency, the new industry considers origin, quality, processing, and cultivation methods as relevant qualities of the bean. It also extends the option of choosing roasts, grinds, and so on to the consumer, thus creating a much richer, personal coffee landscape.

The next step in this industry's development is now taking place. As specialty coffee continues to grow and develop a major presence, it has begun to consolidate into a few major corporate brands. Many regional companies are planning to expand. The market is looking to see what firm will become number two to Starbucks.[7]

The traditional coffee sector has finally taken notice of this boom. The majors have launched their own specialty coffee brands, such as Philip Morris's Gevalia, the world's largest mail-order coffee business, with annual revenues of more than $100 million; Procter & Gamble's Millstone brand, a gourmet whole bean supermarket entry; and Chock Full O'Nuts' short-lived cafes and their Quickava drive-throughs. The majors brought on the poor coffee image prior to the development of the specialty coffee industry. The idea of a Maxwell House or Nescafé gourmet coffee is contradictory—their French and espresso roasts are undermined by their being vacuum packed in cans or instant.

Developed during a time of uncertain affluence, specialty coffee has been part of a larger trend that includes developments such as microbrewed beer, single malt scotch whiskey, and organic vegetables. In each case, a consumer product has been recast as something more authentic, traditional, diverse, flavorful, and healthful than the mass-produced product it supplants. In each case, the new "specialty" product is hyped as the original item that had been debased by mass production and corporatism.

The Specialty Coffee Industry

Specialty coffee is coffee roasted using mainly high-quality Arabica beans. The Arabica bean is widely considered superior to its counterpart, the Robusta, which is used mainly in nonspecialty coffee. Arabica beans usually grow at high elevations, absorb little moisture, and mature slowly. These factors result in beans with a mild aroma and a bright, pleasing flavor that is suitable for specialty coffee.

The specialty coffee industry consists of two distinct business segments: *whole bean,* including ground, coffee sales (for home, office, and restaurant consumption) and *coffee beverage sales.* One major thrust behind the specialty coffee growth is the increase in the number of specialty coffeehouses, which grew from 500 units in 1991 to over 12,000 in 2000. The Specialty Coffee Association of America (SCAA) predicts that approximately 5,000 new coffee bars will open every year in the United States and that this industry will not peak until the year 2015.[8] The National Coffee Drinking Trends survey of 2000 discovered that 79 percent of adults 18 years or older consumed coffee over the past year, compared to 78 percent in 1999 and 75 percent in 1997.[9] Daily consumption in 2000 was 54 percent, an increase of one million new daily drinkers over 1999. Factors contributing to this increase include the development of new quality beverages, an expanding coffee menu, and a new public place for coffee's social consumption: the gourmet coffeehouse. Daily consumption in the gourmet coffee sector has grown from less than 3 percent of the adult population in 1995 to 9 percent in 2000. Occasional consumption in the gourmet coffee sector has increased from 35 percent of the population in 1997 to 53 percent in 2000, while 52 percent of the American adult population (age 18 and over) drink some type of coffee beverage on a daily basis.

In its diversity and focus on quality and distinctiveness, the specialty coffee industry is singularly profitable. Specialty beans that retail for $12 a pound are purchased wholesale before roasting (green) for about $2 per pound. The sale of whole bean coffee has grown in popularity because the increasingly sophisticated consumer grinds the beans at home and brews freshly ground coffee which is palatable even to coffee connoisseurs. According to the 1999 Gallup Survey on Coffee Consumption, nearly 36 percent of all coffee drinkers purchased specialty whole bean coffee for home consumption. In the same survey, consumers stated that 33 percent of those whole bean purchases were made at a retail price of more than $7.00 a pound, reflecting the interest in high-quality, premium-priced coffee.

Consumers favor the supermarket or grocery store for the purchase of whole bean specialty coffee. The 1999 Gallup Survey reported that 61 percent of those consumers did so most frequently in a supermarket or grocery store. Other important purchase locations included specialty coffee stores (14 percent), mail-order catalogs or clubs (4 percent), and gourmet food stores (2 percent).

The whole bean specialty coffee category is highly fragmented and competitive. Green Mountain competes against all sellers; its primary competitors include Gevalia, Illy Café, Millstone, Peet's Coffee & Tea, Seattle's Best, and Starbucks. An estimated 500 smaller and regional brands also compete in this category. In addition, Green Mountain competes indirectly against all other coffee brands on the market.

In the office coffee service (OCS), convenience store, and food service areas, Sara Lee, Kraft, Procter & Gamble,

and New England Coffee are specialty coffee competitors, as are retailers such as Starbucks and Dunkin' Donuts (a subsidiary of Allied Domecq). In fiscal 2002 GMCR acquired a 42 percent ownership in Keurig to focus on the Keurig single-cup Brewer as a way to reach consumers in the office. The Keurig K-Cup allows the office coffee drinker to brew just one cup of coffee from a wide variety of coffee selections. Additionally, Green Mountain competes with "commercial" coffee roasters, to the extent that it is also trying to "upsell" consumers to the specialty coffee segment.

Green Mountain Coffee Roasters expects intense competition, both within its primary geographic territory, the eastern United States, and in other regions of the United States, as it expands its current territories.

Green Mountain Coffee's Growth Strategy

Green Mountain Coffee is focused on building the brand with profitability growing the business. Management believes it can continue to increase sales over the next few years at a rate similar to its historical five-year growth rate (13–18 percent), by increasing market share in existing markets and expanding into new geographic markets.

In recent years, the primary growth in the coffee industry has come from the specialty coffee category, driven by the wider availability of high-quality coffee, the emergence of upscale coffee shops throughout the country, and the general level of consumer education.

Green Mountain coffee is available in various distribution channels and customer categories in its primary geographic area. This multichannel strategy provides widespread exposure to the brand in a variety of settings, ease of access to the products, and many tasting opportunities for consumer trial. Green Mountain coffee is widely available throughout the day: at home in the morning, in hotels, on airplanes and trains, at convenience stores on the way to work, at the office, in restaurants, in supermarkets, and at the movie theater. See Exhibit 4 for sales distribution by channel.

The company believes that the availability of its coffee for consumer trial through convenience stores, office coffee services, and food service establishments is a significant advantage and a key component of its growth strategy. It has been the company's experience that consumer trial of Green Mountain coffee at one level of distribution often leads to a subsequent purchase at another.

As brand awareness increases through trial by consumers of the company's coffee by the cup, demand for whole bean sales of Green Mountain coffee for home consumption also increases. The National Coffee Association's study of coffee drinking trends stated that "over 75 percent of coffee drinkers drink coffee at home." As brand equity is built, wholesale expansion typically continues

Exhibit 4   Coffee Pounds Sold (Whole Bean and Ground) by Sales Channel, 2002–2003

Sales Channel	52 Weeks Ended		Full Year to Year Increase	
	September 27 2003 (%)	September 28 2002 (%)	(lbs.)	(%)
Supermarkets	30.3%	28.0%	930,000	24.6%
Convenience stores	29.1	29.4	559,000	14.1
Other retail	1.9	2.3	(16,000)	−5.2
Restaurants	7.3	8.6	(18,000)	−1.6
Office coffee service	21.4	21.7	394,000	13.4
Other food service	7.4	7.3	171,000	17.3
Consumer direct	2.7	2.7	46,000	12.4
Totals (lbs. sold)	15,569,000	13,503,000	2,066,000	15.3%

Source: Green Mountain Coffee Roasters, Inc., Form 10-K for the fiscal year ended September 27, 2003.

through customers such as supermarkets and specialty food stores, which in turn sell the company's whole bean coffee to consumers. This expansion process capitalizes upon this cup/whole bean interrelationship. The strategy is designed to further increase Green Mountain's market share in the geographic areas where it already operates in order to increase sales density and drive operational and brand-equity efficiencies. Flagship customers such as Amtrak, ExxonMobil, JetBlue Airways, and American Skiing Company are key to the company's geographic expansion strategy, as they provide great visibility and sampling opportunities. See Exhibit 5 for notable wholesale accounts including flagship customers.

Competitor Analysis: Starbucks

Starbucks has a significant presence in supermarkets nationwide. It has a distribution agreement with Kraft Foods, Inc. ("Kraft"), to place Starbucks coffee in supermarkets along with Kraft's Maxwell House brand. Starbucks posted net revenues of $2.5 billion for the 26 weeks ended March 28, 2004, an increase of 28.8 percent from $2.0 billion for the corresponding period of fiscal 2003. During the 26-week period, Starbucks derived approximately 84.5 percent of total net revenues from its company-operated retail stores. Revenues from these stores increased 28.5 percent to $2.1 billion for the 26 weeks ended March 28, 2004, from $1.7 billion for the same period in 2003. The increase was primarily attributable to the opening of 671 new company-operated retail stores in the last 12 months

and comparable store sales growth of 11 percent. The increase in comparable store sales was due to a 10 percent increase in the number of customer transactions and a 1 percent increase in the average dollar value per transaction. Management at Starbucks believes increased traffic in company-operated retail stores continues to be driven by new product innovation, continued popularity of core products, a high level of customer satisfaction, and improved speed of service through enhanced technology, training, and execution at retail stores. All Starbucks stores are located in leased premises. Starbucks derived the remaining 15.5 percent of total net revenues from its specialty operations. Specialty revenues, which include licensing revenues and food service and other revenue, increased 30.9 percent to $391.3 million for the 26 weeks ended March 28, 2004. Licensing revenues, which are derived from retail store licensing arrangements, grocery and warehouse club licensing, and certain other branded-product operations, increased 33.9 percent to $256.0 million for the 26 weeks ended March 28, 2004. The increase was primarily attributable to the opening of 705 new licensed retail stores in the last 12 months, increased grocery revenues as a result of the acquisition of Seattle Coffee Company in the fourth quarter of fiscal 2003, and increased warehouse club revenue due to growth in existing accounts. Food service and other revenue increased 25.5 percent to $135.3 million for the 26 weeks ended March 28, 2004. The increase was primarily attributable to the growth of the food service business as a result of the

Exhibit 5   Green Mountain: Notable Wholesale Accounts

Convenience Stores	Restaurants	Supermarkets	Office Coffee Services	Other Food Services
ExxonMobil convenience stores	Trapp Family Lodge	Fred Meyer—131 stores	Allied Office Products	Amtrak—Northeast corridor
Mirabito Fuel Group doing business as Quickway	Culinary Institute of America	Hannaford Bros.—142 stores	ARAMARK Refreshment Services	American Skiing Company
RL Vallee, Inc., doing business as Maplefields	New England Culinary Institute	Kash n' Karry Food Stores—141 stores	Bostonbean Coffee Company	Columbia University
TETCO	The Harvard Club, New York City	Kings Super Markets—27 stores	Corporate Coffee Systems	JetBlue Airways
Uni-Marts		Price Chopper—105 stores	Crystal Rock/Vermont Pure Springs	Sodexho
		Roche Bros.—14 stores	Dispenser Services Inc.	Stowe Mountain Resort
		Stop & Shop—322 stores (primarily coffee by the cup)	Nestlé Waters of North America	
		Shaw's/Star Market—152 stores		
		Wild Oats Markets—73 stores		

Source: Green Mountain Coffee Roasters, Inc., Form 10-K, 2000–2003.

acquisition of Seattle Coffee Company and the growth in new and existing Starbucks food service accounts.

Starbucks' strategy for expanding its specialty operations is to reach customers where they work, travel, shop, and dine by establishing relationships with prominent third parties who share the company's values. These relationships take various forms, including retail store licensing agreements, wholesale accounts, grocery channel licensing agreements, and joint ventures. Starbucks sells whole bean and ground coffee to several types of wholesale accounts, including office coffee distributors, hotels, airlines, retailers, and restaurants as well as institutional food service companies that handle business, industry, education, and health care accounts. In 1995 Starbucks became the coffee supplier to the 20 million passengers who fly United Airlines each year, and its mail-order sales division accounted for roughly 2 percent of total revenue. Management believes that its direct-response marketing effort helped pave the way for retail expansion into new markets and reinforced brand recognition in existing markets.

In 1998 Starbucks entered into a long-term licensing agreement with Kraft Foods to accelerate growth of the Starbucks brand into the grocery channel in the United States. Pursuant to this agreement, Kraft manages all distribution, marketing, advertising, and promotion for Starbucks coffee in grocery, warehouse club, and mass merchandise stores. By the end of 2003 Starbucks coffee was available in 18,000 supermarkets throughout the United States. It featured distinctive, elegant packaging; prominent positions in grocery aisles; and the same premium quality as that sold in its stores.

Starbucks has spent limited funds on advertising, preferring instead to build the brand cup by cup with customers and depending on word of mouth and the appeal of storefronts. Nevertheless, the company is engaged in a growing effort to extend the Starbucks brand and penetrate new markets, including joint ventures with Dreyer's for a branded ice cream and with Pepsi to distribute bottled Frappuccino; licensee partners; mail-order and specialty sales; and international expansion.

Industry analysts see Starbucks becoming the Nike or Coca-Cola of the specialty coffee segment. It is the only specialty coffee company with a national market coverage. Starbucks's vision is to become the most recognized and respected brand of coffee in the world. The company's efforts to increase its sphere of strategic interest by means of its joint ventures with Pepsi and Dreyer's and its move to sell coffee in supermarkets represents an ongoing drive on CEO Howard Schultz's part to continually reinvent the way Starbucks does business. To sustain the company's growth and make Starbucks a strong global brand, Schultz believes the company must challenge the status quo, be innovative, take risks, and alter its vision of who it is, what it does, and where it is headed.

The Future of Green Mountain Coffee

In fiscal 2002 Green Mountain acquired a 42 percent ownership in Keurig, Incorporated ("Keurig"), by acquiring shares from early investors in Keurig for approximately $15 million. Keurig manufactures brewing equipment that allows users to brew high-quality coffee one cup at a time. As an early investor, Green Mountain has been involved with Keurig since 1994, supporting the development of the brewing system. The appeal of the Keurig K-Cup— perfectly brewing just one cup of coffee from a variety of coffee selections—has contributed to GMCR's success in the office coffee service, or OCS, channel. In fiscal 2003 GMCR introduced Celestial Seasonings tea in K-Cups, contributing further to sales growth. Both Keurig and Green Mountain are undertaking similar endeavors to sell K-Cups to the home consumer. Bob Stiller, president and CEO of Green Mountain Coffee Roasters, stated:

> I believe that the launch of the "Keurig at home" brewer, tied into a Green Mountain K-Cup continuity program, can be a real growth engine for us over the next few years. In fact, over time, we believe the opportunity for Keurig in the home is even bigger than for Keurig in the office. . . . I would like to acknowledge that there is uncertainty concerning the magnitude of Keurig's spending in connection with its own launch of the Keurig Single-Cup Brewer for the home, as well as the time frame for Keurig's return to profitability. [But] when I weigh the risks and the longer-term potential rewards, I am as excited as ever about our compelling prospects both as a roaster selling our coffee in K-Cups and as an equity investor in Keurig.

GMCR was the first roaster to sell its coffee in Keurig's innovative single-cup brewing system and has established a dominant position in the sale of single-cup Keurig portions. GMCR does, however, compete for Keurig sales with three other North American roasters: Diedrich Coffee, Timothy's, and Van Houtte, a vertically integrated roaster and office coffee service distributor in Canada and the United States.

During fiscal 2003, 2002, and 2001, approximately 94 percent, 95 percent, and 96 percent, respectively, of Green Mountain's sales were derived from its wholesale operations located primarily in the eastern United States. Unlike most of its competitors, Green Mountain's wholesale operation services a large variety of establishments, from individual upscale restaurants to major supermarket chains. This strategy enables a deeper penetration in a geographic market, exposing consumers to the brand throughout the day in a variety of locations. The diversity of end users limits the risks of Green Mountain's dependence on any single distribution channel. In the convenience store channel, GMCR's pounds shipped increased by over 14 percent. While the total number of locations serving Green Mountain Coffee increased by about 5 percent over the prior year (to 3,300 at the close of fiscal 2003), the majority of the growth in this channel was driven by improved business with current customers. GMCR's relationship with Exxon Mobil Corporation continues to be a strong driver for growth in this convenience store channel. The supermarket channel experienced growth of more than 24 percent in coffee pounds shipped in fiscal year 2003 versus 2002, a growth driven largely by new distribution. Since the beginning of fiscal 2003, GMCR has added two large customers: Wild Oats Markets, Inc., a leading chain in the rapidly growing natural food category, and Costco Wholesale Corp., a leading buyers' club retailer. GMCR is the exclusive supplier of bulk certified Fair Trade and organic coffee for all Wild Oats locations. Growth in the supermarket channel continued throughout 2003, with the addition of several other chains, including D'Agostino Supermarkets, Harris Teeter, and Wegmans Food Markets. In November 2003 GMCR also began selling to Publix Super Markets.

An important task in global marketing is learning to recognize the extent to which marketing plans and programs can be extended worldwide, as well as the extent to which they must be adapted. Green Mountain cannot afford to replicate Nestlé's marketing blunder. Nestlé sought to transfer its great success with a four-coffee line from Europe to the United States. Nestlé's U.S. competitors were delighted because the transfer led to a decline of 1 percent in Nestlé's U.S. market share.[10]

Green Mountain is focused on the wholesale channel in the gourmet coffee niche. Green Mountain has made trade-offs, divesting its retail store operations to focus on wholesale. GMCR expects intense competition, both within its primary geographic territory and other U.S. regions, as it expands from its current territory. The specialty coffee market is expected to become even more competitive as regional companies expand and attempt to build brand awareness in new markets. Green Mountain competes primarily by providing high-quality coffee, easy access to its products, and superior customer service. GMCR believes that its ability to provide a convenient network of outlets from which to purchase coffee is an important factor in its ability to compete. Through its multichannel distribution network of wholesale and consumer direct operations and its "by the cup" / "by the pound" strategy, GMCR believes it differentiates itself from many of its competitors. Green Mountain also believes that one of the distinctive features of its business is that it is one of the few companies that roasts its coffee individually prior to blending, varying both the degree and timing of the roast to maximize a coffee's particular taste characteristic. GMCR also seeks to differentiate itself by being socially and environmentally responsible. Finally, GMCR believes that being an independent roaster allows it to be better focused and in tune with its wholesale customers' needs than its larger, multiproduct competitors. While the company believes it currently competes favorably with respect to these factors, there can be no assurance that GMCR will be able to compete successfully in the future.

The question for Bob Stiller and Daniel Martin, vice president of sales and marketing at Green Mountain Coffee Roasters, remains what strategic paths GMCR should pursue to achieve its objective of becoming the most recognized and respected brand of coffee in the world. Brand awareness could provide a host of competitive advantages for Green Mountain Coffee.

Endnotes

1. Beverage Marketing Group.
2. Nestlé SA.
3. Datamonitor.
4. *Quarterly Grind,* 2003, October.
5. Slwotzky, Adrian J., & Mundt, Kevin, 1996, Hold the sugar; Starbucks Corp.'s business success, *Across the Board,* 33 (8): 39.
6. Ibid., 39.
7. Peel, Carl, 1997, Los Angeles, a microcosm of the country, *Tea and Coffee Trade Journal* 169 (4): 16–28.
8. Specialty Coffee Association of America.
9. National Coffee Association.
10. Keegan, Warren J., interview with Raymond Viault, vice chairman of General Mills, Inc., *Global Marketing Management,* 7.

Case 19   Growing for Broke*

Look, you've *got* to grow. It's what our economy is all about. Hey, it's what our country is all about! Certainly, it's what drives me. My father, Constantine Anaptyxi, came to America from Greece because he saw big opportunities here. He worked hard, took a few risks, and realized his dreams. I came to this company as CEO five years ago—giving up a senior VP position at a Fortune 500 manufacturer—because I saw big potential for Paragon Tool, then a small maker of machine tools. I didn't make the move so that I could oversee the company's *down*sizing! I didn't intend to create value—for our customers, for our employees, for our shareholders—by thinking small!! I didn't intend to *shrink* to greatness, for God's sake!!!

Okay, so I'm getting a little worked up over this. Maybe I'm just trying to overcome my own second thoughts about our company's growth plans. I know it isn't just about growth; it's about *profitable* growth, as my CFO, William Littlefield, is always happy to remind me. "Nicky," he'll say, "people always talk about getting to the top when they should be focusing on the bottom . . . line, that is." Quite a comedian, that Littlefield. But lame as the quip is, it tells you a lot about Littlefield and what, in my opinion, is his limited view of business. Sometimes you've got to sacrifice profits up front to make *real* profits down the line.

To me, acquiring MonitoRobotics holds just that kind of promise. The company uses sensor technology and communications software to monitor and report real-time information on the functioning of robotics equipment. By adapting this technology for use on our machine tools, we could offer customers a rapid-response troubleshooting service—what consultants these days like to call a "solutions" business. Over time, I'd hope we could apply the technology and software to other kinds of machine tools and even to other kinds of manufacturing equipment. That would make us less dependent on our slow-growing and cyclical machine-tool manufacturing operation and hopefully give us a strong position in a technology market with terrific growth potential. It would also nearly double our current annual revenue of around $400 million—and force Wall Street to pay some attention to us.

What does Littlefield say to this? Oh, he gives a thumbs-down to the acquisition, of course—too risky. But get this: He also thinks we should sell off our existing services division—a "drag on profits," he says. With the help of some outside consultants, the senior management team

has spent the last few months analyzing both our services business and the pros and cons of a MonitoRobotics acquisition. Tomorrow, I need to tell Littlefield whether we should go ahead and put together a presentation on the proposed acquisition for next week's board meeting. If we do move forward on this, I have a hunch a certain CFO might start returning those headhunter calls. And I'd hate to lose him. Whatever our differences, there's no denying that he's capable and smart—in fact, a lot smarter than I am in some areas. On this issue, though, I just don't think he gets it.

Mom and Apple Pie

In 1946, when my father was 21, he left the Greek island of Tinos and came to New York City with his new bride. He worked at a cousin's dry-cleaning store in Astoria, Queens, then started his own on the other side of town. When I was seven, he took his savings and bought a commercial laundry in Brooklyn. Over the next several years, he scooped up one laundry after another, usually borrowing from the bank, sometimes taking another mortgage on the three-family home in Bensonhurst where we had moved. By the time I was a teenager, he was sitting on a million-dollar business that did the linens for all kinds of hotels and hospitals around greater New York. "Nikolas, growth is as American as Mom and apple pie," my father would say to me—he loved using all-American expressions like that. "You gotta get bigger to get better."

My mom was somewhat less expansive in her outlook. She kept my father's accounts, having studied bookkeeping in night school as soon as her English was good enough. And she had her own saying, one that deftly, if inadvertently, bolted together two other platitudes of American slang. "Keep your shirt on," she would say to my father when, arms waving, he would enthusiastically describe some new expansion plan for his business. "Or else you might lose it." My father was the genius behind his company's growth, but I have no doubt that my mother was the one responsible for its profits.

When I was 15, we moved to a nice suburb in Jersey. I never quite fit in: too small for sports, a little too ethnic for the social set, only a middling student. I worked hard, though, and went to Rutgers, where I majored in economics and then stayed on to get an MBA. Something clicked in business school. I seemed to have a knack for solving the real-world problems of the case studies. And I flourished in an environment where the emphasis was on figuring out what you *can* do instead of what you *can't*, on envisioning how things could go right instead of trying to anticipate how they could go wrong. (Thank God I didn't follow my uncle's advice and become a corporate lawyer!)

*Reprinted by permission of Harvard Business Review. "Growing for Broke" by Paul Hemp, September 2002. Copyright © 2002 by the Harvard Business School Publishing Corporation; all rights reserved.

When I graduated, I got a job at WRT, the Cleveland-based industrial conglomerate where I'd interned the summer before. Over the next 15 years or so, I moved up through the ranks, mainly because of my ability to spot new market opportunities. And by the time I was 45, I was heading up the machine-tool division, a $2.3 billion business. Both revenues and profits surged in the three years I was there, it's true. But I still found my job frustrating. Every proposed acquisition or new initiative of any substance had to be approved by people at headquarters who were far removed from our business. And whenever corporate profits flagged, the response was mindless across-the-board cost cutting that took little account of individual divisions' performance.

So when I was offered the opportunity to head up a small but profitable machine-tool maker in southern Ohio, I jumped at the chance.

Sunflower Tableau

I still remember driving to work my first day at Paragon Tool five years ago. Winding through the Ohio countryside, I saw a stand of sunflowers growing in a rocky patch of soil next to a barn. "Now *there's* a symbol for us," I thought, "a commonplace but hardy plant that quickly grows above its neighbors, often in fairly tough conditions." I was confident that Paragon—a solid, unexceptional business operating in an extremely difficult industry and economic environment—had the potential to grow with similarly glorious results.

For one thing, Paragon was relatively healthy. The company was built around a line of high-end machines—used by manufacturers of aerospace engines, among others—that continued to enjoy fairly good margins, despite the battering that the machine-tool industry as a whole had taken over the previous decade and a half. Still, the market for our product was essentially stagnant. Foreign competition was beginning to take its toll. And we continued to face brutal cyclical economic swings.

I quickly launched a number of initiatives designed to spur revenue growth. With some aggressive pricing, we increased sales and gained share in our core market, driving out a number of our new foreign rivals. We expanded our product line and our customer base by modifying our flagship product for use in a number of other industries. We also made a string of acquisitions in the industrial signage and electronic-labeling field, aiming to leverage the relationships we had with our machine-tool customers. No question, these moves put real pressure on our margins. Along with the price cuts and the debt we took on to make the acquisitions, we had to invest in new manufacturing equipment and a larger sales force. But we were laying the foundation for what I hoped would be a highly profitable future. The board and the senior management team, including Littlefield, seemed to share my view.

Indeed, the CFO and I had developed a rapport, despite our differing business instincts. Early on in our working relationship, this sixth-generation Yankee started in with the kidding about my alma mater. "Is that how they taught you to think about it at Rutgers?" he'd say if I was brainstorming and came up with some crazy idea. "Because at *Wharton*, they taught us . . ." I'd just laugh and then tell whoever else was in the room how proud we were that Littlefield had been a cheerleader for the Penn football team—like that was his biggest scholarly accomplishment. One time he "let it slip" that in fact he was Phi Beta Kappa, and we all just groaned. I said, "Give it up, Littlefield. You may have been Phi Beta Kappa, but, despite those letters on your gold pin, you'll never out-*Greek* me." To tell the truth, our skills are complementary, and between us we manage to do a pretty good job for the company.

As Paragon grew, so did the sense of excitement and urgency among our managers—indeed, among the entire workforce. People who once had been merely content to work at Paragon now couldn't wait to tackle the next challenge. And that excitement spread throughout the small Ohio town where we are based. When I'd go with my wife to a party or speak at the local Rotary Club or even stop to buy gas, people would show a genuine interest in the company and our latest doings—it helped that we always mentioned the job-creation impact when announcing new initiatives. There's no doubt it stoked my ego to be one of the bigger fish in the local pond. But even more important for me was the sense that this was business at its best, providing people with a justified sense of well-being about the present and confidence in the future.

Anyway, my point here is that we've grown fast since I arrived, but we still have a long way to go. I've come to think that the real key to our future is in the company's services division. We currently offer our customers the option to buy a standard service contract, under which we provide periodic machine maintenance and respond to service calls. But we've been developing technology and software, similar to MonitoRobotics', that would allow us to respond immediately if a machine at a customer's site goes down. The division currently accounts for less than 10% of our revenue and, because of the cost of developing the new technology, it's struggling to turn a profit.

But I can see in the services division the seeds of a business that will ultimately transform us from a manufacturing company into a high-tech company. Such a transformation, requiring an overhaul of our culture and capabilities, won't be easy. And it will surely require significant additional investments. But the potential upside is huge, with the promise of sales and profit growth that could make our current single-digit gains seem trivial by comparison. Besides, what choice do we have? A number of our competitors have already spotted these opportunities and have begun moving ahead with them. If we don't ramp up quickly, we might well miss out on the action altogether.

A Company in Play

Just over a month ago, I was sitting at my desk preparing a presentation for the handful of analysts who cover our company. Until recently, most of them have had only good things to say about all our growth moves. But last quarter, when we again reported a year-on-year drop in earnings, a few of them started asking pointed questions about our investments and when they could be expected to bear fruit. As I was giving some thought to how I'd answer their questions in the upcoming meeting, the phone rang. It was our investment banker, Jed Nixon.

"Nicky, I think we should talk," he said. I could tell from the sound of his voice he was on to something big, and then he told me what it was: "MonitoRobotics is in play."

We both did some calendar juggling and managed to get together for lunch the very next day at Jed's office in Cincinnati. The rumor was that one of our direct competitors, Bellows & Samson, was about to launch a hostile takeover bid for MonitoRobotics. As it happened, we had just started a conversation with MonitoRobotics' management a few months before, about collaborating on remote servicing technology for machine tools. But Jed's call had had its intended effect, changing my thinking about the company: Why not acquire it ourselves?

Although MonitoRobotics' technology was designed to detect and report operating failures in robotics equipment, managers there had told us when we met that adapting it for use on other industrial machinery was feasible. Indeed, MonitoRobotics had recently licensed the technology to a company that planned to modify it for use on complex assembly lines that experienced frequent breakdowns. Our engineers had confirmed that a version could be developed for our machines—though in their initial assessment they hadn't been exactly sure how long this would take.

Still, the potential benefits of acquiring MonitoRobotics seemed numerous. It would give us a powerful presence in a fast-growing business while preempting a competitor from staking a claim there. Whatever the time lag in adapting MonitoRobotics' technology for use with our products, we would almost certainly be able to offer our customers this valuable troubleshooting service more quickly than if we continued to develop the technology ourselves. And though our products were different, MonitoRobotics and Paragon potentially served many of the same manufacturing customers. "Think of the cross-selling opportunities," Jed said, as he took a bite of his sandwich. The greatest opportunity, though, lay in the possibility that MonitoRobotics' software technology would become the standard means for machine tools—and ultimately a variety of industrial machines—to communicate their service needs to the people who serviced them and to other machines that might be affected by their shutdown.

This was a fairly speculative train of thought. But a MonitoRobotics acquisition had for me the earmarks of a breakthrough opportunity for Paragon. And our earlier conversations with its management team had been cordial, suggesting the company might welcome a friendly offer from us to counter Bellows & Samson's hostile bid. Of course, even if we were able to get MonitoRobotics at a fair price, an acquisition of this size would further delay our return to the margins and profit growth we had known in the past. And that, I knew, wouldn't sit well with everyone.

Management Dissension

The day after my meeting with Jed, I called together members of our senior management team. There was a barely suppressed gasp when I mentioned the potential acquisition, particularly given its size. "Boy, that would be a lot to digest with everything we've got on our plate right now," said Joe McCollum, our senior VP of marketing. "It also might represent the chance of a lifetime," countered Rosemary Witkowski, head of the services division. Then Littlefield spoke up. His skepticism wasn't surprising.

"I was just running a few simple numbers on what the MonitoRobotics acquisition might mean to our bottom line," he said. "Besides the costs associated with the acquisition itself, we'd be looking at some significant expenses in the near term, including accelerated software research, hiring and training, and even brand development." He pointed out that these costs would put further pressure on our earnings, just as our profits were struggling to recover from earlier growth-related investments.

Littlefield did concede that a bold acquisition like this might be just the sort of growth move that would appeal to some of our analysts—and might even prompt a few more securities firms to cover us. But he insisted that if our earnings didn't start bouncing back soon, Wall Street was going to pillory us. Then he dropped his bombshell: "I frankly think this is an opportunity to consider getting out of the services business altogether. Eliminating the continued losses that we've been experiencing there would allow us to begin realizing the profit growth that we can expect from the investments we've made in our still-healthy machine-tool business."

Littlefield argued that, whether we acquired MonitoRobotics or not, it wasn't clear we'd be able to dominate the machine-tool services market because a number of our competitors were already flocking there. Furthermore, the market might not be worth fighting over: Many of our customers were struggling with profitability themselves and might not be willing or able to buy our add-on services. "Last one in, turn out the lights" was the phrase

Littlefield used to describe the rush to dominate a profit-less market.

As soon as she had a chance, Rosemary shot back in defense of her operation. "This is the one area we're in that has significant growth potential," she said. "And we've already sunk an incredible amount of money into developing this software. I can't believe you'd throw all of that investment out the window." But a number of heads nodded when Littlefield argued that we'd recoup much of that investment if we sold the money-losing business.

Several days later, I polled the members of the senior management team and found them split on the issue of the acquisition. And, to be honest, I was beginning to doubt myself on this. I respected Littlefield's financial savvy. And no one had yet raised the issue of whether Paragon, a traditional manufacturing company, had the management capabilities to run what was essentially a software start-up. We decided to hire two highly regarded consulting firms to do quick analyses of the proposed MonitoRobotics acquisition.

The Sunflowers' Successor

Today, the consultants came back to us with conflicting reports. One highlighted the market potential of MonitoRobotics' technology, noting that we might be too far behind to develop similar technology on our own. The other focused on the difficulties both of integrating the company's technology with ours and of adapting it to equipment beyond the robotics field.

So as I drove home tonight, the dilemma seemed no closer to being resolved. In many ways, I am persuaded by the cautionary message of Littlefield's number crunching. At the same time, I firmly believe the pros and cons of such a complex decision can't be precisely quantified; sometimes you just have to go with your instincts—which in my case favor growth. As I turned the issue over in my head, I looked out the car window, half-consciously seeking inspired insight. Sure enough, there was the barn where the sunflowers had been growing five years before. But the bright yellow blossoms, highlighted by the red timbers of the barn, were gone. Instead, a carpet of green kudzu was growing up the side of the increasingly dilapidated building. This fast-growing vine, which already had ravaged much of the South, was now spreading, uncontrolled and unproductive, into southern Ohio.

My mind started to drift and the image of kudzu—a more sinister symbol of growth than the sunflower—began to merge with thoughts of my father, who had died of lung cancer two years before, and my mother, who these days spends most of her time managing her investments. Suddenly, my parents' favorite phrases came to mind. It occurred to me that kudzu was now becoming as American as Mom and apple pie. Even so, its dense foliage certainly seemed like a place where, if you weren't careful, you could easily misplace your shirt.

Should Paragon Tool further its growth ambitions by trying to acquire MonitoRobotics?

One year into the job, Anthony Ruys is trying to breathe new life into the world's third-largest brewer. The Dutch company has been run by three generations of Heineken ancestors whose portraits still adorn the dark-paneled office of the CEO in its Amsterdam headquarters. Ruys was elevated to the position of CEO in 2002, only 10 years after joining the firm. He was asked to take over when Alfred H. "Freddy" Heineken, a hard-nosed businessman with a zest for life, passed away in 2002.

Although the management of Heineken has moved for the first time to an individual who is not a member of the family, Ruys has been well aware of long-standing and well-established traditions that would be difficult to change. "There's a long tradition," he said about the family legacy that he had inherited.[1] Even as he contemplated changes that he must make, Ruys would not dare to dishonor Freddy's memory by claiming that anything as radical as a revolution was in the making at Heineken.

Yet it is not hard to sense that the firm is definitely in the midst of making some long overdue changes. With $11 billion a year in sales, Heineken can lay claim to a brand that may be the closest thing to a global beer brand. But it may no longer be able to take for granted the strengths that have made its squat green bottle the envy of the business. In fact, there have been plenty of signs to indicate that Heineken may have to redouble its efforts to maintain its momentum. Analysts have estimated that the firm's net profit in 2003 would just barely match the $900 million that it had generated in the previous year. See Heineken's income statement and balance sheet in Exhibit 1. This will break a six-year streak of double-digit growth in profits. Consequently, Heineken's stock has lost 10 percent of its value during 2003.

In spite of these setbacks, Heineken has been able to preserve its status as the world's third-largest brewer, with a 7 percent global market share, but its core brand has been losing ground in many markets. There are strong concerns about its decline in the United States because this represents the world's biggest market. Heineken has lost its position as the leading imported beer to Corona, the Mexican beer that is often served garnished with a lime. Corona has managed to overtake Heineken on the basis of its appeal to Hispanic Americans, who represent the country's fastest-growing segment of beer drinkers.

Ruys understands that to build on its previous successes, Heineken needs to prepare itself for widespread changes that are occurring in the $367 billion global market for beer. Beer consumption has been declining in key markets as a result of tougher drunk-driving laws and a growing appreciation for wine. At the same time, the beer markets around the world have become more crowded with a flood of new brands, both domestic and foreign, that have included newly introduced low-carbohydrate brews. As a result of these changes, Ruys believes that Heineken's future success depends on preserving Freddy's spirit, while trying to meet challenges that Freddy may never have anticipated.

Competing in a Global Industry

The beer industry has been relatively fragmented, with an abundance of smaller regional or national brewers dominating each market. Few firms have had significant operations across different countries. Even in 2003, the top four brewing companies controlled less than a third of the global market for beer. Furthermore, many of the leading firms such as Anheuser-Busch and Miller continued to draw most of their revenues from their home markets.

But the industry has been undergoing significant change due to a furious wave of consolidation. Most of the bigger brewers have begun to acquire or merge with their competitors in foreign markets in order to become global players. Anheuser-Busch bought equity stakes and struck partnership deals with Mexico's Grupo Modelo, China's Tsingtao, and Chile's CCU. More significantly, South African Breweries PLC completed the acquisition of U.S.–based Miller Brewing Company to become SAB-Miller, the second-largest global brewer with operations on four continents.

These cross-border deals have provided significant benefits to the brewing giants. To begin with, it has given them ownership of local brands that has propelled them into a dominant position in various markets around the world. Belgium-based Interbrew has acquired brands such as Beck's and Bass, which have a commanding presence in their local markets in Germany and Great Britain, respectively, and have made considerable inroads into foreign markets.

Beyond the domination in certain local markets, acquisitions of foreign brewers might provide firms with the manufacturing and distribution capabilities they need to develop global brands. Anheuser-Busch, for example, has been able to use the facilities of its acquired firms to push the sales of its Budweiser brand in more and more markets. Similarly, the newly formed SABMiller has been attempting to develop the Czech brand Pilsner Urquell into a global brand. Exports of this pilsner have doubled since SAB acquired it in 1999. "The era of global brands is coming," said Alan Clark, Budapest-based managing director of SABMiller Europe.[2]

*This case was prepared by Professor Jamal Shamsie of Michigan State University. This case was developed from published sources as a basis for class discussion rather than to illustrate either effective or ineffective handling of an administrative situation. Material was drawn from published sources. Copyright © 2004 Jamal Shamsie.

Exhibit 1   Heineken's Income Statement and Balance Sheet

	Income Statement (In millions of euros)			
	2002	**2001**	**2000**	**1999**
Total revenue	€10,293	€9,333	€8,107	€7,148
Operating profit	1,282	1,125	921	799
Net profit	795	715	621	516

	Balance Sheet (In millions of euros)			
	2002	**2001**	**2000**	**1999**
Long-term borrowings	€ 1,215	€ 797	€ 875	€ 490
Current liabilities	2,649	2,235	1,892	1,860
Shareholders equity	2,543	2,758	2,396	2,618
Total liabilities and equity	7,781	7,195	6,263	5,986

Source: Heineken annual reports.

Heineken has been a pioneer of this global strategy, using cross-border deals to extend its operations to 170 countries around the globe. Heineken ranked second only to Budweiser in a global brand survey jointly undertaken by *BusinessWeek* and Interbrand in 2004. Heineken has achieved worldwide recognition according to Kevin Baker, director of alcoholic beverages at British market researcher Canadean Ltd. Its success as a global brand has been remarkable. A U.S. wholesaler recently asked a group of marketing students to identify an assortment of beer bottles that had been stripped of their labels. The stubby green Heineken container was the only one that brought instant recognition among the group.

Revitalizing a Global Brand

Heineken had long enjoyed a leading position among the beers in many markets around the world. It had been the best-selling imported beer in the United States for several decades, giving it a steady source of revenues and profits from the world's biggest market. But Heineken's appeal has been difficult to maintain as consumers in many of its markets have been turning away from beer while those sticking with beer are faced with many more choices. U.S. beer consumption has declined by about 1 percent since 2000, while the number of imports that are available to consumers have risen by about 16 percent over the same period.

The $67 billion U.S. market has gradually become the most keenly contested of them all. SABMiller has been pushing its Czech-brewed Pilsner Urquell, while Brussels-based Interbrew has been making inroads with Stella Artois. Even Anheuser-Busch has made moves to enter the market for imports with the launch of Anheuser World Select which is fashioned from imported hops and comes in a green bottle that looks suspiciously similar to Heineken's. Exhibit 2 provides a survey of the world's leading brewers.

Ruys has been especially concerned about the decline in sales of its flagship Heineken brand. By the late 1990s, Heineken had been overtaken by Corona as the top selling imported beer. In 2003 Corona captured about 29 percent of the U.S. imported beer market, far ahead of Heineken's 19 percent share. Corona has reached out to Hispanic Americans who represent one of the fastest-growing segments of beer drinkers. Other Americans have also developed a taste for thirst-quenching Corona while vacationing on Mexican beaches.

Heineken's managers have been trying hard to increase awareness of their flagship brand. While Heineken has become very well known on the East Coast, it has lagged behind other foreign beers in the West. Consequently, the firm has been spending about $51 million a year on marketing the brand throughout the United States, much higher than the $35 million being spent by the Mexican firm that sells Corona. "Heineken has one of the best marketing machines in the industry, but it has been around a long time so it has to work hard to stay relevant with

Exhibit 2   The Top 10 Global Brewers (by Volume)

1. **Anheuser-Busch, Inc.**   St. Louis, Missouri
   Volume: 132.4 million hl   *Sales:* US$13,566 million
   Major Brands: Budweiser, Bud Light, Michelob, Busch

2. **SABMiller PLC**   London, U.K.
   Volume: 120.0 million hl   *Sales:* US$8,426 million
   Major Brands: Castle Lager, Miller Genuine Draft, Miller Lite, Pilsner Urquell

3. **Heineken**   Amsterdam, Netherlands
   Volume: 108.9 million hl   *Sales:* US$10,788 million
   Major Brands: Heineken, Amstel, Murphy's

4. **Interbrew**   Louvain, Belgium
   Volume: 102.0 million hl   *Sales:* US$7,328 million
   Major Brands: Labatt, Bass Ale, Stella Artois, Jupiter

5. **Carlsberg Breweries A/S**   Valby, Denmark
   Volume: 78.6 million hl   *Sales:* US$5,105 million
   Major Brands: Carlsberg, Tuborg, Pripps, Falcon

6. **Ambev**   São Paulo, Brazil
   Volume: 65.0 million hl   *Sales:* US$1,939.2 million
   Major Brands: Brahma Chopp, Skol, Antartica

7. **Scottish & Newcastle**   Edinburgh, U.K.
   Volume: 45.0 million hl   *Sales:* US$4,998 million
   Major Brands: Scottish Courage, Foster's, Kronenbourg, Baltika

8. **Grupo Modelo**   Mexico City, Mexico
   Volume: 38.4 million hl   *Sales:* US$3,503.2 million
   Major Brands: Corona, Pacifico, Estrella, Negra Modelo

9. **Coors**   Golden, Colorado
   Volume: 37.4 million hl   *Sales:* US$3,776.3 million
   Major Brands: Coors Light, Coors, Carling Lager

10. **Kirin**   Tokyo, Japan
    Volume: 32.7 million hl   *Sales:* US$11,837.0 million
    Major Brands: Kirin Lager, Ichiban Shibori, Tanrei

Source: *Beverage World.*

hl = hectoliter, 1 gallon = 0.0378 hectoliters.

young, hip consumers," said Nicole van Putten, beer analyst at Fortis Bank in Amsterdam.[3]

Even as Ruys and his marketing team have been working hard to maintain Heineken's relevance in the changing market, they want to maintain a fair degree of consistency across global markets. "The cliché 'think global, act local' is applicable to our situation," said Frans van der Minne, president and CEO of Heineken USA. But he added: "We wouldn't do anything with the brands that would be totally different from the initiatives that are taken by our colleagues in other parts of the world. We have global brand managers and they are gatekeepers so that all of our commercial initiatives are consistent with the integrity and quality of the brand."[4]

In spite of these challenges, Ruys is confident that Heineken will achieve its target of a 7 percent growth in volume in the United States. Joseph J. Fisch, Jr., who imports rival Dutch lager Grolsch into the United States, recently proclaimed: "The brand Heineken is as healthy as it has ever been."[5] Marketing executives have also pointed out that Heineken is able to squeeze higher profit margins even at lower volumes because of its premium status.

Reinventing the Brand Image

In large part, Heineken's decline in the United States could be attributed to growing problems with its brand image. Potential consumers, such as Véronique dos Santos, a 29-year-old human resources assistant in Paris, prefer more trendy beers such as Corona, imported from Mexico, or Desperados, a tequila-flavored concoction. Many young drinkers tend to regard Heineken as an obsolete brand. John A. Quelch, a professor at Harvard Business School who has studied the beer industry, said of Heineken: "It's in danger of becoming a tired, reliable, but unexciting brand."[6]

Ruys and his managers are well aware of this problem. They have been trying hard to liven up the image of Heineken through tie-ins with big-budget youth films, such as the *Austin Powers* and *Matrix* sequels. At the time of the release of *The Matrix Reloaded,* the firm aired a TV commercial written by the Wachowski brothers, who wrote and directed the movie. In the beer spot, when an obnoxious customer smacks a waitress's behind, the waitress throws a tray of Heineken beer in the air, where it remains suspended. She then uses a Matrix-style kick to knock the customer against the wall. The commercial was well received in the United States as well as in several countries in Europe.

Although some people within the firm felt the commercial was a bit too racy, Ruys and his team were able to win them over. Indeed, Ruys believes that Heineken's advertising has remained refreshingly offbeat, which represents a nod to Freddy's wry sense of humor. One U.S. commercial showed a young man plunging his arm deep into a barrel filled with ice and bottled beer. He gropes around fruitlessly until his whole body begins to shiver. Finally, he hauls out a Heineken. Popping it open, he joins a group of friends, who are also gripping Heinekens and shivering. "They've done a very good job of not being snooty, using accessible jokes and imagery to convey the idea that this beer is a cut above," said Bob Garfield, ad critic of trade weekly *Advertising Age.*[7]

To complement this new image in its commercials, Heineken's marketing team has also sponsored youth-oriented events to keep its brand relevant with young, hip consumers. It got a much-needed boost from a sweepstakes that it sponsored where winners got to attend a Heineken house party in Jamaica. The firm was also the official beer of Gen Art 2002, a nonprofit organization that showcases cutting-edge film, fashion, music, and entertainment for the 21- to 34-year-old demographic.

Finally, the Dutch brewer has been stepping up its marketing to Hispanics, who account for one-quarter of Heineken's U.S. sales. A new Spanish-language spot shows a group of men playing dominoes. They pause for a moment as one of them demonstrates how to pour a glass of beer without stirring up too much foam. "Heineken is for professionals—in beer," says a voice-over. "We want to bring over the values of the brand in a different way," said van der Minne.[8]

The strategy has started to pay off in the United States. Steve Davis, the firm's senior vice president of marketing, has seen a significant shift in the brand's image. "We pretty much reinvented the brand, injected some energy, some vitality, some excitement into it," he said.[9] As a result of this makeover, the average age of the Heineken drinker has fallen from about 40 in the mid-1990s to the early 30s today. Ruys's goal is to push that down into the high-20s in coming years. But he wants to be careful that in reaching out to younger customers he does not alienate the middle-aged beer drinkers who have been Heineken's core customers.

Picking Up on Its Global Efforts

Ruys does not want to rely entirely on a single brand, no matter how successfully it could be marketed around the world. He understands the importance of making deals with or acquiring brewers in various parts of the world. Heineken had been one of the first brewers to recognize the value of cross-border deals; for years, Freddy Heineken had been picking up small brewers from several countries to add more brands and to get better access to more markets. Exhibit 3 lists Heineken's brands in a number of markets.

For the most part, however, Heineken has limited itself to snapping up small national brewers such as Italy's Moretti to Spain's Cruzcampo that have provided it with small, but profitable avenues for growth. In 1996, for example, Heineken had acquired Fischer, a small French brewer, whose Desperados brand has been quite successful in niche markets. Similarly, Paulaner, a wheat beer that the firm picked up in Germany a few years ago, has been making inroads into the U.S. market.

But as other brewers have been reaching out to make acquisitions from around the globe, Heineken runs the risk of falling behind its more aggressive rivals. Over the last two years, Belgium's Interbrew has dished out $5.5 billion for brands such as Germany's Beck's and Britain's Whitbread and Bass. To deal with this growing challenge, Ruys has been pushing Heineken to break out of its play-it-safe corporate culture. Freddy had been reluctant to spend heavily on big-ticket acquisitions.

Already, Ruys has managed to pull off one of Heineken's biggest deals in some time. He spent $2.1 billion to acquire BBAG, a family-owned company based in Linz, Austria. Because of BBAG's extensive presence in central Europe, Heineken has become the biggest brewer in seven countries across eastern Europe.

At the same time, Ruys does not plan to stop acquiring smaller brewers that show promise. During the year that he has been in charge, Ruys has shelled out another

Exhibit 3   **Significant Heineken Brands in Various Markets**

Markets	Brands
United States	Heineken, Amstel Light, Paulaner,[1] Moretti
Netherlands	Heineken, Amstel, Kylian, Lingen's Blond, Murphy's Irish Red
France	Heineken, Amstel, Buckler,[2] Desperados[3]
Germany	Paulaner,[1] Kulmbacher, Thurn und Taxis
Italy	Heineken, Amstel, Birra Moretti
Poland	Heineken, Zywiec
China	Tiger, Reeb*
Singapore	Heineken, Tiger
Kazakhstan	Tian Shan, Amstel
Egypt	Fayrouz[2]
Israel	Maccabee, Gold Star*
Nigeria	Amstel Malta, Maltina
Panama	Soberana, Panama

*Minority interest

[1]Wheat beer

[2]Nonalcoholic beer

[3]Tequila-flavored beer

Source: Heineken annual reports.

$1 billion to acquire almost a dozen other firms. He has added several labels to Heineken's shelf, pouncing on brewers in places like Panama, Egypt, and Kazakhstan. In Egypt, Ruys bought a majority stake in Al Ahram Beverages Co. and hopes to use the Cairo-based brewer's fruit-flavored, nonalcoholic malts as an avenue into other Muslim countries.

However, Ruys believes that his firm can get much more growth out of cross-border deals, which he wants to use to get his managers to become better informed about different markets. Heineken's boss has even resorted to tough tactics to stir his troops out of their complacency. Ruys and his top lieutenants have traveled to places like Madrid and Shanghai to down a cold one with groups of randomly selected young people in order to find out more about their tastes. They meet regularly to think about the steps that they need to take to win over customers across different markets that have not yet developed a strong loyalty to a particular beverage.

Transitioning from the Past into the Future

Even as Ruys tries to develop Heineken into a major global player, he must appear to adhere to the core values and traditions that have guided the family-controlled firm.

With Freddy out of the picture, control of the firm has passed to his only child and heir, Charlene de Carvalho, a housewife and mother of five who resides in London. She has insisted on having a say in all of the major decisions, but she has left Ruys with the day-to-day responsibilities of running the firm. Her husband, Michel de Carvalho, can also exert considerable influence as a prominent member of the board. Speaking on behalf of the family, he emphasized the need to maintain a strong sense of continuity: "We won't deviate from the old man's principle."[10]

If that extends to Heineken's financially conservative style of running the business, this may not allow much room for Ruys to find avenues of growth. Heineken needs to spend heavily to build its presence in various markets if it doesn't want to cede them to its more aggressive global rivals. But it has been constrained in its ability to either buy out or merge with other firms because of concerns about the dilution of the family's control.

Ruys may gain more flexibility if Freddy's family decides to sell their stake. A hostile takeover would be almost impossible to pull off under the current ownership structure. Publicly, de Carvalho has stated that they remain committed to the firm's past, present, and future. "Our mission is to hand a healthy company to the next generation," she recently announced.[11] Nevertheless, there has been considerable speculation that the family might sell if they get the right price.

If the family grip is loosened, Ruys may be able to take more aggressive steps to build Heineken into a more formidable global competitor. "This could be Heineken unchained," said Michael Kraland, the Dutch president of Trinity Capital Partners, a Paris investment firm.[12] But the firm will have to work hard if it wants to catch up with the recent moves of the other major global players. Karel Vuursteen, who retired in 2002 from a top management post at the firm, acknowledged that "in the long run, nobody knows what will happen."[13]

Endnotes

1. Ewing, Jack, & Khermouch, Gerry, 2003, Waking up Heineken, *BusinessWeek,* September 8: 68.
2. Ibid., 70.
3. Bilefsky, Dan, 2003, Heineken brews comeback plans for U.S. market, *Wall Street Journal,* May 27: B1.
4. Theodore, Sarah, 2002, Rising star, *Beverage Industry,* July: 40.
5. Ewing & Khermouch, Waking up Heineken, 69.
6. Ibid.
7. Ibid., 72.
8. Ibid.
9. Theodore, Rising Star, 39.
10. Baker, Stephen, White, Christina, & Khermouch, Gerry, 2002, Freddy Heineken's recipe may be scrapped, *BusinessWeek,* January 28: 56.
11. Ewing & Khermouch, Waking up Heineken, 70.
12. Ibid., 56.
13. Ibid.

Thomas Howe felt good as he reviewed the results of his four years as president of Jays Foods LLC, a regional salty snack foods company. In 1994, when the original owners repurchased the company from Borden, Jays was losing $15 million annually on sales of $75 million. Howe's drive and imagination had led the turnaround of one of the Chicago area's best-known brands. Within four months of the purchase, the company made a profit and has remained in the black ever since. However, Frito-Lay, a powerful competitor, and consolidations among buyers within the grocery industry required new strategies. Howe had to make decisions concerning staffing, marketing, product development, and financing that would ensure his company's long-term profitability.

Jays Foods, with revenues of more than $125 million in 1998, was a privately-held corporation offering a full line of snack food. Sixty-five percent of the 350 product varieties were produced at its Chicago plant where the smell of potato chips brought smiles to drivers along the nation's busiest expressways. More than 1,000 employees were engaged in the manufacture and marketing of its snack food lines whose major brands were Jays, O-Ke-Doke, and Krunchers. Jays relied on co-packers (food manufacturers who produce according to specifications for brand and private labels) for pretzels, corn chips, popcorn, and extruded cheese products. A direct store delivery system composed of 400 route sales people and 40 branch offices delivered snack food to 24,000 customers serving consumers in its primary trade area of Illinois, Wisconsin, Indiana, and Michigan.

Competing against Frito-Lay, the market leader in the salty snack food category, was a challenge that had destroyed many family potato chip manufacturers as well as public corporations with deep pockets. Therefore, Howe knew that to be successful he had to be better than the competition, which had advantages of economies of scale, multimillion dollar advertising campaigns, and the ability to sponsor major sporting events. Jays' abilities to satisfy the regional taste preferences of consumers and to move quickly were strengths of the firm. Howe's continuing test was how well he could use these competitive advantages against Frito-Lay.

History

In 1927, Leonard Japp Sr. recognized the growing popularity of potato chips as a snack food. After operating a chip distributorship, Japp joined with a friend to produce their own chips and within two years the business had grown dramatically, fielding a fleet of 15 trucks to deliver chips to hungry consumers. In 1929, at the onset of the

*Reprinted with permission of Benjamin Weeks and Charles Shanabruch.

Depression, Japp sold his interest to his partner and returned to the distribution business only to start up another company a few years later with George Johnson, a longtime friend. The new firm manufactured and marketed chips under the label "Mrs. Japps Potato Chips." According to the company historian, its big breakthrough came with the invention of the continuous fryer that made chips that were far lighter and had less oil content than other competitors.[1]

In 1941, the company changed its name to Jays Potato Chips to avoid any negative sentiment associated with the Japanese bombing of Pearl Harbor (The owners used the "J's" of Japp and Johnson to create the new name, "Jays"). After World War II, the company grew rapidly because of the ever-growing demand for chips and Jays' providing recipes on the packages that encouraged the use of potato chips as meal extenders and taste enhancers in such recipes as tuna casserole.

Jays built its current plant in Chicago in 1955 to keep up with demand. Today the 124,000-square-foot facility remains one of the largest in the country. During the 1960s, when Leonard Japp Sr. served as president of the Potato Chip Institute, now the Snack Food Association, President John F. Kennedy asked him to lead a delegation to Russia to show the Soviet Union how to set up potato chip plants.[2]

Through the '60s and '70s Jays was a Midwest regional leader in the snack food industry. Its name was associated with quality. Jays' "Can't stop eating 'em" jingle was on the lips of children and adults; its blue and white logo was on the doors of thousands of grocery stores; and its pencils and calendar premiums were given out to kids in the schools. These were the golden years for Jays and its 900 employees.

The marketplace changed in the 1980s and Jays' dominance was threatened by Frito-Lay. At the beginning of the decade, Jays controlled nearly 50 percent of the Chicago market. Five years later the headline of *Crain's Chicago Business* reported: "Jays losing ground to Frito in chip war." Even though the revenues increased from $50 million to $58 million between 1981 and 1984, Frito-Lay made tremendous inroads on Jays' market share. Between 1980 and 1985, Frito-Lay's share of the Chicago market had grown from 29.1 percent to nearly 36.8 percent while Jays had dropped from 48.3 percent to 33.3 percent. This change was devastating as Chicago represented 60 percent of the company's estimated sales of $65 million in 1985.[3]

In addition, start-ups entered the industry. Deep price discounting by the smaller firms and the heavy advertising of Frito-Lay hurt Jays. It did not have funds to counter the ad campaigns. (In 1985, Frito-Lay spent $10 million on its national campaign compared with Jays' $1 million on TV advertising and an additional $228,000 on other media). Equally important, Jays did not discount its prices. Because of a sense of loyalty to the many small stores that accounted for its initial successes, Jays refused to cut special deals with large retailers even though the chain stores accounted for more than 50 percent of the Chicago area's entire food purchases.[4]

Jays weeded out poor performing products, aggressively sought expansion in Detroit and central Illinois, and held fast to its market share lead in Milwaukee. However, the company could not match Frito-Lay's marketing expenditures and trade discounts to major retailers. According to a snack food buyer of one of the major supermarket chains, the company ". . . relied too much on the quality of their product, their name and reputation did not keep up with what other people were doing. They were slow to get to their feet."[5]

To stem further erosion of market share was expensive. For nine years, Leonard Japp Sr. had rebuffed the offers of Borden Inc., a national food and chemical company that had made its mark in the dairy business. The 80-year-old Japp Sr. told a reporter that he had rejected an offer of $30 million the year before and stated that "the family wants to hang in here." Within six months of his denial, Leonard Japp agreed to sell Jays to Borden. When the purchase was announced in the summer of 1986, Joseph Whalen, Jay's executive vice president, acknowledged: "Growth requires a great deal of money. We just ran into some limits."[6]

The acquisition, estimated at $35 million, was regarded as good for Jays' customers and employees. Borden had the resources to expand production, increase advertising, and take back the market share recently given up to Frito-Lay. Borden's strategy was to diversify its holdings from the snack cake industry to the fast-growing salty snack food category by buying up regional snack food makers and to launch a national brand to compete with Frito-Lay.

Within a year, Jays reestablished its Chicago dominance under the ownership of Borden, which dramatically boosted ad spending, offered more aggressive discounts to supermarkets, and introduced an array of new products. Borden's strategy was to emphasize core brands such as potato chips and to allow many of the marketing decisions to be made on a regional, rather than a centralized, basis, to compete more effectively against regional brands.[7] Additionally, the new owner made a major capital investment in the Chicago plant, which enabled Jays to produce a wider variety of products at lower costs than before. Borden also made plans to introduce some of its own cheese snacks and corn-based products to the Chicago market through the Jays route distribution system. The corn products were intended to compete with Frito-Lay's successful Doritos and Fritos.

Initially, the Borden plan seemed to work; however, the decentralization in marketing was offset by the centralization of many decisions in the corporate headquarters. Quality, which was once Jays' hallmark, was sacrificed to volume and discounting. Borden, which had acquired and grouped together regional salty snack food companies, had miscalculated the market. Its efforts to assemble regional brands had failed. By 1993, Jays' revenues had increased to approximately $93 million but its operating losses were in the $13 to $15 million range. Rumors circulated that the Jays facility would be closed and production moved out of state.

At the 90th birthday party for Leonard Japp Sr., the idea for creating Jays Foods, LLC, was born. A party guest informed the birthday honoree and his son, Leonard Japp Jr., that Borden was preparing to spin off its troubled snack group. The father and son looked at each other and Japp Jr. asked his father, "You want to go back to work?" Two days later the Japps met to discuss the possibility of a buyback and set the wheels in motion. Six months later the Japps had their team in place and started the Jays comeback.[8]

The Salty Snack Food Industry

Scale and Scope   The potato chip is a symbol of snacking. According to the Snack Food Association, in 1997, the per capita consumption of the crispy, salty, and fatty chips reached 6.7 pounds, which accounted for 31 percent of the pounds of all salty snack foods consumed. Americans spent $66 billion on all snack foods, with salty snacks accounting for nearly 25 percent of the expenditures.[9]

The salty snack industry had slow growth in volume and increased consolidation. While the growth in volume had been slow (2.8 percent in 1997), the revenues increased more rapidly (6.8 percent). Large publicly traded companies including PepsiCo's Frito-Lay Company, GoodMark Foods, Inc., Lance Inc., and Golden Enterprises all reported increased sales in 1997. According to a survey by the Snack Food Association, the sales did not come easily. Competitive pressures were intense. Additionally, the trend of people eating out and supermarkets selling meals to take home had adversely affected the snack industry.[10]

The salty snack food industry was composed of full-line manufacturers that competed nationally and regionally in a variety of segments as well as national and regional firms that competed within very narrow niches. For example, Cape Cod Potato Chips of Hyannis, Massachusetts, sold its "kettle chips" product in 42 states.

In 1997, the per capita consumption of snack foods in the United States was 21.6 pounds, including 15 snack segments. Sales volume was: potato chips, 6.7 pounds; tortilla chips, 4.9 pounds; pretzels, 2.5 pounds; and microwave popcorn and salty nuts each at 1.5 pounds. Exhibit 1 shows these segments and per capita consumption for the 1995–1997 period.

Exhibit 1   Pounds Per Capita Snack Food Consumption, 1995–1997

Product	1995	1996	1997
Potato Chips	6.5	6.5	6.7
Tortilla Chips	5.0	4.9	4.9
Corn Chips	0.8	0.9	0.8
Ready-to-Eat Popcorn	0.5	0.6	0.6
Microwave Popcorn	1.4	1.3	1.5
Unpopped Popcorn	0.4	0.4	0.4
Extruded Snacks	1.1	1.2	1.2
Pretzels	2.6	2.5	2.5
Pork Rinds	0.2	0.2	0.2
Party Mix	0.4	0.4	0.4
Variety Packs	0.3	0.3	0.3
Snack Nuts	1.6	1.5	1.5
Meat Snacks	0.3	0.2	0.2
Multigrain Chips	0.2	0.2	0.1
Other Snacks	0.3	0.2	0.2

Total 1997 per capita consumption of 21.6 pounds in 1997 (1.9% increase over 1996).
Based on U.S. population of 265,540,600.

Source: *1998 Snack Food Association State of the Snack Food Industry Report,* SW 6.

Patterns and Trends   The sales revenue generated by snack foods had grown on an average of 4.5 percent each year between 1988 and 1997. Revenues were $10.95 billion in 1988, $13.8 billion in 1992, and $16.44 billion in 1997. The pound volume consumed increased from 4.3 billion to 5.7 billion in the same period producing an average annual gain of 3.12 percent.[11]

Manufacturers had been able to increase revenues by producing more premium products and increasing sales in outlets that charge premium prices. In 1997, the average price per pound of snack food sold by convenience stores was $3.87; drug stores, $2.85; supermarkets, $2.74; mass merchandisers, $2.30; and warehouse clubs, $2.00.

The sale of snack foods was not cyclical; the difference between the highest sales month of July was only 10 percent greater than the lowest sales month of March.[12] However, consumption of salty snacks did vary by product segment and by geographic region. Potato chips were most popular in the east central region of the United States where the per capita consumption was 8.8 pounds, 23 percent greater than the national average. The west central region had the highest salty snack food consumption, 24.5 pounds, 13 percent over the national average. While the east and west central regions had a love for potato chips and pretzels, Pacific coast residents preferred tortilla chips.[13]

The dollar share of the snack food market ranged from 31.7 percent for potato chips to 0.1 percent for multigrain chips. Exhibit 2 lists the 1997 dollar and pounds volume for each segment and the percent change from 1996.

Distribution   Each segment had its own channels of distribution profile. In the potato chip segment, supermarkets accounted for 46.0 percent of sales; convenience stores, 13.5 percent; and mass merchandisers, 9.2 percent. Tortilla chips were similar in volume patterns with supermarkets' sales accounting for 46.0 percent; convenience stores, 12.4 percent; and mass merchandisers, 10.4 percent. Ready-to-eat popcorn was quite different with mass merchandisers selling 32.3 percent; supermarkets, 32.0 percent; and drugstores, 9.5 percent. Exhibit 3 provides a breakdown of major segment sales by type of outlet.

Competitive Rivalry   Competition among snack food producers and distributors was intense. Frito-Lay dominated the national market in sales in most segments. Its power nationally had caused regional players to compete by using product innovation, price, service, and exploitation

Exhibit 2   1997 Snack Segment Share of Dollar Sales and Percent Change from 1996

Product	Dollar Sales ($ millions)	Percent Annual Increase	Pounds Volume (millions)	Percent Annual Change
Potato Chips	5,220.0	6.1	1,775	3.3
Tortilla Chips	3,428.5	7.5	1,305	1.5
Pretzels	1,341.3	7.7	658	0.9
Snack Nuts	1,350.7	8.7	403.8	4.2
Extruded Snacks	931.9	9.3	324.6	4.2
Meat Snacks	896.1	4.1	62.7	2.7
Microwave Popcorn	836.5	8.7	386.7	7.8
Corn Chips	589.3	5.3	219.1	3.6
Ready-to-Eat Popcorn	413.0	−4.6	153.3	3.6
Party Mix	358.9	13.4	116.9	8.4
Pork Rinds	308.2	15.6	47.2	7.6
Unpopped Popcorn	84.7	−1.5	100.8	−10.1
Other Snacks	254.2	3.2	60.6	4.7
Variety Packs	290.2	9	80.7	9.1
Multigrain Chips	133.5	−3.4	37.4	−6.4

Source: *1998 Snack Food Association State of the Snack Food Industry Report,* SW 7.

Exhibit 3   Segment Sale by Outlet, 1997

Outlet	Potato Chip	Tortilla Chip	Ready-to-Eat Popcorn	Pretzels	Snack Nuts
Supermarket	46.7%	46.0%	32.2%	43.7%	45.1%
Convenience Stores	13.5	12.4	6.9	11.1	12.7
Mass Merchandiser	9.2	10.4	32.2	6.8	14.0
Grocery Store	8.8	8.7	6.9	14.8	11.7
Other	8.3	8.6	5.8	7.4	3.5
Warehouse Club	4.9	7.6	6.6	8.9	4.8
Vending	4.7	3.4	—	3.3	2.3
Drug Store	3.9	2.9	9.5	4.0	5.9

Source: *1998 Snack Food Association State of the Food Industry Report,* SW 8, 10, 12, 16, and 19.

of niche opportunities. Examples of innovations was Garden of Eat'n's development of organic chip products and LaPreferida's venture with Sargento to launch *Nacho Express,* the first shelf-stable microwaveable nacho kit. More traditional innovations had been in the creation of new flavors and consistency of chips.[14]

To keep up with the health conscious baby-boomers, companies had introduced "better for you" varieties of snack foods. These met with mixed reactions, as the largest group of snackers was males who seem least likely to give up the salty and fatty tastes of traditional snacks. The introduction of Olestra chips by Frito-Lay by special arrangement with Procter & Gamble proved successful in 1997 and 1998. In 1999, many regional potato chip manufacturers cautiously planned their own roll-out of Olestra-based products to round out their product line. Fear about the possible side effects of the fat-free product accounted for this caution.

Innovation in packaging had also been helpful to regional companies. Because snacks had a very short shelf life in the consumer's home—they were eaten rather than stored—a trend toward larger bags helped increase sales. For example, Shearer's Food Inc. recently introduced a two-pound package of rippled chips in a large heavy gauge corrugated box and marketed it as a "value pak."[15]

Competitors   Frito-Lay Company dominated the salty snack food industry with sales of $6.67 billion in North America in 1997. Eight of its brands were among the ten best selling in the snack food section of U.S. supermarkets. With 42 manufacturing plants, 4,000 distribution points, and 12,000 route sales drivers across the United States, it controlled supermarket shelves.

In the potato chip category, Frito-Lay ranked first with sales of $1.14 billion, 60.2 percent of the market. Its nearest branded competitors were Utz of Hanover, Pennsylvania, with sales of $61.6 million, Wise with $61.2 million, Herr Foods, $40.2 million, and Jays Foods, LLC, $37.2 million. Private label potato chips sales were $174.9 million. In the tortilla chip category, Frito-Lay's brands, Doritos and Tostitos, had combined sales of $1.178 billion accounting for nearly 76 percent of the market share. Jays ranked 13th with sales of $7.1 million. In the extruded food category, Frito-Lay's brand, Cheetos, had sales of $201 million and accounted for 57 percent of the category. Its Rold Gold brand led the pretzel category with a 27.9 percent market share.

In the Chicago region, smaller regional salty snack food companies competed with Frito-Lay. Among them were Vitners and Jays in Chicago, McCleary in South Beloit, Illinois, and Seyfert's (Chesty brand) in Fort Wayne, Indiana. Vitners, McCleary, and Seyfert produced snack foods for their own label and co-packed for private labels. For example, Vitner produced for its own route drivers and distributors as well as for major supermarket brands and national food distributors.

Frito-Lay   The dominant competitor in the U.S. salty snack industry is Frito-Lay with over 50 percent of the market. Frito-Lay was created in 1961 by the merger of two successful companies: Frito, the Texas-based corn chip maker, and H.W. Lay and Co., a Georgia potato chip firm. In 1965, Pepsi-Cola and Frito-Lay merged to create PepsiCo, Inc. In 1998, PepsiCo achieved revenues of nearly $29 billion, employed approximately 140,000, and was ranked 31st on the Fortune 500. The company operated with three divisions: Pepsi-Cola (beverages), Frito-Lay (snack chips), and Tropicana (branded juices).[16]

Frito-Lay's mission was: "To be the world's favorite snack and always within arm's reach."[17] In 1966, Frito-Lay went international with snack foods and is the leading company in the world with approximately 20 percent of the market. Major Frito-Lay brands in North America include Lay's and Ruffles brand potato chips, Doritos and Tostitos brand tortilla chips, Fritos brand corn chips, Cheetos brand cheese flavored snacks, and Rold Gold brand pretzels. In 1998, Frito-Lay's worldwide volume was up 5 percent, North American volume was up 5 percent, and international volume was up 6 percent (without acquisitions).[18]

One of the strategies that Frito-Lay employed was the acquisition of brands to supplement their array of products. For example, Frito-Lay recently acquired Cracker Jack, a Chicago maker of candy-coated popcorn and peanut snacks made famous by the toy prize contained in the box and the song "Take Me Out To The Ball Game." According to Steve Reinemuna, chairman and CEO of Frito-Lay: "Cracker Jack is an American icon with universal appeal and tremendous brand equity. Our goal is to reinvigorate the Cracker Jack brand by providing product improvement news, expanded distribution, and creating exciting national marketing and advertising programs. This brand logically extends our business into sweet snacks while complementing our core business."[19]

A Frito-Lay advantage had been its ability to achieve economies of scale in both advertising and manufacturing. For example, in January 1999 the Tostitos brand was the sponsor of the Fiesta Bowl, a national television event in which the "mythical" national championship of the 1998 intercollegiate football season was decided.

Frito-Lay took advantage of a large production capability and produced its snack foods cheaper than most of its competitors. Also, Frito-Lay introduced a number of changes in its North American operations to improve plant efficiencies. In early 1999, the company reported that production was consolidated in its most efficient plants to eliminate production redundancies throughout the system and to streamline logistics and transportation systems. Four plants were scheduled to be closed and five plants to be expanded. As a result of these changes, Frito-Lay incurred charges of $120 million.[20]

Frito-Lay led the ranks of producers who are marketing potato chips that contain Olestra. In a 1998 press release, Brock Leach, president of the Frito-Lay Development Group, stated millions of customers were trying WOW. "Since its national rollout in February, WOW chips have been the most successful new product launch of the decade and today rank among the top five selling snack brands."[21]

Anheuser-Busch and Eagle Brand Snacks   In 1979, Anheuser-Busch, the St. Louis, Missouri, brewer, founded Eagle Snacks, and for 16 years competed in the salty snack industry without ever posting a profit. Although it rose to number two with a market share of 6 percent in the industry, it was never really successful in competing with Frito-Lay. When Anheuser-Busch finally decided to pull the plug on its Eagle division in 1996 and focus on beer and theme parks, the unit was annually losing $25 million on sales of $400 million. Unable to find a buyer, Anheuser-Busch simply shut the unit down with a loss of $206 million and sold four plants to Frito-Lay.

When Anheuser-Busch entered the snack business in 1979, the company believed that it could deliver its products through beer distributors. Although it was assumed that beer and snacks go together, the expected synergies failed to materialize. The distributors were not enthusiastic about carrying low-margin snacks. The two products were located in different areas of the store and were often not purchased by the same customer. As a result, distribution was much more complicated than Anheuser-Busch thought.

Another problem was the sheer size and marketing power of Frito-Lay. When Eagle started to expand in the late 1980s into potato and tortilla chips, Frito-Lay launched a number of new products, cut costs, and improved distribution. In addition, a price war in potato chips put the squeeze on Eagle and some of the smaller regional brands. As a result Eagle snacks never really caught on.[22]

Substitute Products and New Entrants

In 1997, American consumers spent $66 billion to satisfy their snacking desires according to the data collected by AC Nielsen. Pizza flavored English muffins, fun flavored junior bagels, and tropical flavored snack cakes competed with candy and salted snack creations in an intense battle for consumer dollars. That year, sales by snack food as a percent of market by category were: bakery foods, 41.2 percent; salted snacks, 22.2 percent; confectionery snacks, 20.5 percent; and specialty snacks, 16.1 percent.[23] Product innovations in the substitute product lines, plus the greater convenience of the supermarket deli section and the fast-food drive-thru lane continued to make the salty snack industry even more imaginative.

Suppliers and Buyers

Commodities and ingredients represented approximately 30 percent of the cost of snack food. Salaries and direct labor accounted for 17.8 percent, delivery, 8.8 percent, and promotions, 8 percent.[24] The costs of the potatoes and corn and most ingredients as well as labor were set by the market.

Buyers, especially supermarkets, which accounted for nearly 50 percent of the snack food sales, were becoming more powerful as the grocery industry consolidated in the 1990s. The national headquarters controlled the purchasing decisions in regional and local markets. The competition for shelf space and slotting allowances was ranked third in a 1998 survey of the biggest challenges that members of the snack food association would face.[25]

Jays Foods LLC

After the Buyback

In August 1994, when the Japp family completed the repurchase of Jays for reportedly half of their sales price to Borden only eight years earlier, they found a company in need of intensive care. The company they sold had a net income of $2 million compared to one with losses of $15 million. Decisive action and sophisticated management was needed to save the patient. The intensely competitive salty snack food industry was in transition. Powerful buyers were making it harder to get shelf space while demanding more and more in advertising and promotion commitments. Jays' powerful name had been tarnished. Its reputation for quality had been hurt by the failure to put quality first—both in production and distribution.

The responsibility to turn the company around was taken up by Thomas Howe, a food industry veteran who knew both the financial and operating side of manufacturing and marketing a branded product. Howe was introduced to the Japps by their attorney and a mutual friend who knew his extensive experience in the food business would be essential. After earning his BS in accounting in 1973, he joined Swift and Company and rapidly progressed to the position of vice president and controller, and then was named senior vice president and chief financial officer. In 1987, he was promoted to senior vice president of operations for Armour Swift-Eckrich, and in 1991 became president of Butterball Company, a division of ConAgra. At Butterball he managed a $750 million business and increased earnings from $13 million to $30 million in just two years. In September 1994, he joined with the Leonard Japp family to repurchase the company and become the President and co-owner.[26]

Tom Howe summarized for a reporter the situation and the task 11 months into the turnaround: "Our first focus was to put the train back on track and turn it in the right direction."[27] The Jays team focused on quality and on growing the business with existing customers. The original family recipe was once again put back into production and improvements were made to the plant to produce a consistent, quality product. Oil and water filtration systems were improved, fatty acids were controlled, and a radical breakage reduction program was put into place. Half a million dollars was spent to improve production.[28]

Simultaneously, a new marketing and public relations program was put into place. The company's famous slogan, "Can't stop eating 'em," which was all but forgotten under Borden, was revitalized. Japp and Howe went directly to the customers to get a feel for the market and to tell the customers that Jays' focus was now on quality and not the bottom line. They emphasized that they would be accountable to the customers as Jays had been before Borden and that quality and service would be at the highest level.

The payoff was soon in coming. Within four months the red ink ceased to flow and customers returned. The number one customer complaint had been breakage and that had been corrected. Howe told an interviewer that he was getting a tremendous amount of positive feedback about the product. The most important comment was that: "Jays is now what it used to be." Consumer complaints declined by 85 percent and calls to the company were equally divided between compliments and complaints.[29]

Strategy   In a meeting with the authors, Howe drew a map showing the trade area around Lake Michigan, and stated, "I see plenty of room for growth." He noted the company could increase sales to existing customers through better service and a wider array of products. In the first two years since the repurchase, Jays had introduced 150 new products and was seeking to develop new products in each of the Jays, Krunchers, and O-Ke-Doke lines.

Howe explained that the snack food market was full of opportunity. Only 15 percent of American consumers ate three meals each day, most getting their calories and nutrition by eating several smaller meals. Convenience and changing lifestyles had made snacking a way of life. Snack foods accounted for 10 percent of all grocery sales. Most important, grocers knew that snacks' weighted retail margin was 24.7 percent, one-third higher than the grocery margin of 17.8 percent. These facts gave him optimism about the future as he began to focus a two-pronged strategy of new product development and geographic expansion.[30]

Operations   The key to success at Jays was quality assurance. Relentlessly the team refocused the company on the issue of quality in each and every bag of Jays. At the center of the refocusing was the customer. Howe and his team drove thousands of miles in the first few months to meet with the customers to learn firsthand what they had to say about the product. As a result of the feedback, operations addressed the concerns systematically. Chips were once again prepared according to the original family recipe despite the increased costs. Breakage, the single biggest complaint, became the concern of everyone in manufacturing and distribution. Howe emphasized that "People buy chips, not crumbs."[31]

Because the taste and appearance of the chips were determined by the quality of inputs, a higher quality of oil was used and the chipping potatoes were purchased for their freshness. Specially grown potatoes with thin skins were used to speed production, reduce waste, and eliminate the dark brown spots that annoy consumers. Water and oil filtration systems were upgraded. By sorting the potatoes by size so that the smaller potatoes would be used for the smaller-sized bags and the larger potatoes for the larger-sized bags, breakage was radically reduced.

Because poor and split potatoes absorb greater amounts of oil and ultimately would be discovered later in the process, they were pulled off the conveyor belt before chipping. The potatoes were maintained at a specific temperature prior to frying to reduce the amount of oil that was absorbed and to give them the lightness that people identify with the Jays brand. As the chips left the frying vats, the conveyor belt carried them over an optical scanner that shot a jet of air under any dark chip, blowing it aside. Finally, the workers inspected the chips as they ascended the last conveyor before bagging. Before dropping into the bag for packaging, the chips passed over a magnetic field to ensure that no metal objects were bagged.[32]

Quality became everyone's responsibility. Borden's 12-person inspection team was disbanded and all of the production workers were trained to be their own inspectors at every stage of the production process. Weekly, Jays' and competitor's products were purchased off the shelf from area stores and brought to the headquarters, opened, and examined. Recently, when a Monday inspection turned up a great deal of breakage, Howe wrote a letter to all employees urging each individual to make the special effort to correct the situation. The letter was inserted into their paycheck envelope.[33]

Product Mix   At the time of the buyback, Jays relied almost exclusively on potato chip sales but needed to diversify to better meet the needs of its customers. In 1995, chips represented 74.5 percent of sales; popcorn, 12.0 percent; tortilla chips, 4.6 percent; pretzels, 3.1 percent; extruded cheese products, 2.2 percent; and all others, 4.6 percent. Through effective advertising and distribution, Jays was able to maintain its volume and increase market share and decrease its reliance on chips. Potato chips' share of revenues decreased to 64.2 percent and tortilla chips increased to 8.0 percent, pretzels to 7.0 percent, cheese to 3.0 percent, and all others to 7.8 percent. Popcorn's share fell to 2.0 percent.[34]

Jays made adjustments in packaging. Because 85 percent of snack food purchases were by impulse buyers, it was essential to have the right sizes and price points of the product available on the shelf. For example, Jays' sales literature listed 115 choices of potato chips.[35]

In 1998, Jays expanded the number of O-Ke-Doke cheese products, added new flavors of potato chips and cheese dip, as well as introduced new-sized packages of Krunchers and variety packs. Cotton candy and meat snacks were also introduced. In 1999, Jays planned to market several new co-branded products including a salsa flavored tortilla chip with Pace, the nation's largest seller of salsa. Two new lines of pretzels—sourdough nuggets and soft bite sourdough twists—were developed and plans were made for the launch of no-fat potato chips.

The most dramatic product development for Jays came in spring of 1999 with the rollout of its new snack product, E-Z Dippins. Both chips and a dip were contained in one package. The chips and dip were in the sealed separate units of one container and had an extended shelf life. The packages were not to be placed on the salty snack shelves of the supermarkets. Rather, they were to be strategically located in parts of the store where consumers make impulse purchases for snacks or meal substitutes. Howe hoped to have E-Z Dippins mounted on racks near the checkouts, where candy and cupcake-like products dominate, and in other locations in the store where consumers go for a quick hunger fix. The price of E-Z Dippins was set at $1.79 in expectation that customers would pay a premium for the convenience of having the two elements of the snack combined.

Channels of Distribution

One of the strengths of Jays at the time of the buyback was the existence of 350 direct store delivery routes. Route drivers were sales people, merchandisers, and delivery persons, all rolled into one. Their job was to listen and help the customers achieve their sales goals for the snack food category in their store. Because the route system was such a critical element of the turnaround, Jays made a large investment of time and funds in the route staff. Howe and the sales management staff visited the branch offices at the beginning or end of the day to share the vision and mission, to learn what the route people were hearing about the product, to find out what support they needed, and to give them advice on new strategies.

Each route person was provided with a handheld computer to place orders and keep track of inventory. The most important part of the business was to increase sales by improving service to existing accounts and to develop new business. With a computer, each driver was able to reduce paperwork and allocate at least one more hour a day to the fundamentals of his or her job. According to Howe, "We wanted to free the route workers up so they could increase sales and their commissions too."[36]

The route system was divided into approximately 40 sales districts supported by branch offices in 25 locations. Supporting the route sales staff were 40 district sales managers who supervised and supported their people. Northern Illinois had 5 branches, northern Indiana 1, Michigan 7, and Wisconsin 4. As Jays' volume grew the number of routes increased from 350 to 400. Where the route system was underdeveloped, Jays worked with independent food distributors: 7 in northern Illinois, 4 in northern Indiana, 3 in Wisconsin, 7 in Michigan, 2 in Minnesota, and 1 each in Iowa and Missouri.

Pricing

Jays, LLC, ended Borden's pricing strategy, which allowed the branch managers the discretion to raise and lower prices and to support promotions. Howe believed that it would be impossible to reposition the brand if pricing were not unified, so he designated himself as the sole person in the organization to give a price quote other than the published price. "When I took control of pricing,

I told everyone that our pricing was not inflexible; however, only I would decide what was acceptable." He committed to respond to all calls on pricing within 24 hours or sooner.[37]

John Plys, who directs the sales force in the field, explained that Jays does not discount. He stated that "Jays prices its products on a par with Frito-Lay because our quality is better and we can beat them with service."[38]

Marketing

In the first few months after the buyback, Howe, accompanied by Leonard Japp and his vice president of sales, met with all of the key accounts and conveyed one message: "Come Home to Jays." They wanted to tell customers that the original owners were back and that the quality would be back too. Besides these visits, the firm placed a number of public relations stories in food trade journals and Chicago area newspapers to get the Jays' message out to the consumers.

According to Howe, Jays was not like Frito-Lay, which rolled out a marketing plan and gave it to customers. When Howe and his vice president of sales first met with larger customers and were asked what Jays' marketing plan was, he surprised them by handing them a blank piece of paper. "I told them our marketing plan was for each individual customer and what Jays would do would be based upon what the customer wanted to happen in the snack food section of his store." His message to the route sales force was: "People sell Jays." He told all sales people to see the customer, talk with the customer, and ask the customer what was needed so that Jays could design a program to address them.

Jays had a limited advertising budget. John Plys conceded that Jays could not go head to head with Frito-Lay on advertising. He did note that when Frito-Lay's advertising increased demand in the category, Jays took advantage of the expansion of sales in the snack food category. "Because 81–83 percent of salty snack foods sales are by impulse as people walk through the store, the choices are based less upon television advertising than they are for other products. When is the last time you put potato chips on your grocery shopping list? What is essential is to have your product well displayed where people are making choices in the grocery or convenience store," he said.[39]

Rather than try to advertise products, Plys said Jays tried to keep up enthusiasm for its products through cobranding strategies. For example, in the past year Jays had tie-in promotions for major holidays with Miller beer, Coca-Cola, and Budweiser beer.

Packaging was critical to the preservation of the quality and to the presentation of the product. Jays quickly tried to revitalize its name by providing consistency for the brand on the store shelves that had been lost under Borden ownership. The packaging was a key to the marketing strategy to recreate the image that went along with the original taste of Jays. Howe said that focusing on packaging helped to unify the brand for the people who rolled the grocery cart down the aisle of their local supermarket.

Financial and Operating Strategies   Jays was privately held and Tom Howe did not share its bottom-line results. However, he noted that the $13 million loss that Jays experienced the year before the buyback was quickly ended and that under the Japp/Howe ownership the company became profitable. One key was to focus on cost cutting. Howe stated that Jays once again had operating ratios relatively similar to the snack food industry. In the 1998 study prepared for the Snack Food Association, *State of the Snack Food Industry Report,* the following were expense categories and percentages:

Benefits	4.8%
Administrative	9.0
Salaries & Direct Labor	17.8
Commodities & Ingredients	29.9
Packaging	13.8
Delivery	8.8
Promotions	8.0
Gross Margin	8.0

Jays did not have the economies of scale that major competitors such as Frito-Lay had with individual plants dedicated to specific products. Shorter product runs required lost production time for line changeovers and Jays' older plant needed a good deal of ongoing maintenance. In January 1999, the plant was running at full capacity 24 hours a day, five days a week. In the critical areas of supply, nearly all of the inputs were commodities, and swings in the market prices affected all competitors similarly. Administrative costs were lean and outsourcing was used to manage overhead costs.

Rather than build manufacturing capacity for the Jays pretzels and tortilla chip products and its O-Ke-Doke cheezelet products, Jays continued to rely on co-packing. Subcontracting the production and packaging work to specialists in the region gave Jays flexibility to adjust output with minimum investment. Quality control was exercised by testing and frequent visits to co-packer plants. "We are in those plants almost on a daily basis. We share the throttle and demand a high degree of accountability," Howe noted.[40] Outsourcing enabled the company to focus on its flagship potato chip products and marketing as well as provide flexibility.

Organization and Culture   Under Borden, the decision-making process had become rigid in some areas and impossibly loose in others. For example, route drivers adjusted the established prices and gave discounts without checking with management. However, supervisors on the production line waited days for answers from the Columbus, Ohio, corporate offices before making corrections. Volume and pricing had become greater priorities than quality, according to Howe.

Jays had no organization chart by intention. Howe did not want to repeat the problems of centralized management he experienced at large food processing companies. "I did not want the chart to become a crutch that freed people from making decisions and ducking accountability," he emphasized. He focused on performance and spent his time meeting with key personnel to set measurable goals for the short term and to identify the resources that each manager needed to achieve the goals. "The only bureaucracy we have here is what we put in. If we don't like it, we change it."[41]

The team that Howe carefully assembled to handle the turnaround changed as the company took on new and more sophisticated challenges. Howe sought new talent to take the company to the next level. (See Exhibit 4 for a list of key managers.)

Howe communicated directly and often with all of the employees. Quarterly goal-setting meetings with the senior staff were held to define tactical goals that could be achieved quickly to advance the organization toward greater market share and profitability. The same attention to employees in the production facility was also obvious. On a tour of the plant, workers smiled when they saw Howe and he called on them by name. Forklift drivers, conveyor belt pickers, and box packers alike were asked how they were doing and how production was going.[42] Howe noted that he spent two days a week in the field where he shared his vision and values with the route personnel. After attending a conference at Harvard Business School on managing change and motivation, Howe put even more focus on meeting with his employees.

Howe acknowledged that his most formidable work was the maintenance and development of the route system. The system was costly to operate but it met the needs of the customer. (The average Direct Store Delivery, or DSD, system has a 24.1 percent gross margin versus 25.6 percent for the warehouse system. However, it was attractive to the retailer because it provided a much higher total retailer margin: 23.0 percent versus 17.5 percent.) In the DSD system, the vendor assumed many customer costs such as moving, slotting, storage, picking store orders, transportation and fleet, unloading, merchandising labor, and ordering. In return the DSD gave the vendor a partner relationship with the buyers, control over the merchandise presentation, and the chance to help more directly market the product in the store.[43]

When Howe was asked to identify the greatest challenge for Jays, he listed retention of quality workers. For this reason, in the past year new recognition and training

Exhibit 4   **Jays Officers**

Leonard Japp Jr., Chairman

Thomas E. Howe, President and Chief Operating Officer
Bachelor of Science and Commerce Degree, De Paul University, 1973, Certified Public Accountant.
From 1973 through 1994 Howe directed financial and operating divisions of major food processors of branded meat products.

Thomas J. Raleigh, Executive Vice President of Sales
Bachelor of Arts, Marquette University, 1973, and MBA, University of Dallas, 1975.
Extensive experience in food sales as Vice President of Nestlé-Beich, National Sales Manager of Azteca Foods, Inc., and sales management positions with Frito-Lay, Inc., including Senior Division Sales Manager for the 600 employees in the Midwest.

Thomas A. Zwartz, Vice President and Chief Financial Officer
Bachelor of Arts, Graham School of Management, Saint Xavier University, 1989, Certified Public Accountant.
Nine years' experience with Coopers and Lybrand, LLP, Chicago office, including Senior Manager with the Entrepreneurial Advisory Services group.

David Madigan, Vice President of Production
Bachelor of Science, Ohio State University, 1975, and MBA, University of Wisconsin.
Sixteen years' experience in food industry including positions with Frito-Lay, Tombstone Pizza, and recently plant manager for cookie and pastry manufacturer Parco Foods.

Greg Spear, Vice President of Sales Operations
Twenty-three years' experience in the food industry including numerous positions with Armour-Swift Eckrich such as Route Sales Representative, Route Supervisor, Branch Manager, Category Manager and General Manager of DSD.

Source: Jays Foods, L.L.C.

---

and mentoring programs were established. The problem was particularly acute in the hiring and retention of route sales people who were required to work a six-day week schedule. Many individuals with working spouses and children had to balance the obligations of work with family needs. As a result, Jays experimented with a five-day week and hired more drivers.

Challenges   Tom Howe had succeeded in turning the company around but challenges remained. Consolidating Jays' presence in the region still remained a work in progress. Looking at the map of the Midwest, Howe noted that the company had major markets around Lake Michigan and described the areas running in a second loop from St. Paul to St. Louis to Indianapolis to Detroit as "opportunity markets" that he wanted the company to grow into.

Unable to undertake multimillion advertising programs and sponsorship of major events, Jays depended on competitors to build the snack food category. Also, competing for shelf space was becoming more and more formidable as customers changed and became more powerful. For example, in 1998, Chicago's two dominant supermar-

ket chains were acquired (Jewel, a division of American Stores, by Albertson, and Dominick's Finer Foods by Safeway), potentially affecting access to their shelf space. Also, the traditional lines of competition between grocery and soft goods retailers were being blurred by hyperstores such as Wal-Mart and Super-K which have created new ways to shop.

As Tom Howe reflected upon the ever-increasing competitive pressures facing Jays, he realized that the only option open to the company was change.

Endnotes

1. Jays Foods, LLC's Internet Web site (www.jaysfoods.com) provides some background to the company's early history.
2. Jays Foods, company brochures and www.jaysfoods.com.
3. Jays losing ground to Frito in chip war, 1985, *Crain's Chicago Business*, December 16.
4. 1986, *Crain's Chicago Business*, July 7.
5. Ibid.

6. 1998, *Crain's Chicago Business,* July 7.
7. 1987, *Crain's Chicago Business,* May 18.
8. Jays Foods, L.L.C, 1995, *Snack Food,* January.
9. *1998 Snack Food Association State of the Snack Food Industry Report* (hereafter *1998 Snack Report*), SW 3–6; and Going to extremes: State of the industry 1998 (hereafter, State of the industry), *Snack Food and Wholesale Bakery,* SI 5.
10. *1998 Snack Report,* SW 3–6.
11. Ibid., SW 8.
12. Ibid., SW 4–5.
13. Ibid., SW 35.
14. State of the industry, SI 29–30.
15. Ibid., SI 27, 29, and 33.
16. American snackers get a taste of what they want, 1997, Frito-Lay press release, January 20.
17. PepsiCo, Inc., 1997, Annual Report.
18. News from PepsiCo, Inc., 1999, February.
19. Frito-Lay, 1997, press release, October 8.
20. News from PepsiCo, Inc., 1999, January 25.
21. Betcha can't taste the difference or it's free, 1998, Frito-Lay press release September 14.
22. Melcher, Richard, 1996, How Eagle became extinct, *BusinessWeek,* March 4; 68–69; and Benezra, Karen, 1995, Can Poldoian fly Eagle? *Brandweek,* September 18: 25–29.
23. State of the industry, SI 5.
24. *1998 Snack Report,* SW 38.
25. Ibid., SW 42.
26. Howe, Thomas, 1997, interview. All information about the company that is not directly endnoted is based upon information provided and conveyed by Howe (hereafter referred to as "Howe interview").
27. Quoted in *Food R & D,* June 1995.
28. Ibid.
29. Ibid.
30. Howe interview, 1997.
31. Ibid.
32. Howe interview, 1997; and plant tour, November 1997.
33. Howe interview, 1997.
34. Jays Foods, LLC, company sales data.
35. See www.jaysfoods.com for product line and packaging.
36. Howe interview, 1997.
37. Ibid.
38. Plys, John, 1999, interview, July 30.
39. Ibid.
40. Howe interview, 1997.
41. Ibid.
42. 1998, Plant tour by author November.
43. Howe interview, 1997; and Jays worksheet.

Case 22   JetBlue Airways*

Is "High Touch Service" the Key Driver for JetBlue's Future Success?

On December 4, 2003, JetBlue withdrew its services from Atlanta in the wake of a huge retaliation from the airline majors, Delta Air Lines and United Airlines. Following JetBlue's May 2003 entry into Atlanta, both Delta and United (ranking number 2 and number 3, respectively, in the U.S. airline industry) slashed their prices by more than half and boosted their flight schedules. JetBlue's withdrawal raised questions in the minds of both airline travelers and investors alike about the growth and profitability of low-cost carriers. The low-cost carriers grew from carrying less than 10 percent of domestic air traffic in 1990 to carrying about 25 percent in 2003. However, rapid growth and increased entries also meant that the market was getting crowded and further growth was becoming constrained.[1] Could JetBlue continue its spectacular growth? Were its competitive advantages sustainable?

During the five years since its inception, JetBlue had become the 11th largest airline in the United States (based on revenue passenger miles).[2] The firm posted a profit for its 12th consecutive quarter on January 29, 2004. Exhibit 1 provides a comparative statement of JetBlue's operating performance (see the Appendix on page 709 for a description of key terms) on a few key indicators:

Several analysts downgraded the stock because they were skeptical about the costs of expansion as well as the increased competition in the discount segment by major carriers.[3] Even business travelers, an important segment for the company, were becoming more price-sensitive. However, David Neeleman, the CEO and chairman of JetBlue, was optimistic. He said, "In light of the difficult competitive environment we faced in the fourth quarter, we're pleased to report a double-digit operating margin. We begin 2004 from a strong position characterized by excellent cost control diligence, a healthy balance sheet, and a top-rated product offering delivered by dedicated Crewmembers. These key advantages give us tremendous

confidence in our continued growth through what is expected to be a very competitive year."[4]

The United States Airline Industry[5]

Deregulation of the U.S. airline industry in 1978 ushered in competition in the hitherto protected industry. Several low-cost, low-fare operators entered the competitive landscape which Southwest pioneered. In 1971 Southwest initiated service as a regional carrier, but by 1990 it became a major airline when its revenues crossed the $1 billion mark.[6] The Southwest model was based on operating a single-type aircraft fleet with high utilization, a simplified fare structure with single-class seating, and high productivity from its human and physical assets. On the other hand, the "hub-and-spoke" system, increased labor costs, and increases in multitype aircraft fleets bloated the cost structure of the major airlines.

There are three primary segments in the airline industry: major airlines, regional airlines, and low-fare airlines. Major U.S. airlines, as defined by the Department of Transportation, are those with annual revenues of over $1 billion. Eleven passenger airlines belong to this category, the largest of whom include American Airlines, Continental Airlines, Delta Air Lines, Northwest Airlines, and United Airlines. These airlines offer scheduled flights to most large cities within the United States and abroad and also serve numerous smaller cities. Most major airlines adopted the hub-and-spoke route system. In this system, the operations are concentrated in a limited number of hub cities while other destinations are served by providing one-stop or connecting service through the hub.

Regional airlines typically operated smaller aircraft on lower-volume routes than major airlines. Unlike the low-fare airlines, the regional airlines do not have an independent route system. They typically enter into relationships with major airlines and carry their passengers on the "spoke"—that is, between a hub or larger city and a smaller city.

The low-fare airlines, on the other hand, operate from "point to point" and have their own route system. The target segment of low-fare airlines is fare-conscious leisure and business travelers who might otherwise have used al-

---

*This case study was prepared by Naga Lakshmi Damaraju of the University of Texas at Dallas, John R. Gaetz, former graduate student of the University of Texas at Dallas, Marilyn L. Taylor of the University of Missouri at Kansas City, and Gregory G. Dess of the University of Texas at Dallas. All rights reserved to the authors. This case study has been developed purely from secondary sources. The purpose of the case is to stimulate class discussion rather than illustrating effective or ineffective handling of a business situation. The authors thank Dr. Michael Oliff, the University of Texas at Dallas, and Dr. Alan Eisner for their comments on an earlier version of this case.

[1]Isidore, C., 2003, Too much of a cheap thing? *CNN Money,* December 4; http://money.cnn.com/2003/12/04/news/companies/discount_airlines/.

[2]JetBlue, 10-K reports.

[3]Spitz, J., 2004, Downgrades hit Delta and JetBlue; www.marketwatch.com; Barker, R., 2004, Some of my pans should have been picks, *BusinessWeek,* January 19: 90.

[4]JetBlue, 2004, company press release, January 29; www.jetblue.com/learnmore/pressDetail.asp?newsId=230.

[5]This section draws heavily from the SEC filings of JetBlue for the year 2002. Other sources include: Zellner, W., 2003, Look who's buzzing the discounters, *BusinessWeek,* November 24; Zellner, W., 2004, Folks are finally packing their bags, *BusinessWeek,* January 12; and a joint study by Kearney, A.T., & the Society of British Aerospace Companies, The emerging airline industry; www.atkearney.com/shared_res/pdf/Emerging_Airline_Industry_S.pdf.

[6]www.southwest.com/about_swa/airborne.html.

Exhibit 1   JetBlue's Operating Statistics (unaudited)

	Year Ended December			
	2003	**2002**	**2001**	**2000**
Revenue passengers	9,011,552	5,752,105	3,116,817	1,144,421
Revenue passenger miles (000)	11,526,945	6,835,828	3,281,835	1,004,496
Available seat miles (000)	13,639,488	8,239,938	4,208,267	1,371,836
Load factor	84.5%	83.0%	78.0%	73.2%
Breakeven load factor	72.5%	71.5%	73.7%	90.6%
Aircraft utilization (hours per day)	13	12.9	12.6	12
Average fare	$107.09	$106.95	$99.62	$ 88.84
Yield per passenger mile	$ .0837	$ .0900	$ .0946	$ .1012
Passenger revenue per available seat mile	$ .0708	$ .0747	$ .0738	$ .0741
Operating revenue per available seat mile	$ .0732	$ .0771	$ .0761	$ .0763
Operating expense per available seat mile	$ .0608	$ .0643	$ .0698	$ .0917
Airline operating expense per available seat mile	$ .0607	$ .0643	$ .0698	$ .0917
Departures	66,920	44,144	26,334	10,265
Average stage length (miles)	1,272	1,152	986	825
Average number of operating aircraft during period	44	27	14.7	5.8
Full-time equivalent employees at period end	4,892	3,572	1,983	1,028
Average fuel cost per gallon	$ .8508	$ .7228	$ .7563	$ .9615
Fuel gallons consumed (000)	173,157	105,515	55,095	18,340
Percent of sales through jetblue.com during period	73.0%	63.0%	44.1%	28.7%

Source: JetBlue annual reports.

ternative forms of transportation or not traveled at all. Low-fare airlines stimulated demand in this segment and have also been successful in weaning business travelers from the major airlines. The main bases of competition in the airline industry are fare pricing, customer service, routes served, flight schedules, types of aircraft, safety record and reputation, code-sharing relationships, in-flight entertainment systems, and frequent flyer programs.

The economic downturn in the late 1990s and the terrorist attacks on the World Trade Center and the Pentagon on September 11, 2001, severely affected the airline industry. The demand for air travel dropped significantly and led to a reduction in traffic and revenue. Security concerns, security costs, and liquidity concerns increased. The major U.S. airlines reported operating losses of $10 billion for two consecutive years, 2001 and 2002. Several major airlines filed for bankruptcy under Chapter 11 during 2001 and 2002. Many airlines significantly decreased

their capacity, reduced their routes, and postponed purchases of new aircraft. More than 1,000 planes were grounded in the six months following September 11, 2001, and some airlines reported a 50 percent reduction in routes and flight frequency. For example, on the East Coast, US Airways eliminated its MetroJet operation, which was designed to compete with low-cost, low-fare airlines such as Southwest and JetBlue. Delta Air Lines significantly reduced the capacity of Delta Express service, its low-fare, leisure-oriented service provider in the Northeast and Midwest to Florida. In November 2002 National Airlines ceased operations, which opened up the New York–Las Vegas market to other discounters much earlier than originally anticipated. All these events provided opportunities for the low-cost carriers not only to increase the number of flights but also to introduce services on new routes.

The economy started rebounding by the end of 2003, which boosted demand for business and leisure travel.

Industrywide capacity was expected to grow by 7 percent after three years of flight reductions and fewer routes. Low-cost operators such as Southwest and JetBlue were expected to benefit from this trend. On the other hand, the major airlines saw their revenues stabilize after the three-year retreat, made deep cost reductions in their operations, and renewed their confidence to fight back. The majors and their regional partners were expected to boost their domestic capacity by 5 percent in 2004. Much of this expansion was aimed at markets with low-cost competition. And much of this expansion was to come at lower costs, that is, by increasing the utilization of existing aircraft in terms of the number of flights per aircraft, not by new purchases of aircraft.

David Neeleman and JetBlue Airways[7]

Born in São Paulo, Brazil, and brought up in Salt Lake City, David Neeleman dropped out of the University of Utah after his freshman year to move back to Brazil and become a missionary. After two years of missionary work, he made his modest beginning in establishing his own business by renting out condominiums in Hawaii. He then established his own travel agency and began chartering flights from Salt Lake City to the islands to bring in prospective clients for his rental services.

Neeleman's sales prowess caught the attention of June Morris, who owned one of Utah's largest corporate travel agencies. Soon after, in 1984, Neeleman and Morris launched the Utah-based "Morris Air," a charter operation. Morris Air was closely modeled after Southwest Airlines, the legendary discount airlines in the United States. Neeleman considered Herb Kelleher, Southwest's founder, his idol. He studied everything Kelleher accomplished and tried to do it better which meant keeping costs low and turning planes around quickly among a host of other operational and strategic activities/choices. While following the Southwest model, Neeleman brought his own innovations into the business. He pioneered the use of "at-home reservation agents"—routing calls to agents' homes to save money on office rent and infrastructure expense. He also developed the first electronic ticketing system in the airline industry. By 1992 Morris Air had grown into a regularly scheduled airline and was ready for an initial public offering (IPO) when Southwest, impressed by Morris's low costs and high revenue, bought the company for $129 million. Neeleman became the executive vice-president of Southwest. However, Neeleman could not adjust to Southwest's pace of doing things. By 1994, he was at odds with the top executives and left after signing a five-year noncompete agreement.

In the interim between leaving Southwest and establishing JetBlue, Neeleman developed the electronic ticketing system he initiated at Morris Air into one of the world's simplest airline reservation systems: Open Skies. He sold Open Skies to Hewlett-Packard in 1999. During the same period, he was also a consultant to a low-fare Canadian start-up airline, WestJet Airlines.[8] After the completion of the noncompete agreement with Southwest Airlines in 1999, Neeleman launched his own airline. He raised about $130 million of capital in a span of two weeks, an unprecedented amount for a start-up airline.[9] Weston Presidio Capital and Chase Capital, venture capital firms that backed Neeleman's prior ventures, were return investors, and financier George Soros was also brought into the deal. "David's a winner, I knew anything David touched would turn to gold," said Michael Lazarus of Weston Presidio Capital that had earlier funded Morris Air. "We were intrigued with his ideas about a low-cost airline."[10] With such strong support from venture capitalists, JetBlue began as the highest funded start-up airline in U.S. aviation history.

In "JetBlue" Skies

Incorporated in Delaware in August 1998, JetBlue commenced operations in August 2000, with John F. Kennedy International Airport (JFK) as its primary base of operations. In 2001 JetBlue extended its operations to the West Coast from its base at Long Beach Municipal Airport which served the Los Angeles area. In 2002 the company went public with its IPO and was listed on the Nasdaq as JBLU. JetBlue had expected to sell 5.5 million shares at about $24–$26 in its initial public offering. Instead, it sold 5.87 million shares at $27 per share through its lead underwriters Morgan Stanley and Merrill Lynch. The shares closed at $47, up by $18, on the first day of trading. JetBlue's stock offering was one of the hottest IPOs of the year.[11]

JetBlue was established with the goal of being a leading low-fare passenger airline that offered customers a differentiated product and high-quality customer service. It was positioned as a low-cost, low-fare airline providing quality customer service on point-to-point routes. JetBlue had a geographically diversified flight schedule that included both short-haul and long-haul routes.

The mission of the company, according to David Neeleman, was "to bring humanity back to air travel." The airline focused on underserved markets and large metropolitan areas that had high average fares in order to stim-

---

[7]This section draws from Gajilan, A. T., 2004, The Amazing JetBlue, *Fortune Small Business;* www.fortune.com/fortune/smallbusiness/articles/0,15114,444298-2,00.html.

[8]Brazilian-Amercian Chamber of Commerce of Florida, 2004, Chamber News, 2004 Excellence Award; www.brazilchamber.org/news/chambernews/ExcellenceAward2004.htm.

[9]JetBlue Airways Corporation, *International Directory of Company Histories;* http://galenet.galegroup.com.

[10]Gajilan, 2004, Amazing JetBlue; DiCarlo, L., 2001, Management and trends, Jet Blue skies, *Forbes.com,* January 31; www.forbes.com/2001/01/31/0131jetblue.html.

[11]JetBlue IPO soars, 2002, *CNNmoney,* April 12; http://money.cnn.com/2002/04/12/markets/ipo/jetblue/.

Exhibit 2   The JetBlue Effect

Route	Increase in Daily Passengers %	Decrease in Average Fare %	JetBlue's Share of Local Traffic %
New York to Miami/Ft. Lauderdale	14%	17% (to $121.50)	23.1%
New York to Los Angeles basin	2	26 (to $219.31)	18.0
New York to Buffalo	94	40 (to $86.09)	61.2

Figures as of second quarter, 2003.

Source: Data from Back Aviation Solutions; adapted from W. Zellner, "Is JetBlue's Flight Plan Flawed?" *BusinessWeek,* February 16, 2004.

ulate demand. The "JetBlue effect" aspired to create fares going down, traffic going up, and JetBlue ending up with a big chunk of business. Exhibit 2 shows the JetBlue effect in the markets it served.

JetBlue was committed to keeping its costs low. To achieve this objective, the company operated a single-type aircraft fleet comprising Airbus A320 planes as opposed to the more popular but costly Boeing 737. The A320s had 162 seats compared to 132 seats in the Boeing 737. According to JetBlue, the A320 was thus cheaper to maintain and also was more fuel-efficient. Since all of JetBlue's planes were new, the costs of maintenance were also lower. In addition, the single type of aircraft kept training costs low and increased manpower utilization. JetBlue was the first to introduce the "paperless cockpit" in which pilots, equipped with laptops, had ready access to flight manuals that were constantly updated at headquarters. As a result, pilots could quickly calculate the weight and balance and take-off performance of the aircraft instead of having to download and print the manuals for making the calculations. The paperless cockpit thus ensured faster take-offs by reducing paperwork and helped in achieving quicker turnarounds and higher aircraft utilization.[12] There were no meals served on the planes, and pilots even had to be ready, if need be, to do the cleanup work on the plane to keep the time the aircraft was on the ground as short as possible. Innovation was everywhere; for example, there were no paper tickets to lose and no mileage statements to mail to frequent fliers.

JetBlue also deliberately chose underutilized airports for its operations. In large metropolitan areas with multiple airports, there typically was an airport, or even two, that received little attention in terms of domestic air traffic. JetBlue chose to operate in such airports. The reason,

according to Neeleman, was that, with less congestion, it was far easier to get planes in and out of such airports more quickly. Also, when runways were too close, even with a bit of adverse weather, the flights at major airports might be delayed for a couple of hours. However, JetBlue could minimize all such problems by simply not choosing to go to the most popular airports.[13]

Differentiation was another key part of JetBlue's strategy. The airline offered its passengers a unique flying experience by providing new aircraft, leather seats, simple and low fares, free live satellite television with up to 24 channels of DIRECTV programming free of charge at every seat, preassigned seating, and reliable performance.[14] Unlike Southwest, which ferried business travelers on short hauls, JetBlue flew larger planes on typically longer routes. This enabled JetBlue to set its fares even lower than Southwest on a per mile basis.[15] JetBlue also offered more legroom than any other airline, even though it meant having fewer seats per plane. In each of its A320s, the company removed one row of seats, bringing down the number of seats from 162 to 156. That created greater legroom by extending seat pitch—the space from the back of one seat to the back of the seat behind it—to 34 inches on 65 percent of its seats, with the exception of nine rows in the front that remained at 32 inches. Customers could check online at the airline's Web site for more information and assistance in selecting their preferred seat location. "We've always offered an award-winning and very comfortable product but now we've figured out a way to give more customers even more room without changing our fare

---

[12]WEBSMART50, 2003, *BusinessWeek,* November 24: 92.

[13]Interview with David Neeleman by Willow Bay of CNN Business Unusual, 2002, aired June 23; www.cnn.com/TRANSCRIPTS/0206/23/bun.00.html.

[14]JetBlue, 10-K Reports.

[15]Wells, M., 2002, Lord of the skies. *Forbes.com,* November 14.

structure," said David Neeleman.[16] To reward its loyal customers, JetBlue started the "True Blue" program that gave its customers points rather than miles. Points were earned depending on whether the trip is a short (2 points if booked by phone; 4 points if booked online), medium (4 points) or long (6 points) haul. Customers earned double points if they booked their tickets through the company's Web site. For every 100 points earned, customers earned a free round-trip flight to any destination that JetBlue served.

Another important feature is that JetBlue never overbooked its flights. Other airlines routinely overbooked their flights to ensure that they would not fly empty even if it meant significant inconvenience to customers who were bumped. At JetBlue, a customer would never be left behind, except in a rare circumstance such as the need to get to a family member in distress. Even in such situations, it would be the voluntary choice of another customer to opt out of the particular flight. Despite this policy, JetBlue had a smaller percentage of empty seats than its competitors—only 20 percent in September 2003, which was about 13 percent lower than all its larger competitors. JetBlue, in essence, made overbooking redundant by better inventory management. What it gave customers was peace of mind that they would not be bumped when they were expecting to fly. For those who valued their time and appointments, this was a key feature of JetBlue's service.[17]

Passengers were encouraged to book directly through the company's Web site instead of through agents. All tickets were nonrefundable. Passengers were required to call the airline in advance if they were to miss a flight and could rebook another flight at a charge of $25.[18] According to JetBlue officials, passengers holding nonrefundable tickets were more likely to show up for a flight. With these simple methods, JetBlue achieved near total control of its seat sales.

The core of JetBlue's culture was safety, caring, integrity, fun, and passion. Service was top priority at JetBlue and Neeleman referred to JetBlue as "a service company . . . *not* just another airline." For example, even Neeleman sometimes hauled luggage alongside his crews to help meet schedules. On one occasion, he and his crew made phone calls at 3:00 a.m. to alert passengers that their 6:00 a.m. flight was delayed and they need not reach the airport early. JetBlue's policy was to communicate openly and honestly with customers in case of delays. On one Ontario, California, to New York flight, there was a slight skid during the landing at JFK; JetBlue gave out free round-trip tickets to all onboard, even though no one was injured.[19] Neeleman himself flew at least once a week on JetBlue flights and served snacks to get firsthand information and feedback from customers. He expected this service formula to percolate down to all levels of the organization. In his words, "We don't want jaded people working here. If you don't like people or can't deal with customers, you'll be fired."

Neeleman understood the importance of employees in delivering service excellence. JetBlue invested in selecting, training, and maintaining a productive workforce of caring, passionate, fun, and friendly people who wanted to provide customers with the best flying experience possible. Employees were called "Crewmembers" and were offered flexible work hours, initial paid training, free uniforms (unheard of in the industry), and benefits that began the day they started work. Training that emphasized the importance of safety was provided for pilots, flight attendants, technicians, customer service agents, dispatchers, and reservation agents. JetBlue shared its success with employees by providing compensation packages that included competitive salaries, benefits, profit sharing, and a discounted Crewmember stock purchase plan. In addition, a significant number of Crewmembers also participated in the stock option plan. Compensation packages were reviewed regularly to make them competitive so that JetBlue hired and retained the best people possible. JetBlue salary expenses were still less than those of its competitors. Other aspects such as job security, overtime pay, and opportunities for advancement helped offset the purely monetary component of rewards. In Neeleman's opinion, "great People drive solid operating Performance which yields continued Prosperity."[20] He strongly believed that his people were the foundation upon which the company's success was built.[21] To support him in running the company, Neeleman handpicked some noted industry veterans:

- David Barger, president and CEO, who was earlier the vice-president in charge of Continental Airlines' Newark hub from 1994 to 1998 and had extensive experience in airline operations in the New York area.
- John Owen, the chief financial officer, who earlier served as treasurer of Southwest Airlines, 1984–1998, with expertise in aircraft purchase, leasing, and finance transactions.
- Thomas Kelly, executive vice-president and secretary who had worked with Neeleman for more than 18 years as executive vice-president and general counsel at Morris Air, Open Skies.

[16]JetBlue, 2003, Company press release, November 13; www.jetblue.com/learnmore/pressDetail.asp?newsId=213.

[17]Woodyard, C., 2003, Unlike rivals, JetBlue won't do the bump, *USA Today*, October 24; www.upgradebuddy.com/docs/jetblue.html.

[18]Ibid.

[19]DiCarlo, 2001, Management and trends, Jet Blue Skies.

[20]Neeleman, David, 2002, Letter to shareholders, JetBlue annual report; www.jetblue.com/onlineannualreport/letter.html.

[21]JetBlue, www.jetblue.com/onlineannualreport/our-people.html.

Exhibit 3   **Direct Competitor Comparison**

	JetBlue	American Airlines	Southwest Airlines	United Airlines	Delta Air Lines	Industry
Market capitalization ($ billions)	$2.53	$2.45	$11.43	$.166	$1.13	$.931
Employees	4,704	96,400	32,847	63,000	75,100	10,770
Revenue growth (%)	57.20%	(8.80)%	7.50%	(11.50)%	(4.10)%	3.30%
Revenue ($ millions)	$998	$17,440	$5,940	$13,720	$13,300	$1,520
Gross margin (%)	41.31%	17.26%	29.97%	7.72%	8.18%	19.74%
EBITDA ($ millions)	$219.23	$533.00	$867.00	$(392.00)	$336.00	$140.93
Operating margins (%)	16.91%	(4.84)%	8.14%	(9.91)%	(6.40)%	2.73%
Net income ($ millions)	$103.90	(1,230.00)	$443.00	$(2,820.00)	$785.00	$7.30
Earnings per share	$0.969	$(7.855)	$0.538	$(28.213)	$(6.46)	$0.21
Price/earnings ratio	25.59		26.91			17.28

Sources: Company annual reports.

JetBlue's initiatives translated into superior operational performance. Compared to its competitors, the company enjoyed a better completion factor (i.e., the number of flights scheduled versus the number of flights operated), on-time performance, fewer mishandled bags, fewer customer complaints, and virtually no customers denied boarding. In terms of operational efficiency, JetBlue's planes flew 12 hours a day compared with 11 hours at Southwest and 9 at United, US Airways, and American.[22] In its own internal customer surveys, 94 percent ranked their JetBlue experience as "much better" than other airlines and 99 percent said they "definitely would" recommend the airline to others.[23] In 2002 JetBlue was one of only two airlines that made money when all others experienced losses.[24] JetBlue has won numerous awards since it commenced operations in 2000. The company was voted the number one domestic airline in both *Conde Nast Traveler* for 2003 and Readers' Choice Awards in 2002 of all U.S. airlines, and it received the highest score of any airline in the 2003 *Conde Nast Traveler* Business Traveler Awards "coach-only" category. During 2003 JetBlue was also named the number two domestic airline in *Travel and Leisure*'s 2003 World's Best Awards and the "best value for cost." The airline enjoyed an increasing customer base of about 18 million and became the 11th largest passenger carrier in the United States by December 2003.[25] (See Exhibit 3 for a comparison of JetBlue with its competitors, Exhibit 4 for a comparison of JetBlue's stock price with the S&P 500, and Exhibits 5 and 6 for JetBlue's income statements and balance sheets, 1999–2003).

Competitive Reaction

The success of low-cost players in general and JetBlue in particular invoked strong competitive responses. The big players reacted. In April 2003 Delta launched its discount spin-off "Song" airlines to compete directly on JetBlue's routes, with daily flights to West Palm Beach from all three major New York airports. Like JetBlue, Song had all-leather seats, more legroom, and a high-tech in-flight entertainment system. The airline promised to add many more features, including MP3 music and Internet access by early 2004.[26] In addition, Song developed a frequent-flier program that it planned to share with Delta and its partners. Delta Air Lines also strongly retaliated when JetBlue launched its service from Atlanta in May 2003. Delta slashed fares and increased its capacity to Los Angeles airports by nearly 50 percent. United, the number three airline in the United States, also reacted similarly. As a result, JetBlue had to withdraw from Atlanta in December 2003.[27]

[22]Wells, 2002, Lord of the skies.

[23]The Motley Fool (fool.com), 2003, June 20.

[24]Wells, 2002, Lord of the skies.

[25]JetBlue, www.jetblue.com/learnmore/index.html; 10-K report, 2003.

[26]Delta Air Lines Song—News and Information, www.upgradebuddy.com/docs/song.html; Song Web site www.flysong.com/song_and_you/experience/index.jsp.

[27]Isidore, 2003, Too much of a cheap thing?

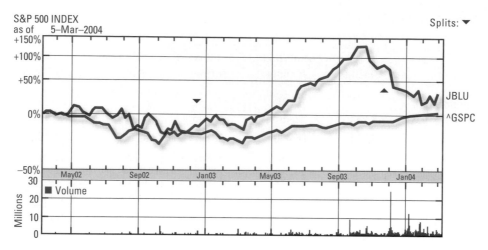

Exhibit 4   Stock Performance of JetBlue versus S&P 500 (March 2002–March 2004)

Source: http://finance.yahoo.com/.

In early 2004, retaliation by other big players appeared imminent. "We're not running from these carriers anymore," vowed the CEO of American Airlines, Gerard J. Arpey, in November 2003. In the same month, United Airlines, the number three player, unveiled plans to launch its low-cost carrier "Ted," (as in UniTED), mainly from Denver.[28] Virgin Airlines' chief executive Richard Branson, who tried to establish a joint venture with Neeleman as early as 1998, was again becoming more interested in entering the U.S. market and had plans to launch Virgin there by early 2005.[29]

Southwest had a clear lead over upstart JetBlue and had been profitable for over 30 straight years. However, Southwest's executives took Neeleman very seriously. "We've got to be prepared for intense competition," said Southwest's CFO, Gary Kelly. Southwest started automating its baggage-handling and boarding pass processes in 2003, aspects that Neeleman had originally pushed for while he worked there. It was also reported that in 2003, Southwest's Kelly sent model JetBlue planes to his executives with a note reading "Know Your Enemy," even though the two airlines did not compete directly at many of the same airports.[30]

According to some analysts, the low-cost carriers seemed to have pretty clear geographic niches. However, further growth initiatives such as expanding into newer routes were likely to bring them into head-on competi-

tion.[31] For JetBlue, growth into any of the other "fortress hubs"—for example, Chicago (United and American), Dallas (American), and Detroit (Northwest)—could provoke strong retaliation from other large players. JetBlue had already experienced such retaliation from Delta in Atlanta and with American in New York. In January 2004 American Airlines initiated an aggressive offer of one trip free for every two trips made on a route in which American competed against JetBlue. The offer was primarily aimed at keeping its customers in New York and Boston from switching to JetBlue.[33] Also, the domestic airline segment was becoming crowded. However, officials of low-cost airlines had a different opinion. According to Southwest's Kelly, "You say, 'Is it getting crowded?' but this is a big country. There's bound to be some competition in the future, but right now there's relatively little overlap." He said that even without adding new cities, the carriers could still grow by adding flights between the existing airports they served.[34]

JetBlue believed that its continued growth would be accomplished by adding additional frequencies on existing routes, connecting new city pairs among the destinations it already served, and through entering new mar-

---

[28]Zellner, 2003, Look who's buzzing the discounters.

[29]Capell, K., & and Zellner, W., 2004, Richard Branson's next big adventure, *BusinessWeek,* March 8.

[30]Gajilan, 2004, The amazing JetBlue.

[31]Ibid.

[32]Donnelly, S. B., 2003, Blue skies: Is JetBlue the next great airline—or just a little too good to be true? *Time Online edition,* May 2; www.time.com.

[33]McGinnis, C., 2004, Wherever JetBlue goes goodies follow, CNN.com, January 27; www.cnn.com. Gillin, E., 2004, AMR takes aim at JetBlue, *The Street.com.* January 7; www.thestreet.com/_yahoo/markets/ericgillin/10135607.html.

[34]Isidore, 2003, Too much of a cheap thing?

Exhibit 5   Income Statements of JetBlue, 1999–2003

	2003	**2002**	**2001**	**2000**	**1999**
			Year Ended December 31		
			(in $ thousands, except per share data)		
Statements of Income Data					
Operating revenues	$998,351	$635,191	$320,414	$104,618	$ —
Operating expenses:					
Salaries, wages and benefits	267,334	162,191	84,762	32,912	6,000
Aircraft fuel	147,316	76,271	41,666	17,634	4
Landing fees and other rents	68,691	43,881	27,342	11,112	447
Aircraft rent	59,963	40,845	32,927	13,027	324
Sales and marketing	53,587	44,345	28,305	16,978	887
Depreciation and amortization	50,397	26,922	10,417	3,995	111
Maintenance materials and repairs	23,114	8,926	4,705	1,052	38
Other operating expenses	159,116	126,823	63,483	29,096	6,405
Total operating expenses	**829,518**	**530,204**	**293,607**	**125,806**	**14,216**
Operating income (loss)	168,833	104,987	26,807	(21,188)	(14,216)
Government compensation[a]	22,761	407	18,706	—	—
Other income (expense)	(16,155)	(10,370)	(3,598)	(381)	685
Income (loss) before income taxes	175,439	95,024	41,915	(21,569)	(13,531)
Income tax expense (benefit)[b]	71,541	40,116	3,378	(239)	233
Net income (loss)	**103,898**	**54,908**	**38,537**	**(21,330)**	**(13,764)**
Earnings (loss) per common share:					
Basic	1.07	0.73	4.39	(11.85)	(16.36)
Diluted	0.97	0.56	0.51	(11.85)	(16.36)
Other Financial Data:					
Operating margin	16.90%	16.50%	8.40%	(20.30)%	—
Ratio of earnings to fixed charges[c]	3.2x	2.7x	1.9x	—	—
Net cash provided by (used in) operating activities	286,337	216,477	111,279	2,824	(6,556)
Net cash used in investing activities	(751,530)	(744,461)	(289,855)	(241,130)	(67,452)
Net cash provided by financing activities	789,136	657,214	261,695	254,463	80,740

[a]Note 14 to the consolidated financial statements on Form 10-K provides a detailed discussion.

[b]In 2001 JetBlue's income tax expense was reduced due to the full reversal of its deferred tax asset valuation allowance. JetBlue does not expect any similar reductions in the future. Note 9 to JetBlue's consolidated financial statements provides details.

[c]According to Form 10-K, earnings were inadequate to cover fixed charges by $26.0 million and $14.2 million for the years ended December 31, 2000 and 1999, respectively.

Source: JetBlue 10-K reports.

kets.[35] JetBlue announced its intention to extend its route network overseas to Caribbean destinations.[36]

Although JetBlue continued looking ambitious, its bases of competitive advantage would not be unchallenged. Competition and imitation followed on the heels

[35]JetBlue, 2003, 10-K report.

[36]JetBlue continuing expansion plan, looking overseas, 2004, *USAToday*, March 3; www.usatoday.com/travel/news/2004-03-03-jetblue-growth_x.htm.

of this advantage and eroded differentiation. On the other hand, JetBlue's cost advantages were not fully developed either. Low labor costs were unlikely to last long given the possibility of unionization of the workforce as the company grew. The aging of its aircraft made the increase in maintenance costs inevitable. The growth in the size of the company and consequently the increase in the number of employees posed challenges to maintaining JetBlue's core culture. Amidst these challenges, in June 2003

Exhibit 6 **JetBlue's Balance Sheet Information, 1999–2003**

	Year Ended December 31				
	2003	**2002**	**2001** (in $ thousands)	**2000**	**1999**
Cash and cash equivalents	$ 570,695	$ 246,752	$117,522	$ 34,403	$ 18,246
Total assets	2,185,757	1,378,923	673,773	344,128	138,182
Total debt	1,108,595	711,931	374,431	177,048	14,577
Convertible redeemable preferred stock	—	—	210,441	163,552	133,478
Common stockholders' equity (deficit)	671,136	414,673	(32,167)	(54,153)	(18,893)

Source: JetBlue 10-K reports.

JetBlue placed an order for 100 new Embraer 190 jet aircraft (from Embraer, the Brazilian jetmaker) with options for another 100. These planes were smaller than the Airbus A320s. They had 100 seats compared to the 156-seat configuration of the A320s and could be used to penetrate midsized markets that the low-cost carriers had largely ignored.[37] JetBlue CFO John Owen said that the planes could be used to connect midsized cities such as Columbus, Ohio, in the midwest with the eastern markets that JetBlue served.[38] Cities such as Austin, Texas, would also be attractive targets because passengers who disliked making connections at Dallas/Fort Worth International Airport for American Airlines or other carriers would like a nonstop flight to New York. Passengers would be willing to pay more on average for such nonstop service, ac-

cording to Dave Barger, JetBlue's president and chief operating officer.[39] However, the move meant a change in JetBlue's one-type aircraft operations model that was at the heart of its low-cost strategy. The change imminently meant added complexities and costs to maintenance, pilot training, and scheduling. It could also complicate labor relations since pilots on smaller planes would be paid less. Also, the smaller Embraer aircraft would have higher expenses per each seat mile, the standard way of measuring expenses in the industry.[40] Even without the Embraer, strains to JetBlue's business model were evident in the decrease in operating margins with increased haul distances. One must ask: Are JetBlue's competitive advantages sustainable? Can it sustain its growth momentum?

[37]Zellner, W., 2003, Strafing the big boys—again, *BusinessWeek,* June 23.

[38]Souder, E., JetBlue plans Carribean services expansion, 2004, DowJones Business News, March 2;
http://biz.yahoo.com/djus/040302/1232000698_2.html.

[39]Torbenson, E., Breaking from formation, 2004, *Dallas Morning News,* February 22: 1-D.

[40]Zellner, 2003, Strafing the big boys.

Appendix   Key Terms Used

Aircraft utilization. The average number of block hours operated per day per aircraft for the total fleet of aircraft.

Available seat miles. The number of seats available for passengers multiplied by the number of miles the seats are flown.

Average fare. The average one-way fare paid per flight segment by a revenue passenger.

Average stage length. Average number of miles flown per flight.

Breakeven load factor. The passenger load factor that will result in operating revenues being equal to operating expenses, assuming constant revenue per passenger mile and expenses.

Load factor. The percentage of aircraft seating capacity that is actually utilized (revenue passenger miles divided by available seat miles).

Operating expense per available seat mile. Operating expenses divided by available seat miles.

Operating revenue per available seat mile. Operating revenues divided by available seat miles.

Passenger revenue per available seat mile. Passenger revenue divided by available seat miles.

Revenue passenger miles. The number of miles flown by revenue passengers.

Revenue passengers. The total number of paying passengers flown on all flight segments.

Yield per passenger mile. The average amount one passenger pays to fly one mile.

Source: JetBlue, SEC filings for 2003.

As 2003 was drawing to a close, William C. Weldon looked back at his first year at the helm of Johnson & Johnson (J&J). The company that he had inherited from his predecessor, Ralph S. Larsen, has for years been one of the most consistent, successful health care companies. J&J has become well known for delivering at least a 10 percent earnings growth year in and year out going back nearly two decades. As a result of this steady performance, the firm's stock price had increased from less than $3, split-adjusted, in the mid-1980s to almost 20 times that now. Even through the recent economic downturn, when the Standard & Poor's 500 stock index fell by 28.1 percent, J&J stock increased by as much as 19.4 percent.

As it has grown, the 117-year-old company has developed into an astonishingly complex enterprise, made up of 204 different businesses organized into three different divisions (see Exhibit 1). The most widely known of these has been the consumer products division that makes Band-Aid adhesive strips, Aveeno skin-care lotions, and various baby products. However, most of J&J's recent growth has come from the divisions responsible for prescription drugs and for medical devices and diagnostics. Drugs alone accounted for almost half of the firm's sales and 61 percent of its operating profits during the last year. With revenues of $36 billion, J&J has already become one of the largest health care companies in the United States.

By the time Weldon took over, however, J&J's crucial businesses were beginning to feel the pressures that have been slowing down the rest of the health care industry. Sales of Procrit, one of the firm's best-selling drugs has failed to show any significant growth over the last year because of the introduction of a new drug by a rival firm. The anticipated slowdown in the growth of Procrit was enough to push the firm's stock down by 3 percent in just one day. Meanwhile, the Food & Drug Administration has recently issued a warning about serious clots that can result from the use of Cypher, J&J's best-selling drug-coated stent launched in the spring of 2003.

Weldon is likely to face his greatest challenge in trying to maintain J&J's growth record even as it begins to run into tougher competition. Over the past decade, a considerable amount of the firm's growth has come from 52 businesses that it bought for $30 billion. As much as 10 percent to 15 percent of its top-line growth each year has come from such investments. But using acquisitions for further growth is likely to become much harder. In order to maintain its 10 percent growth rate, Weldon will have

*This case was prepared by Professor Jamal Shamsie of Michigan State University. This case was developed from published sources as a basis for class discussion rather than to illustrate either effective or ineffective handling of an administrative situation. Copyright © 2004 Jamal Shamsie.

Exhibit 1   Johnson & Johnson Segment Information

Johnson & Johnson is made up of 204 different companies, many of which it has acquired over the years. These individual companies have been assigned to three different divisions:

Pharmaceuticals

Share of firm's sales: 47.2%

Share of firm's operating profits: 60.9%

The most profitable and the fastest-growing division, but its best-known drugs are facing increased competition. Further growth could come from the use of drug delivery devices to develop new formulations of existing products.

Devices & Diagnostics

Share of firm's sales: 34.7%

Share of firm's operating profits: 26.2%

A growing division that has been successful with some recent product introductions, such as the drug-coated stent. May experience more growth with new gene-based tests.

Consumer Products

Share of firm's sales: 18.1%

Share of firm's operating profits: 12.9%

The best-known division, but the least profitable and has the slowest growth. Prospects could improve with over-the-counter versions of drugs that lose their patents.

Source: Johnson & Johnson.

to find ways to increase revenues by almost $4 billion a year. UBS Warburg analyst David Lothson pointed out that to buy something that really affects overall performance is a different proposition for a $36 billion company than it is for a $10 billion company. "You get to a point where finding acquisitions that fit the mold and make a contribution becomes increasingly difficult," Lothson warned. "This puts pressure on the sustainability of this strategy, and ultimately it could break down."[1] Exhibits 2 and 3 illustrate J&J's income statement and balance sheet, 2001–2003.

Creating Autonomous Business Units

Most consumers have known Johnson & Johnson for its Band-Aid adhesives and its baby products, but these consumer products have shown the least profits and the slow-

Exhibit 2   Income Statement
(All numbers in thousands)

	Period Ending		
	December 28, 2003	**December 29, 2002**	**December 30, 2001**
Total Revenue	$41,862,000	$36,298,000	$33,004,000
Cost of revenue	12,176,000	10,447,000	9,536,000
Gross Profit	29,686,000	25,851,000	23,468,000
Operating expenses			
Research development	4,684,000	3,957,000	3,696,000
Selling general and administrative	14,131,000	12,216,000	11,992,000
Nonrecurring	918,000	189,000	—
Total operating expenses	—	—	—
Operating Income or Loss	9,953,000	9,489,000	7,780,000
Income from continuing operations			
Total other income/expenses, net	562,000	(38,000)	271,000
Earnings before interest and taxes	10,515,000	9,451,000	8,051,000
Interest expense	207,000	160,000	153,000
Income before tax	10,308,000	9,291,000	7,898,000
Income tax expense	3,111,000	2,694,000	2,230,000
Net income from continuing operations	7,197,000	6,597,000	5,668,000
Net Income	$ 7,197,000	$ 6,597,000	$ 5,668,000

Source: Johnson & Johnson annual reports.

est growth among J&J's three divisions. In the last year this division accounted for only 18.1 percent of the firm's sales and 12.9 percent of its operating profits. Nevertheless, the firm values this business because it helps build a strong image among the public that helps with the sales in its other divisions.

The majority of J&J's revenues and profits have come from its pharmaceuticals and medical devices. These two divisions have accounted for 81.9 percent of the firm's sales and 87.1 percent of its operating profits over the last year. Its competitors in this field are well aware of J&J's rare combination of scientific expertise and marketing savvy that have helped it to gain a leading position. It has developed a strong reputation for regularly developing or acquiring innovative products and then selling them more aggressively than almost any other company.

To a large extent, however, J&J's success across its three divisions and many different businesses has hinged on its unique structure and culture. Each of its far-flung units has operated pretty much as an independent enterprise. The firm has been able to turn itself into a powerhouse precisely because each of the businesses that it either buys or starts has always been granted virtual autonomy. That independence has fostered an entrepreneurial attitude that has kept J&J intensely competitive as others around it have faltered.

In other words, every business has been given considerable freedom to set its own strategy. Besides developing their strategies, these units are allowed to plan for their own resources; many even have their own finance and human resources departments. While this degree of decentralization makes for relatively high overhead costs, none of the executives who have run J&J, Weldon included, have ever thought that this was too high a price to pay.

In spite of the benefits that J&J has derived from giving considerable autonomy to its various enterprises, there

Exhibit 3   **Balance Sheet**
(All numbers in thousands)

	Period Ending		
	December 28, 2003	December 29, 2002	December 30, 2001
Assets			
Current assets			
Cash and cash equivalents	$ 5,377,000	$ 2,894,000	$ 3,758,000
Short-term investments	4,146,000	4,581,000	4,214,000
Net receivables	8,100,000	6,818,000	5,822,000
Inventory	3,588,000	3,303,000	2,992,000
Other current assets	1,784,000	1,670,000	1,687,000
Total Current Assets	22,995,000	19,266,000	18,473,000
Long-term investments	84,000	121,000	969,000
Property, plant, and equipment	9,846,000	8,710,000	7,719,000
Goodwill	5,390,000	4,653,000	—
Intangible assets	6,149,000	4,593,000	9,077,000
Other assets	3,107,000	2,977,000	1,962,000
Deferred long-term asset charges	692,000	236,000	288,000
Total Assets	48,263,000	40,556,000	38,488,000
Liabilities			
Current liabilities			
Accounts payable	12,309,000	9,332,000	7,479,000
Short/current long-term debt	1,139,000	2,117,000	565,000
Total Current Liabilities	13,448,000	11,449,000	8,044,000
Long-term debt	2,955,000	2,022,000	4,087,000
Other liabilities	4,211,000	3,745,000	1,631,000
Deferred long-term liability charges	780,000	643,000	493,000
Total Liabilities	21,394,000	17,859,000	14,255,000
Stockholders' Equity			
Common stock	3,120,000	3,120,000	3,120,000
Retained earnings	30,503,000	26,571,000	23,066,000
Treasury stock	(6,146,000)	(6,127,000)	(1,393,000)
Other stockholder equity	(608,000)	(867,000)	(560,000)
Total Stockholder Equity	26,869,000	22,697,000	24,233,000
Net Tangible Assets	$15,330,000	$13,451,000	$15,156,000

Source: Johnson & Johnson annual reports.

is a growing feeling that they can no longer operate in near isolation. Weldon has begun to realize, as do most others in the industry, that some of the most important breakthroughs in 21st-century medicine are likely to come from the ability to apply scientific advances in one discipline to another. The treatment of many diseases is becoming vastly more sophisticated: Sutures are coated with drugs to prevent infections; tests based on genomic research could determine who will respond to a certain cancer drug; defibrillators may be linked to computers that alert doctors when patients have abnormal heart rhythms.

Pushing for Synergies

Weldon strongly believes that J&J is perfectly positioned to profit from this shift toward combining drugs, devices, and diagnostics since few companies can match its reach and strength in these basic areas. According to Weldon, "There is a convergence that will allow us to do things we haven't done before."[2] Indeed, J&J has top-notch products in each of those categories. It has been boosting its research and development budget by more than 10 percent annually for the past few years, which puts it among the top spenders, and now employs 9,300 scientists in 40 laboratories around the world.

But Weldon feels that J&J can profit from this convergence only if its fiercely independent businesses can be made to work together. Through pushing these units to pool their resources, Weldon believes that the firm could become one of the few that might be able to attain that often-promised, rarely delivered idea of synergy. Some of the firm's new products, such as the new drug-coated stent, have clearly resulted from the collaborative efforts and sharing of ideas between its various far-flung divisions.

Weldon's vision for the new J&J may well have emerged from the steps that he took to reshape the pharmaceutical operation shortly after he took it over in 1998. At the time, J&J's drug business had been making solid gains as a result of popular products such as the anemia drug Procrit and the antipsychotic medication Risperdal. But the pipeline of new drugs was beginning to sputter after several potential treatments had failed in late-stage testing.

Weldon's solution was to create a new post to oversee all of the pharmaceutical division's R&D efforts. He also formed a divisional committee that brought together executives from R&D with those from sales and marketing to decide which projects to green-light. Until then, the R&D groups had made these critical decisions on their own. No one had thought it might be beneficial to involve any other departments in these decisions. "Some people may have thought Bill curtailed their freedom," said Dr. Per A. Peterson, who oversees all pharmaceutical research and development. "But we've improved the decision making to eliminate compounds that just won't make it."[3]

In order to promote this idea of synergy, however, Weldon has to create this kind of cooperation throughout the company. He needs to push for this collaboration between J&J's units without quashing the entrepreneurial spirit that has spearheaded most of the growth of the firm to date. Jerry Caccott, managing director of the consulting firm Strategic Decisions Group, emphasized that cultivating those alliances "would be challenging in any organization, but particularly in an organization that has been so successful because of its decentralized culture."[4]

Shifting the Company Culture

Weldon, like every other leader in the company's history, has worked his way up through the ranks. His long tenure within the firm has turned him into a true believer in the J&J system. He certainly does not want to undermine the entrepreneurial spirit that has resulted from the autonomy that had been given to each of the businesses. Consequently, even though Weldon may talk incessantly about synergy and convergence, he has been cautious in the actual steps he has taken to push J&J's units to collaborate with each other.

For the most part, Weldon has confined himself to the development of new systems to foster better communication and more frequent collaboration among J&J's disparate operations. Among other things, he has worked with James T. Lenehan, vice-chairman and president of J&J, to set up groups that draw people from across the firm to focus their efforts on specific diseases. Each of the groups is expected to report every six months on potential strategies and projects.

Although most of the changes that Weldon has instituted at J&J are not likely to yield real results for some time, there is already evidence that this new collaboration is working. Perhaps the most promising result of this approach has been J&J's drug-coated stent Cypher. The highly successful new addition to the firm's lineup was a result of the efforts of teams that combined people from the drug business with others from the medical device business. They collaborated on manufacturing the stent, which props open arteries after angioplasty. Weldon claims that if J&J had not been able to bring together people with different types of expertise, it could not have developed the stent without getting assistance from outside the firm.

Even the company's fabled consumer brands have been starting to take on a scientific edge. Its new liquid Band-Aid is based on a material used in a wound-closing product sold by one of J&J's hospital supply businesses. And J&J has used its prescription antifungal treatment Nizoral to develop a dandruff shampoo. Products developed out of such a form of cross-fertilization have allowed the firm's consumer business to increase its operating margins from 13.8 percent in 2000 to 18.7 percent in 2002.

Some of the projects that J&J is currently working on could produce even more significant results. Researchers working on genomic studies in the firm's labs were building a massive database using gene patterns that correlate to a certain disease or to someone's likely response to a particular drug. Weldon encouraged them to share this data with the various business units. As a result, the diagnostics team has been working on a test that the drug R&D folks could use to predict which patients would benefit from an experimental cancer therapy. If the test works, it could significantly cut J&J's drug-development costs.

Maintaining the Pressure

Even as Weldon moves carefully to encourage collaboration between the business units, he has continued to push for the highest possible levels of performance. Those who know him well would say that he is compulsively competitive. As Weldon has been known to state on more than one occasion, "It's no fun to be second."[5] He is such an intense athlete that he was just a sprint away from ruining his knee altogether when he finally decided to give up playing basketball.

In order to make J&J more competitive, Weldon has made some aggressive moves. Two years ago, he pushed for the company's biggest acquisition ever with the $13.2 billion purchase of drug-delivery player Alza Corporation. But Weldon has been trying to let his managers get more involved in J&J's dealings with other firms. He has been closely following the negotiations that his firm has periodically been holding with Guidant Corporation, which makes implantable defibrillators. A deal with Guidant would allow J&J to move into the growing field of cardiovascular medicine that would appear to be perfectly suited for some of the emerging combination therapies. But Weldon is clearly taking a back seat and letting his managers take the lead in these talks.

It is not always easy, however, for Weldon to keep a respectable distance from his managers. For example, he has entrusted the drug business to Christine A. Poon, whom he recruited from Bristol-Myers Squibb Company. Nevertheless, when several senior executives were hammering out details on the $2.4 billion acquisition of Scios Incorporated, a biotech company that has a drug for congestive heart failure, Weldon showed up to join the group. Weldon says he wanted to make an appearance because it was Poon's first major acquisition. "I wanted to be there, if nothing else, to give her some moral support," he said.[6]

Weldon is also letting his managers make their own decisions on the teams where they are working with each other on various projects. He usually likes to be briefed once a month on the progress being made on these projects. Beyond that, Weldon claims that he likes to trust his people. "They are the experts who know the marketplace, know the hospitals, and know the cardiologists," Weldon said about the team that has been working on the Cypher stent. "I have the utmost confidence in them."[7]

Even as Weldon tries to let his managers handle their own affairs, he clearly expects them to seek results with the same tenacity that he displayed in his climb to the top.

As he rose through the ranks at J&J, Weldon became famous for setting near-impossible goals for his people and holding them to it. And for those executives who fall short, Weldon usually has no difficulty in making it clear that he does not like to be disappointed. When a new J&J drug business, Centocor Incorporated, failed to meet the aggressive sales goals it had set for 2000, Weldon was at its headquarters before the week was out. Everyone at the firm knew they could not allow their performance to fall below the targeted level for the next year.

Is There a Cure Ahead?

Weldon will need to draw on all of his competitive spirit to maintain Johnson & Johnson's growth trajectory. At this point, most of J&J's important drugs are under assault from competitors. Growth of the company's biggest-selling product, the $4.3 billion Procrit franchise, has stalled in the face of Aranesp, a drug from archrival Amgen Inc. And its European version called Eprex has been plagued by side-effect problems. J&J's $1.3 billion rheumatoid arthritis drug Remicade is also having to deal with a strong challenge from competing products launched by Amgen and Abbott Laboratories. Even its successful stent Cypher will soon have to deal with a rival offering from Boston Scientific Corporation, which some experts are already claiming to be better.

Weldon has cut costs wherever possible and increased spending on the development of new drugs. But he recognizes that no major new products are likely to come out before 2006. New drugs for diabetes and multiple sclerosis that could have been launched earlier have not been able to make it through clinical trials. CFO Robert J. Darretta Jr. admits, "We've been going through a period well above historic averages. The next couple of years look tougher."[8]

To make matters worse, Weldon is also aware that it will not be easy to grow through acquiring companies with promising drugs that could become blockbusters. To begin with, all of the pharmaceutical firms have been seeking the same kinds of deals. And there are relatively few companies with products far enough along and important enough to make a real difference to J&J.

Nonetheless, Weldon and his team are confident that J&J will be able to find ways to maintain its 10 percent annual growth rate over the long haul. Weldon argues that Procrit will continue to dominate the anemia market and Remicade still has considerable potential because it can be used to treat many other conditions. He is also confident that the heavier investments in developing new drugs will pay off and that J&J will still be able to make the acquisitions that would be a good fit for the firm. According to Poon, who heads the firm's pharmaceutical group, "We'll deal with these external challenges as we have always."[9]

Beyond these, Weldon has high hopes for strong results from his efforts to get different parts of J&J to work together. Already, a team of employees is combining the slow release technology from Alza Corporation with an antipsychotic drug from Centocor Corporation. Other cross-divisional teams are working on possible new treatments for diabetes and stroke.

As Weldon struggles to maintain J&J's performance record, he realizes that he will need to encourage its businesses to work more closely together than they have ever done in the past. At the same time, he is acutely aware that much of the firm's success has resulted from the relative autonomy that it has granted to each of its business units. Weldon knows that even as he strives to push for more collaborative effort, he does not want to threaten the entrepreneurial spirit that has served J&J so well.

Endnotes

1. Barrett, Amy, 2003, Staying on top, *BusinessWeek,* May 5: 61.
2. Ibid., 62.
3. Ibid., 63.
4. Ibid., 62.
5. Ibid.
6. Ibid., 68.
7. Ibid., 66.
8. Barrett, Amy, 2004, Toughing out the drought, *BusinessWeek,* January 26: 84.
9. Ibid., 85.

People are our most valuable asset. They must feel
secure, important, challenged, in control of their destiny,
confident in their leadership, be responsive to common
goals, believe they are being treated fairly, have easy
access to authority and open lines of communication in
all possible directions. Perhaps the most important task
Lincoln employees face today is that of establishing an
example for others in the Lincoln organization in other
parts of the world. We need to maximize the benefits of
cooperation and teamwork, fusing high technology with
human talent, so that we here in the USA and all of our
subsidiary and joint venture operations will be in a
position to realize our full potential.

George Willis, CEO, The Lincoln Electric Company

The Lincoln Electric Company was the world's largest
manufacturer of arc-welding products and a leading producer of industrial electric motors. The firm employed
2,400 workers in two U.S. factories near Cleveland and an
equal number in eleven factories located in other countries. This did not include the field sales force of more than
200. The company's U.S. market share (for arc-welding
products) was estimated at more than 40 percent.

The Lincoln incentive management plan had been
well known for many years. Many college management
texts referred to the Lincoln plan as a model for achieving
higher worker productivity. Certainly, the firm was successful according to the usual measures.

When James F. Lincoln died in 1965, there had been
some concerns even among employees, that the management system would fall into disarray, that profits would
decline, and that year-end bonuses might be discontinued.
Quite the contrary, 24 years after Lincoln's death, the
company appeared to be as strong as ever. Each year, except the recession years 1982 and 1983, saw high profits
and bonuses. Employee morale and productivity remained
very good. Employee turnover was almost nonexistent except for retirements. Lincoln's market share was stable.
The historically high stock dividends continued.

A Historical Sketch

In 1895, after being "frozen out" of the depression-ravaged
Elliott-Lincoln Company, a maker of Lincoln-designed
electric motors, John C. Lincoln, took out his second patent
and began to manufacture his improved motor. He opened
his new business, unincorporated, with $200 he had earned

*By Arthur D. Sharplin, McNeese State University.

Reprinted by permission from the *Case Research Journal*. Copyright © 1989
by Arthur D. Sharplin and the North American Case Research Association.
All rights reserved.

redesigning a motor for young Herbert Henry Dow, who
later founded the Dow Chemical Company.

Started during an economic depression and cursed by
a major fire after only one year in business, the company
grew, but hardly prospered, through its first quarter-
century. In 1906, John C. Lincoln incorporated the business and moved from his one-room, fourth-floor factory
to a new three-story building he erected in east Cleveland.
He expanded his workforce to 30 and sales grew to over
$50,000 a year. John preferred being an engineer and in-
ventor rather than a manager, though, and it was to be left
to another Lincoln to manage the company through its
years of success.

In 1907, after a bout with typhoid fever forced him to
leave Ohio State University in his senior year, James R.
Lincoln, John's younger brother, joined the fledgling
company. In 1914 he became active head of the firm, with
the titles general manager and vice president. John remained president of the company for some years but became more involved in other business ventures and in his
work as an inventor.

One of James Lincoln's early actions was to ask the
employees to elect representatives to a committee (called the
"Advisory Board"), which would advise him on company
operations. The Advisory Board met with the chief executive officer every two weeks. This was only the first of a series of innovative personnel policies which, over the years,
distinguished Lincoln Electric from its contemporaries.

The first year the Advisory Board was in existence,
working hours were reduced from 55 per week, then standard, to 50 hours a week. In 1915, the company gave each
employee a paid-up life insurance policy. A welding
school, which continues today, was begun in 1917. In
1918, an employee bonus plan was attempted. It was not
continued, but the idea was to resurface later.

The Lincoln Electric Employees' Association was
formed in 1919 to provide health benefits and social activities. Over the years, it assumed several additional
functions. In 1923, a piecework pay system was in effect,
employees got two weeks' paid vacation each year, and
wages were adjusted for changes in the consumer price
index. Approximately 30 percent of the common stock
was set aside for key employees in 1914. A stock purchase
plan for all employees was begun in 1925.

The board of directors voted to start a suggestion system in 1929. Cash awards, a part of the early program,
were discontinued in the mid-1980s. Suggestions were rewarded by additional "points," which affected year-end
bonuses.

The legendary Lincoln bonus plan was proposed by
the Advisory Board and accepted on a trial basis in 1934.
The first annual bonus amounted to about 25 percent of

wages. There was a bonus every year after that. The bonus plan became a cornerstone of the Lincoln management system, and recent bonuses approximated annual wages.

By 1944 Lincoln employees enjoyed a pension plan, a policy of promotion from within, and continuous employment. Base pay rates were determined by formal job evaluation, and a merit rating system was in effect.

In the prologue of James R. Lincoln's last book, Charles G. Herbruck wrote regarding the foregoing personnel innovations:

> They were not to buy good behavior. They were not efforts to increase profit and were not antidotes to labor difficulties. They did not constitute a "do-gooder" program. They were expressions of mutual respect for each person's importance to the job to be done. All of them reflect the leadership of James Lincoln, under whom they were nurtured and propagated.

During World War II, Lincoln prospered as never before. By the start of the war, the company was the world's largest manufacturer of arc-welding products. Sales of about $4 million in 1934 grew to $24 million by 1941. Productivity per employee more than doubled during the same period. The Navy's Price Review Board challenged the high profits. The Internal Revenue Service questioned the tax deductibility of employee bonuses, arguing they were not "ordinary and necessary" costs of doing business, but the forceful and articulate James Lincoln was able to overcome the objections.

Certainly after 1935 and probably for several years before that, Lincoln productivity was well above the average for similar companies. The company claimed levels of productivity more than twice those for other manufacturers from 1945 onward. Information available from outside sources tended to support these claims.

Company Philosophy

James R. Lincoln was the son of a Congregational minister, and Christian principles were at the center of his business philosophy. The confidence that he had in the efficacy of Christ's teachings was illustrated by the following remark taken from one of his books:

> The Christian ethic should control our acts. If it did control our acts, the savings in cost of distribution would be tremendous. Advertising would be a contact of the expert consultant with the customer, in order to give the customer the best product available when all of the customer's needs are considered. Competition then would be in improving the quality of products and increasing efficiency in producing and distributing them, not in deception, as is now too customary. Pricing would reflect efficiency of production; it would not be a selling dodge that the customer may well be sorry he accepted. It would be proper for all concerned and rewarding for the ability used in producing the product.

There was no indication that Lincoln attempted to evangelize his employees or customers—or the general public, for that matter. Neither the chairman of the board and chief executive, George Willis, nor the president, Donald F. Hastings, mentioned the Christian gospel in speeches and interviews. The company motto, "The actual is limited, the possible is immense," was prominently displayed, but there was no display of religious slogans and no company chapel.

Attitude toward the Customer   James Lincoln saw the customer's needs as the raison d'être for every company. "When any company has achieved success so that it is attractive as an investment," he wrote, "all money usually needed for expansion is supplied by the customer in retained earnings. It is obvious that the customer's interests, not the stockholder's, should come first." In 1947 he said, "Care should be taken . . . not to rivet attention on profit between 'How much do I get?' and 'How do I make this better, cheaper, more useful?'; the difference is fundamental and decisive." Willis, too, ranked the customer as management's most important constituency. This was reflected in Lincoln's policy to "at all times price on the basis of cost and at all times keep pressure on our cost." Lincoln's goal, often stated, was "to build a better and better product at a lower and lower price." "It is obvious," James Lincoln said, "that the customer's interests should be the first goal of industry."

Attitude toward Stockholders   Stockholders were given last priority at Lincoln. This was a continuation of James Lincoln's philosophy: "The last group to be considered is the stockholders who own stock because they think it would be more profitable than investing money in any other way." Concerning division of the largess produced by incentive management, he wrote, "The absentee stockholder also will get his share, even if undeserved, out of the greatly increased profit that the efficiency produces."

Attitude toward Unionism   There was never a serious effort to organize Lincoln employees. While James Lincoln criticized the labor movement for "selfishly attempting to better its position at the expense of the people it must serve," he still had kind words for union members. He excused abuses of union power as "the natural reactions of human beings to the abuses to which management has subjected them." Lincoln's idea of the correct relationship between workers and managers was shown by this comment: "Labor and management are properly not warring camps; they are parts of one organization in which they must and should cooperate fully and happily."

Beliefs and Assumptions about Employees   If fulfilling customer needs was the desired goal of business, then employee performance and productivity were the means by which this goal could best be achieved. It was the Lincoln attitude toward employees, reflected in the following comments by James Lincoln, which was credited by many with creating the success the company experienced:

> The greatest fear of the worker, which is the same as the greatest fear of the industrialist in operating a company, is the lack of income . . . The industrial manager is very conscious of his company's need of uninterrupted income. He is completely oblivious, evidently, of the fact that the worker has the same need.
>
>   [The worker] is just as eager as any manager is to be part of a team that is properly organized and working for the advancement of our economy . . . He has no desire to make profits for those who do not hold up their end in production, as is true of absentee stockholders and inactive people in the company.
>
>   If money is to be used as an incentive, the program must provide that what is paid to the worker is what he has earned. The earnings of each must be in accordance with accomplishment.
>
>   Status is of great importance in all human relationships. The greatest incentive that money has, usually, is that it is a symbol of success . . . The resulting status is the real incentive . . . Money alone can be an incentive to the miser only.
>
>   There must be complete honesty and understanding between the hourly worker and management if high efficiency is to be obtained.

Lincoln's Business

Arc welding had been the standard joining method in shipbuilding for decades. It was the predominant way of connecting steel in the construction industry. Most industrial plants had their own welding shops for maintenance and construction. Manufacturers of tractors and all kinds of heavy equipment used arc welding extensively in the manufacturing process. Many hobbyists had their own welding machines and used them for making metal items such as patio furniture and barbecue pits. The popularity of welded sculpture as an art form was growing.

While advances in welding technology were frequent, arc-welding products, in the main, hardly changed. Lincoln's Innershield process was a notable exception. This process, described later, lowered welding cost and improved quality and speed in many applications. The most widely used Lincoln electrode, the Fleetweld 5P, was virtually the same from the 1930s to 1989. For at least four decades, the most popular engine-driven welder in the world, the Lincoln SA-200, had been a gray-colored assembly, including a four-cylinder Continental "Red Seal" engine and a 200-ampere direct current generator with two current-control knobs. A 1989 model SA-200 even weighed almost the same as the 1950 model, and it certainly was little changed in appearance.

The company's share of the U.S. arc-welding products market appeared to have been about 40 percent for many years. The welding products market had grown somewhat faster than the level of industry in general. The market was highly price-competitive, with variations in prices of standard items normally amounting to only 1 or 2 percent. Lincoln's products were sold directly by its engineering-oriented sales force and indirectly through its distributor organization. Advertising expenditures amounted to less than 0.75 percent of sales. Research and development expenditures typically ranged from $10 million to $12 million, considerably more than competitors spent.

The other major welding process, flame welding, had not been competitive with arc welding since the 1930s. However, plasma arc welding, a relatively new process which used a conducting stream of superheated gas (plasma) to confine the welding current to a small area, had made some inroads, especially in metal tubing manufacturing, in recent years. Major advances in technology which would produce an alternative superior to arc welding within the next decade or so appeared unlikely. Also, it seemed likely that changes in the machines and techniques used in arc welding would be evolutionary rather than revolutionary.

Products

The company was primarily engaged in the manufacture and sale of arc-welding products—electric welding machines and metal electrodes. Lincoln also produced electric motors ranging from 0.5 to 200 horsepower. Motors constituted about 8 to 10 percent of total sales. Several million dollars had recently been invested in automated equipment that would double Lincoln's manufacturing capacity for 0.5- to 20-horsepower electric motors.

The electric welding machines, some consisting of a transformer or motor and generator arrangement powered by commercial electricity and others consisting of an internal combustion engine and generator, were designed to produce 30 to 1,500 amperes of electrical power. This electrical current was used to melt a consumable metal electrode, with the molten metal being transferred in superhot spray to the metal joint being welded. Very high temperatures and hot sparks were produced, and operators usually had to wear special eye and face protection and leather gloves, often along with leather aprons and sleeves.

Lincoln and its competitors marketed a wide range of general-purpose and specialty electrodes for welding mild steel, aluminum, cast iron, and stainless and special steels. Most of these electrodes were designed to meet the standards of the American Welding Society, a trade association. They were thus essentially the same as to size and composition from one manufacturer to another. Every electrode manufacturer had a limited number of unique products, but these typically constituted only a small percentage of total sales.

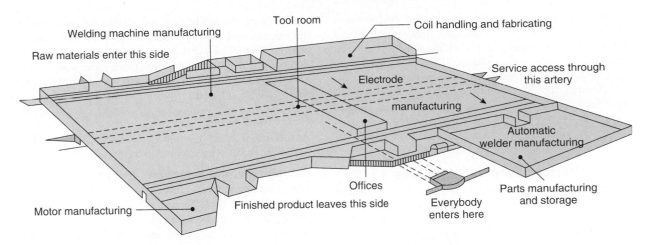

Welding machine manufacturing

Raw materials enter this side

Tool room

Coil handling and fabricating

Electrode

Service access through
this artery

manufacturing

Automatic
welder manufacturing

Offices

Motor manufacturing

Finished product leaves this side

Everybody
enters here

Parts manufacturing
and storage

Exhibit 1   Main Factory Layout

Welding electrodes were of two basic types:

1. Coated "stick" electrodes, usually 14 inches long and smaller than a pencil in diameter, were held in a special insulated holder by the operator, who had to manipulate the electrode in order to maintain a proper arc width and pattern of deposition of the metal being transferred. Stick electrodes were packaged in 6- to 50-pound boxes.

2. Coiled wire, ranging in diameter from 0.035 to 0.219 inch, was designed to be fed continuously to the welding arc through a "gun" held by the operator or positioned by automatic positioning equipment. The wire was packaged in coils, reels, and drums weighing from 14 to 1,000 pounds and could be solid or flux-cored.

Manufacturing Processes

The main plant was in Euclid, Ohio, a suburb on Cleveland's east side. The layout of the plant is shown in Exhibit 1. There were no warehouses. Materials flowed from the ½-mile-long dock on the north side of the plant through the production lines to a very limited storage and loading area on the south side. Materials used on each workstation were stored as close as possible to the workstation. The administrative offices, near the center of the factory, were entirely functional. A corridor below the main level provided access to the factory floor from the main entrance near the center of the plant. *Fortune* magazine declared the Euclid facility one of America's 10 best-managed factories,[1] and compared it with a General Electric plant also on the list:

Stepping into GE's spanking new dishwasher plant, an awed supplier said, is like stepping "into the Hyatt Re-

[1]Bylinsky, Gene, 1984, America's best-managed factories, *Fortune,* May 28: 16.

gency." By comparison, stepping into Lincoln Electric's 33-year-old, cavernous, dimly lit factory is like stumbling into a dingy big-city YMCA. It's only when one starts looking at how these factories do things that similarities become apparent. They have found ways to merge design with manufacturing, build in quality, make wise choices about automation, get close to customers, and handle their workforces.

A new Lincoln plant in Mentor, Ohio, housed some of the electrode production operations, which had been moved from the main plant.

Electrode manufacturing was highly capital-intensive. Metal rods purchased from steel producers were drawn down to smaller diameters, cut to length, coated with pressed-powder "flux" for stick electrodes or plated with copper (for conductivity), and put into coils or spools for wire. Lincoln's Innershield wire was hollow and filled with a material similar to that used to coat stick electrodes. As mentioned earlier, this represented a major innovation in welding technology when it was introduced. The company was highly secretive about its electrode production processes, and outsiders were not given access to the details of those processes.

Lincoln welding machines and electric motors were made on a series of assembly lines. Gasoline and diesel engines were purchased partially assembled, but practically all other components were made from basic industrial products (e.g., steel bars and sheets and bar copper conductor wire).

Individual components, such as gasoline tanks for engine-driven welders and steel shafts for motors and generators, were made by numerous small "factories within a factory." The shaft for a certain generator, for example, was made from a raw steel bar by one operator who used five large machines, all running continuously. A saw cut the bar to length, a digital lathe machined different sections to varying diameters, a special milling machine cut a slot for the keyway, and so forth, until a finished shaft was produced. The operator moved the shafts from machine to machine and made necessary adjustments.

Another operator punched, shaped, and painted sheet-metal cowling parts. One assembled steel laminations onto a rotor shaft, then wound, insulated, and tested the rotors. Finished components were moved by crane operators to the nearby assembly lines.

Worker Performance and Attitudes

Exceptional worker performance at Lincoln was a matter of record. The typical Lincoln employee earned about twice as much as other factory workers in the Cleveland area. Yet the company's labor cost per sales dollar in 1989, 26 cents, was well below the industry average. Worker turnover was practically nonexistent except for retirements and departures by new employees.

Sales per Lincoln factory employee exceeded $150,000. An observer at the factory quickly saw why this figure was so high. Each worker was proceeding busily and thoughtfully about the task at hand. There was no idle chatter. Most workers took no coffee breaks. Many operated several machines and made a substantial component unaided. The supervisors were busy with planning and record-keeping duties and hardly glanced at the people they "supervised." The manufacturing procedures appeared to be efficient—no unnecessary steps, no wasted motions, no wasted materials. Finished components moved smoothly to subsequent workstations.

The Appendix (page 726) gives summaries of interviews with employees.

Organizational Structure

Lincoln never allowed development of a formal organizational chart. The objective of this policy was to ensure maximum flexibility. An open-door policy was practiced throughout the company, and personnel were encouraged to take problems to the persons most capable of resolving them. Once, Harvard Business School researchers prepared an organizational chart reflecting the implied relationships at Lincoln. The chart became available within the company, and management felt that the chart had a disruptive effect. Therefore, no organizational chart appears in this report.

Perhaps because of the quality and enthusiasm of the Lincoln workforce, routine supervision was almost nonexistent. A typical production foreman, for example, supervised as many as 100 workers, a span of control which did not allow more than infrequent worker-supervisor interaction.

Position tides and traditional flows of authority did imply something of an organizational structure, however. For example, the vice-president, sales, and the vice-president, electrode division, reported to the president, as did various staff assistants such as the personnel director and the director of purchasing. Using such implied relationships, it was determined that production workers had two, or at most three, levels of supervision between themselves and the president.

Personnel Policies

As mentioned earlier, Lincoln's remarkable personnel practices were credited by many with the company's success.

Recruitment and Selection　Every job opening was advertised internally on company bulletin boards, and any employee could apply for any job so advertised. External hiring was permitted only for entry-level positions. Selection for these jobs was done on the basis of personal interviews; there was no aptitude or psychological testing. Not even a high school diploma was required—except for engineering and sales positions, which were filled by graduate engineers. A committee consisting of vice-presidents and supervisors interviewed candidates initially cleared by the Personnel Department. Final selection was made by the supervisor who had a job opening. Out of over 3,500 applicants interviewed by the Personnel Department during one period, fewer than 300 were hired.

Job Security　In 1958 Lincoln formalized its guaranteed continuous employment policy, which had already been in effect for many years. There had been no layoffs since World War II. Since 1958, every worker with over 2 years' longevity had been guaranteed at least 30 hours per week, 49 weeks per year.

The policy was never so severely tested as during the 1981–1983 recession. As a manufacturer of capital goods, Lincoln had business that was highly cyclical. In previous recessions the company had been able to avoid major sales declines. However, sales plummeted 32 percent in 1982 and another 16 percent the next year. Few companies could withstand such a revenue collapse and remain profitable. Yet, not only did Lincoln earn profits, but no employee was laid off and year-end incentive bonuses continued. To weather the storm, management cut most of the nonsalaried workers back to 30 hours a week for varying periods of time. Many employees were reassigned, and the total workforce was slightly reduced through normal attrition and restricted hiring. Many employees grumbled at their unexpected misfortune, probably to the surprise and dismay of some Lincoln managers. However, sales and profits—and employee bonuses—soon rebounded, and all was well again.

Performance Evaluations　Each supervisor formally evaluated subordinates twice a year using the cards shown in Exhibit 2. The employee performance criteria—"quality," "dependability," "ideas and cooperation," and "output"—were considered to be independent of each other.

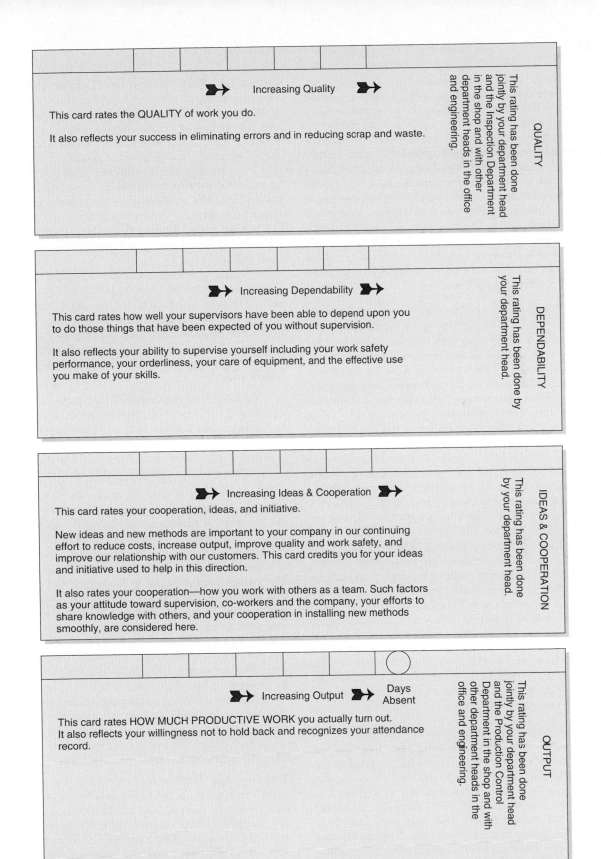

QUALITY

→→ Increasing Quality →→

This card rates the QUALITY of work you do.

It also reflects your success in eliminating errors and in reducing scrap and waste.

This rating has been done jointly by your department head and the Inspection Department in the shop and with other department heads in the office and engineering.

DEPENDABILITY

→→ Increasing Dependability →→

This card rates how well your supervisors have been able to depend upon you to do those things that have been expected of you without supervision.

It also reflects your ability to supervise yourself including your work safety performance, your orderliness, your care of equipment, and the effective use you make of your skills.

This rating has been done by your department head.

IDEAS & COOPERATION

→→ Increasing Ideas & Cooperation →→

This card rates your cooperation, ideas, and initiative.

New ideas and new methods are important to your company in our continuing effort to reduce costs, increase output, improve quality and work safety, and improve our relationship with our customers. This card credits you for your ideas and initiative used to help in this direction.

It also rates your cooperation—how you work with others as a team. Such factors as your attitude toward supervision, co-workers and the company, your efforts to share knowledge with others, and your cooperation in installing new methods smoothly, are considered here.

This rating has been done by your department head.

OUTPUT

→→ Increasing Output →→ Days Absent

This card rates HOW MUCH PRODUCTIVE WORK you actually turn out.
It also reflects your willingness not to hold back and recognizes your attendance record.

This rating has been done jointly by your department head and the Production Control Department in the shop and with other department heads in the office and engineering.

Exhibit 2   Merit Rating Cards

Marks on the cards were converted to numerical scores which were forced to average 100 for each evaluating supervisor. Individual merit rating scores normally ranged from 80 to 110. Any score over 110 required a special letter to top management. These scores (over 110) were not considered in computing the required 100-point average for each evaluating supervisor. Suggestions for improvements often resulted in recommendations for exceptionally high performance scores. Supervisors discussed individual performance marks with the employees concerned. Each warranty claim was traced to the individual employee whose work caused the defect. The employee's performance score might be reduced, or the worker might be required to repay the cost of servicing the warranty claim by working without pay.

Compensation   Basic wage levels for jobs at Lincoln were determined by a wage survey of similar jobs in the Cleveland area. These rates were adjusted quarterly in accordance with changes in the Cleveland area wage index. Insofar as possible, base wage rates were translated into piece rates. Practically all production workers and many others—for example, some forklift operators—were paid by piece rate. Once established, piece rates were never changed unless a substantive change in the way a job was done resulted from a source other than the worker doing the job.

In December of each year, a portion of annual profits was distributed to employees as bonuses. Incentive bonuses since 1934 had averaged about 90 percent of annual wages and somewhat more than after-tax profits. The average bonus for 1988 was $21,258. Even for the recession years 1982 and 1983, bonuses averaged $13,998 and $8,557, respectively. Individual bonuses were proportional to merit rating scores. For example, assume the amount set aside for bonuses was 80 percent of total wages paid to eligible employees. A person whose performance score was 95 would receive a bonus of 76 percent (0.80×0.95) of annual wages.

Vacations   The company was shut down for two weeks in August and two weeks during the Christmas season. Vacations were taken during these periods. For employees with over 25 years of service, a fifth week of vacation could be taken at a time acceptable to superiors.

Work Assignment   Management had authority to transfer workers and to switch between overtime and short time as required. Supervisors had undisputed authority to assign specific parts to individual workers, who might have their own preferences due to variations in piece rates. During the 1982–1983 recession, 50 factory workers volunteered to join sales teams and fanned out across the country to sell a new welder designed for automobile body shops and small machine shops. The result—$10 million in sales and a hot new product.

Employee Participation in Decision Making

Thinking of participative management usually evokes a vision of a relaxed, nonauthoritarian atmosphere. This was not the case at Lincoln. Formal authority was quite strong. "We're very authoritarian around here," said Willis. James R. Lincoln placed a good deal of stress on protecting management's authority. "Management in all successful departments of industry must have complete power," he said. "Management is the coach who must be obeyed. The workers, however, are the players who alone can win the game." Despite this attitude, there were several ways in which employees participated in management at Lincoln.

Richard Sabo, assistant to the chief executive officer, related job enlargement/enrichment to participation. He said, "The most important participative technique that we use is giving more responsibility to employees. We give a high school graduate more responsibility than other companies give their foremen." Management put limits on the degree of participation which was allowed, however. In Sabo's words:

> When you use "participation," put quotes around it—because we believe that each person should participate only in those decisions he is most knowledgeable about. I don't think production employees should control the decisions of the chairman. They don't know as much as he does about the decisions he is involved in.

The Advisory Board, elected by the workers, met with the chairman and the president every two weeks to discuss ways of improving operations. As noted earlier, this board had been in existence since 1914 and had contributed to many innovations. The incentive bonuses, for example, were first recommended by this committee. Every employee had access to Advisory Board members, and answers to all Advisory Board suggestions were promised by the following meeting. Both Willis and Hastings were quick to point out, though, that the Advisory Board only recommended actions. "They do not have direct authority," Willis said, "and when they bring up something that management thinks is not to the benefit of the company, it will be rejected."

Under the early suggestion program, employees were awarded one-half of the first year's savings attributable to their suggestions. Later, however, the value of suggestions was reflected in performance evaluation scores, which determined individual incentive bonus amounts.

Training and Education   Production workers were given a short period of on-the-job training and then placed on a piecework pay system. Lincoln did not pay for off-site education, unless very specific company needs were identified. The idea behind this policy, according to Sabo, was that not everyone could take advantage of such a program, and it was unfair to expend company funds for an advantage to which there was unequal access. Recruits for sales jobs, already college graduates, were given on-the-job training in the plant, followed by a period of work and training at one of the regional sales offices.

Fringe Benefits and Executive Perquisites   A medical plan and a company-paid retirement program had been in effect for many years. A plant cafeteria, operated on a break-even basis, served meals at about 60 percent of usual costs. The Employee Association, to which the company did not contribute, provided disability insurance and social and athletic activities. The employee stock ownership program resulted in employee ownership of about 50 percent of the common stock. Under this program, each employee with more than two years of service could purchase stock in the corporation. The price of the shares was established at book value. Stock purchased through this plan could be held by employees only.

Dividends and voting rights were the same as for stock which was owned outside the plan. Approximately 75 percent of the employees owned Lincoln stock.

As to executive perquisites, there were none. Executives had crowded, austere offices; no executive washrooms or lunchrooms; and no reserved parking spaces. Even the top executives paid for their own meals and ate in the employee cafeteria. On one recent day, Willis arrived at work late due to a breakfast speaking engagement and had to park far away from the factory entrance.

Financial Policies

James R. Lincoln felt strongly that financing for company growth should come from within the company—through initial cash investment by the founders, through retention of earnings, and through stock purchases by those who worked in the business. He saw the following advantages to this approach:

1. Ownership of stock by employees strengthened team spirit. "If they are mutually anxious to make it succeed, the future of the company is bright."
2. Ownership of stock provided individual incentive because employees felt that they would benefit from company profitability.
3. "Ownership is educational." Owner-employees "will know how profits are made and lost; how success is won and lost . . . There are few socialists in the list of stockholders of the nation's industries."
4. "Capital available from within controls expansion." Unwarranted expansion would not occur, Lincoln believed, under his financing plan.
5. "The greatest advantage would be the development of the individual worker. Under the incentive of ownership, he would become a greater man."
6. "Stock ownership is one of the steps that can be taken that will make the worker feel that there is

less of a gulf between him and the boss . . . Stock ownership will help the worker to recognize his [or her] responsibility in the game and the importance of victory."

Until 1980, Lincoln Electric borrowed no money. The company's liabilities consisted mainly of accounts payable and short-term accruals.

The unusual pricing policy at Lincoln was succinctly stated by Willis: "At all times price on the basis of cost, and at all times keep pressure on our cost." This policy resulted in the price for the most popular welding electrode going from 16 cents a pound in 1929 to 4.7 cents in 1938. More recently, the SA-200 welder, Lincoln's largest-selling portable machine, had decreased in price from 1958 through 1965. According to Dr. C. Jackson Grayson of the American Productivity Center in Houston, Texas, Lincoln's prices had increased only one-fifth as fast as the consumer price index from 1934 to about 1970. This resulted in a welding products market in which Lincoln became the undisputed price leader for the products it manufactured. Not even the major Japanese manufacturers, such as Nippon Steel for welding electrodes and Osaka Transformer for welding machines, were able to penetrate this market.

Substantial cash balances were accumulated each year preparatory to paying the year-end bonuses. The bonuses totaled $54 million for 1988. The money was invested in short-term U.S. government securities and certificates of deposit (CDs) until needed. Financial statements are shown in Exhibit 3. Exhibit 4 shows how company revenue was distributed in the late 1980s.

How Well Did Lincoln Serve Its Stakeholders?

Lincoln Electric differed from most other companies in the importance it assigned to each of the groups it served. Willis identified these groups, in the order of priority ascribed to them, as (1) customers, (2) employees, and (3) stockholders.

Certainly the firm's customers had fared well over the years. Lincoln prices for welding machines and welding electrodes were acknowledged to be the lowest in the marketplace. Quality was consistently high. The cost of field failures for Lincoln products had recently been determined to be a remarkable 0.04 percent of revenues. The Fleetweld electrodes and SA-200 welders had been the standard in the pipeline and refinery construction industry, where price was hardly a criterion, for decades. A Lincoln distributor in Monroe, Louisiana, said that he had sold several hundred of the popular AC-223 welders, which were warranted for one year, but never handled a warranty claim.

Perhaps best served of all management constituencies were the employees. Not the least of their benefits, of course, were the year-end bonuses, which effectively

Exhibit 3   **Condensed Comparative Financial Statements ($000,000)***

	1979	1980	1981	1982	1983	1984	1985	1986	1987
Balance Sheets									
Assets									
Cash	$ 2	$ 1	$ 4	$ 1	$ 2	$ 4	$ 2	$ 1	$ 7
Bonds and CDs	38	47	63	72	78	57	55	45	41
Notes and accounts receivable	42	42	42	26	31	34	38	36	43
Inventories	38	36	46	38	31	37	34	26	40
Prepayments	1	3	4	5	5	5	7	8	7
Total current assets	121	129	157	143	146	138	135	116	137
Other assets†	24	24	26	30	30	29	29	33	40
Land	1	1	1	1	1	1	1	1	1
Net buildings	22	23	25	23	22	21	20	18	17
Net machinery and equipment	21	25	27	27	27	28	27	29	33
Total fixed assets	44	49	53	51	50	50	48	48	50
Total assets	189	202	236	224	227	217	213	197	227
Claims									
Accounts payable	17	16	15	12	16	15	13	11	20
Accrued wages	1	2	5	4	3	4	5	5	4
Accrued taxes	10	6	15	5	7	4	6	5	9
Accrued dividends	6	6	7	7	7	6	7	6	7
Total claims	33	29	42	28	33	30	31	27	40
Long-term debt		4	5	6	8	10	11	8	8
Total debt	33	33	47	34	41	40	42	35	48
Common stock	4	3	1	2	0	0	0	0	2
Retained earnings	152	167	189	188	186	176	171	161	177
Total shareholders' equity	156	170	190	190	186	176	171	161	179
Total claims	189	202	236	224	227	217	213	197	227
Income Statements									
Net sales	374	387	450	311	263	322	333	318	368
Other income	11	14	18	18	13	12	11	8	9
Income	385	401	469	329	277	334	344	326	377
Cost of goods sold	244	261	293	213	180	223	221	216	239
Selling, general and administrative expenses‡	41	46	51	45	45	47	48	49	51
Incentive bonus	44	43	56	37	22	33	38	33	39
Income before taxes	56	51	69	35	30	31	36	27	48
Income taxes	26	23	31	16	13	14	16	12	21
Net income	30	28	37	19	17	17	20	15	27

* Columns totals may not check, and amounts less than $500,000 (0.5) are shown as zero, due to rounding.

† Includes investment in foreign subsidiaries, $29 million in 1987.

‡ Includes pension expense and payroll taxes on incentive bonus.

doubled an already above average compensation level. The foregoing description of the personnel program and the comments in the Appendix further illustrate the desirability of a Lincoln job.

While stockholders were relegated to an inferior status by James F. Lincoln, they did very well indeed. Recent dividends had exceeded $11 a share, and earnings per share approached $30. In January 1980, the price of restricted stock, committed to employees, had been $117 a share. By 1989, the stated value at which the company would repurchase the stock if tendered was $201. A check with the New York office of Merrill Lynch, Pierce, Fenner

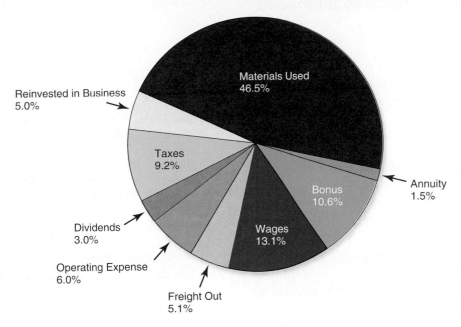

Exhibit 4   **Revenue Distribution**

and Smith at that time revealed an estimated price on Lincoln stock of $270 a share, with none being offered for sale. Technically, this price applied only to the unrestricted stock owned by the Lincoln family, a few other major holders, and employees who purchased it on the open market. Risk associated with Lincoln stock, a major determinant of stock value, was minimal because of the small amount of debt in the capital structure, because of an extremely stable earnings record, and because of Lincoln's practice of purchasing the restricted stock whenever employees offered it for sale.

A Concluding Comment

It was easy to believe that the reason for Lincoln's success was the excellent attitude of the employees and their willingness to work harder, faster, and more intelligently than other industrial workers. However, Sabo suggested that appropriate recognition be given to Lincoln executives, whom he credited with carrying out the following policies:

1. Management limited research, development, and manufacturing to a standard product line designed to meet the major needs of the welding industry.
2. New products had to be reviewed by manufacturing and all producing costs verified before the products were approved by management.
3. Purchasing was challenged not only to procure materials at the lowest cost but also to work closely with engineering and manufacturing to ensure that the latest innovations were implemented.
4. Manufacturing supervision and all personnel were held accountable for reduction of scrap, energy conservation, and maintenance of product quality.
5. Production control, material handling, and methods engineering were closely supervised by top management.
6. Management made cost reduction a way of life at Lincoln, and definite programs were established in many areas, including traffic and shipping, where tremendous savings could result.
7. Management established a sales department that was technically trained to reduce customer welding costs. This sales approach and other real customer services eliminated nonessential frills and resulted in long-term benefits to all concerned.
8. Management encouraged education, technical publishing, and long-range programs that resulted in industry growth, thereby assuring market potential for The Lincoln Electric Company.

Sabo wrote, "It is in a very real sense a personal and group experience in faith—a belief that together we can achieve results which alone would not be possible. It is not a perfect system, and it is not easy. It requires tremendous dedication and hard work. However, it does work, and the results are worth the effort."

Appendix   Employee Interviews

Typical questions and answers from employee interviews are presented below. The employees' names have been changed to protect their privacy.

Interview 1

Betty Stewart, a 52-year-old high school graduate who had been with Lincoln 13 years and who was working as a cost accounting clerk at the time of the interview.

Q.   What jobs have you held here besides the one you have now?

A.   I worked in payroll for a while, and then this job came open and I took it.

Q.   How much money did you make last year, including your bonus?

A.   I would say roughly around $25,000, but I was off for back surgery for a while.

Q.   You weren't paid while you were off for back surgery?

A.   No.

Q.   Did the Employees Association help out?

A.   Yes. The company doesn't furnish that, though. We pay $8 a month into the Employee Association. I think my check from them was $130 a week.

Q.   How was your performance rating last year?

A.   It was around 100 points, but I lost some points for attendance [because of] my back problem.

Q.   How did you get your job at Lincoln?

A.   I was bored silly where I was working, and I had heard that Lincoln kept their people busy. So I applied and got the job the next day.

Q.   Do you think you make more money than similar workers in Cleveland?

A.   I know I do.

Q.   What have you done with your money?

A.   We have purchased a better home. Also, my son is going to the University of Chicago, which costs $13,000 a year. I buy the Lincoln stock which is offered each year, and I have a little bit of gold.

Q.   Have you ever visited with any of the senior executives, like Mr. Willis or Mr. Hastings?

A.   I have known Mr. Willis for a long time.

Q.   Does he call you by name?

A.   Yes. In fact, he was very instrumental in my going to the doctor that I am going to with my back. He knows the director of the clinic.

Q.   Do you know Mr. Hastings?

A.   I know him to speak to him, and he always speaks, always. But I have known Mr. Willis for a good many years. When I did Plant Two accounting, I did not understand how the plant operated. Of course you are not allowed in Plant Two, because that's the Electrode Division. I told my boss about the problem one day and the next thing I knew Mr. Willis came by and said, "Come on, Betty, we're going to Plant Two." He spent an hour and a half showing me the plant.

Q.   Do you think Lincoln employees produce more than those in other companies?

A.   I think with the incentive program the way that it is, if you want to work and achieve, then you will do it. If you don't want to work and achieve, you will not do it no matter where you are. Just because you are merit-rated and have a bonus, if you really don't want to work hard, then you're not going to. You will accept your 90 points or 92 or 85 because, even with that, you make more money than people on the outside.

Q.   Do you think Lincoln employees will ever join a union?

A.   I don't know why they would.

Q.   So you say that money is a very major advantage?

A.   Money is a major advantage, but it's not just the money. It's the fact that having the incentive, you do wish to work a little harder. I'm sure that there are a lot of men here who, if they worked some other place, would not work as hard as they do here. Not that they are overworked—I don't mean that—but I'm sure they wouldn't push.

Q.   Is there anything that you would like to add?

A.   I do like working here. I am better off being pushed mentally. In another company if you pushed too hard, you would feel a little bit of pressure, and someone might say, "Hey, slow down; don't try so hard." But here you are encouraged, not discouraged.

Interview 2

Ed Sanderson, a 23-year-old high school graduate who had been with Lincoln four years and who was a machine operator in the Electrode Division at the time of the interview.

Q.   How did you happen to get this job?

A.   My wife was pregnant, and I was making three bucks an hour and one day I came here and applied.

That was it. I kept calling to let them know I was still interested.

Q. Roughly what were your earnings last year including your bonus?

A. $45,000.

Q. What have you done with your money since you have been here?

A. Well, we've lived pretty well, and we bought a condominium.

Q. Have you paid for the condominium?

A. No, but I could.

Q. Have you bought your Lincoln stock this year?

A. No, I haven't bought any Lincoln stock yet.

Q. Do you get the feeling that the executives here are pretty well thought of?

A. I think they are. To get where they are today, they had to really work.

Q. Wouldn't that be true anywhere?

A. I think more so here because seniority really doesn't mean anything. If you work with a guy who has 20 years here, and you have two months and you're doing a better job, you will get advanced before he will.

Q. Are you paid on a piece-rate basis?

A. My gang does. There are nine of us who make the base electrode, and the whole group gets paid based on how many electrodes we make.

Q. Do you think you work harder than workers in other factories in the Cleveland area?

A. Yes, I would say I probably work harder.

Q. Do you think it hurts anybody?

A. No, a little hard work never hurts anybody.

Q. If you could choose, do you think you would be as happy earning a little less money and being able to slow down a little?

A. No, it doesn't bother me. If it bothered me, I wouldn't do it.

Q. Why do you think Lincoln employees produce more than workers in other plants?

A. That's the way the company is set up. The more you put out, the more you're going to make.

Q. Do you think it's the piece rate and bonus together?

A. I don't think people would work here if they didn't know that they would be rewarded at the end of the year.

Q. Do you think Lincoln employees will ever join a union?

A. No.

Q. What are the major advantages of working for Lincoln?

A. Money.

Q. Are there any other advantages?

A. Yes, we don't have a union shop. I don't think I could work in a union shop.

Q. Do you think you are a career man with Lincoln at this time?

A. Yes.

Interview 3

Roger Lewis, a 23-year-old Purdue University graduate in mechanical engineering who had been in the Lincoln sales program for 15 months and who was working in the Cleveland sales office at the time of the interview.

Q. How did you get your job at Lincoln?

A. I saw that Lincoln was interviewing on campus at Purdue, and I went by. I later came to Cleveland for a plant tour and was offered a job.

Q. Do you know any of the senior executives? Would they know you by name?

A. Yes, I know all of them—Mr. Hastings, Mr. Willis, Mr. Sabo.

Q. Do you think Lincoln salespeople work harder than those in other companies?

A. Yes. I don't think there are many salespeople for other companies who are putting in 50- to 60-hour weeks. Everybody here works harder. You can go out in the plant, or you can go upstairs, and there's nobody sitting around.

Q. Do you see any real disadvantage to working at Lincoln?

A. I don't know if it's a disadvantage, but Lincoln is a spartan company, a very thrifty company. I like that. The sales offices are functional, not fancy.

Q. Why do you think Lincoln employees have such high productivity?

A. Piecework has a lot to do with it. Lincoln is smaller than many plants, too; you can stand in one place and see the materials come in one side and the product go out the other. You feel a part of the company. The chance to get ahead is important, too. They have a strict policy of promoting from within, so you know you have a chance. I think in a lot of other places you may not get as fair a shake as you do here. The sales offices are on a smaller scale, too. I like that when I tell someone that we have two people in the Baltimore office, and they say "You've got to be kidding." It's smaller and more personal. Pay is the most important thing. I have heard that this is the highest-paying factory in the world.

Interview 4

Jimmy Roberts, a 47-year-old high school graduate who had been with Lincoln 17 years and who was working as a multiple-drill press operator at the time of the interview.

Q. What jobs have you had at Lincoln?

A. I started out cleaning the men's locker room in 1967. After about a year I got a job in the flux department, where we make the coating for welding rods. I worked there for seven or eight years and then got my present job.

Q. Do you make one particular part?

A. No, there are a variety of parts I make—at least 25.

Q. Each one has a different piece rate attached to it?

A. Yes.

Q. Are some piece rates better than others?

A. Yes.

Q. How do you determine which ones you are going to do?

A. You don't. Your supervisor assigns them.

Q. How much money did you make last year?

A. $53,000.

Q. Have you ever received any kind of award or citation?

A. No.

Q. Was your rating ever over 110?

A. Yes. For the past five years, probably, I made over 110 points.

Q. Is there any attempt to let the others know . . . ?

A. The kind of points I get? No.

Q. Do you know what they are making?

A. No. There are some who might not be too happy with their points and they might make it known. The majority, though, do not make it a point of telling other employees.

Q. Would you be just as happy earning a little less money and working a little slower?

A. I don't think I would—not at this point. I have done piecework all these years, and the fast pace doesn't really bother me.

Q. Why do you think Lincoln productivity is so high?

A. The incentive thing—the bonus distribution. I think that would be the main reason. The paycheck you get every two weeks is important too.

Q. Do you think Lincoln employees would ever join a union?

A. I don't think so. I have never heard anyone mention it.

Q. What is the most important advantage of working here?

A. Amount of money you make. I don't think I could make this amount of money anywhere else, especially with only a high school education.

Q. As a black person, do you feel that Lincoln discriminates in any way against blacks?

A. No. I don't think any more so than any other job. Naturally, there is a certain amount of discrimination, regardless of where you are.

Interview 5

Joe Trahan, a 58-year-old high school graduate who had been with Lincoln 39 years and who was employed as a working supervisor in the tool room at the time of the interview.

Q. Roughly what was your pay last year?

A. Over $56,000; salary, bonus, stock dividends.

Q. How much was your bonus?

A. About $26,000.

Q. Have you ever gotten a special award of any kind?

A. Not really.

Q. What have you done with your money?

A. My house is paid for—and my two cars. I also have some bonds and the Lincoln stock.

Q. What do you think of the executives at Lincoln?

A. They're really top-notch.

Q. What is the major disadvantage of working at Lincoln Electric?

A. I don't know of any disadvantage at all.

Q. Do you think you produce more than most people in similar jobs with other companies?

A. I do believe that.

Q. Why is that? Why do you believe that?

A. We are on the incentive system. Everything we do, we try to improve to make a better product with a minimum of outlay. We try to improve the bonus.

Q. Would you be just as happy making a little less money and not working quite so hard?

A. I don't think so.

Q. Do you think Lincoln employees would ever join a union?

A. I don't think they would ever consider it.

Q. What is the most important advantage of working at Lincoln?

A. Compensation.

Q. Tell me something about Mr. James Lincoln, who died in 1965.

A. You are talking about Jimmy, Sr. He always strolled through the shop in his shirt sleeves. Big fellow. Always looked distinguished. Gray hair. Friendly sort of guy. I was a member of the Advisory Board one year. He was there each time.

Q. Did he strike you as really caring?

A. I think he always cared for people.

Q. Did you get any sensation of a religious nature from him?

A. No, not really.

Q. And religion is not part of the program now?

A. No.

Q. Do you think Mr. Lincoln was a very intelligent man, or was he just a nice guy?

A. I would say he was pretty well educated. A great talker—always right off the top of his head. He knew what he was talking about all the time.

Q. When were bonuses for beneficial suggestions done away with?

A. About 18 years ago.

Q. Did that hurt very much?

A. I don't think so, because suggestions are still rewarded through the merit rating system.

Q. Is there anything you would like to add?

A. It's a good place to work. The union kind of ties other places down. At other places, electricians only do electrical work, carpenters only do carpenter work. At Lincoln Electric we all pitch in and do whatever needs to be done.

Q. So a major advantage is not having a union?

A. That's right.

Case 25   McDonald's*

On April 19, 2004, James R. Cantalupo, the chairman and CEO of McDonald's, died unexpectedly of a heart attack on his way to a biennial meeting of the firm's executives, franchisees, and suppliers in Orlando, Florida. Cantalupo had come out of retirement only the year before to help improve upon McDonald's lackluster performance. During his brief tenure, he had started to turn things around, as reflected in strong growth in sales over the last three quarters. Reflecting on Cantalupo's performance, Peter Oakes, an analyst at Piper Jaffray, stated: "His impact over the 16-month period was as meaningful as any chief executive's at McDonald's who preceded him and that includes the big guy, Ray Kroc."[1]

The turnaround at McDonald's could partly be attributed to some new additions that Cantalupo had made to its menu. The chain had had a positive response to its increased emphasis on healthier foods, lead by a revamped line of fancier salads. But a bigger success came in the form of the McGriddles breakfast sandwich which was launched nationwide in June 2003. A couple of syrup-drenched pancakes, stamped with the Golden Arches, acted as the top and bottom of the sandwich to hold eggs, cheese, sausage, and bacon in three different combinations. McDonald's has estimated that the new breakfast addition has been bringing in about one million new customers every day.

However, Cantalupo's efforts were not limited to changes in the firm's product offerings. He understood that unless he could address more fundamental issues, McDonald's might be at the end of a long run as a growth company. In fact, Cantalupo was attempting to lay the groundwork for the revival of this growth by tackling some of the firm's more pressing problems. He had cut back on McDonald's expansion plans, trying instead to concentrate on improving the firm's relationships with existing franchisees. He had also forced the firm to focus on its core hamburger business and to get rid of the other underperforming subsidiaries.

It was clear to Cantalupo that the problems at McDonald's went well beyond cleaning up restaurants and revamping the menu. The chain has been squeezed by long-term trends that threaten to leave it marginalized. It was facing a rapidly fragmenting market, where changes in the tastes of consumers have made once-exotic foods like sushi and burritos everyday options. Furthermore, competition has been coming from quick meals of all sorts that can be found in supermarkets, convenience stores, and even vending machines.

*This case was prepared by Professor Jamal Shamsie of Michigan State University. This case was developed from published sources as a basis for class discussion rather than to illustrate either effective or ineffective handling of an administrative situation. Copyright © 2004 Jamal Shamsie.

Amid these changes, McDonald's may be facing its greatest challenge from the "fast-casual" restaurant category. This fast-growing segment includes several newcomers such as Cosi, a sandwich shop, or Quizno's, a gourmet sub sandwich chain, where customers find the food healthier and better tasting. According to Mats Lederhausen, recently appointed to revamp the menu at McDonald's: "We are clearly living through the death of the mass market."[2]

Experiencing a Downward Spiral

Since it was founded more than 50 years ago, McDonald's has been defining the fast-food business. It provided millions of Americans their first jobs even as it changed their eating habits. It rose from a single outlet in a Chicago suburb to become one of the largest chain of outlets spread around the globe. But the company had been stumbling over the past decade. See Exhibit 1 for milestones in the history of McDonald's.

The decline in McDonald's once-vaunted service and quality can be traced to its expansion of the 1990s, when headquarters stopped grading franchises for cleanliness, speed, and service. By the end of the decade, the chain ran into more problems because of the tighter labor market. McDonald's began to cut back on training as it struggled hard to find new recruits, leading to a dramatic falloff in the skills of its employees. According to a 2002 survey by market researcher Global Growth Group, McDonald's came in third in average service time behind Wendy's and sandwich shop Chick-fil-A Inc.

McDonald's also began to fail consistently with its new product introductions, such as the low-fat McLean Deluxe and Arch Deluxe burgers, both of which were meant to appeal to adults. It did no better with its attempts to diversify beyond burgers, often because of problems with the product development process. Consultant Michael Seid, who manages a franchise consulting firm in West Hartford, Connecticut, pointed out that McDonald's offered a pizza that didn't fit through the drive-through window and salad shakers that were packed so tightly that dressing couldn't flow through them.

In 1998, after McDonald's posted its first-ever decline in annual earnings, CEO Michael R. Quinlan was forced out and replaced by Jack M. Greenberg, a 16-year veteran of the firm. Greenberg tried not only to cut back on McDonald's expansion but also to deal with some of the company's growing problems. But his efforts to deal with the decline of McDonald's were slowed by his acquisition of other fast-food chains such as Chipotle Mexican Grill and Boston Market Corporation.

On December 5, 2002, after watching McDonald's stock slide 60 percent over three years, the board ousted

Exhibit 1   McDonald's Milestones

1948 Brothers Richard and Maurice McDonald open the first restaurant in San Bernadino, California, that sells hamburgers, fries, and milk shakes.

1955 Ray A. Kroc, 52, opens his first McDonald's in Des Plaines, Illinois. Kroc, a distributor of milk-shake mixers, figures he can sell a bundle of them if he franchises the business and install his mixers in the new McDonald's.

1961 Kroc buys out the McDonald brothers for $2.7 million.

1963 Ronald McDonald makes his debut as corporate spokesclown using future NBC-TV weatherman Willard Scott. During the year, the company also sells its 1 billionth burger.

1965 McDonald's stock goes public at $22.50 a share. It will split 12 times in the next 35 years.

1967 The first McDonald's restaurant outside the United States opens in Richmond, British Columbia. Today there are 31,108 McDonald's in 118 countries.

1968 The Big Mac, the first extension of McDonald's basic burger, makes its debut and is an immediate hit.

1972 McDonald's switches to the frozen variety for its successful french fries.

1974 Fred L. Turner succeeds Kroc as CEO. In the midst of a recession, the minimum wage rises to $2 per hour, a big cost increase for McDonald's, which is built around a model of young, low-wage workers.

1975 The first drive-through window is opened in Sierra Vista, Arizona.

1979 McDonald's responds to the needs of working women by introducing Happy Meals. A burger, some fries, a soda, and a toy give working moms a break.

1987 Michael R. Quinlan becomes CEO.

1991 Responding to the public's desire for healthier foods, McDonald's introduces the low-fat McLean Deluxe burger. It flops and is withdrawn from the market. Over the next few years, the chain will stumble several times trying to spruce up its menu.

1992 The company sells its 90 billionth burger, and stops counting.

1996 To attract more adult customers, the company launches its Arch Deluxe, a "grown-up" burger with an idiosyncratic taste. Like the low-fat burger, it also falls flat.

1997 McDonald's launches Campaign 55, which cuts the cost of a Big Mac to $0.55. It is a response to discounting by Burger King and Taco Bell. The move, which prefigures similar price wars in 2002, is widely considered a failure.

1998 Jack M. Greenberg becomes McDonald's fourth CEO: a 16-year company veteran, who vows to spruce up the restaurants and menu.

1999 For the first time, sales from international operations outstrip domestic revenues. In search of other concepts, the company acquires Aroma Cafe, Chipotle, Donatos, and, later, Boston Market.

2000 McDonald's U.S. sales peak at an average of $1.6 million annually per restaurant, a figure that has not changed since. It is still greater than the sales at any other fast-food chain.

2001 Subway surpasses McDonald's as the fast-food chain with the most U.S. outlets. At the end of the year it had 13,247 stores, 148 more than McDonald's.

2002 McDonald's posts its first-ever quarterly loss, of $343.8 million. The stock drops to around $13.50, down 40% from five years ago.

2003 James R. Cantalupo returns to McDonald's in January as CEO. He immediately pulls back from the company's 10–15% forecast for per share earnings growth.

2004 Charles H. Bell takes over the firm after the sudden death of Cantalupo, stating he will continue the strategies developed by his predecessor.

Source: McDonald's.

Greenberg. His short tenure had been marked by the introduction of 40 new menu items, none of which caught on big, and the purchase of a handful of nonburger chains, none of which helped the firm to sell more burgers. Indeed, critics said that by trying so many different things and executing them poorly, Greenberg allowed the burger business to continue with its decline. According to Los Angeles franchisee Reggie Webb, "We would have been better off trying fewer things and making them work."[3]

Managing a Troubled Franchise

Until a few years ago, franchisees had clamored to become part of McDonald's growing empire. But during 2002, 126 franchisees left the system in an exodus that had been unheard of in the past. Of these, 68, representing 169 restaurants, were forced out for poor performance. The rest left because they were unhappy with the profits they were making. Since then, as many as 20 franchisees have been leaving McDonald's every month, according to Richard Adams, a former franchisee and a food consultant. The firm buys back franchises if they cannot be sold; thus, forcing out a franchisee can be expensive. McDonald's took a pretax charge of $292 million to close 719 restaurants during 2002 and 2003.

In many cases, franchisees that have seen the chain as stuck in a rut have been jumping ship to faster-growing rivals. Paul Saber, a McDonald's franchisee for 17 years, sold his 14 restaurants back to the company in 2000 when he realized that eating habits were shifting away from McDonald's burgers to fresher, better-tasting food. He moved to rival Panera Bread Company, a fast-growing national bakery cafe chain. "The McDonald's-type fast food isn't relevant to today's consumer," said Saber.[4]

One of the biggest sore points for franchisees has been the top-down manner in which Greenberg and other past CEOs have attempted to fix pricing and menu problems. Many owner-operators still grumble over the $18,000 to $100,000 they had to spend in the late 1990s to install company-mandated "Made for You" kitchen upgrades in each restaurant. The new kitchens were supposed to speed up orders and accommodate new menu items. In the end, they actually slowed service.

Webb, who operates 11 McDonald's restaurants in Los Angeles, claimed that his sales have dipped by an average of $50,000 at each of his outlets over the past 15 years. "From my perspective, I am working harder than ever and making less than I ever had on an average-store basis," said Webb.[5] Most franchisees have seen their margins dip to a paltry 4 percent, from 15 percent when McDonald's was at its peak.

Franchisees have also complained about McDonald's addiction to cutting prices in order to drive up sales. When McDonald's cut prices in a 1997 price war, sales actually fell over the next four months. "Pulling hard on the price lever is dangerous. It risks cheapening the brand," said

Sam Rovit, a partner at Chicago consultant Bain & Company.[6] Yet McDonald's has been sticking with the $1 menu program that it had introduced in 2002. Although the tactic has been squeezing the sales of its rivals, the $1 menu has done little to improve McDonald's results.

Pinning Hopes on a New Team

By the beginning of 2003, consumer surveys were indicating that McDonald's was headed for serious trouble. Measures for the service and quality of the chain were beginning to lag far behind those of its rivals. To deal with its deteriorating performance, the firm decided to bring back retired vice-chairman James R. Cantalupo, 59, who had overseen McDonald's successful international expansion in the 1980s and 1990s. Cantalupo, who had retired only a year earlier, was perceived to be the only candidate with the necessary qualifications, despite shareholder sentiment for an outsider. The board of directors, however, believed that the company needed someone who knew the company well and could move quickly to turn things around.

A few weeks after Cantalupo had taken control, he had to announce McDonald's first quarterly loss in its 47-year history. There were clear indications that sales at outlets open at least a year were continuing to drop after showing a decline of 2.1 percent in 2002. See Exhibits 2 and 3 for the company's income statement and balance sheet, 2001–2003. Cantalupo clearly realized he had no time to lose.

One of the first steps that Cantalupo took was to assemble a fresh team to help McDonald's work itself out of its rut. He chose to bring up younger McDonald's executives, who he felt would bring energy and fresh ideas to the table. "Any company today has to be very vigilent about their business model and willing to break it, even if it's successful, to make sure they stay on top of the changing trends," said Alan Feldman, who had just quit as COO for domestic operations at McDonald's.[7]

For starters, Cantalupo appointed as chief operating officer Charles Bell, 42, an Australian who was also designated as his successor. Bell had become a store manager in his native Australia at 19 and then risen through the ranks. He eventually launched a coffeehouse concept called McCafe that attained considerable success. When he became president of McDonald's Europe, he similarly abandoned McDonald's cookie-cutter orange-and-yellow stores for individualized ones that offer local fare like the ham-and-cheese Croque McDo.

The second top executive Cantalupo recruited was a bona fide outsider, at least by company standards. Mats Lederhausen, a 39-year-old Swede, held an MBA from the Stockholm School of Economics and worked with Boston Consulting Group for two years. However, he jokes that he grew up in a french-fry vat because his father introduced McDonald's to Sweden in 1973. Lederhausen was given charge of growth and menu development.

Exhibit 2   Income Statement
(All numbers in thousands)

	Period Ending December 31		
	2003	**2002**	**2001**
Total Revenue	$17,140,500	$15,405,700	$14,870,000
Cost of revenue	11,943,700	10,746,700	10,253,900
Gross Profit	5,196,800	4,659,000	4,616,100
Operating expenses			
Selling general and administrative	2,048,400	2,546,100	1,719,100
Nonrecurring	316,200	—	200,000
Operating Income or Loss	2,832,200	2,112,900	2,697,000
Income from continuing operations			
Total other income/expenses, net	(97,800)	(76,700)	85,100
Earnings before interest and taxes	2,734,400	2,036,200	2,782,100
Interest expense	388,000	374,100	452,400
Income before tax	2,346,400	1,662,100	2,329,700
Income tax expense	838,200	670,000	693,100
Net income from continuing operations	1,508,200	992,100	1,636,600
Effect of accounting changes	(36,800)	(98,600)	—
Net Income	$ 1,471,400	$ 893,500	$ 1,636,600

Source: McDonald's annual reports.

Besides assembling a management team with a fresh perspective, Cantalupo also searched for new ideas from some of the better-performing franchisees. McDonald's best hope for revival may lie with its most innovative franchisees. One of these, Irwin Kruger, opened a 17,000-square-foot showcase unit in New York's Times Square with brick walls, theatrical lighting, and video monitors showing movie trailers. "We're slated to have sales of over $5 million this year and profits exceeding 10 percent," said Kruger.[8]

Scrambling for a New Strategy

Cantalupo realized that McDonald's often tended to miss the mark on delivering the critical aspects of consistent, fast, and friendly service, and an all-around enjoyable experience for the whole family. He understood that its franchisees and employees alike needed to be inspired as well as retrained on their role in putting the smile back into the McDonald's experience. When Cantalupo and his team laid out their plan for McDonald's in the spring of 2003, they stressed getting the basics of service and quality right, in part by reinstituting a tough "up or out" grading

system that would kick out underperforming franchisees. "We have to rebuild the foundation. It's fruitless to add growth if the foundation is weak," said Cantalupo.[9]

New product additions to the menu were one of the key elements of Cantalupo's new strategy for McDonald's. His team began to add new items such as the McGriddles breakfast sandwich that would draw in new customers and lure back old ones. Lederhausen was working on other possible items that could be added to the chain's menu. The revamped menu was promoted through a new worldwide ad slogan "I'm loving it," which was delivered by pop idol Justin Timberlake through a set of MTV-style commercials.

But Cantalupo had also been keen to build upon the ideas that Bell had tried out in Australia and Europe. The chain had been developing plans to test some outlets in Coral Gables, Florida, with much fancier contemporary decor. Modeled after the stores that Bell had opened in Paris, the seats would have cushions and wood composite tabletops instead of plastic. The walls were to be decorated with colorful art instead of Ronald's face. "This is all part of becoming more relevant to our consumers,"

Exhibit 3   Balance Sheet
(All numbers in thousands)

	Period Ending December 31		
	2003	2002	2001
Assets			
Current assets			
Cash and cash equivalents	$ 492,800	$ 330,400	$ 418,100
Net receivables	734,500	855,300	881,900
Inventory	129,400	111,700	105,500
Other current assets	528,700	418,000	413,800
Total Current Assets	1,885,400	1,715,400	1,819,300
Long-term investments	1,089,600	1,037,700	990,200
Property, plant, and equipment	19,924,700	18,583,400	17,289,500
Goodwill	1,665,100	1,559,800	1,419,800
Other assets	960,300	1,074,200	1,015,700
Total Assets	25,525,100	23,970,500	22,534,500
Liabilities			
Current liabilities			
Accounts payable	2,097,800	2,146,800	2,070,700
Short/current long-term debt	388,000	275,500	177,600
Total Current Liabilities	2,485,800	2,422,300	2,248,300
Long-term debt	9,342,500	9,703,600	8,555,500
Other liabilities	699,800	560,000	629,300
Deferred long-term liability charges	1,015,100	1,003,700	1,112,200
Total Liabilities	13,543,200	13,689,600	13,046,100
Stockholders' Equity			
Miscellaneous stock options, warrants	—	—	500,800
Common stock	16,600	16,600	16,600
Retained earnings	20,172,300	19,204,400	18,608,300
Treasury stock	(9,318,500)	(8,987,700)	(8,912,200)
Capital surplus	1,837,500	1,747,300	1,591,200
Other stockholder equity	(726,000)	(1,699,700)	(1,815,500)
Total Stockholder Equity	11,981,900	10,280,900	9,488,400
Net Tangible Assets	$10,316,800	$ 8,721,100	$ 8,068,600

Source: McDonald's annual reports.

said company spokesman Walt Riker. "When a customer enters our restaurant, they enter our brand."[10]

Cantalupo was also thinking about experimenting with some local variations on the McDonald's theme. Based on the success that Bell had with McCafe in Australia, he wanted to adapt some of McDonald's outlets to local themes. An example of this is the Arch Bistro, complete with chandeliers, leather couches, and soft lighting that McDonald's opened in downtown New Orleans. The menu offers everything from Louisiana shrimp to panini bread filled with chicken Cordon Bleu.

McDonald's was also planning to exploit its brand name by globally relaunching its marginally successful McKids line and to expand it well beyond children's clothing and toys into interactive videos and books. Under Cantalupo, the firm was in the process of making deals to get some royalties for these items from Mattel, Hasbro, and Creative Designs. While McDonald's was expected to make some money on these offerings, they were designed to keep the brand prominent in the minds of kids. "McDonald's wants to be seen as a lifestyle brand, not just a place to go to have a burger," said Marty Brochstein, executive editor of the *Licensing Letter.*[11]

As the firm moves into these new areas that build upon its brand, Cantalupo was thinking of divesting the nonburger chains acquired by his predecessor. Collectively lumped under the Partner Brands, these consisted of Chipotle Mexican Grill, Donatos Pizza, and Boston Market. The purpose of these acquisitions had been to find new growth and to offer the best franchises new opportunities for expansion. But these acquired businesses had not fueled much growth and had actually posted considerable losses in recent years.

Continuing with Its Turnaround

During his 16-month tenure, Cantalupo had attempted to turn McDonald's around by cutting back on expansion plans, reducing operating costs, and introducing new products. By taking these steps, he had managed to boost the firm's financial performance, particularly in the domestic market. But McDonald's was still working hard to improve on the basics of providing tastier burgers, faster service, and cleaner restaurants. "We haven't made as much progress as we could on service," Cantalupo had acknowledged.[12]

Just months before he died, Cantalupo had announced one of McDonald's most controversial changes. In response to concerns about growing obesity among Americans, Cantalupo had stated that the firm would phase out supersizing by the end of 2004. The supersizing option allowed customers to get a larger order of french fries and a bigger soft drink by paying a little bit extra.

Within hours of the announcement of Cantalupo's unexpected death, McDonald's announced the appointment of Charles Bell as the new CEO. As president and chief operating officer, he had been selected by Cantalupo as his successor. A 43-year-old Australian, Bell was the youngest and the first non-American to head the firm. He generally shared Cantalupo's focus on customer experience and stated that he intended to adhere closely to the strategy developed by his predecessor.

Above all, Bell must try to build on the moves that Cantalupo had been making in McDonald's core burger business. Winning back customers for its burgers may even be getting more difficult as a result of increased competition from newer entrants such as the California-based In-N-Out chain. The long-term success of the firm may depend on its ability to compete with rival burger chains. "The burger category has great strength," added David C. Novak, chairman and CEO of Yum! Brands, parent of KFC and Taco Bell. "That's America's food. People love hamburgers."[13]

At the same time, Bell must deal with some of the other critical issues facing the firm. He must figure out how to continue to build sales after the initial excitement generated by new products such as the McGriddles sandwich has worn off. Some franchisees are also upset that recent steps taken by McDonald's have had little effect on the steady decline in their profit margins. Finally, McDonald's efforts to move into children's clothing and toys is risky, given that the firm had little success with its previous attempt to launch the McKids line.

Like Cantalupo, Bell realizes that McDonald's may not have many shots at trying to get its strategy working. The firm needs to figure out what steps it must take to get its sales and profits growing again. "They are at a critical juncture and what they do today will shape whether they just fade away or recapture some of the magic and greatness again," said Robert S. Goldin, executive vice-president at food consultant Technomic Incorporated.[14]

Endnotes

1. Day, Sherri, 2004, McDonald's moves quickly to cover its loss, *New York Times,* April 20: C8.
2. Gogoi, Pallavi, & Arndt, Michael, 2003, Hamburger hell, *BusinessWeek,* March 3: 104.
3. Ibid., 108.
4. Ibid.
5. Ibid.
6. Ibid.
7. Ibid., 108.
8. Ibid.
9. Ibid., 105.
10. Horovitz, Bruce, 2003, You want ambiance with that? *USA Today,* October 30: 3B.
11. Horovitz, Bruce, 2003, McDonald's ventures beyond burgers to duds, toys. *USA Today,* November 14: 6B.
12. Leung, Shirley, 2003, McDonald's net increases 12.5%, bolstered by strong U.S. sales, *Wall Street Journal,* October 23: A3.
13. Pallavi & Arndt, Hamburger hell, 108.
14. Ibid.

Case 26   Microsoft's Battle for the Living Room: The Trojan Horse—The Xbox

On March 10, 2000, Microsoft's chairman Bill Gates stepped onto a stage in the San Jose, California, Convention Center to give the most anticipated speech of the Game Developers Conference. Thousands of people packed the room, and the event was televised all over the world. Gates, dressed in a leather jacket with a large green "X," talked about the future of gaming as he prepared to unveil what he called a "secret, a very deep secret":

> It's very exciting to be here today and have the opportunity to announce a whole new platform. A platform that all of you are going to take in directions that we can't even imagine. Thanks to months of rumors, everyone was in the know: The secret was the Xbox, Microsoft's new video game console.

After this dramatic speech, Gates invited one of the Xbox product launch team, Jonathan "Seamus" Blackley, the chief Xbox technical officer, to the stage to demonstrate the excellent performance of this brand-new machine. Blackley offered several 3-D animation demonstrations to excite the crowd who roared with applause. In developing the Xbox, Blackley said that "the Xbox was Microsoft's weapon to take on the Japanese in the video game business and make gaming the premier entertainment medium."

Due to the prosperity of its software business, Microsoft had a lock on the PC market to such an extent that "Microsoft" became nearly synonymous with "computer software" in many consumers' minds. As an ambitious entrepreneur, however, Gates was never satisfied with the status quo. He wanted to use the television as he had used the personal computer to sell his products and services, and by doing so, expand his Microsoft kingdom from the den to the living room. The Xbox was the console that Gates needed in order to create a new era of Microsoft.

However, manufacturing and selling this brand-new console became a larger-than-anticipated challenge for both Gates and Microsoft for two reasons. First, without any experience in manufacturing family video game consoles, how could Microsoft integrate its business and capital resources in order to introduce the Xbox successfully? Second, since Japanese firms had dominated the video game market since the 1980s, how would Microsoft's rivals respond to its late entry into the video game industry?

This case study was prepared by Professors Armand Gilinsky, Jr., and Zachary Wong at Sonoma State University, with the research assistance of MBA student Yu-Bin Chiou, as a basis for class discussion rather than the effective or ineffective handling of an administrative situation.

© 2004 by Armand Gilinsky, Jr., and Zachary Wong. Not for reproduction or distribution without permission of the authors. All rights reserved.

Third, how would Microsoft's investors respond to its entry into an industry that promised sustained short-term losses as development costs were recouped, not to mention uncertain long-term profitability?

Since Microsoft had neither the arcade gaming expertise of Nintendo and SEGA, nor the extensive consumer electronics experience possessed by Sony, many industry analysts questioned its motives of entering such an unfamiliar territory. Did Bill Gates view the video game console a threat to Microsoft's PC operating system business? After all, Microsoft's major competitors had engineered their consoles to enable Internet access. Due to the decreasing cost of computer memory chips and other devices, the idea of incorporating operating systems other than Microsoft's into their consoles to also serve as personal computers was not inconceivable.

Early Attempts to Enter the Game Business

Microsoft was founded in 1975 by Paul Allen and Bill Gates as a partnership and was incorporated in 1981 (Exhibit 1). The company had a clear mission: "to enable people and businesses throughout the world to realize their full potential." Microsoft also had a company vision, to empower people through great software—any time, any place, and on any device.

Microsoft had begun its business by developing personal computer software. The world famous DOS and Windows series became the backbone of Microsoft's business. Riding the success of its Windows and Office tools, Microsoft quickly expanded its products and services to cover and compete in a wide variety of areas under its seven major business divisions (Exhibit 2). Microsoft now stands as one of the largest companies in the world, enjoying sales exceeding $32 billion and profits approaching $10 billion in fiscal year 2003 (Exhibits 3 and 4).

The history of Microsoft's games business could be tracked to 1983. Although Microsoft's games business since had grown modestly from year to year, it was never profitable, especially compared with other successful divisions within the corporation. Despite repeated attempts, Microsoft's games business failed to meet expectations.

In 1983 Microsoft teamed up with several consumer electronics companies to launch its own hybrid PC-console, which was called MSX, in Asian markets. Unfortunately, because it lacked good games, MSX quickly failed.

To increase revenue in the mid-1990s, Microsoft's games division designed games for Sony's PlayStation. Although the initial PlayStation product sold more than 5 million units in the U.S. market, the games published by Microsoft did not become as popular as other PlayStation games, nor meet expected revenue goals.

Exhibit 1   Microsoft's History

Year	Event
1975	Founded by Paul Allen and Bill Gates.
1978	Fiscal reports showed annual sales exceeded $1 million dollars.
1981	IBM introduced its PC, which used Microsoft's 16-bit operating system, MS-DOS 1.0.
1983	Unveiled the first version of Microsoft Windows.
1984	Formed a partnership with IBM.
1986	Moved its headquarters to Redmond, Washington. Went public at $21 per share. The initial offering raised approximately $61 million. Employed 1,442 workers at the end of this year.
1989	Created a new multimedia division dedicated to developing and producing multimedia systems software and consumer products.
1990	Annual sales exceeded $1 billion.
1992	The new version Windows 3.1 was available worldwide. Merger with Fox Software Inc.
1994	Acquired SOFTIMAGE Inc., the leading developer of high-performance computer animation software and digital video.
1995	Launched Windows 95. Established MSNBC with NBC as an all-news cable TV channel. Established DreamWorks Interactive with DreamWorks SKG.
1996	Formed Interactive Media Group.
1997	Invested $150 million in Apple. Bought Hotmail for $650 million. Launched Internet Explorer 4.0.
1998	Bought Firefly Network.
1999	Invested $5 billion in AT&T.
2000	Bill Gates stepped aside as Microsoft chief executive.
2001	Announced the Xbox entertainment system. Purchased Great Plains software.
2002	Purchased Navision for $1.34 billion.

Sources: Microsoft Web site—www.microsoft.com—and ketupa.com.

In 1995 Microsoft expanded its games division. After the reorganization, the games department was a 150-person division with four development teams. At the same time, Ed Fries, the current vice president of games at Microsoft and one of the Xbox creators, was named head of the games department.

In 1997 Gates convinced Japan's SEGA Corporation to put Microsoft's Windows CE operating system into the SEGA Dreamcast console. The move was intended to enter Microsoft into the console business by partnering with a seasoned video game company. If the Dreamcast console succeeded, Microsoft could dominate the video game market indirectly by capitalizing on its sophisticated technology in software design. However, by the fall of 2000 the Dreamcast market share in the United States was barely 25 percent and started to decrease exponentially

Exhibit 2   Microsoft's Products and Services

Divisions	Product (Service)	Business Content
Client	Windows XP	Microsoft launched Windows XP in October 2001 as the newest version of the Windows family. XP extends the personal computing experience by uniting PCs, devices, and services, while enhancing reliability, security, and performance. Currently, the Windows operating system is the standard desktop application for PC users worldwide.
	Windows 2000 Professional	The new generation of Windows NT Workstation. Windows 2000 Professional operating system combines features to create a mainstream operating system for desktop and notebook computing in all organizations.
	Windows CE	A robust real-time embedded operating system targeted at mobile 32-bit devices. This embedded operating system offers integrated tool sets to enable embedded system developers to quickly create sophisticated embedded device and application solutions.
	Other OSs	Includes Windows NT Workstation, Windows Millennium Edition, and Windows 98.
	Hardware	The Hardware Group develops and markets several PC accessories including the Microsoft IntelliMouse family of handheld pointing devices using IntelliEye optical technology.
Server and Tools	Server Licenses	A client access license gives its holder the legal right to access a computer that runs a Microsoft server product and access to the services supported by the server.
	SQL Server	A comprehensive data management and analysis platform that enables rapid delivery, dependable performance, and secure operation of connected applications.
	Exchange Server	A messaging and collaboration server that provides e-mail, group scheduling, task management, contact management, and document routing capabilities.
Information Worker	Microsoft Office	A software product that features commonly used desktop functionality. The product is based upon a document-centric concept, with common commands and extensive use of cross-application capabilities.
	Other Desktop Applications	Offers other stand-alone desktop application products. Microsoft Project is a project management program for scheduling, organizing, and analyzing tasks, deadlines, and resources. Visio is a diagramming program that helps people visualize and communicate ideas, information, and systems.
Microsoft Business Solutions	Great Plains	Great Plains offers a range of integrated business and accounting products, including Dynamics, Solomon, and eEnterprise. These products provide Internet-ready accounting and business management capabilities, a full range of e-business and accounting applications, and a collaborative environment for information management and sharing for any size company.
	bCentral	Includes Site Manager, a Web site management and hosting service which empowers small businesses to easily create and manage their own Web sites.

Sources: Microsoft's Web site and 2003 Annual Report.

(continued on facing page)

Exhibit 2   Microsoft's Products and Services (continued)

Divisions	Product (Service)	Business Content
MSN	MSN Internet Access	MSN Internet access is Microsoft's service for accessing the Web and experiencing a wide range of rich online services and content. MSN Internet access subscribers can access their account from multiple sources, including a computer, television, Internet appliances, and personal digital assistants.
	MSN Network Service	The MSN network provides services, content, and advertising on the Internet, including MSN Search, Messenger, eShop, Hotmail, Money, and Music, as well as other services and content. MSN Search makes Web searches more useful by providing users with the most relevant results for the most popular search queries on the Web. MSN Messenger is a free Internet messaging service that enables users to see when others are online and exchange instant messages with them. MSN eShop is a one-stop online shopping resource. MSN Hotmail is the world's leading free Web-based e-mail service. MSN Money is a complete online personal financial service that combines finance tools and content from Microsoft with exclusive investment news and analysis from CNBC. MSN Music provides consumers with one place online to find old favorites, as well as discover new music, and delivers a high-quality listening experience.
Mobile and Embedded Devices	CarPoint online automotive service	The CarPoint online automotive service is the leading online automotive marketplace, visited by more than 7 million consumers each month. With details on more than 10,000 car models and 100,000 used vehicles, users can research and compare cars of virtually every make and model, identify local dealers, and receive instructions for post-purchase service and maintenance.
	Pocket PC	Licensed the right to manufacture the handheld device with a Windows CE OS.
Home and Entertainment	PC and Online Games	Microsoft offers a line of entertainment products from classic software games to online games, simulations, sport products, and strategy games. Zone.com is a gaming community on the Internet, which allows multiplayer gaming competitions of Microsoft's popular CD-ROM games and classic card, board, and puzzle games.
	Xbox	Microsoft's next-generation video game console system delivers high-quality graphics and audio gameplay experiences. Games for the Xbox are developed by Microsoft Game Studios and by third-party game development partners. Xbox Live, an online service available to owners of Xbox systems, was launched in the forth quarter of 2002 and allows online game play among users of online-enabled Xbox games.
Other	Expedia, Inc.	Expedia, Inc., operates Expedia.com, a leading online travel service. Expedia.com provides air, car, and hotel booking, vacation packages and cruise offerings, destination information, and mapping.
	Microsoft Press	Microsoft Press offers comprehensive learning and training resources to help new users, power users, and professionals get the most from Microsoft technology through books, CDs, self-paced training kits, and videos that are created to accommodate different learning styles and preferences.

Exhibit 3   Microsoft Corporation's Income Statements, 2001–2003
($ millions)

	2003	2002	2001
Revenue	$32,187.0	$28,365.0	$25,296.0
Cost of goods sold	4,247.0	4,107.0	1,919.0
Gross profit	27,940.0	24,258.0	23,377.0
Gross profit margin	86.8%	85.5%	92.4%
SG&A expense	13,284.0	11,264.0	10,121.0
Depreciation & amortization	1,439.0	1,084.0	1,536.0
Operating income	13,217.0	11,910.0	11,720.0
Operating margin	41.1%	42.0%	46.3%
Nonoperating income	1,509.0	(397.0)	(195.0)
Nonoperating expenses	0.0	0.0	0.0
Income before taxes	14,726.0	11,513.0	11,525.0
Income taxes	4,733.0	3,684.0	3,804.0
Net Income after taxes	$ 9,993.0	$ 7,829.0	$ 7,721.0

Source: Microsoft annual reports.

Exhibit 4   Microsoft's Revenue and Operating Income by Division, 2002–2003
($ millions)

Division	Revenue		Operating Income	
	2003	2002	2003	2002
Client	$10,394	$ 9,360	$ 8,400	$ 7,576
Server and Tools	7,140	6,157	2,457	2,048
Information Worker	9,229	8,212	7,037	6,448
Business Solutions	567	308	(254)	(176)
MSN	1,953	1,571	(299)	(641)
Mobile and Embedded Devices	156	112	(157)	(157)
Home and Entertainment	2,748	2,453	(924)	(874)
Other	—	192	(3,043)	(2,314)
Consolidated	$32,187	$28,365	$13,217	$11,910

Source: Microsoft 2003 Annual Report.

beginning in November when Sony launched its much anticipated PlayStation 2. SEGA eventually discontinued the Dreamcast console in 2001, adding to Microsoft's failed attempts to expand its games business.

In October 1997 Microsoft's games business received encouraging news. Its new real-time strategy game, *Age of Empires,* sold millions of copies in the United States, and earned more than $40 million for Microsoft. Spokesperson

Exhibit 5   Acquisition of Game Companies by Microsoft

Year	Company Name	Location	Game Concentration
1995	Ensemble Studio	Dallas, TX	Real-time strategy games
1998	Virtual House	San Jose, CA	Action games
	Digital Anvil	Austin, TX	Flying and shooting games (Created *Wing Commander* in 1990)
1999	Fasa Interactive	Chicago, IL	Robot games
	Access Software	Seattle, WA	Sports games (*Golf*)

Source: D. Takahashi, *Opening the Xbox* (Roseville, CA: Prima Publishing, 2002).

Ed Fries said, "*Age of Empires* helped us finance our growth, but what's been good about the growth was that it is mostly organic." *Age of Empires* gave Microsoft respect among hard-core gamers and developers. It became a vehicle Gates and Fries could build upon to continue expanding Microsoft's games business.

In 1999 Gates approached Sony's CEO Nobuyuki Idei before Sony's PlayStation 2 announcement. Gates wanted Idei to use Microsoft's programming tools, which would make it easier to develop games for the upcoming PlayStation 2. Idei turned Gates down because he preferred to use (and protect) Sony's proprietary programming tools.

Approaching Sony's CEO unsuccessfully turned out to be Gates's final attempt to make his games dream come true through partnerships with other game platform manufacturers. Gates then made the determination that Microsoft had sufficient capital, technology, human resources, and experience to launch its own video game console. He then decided to capitalize on a series of recent acquisitions (Exhibit 5).

The development and deployment of Microsoft's own game console, the Xbox, was enabled by the creation of a new division, Home and Entertainment, headed by senior vice-president, Robert Bach. The Home and Entertainment division was designed from the start to be autonomous, and it had its own functional units in marketing, operations, and technical deployment.

The U.S. Video Game Industry

The Dawn. Video games had a long history in the United States. In 1961 an MIT student named Steve Russell created *Spacewar,* the first interactive computer game in U.S. video game history. From 1965 to 1980, many famous video game companies, including Service Games (SEGA), Nintendo, Midway, and Namco, began releasing arcade games.

The most well-known arcade games, like *Pac-Man, Donkey Kong,* and *Pong,* also appeared during these 15 years. The first period of the U.S. video game history focused on commercial arcade games.

The Warring States. The first family console emerged in the middle of the 1980s. In 1986 Nintendo of America released the Nintendo Entertainment System (NES or Famicom, Family Computer) nationwide. The NES was the first game console designed for family use. The appearance of the NES not only advanced video game evolution to the next stage, but introduced a new style of home entertainment. This evolution formed a new profitable industry.

After the introduction of the NES, more companies devoted themselves to developing new consoles to attract consumers into this fantasy world (see Exhibit 6). Nintendo maintained the lead position and earned considerable revenue from the growing home video game market until a strong competitor, SEGA, joined the arena. SEGA unveiled its high-performing Mega Drive Genesis (MD) in 1989. This 16-bit console had much higher capability in game and sound performance than the NES, which meant that more exciting game factors could be added into this new system. Soon, the sales of the SEGA MD rose sharply in the United States and the MD caught the eye of many Nintendo players. By the summer of 1990, MD had taken more than 55 percent of new console sales, effectively eroding Nintendo's share by as much as 20 percent. Many third-party game developers also started dropping their Nintendo accounts to begin working with SEGA. In order to survive SEGA's severe competition, Nintendo devoted its business to a new video game niche, the pocket game system. Nintendo created the Game Boy, a pocket game system and the most popular console in gaming history, selling more than 115 million units worldwide. With the success of the Game Boy, Nintendo raised the funds needed to allow it to redevelop its new family console.

Nintendo was very ambitious in the home video game market that it had created. In 1991 Nintendo announced the Super NES, the second generation of its original console. Although the Super NES was a 16-bit console like the SEGA MD, with more game developers and therefore more games available with the system, Nintendo

Exhibit 6   Video Game Console Evolution in the United States, 1986–2001

Year	Console Name	Company	Console Introduction
1986	NES	Nintendo	NES had an 8-bit performance. Also adopted the famous Super Mario Brother as its Mascot.
1989	PC Engine	NEC	The first console with CD-ROM medium.
1989	Mega Drive Genesis	SEGA	Helped SEGA take control of the U.S. console market in 1992.
1989	Game Boy	Nintendo	The most successful pocket console. Sold more than 115 million worldwide.
1990	NeoGeo	SNK	The first 24-bit console.
1991	Super NES	Nintendo	Helped Nintendo take control of the U.S. console market in 1994.
1991	Game Genie	Galoob Toys	Discontinued in 1993.
1993	3DO Multiplayer	Panasonic	The first 32-bit console. Without good software support, discontinued in 1994.
1993	Jaguar	Atari	Discontinued in 1994.
1995	Saturn	SEGA	The first 64-bit console. Discontinued in 1997.
1995	PlayStation	Sony	Established Sony's foundation in the video game business.
1995	Virtual Boy	Nintendo	Discontinued in 1996.
1996	Nintendo 64	Nintendo	Nintendo's first 64-bit console. The last console that used cartridges as the medium.
1999	NeoGeo Pocket	SNK	The Japanese-owned SNK was bought by a Korean company in 2000.
1999	Dreamcast	SEGA	The first console that came with DVD medium.
2000	PlayStation 2	Sony	Took the major market share of console business since its introduction.
2001	Game Boy Advance	Nintendo	The new generation pocket console with a color screen.
2001	GameCube	Nintendo	Nintendo's first step to change its console into mainstream DVD medium.
2001	Xbox	Microsoft	Microsoft's first 128-bit video game console.

Source: Steven L. Kent, *The Ultimate History of Video Games* (Roseville, CA: Prima Publishing, 2001).

dominated the U.S. console market again by 1994. The competition between Nintendo and SEGA escalated again in 1995 when SEGA introduced its new 64-bit console, the Saturn, in the U.S. market. Because the Super NES had less than half of the performance quality and capacity of the brand new Saturn, most people believed SEGA would beat Nintendo quickly and take control of the video game market. SEGA was confident that it could take the market leader position back; however, a video game novice smashed SEGA's gaming dream.

New Competitors Enter. A previously ignored new entrant was Sony, a manufacturer that focused on consumer electronics. Sony entered the video game market in 1995 with its secret weapon—the PlayStation. Like the SEGA Saturn, the PlayStation was a 64-bit console with a CD-ROM game medium. Although there was no obvious difference in the hardware sections of these two systems, the volume of available game software became the advantage Sony needed to beat its powerful rival. Sony positioned its PlayStation as a software provider. Before unveiling this new console, Sony contracted with game developers, so that when the PlayStation premiered, it came with more than a hundred games, approximately half the number of games that Saturn offered. One year later, in 1996, the PlayStation had more than 250 games, exceeding Saturn's titles. Without the competitive advantage of having more games than its competitor, SEGA gradually lost its market share and discontinued the Saturn in 1997, recognizing that it had lost the console war again.

Having high-performing hardware and plenty of supporting software, the PlayStation became unbeatable in the U.S. video game market. The original video game giant, Nintendo, reentered this market in 1996 with its well-designed 64-bit console, Nintendo 64, and attempted to compete against the PlayStation, which was the market leader. With the assistance of some famous game series, like *Super Mario Brothers* and *Pokémon*, the Nintendo 64 sold very well in the beginning. However, the Nintendo 64 had a fatal design flaw. Nintendo used its familiar high-cost cartridges as the game medium instead of adopting the new cheaper CD-ROM game format. The high-cost cartridge became a heavy burden for both developers and consumers and because of this design flaw, Nintendo quickly lost both its game developers and its market share. Nintendo discontinued this console in 1999 and became another victim of Sony's PlayStation.

In 1999 SEGA invested considerable capital in creating the state-of-the-art console—Dreamcast. SEGA was aware of Sony's pending next-generation console, so it introduced the first console of the 21st century before other companies could. The Dreamcast, a high-performance console, earned lots of applause and praise at the Game Developers Conference in 1999. Many TV programs and gaming professional magazines introduced and reviewed the Dreamcast console. However, the thousands of positive reports did not generate the sales that SEGA anticipated. Since the Dreamcast provided higher capacity for software conducting, it was expensive to produce and difficult for developers to design its games. The available software was limited and expensive. Most consumers were still willing to purchase the cheaper PlayStation games with more titles rather than buy the more expensive Dreamcast console and games. The Dreamcast's market share never exceeded 10 percent of the U.S. console market. In 2001 SEGA admitted the failure of Dreamcast, and announced that it was leaving the console business. Since then, SEGA has only been a game-developing company and not a console manufacturer.

After beating SEGA twice, Sony stood alone as the market leader of the U.S. video game industry. Sony did not rest on its laurels, however, and in 2000 it announced its brand-new console, the PlayStation 2. Able to support the games made for the original PlayStation, PlayStation 2 sold more than 10 million units in the United States in November 2001, before the Xbox became available.

In 2001 Nintendo rejoined the video game race with Sony by introducing the new family console, GameCube, and the new pocket system, Game Boy Advance, in the United States.

After several lessons in failure from SEGA and its own history, Nintendo decided to enter the video game market through a niche market rather than competing directly with Sony's PlayStation 2. While most game companies had chosen not to compete directly with Sony, Microsoft introduced its Xbox to challenge Sony's stable market position and profit from this consistently growing industry (Exhibit 7).

Entering the new millennium, the number of U.S. households with a video game console had risen by 13 percent since 1995—from 31.4 million to 35.5 million in 2001. Video game homes had also penetrated urban areas and became popular among minorities and homes without

Exhibit 7   Video Game Sales in the United States, 1998–2003

Year	Sales ($ billions)	Change in Sales Volume (%)	Change in Units Sold (%)
2003	$14.0		
2002	10.3	+9.57%	+8.21%
2001	9.4	+9.30	+6.33
2000	8.6	+4.88	+3.42
1999	8.2	+6.49	+4.17
1998	7.7		

Sources: The NPD Group/NPD Funworld.

children. Contrary to popular belief regarding the demographics of video game players, studies showed that video gaming was primarily an adult-oriented form of entertainment. Video games were no longer child's play; gamers were predominantly adults, both male and female. Research conducted by the Entertainment Software Association in 2004 revealed that 75 percent of console game players were male and 25 percent were female, 46 percent were under 18 years old, 35 percent were 18 to 35, 11 percent were 36 to 45 years old, and 8 percent were over 46.

Competition

Microsoft's Xbox had two competitors: the major one was Sony's PlayStation 2, and the minor one was Nintendo's GameCube. (See Exhibits 8 and 9 for the financial statements of Sony and Nintendo.) Since SEGA had withdrawn from the video game console market, it would not be a major competitor for Microsoft's Xbox.

Nintendo   Nintendo introduced two new gaming systems in 2001, a console and a pocket system. The GameCube, the console, had games that appealed to young players who were less than 20 years old through cute graphics and rich content. Every published game was subject to strict quality control by Nintendo Corporation. Although the GameCube had only one-sixth the number of titles of PlayStation 2, each game was high quality. Nintendo's pocket system was Game Boy Advance, a portable console that appealed to school students. Most of Game Boy Advance's games were easy to play and contained less violence than the games of other consoles. Both of Nintendo's consoles were successful in their own niche markets, the youth market. On average, Nintendo's major consumers were much younger than those of PlayStation 2. After unsuccessfully competing with Sony for six years, Nintendo had decided not to compete directly with this new giant. It focused instead on the young consumer and did well in this niche market. Compared with PlayStation 2's games for teenagers, most of Nintendo's games were easier to design. Nintendo also saved significant cost by developing both the system and the software. Thus, Nintendo made considerable profits in the niche segment, and monopolized the portable console market.

Sony   Sony Entertainment Corporation America (SECA) used a "Trojan horse" strategy to release the moderately priced PlayStation 2. This new console would be the hub of a complete entertainment concept that merged television viewing, movie watching, video game playing, and Internet surfing into one device. In order to fulfill this strategy, Sony designed a new console that was not simply a video game player.

PlayStation 2 was the first console in the 21st century that could play DVD movies. In November 2000 the PlayStation 2 was available for $349.99, a low price compared with other DVD players. Thus, by the end of 2000, only two months after the new console was launched, PlayStation 2 had already sold more than 1 million units in the

Exhibit 8   **Sony Corporation Income Statements, 2001–2003 ($ millions)**

	2003	2002	2001
Revenue	$63,264.0	$57,117.0	$58,518.0
Cost of goods sold	40,672.0	34,993.0	38,901.0
Gross profit	22,592.0	22,124.0	19,617.0
Gross profit margin	35.7%	38.7%	33.5%
SG&A expense	15,402.0	16,612.0	13,071.0
Depreciation & amortization	5,621.0	4,498.0	4,743.0
Operating income	1,569.0	1,014.0	1,803.0
Operating margin	2.5%	1.8%	3.1%
Nonoperating income	379.0	(301.0)	79.0
Nonoperating expenses	231.0	275.0	344.0
Income before taxes	1,717.0	438.0	1,771.0
Income taxes	684.0	491.0	924.0
Net income after taxes	$ 1,033.0	$ (53.0)	$ 847.0

Source: Sony Corporation annual reports.

Exhibit 9   **Nintendo Corporation Income Statements, 2001–2003**
($ millions)

	2003	2002	2001
Revenue	$4,206.5	$4,183.3	$3,661.2
Cost of goods sold	2,574.3	2,522.7	2,204.3
Gross profit	1,632.2	1,660.6	1,456.9
Gross profit margin	38.8%	39.7%	39.8%
SG&A expense	796.8	762.3	786.4
Depreciation & amortization	—	—	—
Operating income	835.4	898.3	670.5
Operating margin	19.9%	21.5%	18.3%
Nonoperating income	312.9	527.7	867.1
Nonoperating expenses	202.8	46.2	202.5
Income before taxes	945.5	1,379.8	1,335.0
Income taxes	383.6	560.5	572.7
Net income after taxes	$ 561.9	$ 819.3	$ 762.3

Source: Nintendo Corporation annual reports.

U.S. market. According to research by NPD FunWorld in December 2000, 32 percent of PlayStation 2 buyers treated this new system as only a DVD player. The DVD player function, part of Sony's Trojan horse strategy, helped Sony sell its video game console to nongaming players.

PlayStation 2 was launched in the United States in November 2000, a year before the official launch of the Xbox. Unlike the launch of the original PlayStation, Sony offered only 19 games for its game console; however, the new PlayStation 2 was completely compatible with the original PlayStation. This meant that PlayStation 2 could not only play the 19 new games, but also play more than 700 original PlayStation games. Original PlayStation users were willing to purchase this new system because they didn't have to abandon their favorite old games. This backward-compatible design became another selling point for PlayStation 2, adding to PlayStation 2's unique competitive advantage.

PlayStation 2 was also the first console with the ability to work with a hard drive and access a dial-up or broadband Internet connection. This design was one part of the Trojan horse concept. With the capability to expand this system, PlayStation 2 could do much more than other consoles. However, since both the hard drive and Internet access were optional accessories instead of built-in functions, they were not commonly applied. By the end of 2001, less than 3 percent of games supported the hard drive function. In addition, before the launch of Xbox, only 8 of 372 PlayStation 2 games could be played through the Internet.

The launch of PlayStation 2 was thought by industry observers to be well timed and well planned. One timing factor was seasonality; console sales more than tripled during November and December in the United States compared to other months of the year. According to research implemented by NPD FunWorld, PlayStation 2 was the top Christmas present that parents in North America wanted to buy for their children in 2000. Because of PlayStation 2's well-timed introduction during the holiday shopping season, by the end of the year its sales exceeded 1 million units and the console took 24 percent of the market share.

The second timing factor was competition. After SEGA's Dreamcast failed, there were no new products on the video game market for a long time. The appearance of PlayStation 2 offered consumers a chance to renew their gaming life with a new generation of video games. The emergence of PlayStation 2 was like a light in the darkness, and it caught everyone's eye.

The third timing factor was game development. Gaming developer companies depended on a good console in order to survive, and PlayStation 2 was the most attractive console. After selling for five years, the Nintendo 64 was already out of date, and no programmers wanted to develop new games for an old system. With sales of only 0.3 million units, the newcomer, SEGA Dreamcast, didn't sell well in the U.S. console market.

There were no economies of scale for the unpopular consoles. PlayStation 2 was the only popular system at that time. Most gaming development companies believed that there were many potential business opportunities behind the PlayStation 2, since they had already had successful experiences with the PlayStation. Thus, PlayStation 2 won considerable contracts with gaming developers, and the number of its games quickly increased in the first quarter of 2001. The variety of games increased the sales of PlayStation 2 more than ever.

Although Sony's PlayStation 2 was largely successful, it had two significant shortcomings. The first was the Trojan horse strategy. The idea of selling a console as a home entertainment hub was a good one. However, Sony was a consumer electronics corporation and did not have many internal resources it could apply to capitalize on its Trojan horse plan. If Sony really wanted to make PlayStation 2 the home entertainment hub, it needed cooperation and resources from a third party, which would increase Sony's cost and risk. Since Sony was the current leader of the U.S. video game industry, it didn't put much effort into transforming PlayStation 2 from a video game console into a home entertainment hub. The second shortage was game development. Many game programmers complained that Sony had created insufficient tools to support PlayStation 2. Shinji Mikami, a seasoned game designer who created best-selling games for Dreamcast, Saturn, Nintendo 64, and PlayStation, said that PlayStation 2 was the most difficult system he had ever worked with. While most game developers recognized the powerful performance capability of the PlayStation 2, they also complained that the PlayStation 2 game-creation process was a nightmare for them.

Entry Wedges and Alternatives

In order to introduce the Xbox into the console market, Microsoft invested $300 million to design the console, $500 million in marketing, and $200 million to build the machines. For Bill Gates, the Xbox was the real "Trojan horse" for Microsoft. By selling the Xbox, Gates not only anticipated considerable profits in the growing video game industry, but expected to sell extra products and services related to the home entertainment industry.

Although Microsoft was not the first company to use the Trojan horse strategy to sell its console, Microsoft had more related products and services that could be added.

Release Timing The idea of the Xbox had been initially proposed in March 1999, and was quickly approved by Bill Gates and Microsoft's board of directors within three months. According to Kevin Bachus, one of the Xbox creators, the Xbox could be released before the end of 2000, when Sony's PlayStation 2 was released. However, the Xbox was the first console that Microsoft designed and sold in the video game market, and top man-

agement teams believed that Microsoft required more time to evaluate the market, consumers, and competitors. Finally, they decided to postpone the release date until November 2001, a year after the release of PlayStation 2.

Another reason for the delay was the cost of the hardware. After evaluating the performance of PlayStation 2, the Xbox development team realized they needed a console with newer graphics technology and a higher capability processor to beat their strong competitor. In order to create an ultimate gaming system, the Xbox developers decided to put the most advanced units into the console. Since they had just been developed, these new units were expensive. However, after a few months, the price of the units could fall significantly due to economies of scale or the maturity of unit technology. For this reason, Microsoft decided to postpone the release date of the Xbox in order to possibly lower the cost of the units.

Price In the U.S. console market, price alone was not a critical factor for consumers when making their purchasing decisions. Since video games were recreational products, most console buyers were less sensitive to the console's price than its features, quantity and quality of games, and their confidence in the products. For example, at the end of 2000 and the first three quarters of 2001, PlayStation 2 monopolized the family console market. Pricing was not important during this period in which one product, PlayStation 2, was clearly superior to its competitors. Consumers could only choose to buy it or not, rather than choose between PlayStation 2 and a different product.

On the other hand, price became a deciding factor for consumer purchasing decisions when there were two or more similar products existing in the same market. For example, since the market segment of Xbox was very similar to that of PlayStation 2, focusing on male consumers from age 15 to 35 and appealing to the concept of a home entertainment hub, the Xbox was sold with a price similar to the price of the PlayStation 2. To compete with the powerful newcomer, Sony cut the price of PlayStation 2 from $349.99 to $299.99 one month before the Xbox's official release. In response, Microsoft had no choice but to sell its Xbox for $299.99. According to Microsoft, the initial cost of the Xbox was estimated to be approximately $400. This meant that for each console sold, Microsoft incurred a $100 loss on its income statement. Microsoft understood this situation; however, it hoped to make the Xbox as popular as possible without worrying about the losses. As Nat Brown, one of the four Xbox creators, said:

> The goals of the Xbox are to make money, expand Microsoft's technology into the living room, and create the perception that Microsoft is leading the charge in the new era of consumer appliances. We are looking for long-term benefits, thus, we know that painful short-term money losses are inevitable.

Hardware   The Xbox was as outstanding as the developers expected. More than just a video game console, the Xbox could be used as another personal computer. The machine used a 733MHz microprocessor from Intel, which made the Xbox the first console containing a computer processor. The Xbox had a graphics chip from Nvidia that had three times more capacity than the graphics processing unit in PlayStation 2 and an 8-gigabyte hard drive from IBM, which was an add-on component for PlayStation 2. In addition, the Xbox had twice as much memory as PlayStation 2 and a built-in Ethernet card and DVD ROM. As many of these components were made by Microsoft's PC manufacturing partners—including Intel, Nvidia, and IBM—this tended to strengthen Microsoft's bargaining position in negotiations for component costs.

DVD Player   The Xbox had a DVD ROM which played the games and, like PlayStation 2, offered a DVD player kit. However, unlike PlayStation 2, the DVD player of the Xbox was not a default function, and Xbox owners had to spend an additional $29.99 to buy a DVD playback kit in order to play DVD movies on their Xbox. Microsoft cut the built-in DVD player function because it saved $25 in each Xbox produced. However, many Xbox purchasers later complained about the DVD design, feeling that the built-in DVD player function should be a basic part of new consoles. Therefore, the Xbox's DVD design frustrated some consumers.

Internet Connection   Microsoft believed that playing games through the Internet was the future trend of the video game industry, so it made the Ethernet card a built-in part of the Xbox. However, since it did not support a dial-up connection, the Xbox became a device that was designed only for users with broadband Internet access. The Xbox developers had three reasons for this broadband-only design. First, this design simplified the process for game developers, who would not have to worry about designing games for play over both phone lines and high-speed Internet connections such as cable modems or DSL. Second, it was a concept issue. As Ted Hase, one of the Xbox creators, said, "Putting a 56k modem on the Xbox would be akin to putting cloth seats in a Ferrari." Third, since PlayStation 2 provided both dial-up and Ethernet adapters, this was an important way to make the Xbox different from its competitors and prove the high performance of the Xbox. For these reasons, the developers did not add the phone-line modem in the Xbox. Unfortunately, at the end of 2002 only 15 percent of U.S. households had broadband Internet connections. However, Dataquest reported that the rate of broadband Internet use nearly tripled from 2001 to 2002. As of December 2003, about 21 percent of U.S. homes already had high-speed access. This figure translated to approximately 43 percent

of the Internet-connected households in the United States. About 57 percent of the Internet-connected households remained dependent on narrowband connections of 56.6 kb/s or lower. According to a report by cNet, the number of U.S. homes with a broadband connection was forecasted to reach 33.5 million by the end of 2004, adding another 8.5 million households. Microsoft, which also operated the MSN Internet service business, believed that after some "blockbuster" online Xbox games became available, it could benefit from both online gaming and add-on Internet services such as e-mail, Web site hosting, and licensed downloads of music and other digital entertainment. (See Exhibit 10 for a comparison of online gaming platforms.)

Direct X   Although developing games for PlayStation 2 had been a nightmare for many programmers, the development process was easier for the Xbox because it involved the use of Microsoft's well-developed program Direct X as the major programming tool. Direct X was a collection of applications programming interfaces, or APIs, that enabled software developers to write code to exploit any type of PC hardware. The technology was crucial to the games business because it allowed software developers to standardize game programs. With the application of Direct X, it was easier for game programmers to design games for the Xbox than for PlayStation 2. Also, since Direct X became the programming standard for PC gaming developers, it was not very difficult for these companies to convert PC games into Xbox games. By using Direct X, Microsoft expected to attract plenty of software developers to design Xbox games or even change their developing platform from PlayStation 2 to the Xbox.

Expanding the Xbox's game titles would be a critical method for increasing Xbox sales. However, since PlayStation 2 had sold more than 8 million units and took more than 50 percent of the market share before the Xbox even joined the race, most game developers could not neglect this huge market. Thus, many developers designed games for PlayStation 2, and then transferred the same title into the Xbox's easier-designed platform. The number of the Xbox's games increased, but most of them were also published for the PlayStation 2 console with the same title and the same content. In addition, since these games were primarily designed for PlayStation 2, they tended not to be optimized for the Xbox platform in terms of performance and features.

Product Launch and Aftermath

On the night of November 14, 2001, Microsoft successfully launched the Xbox in New York City's Times Square. With the success of this first step, Bill Gates realized that the toughest and severest competition was just beginning between the three horses (PlayStation 2, the GameCube, and the Xbox) and the pony (the Game Boy Advance).

Exhibit 10   Comparison of Online Gaming Platforms

Features	Xbox	PlayStation 2
Built-in Ethernet port	Yes	No—add-on, $40 or $20 with a console purchase
Built-in hard disk for content downloads and multiplayer games	Yes	No—add-on, $80 to $100
All online games under one service	Yes	No
One unique identity	One password for all games	Varies by publisher
Connection	Broadband	Broadband or 56k modem
Find friends across service	Yes	No
Worldwide matchmaking	Yes	Yes
Voice in all games	All games	SOCOM only
Single list for all games	Yes	No
Invite friends to your game	Yes	No
Find and join your friends	Yes	No
Parental controls	Yes	No
Content downloads	Yes	HDD required
Hardware price	Ethernet adapter included with Xbox hardware. Xbox Communicator (free with Xbox *Live* subscription)	Network adapter: $40 Headset: $10 when gamers purchase SOCOM ($59.99) Service pricing options determined by each publisher
Service charge	Initial starter kit: $49.95 for one-year subscription, minigame(s) and an Xbox Communicator	Pricing options determined by each publisher
Ranking against friends	Yes	Not available
Third-party developers	61	16
Number of launch titles	7	5

Source: Gamespot.com.

Since the launch of the console, the award-winning lineup of software for the Xbox had reached a number of key sales milestones. According to independent data from the NPD Group, the definitive source of sales and market data on the video game industry, the Xbox had sold more than 10 million units of software in the first eight months the console had been on the market in the United States. That's the most software ever sold for a new video game system in the United States in the same period of time.

In May 2002 all three major game console manufacturers announced price cuts. The Xbox, with a cut of $100, experienced the largest percentage gains, with sales having spiked approximately 131 percent in the United States

within the first two months, according to NPD. However, initial market enthusiasm in the Xbox soon died down.

Although the Xbox offered the state-of-the-art of what game consoles could deliver and would pleasantly surprise its customers, the features were not the keys for Microsoft to attract consumers and beat opponents. During the second half of 2002, sales of the Xbox were well short of the launch team's forecasts. Microsoft announced that sales barely hit the bottom end of its previous forecast, and the company alerted suppliers that it was lowering sales projections for 2003 and, as a result, would buy fewer parts. Microsoft informed its Xbox parts suppliers not to expect any orders in the first half of 2003 so that the company could deplete existing console supplies. Nvidia, a key partner of Microsoft that made the Xbox's video controller, suffered the most. Adding to the soured relationship, Microsoft and Nvidia were in court over a disagreement regarding the price Microsoft was supposed to pay per unit for the video controllers.

As of June 2003 Sony's PlayStation 2 had captured 74 percent of the market, leaving Nintendo's GameCube to split the remainder of the market with console newcomer Microsoft and its Xbox at 13 percent each. It was now a nearly $30 billion industry, which made it larger than the film entertainment business upon which most of its best-selling titles were based! As of May 2004, PlayStation 2 continued to dominate the market, with more than 70 million consoles sold worldwide, maintaining its market share lead of five times that of the Xbox or GameCube.

Looking Forward

Although the video game industry by 2004 was dominated by only a few major players, Microsoft remained keenly aware that the video gaming console business would be highly competitive and continue to be characterized by limited platform life cycles, frequent introductions of new hit titles, and the development of new technologies. (See Exhibit 11 for the best-selling game titles in the first quarter of 2004.) Industry observers felt that Microsoft would have to outdistance its competitors in terms of price, product quality and variety, timing of releases, and effectiveness of distribution and marketing.

As announced at the 10th Annual E3 Video-Game Convention in Los Angeles in May 2004, Sony cut the price of its PlayStation 2 console to under $150, matching Microsoft's earlier reduction in the price of its Xbox console. By contrast, Nintendo had been selling its GameCube console for $99 since 2003. To mark the 10th anniversary of its founding, the Entertainment Software Association (ESA), an industry trade group representing video and computer game manufacturers, asked gamers what they considered to be the three biggest advancements made by the game industry in the past 10 years. Ninety-one percent said the increased quality of game graphics represented the biggest advancement. Respondents also indicated that the following milestones were significant: the increase in the variety of content (37 percent); the introduction of multiplayer game playing (27 percent); and the introduction of better story lines and more character development into games (28 percent). Over half (53 percent) of all game players expressly stated they were currently playing games as much as or more than they did 10 years ago.

The ESA also asked respondents to pick the three most important goals for the industry in the coming decade. Not surprisingly, most often mentioned (87 percent) was to reduce the price of games. Other goals included offering additional levels, characters, and other content in games (53 percent); creating more games for women (42 percent); decreasing reliance on licensed content (i.e., from films) and increasing reliance on original stories (36 percent); offering more games for purchase via download (21 percent); and making more games playable online (17 percent). The three major video game platform manufacturers also announced that they intended to introduce new consoles in 2005 or 2006.

Exhibit 11   Best-Selling Video Game Titles Ranked by Total U.S. Units, 1st Quarter 2004

Rank	Title	Platform	Publisher	Release Date	ARP*
1	*NFL Street*	PlayStation 2	Electronic Arts	Jan. 04	$49
2	*Need Speed: Underground*	PlayStation 2	Electronic Arts	Nov. 03	49
3	*Ninja Gaiden*	Xbox	Tecmo	Mar. 04	50
4	*Pokémon Colosseum*	GameCube	Nintendo	Mar. 04	48
5	*Sonic Heroes*	GameCube	SEGA	Jan. 04	49
6	*MVP Baseball 2004*	PlayStation 2	Electronic Arts	Mar. 04	49
7	*Final Fantasy Crystal*	GameCube	Nintendo	Feb. 04	49
8	*Halo*	Xbox	Microsoft	Nov. 01	30
9	*Mario Kart: Double*	GameCube	Nintendo	Nov. 03	49
10	*Bond 007: Everything*	PlayStation 2	Electronic Arts	Feb. 04	49

*ARP = Average retail price

Source: NPD.com.

Microsoft's supreme capital resources, unsurpassed reputation, and immense dominance in the software industry may have a significant influence on its ability to enlist third-party game developers and equipment manufacturers for the Xbox and acquire some video game development companies. However, unlike its past ventures, battling for the living room has been a fundamentally different kind of business for Microsoft. Would Bill Gates and his team be able to dominate the video game industry as they had previously done in their operating systems and software application markets? The answer seemed to depend on their future capability to set industry standards, dictate future strategic moves, and continue to manage "outside the box."

Bibliography

Alexander & Associates, 2001, Comparing generations of console gaming, www.alexassox.com.

Bishop, T., 2004, Video game console wars getting hotter, http://seattlepi.nwsource.com.

Boulding, A., 2002, State of the Xbox interview: Ed Fries, http://xbox.ign.com.

Chiu, B., 1998, *Microsoft Internet gaming zone: Fighter ace: Inside moves* (Redmond, WA: Microsoft Press).

DeMaria, R., & Wilson, J. L., 2002, *High score! The illustrated history of electronic games* (New York: McGraw-Hill Osborne Media).

Entertainment Software Associates, 2004, Demographic information, www.theesa.com.

Frederick, J., 2003, The console wars: Game on, www.time.com.

Games-Advertising.com, 2000, Gaming demographics: Gaming is an adult thing, www.games-advertising.com.

Gameinfowire.com, 2004, Americans playing more games, watching less movies and television, www.gameinfowire.com.

GIGnews.com, 2001, US video game industry ahead of its game despite recession, www.gignews.com.

Herman, L., 1994, *Phoenix: The fall & rise of home videogames* (Union, NJ: Rolenta Press).

Herz, J. C., 1997, *Joystick nation: How videogames ate our quarters, won our hearts, and rewired our minds* (New York: Little, Brown).

Hesseldahl, A., 2001, Xbox success? Not so fast, www.forbes.com.

Hopkins, J., 2004, Other nations zip by USA in high-speed net race, www.usatoday.com.

Kent, S. L., 2001, *The ultimate history of video games* (Roseville, CA: Prima Publishing).

Ketupa.com, 2002, Media profiles of Microsoft, www.ketupa.net.

Kovsky, S., 2002, High-tech toys for your TV (Indianapolis: Que Publishing).

Microsoft, 2002, Microsoft's solution for Internet business helps build early Xbox success, www.microsoft.com.

NPD Group, 2004, The NPD Group reports console video games industry sales fall slightly in first quarter 2004 over same period last year, www.npd.com.

———, 2003, Annual 2002 U.S. video game sales break record, www.npd.com.

Poole, S., 2000, *Trigger happy: Videogames and the Entertainment Revolution* (New York: Arcade Publishing).

Redmond, W., 2002, Xbox hits major sales milestones for console and games, www.microsoft.com.

———, 2002, New price is expected to expand market for world's most powerful video game console, www.microsoft.com.

———, 2003, Xbox live bursts through 350,000-subscriber mark as players rush for fresh downloadable content, www.microsoft.com.

Sheff, D., 1993, *Game over: How Nintendo zapped an American industry, captured your dollars, & enslaved your children* (Collingdale, PA: Diane Publishing).

SINA.com, 2004, US broadband connection to reach 33.5 million homes in 2004, http://english.sina.com.

Takahashi, D., 2002, *Opening the Xbox* (Roseville, CA: Prima Publishing).

TeamXbox.com, 2002, Xbox sales soaring, http://news.teamxbox.com.

Thurrott, P., 2003, Xbox sales worse than expected, www.winnetmag.com.

Underdahl, B., 2002, Xbox: Blow the lid off! (New York: McGraw-Hill Osborne Media).

Case 27 Nokia's Strategic Intent for the 21st Century

Sitting in the corporate conference room on top of the Espoo Tower in Finland in March 2003, K. P. Wilska, president Nokia Americas, gazed out the window over a frozen lake at a glaringly visible Sony-Ericsson logo on the adjacent office tower. "Sony-Ericsson was started by some of our people with some of our ideas . . . With over 60,000 people and $33 billion in sales we are on top of the wireless communication industry today but it seems like there are more challenges and obstacles than when we began this journey over a decade ago." Pekka Ali-Peitella, global president, added, "we have helped create a fundamentally new global market in less than ten years—and an organization that has consistently created value with a track record of successful product innovation, rapid response and growing brand recognition." Holstein Moerk, executive vice president, Human Resources, added, "We are continually in a state of reorganization and resource reallocation, targeting new customers and markets while focusing on building high performance teams and making sure that our associates' life strategies coincide with our corporate strategy and vision."

By the end of 2003, Nokia was the world's largest, most profitable maker of cellular phones—ahead of Motorola, Ericsson, Siemens, Samsung, and a host of others (Exhibit 1). Its products included mobile phones (wireless voice and data devices for personal, business, and entertainment uses) and networks (wireless switching and transmission equipment used by carriers). Nokia's other products included set-top boxes, home satellite systems, wireless network software, and cell phone displays. The company's Nokia Ventures division invested in technology-related start-ups.

Chairman and CEO since 1992, Jorma Ollila's vision for the next decade was clear: Nokia would dominate the wireless communication space by expanding voice communications to developing markets, by delivering extended mobility to the enterprise, and by driving consumer mobile multimedia. The management team would face both old and new competitors and consortia alike in carving out their strategic intent in hopes of redefining a new information-communication-entertainment industry space.

Nokia Mobile Phones and the Early 1990s

In 1990, as newly appointed president of Nokia Mobile Phones (the smallest of five Nokia Group divisions, with just over 3,000 employees and sales of $500 million), Jorma Ollila would oversee the upstart mobile telephone division's ascendance within the group and, more importantly, within the industry at large. By mid-1991 his division had become the world's second largest producer of mobile telephones (a 13 percent market share), nearly half the size of number one Motorola (22 percent market share). Motorola, a fully integrated manufacturer of mobile telephony with $10 billion revenues, had fully owned operations in each phase of the value chain, from semiconductors to handsets to cellular infrastructure equipment and satellites. A close third was NEC Corporation (10 percent market share), a formidable competitor with $26 billion in revenues and vast financial resources. Both Motorola and NEC were poised to dominate the burgeoning cellular phone market (Exhibit 2).

In the early 1990s the cellular market had grown rapidly with significant top-line and bottom-line growth. The consumer of choice was primarily the business user willing to pay for the functional mobility of cellular phones despite their high prices. These prices were unattractive to the mass-market consumer and cellular phone design remained bulky and functionally limited. Asia-Pacific manufacturers began to drive down the high initial margins of the leading competitors. Concurrently, cellular phone sales were expected to grow up to 20 percent annually for the next few years. These factors created considerable uncertainty and blurred the future of cellular phones as a mass communication medium.

At this time, communication standards for cellular phones had yet to evolve. There were multiple proprietary

Exhibit 1 Worldwide Market Share of Cellular Handset Manufacturers by Units (%)

	1990	2003
Nokia	13.00%	34.10%
Motorola	22.00	14.80
Ericsson/Sony	3.00	7.70
Samsung	0.00	7.20
Siemens	0.00	7.20
Kyocera	0.00	4.30
Panasonic	6.00	4.10
Others	56.00	20.60
Total	100.00%	100.00%

Source: Micrologic Research.

This case was prepared by research associate Dev Krishnan, under the supervision of Professor Michael D. Oliff, as a basis for classroom discussion rather than to illustrate the effective or ineffective handling of a business situation. It was developed within the scope of Enterprise 2020, a development program conducted with global enterprises. Copyright © School of Management, University of Texas, Dallas, 2004.

Exhibit 2   Cellular Handset Sales by Technology
(In millions of units)

	Actual 2001	Projected 2006
Analog	13.5	0.8
Other	47.6	19.1
GSM	274.3	391.5
CDMA One	49.0	23.5
W-CDMA	0.1	102.7
CDMA 2000	2.4	196.9
Total	386.9	734.5

Technology

	2001 Sales (%)	2006 Sales (%)
Generation 1	15.79%	2.71%
Generation 2	83.56	56.50
Generation 3	0.65	40.79
Totals	100.00%	100.00%

Source: Micrologic Research; 3G Technologies.

standards across, and often within, markets. These standards gave firms the ability to own the value chain by developing proprietary hardware and software for cellular service providers. Communication standards consisted broadly of two disparate categories, analog and digital, with each player in the cellular industry committed to a variant of one or the other. Analog was a legacy system, with digital standards only gradually emerging at that time as the potential universal standard of the future. From their inception, digital communication standards increased network utilization by enabling higher data transmission on the same bandwidth. As an open communication standard, digital allowed cellular providers to mix and match equipment of different manufacturers. Consequently, these emerging standards provided marginalized cellular players with "the right to play," especially those who had been previously shut out of the cellular market because of the proprietary technology and equipment that analog standards required. Firms had to make the tough choice of which communication standard to back as it involved significant resource commitments no matter which path was chosen. The stage was set for the first war for the cellular phone industry.

The Road to 2002

Lacking the resources to compete head-on with either Motorola or NEC, Nokia focused on creating strong alliances across the value chain. Ollila bet on a rapid emer-

gence of digital standards and signed an agreement with AT&T to design new semiconductors for the coming digital cellular phones to which he had committed the company. Nokia also entered a consortium with Alcatel and AEG to design cellular systems for European digital markets. They initiated and signed an agreement with the consumer electronics retailer Tandy/Radio Shack to distribute a custom-made Nokia phone, called the Tandy Mobira, in the U.S. market. Nokia also acquired key resources to provide added impetus to its development efforts. In late 1991, the company bought Technophone, the number two European cellular phone manufacturer, which led to increased economies of scale, greater market share, and increased access to R&D resources.

Committed to pursue and propagate digital technology, Nokia determined that players in the cellular phone market needed a uniform standard for communication and network interface. The firm leveraged its strength in building partnerships and entered into industrywide alliances with network equipment manufacturers to adopt a common communication standard. With its extensive digital technology experience, Nokia propelled the establishment of its global system for mobile communications (GSM) digital standard. Its alliances and industrywide consortiums were such effective platforms to propagate the standard that by 2001, three out of every four phones sold were GSM compatible.

Ollila and his team realized that the keys to serving the changing markets were the new distribution channels that would open up as digital cellular phones became easier to configure with smart cards. Nokia entered into distribution alliances with key electronic retailers and significantly increased its penetration in key markets, resulting in higher visibility shelf space among trade channels compared to their competitors. Nokia grabbed the initial lead in the mid-90s and built the momentum critical for its meteoric rise. Forecasts made a year earlier of 400,000 units for 1993 turned into year-end sales in excess of 20 million digital phones.

At the same time, production planning at Nokia was ill-equipped to handle the explosion in cellular phone sales. The turbulent market and plethora of communication standards required a multitude of proprietary parts for each mobile phone assembled, with some parts having lead times in excess of internal planning horizons. Consequently, Nokia's stockpile of work-in-process inventory grew out of control and became financially burdensome. This situation was further compounded by the lack of adequate information systems to help predict or prevent blockages in the supply chain.

Nokia believed the key to success was the ability to drastically ramp up production to meet and exceed customer expectations, that is, the various channel partners. Consequently, the firm invested in a reliable information system that served the needs of production planning, accurate forecasting, reliable sales reporting, and supplier integration to accurately assess bottlenecks in the supply chain and reduce inventory levels. By 1993 Nokia Mobile Phones had reduced its distribution sites from 18 to 9, decreased the number of suppliers from 300 to 150, and closed three plants in Finland—drastically reducing complexity. Overall lead times were reduced by 50 percent through a number of related initiatives: R&D focus on the standardization of component parts, assembly process improvements, purchasing lead-time emphasis and measurement, and so forth. Developing a distinctive competency in rapid response proved successful and increased profits substantially while providing the much needed flexibility demanded by a turbulent market.

Nokia also recognized early that increased price pressures would render cell phones a commodity in the near future and began to "think like a consumer products company" well ahead of its competitors. They advertised aggressively, reallocated significant resources, and built brand image among the end consumers who they felt would increasingly dictate the choice of phones bought in the market. This brand competency was executed on a global scale as Nokia expanded its reach both east and west. By 1999, after several years of sponsoring the NCAA Sugar Bowl, over 90 percent of North Americans finally recognized the firm as "Scandinavian and not Japanese." Recognition of Nokia's distinctive competency in global brand management was indicated by *Business-Week* Interbrand's report* in which Nokia was ranked number six on the list of the "World's most admired brands" among heavyweights like Coca-Cola and Intel.

Nokia spent the rest of the decade allocating significant resources to build a distinctive competency in product innovation. Like Sony and 3M, the company further complemented its brand image with superior product offerings. The firm repeatedly and consistently exceeded consumer expectations with unique, appealing ergonomic designs, user-friendly interfaces, and easy-to-use phone services.

With established distinctive competencies in rapid response, global brand management, and product innovation, Nokia signed deals in 1999 to put its wireless application protocol (WAP) software into network servers produced by Hewlett-Packard and IBM. The company, which also unveiled several WAP-enabled phones designed to access the Internet, widened its lead as the world's biggest seller of mobile phones and made several acquisitions to strengthen its Internet protocol networks business. Extending its push into Internet capability, Nokia also bought several smaller companies that developed e-commerce and telephony technologies.

"Life went mobile"[1] as cellular communications came of age with cellular phones exceeding fixed tele-

phone lines worldwide (1.2 billion versus 1.0 billion, respectively). Continued reductions in cost of use (both handset and network charges) would continue to drive growth. Cellular phones provided consumers worldwide with mobility and connectivity never imagined even a decade before. Studies showed that a significant number of North American families were doing away with fixed-line phones and using wireless exclusively for the home and family. At the same time the majority of the world's population (outside of the G8 countries) had yet to have access to any form of telephony, providing Nokia and other mobile phone manufacturers with the opportunity to reach vast numbers of the world's population.

New Industries and Markets

As it entered the second millennium, Nokia was well ahead of its rivals in wireless digital phones and dominated the European GSM market. It lagged slightly in the U.S. market where many large carriers adopted Qualcomm's code division multiple access (CDMA) standard. In 2000 Nokia began to cover the bases for the third generation by offering products to bridge the gap between generations. In an effort to jump-start declining handset sales as the cell phone market in the West and Japan approached saturation, Nokia set its sights on becoming the leader in third-generation (3G) wireless network equipment. The company teamed with other phone makers and wireless service providers to develop a common global standard for 3G phone software. The effort was backed by Motorola, Sony-Ericsson, and Japan's NTT DoCoMo.

Nokia's management team had browsed through a University of Texas at Dallas *Enterprise 2020* executive report during the first quarterly review for 2003. Broadly, the report predicted and described a set of forces and value drivers that would likely reshape the future of commercial and individual life concurrently. More specifically, it outlined emerging customer and consumer expectations, trends, and potential discontinuities that would impact the wireless industry directly. The future relevance of Nokia's global leadership in cellular handset production and the past decade of historic telecom success were put in question by the *Enterprise 2020* executive report's focus on other rapidly converging global industries and markets. Nokia's management team was particularly interested in the commercial and consumer developments in:

Information communication and knowledge commerce.

Innovation and performance improvement.

Education and entertainment.

Lifestyle enhancement and extension.

Info-know-com, Inno-formance, Edu-tainment, and Life-enrichment were emerging as related but distinct global industries that would encompass over a trillion

---

*Khermooch, Gerry, 2003, "Brands in an age of anti-Americanism," *BusinessWeek*, August 4: 69.

[1]Ollila, Jorma, 2003, Life goes mobile, Nokia Corporation.

**Exhibit 3   2002 Financial Information for Leading Global Cellular Service Providers
(All figures are $ millions, unless otherwise indicated)**

Income Statement			
	Vodafone	**NTT DoCoMo**	**Cingular**
Revenue	$48,005.0	$40,730.8	$14,727.0
Cost of goods sold	21,911.0	13,793.8	4,930.0
Gross profit	26,094.0	26,937.0	9,797.0
Gross profit margin (%)	54.4%	66.1%	66.5%
Selling, general, and administrative expense	8,539.0	11,641.7	7,276.0
Depreciation and amortization	25,139.0	6,345.4	1,850.0
Operating income	(7,584.0)	8,949.9	2,521.0
Operating margin (%)	0.0%	22.0%	17.1%
Nonoperating income	(1,029.0)	(2,719.8)	29.0
Nonoperating expenses	1,188.0	142.9	1,299.0
Income before taxes	(9,809.0)	6,087.2	1,251.0
Income taxes	4,672.0	3,849.3	12.0
Net income after taxes	(14,481.0)	2,237.9	1,239.0
Continuing operations	(15,518.0)	2,102.2	1,239.0
Discontinued operations	—	—	—
Total operations	(15,518.0)	2,102.2	1,239.0
Total net income	$(15,518.0)	1,799.7	1,207.0
Net profit margin (%)	0.0%	4.4%	8.2%

Source: www.hoovers.com.   (continued on facing page)

U.S. dollars of annual value in the foreseeable future. Excerpts from the 2020 report on the following subjects follow: new distribution channels, changing markets, cellular standards, customer revenue requirements, consumer expectations, and the convergence of appliances, as well as performance improvement.

New Distribution Channels   In the early 1990s, fragmented cellular standards, requiring proprietary products, gave cellular phone users limited choice of cellular handsets. As cellular communication standards converged and dominant cellular service providers (CSPs) emerged in each market, consumers were faced with an increasing array of cellular handsets. Initially, individual phones were configured at the point of sale by appliance store representatives and primed before use. As technology improved and standards emerged, phones came preconfigured and "ready-to-use." CSPs used this improvement in technology as an opportunity to gain control of both the point of sale and the end consumer. Cellular phone manufacturers were increasingly pressured to introduce discounted custom-made phones which were provided at subsidized rates to consumers.[2] Manufacturers in the Asia-Pacific region drove down prices faster than expected for lower-end, feature-sparse phones used by entry-level cellular consumers. By the turn of the century, CSPs worldwide had gone through a tumultuous process of expansion, acquisition, and consolidation in cellular markets. Three CSPs emerged as formidable players (see Exhibit 3 and Exhibit 4) in the global wireless cellular-scope of 2004.

[2]CSPs were getting into the practice of running promotions on the latest cellular models, offering them at discounted prices. Low-end or entry-level phones were being given away at heavily discounted prices, in some cases free, to the end consumer upon signing an extended service plan. Extended service plans locked in consumers to the cellular carrier to the life of the plan, with penalties to the consumer for premature termination.

Exhibit 3   2002 Financial Information (continued)

Balance Sheet			
	Vodafone	**NTT DoCoMo**	**Cingular**
Assets			
Cash	751.0	5,767.4	908.0
Net receivables	10,171.0	6,130.3	1,520.0
Inventories	577.0	570.1	126.0
Other current assets	2,078.0	1,414.0	177.0
Total current assets	13,577.0	13,881.8	2,731.0
Net fixed assets	30,935.0	22,665.6	10,146.0
Other noncurrent assets	213,536.0	14,761.3	11,245.0
Total assets	258,048.0	51,308.6	24,122.0
Liabilities and shareholders' equity			
Current Liabilities			
Accounts payable	3,946.0	5,409.2	1,043.0
Short-term debt	2,260.0	1,158.1	90.0
Other current liabilities	16,382.0	2,345.5	1,654.0
Total current liabilities	22,589.0	8,912.8	2,787.0
Long-term debt	20,822.0	10,261.9	12,546.0
Other noncurrent liabilities	6,761.0	2,693.8	1,248.0
Total liabilities	54,696.0	21,872.5	16,581.0

Shareholders' Equity			
Preferred stock equity	—	—	—
Common stock equity	203,352.0	29,436.0	7,541.0
Total equity	203,352.0	29,436.0	7,541.0
Shares outstanding (millions of shares)	6,816.5	5,017.0	—

Cash Flow Statement			
Net operating cash flow	16,515.0	13,420.9	3,592.0
Net investing cash flow	(16,204.0)	(7,380.6)	(3,585.0)
Net financing cash flow	310.0	(2,822.7)	334.0
Net change in cash	621.0	3,217.6	341.0

Other Information			
Depreciation and amortization	25,139.0	6,345.4	1,850.0
Capital expenditures	(16,227.0)	(5,932.7)	(3,085.0)

Exhibit 4   Key Financial Indicators of Cellular Phone Manufacturers, 2002
(All figures are $ millions, unless otherwise indicated)

	Vodafone	DoCoMo	Cingular	Industry	Market
Key Numbers					
Annual sales	$ 48,005.0	$40,730.8	$14,727.0		
Employees	66,667	23,310	39,400		
Market capitalization	163,522.0	90,464.0	NA		
No. of shares outstanding	6,816.5	5,018.0	NA		
Profitability (%)					
Gross profit margin	54.4%	66.1%	66.5%	51.05%	48.51%
Net profit margin	0.0	4.4	8.2	(4.63)	5.25
Return on equity	0.0	15.5	16.43	—	10.6
Return on assets	(5.8)	9.1	5.14	(1.5)	1.8
Return on invested capital	(7.5)	12.0	16.43	(2.0)	5.0
Valuation					
Price/sales ratio	3.41	2.03	NA	2.83	1.25
Price/earnings ratio	(11.29)	17.57	NA	NA	25.9
Price/book ratio	0.79	2.68	NA	1.49	2.52
Operations					
Days of sales outstanding	89.61	64.84	37.16	67.89	56.18
Inventory turnover	83.20	71.45	116.88	23.60	8.40
Days cost of goods sold in inventory	9.48	14.88	9.20	15.00	43.00
Asset turnover	0.19	0.79	0.61	0.40	0.40

Source: www.hoovers.com.

The Vodafone Group, based in the United Kingdom and, with its subsidiaries, the world's largest cellular service provider, catered to 123 million cellular service subscribers.[3] The company owned stakes in leading wireless carriers around the globe. It held an interest in leading mobile phone operators in the United States (45 percent-owned Verizon Wireless), Germany (D2), and the U.K. (Vodafone). The Vodafone Group owned stakes in operating affiliates in Europe, the Americas, the Asia-Pacific region, the Middle East, and Africa. It also held stakes in wireless carriers in several other European countries, including France, the Netherlands, and Spain. In 2002 Vodafone entered into a partnership with software giant Microsoft to develop better cellular services for consumers worldwide.

By 2004 NTT DoCoMo had over 44 million digital network subscribers, second only to Vodafone.[4] The company enjoyed a major commercial success with the rollout of the "i-mode" service in the second quarter of 2001 within the Japanese market.[5] For the first time, the i-mode service provided consumers with the ability to access the World Wide Web through wireless handsets and, concurrently, the ability to use their handsets to purchase products and services directly. In 2003 nearly 38 million customers subscribed to DoCoMo's i-mode service. The company also offered paging, maritime, and in-flight phone services, and sold handsets and pagers. DoCoMo (which means "anywhere") cornered nearly 60 percent of

[3]Vodafone overview, 2004, February 29, www.hoovers.com.

[4]NTT DoCoMo overview, 2004, March 11, www.hoovers.com.

[5]"i-mode" is a registered trademark of NTT DoCoMo.

Exhibit 5   Financial Performance of Global Cellular Phone Manufacturers, 2002

	Nokia	Ericsson	Motorola	Industry	Market
Key Numbers					
Annual sales ($ millions)	31,526.00	16,808.00	26,679.00		
Employees	51,748	64,621	97,000		
Market value ($ millions)	80,546.60	27,022.30	31,487.60		
Profitability (%)					
Gross profit margin	41.95%	36.11%	41.50%	38.81%	49.07%
Pretax profit margin	17.30	−19.48	3.25	−2.91	5.43
Net profit margin	11.70	−16.01	2.17	−3.79	2.50
Return on equity	23.40	—	4.90	0.00	5.10
Return on assets	14.70	−10.30	1.90	−2.70%	0.80
Return on invested capital	23.40	−19.80	3.10	−4.20	2.40
Valuation					
Price/sales ratio	2.36	1.78	1.18	2.11	1.23
Price/earnings ratio	20.47	—	54.12	—	50.76
Price/book ratio	4.73	3.29	2.65	3.54	2.50
Price/cash flow ratio	15.04	−16.11	13.01	71.14	13.92
Operations					
Days of sales outstanding	—	169.11	49.11	88.03	56.80
Inventory turnover	12.40	4.60	6.00	6.60	7.80
Days cost of goods sold in inventory	—	78.00	60.00	55.00	46.00
Asset turnover	1.40	0.60	0.90	0.70	0.40
Net receivables turnover flow	6.30	1.90	6.80	3.90	7.00
Financial					
Current ratio	2.20	2.45	1.87	2.30	1.46
Quick ratio	1.90	2.20	1.20	1.90	1.00
Leverage ratio	1.60	2.88	2.52	2.33	6.03
Total debt/equity	0.03	0.49	0.67	0.51	1.45

Source: Company annual reports.

the Japanese market for mobile phones through its eight majority-owned regional operating subsidiaries. The company licensed its i-mode technology through a subsidiary to the telecom units in France, Italy, and Spain. As of the fourth quarter of 2003, DoCoMo Europe Ltd. had secured major bids on European next-generation mobile phone licenses as well.

Two regional Bell companies combined assets to create the number two wireless carrier, after Verizon Wireless, in the United States: Cingular Wireless Communica-

tions.[6] By January 2004, it had over 25 million customers, including subscribers to its Mobitex wireless data services network. Cingular operated primarily in the U.S. market. Soon after, Cingular bought domestic rival AT&T Wireless when it won a bidding war with the Vodafone Group. The deal, valued at $41 billion, created the leading U.S. wireless carrier with 46 million customers, topping the leader at the time, Verizon Wireless. Exhibit 5 illustrates the

[6]Cingular Wireless overview, 2004, March 11, www.hoovers.com.

Exhibit 6   Sales of Nokia Operations and Business Groups, 2002

	$ Millions	% of Total
Nokia Operations		
United States	4,900	16%
United Kingdom	3,268	10
China	2,943	9
Germany	1,942	6
Finland	371	2
Other regions	18,103	57
Total	31,526	100%
2002 Sales		
Nokia Mobile Phones	24,379	77%
Nokia Networks	6,868	21
Nokia Ventures Organization	482	2
Total	31,729	100%

Source: Nokia annual reports.

financial performance of leading cell phone manufacturers. Exhibits 6 and 7 provide details on Nokia's sales and organization.

The Changing Nature of Markets   The resolution of the analog versus digital standard battle of the early 1990s gave way to the frenzied jockeying for market position in emerging cellular service markets—North America, Europe, and Asia-Pacific—to own various parts of the cellular value chain. Gradually, these markets were saturated from the slowing economic growth in these regions. Moreover, the face of global trade was changing as trading blocs emerged—the European Union, North American Free Trade Agreement (NAFTA)—nations adopted liberalized trading policies (India, China), and many countries embraced world trade (under the auspices of the World Trade Organization). Two key emerging markets that showed potential for extensive deployment of cellular services were China and India (see Exhibit 8).

China   By the mid-1990s China had gradually embraced the free market model. At the turn of the century, the Chinese government opened up many sectors of the economy for foreign investment, including cellular communications infrastructure. Until 1997 China Telecom was the only organization allowed to operate cellular services. To foster competition the Chinese government set up another organization that was allowed to offer cellular services, China Unicom. Cellular services has grown at a feverish pace since the formation of these organizations. Before 2000 came to a close, China overtook the United States as the largest cellular communications market.[7] In 2003 the Chinese government awarded licenses to cellular infrastructure providers to provide 3G infrastructure to China Unicom and China Telecom for WCDMA and CDMA 2000-compliant hardware. At the end of the third quarter of 2003, it was estimated that for every CDMA 2000 phone sold, seven GSM-based WCDMA phones were sold.[8]

India   The Indian economy emerged from its socialist past to embrace the global economy in the early 1990s. In 1996 the Indian government awarded cellular licenses to private firms allowing them to offer and operate cellular services. With its large population and underdeveloped telecommunications market, this represented an ideal potential market for cellular phones. Since 2000 many large foreign cellular operators have invested in India, building on the early successes of other cellular operators and the liberalized trade policies in place. Following entry, players in the cellular industry were faced with significant implementation issues. Geographic disparity led to logistic issues while linguistic diversity led to higher than antici-

[7]China Unicom overview, 2004, February 29, www.hoovers.com.

[8]Vodafone overview.

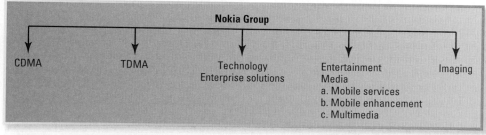

Exhibit 7   Organizational Structure of the Nokia Group, 2002 Resource Allocation Model

Exhibit 8   Potential Cellular Markets Based on Population and Telecommunication Penetration

Number	Markets	Population (In millions) (a)	Fixed + Cellular Lines (In millions) (b)	Market Potential (a) – (b)
1	India	1,046	36	1,010
2	China	1,284	327	957
3	Indonesia	231	15	216
4	Pakistan	148	4	144
5	Bangladesh	133	1	132
6	Nigeria	130	2	128
7	Brazil	176	48	128
8	Russia	145	44	101
9	Vietnam	81	4	77
10	Philippines	85	17	68
11	Ethiopia	68	0	68
12	Mexico	103	38	65
13	Egypt	71	8	63
14	Iran	67	8	59
15	Democratic Republic of the Congo	55	0	55
16	Myanmar (Burma)	42	0	42
17	Thailand	62	21	41
18	Tanzania	37	1	36
19	Sudan	37	1	36
20	Ukraine	48	13	35

Source: *Plunkett's Telecommunication Industry Almanac 2003.*

pated marketing costs. To overcome consumer uncertainty concerning the cost of ownership of cellular handsets, manufacturers introduced inexpensive mobile phone models throughout India.[9] Indian cellular infrastructure had been largely based on GSM standards. In 2003, however, cellular service providers started offering CDMA 2000-compatible phones as well.

Emerging Cellular Standards   As the 1990s came to a close, voice usage revenues leveled, limiting growth for cellular service providers worldwide. The prevalent CDMA and GSM standards had limitations on the bandwidth available to individual users and the amount of data they could support on a communications network. In ad-

dition, cellular phone users increasingly looked for a richer, more interactive cellular phone experience that required higher bandwidths than those then available.

These factors led to a worldwide initiative to create the next generation cellular communication standard—3G—the third iteration. The 3G peer-to-peer open standard was created to support higher data transmission levels across cellular networks and improve the communication experience of wireless terminal users through new data-rich services—games, photo and video messaging, and mapping. The open standard left many organizations vying to own strategic parts of the 3G pie[10] content development, wireless terminal communication, and interface standards for phones (displays, operating systems, and network traffic

[9]Nokia launches entry-level phones for new growth markets, 2003, Asia Intelligence Wire, August 31.

[10]Heads we win, tails we win, 2003, *Fortune* (Europe), March 3: 50.

Exhibit 9   Expected Value Chain for 3G Services

	CSP 1	CSP 2	CSP 3
Network applications	Tailored network application for CSP 1	Tailored network application for CSP 2	Tailored network application for CSP 3
Middleware	Numerous middleware vendors	Numerous middleware vendors	Numerous middleware vendors
Hardware	Numerous hardware vendors	Numerous hardware vendors	Numerous hardware vendors

Source: Nokia Corporation, 2003.

management). (See Exhibit 9.) Cellular service firms were eager to be the first to offer fully integrated 3G services to their customers. In 2002 European carriers spent upward of $100 billion on licenses for the radio spectrum necessary to offer 3G services.

Adding to the allure of 3G service was the emergence of the Internet as the information backbone for a variety of information-related functions—personal, financial, social, to name a few. Cellular providers then faced the opportunity of seamlessly linking consumers with the Internet on their wireless terminals. The Internet provided the seemingly limitless databank for multimedia messaging services (MMSs), 3G's unique proposition to enhance the communications of cellular users with other contacts. MMSs enhanced the use of the wireless terminal as a communication tool by incorporating pictures, video, and streaming audio to enrich the effectiveness of the message sent. Content formatted for mobile terminals, standards for transmission of media over wireless terminals, and revenue/profit models for content and carriers emerged as key concerns in integrating Internet-based services into wireless handsets.

However, in the race for the dominant 3G cellular communication standard, a new battle loomed on the horizon. From the early 1990s GSM had come to dominate the world as the cellular communication standard of choice (three of every four cellular callers worldwide used a GSM-compatible phone on a GSM-based network). At the heart of the race stood two opposing network communication standards to offer 3G services. On one side were all the carriers who relied on the CDMA communication standard—most U.S.-based carriers, all of South Korea, and a host of other global carriers. On the other, much larger side adhering to the GSM communication standard were most of Europe, some U.S.-based carriers, and most of China and India. Each group offered its version of 3G; CDMA 2000 in the CDMA world and WCDMA among the GSM proponents. The outcome remained unclear as to

which standard would prevail. Most industry observers predicted that WCDMA would eventually become the dominant 3G network standard largely due to the GSM market share advantage. The actual number would ultimately depend on the emerging standard in developing cellular markets. As of the second quarter of 2003, 37 CDMA 2000 networks were up and running around the world, compared with 2 WCDMA networks. Implementing 3G-compliant networks based on CDMA 2000 outpaced equivalent 3G-compliant WCDMA implementations as CDMA 2000 chipset design licenses became easier to integrate across markets.[11] By the end of 2003, problems with equipment and the rollout of worldwide technical upgrades had set back overall industry 3G projections by 12 to 24 months.

The following issues remained key concerns in the rollout of 3G worldwide:

1. With content across wireless networks digitally stored, owned, and consumed, digital rights management (DRM) emerged as a primary concern for promoting wireless content and its lawful use.[12] DRM promoted lawful distribution and usage of copyrighted material by giving licenses for the requesting party to use or view the material for a limited period of time or indefinitely. An industry alliance was under way to speed the propagation of digital content to mobile terminals in an efficient, profitable, and effective manner.

[11]U.S.-based Qualcomm, a forerunner in CMDA technology, owns much of the chipset technology design patents, and licenses for 3G-compliant CDMA 2000 networks, which require CSPs to purchase technology licenses from this firm. The resultant standardization of technology and related designs has increased portability of CDMA 2000-compliant technologies across markets. As of 2003, WCDMA had multiple design standards prevalent that sometimes limit portability across markets.

[12]MMS entering into the next phase, 2003, White paper by Nokia Corporation, 11–12.

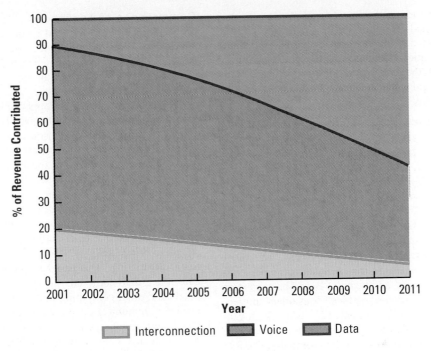

Exhibit 10   Projected Sources of Revenue for Mobile Operators

2. Security remained a prime concern for mobile users; its impact had already been felt on application developers. New standards on the existing transfer of sensitive data, personal information, and privacy had not yet reached the required security levels because networks were constrained by the amount of volume-heavy encrypted information they could support. Additionally, smart cards had been embedded in some cellular handsets, giving handset users the ability to purchase goods and services (from objects with embedded smart cards) by authenticating purchases through their cellular handsets. The key concerns of security and authentication for this technology remained unanswered as 2004 began.

Customers—Revenue Growth Requirements   At the turn of the 21st century most cellular carriers faced worldwide declines in revenue growth, resulting from the saturation of key markets in North America, Europe, and the Asia-Pacific region. At the time players in the telecommunications industry had made capital expenditures to upgrade or maintain aging infrastructure, resulting in a profits squeeze in the industry. Additionally, voice services, the bread and butter for most carriers, were fast becoming commodity products, and voice usage rates were peaking as well (see Exhibit 10). The near simultaneous squeeze in top-line and bottom-line growth from these factors left many carriers scrambling for new sources of growth or profits. Key initiatives were sought to widen the subscriber base and improve network utilization.

Cellular service providers also planned to widen their subscriber base by entering new emerging markets. CSPs fast discovered that cellular customers in different markets had divergent needs. In most emerging markets, offering low-cost options to consumers was the most important factor. According to consumer behavior studies in these markets, the prevailing price sensitivity associated with consumers switching to cellular phones from other forms of telecommunication indicated that halving the total cost of ownership would more than double penetration. As a method of inducing cellular subscribers to try out cellular phones, prepaid cellular services seemed to be the model of choice for consumers in emerging markets. Furthermore, the lagging infrastructure and diverse geographic conditions in those markets required cellular infrastructure providers to introduce low-cost options to help carriers deploy their networks cost-effectively. Cellular infrastructure providers started offering network base station planning and alternative base station designs as add-on services to reduce implementation costs of CSPs in emerging markets.

The cellular industry responded to the limited potential voice services offered for differentiation by investing in new technology that allowed users to communicate over cellular networks using rich media like pictures, streaming audio, and video. Rich media carried over 3G networks that tap into the Internet were being pushed actively by major carriers worldwide as the next "star service." CSPs then had the opportunity to differentiate these services and drive bottom-line growth. CSPs intensified work with application designers to deliver technologies that would enrich the lives of mobile handset users. Key challenges remained with the seamless transition from old to new technologies.

Consumer Expectations—Phones, Mobility, Usage, and Lifestyle

For many consumers, cellular phones had moved far beyond a one-dimensional instrument for voice conversation. To them the cellular phone had become a tool for entertainment (e.g., gaming, audio, imaging, media), personal expression, and extended communication. These diverse applications had ushered in the age of the "wireless terminal." The ability to perform multiple functions in addition to voice and data transmission had become a basic consumer requirement. The most common uses for wireless terminals were voice, personal expression, active usage, and fashion. Based on consumer usage statistics and psychographics, consumers' preferences could be effectively segmented by usage (high versus low usage), lifestyle (activity-specific terminals), and product category (application-specific terminals). The following trends had emerged in consumer preferences related to the performance of their mobile terminals:

- *Content from a strong or trusted brand*—consumers were interested in browsing for content on their mobile terminals. Furthermore, consumers were willing to accept content only from a trusted brand or portal.
- *Targeted content*—the content needed to appeal to a specific consumer group and ideally would be selected based on the consumer's preset preferences—for example, "mobile wallets" for financial applications.
- *Friendly portal navigation*—consumers preferred the richer browsing experience afforded by color browsers built in to their wireless terminals. Navigating between portals was often cumbersome with traditional terminal design.
- *Consumer "mobile personality"*—users sought a wireless terminal as an extension of their personality, a communicator to and from their friends and peers.

The last trend posed immense potential in segmenting consumers, building applications, and delivering services in the new wired world. However, the "mobile personality" concept raised issues in the creation and completion of cellular transactions—identity, authentication, user profile, and privacy. Players in the cellular industry scrambled to address these issues in the race to offer consumers the "killer app" of 3G services.

Convergence of Appliances

The early 1990s saw a proliferation in the form and nature of electronic appliances. Not only did appliances get smaller and more portable, but they became increasingly multifunctional. Consumers began to expect an appliance to perform beyond its primary functional use. The rise of the Internet brought a hitherto untapped opportunity for interconnectivity among appliances. In the past data was stored, consumed, or retrieved from the source appliances with little or no interconnectivity between the appliances themselves. The Internet provided the ability to link seemingly incongruent devices that stored, disseminated, or captured information. The influence on consumers' lifestyles from these trends—multifunctionality among appliances and the sustained need for computing power—spawned new genres of information-friendly portable devices that sought to bridge the gap between mobility and multifunctional computing. The personal digital assistant (PDA) and other smart terminals provided links between computers and other computing devices to share information. Device communication protocols like Bluetooth further aided and encouraged information exchange between seemingly incompatible devices.[13] The lines between pure computing devices and mobile terminals became increasingly blurred.

These trends fueled the emergence of "smart phones" that allowed for word processing, spreadsheet manipulation, e-mail and Internet browsing, and personal information management as well as data synchronization to desktop applications. By 2003 smart phones were growing at the expense of nonconnected PDAs which recorded their second consecutive year of decline that year—down 8.4 percent to 11.35 million units—according to IDC, an independent research firm. Of the 118 million mobile handsets shipped during the first quarter of 2003, 2 million were smart phones. A wireless handset market analyst at IDC opined that, by 2007, 75 percent of all mobile phones would be converged devices, with a major segment from the smart phones category.[14] With its 61 percent share, Nokia continued to dominate in converged devices, trailed far behind by Sony-Ericsson and Motorola with a 10.2 and 5.6 percent share, respectively. Smart handsets had begun the race to own the operating systems on which wireless terminals ran. Microsoft, not surprisingly, had made a concerted effort to promote its operating system for such wireless terminals.

Digital TV (DTV) had increased its reach as a medium to propagate digital content with increased presence in Europe and the Asia-Pacific region.[15] DTV pro-

---

[13]Bluetooth is the registered trademark of Bluetooth SIG Limited, www.bluetooth.com.

[14]IDC, 2003, September 12, www.idc.com.

[15]Nokia Corporation, 2003, *Digital convergence in the home,* slides.

vided the opportunity to facilitate interoperability among electronics devices in the consumer's home. New appliances emerged to facilitate this integration and provide a unique arena where wireless terminals networked between linked appliances. Firms across diverse industries competed in the development of consumer "devices" that networked home appliances which stored, captured, or disseminated digital information for the consumer's entertainment and basic lifestyle support.

Selected Responses of Nokia to the Challenges Ahead   By 2003 Nokia had developed and introduced the Vertu Premium Phone at prices listed between $4,900 and $19,450 each. These stylish handsets featured a sapphire-crystal screen and ruby bearings and were available in stainless steel, gold, and platinum finishes. Singer Jennifer Lopez and actress Gwyneth Paltrow were two of the first celebrity consumers to match their Rolex watches and Chanel accessories with Nokia's "designer earpiece."

Also in 2003, Nokia acquired Sega.com to improve its online games and services. Coupled with its internally developed mobile N-Gage gaming console, Nokia penetrated the multiplayer gaming environment and a niche of consumers willing to pay to play over 3G networks.

Purposing to "drive voice totally wireless," Nokia placed a heavy focus on less developed markets. The development of a range of entry-level wireless terminals and innovative solutions to reduce carrier fixed costs also had become a high priority by this time.

The Nokia Image Viewer was introduced in Europe and Asia-Pacific markets during 2003 to support DTV's "digital presence in the home." The product addressed interoperability among home electronics devices and provided management and distribution of digital content, linking personal computers, televisions, and wireless terminals to share content. A 16-member alliance between Nokia and leading computing, consumer appliance, and mobile device enterprises was established concurrently to explore other products and services in the same user space.

Next Steps and a Strategic Intent for 2010
As Nokia's top management team reconvened in Espoo in March 2004, they were convinced that dramatic change was ahead. The most recent market share results for wireless handsets were less than encouraging (see Exhibit 11). Both Motorola and Samsung had gained significant ground over the previous 12 months. As foreseen, Nokia's bread-and-butter products—wireless handsets—were not likely to provide the double-digit, year-to-year revenue and profit growth required to sustain the firm's dominance in the coming decade. They began to discuss a "new" view of Nokia's "chosen markets" and the distinctive competencies required to sustain the company's influence in them.

Exhibit 11   **Worldwide Handset Sales and Market Shares**

Company	Sales (In millions)		Market Share (%)	
	Q1 2004	Q1 2003	Q1 2004	Q1 2003
Nokia	44.2	39.5	28.9%	34.6%
Motorola	25.1	16.7	16.4	14.7
Samsung	19.1	12.3	12.5	10.8
Siemens	12.3	8.6	8.0	7.6
Sony-Ericsson	8.5	5.4	5.6	4.7
Lucky Goldstar	8.1	5.6	5.3	4.9
Others	35.7	25.9	23.3	22.7
Total	**153.0**	**114.0**	**100%**	**100%**

Source: Gartner Inc.

Case 28　Outback Steakhouse Goes International*

In early 1995 Outback Steakhouse enjoyed the position as one of the most successful restaurant chains in the United States. Entrepreneurs Chris Sullivan, Bob Basham, and Tim Gannon, each with more than 20 years' experience in the restaurant industry, started Outback Steakhouse with just two stores in 1988. In 1995 the company was the fastest growing U.S. steakhouse chain with over 200 stores throughout the United States.

Outback achieved its phenomenal success in an industry that was widely considered as one of the most competitive in the United States. Fully 75 percent of entrants into the restaurant industry failed within the first year. Outback's strategy was driven by a unique combination of factors atypical of the food service industry. As Chairman Chris Sulllivan put it, "Outback is all about a lot of different experiences that has been recognized as entrepreneurship." Within six years of commencing operations, Outback was voted as the best steakhouse chain in the country. The company also took top honors along with Olive Garden as America's favorite restaurant. In December 1994, Outback was awarded *Inc.*'s prestigious Entrepreneur of the Year award. In 1994 and early 1995, the business press hailed the company as one of the biggest success stories in corporate America in recent years.

In late 1994 Hugh Connerty was appointed president of Outback International. In early 1995 Connerty, a highly successful franchisee for Outback, explained the international opportunities facing Outback Steakhouse as it considered its strategy for expansion abroad:

> We have had hundreds of franchise requests from all over the world. (So) it took about two seconds for me to make that decision [to become President of Outback International] . . . I've met with and talked to other executives who have international divisions. All of them have the same story. At some point in time the light goes off

and they say, "Gee, we have a great product. Where do we start?" I have traveled quite a bit on holiday. The world is not as big as you think it is. Most companies who have gone global have not used any set strategy.

Despite his optimism, Connerty knew that the choice of targeted markets would be critical. Connerty wondered what strategic and operational changes the company would have to make to assure success in those markets.

History of Outback Steakhouse, Inc.

Chris Sullivan, Bob Basham, and Tim Gannon met in the early 1970s shortly after they graduated from college. The three joined Steak & Ale, a Pillsbury subsidiary and restaurant chain, as management trainees as their first post-college career positions. During the 1980s Sullivan and Basham became successful franchisees of 17 Chili's restaurants in Florida and Georgia with franchise headquarters in Tampa, Florida.[1] Meanwhile, Gannon played significant roles in several New Orleans restaurant chains. Sullivan and Basham sold their Chili's franchises in 1987 and used the proceeds to fund Outback, their start-from-scratch entrepreneurial venture. They invited Gannon to join them in Tampa in fall 1987. The trio opened their first two restaurants in Tampa in 1988.

The three entrepreneurs recognized that in-home consumption of meat, especially beef, had declined.[2] Nonetheless, upscale and budget steakhouses were extremely popular. The three concluded that people were cutting in-home red meat consumption, but were still very interested in going out to a restaurant for a good steak. They saw an untapped opportunity between high-priced and budget steakhouses to serve quality steaks at an affordable price.

Using an Australian theme associated with the outdoors and adventure, Outback positioned itself as a place providing not only excellent food but also a cheerful, fun, and comfortable experience. The company's Statement of Principles and Beliefs referred to employees as "Outbackers" and highlighted the importance of hospitality, sharing, quality, fun, and courage.

Catering primarily to the dinner crowd,[3] Outback offered a menu that featured specially seasoned steaks and prime rib. The menu also included chicken, ribs, fish, and pasta entrees in addition to the company's innovative appetizers.[4] CFO Bob Merritt cited Outback's food as a prime reason for the company's success. As he put it:

> One of the important reasons for our success is that we took basic American meat and potatoes and enhanced the flavor profile so that it fit with the aging population . . . Just look at what McDonald's and Burger King did in their market segment. They (have) tried to add things

*The authors express deep appreciation to the following individuals at the Ewing Marion Kauffman Foundation which underwrote the expenses for the development of the case and a video on the company: Dr. Ray Smilor, Vice-President, and Dr. Mabel Tinjacha, Program Specialist for the Center for Entrepreneurial Leadership. In addition, the authors also wish to express special appreciation to Outback executives Bob Merritt, CFO and Treasurer; Nancy Schneid, Vice President of Marketing; and Hugh Connerty, President (of Outback International) who contributed special time and attention to this particular case. The research team has had sustained commitment from all the senior executives including Chris Sullivan, Chairman and CEO; Bob Basham, President and COO; Tim Gannon, Sr. Vice President; and Ava Forney, Assistant to the Chairman and CEO; as well as other Outback officers, executives, and employees. Numerous "Outbackers" have given generously of time, knowledge, and skills to make this case study possible.

Reprinted with permission of Marilyn L. Taylor, Gottlieb-Missouri Chair of Strategic Management, Bloch School of Business and Public Administration, 5110 Cherry, University of Missouri at Kansas City, Kansas City, MO 64110, 816-235-5530, FAX 816-235-2312, e-mail: mltaylor@cctr.umkc.edu

to their menu that were more flavorful (for example) McDonald's put the Big Mac on the menu . . . as people age, they want more flavor . . . higher flavor profiles. It's not happenstance. It's a science. There's too much money at risk in this business not to know what's going on with customer taste preferences.

The company viewed suppliers as "partners" in the company's success and was committed to work with suppliers to develop and maintain long-term relationships. Purchasing was dedicated to obtaining the highest quality ingredients and supplies. Indeed, the company was almost fanatical about quality. As Tim Gannon, vice-president and the company's chief chef, put it, "We won't tolerate less than the best." One example of the company's quality emphasis was its croutons. Restaurant kitchen staff made the croutons daily on-site. The croutons had 17 different seasonings, including fresh garlic and butter. The croutons were cut by hand into irregular shapes so that customers would recognize they were handmade. At about 40 percent of total costs, Outback had one of the highest food costs in the industry. On Friday and Saturday nights customers waited up to two hours for a table. Most felt that Outback provided exceptional value for the average entree price of $15 to $16.

Outback focused not only on the productivity and efficiency of "Outbackers" but also their long-term well-being. Executives referred to the company's employee commitment as "tough on results, but kind with people." A typical Outback restaurant staff consisted of a general manager, an assistant manager, and a kitchen manager plus 50 to 70 mostly part-time hourly employees. The company used aptitude tests, psychological profiles, and interviews as part of the employee selection process. Every applicant interviewed with two managers. The company placed emphasis on creating an entrepreneurial climate where learning and personal growth were strongly emphasized. As Chairman Chris Sullivan explained:

> I was given the opportunity to make a lot of mistakes and learn, and we try to do that today. We try to give our people a lot of opportunity to make some mistakes, learn, and go on.

In order to facilitate ease of operations for employees, the company's restaurant design devoted 45 percent of restaurant floor space to kitchen area. Waitstaff were assigned only three tables at any time. Most Outback restaurants were only open 4:30–11:30 p.m. daily. Outback's waitstaff enjoyed higher income from tips than in restaurants that also served lunch. Restaurant management staff worked 50–55 hours per week in contrast to the 70 or more common in the industry. Company executives felt that the dinner-only concept had led to effective utilization of systems, staff, and management. Outbackers reported that they were less worn out working at Outback

and that they had more fun than when they worked at other restaurant companies.

Outback executives were proud of their "B-locations (with) A-demographics" location strategy. They deliberately steered clear of high-traffic locations targeted by companies that served a lunch crowd. Until the early 1990s most of the restaurants were leased locations, retrofits of another restaurant location. The emphasis was on choosing locations where Outback's target customer would be in the evening. The overall strategy payoff was clear. In an industry where a sales-to-investment ratio of 1.2-to-1 was considered strong, Outback's restaurants generated $2.10 for every $1 invested in the facility. The average Outback restaurant unit generated $3.4 million in sales.

In 1995 management remained informal. Headquarters were located on the second floor of an unpretentious building near the Tampa airport. There was no middle management—top management selected the joint venture partners and franchisees who reported directly to the president. Franchisees and joint venture partners in turn hired the general managers at each restaurant.

Outback provided ownership opportunities at three levels of the organization: at the individual restaurant level, through multiple store arrangements (joint venture and franchise opportunities), and through a stock ownership plan for every employee. Health insurance was also available to all employees, a benefit not universally available to restaurant industry workers. Outback's restaurant-level general managers' employment and ownership opportunities were atypical in the industry. A restaurant general manager invested $25,000 for a 10 percent ownership stake in the restaurant, a contract for five years in the same location, a 10 percent share of the cash flow from the restaurant as a yearly bonus, opportunity for stock options, and a 10 percent buyout arrangement at the end of the five years. Outback store managers typically earned an annual salary and bonus of over $100,000 as compared to an industry average of about $60,000–$70,000. Outback's management turnover of 5.4 percent was one of the lowest in its industry in which the average was 30–40 percent.

Community involvement was strongly encouraged throughout the organization. The corporate office was involved in several nonprofit activities in the Tampa area and also sponsored major national events such as the Outback Bowl and charity golf tournaments. Each store was involved in community participation and service. For example, the entire proceeds of an open house held just prior to every restaurant opening went to a charity of the store manager's choice.

Early in its history the company had been unable to afford any advertising. Instead, Outback's founders relied on their strong relationships with local media to generate public relations and promotional efforts. One early relationship developed with Nancy Schneid who had extensive experience in advertising and radio. Schneid later became

Outback's first vice-president of marketing. Under her direction, the company developed a full-scale national media program that concentrated on television advertising and local billboards. The company avoided couponing and its only printed advertising typically came as part of a package offered by a charity or sports event.

Early financing for growth had come from limited partnership investments by family members, close friends, and associates. The three founders' original plan did not call for extensive expansion or franchising. However, in 1990 some friends, disappointed in the performance of several of their Kentucky-based restaurants, asked to franchise the Outback concept. The converted Kentucky stores enjoyed swift success. Additional opportunities with other individuals experienced in the restaurant industry arose in various parts of the country. These multi-

store arrangements were in the form of franchises or joint ventures. Later in 1990 the company turned to a venture capital firm for financing for a $2.5 million package. About the same time, Bob Merritt joined the company as CFO. Merritt's previous IPO[5] experience helped the company undertake a quick succession of three highly successful public equity offerings. During 1994 the price of the company's stock ranged from $22.63 to a high of $32.00. The company's income statements, balance sheets, and a summary of the stock price performance appear as Exhibits 1, 2, and 3, respectively.

Outback's International Rollout

Outback's management believed that the U.S. market could accommodate at least 550–600 Outback steakhouse restaurants. At the rate the company was growing (70 stores

Exhibit 1   Outback Steakhouse, Inc.
Consolidated Statements of Income

	Years Ended December 31		
	1994	1993	1992
Revenues	$451,916,000	$309,749,000	$189,217,000
Costs and Expenses			
Costs of revenues	175,618,000	121,290,000	73,475,000
Labor and other related expenses	95,476,000	65,047,000	37,087,000
Other restaurant operating expenses	93,265,000	64,603,000	43,370,000
General & administrative expenses	16,744,000	12,225,000	9,176,000
(Income) from oper. of unconsol. affl.	(1,269,000)	(333,000)	
	379,834,000	262,832,000	163,108,000
Income from Operations	72,082,000	46,917,000	26,109,000
Nonoperating Income (Expense)			
Interest income	512,000	1,544,000	1,428,000
Interest expense	(424,000)	(369,000)	(360,000)
	88,000	1,175,000	1,068,000
Income before Elimination			
Minority partnerships' interest and income taxes	72,170,000	48,092,000	27,177,000
Elimination of minority partners' interest	11,276,000	7,378,000	4,094,000
Income before provision for income taxes	60,894,000	40,714,000	23,083,000
Provision for income taxes	21,602,000	13,922,000	6,802,000
Net income	$ 39,292,000	$ 26,792,000	$ 16,281,000
Earnings per common share	$ 0.89	$ 0.61	$ 0.39
Weighted average number of common shares outstanding	43,997,000	43,738,000	41,504,000
Pro forma:			
Provision for income taxes	22,286,000	15,472,000	8,245,000
Net income	$ 38,608,000	$ 25,242,000	$ 14,838,000
Earnings per common share	$ 0.88	$ 0.58	$ 0.36

Exhibit 2   **Outback Steakhouse, Inc.**
Consolidated Balance Sheets

	December 31				
	1994	**1993**	**1992**	**1991**	**1990**
Assets					
Current assets					
Cash and cash equivalents	$ 18,758,000	$ 24,996,000	$ 60,538,000	17,000,700	2,983,000
Short-term municipal securities	4,829,000	6,632,000	1,316,600		
Inventories	4,539,000	3,849,000	2,166,500	1,020,800	319,200
Other current assets	11,376,000	4,658,000	2,095,200	794,900	224,100
Total current assets	39,502,000	40,135,000	66,116,700	18,816,400	3,526,300
Long-term municipal securities	1,226,000	8,903,000	7,071,200		
Property, fixtures and equipment, net	162,323,000	101,010,000	41,764,500	15,479,000	6,553,200
Investments in and advances to unconsolidated affiliates	14,244,000	1,000,000			
Other assets	11,236,000	8,151,000	2,691,300	2,380,700	1,539,600
	$228,531,000	$159,199,000	$117,643,700	36,676,100	11,619,100
Liabilities and Stockholders' equity					
Current liabilities					
Accounts payable	$ 10,184,000	$ 1,053,000	$ 3,560,200	643,800	666,900
Sales taxes payable	3,173,000	2,062,000	1,289,500	516,800	208,600
Accrued expenses	14,961,000	10,435,000	8,092,300	2,832,300	954,800
Unearned revenue	11,862,000	6,174,000	2,761,900	752,800	219,400
Current portion of long-term debt	918,000	1,119,000	326,600	257,000	339,900
Income taxes payable			369,800	1,873,200	390,000
Total current liabilities	41,098,000	20,843,000	16,400,300	6,875,900	2,779,600
Deferred income taxes	568,000	897,000	856,400	300,000	260,000
Long-term debt	12,310,000	5,687,000	1,823,700	823,600	1,060,700
Interest of minority partners in consolidated partnerships	2,255,000	1,347,000	1,737,500	754,200	273,000
Total liabilities	56,231,000	28,774,000	20,817,900	8,753,700	4,373,300
Stockholders equity					
Common stock, $0.01 par value, 100,000,000 shares authorized for 1994 and 1993; 50,000,000 authorized for 1992; 42,931,344 and 42,442,800 shares issued and outstanding as of December 31, 1994 and 1993, respectively; 39,645,995 shares issued and outstanding as of December 31, 1992	429,000	425,000	396,500	219,000	86,300
Additional paid-in capital	83,756,000	79,429,000	74,024,500	20,296,400	4,461,100
Retained earnings	88,115,000	50,571,000	22,404,800	7,407,000	2,698,400
Total stockholders' equity	172,300,000	130,425,000	96,825,800	27,922,400	7,245,800
	$228,531,000	$159,199,000	$117,643,700	36,676,100	11,619,100

Exhibit 3   Outback Steakhouse, Inc., Selected Financial and Stock Data

Year	Systemwide Sales*	Company Revenues*	Net Income*	EPS	Company Stores	Franchises & JVs	Total
1988	$ 2,731	$ 2,731	$ 47	$0.01	2	0	2
1989	13,328	13,328	920	0.04	9	0	9
1990	34,193	34,193	2,260	0.08	23	0	23
1991	91,000	91,000	6,064	0.17	49	0	49
1992	195,508	189,217	14,838	0.36	81	4	85
1993	347,553	309,749	25,242	0.58	124	24	148
1994	548,945	451,916	38,608	0.88	164	50	214

Outback Stock Data

	High	Low		High	Low
1991			**1993**		
Second quarter	$ 4.67	$ 4.27	First quarter	$22.00	$15.50
Third quarter	6.22	4.44	Second quarter	26.16	16.66
Fourth quarter	10.08	5.50	Third quarter	24.59	19.00
			Fourth quarter	25.66	21.16
1992			**1994**		
First quarter	$13.00	$ 9.17	First quarter	$29.50	$23.33
Second quarter	11.41	8.37	Second quarter	28.75	22.75
Third quarter	16.25	10.13	Third quarter	30.88	23.75
Fourth quarter	19.59	14.25	Fourth quarter	32.00	22.63

*In thousands of dollars.

EPS = earnings per share; JV = joint venture.

annually), Outback would near the U.S. market's saturation within 4–5 years. Outback's plans for longer-term growth hinged on a multipronged strategy. The company planned to roll out an additional 300–350 Outback stores, expand into the lucrative Italian dining segment through its joint venture with the successful Houston-based Carrabba's Italian Grill, and develop new dining themes.

At year-end 1994 Outback had 164 restaurants in which the company had a direct ownership interest. The company had six restaurants which it operated through joint ventures in which the company had a 45 percent interest. Franchisees operated another 44 restaurants. Outback operated the company-owned restaurants as partnerships in which the company was general partner. The company owned from 81 percent to 90 percent. The remainder was owned by the restaurant managers and joint venture partners. The six restaurants operated as joint ventures were also organized as partnerships in which the company owned 50 percent. The company was responsible for 50 percent of the costs of these restaurants.

The company organized the joint venture with Carrabba's in early 1993. The company was responsible for 100 percent of the costs of the new Carrabba's Italian Grills although it owned a 50 percent share. As of year-end 1994 the joint venture operated 10 Carrabba's restaurants.

The franchised restaurants generated 0.8 percent of the company's 1994 revenues as franchise fees. The portion of income attributable to restaurant managers and joint venture partners amounted to $11.3 million of the company's $72.2 million 1994 income.

By late 1994 Outback's management had also begun to consider the potential of non-U.S. markets for the Outback concept. As Chairman Chris Sullivan put it:

> . . . we can do 500–600 (Outback) restaurants, and possibly more over the next five years . . . [However,] the world is becoming one big market, and we want to be in place so we don't miss that opportunity. There are some problems, some challenges with it, but at this point there have been some casual restaurant chains that have gone [outside the United States] and their average unit sales are way, way above the sales level they enjoyed in the United States. So the potential is there. Obviously, there are some distribution issues to work out, things like that. But we are real excited about the future internationally. That will give us some potential outside the United States to continue to grow as well.

In late 1994 the company began its international venture by appointing Hugh Connerty as president of Outback International. Connerty, like Outback's three founders, had extensive experience in the restaurant industry. Prior to joining Outback he developed a chain of successful Hooter's restaurants in Georgia. He used the proceeds from the sale of these franchises to fund the development of his franchise of Outback restaurants in northern Florida and southern Georgia. Connerty's success as a franchisee was well recognized. Indeed, in 1993 Outback began to award a large crystal trophy with the designation "Connerty Franchisee of the Year" to the company's outstanding franchisee.

Much of Outback's growth and expansion were generated through joint venture partnerships and franchising agreements. Connerty commented on Outback's franchise system:

> Every one of the franchisees lives in their areas. I lived in the area I franchised. I had relationships that helped with getting permits. That isn't any different than the rest of the world. The loyalties of individuals that live in their respective areas [will be important]. We will do the franchises one by one. The biggest decision we have to make is how we pick that franchise partner. . . . That is what we will concentrate on. We are going to select a person who has synergy with us, who thinks like us, who believes in the principles and beliefs.

Outback developed relationships very carefully. As Hugh Connerty explained:

> . . . trust . . . is foremost and sacred. The trust between (Outback) and the individual franchisees is not to be violated . . . Company grants franchises one at a time.[6] It takes a lot of trust to invest millions of dollars without any assurance that you will be able to build another one.

However, Connerty recognized that expanding abroad would present challenges. He described how Outback would approach its international expansion:

> We have built Outback one restaurant at a time. . . . There are some principles and beliefs we live by. It almost sounds cultish. We want international to be an opportunity for our suppliers. We feel strongly about the relationships with our suppliers. We have never changed suppliers. We have an undying commitment to them and in exchange we want them to have an undying commitment to us. They have to prove they can build plants (abroad) . . .

He explained:

> I think it would be foolish of us to think that we are going to go around the world buying property and understanding the laws in every country, the culture in every single country. So the approach that we are going to take is that we will franchise the international operation with company-owned stores here and franchises there so that will allow us to focus on what I believe is our pure strength, a support operation.

U.S. Restaurants in the International Dining Market

Prospects for international entry for U.S. restaurant companies in the early 1990s appeared promising. Between 1992 and 1993 alone international sales for the top 50 restaurant franchisers increased from US$15.9 billion to US$17.5 billion. Franchising was the most popular means for rapid expansion. Exhibit 4 provides an overview of the top U.S. restaurant franchisers including their domestic and international revenues and number of units in 1993 and 1994.

International expansion was an important source of revenues for a significant number of players in the industry. International growth and expansion in the U.S. restaurant industry over the 1980s and into the 1990s was largely driven by major fast-food restaurant chains. Some of these companies, for example, McDonald's, Wendy's, Dairy Queen, and Domino's Pizza, were public and freestanding. Others, such as Subway and Little Caesars, remained private and freestanding. Some of the largest players in international markets were subsidiaries of major consumer products firms such as PepsiCo[7] and Grand Metropolitan PLC.[8] In spite of the success enjoyed by fast-food operators in non–U.S. markets, casual dining operators were slower about entering the international markets. (See Appendix A on page 775 for brief overviews of the publicly available data on the top ten franchisers and casual dining chains that had ventured abroad as of early 1995.)

One of the major forces driving the expansion of the U.S. food service industry was changing demographics.

Exhibit 4   Top 50 U.S. Restaurant Franchises Ranked By Sales ($ in Millions)

Rank	Firm	Total Sales		International Sales		Total Stores		International Stores	
		1994	1993	1994	1993	1994	1993	1994	1993
1	McDonald's	$25,986	$23,587	$11,046	$9,401	15,205	13,993	5,461	4,710
2	Burger King	7,500	6,700	1,400	1,240	7,684	6,990	1,357	1,125
3	KFC	7,100	7,100	3,600	3,700	9,407	9,033	4,258	3,905
4	Taco Bell	4,290	3,817	130	100	5,615	4,634	162	112
5	Wendy's	4,277	3,924	390	258	4,411	4,168	413	377
6	Hardee's	3,491	3,425	63	56	3,516	3,435	72	63
7	Dairy Queen	3,170	2,581	300	290	3,516	3,435	628	611
8	Domino's	2,500	2,413	415	275	5,079	5,009	840	550
9	Subway	2,500	2,201	265	179	9,893	5,009	944	637
10	Little Caesars	2,000	2,000	70	70	4,855	4,754	155	145
Average of firms 11–20		1,222	1,223	99	144	2,030	1,915	163	251
Average of firms 21–30		647	594	51	26	717	730	37	36
Average of firms 31–40		382	358	7	9	502	495	26	20
Average of firms 41-50		270	257	17	23	345	363	26	43

Non-Fast-Food in Top 50

Rank	Firm	Total Sales		International Sales		Total Stores		International Stores	
		1994	1993	1994	1993	1994	1993	1994	1993
11	Denny's	$1,779	$ 1,769	$ 63	$ 70	1,548	1,515	58	63
13	Dunkin' Donuts	1,413	1,285	226	209	3,453	3,047	831	705
14	Shoney's	1,346	1,318	0	0	922	915	0	0
15	Big Boy	1,130	1,202	100	0	940	930	90	78
17	Baskin-Robbins	1,008	910	387	368	3,765	3,562	1,300	1,278
19	TGI Friday's	897	1,068	114	293	314	NA	37	NA
20	Applebee's	889	609	1	0	507	361	2	0
21	Sizzler	858	922	230	218	600	666	119	116
23	Ponderosa	690	743	40	38	380	750	40	38
24	Int'l House of Pancakes	632	560	32	29	657	561	37	35
25	Perkins	626	588	12	10	432	425	8	6
29	Outback Steakhouse	549	348	0	0	NA	NA	NA	NA
30	Golden Corral	548	515	1	0	425	425	2	1
32	TCBY	388	337	22	15	2,801	2,474	141	80
37	Showbiz/Chuck E. Cheese	370	373	7	8	332	NA	8	NA
39	Round Table Pizza	357	340	15	12	576	597	29	22
40	Western Sizzlin	337	351	3	6	281	NA	2	NA
41	Ground Round	321	310	0	0	NA	NA	NA	NA
42	Papa John's	297	NA	0	NA	632	NA	0	NA
44	Godfather's Pizza	270	268	0	0	515	531	0	0
45	Bonanza	267	327	32	47	264	NA	30	NA
46	Village Inn	266	264	0	0	NA	NA	NA	NA
47	Red Robin	259	235	27	28	NA	NA	NA	NA
48	Tony Roma's	254	245	41	36	NA	NA	NA	NA
49	Marie Callender	251	248	0	0	NA	NA	NA	NA

NA: Not ranked in the top 50 for that category.

Source: "Top 50 Franchisers," *Restaurant Business*, November 1, 1995, pp. 35–41.

In the United States prepared foods had become a fastest-growing category because they relieved the cooking burdens on working parents. By the early 1990s, U.S. consumers were spending almost as much on restaurant fare as for prepared and nonprepared grocery store food. U.S. food themes were very popular abroad. U.S. food themes were common throughout Canada as well as western Europe and East Asia. As a result of the opening of previously inaccessible markets like eastern Europe, the former Soviet Union, China, India, and Latin America, the potential for growth in U.S. food establishments abroad was enormous.

In 1992 alone, there were more than 3,000 franchisers in the United States operating about 540,000 franchised outlets—a new outlet of some sort opened about every 16 minutes. In 1992 franchised business sales totaled $757.8 billion, about 35 percent of all retail sales. Franchising was used as a growth vehicle by a variety of businesses including automobiles, petroleum, cosmetics, convenience stores, computers, and financial services. However, food service constituted the franchising industry's largest single group. Franchised restaurants generally performed better than freestanding units. For example, in 1991 franchised restaurants experienced per store sales growth of 6.2 percent versus an overall restaurant industry growth rate of 3.0 percent. However, despite generally favorable sales and profits, franchisor-franchisee relationships were often difficult.

Abroad franchisers operated an estimated 31,000 restaurant units. The significant increase in restaurant franchising abroad was driven by universal cultural trends, rising incomes, improved international transportation and communication, rising educational levels, an increasing number of women entering the workforce, demographic concentrations of people in urban areas, and the willingness of younger generations to try new products.[9] However, there were substantial differences in these changes between the United States and other countries and from country to country.

Factors Impacting Country Selection

Outback had not yet formed a firm plan for its international rollout. However, Hugh Connerty indicated the preliminary choice of markets targeted for entry:

> The first year will be Canada . . . Then we'll go to Hawaii . . . Then we'll go to South America and then develop our relationships in the Far East, Korea, Japan, . . . the Orient. At the second year we'll begin a relationship in Great Britain and from there a natural progression throughout Europe. But we view it as a very long-term project. I have learned that people think very different than Americans.

There were numerous considerations which U.S. restaurant chains had to take into account when determining which non–U.S. markets to enter. Some of these factors are summarized in Exhibit 5. Issues regarding infrastructure and demographics are expanded below. Included are some of the difficulties that U.S. restaurant companies encountered in various countries. Profiles of Canada, South Korea, Japan, Germany, Mexico, and Great Britain appear in Appendix B on page 780.

Infrastructure A supportive infrastructure in the target country is essential. Proper means of transportation, communication, basic utilities such as power and water, and locally available supplies are important elements in the decision to introduce a particular restaurant concept. A restaurant must have the ability to get resources to its location. Raw materials for food preparation, equipment for manufacture of food served, employees, and customers must be able to enter and leave the establishment. The network that brings these resources to a firm is commonly called a supply chain.

The level of economic development is closely linked to the development of a supportive infrastructure. For example, the U.S. International Trade Commission said:

> Economic conditions, cultural disparities, and physical limitations can have substantial impact on the viability of foreign markets for a franchise concept. In terms of economics, the level of infrastructure development is a significant factor. A weak infrastructure may cause problems in transportation, communication, or even the provision of basic utilities such as electricity . . . International franchisers frequently encounter problems finding supplies in sufficient quantity, of consistent quality, and at stable prices . . . Physical distance also can adversely affect a franchise concept and arrangement. Long distances create communication and transportation problems, which may complicate the process of sourcing supplies, overseeing operations, or providing quality management services to franchisees.[10]

Some food can be sourced locally, some regionally or nationally, and some must be imported. A country's transportation and distribution capabilities may become an element in the decision of the country's suitability for a particular restaurant concept.

Sometimes supply chain issues require firms to make difficult decisions that affect the costs associated with the foreign enterprise. Family Restaurants Inc. encountered problems providing brown gravy for its CoCo's restaurants in South Korea. "If you want brown gravy in South Korea," said Barry Krantz, company president, "you can do one of two things. Bring it over, which is very costly. Or, you can make it yourself. So we figure out the flavor profile, and make it in the kitchen." Krantz concedes that a commissary is "an expensive proposition but the lesser of two evils."[11]

In certain instances a country may be so attractive for long-term growth that a firm dedicates itself to creating a

Exhibit 5　Factors Affecting Companies' Entry into International Markets

External Factors

Country Market Factors

Size of target market, competitive structure—atomistic, oligopolistic to monopolistic, local marketing infrastructure (distribution, etc.).

Country Production Factors

Quality, quantity, and cost of raw materials, labor, energy, and other productive agents in the target country as well as the quality and cost of the economic infrastructure (transportation, communications, port facilities, and similar considerations).

Country Environmental Factors

Political, economic, and sociocultural character of the target country—government policies and regulations pertaining to international business.

Geographical distance—impact on transportation costs.

Size of the economy, absolute level of performance (GDP per capita), relative importance of economic sectors—closely related to the market size for a company's product in the target country.

Dynamics including rate of investment, growth in GDP, personal income, changes in employment. Dynamic economies may justify entry modes with a high break-even point even when the current market size is below the break-even point.

Sociocultural factors—cultural distance between home country and target country societies. The closer the cultural distance, the quicker the entry into these markets (e.g., Canada).

Home Country Factors

Big domestic market allows a company to grow to a large size before it turns to foreign markets. Competitive structure. Firms in oligopolistic industries tend to imitate the actions of rival domestic firms that threaten to upset competitive equilibrium. Hence, when one firm invests abroad, rival firms commonly follow the lead. High production costs in the home country are an important factor.

Internal Factors

Company Product Factors

Products that are highly differentiated with distinct advantages over competitive products give sellers a significant degree of pricing discretion.

Products that require an array of pre- and post-purchase services make it difficult for a company to market the product at a distance.

Products that require considerable adaptation.

Company Resource/Commitment Factors

The more abundant a company's resources in management, capital, technology, production skills, and marketing skills, the more numerous its entry mode options. Conversely, a company with limited resources is constrained to use entry modes that call for only a small resource commitment. Size is therefore a critical factor in the choice of an entry mode. Although resources are an influencing factor, it must be joined with a willingness to commit them to foreign market development. A high degree of commitment means that managers will select the entry mode for a target from a wider range of alternative modes than managers with a low commitment.

The degree of a company's commitment to international business is revealed by the role accorded to foreign markets in corporate strategy, the status of the international organization, and the attitudes of managers.

Source: Franklin Root, *Entry Strategies for International Markets* (Lexington, MA: D. C. Heath, 1987).

supply chain for its restaurants. An excellent illustration is McDonald's expansion into Russia in the late 1980s:

> . . . [S]upply procurement has proved to be a major hurdle, as it has for all foreign companies operating in Russia. The problem has several causes: the rigid bureaucratic system, supply shortages caused by distribution and production problems, available supplies not meeting McDonald's quality standards . . . To handle these problems, McDonald's scoured the country for supplies, contracting for such items as milk, cheddar cheese, and beef. To help ensure ample supplies of the quality products it needed, it undertook to educate Soviet farmers and cattle ranchers on how to grow and raise those products. In addition, it built a $40 million food-processing center about 45 minutes from its first Moscow restaurant. And because distribution was (and still is) as much a cause of shortages as production was, McDonald's carried supplies on its own trucks.[12]

Changing from one supply chain to another can affect more than the availability of quality provisions—it can affect the equipment that is used to make the food served. For example:

> . . . Wendy's nearly had its Korean market debut delayed by the belatedly discovered problem of thrice-frozen hamburger. After being thawed and frozen at each step of Korea's cumbersome three-company distribution channel, ground beef there takes on added water weight that threw off Wendy's patty specifications, forcing a hasty stateside retooling of the standard meat patty die used to mass-produce its burgers.[13]

Looking at statistics such as the number of ports, airports, quantity of paved roads, and transportation equipment as a percentage of capital stock per worker can give a bird's-eye view of the level of infrastructure development.

Demographics   Just like the domestic market, restaurants in a foreign market need to know who their customers will be. Different countries will have different strata in age distribution, religion, and cultural heritage. These factors can influence the location, operations, and menus of restaurants in the country.

A popular example is India, where eating beef is contrary to the beliefs of the 80 percent of the population that is Hindu.[14] Considering India's population is nearly one billion people, companies find it hard to ignore this market even if beef is a central component of the firm's traditional menu. "We're looking at serving mutton patties," says Ann Connolly, a McDonald's spokeswoman.[15]

Another area where religion plays a part in affecting the operation of a restaurant is the Middle East. Dairy Queen expanded to the region and found that during the Islamic religious observance of Ramadan no business was conducted; indeed, the windows of shops were boarded up.[16]

Age distribution can affect who should be the target market. "The company [McDonald's in Japan] also made modifications [not long after entering the market], such as targeting all advertising to younger people, because the eating habits of older Japanese are very difficult to change."[17] Age distribution can also impact the pool of labor available. In some countries over 30 percent of the population is under 15 years old; in other countries over 15 percent is 65 or older. These varying demographics could create a change in the profile for potential employees in the new market.

Educational level may be an influence on both the buying public and the employee base. Literacy rates vary, and once again this can change the profile of an employee as well as who comprises the buying public.

Statistics can help compare countries using demographic components like literacy rates, total population and age distribution, and religious affiliations.

Income   Buying power is another demographic that can provide clues to how the restaurant might fare in the target country, as well as how the marketing program should position the company's products or services. Depending on the country and its economic development, the firm may have to attract a different segment than in the domestic market. For example, in Mexico:

> . . . major U.S. firms have only recently begun targeting the country's sizable and apparently burgeoning middle class. For its part, McDonald's has changed tactics from when it first entered Mexico as a prestige brand aimed almost exclusively at the upper class, which accounts for about 5 percent of Mexico's population of some 93 million. With the development of its own distribution systems and improved economies of scale McDonald's lately has been slashing prices to aid its penetration into working-class population strongholds. "I'd say McDonald's pricing now in Mexico is 30 percent lower, in constant dollar terms, than when we opened in '85," says Moreno [Fernando Moreno, now international director of Peter Piper Pizza], who was part of the chain's inaugural management team there.[18]

There are instances where low disposable income does not translate to a disinterest in dining out in a Western-style restaurant. While Americans dine at a fast-food establishment such as McDonald's one or two times per week, lower incomes in the foreign markets make eating at McDonald's a special, once-a-month occurrence. "These people are not very wealthy, so eating out at a place like McDonald's is a dining experience."[19] China provides another example:

> . . . at one Beijing KFC last summer, [the store] notched the volume equivalent of nine U.S. KFC branches in a single day during a $1.99 promotion of a two-piece meal with a baseball cap. Observers chalk up that blockbuster

business largely to China's ubiquitous "spoiled-brat syndrome" and the apparent willingness of indulgent parents to spend one or two months' salaries on splurges for the only child the government allows them to rear.[20]

Statistics outlining the various indexes describing the country's gross domestic product, consumer spending on food, consumption and investment rates, and price levels can assist in evaluating target countries.

Trade Law   Trade policies can be friend or foe to a restaurant chain interested in expanding to other countries. Trade agreements such as NAFTA (North American Free Trade Agreement) and GATT (General Agreement on Tariffs and Trade) can help alleviate the ills of international expansion if they achieve their aims of "reducing or eliminating tariffs, reducing nontariff barriers to trade, liberalizing investment and foreign exchange policies, and improving intellectual property protection . . . The recently signed Uruguay Round Agreements [of GATT] include the General Agreement on Trade in Services (GATS), the first multilateral, legally enforceable agreement covering trade and investment in the services sector. The GATS is designed to liberalize trade in services by reducing or eliminating governmental measures that prevent services from being freely provided across national borders or that discriminate against firms with foreign ownership."[21]

Franchising, one of the most popular modes for entering foreign markets, scored a win in the GATS agreement. For the first time franchising was addressed directly in international trade talks. However, most countries have not elected to make their restrictions on franchising publicly known. The U.S. International Trade Commission pointed out:

> Specific commitments that delineate barriers are presented in Schedules of Commitments (Schedules). As of this writing, Schedules from approximately 90 countries are publicly available. Only 30 of these countries specifically include franchising in their Schedules . . . The remaining two-thirds of the countries did not schedule commitments on franchising. This means that existing restrictions are not presented in a transparent manner and additional, more severe restrictions may be imposed at a later date . . . Among the 30 countries that addressed franchising in the Schedules, 25 countries, including the United States, have committed themselves to maintain no limitations on franchising except for restrictions on the presence of foreign nationals within their respective countries.[22]

Despite progress, current international restaurant chains have encountered a myriad of challenges because of restrictive trade policies. Some countries make the import of restaurant equipment into their country difficult and expensive. The Asian region possesses "steep tariffs and [a] patchwork of inconsistent regulations that impede imports of commodities and equipment."[23]

Outback's Growth Challenge

Hugh Connerty was well aware that there was no mention of international opportunities in Outback's 1994 Annual Report. The company distributed that annual report to shareholders at the April 1995 meeting. More than 300 shareholders packed the meeting to standing room only. During the question and answer period a shareholder had closely questioned the company's executives as to why the company did not pay a dividend. The shareholder pointed out that the company made a considerable profit in 1994. Chris Sullivan responded that the company needed to reinvest the cash that might be used as dividends in order to achieve the targeted growth. His response was a public and very visible commitment to continue the company's fast-paced growth. Connerty knew that international had the potential to play a critical role in that growth. His job was to help craft a strategy that would assure Outback's continuing success as it undertook the new and diverse markets abroad.

Appendix A   Profiles of Casual Dining and Fast-Food Chains*

This appendix provides summaries of the 1995 publicly available data on: 1) the two casual dining chains represented among the top 50 franchisers that had operations abroad (Applebee's and TGI Friday's/Carlson Companies, Inc.) and 2) the top 10 franchisers in the restaurant industry, all of which are fast-food chains (Burger King; Domino's; Hardee's; International Dairy Queen, Inc.; Little Caesars; McDonald's; PepsiCo, including KFC, Taco Bell, and Pizza Hut; Subway; and Wendy's).

(1) Casual Dining Chains with Operations Abroad

Applebee's   Applebee's was one of the largest casual dining chains in the United States. It ranked 20th in sales and 36th in stores for 1994. Like most other casual dining operators, much of the company's growth had been fueled by domestic expansion. Opening in 1986, the company experienced rapid growth and by 1994 had 507 stores. The mode of growth was franchising, but in 1992 management began a program of opening more company-owned sites and buying restaurants from franchisees. The company positioned itself as a neighborhood bar and grill and offered a moderately priced menu including burgers, chicken, and salads.

In 1995 Applebee's continued a steady program of expansion. Chairman and CEO Abe Gustin set a target of 1,200 U.S. restaurants and had also begun a slow push into international markets. In 1994 the company franchised restaurants in Canada and Curaçao and signed an agreement to franchise 20 restaurants in Belgium, Luxembourg, and the Netherlands.

Year	1989	1990	1991	1992	1993	1994**
Sales*	29.9	38.2	45.1	56.5	117.1	208.5
Net Income*	0.0	1.8	3.1	5.1	9.5	16.9
EPS($)	(0.10)	0.13	0.23	0.27	0.44	0.62
Stock Price Close($)	4.34	2.42	4.84	9.17	232.34	13.38
Dividends($)	0.00	0.00	0.01	0.02	0.03	0.04
# Employees	1,149	1,956	1,714	2,400	46,600	8,700

*$ millions.

**1994: Debt ratio 20.1%; ROE 19.2; Cash $17.2 million; Current ratio 1.13; LTD $23.7.

*Unless otherwise noted the information from this appendix was drawn from: "Top 50 Franchisers," *Restaurant Business,* November 1, 1995, pp. 35–41; and Hoover's Company Profile Database, Austin, TX: The Reference Press, 1996 (from American Online Service), various company listings.

TGI Friday's/Carlson Companies, Inc.   TGI Friday's was owned by Carlson Companies, Inc., a large, privately held conglomerate that had interests in travel (65 percent of 1994 sales), hospitality (30 percent), plus marketing, employee training, and incentives (5 percent). Carlson also owned a total of 345 Radisson Hotels and Country Inns plus 240 units of Country Kitchen International, a chain of family restaurants.

Most of Carlson's revenues came from its travel group. The company experienced an unexpected surprise in 1995 when U.S. airlines announced that they would put a cap on the commissions they would pay to book U.S. flights. Because of this change, Carlson decided to change its service to a fee-based arrangement and expected sales to drop by US$100 million in 1995. To make up for this deficit, Carlson began to focus on building its hospitality group of restaurants and hotels through expansion in the United States and overseas. The company experienced significant senior management turnover in the early 1990s and founder Curtis Carlson, age 80, had announced his intention to retire at the end of 1996. His daughter was announced as next head of the company.

TGI Friday's grew 15.7 percent in revenue and 19.4 percent in stores in 1994. With 37 restaurants overseas, international sales were 12.7 percent of sales and 11.8 percent of stores systemwide. Carlson operated a total of 550 restaurants in 17 countries. About one-third of overall sales came from activities outside the U.S.

Year	1985	1986	1987	1988	1989	1990	1991	1992	1993	1994
Sales*	0.9	1.3	1.5	1.8	2.0	2.2	2.3	2.9	2.3	2.3

* $ billions; no data available on income; excludes franchisee sales.

(2) The Top Ten Franchisers in the Restaurant Industry

Burger King   In 1994 Burger King was number two in sales and number four in stores among the fast-food competitors. Burger King did not have the same presence in the global market as McDonald's and KFC. For example, McDonald's and KFC had been in Japan since the 1970s. Burger King opened its first Japanese locations in 1993. By that time, McDonald's already had over 1,000 outlets there. In 1994 Burger King had 1,357 non-U.S. stores (17.7 percent of systemwide total) in 50 countries, and overseas sales (18.7 percent) totaled US$1.4 billion.

Burger King was owned by the British food and spirits conglomerate Grand Metropolitan PLC. Among the company's top brands were Pillsbury, Green Giant, and

Year (Burger King)	1985	1986	1987	1988	1989	1990	1991	1992	1993	1994
Sales*	5,590	5,291	4,706	6,029	9,298	9,394	8,748	7,913	8,120	7,780
Net Income*	272	261	461	702	1,068	1,069	616	412	450	432
EPS($)	14	16	19	24	28	32	33	28	30	32
Stock Price—Close($)	199	2,282 25	215	314	329	328	441	465	476	407
Dividend/Share($)	5.0	5.1	6.0	7.5	8.9	10.2	11.4	12.3	13.0	14.0
Employees (thousands)	137	131	129	90	137	138	122	102	87	64

*Millions of Sterling; 1994: Debt ratio 47.3%; ROE 12.4%; Cash (Ster.) 986M; LTD (Ster.) 2,322 million.

1994 Segments Sales (Profit): North America: 62% (69%); U.K. & Ireland 10% (10%); Africa & Middle East 2% (1%); Other Europe: 21% (18%); Other Countries: 5% (2%).

Segment Sales (Profits) by Operating Division: Drinks 43% (51%); Food 42% (26%); Retailing 14% (22%); Other 1% (1%).

Häagen-Dazs. Grand Met's situation had not been bright during the 1990s, with the loss of major distribution contracts like Absolut vodka and Grand Marnier liqueur, as well as sluggish sales for its spirits in major markets. Burger King was not a stellar performer, either, and undertook a major restructuring in 1993 to turn the tide including reemphasis on the basic menu, cuts in prices, and reduced overhead. After quick success, BK's CEO James Adamson left his post in early 1995 to head competitor Flagsston Corporation.

Domino's   Domino's Pizza was eighth in sales and seventh in stores in 1994. Sales and store unit growth had leveled off; from 1993 to 1994 sales grew 3.6 percent, and units only 1.4 percent. The privately held company registered poor performance in 1993, with a 0.6 percent sales decline from 1992. Observers suggested that resistance to menu innovations contributed to the share decline. In the early 1990s the company did add deep dish pizza and buffalo wings.

Flat company performances and expensive hobbies were hard on the owner and founder Thomas Monaghan. He attempted to sell the company in 1989 but could not find a buyer. He then replaced top management and retired from business to pursue a growing interest in religious activities. Company performance began to slide, and the founder emerged from retirement to retake the helm in the early 1990s. Through extravagant purchases of the Detroit Tigers, Frank Lloyd Wright pieces, and antique cars, Monaghan put the company on the edge of financial ruin. He sold off many of his holdings (some at a loss), reinvested the funds to stimulate the firm, and once again reorganized management.

Despite all its problems, Domino's had seen consistent growth in the international market. The company opened its first foreign store in 1983 in Canada. Primary overseas expansion areas were Eastern Europe and India. By 1994 Domino's had 5,079 stores with 823 of these in 37 major international markets. International brought in 17 percent of 1994 sales. Over the next 10–15 years the company had contracts for 4,000 additional international units.[24] These units would give Domino's more international than domestic units. International sales were 16.6 percent of total, and international stores were 16.5 percent of total in 1994.

Hardee's   Hardee's was number six in sales and eleven in stores for 1994. In 1981 the large diversified Canadian company, Imasco, purchased the chain. Imasco also owned Imperial Tobacco (Player's and du Maurier, Canada's top two sellers), Burger Chef, two drugstore chains, the development company Genstar, and CT Financial.

Hardee's had pursued growth primarily in the U.S. Of all the burger chains in the top 10 franchises, Hardee's had the smallest international presence with 72 stores generating US$63 million (1.8 percent and 2.0 percent of sales and stores, respectively) in 1994.

Hardee's sales grew by about 2 percent annually for 1993 and 1994. A failed attempt by Imasco to merge its Roy Rogers' restaurants into the Hardee's chain forced the parent company to maintain both brands. Hardee's attempted to differentiate from the other burger chains by

Years (Domino's)	1985	1986	1987	1988	1989	1990	1991	1992	1993	1994
Sales*	1,100	1,430	2,000	2,300	2,500	2,600	2,400	2,450	2,200	2,500
Stores	2,841	3,610	4,279	4,858	5,185	5,342	5,571	5,264	5,369	5,079
Employees (thousands)	NA	NA	NA	NA	NA	100	NA	NA	NA	115

*Millions.

Years (Hardee's)	1985	1986	1987	1988	1989	1990	1991	1992	1993	1994
Sales*	3,376	5,522	6,788	7,311	8,480	9,647	9,870	9,957	9,681	9,385
Net Income*	262	184	283	314	366	205	332	380	409	506
EPS($)	1.20	0.78	1.12	1.26	1.44	1.13	0.64	0.68	0.74	0.78
Stock Price—Close($)	13.94	16.25	12.94	14.00	18.88	13.81	18.25	20.63	20.06	19.88
Dividends($)	0.36	0.42	0.48	0.52	0.56	0.64	0.64	0.68	0.74	0.78
Employees (thousands)	NA	NA	NA	NA	190	190	180	NA	200	200

*$ millions—all $ in Canadian; 1994: Debt ratio 38.4%; ROE 16.1%; Current ratio: 1.37; LTD (millions): $1,927.

1994 Segment Sales (Operating Income): CT Financial Services 47% (28%); Hardee's 32% (11%); Imperial Tobacco 16% (0%); Shoppers Drug Mart 2% (9%); Genstar Development 1% (2%).

Years (Dairy Queen)	1985	1986	1987	1988	1989	1990	1991	1992	1993	1994
Sales*	158	182	210	254	282	287	287	296	311	341
Net Income*	10	12	15	20	23	27	28	29	30	31
EPS($)	0.33	0.42	0.51	0.70	0.83	0.97	1.05	1.12	1.79	1.30
Stock Price—Close($)	5.20	7.75	8.00	11.50	14.75	16.58	21.00	20.00	18.00	16.25
Dividends($)	-0-	-0-	-0-	-0-	-0-	-0-	-0-	-0-	-0-	-0-
Employees (thousands)	430	459	503	520	549	584	592	672	538	564

* $ millions; 1994: Debt ratio 15.3%; ROE 24.4%; Current ratio 3.04; LTD $23 million.

1994 Restaurants: U.S. 87%; Canada 9%; Other 4%; Restaurants by type: DQs: franchised by company: 62%; franchised by territorial operators 27%; foreign 3%; Orange Julius 7%; Karmelkorn 1%, Golden Skillet (less than <1%); Sales by Source: Good supplies & equipment to franchises 78%; service fees 16%; franchise sales & other fees 3%; real-estate finance & rental income 3%.

offering an upscale burger menu, which received a luke-warm reception by consumers.

International Dairy Queen, Inc.   Dairy Queen was one of the oldest fast-food franchises in the United States: the first store was opened in Joilet, Illinois, in 1940. By 1950, there were over 1,100 stores, and by 1960 Dairy Queen (DQ) had locations in 12 countries. Initial franchise agreements focused on the right to use the DQ freezers, an innovation that kept ice cream at the constant 23 degrees Fahrenheit necessary to maintain the soft consistency. In 1970 a group of investors bought the franchise organization, but the group has been only partly successful in standardizing the fast-food chain. In 1994 a group of franchisees filed an antitrust suit in an attempt to get the company to loosen its control on food supply prices and sources. DQ franchises cost $30,000 initially plus continuing payments of 4 percent of sales.

The company's menu consisted of ice cream, yogurt, and Brazier (hamburgers and other fast food) items. Menu innovations included Blizzards (candy and other flavors mixed in the ice cream). The company had also acquired several companies including Golden Skillet (1981), Karmelkorn (1986), and Orange Julius (1987).

In 1994 Dairy Queen ranked number seven in sales and six in stores. By that same year the company had expanded its presence into 19 countries with 628 stores and US$300 million in international sales. 1994 was an excellent year for DQ: sales were up 22.8 percent over 1993. This dramatic change (1993 scored an anemic 3.0 percent gain) was fueled by technology improvements for franchisees and international expansion. In 1992 Dairy Queen opened company-owned outlets in Austria, China, Slovenia, and Spain. DQ announced in 1995 that it had a plan to open 20 stores in Puerto Rico over a four-year period.

Little Caesar's   Little Caesar's ranked 10th in sales and eighth in stores for 1994. Sales growth had slowed to a halt: a 1992–93 increase of 12.2 percent evaporated into no increase for 1993–94.

These numbers were achieved without a significant overseas presence. Of the top 10 franchises, only Hardee's had a smaller number of stores in foreign lands. Little Caesar's received 3.5 percent of sales from foreign stores. Only 3.2 percent of the company's stores were in non-U.S. locations, namely, Canada, the Czech and Slovak republics, Guam, Puerto Rico, and the U.K.

McDonald's   At the top in 1994 international sales and units, McDonald's Inc. was the most profitable retailer in the U.S. during the 1980s and into the 1990s. The company opened its first store in California in 1948, went public in 1965, and by 1994 had over 20 percent of the U.S. fast-food business. McDonald's opened its first

Years (Little Caesars)	1985	1986	1987	1988	1989	1990	1991	1992	1993	1994
Sales*	340	520	725	908	1,130	1,400	1,725	2,050	2,150	2,000
# of stores	900	1,000	1,820	2,000	2,700	3,173	3,650	4,300	5,609	4,700
Employees	18,000	26,160	36,400	43,600	54,000	63,460	73,000	86,000	92,000	95,000

*$Millions.

international store in Canada in 1967. Growing domestic competition in the 1980s gave impetus to the company's international expansion. By 1994 there were over 15,000 restaurants under the golden arches in 79 countries. The non–U.S. stores provided about one-third of total revenues and half of the company's profits. McDonald's planned to open 1,200–1,500 new restaurants in 1995, most outside the United States. International markets had grown into an attractive venue for the burger giant because there was "less competition, lighter market saturation, and high name recognition" in international markets.

The company's growth was fueled by aggressive franchising. In the early 1990s two-thirds of the McDonald's locations were franchised units and franchisees remained with the company an average of 20 years. McDonald's used heavy advertising ($1.4 billion in 1994) and frequent menu changes and other innovations—1963: Filet-O-Fish sandwich and Ronald McDonald; 1968 Big Mac and first TV ads; 1972: Quarter Pounder, Egg McMuffin (breakfast); 1974: Ronald McDonald House; 1975: drive-thru; 1979: Happy Meals; 1983: Chicken McNuggets; 1986: provided customers with list of products' ingredients; 1987: salads; 1980s: "value menus"; 1991: McLean DeLuxe, a low-fat hamburger (not successful) and experimentation with decor and new menu items at local level; 1993: first restaurants inside another store (Wal-Mart). The company planned to open its first restaurants in India in 1996 with menus featuring chicken, fish sandwiches, and vegetable nuggets. There would be no beef items.

From 1993–1994 McDonald's grew 10.2 percent in sales and 8.7 percent in stores. Because of its extensive experience in international markets, international sales had grown to 42.5 percent of its total revenues, and half

its profits. Indeed, McDonald's was bigger than the 25 largest full-service chains put together.

PepsiCo: KFC and Taco Bell—also includes Pizza Hut (latter is not in the top 50)   PepsiCo owned powerful brand names such as Pepsi-Cola and Frito-Lay and was also the world's number one fast-food chain—with its ownership of KFC, Taco Bell, and Pizza Hut.

KFC was third in sales and stores of the top 50 franchises in 1994. Active in the international arena since the late 1960s, KFC had been a major McDonald's competitor in non–U.S. markets. In 1994 the company had US$3.6 billion in sales and 4,258 stores in other countries. McDonald's had been commonly number one in each country it entered, but KFC had been number two in international sales and had the number one sales spot in Indonesia. In 1994, KFC international revenues were 50.7 percent of sales with 45.3 percent of stores in international locations.

Taco Bell was fourth in sales and fifth in stores of the top 50 franchises in 1994. This ranking had been achieved with minimal international business to date. Taco Bell had US$130 million sales and 162 stores internationally. The company attempted to enter the Mexican market in 1992 with a kiosk and cart strategy in Mexico City. The venture did not fare well, and Taco Bell soon pulled out of Mexico.[25] In 1994 international revenues were 3.0 percent of sales and 2.9 percent of stores were international locations.

Subway   Founded more than 29 years ago, Subway remained privately held in 1994.[26] The company had experienced explosive growth during the 1990s. It ranked ninth in sales and second in stores for 1994. Sales grew 13.6 percent from 1993 to 1994, and 26 percent from 1992 to 1993. Stores grew 17.1 percent from 1993 to

Years (McDonald's)	1985	1986	1987	1988	1989	1990	1991	1992	1993	1994
Sales*	3,695	4,144	4,894	5,566	6,142	6,640	6,695	7,133	7,408	8,321
Net Income*	433	480	549	656	727	802	860	959	1,083	1,224
EPS($)	0.56	0.63	0.73	0.86	0.98	1.10	1.18	1.30	1.46	1.68
Stock Price—Close($)	9.00	10.16	11.00	12.03	17.25	14.56	19.00	24.38	28.50	29.25
Dividends($)	0.10	0.11	0.12	0.14	0.16	0.17	0.18	0.20	0.21	0.23
Employees (thousands)	148	159	159	169	176	174	168	166	169	183

* $ million; 1994: Debt ratio 41.2%; ROE 20.7%; Cash $180 million; Current ratio 0.31; LTD $2.9 million; Market value $20 billion.

Years (PepsiCo)	1985	1986	1987	1988	1989	1990	1991	1992	1993	1994
Sales*	8,057	9,291	11,485	13,007	15,242	17,803	19,608	21,970	25,021	28,474
Net Income*	544	458	595	762	901	1,077	1,080	1,302	1,588	1,784
EPS($)	0.65	0.58	0.76	0.97	1.13	1.35	1.35	1.61	1.96	2.22
Stock Price—Close($)	8.06	8.66	11.11	13.15	21.31	26.00	22.88	3.40	40.88	36.25
Dividends/Share($)	0.15	0.21	0.22	0.25	0.31	0.37	0.44	0.50	0.58	0.68
Employees (thousands)	150	214	225	235	266	308	338	372	423	471

*$ millions; 1994: Debt ratio 48.1%; ROE 27.0%; Cash (millions) $1,488; Current ratio 0.96; LTD (millions) $8,841.

1994 Segment Sales (Operating Income): Restaurants 37% (22%); Beverages 34% (37%); Snack foods 29% (41%).

1994, and 15.3 percent from 1992 to 1993. In 1994 Subway overtook KFC as the number two chain in number of stores behind McDonald's. The company attributed its growth at least partially to an exceptionally low-priced and well-structured franchise program. In addition, store sizes of 500–1,500 square feet were small. Thus, the investment for a Subway franchise was modest.

The company's growth involved a deliberate strategy. The formula involved no cooking on-site, except for the baking of bread. The company promoted the "efficiency and simplicity" of its franchise and advertised its food as "healthy, delicious, (and) fast." The company advertised regularly on TV with a $25 million budget and planned to increase that significantly. All stores contributed 2.5 percent of gross sales to the corporate advertising budget. Subway's goal was to equal or exceed the number of outlets operated by the largest fast food company in every market that it entered. In most cases the firm's benchmark was burger giant McDonald's.

International markets played an emerging role in Subway's expansion. In 1994 international sales were 10.6 percent of sales, compared to 8.9 percent the previous year. International stores were 9.5 percent of total in 1994, and 7.5 percent in 1993. Subway boasted a total of 9,893 stores in all 50 states and 19 countries.[27]

Wendy's   Wendy's was number five in sales and number nine in stores for 1994. In 1994 after 25 years of operation, Wendy's had grown to 4,411 stores. This growth had been almost exclusively domestic until 1979, when Wendy's ventured out of the United States and Canada to open its first outlets in Puerto Rico, Switzerland, and West Germany. Wendy's granted J. C. Penney the franchise rights to France, Belgium, and Holland, and had one store open in Belgium by 1980.

Wendy's still saw opportunities for growth in the United States. Industry surveys had consistently ranked Wendy's burgers number one in quality, but poor in convenience (Wendy's had one store for every 65,000 people while McDonald's, in contrast, had one for every 25,000). Growth was driven primarily by franchising. In 1994, 71 percent of the stores were operated by franchisees and 29 percent by the company. Company restaurants provided 90 percent of total sales while franchise fees provided 8 percent. The company had made menu and strategic changes at various points in its history. For example, in 1977 the company first began TV advertising; 1979, introduced its salad bar; 1985, experimented with breakfast; 1986 and 1987, introduced Big Classic and SuperBar buffet (neither very successful); 1990, grilled chicken sandwich and 99¢ Super Value Menu items; and 1992, packaged salads.

Wendy's planned to add about 150 restaurants each year in foreign markets. With a presence of 236 stores in 33 countries in 1994, international was 9.1 percent of sales and 9.4 percent of stores in 1994.

Year (Wendy's)	1985	1986	1987	1988	1989	1990	1991	1992	1993	1994
Sales*	1,126	1,140	1,059	1,063	1,070	1,011	1,060	1,239	1,320	1,398
Net Income*	76	(5)	4	29	24	39	52	65	79	97
EPS($)	0.82	(0.05)	0.04	0.30	0.25	0.40	0.52	0.63	0.76	0.91
Stock price—Close($)	13.41	10.25	5.63	5.75	4.63	6.25	9.88	12.63	17.38	14.38
Dividends/Share($)	0.17	0.21	0.24	0.24	0.24	0.24	0.24	0.24	0.24	0.24
Employees (thousands)	40	40	45	42	39	35	39	42	43	44

* $ millions; 1994: Debt ratio 36.6%; ROE 5.2%; Current ratio 0.98; LTD (millions) $145.

Appendix B   Country Summaries

Canada

In the 1990s Canada was considered an ideal first stop for U.S. business seeking to begin exporting. Per capita output, patterns of production, market economy, and business practices were similar to those in the U.S. U.S. goods and services were well received in Canada: 70 percent of all Canadian imports were from the United States. Canada's market conditions were stable, and U.S. companies continued to see Canada as an attractive option for expansion.

Canada had one of the highest real growth rates among the OECD during the 1980s, averaging about 3.2 percent. The Canadian economy softened during the 1990s, but Canadian imports of U.S. goods and services were expected to increase about 5 percent in fiscal year 1996.

Although Canada sometimes mirrored the United States, there are significant cultural and linguistic differences from the United States and between the regional markets in Canada. These differences were evident in the mounting friction between the English- and French-speaking areas of Canada. The conflict had potential for splitting of territory between the factions, slicing Canada into two separate countries. The prospect of this outcome left foreign investors tense.

Germany

In the mid-1990s Germany was the largest economy in Europe, and the fifth largest overall importer of U.S. goods and services. Since reunification in 1990, the eastern part of Germany had continued to receive extensive infusions of aid from western Germany, and these funds were only just beginning to show an impact. The highly urbanized and skilled West German population enjoyed a very high standard of living with abundant leisure time. In 1994, Germany emerged from a recession, and scored a GDP of US$2 trillion.

A unique feature of Germany was the unusually even distribution of both industry and population—there was no single business center for the country. This was a challenge for U.S. firms. They had to establish distribution networks that adequately covered all areas of the country. In Germany there was little opportunity for regional concentration around major population centers as in the United States.

The country was a good market for innovative high-tech goods and high-quality food products. Germans expected high-quality goods, and would reject a less expensive product if quality and support were not in abundance. Strongest competition for U.S. firms were the German domestic firms not only because of their home-grown famil-

iarity of the market, but also because of the consumers' widely held perception that German products were "simply the best."

A recurring complaint from Germans was the prevalent "here today, gone tomorrow" business approach of American firms. Germans viewed business as a long-term commitment to support growth in markets, and did not always receive the level and length of attention necessary from U.S. companies to satisfy them.

Conditions in the former area of East Germany were not the doomsday picture often painted, nor were they as rosy as the German government depicted. It would take 10–15 years for the eastern region of the country to catch up to the western region in terms of per capita income, standard of living, and productivity.

Japan

Japan had the second largest economy in the world. Overall economic growth in Japan over the past 35 years had been incredible: 10 percent average annual growth during the 1960s, 5 percent in the 1970s and 1980s. Growth ground to a halt during the 1990s due to tight fiscal policy. The government tightened fiscal constraints in order to correct the significant devaluation of the real estate markets. The economy posted a 0.6 percent growth in 1994 largely due to consumer demand. The overall economic outlook remained cloudy, but the outlook for exports to Japan remained positive.

Japan was a highly homogeneous society with business practices characterized by long-standing close relationships among individuals and firms. It took time for Japanese businessmen to develop relationships, and for non-Japanese businesspeople the task of relationship building in Japan was formidable. It was well known that Japan's market was not as open as the United States but the U.S. government had mounted multifaceted efforts to help U.S. businesspeople to "open doors." While these efforts were helpful, most of the responsibility in opening the Japanese market to U.S. goods or services remained with the individual firm. Entering Japan was expensive and generally required four things: 1) financial and management capabilities and a Japanese-speaking staff residing within the country, 2) modification of products to suit Japanese consumers, 3) a long-term approach to maximizing market share and achieving reasonable profit levels, and 4) careful monitoring of Japanese demand, distribution, competitors, and government. Despite the challenges of market entry, Japan ranked as the second largest importer of U.S. goods and services.

Historically Japanese consumers were conservative and brand conscious, although the recession during the '90s nurtured opportunities for "value" entrants. Tradi-

* The material in this appendix is adapted from the Department of Commerce Country Commercial Guides and the *CIA World Fact Book*.

tional conformist buying patterns were still prominent, but more individualistic habits were developing in younger Japanese aged 18–21. This age cohort had a population of 8 million people, and boasted a disposable income of more than US$35 billion.

Japanese consumers were willing to pay a high price for quality goods. However, they had a well-earned reputation for having unusually high expectations for quality. U.S. firms with high-quality, competitive products had to be able to undertake the high cost of initial market entry. For those that were willing, Japan could provide respectable market share and attractive profit levels.

Mexico

Mexico had experienced a dramatic increase in imports from the United States since the late 1980s. During 1994 the country experienced 20 percent growth over 1993. In 1994, Mexico's peso experienced a massive devaluation brought on by investor anxiety and capital flight. Although the Mexican government implemented tight fiscal measures to stabilize the peso, its efforts could not stop the country from plunging into a serious recession.

Inflation rose as a result of the austerity policies and it was expected to be between 42–54 percent in 1995. Negative economic growth was anticipated in 1995 as well. The U.S. financial assistance package (primarily loans) provided Mexico with nearly US$50 billion and restored stability to the financial markets by mid-1995. The government was taking measures to improve the country's infrastructure. Mexico's problems masked that its government had, on the whole, practiced sound economic fundamentals.

Mexico was still committed to political reform despite the current economic challenges. After ruling the government uninterrupted for 60 years, the PRI party had begun to lose some seats to other political parties. Mexico was slowly evolving into a multiparty democracy.

Despite the economic misfortunes of recent years, Mexico remained the United States' third largest trading partner. Mexico still held opportunities for U.S. firms able to compete in the price-sensitive recessionary market. Mexico had not wavered on NAFTA since its ratification and in the mid-1990s 60 percent of U.S. exports to Mexico entered duty free.

South Korea

South Korea had been identified as one of the U.S. Department of Commerce's 10 "Big Emerging Markets." The country's economy overcame tremendous obstacles after the Korean War in the 1950s left the country in ruins. The driving force behind South Korea's growth was export-led development and energetic emphasis on entrepreneurship. Annual real GDP growth from 1986 to 1991 was over 10 percent. This blistering pace created inflation, tight labor markets, and a rising current account deficit. Fiscal policy in 1992 focused on curbing inflation and reducing the deficit. Annual growth, reduced to a still enviable 5% in '92, rose to 6.3 percent in 1993. Fueled by exports, 1994's growth was a heady 8.3 percent. South Korea's GDP was larger than Russia, Australia, or Mexico.

The American media had highlighted such issues as student demonstrations, construction accidents, and North Korean nuclear problems and trade disputes. Investors needed to closely monitor developments related to North Korea. However, the political landscape in South Korea had been stable enough over the 1980s to fuel tremendous economic expansion. The country was undertaking significant infrastructure improvements. Overall, South Korea was a democratic republic with an open society and a free press. It was a modern, cosmopolitan, fast-paced, and dynamic country with abundant business opportunities for savvy American businesses.

There had been a staggering development of U.S. exports to South Korea: US$21.6 billion in 1994 and over US$30 billion expected in 1995. While South Korea was 22 times smaller than China in terms of population, it imported two times more U.S. goods and services than China in 1994!

Although South Korea ranked as the United States' sixth largest export market, obstacles for U.S. firms still remained. Despite the country's participation in the Uruguay Round of GATT and related trade agreements, customs clearance procedures and regulations for labeling, sanitary standards, and quarantine often served as significant nontariff barriers.

The United Kingdom (or Great Britain)

The United Kingdom (U.K.) was the United States' fourth largest trading partner and the largest market for U.S. exports in Europe. Common language, legal heritage, and business practices facilitated U.S. entry into the British market.

The U.K. had made significant changes to its taxation, regulation, and privatization policies that changed the structure of the British economy and increased its overall efficiency. The reward for this disciplined economic approach had been sustained—modest growth during the 1980s and early 1990s. GDP grew 4.2 percent in 1994, the highest level in six years. The U.K. trimmed its deficit from US$75 billion in fiscal 1994 to US$50 billion in fiscal 1995.

The U.K. had no restrictions on foreign ownership and movement of capital. There was a high degree of labor flexibility. Efficiencies had soared in the U.K. and in the mid-1990s the country boasted the lowest real per unit labor cost of the Group of Seven (G7) industrialized countries.

The U.K.'s shared cultural heritage and warm relationship with the United States translated into the British finding U.S. goods and services as attractive purchases. These reasons, coupled with British policy emphasizing free enterprise and open competition, made the U.K. the destination of 40 percent of all U.S. investment in the European Union (EU).

The U.K. market was based on a commitment to the principles of free enterprise and open competition. Demand for U.S. goods and services was growing. The abolition of many internal trade barriers within the European Common Market enabled European-based firms to operate relatively freely. As a result, U.S. companies used the U.K. as a gateway to the rest of the EU. Of the top 500 British companies, one in eight was a U.S. affiliate. Excellent physical and communications infrastructure combined with a friendly political and commercial climate were expected to keep the U.K. as a primary target for U.S. firms for years to come.

Endnotes

1. All three Outback founders credited casual dining chain legend and mentor Norman Brinker with his strong mentoring role in their careers. Brinker played a key role in all of the restaurant chains Sullivan and Basham were associated with prior to Outback.

2. American consumption of meat declined from the mid-1970s to the early 1990s primarily as a result of health concerns about red meat. In 1976 Americans consumed 131.6 pounds of beef and veal, 58.7 pounds of pork, and 12.9 pounds of fish. In 1990 the figures were 64.9 pounds of beef and veal, 46.3 of pork, and 15.5 of fish. The dramatic decrease was attributed to consumer attitudes toward a low-fat, healthier diet. Menu items that gained in popularity were premium baked goods, coffees, vegetarian menu items, fruits, salsa, sauces, chicken dishes, salad bars, and spicy dishes. Kurian, George Thomas, 1994, *Datapedia of the United States* 1790–10000 (Maryland: Bernan Press: 113.)

3. Outback's original Henderson Blvd. (Tampa, Florida) Restaurant was one of the few open for lunch. By 1995 the chain had also begun to open in some locations for Sunday lunch or for special occasions such as Mother's Day lunch.

4. Outback's signature trademark was its best-selling "Aussie-Tizer," the "Bloomin' Onion." The company expected to serve 9 million Bloomin' Onions in 1995.

5. Merritt had worked as CFO for another company, which had come to the financial markets with its IPO (initial public offering).

6. Outback did not grant exclusive territorial franchises. Thus, if an Outback franchisee did not perform, the company could bring additional franchisees into the area. Through 1994 Outback had not had territorial disputes between franchisees.

7. PepsiCo owned Kentucky Fried Chicken, Taco Bell, and Pizza Hut.

8. Grand Met owned Burger King.

9. Ref. AME 76 (KR).

10. Industry and trade summary: Franchising, 1995, Washington, DC: U.S. International Trade Commission: 15–16.

11. World hunger, 1994, *Restaurant Hospitality,* November: 97.

12. *International Business Environments and Operations,* 7th ed., 1995: 117–19.

13. U.S. restaurant chains tackle challenges of Asian expansion, 1994, *Nation's Restaurant News,* February 14: 36.

14. *CIA World Factbook,* 1995, India.

15. Big McMuttons, 1995, *Forbes,* July 17: 18.

16. Interview with Cheryl Babcock, 1995, University of St. Thomas, October 23.

17. Franchise management in East Asia, 1990, *Academy of Management Executive,* 4 (2): 79.

18. U.S. operators flock to Latin America, 1994, *Nation's Restaurant News,* October 17: 47.

19. Interview with Cheryl Babcock, 1995.

20. U.S. restaurant chains tackle challenges of Asian expansion, 1994, 36.

21. Industry and trade summary: Franchising, 1995, 30.

22. Ibid.

23. U.S. restaurant chains tackle challenges of Asian expansion, 1994, 36.

24. Big news over there!, 1994, *Restaurants and Institutions,* July 1.

25. U.S. operators flock to Latin America, 1994.

26. There is, thus, no publicly available financial data on Subway.

27. Subway, 1996, the Internet, accessed March 24.

Case 29   Panera Bread Company

An exciting new segment in the restaurant industry, the fast-casual market, is growing 15–20 percent each year, despite the slowdown in consumer spending, changing economic conditions, and increases in gas prices.[1] The restaurant industry is extremely competitive with existing companies planning major expansion efforts and new concept restaurants opening every day. In addition, media headlines highlight the low-carb trend among consumers. In May 2004 the managers of Krispy Kreme Doughnuts, Inc., a competitor of Panera Bread, announced they were reducing the profit projection for the year because of lower demand for its high-calorie doughnuts. Scott Livengood, chief executive and chairman of Krispy Kreme, stated, "The popularity of low-carb diets has captured the consumer's attention. It's impossible to predict if low-carb is a passing fad or will have a lasting impact."

Panera's management team plans to open between 140 and 150 new bakery-cafes in 2004, expects increases in systemwide sales, and hopes to maintain its leadership position in the very competitive restaurant industry. Can these goals be obtained despite the dynamic characteristics of this industry?

The Restaurant Industry

There are approximately 8 million restaurants in the world and about 300,000 restaurant companies. The industry has two major segments: The full-service segment includes family-style restaurants, dinner houses, and grill/buffet restaurants. The fast-food segment includes sandwiches, hamburgers, Mexican food, pizza, and chicken and is represented by companies such as Burger King, Taco Bell, KFC, Pizza Hut, McDonald's, Popeye's, Subway, and Wendy's.[2] With high competition, a mature market, a decline in the supply of workers age 16 to 24, and low profit margins, this is a difficult industry in which to excel. Overall restaurant sales have been rising about 5 percent annually.

In a recent report on the Top 100 chain restaurant companies, Technomic reported annual growth of 5.1 percent and 2001 systemwide sales of $136.5 billion, an increase of $6.6 billion over 2000.[3] The other sandwich category of the Top 100 chain restaurants grew at 12.8 percent, doughnuts at 12.3 percent, and the full-service, varied menu, Italian, and steak categories each grew more than 8 percent. The 10 fastest-growing chains with sales over $200 million in 2001 were Panera Bread, Krispy Kreme, Quizno's Classic Subs, Culver's, P.F. Chang's

China Bistro, Chevys, Carrabba's Italian Grill, Buffalo Wild Wings, Starbucks, and the Cheesecake Factory. Exhibit 1 shows restaurant chains with the highest three-year sales growth rates as of June 2004.

International sales for the Top 100 chain restaurants increased only 1.8 percent in 2001, down from 6.4 percent in 2000. Technomic analysts suggest that the U.S. restaurant industry is somewhat insulated from economic swings.

There is an exciting new restaurant market segment developing—the fast-casual market—and these restaurants are becoming key players in the industry. The fast-casual market is a combination of the quick service of traditional fast-food restaurants with the higher-quality food products found in sit-down restaurants. The fast-casual market is a $6 billion industry growing 15 to 20 percent each year. It represented about 2 percent of the restaurant market in 2003. Sales growth is expected to double to $12 billion during the next five years and grow to $30 billion by 2010.[4]

What has led to the success of this restaurant segment? Many people are tired of fast food, and the fast-casual restaurant offers a new alternative; baby boomers' children have left home and this group is weary of cooking; young professionals do not want to cook every night; many Americans are concerned about eating more healthy foods; and more individuals want to spend little time

This case was prepared by Professors Debora J. Gilliard and Rajendra Khandekar of Metropolitan State College—Denver as a basis for class discussion rather than to illustrate either effective or ineffective handling of an administrative situation. Copyright © 2004 Debora J. Gilliard and Rajendra Khandekar. All rights reserved.

Exhibit 1   **Restaurant Chains with Highest Three-Year Sales Growth Rates, June 2004**

Restaurant	Three-Year Sales Growth Rate (%)
New World Restaurants (Einstein Bagels)	85.862%
P.F. Chang's	33.527
Buffalo Wild Wings	33.493
Panera Bread	32.965
Krispy Kreme Doughnuts	30.322
Landry's Restaurants	28.513
BUCA Inc.	25.580
Chicago Pizza & Brewery	25.293
Starbucks	23.235
Cheesecake Factory, Inc.	20.864
Industry Average	**11.635%**

Source: Reuters.com.

eating a meal. In addition, these restaurants tend to have strong sales in multiple parts of the day and develop a narrow menu focus.[5] Restaurants commonly included in the fast-casual segment include Panera Bread, Moe's Southwest Grill, Firehouse Subs, Chipotle, Sweet Tomatoes, Baja Fresh Mexican Grill, Rubio's Fresh Mexican Grill, Atlanta Bread Company, McAlister's Deli, Wingstop, and Crescent City Beignets. Exhibit 2 shows the leaders in the fast-casual category in 2002.

There are a number of trends that are influencing the restaurant industry:

♦ Increasing sales of chicken entrees. Many people perceive chicken to be a healthy food. Antonio Swad, founder of Wingstop Restaurants, states, "I was seeing that even people who say, 'I don't eat meat,' really mean that they don't eat red meat or pork. It just shows you what a position poultry has! It's almost the meat that non-meat eaters eat."[6]

♦ Consumers are showing an increased interest in more healthful foods. Organic foods are becoming more common as are healthy finger foods, such as sushi. Chefs are including more nuts (good sources of protein, fiber, vitamins, and minerals) in salads and entrees.

♦ Low-carb diets are affecting restaurant sales. The National Bread Leadership Council reported that U.S. consumers are eating 63 percent less bread in 2003 than they did in 2002. The council predicts this number will increase in 2004. Many restaurants are reporting changes in consumer eating habits: fewer bread requests and greater numbers of meat and vegetable requests. A Harris Poll conducted in the summer of 2003 indicated that 32 million Americans reported they were on a high-protein, low-carb diet.[7]

♦ More restaurants are allowing customers to customize their meals. For example, Peninsula Grill offers four steaks and five fish that guests can customize by choosing from 10 sauces. Executive Chef Robert Carter stated, "People can choose what they want to go together. What it creates is the

Exhibit 2   Leading Fast-Casual Concepts

	Sales ($ Millions)	$ Change 2001–2002 %	Total Units	Unit Change 2001–2002 %
		2002 Estimates		
Panera Bread	$ 755	42%	478	29%
Boston Market	650	4	662	1
Fazoli's	430	6	401	2
Baja Fresh	249	41	210	39
Chipotle	225	55	232	31
Buca di Beppo	240	37	82	21
Sweet Tomatoes/Souplantation	214	8	97	3
Taco Cabana	175	(1)	126	2
Atlanta Bread Company	160	59	153	27
Corner Bakery	138	17	81	17
La Madeleine	125	3	62	3
Rubio's Fresh Mexican Grill	119	6	143	6
McAlister's	107	34	103	34
Cosi	84	20	91	28
Pick Up Stix	75	15	75	32
Noodles & Company	59	69	58	61
Wolfgang Puck Express	52	53	39	105
Qdoba	58	13	85	13
Est. All Others	823	28	686	25
Total	$4,742	23%	3,864	17%

Source: Hale Group, Ltd.

ability for someone to be able to create their own dish. We wanted to have some options and give people what they wanted. . . . I think that the biggest trend is giving customers some options. . . . Restaurants that aren't willing to give customers choices are being perceived as stuffy or snooty."[8]

♦ Decor sets a restaurant apart from its competition and can be a defining aspect and enhance a restaurant's theme. A majority of restaurant owners/managers indicated they had remodeled their dining areas at least once since 1996 when responding to a National Restaurant Association survey.

♦ Today's customer is demanding better-quality food, better service, and better food safety. Restaurateurs must meet these demands with innovative food preparation and service.

♦ About half of 18- to 34-year-olds, who represent 37 percent of fast-food customers, are also eating at fast-casual chains.[9]

Restaurant and Institutions reported that in the rapidly changing restaurant environment, it is imperative for restaurants to engage in brand reengineering.[10] Restaurants do this by changing their name to reflect changes in concepts, changes in menus, new signage, and new decor. Lee Peterson, executive director of the design group at WD Partners, a firm that works with chain restaurants, said that restaurants do not have set shelf lives, but they do have life cycles. He further indicated that concepts are destined to die out, but they do require refurbishing to survive. Peterson stated, "Birth of the fast-casual segment made the quick-service industry realize it was aging. But that is healthy because it spurs reflection and improvement."

The quick-services restaurants are responding to trends by refreshing their menus and expanding into fast-casual concepts. The Hale Group reported that McDonald's and Jack in the Box have introduced premium salads, Burger King has "fire-grilled" burgers, Arby's has been successful with its Market Fresh Sandwiches, Subway is repositioning itself as a provider of healthy foods, and Schlotzsky's has introduced a health menu. Casual dining restaurants are also responding by offering convenient options such as Chili's To Go service, Outback's and Applebee's curbside delivery, and Applebee's fast-lunch menus. TGI Friday's, Ruby Tuesday's, and Chili's are adding low-carb options to their menus, and the Don Pablo's chain of Mexican restaurants added Low-Carb Lettuce Wrap Fajitas to its menu.[11]

History of Panera Bread Company

Ron Shaich cofounded Au Bon Pain Co. in 1981 with the opening of three bakery-cafes and one cookie store. The company continued to grow throughout the 1980s and 1990s. By the end of 1997, the company had 160 bakery-cafes in the United States, mostly located on the East Coast, and 96 bakery-cafes outside the country in Chile, the Philippines, Indonesia, Thailand, Brazil, and the United Kingdom. The company had bakery-cafes located in 9 domestic airports and 14 DoubleTree Hotels.

Twenty-five years ago Ken Rosenthal first tasted the sourdough bread that would become a vital part of Panera Bread. He was so taken by the bread's texture and flavor that he persuaded the family that made it to sell him the sourdough starter. In October 1987 Ken packed the starter in a cooler and brought it back to St. Louis where he started the St. Louis Bread Co. The handcrafted bread became a favorite among local citizens and the concept soon evolved to include other breads, bagels, pastries, sandwiches, salads, and espresso beverages.

On December 22, 1993, Au Bon Pain Co. purchased the St. Louis Bread Co. At the time, the St. Louis Bread Co. consisted of 19 company-owned bakery-cafes and one franchised bakery-cafe located primarily in the St. Louis area. Au Bon Pain Co. consisted of over 300 quick-service bakeries in the East. In 1998 Au Bon Pain Co.'s CEO, Ron Shaich, decided to build St. Louis Bread Co. into a national brand under the name Panera Bread. Panera, derived from Latin, means "time of bread" and the name change reflected the vision and focus of expanding the company: "The time of bread was dawning in America."[12] In May 1999 all of Au Bon Pain Co.'s business units were sold except the bakery-cafe business unit, which was officially renamed Panera Bread Company. Today the Panera bakery-cafes produce among the highest average retail unit volumes of any concept outside of casual dining. In 2003 the company reported company bakery-cafe sales of $265.9 million and franchise bakery sales of $711.0 million. As of December 2003 the company had over 602 bakery-cafes with average unit volumes of $1.85 million. It is ranked as one of the top growth companies in the food service industry.

Company Concept and Strategy

The Panera Bread Company brings the tradition of freshly baked bread to neighborhoods. Only the highest-quality ingredients are used—only fresh dough and no preservatives—and the bread is baked fresh everyday. Panera Bread bakes more fresh bread each day than any other bakery-cafe operation in the United States, which helps fulfill the company's mission of putting "a loaf of bread in every arm."

Panera Bread serves 18 kinds of breads, bagels, muffins, scones, rolls and sweet goods, made-to-order sandwiches, hearty soups, custom-roasted coffees, and cafe beverages such as espresso and cappuccino drinks. The company regularly reviews its product offerings to ensure it is satisfying changing customer preferences. Two customer groups have been identified: the "bread-loving trendsetters" who embrace new and nutritional items, and the "bread-loving traditionalists." In 2002 the company introduced a new artisan bread that is an all-natural, handcrafted bread baked on a stone deck. In spring of 2003 the company introduced a line of ciabatta bread sandwiches. Kevin Ament, a company spokesperson, stated, "People want high-quality handcrafted foods that are made with the best ingredients and that are fresh. What Panera is doing with bread is similar to what Starbucks did with coffee: educating customers about a staple people took for granted."[13] Ron Shaich announced in August 2003 that the company was in the process of equipping its bakery-cafes with free Wi-Fi access. He stated, "Panera is the first national chain to take substantial steps forward in meeting growing consumer demand for high-speed Internet access without charging for the service. By offering this extra amenity, we hope to more fully meet the needs of our sophisticated and diverse consumer base." In December 2003 Panera Bread and Viking Culinary Arts Centers announced they were teaming up to offer monthly classes on how to prepare fresh baked breads at home. Panera artisan bakers will conduct classes at Viking Culinary Arts Centers in Atlanta, Cleveland, Dallas, Long Island, Philadelphia, and St. Louis. Other initiatives the company is introducing in an effort to increase sales growth are: Via Panera, an off-premises sales concept to improve convenience to customers; new and seasonal food items; and a debit card program similar to that offered by Starbucks.

Shaich indicated that consumer interest in the low-carbohydrates diets "served to temper our comparable stores' sales' increases, which totaled a modest 0.2 percent systemwide in 2003."[14] He indicated that Panera's diverse menu has always offered choices to customers. However, to address the low-carb trend, Panera introduced a new line of low-carb breads, bagels, and breadsticks in June 2004.

The menu, operating system, and design allow Panera Bread to operate in several successful times of the day: breakfast, lunch, and daytime "chill out" (between breakfast and lunch and between lunch and dinner when customers take a break from their daily activities to visit bakery-cafes). In addition, the company sells bread to take home.

The bakery-cafes are primarily located in suburban, strip mall, and regional mall locations. As of December 27, 2003, the company operated 602 Panera Bread bakery-cafes in 35 states (see Exhibit 3).

The company has been successful because of its unit economies, its fine premium food, and its loyal customer base. Panera Bread serves its food on china, has well-spaced tables, and the decor reflects that of a French cafe. The environment is very important since about half of its customers eat on-site. Kevin Ament recently stated, "It's very much a gathering place where people can go and relax and enjoy the food."[15] The company also delivers what its sophisticated customers desire: fresh sandwiches, bagels, salads, soups, pastries, and alternatives to fast food.[16]

Exhibit 3   Panera Bread/St. Louis Bread Co. Bakery-Cafes

State	Company Bakery-Cafes	Franchise-Operated Bakery-Cafes	Total Bakery-Cafes
Alabama			4
Arkansas		2	2
California		5	5
Colorado		14	14
Connecticut	1	4	5
Delaware		1	1
Florida	5	43	48
Georgia	8	6	14
Iowa		13	13
Illinois	34	32	66
Indiana	3	15	18
Kansas		14	14
Kentucky	4	1	5
Massachusetts	2	18	20
Maryland		18	18
Maine		2	2
Michigan	32	8	40
Minnesota		20	20
Missouri	36	16	52
North Carolina	1	17	18
Nebraska		7	7
Nevada		2	2
New Hampshire		7	7
New Jersey		25	25
New York	5	3	8
Ohio	6	55	61
Oklahoma		15	15
Pennsylvania	7	27	34
Rhode Island		3	3
South Carolina	2		2
Tennessee	1	9	10
Texas	2	9	11
Virginia	20	1	21
West Virginia		2	2
Wisconsin		15	15
Totals	173	429	602

Source: Panera Bread Co. 2003 Annual Report.

In order to achieve the goals for this business, Chairman Ron Shaich indicated the company must:[17]

◆ Ensure the concept remains special.

◆ Deliver spectacular execution every day.

◆ Effectively execute a growth strategy through committed franchisees/area development partners, company operators, and joint venture partners.

◆ Evolve the information systems, management practices, and culture to drive focus, accountability, and transparency.

◆ Encourage evolution and change consistent with our commitment to bread leadership and our concept essence.

Throughout 2003 Panera Bread Company's breads, bakery products, soups, and sandwiches were often voted "best of" in many regional markets. A few of the awards Panera received include: "Best Bakery" in Chattanooga, Franklin (Massachusetts), Kansas City, Knoxville, Sarasota, Boulder, and Highlands Ranch (Colorado); "Best Bread" in Cincinnati, Cleveland, Hyde Park, and St. Louis; "Best Bagels" in Columbus, Iowa City, Sarasota, and Oak Ridge (Tennessee); and "Best Sandwiches" in Minneapolis/St. Paul, Rochester, and Milwaukee.[18] In the spring of 2003, Panera was ranked as the top-performing company in Standard & Poor's Small Cap 600 Index.[19] Also in that year, Panera Bread received, for the second consecutive year, top ranking in the "Choice of Chains" awards sponsored by *Restaurant and Institutions* magazine. The award is based on consumer rankings of food quality, menu variety, value, service, atmosphere, cleanliness, and convenience. Panera was also ranked number one for food quality among all 95 competitors. *Nation's Restaurant News* announced Panera Bread was ranked number one in a national consumer satisfaction survey of more than 71,000 consumers.[20]

In 1992 the company established Operation Dough-Nation, a program that allows Panera Bread to contribute back to the community. The cash donations received at the bakery-cafes are matched with bread and cash and distributed to local food pantries. At the end of each day, any unsold loaves of bread are taken to a local hunger relief agency. The company has also developed a Dough for Funds program that allows nonprofit groups to sell special coupons for Panera Bread products and keep half the proceeds for their causes.

Management

The management team at Panera Bread Company is filled with individuals with a great deal of food service experience (see Exhibit 4).

Company Operations

Management Information Systems   The cash registers at each bakery-cafe collect point-of-sale transaction data that is used to generate marketing information, product mix, and average check amount. The in-store system is designed to assist managers in scheduling labor, managing food costs, and providing access to retail data. The sales, bank deposit, and variance data for each bakery-cafe are submitted to the company's accounting department daily and the information is then used to generate weekly reports and monthly financial data.

Distribution   Independent distributors are used to distribute sweet goods products and other materials to the bakery-cafes. This allows Panera to eliminate an investment in distribution systems and focus on its retail operations. Fresh dough products are provided by the commissaries, and all other products and supplies (e.g., paper goods and coffee) are contracted for by the company and delivered by vendors to the independent distributors.

Franchise Operations   Panera Bread began its franchising program in 1996. The company prefers to establish area development agreements (ADAs) rather than individual franchises. The ADA requires a franchise to develop a specified number of bakery-cafes on or before specific dates as designated in each agreement. Franchisee-owned bakery-cafes must meet the same standards for product quality, menu, site selection, and construction as company-owned bakery-cafes. Franchisees are required to purchase all dough products from company-approved sources and the company's commissary supplies all fresh dough products. The franchise fee is $35,000 with the total investment in a bakery-cafe ranging from $564,000 to $910,725. A royalty fee of 4 percent to 5 percent on gross sales is payable each week. As of December 28, 2003, the company was working with 32 franchisee groups, had 429 franchised bakery-cafes open, and had commitments to open 409 additional franchised bakery-cafes. The manager and head baker of each franchise are required to attend Panera Bread's training program. The classroom portion of the management training course lasts five days and the in-store training portion lasts four to six weeks. Topics discussed during the training program include area and shift management, administration, customer service, quality assurance, company history, safety procedures, and human resources.

Bakery Supply Chain   All bakery-cafes use fresh dough for the sourdough bread, artisan breads, and bagels which is supplied daily by a regional commissary of the company. As of December 27, 2003, the company had 17 regional fresh dough facilities. Although the distribution system requires a major commitment of capital, it provides cost efficiencies and assures consistent quality and supply of dough to the bakery-cafes. These give Panera Bread a competitive advantage. Product consistency enhances brand identity. The company distributes the dough using a leased fleet of temperature-controlled trucks. The optimal distribution limit is within 200 miles of the commissary and the average distribution route delivers dough to six bakery-cafes.

Exhibit 4   Panera Bread Company Officers

Name and Title	Background
Ronald Schaich Chairman and Chief Executive Officer	Cofounder of Au Bon Pain Co., 1981 MBA, Harvard Business School
Paul E. Twohig Executive Vice-President and Chief Operating Officer; joined Panera in January 2003	30 years' experience in food industry; Starbucks, 9 years; Burger King
Neal Yanofsky Executive Vice-President, Chief Administrative and Corporate Staff Officer, joined Panera in June 2003	Graduate of Harvard College and Harvard Business School; research fellow, London School of Economics; independent business consultant
Scott G. Davis Senior Vice-President and Chief Concept Officer	Started with Au Bon Pain in 1987
Mike J. Kupstas Senior Vice-President and Chief Franchise Officer; joined Panera in January 1996	Long John Silver's Inc. and Red Lobster
John Maguire Senior Vice-President, Chief Company and Joint Venture Operations Officer; joined Panera in 1994	15 years of bakery experience
Michael J. Nolan Senior Vice-President and Chief Development Officer; joined Panera in 2001	
Mark Borland Senior Vice-President and Chief Supply Chain Officer	With Au Bon Pain since 1986
Mark E. Hood Senior Vice-President and Chief Financial Officer; joined Panera in August 2002	U.S. Loyalty Corp. and Saks Holding Inc.

In May 2003 Panera opened its first bakery-cafe in Las Vegas using a new concept. In addition to the 5,600-square-foot bakery-cafe, a 500-square-foot fresh dough facility was included. This on-site commissary will produce fresh dough daily and customers are able to observe the baking process.

Other baked goods served at the bakery-cafes are prepared with frozen dough. In 1996 a state-of-the-art production facility was built in Mexico, Missouri, which the company sold to Bunge Food Corporation in 1998 for $13 million. At the time of sale, the company entered into a five-year (1998–2003) supply agreement with Bunge for the supply of its frozen dough needs. The sale of the production facility provided economies of scale in plant production and allowed the company to take advantage of Bunge's significant purchasing power.

In April 2003 the company signed an agreement with Dawn Food Products, Inc., to provide sweet goods for the 2003–2008 period. The company believes cost savings will be achieved by making the switch from Bunge to Dawn.

Financial Information

Exhibits 5 and 6 provide income and expense figures, and a consolidated balance sheet, respectively, for the most recent 12-month period.

Exhibit 7 provides key statistics for Panera Bread for the 12 months ended April 30, 2004.

For the 52-week period from May 2003 to May 2004 the stock price reached a high of $47.79 and a low of $32.65.

First quarter 2004 net income increased 26 percent over the same period in 2003. By April 17, 2004, the company had 637 bakery-cafes. During the 16 weeks ended April 17, 2004, Panera Bread opened 36 new bakery-cafes and closed one.

The company expects price increases in 2004 of about 2 percent for major ingredients such as butter, milk, hard cheeses, and cream cheese. Some of the price in-

Exhibit 5 **Panera Bread Company, Income and Expenses**

	For the Fiscal Years Ended[1]				
	December 27, 2003	December 28, 2002	December 29, 2001	December 30, 2000	December 25, 1999[2]
	(in thousands, except per share and bakery-cafe data)				
Costs and expenses:					
Bakery-cafe expenses:					
Cost of food and paper products	$ 73,727	$ 63,255	$ 48,253	$ 40,998	$ 52,362
Labor	81,152	63,172	45,768	36,281	45,167
Occupancy	17,990	14,619	11,345	9,313	15,552
Other operating expenses	36,804	27,971	20,729	16,050	18,740
Total bakery-cafe expenses	209,673	169,017	126,095	102,642	131,821
Fresh dough cost of sales to franchisees	47,151	33,959	21,965	12,261	6,490
Depreciation and amortization	19,487	13,965	10,839	8,412	6,379
General and administrative expenses	28,140	24,986	19,589	16,381	17,104
Pre-opening expenses	1,531	1,051	912	414	301
Nonrecurring charge[3]	—	—	—	494	5,545
Total costs and expenses	305,982	242,978	179,400	140,604	167,640
Operating profit	49,904	34,774	21,717	10,785	3,719
Interest expense	48	32	72	164	2,745
Other expense (income), net	1,227	287	213	(409)	735
Loss from early extinguishment of debt[4]	—	—	—	—	579
Minority interest	365	180	8	—	(25)
Income (loss) before income taxes and cumulative effect of accounting change	48,264	34,275	21,424	11,030	(315)
Provision for income taxes	17,616	12,510	8,272	4,177	314
Income (loss) before cumulative effect of accounting change	30,648	21,765	13,152	6,853	(629)
Cumulative effect to December 28, 2002, of accounting change, net of tax benefit	239	—	—	—	—
Net income (loss)	$ 30,409	$ 21,765	$ 13,152	$ 6,853	$ (629)

(continued on next page)

creases will be passed along to consumers, but company leaders also expect their margins to experience pressure.

In a press release on May 13, 2004, Ron Shaich, chairman and CEO, reported: "We are very pleased with our performance to date and are enthusiastic about the company's prospects. Sales in both new and mature bakery-cafes are robust and new store development is proceeding at a record pace. These two leading indicators of our per-formance indicate the stability of our business and the depth of consumer demand for the brand."

To date, Panera Bread's performance has been above industry averages. How can the company continue to achieve high growth rates in the future with the low-carb diet gathering momentum, new restaurants opening in the fast-casual segment, changes in the economic environ-ment, and changes in the demographic market?

Exhibit 5   Income and Expenses (continued)

	For the Fiscal Years Ended[1]				
	December 27, 2003	December 28, 2002	December 29, 2001	December 30, 2000	December 25, 1999[2]
	(in thousands, except per share and bakery-cafe data)				
Per common share:					
Basic:					
Income (loss) before cumulative effect of accounting change	$ 1.03	$ 0.75	$ 0.47	$ 0.27	$ (0.03)
Cumulative effect of accounting change	(0.01)	—	—	—	—
Net income (loss)	$ 1.02	$ 0.75	$ 0.47	$ 0.27	$ (0.03)
Diluted:					
Income (loss) before cumulative effect of accounting change	$ 1.01	$ 0.73	$ 0.46	$ 0.26	$ (0.03)
Cumulative effect of accounting change	(0.01)	—	—	—	—
Net income (loss)	$ 1.00	$ 0.73	$ 0.46	$ 0.26	$ (0.03)
Weighted average shares of common stock outstanding:					
Basic	29,733	28,923	27,783	25,114	24,274
Diluted	30,423	29,891	28,886	26,267	24,274
Comparable bakery-cafe sales percentage increases for:					
Company-owned bakery-cafes	1.7%	4.1%	5.8%	8.1%	3.3%
Franchise-operated bakery-cafes	(0.4)%	6.1%	5.8%	10.3%	(7)
Systemwide	0.2%	5.5%	5.8%	9.1%	(7)
Consolidated balance sheet data:					
Cash and cash equivalents	$ 42,402	$ 29,924	$ 18,052	$ 9,011	$ 1,936
Total assets	$245,943	$188,440	$143,934	$111,689	$ 91,029
Stockholders' equity	$195,937	$153,656	$119,872	$ 91,588	$ 73,246
Bakery-cafe data:					
Company-owned bakery-cafes open	173	132	110	90	81
Franchise-owned bakery-cafes open	429	346	259	172	100
Total bakery-cafes open	602	478	369	262	181

[1]Fiscal year 2000 consists of 53 weeks. Fiscal years 2003, 2002, 2001, and 1999 were comprised of 52 weeks.

[2]Includes the results of the Au Bon Pain Division (ABP) until it was sold on May 16, 1999.

[3]In 1999 the company recorded a $5.5 million impairment charge to reflect the May 1999 sale of ABP. In 2000 the company received a payment of $0.9 million as consideration for amending the ABP sale agreement to permit a subsequent sale. This nonrecurring gain was offset by a $0.9 nonrecurring charge related to the sale and a $0.5 million charge for asset impairment relating to closure of four Panera Bread bakery-cafes.

[4]Loss from extinguishment of debt was reclassified from an extraordinary item in accordance with the provisions of SFAS No. 145, "Rescission of FASB Statements No. 4, 44, and 64, Amendment of FASB Statement No. 13, and Technical Corrections."

Exhibit 6   Panera Bread Company, Balance Sheet

Consolidated Balance Sheets (in thousands, except share and per share information)		
	December 27, 2003	**December 28, 2002**
Assets		
Current Assets:		
Cash and cash equivalents	$ 42,402	$ 29,924
Investments in government securities	5,019	4,102
Trade accounts receivable, less allowance of $53 in 2003 and $33 in 2002	9,646	7,462
Other accounts receivable	2,748	2,097
Inventories	8,066	5,191
Prepaid expenses	1,294	1,826
Deferred income taxes	1,696	8,488
Other	—	172
Total current assets	70,871	59,262
Property and equipment, net	132,651	99,313
Other assets:		
Investments in government securities	4,000	5,047
Goodwill	32,743	18,970
Deposits and other	5,678	5,554
Deferred income taxes	—	294
Total other assets	42,421	29,865
Total assets	$ 245,943	$ 188,440
Liabilities and Stockholders' Equity		
Current liabilities:		
Accounts payable	$ 8,072	$ 5,987
Accrued expenses	35,552	24,935
Current portion of deferred revenue	1,168	1,403
Total current liabilities	44,792	32,325
Deferred income taxes	328	—
Other long-term liabilities	1,115	262
Total liabilities	46,235	32,587
Minority interest	3,771	2,197
Commitments and contingencies		
Stockholders' equity:		
Common stock, $.0001 par value:		
Class A, 75,000,000 shares authorized; 28,296,581 issued and 28,187,581 outstanding in 2003; and 27,446,448 issued and 27,337,448 outstanding in 2002	3	3
Class B, 10,000,000 shares authorized; 1,847,221 issued and outstanding in 2003 and 1,977,363 in 2002	—	—
Treasury stock, carried at cost	(900)	(900)
Additional paid-in capital	121,992	110,120
Retained earnings	74,842	44,433
Total stockholders' equity	195,937	153,656
Total liabilities and stockholders' equity	$ 245,943	$ 188,440

Exhibit 7   Panera Bread Company: Key Statistics for the 12-Month Period Ended April 30, 2004

	$ in millions except per share data
Profitability	
Profit margin (ttm):	8.41%
Operating margin (ttm):	14.02%
Management Effectiveness	
Return on assets (ttm):	14.78%
Return on equity (ttm):	18.12%
Income Statement	
Revenue (ttm):	387.15
Revenue per share (ttm):	12.692
Revenue growth (lfy):	28.10%
Gross profit (ttm):	99.06
EBITDA (ttm):	69.39
Net income* (ttm):	32.57
Diluted earnings per share (ttm):	1.07
Earnings growth (lfy):	39.70%
Balance Sheet	
Total cash (mrq):	47.42
Total cash per share (mrq):	1.57
Total debt (mrq):	0
Total debt/equity (mrq):	0
Current ratio (mrq):	1.582
Book value per share (mrq):	6.524
Cash Flow Statement	
From operations (ttm):	68.53
Free cash flow (ttm):	27.34

ttm = trailing 12 months

mrq = most recent quarter

lfy = last fiscal year

*Net income available to common shareholders

Source: Yahoo Finance, 2003–2004, http://biz.yahoo.com.

References

1. Zganjar, L., 2003, "Quick-casual" restaurants gain healthy ground, *Birmingham Business Journal,* April 21.
2. Hoover's Online, 2003–2004, www-2.hoovers.com.
3. Technomic Annual Report shows solid performance among the top 100 chain restaurant companies, 2002, www.technomic.com/news, May 22.
4. Zganjar, "Quick-casual" restaurants; Rothstein, Kim, 2003, Fast casual sends a strategic signal, *Strategic Initiative* 18 (3); www.halegroup.com.
5. Franchise Help Online 2003, online newsletter; Hamaker, S. S., & Panitz, B., 2002, In vogue: What's hot in the restaurant industry, *Restaurants USA,* May; www.restaurant.org/rusa/magArticle.
6. Hamaker & Panitz, 2002, In vogue.
7. www.cyberflexing.com, 2004; Mexican restaurants capitalize on the low-carb craze, 2004, Maiden Name Press, www.restmex.com.
8. Hamaker & Panitz, 2002, In vogue.
9. Fast casual, 2004, Trendscape; 222.trendsetters.com/food-trend/8001,1,fast-casual.html.
10. Hume, Scott, 2004, Reinventing the wheels: Impact of fast casual, *Restaurants and Institutions,* April 1; www.keepmedia.com/jsp/article.
11. Rothstein, 2003, Fast casual; Nelson, R., 2004, Is the low-carb craze affecting bakeries, restaurants? *Minneapolis Star Tribune,* February 12; www.startribune.com/stories/438/4362434.html; Mexican restaurants capitalize on the low-carb craze, 2004.
12. Panera Bread Company, 2003 Annual report, www.panerabread.com.
13. Zganjar, 2003, "Quick-casual" restaurants.
14. Panera Bread Company, 2003, Annual report.
15. Zganjar, 2003, "Quick-casual" restaurants.
16. Suhr, J., 2003, Panera food not fast; its growth is, *Denver Post,* April 6: 16.
17. Panera Bread Company, 2003, Annual report.
18. Panera Bread Company, 2003, www.panerabread.com.
19. Suhr, 2003, Panera food not fast.
20. Yahoo Finance, 2003–2004, http://biz.yahoo.com; Panera Bread Company, 2003, Annual report.

Case 30   Pixar Animation Studios

Basking in the success of its latest release, *Finding Nemo,* Pixar Animation Studios announced in late January 2004 that it had decided to end its talks with Walt Disney on continuing their 12-year-old partnership. The current agreement is set to expire after Pixar has delivered its next two films by the end of 2005. "After 10 months of trying to strike a deal with Disney, we're moving on," stated Steve Jobs, the Apple Computer chief executive who also heads the animation firm. "We've had a great run together —one of the most successful in Hollywood history—and it's a shame that Disney won't be participating in Pixar's future success."[1]

Since Pixar signed its first distribution pact with Disney, it has delivered a string of five straight hits: *Toy Story, A Bug's Life, Toy Story 2, Monsters, Inc.,* and *Finding Nemo.* Including estimates for the revenues from its latest hit, Pixar films will have earned well over $2.75 billion at the box office worldwide and sold more than 200 million DVDs and videos, making it one of the world's most successful animation companies (see Exhibit 1 for the top 10 animated films). "They're the ultimate pure-play media company," said Merrill Lynch analyst Andrew Slabin.[2]

But Jobs has been trying to negotiate with Michael Eisner, Disney's chief executive, about the share of profits that Pixar would get and the amount of control that it would maintain over its films. Under their current agreement, Disney has given Pixar half of the profits that are generated by each of its films from ticket sales, video sales, and merchandising royalties. But Disney has also charged Pixar a fee of 12.5 percent of total revenues for distributing its movies, which is deducted before any profits are assessed. Furthermore, although Pixar has shared with Disney the cost of producing and marketing its films, Disney has retained the rights to the use of all of the characters and the rights to any sequels that would be developed.

Jobs had made it clear that he wants Pixar to finance and market its own movies and to retain all of the profits that they generate. He was willing to give Disney a distribution fee that would run between 7 percent and 10 percent of a film's revenues. Clearly, Pixar has the funds to produce and market its own films because its successes have provided it with a strong balance sheet, with over $500 million in cash and no debt. Eisner felt that Disney would not stand to gain much from making such a deal with Pixar. See Exhibits 2 and 3 for Pixar's income statement and balance sheet.

However, many analysts believe that Jobs should be able to get one of the Hollywood studios to agree to his

This case was prepared by Professor Jamal Shamsie of Michigan State University. This case was developed from published sources as a basis for class discussion rather than to illustrate either effective or ineffective handling of an administrative situation. Copyright © 2004 Jamal Shamsie.

terms. The prospect of a new deal has raised expectations for the firm's future. Pixar posted profits of $90 million in 2002 on sales of $202 million. Prudential Securities expects that, with a contract for 100 percent of profits after distribution fees, Pixar's net income would surge to $163 million in 2007 on sales of $361 million. Such hopes have lifted the firm's stock to just over $70, a rise of just more than 50 percent from the beginning of 2002 (see Exhibit 4).

Pushing for Computer Animated Films

The roots of Pixar stretch back to 1975 with the founding of a vocational school in Old Westbury, New York, called the New York Institute of Technology. It was there that Edwin E. Catmull, a straitlaced businessman from Salt Lake City who loved animation but couldn't draw, teamed up with the people who would later form the core of Pixar. "It was artists and technologists from the very start," recalled Alvy Ray Smith, who worked with Catmull during those years. "It was like a fairy tale."[3]

By 1979 Catmull and his team decided to join forces with famous Hollywood director George W. Lucas, Jr. They were hopeful that this would allow them to pursue their dream of making animated films. As part of Lucas's filmmaking facility in San Rafael, California, Catmull's group of aspiring animators was able to make substantial progress in the art of computer animation. But the unit was not able to generate any profits and Lucas was not willing to let it grow beyond using computer animation for special effects.

Catmull finally turned in 1985 to Jobs, who had just been ousted from Apple. Jobs was reluctant to invest in a firm that wanted to make full-length feature films using computer animation. But a year later, Jobs decided to buy Catmull's unit for just $10 million, which represented a third of Lucas's asking price. While the newly named Pixar Animation Studios tried to push the boundaries of computer animation over the next five years, Jobs ended up having to invest an additional $50 million—more than 25 percent of his total wealth at the time. "There were times that we all despaired, but fortunately not all at the same time," said Jobs.[4]

Still, Catmull's team did continue to make substantial breakthroughs in the development of computer generated full-length feature films. In 1991 Disney ended up giving Pixar a three-film contract that started with *Toy Story.* When the movie was finally released in 1995, its success surprised everyone in the film industry. Rather than the nice little film Disney had expected, *Toy Story* became the sensation of 1995. It rose to the rank of the third highest grossing animated film of all time, earning $362 million in worldwide box office revenues.

Exhibit 1   Leading Animated Films

All five of Pixar's films released to date have ended up among the top 10 animated films of all time based on worldwide box office revenues.

Title	Year Released	Box Office Gross (In $ millions)	Studio
1. *The Lion King*	1994	$768	Disney
2. *Finding Nemo*	2003	740	*Pixar*
3. *Monsters, Inc.*	2001	523	*Pixar*
4. *Aladdin*	1992	502	Disney
5. *Toy Story 2*	1999	485	*Pixar*
6. *Shrek*	2001	477	Dreamworks
7. *Tarzan*	1999	435	Disney
8. *Toy Story*	1995	362	*Pixar*
9. *A Bug's Life*	1998	361	*Pixar*
10. *Beauty and the Beast*	1991	352	Disney

Source: Adapted from *Variety*.

Within days, Jobs decided to take Pixar public. When the shares, priced at $22, shot past $33, Jobs called his best friend, Oracle CEO Lawrence J. Ellison, to tell him he had company in the billionaire's club. With Pixar's sudden success, Jobs returned to strike a new deal with Disney. Early in 1996, at a lunch with Walt Disney chief Michael Eisner, Jobs made his demands: an equal share of the profits, equal billing on merchandise and on-screen credits, and guarantees that Disney would market Pixar films as it did its own.

Boosting the Creative Component

With the success of *Toy Story*, Jobs realized that he had hit something big. He had obviously tapped into his Silicon Valley roots and turned to computers to forge a unique style of creative moviemaking. In each of its subsequent films, Pixar has continued to develop computer animation that has allowed for more lifelike backgrounds, texture, and movement than ever before. For example, since real leaves are translucent, Pixar's engineers developed special software algorithms that both reflect and absorb light, creating luminous scenes among jungles of clover.

In spite of the significance of these advancements in computer animation, Jobs was well aware that successful feature films would require a strong creative spark. He understood that it would be the marriage of technology with creativity that would allow Pixar to rise above most of its competition. To get that, Jobs fostered a campuslike environment within the newly formed outfit similar to the freewheeling, charged atmosphere in the early days of his beloved Apple, where he also returned as acting CEO. "It's not simply the technology that makes Pixar," said Dick Cook, president of Walt Disney Studios.[5]

Even though Jobs has played a crucial supportive role, it is Catmull, now elevated to the position of Pixar's president, who has been mainly responsible for ensuring that the firm's technological achievements help to pump up the firm's creative efforts. He has been the keeper of the company's unique innovative culture, which has blended Silicon Valley techies, Hollywood production honchos, and artsy animation experts. In the pursuit of Catmull's vision, this eclectic group has transformed their office cubicles into tiki huts, circus tents, and cardboard castles with bookshelves stuffed with toys and desks adorned with colorful iMac computers.

Catmull has also been working hard to build upon this pursuit of creative innovation by establishing programs to develop the employees. Each new hire is expected to spend 10 weeks at Pixar University, an in-house training program that includes courses in live improvisation, drawing, and cinematography. The school's dean is Randall E. Nelson, a former juggler who has been known to perform his act using chain saws so students in animation classes have something compelling to draw.

It is this emphasis on the creative use of technology that has kept Pixar on the cutting edge. The firm has turned out ever more lifelike short films, including 1998's Oscar-winning *Geri's Game*, which used a technology

Exhibit 2   **Pixar's Income Statement**
(All numbers in thousands)

	Period Ending		
	January 3, 2004	December 28, 2002	December 29, 2001
Total Revenue	$262,498	$201,724	$70,223
Cost of revenue	38,058	41,534	12,318
Gross Profit	224,440	160,190	57,905
Research & development	15,311	8,497	6,341
Selling, general, and administrative	15,205	11,011	10,048
Operating Income or Loss	193,924	140,682	41,516
Income from continuing operations			
Total other income/expenses, net	10,517	10,342	14,355
Earnings before interest and taxes	204,441	151,024	55,871
Interest expense	—	—	—
Income before tax	204,441	151,024	55,871
Income tax expense	79,673	61,074	19,865
Net income from continuing operations	124,768	89,950	36,006
Discontinued operations	—	—	211
Extraordinary items	—	—	—
Effect of accounting changes	—	—	—
Other items	—	—	—
Net Income	124,768	89,950	36,217
Preferred stock and other adjustments	—	—	—
Net Income Applicable to Common Shares	$124,768	$ 89,950	$36,217

Source: Pixar annual reports.

called subdivision surfaces. This makes realistic simulation of human skin and clothing possible. "They're absolute geniuses," gushed Jules Roman, cofounder and CEO of rival Tippett Studio. "They're the people who created computer animation really."[6]

Becoming Accomplished Storytellers

A considerable part of the creative energy goes into story development. Jobs understands that a film works only if its story can move the hearts and minds of families around the world. His goal is to develop Pixar into an animated movie studio that becomes known for the quality of its storytelling above everything else. "We want to create some great stories and characters that endure with each generation," Jobs has stated.[7]

For story development, Pixar relies heavily on 41-year-old John Lasseter, who goes by the title of vice-president of the creative. Known for his Hawaiian shirts and irrepressible playfulness, Lasseter has been the key to the appeal of all of Pixar's films. Lasseter gets very passionate about developing great stories and then harnessing computers to tell these stories. Most of Pixar's employees believe it is this passion that has allowed the studio to ensure that each of its films has been a commercial hit. In fact, Lasseter is being regarded as the Walt Disney of the 21st century.

When it's time to start a project, Lasseter isolates a group of eight or so writers and directs them to forget about the constraints of technology. While many studios try to rush from script to production, Lasseter takes up to

Exhibit 3   Pixar's Balance Sheet
(All numbers in thousands)

	Period Ending		
	January 3, 2004	**December 28, 2002**	**December 29, 2001**
Assets			
Current assets			
Cash and cash equivalents	$48,320	$44,431	$56,289
Short-term investments	—	294,652	222,310
Net receivables	203,794	136,911	20,660
Inventory	107,667	—	—
Other current assets	—	13,826	—
Total Current Assets	**359,781**	**489,820**	**299,259**
Long-term investments	473,603	—	—
Property, plant, and equipment	115,026	117,423	111,995
Intangible assets	—	92,104	86,839
Other assets	1,047	—	3,528
Deferred long-term asset charges	51,496	32,719	21,673
Total Assets	**1,000,953**	**732,066**	**523,294**
Liabilities			
Current liabilities			
Accounts payable	52,405	11,663	15,495
Other current liabilities	—	7,341	2,113
Total Current Liabilities	**52,405**	**19,004**	**17,608**
Other liabilities	8,038	—	—
Total Liabilities	**60,443**	**19,004**	**17,608**
Stockholders' Equity			
Common stock	546,999	442,477	325,362
Retained earnings	393,197	268,429	178,479
Other stockholder equity	314	2,156	1,845
Total Stockholder Equity	**940,510**	**713,062**	**505,686**
Net Tangible Assets	**$940,510**	**$620,958**	**$418,847**

Source: Pixar annual reports.

two years just to develop the story. Once the script has been developed, artists create storyboards and copy them onto videotapes called reels. Even computer-animated films must begin with pencil sketches that are viewed on tape. "You can't really shortchange the story development," Lasseter has emphasized.[8]

Only after the basic story has been set does Lasseter begin to think about what he'll need from Pixar's technologists—and it's always more than the computer animators expect. Lasseter, for example, demanded that the crowds of ants in *A Bug's Life* not be a single mass of look-alike faces. To solve the problem, computer expert

Exhibit 4   **Pixar's Stock Performance and Annual Projections**

Stock Price, October 2003	
Stock price	$71
Rise during year	34%
Market value	$4.0 billion
Net cash	$502.0 million

Current & Projected Annual Figures	
2002 Profits per share	$1.68
2002 Price/earnings ratio	42.2
2003 Profits per share	$1.75 Projected
2003 Price/earnings ratio	40.6 Projected
2004 Profits per share	$1.30 Projected
2004 Price/earnings ratio	54.6 Projected

Sources: Pixar annual reports, Thompson Financial, *Barron's.*

William T. Reeves developed software that randomly applied physical and emotional characteristics to each ant. In another instance, writers brought a model of a butterfly named Gypsy to researchers, asking them to write code so that when she rubs her antennae, you can see the hairs press down and pop back up.

At any stage during the process, Lasseter may go back to potential problems that he may see with the story. In *A Bug's Life,* for example, the story was totally revamped after more than a year of work had been completed. Originally, it was about a troupe of circus bugs run by P.T. Flea that tries to rescue a colony of ants from marauding grasshoppers. But because of a flaw in the story—why would the circus bugs risk their lives to save stranger ants?—codirector Andrew Stanton recast the story to be about Flik, the heroic ant who recruits Flea's troupe to fight the grasshoppers. "You have to rework and rework it," explained Lasseter. It is not rare for a scene to be rewritten as much as 30 times.[9]

Pumping Out the Hits

In spite of its formidable string of hits, Pixar has had difficulty in stepping up its pace of production. Although they may cost 30 percent less than traditional animated films, computer-generated animated films still take considerable time to develop. Furthermore, because of the emphasis on every single detail, Pixar used to complete most of the work on a film before moving on to the next one. Catmull and Lasseter have since decided to work on several projects at the same time, but it still took 18 months for the studio to follow up *Monsters, Inc.* with *Finding*

Nemo. Jobs has stated he would like Pixar to release a movie each year.

In order to push for this ambitious goal, Pixar has nearly doubled in size since 1998, to 750 employees. It is also turning to a stable of directors to oversee its movies. Lasseter, who directed Pixar's first three films, is supervising other directors who are taking the helm of various films that the studio chooses to develop. *Monsters, Inc.* and *Finding Nemo* were directed by some of this new talent. But there are concerns about the number of directors that Pixar can rely upon to turn out high-quality animated films. Michael Savner of Bank of America Securities has commented: "You can't simply double production. There is a finite amount of talent."[10]

To meet the faster production pace, Catmull has also added new divisions including one to help with the development of new movies and one to oversee movie development shot by shot. The eight-person development team has helped to generate more ideas for new films. "Once more ideas are percolating, we have more options to choose from so no one artist is feeling the weight of the world on their shoulders," said Sarah McArthur, Pixar's vice president of production.[11]

Finally, Catmull is turning to new technology to help ramp up production. His goal is to reduce the number of animators to no more than 100 per film. Toward this end, Catmull has been overseeing the development of new animation software, called Luxo, which will allow fewer people to do more work. While the firm's old system allowed animators to easily make a change to a specific character, Luxo adjusts the environment as well. For example, if an animator adds a new head to a monster, the system would automatically cast the proper shadow.

Above all, Catmull has been working hard to retain Pixar's commitment to quality even as it grows. He has been using Pixar University to encourage collaboration among all employees so that they can develop and retain the key values that are tied to their success. And he has helped devise ways to avoid collective burnout. A masseuse and a doctor now come to Pixar's campus each week, and animators must get permission from their supervisors if they want to work more than 50 hours a week.

Jobs is well aware of the dangers of growth for a studio whose successes came out of a lean structure that wagered everything on each film. It remains to be seen whether Pixar is able to draw on its talent to increase production without compromising the high standards set by Catmull and Lasseter. The question is whether the company can keep making hits if it's doubling the number of films it makes. "You wonder, are they at risk of becoming formulaic?" asked Merrill Lynch analyst Andrew Slabin.[12]

To Infinity and Beyond?

Job's decision to break off talks with Disney took industry observers by surprise. It is clear that Disney has been relying heavily on Pixar since its own animated films have not performed well. But there are questions about the ability of Pixar to continue with its success without any support from Disney. Pixar may no longer need Disney's assistance with the financing and production of its films, but Disney has provided much more critical support for the marketing and distribution of these films and any associated merchandise such as toys and videos.

Pixar may not have sufficient experience to handle these marketing and distribution functions. It has managed to release just five films so far, even though they have managed to rise to the list of box office leaders among animated films. Most observers believe that Pixar relied heavily upon Disney's capabilities in order to achieve its early success. It was Disney that had the marketing might that helped to transform characters such as Woody or Nemo from mere images on the big screen into household names.

Furthermore, Pixar stands to lose some revenue over the next two years by not maintaining its relationship with Disney. Under its present contract, Disney will still distribute the next two Pixar films: *The Incredibles,* due later in 2004, and *Cars,* due sometime in 2005. Disney had been willing to adjust the profit split on these two films if Pixar chose to continue with the present arrangement. By deciding to make a deal with another Hollywood studio, Pixar will have to wait until 2006 before it can keep more of the profits from its own films.

Even if Pixar is able to get a greater share of the profits from its films, it will still have to keep generating hits.

But Catmull and Lasseter are confident that they have the talent that will allow them to keep pushing out great animated films. "We're not jumping on the bandwagon, we're making it," claimed Catmull.[13] Sarah McArthur echoes this feeling: "There's an atmosphere of building something. There's energy, camaraderie, creativity. We're trying to make this work."[14]

Furthermore, Pixar's talent does not have Hollywood-style costs attached to them. Employees are happy to receive stock options and no one in the firm has long-term contracts. Even under these conditions, the firm has little turnover. "We have the lowest turnover rate in Hollywood history," said Lasseter. "We created the studio we want to work in. We have an environment that's wacky. It's a creative brain trust: It's not a place where I make my movies —it's a place where a group of people makes movies."[15]

Pixar certainly comes as close to a sure thing as exists in the unpredictable movie business, but no one expects it to have an endless winning streak. "It's hard to put a string of 10 megablockbusters together," said Michael Savner of Bank of America Securities.[16] The risk of a failure is likely to rise as Pixar tries to ramp up production. "Things like creativity don't necessarily scale up," said Sasa Zorovic, an analyst at Robert Stephens in San Francisco.[17]

Endnotes

1. Holson, Laura M., 2004, Pixar, creator of *Finding Nemo,* sees end to its Disney partnership, *New York Times,* January 30: A1.
2. Burrows, Peter, 2003, Pixar's unsung hero, *BusinessWeek,* June 30: 68.
3. Burrows, Peter, & Grover, Ronald, 1998, Steve Jobs: Movie mogul, *BusinessWeek,* November 23: 150.
4. Ibid., 150.
5. Ibid., 146.
6. Ibid.
7. Graser, Marc, 1999, Pixar run by focused group, *Variety,* December 20: 74.
8. Ibid.
9. Burrows & Grover, 1998, 146.
10. Bary, Andrew, 2003, Coy story, *Barron's,* October 13: 21.
11. Tam, Pui-Wing, 2001, Will quantity hurt Pixar's quality? *Wall Street Journal,* February 15: B4.
12. Burrows, 2003, 69.
13. Burrows & Grover, 1998, 146.
14. Graser, 1999, 74.
15. Ibid.
16. Bary, 2003, 21.
17. Tam, 2001, B1.

Case 31 Procter & Gamble

On August 1, 2003, Procter & Gamble, the Cincinnati-based consumer products firm announced that it was ending its restructuring program a full year ahead of schedule. The program had been initiated in 1999 with the appointment of Durk I. Jager as the firm's new CEO. But it was completed by Alan G. "A.G." Lafley who took over the helm in June 2000 after Jaeger was pressured to resign. A 23-year P&G veteran, Lafley moved quickly to shift the focus of the firm back to building upon its past accomplishments.

Under Lafley, P&G turned to its old and reliable brands such as Tide, Pampers, and Crest in order to gain back lost market share. The market share gains that the firm was able to extract from these well-established products have attracted a lot of attention. The company's stock price has climbed 58 percent, to $92 a share, since Lafley started, even as the Standard & Poor's 500 stock index declined by 32 percent. Banc of America analyst William H. Steele has estimated that P&G's profits for the fiscal year, which ended June 30, 2003, will rise by 13 percent, to $5.57 billion, on an 8 percent increase in sales, to $43.23 billion. Growth in sales has averaged 7 percent over the past six quarters, excluding acquisitions, well above Lafley's goal and the industry average. See Exhibits 1 and 2 for Procter & Gamble's income statement and balance sheets, 2001–2003.

According to industry analysts, this shift back to P&G's roots by the soft-spoken Lafley was exactly the antidote the firm may have needed after Jager's disastrous reign. Jager had moved with considerable speed to try to rip apart P&G's insular culture and remake it from the bottom up. Instead of pushing P&G to excel, however, the steps that he took during his 17-month term nearly brought the venerable company to a grinding halt. His companywide reorganization left many employees confused and paralyzed, leading to disastrous results.

In the wake of the chaos that had resulted from Jager's attempt to drastically change every aspect of the firm's operations, Lafley was simply asked to restore some degree of stability. Since he has taken over, the mild-mannered 56-year-old chief executive has worked hard to create some new momentum and revive employee morale. P&G did need some urgent action because the Swiffer dust mop was the only successful new brand that it had managed to develop over the previous 15 years. At the same time, the employees needed some reassurance that the old way of doing things would still have some value.

This case was prepared by Professor Jamal Shamsie of Michigan State University. This case was developed from published sources as a basis for class discussion rather than to illustrate either effective or ineffective handling of an administrative situation. Copyright © 2004 Jamal Shamsie.

What's less obvious is that, in his quiet way, Lafley has proved to be even more of a revolutionary than the flamboyant Jager. Long before he took over the firm, Lafley had been pondering how to make P&G relevant in the 21st century, as speed and agility would become necessary for competitive advantage. As president of North American operations, he had even spoken with Jager about the need to remake the company. Now as CEO, Lafley has been leading the most sweeping transformation of the company since it was founded by William Procter and James Gamble in 1837 as a maker of soap and candles.

An Attempted Turnaround

For most of its 166 years, P&G has been one of America's preeminent companies. The firm has developed several well-known brands such as Tide, one of the pioneers in laundry detergents, which was launched in 1946, and Pampers, the first disposable diaper, which was introduced in 1961. P&G built its brands through its innovative marketing techniques. In the 1880s, it was one of the first companies to advertise nationally. Later, P&G invented the soap opera by sponsoring *Ma Perkins* when radio caught on and *Guiding Light* when television took hold. In the 1930s P&G was the first firm to develop the idea of brand management, setting up marketing teams for each brand and urging them to compete against each other.

By the 1990s, however, P&G was in danger of becoming another Eastman Kodak or Xerox, a once-great company that might have lost its way. Sales on most of its 18 top brands were slowing as the company was being outhustled by more focused rivals such as Kimberly-Clark and Colgate-Palmolive. The only way P&G kept profits growing was by cutting costs, which would hardly work as a strategy for the long term. At the same time, the dynamics of the industry were changing as power shifted from manufacturers to massive retailers. Retailers such as Wal-Mart were starting to use their size to get better deals from P&G, further squeezing its profits.

When Jager took over in January 1999, he understood that big changes were needed to get P&G back on track. But the moves that he made generally misfired, sinking the firm into deeper trouble. He introduced expensive new products that never caught on while letting existing brands drift. He wanted to buy two huge pharmaceutical companies, a plan that threatened P&G's identity but never was carried out.

At a company prized for consistent earnings, Procter & Gamble under Jager missed forecasts twice in six months. During the fiscal year when he was in charge, earnings per share rose by just 3.5 percent instead of an estimated 13 percent. And during that time, the share

Exhibit 1   Procter & Gamble's Income Statement
(All numbers in thousands)

	Period Ending June 30		
	2003	2002	2001
Total Revenue	$43,377,000	$40,238,000	$39,244,000
Cost of revenue	22,141,000	20,989,000	22,102,000
Gross Profit	21,236,000	19,249,000	17,142,000
Operating expenses			
Selling, general, and administrative	13,383,000	12,571,000	12,406,000
Operating Income or Loss	7,853,000	6,678,000	4,736,000
Income from continuing operations			
Total other income/expenses, net	238,000	308,000	674,000
Earnings before interest and taxes	8,091,000	6,986,000	5,410,000
Interest expense	561,000	603,000	794,000
Income before taxes	7,530,000	6,383,000	4,616,000
Income tax expense	2,344,000	2,031,000	1,694,000
Net income from continuing operations	5,186,000	4,352,000	2,922,000
Net Income	**$5,186,000**	**$4,352,000**	**$2,922,000**

Source: Procter & Gamble Co. annual reports.

price slid 52 percent, cutting P&G's total market capitalization by $85 billion. The effects were widely felt within the firm, where employees and retirees hold about 20 percent of the stock.

But Jager's greatest failing was his scorn for the family. Jager, a Dutchman who had joined P&G overseas and worked his way to corporate headquarters, pitted himself against P&G culture. Susan E. Arnold, president of P&G's beauty and feminine care division, said that Jager tried to make the employees turn against the prevailing culture, contending that it was burdensome and insufferable. Some go-ahead employees even wore buttons that read "Old World/New World" to express disdain for P&G's past.

A New Style of Leadership

On June 6, 2000, the day of his 30th wedding anniversary, Alan G. Lafley received a call from John Pepper, a former CEO who was now a board member. Pepper asked Lafley to take over the reins of P&G from Jager; this represented a boardroom coup unprecedented in the firm's history. In a sense, Lafley had been preparing for this job his entire adult life. He never hid the fact that he wanted to run P&G one day. Hired in 1977 as a brand assistant for Joy dishwashing detergent, Lafley climbed quickly to head P&G's

soap and detergent business, where he introduced Liquid Tide in 1984. A decade later, he moved to Kobe, Japan, to head the Asian division, returning to Cincinnati in 1998 to run the company's North American operations.

By the time he had taken charge of P&G, Lafley had developed a reputation as a boss who steps back to give his staff plenty of responsibility. He also asks them a series of keen questions to help him shape decisions. As CEO, Lafley refrained from making any grand pronouncements on the future of P&G. Instead, he has been spending an inordinate amount of time patiently communicating to his employees about the types of changes that he would like to see at the company.

Lafley began his tenure by breaking down the walls between management and employees. Since the 1950s, all of the senior executives at P&G used to be located on the 11th floor of the firm's corporate headquarters. Lafley changed this setup, moving all five division presidents to the same floors as their staff. Then he turned some of the emptied space into a leadership training center. On the rest of the floor, he knocked down the walls so that the remaining executives, including himself, would share open offices. Lafley sits next to the two people he talks to the most, which, in true P&G style, was officially established by a

Exhibit 2   **Procter & Gamble's Balance Sheet**
                (All numbers in thousands)

	Period Ending June 30		
	2003	**2002**	**2001**
Assets			
Current assets			
Cash and cash equivalents	$5,912,000	$3,427,000	$2,306,000
Short-term investments	300,000	196,000	212,000
Net receivables	3,881,000	3,611,000	3,328,000
Inventory	3,640,000	3,456,000	3,384,000
Other current assets	1,487,000	1,476,000	1,659,000
Total Current Assets	**15,220,000**	**12,166,000**	**10,889,000**
Long-term investments	—	—	—
Property, plant, and equipment	13,104,000	13,349,000	13,095,000
Goodwill	11,132,000	10,966,000	8,805,000
Intangible assets	2,375,000	2,464,000	1,331,000
Accumulated amortization	—	—	1,836,000
Other assets	1,875,000	1,831,000	2,103,000
Total Assets	**43,706,000**	**40,776,000**	**34,387,000**
Liabilities			
Current liabilities			
Accounts payable	10,186,000	8,973,000	7,613,000
Short/current long-term debt	2,172,000	3,731,000	2,233,000
Total Current Liabilities	**12,358,000**	**12,704,000**	**9,846,000**
Long-term debt	11,475,000	11,201,000	9,792,000
Other liabilities	2,291,000	2,088,000	1,845,000
Deferred long-term liability charges	1,396,000	1,077,000	894,000
Total Liabilities	**27,520,000**	**27,070,000**	**22,377,000**
Stockholders' Equity			
Preferred stock	1,580,000	1,634,000	1,701,000
Common stock	1,297,000	1,301,000	1,296,000
Retained earnings	13,692,000	11,980,000	10,451,000
Capital surplus	2,931,000	2,490,000	2,057,000
Other stockholder equity	(3,314,000)	(3,699,000)	(3,495,000)
Total Stockholder Equity	**16,186,000**	**13,706,000**	**12,010,000**
Net Tangible Assets	**$2,679,000**	**$276,000**	**$1,874,000**

Source: Procter & Gamble Co. annual reports.

flow study. They are head of human resources Ricard L. Antoine and vice-chairman Bruce Byrnes.

Lafley has established a tradition of meeting with Antoine every Sunday evening to review the performance of the firm's 200 most senior executives. This reflects Lafley's determination to make sure the best people rise to the top. And Byrnes, whom Lafley refers to as "Yoda," the sage-like *Star Wars* character, gets a lot of face time because of his marketing expertise. As Lafley says, "The assets at P&G are what? Our people and our brands."[1]

Lafley's leadership style has also been visible in P&G's new conference room, where he and the firm's 12 other top executives meet every Monday at 8 a.m. to review results, plan strategy, and set the drumbeat for the week. The table is now round instead of rectangular. Instead of sitting where they were told, the executives now sit where they like. True to his character, Lafley maintains a low profile at most of these meetings. He occasionally joins in the discussion, but most of the time the executives talk as much to each other as to Lafley.

Indeed, Lafley's charm offensive has so disarmed most P&G employees that he has been able to change the company profoundly. He has replaced more than half of the company's top 30 officers, more than any P&G boss in memory, and trimmed its workforce by some 9,600 jobs. And he has moved more women into senior positions; Lafley skipped over 78 general managers with more seniority to name 42-year-old Deborah A. Henretta to head P&G's then-troubled North American baby care division. "The speed at which A.G. has gotten results is five years ahead of the time I expected," said Scott Cook, founder of software maker Intuit Incorporated, who joined P&G's board shortly after Lafley's appointment.[2]

A New Strategic Focus

Lafley is intent on shifting the focus of P&G back to its consumers. At one of his weekly meetings with Antoine, Lafley rose from his chair to look more closely at a spreadsheet detailing the firm's seven layers of management. "It's not being felt strongly enough in the middle of the company," he said in his slightly high-pitched voice. "They don't feel the hot breath of the consumer."[3]

At every opportunity, Lafley has tried to drill his managers and employees to not lose sight of the consumer. He feels that P&G has often let technology rather than consumer needs dictate its new products. He would like to see the firm work more closely with retailers, the place where consumers first see the product on the shelf. And he would like to see much more concern with the consumer's experience at home. At the end of a three-day leadership seminar, Lafley was thrilled when he heard the young marketing managers declare: "We are the voice of the consumer within P&G, and they are the heart of all we do."[4]

In order to better focus on serving the needs of its consumers, Lafley is putting a tremendous amount of em-

phasis on the firm's brands. When describing the P&G of the future, he said, "We're in the business of creating and building brands."[5] (See Exhibit 3 for P&G's product segments.) This has been most noticeable in the firm's beauty care business. Under Lafley, P&G has made some costly acquisitions to complement its Cover Girl and Oil of Olay brands. After purchasing Clairol in 2001 for $5 billion, he is now set to purchase hair care manufacturer Wella for a price that may exceed $7 billion.

But Lafley is not just buying brands to build upon P&G's consumer base. He has also been pushing the firm to approach its brands more creatively. Crest, for example, which used to be marketed as a toothpaste brand, is now defined as an oral care brand. The firm now sells Crest brand toothbrushes and whitening products. There's even an electric toothbrush, SpinBrush, which was added to the Crest line after P&G acquired it in January 2001.

Although P&G has tried to push for an increased number of higher-margin products, Lafley has argued that the firm does not have to stick to producing more premium-priced goods. The firm has recently introduced a cheaper formulation for Crest in China. The Clairol deal has given P&G bargain shampoos such as Daily Defense. And with Lafley's encouragement, managers have looked at their most expensive products to make sure they aren't too costly. In many cases, they've actually lowered the prices on several of their core categories such as laundry detergents and tampons.

P&G is also willing to license its own technologies to get them to the marketplace faster. It joined with the Clorox Company, maker of Glad Bags, last October to share a food-wrap technology it had developed. It was unprecedented for P&G to work with a competitor, says licensing head Jeffrey Weedman. The overall effect is undeniable. "Lafley has made P&G far more flexible," said Banc of America's Steele.[6]

A Revolution Still in the Making

Although Lafley has managed to give a tremendous push to Procter & Gamble to rethink its business model, it is quite clear he has more revolutionary changes in mind. A confidential memo was circulated among P&G's top brass in late 2001 that even drew a sharp response from some of its board members. It argued that P&G could be cut to 25,000 employees, a quarter of its current size. Lafley admitted that the memo had drawn a strong reaction: "It terrified our organization."[7]

Even though it turned out that Lafley did not write this infamous memo, it nonetheless reflected the central tenet of his vision that P&G should do only what it does best and nothing more. He clearly wants a more outwardly focused, flexible company. This means that P&G does not have to do everything in-house. If there are no clear benefits stemming from doing something within the firm, it should be contracted out. Such a philosophy has

Exhibit 3   Procter & Gamble Segment Information

Estimates for Fiscal Year Ending June 30, 2003

Fabric & Home Care

Contribution: Share of total sales: 29%
Operating profit margin: 25%

Outlook: Very Good
Firm has cut costs to deal with lower-priced products from competitors; it has also introduced new higher-margin products, such as the Swiffer duster.

Beauty Care

Contribution: Share of total sales: 28%
Operating profit margin: 23%

Outlook: Good
Firm has expanded this business through acquisition of Clairol and Wella; it is trying to seek more internal growth.

Baby & Family Care

Contribution: Share of total sales: 23%
Operating profit margin: 17%

Outlook: Good
Firm has increased sales to share disposable diaper market with Kimberly-Clark; it is trying to deal with price competition from rivals in this business.

Health Care

Contribution: Share of total sales: 13%
Operating profit margin: 18%

Outlook: Mixed
Firm has regained the lead from Colgate in oral care; its pharmaceutical business is heavily dependent on Actonel, a drug for osteoporosis, but could get a boost from over-the-counter sales of heartburn drug Prilosec.

Snacks & Beverages

Contribution: Share of total sales: 7%
Operating profit margin: 15%

Outlook: Weak
Firm has already sold Crisco and Jif to J.M. Smucker; it is expected to get out of this business.

Source: Banc America Securities.

serious implications for every facet of P&G's operations from R&D to manufacturing.

Lafley has clearly challenged the supremacy of P&G's research and development operations. He has confronted head-on the stubbornly held notion that everything must be invented within P&G by asserting that half of its new products should come from the outside. Under his tenure, the firm has begun to get about 20 percent of its new product ideas from outside the firm. This is double the 10 percent that existed at P&G when he took over.

A variety of other activities are also being driven out of the firm. In April 2003 Lafley turned over all bar-soap manufacturing, including Ivory, P&G's oldest surviving brand, to a Canadian contractor. One month later, he outsourced P&G's information technology operation to Hewlett-Packard (HP). While Lafley shies away from saying just how much of P&G's factory and back-office operations he may hand over to someone else, he admits that facing up to the realities of the marketplace may force some hardships on its employees.

Lafley is well aware that nearly one-half of the firm's 102,000 employees work in its plants. So far, he has taken concrete steps to ease the hardships that may be caused by cutting back on P&G's operations. "Lafley has deftly handled the outsourcing deals, which has lessened fear within P&G," said Roger Martin, a close adviser of Lafley's and dean of the University of Toronto's Joseph L. Rotman School of Management.[8] At the bar-soap operations, based entirely in Cincinnati, 200 of the 250 employees went to work for the Canadian contractor. Similarly, all 2,000 of the information technology workers were moved over to HP. No one would dispute that such moves are clearly revolutionary for a firm such as P&G. "He's absolutely breaking many well-set molds at P&G," said eBay's CEO, Margaret C. Whitman, whom Lafley had recently appointed to the board.[9]

Daunting Challenges

Precisely because of his achievements, Lafley has come under enormous pressure to restore P&G to a company that is admired, imitated, and uncommonly profitable. Nowhere are those expectations more apparent than on the second floor of headquarters, where three of its former chief executives are still active. John Pepper, a popular former boss who returned briefly as chairman when Jager left but then gave up the post to Lafley last year, has stated, "It's now clear to me that A.G. is going to be one of the great CEOs in this company's history."[10]

But Lafley still faces daunting challenges. Keeping up the earnings growth, for example, will get tougher as competitors fight back and as P&G winds down a large restructuring program. "What has to happen is that they make sure that they can be self-supporting when the cost savings diminish," said Simon Burton, an analyst at Banc of America Capital Management.[11]

There are also serious concerns about Lafley's use of acquisitions to make P&G grow. The deals make it harder for investors to decipher earnings growth from existing operations. Then there's the risk of fumbling the integration, as noted by Arthur B. Cecil, an analyst at T. Rowe Price Group. These risks can be higher because Lafley has been looking to pharmaceuticals and beauty care for growth, where the margins are high but where P&G has considerably less experience than rivals. Already, Clairol hair color, the most important product in P&G's recent purchase, has lost five points of market share to the French firm L'Oréal in the United States, according to ACNielsen Corp.

The reliance on external sources for new products can also be problematic. As any scientist will attest, decisions to purchase a new product idea often tend to be extremely hard to make. The process of picking winners from other labs is likely to be both difficult and expensive. P&G already missed a big opportunity by passing up the chance to buy water-soluble strips that contain mouthwash. Listerine managed to grab the product and has profited handsomely from the deal.

But finding new avenues to grow could be the only way to balance P&G's growing reliance on Wal-Mart. Former and current P&G employees say the discounter could account for one-third of P&G's global sales by the end of the decade. Meanwhile, the pressure from consumers and competitors to keep prices low will only increase. "P&G has improved its ability to take on those challenges, but those challenges are still there," said Lehman analyst Ann Gillin.[12]

The biggest risk, though, is that Lafley will lose the people at P&G. The firm's insular culture has been famously resistant to new ideas. Employees form a tightly knit family because most of them start out and grow up together at P&G, which only promotes from within. Over the years, these people have gradually adopted the culture of the firm and come to believe in it. Lafley is well aware of his predicament. He recently admitted, "I am worried that I will ask the organization to change ahead of its understanding, capability, and commitment."[13]

Endnotes

1. Berner, Robert, 2003, P&G: New and improved, *BusinessWeek,* July 7: 62.
2. Ibid., 55.
3. Ibid., 54.
4. Ibid., 62.
5. Ibid., 63.
6. Ibid.
7. Ibid., 55.
8. Ibid., 63.
9. Ibid., 58.
10. Ibid., 55.
11. Ellison, Sarah, 2003, P&G net rises 4.9% on solid sales. *Wall Street Journal,* August 1: B2.
12. Berner, 2003, P&G: New and improved, 63.
13. Ibid., 58.

Case 32   Robin Hood

It was in the spring of the second year of his insurrection against the High Sheriff of Nottingham that Robin Hood took a walk in Sherwood Forest. As he walked he pondered the progress of the campaign, the disposition of his forces, the Sheriff's recent moves, and the options that confronted him.

The revolt against the Sheriff had begun as a personal crusade, erupting out of Robin's conflict with the Sheriff and his administration. Alone, however, Robin Hood could do little. He therefore sought allies, men with grievances and a deep sense of justice. Later he welcomed all who came, asking few questions, and only demanding a willingness to serve. Strength, he believed, lay in numbers.

He spent the first year forging the group into a disciplined band, united in enmity against the Sheriff, and willing to live outside the law. The band's organization was simple. Robin ruled supreme, making all important decisions. He delegated specific tasks to his lieutenants. Will Scarlett was in charge of intelligence and scouting. His main job was to shadow the Sheriff and his men, always alert to their next move. He also collected information on the travel plans of rich merchants and tax collectors. Little John kept discipline among the men, and saw to it that their archery was at the high peak that their profession demanded. Scarlock took care of the finances, converting loot into cash, paying shares of the take, and finding suitable hiding places for the surplus. Finally, Much the Miller's son had the difficult task of provisioning the ever-increasing band of Merrymen.

The increasing size of the band was a source of satisfaction for Robin, but also a source of concern. The fame of his Merrymen was spreading, and new recruits poured in from every corner of England. As the band grew larger, their small bivouac became a major encampment. Between raids the men milled about, talking and playing games. Vigilance was in decline, and discipline was becoming harder to enforce. "Why," Robin reflected, "I don't know half the men I run into these days."

The growing band was also beginning to exceed the food capacity of the forest. Game was becoming scarce, and supplies had to be obtained from outlying villages. The cost of buying food was beginning to drain the band's financial reserves at the very moment when revenues were in decline. Travelers, especially those with the most to lose, were now giving the forest a wide berth. This was costly and inconvenient to them, but it was preferable to having all their goods confiscated.

Robin believed that the time had come for the Merrymen to change their policy of outright confiscation of goods to one of a fixed transit tax. His lieutenants strongly resisted this idea. They were proud of the Merrymen's famous motto: "Rob the rich and give to the poor." "The farmers and the townspeople," they argued, "are our most important allies. How can we tax them, and still hope for their help in our fight against the Sheriff?"

Robin wondered how long the Merrymen could keep to the ways and methods of their early days. The Sheriff was growing stronger and better organized. He now had the money and the men, and was beginning to harass the band, probing for its weaknesses.

The tide of events was beginning to turn against the Merrymen. Robin felt that the campaign must be decisively concluded before the Sheriff had a chance to deliver a mortal blow. "But how," he wondered, "could this be done?"

Robin had often entertained the possibility of killing the Sheriff, but the chances for this seemed increasingly remote. Besides, while killing the Sheriff might satisfy his personal thirst for revenge, it would not improve the situation. Robin had hoped that the perpetual state of unrest, and the Sheriff's failure to collect taxes, would lead to his removal from office. Instead, the Sheriff used his political connections to obtain reinforcement. He had powerful friends at court, and was well regarded by the regent, Prince John.

Prince John was vicious and volatile. He was consumed by his unpopularity among the people, who wanted the imprisoned King Richard back. He also lived in constant fear of the barons, who had first given him the regency, but were now beginning to dispute his claim to the throne. Several of these barons had set out to collect the ransom that would release King Richard the Lionheart from his jail in Austria. Robin was invited to join the conspiracy in return for future amnesty. It was a dangerous proposition. Provincial banditry was one thing, court intrigue another. Prince John's spies were everywhere. If the plan failed, the pursuit would be relentless and retribution swift.

The sound of the supper horn startled Robin from his thoughts. There was the smell of roasting venison in the air. Nothing was resolved or settled. Robin headed for camp promising himself that he would give these problems his utmost attention after tomorrow's raid.

Prepared by Joseph Lampel, City University, London. Copyright Joseph Lampel © 1985, Revised 1991. Reprinted with permission.

In January 2004, Samsung Electronics of South Korea used the Consumer Electronics Show in Las Vegas to show off two of the world's largest flat-panel televisions that it had designed for the home. These consisted of an expensive 80-inch plasma model and a boundary-breaking 57-inch liquid crystal display (LCD) set. Previous plasma display television sets have not exceeded 63 inches and liquid display sets sold to date have not measured more than 46 inches.

Such breakthrough products suggested that Samsung has come a long way from its brush with bankruptcy just six years ago. For years, it had squeezed out profits by producing cheap television sets and microwave ovens based on technology developed by other firms. Since then, Samsung has transformed itself into a much more innovative firm, creating cutting-edge technology across a spectrum of product lines. Its feature-jammed gadgets have been racking up design awards, and the company has been rapidly muscling its way to the top of consumer-brand awareness surveys.

In the process, Samsung's profits have surged as it has grown to become a global leader in 19 different products ranging from dynamic random-access memory (DRAM) chips to flat-screen televisions. Since 1997 Samsung has been able to reduce its debt from an unsustainable $10.8 billion to $1.4 billion, leaving it in a healthy net cash position. The global consulting firm Interbrand recently declared Samsung to be the world's fastest-growing brand, setting its brand value at a staggering $10.8 billion. Even during periods of weak demand, Samsung has been able to earn more than most of its rival technology firms. Exhibit 1 shows Samsung's income statement, 1999–2002.

Samsung's earning power can be attributed in large part to its decision to focus on niches that command higher prices and fatter margins. In cell phones, for example, the firm has kept its average selling price at $191, compared with $154 for Nokia and $147 for Motorola, according to Technology Business Research. Even in components that Samsung manufactures for others, it has focused on higher-margin specialty products. Some 70 percent of its memory revenues stem from graphic chips for game consoles, high-density memory products for powerful servers, and flash memory for handheld computers, cell phones, and camcorders.

But Samsung continues to be hounded by many doubts about the sustainability of its business model. Most industry observers insist that high-technology firms

This case was prepared by Professor Jamal Shamsie of Michigan State University. This case was developed from published sources as a basis for class discussion rather than to illustrate either effective or ineffective handling of an administrative situation. Copyright © 2004 Jamal Shamsie.

must focus upon developing proprietary content in order to maintain higher margins and hold off the competition. Yet Samsung has defiantly stuck with its focus on hardware, choosing to partner with software firms. Furthermore, it insists on developing and manufacturing all of the components—ranging from chips to displays—that are used in its own products. "If we get out of manufacturing," said recently installed CEO and vice-chairman Jong Yong Yun, "we will lose."[1]

Discarding a Failing Strategy

The transformation of Samsung into a premier brand has been the result of the ceaseless efforts of Jong Yong Yun, who was appointed president and CEO in 1996. When Yun took charge, Samsung was still making most of its profits from lower-priced appliances that consumers were likely to pick up if they could not afford higher-priced brands such as Sony or Mitsubishi. It had also become an established low-cost supplier of various components to such larger and better-known manufacturers around the world.

Although the firm was making profits, Yun was concerned about the future prospects of a firm that was relying on a strategy of competing on price with products based on technologies that had been developed by other firms. The success of this strategy was tied to the ability of Samsung to continually scout for locations that would allow it to keep its manufacturing costs down. At the same time, it would need to keep generating sufficient orders to maintain a high volume of production. In particular, he was concerned about the growing competition that the firm was likely to face from the many low-cost producers springing up in other countries such as China.

Yun's concerns were well founded. Within a year of his takeover, Samsung was facing serious financial problems that threatened its very survival. The company was left with a huge debt as an economic crisis engulfed most of Asia in 1997, leading to a drop in demand and a crash in the prices of many electronic goods. In the face of such a deteriorating environment, Samsung continued to push for maintaining its production and sales records even as much of its output was ending up unsold in warehouses.

By July 1998 Samsung Electronics was losing millions of dollars each month. "If we continued, we would have gone belly-up within three or four years," Yun recalled.[2] He knew that he had to make some drastic moves to turn things around. Yun locked himself in a hotel room with nine other senior managers for a whole day to find a way out. They all wrote resignation letters and pledged to resign if they failed.

After much deliberation, Yun and his management team decided to take several steps to push Samsung out of its precarious financial position. To begin with, they laid

Exhibit 1   Samsung Electronics Income Statement
(In billions of Korean won)

	2002	2001	2000	1999
Net sales	₩ 59,569	₩ 46,444	₩ 43,528	₩ 32,088
Gross profit	22,616	13,787	15,889	10,611
Operating profit	9,246	3,951	9,060	5,376
Net income	7,053	3,055	6,003	3,175

Source: Samsung Electronics annual reports.

$1 = ₩1200

off about 30,000 employees, representing well over a third of its entire workforce. They also closed many of Samsung's factories for two months so they could get rid of the company's large inventory. Finally, they sold off about $2 billion worth of businesses like pagers and electric coffeemakers that were perceived to be of marginal significance for the firm's future. Exhibit 2 provides the revenue breakdown by product for Samsung Electronics for year-end 2002.

Developing a Premium Brand

Having managed to stem the losses, Yun wanted to move Samsung away from its strategy of competition based largely on the lower price of its offerings. Consequently, he began to push the firm to develop its own products rather than to copy those developed by other firms. In par-

ticular, Yun placed considerable emphasis on the development of products that would impress consumers with their attractive designs and advanced technology. By focusing on such products, Yun hoped that he could develop Samsung into a premium brand that would allow him to charge higher prices.

To achieve this, Yun had to reorient the firm and help it to develop new capabilities. He recruited new managers and engineers, many of whom had developed considerable experience in the United States. Once they had been recruited, Yun got them into shape by putting them through a four-week boot camp that consisted of martial drills at the crack of dawn and daylong mountain hikes. To create incentives for this new talent, Yun discarded Samsung's rigid seniority-based system for advancement and replaced it with one based on merit.

Exhibit 2   Samsung Electronics: Revenue Breakdown (In $ billions)

Year Ending December 31, 2002		
	Sales	**Profits**
Semiconductors Including DRAMS, SRAMS, and NAND flash chips	$10.7	$ 3.2
Telecommunications Including digital phones and handsets	10.4	2.5
Digital Media Including thin film LCD, plasma, and projection displays, and televisions	8.2	32.0
Digital Appliances Including "intelligent" refrigerators, microwave ovens, air conditioners	3.1	11.0

Source: Samsung Electronics annual reports.

As a result of these efforts, Samsung began launching an array of products designed to make a big impression on consumers. These included large flat-panel televisions, cell phones with a variety of features such as cameras and PDAs, ever-thinner notebook computers, and speedier and richer semiconductors. Samsung's image was helped by the dozens of awards that its new products began to rack up. The firm called them "wow products" and they were designed to elevate Samsung in the same way the Triniton television and the Walkman had helped plant Sony in the minds of consumers.

A large part of the success of Samsung's products can be attributed to the company's efforts to focus on the specific needs of prospective customers. Mike Linton, executive vice-president of Best Buy, stated that Samsung regularly gets information from retailers about the new features that customers want to see in their electronic devices. This close link with retailers has helped Samsung to come up with two of its recent best-selling products: a combined DVD/VCR player and a cellular phone that also works as a personal digital assistant (PDA). According to Graeme Bateman, head of research for the Japanese investment bank Nomura Securities, "Samsung is no longer making poor equivalents of Sony products. It is making things people want."[3]

Finally, to help Samsung change its image among consumers, Yun hired a marketing whiz, Eric Kim, to be the firm's global marketing director. Kim has worked hard to create a more upscale image of the firm and its products. He moved Samsung's advertising away from 55 different advertising agencies worldwide and placed this business with one firm, Madison Avenues's Foote, Cone & Belding Worldwide, in order to create a consistent global brand image for its products. He has also begun to pull Samsung out of big discount chains like Wal-Mart and Kmart and placed more of its products with specialty stores such as Best Buy and Circuit City.

Pushing for New Products

Yun has taken many steps to speed up Samsung's new product development process. He is well aware that he will only be able to maintain the higher margins as long as his firm can keep introducing new products into the market well ahead of its established rivals. Samsung managers who in the past worked for big competitors say they now go through far fewer layers of bureaucracy to win approval for new products, budgets, and marketing plans, speeding up their ability to seize opportunities. In a recent speech, Sony chairman Nobuyuki Idei referred specifically to Samsung's efforts to undertake "aggressive restructuring."

Apart from removing the bureaucratic obstacles, Yun has also forced Samsung's own units to compete with outsiders in order to speed up the process for developing innovative new products. In the liquid crystal display business, Samsung buys half of its color filters from Sumitomo Chemical Company of Japan and sources the other half internally, pitting the two teams against each other. "They really press these departments to compete," said Sumitomo's president, Hiromasa Yonekura.[4]

Samsung says it has been able to reduce the time from the conception of a new product to rollout to as little as 6 months, compared to the 14 months it used to take the firm just six years ago. For example, after Samsung persuaded T-Mobile, the German-U.S. cell phone carrier, to market a new camera phone in April 2002, it quickly assembled 80 designers and engineers from its chip, telecom, display, computing, and manufacturing operations. In four months, they had a prototype for the V205, which has an innovative lens that swivels 270 degrees and transmits photos wirelessly. By October the phones had begun to roll out of Samsung's plants after some engineers had flown to Seattle to field-test the phone on T-Mobile's servers and networks.

Because of the greater speed of its development process, Samsung was able to launch 95 new products in the United States during 2003. In cell phones alone, the firm introduced 20 new models, almost twice as many as any rival. Furthermore, the 130 models Samsung introduced globally last year were based on 78 different platforms. Whereas Motorola completely changes its product line every 12 to 18 months, Samsung manages to refresh its lineup every 9 months.

Samsung has already introduced the first voice-activated phones, handsets with MP3 players, and digital camera phones that send photos over global system for mobile communications (GSM) networks. The firm has been just as fast in digital televisions, becoming the first to market projection TVs using new chips from Texas Instruments that employed digital light processing (DLP). DLP chips contain 1.3 million micromirrors that flip at high speeds to create a sharper picture. Texas Instruments had given Japanese companies the technology early in 1999, but they never figured out how to manufacture the sets economically. Samsung entered the scene in late 2001, and already has seven DLP projection sets starting at $3,400 that have become the hottest-selling sets in their price range. "They'll get a product to market a lot faster than their counterparts," says George Danko, Best Buy's senior vice-president for consumer electronics.[5]

Competing for the Digital Home

Yun is hoping that Samsung's advances in digital technologies will increase its chances of dominating the digital home. He believes that his firm is in a better position to benefit from the day that all home appliances from handheld computers to intelligent refrigerators will be linked to each other and adapt to the personal needs of consumers. In particular, Samsung appears to be well placed to take advantage of its capabilities to design and manufacture a wide array of products that straddle traditional categories of technology. "We have to combine computers, consumer electronics, and communications as Koreans mix their rice with vegetables and meats," said Dae Je Chin, the head of Samsung's digital media division.[6]

Yun has worked closely with Chin to summon engineers and designers from across the firm to mix wireless, semiconductor, and computer expertise in order to pursue their vision of domination of the digital home. One such product from the firm has been NEXiO, a combined cell phone and handheld computer. The device has a five-inch screen, large enough for a user to run a spreadsheet or to browse the Web. Another new offering is a refrigerator called Zipel that has a 15-inch flat-panel touch screen tucked into the door. The display can be used to surf the Internet and to send or receive e-mail.

Samsung has already displayed a version of its networked home in Seoul's Tower Palace apartment complex, where 2,400 families could operate appliances from washing machines to air conditioners by tapping on a wireless "Web pad" device, which doubles as a portable flat-screen TV. It may sound a bit futuristic, but when the digital home does become more realistic, Samsung has a chance. "They've got the products, a growing reputation as the innovator, and production lines to back that up," said In-Stat/MDR consumer electronics analyst Cindy Wolf.[7]

Samsung's status in chips and displays, which can make up 90 percent of the cost of most digital devices, gives it an edge in handsets and other products. It has long held the lead in the global market for DRAM semiconductors, the memory chips that are vital to almost every digital product that we use. Samsung also leads in static random access memory (SRAM) and controls 55 percent of the $2 billion market for NAND flash memory, a technology mainly used in removable cards that store large music and color-image files. The company's breadth in displays gives it a similar advantage. It leads in thin-film liquid crystal displays (LCDs) which are becoming the favored format for PCs, normal-size TVs, and all mobile devices.

The vision of dominating the digital home has been fueled by the growing belief among many of Samsung's top executives that they may soon be able to unseat Sony as the most valuable electronics brand and most important shaper of digital trends. "We believe we can be number one," said Samsung America chief executive Oh Dong Jin.[8] Even Sony CEO Nobuyuki Idei privately admitted that Samsung may be on the verge of overtaking his firm in the consumer electronics race. "Sony is now only strong in audio and video like DVDs and TVs," added Jin. "We are much stronger now in other fields."[9] Exhibit 3 shows the market share and rank of leading companies in a number of important products.

Creating a Sustainable Model?

Yun's strategy to focus on higher-end products has clearly enhanced the firm's brand image and led to a sharp increase in its revenues and profits. Samsung's brand value has risen rapidly over the past few years, according to Interbrand, a New York research firm that has developed a formula to measure brand value. Many executives in the U.S. retail market said they have been astounded by the firm's ability to generate a superior brand image. "Samsung is going to be the first Korean company to create a true global brand," according to Samsung's marketing head, Eric Kim.[10]

But serious questions remain about the ability of Samsung to rely exclusively on its hardware to continue to generate high margins. Many U.S., Japanese, and European companies have failed to sustain their profitability through the pursuit of a strategy devoted to the designing and manufacturing of electronics products. Even Sony has

Exhibit 3   Global Market Share, 2002

Product Category	Market Share %	Samsung's Market Rank	Market Leader
DRAM chips	32%	1	Samsung
Flash memory	14	2	Intel
Cell phones	15	2	Nokia
LCDs	18	1	Samsung
Big screen TVs*	32	1	Samsung
DVD players	11	3	Toshiba
MP3 players	13	3	SonicBlue
Microwave ovens	25	1	Samsung

*Priced at $3,000 and above.

Sources: iSupply, IC Insights, Gartner, Display Search, NPD Techworld, In-Stat/MDR, Samsung Corporation.

seen its margins drop on most of its hardware. Most of Sony's profits over the past decade have come from its PlayStation console and games.

Most of Samsung's rivals have realized that the life cycle of most electronics products tends to be brutally short. Furthermore, it is hard to prevent the prices of these products from dropping sharply over time. An average DVD player currently sells for less than a quarter of the price it fetched five years ago. By comparison, television sets have done better, with prices dropping by only 30 percent over the same period.

Yun appears to be well aware of the challenges that lie ahead for Samsung. He understands that his firm must keep investing heavily in R&D and developing new factories in locations that offer lower costs. Yun points out that Samsung has maintained technological leadership in digital technology, allowing it to keep turning out advanced products with desirable features that can fetch higher margins. The firm has also sunk over $20 billion into expanding its production capacity over the past five years.

In spite of these achievements, several industry experts argue that Samsung will remain vulnerable if it does not branch out into software and content. But Yun has decided against branching out like Sony or Apple into music, movies, and games. He has decided against such a move in spite of growing evidence that the content subscription business can provide a firm with a more lucrative source of revenue. Instead, Yun has chosen to collaborate with various content and software providers such as Microsoft and Time Warner.

By choosing to focus on hardware, Yun has placed his faith in the ability of Samsung to stay at the forefront of core technologies and to master its manufacturing capabilities. "Everyone can get the same technology now," he recently commented. "But that doesn't mean they can make an advanced product."[11] In effect, Yun is betting Samsung's future on an unwavering commitment to the ability to keep putting out exceptional products. Eric Kim said: "During the 1980s and 1990s, the Japanese and Europeans dominated the electronics industry. But now we believe Samsung can dominate any market, including the U.S."[12]

References

1. Edwards, Cliff, Ihlwan, Moon, & Engardio, Pete, 2003, The Samsung way, *BusinessWeek*, June 16: 58.
2. Holstein, William J., 2002, Samsung's golden touch, *Fortune*, April 1: 32.
3. Gibney, Frank, Jr., 2002, Samsung moves upmarket, *Time*, March 25: 49.
4. Edwards, Ihlwan, & Engardio, 2003, 60.
5. Ibid., 61.
6. Stone, Brad, 2002, Samsung in bloom, *Newsweek*, July 15: 34.
7. Edwards, Ihlwan, & Engardio, 2003, 61, 64.
8. Ibid., 58.
9. Solomon, Jay, 2002, Seoul survivors: Back from the brink, *Wall Street Journal*, June 13: A1.
10. Ibid.
11. Edwards, Ihlwan, & Engardio, 2003, 64.
12. Solomon, 2002, A2.

The supply of grapes crushed in California's 2003 harvest was an all-time record and it followed a record 2002 harvest. Quality is excellent—yet thousands of acres of vines are being pulled up across California with replanting of fruit trees. The *Santa Rosa Press Democrat* reported that Mondavi was cutting 10 percent of its workforce due to a reduced demand for wines selling above $25.00 per bottle at retail and to a projected quarterly operating loss for the first time since they became a public company in 1993. Several small wineries here in Sonoma County, notably DeLoach and Roshambo, have gone bankrupt in the last year. How are things going for you on the East Coast, Jan?

Janess (Jan) Thaw had trouble responding to the information she had just received from her cousin, Stan White, during their telephone conversation in late May 2004. She had recently prepared a business plan for the expansion of her Schoolhouse Lane Estates winery, located in Cutchogue on the North Fork of Long Island. Her plans included the purchase of grape-growing acreage as well as expansion of the winery and construction of a retail store, new tasting room, and renovation of a special events facility. The estimated cost of these initiatives was $2.4 million and new construction would take approximately a year to complete. Her cousin Stan's information created a wave of uncertainty concerning not only these plans, but also the outlook for her current business strategy. Regardless of the financing options available to her, Jan knew that she'd first have to get the strategy right.

Company History

Jan and her twin brother Nick grew up on a 35-acre potato farm adjacent to Schoolhouse Lane, located on the North Fork of Long Island. Owned by her parents, the farm barely provided for family living expenses. While her father Harry plowed the fields, her mother Suzanne taught fourth grade at a nearby public school.

The experience of growing up on a farm had a very different impact on the adult lifestyles of the children. Jan loved the land. She enjoyed walking the fields with her Dad and seeing the animals that lived on the land, especially the birds nesting in the tall oaks on the periphery of the family property.

This case was prepared by Professors Raymond H. Lopez of Pace University and Armand Gilinsky, Jr., at Sonoma State University as a basis for class discussion rather than to illustrate either effective or ineffective handling of an administrative situation. All individuals and events have been disguised at the request of the host organization.

Copyright © 2004 by Raymond H. Lopez and Armand Gilinsky, Jr. This case may not be reproduced without the express written permission of the authors. All rights reserved.

Jan attended the agricultural school at Cornell University. She worked during the summer at small wineries in the Finger Lakes region in upstate New York. Upon graduation in 1985, she was offered an assistant winemaker position at the Glenora Winery in Hammondsport, New York. For three years she experienced all aspects of the wine-making process and saw a chance to combine her love for the land with a career path in this industry.

By contrast, her brother Nick, an avid reader and athlete, could not wait to leave the farm for college. With a full athletic scholarship to Yale, Nick thrived in what he thought was a "big city" (New Haven, Connecticut). After completing his BA in economics, he then went on to Columbia University for an MBA with a concentration in finance.

A few years later Harry and Suzanne told their children that they were ready to retire and move to Sedona, Arizona. They sold their farm to Jan and Nick for one dollar in 1988 and headed west.

In January 1989 Jan and Nick each unexpectedly inherited $3 million after the death of their uncle Garry. They had very different uses for these funds. Jan paid off her student loans and immediately embarked on a long-held plan to convert the potato fields to the growing of wine grapes. Nick paid off his loans and started a financial consulting firm for private equity investors in Manhattan. Although they spoke often on the phone, Nick had not been out to the farm for more than three years. Jan would occasionally meet him for dinner in Manhattan.

During the spring of 1989 Jan planted 20 acres of grapevines on the property and named her new business Schoolhouse Lane Estates. By fall 1994 her first harvest was completed and the grapes were crushed at a local winery. Production was 60 tons of grapes, resulting in 5,000 cases of bottled wine. Within six months, they were all sold locally to restaurants, catering firms, and local businesses for gifts and promotions. Revenues from cases sold were just over $250,000. The business seemed poised for growth.

Schoolhouse Lane Estates' wines—Cabernet Sauvignon, Merlot (red varietals), Meritage (a blend of red varietals), and Chardonnay (white wine)—were well received on their introduction to the local marketplace. Jan sold her wines at retail prices ranging from $10 per bottle for Merlot ($120 per 12-bottle case) to $36 per bottle for the Meritage ($432 per case). As demand grew, Jan decided to operate her own winery. There was a small winery on six acres of land just east of her vineyards. She had been speaking with the owner and sensed that he was ready to retire and move to Weaverville, North Carolina. After only three meetings, they agreed upon the terms of a sale and in the fall of 1996, Jan was now the proud owner of a winery. She invested $2.2 million, financed with a mortgage from a local Long Island bank, and was ready to oversee her first wine production in the fall of 1997. Having expanded its acreage, producing quality grapes, and using grape purchases from other vineyards, the renamed Schoolhouse Lane Estates generated just over $1.5 million in revenue.

Over the next five years through 2002, Schoolhouse Lane Estates expanded its presence in the local wine markets. About 35 percent of sales were to off-premises accounts, such as wholesalers and retailers, and 45 percent to on-premises accounts, such as restaurants and caterers. These trade intermediaries handled her products before they were resold to the final consumer, with a retail markup of 100 percent. Direct sales to consumers at retail prices by way of the tasting room accounted for the remaining 20 percent of Schoolhouse Lane's sales. Product acceptance translated into growing net revenues (Exhibit 1). Although her operating expenses for marketing and sales had grown rapidly, Jan felt that these expenditures were needed to differentiate her portfolio of fine wines from competitors' offerings and to stimulate demand from trade intermediaries.

Schoolhouse Lane's balance sheets (Exhibit 2) and statements of cash flow (Exhibit 3) reflected her efforts as well as the challenges of growing her business. Most significant among these challenges was the rapid and continuing expansion of inventories, as premium red wines and red wine blends require longer aging periods in oak barrels. Growing inventories were financed with an expanding line of credit from Goose Creek Savings, a local lending bank. Goose Creek Savings, however, maintained a lending limit for a business her size of up to $3 million based on the replacement value of fixed assets. Goose Creek Savings was also financing a small percentage of her inventories through a revolving line of credit. Either a larger bank would be needed within the year, or perhaps a more permanent source of financing would be needed. Laurel Durst, Jan's accountant and financial manager, had recently been exploring a number of working capital financing options with the North Fork Bancorp.

Evolution of Long Island's Wine Industry

How did it all begin? A small band of hesitant artisans and amateurs had pioneered the wine industry in converted barns and potato fields in the 1970s, in many cases because they sought a simpler agrarian lifestyle, or so they thought. In less than a third of a century, the profile of

Exhibit 1   Schoolhouse Lane Estates Income Statements, 1999–2003 ($ thousands)

	2003	2002	2001	2000	1999
Net Sales	$5,416.4	$4,924.7	$4,296.6	$3,646.5	$3,040.4
Cost of Goods Sold	3,566.2	3,152.6	2,744.5	2,318.8	1,788.6
Gross Profit	1,850.2	1,772.1	1,552.1	1,327.7	1,251.8
Operating Expenses					
Marketing & Advertising	145.2	130.9	116.6	101.2	89.1
Selling & Administration	935.0	811.8	711.7	572.0	358.6
Total Operating Expenses	1,080.2	942.7	828.3	673.2	447.7
Operating Income (EBIT)	770.0	829.4	723.8	654.5	804.1
Interest Expense[a]	376.2	326.7	295.9	282.7	259.6
Net Income before Taxes	393.8	502.7	427.9	371.8	544.5
Income Taxes[b]	157.3	201.3	171.6	148.5	217.8
Net Income (Loss)	$ 236.5	$ 301.4	$ 256.3	$ 223.3	$ 326.7
Number of cases sold	36,109	32,831	28,644	24,310	20,269
Average wholesale FOB price per 12-bottle case	$ 150.00	$ 150.00	$ 150.00	$ 150.00	$ 150.00
Average retail price per 12-bottle case	$ 300.00	$ 300.00	$ 300.00	$ 300.00	$ 300.00

[a]Prime + 2% on average balance for a line of credit.

[b]Federal and state income tax rate of 40%.

Exhibit 2   Schoolhouse Lane Estates Balance Sheets, 1999–2003
         ($ thousands)

	2003	2002	2001	2000	1999
Assets					
Current Assets					
Cash	$ 244.2	$ 218.9	$ 231.0	$ 216.7	$ 210.1
Accounts Receivable	268.4	277.2	294.8	269.5	235.4
Inventories	3,279.1	2,839.1	2,568.5	2,183.5	1,925.0
Prepaid and Other Expenses	48.4	44.0	46.2	41.8	40.7
Total Current Assets	3,840.1	3,379.2	3,140.5	2,711.5	2,411.2
Property, Plant and Equipment	3,578.3	3,440.8	3,291.2	3,254.9	3,172.4
Less: Accumulated Depreciation and Amortization	216.7	191.4	183.7	191.4	216.7
Net Property, Plant and Equipment	3,361.6	3,249.4	3,107.5	3,063.5	2,955.7
Other Assets (Net)	16.5	15.4	16.5	15.4	13.2
Total Assets	$7,218.2	$6,644.0	$ 6,264.5	$5,790.4	$5,380.1
Liabilities and Capital					
Current Liabilities					
Accounts Payable	$ 298.1	$ 256.3	$ 217.8	$ 194.7	$ 170.5
Accrued Expenses	268.4	222.2	193.6	169.4	150.7
Line of Credit (bank)d	1,282.6	999.9	955.9	757.9	565.4
LTD (current portion)	33.0	33.0	33.0	33.0	33.0
Total Current Liabilities	1,882.1	1,511.4	1,400.3	1,155.0	919.6
Long-Term Debt Mortgagec	2,288.0	2,321.0	2,354.0	2,381.5	2,429.9
Equity					
Class A Commona	1,661.0	1,661.0	1,661.0	1,661.0	1,661.0
Class B Commonb	0.0	0.0	0.0	0.0	0.0
Retained Earnings (Loss)	1,387.1	1,150.6	849.2	592.9	369.6
Total Equity	3,048.1	2,811.6	2,510.2	2,253.9	2,030.6
Total Liabilities and Equity	$7,218.2	$6,644.0	$ 6,264.5	$5,790.4	$5,380.1

dClass B Common Stock—1 vote.

cClass A Common Stock—10 votes.

aPrime + 2% on average balance for line of credit.

bLong-term debt (mortgage) at 7%.

Long Island wine moguls had morphed to that of self-assured professionals backed by deep-pocketed investors who were also seeking a different lifestyle.

The migration to become owners of Long Island wineries was not unlike the one followed by "refugees" from the high-tech world of Silicon Valley, who bought or developed new Napa and Sonoma wineries in California in the late 1990s. Similar to what their California counterparts had accomplished in the prior decade, the showcase Long Island wineries of the early 2000s burst on the New York culinary scene by making prize-winning and sought-after wines. While the production of world-class

Exhibit 3   Schoolhouse Lane Estates Statements of Cash Flow, 2000–2003
($ thousands)

	2003	2002	2001	2000
Cash Flows from Operating Activities				
Net Income	$ 236.5	$ 301.4	$ 256.3	$ 223.3
Depreciation	25.3	7.7	34.1	24.2
Increase in Receivables (Net)	8.8	17.6	(25.3)	(34.1)
Increase in Inventories	(440.0)	(270.6)	(385.0)	(258.5)
Increase in Prepaid and Other Expenses	(4.4)	2.2	(4.4)	(1.1)
Increase in Accounts Payable	41.8	38.5	23.1	24.2
Increase in Accrued Expenses	46.2	28.6	24.2	18.7
Net Cash Provided (Used) by Operating Activities	(85.8)	125.4	(77.0)	(3.3)
Cash Flows from Investing Activities				
Purchase of Property, Plant and Equipment	(137.5)	(149.6)	(78.1)	(132.0)
Other Assets (Net)	(1.1)	1.1	(1.1)	(2.2)
Net Cash Used for Investing Activities	(138.6)	(148.5)	(79.2)	(134.2)
Cash Flows from Financing Activities				
Increase (Decrease) from Bank Line of Credit	282.7	44.0	198.0	192.5
Increase (Decrease) in Long-Term Debt (current portion)	0.0	0.0	0.0	0.0
Increase (Decrease) in Mortgage	(33.0)	(33.0)	(27.5)	(48.4)
Net Cash Provided (Used) in Financing Activities	249.7	11.0	170.5	144.1
Net Increase in Cash	25.3	(12.1)	14.3	6.6
Cash at the Beginning of the Year	218.9	231.0	216.7	210.1
Cash at the End of the Year	244.2	218.9	231.0	216.7

wines was still said to be some years away, the money, the wine-making talent, and the will to make them were now in place. It seemed just a matter of time before Long Island winemakers were regarded with the same status as their California counterparts, according to the Long Island Wine Council.

The land of the North Fork, where most wineries were located, was flat to slightly rolling, planted not only with grapes but also with potatoes, sod, and fruit trees. Craggy oaks shaded the villages of Greenport, Southold, and Cutchogue, small and quaint with 200-year-old houses and 100-year-old churches and plaques to show where the Pilgrims' punishment stocks used to stand on the village green. The water was never more than a few miles away, as the Long Island Sound lay to the north, and Peconic Bay and the Atlantic Ocean to the south.[1]

[1]On the North Fork, dreams of Napa, 2000, *New York Times,* July 26: F1.

From its humble beginnings in 1973, the Long Island wine industry had developed steadily with growing numbers of vineyards, wineries, and acreage to produce quality wine products. Long Island wineries produced a broad variety of red varietals including Cabernet Sauvignon, Cabernet Franc, Merlot, Pinot Noir, and Shiraz, as well as white varietals such as Chardonnay, Gewürztraminer, Riesling, and Sauvignon Blanc. A few wineries, like Schoolhouse Lane, produced a Bordeaux-style blend of red wines called Meritage. All Long Island winery owners and their trade association, the Long Island Wine Council, anticipated continued growth and expansion into the 21st century.

Grape growing and wine production were located primarily on the eastern end of Long Island, which jutted more than 100 miles into the Atlantic Ocean, parallel to the coastlines of Connecticut and Rhode Island. The North and South Forks of eastern Long Island were a maritime region with a unique combination of climate, soil characteristics, and growing conditions ideal for quality wine production. Bays bordering the North and South Forks insulated the vineyards and trapped moist warm air. Along with rich sandy glacial soil, this combination created the perfect environment for growing grapes. Growing seasons were quite long (averaging approximately 200 days) and relatively mild winters encouraged the planting of Europe's noble vinifera grapes on almost all acres planted.

The Long Island wineries represented three appellations (American Viticultural Areas or AVA) approved by the Bureau of Alcohol, Tobacco and Firearms (BATF)—the North Fork of Long Island, the Hamptons, and, as of April 2001, Long Island AVA. This latest designation allowed for further expansion beyond the two forks of Long Island's east end, while at the same time protecting the overall integrity of the region's wines.[2]

New York State ranked third nationally in wine production. According to the New York Farm Bureau, the state had almost 1,000 family-owned vineyards that produced 175,000 tons of grapes annually—a $40 million industry. There were 160 wineries in the four main wine-producing regions of the state: the Finger Lakes, the Lake Erie region, the Hudson River Valley, and the Long Island region. All told, these regions produced over 100 million bottles of wine each year and attracted approximately one million tourists.[3]

Long Island wines were sold primarily in the New York metropolitan region. Products were found at most vineyards and in local wine retail stores, as well as in a broad variety of restaurants and catering establishments. Quality had been enhanced, resulting in higher ratings by wine magazines and in national taste tests, and the market broadened up and down the East Coast. Large regional distributors had in recent years shown a growing interest in carrying these wines. Several wineries already distributed their products in Florida, California, and Texas.

Anticipating that this trend would accelerate as knowledge spread of the rising quality of Long Island wines, the Long Island wine producers hoped that recent support from a New York U.S. congressional delegation would help to overturn the ban on direct shipments outside the state.[4] New York remained the nation's largest wine producing state that did not allow direct shipments. Current law prohibited wine producers from shipping wine directly to consumers in other states. Thirteen states already had reciprocal wine shipment laws enabling out-

of-state shipments of wine, and eight had laws allowing the direct shipment of wine to customers.

Recent Developments and Industry Maturation

By 2003 Long Island boasted 56 vineyards and 30 wineries.[5] The remaining 26 vineyard owners who lacked production capacity either sold their grapes to other wineries or contracted with other wineries to produce wine.

A sure sign of the maturation of the industry on Long Island came with the announcement of a custom-crush facility to be constructed in Mattituck. This facility would cater to independent vineyard owners and grape buyers who lacked their own wine-making facilities.[6] The new custom-crush venture was led by Russell Hearn, the winemaker at Pellegrini Vineyards, along with investors Mark Lieb, a Connecticut money manager and owner of the 50-acre Lieb Vineyard, and Bernard Sussman, also a money manager and an associate of Lieb. The partners expected to fund 40 to 50 percent of the new winery with equity, borrowing the rest from a Long Island bank.

"The primary purpose of this venture is to make wines for a number of small and large producers which choose not to, or are unable to, build their own wineries," Hearn said. "Our service would allow someone to have small amounts of wine made and bring in their own consultant [winemaker] to set the style. The number of wineries that offered custom services in the past are approaching their maximum," Hearn added. Moreover, vineyards for commercial wine production in Long Island were expected to double in the next two decades, further expanding the customer base.[7]

The Long Island wineries drew more than 500,000 visitors in 2003 for wine tours. Although traffic congestion was increasing on the two roads that fed the North Fork, some locals felt that the trade-off was worth the price. Several local residents credited the vineyards as having preserved open space that might otherwise have been developed for housing.[8]

Wine Production in the United States

The internal structure of the U.S. wine industry similarly underwent fundamental changes after the early 1980s. In terms of product, the most significant developments were observed in table wine. After 1992 table wines represented the largest segment of production and value of shipments, and accounted for more than 85 percent of total shipments annually. At the same time, table wine

---

[2]To put this information in perspective, the California wine industry has been in business for more than 200 years and currently has 86 AVAs, www.wineinstitute.org.

[3]States News Service, 2004, Washington, DC, February 5.

[4]On January 29, 2004, U.S. Senators Hilary Rodham Clinton and Charles Schumer, along with U.S. Representatives Louise Slaughter, Tim Bishop, Maurice Hinchey, Sherwood Boehlert, Jack Quinn, and Arno Houghton, signed a letter calling on Governor Pataki and the New York State Legislature to overturn the direct shipping ban.

[5]Canavor, N., 2003, Long Island continues to gain notoriety as wine-making region, *Long Island Business News*, April 4.

[6]In contrast, nine custom-crush facilities served California's wine industry.

[7]Walzer, R., 1999, Hearn pressing for $2M winery, *Long Island Business News*, October 1: 5A.

[8]Johnson, K., 2003, Success is in the grapes; from a scruffy past, a winemaking capital emerges, *New York Times*, August 30: B1.

products responded to changes in the tastes and preferences of consumers for higher-quality premium wines.

Grapes used in the production of table wines were of varying quality. Varietals were delicate thin-skinned grapes whose vines usually took approximately four years to begin bearing fruit. As defined by the "truth in labeling" standards of the Bureau of Alcohol, Tobacco, and Firearms, one varietal—the name of a single grape—had to be used if more than 75 percent of the wine was derived from grapes of that variety, and the entire 75 percent was grown in the labeled appellation of origin. Appellation denoted that "at least 75 percent of a wine's volume was derived from fruit or agricultural products and grown in the place or region indicated."[9] Developing the typical varietal characteristics that resulted in enhanced flavor, taste, and finish could take another two to three years after the four years required for newly planted vines to bear fruit. These additional growing periods, in the pursuit of enhanced quality and value, increased both investment levels and operating expenses.

The wine industry was capital intensive. In addition to land and vineyards, a fully integrated firm needed investments in crushing facilities, fermentation tanks, barrels for aging their product, and warehouses to store the bottled and cased wine. Ownership was not essential for any of these activities. However, to control the quality and quantity of production, these investments became essential as a firm developed its brands and expanded its markets.

Since the wine industry was inherently capital intensive, as well as seasonal and cyclical, winery owners generally experienced low profit margins and limited options for outside capital, according to Dan Aguilar of Silicon Valley Bank, a major lender to the wine industry in Napa and Sonoma counties in California. Even under the best of conditions, working capital was under some pressure. Winery owners typically sought to fund continuing operations and business growth/inventory growth from limited retained earnings and bank debt, while at the same time satisfy the voracious appetites of their wineries for funds to finance some mixture of vineyards, production facilities, equipment, barrels, and tasting room and visitor facilities.[10]

Business risks were also substantial. Weather conditions could affect the quality and quantity of grape production. Insect damage and disease could affect the vines. Replanting of new vines required four to five years before commercial quantities of grapes could be expected.

In the fall of the year, usually late September to early November, depending on the weather, grapes were picked and carefully brought from the fields to the crushing fa-cility. There was only one crop per year and crushing took from one to two months. Consequently, the investment in this facility stood idle at least 10 months of the year. Since all the grapes in a region matured at approximately the same time, there was no way to rent out crushing capacity to other wineries at other times of the year.

After crushing, the juice was pumped into the fermentation tanks. These stainless steel vessels were temperature controlled to balance the heat generated by the natural fermentation process. Fermentation lasted only a few weeks after the crush, so this investment was also idle more than 85 percent of the time.

From the fermentation tanks, the wine was pumped into oak barrels for aging. These barrels were expensive, costing $600 to $700 each. Due to quality concerns, they were used for only four or five years at which time their value was negligible (some were cut in half and sold as planters). A barrel-aging facility was a large open space that also had to be climate controlled. During the aging process, some wine was lost due to evaporation through the porous oak barrel. Every two weeks each barrel was refilled up to 3 inches from its top. For premium red wines that aged in barrels for two years or longer, about 5 percent of the original wine was typically lost to evaporation.

Table wines were defined as those with 7 to 14 percent alcohol content by volume and were traditionally consumed with food. In contrast, other wine products such as sparkling wine (champagnes), wine coolers, pop wines, and fortified wines were typically consumed as stand-alone beverages. Table wines that retailed for less than $3 per 750 ml bottle were generally considered to be generic or "jug" wines, while those selling for more than $3 per bottle were considered premium wines.

Premium wines generally had a vintage date on their labels. This designation signified that the product had been made with at least 95 percent of the grapes harvested, crushed and fermented in the calendar year shown on the label, and used grapes from an appellation of origin (i.e., Napa Valley, Sonoma Valley, Central Coast in California; North Fork, the Hamptons, or Long Island AVA on Long Island). Within the premium wine category, a number of market segments emerged based on retail price points. "Popular premium" wines generally sold for $3 to $7 per bottle, while "super premium" wines retailed for $7 to $14. The "ultra premium" category sold for $14 to $20 per bottle, while any retail price above $20 per bottle was considered by the industry to be "luxury premium."

Changing Dynamics of the U.S. Wine Market

The value of alcoholic and nonalcoholic beverages consumed by Americans grew modestly from 1995 to 2002, according to figures compiled in *Adams' Wine Handbook, 2003*. For purposes of comparison, the largest beverage category was soft drinks, which in 2002 achieved almost

[9]Bureau of Alcohol, Tobacco and Firearms, Regulatory Agency, U.S. Department of the Treasury, Title 27, Part 4 of the Code of Federal Regulations.

[10]Aguilar, D., 2003, Working capital analysis for wine industry clients, working paper, Silicon Valley Bank Wine Group, December 26.

double the dollar value of the next largest category, coffee. The consumption of wine produced domestically, as well as imports, grew steadily over the same period, but its volume remained significantly smaller, at less than 4 percent of soft drink volume in 2002. Wine consumption increased by 2.8 percent per year since 1996, trailing only bottled water at 10.8 percent per year and hard cider (an alcoholic beverage) at 8.8 percent per year. By contrast, overall beverage consumption grew at only 1.8 percent per year from 1996 to 2002. On a per capita basis, wine consumption rose steadily from 1.8 gallons per person per year in 1996, to just over 2.0 gallons in 2002.

Total wine consumption in the United States also reached an all-time high in 2002. At 595 million gallons, it exceeded the record consumption of 587 million gallons reached in 1986 (Exhibit 4). From those peak years in the mid-1980s, total consumption as well as per capita consumption trended downward for more than a decade. Since the early 1990s growth rebounded to record consumption and sales levels for table wine (Exhibit 5).

Reflecting the changing tastes and preferences of the American consumer, the growth performance of table wine sales by color also underwent dramatic changes. In 1991 white wine volume accounted for almost one-half of

Exhibit 4   U.S. Wine Consumption, 1980–2002 (estimated)

Years	Total Wine (millions of gallons)[1]	Total Wine (per capita)[3]	Total Table Wine (millions of gallons)[2]	Total Table Wine (per capita)[3]
2002 (est.)	595	2.06	532	1.84
2001	561	1.96	503	1.76
2000	558	1.97	498	1.76
1999	551	2.02	482	1.76
1998	526	1.95	466	1.72
1997	520	1.94	461	1.72
1996	505	1.90	443	1.67
1995	469	1.79	408	1.56
1994	459	1.77	395	1.52
1993	449	1.74	381	1.48
1992	476	1.87	405	1.59
1991	466	1.85	394	1.56
1990	509	2.05	423	1.70
1989	524	2.11	432	1.74
1988	551	2.24	457	1.86
1987	581	2.39	481	1.98
1986	587	2.43	487	2.02
1985	580	2.43	378	1.58
1984	555	2.34	401	1.69
1983	528	2.25	402	1.71
1982	514	2.22	397	1.71
1981	506	2.20	387	1.68
1980	480	2.11	360	1.58

[1]All wine types including sparkling wine, dessert wine, vermouth, and other special natural and table wines.

[2]Table wines include all "still" wines not over 14% alcohol content.

[3]Per capita consumption in gallons based on the resident population of the United States.

Sources: The Wine Institute, www.wineinstitute.org; Gomberg, Fredricksen & Associates.

Exhibit 5   Wine Sales in the United States (Millions of gallons):
Domestic Shipments and Foreign Producers Entering U.S. Distribution Channels,
1991–2003 (estimated)

Year	Table Wine[1]	Dessert Wine[2]	Champagne, Sparkling Wine	Total Wine	Total Retail Value (in $ billions)
2003 (est.)	558	41	28	627	$21.6
2002	532	37	27	595	21.1
2001	503	34	25	561	19.8
2000	499	32	28	558	19.0
1999	475	31	37	543	18.1
1998	466	31	29	526	17.0
1997	461	29	29	519	16.1
1996	439	31	29	500	14.3
1995	404	30	30	464	12.2
1994	394	33	31	458	11.5
1993	381	35	33	449	11.0
1992	405	37	33	476	11.4
1991	394	39	33	466	10.9

[1]Includes all still wines not over 14% alcohol; excludes Canadian Coolers (made from malt).

[2]Includes all still wines over 14% alcohol.

Source: The Wine Institute, http://www.wineinstitute.org.

all wine sold in supermarkets, which sold 78 percent of all wine purchased in the United States (the remaining 22 percent of wine shipments were sold through specialty wine shops, tasting rooms, the Internet, or on-premises accounts such as hotels and restaurants). Approximately one-third of total wine sales by dollars in 1991 were blush/rosé, while only 17 percent were red (Exhibit 6). By 2003 the market share of white wine and blush/rosé had declined to about 40 percent and 21 percent of total sales, respectively, but red wine grew to nearly 40 percent. Still, most red wines were more expensive to produce and thus sold for higher prices than either white or blush/rosé. The net result was that revenues at the wholesale and consumer levels had grown more rapidly than the increase in case wine volume that was produced and then sold.

The latest forecasts from *Impact Databank 2003* indicated that strong advances from imported wine could be expected to drive much of the growth for the U.S. wine market through 2010. Forecast growth in consumption of domestic wines was 3.3 percent to 193 million cases in 2003, 198 million cases in 2005, and about 211 million cases by 2010. For imports, a 12 percent increase to 65 million cases was projected for 2003, and case volume was projected to reach 90 million cases by 2010. California's dominant U.S. market share of domestic table wines was

Exhibit 6   Table Wine Volume Share by Color
(in U.S. supermarkets)

Color	1991	1995	2002	2003
Red	17%	25%	39%	40%
White	49	41	40	40
Blush/Rosé	34	34	21	20
Total	100%	100%	100%	100%

Source: U.S. supermarket data from ACNielsen Beverage Alcohol Team.

forecast to slip from 67 percent in 2003 to 63 percent in 2010, due in part to strong growth from imported varietals such as Shiraz/Syrah, Chardonnay, and Pinot Grigio. *Impact Databank* also forecast that the share of red wine in the U.S. market was expected to continue to gain at a more rapid pace than white or blush wine. Late projections held that red wine consumption would grow to 98 million cases in 2003 and 128 million cases by 2010. Projected annual compound growth rates for red wines were 5.9 percent for 2000–2005, and 3.5 percent for 2005–2010. White wine consumption was forecast to grow to 90 million cases by

2003 and 100 million cases by 2010. This translated into annual compound growth rates for white wines of 4.3 percent for 2000–2005, and further 1 percent annual increases from 2005 to 2010.

Competition

Since the 1960s there had been a substantial increase in the number of firms producing wine products in the United States. From hundreds of companies in the 1970s, the number exceeded 1,800 wineries by the turn of the century. Most were relatively small, each of the 50 states already had at least one winery, and about 800 were located in California. By 2004 the 20 largest firms produced approximately 90 percent of all American wines by volume and 85 percent by value at wholesale.[11]

The competitive structure of the industry could be classified into 3 types of stand-alone wineries: public conglomerates. private conglomerates, and multi-industry firms (primarily public). The largest publicly traded winery was Robert Mondavi, along with Chalone, a much smaller firm. Privately held wineries included the industry giant E&J Gallo, Kendall-Jackson, The Wine Group, and more than a thousand small- to medium-size wineries. The final group of competitors consisted of large publicly traded multi-industry firms. These included Allied Domecq, Brown Forman (Wine Estates Division), Foster's Group (Beringer Blass), Constellation Brands (Canandaigua Division), Diageo (Chateau and Estates Division), Fortune Brands, Louis Vuitton Moët Hennessey (LVMH), and UST (formerly known as U.S. Tobacco).

In addition to domestic competition, a growing percentage share of the U.S. wine market had been gained by imports. In addition to the traditional "Old World" supplies from France, Italy, Germany, Spain, and Portugal, a new group of countries had experienced growing acceptance of their wine production. Australia, Chile, and Argentina (the "New World" suppliers) increased their market share in the last decade, offering high-quality wines at very competitive prices.

Consolidation among wineries began to accelerate in the early 1990s, as larger producers decided to purchase smaller ones in order to achieve greater economies of scale in marketing and economies of scope in gaining access to more varied channels of distribution. These larger wineries could then become more effective in negotiating favorable selling terms with an increasingly small number of large regional distributors.[12] The "consolidators" were generally public firms that were able to offer predominantly family-run wine businesses a means to greater liq-

uidity of their investment in larger, more diversified firms. Concurrently, the attractiveness of wine production across the United States resulted in a growing number of entrepreneurs purchasing or starting new, small operations.

Jan Meets with Her Team

The day after her conversation with cousin Stan, Jan set up a meeting with her operations manager Dan Henning and her accountant Laurel Durst. She also invited the executive director of the 14-year-old Long Island Wine Council, Nanette Hansen, to get her broader perspective of local conditions.

Jan began the meeting by presenting her plans for the expansion:

> We have an opportunity to purchase additional grape-producing acreage across Schoolhouse Lane from our vineyard, that is, to buy 28 acres for $900,000. We have been farming that land and now have the opportunity to purchase it. The winery needs expanded capacity, and I have estimates between $800,000 and $900,000 for the land. Our tasting room is overcrowded—even on weekdays—and its expansion would require $250,000. Finally, many of our neighboring competitors already have facilities for special events (weddings, birthday parties, anniversaries, business meetings, etc.), but I have a design in mind that is expected to cost $450,000. I estimate another $700,000 to $800,000 in working capital will be necessary as well, bringing the total investment up to about $2.4 million.

Dan supported Jan's plans:

> The winery is operating at 100 percent capacity and I still had to ship some grapes over to the custom-crush facility in Mattituck. I'd like to bring all our production back here under our complete control.

The Schoolhouse Lane team was eager to hear Nanette's perspective, as she represented a broader regional industry viewpoint. Nanette was prepared for their questions, distributing copies of the information on Long Island wineries (see Exhibits 7 and 8) to the rest of the group.

> At the Long Island Wine Council, our prime focus is the local producers and their markets. I can't tell you much about conditions in California such as how long the "glut" of grapes will last, but we have studied the markets extensively in the East Coast.
>
> On the supply side, acreage and production have grown steadily over the last seven years through the harvest of 2003. Grape quality has risen consistently and yields per acre have grown slowly. A number of new owners have come to the area, bringing strong financial support to many vineyards and wineries. On the demand side, a major segment is event driven—celebrations of

[11]The Wine Institute, www.wineinstitute.org.

[12]According to Vic Motto of Motto Kryla Fisher, a Napa, California, consultant to the wine industry, there were 10,940 distributors of wine in 1990 and 5,134 in 2000, but only two to three major distributors per state. The top 10 distributors accounted for 33 percent of wine sales in 1993 and 60 percent in 2003.

Exhibit 7   Long Island Wine Industry Statistics
(Selected years)

Year	Number of Vineyards	Number of Wineries	Planted Acres	Total Acres Owned	Value Per Acre ($)	Wine Production (Cases)
2004	56	30				
2002	52	29	3,000	4,000		500,000
2000		21	2,200	2,800	$20,000	400,000
1999		21	2,100			
1998		21				200,000
1996	40			1,800		
1995		23	1,055		15,000	200,000
1989		14				
1987		12				
1985	16	7	600			
1984	12	4	700			
1975		1				
1973	1			17	4,000	

Sources: *The Wine Press, Underground Wine Journal, Wine East, Long Island Business News, Newsday,* and the Long Island Wine Council.

Exhibit 8   Estimated Values of Vineyards and Wineries on Long Island
(Selected years)

Year	Name	Location	Winery Capacity (cases)	Total Planted Acres	Estimated Value ($)
2001	Raphael	Peconic	10,000	70	$6,000,000
2000	Gristina	Cutchogue	10,000	44	5,200,000
	Bedell Cellars	Cutchogue	8,000	50	5,000,000
	Pindar Vineyards	Peconic	80,000	42.5	
	Comtesse Thérèse	Mattituck		40	400,000
1999	Hargrave	Cutchogue	7,000	84	4,000,000
	Laurel Lake Vineyards	Laurel	5,500	23	2,000,000
	Corey Creek	Southold	4,000	30	2,500,000
	Peconic Bay Vineyards	Cutchogue		35	2,200,000
	Bidwell Vineyards	Cutchogue	15,000	34	2,900,000
1997	Laurel Lake Vineyards	Laurel		23	3,000,000
1993	Dzugas-Smith Vineyards	Cutchogue		29	245,000

Sources: *The Wine Press, Underground Wine Journal, Wine East, Long Island Business News, Newsday,* and the Long Island Wine Council.

either a personal or business nature. For many local wineries, this represents 40 percent or more of their revenues and any weakness in pricing or volume will be felt quickly on cash inflows.

There has been a weakening in the last three years in business spending for events. While volume has held up reasonably well, the price points have deteriorated—moderately priced premium products ($10–$15 per bottle) have been substituted for deluxe premium wines ($25 and up per bottle). Corporate and business budgets have been tightened and it is unlikely that this trend will be reversed in the next few years. On a brighter note, on-premises sales have finally begun to rise this spring, as restaurant patrons are spending more on fine wine.

Will the Long Island wine industry be adversely or positively affected by these national trends? Will the regional extent of our markets shelter us from cyclical slowdowns in demand? From conversations with our members, the next few years are still likely to be quite challenging for our industry here on the East End.

Since 2001 New York City's financial services industry had experienced some of the largest declines in employment as well as reductions in salaries and bonuses. Special events sales volumes had also slowed, due to cost containment at parties and declining expenditures for high-end wines at restaurants. Still, overall volume and revenues had been rising due to expansion of the geographic market for Long Island wines on the East Coast and growth westward through New York, Pennsylvania, Maryland, and Virginia. This geographic expansion, it was hoped by many local producers, could help offset the local trend toward lower prices to bolster sagging sales.

In response to Nanette's overview, Jan mentioned that she'd come across a *BusinessWeek* article concerning the consumption profile of wine drinkers in the United States.[13] Forecasted trends for growth in U.S. wine consumption were hardly spectacular:

> One statistic I picked up was that in many European countries such as France, Germany, Italy, and Spain, wine is almost a necessity with meals—this is not the case here in the United States. Just over 10 percent of American adults account for 86 percent of wine consumed annually! We have not yet been successful at stimulating wine consumption to broader segments of the population. Until this occurs, perhaps our market strategy should be directed towards those consumers who are already drinking wine on a *regular* basis.

Ending the meeting, Jan thanked all present for sharing their ideas and expertise. She knew that she would have to prioritize each projected cost item and defend these ex-

[13]Himelstein, L., 2002, This Merlot's for you, *BusinessWeek*, September 30. 65–68.

penditures when making a formal proposal for financing. Financing the proposed expansion as well as incremental working capital might have to be sourced by some form of equity, meaning that Jan would no longer own 100 percent of the Schoolhouse Lane Estates!

Jan Seeks Help

Jan decided it was time to call her brother Nick. Although he hadn't visited the North Fork in years, he had been to the Hamptons each summer, driving to his family's summer home on the beach. Jan began the call by saying, "Nick, how has your business and career been going this last year? I heard about all the reductions in financial services employment. Have you been affected?"

"My firm has maintained its competitiveness in these uncertain times," Nick assured her. "We are also diversifying our clients' portfolios from real estate and annuities into private and public equity positions. If you know of any interesting investment opportunities, we would examine the financial data."

Somewhat surprised, Jan responded, "Nick, did you know that at Schoolhouse Lane Estates, we have a financial proposal on the table? We need an equity investment of approximately $2 million. Although the equity in the business is currently low, I will not be willing to give up control."

"Send me your business plan and financial statements," Nick replied, "and I'll contact you in two weeks with a proposal. The amount you are looking for is well within the range of my clients."

"Thanks, Nick," said Jan. "I'll fax you the documents tomorrow."

Two Weeks Later

"Jan, this is your brother. I received your materials and have a proposal for an investment of $2 million. Can we meet for lunch this Wednesday and I'll present the details? I also would like my wife to be at our meeting. As an equity strategist for a large investment banking house in Manhattan, Monica can provide some insight into the workings of the private equity market. She would also like to visit the winery."

Jan agreed and the three met for a long lunch at the Old Mill House in Peconic. After the salad, Nick presented details of his $2 million proposal to Jan.

"Although investment returns are low these days for fixed-income instruments, venture capital is still expensive. I could offer you a 10-year convertible note with interest at 6 percent," Nick began.

Sipping a glass of locally produced Gallucio Reserve Merlot, Monica added, "The note would provide the investor with potential capital gains up to his or her required return of between 20 and 25 percent per year, and then be converted into common stock with a par value of $1 per share. The holder would have the option over the next five years to convert the note into company stock at today's book value. If conversion did not occur, the note would be amortized from year 6 through year 10."

"Thanks," replied Jan, "I will have to speak with my accountant concerning the number of shares that would be granted should the note be converted, so that the required rate of return will be realized by your investor. By the way, who is this investor and when can I meet her or him?"

Nick smiled as Monica said, "Jan, you have known him all your life!"

The Bank Responds

The next day, Jan's accountant Laurel took Jan's projected capital expenditures of $2.4 million for expansion of the Schoolhouse Lane Estates operations, along with the business plan for the next five years, to the North Fork Bank. The projections included two scenarios: a "best case" for a revenue growth rate of 20 percent and a "base case" at a 15 percent growth rate. Both forecasts assumed enhanced operating efficiencies and expanded profit margins with no changes in prices and no introduction of new wine products.

The bank officer was skeptical of the most optimistic case, especially after speaking with a number of other winery operators in the area. North Fork's initial proposal was for a maximum $400,000 term loan with a small increase in the revolving line of credit to $3 million. The banker's implications and position were clear—Schoolhouse Lane needed permanent equity capital to sustain its growth plans. While the longer-term outlook for the industry was quite favorable, the banker was cautious about the trading conditions for wine over the next two years (2005 and 2006).

As she walked through the parking lot at North Fork Bank, Laurel relayed this disappointing news to Jan on her mobile phone. Although Jan understood why permanent capital was needed to support her growth strategy, she was not able to add to her personal investment in the business. Her husband, Tom, a professor of history at Stony Brook University, also believed that too large a percentage of the family's assets were already tied up in the business.

Nick's Position

After receiving Jan's fax, Nick responded by e-mail with some questions concerning the timing of the expenditures outlined in Jan's proposal. He was concerned about the "grape glut" and its impact on product pricing. In addition, the economic outlook in the near term appeared to be neither clearly defined nor strong. Therefore, could Jan construct forecasts using average annual growth rates in revenues of between 5 and 10 percent (less optimistic than Jan's 15 to 20 percent)? Nick did, however, agree with his sister that enhanced efficiencies could generate faster growth in net income than the growth in revenues.

With respect to Jan's concerns over maintaining ownership control, Nick was nevertheless very understanding. Monica had gently but firmly reminded him that the "last thing he should ever do was take over the operations of Schoolhouse Lane Estates." He thus approached this deal from a strictly financial point of view. Nick was looking for a viable and profitable investment of $2 million that would fit nicely into his portfolio. A current return of 6 percent, with a total expected return of 20 percent over at least a five-year holding period, was quite acceptable to him. While he might have expected a 25 percent total return on an investment with this risk profile some years ago, equity risk premiums had been trending downward in late May 2004, so a 20 percent return would meet or exceed his current portfolio needs.

Nick was aware of the lack of liquidity of an investment in Schoolhouse Lane Estate's operations. This investment would definitely have a "buy-and-hold" profile. Selling a private equity investment was traditionally accomplished through an initial public offering or an acquisition by another wine business, often years after the venture had developed into a viable, competitive, and profitable business. In evaluating his potential position in Schoolhouse Lane Estates, he was not confident that either of these scenarios would occur in the near term.[14] His only hope for monetizing his investment in the next five years would be to sell his shares back to Jan at a reasonable value or try to sell them to another private investor.

One More Meeting

After receiving her brother's proposal, Jan again met with Dan and Laurel. She opened the meeting by saying:

> I can't believe how expensive this funding could be even under the lowest cost presentation. Even given my most optimistic forecast of earnings growth for Schoolhouse Lane Estates and Nick's "cheapest" financing alternative, I will lose more than one-half ownership in the company. I surely do not want that to happen! Maybe we should defer our expansion plans or explore other options.

Dan countered by reiterating his desire to purchase the vineyard across the road and expand the winery's capacity:

> . . . that property has been owned by the O'Reilly family for 55 years. We may never get an opportunity to

---

[14]Nick had recently read a *New York Times* article about the Gallucio Family Cellars in Cutchogue. That winery had been on the market for $7.5 million in the fall of 2003 with no takers. Gallucio had 82.5 acres, about 44 of them under vines, and had a 10,000-case annual production capacity. The Gallucios had purchased the property from Gristina Vineyards for $5.2 million in 2000. Vincent and Judy Gallucio had announced an ambitious expansion plan but in 2002 reversed their plan to transform the property from a boutique to a larger-scale winery. See Goldberg, H. G., 2004, Winery to feature state wines, *New York Times,* March 21: sec. 14LI, 12.

Exhibit 9   Report of the Appraisal of Assets of the Schoolhouse Lane Estates

In response to the request of Ms. Janess Thaw, sole owner of the Schoolhouse Lane Estates, we hereby enclose our estimates of current market values for the firm's wine inventory as well as its fixed-asset position. Our personnel have carefully examined your inventories, land, winery building, and equipment and compared these assets with current market values that we have observed over the last six months. We are pleased to report to you that the quality of your inventory is excellent and your assets are in top operating condition.

With your firm's growing emphasis on the production of premium red wines (Meritage, Cabernet Sauvignon, and Merlot), our appraisal estimates that 30 percent of wine in barrels by volume has been stored for more than two years, resulting in a doubling of its book value at the time fermentation was completed in early 2003. Another 40 percent, also red wine and mostly from the 2003 harvest, has been in barrels for 14 months. Remaining wine volumes are a mixture of younger reds and white Chardonnay. We conclude that as of May 2004 the value of inventory, if sold in the local wholesale market, would result in receipts of $5.12 million.

In a separate analysis of property, plant, and equipment, our real estate expert on current market conditions estimates the value of company-owned land at $1,088,000 or $32,000 per acre on the 34 acres under cultivation by Peconic Bay. This is in contrast to $720,000, which is the current book value of this land on a historical cost basis.

The remaining $2,641,600 of depreciated book value of the winery plant and equipment has also increased in value since its original purchase. Its current replacement value is $3.35 million, according to our appraiser.

In summary, upon a sale of these three major asset categories, it is estimated that they would bring to the firm a total of $9,550,233, or $2,909,533 more than their current book value of $6,640,700. This additional value could be added to the firm's equity account of $3,048,100 at year-end 2003, bringing its total up to $5,957,633.

Summary Data			
Asset	Book Value December 31, 2003	Adjusted Market Value April 30, 2004	Appraisal Difference
Land—34 planted acres	$ 720,000	$1,088,000	$ 368,000
Plant & Equipment	2,641,600	3,347,233	705,633
Inventory	3,279,100	5,115,000	1,835,900
Totals	$6,640,700	$9,550,233	$2,909,533
Less: Liabilities	4,170,100	4,170,100	—
Equity Value	$2,470,600	$5,380,133	$2,909,533

It was a pleasure to provide you with the above data. If there is any additional information or clarifications that you may require, do not hesitate to contact us.

Respectfully submitted,

Sharon Brown, President
East End Associates
May 4, 2004

purchase it again if it is bought by another winery. We have managed it for the last six years and know the quality of grape production.

Laurel had planned what she would recommend. An integral component of her presentation was a summary of an appraisal report that had been prepared for Schoolhouse Lane Estates by a local firm specializing in wine industry asset valuations on Long Island (Exhibit 9). The appraisal clearly showed that the current value of the firm's two largest asset categories was considerably higher than their book values (approximately $9.5 million versus book values of $6.6 million). Adding the difference of nearly $2.9 million to the firm's equity value would surely enhance Jan's bargaining position in negotiating for new funds, possibly with other investors besides her brother. Laurel then summarized and prioritized the three components of the Schoolhouse Lane Estates' expansion plans:

> I agree with Dan that our highest priority at this time is the land purchase. We can produce larger volumes of wine, if the market so demands, at the new custom-crush facility. By postponing the other projects, Jan, you would reduce the volume of funds needed from your brother and, consequently, the dilution of your ownership position. If you really want to spend the entire $2.4 million in the next year, remember you can sell the Class B common stock that you already carry on the balance sheet.

After the meeting ended, Jan walked slowly back to her office. Almost there, she abruptly turned around, walked out of the building, and proceeded toward the vineyard. Strolling leisurely past the old oak trees with birds perching in the branches, she then ambled all the way down Schoolhouse Lane to the shore of Peconic Bay. Sitting on a large rock near the shore, she spent the next hour considering her alternatives. Should she continue the current strategy and focus on internal growth, borrow some money from the North Fork Bank, sell equity, and complete the expansion in order to sell the winery later down the road, or maybe sell all of Schoolhouse Lane Estates now? Jan knew that when she returned to the office, Dan and Laurel would be awaiting her decision.

In December 2001, Dean Kamen unveiled his self-proclaimed revolutionary product—the Segway Human Transporter (HT). Prior to its release, there was a tremendous amount of speculation surrounding the Segway HT. News of a revolutionary new product invented by Kamen had leaked to the public. Several newspapers, technology authors, and science enthusiasts speculated on what the product might be, referring to the mysterious invention as "IT" although its internal code name was "Ginger." Kamen first revealed his Segway HT in Silicon Valley, to officials from San Francisco International Airport, the California Department of Transportation, the City of Palo Alto, Stanford University, and John Chambers of Cisco Systems.[1] On December 2, 2001, Kamen went national with an official unveiling and demonstration of the Segway HT on *Good Morning America.*

Kamen's inspiration for the name Segway came from the word *segue,* which means "to transition smoothly from one state to another." The Segway HT is described as "a self-balancing, personal transportation device designed to go anywhere people do."[2] Kamen, Segway LLC's original chairman, worked with a number of engineers and designers to create the Segway HT's technology and design. And while this is not Kamen's first invention, it is the first product that Segway LLC is producing, manufacturing, and marketing on its own. Kamen invented the Segway with the idea that the device could eventually replace some of the short car trips that people take. The Segway HT is battery powered, has no engine, no brakes, no throttle, no gearshift, and no steering wheel, and can run all day, nonstop, on ten cents worth of electricity per charge.[3]

Kamen had been very successful with his previous revolutionary inventions, including the INDEPENDENCE IBOT Mobility System, which enables wheelchair-bound individuals to navigate rough terrain (which is where the technology for the Segway was created); the first portable insulin pump; the first portable dialysis machine; and advanced heart stents, one of which is currently implanted in U.S. Vice President Dick Cheney's heart. Despite Kamen's obvious success as an innovator, the question arises—can Kamen maintain his successfulness with the Segway as the manufacturer, distributor, and marketer?

Will the product revolutionize modern-day transportation? And can inventors of a product effectively take a significant role in successfully marketing their product?

Dean Kamen

Dean Kamen was born in 1951 on Long Island, New York, the son of the 1950s comic book artist Jack Kamen. Today Kamen lives near Manchester, New Hampshire, in a hexagon-shaped, 32,000-square-foot home which he designed. The grounds of his estate include a baseball diamond, and his possessions include a Hummer, a Porsche, and two helicopters—"both of which he helped design and one of which he uses to commute to work each day."[4] Kamen also owns a small island off the coast of Connecticut, which he calls "North Dumpling" and considers to be "a sovereign state." North Dumpling has its own flag, navy, currency (all of which he of course created), and a "mutual nonaggression pact" with the United States signed by Kamen and President George H. W. Bush.[5]

Kamen's innovative spirit was first evident in high school, when he developed an audiovisual control system for New York's Hayden Planetarium.[6] His career really took off while he was attending Worcester Polytechnic Institute. Kamen's brother, a medical student at the time, told him how difficult it was to administer intravenous drugs to cancer patients and diabetics. Kamen's imagination was sparked and, while still in his twenties, he tackled the problem by inventing the first portable infusion pump which enables patients to receive their medication without having to stay in a hospital. And while Kamen never graduated from Worcester Polytechnic, he pursued a successful career as a physicist and mechanical engineer, becoming a millionaire as a self-taught inventor, and receiving several honorary doctorates along the way.

As of 2004 Dean Kamen held more than 150 U.S. and foreign patents related to medical devices, climate-control systems, and helicopter design. In 1982 Kamen founded a company called DEKA Research and Development, which originally "consisted of a relatively small group of individuals and lots of innovative ideas."[7] DEKA grew to include almost 200 engineers, technicians, and machinists who worked in electronics and software engineering labs, machine shops, and computer-aided design (CAD) stations. DEKA's mission was to foster innovation as "a company where the questioning of conventional thinking is encouraged and practiced by everyone—engineers and nonengineers alike—because open minds are

---

*This case was prepared by graduate student Alanna Tracey and Professor Alan B. Eisner of Pace University as a basis for class discussion rather than to illustrate either effective or ineffective handling of an administrative situation. Copyright © 2004 Alan B. Eisner.

[1]Heilemann, John, 2001, Reinventing the wheel, *Time,* December 10, vol. 158): 50.

[2]Segway, www.segway.com.

[3]Ibid.

[4]Heilemann, 2001, Reinventing the wheel.

[5]Ibid.

[6]Segway, http://origin.www.segway.com/aboutus/dean_kamen.html.

[7]www.thefutureschannel.com/kamen_conversation.htm.

more likely to arrive at workable solutions."[8] Kamen also founded FIRST (*For Inspiration and Recognition of Science and Technology*) in the early 1990s, to "inspire young people, their schools, and communities in an appreciation of science and technology, and how mastering these can enrich the lives of all."[9]

Over the years, Kamen has been honored with several awards, some of which are listed below.[10]

- The Juvenile Diabetes Research Foundation—New England Chapter, New Hampshire Branch, named Dean Kamen "2002 Person of the Year."
- President Clinton awarded the National Medal of Technology to Kamen in 2000, for inventions that have advanced medical care worldwide, and for innovative and imaginative leadership in awakening America to the excitement of science and technology.
- The Heinz Award was given to Kamen in 1998 in technology, the economy, and employment for a set of inventions that have advanced medical care worldwide.
- In 1994 Kamen received the Kilby Award, which celebrates those who make extraordinary contributions to society through science, technology, innovation, invention, and education.

In 2001 Kamen unveiled his Segway HT invention to the world and made it available for purchase by business consumers (see photo this page). As explained by Kamen to *Time* magazine in 2002, "the big idea is to put a human being into a system where the machine acts as an extension of your body."[11]

How the Segway HT Works

A Segway HT is made up of eight critical parts: inertial rate sensors, tilt sensors, motors, batteries, control shaft, tires, controller boards, and chassis. The inertial rate sensors contain the five gyroscopes and tilt sensors, which work together to determine shifts in body weight and changes in terrain. "A basic gyroscope is a spinning wheel inside a stable frame . . . because of its resistance to outside force, a gyroscope wheel will maintain its position in space (relative to the ground), even if you tilt it."[12] Segway HTs use solid-state angular rate sensors constructed of silicon. This sort of gyroscope determines an object's rotation using the apparent turning of an object in relation to another rotating object on a very small scale. Although the Segway HT has five gyroscopic sensors, it only needs three to detect forward and backward "pitch," or tilt away

Source: Segway LLC

from a vertical position, as well as leaning to the left or right (termed "roll"). The extra sensors exist to make the vehicle more reliable. The balance sensors are two "tilt sensors filled with electrolyte fluid. Like your inner ear, this system figures out its own position relative to the ground based on the tilt of the fluid surface."

Two motors work independently to drive each wheel. The motors are completely emission free and are able to transfer power even if one motor fails. There are two types of batteries available for the Segway: NiCd and NiMH. The control shaft is height adjustable and is made of die-cast aluminum.

The Segway HT contains two controller boards, or circuit boards that send commands to the motors based on input from sensors. If one of the boards fails, the other can completely function alone. The Segway's controller boards are extremely important because they need to make very precise adjustments to keep the HT from falling over. In normal operation, these boards check the position sensors about 100 times a second. There are two tubeless tires attached to the Segway HT, which are resistant to flats, treated for enhanced traction on wet surfaces, and treated to leave no marks on indoor surfaces. The rubber diaphragms are located under the rider platform where they engage the machine in its self-balancing system. The chassis houses the electronic components of the Segway and has been tested to withstand seven tons of force.

Products

In 2004 Segway offered three main product lines, the *e Series,* the *i Series,* and the *p Series* (see Exhibit 1 for a comparison of the features of each model). The *e Series,*

[8]Ibid.

[9]www.usfirst.org/about/bio_dean.htm.

[10]Ibid.

[11]Heilemann, 2001, Reinventing the wheel.

[12]Harris, Tom, *How Segways work,* www.howstuffworks.com.

which was only available to business and commercial users, contained three storage cases and had an electronic parking stand so the Segway HT could balance alone. The machine had three keys that determined the maximum speed a rider could drive. The beginner key (black) had a maximum speed of 6 miles per hour, with a slower turning rate. The "sidewalk operation key" (yellow) had a maximum speed of 8 miles per hour, and a medium turning rate. And the "open environment key" (red) had a maximum speed of 12.5 miles per hour, with the most responsive turning rate. A single battery charge for an HT could last for a range of 5 to 15 miles of use, with the actual distance based on the terrain over which the rider traveled (i.e., on a smooth flat terrain, the battery charge would carry a further distance). The *e Series* had two 60-cell NiMH battery packs, and could be recharged by 90 to 260 volt and 50 to 60 Hz AC outlets. A complete cycle charge would take four to six hours, at a cost of less than 10 cents of electricity. The model also had a redundant balancing and electrical system to ensure the safety of the rider in case the first system failed. "If any system begins operating at diminished capacity, the other is programmed to assume responsibility while maintaining balance and bringing the Segway HT to a safe stop."[13]

The *e Series* was only available to businesses and not to the general public. The machine cost $5,500 and could be purchased by contacting Segway LLC directly. By early 2004, several companies and governments were using the Segway HT *e Series*, including the City of Seattle, the U.S. Postal Service, Michelin of North America, GE Plastics, Delphi, the City of Atlanta, Georgia Power, Walt Disney Co., and the Boston and Chicago police departments. The New York City Police Department had also purchased a small fleet to evaluate.

The *i Series* was intended for individual consumers, but could also be purchased by business customers. The *i Series* was available for preorder in November 2002 and became available for shipment in March 2003. In 2004 the price of an *i Series* model was $4,495, which reflected a $500 price reduction made when the *p Series* was released.

The last Segway HT model released was the *p Series,* which cost $3,995. The *p Series* could be preordered in October 2003 and was available for shipment in mid-November 2003. The *p Series* was the smallest and lightest weight Segway HT, weighing 13 lbs. less than the commercial *i Series*. The *p Series* had a shorter riding range, a smaller temperature range in which it could be used, and a smaller platform and footprint than either the *e Series* or *i Series* models. Finally, the battery requirement for the *p Series* was also smaller, requiring two 48-cell NiMH batteries, rather than the two 60 cells needed by the other two models.

All three Segway HT models came with "power assist mode," which was designed to help maneuver the Segway HT when the consumer was not on the machine. "In this mode, the Segway HT's motors are used to assist the user in moving the unit forward or backward. This motion is controlled by the steering grip, which becomes a speed control when in power assist mode. This allows you to ascend or descend stairs more easily and better navigate challenging terrain."[14]

Purchasing a Segway: Distribution Channels

When the Segway HT was first announced in December 2001, the product was available only to commercial consumers. In November 2002, the *i Series* product was made available for preorder for individual consumers through Amazon.com or through Segway directly. Most orders were received during late February through March 2003; however, there was one promotional exception. On December 25, 2002, 30 Amazon winners received their Segway two and one-half to three months before other consumers. The one-year time period between the announcement and release of the Segway HT product was due to Segway LLC's need to conduct further testing on the safety and reliability of the product, as well as an attempt to create legislation that would allow for the Segway HT's use.

Methods for purchasing a Segway HT varied depending on the model desired. Purchasing an *e Series* could only be done through Segway itself. However, to purchase an *i Series* or *p Series,* consumers had four options: contact Segway directly; go to an authorized dealer; order through Amazon.com; or purchase through Brookstone. In early 2004 Segway HTs could be tried, purchased, or rented from retailers in 22 states (see Exhibit 2).

Segway's corporate headquarters was located in Bedford, New Hampshire, which is also its manufacturing and training facility. Consumers could contact the company itself by calling 1-866-4SEGWAY. The facility was open from 8 a.m. to 5 p.m. eastern standard time for orders, and until 8 p.m. for technical support issues.

Amazon was the first outside organization to carry Segway HTs, and until mid-2003, consumers could purchase a Segway HT only through Amazon and Segway. In the fall of 2003, however, Brookstone stores decided to offer customers the opportunity to purchase the product. The negotiations between Segway and Brookstone were protracted. Brookstone, although known for its technologically advanced products, did not want to carry the Segway HT because of the extremely high carrying costs associated with the product. Segway and Brookstone eventually came to an agreement that Segway HTs would

[13]Ibid.   [14]www.segway.com.

Exhibit 1   Comparison of the Segway HT Models

	e Series	*i Series*	*p Series*
Speed	12.5 mph (20 km/h)	12.5 mph (20 km/h)	10 mph (16 km/h)

Speed can easily be controlled by the user and each Segway HT comes with three distinct keys that allow the top speed to be set according to the riding environment.

	e Series	*i Series*	*p Series*
Range (on a single charge)	8–12 miles (13–19 km)	8–12 miles (13–19 km)	6–10 miles (9–16 km)

The range for each model varies with terrain, payload, and riding style. Under normal riding conditions, you can expect to ride about 10 miles on a single charge for the *i* and *e Series,* and about 8 miles for the *p Series*. Proper battery care, riding on flat surfaces, and riding at a constant speed will help increase your range.

	e Series	*i Series*	*p Series*
Temperature	32°F (0°C) to 122°F (50°C)	32°F (0°C) to 122°F (50°C)	40°F (5°C) to 122°F (50°C)

When stored and charged at room temperature, the Segway HT can operate in a wide range of temperatures. Actual performance is dependent on battery temperature, terrain, and riding style.

	e Series	*i Series*	*p Series*
Terrain	Variable, rugged	Variable, rugged	Smooth, even

The larger tires and wider profile of both the *i* and *e Series* make them ideal for varied terrain and rugged environments. The *p Series* is designed to operate on smooth, even surfaces. The Segway HT's inertial sensors constantly monitor the rider's position relative to gravity. This allows the Segway HT to adjust for changes in terrain while keeping the rider upright.

	e Series	*i Series*	*p Series*
Payload	*Rider:* 100–250 lbs (45–113 kg) *Rider & Cargo:* 260 lbs (118 kg)	*Rider:* 100–250 lbs (45–113 kg) *Rider & Optional cargo:* 260 lbs (118 kg)	*Rider:* 100–200 lbs (45–91 kg) *Optional cargo:* 10 lbs (4.5 kg)

Depending upon rider size and expected use, choose the machine that fits your needs. While the *e Series* comes with side cargo bags, Segway offers optional cargo accessories for both the *i* and *p Series*.

	e Series	*i Series*	*p Series*
Space	*Platform height:* 8.3 in (21 cm) *Footprint:* 19 × 25 in (48 × 64 cm)	*Platform height:* 8.3 in (21 cm) *Footprint:* 19 × 25 in (48 × 64 cm)	*Platform height:* 6.7 in (17 cm) *Footprint:* 16 × 21.8 in (41 × 55 cm)

We designed the Segway HT to take up no more space than the average person. The smaller size and lower platform of the *p Series* allows a rider to easily maneuver crowded sidewalks, buildings, and other tight spaces.

	e Series	*i Series*	*p Series*
Weight	95 lbs (43 kg)	83 lbs (38 kg)	70 lbs (32 kg)

The Segway HT was designed to be easily stored and to seamlessly combine with other forms of transportation. The smaller *p Series* is lighter and can easily fit in the trunk of most cars.

Turning Radius: zero

One characteristic of a pedestrian is the ability to turn in place without impacting any nearby person or object, something few vehicles can do. By balancing on a single axle, Segway HT users can also turn in place.

Source: Segway, www.segway.com/segway/specs_compare.html.

only be available to "test-drive" in certain Brookstone locations, and that Brookstone would not carry any Segway HTs in its inventory. However, a customer could purchase the Segway HT through Brookstone's 1-866-4SEGWAY number, or a Brookstone store associate could make the phone call for the customer.

The price of a Segway HT included customer orientation with a first ride, if desired, and a limited warranty. Product orientation for one person was included no matter where the product was purchased (authorized dealer, Brookstone, Amazon.com, or Segway itself). Orientation was not a requirement of the purchase, but was offered for

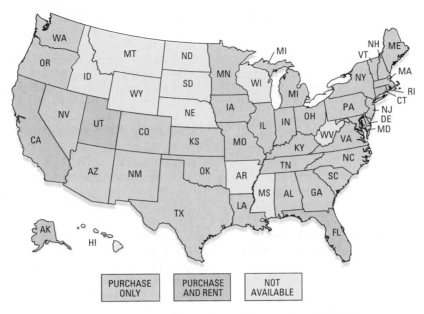

Locations where you can try, rent, or purchase the Segway HT are currently available in 22 states:

Alaska – Arizona – California – Florida – Hawaii – Illinois – Maine – Maryland
Massachusetts – Michigan – Minnesota – Nevada – New Hampshire – New Jersey
New York – Ohio – Rhode Island – Texas – Utah – Vermont – Virginia – Washington

Exhibit 2   Locations of Segway HT Retailers

Source: Segway, 2004, www.segway.com/connect/locator.

free; new owners were taught how to maneuver their product and use all of its features. Usually orientation was scheduled through a Segway representative, five days after the consumer received the product. Products could be returned only if the Segway was not used within 10 days of receipt and the product was still in its original packaging. The consumer was also responsible for return shipping costs, and a 10 percent (of the total purchase price) restocking fee. All Segway HTs were shipped through BAX, a freight carrier, at a cost of $100 for standard shipping (5–10 business days) or $250 for expedited shipping (3 business days).

Management and Organizational Structure

As the inventor of the Segway HT, Dean Kamen initially helped to manage the affairs of the company. He was both the founder of the company and its chairman. During its first two years, the face of the company's top commander changed frequently, with three different presidents in charge.[15] Tim Adams, a former Chrysler executive, was the first company president, followed soon by a former Subaru executive, but neither of these gentlemen was a good fit for the small start-up company. Vernon Loucks

Jr., former CEO of Baxter International, was brought in as Segway's new CEO in January 2003, followed in November of that year by Ronald Bills, who assumed the role of president and CEO. Bills was a board member and former general manager of the Polaris Marine division. Polaris Industries, Inc., was a leader in the snowmobile industry, a manufacturer of personal watercraft, and one of the largest manufacturers of all-terrain vehicles in the world. As of 2004 Segway LLC had no declared vision or organizational goals available to the public.

Segway LLC was comprised of several "teams."[16]

♦ The User Interface Design Team designed the display that makes the Segway HT easy to use.

♦ The Power Base Design Team implemented Segway HT's mechanical design and determined all the components to ensure design and performance specifications were met.

♦ The Embedded Design Team created and tested the electronics and software responsible for the functioning and balancing of the Segway HT.

♦ The Industrial Design Teams helped develop the physical characteristics of the Segway HT.

[15]Rivlin, Gary, 2003, Segway's breakdown, *Wired Magazine*, March.

[16]www.segway.com/aboutus/the_people.html.

- The Dynamics Team wrote the software that the Segway HT used to balance and maneuver.
- The Mechanical Integrity Team was responsible for testing the conditions a Segway HT could withstand.
- The Electrical Integrity Team tested the electronic components that made up the Segway HT.
- The Supply Chain Team researched and created partnerships with current suppliers, and ensured that the manufacturing entity was constantly stocked.
- The Manufacturing Team assembled the Segway HTs.
- The Technical Service Team assisted customers and the factories that produced the Segway HTs.
- The Regulatory Team worked with national and municipal authorities to ensure that Segway was viewed as an "extension of the pedestrian."
- The Marketing Team was responsible for building the company's identity. "They manage a multifaceted strategic approach to brand creation, including carrying out an opportunity assessment, developing a marketing vision, and helping to define a new category of human transportation."[17] Segway's marketing was the liaison with commercial consumers; it also included the Web Team, which designed Segway's Web site with the goal of being "scalable and reliable." Most of the marketing was done in-house, but certain projects were contracted out, and the projects and the name of the marketing group were not disclosed.
- The Sales Team was responsible for selling the Segway HTs to commercial consumers only.
- The Information Technology (IT) Team of Segway helped to run the Web site and channeled questions and orders appropriately.

Partners

While the Segway HT was invented and developed by Kamen and his teams, bringing the product to realization was not accomplished without the significant contributions of companies and individuals outside the Segway family. Segway was assisted by a number of supply partners, which invested their money and time into the design process and worked closely with Segway "to ensure that exacting specifications and deadlines were met and that the soul of the Segway HT was maintained."[18] (See Exhibit 3 for a list of Segway's supply partners and their contributions to the Segway HT.)

Laws and Legislation

Prior to the release of the Segway *i Series* and *p Series,* the Segway organization's regulatory department spent a considerable amount of time and energy lobbying to have the product legally allowed to operate on sidewalks, bike paths, parks, and roads. By early 2004, some 40 states within the United States and the District of Columbia had "permissive legislation," which allowed Segway HTs to be operated on sidewalks, bike paths, and specific roads. The laws varied from state to state, and local governments were permitted to create additional regulations or rules concerning where Segway HTs could be operated legally. The 40 states were Alabama, Alaska, Arizona, California, Delaware, Florida, Georgia, Hawaii, Iowa, Idaho, Illinois, Indiana, Kansas, Maryland, Maine, Michigan, Minnesota, Missouri, Mississippi, Nevada, North Carolina, Nebraska, New Hampshire, New Jersey, New Mexico, Ohio, Oklahoma, Oregon, Pennsylvania, Rhode Island, South Carolina, South Dakota, Tennessee, Texas, Utah, Virginia, Vermont, Washington, Wisconsin, and West Virginia.

Connecticut, Massachusetts, New York, North Dakota, and Wyoming had not enacted legislation permitting Segway HTs in pedestrian areas. This did not mean that Segway HTs were prohibited; it simply meant there was no official state legislation regarding their use.

Competition

Kamen's dream was for the Segway HT to replace the automobile—eventually. The automotive industry remained a giant industry; most people saw its function as invaluable, especially in the United States. The auto industry was also moving toward hybrid cars, which are more environmentally friendly. Hybrids release less carbon dioxide, which in turn creates less air pollution from emissions. Hybrid cars are powered by a combination of gasoline and electric components. The benefits of hybrid cars are fewer tailpipe emissions and improved mileage. Several automakers have produced hybrid cars within the United States—namely, the Honda Insight and the Toyota Prius. Several other manufacturers had already built hybrids and were planning to introduce them into the U.S. market in the future.

The C5

In 1985 Sir Clive Sinclair, a famous inventor, released his Sinclair C5, touted as "the last futuristic transport."[19] Until the release of the Segway HT, the C5 was the latest public attempt at a solution to moving around cities, perhaps even a replacement of the automobile. It lasted only 10 months in the U.K. before it was scrapped. The C5 was a battery- and pedal-powered, three-wheeled vehicle which cost £399 ($700). The C5 was significantly smaller and lower than an automobile. Five thousand units of the C5 were sold, 1,000 in the first month, before its dissolution. The main cause of the Sinclair C5's flop was that it was "too extreme for the British public. It received a bad press,

[17]Ibid.

[18]www.segway.com/aboutus/development_partnerships.html.

[19]Duffy, Jonathan, 2003, Move over Segway, I'm planning the C6, BBC News: U.K. ed., August 5.

Exhibit 3   Segway HT's Supply Partners and Their Contributions

Supply Partners	Contributions
Silicon Sensing Systems is the world's leading provider of Silicon Micro-Machined sensors to the automotive, commercial, and aerospace sectors.	It collaborated with Segway to develop and perfect the human transporter's gyro and tilt sensor systems, a key component of the machine's self-balancing capability.
Michelin is a recognized leader in innovative mobility solutions. The company manufactures and sells tires for every type of vehicle, including airplanes, automobiles, bicycles, earthmovers, farm equipment, heavy-duty trucks and motorcycles.	Michelin engineers worked with Segway to develop the Michelin Balance tire which has the proper compound, unique tread design, rolling resistance, and handling to work with this new form of personal transportation.
Pacific Scientific, a Danaher Motion company, manufactures high-performance electric motors and drive systems for semiconductor, electronic assembly, medical/fitness, packaging, and other precision automation applications.	It specially designed the Segway HT's compact, brushless, electric servo motor.
Delphi Corporation manufactures integrated circuits, smart sensors, and software algorithms for the transportation, aerospace, telecommunications, and heavy equipment industries.	Delphi assisted in the development of the Segway HT's integrated circuit boards to meet the standards used for automotive reliability levels in extreme environments.
Saft, a leader in the worldwide marketplace for self-contained energy solutions, serves customers with rechargeable battery-power solutions that resist environmental swings for portable household appliance and hand tool, defense, mobility, and professional electronics applications.	Saft helped Segway develop smart-charging, self-contained NiCd and NiMH batteries that require no external charger.
Magnetek engineers systems that supply and control power for both home and industrial applications, including elevators, computer and telecommunications systems, graphic arts and medical imaging, robotics, and compressor motors.	It helped Segway create the power supply that receives normal wall current and charges the batteries.
Axicon is a leading designer and developer of quiet gear systems.	Axicon worked collaboratively with Segway to optimize the performance of their quiet helical gear systems and is the exclusive supplier of the Segway HT transmissions.
GE Plastics manufactures high-performance engineering thermoplastics, with manufacturing facilities and technology and innovation centers around the world.	It provided Segway with a host of durable and environmentally friendly materials for the Segway HT, the first commercial application for its game-changing SOLLX™ polymer, a weather-resistant film that offers an alternative to paint.
Microprocessor Designs (µPD) is a product design and development firm specializing in embedded microcomputer hardware and firmware.	The team at µPD worked closely with Segway's product development team throughout the HT's development, including system, hardware, firmware design, integration, test, and transfer to key manufacturers.
C&J Industries is a leading precision injection molding company.	It manufactured many of the plastic components on the Segway HT and helped create a wheel assembly to withstand the vigorous environmental and load requirements of the Segway HT.
Appshop, the largest independent Oracle Application Service Provider, provides end-to-end integrated managed solutions including professional services, hosting, ongoing maintenance, and functional and technical 24/7 support.	Segway worked with Appshop to develop the enterprise application solutions for its e-commerce, customer care, supply chain, manufacturing, and finance processes.
Jager Di Paola Kemp Design (JDK) uses design strategically to build brand distinction through product, packaging, merchandising, and marketing communication.	JDK worked with Segway to create the brand platform, identity, business papers, packaging, and marketing/promotional materials. It also collaborated with the industrial design team on product color, graphics, and finishes.

Source: Segway, www.segway.com/aboutus/development_partnerships.html.

being widely condemned as unsafe and impractical," and "was declared a death trap by the Automobile Association because it was too small to be seen by lorry drivers."[20] Sir Clive claimed he would release a C6 sometime in 2004, and that it would compete with the Segway HT.

Strategies and Goals

With the creation of the Segway HT, Dean Kamen stated that the goal was "building something that would make a unique and lasting contribution to society."[21] Financing for Segway's manufacturing, production, and marketing came partially from Credit Suisse, First Boston Private Equity, Kleiner Perkins Caulfield & Byers (which reportedly invested $38 million), and individual investors. Venture capitalist John Doerr, of Kleiner Perkins Caulfield & Byers, predicted Segway would reach $1 billion in sales faster than any company in history.[22]

Although Kamen had invented earlier products that were successfully manufactured by other companies, he was unwilling to turn over the manufacturing of the Segway HT to any other company. Kamen said, "It's a new idea. That's what's so exciting, but that's also why I couldn't license the technology." He also stated, "If I had partnered up with somebody, we wouldn't have the thrill, frankly, of helping to add this new dimension of transportation to the world."[23] That explains why Kamen would not license the manufacturing, distribution, and selling to any other organization. Segway was truly under the control of Kamen and his board members.

Kamen determined that Segway would change the way society viewed and used transportation. "I want to make a product that really has a serious impact on the environment, that can bring energy back to our inner cities."[24] He forecast that Segway would be "stamping out 10,000 machines a week" by year-end 2002. But Professor Karl Ulrich of the University of Pennsylvania estimated production by the end of 2002 would be 10 a week. Clearly, there was a wide discrepancy in the forecasts of those involved with Segway's creation and financing and those outside its operations.

With the millions invested—an estimated $90 million, with Segway LLC worth an estimated $650 million[25]—and with sales far from the billion dollar mark, Segway could be marked as a substantial letdown.

The Future

Kamen's aspirations for the Segway HT were great—he believed Segway would "be to the car what the car was to the horse and buggy."[26] For a future so great, there were several options ahead for the company.

First, the organization could continue to progress as it had thus far. The company had made slow progress since the release of the HT. However, this progress was consistent with Kamen's desire to "protect" the Segway HT from being marketed or sold as a toy or recreational product. Kamen had invested and financed Segway's manufacturing facility through his own resources and those of outsiders. Both he and his financiers seemed confident that the strategy they were pursuing was the best available option.

Or Kamen could sell the rights and manufacturing facility of Segway to an outside manufacturer. Kamen was a seasoned inventor who previously had licensed all of his other inventions to experienced organizations; nevertheless, he had decided to keep the Segway HT completely in-house. This decision served as the main criticism of the strategy. While many have said that Kamen was a genius inventor, they criticized his ability to be a part of effective product marketing and production. If Kamen sold the licensing of the Segway HT, he would relinquish control over the day-to-day operations of the company. However, Kamen could buy a share of ownership in the organization to whom he sold the rights in order to continue his involvement with the Segway product.

Still another option was for Segway to hire an outside marketing firm that could help it develop an effective marketing strategy for Segway products. That would allow Kamen the final say on all matters having to do with the marketing and selling of Segway, while gaining a professional opinion and guidance on how to develop demand and to market the product.

The action Kamen finally chose in 2004 was to hire Gary Pietruszewski as vice-president of sales and customer support. Pietruszewski, a former executive at Bentley Motor Cars Inc., was working to expand the number of locations where customers could test-drive and purchase a Segway HT. He hoped to accomplish this by building a national network of Segway dealers, modeled after the automobile dealerships he was accustomed to working with.

The future of Segway was uncertain. Sales reported through September 2003 were a mere 6,000 units, after which a software problem that was reportedly causing riders to fall off the device prompted the Consumer Products Safety Commission to issue a recall of all Segways on the market. In addition, the need for new cash forced Kamen to mortgage Segway's Bedford, New Hampshire, facility

[20]Profile of Sir Clive Sinclair, MENSA, www.mensa.org.uk/mensa/clivesinclair.html; Duffy, 2003, Move over Segway.

[21]www.segway.com/aboutus.

[22]Rivlin, Segway's breakdown.

[23]Dumaine, Brian, 2002, Profile of an entrepreneur on a roll: Dean Kamen, *Fortune Small Business,* July 9.

[24]Ibid.

[25]Rivlin, 2003, Segway's breakdown.

[26]Heilemann, 2001, Reinventing the wheel.

for $3.2 million and raise additional funds from his network of personal contacts. One of the new investors, John S. Weston, former chairman and chief executive of Automatic Data Processing Inc., reportedly made an investment on a "what-the-hell friendship basis," helping Kamen net around $31 million in additional cash.[27]

Kamen, as the inventor of the human transporter, had taken on a huge responsibility with Segway. Until the Segway HT, he had invented and then licensed his products to large, established manufacturers to produce and sell. Now he would not release the license of the Segway.

While Ronald Bills has been given more power over spending and strategic matters than his predecessors, Kamen is still in the picture.

[27]Armstrong, David, 2004, The Segway: Bright idea, wobbly business, *Wall Street Journal,* February 12: B1.

"David," Donna Cooper exclaimed. "You won't believe it, but these look like love letters! And look, they're from when he was in the service!"

David Fisher, the corporate archivist for GPC Incorporated, hastened toward the young woman sprawled on his dusty floor but cheerily holding aloft a packet of yellowed envelopes. Unaccustomed to so much commotion in this room, he was still trying to process what had just happened. A moment ago, he'd been giving Miss Cooper, the writer hired to pen GPC's 75th anniversary book, a tour of his admittedly cluttered storeroom. Following at some distance, she'd chosen another path through the debris, only to reach an impasse. He'd glanced back just in time to see her give a shove to—of all things—the founder's writing desk. The brittle wooden legs, now in their 100th year at least, could hardly have been expected to scoot across the rough cement swirls of the basement floor. One had snapped immediately, the desk had toppled, and Miss Cooper had followed the whole wreck down.

Which was when, even through the air of the old storeroom, semiopaque with suspended dust, and even despite the early-stage cataract in his left eye, David spotted something that made his historian's heart leap. The back of the desk, now splintered, had mysteriously yielded a drawer, one he had never discovered in his years of puttering around it. Visible inside were some papers. Following his wondering gaze, the infuriating, wonderful Miss Cooper had spied, and snatched out, the treasure.

A Bittersweet Discovery

She was right, of course. They were letters composed to a sweetheart by Hudson Parker after he'd shipped out with Company K, the 137th U.S. Infantry unit made up of recruits from Kansas and Missouri. The first was dated August 6, 1917—a full decade before he'd founded General Parkelite Company. David took quick note of the addressee: Mary Beatrice White. Not a name he'd heard before. Clearly this romance preceded Virginia, the woman Hud had married. David was faintly scandalized to realize that old Hud had squirreled away these letters, no doubt unbeknownst to his wife. At the same time, he was touched at the thought of an unforgotten first love. And although his first instinct would usually have been to don cotton gloves and carry the letters into better light, he instead cleared a bit of floor space near Miss Cooper and sat. There was an undeniable charm in having this young

Harvard Business Review's cases, which are fictional, present common managerial dilemmas and offer concrete solutions from experts.

Reprinted by permission of Harvard Business Review. "The Skeleton in the Corporate Closet" by Julia Kirby, June 2002. Copyright © 2002 by the Harvard Business School Pubolishing Corporation; all rights reserved.

woman eagerly extract letters from envelopes and read them aloud.

"My dearest Mary," she recited. "It began raining here this morning, and it is still at it. No drill today, so I will have time to write a letter or two." Impatient to find something juicier, she scanned the rest of the letter before handing it over. "Oh, look, David, how he signs it: 'With best of love to my own little girl.'" David accepted the letter and pushed his glasses down on his nose to peer over them. As always, he took a moment to appreciate the superior penmanship of an earlier age. Then his trained eye went to work on the page, drilling for facts that could be cataloged and cross-referenced with other accounts of the founder's war years. Donna, meanwhile, merrily called out other quaint snippets.

A half-hour passed in this way before David's joints, chilled by the bare floor, started to protest, and he suggested a change of venue. "Yeah," said Donna. "It's pretty musty in here, isn't it?" But as David took a moment to prop up the damaged desk and replace its drawer, Donna pulled another paper from an envelope. "Oh, this is the kind of thing you'll like," she noted, unfolding what looked, curiously, like drafting paper. She thrust it toward him and promptly launched into the accompanying letter. "You will recall from my last letter that we expect to see action this week, Mary darling. Enclosed is a document I hardly expect you to find interesting but entreat you to keep safe till my return." Indeed, it didn't interest Donna, so she rose to her feet and briskly dusted her skirt. "Honestly, David, I don't know how you work in here. My eyes are beginning to burn." But when she turned toward him, she was dismayed to see him staring at the paper he was clutching, his own eyes filling with tears.

Our Founder, a Thief?

A day passed before David appeared at the door of Jill Pierce, the communications VP who was his boss, and asked for a meeting at her convenience. Masking her surprise (in her seven years as his superior, she couldn't recall his ever initiating contact), she invited him in on the spot. Soon she was holding the letter herself and listening to David explain its import. Shockingly, it proved that the formula for Parkelite—the miracle plastic that was the company's first patent and its bread and butter for two full decades—had been someone else's innovation, not Hud Parker's. Not to put too fine a point on it, GPC's revered founder was a thief.

David filled in the parts of the story she didn't know. Of course, she needed no reminder of what Parkelite was. Although it had long since been superseded by better materials, it had been a huge technological advance in its day. A dense synthetic polymer, it could be molded or extruded and had the advantage of not changing shape after being mixed and heated. Most important, it wasn't flammable like earlier celluloid plastics. Manufacturers had used it to make things like engine parts, radio boxes, switches—even costume jewelry and inexpensive dinnerware. At the height of its popularity, General Parkelite was producing some 200,000 tons of the stuff per year.

What Jill had never heard was that in 1938, a lawsuit had been brought against Hud Parker and General Parkelite by the father of Karl Gintz, claiming that his son had been the true, sole inventor of Parkelite. Hud and Karl had studied chemistry together at Princeton, David explained, and had been star pupils who had egged each other on. But as well as being competitors, they were close friends, even to the extent that when war broke out in Europe, they enlisted together. Both dreamed of becoming pilots in the Army's Signal Corps, and both easily made the grade. They were transferred to the 94th Pursuit Group and posted to France. But in August 1918—just a week, Jill noted with a shiver, prior to the postmark on the envelope she held—Karl had been killed in maneuvers when the wing of his French-built trainer had collapsed. David pointed out that the formulas and diagrams neatly lettered on the graph paper were clearly the genesis of Parkelite, which Hud Parker had patented in 1920. Just as clearly, they were the work of Karl Gintz. "This is the document," David concluded, "that would have allowed the Gintz family to win its case."

Unprepared for the Worst

Jill had kept her composure while David was in her office, but as soon as he left, she opened her desk drawer, fished out a bottle of liquid antacid, and took a slug. David's chief concern seemed to be who would tell Hap—that is, Hudson Parker III, GPC's longtime CEO and the grandson of the founder. But that was the least of her worries. Clearly, this was a potential PR disaster, and her mind raced through the various ways it might play out. In honor of GPC's 75th anniversary, she'd introduced a heavy dose of nostalgia into this year's advertising. Hud Parker's image was splashed everywhere, along with the tag line, "He started it all." More like he *stole* it all, Jill thought bitterly, then felt guilty that such a remark would even occur to her. What a contrast to the pride she'd felt last summer when some focus groups she'd observed had come up with words like "trusted," "straight shooting," and "dependable" to describe the GPC brand. This was a catastrophe. And with all the extra planning that the special anniversary promotions required, she was already working flat out.

On her way to the CEO's office that afternoon, she lost her nerve at least three times. The fourth time, she even had Hap's doorway in sight, only to detour to the elevator lobby instead. She had a sudden determination to go down to the archives and urge David to destroy the incriminating paper and forget about it. But the fantasy died quickly as she recalled his haggard look in her office that morning. He'd already struggled with whether he could do that, she now realized, and decided he couldn't. She stopped short of hitting the down button and turned back toward the corner office.

History in the Remaking

Three days later, it was Hap Parker who was deciding what to do with the unwelcome news and 80-year-old graph paper now in his possession.

He'd been shocked, of course, and indeed had lost an entire weekend working through the implications on a purely personal level. On Saturday morning, he'd driven the two hours to the lakeside cottage where he'd spent summer days with his grandfather half a century before. He sat cross-legged on the dock, looked across the glittering water, then put his face in his hands and wept. First for his grandfather, who regardless of this incident didn't deserve to be impugned. The Parkelite patent, after all, was only a formula. It still took a great man to build a great company—and he had. And he had hardly coasted on that initial success. Instead, he'd infused the whole organization with the importance and excitement of constant innovation. It was his continuing attention to R&D that had led to General Parkelite's next generation of products, which, along with those of competitors, had made Parkelite obsolete. He'd won the respect of business leaders—indeed, of his country. He was a World War I ace, for God's sake! And a fair-dealing businessman, philanthropist, and community leader. A compassionate employer, certainly. And a dear grandfather, revered no less by his grandchildren for his tendency to dote on them.

This line of thought led Hap directly to self-pity. For neither did he, who had always held himself to the highest standard—with his grandfather's example as his North Star—deserve to have his name smeared. What was that line from Exodus about the sins of the fathers? He struggled to retrieve a long-forgotten catechism. Something about being visited on even the third and fourth generations. And now a fresh horror occurred to him: How much would Chip suffer, and even little Teddy, if this became known?

If. Had he really allowed himself to think "if"? He meant "when."

Reputation—or Reparation?

By Monday, Hap's thoughts were back with GPC and its employees, shareholders, and customers. He was listening to Newland Lowell, GPC's legal counsel, weigh in on the matter. No doubt about it, Newland was sharp. He'd come up with angles on this thing Hap hadn't anticipated.

As soon as he'd pressed the door shut behind him, in fact, Newland had broken into an improbable grin. "I know you're upset, Hap, so I'm going to get to the bottom line first," he said. "We haven't been able to turn up an heir to Karl Gintz." When he got no reaction, he hastened to pull out his other notes. "So. Let's take this from the top."

Newland first outlined a carefully reasoned argument that the letter, had it been introduced at trial long ago, would not necessarily have changed the verdict. The jury, he managed to persuade Hap, was fundamentally sympathetic to Hud Parker and not a little suspicious of Gintz's family. "If there's one thing I've learned," Newland said, "it's that jurors vote with their hearts and then find the legal hook to hang their emotions on." Besides, there would have been no proof that Karl hadn't meant to give the intellectual property to his friend and fellow soldier. "After all, no one else in his family was a chemist. They wouldn't have been able to make heads or tails of his notes. How do we know it wasn't his intent to let your grandfather take it forward? Maybe they were collaborating on it."

"But, Newland," Hap interjected. "If that had been the case, why wouldn't Hud have simply said so?"

"We're talking about a court case," Lowell reminded him. "His legal counsel would never have let him say that."

Hap fell silent again and let Newland continue to lay out his next argument: that there was no way of knowing when the letters Hud had sent to Mary Beatrice White had come back into his possession. It could have been years after the court case. "Not to mention," Newland added, "that if he needed this paper to fudge his own documentation for the patent, then why was it still in that envelope? Isn't it conceivable that the innovation was essentially your grandfather's but that Karl had taken careful notes on it to study and perhaps improve upon?"

Believing his arguments were carrying the day, Newland finally plunged into his last set of notes. These were legal strategies for "containing the discovery"—in essence placing a gag order on the few people in the organization who knew the truth. But Hap had already begun to chafe at what were sounding increasingly like elaborate rationalizations, and this was a bridge too far. He stood up from his desk and nodded to Newland. "Thank you, that's as much as I care to hear this afternoon."

Newland Lowell had known Hap Parker long enough not to mistake his tone, courteous though it might have seemed to others. He sighed as he swept his files back into his briefcase and rose from his chair. "Look, Hap. I'll be straight with you. I know you have a strong sense of what's ethical here. But you also have an organization to take care of. Your employees will be better off, not to mention your shareholders—hell, the *world* is better off if Hud Parker remains a hero. Don't be overly fastidious about this."

Doing the Right Thing

Packing up for the day, Hap had made up his mind. It was absurd that a company whose culture was all about honesty and integrity would tolerate a lie at its core. Maybe there was no one deserving of reparations out there, but surely the company deserved to pay some. He'd find some heir, somewhere.

He wasn't 20 yards down the hall, though, before he encountered a group of three GPC managers, two of them quite new to the company and the other a veteran. As he approached, he overheard the veteran, whose back was to Hap, saying patiently to one of the others, "Well, but, of course, Kevin, that just wouldn't be right." Then, catching sight of Hap, he fell into step with him, hoping to sound out the boss on some other matter.

Just out of earshot, Hap tilted his head back toward where the three had been standing and asked, "What was that about?" The manager explained that Kevin had proposed a marketing idea that seemed a little, well, not exactly underhanded, but. . . . The kid had come to GPC from a competitor with a certain industry reputation. "You know, people there learn to work all the angles and do a lot of things with a wink," he shrugged. "Don't worry, though. He wasn't comfortable there—that's why we got him."

"So you think he's got the potential to be a GPC'er?" Hap pressed.

"Well, that's the great thing about a strong culture, isn't it, Hap? It rubs off. He'll soon pick up on how things are done around here."

The unintended irony of those words made Hap queasy. Suddenly, he couldn't imagine damaging the strong belief in GPC held by this decent man and his 8,000 coworkers. Maybe Newland was right, he thought, and he was being too narrow in his ethics—even self-indulgent.

Was it possible for the right thing to be a lie?

Case 37 Southwest Airlines: How Much Can "LUV" Do?*

Southwest Airlines (SWA) did it again in 2004. For eight years in a row, and even three years after its celebrity CEO Herb Kelleher stepped down in 2001, the company retained its grip on the Fortune Top Ten list of America's most admired companies.[1] Also, Southwest posted a profit for the 31st consecutive year and for 51 consecutive quarters by the fourth quarter of 2003—both of which were achievements unsurpassed in the airline industry. All this was achieved while the airline industry as a whole was experiencing losses for three straight years and when several larger airlines underwent or continued to restructure their business, gain wage concessions from their employees, and slash costs in efforts to avoid bankruptcy or emerge from bankruptcy.[2]

While these were admirable achievements, there seemed to be some emerging chinks in Southwest's low-cost, fun-culture armor. In 2002, its employee groups started calling for federal mediation for the first time. This was a result of their negotiations for pay raises which represented brewing tension between management and workers over the sharing of the spoils.[3] As the company grew to over 35,000 employees, there were challenges to keep the "LUV" culture intact (LUV was Southwest's ticker symbol on the New York Stock Exchange, signifying the company's operations from Love Field in Dallas as well as its emphasis on "love" to its customers and employees). Further, competition in the discount segment was heating up with the entry of several new low-cost, high-frill carriers such as JetBlue, Song, and Ted, though they were not at that moment direct competitors in Southwest's markets. And, the effect of leadership change was too early to gauge with Herb Kelleher still playing a dominant role making strategy for the company. With the spirit of the "underdog" becoming irrelevant, was there a dominant vision for the company to propel it to success in the future?

Background and Growth

The inconvenience and expense of ground travel by bus or automobile between the cities of Houston, Dallas, and San Antonio—the Golden Triangle that was experiencing rapid economic and population growth during the late 1960s—offered an opportunity for an intrastate airline. The idea was suggested by Rollin King, a San Antonio entrepreneur who owned a small commuter air service, when his banker, John Parker, complained about the issue. King then talked to Herb Kelleher—a New Jersey born, New York University Law School graduate who moved to San Antonio in 1967 to practice law. They soon pooled the seed money to start Southwest Airlines. The infant Southwest Airlines (SWA) fought long-drawn legal battles, primarily engineered by the major airline carriers, for over four years before it got its first flight off the ground in 1971. Later on, the company had to work around a regulation intended to penalize SWA's decision to operate out of Dallas Love Field instead of moving to the new Dallas–Fort Worth (DFW) airport. With Herb's brilliant legal expertise and extensive lobbying with the House of Representatives, the issue was settled and SWA was allowed to operate out of Love Field in 1979. The struggle for existence in the initial years worked to the advantage of the company as it created the esprit de corps for which it became so well known. The employees were caught up fighting for the "SWA cause" that created "the warrior mentality, the very fight to survive," according to Colleen Barrett, who became the president and chief operating officer of SWA in 2001.[4]

Kelleher, however, was not the first chief executive officer of Southwest. Lamar Muse, an airline veteran who worked earlier with Trans Texas, Central and Universal Airlines was brought in to get the company off to a good start. That was followed by the brief tenure of Howard Putnam, another airline veteran hired from United Airlines, from 1978 to 1982. Herb Kelleher served as the chairman of the board during that period, then took the CEO position in 1982 and championed Southwest's expansion (at that time the company had only 27 planes, $270 million in revenues, and flew only to 14 cities).[5] SWA was one of a kind right from its beginning. It was the pioneer of the "low-cost strategy." It flew planes point-to-point—short-haul flights bypassing the expensive hub-and-spoke operations. It chose less popular, less congested airports to achieve quicker turnarounds.

*This case study was prepared by Ms. Naga Lakshmi Damaraju of the University of Texas at Dallas, Professor Gregory G. Dess at University of Texas at Dallas, Professor Alan B. Eisner at Pace University, and Vasudev Krishnan, former graduate student at the University of Texas at Dallas. The purpose of the case is to stimulate class discussion rather than illustrating effective or ineffective handling of a business situation. The authors thank Professor Michael Oliff at the University of Texas at Dallas, for his valuable comments on an earlier version of this case.

[1] Serwer, B., 2004, Southwest Airlines: The hottest thing in the sky, *Fortune*, March 8: 88–106.

[2] Southwest Airlines, 2003, SEC filings, Form 10-K for 2003.

[3] Roman, M., 2002, Southwest Air's family feud, *BusinessWeek*, July 15: 48.

[4] Freiberg, K., & Freiberg, J., 1996, Nuts! Southwest Airlines' crazy recipe for personal and business success (Austin, TX: Bard Press): 20–27; http://archives.californiaaviation.org/airport/msg15249.html.

[5] Ibid.

SWA offered airfares so low that it gave the bus and car travel companies a run for their money. It served no meals on its airlines and provided only a snack of peanuts. That saved plenty of money and manpower. There was no assigned seating which reduced boarding times and helped planes turn around faster. The average turnaround time for planes was around 25 minutes. Faster turnaround times and higher aircraft utilization also meant a reduced number of aircraft and gate facilities than would otherwise have been necessary. SWA's attractive flight attendants in hot pants were a source of live entertainment on flights (e.g., the flight attendants made funny presentations of the otherwise routine and boring safety instructions or performed preflight tricks such as popping out of overhead bins).[6] It was the first major airline that introduced ticketless travel and one of the first to put up a Web site and offer online booking.[7] It operated a single aircraft type, Boeing 737, that kept its training costs low and manpower utilization high as it offered great flexibility in manpower deployment. Starting with three Boeing 737s in 1971, the company fleet grew to 388 Boeing 737 aircraft, providing service to 59 airports in 58 cities in 30 states throughout the United States by the end of 2003 (see Exhibits 1, 2, and 3). It topped the monthly domestic passenger traffic rankings for the first time in May 2003. From May through August 2003, Southwest Airlines was the largest carrier in the United States based on originating domestic passengers boarded, and scheduled domestic departures.[8]

The SWA Leadership and Culture

There are many stories about Herb Kelleher's flamboyant style for a CEO. He smoked cigars, loved Wild Turkey whiskey, was often seen dressed up as Elvis Presley, and publicly arm-wrestled and won over a rival company CEO to settle a dispute over an advertisement slogan.[9] Kelleher truly believed that business could and should be fun—at too many companies, people put on a mask when they came to their office. People would not be their natural selves and would be overly serious, which explained why most business encounters were bland and impersonal. Therefore, SWA tried not to hire people who were humorless, self-centered, or complacent. Not surprisingly, there was no human resources department but a People Department at Southwest. The guiding principle for recruitment at SWA was "Hire for attitude and train for skills." Herb believed that to be the most important principle. When a person from the People Department said to

him: "Herb, I'm getting a little embarrassed because I've interviewed 34 people for a ramp agent position in Amarillo," Herb replied: "If you have to interview 134 people to find the appropriate person to be a ramp agent in Amarillo, do it. Because the most important thing is to get the right people, and if you get the wrong ones they start poisoning everybody else."[10]

Kelleher's penchant for laughter and fun became a part of Southwest's culture. Prospective employees were asked how humor helped them out of a difficult situation. Prospective pilots were sometimes asked to pull on shorts and the ones who saw fun in it passed the interview. All people at the company were to be treated with dignity and respect and Herb did not believe in hierarchical barriers. When a vice-president complained to the CEO that customers, gate agents, pilots, and baggage handlers had more access to him than he did, Kelleher said to him, "Let me explain this: They're more important than you are." Herb recognized the key to satisfied customers was having satisfied employees. So employees came first and that orientation was embodied in the mission statement (Exhibit 4).

The culture was put into operation through a number of policies and programs. The casual dress policy reinforced the company's desire that people be themselves on the job. Celebrations such as "Spirit Parties," culture parties, and weekly deck parties were organized at headquarters regularly to bring employees together. Activities at the events included gong shows, talent shows, dance contests, limbo contests, and famous person look-alike themes. The culture committee at SWA welcomed new employees with a "New Hire Welcome Kit" that included a bag, T-shirt, badge holder, pen, and a welcome letter. To build solidarity across all departments, there was an employee recognition program in which employees recognized each other's achievements. Such a practice helped community building within and across departments. For example, one work group committee recognized flight attendants 10 times a year with "Hokey Days," named for the broom apparatus used by flight attendants to sweep the cabin after the flights. Committee members chose two locations at which to honor flight attendants, greeted each arriving plane, waited until passengers got off, and then boarded with goodies. Flight attendants were asked to relax while the committee members cleaned the plane for them. There were similar programs to honor other departments as well.[11] There was also a "Walk a Mile Program" designed to foster problem solving and cooperation, in

[6]Freiberg, & Freiberg, 1996, Nuts! Southwest Airlines crazy recipe, 6.

[7]Greylock Associates, 2003, Herb Kelleher, chairman, CEO and president, Southwest Airlines.

[8]Southwest Airlines, SEC filings, Form 10-K for 2003.

[9]McConnell, B., 2001, The wild, flying turkey with wings: Creating customer evangelists—A profile of Herb Kelleher; www.creatingcustomerevangelists.com/resources/evangelists/herb_kelleher.asp.

[10]Kelleher, Herb, 2003, Interview with Mark Morrison of *BusinessWeek* at Texas McComb's School of Business, December 23; www.businessweek.com.

[11]Southwest Airlines, 2003, Great Place to Work Institute—Innovation Awards; www.greatplacetowork.com/education/innovate/honoree-2003-southwest.htm.

Exhibit 1   Financial and Operating Data for Southwest Airlines, 1999–2003*

	2003	2002	2001	2000	1999
	Year Ended December				
	(In $ millions, except per share amounts)				
Financial Data					
Operating revenues	$ 5,937	$ 5,522	$ 5,555	$ 5,650	$ 4,736
Operating expenses	5,454	5,104	4,924	4,628	3,954
Operating income	483	418	631	1,022	782
Other expenses/income, net	−225	25	−197	4	8
Income before income taxes	708	393	828	1,018	774
Provision for income taxes	266	152	317	392	299
Net Income	442	241	511	626	475
Net income per share, basic	$ 0.56	$ 0.31	$ 0.67	$ 0.84	$ 0.63
Net income per share, diluted	$ 0.54	$ 0.30	$ 0.63	$ 0.79	$ 0.59
Cash dividends per common share	$ 0.02	$ 0.02	$ 0.02	$ 0.01	$ 0.01
Total assets at period-end	$9,878.00	$ 8,954.00	$ 8,997.00	$ 6,670.00	$ 5,654.00
Long-term obligations at period-end	$1,332.00	$ 1,553.00	$ 1,327.00	$ 761.00	$ 872.00
Stockholders' equity at period-end	$5,052.00	$ 4,422.00	$ 4,014.00	$ 3,451.00	$ 2,836.00
Operating Data					
Revenue passengers carried	65,673,945	63,045,988	64,446,773	63,678,261	57,500,213
Revenue passenger miles (RPMs) (000s)	47,943,066	45,391,903	44,493,916	42,215,162	36,479,322
Available seat miles (ASMs) (000s)	71,790,425	68,886,546	65,295,290	59,909,965	52,855,467
Load factor	66.8%	65.9%	68.1%	70.5%	69.0%
Average length of passenger haul (miles)	730	720	690	663	634
Trips flown	949,882	947,331	940,426	903,754	846,823
Average passenger fare	$ 87.42	$ 84.72	$ 83.46	$ 85.87	$ 79.35
Passenger revenue yield per RPM	$ .1197	.1177	.1209	.1295	.1251
Operating revenue yield per ASM	.0827	.0802	.0851	.0943	.0896
Operating expenses per ASM	.0760	.0741	.0754	.0773	.0748
Operating expenses per ASM, excluding fuel	.0644	.0630	.0636	.0638	.0655
Fuel cost per gallon (average)	.723	.680	.709	.787	.527
Number of employees at year-end	32,847	33,705	31,580	29,274	27,653
Size of fleet at year-end	388	375	355	344	312

* Refer to the Appendix for a list of terms used in the airline industry.

Source: Southwest Airlines, SEC filings, Form 10-K for 2003, www.sec.gov/Archives/edgar/data/92380/000095013404000842/d11818e10vk.htm.

which an employee could do somebody else's job for a day (while operations people obviously could not fly the airplanes, pilots could do the work as operations agents).[12] Further, the company had the "Star of the Month"—outstanding employees would be chosen to appear in *Spirit*,

the in-flight magazine of Southwest—which recognized the distinct contributions of employees toward excellence in customer service.[13]

The warmth toward employees was also expressed by other modes. At Southwest's headquarters in Dallas, the walls were covered with more than 10,000 picture

[12]Kelleher, Herb, 1997, *Leader to Leader,* No. 4; www.pfdf.org/leaderbooks/L2L/spring97/kelleher.html.

[13]Southwest Airlines, www.southwest.com/careers/stars/stars.html.

Exhibit 2   Cities Served by Southwest Airlines

Source: Southwest Airlines Web site, with permission from the company; www.southwest.com/swatakeoff/cities_states_airports.html.

frames that contained photos of employees' pets, of stewardesses in miniskirts, of Southwest planes gnawing on competitor's aircraft. Also there were teddy bears, jars of pickled hot peppers, and pink flamingos. There was cigarette smoking and lots of chuckling. "To me, it's comfortable," said Colleen Barrett, who was most responsible for nurturing Southwest culture from its early days. "This is an open scrapbook. We aren't uptight. We celebrate everything. It's like a fraternity, a sorority, a reunion. We are having a party!" she said. Barrett also regularly traveled to meet the employees and personally sent them birthday cards, not so much to win their loyalty as to communicate the true spirit of a family. The company celebrated with its employees when good things happened and grieved with

Exhibit 3   Growth in the Number of Cities Served by Southwest Airlines, 1994–2003

Year Ended	No. of Cities Served
1994	44
1995	45
1996	49
1997	51
1998	52
1999	56
2000	57
2001	58
2002	58
2003	58

Source: Southwest Airlines, Form 10-Ks filed with SEC.

Exhibit 4   The Mission of Southwest Airlines

The mission of Southwest Airlines is dedication to the highest quality of Customer Service delivered with a sense of warmth, friendliness, individual pride, and Company Spirit.

To Our Employees

We are committed to provide our Employees a stable work environment with equal opportunity for learning and personal growth. Creativity and innovation are encouraged for improving the effectiveness of Southwest Airlines. Above all, Employees will be provided the same concern, respect, and caring attitude within the organization that they are expected to share externally with every Southwest Customer.

Source: Southwest Airlines, www.southwest.com/about_swa/mission.html.

them when they had a devastating experience.[14] She said, "What we do is very simple, but it's not simplistic. We really do everything with passion. We scream at each other and we hug each other."[15]

Cost consciousness was another important part of the culture. "Yes, our culture is almost like a religion," said Gary Kelly, CFO of Southwest, "but it's a dichotomy. In many ways we are conservative. Financially, for instance."[16] According to Herb Kelleher, close attention to costs had produced the kind of financial success Southwest had seen. He said, "Even in the best of times, we kept our costs low and questioned every expenditure. For years, I used to approve every expenditure over $1,000. Why? To encourage a cost-conscious culture. I couldn't look at all of them, of course. But I would question them selectively, and that kept people paying attention."[17]

Treating employees well at Southwest did not mean that they were paid high salaries. By creating value through intangibles, the company kept wages lower than those of competitors. Officers at Southwest were paid about 30 percent less, on average, than their counterparts at other airlines. But the airline made stock options widely available, so all employees—not just executives—could share in the company's financial success. Southwest even had a policy that its officers received pay increases that were no larger, proportionally, than what other employees received. But employees were also expected to take pay reductions when times were not good. Job security was ensured, however, with a "no-furlough policy" and Southwest did not lay off a single employee during the economic downturn after the terrorist attacks on September 11, 2001, while many of its competitors did.[18] Caring for employee happiness showed positive results. Southwest had less employee turnover than its competitors. For years, Southwest enjoyed the loyalty of its employees despite the high level of employee unionization. "Once labor leaders realize that you're trying to take care of your people, most of the edge [in contract negotiations] is gone," said Kelleher.[19]

Southwest's employees worked more hours than their counterparts at other airlines. Southwest pilots flew nearly 80 hours a month compared to United's 50 hours. Southwest pilots were paid by trip, not per hour, which created a strong interest in keeping flights on schedule. Also, pilots tended to be cost conscious because a big part of their compensation came from stock options. On some occasions, pilots even pitched in to help ground crews move luggage to ensure on-time flights—something virtually unheard of at Southwest's bigger rivals. Flight attendants at Southwest worked about 150 hours a month, compared with 80 hours at many other airlines, according to union president Thom McDaniel. Southwest attendants were required by contract to make a reasonable effort to tidy the airplane between flights, a job performed by maintenance personnel at rival airlines. According to an airline labor expert, senior flight attendants at United got as many as 52 vacation days a year (compared with 35 days for veterans at Southwest) and they never had to clean up after the passengers.[20]

Maintaining focus on the core business was another element for both cost control and pursuing a niche strategy. Kelleher consciously ensured that the company did not diverge into allied businesses such as car rentals or reservations. Most of Southwest's growth had been organic, that is, by adding more flights on its existing routes and by connecting more dots (adding cities). The airline started complementing its short-haul flights with long-haul flights and began transcontinental services. According to Kelleher, the airline did not plan for international flights as it meant a total change in the way it operated and involved training its 35,000 employees to handle that change.[21]

The cost consciousness and employee commitment translated into operational excellence and increased profitability. Southwest's planes flew about 10.9 hours per day, much more than any other airline except for that of JetBlue, which flew close to 13.0 hours per day. Southwest could offer lower fares—as much as 50 percent lower than its major rivals—and still remain profitable. With such low costs, it created what was called the "Southwest effect," an explosion in the traffic and nabbing of customers who would have driven before.[22] The term Southwest effect was coined by the U.S. Department of Transportation to refer to the consistent phenomenon of a decrease in average fares and stimulation of demand that occurred when Southwest Airlines entered any market.[23]

In May 1988 Southwest became the first airline to win the coveted "Triple Crown" for a month: Best On-Time Record, Best Baggage Handling, and Fewest Customer Complaints. Since then, Southwest has won it more than 30 times, as well as five annual Triple Crowns for 1992, 1993, 1994, 1995, and 1996. Southwest crossed its $1 billion revenue mark in 1990 to become a major airline and continued its profitable operations to emerge as

[14]Shinn, S., 2003, LUV, Colleen, *BizEd.,* March–April.

[15]Serwer, 2004, Southwest Airlines: The hottest thing in the sky.

[16]Ibid.

[17]What makes Southwest Airlines fly?; http://knowledge.wharton.upenn.edu/articles.cfm?catid=2&articleid=753.

[18]Ibid.; Kelleher, 1997, *Leader to Leader;* Freedman, M., 2002, Non-stop growth? ABCNews.com, July 2.

[19]What makes Southwest Airlines fly?

[20]Donnelly, S. B., 2002, One airline's magic, *Time,* October 28: 45–47.

[21]Kelleher, 2003, Interview with Mark Morrison; McConnell, 2001, The wild, flying turkey with wings.

[22]Zellner, W., 2001, Southwest: After Kelleher, more blue skies, *BusinessWeek,* April 2: 45.

[23]Southwest Airlines, www.southwest.com/swatakeoff/southwest_effect.html.

number seven among major airlines based on revenue in 2003. Stories of Southwest employees providing excellent customer service abound and Southwest had even set up a direct TV to show how its employees treated customers.[24]

The Changing Times and Challenges

Southwest Airlines had a change in leadership in August 2001 when Herb Kelleher relinquished power to two of his close aides. Colleen C. Barrett, vice-president for customers, became the president and chief operating officer; and James F. Parker, general counsel, became the chief executive officer. Barrett and Parker had each worked together for over 22 years and for much longer with Kelleher from the time he was a lawyer. In contrast to Kelleher's obtrusive personality, Parker was a quiet diplomat. He had been the company's lead labor negotiator for years, and his opponents said he pursued the company line quite forcefully, if politely, in talks. "He will surprise you because he doesn't look like he's tough, but he doesn't give anything away," said a former vice president of the airline's pilot association.[25] Unlike Kelleher, Parker was not as fond of celebrations because he didn't see them as contributing to productivity. But he came to realize that the party preparations were a model of teamwork and employee bonding and he started participating in the celebrations in 2002.[26]

Barrett, on the other hand, had been the culture keeper of Southwest since the earliest days of the company. However, she was a reluctant public speaker. Thus, she let Parker take the lead with Wall Street and the media. How far the lieutenants replaced the "rock star" personality of Kelleher, who exuded warmth to his employees, was too early to guess. Kelleher remained chairman of the board and focused on long-range strategy and government affairs. He maintained control of schedule planning and aircraft acquisitions, the backbone of Southwest's strategy during the period of transition.[27] Whether things would be the same after Kelleher left the scene completely was another important question facing Southwest.

The growth of the company and the consequent increase in the number of employees also posed challenges to keeping the culture intact. The distance between the rank-and-file and top management was growing. While Colleen Barrett could reach all the employees through personally signed birthday cards when the company was small, such a task was becoming increasingly unrealistic.

Even though she continued to do so, she could reach only a fraction of Southwest's 35,000 employees dispersed over different cities. Keeping in close touch with employees was becoming an increasingly challenging task. In earlier times of difficulty, Herb Kelleher personally addressed and rallied his troops, but such an exercise was no longer easy.

In addition, the otherwise warm employee relations at Southwest seemed to chill over time. Unions were becoming more aggressive in expressing their frustration, in contrast to earlier days when disputes were resolved more amicably and peacefully. In the summer of 2001, ramp workers picketed near company headquarters with signs that read, "Record Profits Empty Pockets." They complained that staff shortages, combined with Southwest's record passenger loads, and a drive to improve on-time performance, meant they had to lift more bags and had to do so more quickly which put them at risk of injury.[28] And, for the first time in company history, in July 2002 Southwest's mechanics union asked federal mediators to intervene to break a contract deadlock over pay. While the company was nowhere near a strike, the incident clearly signaled the strains appearing in employee relations.[29]

Since 2002 the company was also engaged without much success in a contract renegotiation with flight attendants. In July 2003 a group of flight attendants staged a demonstration at the headquarters with signs "Spread the LUV" and handed out cards to travelers reading "Give our flight attendants a break." The move was an expression of frustration toward management's idea of increasing their work hours. Also, workers who had been working hard to boost the productivity of the company were not seeing much return from profit sharing and a pummeled stock. After years of hard work, some long-time employees felt that they had no more to give. Karen Amos, a 26-year Southwest veteran, said, "We have been there for them. There comes a time when it becomes too much."[30] The company had to drop the move to increase work hours, but still could not get a deal made with the flight attendants. Some workers perceived that the company had been fairer in its negotiations in past years.

In November 2003, after 11 rounds of talks without success, the flight attendants threw a Thanksgiving party at Salt Lake City International Airport, primarily as a means of putting pressure on management to accept their demands for holiday pay and better working conditions. Kevin Onstead, a Southwest negotiator and flight attendant, said:

---

[24]www.southwest.com; Serwer, 2004, Southwest Airlines: The hottest thing in the sky, 88–106.

[25]Freedman, 2002, Non-stop growth?

[26]Trotman, M., 2003, Inside Southwest Airlines, storied culture feels strains, *Wall Street Journal Online,* July 11; http://online.wsj.com.

[27]Zellner, 2001, Southwest: After Kelleher, more blue skies; Zellner, W., & Arndt, M., 2003, Holding steady, *BusinessWeek,* February 3: 66–68.

[28]Trotman, 2003, Inside Southwest Airlines.

[29]Roman, 2002, Southwest Air's family feud, 48.

[30]Trotman, 2003, Inside Southwest Airlines.

Exhibit 5   **Southwest Airline's Operating Expenses per Average Seat Mile, 1995–2003 (In cents)**

Expense Category	2003	2002	2001	2000	1999	1998	1997	1996	1995
Salaries, wages & benefits (including employee retirement plans)	3.10	2.89	2.84	2.81	2.75	2.70	2.56	2.45	2.40
Fuel and oil	1.16	1.11	1.18	1.34	.93	.82	1.11	1.19	1.01
Maintenance materials and repairs	.60	.57	.61	.63	.70	.64	.58	.62	.60
Agency commissions	.07	.08	.16	.27	.30	.33	.35	.35	.34
Aircraft rentals	.25	.27	.29	.33	.38	.43	.45	.47	.47
Landing fees and other rentals	.52	.50	.48	.44	.46	.45	.46	.46	.44
Depreciation	.53	.52	.49	.47	.47	.47	.44	.45	.43
Other expenses	1.37	1.47	1.49	1.44	1.49	1.48	1.45	1.51	1.38
Total	7.60	7.41	7.54	7.73	7.48	7.32	7.40	7.50	7.07

Source: Southwest Airlines annual reports and 10-K reports.

We are concerned about the culture of the airline. We are fighting for the recognition of our contribution to that culture. We've been key in Southwest Airlines' success. Flight attendants are prepared to strike as a last resort. We are willing to do whatever it takes to get a fair contract.[31]

The negotiations had not borne fruit by early 2004. Thom McDaniel, president of the TWU, said that flight attendants were willing to return to the negotiating table. However, he made the point that the latest management offer fell short of their expectations. "We feel that our culture is at risk because of the actions taken by Southwest's management during these negotiations."[32]

Pressure on Southwest for pay increases was also likely to mount from the pilots' union whose contract was due to expire in 2006. Many of the employee groups started feeling that Southwest Airlines was no longer the underdog and that their pay should match the profitability of the company. Love (LUV) alone no longer seemed to be enough. That meant a twin challenge in terms of culture and costs.

Southwest was already experiencing cost increases per average seat mile (ASM), a key metric used to measure performance in the industry, primarily due to increases in fuel costs and wages. The cost per ASM went up from 7.07 cents in 1995 to 7.60 cents in 2003, with fuel

costs, wages, and benefits as the major contributors (Exhibit 5). Southwest's cost per average seat mile remained below that of the big carriers whose costs ranged between 9.0 and 13.0 cents. The company was already working hard on controlling costs. With more of its customers making reservations online, it closed three call centers in 2003, saving about $20 million annually.[33] Further cost squeezing appeared to be a difficult proposition. Some industry experts, however, believed that even if Southwest raised employee pay, it would still remain profitable because it had the lowest unit labor costs compared to other major airlines.

Intensifying competition in the low-fare segment was another factor that had become difficult to ignore. While the newly launched competitors such as JetBlue, AirTran, Delta's Song, and United's Ted were not a direct threat to Southwest on its existing routes, further expansion of those carriers could bring them head-on with Southwest. JetBlue's intentions, as expressed in early 2004, indicated that it was exploring the possibility of launching a service from Austin (and later from Dallas–Fort Worth) to New York.[34] These new airlines offered far more attractive services such as leather seats and in-flight entertainment systems, for almost the same fare. Therefore, these rivals could make the no-frills approach of Southwest pale before them (Exhibit 6). Whether Southwest's loyal customers would still stick with the airline when they could get more value for their money elsewhere was another

[31]Warchol, G., 2003, Southwest crews rally for their cause, *Salt Lake Tribune*, November 26; www.sltrib.com/2003/Nov/11262003/Business/Business.asp.

[32]Southwest flight attendants may resume contract talks, 2004, AIRwise News, February 18; www.airwise.com/news/airlines/southwest.html.

[33]Serwer, 2004, Southwest Airlines: The hottest thing in the sky.

[34]Torbenson, E., 2004, Breaking from formation, *Dallas Morning News*, February 22: 1-D.

Exhibit 6   A Comparison of Southwest and Its New "Low-Cost" Rivals

Airline	Year Founded	Aircraft Fleet	Hubs	Unions	Assigned Seats	Ticket Change Fee	Food	In-Flight Entertainment	No. of Cities Served*
Southwest	1971	Boeing 737s	No	Yes	No	No	Snacks only	Wisecracking flight attendants	58
AirTran	1993	Varied	Yes	Yes	Yes	$50	Snacks only	Nothing at the time	45
JetBlue	2000	Airbus A320s	No	No	Yes	$25	Snacks only	DirectTV at each seat	27
Song (Delta)	2003	Boeing 757s	No	Pilots only	Yes	$25	Meals for sale	Satellite TV at each seat; pay-per-view movies; videogames	13
Ted (United)	2004	Airbus A320s	Yes	Yes	Yes	$100	Meals for sale	Nothing at the time	13

*Obtained from destinations served as shown on their respective Web sites as of April 2004.

Source: B. Serwer, Southwest Airlines: The Hottest Thing in the Sky, *Fortune,* March 8, 2004, pp. 88–106.

significant question. Southwest's investments to automate and significantly streamline the ticketing and boarding process with computer-generated bag tags, automated boarding passes, self-service boarding pass kiosks, and so forth, and its investments to increase the functionality of its Web site, along with its moves to enhance aircraft interiors with leather seats, can hardly be described as *not* motivated by competition.[35] That JetBlue caught Southwest's attention was clear by Parker's comment that Southwest was studying the possibility of introducing an in-flight entertainment system, though at the moment it was too costly to adopt. Thus, matching amenities with the newly emerging competition could pose additional challenges to the low-cost strategy. Kelleher's reaction to the emerging competition was simple—he had seen that movie before.

Meanwhile, Southwest announced plans to enter the Philadelphia market, a stronghold of US Air, by May 9, 2004. The Philadelphia market was one of the most overpriced and underserved. Southwest aimed at capturing the market with its tried and tested low-cost, no frills formula. US Air responded, "We will be a vigorous competitor to Southwest in Philadelphia on every route they fly."[36] Southwest could perhaps sustain its advantage over its major rivals, but could it face the prospect of sustaining its advantage over its low-cost rivals if they chose to enter the same market? One must ask: Would Southwest's further flight to success be smooth enough given the triple challenge of managing leadership change, maintaining culture in the face of growth, and increasing competition?

[35]Southwest Airlines, SEC filings of Form 10-K for 2003.

[36]Serwer, 2004, Southwest Airlines: The hottest thing in the sky.

Appendix   Key Terms Used

Aircraft utilization. The average number of block hours operated per day per aircraft for the total fleet of aircraft.

Available seat miles. The number of seats available for passengers multiplied by the number of miles the seats are flown.

Average fare. The average one-way fare paid per flight segment by a revenue passenger.

Average stage length. The average number of miles flown per flight.

Breakeven load factor. The passenger load factor that will result in operating revenues being equal to operating expenses, assuming constant revenue per passenger mile and expenses.

Load factor. The percentage of aircraft seating capacity actually utilized (revenue passenger miles divided by available seat miles).

Operating expense per available seat mile. Operating expenses divided by available seat miles.

Operating revenue per available seat mile. Operating revenue divided by available seat miles.

Revenue passenger miles. The number of miles flown by revenue passengers.

Revenue passengers. The total number of paying passengers flown on all flight segments.

Yield per passenger mile. The average amount one passenger pays to fly one mile.

Source: JetBlue 10-K reports.

Case 38   Starbucks Corporation: Competing in a Global Market

Starbucks Corporation is a coffee company based in Seattle, Washington. It buys, roasts, and sells whole bean specialty coffees and coffee drinks through an international chain of retail outlets. From its beginnings as a seller of packaged, premium specialty coffees, Starbucks has evolved into a firm known for its coffeehouses, where people can purchase beverages and food items as well as packaged whole bean and ground coffee. Starbucks is credited with changing the way Americans—and people around the world—view and consume coffee, and its success has attracted global attention.

Starbucks has consistently been one of the fastest-growing companies in the United States. Over a 10-year period starting in 1992, the company's net revenues increased at a compounded annual growth rate of 20 percent, to $3.3 billion in fiscal 2002. Net earnings have grown at an annual compounded growth rate of 30 percent to $218 million in fiscal 2002, which is the highest reported net earnings figure in the company's history (see Exhibit 1). As *BusinessWeek* tells it:

> On Wall Street, Starbucks is the last great growth story. Its stock, including four splits, has soared more than 2,200 percent over the past decade, surpassing Wal-Mart, General Electric, PepsiCo, Coca-Cola, Microsoft, and IBM in total return. Now at $21 [September 2002], it is hovering near its all-time high of $23 in July [2002], before the overall market drop.[1]

To continue this rapid pace of growth, the firm's senior executives are looking to expand internationally. Specifically, they are interested in further expansion in Europe (including the Middle East), Asia-Pacific (including Australia and New Zealand), and Latin America. Expanding in these three continents represents both a challenge and an opportunity to Starbucks. While the opportunity of increased revenues from further expansion is readily apparent to the company's top management, what is not clear is how to deal with growing "antiglobalization" sentiment around the world.

This case looks at issues that are arising as Starbucks seeks to dominate specialty coffee markets around the world and explores what changes in strategy might be required.

Suresh Kotha and Debra Glassman, both from the University of Washington, prepared this case for the basis of class discussion rather than to illustrate either effective or ineffective handling of an administrative situation. The case was originally developed for the 2003 Global Business Challenge case competition at the University of Washington Business School. The authors thank the Global Business Center, the University of Washington, and the Starbucks Corporation for their generous support in preparing the case. All rights reserved to the authors. Copyright © 2003 Kotha & Glassman.

Background

In 1971, three Seattle entrepreneurs—Jerry Baldwin, Zev Siegl, and Gordon Bowker—started selling whole bean coffee in Seattle's Pike Place Market. They named their store Starbucks, after the first mate in *Moby Dick*.[2] By 1982 the business had grown to five stores, a small roasting facility, and a wholesale business selling coffee to local restaurants. At the same time, Howard Schultz had been working as vice-president of U.S. operations for Hammarplast, a Swedish housewares company in New York, marketing coffeemakers to a number of retailers, including Starbucks. Through selling to Starbucks, Schultz was introduced to the three founders, who then recruited him to bring marketing savvy to their company. Schultz, 29 and recently married, was eager to leave New York. He joined Starbucks as manager of retail sales and marketing.

A year later, Schultz visited Italy for the first time on a buying trip. He noticed that coffee is an integral part of the culture in Italy; Italians start their day at an espresso bar and later in the day return with their friends. There are 200,000 coffee bars in Italy, and about 1,500 in Milan alone. Schultz believed that, given the chance, Americans would pay good money for a premium cup of coffee and a stylish place to enjoy it. Enthusiastic about his idea, Schultz returned to tell Starbucks' owners of his plan for a national chain of cafes styled on the Italian coffee bar. The owners, however, did not want to be in the restaurant business. Undaunted, Schultz wrote a business plan and began looking for investors. By April 1985 he had opened his first coffee bar, Il Giornale (named after the Italian newspaper), where he served Starbucks coffee. Following Il Giornale's immediate success, he expanded to three stores. In 1987 the owners of Starbucks agreed to sell the firm to Schultz for $4 million. The Il Giornale coffee bars took on the name of Starbucks.

Convinced that Starbucks would one day be in every neighborhood in America, Schultz focused on growth. At first, the company's losses almost doubled (to $1.2 million in fiscal 1990), as overhead and operating expenses ballooned with the expansion. Starbucks lost money for three years running, and the stress was hard on Schultz, but he stuck to his conviction not to "sacrifice long-term integrity and values for short-term profit."[3] In 1991 sales shot up 84 percent, and the company turned profitable. In 1992 Schultz took the firm public at $17 a share.

Believing that market share and name recognition were critical to the company's success, Schultz continued to expand the business aggressively. Schultz observed, "There is no secret sauce here. Anyone can do it." From the beginning, Schultz has professed a strict growth policy. Although many other coffeehouses or espresso bars are

Exhibit 1   Starbucks Selected Financial and Store Data
(In thousands, except earnings per share and store operating data)

	As of and for the Fiscal Year Ended[1]				
	Sept. 29, 2002 (52 Wks)	Sept. 30, 2001 (52 Wks)	Oct. 1, 2000 (52 Wks)	Oct. 3, 1999 (53 Wks)	Sept. 27, 1998 (52 Wks)
Results of Operations Data					
Net revenues:					
Retail	$ 2,792,904	$ 2,229,594	$ 1,823,607	$ 1,423,389	$ 1,102,574
Specialty	496,004	419,386	354,007	263,439	206,128
Total net revenues	3,288,908	2,648,980	2,177,614	1,686,828	1,308,702
Merger expenses[2]	—	—	—	—	8,930
Operating income	318,725	281,094	212,252	156,711	109,216
Internet-related investment losses	—	2,940	58,792	—	—
Gain on sale of investment	13,361	—	—	—	—
Net earnings	$ 215,073	$ 181,210	$ 94,564	$ 101,693	$ 68,372
Net earnings per common share—diluted	$ 0.54	$ 0.46	$ 0.24	$ 0.27	$ 0.19
Balance Sheet Data					
Working capital	$ 310,048	$ 148,661	$ 146,568	$ 135,303	$ 157,805
Total assets	2,292,736	1,846,519	1,491,546	1,252,514	992,755
Long-term debt (including current portion)	5,786	6,483	7,168	7,691	1,803
Shareholders' equity	1,726,638	1,375,927	1,148,399	961,013	794,297
Store Operating Data					
Percentage change in comparable store sales[3]					
North America	7%	5%	9%	6%	5%
International	(3)%	2%	23%	20%	28%
Consolidated	6%	5%	9%	6%	5%
Systemwide retail store sales[4]	$ 3,796,000	$ 2,950,000	$ 2,250,000	$ 1,633,000	$ 1,190,000
Systemwide stores opened during the year:[5]	1,177	1,208	1,003	612	474
Systemwide stores open at year end:					
Continental North America					
Company-operated stores	3,496	2,971	2,446	2,038	1,622
Licensed stores	1,078	809	530	179	133
International					
Company-operated stores	384	295	173	97	66
Licensed stores	928	634	352	184	65
Total	5,886	4,709	3,501	2,498	1,886

[1]The company's fiscal year ends on the Sunday closest to September 30. All fiscal years presented include 52 weeks, except fiscal 1999, which includes 53 weeks.

[2]Merger expenses relate to the business combination with Seattle Coffee Holdings Limited.

[3]Includes only company-operated stores open 13 months or longer.

[4]Systemwide retail store sales include sales at company-operated and licensed stores and are believed by management to measure global penetration of Starbucks retail stores.

[5]Systemwide store openings are reported net of closures.

Source: Starbucks Corporation.

franchised, Starbucks owns all of its North American stores outright, with the exception of license agreements in airports. Further, rather than trying to capture all the potential markets as soon as possible, Starbucks goes into a geographic market and tries to dominate it completely before setting its sights on further expansion. Using this strategy, Starbucks has grown from 17 coffee shops in 1987 to 5,688 outlets in 28 countries by the end of fiscal 2002 (see Exhibit 2). It also employed over 60,000 individuals, including approximately 50,000 in retail stores, at the end of 2002.

Starbucks Corporation is organized into two business units that correspond to the company's operating segments: North American and International. In 1995 Starbucks Coffee International, a wholly owned subsidiary of Starbucks Coffee Company, was set up to build Starbucks' businesses outside North America, including opening company-owned, licensed, and joint-venture-based retail stores worldwide.

A recent article in *BusinessWeek* noted:

> Starbucks also has a well-seasoned management team. Schultz, 49, stepped down as chief executive in 2000 to become chairman and chief global strategist. Orin Smith, 60, the company's numbers-cruncher, is now CEO and in charge of day-to-day operations. The head of North American operations is Howard Behar, 57, a retailing expert who returned last September, two years after retiring. The management trio is known as H$_2$O, for Howard, Howard, and Orin."[4]

Exhibit 3 provides a partial list of Starbucks' top management, and the Appendix on page 863 provides a timeline and history of Starbucks.

The Starbucks Model

Howard Schultz's goal was to: "Establish Starbucks as the premier purveyor of the finest coffee in the world while maintaining uncompromising principles as we grow." The company's 25-year goal is to "become an enduring, great company with the most recognized and respected brand in the world, known for inspiring and nurturing the human spirit." The company's mission statement articulates several guiding principles to measure the appropriateness of the firm's decisions (see Exhibit 4). In describing Starbucks' unique approach to competition, *Fortune* noted:

> The strategy is simple: Blanket an area completely, even if the stores cannibalize one another's business. A new store will often capture about 30% of the sales of a nearby Starbucks, but the company considers that a good thing: The Starbucks-everywhere approach cuts down on delivery and management costs, shortens customer lines at individual stores, and increases foot traffic for all the stores in an area. Last week 20 million people bought a cup of coffee at a Starbucks. A typical customer stops by 18 times a month; no American retailer has a higher frequency of customer visits. Sales have climbed an average of 20% a year since the company went public. Even in a down economy, when other retailers have taken a beating, Starbucks store traffic has

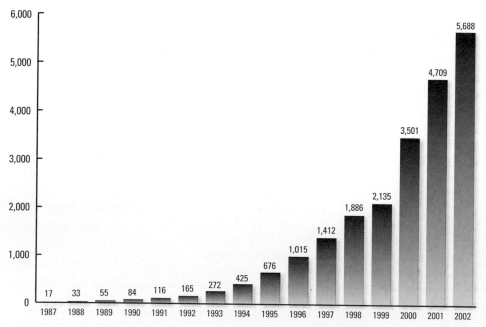

Exhibit 2   **Number of Starbucks Store Locations (As of November 2002)**

Source: Starbucks Corporation.

Exhibit 3   Starbucks Top Management Team

Howard Schultz is the founder of the company and has been chairman of the board since its inception in 1985. Mr. Schultz served as chief executive officer from 1985 until June 2000, when he transitioned into the role of chief global strategist. From 1985 to June 1994, Mr. Schultz was also the company's president. From September 1982 to December 1985, Mr. Schultz was the director of Retail Operations and Marketing for Starbucks Coffee Company, a predecessor to the company; and from January 1986 to July 1987, he was the chairman of the board, chief executive officer, and president of Il Giornale Coffee Company, a predecessor to the company.

Orin C. Smith joined Starbucks Corporation in 1990 and has served as president and chief executive officer of the company since June 2000. From June 1994 to June 2000, Mr. Smith served as the company's president and chief operating officer. Prior to June 1994, Mr. Smith served as the company's vice-president and chief financial officer and later, as its executive vice-president and chief financial officer.

Peter Maslen joined Starbucks in August 1999 as president, Starbucks Coffee International, Inc. Prior to joining Starbucks, Mr. Maslen served in various executive positions within Asia-Pacific and Europe with Mars Inc., PepsiCo, Inc., and Tricon Global Restaurants. From 1992 to 1999, as senior vice-president with Tricon, he served as president of its German, Swiss, Austrian, and Central Europe divisions.

Jim Donald joined Starbucks in November 2002 as president, Starbucks North America. He is responsible for managing Starbucks North America company-owned and licensed stores, business alliances (food service, grocery, club channels of distribution, joint venture partnerships with Pepsi-Cola Company and Dreyer's Grand Ice Cream, Inc.) in the United States and Canada, store development, retail systems, administration, and retail partner resources. Mr. Donald brings 32 years of experience in the retail and food industry. Prior to joining Starbucks, he was chairman, president and chief executive officer at Pathmark Stores, Inc., since 1996. In addition, he has held several senior leadership positions at top-tier retail companies including Safeway, Wal-Mart, and Albertson's.

Michael Casey joined Starbucks in August 1995 as senior vice-president and chief financial officer and was promoted to executive vice-president, chief financial officer, and chief administrative officer in September 1997. Prior to joining Starbucks, Mr. Casey served as executive vice-president and chief financial officer of Family Restaurants, Inc., from its inception in 1986. During his tenure there, he also served as a director from 1986 to 1993, and as president and chief executive officer of its El Torito Restaurants, Inc., subsidiary from 1988 to 1993.

Eduardo R. (Ted) Garcia joined Starbucks in April 1995 as senior vice-president, Supply Chain Operations, and was promoted to executive vice-president, Supply Chain and Coffee Operations, in September 1997. From May 1993 to April 1995, Mr. Garcia was an executive for Gemini Consulting. From January 1990 until May 1993, he was the vice-president of Operations Strategy for Grand Metropolitan PLC, Food Sector.

Source: Starbucks Corporation, November 2002.

---

risen between 6% and 8% a year. Perhaps even more notable is the fact that Starbucks has managed to generate those kinds of numbers with virtually no marketing, spending just 1% of its annual revenues on advertising. (Retailers usually spend 10% or so of revenues on ads.)[5]

BusinessWeek added:

Clustering stores increases total revenue and market share, [CEO] Orin Smith argues, even when individual stores poach on each other's sales. The strategy works, he says, because of Starbucks' size. It is large enough to

absorb losses at existing stores as new ones open up, and soon overall sales grow beyond what they would have with just one store. Meanwhile, it's cheaper to deliver to and manage stores located close together. And by clustering, Starbucks can quickly dominate a local market.[6]

And Schultz pointed out:

The market is much larger than we originally thought. . . . In most cases local competitors benefit from our arrival because of the expansion of the marketplace. Our strategy is never to eliminate or hurt the competition.

Exhibit 4   Starbucks Mission Statements and Guiding Principles

---

Mission Statement

Establish Starbucks as the premier purveyor of the finest coffee in the world while maintaining our uncompromising principles while we grow.

The following six guiding principles will help us measure the appropriateness of our decisions:

- Provide a great work environment and treat each other with respect and dignity.
- Embrace diversity as an essential component in the way we do business.
- Apply the highest standards of excellence to the purchasing, roasting, and fresh delivery of our coffee.
- Develop enthusiastically satisfied customers all of the time.
- Contribute positively to our communities and our environment.
- Recognize that profitability is essential to our future success.

Environmental Mission Statement

Starbucks is committed to a role of environmental leadership in all facets of our business.

We fulfill this mission by a commitment to:

- Understanding environmental issues and sharing information with our partners.
- Developing innovative and flexible solutions to bring about change.
- Striving to buy, sell, and use environmentally friendly products.
- Recognizing that fiscal responsibility is essential to our environmental future.
- Instilling environmental responsibility as a corporate value.
- Measuring and monitoring our progress for each project.
- Encouraging all partners to share in our mission.

Source: Starbucks Corporation.

We never under-price our coffee and it's clear that we position ourselves so as not to undercut the pricing structure in the marketplace.

Schultz observed that the company is still in its early days of growth worldwide. "We are opening three or four stores every day," he noted. "We feel strongly that the driver of the equity of the brand is directly linked to the retail experience we create in our stores. Our commitment to the growth of the company is significant and will continue to be based on the long-term growth potential of our retail format."

Securing the Finest Raw Materials   Starbucks' coffee quality begins with the purchase of high-quality *arabica* coffee beans. Although many Americans were raised on a commodity-like coffee made from lower-quality *robusta* beans (or arabica beans mixed with less-expensive filler beans), Starbucks coffee is strictly arabica, and the company ensures that only the highest-quality beans are used. Dave Olsen, the company's then senior

vice-president and chief coffee procurer, scoured mountain trails in Indonesia, Kenya, Guatemala, and elsewhere in search of Starbucks' premium bean. His standards were demanding, and he conducted exacting experiments in order to get the proper balance of flavor, body, and acidity.

From the company's inception, it has worked on developing relationships with the countries from which it buys coffee beans. Traditionally, Europeans and Japanese bought most of the premium coffee beans. Olsen sometimes had to convince coffee growers to sell to Starbucks—especially since American coffee buyers are notorious purchasers of the "dregs" of the coffee beans. In 1992 Starbucks set a new precedent by outbidding European buyers for the exclusive Narino Supremo bean crop.[7] Starbucks collaborated with a mill in the tiny town of Pasto, located on the side of the Volcano Galero. There they set up a special operation to single out the particular Narino Supremo bean, and Starbucks guaranteed to purchase the entire yield. This enabled Starbucks to be the exclusive purveyor of Narino Supremo, purportedly one of the best coffees in the world.[8]

Roasting Roasting the coffee bean is close to an art form at Starbucks. Starbucks currently operates multiple roasting and distribution facilities. Roasters are promoted from within the company and trained for over a year, and it is considered quite an honor to be chosen. The coffee is roasted in a powerful gas-fired drum roaster for 12 to 15 minutes while roasters use sight, smell, hearing, and computers to judge when beans are perfectly done. The color of the beans is even tested in an Agtron blood-cell analyzer, with the whole batch being discarded if the sample is not deemed perfect.

The Starbucks Experience According to Schultz, "We're not just selling a cup of coffee, we are providing an experience." In order to create American coffee enthusiasts with the dedication of their Italian counterparts, Starbucks provides a seductive atmosphere in which to imbibe. Its stores are distinctive and sleek, yet comfortable. Though the sizes of the stores and their formats vary, most are modeled after the Italian coffee bars where regulars sit and drink espresso with their friends.

Starbucks stores tend to be located in high-traffic locations such as malls, busy street corners, and even grocery stores. They are well lighted and feature plenty of light cherry wood and artwork. The people who prepare the coffee are referred to as "baristas," Italian for bartender. Jazz or opera music plays softly in the background. The stores range from 200 to 4,000 square feet, with new units tending to range from 1,500 to 1,700 square feet. In 2003 the average cost of opening a new store (including equipment, inventory, and leasehold improvements) is in the neighborhood of $350,000; a "flagship" store costs much more.

Building a Unique Culture While Starbucks enforces almost fanatical standards about coffee quality and service, the policy at Starbucks toward employees is laid-back and supportive. They are encouraged to think of themselves as partners in the business. Schultz believes that happy employees are the key to competitiveness and growth.

> We can't achieve our strategic objectives without a workforce of people who are immersed in the same commitment as management. Our only sustainable advantage is the quality of our workforce. We're building a national retail company by creating pride in—and stake in—the outcome of our labor.[9]

On a practical level, Starbucks promotes an empowered employee culture through generous benefits programs, an employee stock ownership plan, and thorough employee training, Each employee must have at least 24 hours of training. Classes cover everything from coffee history to a seven-hour workshop called "Brewing the Perfect Cup at Home." This workshop is one of five classes that all employees must complete during their first six weeks with the company. Reports *Fortune:*

It's silly, soft-headed stuff, though basically, of course, it's true. Maybe some of it sinks in. Starbucks is a smashing success, thanks in large part to the people who come out of these therapy-like training programs. Annual barista turnover at the company is 60 percent compared with 140 percent for hourly workers in the fast-food business.[10]

Starbucks offers its benefits package to both part-time and full-time employees. The package includes medical, dental, vision, and short-term disability insurance, as well as paid vacation, paid holidays, mental health/chemical dependency benefits, an employee assistance program, a 401(k) savings plan, and a stock option plan. It also offers dependent coverage that includes same-sex partners.[11] Schultz believes that without these benefits, people do not feel financially or spiritually tied to their jobs. He argued that stock options and the complete benefits package increase employee loyalty and encourage attentive service to the customer.[12]

Employee turnover is also discouraged by Starbucks' stock option plan known as the Bean Stock Plan. Implemented in August 1991, the plan made Starbucks the only private company to offer stock options unilaterally to all employees.

Starbucks' concern for employee welfare extends beyond its retail outlets to coffee producers. The company's guidelines call for overseas suppliers to pay wages and benefits that "address the basic needs of workers and their families" and to allow child labor only when it does not interrupt required education.[13] This move has set a precedent for other importers of agricultural commodities.

Leveraging the Brand *Multiple Channels of Distribution* Besides its stand-alone stores, Starbucks has set up cafes and carts in hospitals, banks, office buildings, supermarkets, and shopping centers. Other distribution agreements have included office coffee suppliers, hotels, and airlines. Office coffee is a large segment of the coffee market. Associated Services (an office coffee supplier) provides Starbucks coffee exclusively to thousands of businesses around the United States. Starbucks has deals with airlines, such as an agreement with United Airlines to provide Starbucks coffee to United's nearly 75 million passengers a year. Starbucks, through a licensing agreement with Kraft Foods Inc., offers its coffee in grocery stores across the United States.

Brand Extensions In 1995 Starbucks launched a line of packaged and prepared teas in response to growing demand for teahouses and packaged tea. Tea is a highly profitable beverage for restaurants to sell, costing only 2 cents to 4 cents a cup to produce.[14] As its tea line became increasingly popular, the company in January 1999 acquired Tazo, a tea company based in Portland, Oregon.

Starbucks coffee is also making its way onto grocery shelves by way of a carefully planned series of joint ventures.[15] An agreement with PepsiCo Inc. brought a bottled version of Starbucks Frappuccino (a cold, sweetened coffee drink) to store shelves in August 1996. In another 50–50 partnership, Dreyer's Grand Ice Cream Inc. distributes seven quart-product and two bar-product varieties of Starbucks coffee ice cream.

Other partnerships by the company are designed to form new product associations with coffee. For instance, the company's music subsidiary, Hear Music, regularly releases CDs, some in collaboration with major record labels, that are then sold through Starbucks retail stores.

While Starbucks is the largest and best known of the coffeehouse chains and its presence is very apparent in metropolitan areas, the firm's estimates indicate that only a small percentage (about 7 percent) of the U.S. population has tried its products. Through distribution agreements and the new product partnerships, Starbucks hopes to capture more of the U.S. market.

International Expansion

For many years analysts have observed that the U.S. coffee bar market may be reaching saturation. They have pointed to market consolidation, as bigger players snapped up some of the smaller coffee bar competitors.[16] Further, they have noted that Starbucks' store base is also maturing, leading to a slowdown in the growth of unit volume and firm profitability. In response, some have argued, Starbucks has turned its attention to foreign markets for continued growth. For instance, *BusinessWeek* noted:

> To duplicate the staggering returns of its first decade, Starbucks has no choice but to export its concept aggressively. Indeed, some analysts give Starbucks only two years at most before it saturates the U.S. market. The chain now [in August 2002] operates 1,200 international outlets, from Beijing to Bristol. That leaves plenty of room to grow. Indeed, about 400 of its planned 1,200 new stores this year will be built overseas, representing a 35 percent increase in its foreign base. Starbucks expects to double the number of its stores worldwide, to 10,000 in three years.[17]

However, of the predicted three or four stores that will open each day, the majority will continue to be in the United States.

Early Expansion   In 1995 the firm established a subsidiary called Starbucks Coffee International, Inc. At that time, the subsidiary consisted of 12 managers located in Seattle. Today this subsidiary is led by Australian expatriate Peter Maslen and is staffed with about 180 experienced multinational and multilingual managers located in Seattle and three regional offices around the world. This group is responsible for all of Starbucks' business development outside North America, including developing new businesses, financing and planning stores, managing operations and logistics, merchandising, and training and developing Starbucks' international managers.

Starbucks' first non-North American store was opened in 1996 in Tokyo. In reflecting on this early step in internationalizing the chain, Schultz noted:

> Two years prior to opening up in Japan, we hired this blue-chip consulting firm to guide us to succeed here. Basically, they said we would not succeed in Japan. There were a number of things they told us to change. [They said] we had to have smoking, but that was a nonstarter for us. They also said no Japanese would ever lose face by drinking from a cup in the street. And third, they said that given the [high] rent, stores couldn't be larger than 500 square feet . . . Well, our no-smoking policy made us an oasis in Japan. As for our to-go business, you can't walk down a street in Tokyo today and not see someone holding a cup of Starbucks coffee. And our store size in Japan is identical to our store size in the United States, about 1,200 to 1,500 square feet. It just shows the power of believing in what you do. And also that Starbucks is as relevant in Tokyo, Madrid, or Berlin as it is in Seattle.[18]

The Starbucks Way   According to *US News and World Report*:

> When venturing overseas, there is a Starbucks way. The company finds local business partners in most foreign markets . . . It tests each country with a handful of stores in trendy districts, using experienced Starbucks managers. It sends local baristas to Seattle for 13 weeks of training. Then it starts opening stores by the dozen. Its coffee lineup doesn't vary, but Starbucks does adapt its food to local tastes. In Britain, it won an award for its mince pie. In Asia, Starbucks offers curry puffs and meat buns. The company also fits its interior decor to the local architecture, especially in historic buildings. "We don't stamp these things out cookie-cutter style," says Peter Maslen, president of Starbucks Coffee International.[19]

Although Starbucks is committed to owning its North American stores, it has sought partners for much of its overseas expansion. As Kathy Lindemann, senior vice-president of Operations for Starbucks International, describes it:

> Our approach to international expansion is to focus on the *partnership first, country second*. We rely on the local connection to get everything up and working. The key is finding the right local partners to negotiate local regulations and other issues. We look for partners who share our values, culture, and goals about community development. We are primarily interested in partners who can guide us through the process of starting up in a foreign location. We look for firms with: (1) a similar philosophy to ours in terms of shared values, corporate

citizenship, and commitment to be in the business for the long haul, (2) multiunit restaurant experience, (3) financial resources to expand the Starbucks concept rapidly to prevent imitators, (4) strong real-estate experience with knowledge about how to pick prime real estate locations, (5) knowledge of the retail market, and (6) the availability of the people to commit to our project.

In an international joint venture, it is the partner that chooses store sites. These are submitted for approval to Starbucks, but the partner does all the preparatory and selection work. Cydnie Horwat, vice-president for International Assets Development Systems & Infrastructure, explains how a Starbucks market entry plan starts with brand building, which then facilitates rapid further expansion in a country:

When first entering a market, we're looking for different things in the first one to three years than later on. During these early years, we're building our brand. Our stores are the biggest source of advertising, since we do not do a lot of separate advertising. So we have a higher investment in stores in the first three years. About 60–70 percent of stores opened in these first three years are our high brand-builders.

Horwat added:

First, we look for extremely visible sites in well-trafficked areas and focus on three major factors: demographics, branding potential, and financials. Second, we categorize sites on an A to D scale. "A" sites are "signature" sites that are qualitatively superior to all other sites within the trade area [an area within which Starbucks chooses to locate one store]. We rarely take a "C" or "D" store.[20] Third, we ask our international Market Business Unit[21] (MBU) to send in the "site" submittal package with quantitative and qualitative measures, such as how the site meets Starbucks' established criteria and the partner's agreed-upon criteria. This package is reviewed by a number of functional units—operations, finance, and real estate—within the International Group. Fourth, we move into the design phase, which is done in Seattle using information provided by the partner. Next we negotiate the lease with the landlord and initiate the construction when the appropriate permits are obtained. Finally, we turn over the store to operations. The whole process takes about 13–16 weeks from start to finish.

Establishing Starbucks as a Global Brand

Based on the success in Japan and other locations, Schultz's goal is for Starbucks to have a ubiquitous image as one of the most respected brands in the world. He noted:

Whenever we see the reception we're getting in markets in places such as China, the Philippines, Malaysia, the U.K., and most recently Spain and Germany, we recognize that the growth potential for the company [overseas]

is very significant. We want to accelerate that growth, maintain our leadership position, and, ultimately, become one of the most respected brands in the world.[22]

Since its early foray into the Japanese market, the pace of international expansion has picked up significantly. In 1998 Starbucks acquired Seattle Coffee Company in the United Kingdom, a chain with more than 38 retail locations. That same year, it opened stores in Taiwan, Thailand, New Zealand, and Malaysia. In 1999 Starbucks opened in China (Beijing), Kuwait, South Korea, and Lebanon. In 2000 it entered another seven markets (China—Hong Kong and Shanghai, Dubai, Australia, Qatar, Saudi Arabia, and Bahrain). It added three markets in 2001 (Switzerland, Israel, and Austria). Last year, another nine markets were opened (Oman, Spain, Indonesia, Germany, Southern China—Macau and Shenzhen, Mexico, Puerto Rico, and Greece). Exhibit 5 highlights the growth of international stores, and Exhibit 6 provides the list of countries where Starbucks has a presence.

Schultz says that this expansion is only beginning and confidently predicts more to come:

Ten years ago, we had 125 stores and 2,000 employees. Today we have 62,000 people working in 30 countries outside of North America, serving approximately 22 million customers a week. Our core customer is coming in about 18 times a month. With the majority of adults around the world drinking two cups of coffee a day and with Starbucks having less than a 7 percent share of total coffee consumption in the United States and less than 1 percent worldwide, these are the early days for the growth and development of the company. We've got a model that has been well tested from market to market.

Starbucks is well on its way to becoming a global brand. According to *BusinessWeek:*

[T]he Starbucks name and image connect with millions of consumers around the globe. It was one of the fastest-growing brands in a *BusinessWeek* survey of the top 100 global brands published August 5 [2002]. At a time when one corporate star after another has crashed to earth, brought down by revelations of earnings misstatements, executive greed, or worse, Starbucks hasn't faltered.[23]

But becoming a global company is not without risks. As *BusinessWeek* pointed out,

Global expansion poses huge risks for Starbucks. For one thing, it makes less money on each overseas store because most of them are operated with local partners. While that makes it easier to start up on foreign turf, it reduces the company's share of the profits to only 20 percent to 50 percent."[24]

In addition, the firm is becoming a target for antiglobalization activists around the world.

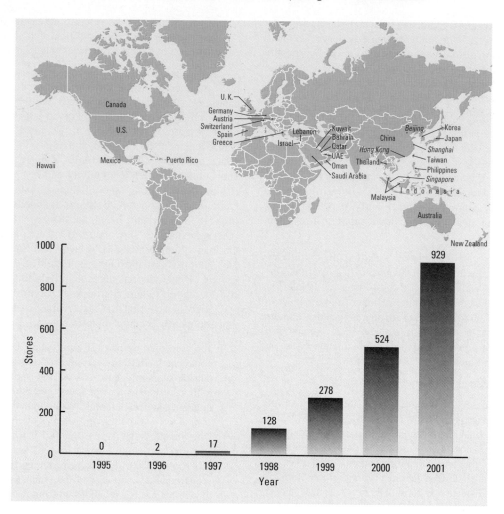

Exhibit 5   Growth of International Stores, 1995–2001

Source: Starbucks International Group.

Perils of Globalization

As Starbucks establishes a global presence, its growing ubiquity has not gone unnoticed by antiglobalization activists. A clear manifestation of this came in November 1999, as tens of thousands of protesters took to the streets of downtown Seattle when the World Trade Organization (WTO) held its third ministerial conference there. Although nongovernmental organizations (NGOs) and activists had gathered to oppose the WTO, some activists deliberately targeted multinationals like Starbucks, Nike, and McDonald's.[25] A small, but vocal, percentage of these protestors garnered international press coverage by committing acts of vandalism against carefully chosen targets.

Protesters flooded Seattle's streets, and among their targets was Starbucks, a symbol, to them, of free-market capitalism run amok, another multinational out to blan-

ket the earth. Amid the crowds of protesters and riot police were black-masked anarchists who trashed the store, leaving its windows smashed and its tasteful green-and-white decor smelling of tear gas instead of espresso.[26]

Recalling this incident against his firm, Schultz said: "It's hurtful. I think people are ill-informed. It's very difficult to protest against a can of Coke, a bottle of Pepsi, or a can of Folgers. Starbucks is both a ubiquitous brand and a place where you can go and break a window. You can't break a can of Coke."

Antiglobalization protesters target recognizable global brands because they are convenient symbols. The following excerpt from "The Ruckus Society's Action Planning Manual" illustrates the close ties between global brands and the principles of direct action against them:[27]

Exhibit 6 **Licensed Starbucks International Stores (as of September 2002)**

Asia-Pacific		Europe/Middle East/Africa		Latin America/ International	
Japan	397	United Arab Emirates	23	Hawaii	30
Taiwan	99	Saudi Arabia	22	Mexico	1
China	88	Kuwait	16	Puerto Rico	1
South Korea	53	Switzerland	12		
Philippines	49	Lebanon	11		
New Zealand	34	Israel	6		
Singapore	32	Austria	5		
Malaysia	26	Spain	5		
Indonesia	5	Germany	4		
		Qatar	3		
		Bahrain	2		
		Greece	2		
		Oman	2		
Total	783		113		32

Product sales to, and royalty and license fee revenues from, licensed international retail stores accounted for approximately 17% of specialty revenues in fiscal 2002.

These figures do not include company-operated stores.

Source: Starbucks 10-K report.

First, [we] use direct action to reduce the issues to symbols. These symbols must be carefully chosen for their utility in illustrating a conflict: an oil company vs. an indigenous community, a government policy vs. the public interest. Then we work to place these symbols in the public eye, in order to identify the evildoer, detail the wrongdoing and, if possible, point to a more responsible option.

The message that activists want to communicate focuses on the overseas activities of corporations. They accuse multinationals of paying less than a living wage to workers in the Third World, of engaging in labor and environmental practices that would be outlawed in their home countries, of driving local competitors out of business, and of furthering "cultural imperialism." As one Global Trade Watch field organizer described it:

The rules by which trade is governed need to have more to do with the interests of citizens than with the back pockets and cash wads of a couple of corporate CEOs. And we want to make sure that there is a balance consideration. Obviously people are always going to be concerned with their profits—it's business, we understand that, we accept that. But we think that needs to be balanced with concern for the rights of workers, basic human rights, [and] protecting the environment.[28]

Critics further accuse international organizations like the WTO, World Bank, and the International Monetary Fund (IMF) of promoting corporate globalization by supporting trade liberalization, by promoting export-based economic development, and by facilitating foreign direct investment. According to an organization that bills itself as Mobilization for Global Justice:

Most of the world's most impoverished countries have suffered under IMF/World Bank programs for two decades: They've seen debt levels rise, unemployment skyrocket, poverty increase, and environments devastated. Urged to export, they focus on cash crops like coffee instead of food for their own people, and allow foreign governments to build sweatshops—which also puts pressure on jobs in the U.S.[29]

When Starbucks opened its first store in Mexico in September 2002, it chose a site in the Sheraton Hotel on the Paseo de la Reforma (Boulevard of the Reform) in Mexico City. This was Starbucks' first store in Latin America and its first in an "origin country," that is, a coffee-producing country. An article on the Organic Consumers Association Web site described Starbucks' Mexican flagship store:

> The new Starbucks on Reforma features soft lighting and an aromatic ambiance. . . . Behind the counter, well-groomed employees whip out the signature Frappuccinos and lattes. Indeed, the only jarring note is the 36 pesos ($3.60) the young woman at the register wants for a double latte, 10 times the price Indian farmers are getting for a pound of their product in Chiapas, Oaxaca, and other coffee-rich states of southern Mexico. . . . There is no starker contrast in the economics of coffee these days than between the cushy comforts and gourmet blends of the Starbucks "Experiencia" and the grim, daily existence of 360,000 mostly Indian coffee farmers who work small plots carved from the jungle mountains of southern Mexico.[30]

Multinational corporations and their supporters responded that the effects of—and solutions for—globalization are more complicated than the critics contend. They noted that multinationals create jobs, pay better prices and wages than domestic firms, and conform to *local* labor and environmental regulations.

> The skeptics are right to be disturbed by sweatshops, child labor, bonded labor and the other gross abuses that go on in many poor countries (and in the darkest corners of rich ones, too). But what makes people vulnerable to these practices is poverty. . . . The more thoroughly these companies [multinationals] penetrate the markets of the Third World, the faster they introduce their capital and working practices, the sooner poverty will retreat and the harder it will be for such abuses to persist.[31]

Moreover, multinationals argued, they have responded to the criticism of profit-driven behavior by developing corporate codes of conduct, corporate social responsibility programs, and partnerships with nongovernmental organizations.[32] They pointed out, however, that they are in a no–win situation vis-à-vis their critics, because they can always be criticized for not doing enough.

Starbucks has found that global concerns often get mixed up with and intertwined with local issues. Even the mere act of opening a Starbucks retail store in a neighborhood can result in local activism and community "push-back" against the Starbucks brand. For example, when Starbucks opened a store in Cambridge, Massachusetts, in 1998, it was greeted by picketers carrying signs that read, "Don't Let Corporate Greed Destroy Our

Neighborhood." A lawyer who helps communities keep national chains out, said: "It's part of the growing tension in the world between the mass-market economy and people's desire to retain self-control and some local culture. . . . If you've got a beef with Starbucks, you've got a beef with capitalism."[33]

Starbucks has faced a variety of "community push-back" situations around the world. Soon Beng Yeap, one of Starbucks International brand reputation managers, noted: "This [community push-back] is a live issue and Starbucks manages each push-back incident case by case. In some markets [we] have gone in and in some [we] have pulled out." He cited two recent examples, one in London, where Starbucks decided to withdraw its efforts to open a store after local activists actively campaigned against the firm, and the other in Beijing, where the firm opened a store in a historic district and, following subsequent and significant adverse comment reported in local and international media, decided to stay put.

Primrose Hill and Starbucks' Decision to Withdraw   In 2002 Starbucks made plans to open a store in Primrose Hill, a London suburb. Located in North West London, Primrose Hill is a well-known historical and picturesque area comprised of a public park, a shopping "village" area, and attractive Victorian residential housing. Residents of Primrose Hill—many of whom are writers, photographers, actors, and musicians—take great pride in the area and are protective of their local environment, acting to ensure that no chain stores operate in the area.[34]

In early 2002 Starbucks selected Primrose Hill as a potential site for a store and submitted an application to the local council. When this information was published in the local papers, it received considerable negative feedback from the residents, in particular from the Primrose Hill Conservation Area Advisory Committee. This committee claimed that litter, noise, and disruption from deliveries to Starbucks store in Primrose Hill would ruin the village ambience and contribute to the "homogenization of the high street." The opposition surprised Starbucks because Primrose Hill residents, associations (including the Primrose Hill Conservation Area Advisory Committee), and businesses had been contacted as part of consultation period for the potential site. Although the objections to Starbucks' entry focused on local planning issues, there was an antiglobalization element as well. One critic was quoted saying that Starbucks was "renowned for not paying proper money to coffee growers."[35]

In response to the critics, Starbucks offered to arrange meetings between the planning committee, local councillors, and its representatives to discuss the issue and hear their concerns. Despite Starbucks' efforts, no meeting offers were accepted and minimal responses were received.

In the meantime, the Primrose Hill Conservation Area Advisory Committee began to campaign strongly against Starbucks. It collected more than 1,300 letters of objection, which it then presented to the local council. Many celebrities, such as the actor Jude Law, National Theatre director Nicholas Hytner, broadcaster Joan Bakewell, singer Neneh Cherry, author Jeanette Winterson, and artist Patrick Caufield, lent their support by opposing the Starbucks application. Media coverage that was initially local became national when celebrities became involved. According to Horwat, the vice-president for International Assets Development Systems for Starbucks:

> Primrose Hill was an "A" site. A very affluent neighborhood, little or no competition and we knew it would be a winner. Everyone [at Starbucks Coffee International] loved it. The real estate people, the finance people, and others signed off on the deal. Opposition came only when city council was about to approve [our application]. The opposition claimed that our entry would raise rents in the community. So we went back to city council to argue our case. But activists brought in movie stars and got local and national media attention.

In early June 2002, when it was apparent that Starbucks was not welcome in Primrose Hill, the company decided against opening the store. Reflecting on the decision to withdraw, Horwat explained:

> We care about the views of the communities of which we are a part. We try to have our stores be part of a community. We had hoped to make a positive contribution for people to get together in Primrose Hill. If the community does not welcome us, it's not someplace we want to be.

Soon Beng Yeap added:

> You have to understand the bigger picture in the U.K. to appreciate what was going on locally at that time—Starbucks was seen as an American chain coming into the British market and the British media tend to be very cynical. The specialty coffee market was becoming crowded and extremely competitive with several other chains such as Café Nero, Coffee Republic, and Costa Coffee making a strong push for market share. The Starbucks team reviewed all the factors involved as well as listened carefully to the community concerns. At the end of the day, we decided to withdraw our application.

Beijing and Starbucks' Decision to Stay   Starbucks opened its first outlet in Beijing in January 1999 and has over 100 stores in China today. However, Starbucks touched a nationalist nerve in 2000 when it opened a small coffee shop in Beijing's Forbidden City.[36] In highlighting this particular store, the *New York Times* noted:

> If ever there was an emblem of the extremes to which globalization has reached, this is it: mass-market American coffee culture in China's most hallowed historic place. Even a McDonald's in the Kremlin would not come as close. Starbucks opened its Forbidden City shop a month ago [September 2000] with a signature menu board advertising the usual Americano and decaf latte coffee and a glass display case filled with fresh glazed donuts, cinnamon rings, and banana walnut muffins.[37]

Starbucks, for its part, had taken extraordinary care to ensure that its presence was unobtrusive. To avoid ruining the atmosphere of the Forbidden City, the signs and brand images were placed inside for this store. This small store (barely a closet according to some reports) had only two small tables and few chairs. It was located on the edge of the Forbidden City, among 50 other retailers, including some selling souvenirs and trinkets. Despite such a low-key presence, this store ignited controversy. Dozens of Chinese newspapers reported on reactions to the shop. According to one report in the *People's Daily:*

> The reason for the uproar is due to the cafe's location: the Forbidden City, the world's largest imperial palace . . . First constructed in 1406, the Forbidden City is China's best-preserved ancient architecture encircled by a rampart of three kilometers. The cafe, named Starbucks, is situated in the southeastern corner of the Hall of Preserving Harmony (Baohedian), one of the three most impressive buildings on the palace ground. The hall used to be the venue to hold feasts by emperors and nobles of ethnic groups on New Year's Eve of China's lunar calendar. . . . Debates over the mini-cafe took place first on the Web. A survey by Sina.com showed that over 70 percent of nearly 60,000 people surveyed were opposed to the cafe's entry into the Forbidden City, the main reason being the damaging effects to the Chinese cultural heritage and its atmosphere.[38]

The administrators of the Forbidden Palace and other government officials took note of the controversy but were supportive of Starbucks. Chen Junqi, a spokesperson for the Forbidden City Museum, maintained that allowing Starbucks into the Forbidden City was part of their efforts to improve services in the area. Moreover, Chen added: "The reaction has been very intense. Some people say this is a gem of Chinese culture and that foreign brands should not be allowed in. . . . We can't give up eating for the fear of choking."[39]

According to Horwat:

> The Forbidden City location was a "C" site at best. But definitely not a "D" site, because there was still the benefit of brand presence. But the government said, "We think you should come in," and it was difficult to say no. There was no local community, only tourists.

Following the flurry of articles in the Chinese media, CNN began to run news clips of this story in the United States. Watching this unfold in the U.S. media, some

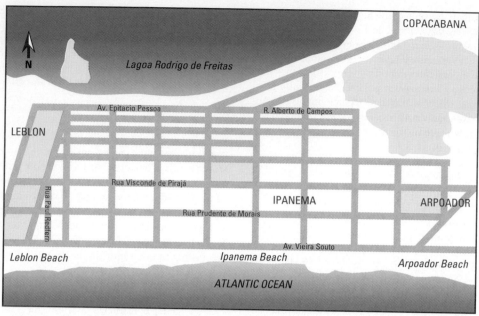

Exhibit 7   Map of the Ipanema Area, Rio de Janeiro, Brazil

Source: www.ipanema.com

senior managers at Starbucks became alarmed at the negative publicity. According to Soon Beng Yeap:

> The immediate reaction was to "close the store!" due to the relentless negative coverage generated by the international media. After serious discussion among the senior executives, we felt as guests in a foreign country, we should be respectful of our hosts—the Forbidden City officials—who invited us to be there in the first place. We decided to not pull out because it was the international media that stirred up the whole controversy. Unlike the Primrose Hill case, there was no real local community "push-back." It was all media-driven. A few reporters got hold of the story and ran with it, all citing the same survey by Sina.com. We were very disappointed by the negative media coverage, which created a false sense of "cultural imperialism" about our intentions in opening the store, especially when we worked very hard to be culturally sensitive and listen to the local community.

The controversy has since died down, as a recent report (February 2003) in the *Straits Times* of Singapore indicated:

> [Today] if anything, the tourists were more upset than the Beijing residents about the presence of Starbucks in the Forbidden City, complaining that it was out of place in a historical site . . . Asked what were the hottest issues of the day for ordinary citizens, taxi driver Liu Zhiming said: "Cars, apartments, and making money. What else?"[40]

Entering Rio De Janeiro, Brazil

Peter Maslen, president of Starbucks Coffee International, hurriedly convened a meeting of his key executives in Starbucks International, including Julio Gutierrez, his president for Latin America. Starbucks' entry into Brazil was in jeopardy, because certain activists opposing Starbucks' presence in the country were gaining momentum.

Brazil is the largest coffee-producing country in the world, and this was Starbucks' second foray into Latin America (after Mexico). The company chose not to seek a joint venture partner to enter Brazil. Since many copycat chains had sprung up in Rio de Janeiro, some imitating Starbucks to the last detail, Maslen felt that his team had to move quickly before any particular group established itself as the premier chain. After several years of work by Gutierrez's Latin America team, no suitable joint venture partner had been identified, and Maslen was considering establishing a 100 percent Starbucks owned MBU (as it had already done in the U.K., Australia, and Thailand).

The business development group, with Gutierrez's team, had picked a site in the Ipanema area of Rio de Janeiro. They proposed that a flagship store be opened on this neighborhood's main commercial street—Rua Visconde de Pirajá (see Exhibit 7). Many of Rio's most traditional boutiques started in Ipanema, later to be exported to the malls and other parts of town. Many world-renowned brands such as Cartier, Louis Vuitton, and Polo Ralph Lauren had stores on the Rua Visconde de Pirajá. It is often said that news in Ipanema makes headlines all over Brazil.

Starbucks had also chosen other sites, four to be specific, where the company could open stores immediately following the opening of the flagship Ipanema store. One of these stores was to be located in the posh neighborhood of Barra de Tijuca; another was slated for Leblon, and two others for shopping malls located in affluent residential neighborhoods in the city. The Real Estate group was ready to sign the lease with the agents of the Ipanema property owner, but was awaiting a formal response from the city council members.

The business development group, led by Troy Alstead, senior vice-president of finance and business development at Starbucks International, was confident that the Ipanema location was an "A" category site. "The demographics of this area are just right for a flagship store. They are affluent, young, and love American brands." The business development group's financial projections indicated that the Ipanema Starbucks store would be profitable in a short time, and Alstead believed that this was a conservative figure. Further, he pointed out:

> Based on the company's experiences of opening flagship stores in similar, high traffic posh neighborhoods in other cites around the world—our store in Ginza, Japan comes to mind—we believe the Ipanema store would be viable for Starbucks. We estimate meeting store level ROI targets in aggregate for the first five stores within two years.

Exhibit 8 provides the finance group's forecast for the Ipanema and the other four stores in Brazil for the first five years of operations.

But Maslen had some concerns. He was troubled by reports of rising levels of violence and street crime in Rio de Janeiro and São Paulo. In response to this growing violence, some of the most fashionable retailers were relocating themselves in shopping malls. He also questioned whether the timing for Starbucks was off. Current world events had generated anti-American feeling in many countries.

Following the standard practice, Starbucks had been working with the local chamber of commerce since January 2003, and with the local city council for the required permits. The members of the city council and local chamber of commerce were positive about granting Starbucks permission to begin construction. While the formal voting had yet to be undertaken, it looked certain that, barring anything unusual, permission would be granted.

But nongovernmental organizations like the Organic Consumers Association and Global Exchange were mobilizing faster than expected to oppose Starbucks' entry into Brazil. They found out about Starbucks' intent to enter Brazil when the Ipanema district chamber of commerce newsletter proudly announced that, "We are extremely pleased to welcome Starbucks into the fashionable district of Ipanema. By opening a store in our neighborhood, they will join other global brands and help enhance further our district's image as *the* place to be in Rio."

The NGOs were recruiting local activists and had informed Starbucks that they would oppose its entry into Brazil by petitioning the local council to reject its application. They also threatened to start picketing in front of the store once construction was initiated. The "brand" group at Starbucks was concerned about the turn of events. Soon Beng elaborated:

> People in Latin America know the brand because of their proximity to the U.S. Potential partners are always contacting us about coming in. Before we go into a place like Brazil, what is the due diligence we have to do? It's an origin country for us [i.e., coffee-producing country]. It's a very vocal place, and there is a love-hate relationship with the United States. Finance people always want to say yes to a store when the numbers look good. Today some in Starbucks, at least in our group, say that maintaining and protecting our strong "brand" reputation is equally important. Others counter: If our brand is strong then why worry about it? This is a discussion we have here every day in the company. While the "push-back" is not totally unexpected, it is hard to gauge to the severity of the situation and its likely impact on our brand.

Maslen asked Alstead's business development group to work with Gutierrez's Latin American team to estimate how the picketing in front of the store might impact the financial projections his group had prepared. Their answer:

> Our financial estimates for the Ipanema store are based on comparables from other flagship stores in locations similar to Rio in other parts of the world. Our financial models are sensitive to the demographics of the area. We project that demand could fall from 5 to 25 percent, because of people picketing in front of the store. We acknowledge it is much harder to guess what the impact on our entire system in Brazil might be as we open new stores. It all depends upon the type of media coverage the activists are able to muster and the issues the media choose to highlight.

Soon Beng Yeap volunteered:

> The tide of public opinion is unpredictable. We review each "push-back" incident the best we can, and we have a reasonable track record of predicting outcomes. But, every time we walk into a potential site somewhere in the world, we potentially face this [push-back]. It would be great to have a foolproof tool or system to help us evaluate these sorts of issues and make the appropriate decisions.

Maslen had to leave Seattle to attend an important meeting in Europe the following day. He called together his key managers and said,

Exhibit 8   Financial Analysis for the First Five Brazilian Stores

Projected Profits and Losses for Ipanema Store (US$)					
	Year 1	**Year 2**	**Year 3**	**Year 4**	**Year 5**
Net sales[1]	$ 1,000,000	$ 1,100,000	$ 1,210,000	$ 1,270,500	$ 1,334,025
Cost of goods sold[2]	350,000	330,000	326,700	343,035	360,187
Gross profit	$ 650,000	$ 770,000	$ 883,300	$ 927,465	$ 973,838
Staff costs	200,000	225,000	250,000	250,000	250,000
Marketing[3]	75,000	50,000	50,000	50,000	50,000
Other costs	75,000	100,000	125,000	125,000	125,000
Occupancy costs	175,000	175,000	175,000	175,000	175,000
Total costs	$ 525,000	$ 550,000	$ 600,000	$ 600,000	$ 600,000
Operating cash flow	$ 125,000	$ 220,000	$ 283,300	$ 327,465	$ 373,838
Depreciation[4]	54,200	54,200	54,200	54,200	54,200
Store pretax profit	$ 70,800	$ 165,800	$ 229,100	$ 273,265	$ 319,638
Construction costs[5]	$ 400,000				
Key money[6]	$ 1,000,000				

Projected Profits and Losses for a "Typical" Store in Locations outside the Ipanema Area (US$)*					
	Year 1	**Year 2**	**Year 3**	**Year 4**	**Year 5**
Net sales[1]	$ 625,000	$ 650,000	$ 700,000	$ 735,000	$ 771,750
Cost of goods sold[2]	218,750	195,000	189,000	198,450	208,373
Gross profit	$ 406,250	$ 455,000	$ 511,000	$ 536,550	$ 563,378
Staff costs	100,000	115,000	135,000	135,000	135,000
Marketing[3]	45,000	30,000	30,000	30,000	30,000
Other costs	60,000	75,000	75,000	75,000	75,000
Occupancy costs	70,000	70,000	70,000	70,000	70,000
Operating cash flow	$ 131,250	$ 165,000	$ 201,000	$ 226,550	$ 253,378
Depreciation[4]	25,000	25,000	25,000	25,000	25,000
Store pretax profit	$ 106,250	$ 140,000	$ 176,000	$ 201,550	$ 228,378
Construction costs[5]	$ 215,000				
Key money[6]	$ 400,000				

*Starbucks intends to open four such stores in Rio, in addition to the one in Ipanema.

[1]Net sales are projected to grow at 10% for years 1 and 2, and at 5% thereafter.

[2]Due to increases in efficiency, the cost of goods sold are estimated at 35% for year 1, 30% for year 2, and 27% thereafter.

[3]Marketing costs are higher for year 1.

[4]Straight-line 10-year depreciation for construction and equipment costs.

[5]These represent initial design and construction costs.

[6]Monies paid to the landlord to secure the site.

Look, we've experienced a variety of "push-backs" and protests before. What lessons have we learned? We've been deciding whether to go into sites or pull out on a case-by-case basis. If we're going to grow to 25,000 stores, we cannot keep taking an ad hoc approach. We need a systematic method to respond to push-back—to decide whether we stay with a site or pull out. I want you to come up with a way to help me decide whether to go into Rio at all. And it's got to be a system or decision process that would work equally well in London or Beijing or anyplace else that we want to open. Let's meet again when I get back to town in a couple days.

The managers of Starbucks Coffee International had their work cut out for them. But they looked forward to tackling the issues raised by Peter Maslen.

Endnotes

1. Planet Starbucks, 2002, *BusinessWeek,* September 9: 100–110.
2. "The name came about when the original owners looked to Seattle history for inspiration and chose the moniker of an old mining camp: Starbo. Further refinement led to Starbucks, after the first mate in *Moby Dick,* which they felt evoked the seafaring romance of the early coffee traders (hence the mermaid logo)." Planet Starbucks, 2002, 103.
3. *Success,* 1993, April.
4. Planet Starbucks, 100–110.
5. Mr. Coffee, 2003, *Fortune,* March 30.
6. Planet Starbucks, 2002, 103.
7. This Colombian coffee bean crop is very small and grows only in the high regions of the Cordillera mountain range. For years, the Narino beans were guarded zealously by Western Europeans, who prized their colorful and complex flavor. It was usually used for upgrading blends. Starbucks was determined to make them available for the first time as a pure varietal. This required breaking western Europe's monopoly over the beans by convincing the Colombian growers that it intended to use "the best beans for a higher purpose."
8. *Canada Newswire,* 1993, March 1.
9. *Inc.,* 1993, January.
10. *Fortune,* 1996, December 9.
11. The decision to offer benefits even to part-time employees (who represent roughly two-thirds of Starbucks' 10,000 employees) has gained a great deal of attention in the press. According to a Hewitt Associates LLC survey of more than 500 employers, only 25 percent of employers offer medical coverage to employees working less than 20 hours a week. It was difficult to get insurers to sign Starbucks up since they did not understand why Starbucks would want to cover part-timers.
12. *Inc.,* 1993, January.
13. *Wall Street Journal,* 1995, October 23.
14. *Nations Restaurant News,* 1995, July 10.
15. The Specialty Coffee Association of America notes that supermarkets account for over 60 percent of all coffee sold in America, followed by gourmet stores (14 percent), mass market (11 percent), mail order (8 percent) and other.
16. *Washington Post,* 1995, August 1.
17. Schultz, however, firmly believes that Starbucks growth is far from saturation both in the United States and overseas: "We have less than 7 percent of the coffee-consuming opportunities in North America. People are still drinking bad coffee." Planet Starbucks, 2002, 102.
18. Online Extra: Q&A with Starbucks' Howard Schultz, 2002, *BusinessWeek,* September 9.
19. *US News and World Report,* 2001, February 19.
20. The difference between an "A" store and a "D" store can be substantial. A "D" store is expected to have about 50–60 percent lower sales. Starbucks classifies a store as "A" if the store location is the focal point of the area, with great visibility, readily available parking, and excellent access to and from the site; cannot be outpositioned by competitors; and fits with Starbucks' desire to build a distinctive image.
21. Starbucks' international businesses are typically joint ventures in which Starbucks holds various levels of equity (ranging from 5 percent to 100 percent). These ventures are referred to as Market Business Units (MBUs). Regardless of the level of equity Starbucks holds, it supports all of its MBUs in an "ownership blind" manner by providing all MBUs with the same level of support.
22. Online Extra: Q&A with Starbucks' Howard Schultz, 2002.
23. Planet Starbucks, 2002, 102.
24. Ibid.
25. The protesters claimed that international organizations like the WTO and International Monetary Fund (IMF) are tools of multinational corporations. Since Seattle, violent protests have been the norm at events such as the annual meetings of the IMF and World Bank, G8 summits, and the World Economic Forum.
26. Planet Starbucks, 2002.
27. Ruckus Society Web site, http://ruckus.org/man/action_planning.html, accessed March 14, 2003.
28. Interview with Alesha Daughtrey, Global Trade Watch field organizer, August 17, 2000; archived in the WTO History Project, University of Washington Center for Labor Studies, http://depts.washington.edu/wtohist/Interviews/Interviews.htm.
29. Mobilization for Global Justice, http://sept.globalizethis.org, accessed March 14, 2003.

30. Ross, John, The unloving cup, Organic Consumers Association, December 12; www.organicconsumers.org/starbucks.

31. Grinding the poor, 1997, *Economist,* November 6.

32. For example, Starbucks' *Commitment to Origins* is a four-part Corporate Social Responsibility program that includes offering Fair Trade certified coffee, organic certified coffee, Farm Direct (single-origin coffees purchased directly from the farmer), and Conservation coffees (emphasizing shade-grown in partnership with the NGO Conservation International). See www.starbucks.com/aboutus/cto_coffees.asp.

33. Brewing a Tempest in a Coffee Cup, 1998, quoting Edward McMahon, *Christian Science Monitor,* February 25.

34. This desire for protection dates back to 1841 when the residents actively campaigned against the area being opened up to the general public. Such actions discouraged further building developments, thus enabling the residents to retain the look and feel of their neighborhood.

35. Stars v. Starbucks: Not a bean for the coffee shop giant, 2002, *Independent on Sunday* (London), June 2.

36. Coffee with your tea?, 2001, *Economist,* October 4.

37. Globalization puts a Starbucks into the Forbidden City in Beijing, *New York Times,* November 25.

38. Starbucks cafe in Forbidden City under fire, 2000, *People's Daily* (Shanghai), November 24.

39. Smith, 2002, Globalization puts a Starbucks into the Forbidden City.

40. Capitalism runs amok, 2003, *Straits Times,* February 16.

1971 Starbucks opens its first location in Seattle's Pike Place Market.

1982 Howard Schultz joins Starbucks as director of retail operations and marketing. Starbucks begins providing coffee to fine restaurants and espresso bars.

1983 Schultz travels to Italy where, impressed with the popularity of espresso bars in Milan, he sees the potential to develop a similar coffee bar culture in Seattle.

1984 Schultz convinces the founders of Starbucks to test the coffee bar concept in a new location in downtown Seattle. This successful experiment is the genesis for a company that Schultz founds in 1985.

1985 Schultz founds Il Giornale, offering brewed coffee and espresso beverages made from Starbucks coffee beans.

1987 With the backing of local investors, Il Giornale acquires Starbucks assets and changes its name to Starbucks Corporation.
Opens in Chicago and Vancouver, B.C. Starbucks location total = 17

1988 Starbucks introduces mail order catalog with service to all 50 states. Starbucks location total = 33

1989 Opens in Portland, Oregon. Starbucks location total = 55

1990 Starbucks expands headquarters in Seattle and builds a new roasting plant. Starbucks location total = 84

1991 Establishes a relationship with CARE, the international relief and development organization, and introduces the CARE coffee sampler.
Becomes the first U.S. privately owned company to offer a stock option program that includes part-time employees.
Opens first licensed airport location with HMS Host at Sea-Tac International Airport.
Opens in Los Angeles. Starbucks location total = 116

1992 Completes initial public offering with common stock traded on the Nasdaq National Market under the trading symbol "SBUX."
Opens in San Francisco; San Diego; Orange County, California; and Denver. Starbucks location total = 165

1993 Begins Barnes & Noble, Inc., relationship.
Opens in Washington, D.C. Starbucks location total = 272

1994 Awarded ITT/Sheraton (now Starwood Hotels) account.
Opens in Minneapolis, Boston, New York, Atlanta, Dallas, and Houston. Starbucks location total = 425

1995 Based on an extremely popular in-house music program, Starbucks begins selling compact disks.
Awarded United Airlines account.
Begins serving Frappuccino blended beverages, a line of low-fat, creamy, iced coffee beverages.
Forms alliance with Canadian bookstore Chapters Inc.
Starbucks Coffee International forms joint venture with SAZABY Inc., to develop Starbucks coffeehouses in Japan.
Opens in Philadelphia, Pittsburgh, Las Vegas, Cincinnati, Baltimore, San Antonio, and Austin, Texas.
Starbucks location total = 676

1996 Starbucks Coffee International opens locations in Japan, Hawaii, and Singapore.
Awarded Westin (now Starwood Hotels) account.
Starbucks and Dreyer's Grand Ice Cream, Inc., introduce Starbucks Ice Cream and Starbucks Ice Cream bars.
Starbucks Ice Cream quickly becomes the number one brand of coffee ice cream in the United States.
North American Coffee Partnership (Starbucks and Pepsi-Cola Company business venture) begins selling a bottled version of Starbucks Frappuccino blended beverage.

Opens in Rhode Island, Idaho, North Carolina, Arizona, Utah, and Ontario, Canada. Starbucks location total = 1,015

1997 Starbucks Coffee International opens locations in the Philippines.

Awarded Canadian Airlines account.

Forms alliance with eight companies to enable the gift of more than 320,000 new books for children through the All Books for Children first annual book drive.

Establishes The Starbucks Foundation, benefiting local literacy programs in communities where Starbucks has coffeehouses.

Opens in Florida, Michigan, and Wisconsin. Starbucks location total = 1,412

1998 Starbucks Coffee International opens locations in Taiwan, Thailand, New Zealand, and Malaysia.

Introduces Tiazzi blended juice tea, a refreshing mixture of tea, fruit juice, and ice.

Acquires Seattle Coffee Company in the United Kingdom with more than 60 retail locations.

Acquires Pasqua Inc., a San Francisco–based coffee retailer.

Forms Urban Coffee Opportunities, a joint venture with Earvin "Magic" Johnson's Johnson Development Corp., to develop Starbucks Coffee locations in underserved, urban neighborhoods throughout the United States.

Signs a licensing agreement with Kraft Foods Inc. to extend the Starbucks brand into grocery channels across the United States.

Launches Starbucks.com.

Opens two new coffeehouse concepts: Cafe Starbucks in Seattle and Circadia Coffee House in San Francisco.

Opens in New Orleans; St. Louis; Kansas City, Missouri; and Portland, Maine. Starbucks location total = 1,886

1999 Starbucks Coffee International opens locations in China, Kuwait, Korea, and Lebanon.

Acquires Tazo, a Portland, Oregon–based tea company.

Partners with Conservation International to promote environmentally sound methods of growing coffee.

Introduces Shade Grown Mexico Coffee.

Acquires Hear Music, a San Francisco–based music company.

Enters agreement with Albertson's, Inc., to open more than 100 Starbucks locations in their supermarkets in the year 2000.

Opens in Memphis and Nashville, Tennessee; and Saskatchewan, Canada. Starbucks location total = 2,135

2000 Enters into licensing agreement with TransFair USA to market and sell Fair Trade Certified coffee.

Introduces a Commitment to Origins coffee category that includes shade-grown, organic, and Fair Trade Certified selections.

Expands contribution to Conservation International to establish conservation efforts in five new sites.

Enters agreement with Host Marriott International to open locations in select properties. Starbucks Coffee International opens in Dubai, Hong Kong, Shanghai, Qatar, Bahrain, Saudi Arabia, and Australia.

Starbucks location total = 3,501

2001 Introduces coffee sourcing guidelines developed in partnership with The Center for Environmental Leadership in Business, a division of Conservation International.

Commits to the purchase of one million pounds of Fair Trade Certified coffee.

Offers $1 million in financial support to coffee farmers through Calvert Community Investments.

Begins to offer high-speed wireless Internet access in stores.

The Starbucks Foundation awards more than 450 grants totaling $4.2 million to literacy, schools, and community-based organizations across North America.

Begins offering the Starbucks Card, a stored value card for customers to use and reload.

Enters agreement with Hyatt Hotels Corp.

Starbucks Coffee Japan introduces a stock option program for eligible full and part-time partners and successfully implements IPO.

Starbucks and international business partners seed Starbucks Cares Fund with $1.2 million contribution to benefit September 11th Fund. Customers and partners contribute more than $1.4 million to Starbucks Cares.

Starbucks opens 300th location in Japan and celebrates fifth year of business in Japan.

Starbucks Coffee International opens in Switzerland, Israel, and Austria. Starbucks location total = 4,709

2002 Signs memorandum of understanding with Fairtrade Labelling Organizations International (FLO) that enables the company to enter into licensing agreements with national FairTrade organizations to sell Fair Trade Certified coffee in the countries where Starbucks does business.

Publishes its first Corporate Social Responsibility Annual Report.

Celebrates 10-year anniversary of Starbucks IPO.

Introduces Starbucks DoubleShot to the ready-to-drink coffee category.

Signs licensing agreement with TransFair Canada to bring Fair Trade Certified coffee to more than 270 retail locations in Canada.

Starbucks Coffee International opens in Oman, Indonesia, Germany, and Spain. Starbucks location total = 5,688

Case 39 Toys "R" Us Moving into 2004*

During 2003, Toys "R" Us and the rest of the specialty toy retailers took a huge bashing from Wal-Mart and other department stores that offered low prices on popular items. Toys sales at toy stores dropped 7.7 percent from 2002, forcing several top stores to file for Chapter 11 protection.[1] FAO Inc., parent of FAO Schwartz toy stores, filed for bankruptcy twice during 2003. After withholding vendor payments in December 2003, KB Toys announced in January 2004 it too had filed for bankruptcy and planned to close almost half of its 1,217 stores. The news wasn't quite as grim for Toys "R" Us, but it also wasn't celebratory. During the first week of January 2004, Toys "R" Us CEO and chairman John Eyler told investors that the company had made a "strategic decision to match Wal-Mart's deep price cuts in order to protect market share," and that the company had suffered as a result of that approach.[2]

One reason Wal-Mart and other discount retailers are able to set their prices so low is because they "use toys as a loss leader, selling them at rock-bottom prices, and making up the profit on sales of other items."[3] This pricing of toys at cost or below cost is destroying the profit margins of stand-alone toy retailers like FAO Inc., KB Toys, and Toys "R" Us.

So what can specialty toy stores do to stay afloat? According to industry analysts they need to differentiate themselves from the discount toy stores. This can be accomplished in several ways, by offering higher-end products, better selection, exceptional service, or a unique "shopping experience." Toys "R" Us has in the past attempted to differentiate itself using several of these methods. USA Today observed that "Shoppers go to discounters for price and to Toys "R" Us for broad selection."[4] Recent differentiation strategies have focused on improving the customer service and creating stores that are a destination for fun, not just shopping. However, the pressure from discounters has been immense and, as a result of a greater than expected $38 million loss, Toys "R" Us announced in November 2003 that it planned to close its Kids "R" Us clothing and Imaginarium educational toys stores and cut 3,800 jobs.[5]

Snapshot of Toys "R" Us

Toys "R" Us, Inc., headquartered in Paramus, New Jersey, became a public company in 1978. At the beginning of 2004, it was an $11.5 billion dollar business with approximately 1,500 stores worldwide. The merchandise mix ranged in price from three dollars to three hundred dollars, and included both children's and adults' toys and games, bicycles, sporting goods, small pools, infant and juvenile furniture, infant and toddler apparel, and children's books, as well as an electronics section, which featured video games, electronic handheld toys, videotapes, audio CDs, and computer software, along with a smattering of small TVs, shelf-stereos, and radios. In early 2004 Toys "R" Us included several divisions: Toys "R" Us—U.S., Toys "R" Us—International, Kids "R" Us, Babies "R" Us, and Toysrus.com. See Exhibit 1 for store types and Exhibit 2 for the company's vision, mission, and goals.

History of Toys "R" Us

Charles Lazarus founded Toys "R" Us in 1948 in Washington, D.C. Lazarus started out in business with a baby furniture store. However, as his customers increasingly requested toys for their children, Lazarus strove to meet their demand and gradually moved into the toy business. In 1957 Lazarus opened the first toy supermarket, during a time when specialty retailing and off-price positioning were revolutionary concepts in the days before malls and discount stores. With the success of these stores, Toys "R" Us became a public company in the late 1970s and by early 2000 had become an $11 billion business. Exhibit 3 provides the company's earnings from January 2000 to January 2004.

In the 1980s Toys "R" Us set out to expand its customer reach to cover not only the greater part of the United States, but also the world market. Toys "R" Us International opened its first stores in 1984 in Singapore and Canada. As of 2004 Toys "R" Us had more than 700 stores in the United States and more than 500 stores elsewhere in 27 countries, including franchised and licensed operations. The company's expansion effort did not stop only at reaching more people, but also endeavored to offer customers a greater variety of items, just as Lazarus had when he first opened his store in 1948. To this end, Kids "R" Us opened its doors in 1983, and offered name-brand children's wear (such as OshKosh B'Gosh) and K.R.U. private-label brands, as well as its own line of "lifestyle products," including fashion accessories, bath and body products, cosmetics, and home decor. Babies "R" Us, which first opened in Westbury, New York, in May 1996, offered baby apparel, furniture, car seats, bedding, strollers, and more. The stores also provided a baby registry system for expecting parents and allowed parents to create, view, and change their personal registry over the Internet. In July 1999 Toys "R" Us, with an interest in the educational and learning toy segment, purchased Imaginarium, the 37th player ranked by sales. Existing stand-

*This case was prepared by Professor Alan B. Eisner and graduate student Keeley Townsend of Pace University as a basis for class discussion rather than to illustrate either effective or ineffective handling of an administrative situation. Copyright © 2004 Alan B. Eisner.

Exhibit 1   Breakdown of Stores by Divisions

	2004	2003	2002	2001	2000	1999	1998	1997	1996	1995
Number of Stores										
Toys "R" Us—U.S.	685	685	701	710	710	704	700	682	653	618
Toys "R" Us—International	574	544	507	491	462	452	441	396	337	293
Kids "R" Us—U.S.	44*	183	165	198	205	212	215	212	213	204
Babies "R" Us—U.S.	198	146	184	145	131	113	98	82	—	—
Imaginarium—U.S.		37	42	37	40	—	—	—	—	—
Total Stores	1501	1595	1599	1,581	1,548	1,481	1,454	1,372	1,203	1,115

Source: Toys "R" Us, Inc., 10-K report.

*All Kids "R" Us stores to close by the end of 2004.

alone Imaginarium stores continued, and Toys "R" Us incorporated in-store Imaginarium World sections in 10 to 20 of its stores in time for Christmas 1999. By early 2004 all stand-alone Imaginarium stores had been closed. Imaginarium Worlds could be found in more than 436 Toys "R" Us stores in the United States. The division continued to operate 185 international locations and guest could shop online.

In the late 1990s convenient online shopping for goods from all Toys "R" Us divisions became one of the company's major objectives. Toysrus.com was founded in 1998 with the goal of becoming a premier online toy, video game, and baby store. However, the division experienced a rocky beginning when, during the 1999 Christmas season, Toysrus.com employees faced a real siege. The company's "Black Sunday" came on November 6, 1999, as 62 million advertising circulars were placed in local newspapers around the country offering free shipping on Christmas toy orders placed over the Internet. When Toysrus.com was unable to fulfill orders in time for Christmas, the firm received numerous consumer complaints and negative publicity from the press and television news about the firm's problems. Toys "R" Us had the toys available in its warehouses, but was unable to pick, pack, and ship customer orders in a timely manner.

Toysrus.com gained momentum again when it formed an alliance with Amazon.com in 2000. The alliance proved successful by more than tripling Toysrus.com sales and the number of orders from the prior year and by providing customers with a favorable online toy-buying experience.

Competition

At the same time that Toys "R" Us was creating its online business unit, it was also facing competitive pressures in its traditional brick-and-mortar business. Its market share had dropped from 25 percent in 1990 to 15.6 percent in 1999. In 1998 Wal-Mart dethroned Toys "R" Us as the number one toy seller after more than a decade of being on top.

The $30.7 billion traditional toy industry had undergone significant changes since the early 1990s (see Exhibit 4 for the growth of the toy industry). General mass merchandise retailers had grown, as had their toy departments. Mall retailers like KB Toys managed to channel a great deal of money into shopping malls with the introduction of their small mall-based toyshops. Exhibit 5 shows the changing market share among retailer types. The Toys "R" Us chain suffered and saw its market share drop from 25 percent in 1990 to 16.8 percent in 1998 and 17 percent in 2004.[6] Toys "R" Us had been the leader for over a decade until ousted in 1998 by Wal-Mart (see Exhibit 6).

Exhibit 2   Toys "R" Us: Vision, Mission, and Goals

Vision:	Put joy in kids' hearts and a smile on parents' faces.
Mission:	A commitment to making each and every customer happy.
Goal:	To be the "Worldwide Authority on Kids, Families, and Fun."

Source: Toys "R" Us, Inc., 2000 Annual Report.

Exhibit 3   Consolidated Statements of Earnings: Toys "R" Us, Inc., and Subsidiaries
(In $ millions except per share data)

	January 2004	February 2003	February 2002	February 2001	January 2000
Net sales	$11,566	$11,305	$11,019	$11,332	$11,862
Cost of sales	7,849	7,799	7,604	7,815	8,321
Gross Profit	3,717	3,506	3,415	3,517	3,541
Selling, general, and administrative expenses	3,022	2,718	2,721	2,832	2,743
Depreciation, amortization, and asset write-offs	348	317	308	290	278
Restructuring	85		186		
Equity in net earnings, Japan				(31)	
Total Operating Expenses	3,455	3,035	3,215	3,091	3,021
Operating income	262	471	200	426	520
Gain from IPO, Japan				315	
Interest expense	(142)	(119)	(117)	(127)	91
Interest and other income	15	9	8	23	(11)
Interest expense, net				80	93
Earnings/Loss before Income Taxes	138	361	91	637	440
Income taxes	50	132	24	233	161
Net Earnings/Loss	88	229	67	404	279
Basic earnings/loss per share	.41	1.10	.34	1.92	1.14
Diluted earnings/loss per share	.41	1.09	.33	1.88	1.14

The Toys "R" Us Strategy

One method for Toys "R" Us to regain its competitive edge in the brick-and-mortar business was through qualitative improvements in its traditional stores. To address retail quality, Toys "R" Us set out to improve the customers' shopping experience within its stores. Initially, most U.S. Toys "R" Us stores conformed to a traditional big-box format, with full-size stores averaging about 46,000 square feet and stores in smaller markets ranging between 20,000 and 30,000 square feet. In 1999, however, the company began converting stores to a new layout called the "C3" format store, which was designed to make Toys "R" Us stores easier to shop in, with wider aisles, more feature opportunities and end-caps, more shops, and logical category layouts.[7] To make the stores more shopper-friendly and better able to compete with the

Exhibit 4   U.S. Toy Industry Sales
(In $ billions)

Industry Segments	1993	1994	1995	1996	1997	1998	1999	2000	2001	2002	2003
Total industry (with video games)	$18.7	$20.1	$20.8	$22.7	$25.6	$27.2	$29.9	$29.4	34.1	$31.6	$30.7
Traditional toys	14.8	17.0	17.7	19.1	20.6	21.0	23.0	23.0	24.7	21.3	20.7
Video games	3.9	3.1	3.1	3.6	5.0	6.2	6.9	6.4	9.4	10.3	10.0

Sources: Toy Manufacturers of America, Inc., New York, and NPD Group, New York.

Exhibit 5   **Distribution of Sales by Retail Type**

Type	Dollar Share (%)					
	1995	1996	1997	1998	1999	2000
Discount stores	41.2	40.7	41.6	41.5	40.0	41.8
National toy stores	23.6	23.6	23.2	21.7	20.8	21.0
All other outlets	13.8	13.4	12.9	12.8	13.8	11.9
Mail order	4.4	4.8	4.6	5.3	5.0	5.1
Card/gift/stationery	0.9	1.2	1.9	3.1	4.2	2.2
All other toy stores	3.6	4.3	3.9	3.7	3.9	3.4
Food/drugstores	3.4	3.4	3.5	3.6	3.4	2.9
Department stores	4.1	3.8	3.4	4.1	3.3	4.0
E-tailers*					1.2	2.1
Hobby/craft stores	2.9	3.1	3.2	2.7	2.8	3.5
Variety stores	2.1	1.7	1.8	1.5	1.7	2.1

*New category.

Sources: Toy Manufacturers of America, Inc., New York, and NPD Group, New York.

more intimate specialty retailers, Toys "R" Us also introduced the merchandise "world" in 1999. Exhibit 7 lists the various "worlds" developed. The company took the quality shopping experience one step further when, in November 2001, Toys "R" Us opened its international flagship store in Times Square in New York City. The multilevel store offered a vast selection of toys and other entertainment, including a 60-foot Ferris wheel, 4,000-square-foot Barbie Dollhouse, and a 20-foot tall animatronic Jurassic Park T-Rex that roared.

Exhibit 6   **Top Toy Sellers: Percent of Annual Industry Sales**

Retailer	1995	1996	1997	1998	1999	2000	2001	2002	2003
Wal-Mart	14.6%	15.3%	16.3%	17.4%	17.4%	19.0%	19.3%	19.6%	20.0%
Toys "R" Us	19.2	18.9	18.3	16.8	15.6	16.5	16.6	16.8	17.0
Kmart	8.5	8.3	8.2	8.0	7.2	7.4	7.0	6.5	6.0
Target	6.1	6.4	7.1	6.9	6.8	7.2	7.4	7.8	8.0
KB Toys/Toy Works	4.3	4.3	4.9	4.9	5.1	4.7	4.8	4.8	5.0
Ames	1.2	1.2	1.1	1.3	1.6	1.0	0.8	.4*	
J. C. Penney	1.5	1.7	1.5	1.6	1.2	1.4	1.4	1.2	1.0
Hallmark				1.0	1.1	0.9	0.9	0.9	0.9
Meijer		1.0	1.1	1.2	1.0	0.9	1.0	1.0	1.0
Shopko				0.9	0.8	0.8	0.8	0.8	0.8
Service Merchandise	1.8	1.6	1.1*						
Hills	1.6	1.3	1.2	1.1*					

Sources: NPD Group, New York, and Toy Manufacturers of America, Inc., New York, and author estimates.

*Exited the toy business.

Exhibit 7   Toys "R" Us Merchandise Worlds

World	Description
R Zone	Video, electronics, computer software, and related products
Action and Adventure	Action figures, die-cast cars, etc.
Girls	Dolls, collectibles, accessories, lifestyle products
Outdoor Fun	Bikes, sports, play sets
Preschool	Toys, accessories
Seasonal	Christmas, Halloween, Summer, etc.
Juvenile	Baby products and apparel
Learning Center	Educational and developmental products
Family Fun	Games and puzzles

Source: Toys "R" Us, Inc., 1999 Annual Report.

To help recapture its number one place from Wal-Mart, Toys "R" Us developed a new corporate strategy and marketing plan. Toys "R" Us hired a new marketing vice-president, Warren Kornblum, who immediately overhauled the company's entire marketing operation. In the past Toys "R" Us had joined in small vendor promotions and managed scattered marketing efforts. Kornblum changed that around, deciding to do fewer but bigger promotions. The company teamed with Major League Baseball as a sponsor for the Diamond Skills Program, a youth skill competition. Then the firm helped a champion women's soccer team travel to 12 U.S. cities with a tie-in from SFX Entertainment to create the Toys "R" Us Victory Tour. Toys "R" Us also carried out a promotional deal with Fox Kids Network and Walt Disney for the feature film *Toy Story 2*. As a result of these marketing efforts, sales increased from $11.2 billion in 1998 to $11.9 billion in 1999.[8] Warren Kornblum's strategy seemed to be working, yet the company was still unable to unseat Wal-Mart. He set up a "Scan and Win" promotion where shoppers held up Universal Product Code (UPC) game pieces to scanners to see if they had won a prize. More than a million consumers were scanned in with this promotion, making this one of the company's most successful programs for store traffic improvement. The mountains of sweepstakes entries and packed venues, however, began causing inventory shortages in the all-important holiday period of 1999. Inventory mishaps were the main reason why fourth-quarter 1999 sales stayed at a flat $5 billion.

When John Eyler came in as the new CEO of Toys "R" Us in January 2000, he slashed expenses across the board, started efforts to provide better customer service, increased the number of employees in stores, and expanded store operating hours. All of the marketing activi-

ties were aimed at bringing customers into the chain's new store design and layout model—C3: customer-driven, cost-effective concept. This easier-to-shop C3 format allowed for 18 percent more selling space through wider aisles, which were to be installed in 75 percent of the stores by the end of 2000. Toys "R" Us hoped this new strategy would take market share back from Wal-Mart, Kmart, Target, and KB Toys. For 2000–2001 the company restructured its budget to allocate more money toward marketing. Toys "R" Us planned to continue with sports and movie entertainment themes for promotions.

Toys "R" Us saw evidence in 2002 that its strategies for marketing and improving the customer experience were working. The company saw increases in both average transaction size and consumer satisfaction research scores in 2002; it received higher marks from customers for service, in-stock position, knowledgeable associates, and competitive pricing.[9] Despite these successes, Toys "R" Us was not satisfied with the comparable store sales performance of its U.S. toy stores in 2002. Seasonal, video, and juvenile businesses experienced negative comparable store sales, but the core toy sales, which included Boys and Girls, Learning, and Preschool toys, outpaced toy industry performance by 4 percent for the year.[10]

Also in 2002, three company divisions—Babies "R" Us, Toys "R" Us International, and Toysrus.com—enjoyed record performances. Toysrus.com achieved operating profitability in the fourth quarter of 2002, a full year ahead of schedule. The Kids "R" Us division had been struggling in its stand-alone stores, but began seeing positive results from sourcing apparel through the division from the Babies "R" Us stores and the Toys "R" Us/Kids "R" Us combo stores. At the end of fiscal year 2002, the Toys "R" Us total apparel business represented approximately $900 million in sales, at above-average profit margins, and continued growth was expected.[11] Approximately 65 percent of those sales came from exclusive products that generated higher margins than nationally branded items.

New Directions?

To compete with Wal-Mart and reach potential customers more often, Toys "R" Us began to test a new concept called *Toys "R" Us Toy Box* in a limited number of grocery stores in 2001. Eyler hoped to offer toys at the place where, he believed, potential customers shopped most frequently: grocery stores. The Toy Box concept consists of approximately 40 to 70 feet of space containing smaller toy items with prices generally below $25. In 2003 Eyler inked a multiyear deal with Albertson's, Inc., to become the exclusive toy provider for its supermarkets and drugstores. Toys "R" Us had opened approximately 900 toy sections across Albertson's store locations and expected to complete the rollout to 2,000 toy sections within the chain in the first half of 2004.

Meanwhile the competitive pressure from discounters and other channels was intense. Wal-Mart was still the dominant toy seller. Toys "R" Us and Amazon.com became embroiled is a series of lawsuits regarding the exclusivity of Toys "R" Us products on the Amazon.com site. In January 2004 Toys "R" Us implemented the closing of the 36 freestanding Imaginarium and 146 freestanding Kids "R" Us stores due to continued declining performance.

Endnotes

1. Moore, Angela, 2004, Sad holiday season for toy stores? Reuters, January 3; www.reuters.com.
2. Verdon, Joan, 2004, Retailer Toys "R" Us posts disappointing holiday results, *Record—Knight Ridder/Tribune Business News,* January 9; http://news.stockselector.com/newsarticle.asp?symbol=TOY&article=62013210.
3. Moore, 2004, Sad holiday season for toy stores?
4. Grant, Lorrie, 2004, KB Toys files for Chapter 11 after cutthroat holiday season, *USA Today,* January 15.
5. Gatlin, Greg, 2003, Toyshops go own way in Wal-Mart fight, *Boston Herald,* November 25; http://business.bostonherald.com.
6. Liebeck, Laura, 1999, TRU follows a new leader, *Discount Store News,* 38(8): 1, 92.
7. C3—customer-driven, cost-effective concept.
8. The real toy story, 2000, *Promo,* 13 (5).
9. Toys "R" Us, 2002, Annual Report 2002, http://media.corporate-ir.net/media_files/irol/12/120622/toysrus/ar2002/index.html.
10. Ibid.
11. Ibid.

Case 40   Trouble in Paradise

From Mike Graves's tall windows, which were draped in red velvet, the view of Shanghai was spectacular: the stately old Western-style buildings, the riot of modern skyscrapers, the familiar needle of the TV tower. But today Mike barely noticed it. Clenching a copy of his Chinese partner's proposal for another acquisition—it would be the company's fourth—he paced the floor and replayed in his mind that morning's unsettling phone call.

He had called his boss, Bill Windler, at headquarters in Ohio, hoping to get a nice quote to inject into the brief remarks he was to make at that day's banquet celebrating the joint venture's tenth anniversary. But as he gave Windler a quick rundown of what he intended to say—mostly about the joint venture's progress toward "world-class quality"—Mike could sense his boss's growing frustration. About five minutes into the call, Windler cut Mike off in midsentence, saying, "Don't throw your shoulder out patting yourself on the back."

Windler reminded Mike about the margins he was looking for across all of Heartland Spindle's businesses. "A 4% ROI is pathetic," Windler said. "We've been in there ten years, Mike. The numbers should look better by now." He said he was looking for a 20% ROI, adding that such a number could surely be achieved through greater efficiency and more automation. And in Windler's view, the company had at least 1,200 employees too many. "That needs to be fixed, fast," he said.

Mike knew his boss wouldn't take no for an answer, but he had also learned that his Chinese partners would never agree to drastic moves such as the layoffs suggested by Windler. It was beginning to look as though the five good years he had spent here as general manager might be destined to come to a painful end. Mike couldn't help but wonder if those harsh words from Ohio were a warning that his contract might not be renewed in six months.

Then, to top things off, just as Mike had extricated himself from the phone conversation, this latest acquisition proposal had arrived from deputy general manager Qinlin Li. The top executive on the Chinese side of the joint venture, Qinlin had been with the JV since its inception. As before, there would be almost irresistible pressure

HBR's cases, which are fictional, present common managerial dilemmas and offer concrete solutions from experts.

Reprinted by permission of Harvard Business Review. "Trouble in Paradise" by Katherine Xin and Vladimir Pucik, August 2003. Copyright © 2003 by the Harvard Business School Publishing Corporation; all rights reserved.

Katherine Xin is a professor of management and holds the Michelin Chair in Leadership and Human Resource Management at China Europe International Business School (CEIBS) in Shanghai; she is also the editor in chief of HBR China. Vladimir Pucik is a professor of international human resources and strategy at the International Institute for Management Development (IMD) in Lausanne, Switzerland.

to go along with the deal. The Chinese side would make it clear yet again that the delicate partnership depended on Mike's support for continuous expansion and protection of jobs. The timing couldn't have been worse: The last thing Windler would want was more growth initiatives eating into the profits.

A knock on the heavy teak door snapped him out of his musings. Feng Chen, Mike's assistant and translator, informed him that his car was waiting.

Enhance Friendly Cooperation

As the car pulled up outside the Shangri-La Hotel, Mike forced himself to smile at the red carpet lined with dozens of lavish flower baskets sent by local government officials, business partners, suppliers, customers, and even competitors. A marching band in full uniform stood at the hotel entrance, and above it stretched a bright red banner that said, in Chinese and English: "Enhance Friendly Cooperation and Ensure Mutual Growth" and "Celebrate the Tenth Anniversary of Zhong-Lian Knitting Co. Ltd."

Mike exchanged greetings with Qinlin, who had been there for an hour already and was still seeing to last-minute details. In the ballroom, an elegant young woman in a red silk *qi-pao*, a traditional dress for formal celebrations, escorted Mike to the round table that was front and center. Two Chinese senior executives, Qinlin's immediate subordinates, stood up and nodded their greetings.

There was a burst of excited applause, and cameras flashed. Qinlin was accompanying three important government officials into the room. They approached Mike's table and politely bickered for several minutes over who should enjoy the most prominent seat at the table, as required by Chinese custom. At last, the eldest and most highly placed official accepted the seat of honor. Qinlin stepped up to the podium, above which hung a huge Chinese knot of red silk, the symbol of cooperation. There was an expectant hush as he tapped the microphone.

"Ladies and gentlemen," Qinlin began, "thank you for joining me to celebrate the tenth anniversary of Zhong-Lian Knitting Company Limited. Those who were with the company at the beginning remember the hardships we endured and the hard work we put in. Since the establishment of Zhong-Lian as a 50/50 joint venture between Suzhou First Textile Company and our U.S. partner, Heartland Spindle Company, Zhong-Lian has faced many difficulties and obstacles. But we succeeded." Mike was listening to the translator's words, but he could hear the passion in Qinlin's voice. "We turned a money-losing company into a money-making company, and we made great headway as a result of support from our government, efforts on the part of both parent companies, and all our managers and employees."

Mike hadn't been there during the early days, but he knew the stories. He was the fourth GM sent by Heartland in ten years. His two most recent predecessors had left before their three-year assignments were complete, one for family reasons—his wife couldn't adapt to China—and the other for a better job offer (allegedly). Mike, a veteran manager with 20 years of international experience, had lived and worked in Japan, Hong Kong, and Australia before Heartland sent him to Shanghai.

Mike's toughest challenge at the outset was the language barrier. He wouldn't have survived without Feng Chen's help. It didn't take long for Mike to learn what *cha-bu-duo* meant: "almost okay." He hated that word! It was baffling to him: Even though his Chinese partners were intelligent and willing to work hard, they weren't exactly obsessed with quality. They cut corners and hardly ever followed operating procedures to the letter. Buttons often fell off sweaters before the garments were even shipped out of the factory. *Cha-bu-duo* is why Mike insisted on introducing Total Quality Management to Zhong-Lian—and TQM was probably why the JV had been so successful. Mike had also felt a small sense of satisfaction when he taught his Chinese colleagues a new term: Six Sigma.

Cha-bu-duo wasn't the only expression Mike heard all too often. He also quickly got used to *yan-jiu-yan-jiu*, which means "Let's review and discuss." When he proposed a new system to deal with sewage disposal three months after he started (he was astonished that his Chinese partner hadn't updated it already), his counterparts said, "Okay, *yan-jiu-yan-jiu*." Two months later, after Mike's repeated prodding, the proposal made it onto a meeting agenda. But at the meeting, the Chinese managers seemed reluctant to discuss the matter, and no one wanted to assume responsibility for solving the problem. When Mike asked managers for feedback individually, they all had ideas, many of them excellent. He couldn't imagine why the managers hadn't spoken up at the meeting.

It didn't make sense to him until months later, when Mike heard someone say, "Keeping silent in a group is safer. You won't get in trouble if you don't do anything. But you will get in trouble if you make a mistake. We are experienced under this system, and we know how it works." At any rate, Mike was relieved when the equipment was set up—even though it took two years and outside pressure from the provincial Environment Protection Bureau to make it happen.

There was another burst of applause. Qinlin's voice reverberated through the room. "We have acquired three money-losing state-owned enterprises and managed to earn an annual profit of between 5% and 6%," he said. "The number of employees increased from 400 to 2,300 in the past decade. Given the slump of the textile industry in these years, Zhong-Lian's achievement is remarkable.

In the coming years, we will further enhance the company and maintain our growth momentum."

Qinlin paused, and his eyes sparkled. "Let me tell you another piece of good news," he said. "We are preparing our fourth acquisition, which is expected to raise our production capacity by 40%. The number of our employees will grow to nearly 3,500. And all this will help us launch our next initiative: building our own *national brand.*"

What little appetite Mike had for the celebration vanished. He had long been trying to quash that kind of talk. Heartland, he knew, would never support launching an apparel brand that would eat up resources and limit profits for years. Qinlin knows this well, Mike thought, so why is he raising expectations in such a public way?

Qinlin thanked the vice mayor and the other government officials without whose "wise supervision," in his effusive words, the joint venture would not have made such great progress. The vice mayor rose to speak and returned the compliments, praising Zhong-Lian's contribution to the local economy—especially to maintaining employment levels—and calling the joint venture a flagship among the city's enterprises.

When it was Mike's turn, he too voiced the expected praise for the officials—it was a ritual whose airy forms and steely seriousness had become almost second nature to him. But throughout his little speech, he felt he was hardly doing more than going through the motions. He was preoccupied by Qinlin's plans and what they would mean for profitability.

Later, the lazy Susan at each table was filled with eight cold dishes, eight hot dishes, and two showpiece dishes: a whole suckling pig and a whole braised mandarin fish in the shape of a squirrel. Qinlin, as the host of his table, proposed a toast. Then he emptied his glass as a sign of his sincerity and joy. Glasses clinked; champagne and Coke bubbled. But Mike had become so attuned to the subtleties of these gatherings that he immediately noticed the response of the officials: Instead of emptying their glasses, they merely took sips. Mike supposed that they must have heard about his opposition, muted though it had been, to the expansion ideas.

Living in Style

Sitting in the backseat of the company car, Mike felt his tension ease when his driver, Lao Li, turned into his neighborhood. The car slipped by a row of cypresses and passed a perfectly manicured golf course. Designed in European country style, the elegant Green Villa was an ideal residence for expatriates. Mike loved this village—its extensive recreational amenities, its first-class service. At very little cost, for example, Mike's family had hired a live-in domestic helper who happened to be a superior cook. His wife, Linda, played golf three times a week with her friends in the village, and she had recently taken up yoga. The company paid $7,800 a month to rent the family's home; it also paid for a chauffeur, a nanny, and the children's education at Concordia International School (the best in Shanghai). Life here was easy and comfortable—a world away from what it would have been like back in Ohio.

But Mike's tension returned when he thought about his meeting the next morning with the people at Hua-Ying, the potential acquisition. He wouldn't be living in Green Villa much longer if he signed off on that deal.

Over dinner, Mike told Linda about the conversation with Windler.

"Don't they understand that the Chinese way of doing business is different from the American way?" Linda asked him sympathetically. "It's not all about squeezing the most out of your workers here. They value stability and long-term employment. You'd think Heartland would've been prepared for this sort of performance. It's not like you're losing money, like so many JVs here do. Just last week on the course, Christie and Maya told me that their husbands' businesses hadn't turned a profit yet."

"I know, but that doesn't seem to be good enough any more," Mike said. He recounted Bill's suggestions about layoffs and investing in more automated equipment. He knew that he would soon have to broach these subjects with his Chinese partners.

Mike's biggest problem was that he could see both sides. Heartland wanted to reposition itself in the U.S. market—selling at discount stores wasn't profitable enough. But to enable Heartland to make the jump to high-end retailers, the joint venture would have to meet much higher standards of quality. Those old dyeing machines, for instance, would have to go; they had cost the company a lot of money over the last few years, not just in shipping and handling charges for returned products but also in terms of the company's reputation. New machines would fix that problem, but they'd create another one: Many jobs would disappear.

The Chinese partners were much more concerned with creating jobs and keeping government officials happy than with improving quality. They wanted to keep growing into new provinces and buying up unprofitable companies, even if turning them around took years. But expansion would require significant additional resources that Heartland Spindle clearly wasn't ready to commit. And now there would be pressure to create a new company to market a national brand, again a drain on cash.

"So what do you think you're going to do?" Linda asked.

"I'm meeting with executives from Hua-Ying tomorrow morning. Maybe they'll surprise me with an operation that won't take forever to turn around—that'd be the best case," Mike said. "After that, I'll have to talk to Qin-lin and the others about Heartland's concerns. But I know how that conversation will play out. They'll say Heartland is being shortsighted and that the JV's history of turning around money-losing businesses should prove that we just need to be more patient.

"I wish Bill and the rest back in the States had a better understanding of how things work here. I was skeptical myself at the beginning. Remember when we first got here and I was fuming at the business expenses? Seemed like every executive on the payroll was wining and dining some key partner or contact. And Robert O'Reilly, our controller, came to me shouting that our Chinese partner spent money like water. But, gradually, we both figured out that those expenses were paying off for us. The Chinese ritual of sharing food—nurturing *guanxi*—is so powerful in making deals that it became one of our hidden assets. I'm afraid we won't get those kinds of results if we focus only on cutting costs and laying off workers, as Ohio wants us to do."

PowerPoint and Green Tea

The chief executive of Hua-Ying, Genfa Wang, sent his own limousine to pick up Mike and Qinlin as a symbol of his sincerity and hospitality. Genfa and his top managers were waiting at the gate when the car pulled up, and one of the men stepped forward to open the car door. Genfa greeted Mike, Qinlin, and Feng Chen with, "My honor! My honor! It is a great pleasure to have you here with us."

The first building they entered looked fairly clean, but the conference room carpet was pocked with cigarette burns. Not exactly a high-class operation, Mike thought. Up on the third floor, there was a disagreeable odor—no flush. He could just imagine the state of the plumbing. And hadn't leaky pipes been responsible for the initial spread of SARS into cities in Hong Kong? He was sure he had read something like that. His unease grew. What other hidden risks were lurking in this facility? There was no way he was going to be able to agree to this acquisition, he thought.

But he was pleasantly surprised to see seven cups of Bi Luo Chun tea, one of the best Chinese green teas, on an elegant redwood table. And a minute later, Genfa pulled out a laptop and began making his presentation using PowerPoint slides. Mike was shocked. He hadn't expected such sophistication from a company this size, especially a company that seemed to lack modern sanitary facilities. Genfa, sensing Mike's reaction, said proudly, "My nephew gave me training on this high-tech stuff. He is a college graduate, a vice GM of our company in charge of technology and engineering."

Great, Mike thought with exasperation. There were probably a few relatives on the board, too. But his mood swung back during Genfa's 40-minute presentation as the CEO spoke precisely and clearly about the numbers—it was obvious he was shrewd about the market. Mike was intrigued.

At the second building, his earlier impressions were reinforced: The machines in here looked old and shabby. Some workers were busy, but others were idly waiting for a product delivery. Bales of goods were stacked high in one corner, and Mike stumbled over a box as he picked his way through the dim light. When he noticed that the record sheets on the desk and walls were handwritten, his heart sank: So much for high-tech.

On his way home that night in his own company's car, Mike gazed out the window, trying to figure out what to do next. Should he recommend the acquisition to Bill? Should he propose rejecting the deal and thus probably bring an end to the partnership? The idea of buying out the JV had occurred to him, but it clearly wouldn't work, not with the Chinese partner dreaming of a national brand. When the Audi came to a stop outside Mike's house, he hadn't reached any conclusions. He knew he was going to have another sleepless night at Green Villa.

Can Mike keep the joint venture from unraveling?

Case 41   Wal-Mart's Strategy for the 21st Century: Sustaining Dominance*

By the turn of the century, Wal-Mart had been named Retailer of the Century by *Discount Store News;* made *Fortune* magazine's lists of the Most Admired Companies in America and the 100 Best Companies to Work For, and was ranked on the *Financial Times'* list of the Most Respected Companies in the World. In 2002 Wal-Mart became number one on the Fortune 500 list and was presented with the Ron Brown Award for Corporate Leadership, a presidential award that recognizes companies for outstanding achievement in employee and community relations.

By the end of 2003, Wal-Mart was the world's largest corporation with a market valuation of more than $400 billion, 1.4 million employees, and 4,700 store locations in the United States and abroad (see Appendixes 1A, 1B, and 2A starting on page 884). Operating the world's biggest private satellite communications system, the firm tracked sales, replenished inventory, processed payments, and regulated individual store temperatures in real-time. Wal-Mart's Retail Link-System was the largest civilian database in the world, slightly smaller than that of the Pentagon, and three times the size of the Internal Revenue Service's database.

The company's combined annual growth rate during 1999–2003 was 15 percent in revenue and 14 percent in earnings before interest and taxes (EBIT). Similar growth rates over the next decade, if sustained, would result in a $1 trillion business generating well over $50 billion EBIT with a workforce in excess of 4 million people (see Appendix 2B). Virtually everybody—industry experts, market analysts, consumers, special interest groups, competitors, and suppliers—questioned not only the sustainability, but also the desirability of such current or projected growth rates and consequent dominance. Global 24-hour visibility and exposure were two things that Sam Walton had strived to avoid. His legacy could no longer hope to escape these.

Wal-Mart's leadership was primarily concerned with sustainability. How do you sustain a projected $40 billion growth in revenue and $20 billion growth in EBIT per year? Aware that the past did not always predict the future reliably, top management must have wondered if the firm's formula for success and its current resource allocation strategy would be sufficient to ensure such astronomical growth. How many more Super Centers could be built in the Americas? Could Wal-Mart build a distinctive competency in international operations to fuel growth when neither it nor any other major retailer had yet succeeded in doing so? Could it transport its distinctive competency in logistics to Europe and China along with its corporate culture? With its increased global presence, the firm was being attacked from all sides. Human resource practices, supplier relationships, and purchasing practices along with community relations were increasingly being targeted. A small group of old-timers in Bentonville, Arkansas (the company's headquarters), reminisced over simpler times when Sam would have just advised them to "Manage one store at a time, respect the individual, and create value with our customers."

Company History—Sam Walton's Era, 1962–1992[1]

With previous retailing experience and expertise, Sam Walton and his brother Bud Walton opened their first Wal-Mart Discount City store in 1962 (the same year that Kmart and Target were founded) in Rogers, Arkansas. They opened 15 department-sized stores in small rural towns throughout the Midwest by the end of the 1960s (see Appendix 3).

While Wal-Mart's huge stores and variety of branded merchandising resembled Kmart and other competitors, Sam's "every day low price" (EDLP) and limited promotional budgets proved unique in the industry. A hub-and-spoke distribution system with wholly owned warehousing and transportation together propelled Wal-Mart to *Forbes*'s number one ranking among U.S. discounters in 1977 (the ranking was based on return on equity, return on capital, sales growth, and earnings growth).

Sam Walton's Four Basic Beliefs and Three Pricing Philosophies[2]   At the heart of Sam Walton's philosophy and Wal-Mart's corporate culture were four basic beliefs: excellence in the workplace, respect for the individual, customer service, and always having the lowest prices. The company had stayed true to these principles since 1962. Sam envisioned customers who trusted Wal-Mart's pricing philosophy and the ability to find the lowest prices with the best possible customer service. Years ago, Sam Walton challenged associates to practice what he called "aggressive hospitality." He said "Let's be the most friendly—offer a smile of welcome and beyond what our customers expect. Why not? You can do it and do it better than any other retailing company in the world . . .

*This case was prepared by Professor Michael D. Oliff with the support of research assistant Isil Kosdere as the basis for class discussion. It was developed within the scope of Enterprise 2020, a development program conducted with global enterprises. The School of Management, University of Texas, Dallas, © 2004.

[1]Wal-Mart Stores, Inc., 1999, *International Directory of Company Histories,* vol. 26 (St. James Press). Reproduced in Business and Company Resource Center, 2003 (Farmington Hills, MI: Gale Group), www.galenet.com/servlet/BCRC.

[2]The material in this section is based on information from the official Wal-Mart Web site, www.walmart.com.

exceed your customers' expectations and they'll come back over and over again."

Perhaps the most unique belief Walton had was that each store should reflect the values of its customers and support the vision they hold for their community. As a result, Wal-Mart's community outreach programs were guided by local associates who grew up in the area and understood its needs.

Sam's initial pricing policies permeated the Wal-Mart culture. His every day low price (EDLP) strategy flew in the face of another competitor's "blue-light specials." Not considered as a "sale," an ongoing process at Wal-Mart would ensure EDLP. Another strategy, the "special buy," resulted from the continuous pressure on costs and the global search for merchandise of exceptional value.

Growth and Increased Visibility Sam's Clubs, established in 1983, marked the entrance into the cash-and-carry discount membership market. It also led to expansion into cities and population centers. Within eight years, 150 clubs would be opened in the United States. Format innovations continued as Sam experimented with France's hypermarket concept—stadium-sized stores with groceries, general merchandise, and a host of satellite services. These ultimately gave way to Wal-Mart Super Centers (a 150,000-square-foot format with foods, more items, and more accessible merchandise) with hundreds built in the 1990s.

Wal-Mart enjoyed a 12-year stretch of 35 percent annual profit growth through 1987. Its internal reengineering of the supply chain did not come without external consequences. The firm's buying and distribution practices and general competitive impact on small, independent businesses repeatedly came under fire. Vendor-direct purchasing led to an "uprising" of more than 100,000 independent sales representatives in 1987. Wal-Mart was accused of "excluding them from the selling process." In towns where it had operated for eight or more years, small businesses—drugstores, hardware, clothing, sporting goods—found it virtually impossible to compete with the firm's economies of scale.

In a public relations effort motivated by good business sense, Wal-Mart sent an open letter to U.S. manufacturers in March 1985, inviting them to take part in a "Buy American" program. The company offered to work with them in producing products that could compete against imports. "Our American suppliers must commit to improving their facilities and machinery, remain financially conservative, and work to fill our requirements and, most importantly, strive to improve employee productivity," Walton told American Business in April 1988.

During the same period, Wal-Mart developed a record for community service that began with awarding $1,000 scholarships to high school students in each community it served. At the same time, the company's refusal to stock dozens of widely circulated adult and teen magazines had some critics claiming that Wal-Mart was willfully narrowing the choices of the buying public and in essence bowing to pressure from conservative special interest groups.

Purchases of upstream businesses—Western Merchandise and the McLane Company—increased economies of scale. The merger of the Wholesale Club (adding 28 stores to the Sam's Clubs) and the introduction of Sam's American Choice, the company's own brand of products, signaled the firm's aggressive posture with regard to both current competitors and suppliers.

In 1991 Wal-Mart expanded outside the United States for the first time when it entered into a joint venture with Mexico's largest retailer, Cifra. The venture developed a price club called Club Aurrera, a store that required an annual membership fee of $25. Shoppers could choose from 3,500 products ranging from frozen vegetables to fur coats.

Founder Sam Walton died of bone cancer on April 5, 1992. At the time of his death, he was the second richest man in the world, after the sultan of Brunei, having built a personal fortune in 30 years based solely on creating value with customers. David Glass, CEO, handpicked as Sam's successor, had led a smooth management transition since 1988 and now began to focus on the decade of challenges ahead.

Wal-Mart after Sam

Glass and his management team accelerated growth immediately. From 1992 to 1993, Wal-Mart opened 161 stores, and closed only one. Another 48 Sam's Clubs and 51 Bud's Warehouse Outlets were also opened with expansions or relocations at 170 existing Wal-Mart stores and 40 Sam's Clubs (the company's 2,138 stores included 34 Wal-Mart Super Centers and 256 Sam's Clubs with a net addition of 34.5 million square feet of retail space).

In January 1993 Wal-Mart's reputation was assaulted when NBC-TV's *Dateline* news reported on child laborers in Bangladesh producing merchandise for Wal-Mart stores. The program showed children working for pennies per hour in a country that lacked child labor laws. The program further alleged that items made outside the United States were being sold under "Made in USA" labels as part of the company's "Buy American" campaign started in 1985. Glass appeared on the program saying that he did not know of any child exploitation by the company, but he apologized for some of the incorrect signage.

In April 1993 Wal-Mart expanded further upstream and introduced its private-label "Great Value," which included a line of 350 packaged food items. In the same year Wal-Mart purchased 91 Pace Membership Warehouse clubs from Kmart and converted the new units into Sam's Clubs. Concurrently, the formation of PriceCostco Inc., later renamed Costco Cos., signaled the emergence of Sam's Clubs' only viable rival—a competitor that would challenge the firm's dominance in the cash-and-carry market over the next decade.

Slowdown in the Mid-1990s Wal-Mart's double-digit comparable store sales rates began falling in 1994 and varied between 4 and 7 percent, which was closer to the retail industry average. The Wal-Mart discount store chain, which reached a peak of 1,995 units in 1996, was reduced to 1,921 units by 1998. Instead, the company staked its domestic future on the Wal-Mart Super Center chain, expanded from 34 units in 1993 to 441 units in 1998. Most of the new Super Centers—377 in total—were converted Wal-Mart discount stores, as the company sought the additional per store revenue that could be gleaned from selling groceries. Meanwhile, the Sam's Club chain was struggling and not as profitable as the company overall. As it attempted to turn this business around, Wal-Mart curtailed its expansion in the United States; only 17 more Sam's Clubs were opened between 1995 and 1998.

International Expansion Continues[3] Faced with lagging domestic sales, an aggressive international expansion ensued. Following its 1991 move into Mexico, Wal-Mart entered into the other North American Free Trade Agreement (NAFTA) market, Canada, three years later, when it purchased 122 Woolco stores from Woolworth Corporation. Over the next six years, Wal-Mart became the largest retailer in both Mexico and Canada and made additional entries into Puerto Rico, Argentina, and Brazil. The firm ventured into Japan and Korea in the late 1990s.

Wal-Mart entered China in August 1996 with the opening of its first Super Center and Sam's Club in Shenzhen, near Hong Kong. As a harbinger of China's economic reform and the fastest-growing coastal city in China, Shenzhen proved to be the best location for Wal-Mart's investment. Four years later Wal-Mart had 28 stores and employed more than 15,000 associates in Shenzhen. Wal-Mart subsequently opened 26 additional joint venture stores including 21 Super Centers and 5 Sam's Club units in China's coastal cities.

ASDA, Britain's best-value food and clothing superstore, became part of the Wal-Mart family in July 1999. The company had 247 stores and 21 depots across the United Kingdom employing 125,000 associates. The Wal-Mart name appeared on a U.K. store for the first time in 2000, when the first ASDA–Wal-Mart Super Center opened in Bristol. ASDA–Wal-Mart Super Centers brought a unique shopping experience to British customers, offering the best products of both organizations. By 2003 the company operated 14 ASDA–Wal-Mart Super Centers throughout the U.K.

International sales accounted for approximately 16.7 percent of total company sales in fiscal 2003, the same percentage as in 2001. During 2003 Wal-Mart International opened 120 units in existing markets. The announced units included two restaurant formats, specialty apparel retail stores, and supermarkets in Mexico. Overall, however, the international division's profitability lagged well behind that of domestic operations.

Germany and Wal-Mart's First International 'War'[4] By the second millennium, Germany accounted for 15 percent of Europe's $2 trillion a year retail market. Yet it suffered from a shrinking percentage of consumer spending. In conditions of near oligopoly, the top five German retailers alone accounted for over 60 percent of market share (see Appendixes 4A, 4B, 4C, and 4D for data on the European and, specifically, German retail markets). With average profits of 0.8 percent of sales, this was the least profitable retail market in the industrial world. Such lackluster profitability could be attributed in part due to the family ownership of a majority of German retailers; zoning regulations that imposed severe limits on the construction of large-scale stores; the euro conversion on January 1, 2002, and subsequent confusion among consumers; and the apparent preponderance of price/value versus service/quality expectations held by much of the population.

The acquisition of the 21-unit Wertkauf hypermarket chain in Germany in December 1997 marked not only Wal-Mart's entry into Europe but also into the most competitive retail battleground in the world. The German chain had annual sales of $1.4 billion and was the eighth largest hypermarket operator in the country. The takeover of Spar and its 74 domestic locations (revenues: $1.1 billion) marked the second wave of Wal-Mart's attack. By many accounts, Wal-Mart Germany was not a success from its inception until the beginning of 2004. Pundits argued that the firm chose wisely with the Wertkauf acquisition but poorly with Spar. The latter, considered by Germans to be the weakest player in the market, posed significant brand and quality challenges from the beginning.[5] Knorr and Arndt claimed Wal-Mart Germany's operations had also suffered from:[6]

- A "hubris and clash of cultures" approach by management to labor relations.
- A failure to deliver on its legendary "we sell for less—always," "every day low prices," and "excellent service" value proposition.
- Bad publicity from its repeated infringement of some important German laws and regulations.

Regardless of the reasons, Wal-Mart Germany had clearly not met top management's profit expectations as 2004 began and it continued to pose both significant challenges and opportunities.

[3]The material in this section comes largely from the official Wal-Mart Web site, www.walmart.com.

[4]Knorr, Andreas, & Arndt, Andreas, 2003, Why did Wal-Mart fail in Germany? IWIM, University of Bremen, June 24.

[5]KPMG/EHI, 2001, 15.

[6]Knorr & Arndt, 2003, Why did Wal-Mart fail in Germany?, 18.

Exhibit 1   Economic Concentration of the Top 10 Retail Companies in the World, 2002

Company	Home Country	Sales (US$ millions)
Wal-Mart Stores, Inc.	U.S.	$229,617.0
Carrefour Group	France	64,762.3
Home Depot, Inc.	U.S.	58,247.0
Kroger Co.	U.S.	51,760.0
Metro AG	Germany	48,124.4
Royal Ahold	Netherlands	47,114.3
Target Corporation	U.S.	42,722.0
Tesco PLC	U.K.	39,517.2
Costco Companies	U.S.	37,993.1
ITM Enterprises	France	36,183.7

The Global Retail Industry

Retailing, the second-largest industry in the United States both in the number of establishments and number of employees, was also one of the largest worldwide. In 2003 the retail industry employed over 23 million Americans and generated more than $3 trillion in sales annually. Single-store businesses accounted for over 95 percent of all U.S. retailers, but generated less than 50 percent of all retail store sales. Wal-Mart was by far the largest retailing entity not only in the United States but in the world, equaling the combined sales of the next four largest global players (see Exhibit 1).

An unstable business environment, weak economic growth, and nervous consumers contributed to minimal growth among the world's 100 largest retailers. The average growth rate for the top 100 retailers from 2001 to 2002 dropped to less than 4 percent, with both the "largest" and "smallest" operators struggling to replicate prior-year growth.[7] While Wal-Mart had held the top spot since 1990, there was significant movement among other leading players—both up and down the list—as tough competitive, political, and economic factors took their toll. Further, unlike in prior years, retailers in the U.K., not the United States, were the strongest performers overall.[8]

[7]Retail Forward, comp., The top 100 retailers worldwide 2002.

[8]"The world's largest retailers cannot expect a stable business environment going forward," commented Geoff Wissman, vice-president with Retail Forward. "Slow economic recovery in the U.S. combined with weak economies in Japan, Latin America, and Western Europe, are forcing many retailers to seek alternative outlets for growth outside their home countries . . . Retailers will find themselves battling for market share rather than relying on growing markets," Wissman stated. "The recent difficulties faced by some of the world's largest retailers—including Kmart, Royal Ahold, and Sears—reinforce the fact that retailers of any size can experience serious financial strain."

Metro, Carrefour, and Royal Ahold were all focused on new store sales and continued expansion internationally while grappling with growth in existing markets.

As of January 2004, the retail industry was still fragmented globally with no single player yet able to prove it could dominate across several continents. Industry experts agreed retailers that could successfully develop China, Southeast Asia, and the former Soviet Republics (in that order) would reap long-term benefits for decades to come.

It was also clear that traditional internationalization strategies that relied on "exports" (of products, processes, or services) across borders had not fared well in an environment characterized by small, immobile, and uninformed consumers. To succeed internationally, Wal-Mart would have to pick its way carefully. What vehicles—joint ventures, strategic alliances, franchising, shareholdings in local retailers, mergers, or acquisitions—and capabilities would it invest in?

The North American Retail Industry

Target Corporation, the number two discounter in the United States, had carved out a niche by offering more upscale, fashionable merchandise than rivals Wal-Mart and struggling Kmart. Target had distinguished itself by employing a strategy that relied on exclusive private-label offerings from big-name designers. The nation's number two discounter was number one when it came to corporate giving. Target topped the *Forbes* list of America's Most Philanthropic Companies in 2001, donating 2.5 percent of its 2000 income (nearly $86 million). By comparison, Wal-Mart gave away $116.5 million in 2001, less than 1 percent of its income in 2000.

In 2003 Kroger was the number one pure grocery chain in the United States. The grocery chain planned to

Exhibit 2   The North American Competitors (In $ millions)

		2002	2001	2000
Target	Revenues	$43,917	$39,826	$36,903
	Net income	1,654	1,410	1,264
Sears	Revenues	41,366	40,990	40,848
	Net income	1,376	735	1,343
Kroger	Revenues	51,760	50,098	49,000
	Net income	1,205	1,043	877

spend $120 million by the end of 2004 to open as many as nine new stores and remodel older ones in Tennessee, where Wal-Mart was introducing its Neighborhood Market stores. Also in response to intense competition from Wal-Mart Super Centers, which captured 13.0 percent of the U.S. grocery market in 2002 compared to Kroger's 7.2 percent share, Kroger had been cutting prices to hang onto customers. Wal-Mart operated Super Centers in more than half of Kroger's markets. Lured by the growing popularity of dollar stores, Kroger was experimenting with the concept in two of its Houston supermarkets.

During the same period, Sears was developing a free-standing off-mall format—Sears Grand—to compete directly with the big discounter chains by selling consumables, health and beauty aids, housewares, and toys, among other offerings. The first store (twice the size of an average Sears store) opened in Utah in September 2003. The second Sears Grand shop was set to open in Chicago in the spring of 2004, followed by a third in Las Vegas in the fall. (See Exhibit 2 for a financial comparison of these three North American competitors.)

The Wal-Mart Culture and Distinctive Competencies

As Wal-Mart continued to grow into new areas and develop new formats, much of its success was attributed to its corporate culture and distinctive competencies (see Appendix 5). Walton wanted all his managers and workers to have a hands-on approach to their jobs and to be totally committed to Wal-Mart's main goal, which he defined as total customer satisfaction. To motivate his employees, Walton created a strategic control system that gave employees at all levels continuous feedback about their performance and the company's.[9]

The culture pushed decision-making authority down to store managers, department managers, and individual employees. Wal-Mart was renowned for treating its employees well, but at the same time, demanding commitment and excellent performance. This culture was backed

up with profit-sharing and stock ownership plans for all employees, including associates, to make every employee "think and behave like an owner of the company." No wonder Wal-Mart had higher employee productivity, less shrinkage (employee theft), and lower costs than industry rivals.

Wal-Mart's Distinctive Competencies   As the number of stores grew, Wal-Mart pioneered the development of a hub-and-spoke distribution system, where central distribution warehouses were strategically located to serve clusters of stores. This system allowed Wal-Mart to rapidly replenish stock in its stores and to keep the amount of unproductive space to a minimum.

The results included higher sales per square foot and more rapid inventory turnover. This combination helped to increase store sales and drive down inventory and logistics costs (see Exhibit 3). The firm was also one of the first to utilize computer-based information systems to track in-store sales and transmit this information to suppliers. This information was used to determine pricing and stocking strategies that optimized inventory management. The combination of state-of-the art information systems and the hub-and-spoke distribution system allowed Wal-Mart to build the leanest supply chain in the industry.[10]

The firm's brand and market management, supply chain management, and customer value focus distinguished it in the industry. These corporate abilities or distinctive competencies, coupled with locational assets and unique cultural attributes, served it well throughout the 1990s. Insiders wondered whether these historical strengths alone were sufficient to build a trillion-dollar enterprise over the next decade—with $200 to $500 billion in sales outside the Americas. Furthermore, how could Wal-Mart appease external stakeholders as its influence magnified? For example, concerns with Wal-Mart's purchasing practices resurfaced in December 2003.[11]

---

[9]Sam Walton's approach to implementing Wal-Mart's strategy, in Walton, Sam, 1992, *Made in America* (NY: Doubleday).

[10]The case "Wal-Mart's Mexican Adventure."

[11]Fishman, Charles, 2003, The Wal-Mart you don't know (Why low prices have a high cost), *Fast Company,* December.

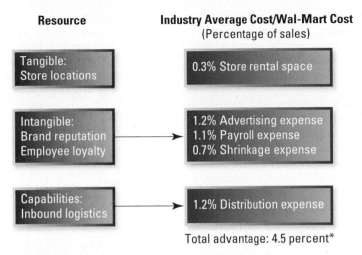

Exhibit 3   Wal-Mart's Competitive Advantage

*Wal-Mart's cost advantage as a percentage of sales. Each percentage point advantage is worth $500 million in net income to Wal-Mart.

Source: Pankaj Ghemawat, "Wal-Mart Stores' Discount Operations," Harvard Business School case 9-387-018.

There is no question that doing business with Wal-Mart can give a supplier a fast, heady jolt of sales and market share. But that fix can come with long-term consequences for the health of a brand and a business.

Wal-Mart is legendary for forcing its suppliers to redesign everything from their packaging to their computer systems. It is also legendary for quite straightforwardly telling them what it will pay for their goods.

Many companies and their executives frankly admit that supplying Wal-Mart is like getting into the company version of basic training with an implacable army drill sergeant. The process may be unpleasant. But there can be some positive results.

Future Questions

CNN described the coming extinction of American malls as the "Death of an American Icon." In 2000 PricewaterhouseCoopers and the Center for the New Urbanism first identified "grey fields," or dying malls, as those with annual sales of less than $150 per square foot—less than a third of sales at successful malls. Their study found that 7 percent of existing regional malls qualified as grey fields, and another 12 percent were headed in that direction. Increasingly, these grey fields were being redeveloped into lifestyle centers or "main street centers," which mimicked traditional villages of the past—with lots of open-air space, attractive landscaping, outdoor sound systems, park benches, artistic fountains, and attractive building facades. Regardless of the fate of American malls, Wal-Mart and its rivals wondered:

- What would the retail industry look like by the year 2010?
- Would the economy return to the growth rates of the mid-'90s?
- Would consumers worry about inflation or deflation?
- Would aging baby boomers still be driving consumer spending or would they be tapped out by their overextended credit card debt and devastated retirement accounts?
- By 2010 would Wal-Mart take a larger share in existing product categories, or leap into new categories like banking and auto retailing?

The five dominant trends that could alter the face of the retailing industry in the remaining years of the decade were:[12]

1. Removal of the "one size fits all" premise which would be replaced by a system in which individual retailers employed a more robust multiformat or portfolio strategy.
2. A very unique concept of "Wal-Mart always smiling" would be even more successful by 2010, with the company's continued focus on the customer shopping experience, customer care, customer intimacy, and customer value.
3. As consumers searched for greater shopping efficiency, their preferences would shift away from

[12]2003, *Retail Merchandiser*, 43 (5): 4.

traditional supermarkets and discount department stores toward Super Centers. Some supermarkets would expand their one-stop shopping appeal while others would tap into emerging trends such as natural/organic, ethnic, gourmet, and health food products.

4. The days of mass-merchandised specialty chains with multitudes of outlets delivering the same narrow and deep assortment of goods to the market, regardless of location, would be over. Specialty retailers would manage a portfolio of different concepts, each operating a small chain of stores in order to address multiple market opportunities.

5. Customers would embrace technologies that gave them more control over the shopping process. These would include Web-enabled store kiosks which give shoppers access to a retailer's full inventory; wireless technology that provides shoppers with product information on handheld devices; smart carts that draw on shoppers' buying history to alert them to products and promotions; radio frequency identification (RFID)-enabled checkout where all items in a cart are scanned at once; and contactless payment solutions that use RFID-enabled smart cards or transponders.

Other Retail Industry Trends

By 2003 the consolidation wave that started in the United States had caught on in Europe too. With the largest retail space per capita, the U.S. market was a prime candidate for consolidation owing to the proliferation of retailers in the previous two decades that led to the paring down of margins and intense undercutting of prices. The inevitable shakeout was precipitated by Wal-Mart's takeover of many small retailers.

Wal-Mart's acquisition of the U.K. food retailer ASDA in 2002 marked the international entry of American retailers into the United Kingdom. Until then, U.S. retailers had concentrated on domestic expansion only. However, globalization had hit Europe much earlier and the French firm Carrefour had long ago struck roots in South America and Mexico. Similarly, Royal Ahold struck firm roots in the U.S. retail arena with its Stop & Shop chain and the takeover of the ailing Peapod.com.

Many retailers had started vending fuel adjacent to their outlets. This not only came as a boon to the time-starved customer but also provided an opportunity for retailers to cross-subsidize merchandise sales with fuel sales. A similar phenomenon happened at gasoline stations where convenience stores catered to the basic needs of customers. "Buying the product from the cheapest and most efficient source" was the retailer credo.

To reduce time in queues, retailers had given self-checkout authorization to customers. Initially, this was done only for frequent shoppers or loyalty cardholders.

The reduction of cycle time (between ordering and physical arrival of the merchandise) was a critical cost driver in the retailing industry. Retailers looked for ways to cut inventories. The most common facilitator was an accurate demand and sales forecast as well as rapid replenishment.

Technology Trends

Enterprise integration, or linking all the different systems used by a retailer to provide seamless information flow and better resource management, was an important trend emerging in the retail industry.

Smart cards that contained detailed customer information provided a wealth of information to the retailer about customers' buying habits and patterns. Also, they helped in tailoring the offering to specific needs. They integrated many operations and one card could be used across locations and functions. To avoid the risk of obsolescence, many retail software vendors provided Web-based packages updated in real-time.

Radio frequency data communication had become a standard in the retail fulfillment industry. Handheld radio frequency devices provided an excellent tool to perform inventory tracking and order-picking activities.

Large retailers had relied on intranets and extranets for information sharing within the organization and with external entities, respectively. Extranets had long been a preferred way of carrying out electronic data interchange with suppliers. However, with the Internet becoming omnipresent, their efficacy would decrease, and virtual private networks that offered a secure pipeline for information flow using the Internet would become increasingly employed for the exchange of information.

Consumer Trends[13]

Single-serve, "easy-pour," and portable packaging had all been on the scene awhile. However, these were expected to become the norm for most products in addition to required enhancements in temperature-control, spill-proof, lifestyle, and alternative-usage packaging.

Obesity and the problems associated with it were expected to increase. Manufacturers and retailers would have to deal with this issue by offering healthier foods and increased information relating to health and nutrition. Products oriented toward wellness and an improved life would continue to emerge in numerous categories beyond the traditional health and beauty aid (HBA) and drug categories. These products made numerous claims and required significant communication with the consumer to ensure their success. This trend began with the aging population, but was fueled by manufacturers seeking any avenue available to develop and market new products ahead of the continued growth of store-controlled brands.

---

[13]The material in this section is provided in large part by MJH & Associates, July 2003.

Shoppers continued to decrease the amount of time they spent on each shopping trip. Grocery shopping continued to be viewed as "need to do" instead of "want to do." As such, consumers desired to travel fewer aisles on any one shopping trip and ultimately spend less time in the store. The implications of these views would be continued modification of store layouts and limits on the absolute size of new stores built.

In future, loyalty card programs and, more importantly, the processing of related data would be performed by third-party companies. These dedicated research firms focused on linking databases across industries. The result would be far more valuable marketing information, both within and outside the grocery industry. Due to the inability of most retailers to provide truly individualized services to loyalty cardholders, their future use would be questioned, if not eliminated, by some retailers and refocused by others. This trend would be exacerbated by consumer privacy concerns or plain indifference.

Wal-Mart's Future

In January 2004 Wal-Mart was at the top of the business world. By anyone's reckoning, it had dominated an industry for two decades and grown into one of the most influential corporate enterprises in history. To maintain its phenomenal growth in the future, it needed to sustain growth in the Americas and address development and profitability issues internationally.

With market saturation looming in the United States and the absence of any truly international retailer, how would Sam's successors allocate future resources to ensure Wal-Mart's global dominance across disparate markets?

Appendix 1A   *Fortune* Rankings of the World's Largest Companies

Rank	Fortune 1992	Value	Rank	Fortune 2003	Value
1	ExxonMobil	$75,800.00	1	Wal-Mart Stores	$246,525.00
2	General Electric	73,900.00	2	General Motors	186,763.00
3	Wal-Mart Stores	73,500.00	3	ExxonMobil	182,466.00
4	Royal Dutch Shell	71,800.00	4	Ford Motor	163,630.00
5	Nippon Telephone & Telegraph	71,400.00	5	General Electric	131,698.00
6	Philip Morris	69,300.00	6	Citigroup	100,789.00
7	AT&T	68,000.00	7	ChevronTexaco	92,043.00
8	Coca-Cola	55,700.00	8	Intl. Business Machines	83,132.00
9	Mitsubishi Bank	53,500.00	9	American Intl. Group	67,722.80
10	Merck	50,300.00	10	Verizon Communications	67,625.00
11	IND Bank of Japan	46,500.00	11	Altria Group	62,182.00
12	Sumitomo Bank	45,600.00	12	Conoco Phillips	58,394.00
13	Toyota Motor	44,100.00	13	Home Depot	58,247.00
14	Fuji Bank	41,800.00	14	Hewlett-Packard	56,588.00
15	Dai-Ichi Kangyo Bank	41,800.00	15	Boeing	54,069.00
16	Sanwa Bank	37,900.00	16	Fannie Mae	52,901.10
17	British Telecom	37,800.00	17	Merck	51,790.30
18	Procter & Gamble	36,400.00	18	Kroger	51,759.50
19	Glaxo Holdings	36,100.00	19	Cardinal Health	51,135.70
20	Bristol-Myers Squibb	35,100.00	20	McKesson	50,006.00

Amounts in $ millions.

Appendix 1B   Wal-Mart Stores: Five-Year Financial Summary

	(Dollar amounts in millions except per share data) Fiscal Years Ending January 31				
	2004	**2003**	**2002**	**2001**	**2000**
Net sales	$256,329	$229,616	$204,011	$180,787	$156,249
Net sales increase	12%	13%	13%	16%	20%
Domestic comparative store sales increase*	4%	5%	6%	5%	8%
Cost of sales	$198,747	$178,299	$159,097	$140,720	$121,825
Operating, selling, general, and administrative expenses	44,909	39,983	35,147	30,822	26,025
Interest expense, net	832	927	1,183	1,196	840
Effective tax rate	36%	35%	36%	36%	37%
Income from continuing operations	$8,861	$7,818	$6,448	$6,087	$5,394
Net income	9,054	7,955	6,592	6,235	5,324
Per share of common stock:					
Income from continuing operations, diluted	2.03	1.76	1.44	1.36	1.21
Net income, diluted	2.07	1.79	1.47	1.39	1.19
Dividends	0.36	0.3	0.28	0.24	0.2
Financial Position					
Current assets of continuing operations	$ 34,421	$ 29,543	$ 26,615	$ 25,344	$ 23,478
Inventories	26,612	24,401	22,053	20,987	19,296
Property, plant and equipment, and capital leases, net	58,530	51,374	45,248	40,461	35,533
Total assets of continuing operations	104,912	92,900	81,549	76,231	68,983
Current liabilities of continuing operations	37,418	32,225	26,795	28,366	25,525
Long-term debt	17,102	16,597	15,676	12,489	13,653
Long-term obligations under capital leases	2,997	3,000	3,044	3,152	3,000
Shareholders' equity	43,623	39,461	35,192	31,407	25,878
Financial Ratios					
Current ratio	0.9	0.9	1	0.9	0.9
Return on assets**	9%	9%	8%	9%	10%
Return on shareholders' equity***	21%	21%	19%	21%	23%

Source: Wal-Mart 2004 Annual Report.

*Comparative store sales are considered to be sales at stores that were open as of February 1 of the prior fiscal year and have not been expanded or relocated since February 1 of the prior fiscal year.

**Income from continuing operations before cumulative effect of accounting change divided by average assets.

***Income from continuing operations divided by average shareholders' equity.

Financial information for all years has been restated to reflect the sale of McLane Company, Inc., ("McLane") that occurred in fiscal 2004. McLane is presented as a discontinued operation.

All years have been restated for the adoption of the expense recognition provisions of Financial Accounting Standards Board Statement No. 123, "Accounting and Disclosure of Stock-Based Compensation." Fiscal 1994 and 1995 were not affected by the adoption.

In fiscal 2003, the company adopted Financial Accounting Standards Board Statement No. 142, "Goodwill and Other Intangible Assets."

In years prior to adoption, the company recorded amortization expense related to goodwill.

Appendix 2A   Number of Wal-Mart Stores

Year	2001		2002		2003	
Store Type	**Domestic**	**International**	**Domestic**	**International**	**Domestic**	**International**
Regular discount stores	1,736	612	1,647	648	1,568	942
Super Centers	888	405	1,066	455	1,258	238
Sam's Club	475	53	500	64	525	71
Neighborhood markets	19	0	31	6	49	37
Total	3,118	1,070	3,244	1,173	3,400	1,288

Appendix 2B   Wal-Mart's EBIT and Net Income, 1987–2003

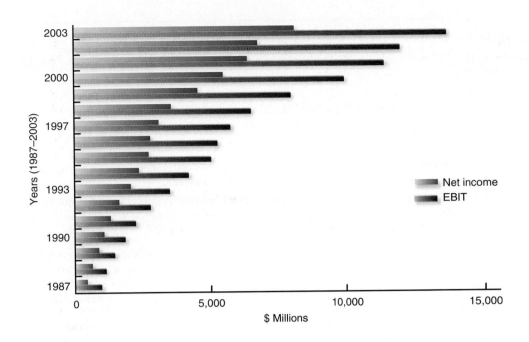

Appendix 3   Wal-Mart Timeline

1962   Sam Walton and his brother opened their first Wal-Mart Discount City in Rogers, Arkansas.

1969   Brothers had opened 18 Wal-Mart stores throughout Arkansas, Missouri, Kansas, and Oklahoma. They still owned 15 Ben Franklin franchises.

1970   Wal-Mart went public.

1972   Company was listed on the New York Stock Exchange for the first time.

1976   The Waltons phased out Ben Franklin Stores.

1977   The company made its first significant acquisition when it bought 16 Mohr-Value stores in Missouri and Illinois.

1977   Based on data from the previous five years, *Forbes* ranked the nation's discount and variety stores. Wal-Mart ranked first in return on equity, return on capital, sales growth, and earnings growth.

1978   Wal-Mart began operating its own pharmacy, auto service center, and jewelry divisions, and acquired Hutchinson Wholesale Shoe Co.

1979   With 276 stores in 11 states, sales rose to $1.25 billion.

1983   The company opened its first three Sam's Wholesale Clubs and began its expansion into markets in larger towns.

1985   "Buy American" program was launched.

1987   Wal-Mart's first Hypermart USA store was opened.

1987   Prices were reduced as much as 40% below full retail level; sales volume averaged $1 million per week.

1987   100,000 independent representatives initiated a public campaign to fight Wal-Mart's effort to remove them from the selling process, claiming that their elimination jeopardized a manufacturer's right to choose how it sells its products.

1988   Concentrated in the South and Midwest, Wal-Mart operated in 24 states.

1990   The first stores opened in California, Nevada, North Dakota, South Dakota, Pennsylvania, and Utah.

1990   Wal-Mart agreed to sell its nine convenience store–gas station outlets to Conoco Inc.

1990   Acquired the McLane Company, Inc., a distributor of grocery and retail products based in Temple, Texas.

1991   A new store brand, Sam's American Choice, was introduced.

1991   The company owned 148 Sam's Clubs.

1992   April 5: Founder Sam Walton died.

1992   The company opened 150 new Wal-Mart stores and 60 Sam's Clubs. Some of these stores represented a change in policy for the company, opening near big cities with large populations.

1992   Wal-Mart entered into a joint venture with Cifra in Mexico.

1993   A television show revealed child laborers in Bangladesh producing merchandise for Wal-Mart for five cents an hour. The program further alleged that foreign-made products were being sold under "Made in USA" labels.

1993   Wal-Mart introduced another private label called Great Value and channeled the proceeds from its American Choice label into the Competitive Edge Scholarship Fund.

1993   Wal-Mart's 1,914 stores included 40 Super Centers in 45 states and Puerto Rico, 208 Sam's Clubs in 42 states, and four Hypermart USAs. Retailers Dayton Hudson, Kmart, and Meijer complained about Wal-Mart's misleading price comparisons.

1994   Purchased 122 Woolco stores in Canada from Woolworth Corporation.

1994   Wal-Mart signed an agreement with the State of Michigan promising various changes in the way it compares prices to those of its competitors.

1994   Announced plans to expand into Argentina and Brazil.

1994   A joint venture was formed to open three to four stores in Hong Kong and to operate discount stores in China.

1995   David Glass received *Chief Executive* magazine's 1995 Chief Executive of the Year Award.

(continued on next page)

(continued)

1996   Tested the sale of stock items on the Internet.

1996   Wal-Mart opened its first Super Center and Sam's Club in Shenzhen, China.

1997   Wal-Mart entered Europe for the first time when it acquired the 21-unit Wertkauf hypermarket chain in Germany.

1998   In an effort to accelerate growth, Wal-Mart began testing a new format, the Wal-Mart Neighborhood Market.

1998   Opened 32 Super Center stores, bringing the total number in operation to 542; opened two stores in New Hampshire. Operations spanned 29 states.

1998   Wal-Mart entered Korea through its acquisition and conversion of four Makro stores.

1998   A Wal-Mart expansion under a franchise agreement into a troubled Indonesia appeared to have stalled.

1999   Purchased the 230-store ASDA Group PLC, the third-largest food retailer in the United Kingdom. Named one of the Most Admired Companies in America by *Fortune*.

2000   Glass stepped down as CEO and president, and was succeeded by H. Lee Scott, Jr.

2000   Became the largest retailer in Mexico and acquired full ownership of 194 stores and 205 restaurants from its former partner Cifra SA.

2000   Became union-free in North America and converted the last of its remaining Hypermarket USA stores to a Wal-Mart Super Center.

2002   Wal-Mart purchased at 34% stake in Seiyu, Ltd., a leading Japanese retailer. Seiyu operated over 400 supermarkets in Japan and employed 30,000 associates.

2002   When fiscal year sales reached $220 billion, Wal-Mart became the largest company in the world.

2002   Planned to invest $2 billion on international expansion.

2003   Was announced No. 1 on *Fortune* magazine's annual survey of Most Admired Companies in America.

Appendix 4A   Store Hours in Selected European Union Countries

Country	Mon.–Fri.	Sat.	Sun./Holidays	Hours per Week
United Kingdom	0000–2400	0000–2400	0000–2400	168
Netherlands	0600–2200	0600–2200	Closed	96
Spain	0000–2400	0000–2400	Closed	144
France	0000–2400	0000–2400	Open*	144
Germany	0600–2000	0600–2000	Closed	84

*Only store owners and their family members, but no employees, are permitted to work on Sundays and holidays.

Source: *KPMG/EHI,* 2001, p. 10.

Appendix 4B Germany's Top 15 Retailers, 2002

Rank	Company	Revenues in Germany (€ billions)
1	Metro AG	€32.0
2	Rewe Group	28.6
3	Edeka/AVA Group	25.2
4	Aldi Group	25.0
5	Schwarz Gruppe	17.2
6	KarstadtQuelle	16.1
7	Tengelmann Group	12.5
8	Lekkerland-Tobaccoland	8.2
9	Spar Group	7.5
10	Schlecker	5.3
11	Globus	3.4
12	Dohle Group	2.9
13	Wal-Mart Germany	2.9
14	Norma	2.4
15	Bartels-Langness	2.1

Source: *KPMG/EHI*, 2001.

Appendix 4C   German Retailers: Productivity per Unit of Sales Floor

Rank	Company	Sales in € per Sq. Meter
1	Aldi Group	€7,500
2	Rewe Group	5,850
3	Globus	5,250
4	Schwarz Group	4,900
5	Metro	4,000
6	Edeka Group	3,600
7	Tengelmann Group	3,600
8	Wal-Mart	3,500
9	Spar Group	3,000

Source: *KPMG/EHI*, 2001, p. 15.

Appendix 4D   German Retailers: Overall Customer Satisfaction

Rank	Company	Satisfaction Index (Maximum: 100)
1	Aldi Group	73.45
2	Globus	71.42
3	Kaufland	71.01
4	Lidl	69.09
5	Norma	68.52
6	Marktkauf	66.96
7	Wal-Mart	64.39
8	Metro	63.97
9	Penny	63.32
10	Real	62.50

Source: *KPMG/EHI*, 2001, p. 15.

Appendix 5　Sam's Rules for Building a Business

Sam's 10 Rules for Building a Business

People often ask, "What is Wal-Mart's secret to success?" In response to this ever-present question, Sam Walton compiled a list of 10 key factors that unlock the mystery in his 1992 book *Made in America*. These factors are known as "Sam's Rules for Building a Business."

Rule 1: Commit to your business. Believe in it more than anybody else. I think I overcame every single one of my personal shortcomings by the sheer passion I brought to my work. I don't know if you're born with this kind of passion, or if you can learn it. But I do know you need it. If you love your work, you'll be out there every day trying to do it the best you possibly can, and pretty soon everybody around will catch the passion from you—like a fever.

Rule 2: Share your profits with all your Associates, and treat them as partners. In turn, they will treat you as a partner, and together you will all perform beyond your wildest expectations. Encourage your Associates to hold a stake in the company. Offer discounted stock, and grant them stock for their retirement. It's the single best thing we ever did.

Rule 3: Motivate your partners. Money and ownership alone aren't enough. Constantly, day by day, think of new and more interesting ways to motivate and challenge your partners.

Rule 4: Communicate everything you possibly can to your partners. The more they know, the more they'll understand. The more they understand, the more they'll care. Once they care, there's no stopping them.

Rule 5: Appreciate everything your Associates do for the business. A paycheck and a stock option will buy one kind of loyalty. But all of us like to be told how much somebody appreciates what we do for them. We like to hear it often, and especially when we have done something we're really proud of. Nothing else can quite substitute for a few well-chosen, well-timed, sincere words of praise.

Rule 6: Celebrate your successes. Find some humor in your failures. Don't take yourself so seriously. Loosen up, and everybody around you will loosen up. Have fun. Show enthusiasm—always.

Rule 7: Listen to everyone in your company. And figure out ways to get them talking. The folks on the front lines—the ones who actually talk to the customer—are the only ones who really know what's going on out there. You'd better find out what they know. This really is what total quality is all about.

Rule 8: Exceed your customers' expectations. If you do, they'll come back over and over. Give them what they want—and a little more. Let them know you appreciate them. Make good on all your mistakes, and don't make excuses—apologize.

Rule 9: Control your expenses better than your competition. This is where you can always find the competitive advantage. For 25 years running—long before Wal-Mart was known as the nation's largest retailer—we ranked No. 1 in our industry for the lowest ratio of expenses to sales.

Rule 10: Swim upstream. Go the other way. Ignore the conventional wisdom. If everybody else is doing it one way, there's a good chance you can find your niche by going in exactly the opposite direction.

Other Important Rules and Policies

The Sundown Rule: One Sunday morning, Jeff, a pharmacist at a Wal-Mart store in Harrison, Arkansas, received a call from his store. A store associate informed him that one of his pharmacy customers, a diabetic, had accidentally dropped her insulin down her garbage disposal. Knowing that a diabetic without insulin could be in grave danger, Jeff immediately rushed to the store, opened the pharmacy and filled the customer's insulin prescription. This is just one of many ways your local Wal-Mart store might honor what is known by our Associates as the Sundown Rule.

The Ten-Foot Rule: One of Wal-Mart's secrets to customer service is our "10-foot attitude," handed down to us by Wal-Mart Founder, Sam Walton. During his many store visits, he encouraged associates to take a pledge with him:　". . . I want you to promise that whenever you come within 10 feet of a customer, you will look him in the eye, greet him, and ask him if you can help him."

Pricing Policy: Sam's adherence to this pricing philosophy was unshakable, as one of Wal-Mart's first store managers recalls:

> Sam wouldn't let us hedge on a price at all. Say the list price was $1.98, but we had paid only 50 cents. Initially, I would say, "Well, it's originally $1.98, so why don't we sell it for $1.25?" And, he'd say, "No. We paid 50 cents for it. Mark it up 30 percent, and that's it. No matter what you pay for it, if we get a great deal, pass it on to the customer." And of course that's what we did.

Source: The official Wal-Mart Web site, www.walmart.com.

In the quarter ending January 31, 2004, World Wrestling Entertainment (WWE) posted a profit of $8.9 million, compared to a loss of $16 million in the same period a year earlier. Although the firm had not shown any growth in its revenues, it had nevertheless managed to generate a decent profit as a result of its cost-cutting measures. "Results for the third quarter exceeded our expectations," stated WWE's president and CEO Linda McMahon. "Improved operating results across our television, advertising, and home video businesses coupled with a continued decrease in our overhead contributed to a strong and profitable quarter."[1]

The results could indicate that WWE was finally pulling out of three years of decline. During the 1990s, WWE's potent mix of shaved, pierced, and pumped-up muscled hunks; buxom, scantily clad, and sometimes cosmetically enhanced beauties; and body-bashing clashes of good versus evil had resulted in an empire that claimed over 35 million fans. Furthermore, the vast majority of these fans were males between the ages of 12 and 34, the demographic segment that makes most advertisers drool. And these guys had driven up WWE's revenues by their insatiable appetite for tickets, broadcasts, books, CDs, games, and other merchandise. See Exhibits 1 and 2 for the company's income statement and balance sheet for 2001 to 2003.

By the end of 1999, WWE had managed to draw on its surge in popularity to raise $170 million through an initial public offering. The husband-and-wife team of Vince and Linda McMahon planned to use these new funds to push aggressively for further growth by moving the firm beyond its wrestling roots. In some ways, the efforts to pursue other opportunities were driven by the firm's desire to reduce its dependence on wrestling, in case its popularity may have peaked.

However, most of WWE's efforts to build on its success with wrestling led to significant losses. The failure of the firm's effort to create a football league folded after just one season, resulting in a $57 million loss. As WWE stumbled in its efforts to diversify, it also began to see a drop in revenues from wrestling. It struggled to create new wrestling stars and to introduce new characters into its shows. Some of WWE's most valuable younger viewers were also turning to new reality-based shows on television such as *Survivor, Fear Factor,* and *Jackass.*

Over the last year, however, things seem to be finally turning around for World Wrestling Entertainment. Vince

McMahon gained a lot of publicity from the show that his crew performed for U.S. troops in Iraq during the 2003 Christmas holidays. The 2004 version of its annual premier live show, *Wrestlemania XX,* sold out almost immediately after tickets went on sale at Madison Square Garden in New York City. And new wrestling stars such as rapper John Cena and Randy Orton began to draw back audiences to WWE's live events and more viewers to its television shows, including pay-per-view events.

Developing a Wrestling Empire

Most of the success of World Wrestling Entertainment can be attributed to the persistent efforts of Vince McMahon. He was a self-described juvenile delinquent who went to military school as a teenager to avoid being sent to a reformatory. Around 1970 Vince joined his father's wrestling company, Capital Wrestling Corporation. He did on-air commentary, developed scripts, and otherwise promoted wrestling matches.

Vince bought Capital Wrestling from his father in 1982, eventually renaming it the World Wrestling Federation (WWF), the name by which it was known until the World Wildlife Fund, which had the same initials, forced a change. At that time, wrestling was managed by regional fiefdoms that avoided encroaching on anyone else's territory. Vince changed all that by paying local television stations around the country to broadcast his matches. His aggressive pursuit of national audiences gradually squeezed out most rivals. "I banked on the fact that they were behind the times, and they were," said McMahon.[2]

Soon after, Vince broke another taboo by admitting to the public that wrestling matches were scripted. Although he made this admission to avoid the scrutiny of state athletic commissions, wrestling fans appreciated his honesty. The WWF began to draw in more fans through the elaborate story lines and the captivating characters of its wrestling matches. The firm turned wrestlers such as Hulk Hogan and Andre the Giant into mainstream icons of pop culture. By the late 1980s, the WWF's *Raw Is War* had become a top-rated show on cable and the firm also began to offer pay-per-view shows.

Vince faced his most formidable competition after 1988, when Ted Turner bought out World Championship Wrestling (WCW), one of the few major rivals still operating. Turner spent millions luring away WWF stars such as Hulk Hogan and Macho Man Randy Savage. He used these stars to launch a show on his TNT channel to go up against WWF's major show, *Raw Is War.* Although Turner's new show caused a temporary dip in the ratings for the WWF's shows, Vince fought back with pumped-up scripts, mouthy muscle-men, and lycra-clad women. "Ted Turner decided to come after me and all of my talent," growled Vince, "and now he's where he should be . . ."[3]

This case was prepared by Professor Jamal Shamsie of Michigan State University. This case was developed from published sources as a basis for class discussion rather than to illustrate either effective or ineffective handling of an administrative situation. Copyright © 2004 Jamal Shamsie.

Exhibit 1   World Wrestling Entertainment: Income Statement
(All figures in thousands)

	Period Ending April 30		
	2003	2002	2001
Total Revenue	$374,264	$425,026	$456,043
Cost of revenue	237,343	260,218	258,103
Gross Profit	136,921	164,808	197,940
Selling, general, and administrative	99,349	109,571	105,779
Others	10,965	13,113	7,180
Operating Income or Loss	26,607	42,124	84,981
Income from continuing operations			
Total other income/expenses, net	1,114	18,202	15,916
Earnings before interest and taxes	27,721	60,326	100,897
Interest expense	783	784	856
Pretax income	26,938	59,542	100,041
Income tax expense	10,836	21,947	37,144
Net income from continuing operations	16,102	37,595	62,897
Discontinued operations	(35,557)	4,638	(46,910)
Net Income	(19,455)	42,233	15,987
Preferred stock and other adjustments	—	—	—
Net Income Applicable to Common Shares	$ (19,455)	$ 42,233	$ 15,987

Source: World Wrestling Entertainment annual reports.

In 2001 Vince was finally able to acquire WCW from Turner's parent firm AOL Time Warner for a bargain price of $5 million. Because of the manner in which he eliminated most of his rivals, Vince had earned a reputation for being as aggressive and ambitious as any character in the ring. Paul MacArthur, publisher of the industry newsletter *Wrestling Perspective,* praised his accomplishments: "McMahon understands the wrestling business better than anyone else. He's considered by most in the business to be brilliant."[4]

Creating a Script for Success
Since taking over the World Wrestling Federation, Vince has changed the entire focus of the wrestling shows. He looked to television soap operas for ways to enhance the entertainment value of his live events. Vince reduced the amount of actual wrestling and replaced it with wacky yet somewhat compelling story lines. He developed interesting characters and story lines by employing techniques similar to those used by many successful television shows. There was great deal of reliance on the themes of "good versus evil" or "settling the score" in the development of the plots for his wrestling matches. The plots and subplots ended up providing viewers with a mix of romance, sex, sports, comedy, and violence against a backdrop of pyrotechnics.

Over time, the scripts for the matches became tighter, with increasingly intricate story lines, plots, and dialogue. All the details of every match were worked out well in advance, leaving the wrestlers themselves to decide only the manner in which they would dispatch their opponents. Vince referred to his wrestlers as "athletic performers" who were selected on the basis of their acting ability in addition to their physical stamina.

Vince's use of characters was well thought out. He was able to exploit the stage characters that he created for each of his wrestlers to develop and sell various kinds of merchandise. Vince also ensured that his firm owned the rights to the characters played by his wrestlers. This allowed him to continue to exploit any character that he developed for his television shows, even after the wrestler who played that character had left the firm.

Exhibit 2 World Wrestling Entertainment: Balance Sheet
(All figures in thousands)

	Period Ending April 30		
	2003	**2002**	**2001**
Assets			
Current assets			
Cash and cash equivalents	$128,473	$ 86,659	$ 45,040
Short-term investments	142,641	207,407	194,631
Net receivables	49,729	63,835	72,337
Inventory	839	1,851	4,918
Other current assets	39,572	15,935	23,581
Total Current Assets	361,254	375,687	340,507
Property, plant, and equipment	59,325	91,759	83,521
Goodwill	—	11,588	—
Intangible assets	4,625	—	—
Other assets	7,447	8,407	19,064
Total Assets	432,651	487,441	443,092
Liabilities			
Current liabilities			
Accounts payable	49,179	64,076	58,434
Short/current long-term debt	777	601	556
Other current liabilities	36,216	24,024	26,340
Total Current Liabilities	86,172	88,701	85,330
Long-term debt	9,126	9,302	9,903
Total Liabilities	95,298	98,003	95,233
Stockholders' Equity			
Common stock	730	729	729
Retained earnings	69,634	93,435	51,202
Treasury stock	(30,569)	(1,139)	—
Capital surplus	297,315	296,938	296,525
Other stockholder equity	243	(525)	(597)
Total Stockholder Equity	337,353	389,438	347,859
Net Tangible Assets	$332,728	$377,850	$347,859

Source: World Wrestling Entertainment annual reports.

By the late 1990s Vince had two weekly shows on television. Besides the original flagship program on the USA cable channel, the WWF had added *Smackdown!* on the UPN broadcast television channel. He developed a continuous story line using the same characters to drive the audience to both the shows. But the acquisition of WCW resulted in a significant increase in the number of wrestling stars under contract. Trying to incorporate more than 200 characters into the story lines for the WWF's shows proved to be a challenging task.

To deal with this challenge, Vince began to develop different plots using a different set of characters for his cable television show *Raw Is Wild* and his broadcast television show *Smackdown!* He also moved *Raw* from the USA channel to Viacom's Spike TV cable channel. The combination of these changes resulted in a significant drop in viewers for both of the WWF's television shows. Attendance at the firm's live events was also hurt by the absence of key wrestling stars such as "Stone Cold" Steve Austin and "The Rock" Dwayne Johnson, who were either out with injuries or making movies.

Managing a Road Show

A typical workweek for the WWF can be grueling for the McMahons, the talent, and the crew. The organization puts on some 200 live shows a year requiring everyone to be on the road most days of the week. The touring crew includes 85 stagehands and 120 other crew members. All of the WWF's live events, including those used for its two weekly shows *Raw* and *Smackdown!,* are held in different cities. Consequently, the crew is always packing up a dozen 18-wheelers and driving hundreds of miles to get from one performance to the next. The live shows also provide material for WWF specials or pay-per-view shows. Since there are no repeats of any WWF shows, the live performances must be held all year-round.

Live shows form the core of all of the WWF's businesses. They give the firm a big advantage in the entertainment world. Most of the crowd show up wearing WWF merchandise and scream throughout the show. Vince and his crew pay special attention to the response of the audience to different parts of the show. The script for each performance is not set until the day of the show and sometimes changes are made even in the middle of a show. Vince boasted, "We're in contact with the public more than any entertainment company in the world."[5]

Although the live shows usually fill up, the attendance fee—on average, around $30—barely covers the cost of the production. But these live performances provide content for nine hours of original television programming as well as additional footage for the WWF Web

site. The shows also create strong demand for WWF merchandise. In addition, the WWF cuts most of its own advertising deals, offering spots on its television shows, its Internet site, or even at the live shows. "It's really one content being repurposed over and over again," explained August Liguori, the firm's chief financial officer.[6]

This road show is managed not only by Vince, but by all of his family. Vince's efforts notwithstanding, the development of the World Wrestling Federation turned into a family affair. While the slick and highly toned Vince could be regarded as the creative muscle behind the growing sports entertainment empire, his wife Linda began quietly to manage its day-to-day operation. Throughout its existence, she has helped to balance the books, make the deals, and handle the details necessary for the growth and development of the WWF franchise.

One of Vince and Linda's greatest pleasures has been to see their kids move into the business. Their son Shane heads wwf.com, the firm's streaming media site, and their daughter Stephanie has just become part of the creative writing team. "This business is my heart and soul and passion and always has been," Stephanie commented. The family's devotion lies behind much of the success of the WWF. "If they are out there giving 110 percent, it's a lot easier to get it from everyone else," said wrestler Steve Blackman.[7]

Pursuing New Opportunities

Flush with this success, the World Wrestling Federation raised $170 million through an initial public offering in late 1999. In its prospectus, the firm stated that it would use the proceeds in part to diversify and thus be less dependent on wrestling. Under the expert guidance of Linda, WWF had already branched into merchandise such as action figures, CDs, home videos, books, magazines, and games (see Exhibit 3).

The most ambitious of the WWF's diversification efforts was the creation of an eight-team football league called the XFL. Promising a fully competitive sport unlike

Exhibit 3   World Wrestling Entertainment: Revenue Breakdown
(All figures in $ millions)

	2003	2002	2001
Live and televised shows	$ 295.4	$ 323.5	$ 335.7
Live events, television shows, pay-per-view shows, advertising			
Branded merchandise	78.9	86.1	102.5
Merchandise, publishing, home videos, Internet			

Source: World Wrestling Entertainment annual reports.

the heavily scripted wrestling matches, Vince tried to make the XFL a faster-paced, more fan-friendly form of football than the National Football League (NFL). Emphasizing that the X stands for extreme, Vince had stated: "This will not be a league for pantywaists or sissies," he said. "The XFL will take you places where the NFL is afraid to go because, quite frankly, we are not afraid of anything."[8] He also introduced several technological enhancements to XFL telecasts, such as wiring coaches with live microphones, placing cameras in the locker rooms, and using plenty of helmet cameras.

In this new league, Vince was able to partner with NBC which was looking for a lower-priced alternative to the televised games of the NFL. The XFL kicked off with great fanfare in February 2001. Although the games were well attended, television ratings dropped steeply after the first week. The football venture was folded after just one season, resulting in a $57 million loss for the WWF. Both Vince and Linda insisted that the venture could have paid off if it had been given enough time. Vince commented, "I think our pals at the NFL went out of their way to make sure this was not a successful venture."[9]

The WWF also failed to generate much business with a $40 million theme restaurant in New York's Times Square. Seating more than 600 patrons, the restaurant was expected to showcase the firm's talent in occasional guest appearances. It was also expected to drive up sales of WWF merchandise. There were also plans to hold some wrestling matches at the restaurant. But the enterprise has racked up losses, running about $8 million over the last year.

The firm is now focusing more heavily on television and film, including a cartoon series for the 2- to 11-year-old crowd that could air as early as 2005. "Television is our base," Linda said. "We want to continue to develop more television programs, made-for-television movies as well as theatrical releases."[10] Vince is also interested in developing a late-night franchise that he claims could be "a little racier and a little more Wild West" than the current programs. Meanwhile, the company has also become involved in movie production with action-adventure or horror films, many of which has its wrestlers such as The Rock or Stone Cold as stars. Linda insisted that they will continue to explore new ventures, though they will be paying much more attention to their potential bottom-line implications.

Poised for a Resurgence?

In 2002 the WWF was hit by a British court ruling that their original "WWF" acronym belonged to the World Wildlife Fund. The firm had to undergo a major branding transition, changing its well-known name and triple logo from WWF to WWE. Although the change in name has been costly, it is not clear that this will hurt the firm in the long run. "Their product is really the entertainment. It's the stars. It's the bodies," said Larry McNaughton, managing director and principal of CoreBrand, a branding consultancy.[11] Linda believes that the new name might actually be beneficial for the firm. "Our new name puts the emphasis on the 'E' for entertainment," she commented.[12]

Vince and his crew are using the name change to try to re-create the buzz that had surrounded his firm in past years before it hit some serious bumps. The firm had launched a new campaign with the message "Get the 'F' out." Linda rejected any suggestion that the fortunes of World Wrestling Entertainment may be driven by a fad that is unlikely to last. She maintained that the interest in their shows will survive in spite of growing competition from newer sources of entertainment such as reality-based television shows. There are signs that WWE's new wrestling stars are beginning to catch on and fans are being drawn back to the different characters and story lines used on the two major television shows, *Raw* and *Smackdown!* *Raw* still continues to be one of the top shows each week among those shown on cable television. *Smackdown!* has maintained its status as the leading show for the UPN network. It draws about 25 percent more viewers than the network's next most popular shows. Exhibit 4 shows figures for WWE's live and televised shows.

Exhibit 4   World Wrestling Entertainment: Live and Television Shows

	Number of Live Events	Total Attendance	Domestic Pay-per-view Buys
2003	327	1,815,100	5,378,100
2002	237	2,032,754	7,135,464
2001	212	2,449,800	8,010,400
2000	206	2,485,100	6,884,600
1999	199	2,273,701	5,365,100

Source: World Wrestling Entertainment annual reports.

Furthermore, Vince and Linda McMahon have claimed that their attempts to diversify were never meant to convey any loss of interest in wrestling. They believe that their experience with staging wrestling shows over the years has provided them with the foundation to move into other areas of entertainment. After all, it was their ability to use wrestling to create a form of mass entertainment that had made the WWF such a phenomenal success. In response to critics who questioned the value of wrestling matches with rigged outcomes, James F. Byrne, senior vice-president for marketing, stated: "Wrestling is 100 percent entertainment. There's no such thing as fake entertainment."[13]

With more characters at their disposal and different characters being used in each of their shows, WWE is planning to ramp up the number of live shows, including more in overseas locations. An increase in the number of shows may also boost the revenues that the firm is able to generate from its merchandise. Andy Rittenberry, an analyst with Gabelli Asset Management who has been following WWE, stated: "Maybe you think it's idiotic, and you don't like the typical wrestler and the people who watch it. But they have built a good brand."[14] Moreover, unlike many other media firms, WWE has little debt and over $270 million in cash. "We make money when we are not hot," remarked Vince. "When we are hot, it's off the charts."[15]

Those who understand don't need an explanation. Those who need an explanation will never understand.

—**Marty,** a 19-year-old wrestling addict quoted in *Fortune,* October 6, 2000.

Endnotes

1. An $8.9 million profit for World Wrestling, 2004, *New York Times,* February 19: C10.
2. McLean, Bethany, 2000, Inside the world's weirdest family business, *Fortune,* October 16: 298.
3. Brady, Diane, 2000, Wrestling's real grudge match, *BusinessWeek,* January 24: 164.
4. Mooradian, Don, 2001, WWF gets a grip after acquisition, *Amusement Business,* June 4: 20.
5. 2000, *Fortune,* October 16: 304.
6. Ibid.
7. Ibid., 302.
8. Fisher, Eric, 2000, A perfect marriage: Football, WWF? *Washington Times,* February 4: B2.
9. Bradley, Diane, 2004, Rousing itself off the mat? *BusinessWeek,* February 2: 73.
10. McConville, Jim, 2000, Taking the WWF off the beat-'em-up path, *Electronic Media,* January 24: 42.
11. Oestricher, Dwight, & Steinberg, Brian, 2002, WW . . . E it is, after fight for F nets new name, *Wall Street Journal,* May 7: B2.
12. Finnigan, David, 2002, Down but not out, WWE is using a rebranding effort to gain strength, *Brandweek,* June 3: 12.
13. Wyatt, Edward, 1999, Pro wrestling tries to pin down a share value, *New York Times,* August 4: C11.
14. Beatty, Sally, 2002, Unusual executive couple fights to save World Wrestling Federation, *Wall Street Journal,* February 21: B1.
15. Bradley, 2004, p. 74.

Case 43   Yahoo!

In the fall of 2003, Yahoo! began to add tools to help Internet surfers make better side-by-side comparisons of products according to criteria such as brand, price, and features. The firm, based in Sunnyvale, California, was revamping its online shopping services to make it easier for users to find merchandise. Yahoo!'s latest move was part of the basic strategy that CEO Terry S. Semel has been pursuing to build the Web site into a digital Disneyland, a souped-up theme park for the Internet age. His goal is to build the Yahoo! site into a self-contained world of irresistible offerings that would grab and keep surfers glued to it for hours at a time.

When Semel was persuaded by Yahoo! cofounder Jerry Yang to come out of retirement to take over the floundering firm, he faced an unenviable task. Advertising revenues at the Internet icon had been plummeting, leading to a precipitous decline in its stock value. Semel replaced the well-liked Timothy Koogle who had been pushed aside by the company's board. To make things worse, leery employees quickly saw that Semel, a retired Hollywood executive, did not really know much about Internet technology and looked stiffly out of place at Yahoo!'s playful, egalitarian headquarters.

Two years after taking control as chairman and CEO, Semel has silenced the doubters. During the short time he has been there, Semel has done nothing less than remake the culture of the quintessential Internet company. The spontaneity that drove the firm's decisions during its go–go days has been replaced by a strong sense of order. By imposing his buttoned-down management approach on Yahoo!, the 60-year-old has engineered one of the most remarkable revivals of a beleaguered dot-com.

Once paralyzed by management gridlock and written off as another overhyped has-been, Yahoo! has been roaring back. The company earned $43 million on revenues of $953 million in 2002, compared with a $93 million loss in 2001 on $717 million in sales. And Yahoo!'s momentum is growing. Analysts predicted that profits for 2003 would quadruple, to more than $200 million, while sales would climb by 33 percent, to $1.3 billion. "What he has done is just phenomenal," said Barry Diller, CEO of USA Interactive, a Yahoo! competitor.[1] Exhibits 1 and 2 show Yahoo! Inc.'s income statement and balance sheet for the years 2001 to 2003.

Semel's new strategy for Yahoo! has also been gaining fans on Wall Street and stoking new fears of a mini-Internet bubble. The company's shares have soared 200 percent in the past eight months to $26. Yahoo!'s market capitalization may still fall far below the all-time high of $127 billion that it had climbed to in early 2000, but its current price-earnings ratio of 79 beats that of the highly successful eBay and is triple that of heavyweight Microsoft. Yet there are some nagging questions about Yahoo!'s future. Will Semel be able to maintain the momentum that he has generated? Can Yahoo! continue to make gains against established rivals such as AOL, MSN, and Google? Are Semel's ambitions to make Yahoo! a digital theme park realistic?

Remaking the Culture

Like many other Internet firms, Yahoo! had attracted visitors by developing a site that would offer a variety of services for free. Those who logged on were able to obtain, among other things, the latest stock quotes and news headlines. The firm relied on online advertising for as much as 90 percent of its revenue. Yahoo! founders David Filo and Jerry Yang were confident that advertisers would continue to pay in order to reach its younger and technologically savvy surfers. In fact, Yahoo! often came across as arrogant to most of its advertisers at the height of the Net bubble. Its attitude, recalled Jeff Bell, a marketing vice-president at DaimlerChrysler, was "Buy our stuff, and shut up."[2]

By the spring of 2001, Yahoo!'s advertising revenue was falling precipitously, its stock was losing most of its value, and some observers were questioning the firm's business model. With the collapse of the dot-com advertisers, the firm's revenue was down by almost a third from the previous year. Semel was asked to help turn the firm around, but he agreed to take on the task only after Koogle had agreed to step down as chairman. Semel's style was in stark contrast to the relaxed, laid-back approach of Koogle. With Koogle out of the way, Semel started to work on replacing Yahoo!'s freewheeling culture with a much more deliberate sense of order.

The changes that Semel has made may not be evident to the casual observer. Visitors to Yahoo!'s headquarters will still see the purple cow in the lobby, be confronted with acres of cubicles, and meet workers clad in jeans. But Semel has dispensed with the hype that once vaulted companies such as Yahoo! into the stratosphere. He moved swiftly to chop down the 44 business units he inherited to 5, stripping many executives of pet projects. He did not care much for the firm's "cubicles-only" policy, finally locating his own office in a cube adjacent to a conference room so he could make phone calls in private.

Semel has even changed Yahoo!'s old freewheeling approach to decision making. When Koogle was in charge, executives would brainstorm for hours, often following hunches with new initiatives. Under Semel, managers

This case was prepared by Professor Jamal Shamsie of Michigan State University. This case was developed from published sources as a basis for class discussion rather than to illustrate either effective or ineffective handling of an administrative situation. Copyright © 2004 Jamal Shamsie.

Exhibit 1   Yahoo! Income Statement
(All figures in thousands)

	Period Ending December 31		
	2003	2002	2001
Total Revenue	$1,625,097	$953,067	$717,422
Cost of revenue	358,103	162,881	157,001
Gross Profit	1,266,994	790,186	560,421
Operating expenses			
Research and development	207,285	143,468	126,090
Selling, general, and administrative	709,669	537,344	466,295
Nonrecurring	—	—	62,221
Others	54,374	21,186	64,085
Total operating expenses	—	—	718,691
Operating Income or Loss	295,666	88,188	(158,270)
Income from continuing operations			
Total other income/expenses, net	95,158	91,588	77,138
Earnings before interest and taxes	384,903	178,225	(81,825)
Pretax income	384,903	178,225	(81,825)
Income tax expense	147,024	71,290	10,963
Minority interest	(5,921)	(1,551)	(693)
Net income from continuing operations	237,879	106,935	(92,788)
Effect of accounting changes	—	(64,120)	—
Net Income	237,879	42,815	(92,788)
Net Income Applicable to Common Shares	$ 237,879	$ 42,815	$ (92,788)

Source: Yahoo! annual reports.

have to make formal presentations of any new ideas in weekly meetings of a group called the Product Council. Championed by Semel and his chief operating officer, Daniel Rosensweig, the Product Council typically includes nine managers from all corners of the company. The group sizes up business plans to make sure all new projects bring benefits to Yahoo!'s existing businesses. "We need to work within a framework," said Semel. "If it's a free-for-all . . . we won't take advantage of the strengths of our company."[3]

There are some indications that Semel's changes may already be starting to pay off. With the focus and discipline that he has imposed on the firm, Semel appears to be making some progress in getting Yahoo! to grow again. Most of the employees, who have been anxious to see the value of their stock rise again, have begun to support Semel in his efforts to remake Yahoo! "People don't always agree with the direction they're getting, but they're

happy the direction is there," said a current Yahoo! manager who requested anonymity.[4]

Rethinking the Business Model

Semel began turning Yahoo! around by wooing traditional advertisers, making gestures to advertising agencies that had been angered with the company's arrogance during the boom. Traditional advertisers such as Coca-Cola, General Motors, and the Gap have been flocking to Yahoo!'s sites. They say they have gravitated to Yahoo! because it has been using technology that goes beyond static banner advertising, offering eye-catching animation, videos, and other rich-media formats. As a result of these efforts, Yahoo! generated more advertising revenue than America Online during the last year. Exhibit 3 shows Internet advertising revenues from 1998 to 2002.

But Semel does not want Yahoo! to rely on advertising revenues. He has been trying to add services that con-

Exhibit 2   Yahoo! Balance Sheet
    (All figures in thousands)

	Period Ending December 31		
	2003	2002	2001
Assets			
Current Assets			
Cash and cash equivalents	$ 713,539	$ 310,972	$ 372,632
Short-term investments	595,978	463,204	553,795
Net receivables	282,415	113,612	68,648
Other current assets	129,777	82,216	56,458
Total Current Assets	1,721,709	970,004	1,051,533
Long-term investments	1,452,629	914,207	967,366
Property, plant, and equipment	449,512	371,272	131,648
Goodwill	1,805,561	415,225	192,987
Intangible assets	445,640	96,252	21,932
Other assets	56,603	23,221	13,880
Total Assets	5,931,654	2,790,181	2,379,346
Liabilities			
Current liabilities			
Accounts payable	515,518	276,313	225,546
Other current liabilities	192,278	135,501	132,971
Total Current Liabilities	707,796	411,814	358,517
Long-term debt	750,000	—	—
Other liabilities	516	—	23,806
Deferred long-term liability charges	72,374	84,540	—
Minority interest	37,478	31,557	30,006
Total Liabilities	1,568,164	527,911	412,329
Stockholders' Equity			
Common stock	678	611	581
Retained earnings	230,386	(7,493)	(50,308)
Treasury stock	(159,988)	(159,988)	(59,988)
Capital surplus	4,288,816	2,430,222	2,067,410
Other stockholder equity	3,598	(1,082)	9,322
Total Stockholder Equity	4,363,490	2,262,270	1,967,017
Net Tangible Assets	$2,112,289	$1,750,793	$1,752,098

Source: Yahoo! annual reports.

sumers would be willing to pay for, a strategy that requires time to put into place. Two former executives said that when Semel took over, he was shocked to find out that Yahoo! did not have the technology in place to handle surging demand for paid services such as online personals. He had to crack down on the firm to whip it into shape to handle the addition of such premium services.

Semel then used the deal-making skills that made him a legend in the movie business to land crucial acquisitions and partnerships that could produce rich new revenues for

Exhibit 3 Internet
Advertising Revenues

Year	$ Billions
2002	$6.3
2001	7.5
2000	8.5
1999	4.1
1998	2.1

Source: PricewaterhouseCoopers,
Interactive Advertising Bureau.

Yahoo! The buyout of HotJobs.com in 2002 moved Yahoo! into the online job-hunting business, adding $80 million to the firm's revenue. Semel also made a deal with phone giant SBC Communications to launch the firm into the business of selling broadband access to millions of American homes. Under the terms of the deal, SBC pays Yahoo! about $5 of the $40 to $60 customers pay each month for service. Yahoo!'s revenues from this deal were projected to jump from $70 million in 2003 to $125 million in 2004.

Of all of Semel's deals, none shines brighter than the partnership with Overture Services, which is expected to add $230 million to Yahoo!'s revenues in 2004. The companies have teamed up to sell advertisements near Yahoo!'s search results, a business known as "paid search." If a user searches for "cookware," for instance, advertisers ranging from Macy's to Sur La Table are able to bid to showcase their links near the results. Overture delivers the advertisers and forks over roughly two-thirds of the revenue. While Yahoo! had debated such a partnership for years under Koogle, Semel managed to push it through in less than a year.

By making such smart deals, Semel has built Yahoo! into a site that can offer surfers many different services, several of which require the customer to pay a small fee. The idea has been to coax Web surfers to spend hard cash on everything from digital music and online games to job listings and premium e-mail accounts with loads of extra storage. Fees from such offerings already account for about one-third of Yahoo!'s annual revenues. Semel hopes that the contribution from such paid services will rise to 50 percent of the firm's revenues during 2004. "We planted a lot of seeds a year and a half ago, and some are beginning to grow," he said.[5]

An Internet Theme Park

In order to build upon the foundation that he has already laid, Semel envisions building Yahoo! into a digital theme park where Web surfers would log on to Yahoo!'s site like customers squeezing through the turnstiles at Disneyland in Anaheim. Instead of being an impartial tour guide to the Web, Yahoo! should be able to entice surfers to stay inside its walls as long as possible.

This vision for Yahoo! represented a drastic change from the model developed by its original founders, Filo and Yang. Koogle had let his executives develop various offerings that operated relatively independently. Managers had built up their own niches around the main Yahoo! site. No one had thought about developing the portal as a whole, much less how the various bits and pieces could work together. "Managers would beg, borrow, and steal from the network to help their own properties," said Greg Coleman, Yahoo!'s executive vice-president for media and sales.[6]

Semel has been pushing to stitch it all together. He has demanded that Yahoo!'s myriad of offerings from e-mail accounts to stock quotes to job listings interact with each other. Semel has called this concept "network optimization" and regards this as a key goal for his firm. To make this concept work, every initiative should not only make money but also feed Yahoo!'s other businesses. Most of the focus of the Product Council meetings has been on the painstaking job of establishing these interconnections between the various services that are offered on the site.

With these constraints, it has become much harder for new projects to get approved. Semel has been determined to have any new offerings tied in with what is already being offered on Yahoo! He claims this makes them easier for customers to find, increasing their chances of success. Of the 79 current ideas for premium services at some stage of planning inside Yahoo!, only a few are likely to be launched over the next year.

A key element of Semel's strategy to build Yahoo! into a digital theme park also lies in his ability to push customers into broadband. Lots of the services that he is banking on, such as music and interactive games, are data hogs that appeal mostly to surfers that have high-speed links. Furthermore, since broadband is always on, many of Yahoo!'s customers are more likely to be lingering in Semel's theme park for hours on end, day after day. "The more time you spend on Yahoo!, the more apt you are to sample both free and paid services," he said.[7]

But Yahoo! is not well positioned to push its services on broadband. Its alliance with SBC Communications allows it to reach only about a third of the country. MSN's deals with Verizon Communications and Qwest Communications give it far greater access to customers around the country. Semel's efforts to land other broadband deals have come up short. This can represent a serious drawback, given the fragile nature of these partnerships. If SBC concludes that the Yahoo! brand does not draw in sufficient customers, it could cut Yahoo! out and save itself millions.

If Semel can overcome these challenges and pull it off, the new Yahoo! could become one of the few enduring powerhouses on the Internet. Based on analysts' predictions, customers who pay for its services could more than triple in number, to 10.0 million in 2005 from the 2.9 million that it presently draws. This could cause profits to soar 75 percent over the next two years to $350 million, and sales could surge 30 percent during the same period to $1.7 billion. "Yahoo! has emerged as a durable digital franchise," said Alberto W. Vilar, president of Amerindo Investment Advisors, which has an undisclosed stake. "If you take the long view, this stock could still double or triple."[8]

Running into Competition

But Yahoo! is not the only player with aspirations to become a digital theme park. Both Time Warner's AOL and Microsoft's MSN have the same goal in mind and they can boast of substantial advantages over Yahoo! AOL, despite its merger headaches, can tap into popular content from the world's largest media company, from CNN to Warner Music. MSN can derive substantial benefits from the software muscle and cash reserves of Microsoft, as well as broadband partnerships that cover 27 percent more lines into homes and businesses than Yahoo!'s SBC deal.

Yahoo! may also have a more difficult time than AOL or MSN in getting a sufficient number of surfers to pay for its new offerings. More of its customers may have become used to getting services without any charge. "Yahoo!'s brand is built on free information services," said MSN group product manager Lisa Gurry.[9] She believes that coaxing Yahoo! customers to pull out their wallets is likely to present a formidable challenge.

Furthermore, Semel's dream of a digital theme park may be threatened by the growing popularity of search engines. In this regard, Yahoo! may have to deal with a recent rise of a newer competitor, Google. In just four years, Google has turned into a global sensation and is now widely regarded as the most prominent search engine in most parts of the world. If search engines continue to attract surfers, they may start turning to Google's uncluttered search offerings to find everything they need instead of flocking to flashy theme parks such as the one Yahoo! is attempting to develop.

In any case, Semel may not be able to realize his dream of transforming Yahoo! into a digital theme park without doing better in the booming Internet search market, where it ranks third behind MSN and Google. Industry analysts say that as Web surfers gain expertise, they visit general-interest sites such as Yahoo! less and instead cut to the chase by typing in keywords on a search engine. According to analytics firm WebSideStory, the percentage of Web site visitors arriving via search engines doubled in the past year, to 13 percent.

Semel has understood the importance of attracting surfers who have been turning to MSN and Google for their Internet searches. He has been moving swiftly to beef up Yahoo!'s search capabilities, including the ability to incorporate information such as weather forecasts into search results, eliminating the need to jump to additional Web pages. He closed a $290 million deal for search company Inktomi in March 2003 because he realized that it was important to own the technology behind this and to manage it internally.

With the search capabilities in place, Semel and the rest of his team have been trying to push Yahoo! as a search engine. The firm must try to build up its brand in order to overcome the established reputations of MSN and Google. Analysts claim that in terms of technology, Inktomi offers a search engine that is better than most. To communicate this, Semel kicked off a national marketing campaign in May 2003 in New York's Times Square with the unveiling of a huge computer-screen ad featuring live searches on the Yahoo! site.

Fulfilled or Shattered Dreams?

It is hard to dispute that Semel has clearly pulled off a stunning revival of a floundering firm by cutting costs, imposing discipline, and making deals. Despite the advantages of AOL and MSN, Yahoo! has kept its position as one of the most popular sites on the Web, according to Nielsen//NetRatings (see Exhibit 4). Semel has used all of his skills to boosting its customer count eightfold from the 375,000 that it drew when he arrived in 2001.

But Yahoo! still has a long way to go before it can become the digital Disneyland that Semel has envisioned. Although Yahoo! has been profiting from its deal with Overture, Semel should be concerned that Microsoft's MSN also has a similar deal. He may have to fork over a hefty sum of money to make a bid for Overture in order to prevent Microsoft from acquiring it. Semel is also still looking to go beyond Yahoo!'s deal with SBC to strengthen the company's position in broadband. And while its acquisition of Inktomi has provided Yahoo! with search capabilities that he could use to battle MSN and Google, Semel is still pushing to build the brand as a search engine.

Exhibit 4   Search Site Rankings, February 2003

	Visitors (In millions)	Time Spent per Person (In minutes)
Google	40.3	25
Yahoo! Search	36.5	11
MSN Search	35.1	8
AOL Search	23.7	34
Ask Jeeves	13.0	11

Source: Nielsen//NetRatings.

Critics also worry that under Semel's careful and laborious screening process for new projects, Yahoo! may run the risk of losing its innovative edge. Semel has responded by pointing to the advantages that he has provided Yahoo! by the reduction of clutter and the focus on a handful of high-performance services that feed each other. For a success story, he points to the company's recently relaunched search capabilities. Any consumers who search for "pizza" and type in their area code end up on Yahoo!'s Yellow Pages which provide them with return addresses and maps showing how to drive to nearby pizza restaurants. Semel boasts that Yahoo! is the only heavyweight portal that integrates content this deeply into its search features.

Yahoo! is clearly back in the running along with the other leaders that have survived from the Internet-driven era. Its accomplishments under Semel have attracted considerable attention. "Yahoo! has reemerged as a potent force," said Derek Brown, an analyst at Pacific Growth Equities. "It's well-positioned to leverage its massive global user base and dominant brand."[10] But it is still not clear whether Semel's efforts will build Yahoo! into a brand that will be able to hold its own against formidable rivals.

Endnotes

1. Elgin, Ben, & Grover, Ronald, 2003, Yahoo!: Act two, *BusinessWeek,* June 2: 71.
2. Ibid., 76.
3. Ibid., 74.
4. Ibid.
5. Ibid., 72.
6. Ibid., 74.
7. Ibid., 72.
8. Ibid.
9. Ibid.
10. Ibid., 73.

Yum! Brands, Inc., was the world's largest fast-food company in 2004. It operated more than 33,000 KFC, Pizza Hut, Taco Bell, Long John Silver's, and A&W restaurants worldwide. It was the market leader in the chicken, pizza, Mexican, and seafood segments of the U.S. fast-food industry. Yum! Brands also operated more than 12,000 restaurants outside the United States. KFC and Pizza Hut accounted for more than 96 percent of the company's international restaurant base and managed restaurants in 116 countries. Among the first fast-food chains to go international in the late 1950s and 1960s, KFC and Pizza Hut were two of the world's most recognizable brands. Both KFC and Pizza Hut expanded through the 1990s by growing their restaurants into as many countries as possible. However, Yum! Brands realized that different countries offered different opportunities to contribute to the company's worldwide operating profits.

By 2004 Yum! Brands began to focus more attention on portfolio management in individual countries. It increasingly focused its international strategy on developing strong market share positions in a small number of high-growth markets such as Japan, Canada, the United Kingdom, China, Australia, Korea, and Mexico. It also hoped to build strong positions in continental Europe, Brazil, and India. Consumer awareness in these markets, however, was still low and neither KFC nor Pizza Hut had strong operating capabilities there. China and India were appealing markets because of their large populations. From a regional point-of-view, Latin America was appealing because of its close proximity to the United States, language and cultural similarities, and the potential for a future World Free Trade Area of the Americas, which would eliminate tariffs on trade within North and South America. The most important long-term challenge for Yum! Brands was to strengthen its position in a set of core international markets while also developing new markets where consumer awareness and operating capabilities were weak.

Company History

Kentucky Fried Chicken Corporation Fast-food franchising was still in its infancy in 1952 when Harland Sanders began his travels across the United States to speak with prospective franchisees about his "Colonel Sanders Recipe Kentucky Fried Chicken." By 1960, "Colonel" Sanders had granted Kentucky Fried Chicken (KFC) franchises to more than 200 take-home retail outlets and restaurants across the United States. Four years later, at the age of 74, he sold KFC to two Louisville businessmen for $2 million. In 1966 KFC went public and was listed on the New York Stock Exchange. In 1971 Heublein, Inc., a distributor of wine and alcoholic beverages, successfully approached KFC with an offer and merged KFC into a subsidiary. Eleven years later, R.J. Reynolds Industries, Inc., (RJR) acquired Heublein and merged it into a wholly owned subsidiary. The acquisition of Heublein was part of RJR's corporate strategy of diversifying into unrelated businesses such as energy, transportation, food, and restaurants to reduce its dependence on the tobacco industry. In 1985 RJR acquired Nabisco Corporation in an attempt to redefine RJR as a world leader in the consumer foods industry. As RJR refocused its strategy on processed foods, it decided to exit the restaurant industry. It sold KFC to PepsiCo, Inc., one year later.

Pizza Hut In 1958 two students at Wichita State University—Frank and Dan Carney—decided to open a pizza restaurant in an old building at a busy intersection in downtown Wichita. To finance their new business, they borrowed $500 from their mother. They called the restaurant the "Pizza Hut," a reference to the old tavern beside the market that they renovated to open the new business. They opened four more restaurants during the next two years. The Pizza Hut concept was so well received by consumers that they were soon licensing the concept to franchises. By 1972 the Carneys had opened 1,000 restaurants and listed the firm on the New York Stock Exchange. In less than 15 years, Pizza Hut had become the number one pizza restaurant chain in the world in terms of sales and number of units. Internationally, they opened their first restaurant in Canada in 1968 and soon established franchises in Mexico, Germany, Australia, Costa Rica, Japan, and the United Kingdom. In 1977 they sold the business to PepsiCo, Inc. Pizza Hut's headquarters remained in Wichita and Frank Carney served as Pizza Hut's president until 1980. (It is interesting to note that Frank opened a Papa John's Pizza franchise in 1994. Today he is one of Papa John's largest franchisees).

PepsiCo, Inc. PepsiCo believed the restaurant business complemented its consumer product orientation. The marketing of fast food followed many of the same patterns as soft drinks and snack foods. Pepsi-Cola and Pizza Hut pizza, for example, could be marketed in the same television and radio segments, which provided higher returns for each advertising dollar. Restaurant chains also provided an additional outlet for the sale of Pepsi soft drinks. In 1978 PepsiCo acquired Taco Bell. After acquiring KFC in 1986, PepsiCo controlled the leading brands

Copyright © 2004 by Jeffrey A. Krug of Appalachian State University, Walker College of Business, Department of Management, 4087 Raley Hall, Boone, NC 28608. Phone: (828) 262-6236. Email: krugja@appstate.edu. All rights reserved.

in the pizza, Mexican, and chicken segments of the fast-food industry. PepsiCo's strategy of diversifying into three distinct but related markets created one of the world's largest food companies.

In the early 1990s, PepsiCo's sales grew at an annual rate of more than 10 percent. Its rapid growth, however, masked troubles in its fast-food businesses. Operating margins at Pepsi-Cola and PepsiCo's Frito-Lay division averaged 12 and 17 percent, respectively. Margins at KFC, Pizza Hut, and Taco Bell, however, fell from an average of 8 percent in 1990 to 4 percent in 1996. Declining margins reflected increasing maturity in the U.S. fast-food industry, intense competition, and the aging of KFC and Pizza Hut restaurants. PepsiCo's restaurant chains absorbed nearly one-half of PepsiCo's annual capital spending but generated less than one-third of its cash flows. Cash had to be diverted from PepsiCo's soft drink and snack food businesses to its restaurant businesses. This reduced PepsiCo's corporate return on assets, made it more difficult to compete effectively with Coca-Cola, and hurt its stock price. In 1997 PepsiCo decided to spin off its restaurant businesses into a new company called Tricon Global Restaurants, Inc.

Yum! Brands, Inc.   The spin-off created a new, independent, publicly traded company that managed the KFC, Pizza Hut, and Taco Bell franchises. David Novak became Tricon's new CEO. He moved quickly to create a new culture within the company. One of his primary objectives was to reverse the long-standing friction between management and franchisees that was created under PepsiCo ownership. Novak announced that PepsiCo's top-down management system would be replaced by a new management emphasis on providing support to the firm's franchise base. Franchises would have greater independence, resources, and technical support. Novak symbolically changed the name on the corporate headquarters building in Louisville to "KFC Support Center" to drive home his new philosophy.

The firm's new emphasis on franchise support had an immediate effect on morale. In 1997, the year of the divestiture, the company recorded a loss of $111 million in net income. In 2003 it recorded net income of $617 million on sales of $7.4 billion, a return on sales of 8.3 percent. In 2002 Tricon acquired Long John Silver's and A&W All-American Food Restaurants. The acquisitions increased Tricon's worldwide system to almost 33,000 units. One week later, shareholders approved a corporate name change to Yum! Brands, Inc. (Exhibit 1). The acquisitions signaled a shift in the company's strategy from a focus on individual to multibranded units. Multibranding combined two brands in a single restaurant such as KFC and Taco Bell, KFC and A&W, Pizza Hut and Taco Bell, and Pizza Hut and Long John Silver's. Multibranded

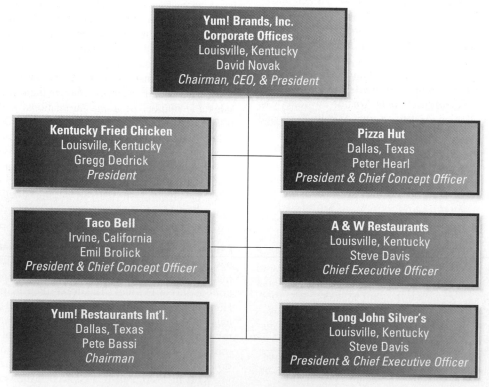

Exhibit 1   Yum! Brands, Inc.: Organizational Chart, 2004

units attracted a larger consumer base by offering them a broader menu selection in one location. By 2004 the company was operating more than 2,400 multibrand restaurants in the United States.

Fast-Food Industry

The National Restaurant Association (NRA) estimated that U.S. food service sales increased by 3.3 percent to $422 billion in 2003. More than 858,000 restaurants made up the U.S. restaurant industry and employed 12 million people. Sales were highest in the full-service, sit-down sector, which grew 3.3 percent to $151 billion. Fast-food sales rose at a slower rate, 2.7 percent to $119 billion. The fast-food sector was increasingly viewed as a mature market. As U.S. incomes rose during the late 1990s and early 2000s, more consumers frequented sit-down restaurants that offered better service and a more comfortable dining experience. Together, the full-service and fast-food segments made up about 64 percent of all U.S. food service sales.

Major Fast-Food Segments Eight major segments made up the fast-food segment of the restaurant industry: sandwich chains, pizza chains, family restaurants, grill buffet chains, dinner houses, chicken chains, non-dinner concepts, and other chains. Sales data for the leading chains in each segment are shown in Exhibit 2. Most striking is the dominance of McDonald's, which had sales of more than $22 billion in 2003. McDonald's accounted for 14 percent of the sales of the top 100 chains. To put McDonald's dominance in perspective, the second largest chain—Burger King—held less than a 5 percent share of the market.

Sandwich chains made up the largest segment of the fast-food market. McDonald's controlled 35 percent of this segment, while Burger King ran a distant second with a 12 percent share. Sandwich chains struggled through early 2003 as the U.S. recession lowered demand and the war in Iraq increased consumer uncertainty. U.S. consumers were also trending away from the traditional hamburger, fries, and soft drink combinations and demanding more healthy food items and better service. Many chains attempted to attract new customers through price discounting. Instead of drawing in new customers, however, discounting merely lowered profit margins. By mid-2003 most chains had abandoned price discounting and began to focus on improved service and product quality. McDonald's, Taco Bell, and Hardee's were particularly successful. They slowed new restaurant development, improved drive-through service, and introduced a variety of new menu items. McDonald's and Hardee's, for example, introduced larger, higher-priced hamburgers to increase value perceptions and ticket prices. The shift from price discounting to new product introductions increased average ticket sales and helped sandwich chains improve profitability in 2004.

Dinner houses made up the second-largest and fastest-growing fast-food segment. Segment sales increased by almost 9.0 percent in 2003, surpassing the average increase of 5.5 percent in the other segments. Much of the growth in dinner houses came from new unit construction in suburban areas and small towns. Applebee's, Chili's, Outback Steakhouse, Red Lobster, and Olive Garden dominated the segment. Each chain generated sales of more than $2 billion in 2003. The fastest-growing dinner houses, however, were newer chains generating less than $700 million in sales, such as P. F. Chang's China Bistro, the Cheesecake Factory, Carrabba's Italian Grill, and LongHorn Steakhouse. Each chain was increasing sales at a 20 percent annual rate. Dinner houses continued to benefit from rising household incomes in the United States. As incomes rose, families were able to move up from quick-service restaurants to more upscale, higher-priced dinner houses. In addition, higher incomes enabled many professionals to purchase more expensive homes in new suburban developments, thereby providing additional opportunities for dinner houses to build new restaurants in unsaturated areas.

Increased growth among dinner houses came at the expense of sandwich chains, pizza and chicken chains, grill buffet chains, and family restaurants. "Too many restaurants chasing the same customers" was responsible for much of the slower growth in these other fast-food categories. Sales growth within each segment, however, differed from one chain to another. In the family segment, for example, Denny's (the segment leader in sales), Shoney's, Perkins, and Big Boy shut down poorly performing restaurants. At the same time, IHOP, Bob Evans, and Cracker Barrel expanded their bases. The hardest-hit segment was grill buffet chains. Declining sales caused both Sizzlin' and Western Sizzlin' to drop out of the list of Top 100 chains, leaving only three chains in the Top 100 (Golden Corral, Ryan's, and Ponderosa). Each of these three chains shut down restaurants in 2003. Dinner houses, because of their more upscale atmosphere and higher-ticket items, were better positioned to take advantage of the aging and wealthier U.S. population.

Yum! Brands: Brand Leadership Exhibit 3 shows sales and restaurant data for the pizza, chicken, and sandwich segments. Yum! Brands generated U.S. sales of $16.3 billion across its five brands. It operated close to 21,000 U.S. and 12,000 non-U.S. restaurants, or more than 33,000 restaurants worldwide. Four of its brands—Pizza Hut (pizza), KFC (chicken), Taco Bell (Mexican), and Long John Silver's (seafood)—were the market leaders in their segments. Taco Bell was the third most profitable restaurant concept behind McDonald's and Starbucks. Profitability at McDonald's was primarily driven by volume; each McDonald's restaurant generated an annual average of $1.6 million in sales compared to an industrywide average of $1.0 million. Starbucks, in contrast, generated

Exhibit 2   Top U.S. Fast-Food Restaurants (Ranked by 2003 Sales, $ millions)

Sandwich Chains	Sales	Change		Dinner Houses	Sales	Change
McDonald's	$22,121	8.9%		Applebee's	$ 3,520	10.6%
Burger King	7,680	−2.8		Chili's	2,505	11.8
Wendy's	7,315	5.2		Outback Steakhouse	2,456	7.1
Subway	5,690	8.8		Red Lobster	2,315	−1.9
Taco Bell	5,346	2.8		Olive Garden	2,165	11.6
Arby's	2,710	0.6		TGI Friday's	1,791	2.6
Jack in the Box	2,360	5.4		Ruby Tuesday	1,450	14.8
Sonic Drive-In	2,359	7.0		Romano's	699	9.4
Dairy Queen	2,165	−1.1		Cheesecake Factory	689	20.6
Hardee's	1,662	−2.3		Hooter's	670	6.5
Other Chains	3,934	9.4		Other Chains	5,277	10.7
Total Segment	$63,342	5.2%		Total Segment	$23,537	8.8%
Pizza Chains				**Chicken Chains**		
Pizza Hut	$ 5,033	−1.3%		KFC	$ 4,936	2.8%
Domino's	3,003	2.6		Chick-fil-A	1,534	11.8
Papa John's	1,719	−2.4		Popeyes	1,274	1.6
Little Caesars	1,200	4.3		Church's	700	−2.5
Chuck E. Cheese's	476	3.5		Boston Market	646	0.8
CiCi's Pizza	380	13.9		El Pollo Loco	396	8.7
Round Table Pizza	378	1.1		Bojangles'	375	8.0
Total Segment	$12,189	0.7%		Total Segment	$ 9,861	3.8%
Family Restaurants				**Other Dinner Chains**		
Denny's	$ 2,132	0.6%		Panera Bread	$ 908	32.0%
IHOP	1,676	14.7		Long John Silver's	777	2.8
Cracker Barrel	1,480	5.3		Disney Theme Parks	707	0.4
Bob Evans	954	9.0		Old Country Buffet	548	−4.5
Waffle House	789	2.7		Captain D's Seafood	506	1.7
Perkins	787	−1.3		Total Segment	$ 3,446	7.0%
Other Chains	2,162	1.2		**Non-Dinner Concepts**		
Total Segment	$ 9,980	4.3%		Starbucks	$ 3,118	25.8%
Grill Buffet Chains				Dunkin' Donuts	2,975	10.2
Golden Corral	$ 1,247	7.8%		7-Eleven	1,410	5.6
Ryan's	814	0.2		Krispy Kreme	957	24.0
Ponderosa	537	−2.1		Baskin-Robbins	510	−2.5
Total Segment	$ 2,598	3.2%		Total Segment	$ 8,970	14.9%

Source: *Nation's Restaurant News.* Sales rankings for contract and hotel chains not included.

Exhibit 3 Leading Pizza, Chicken, and Sandwich Chains, 2003

Pizza Chains	Sales ($ millions)	Growth Rate (%)	Units	Growth Rate (%)	Sales per Unit ($000s)
Pizza Hut	$ 5,033.0	(1.3)%	7,523	(1.0)%	$ 665.7
Domino's Pizza	3,003.4	2.6	4,904	1.2	616.0
Papa John's Pizza	1,718.5	(2.4)	3,035	(0.4)	661.5
Little Caesars Pizza	1,200.0	4.4	2,593	(0.2)	395.1
Chuck E. Cheese's	476.2	3.5	485	5.1	1,070.1
CiCi's Pizza	380.4	13.9	465	11.5	862.6
Round Table Pizza	378.4	1.1	456	(5.6)	757.6
Total	$12,189.9	3.1%	19,461	1.5%	$718.3
Chicken Chains					
KFC	$ 4,936.0	2.8%	5,524	1.0%	$ 897.8
Chick-fil-A	1,534.4	11.8	1,235	4.9	1,394.3
Popeyes Chicken	1,274.0	1.6	1,447	3.8	896.9
Church's Chicken	700.0	(2.5)	1,235	(1.0)	564.1
Boston Market	646.0	0.8	630	(3.1)	1,009.4
El Pollo Loco	395.7	8.7	314	2.6	1,276.5
Bojangles'	374.8	8.0	320	9.6	1,224.8
Total	$ 9,860.9	4.5%	10,705	2.6%	$1,037.7
Sandwich Chains					
McDonald's	$22,121.4	8.9%	13,609	0.9%	$1,632.6
Burger King	7,680.0	(2.8)	7,656	(3.1)	987.1
Wendy's	7,315.0	5.2	5,761	3.8	1,293.5
Subway	5,690.0	8.8	16,499	13.6	366.8
Taco Bell	5,346.0	2.8	5,989	(2.9)	879.7
Arby's	2,710.0	0.6	3,303	1.6	827.1
Jack in the Box	2,360.0	5.4	1,947	4.6	1,239.2
Total	$53,222.4	4.1%	54,764	2.6%	$1,032.3
Long John Silver's	777.0	2.8	1,204	(1.4)	640.8
A&W Restaurants	200.0	NA	576	(13.4)	NA
Yum! Brands Total	16,292.0	NA	20,822	(1.4)	NA

Source: *Nation's Restaurant News.*

Note: Sales per unit are calculated based on a mathematical equation of annual systemwide sales growth and changes in the number of operating units.

less revenue per store—about $660 million each year—but premium pricing for its specialty coffee drinks drove high profit margins. Taco Bell was able to generate greater overall profits because of its lower operating costs. Products such as tacos, burritos, gorditas, and chalupas used similar ingredients. In addition, cooking machinery was simpler, less costly, and required less space than pizza ovens or chicken broilers.

Pizza Hut controlled the pizza segment with a 41 percent share, followed by Domino's (25 percent) and Papa

John's (14 percent). As the pizza segment became increasingly mature, the traditional pizza chains were forced to close old or underperforming restaurants. Only relatively new pizza chain concepts such as CiCi's Pizza, which offered an inexpensive all-you-can-eat salad and pizza buffet, and Chuck E. Cheese's, which focused on family entertainment, were able to significantly grow their restaurant bases during 2003. Most chains could no longer rely on new restaurant construction to drive sales. Another problem was the proliferation of new diets. Many Americans were eating pizza less often as they pursued the Atkins Diet (low carbohydrates), "The Zone" (balanced meals containing equal parts of carbohydrates, protein, and unsaturated fat), or a traditional low-fat diet. Each diet discouraged users from eating pizza, which was high in both fat and carbohydrates.

Operating costs were also rising because of higher cheese and gasoline prices. Pizza chains were forced to develop unique strategies that attracted more customers but protected profit margins. Some chains raised pizza prices to offset higher-priced ingredients or raised home delivery charges to offset higher gasoline costs. Most chains, however, responded with new product introductions. Pizza Hut introduced a low-fat "Fit 'n Delicious" pizza that used one-half the cheese of normal pizzas and toppings with lower fat content. It also introduced a "4forAll" pizza that contained four individually topped six-inch square pizzas in the same box. Domino's introduced a Philly cheese steak pizza, its first new product introduction since 2000. Papa John's introduced a new barbeque chicken and bacon pizza. In addition, it began a campaign that allowed customers to choose one of three free DVDs with the purchase of a large pizza. By matching pizza and movies, Papa John's hoped to encourage customers to eat pizza more often. Pizza Hut quickly responded with its own offer for a free DVD with the purchase of any pizza at the regular price.

KFC continued to dominate the chicken segment with sales of $4.9 billion in 2003, more than 50 percent of sales in the chicken segment. Its nearest competitor, Chick-fil-A, ran a distant second with sales of $1.5 billion. KFC's leadership in the U.S. market was so extensive that it had fewer opportunities to expand its U.S. restaurant base. Despite its dominance, KFC was slowly losing market share as other chicken chains increased sales at a faster rate. Sales data indicated that KFC's share of the chicken segment fell from a high of 64 percent in 1993, a 10-year drop of 14 percent. During the same period, Chick-fil-A and Boston Market increased their combined share by 11 percent. On the surface, it appeared that these market share gains came by taking customers away from KFC. The growth in sales at KFC restaurants, however, had generally remained steady during the last two decades. In reality, the three chains competed for different market groups. Boston Market, for example, appealed to

professionals with higher incomes and health-conscious consumers who didn't regularly frequent KFC. It expanded the chicken segment by offering healthy, "home-style" alternatives to nonfried chicken in a setting resembling an upscale deli. Chick-fil-A concentrated on chicken sandwiches rather than fried chicken and most of its restaurants were still located in shopping mall food courts.

The maturity of the U.S. fast-food industry intensified competition within the chicken segment. As in the pizza segment, chicken chains could not rely on new restaurant construction to build new sales. In addition, chicken costs, which represented about one-half of total food costs, increased dramatically in 2004. A boneless chicken breast, which cost $1.20 per pound in early 2001, cost $2.50 per pound in 2004, an increase of more than 100 percent. Profit margins were being squeezed from both the revenue and cost sides. All chains focused on very different strategies. KFC added new menu boards and introduced new products such as oven roasted strips and roasted twister sandwich wraps. Boston Market experimented with home delivery and began to sell through supermarkets. Chick-fil-A continued to build freestanding restaurants to expand beyond shopping malls. Church's focused on adding drive-through service. The intensity of competition led chicken chains to implement very different strategies for differentiating their product and brand.

Trends in the Restaurant Industry

A number of demographic and societal trends influenced the demand for food eaten outside the home. Rising income, greater affluence among a larger percentage of American households, higher divorce rates, and the marriage of people later in life contributed to the rising number of single households and the demand for fast food. More than 50 percent of women worked outside the home, a dramatic increase since 1970. This number was expected to rise to 65 percent by 2010. Double-income households contributed to rising household incomes and increased the number of times families ate out. Less time to prepare meals inside the home added to this trend. Countering these trends, however, was the slower growth rate of the U.S. population and a proliferation of fast-food chains that increased consumer alternatives and intensified competition.

Baby boomers (ages 35 to 50) constituted the largest consumer group for fast-food restaurants. Generation Xers (ages 25 to 34) and the "mature" category (ages 51 to 64) made up the second and third largest groups, respectively. As consumers aged, they became less enamored of fast food and were more likely to trade up to more expensive restaurants such as dinner houses and full-service restaurants. Sales for many Mexican restaurants, which were extremely popular during the 1980s, began to slow as Japanese, Indian, and Vietnamese restaurants became more fashionable. Ethnic foods were rising in popularity as U.S. immigrants, who constituted 13 percent of the U.S. population in 2004, looked for establishments that sold their native foods.

Labor was the top operational challenge of U.S. restaurant chains. Restaurants relied heavily on teenagers and college-age workers. Twenty percent of all employed teenagers worked in food service, compared to only 4 percent of all employed men over the age of 18 and 6 percent of all employed women over age 18. As the U.S. population aged, fewer young workers were available to fill food service jobs. The short supply of high school and college students meant they had greater work opportunities outside food service. Turnover rates were notoriously high. The National Restaurant Association estimated that about 96 percent of all fast-food workers quit within a year, compared to about 84 percent of employees in full-service restaurants.

Labor costs made up about 30 percent of a fast-food chain's total costs, second only to food and beverage costs. To deal with the decreased supply of employees in the age 16 to 24 category, many restaurants were forced to hire less reliable workers. This affected service and restaurant cleanliness. To improve quality and service, restaurants hired elderly employees who wanted to return to the workforce. To attract more workers, especially the elderly, restaurants offered health insurance, noncontributory pension plans, and profit-sharing benefits. To combat high turnover rates, restaurants turned to training programs and mentoring systems that paired new employees with experienced ones. Mentoring systems were particularly helpful in increasing the learning curve of new workers and providing better camaraderie among employees.

The Global Fast-Food Industry

As the U.S. market matured, more restaurants turned to international markets to expand sales. Foreign markets were attractive because of their large customer bases and comparatively little competition. McDonald's, for example, operated 48 restaurants for every one million U.S. residents. Outside the United States, it operated only one restaurant for every five million residents. McDonald's, Pizza Hut, KFC, and Burger King were the earliest and most aggressive chains to expand abroad beginning in the 1960s. This made them formidable competitors for chains investing abroad for the first time. Subway, TCBY, and Domino's were more recent global competitors. By 2004 each was operating in more than 65 countries. Exhibit 4 lists the world's 35 largest restaurant chains.

The global fast-food industry had a distinctly American flavor. Twenty-eight chains (80 percent of the total) were headquartered in the United States. U.S. chains had the advantage of a large domestic market and ready acceptance by the American consumer. European firms had less success developing the fast-food concept because Europeans were more inclined to frequent midscale restaurants where they spent several hours enjoying multicourse meals in a formal setting. KFC had trouble breaking into the German market during the 1970s and 1980s because Germans were not accustomed to buying takeout or ordering food over the counter. McDonald's had greater success in Germany because it made changes to its menu and operating procedures to appeal to German tastes. German beer, for example, was served in all of McDonald's restaurants in Germany. In France, McDonald's used a different sauce that appealed to the French palate on its Big Mac sandwich. KFC had more success in Asia and Latin America where chicken was a traditional dish.

Yum! Brands operated more than 12,000 restaurants outside the United States (see Exhibit 5). The early international experience of KFC and Pizza Hut put them in a strong position to exploit the globalization trend in the industry. A separate subsidiary in Dallas—Yum! Brands International—managed the international activities of all five brands. As a result, the firm had significant international experience concentrated in one location and a well-established worldwide distribution network. KFC and Pizza Hut accounted for almost all of the firm's international restaurants. Yum! Brands planned to open 1,000 new KFC and Pizza Hut restaurants outside the United States each year, well into the future. This came at a time when both KFC and Pizza Hut were closing units in the mature U.S. market.

Of the KFC and Pizza Hut restaurants located outside the United States, 77 percent were owned by local franchisees or joint venture partners who had a deep understanding of local language, culture, customs, law, financial markets, and marketing characteristics. Franchising allowed firms to expand more quickly, minimize capital expenditures, and maximize return on invested capital. It was also a good strategy for establishing a presence in smaller markets like Grenada, Bermuda, and Suriname where the small number of consumers only allowed for a single restaurant. The costs of operating company-owned restaurants were prohibitively high in these markets. In larger markets such as China, Canada, Australia, and Mexico, there was a stronger emphasis on building company-owned restaurants. Fixed costs could be spread over a larger number of units and the company could coordinate purchasing, recruiting, training, financing, and advertising. This reduced per unit costs. Company-owned restaurants also allowed the company to maintain tighter control over product quality and customer service.

Country Evaluation and Risk Assessment

International Business Risk   Worldwide demand for fast food was expected to grow rapidly during the next two decades as rising per capita income made eating out more affordable for greater numbers of consumers. International business, however, carried a variety of risks not present in the domestic market. Long distances between

Exhibit 4   The World's 35 Largest Fast-Food Chains in 2004

Franchise	Corporate Headquarters	Home Country	Number of Countries with Operations
1. McDonald's	Oak Brook, Illinois	U.S.	121
2. KFC	Louisville, Kentucky	U.S.	99
3. Pizza Hut	Dallas, Texas	U.S.	92
4. Subway Sandwiches	Milford, Connecticut	U.S.	74
5. TCBY	Little Rock, Arkansas	U.S.	67
6. Domino's Pizza	Ann Arbor, Michigan	U.S.	65
7. Burger King	Miami, Florida	U.S.	58
8. TGI Friday's	Dallas, Texas	U.S.	53
9. Baskin-Robbins	Glendale, California	U.S.	52
10. Dunkin' Donuts	Randolph, Massachusetts	U.S.	40
11. Wendy's	Dublin, Ohio	U.S.	34
12. Chili's Grill & Bar	Dallas, Texas	U.S.	22
13. Dairy Queen	Edina, Minnesota	U.S.	22
14. Little Caesars Pizza	Detroit, Michigan	U.S.	22
15. Popeyes	Atlanta, Georgia	U.S.	22
16. Outback Steakhouse	Tampa, Florida	U.S.	20
17. A&W Restaurants	Lexington, Kentucky	U.S.	17
18. PizzaExpress	London	U.K.	16
19. Carl's Jr.	Anaheim, California	U.S.	14
20. Church's Chicken	Atlanta, Georgia	U.S.	12
21. Taco Bell	Irvine, California	U.S.	12
22. Hardee's	Rocky Mount, North Carolina	U.S.	11
23. Applebee's	Overland Park, Kansas	U.S.	9
24. Sizzler	Los Angeles, California	U.S.	9
25. Arby's	Ft. Lauderdale, Florida	U.S.	7
26. Denny's	Spartanburg, South Carolina	U.S.	7
27. Skylark	Tokyo	Japan	7
28. Lotteria	Seoul	Korea	5
29. Taco Time	Eugene, Oregon	U.S.	5
30. Mos Burger	Tokyo	Japan	4
31. Orange Julius	Edina, Minnesota	U.S.	4
32. Yoshinoya	Tokyo	Japan	4
33. IHOP	Glendale, California	U.S.	3
34. Quick Restaurants	Brussels	Belgium	3
35. Red Lobster	Orlando, Florida	U.S.	3

Source: Case author's research.

Exhibit 5   Yum! Brands, Inc.—Largest International Markets, 2004

	KFC	Pizza Hut	Taco Bell	Long John Silver's	A&W	Yum! Brands
			Number of Restaurants			
United States	5,524	7,523	5,989	1,207	579	20,822
International	7,354	4,560	249	31	183	12,377
Worldwide	12,878	12,083	6,238	1,238	762	33,199
International Total (%)	57.1%	37.7%	4.0%	2.5%	24.0%	37.3%
Top Foreign Markets						
1. Japan	1,167	327	24			1,518
2. Canada	733	353	84			1,170
3. U.K.	591	556				1,147
4. China	979	127	1			1,107
5. Australia	516	319	7			842
6. Korea	209	299				508
7. Malaysia	329	106	32	6	26	499
8. Mexico	309	180	1		1	491
9. Thailand	299	77	28		28	432
10. Indonesia	198	85	69		74	426
11. South Africa	360	3				363
12. Philippines	128	113	6		6	253
Other Latin America						
Puerto Rico	95	60	32			187
Ecuador	45	20	4			69
Costa Rica	15	41	11			67
Brazil	3	63				66
Chile	30	28				58
Other Asia						
Taiwan	132	111				242
Singapore	73	34	24	24		155
Other Selected Markets						
France	24	126				150
Germany	45	77				122
Saudi Arabia	50	92	9		9	160
India	2	65				67

Source: Yum! Brands, Inc.

headquarters and foreign franchises made it more difficult to control the quality of individual restaurants. Large distances also caused servicing and support problems, and transportation and other resource costs were higher. In addition, time, cultural, and language differences increased communication problems and made it more difficult to get timely and accurate information.

During the 1970s and 1980s, KFC and Pizza Hut attempted to expand their restaurant bases into as many countries as possible—the greater the number of countries, the greater the indicator of success. By the early years of the 21st century, however, it became apparent that serving a large number of markets with a small number of restaurants was a costly business. If a large number of restaurants could be established in a single market or region, then significant economies of scale could be achieved by spreading fixed costs of purchasing, advertising, and distribution across a larger restaurant base. Higher market share, as a result, was typically associated with greater cash flow and higher profitability.

Country analysis was an important part of the strategic decision-making process. Few companies had sufficient resources to invest everywhere simultaneously. Choices had to be made about when and where to invest scarce capital. Country selection models typically assessed countries on the basis of market size, growth rates, the number and type of competitors, government regulations, and economic and political stability. In an industry such as fast food, however, an analysis of economic and political variables was insufficient. As mentioned earlier, KFC had trouble establishing a presence in Germany because many consumers there didn't accept the fast-food concept. An analysis of Germany's large, stable economy would otherwise have indicated a potentially profitable market.

An important challenge for multinational firms was to accurately assess the risks of doing business in different countries and regions in order to make good choices about where to invest. A useful framework for analyzing international business risk was to separate risk into factors of country, industry, and firm. Country factors, for example, included risks associated with changes in a country's political and economic environment. These included political risk (e.g., war, revolution, changes in government, price controls, tariffs, and government regulations), economic risk (e.g., inflation, high interest rates, foreign exchange rate volatility, balance of trade movements, social unrest, riots, and terrorism), and natural risk (e.g., rainfall, hurricanes, earthquakes, and volcanic activity).

Industry factors addressed changes in industry structure that inhibited a firm's ability to compete successfully in its industry. These included supplier risk (e.g., changes in supplier quality and supplier power), product market risk (e.g., consumer tastes and the availability of substitute products), and competitive risk (e.g., rivalry among competitors, new market entrants, and new product innovations).

Last, firm factors examined a firm's ability to control its internal operations. They included labor risk (e.g., labor unrest, absenteeism, employee turnover, and labor strikes), supplier risk (e.g., raw material shortages and unpredictable price changes), trade secret risk (e.g., protection of trade secrets and intangible assets), credit risk (e.g., problems in collecting receivables), and behavioral risk (e.g., control over franchise operations, product qual-

ity and consistency, service quality, and restaurant cleanliness). Each of these factors—country, industry, and firm—had to be analyzed simultaneously to fully understand the costs and benefits of international investment.[1]

Country Risk Assessment in Latin America

Latin America is comprised of some 50 countries, island nations, and principalities that were settled by the Spanish, Portuguese, French, Dutch, and British during the 1500s and 1600s. Spanish is spoken in most countries, the most notable exception being Brazil where the official language is Portuguese. Despite commonalities in language, religion, and history, however, political and economic policies differ significantly from one country to another.

Mexico　Many U.S. companies considered Mexico to be one of the most attractive investment locations in Latin America in the 1990s. Its population of 105 million was more than one-third as large as the United States, and three times larger than Canada's population of 32 million. Prior to 1994, Mexico levied high tariffs on many goods imported from the United States. As a result, many U.S. consumers purchased less expensive products from Asia or Europe. In 1994 the North American Free Trade Agreement (NAFTA) was signed. NAFTA eliminated tariffs on goods traded between the United States, Canada, and Mexico. It created a trading bloc with a larger population and gross domestic product than the European Union. The elimination of tariffs led to an immediate increase in trade between Mexico and the United States. By 2004, 85 percent of Mexico's exports were purchased by U.S. consumers. In turn, 68 percent of Mexico's total imports came from the United States.

Most Mexicans (70 percent) lived in urban areas such as Mexico City, Guadalajara, and Monterrey. Mexico City's population of 18 million made it one of the most populated areas in Latin America. Many U.S. firms had operations in or around Mexico City. The fast-food industry was well developed in Mexico's cities. The leading U.S. fast-food chains already had significant restaurant bases in Mexico, most importantly KFC (274 restaurants), McDonald's (261), Pizza Hut (174), Burger King (154), and Subway (71). Mexican consumers readily accepted the fast-food concept. Chicken was also a staple product in Mexico and helped explain KFC's wide popularity. Mexico's large population and ready acceptance of fast-food represented a significant opportunity for fast-food chains. Competition, however, was intense.

Brazil　Brazil, with a population of 182 million, was the largest country in Latin America and the fifth largest country in the world. Its land base was almost as large as the United States and bordered 10 countries. It was the

[1]For an in-depth discussion of international business risk, see Miller, Kent D., 1992, A framework for integrated risk management in international business, *Journal of International Business Studies*, 21 (2): 311–31.

Exhibit 6 Latin America: Selected Economic and Demographic Data

	United States	Canada	Mexico	Colombia	Venezuela	Peru	Brazil	Argentina	Chile
Population (millions)	290.3	32.2	104.9	41.7	24.7	28.4	182.0	38.7	15.7
Growth rate (%)	0.9%	0.9%	1.4%	1.6%	1.5%	1.6%	1.5%	1.1%	1.1%
Population Data: Origin									
European (non-French origin)	65.1%	43.0%	9.0%	20.0%	21.0%	15.0%	55.0%	97.0%	95.0%
European (French origin)		23.0%							
African	12.9%			4.0%	10.0%		6.0%		
Mixed African and European				14.0%		37.0%	38.0%		
Latin American (Hispanic)	12.0%								
Asian	4.2%	6.0%							
Amerindian or Alaskan native	1.5%	2.0%	30.0%	1.0%	2.0%	45.0%			3.0%
Mixed Amerindian and Spanish			60.0%	58.0%	67.0%				
Mixed African and Amerindian				3.0%					
Other	4.3%	26.0%	1.0%			3.0%	1.0%	3.0%	2.0%
Total	100.0%	100.0%	100.0%	100.0%	100.0%	100.0%	100.0%	100.0%	100.0%
GDP ($ billions)	$10,400	$ 923	$ 900	$ 268	$ 133	$ 132	$1,340	$ 391	$ 151
Per capita income (US$)	$37,600	$29,400	$9,000	$6,500	$5,500	$4,800	$7,600	$10,200	$10,000
Real GDP growth rate	2.5%	3.4%	1.0%	2.0%	−8.9%	4.8%	1.0%	−14.7%	1.8%
Inflation rate	1.6%	2.2%	6.4%	6.2%	31.2%	0.2%	8.3%	41.0%	2.5%
Unemployment rate	5.8%	7.6%	3.0%	17.4%	17.0%	9.4%	6.4%	21.5%	9.2%
Literacy rate	97.0%	97.0%	92.2%	92.5%	93.4%	90.9%	86.4%	97.0%	96.2%

Source: U.S. Central Intelligence Agency, 2002. *The World Factbook*. Demographic data is 2003 estimate; economic data as of year-end 2002.

world's largest coffee producer and largest exporter of sugar and tobacco. In addition to its abundant natural resources and strong export position in agriculture, Brazil was a strong industrial power. Its major exports were airplanes, automobiles, and chemicals. Its gross domestic product of $1.3 trillion was larger than Mexico's and the largest in Latin America (see Exhibit 6). Some firms viewed Brazil as one of the most important emerging markets, along with China and India.

The fast-food industry in Brazil was less developed than in Mexico or the Caribbean. This was partly the result of the structure of the fast-food industry that was dominated by U.S. restaurant chains. U.S. chains expanded further away from their home base as they gained experience operating in Latin America. As firms gained a foothold in Mexico and Central America, it was a natural progression to move into South America. McDonald's understood the importance of Brazil. It opened its first restaurant in 1979 and by 2004 was operating 1,200 restaurants, ice-cream kiosks, and McCafés there. Many restaurant chains such as Burger King, Pizza Hut, and KFC built restaurants in Brazil in the early- to mid-1990s but eventually closed them because of poor sales. Like Germany, many Brazilians were not quick to accept the fast-food concept.

One problem facing U.S. fast-food chains was eating customs. Brazilians ate their big meal in the early afternoon. In the evening, it was customary to have a light meal such as soup or a small plate of pasta. Brazilians rarely ate food with their hands, preferring to eat with a knife and fork. This included food like pizza, which Americans typically ate with their hands. They also were not accustomed to eating sandwiches; if they did eat sandwiches, they wrapped the sandwich in a napkin. U.S. fast-food chains catered to a different kind of customer who wanted more than soup but less than a full sit-down meal. U.S. fast-food chains were more popular in larger cities such as São Paulo and Rio de Janeiro where business people were in a hurry. Food courts were well developed in Brazil's shopping malls but included sit-down as well as fast-food restaurants. U.S. restaurant chains were, therefore, faced with the challenge of changing the eating habits of Brazilians or convincing Brazilians of the attractiveness of fast-food, American style.

Risks and Opportunities

Yum! Brands faced difficult decisions surrounding the design and implementation of an effective international strategy over the next 20 years. Its top seven markets generated more than 70 percent of its international profits. As a result, it planned to continue its aggressive investments in its primary markets. It was also important, however, to improve brand equity in other regions of the world such as continental Europe, Brazil, and India where consumer acceptance of fast food was still weak and the company had limited operational capabilities. Latin America as a region was of particular interest because of its geographic proximity to the United States, cultural similarities, and NAFTA. The company needed to sustain its leadership position in Mexico and the Caribbean but also looked to strengthen its position in countries such as Brazil, Venezuela, and Argentina. Limited resources and cash flow limited KFC's ability to aggressively expand in all countries simultaneously. Country evaluation and risk assessment would be an important tool for developing and implementing an effective international strategy.

company index

A. T. Kearney, 40, 156, 700
Abbott Laboratories, 714
Abovenet, 632
ABS Multimedia, 532
Accenture, 25, 134; *see also* Andersen Consulting
Accolade, 532
Acer, 381
ACNeilsen Corp., 804
Activision, 534, 535, 538
Adam's Mark, 157
Adelphia, 211, 384
Adolph Coors Company, 499–513, 599, 600, 685
AEP, 407
Aerie Networks, 419
AES, 387
Agilent Technologies, 562, 573
Agillion, Inc., 15
Airbus Industrie, 703
AirTran, 844
AK Steel Corp., 58
Al Ahram Beverages Co., 687
alando.de AG, 633
Alberto-Culver, 172
Albertson's, 149, 653
Alcoa, 600
Aldi Group, 891, 892, 893
Allied Domecq, 819
Allied Office Products, 676
Allied Signal, 78
ALLtech Inc., 615
AltiTunes Partners LP, 458
Altria Group, 672, 884
Alza Corporation, 714, 715
Amazon.com, 460, 621, 635, 636, 827, 828, 867
Ambev, 685
American Airlines, 700, 705, 706
American Can Company, 597, 602, 603, 605, 607, 614
American Capital Strategies, 176
American Express, 31
American International Group, 884
American Skiing Company, 675, 676
American Stores, 698
Ames, 869
Amgen, 714
Amtrak, 675, 676
Anaconda Aluminum, 607
Andersen Consulting, 131; *see also* Accenture
Andersen Windows, 165
Andersen Worldwide, 210
Anderson Consulting, 654

Andrew Corporation, 379
Anheuser-Busch Companies, Inc., 500, 502, 503, 504, 506–508, 512, 599, 600, 606, 685, 694, 696
AOL/Time Warner, 202, 308, 312, 629, 630, 896, 902
Applebee's, 770, 775, 910, 914
Apple Computer, 155, 175, 418, 625, 737
Appshop, 830
Aptus Financial, LLC, 446
ARAMARK Refreshment Services, 676
Arby's, 910, 911, 914
Arcadia, 532
Ariba, Inc., 623
Aroma Cafe, 731
Arthur Andersen, 17, 308
Asea Brown Boveri (ABB), 22, 239
Ashford.com, 635
Astra, 367
Atari, 530–539, 742
Atlanta Bread Company, 784
AT&T, 38, 78, 81, 202, 419, 559, 562, 737, 752, 884
Au Bon Pain Co., 785
Auctions.com, 635, 638
AuctionWatch, 634, 637
Audible, 635
Autobytel.com, 422, 423
Automatic Data Processing Inc., 833
Automation, 31
AutoTrader.com, 631
Avogadro, 131
A&W Restaurants, 911, 914
Axicon, 830

B. Dalton, 89
Bain & Company, 401, 732
Baja Fresh, 784
Ball Corporation, 597, 603–606
Banc of America Capital Management, 804
Bank of America, 448, 797
Barnes & Noble, 863
Bartels-Langness, 891
Baskin-Robbins, 547, 620, 770, 910, 914
Bath & Body Works, 176
Baxter International, 829
BBAG, 686
Beam Software, 532
Beatrice, 436
Beecham Group, 203
Bellows & Samson, 681
Beneficial, 185
Ben Franklin Stores, 888
Ben & Jerry's, 540–554, 616

Berkshire Hathaway, 74, 189, 193, 313
Bertelsmann, 407
Best Buy, 420, 808
Best Practices, LLC., 420
Big Boy, 770, 909
Billpoint, 632
Blockbuster, 537
Bluetooth SIG Limited, 762
BMW, 52, 61, 157, 158, 381, 382, 648
Bob Evans, 909, 910
Boeing, 80, 226, 345, 449, 703, 838, 884
Boise Cascade, 362
Bojangles', 910, 911
Bonanza, 770
Bonogram S. A., 547
Booz, Allen and Hamilton, 311
Borden Inc., 690, 694, 696
Bostonbean Coffee Company, 676
Boston Beer Company, 576, 579
Boston Consulting Group (BCG), 153, 198–201, 732
Boston Market Corporation, 730, 731, 784, 910, 911, 912
Boxlot, 635
BP Amoco, 20, 31, 40, 51
Braniff, 127
Breckenridge Holding Company, 576–588
Brinker International, 29, 336
Bristol-Myers Squibb Company, 714
British Airways, 127, 407
British American Tobacco (BAT), 133
British Petrolem (BP), 440
British Telecom, 884
Brookstone, 827, 828
Brown Foreman, 819
BTR, 197
Buca di Beppo, 784
BUCA Inc., 783
Buffalo Wild Wings, 783
Bunge Food Corporation, 788
Burdines, 75
Burger Chef, 776
Burger King, 770, 775, 783, 910, 911, 914

Cabot Corporation, 200–201
Cadbury Schweppes, 302
Campbell Soup, 74, 75, 81
Canadean Ltd., 684
Cannondale, 157
Canon, 27, 127
Cape Cod Potato Chips, 690
Captain D's Seafood, 910
Card Capture Services, 446

Cardinal Health, 82, 884
CareerMosaic.com, 87
CareerPath.com, 87
Cargill, 86
Caribbean Shipping & Cold Storage, 450
Carling O'Keefe Breweries, 204
Carlsberg Breweries A/S, 685
Carl's Jr., 914
CarMax, 206
CarPoint, 739
Carrabba's Italian Grill, 768, 783, 909
Carrefour, 879, 882
Case, S. M., 22
Casio, 188
Caswell-Massey, 176, 177
Caterpillar, Inc., 157, 170, 338
CBS Sportsline, 637
CCU, 683
Centocor, Inc., 370, 715
Chalone, 819
Champion International, 197
ChannelSpace Entertainment, Inc., 630
Chaparral Steel, 376, 377
Charles Schwab & Co., 15, 184,
    185, 203
Chase/J.P. Morgan, 202
CheckSpace, 131
Cheesecake Factory, 783, 909, 910
Chemical Bank, 302, 390
ChevronTexaco, 27, 122, 884
Chevy's, 783
Chicago Pizza & Brewery, 783
Chick-fil-A, 910, 911, 912
Chili's Grill & Bar, 910, 914
Chipotle Mexican Grill, 730, 731, 784
Chiquita Brands International, 589–596
Chock Full O'Nuts, 673
Christie's, 623
Chrysler Corporation, 175
Chuck E. Cheese's, 910, 911, 912
Church's Chicken, 910, 911, 914
Ciba-Geigy, 187, 200, 223
Ciba Specialty Chemicals, 81
CiCi's Pizza, 910, 911, 912
Cinergy, 123
Cingular Wireless Communications, 754,
    755, 756, 757
Circuit City, 206, 808
Cisco Systems, 87, 202, 292, 293, 378,
    404, 408, 825
CIT Group, 291
Citibank, 21, 184
Citicorp, 235
Citigroup, 125, 884
Citipost, 458
C&J Industries, 830
Claris, 625
Clayton, Dublilier, & Rice, 197
CNET, 623
Cnstar, 602

Coca-Cola Enterprises, Inc., 127, 170,
    227, 231, 232, 316, 321, 599, 696,
    753, 846, 884, 902
Coinstar, Inc., 516, 519
CollegeBytes.com, 623
Commerce One, 50
Compaq Computer Corp., 175, 430, 565,
    629
CompUSA, 637
CompuServe, 630
Computer Associates, 302
Computer Services Corporation, 6, 7
ConAgra, 86, 337, 694
Conoco Phillips, 884, 888
Conseco, 185
Constellation Brands, 819
Context Integration, 136
Continental Airlines, 700
Continental Can, 602, 603, 605, 607
Continental Can Canada (CCC), 614
Cooper Industries, 186, 187, 197
Cooper Software, Inc., 122, 303
Coral Blood Services, 514, 519
CoreBrand, 899
Corel, 39
Corner Bakery, 784
Corning, Inc., 415
Corporate Coffee Systems, 676
Corporate Interns, Inc., 461
Corptech, 379
Cosi, 784
Costco Cos., 651, 653, 877
Covey Leadership Center, 204
CP group of Thailand, 337
Crabtree and Evelyn, 176
Cracker Barrel, 903, 910
Credit Suisse First Boston, 571
Crossgain, 131
Crown Cork & Seal, 597–614
Cruzcampo, 686
Crystal Rock/Vermont Pure Springs, 676
CT Financial, 776
Culvers, 783
Custom Research Inc. (CRI), 158, 159
CVS, 82, 161
Cybercorp Inc., 203
Cypress Semiconductor, 27
Cyveillance, 449

D. H. Brown Associates, 574
Daewoo Motor Co., 244, 311
D'Agostino Supermarkets, 678
Dai-Ichi Kangyo Bank, 884
DaimlerChrysler, 52, 190, 202, 644, 646,
    901
Daiwa Securities Group, 320
Dannon, 547
DataLabs International, 90
Datamonitor, 616
Dawn Food Products, Inc., 788

Dayton Hudson, 888
Deja News, 42
Della.com, 635
Dell Computer Corporation, 134, 135,
    227, 345, 347, 417, 565, 621, 637
DeLoach Winery, 811
Deloitte Touche Tohmatsu, 415
Delphi Corporation, 827, 830
Delta Air Lines, 700, 705, 706, 843, 844
Denny's Restaurants, 382, 770, 909, 910,
    914
Den-O-Tech, 532
Deutsche Telekom, 407
Diageo, 819
Diamond International Corporation, 606
Dickinson, 381
Diedrich Coffee, 677
digiMine, 131
Digital Cities, 630
Digital Cost Partners, 537
Digital Dimensions, Inc., 453
Digital Equipment Corp., 43, 132
Dippin' Dots, 615–620
DIRECTV, 703
The Disney Stores, Inc., 537
Disney Theme Parks, 910
Dispenser Services Inc., 676
Dohle Group, 891
Dole, 547
Domino's Pizza, 769, 770, 775, 776, 904,
    911, 912, 914
Donatos, 731
Dove Bar International, 547
Dow Chemical Corporation, 20, 21, 716
DreamWorks SKG, 379, 737
Dreyer's Grand Ice Cream, Inc., 549,
    551, 616, 852, 863
drugstore.com, 635
Dunkin' Donuts, 620, 770, 910, 914
DuPont, 367, 401
Duracell, 161, 189

Eastman Kodak, 396, 799
eBay, 119, 621–639, 804, 901
edeal, 635
Edeka/AVA Group, 891, 892
Eden Studios, 532
ehammer, 635
E&J Gallo, 819
Electronic Arts (EA), 534, 535, 537, 538,
    539, 749
Electronic Data Systems (EDS), 6–7, 12,
    25, 484, 485
Eli Lilly & Co., 60, 195, 299, 404
Elliott-Lincoln Company, 716
E-Loan, 448
El Pollo Loco, 910, 911
EMC, 162, 163
Emerson Electric, 197, 296, 298
Emerson Electronic, 201

Encyclopaedia Britannica, 43
Energizer, 161
Enron Corp., 17, 210, 211, 308, 318, 319, 382, 384
Equifax, Inc., 631
Ericsson, 234, 751, 757; *see also* Sony-Ericsson
Ernst & Young, 383
eRock.com, 638
E-Stamp, 633
Ethicon Endo Surgery, Inc., 370
E*Trade, 446
eWanted.com, 638
Excite, 637
Exodus Communications, 632
Expedia, Inc., 739
ExxonMobil, 202, 382, 407, 675, 676, 678, 884

f

FairMarket Network, 623, 634, 635, 637
Family Restaurants, Inc., 849
Fannie Mae, 884
FAO Inc., 438, 866
Fazoli's, 784
Federal Express (FedEx), 29, 137, 158, 159, 160, 296, 303, 458, 460
Fenner and Smith, 724–725
Ferrari, 158
Fidelity Investments, 50, 313, 342
Filene's Basement, 176
Firefly Network, 737
Firestone, 382
First Auction, 630
First Tennessee, 129
Fischer, 686
Fisher-Price, 462
Fixx Services, Inc., 456
Flagsston Corporation, 776
Fleet Boston Financial, 129, 448
Fleet Mortgage, 75
Fleming, 653
Food Lion, 14, 137, 148–150, 151, 320
Ford Motor Company, 16, 21, 26, 63, 190, 228, 233, 236, 239, 330, 351, 382, 660, 884
Forest Laboratories, 316
Forrester Research, 70, 172
Fortis Bank, 685
Fortune Brands, 31, 819
Foster-Miller, 441
Foster's Group, 819
Fox Software Inc., 737
Franklin Quest Company, 204
FreeMarkets Online, 57, 161
FreshDirect, 650–659
Frito-Lay, Inc., 689–693
Frusen Gladje, 547
Fuji Bank, 884
Fuld & Co., 41, 42

g

G. Heileman Brewing Company, 501, 504, 506–508
Gabelli Asset Management, 900
Gallucio Family Cellars, 822
Galoob Toys, 742
Game City, 532
Gannett Co., 294, 295
Gap Corporation, 20, 21, 176, 902
Garden of Eat'n, 692
Gartner Group, 421, 621
Gateway, 347, 565
GE Aerospace, 174
Gear.com, 635
GE Medical Systems, 25, 123
Gemini Consulting, 849
General Dynamics, 174
General Electric (GE), 7, 121, 124, 125, 126, 190, 210, 224, 307, 321, 341, 342, 354, 419, 719, 846, 884
General Foods, 547
General Magic, 625
General Mills, 153, 155, 242, 298
General Motors (GM), 21, 52, 63, 92, 119, 163, 210, 244, 316, 321, 335, 430, 644, 646, 660–665, 902
Genstar, 776
Genzyme, 234
GE Plastics, 827, 830
Gerber Products Co., 87
Gibson, 160
GigaMedia, 243
Gillette, 84, 127, 161, 188, 189
Glaxo Holdings, 884
GlaxoSmithKline, 125, 202, 203
Glenora Winery, 811
Global Crossing, 210, 308, 319
Global Growth Group, 730
Globus, 891, 892, 893
GO.com, 630
Godfather's Pizza, 770
Golden Corral, 770, 909, 910
Golden Enterprises, 690
Goldman, Sachs & Co., 80, 531
Golfsmith International, 70
Gomez Advisors, 634
GO Network Auctions, 634, 635, 637
Good Humor–Breyers Ice Cream, 616, 620
GoodMark Foods, Inc., 690
Google, 42, 905
Goose Creek Savings, 812
Grand Metropolitan, PLC, 547, 769, 775, 849
Graybar Electric Co., 422
Great Plains, 737
Greenlight.com, 635
Green Mountain Coffee Roasters (GMCR), 670–678
Green Tree Financial, 185
Gremlin, 532

GroceryWorks, 655
Ground Round, 770
Grupo Modelo, 685
Gryphon, 449
GT Interactive, 532
Gucci, 161
Guidant Corporation, 714

h

Häagen-Dazs, 245, 246, 547, 548, 616, 620
Haggle Online, 635
Hallmark Cards, Inc., 18, 869
Hammarplast, 846
Hanover Insurance, 375
Hanson plc, 197, 198, 306, 307
Hanson Trust, 337
Harbour & Associates, 663
Hardee's, 770, 775, 776, 909, 910, 914
Harley-Davidson, 84, 155, 158, 188
Harris Teeter, 678
Harvard Pilgrim Healthcare, 136, 137
Hasbro Inc., 462, 625
Hasbro Interactive, Inc., 530, 531, 532
HCI Direct, 75
HeadHunter.com, 87
Healthsouth Corp., 384
Heekin Can, Inc., 603, 604, 606
Heineken, 683–688
HemaCare Corporation, 514, 519
Heublein, 907
Hewlett-Packard Co., 79, 128, 132, 133, 205, 225, 227, 296, 344, 347, 407, 559–575, 753, 884
Hills, 869
Hoffman LaRoche, 223
Home Depot, Inc., 297, 304, 365, 884
Homegrocer.com, 635
Honda Motors, 63, 74, 127, 157, 236, 348, 644, 646, 648, 663, 664
Honeywell, 52, 53, 78, 174, 190
Hooters, 910
Hotjobs.com, 87, 904
Hotmail, 737
Household International, 185
Hugger Mugger Yoga Products, 456
Hughes Electronics, 430
Hutchinson Wholesale Shoe Co., 888
Hyatt Hotels Corp., 864
Hyundai, 61, 63, 80, 648

i

IBM, 6, 7, 21, 44, 59, 70, 90, 102, 131, 175, 225, 235, 244, 321, 347, 350, 351, 404, 565, 609, 737, 747, 753, 846, 884
Icos Corp., 60
ICQ, 630
I-Escrow, 632
Ignition Corporation, 131
IKEA, 10, 154, 155
Imaging and Printing Systems, 562

Imasco, 776
ImClone Systems, 17
Imperial Tobacco, 776
IND Bank of Japan, 884
Infogrames Entertainment SA (IESA), 530–539
Information Resources, Inc. (IRI), 616
Infoseek Corporation, 637
Inkjet Imaging Solutions, 562
Inktomi, 905
InnoCentive, 404
Intel Corp., 7, 17, 22, 119, 237, 245, 303, 313, 378, 379, 403, 404, 407, 410, 753
Interactive Media Group, 737
Interbrew, 685
Interface, Inc., 437
International Dairy Queen, Inc., 547, 769, 770, 773, 777, 910, 914
International House of Pancakes (IHOP), 770, 909, 910, 914
Intuit Incorporated, 177, 402, 626, 802
Iowa Beef Processors (IBP), 86
Isuzu, 648
ITT, 337

J. C. Penney Co., 62, 119, 167, 637, 779, 869
J. D. Power & Associates, 158, 160, 663
J. P. Morgan Chase, 302, 390
Jack in the Box, 910, 911
Jager Di Paola Kemp Design (JDK), 830
Jays Foods, L.L.C., 689–699
Jerome Goods, 346
JetBlue Airways Corporation, 78, 675, 676, 843, 844
Jobsearch.com, 87
John Deere, 623
John Hancock Financial Services, Inc., 422
John Labatt, Ltd., 599
Johnson Controls, 413, 602
Johnson & Johnson, 40, 370, 387, 388, 435, 461, 367
Juno Online Services, 75

KarstadtQuelle, 891
Kaufland, 893
KB Toys, 866, 867, 869
Kellogg Company, 234, 562
Kendall-Jackson, 819
Kentucky Fried Chicken Corporation (KFC), 770, 907, 910, 911, 914
Keurig, Incorporated, 674, 677
Kia, 648
Kidder Peabody, 210
Kiehl's, 434
Kingsley Management LLC, 441
Kinko's, 630
Kirin, 685

Kleiner Perkins Caulfield & Byers, 132, 832
Kmart, 61, 171, 172, 304, 808, 869, 876, 879, 888
Kohlberg, Kravis, Roberts & Company, 197
Koos Group, 243
KPMG, 318
Kraft Foods, Inc., 547, 670, 674, 675, 677, 851
Krispy-Kreme Doughnuts, Inc., 435, 436, 783, 910
Kroger, 149, 164, 653, 879, 880, 884
Kruse International, 631
Kwik-Fit, 645
Kyocera Corp., 459

L. A. Gear, 161
La Madeleine, 784
Lance Inc., 690
Lands' End, Inc., 76
LaPreferida, 692
LeapFrog Enterprises, 462
Legend Group, 298
Lego, 44
Lehman Brothers, 173
Lekkerland-Tobaccoland, 891
Leonhardt Plating Company, 377
Levi Strauss, 44, 380, 390
Lexus, 157, 158, 159
Lidl, 893
Lieb Vineyard, 815
The Limited, Inc., 148
Lincoln Electric Company, 716–729
Little Caesars, 769, 770, 775, 777, 910, 911, 914
Litton Industries, 195
living.com, 635
Lloyd's of London, 631
Lockheed Martin, 8, 11, 174, 195, 299, 350, 449
Longhorn Steakhouse, 909
Long John Silver's, 910, 911
Loral Corporation, 195
Lord & Taylor, 176
Lotteria, 914
Lotus Corp., 90, 244
Louis Vitton Möet Hennesey (LVMH), 819
Lowe's, 365
Lucent Technologies, 404, 407, 559, 562
Lycos, 629, 637

Macy's, 904
Magnetek, 830
Mail Boxes Etc. (MBE), 457, 633
Mandalay Entertainment, 27
Marantz, 157
Marie Callender, 770
Marks & Spencer, 84, 85

Marktkauf, 893
Marshall Industries, 366
Mars Inc., 849
Martin Guitar, 157
Martin Marietta; see Lockheed Martin
Matsushita, 170
Mattel, 462
Maxwell House, 673
Mazda, 351
McAllistairs, 784
McCaw Cellular, 202
McDonald's Corporation, 27, 195, 227, 234, 301, 457, 619, 620, 730–735, 765, 769, 770, 773, 775, 777–778, 779, 783, 854, 857, 909, 910, 911, 913, 914
McDonnell Douglas (MD), 195
McKesson, 187, 884
McKinsey & Company, 43, 224, 309, 540
McLane Company, 877
Medtronic, Inc., 27, 126, 127
Meijer, 869, 888
Mercedes-Benz, 23
Mercer Human Resources Consulting, 129
Merck & Co., 23, 87, 118, 125, 209, 367, 562, 884
Merrill Lynch, 122, 184, 309, 448, 724, 798
Metal Box, 614
Metro AG, 879, 891, 893
Michelin, 827, 830
Microprocessor Designs, 830
Microsoft Corporation, 78, 119, 123, 131, 160, 175, 224, 226, 228, 243, 303, 321, 350, 351, 381, 410, 420, 421, 533, 534, 621, 625, 637, 736–750, 810, 846, 901
MicroUnity, Inc., 441
Micro Warehouse, 623
Midway, 741
Miller Brewing Company, 500, 502, 503, 504, 506–508, 512, 683, 696
Mirabito Fuel Group, 676
Mitsubishi, 648
Mitsubishi Bank, 884
Moai Technologies, 623
The Molson Companies, Ltd., 204, 599
MonitoRobotics, 679–682
Monsanto, 75, 127
Monster.com, 87
Moretti, 686
Morgan Stanley, 156, 446
Morris Air, 702
Morrison Knudsen (MK), 16, 362
Mos Burger, 914
Motel 6, 40
Motorola, 14, 27, 38, 124, 381, 412, 416, 440, 463, 751, 752, 753, 757, 763
Motto Kryla Fisher, 819

MSA Aircraft Interior Products, Inc., 300–301
MSN, 739, 905
MusiKube, LLC., 458

n
Nabisco Corporation, 441, 907
Namco, 741
Nartron Corporation, 463
National Can Company, 603, 605, 614
Nationjob.com, 87
Nationwide Recyclers, Inc., 608
Navision, 737
NBC, 537
NEC, 20, 234, 633, 751, 752
Nescafé, 673
Nestlé SA, 190, 232, 238, 616, 672
Nestlé Waters of North America, 676, 678
NetGrocer.com, 655, 656–659
Netpartners Internet Solutions, 446
Netscape, 122, 630
Network Appliance (NA), 162, 163
Network Associates, 8
Newell Rubbermaid, 296
New England Coffee, 674
New York Yankees, 7
NextCard, 635
Nextel, 403
NextJet, Inc., 29, 30
Nike, 228, 234, 347, 348, 854
Nintendo, 61, 533, 534, 535, 736, 741, 742, 744, 746, 749
Nippon Telephone & Telegraph, 884
Nissan, 92, 351, 644, 648, 664
Nokia, 38, 157, 205, 410, 411, 751–763
Noodles & Company, 784
Nordstrom, 61, 76, 157
Norma, 891, 893
Nortel Networks, 205, 406, 410
North Face, 157
North Fork Bancorp, 812
Northrop Grumman, 449
Northstar Group, Inc., 316
Northwest Airlines, 700
Nova Cruz Products LLC, 438
Novartis, 81, 187
Novell, 39, 351
NTT DoCoMo, 243, 753, 754, 755, 756, 884
Nucor, 119, 130, 296, 305
Nvidia, 749
NYCGrocery.com, 656
Nynex, 56

o
Oakshire Mushroom Farm, Inc., 438, 439
Ocean Software, 532
OEP Imaging Operating Corporation, 397
Office Depot, 76, 448
Offshore Heavy Transport, 52
Old Country Buffet, 910

Olive Garden, 910
OpenSite Technologies, 623
Oracle Corporation, 14, 70–71, 102, 175, 228, 308, 316, 794
Orange Julius, 914
Orion Pictures, 537
Outback Steakhouse, Inc., 764–782, 910, 914
Outpost.com, 638
Owens-Illinois, 602
Oxford GlycoSciences, 234
Ozisoft, 532

p
Pabst, 504, 506–508
Pacific Gas and Electric, 321
Pacific Scientific, 830
Panasonic, 410, 742
Panera Bread Company, 436, 732, 783–792, 910
Papa John's, 770, 910, 911, 912
Paradigm Entertainment, 532
Paragon Tool, 679–682
Paramount Communications, 537
Parcel Plus, 632
Parker Pen, 189
Pathmark Stores, Inc., 849
Peapod, 655
Pechiney International, 614
Pellegrini Vineyards, 815
PepsiCo Inc., 155, 192, 226, 227, 321, 602, 689, 693, 769, 775, 778, 783, 846, 849, 852, 863, 907–908
Perkins, 770, 909, 910
Peter Kiewit Sons Inc., 597, 603
Peter Piper Pizza, 773
Pets.com, 635
P.F. Changs China Bistro, 783, 909
Pfizer Inc., 60, 82, 125, 203
Pfizer/Warner-Lambert, 202, 203
Philadelphia 76ers, 373
Philip Morris Companies Inc., 599, 673, 884
Philips Media, 532
Phillips Petroleum, 195
PHPK, 407
Pick Up Stix, 784
Pierce, 724
Pier 1 Imports, 40, 43
Pillsbury Corporation, 547
Pixar Animation Studios, 793–798
PizzaExpress, 908
Pizza Hut, 910, 914
Playing Mantis, 441
Polaris Industries, Inc., 829
Polaroid Corporation, 16, 132, 396, 397
Ponderosa, 770, 909, 910
Popcyc's Chicken, 783, 910, 911, 914
Porsche, 158, 163, 320, 648
Potash Corporation of Saskatchewan, Inc., 156

Premier Automotive Group (PAG), 646, 648
Priceline.com, 85, 210
PricewaterhouseCoopers, 342, 346, 881
Primerica, 603
ProCD, 56, 72
Procter & Gamble, 20, 31, 137, 173, 195, 196, 226, 230, 383, 385, 461, 589, 625, 672, 673, 674, 693, 799–804, 884
Prufrock Corporation, 102–112
Psygnosis, 532
Publix Super Markets, 653, 678
Puritan-Bennett Corporation, 346

q
Qdoba, 784
Quaker Oats, 170
Quest Diagnostics, 129
Quick Restaurants, 914
Quizno's Classic Subs, 783
Qwest Communications, 904

r
R. C. Can, 607
R. J. Reynolds Industries, Inc. (RJR), 907
RadioFrame Networks, 403
Random House, 458
Raytheon, 195
Real, 893
Red Lobster, 910, 914
Red Robin, 770
Reebok, 347, 348
Retail Forward, Inc., 413
Rewe Group, 891, 892
Reynolds Metals, 597, 600, 601, 603
Ritz-Carlton, 301
RL Vallee, Inc., 676
Robert Mondavi, 811, 816, 819
Roberts Express, 159
Rockstar Games, 535
Romano's, 910
Rosa Verde, 207
Rose International, 453
Rosenbluth International, 121
Rosen Motors, 16, 430–431
Roshambo Winery, 811
Roundarch, 415
Round Table Pizza, 770, 910, 911
Royal Ahold, 653, 656, 879
Royal Dutch Shell, 884
Rubbermaid Corporation, 398
Rublos Mexican Grill, 784
Ruby Tuesday, 910
Running Press, 461
Ryan's, 909, 910
Ryder, 165

s
SAB-Miller PLC, 683, 685
Safeway, 653, 698, 849
Saft, 830
Sam's Club, 653

Samsung Electronics, 751, 763, 806–810
Sandoz, 81, 223
Sanford C. Bernstein & Company, 664
Sanwa Bank, 884
SAP, 102, 224, 320
Sapient Health Network (SHN), 473, 474
Sara Lee, 674
Sargento, 692
SAS Institute, 79, 133, 135
Saturn, 125
SAZABY Inc., 863
SBC/Ameritech, 202
SBC Communications, 904
Schlecker, 891
Schlitz, 500, 502, 504, 506–508
Schoolhouse Lane Estates, 811–824
Schwarz Gruppe, 891, 892
SCM, 198
Scottish & Newcastle, 685
The Seagram Company, Ltd., 599
Sears, Roebuck & Co., 39, 157, 389, 879, 880
SEGA Corporation, 533, 736, 737, 741, 742, 743, 745, 749
Segway LLC, 825–833
Semco, Inc., 303
Service Merchandise, 869
7-Eleven, 910
Seven Networks, 451
SG Cowen Securities, 202
Sharp Corporation, 188–189, 306, 333, 341, 342
Sharper Image, 438, 623
Shaw Industries, 74, 187, 189, 193
Shearer's Food Inc., 693
Shell Oil Company, 20, 44, 127
Shiny Entertainment, 531, 532
Shoney's, 770, 909
Shopko, 869
Showbiz/Chuck E. Cheese, 770
Siebel Systems, Inc., 137, 158, 160, 235, 293
Siemens, 407, 751
Silgan Plastics, 602
Silicon Graphics, Inc. (SGI), 8
Silicon Sensing Systems, 830
Silicon Valley Bank, 816
Sizzler, 770, 914
Sizzlin', 909
Skylark, 914
SkyTower Telecommunications, 455, 456
SmithKline Beecham, 203, 342
SNK, 742
Sodexho, 676
Sodima, 242
SOFTIMAGE Inc., 737
Solectron, 123
Sonic Drive-In, 910
Sonoco Products Co., 602

Sony Corporation, 206, 408, 410, 419, 434, 533, 534, 535, 740, 741, 742, 743, 744, 745, 746, 747, 808
Sony-Ericsson, 751, 753; see also Ericsson
Sotheby's, 623, 635
South African Breweries Plc, 683
Southwest Airlines (SWA), 7, 9, 80, 121, 122, 127, 296, 297, 705, 837–845
Spar Group, 878, 891, 892
Spelling Entertainment, 537
Springfield ReManufacturing Corporation (SRC), 376, 377
Sprint Corporation, 18, 383
Spry Learning Co., 460
Square ENIX USA, 535
St. Louis Bread Co., 785
Stacy's Pita Chip Co., 444
Staples, 75, 76, 448
Starbucks, 436, 438, 626, 670, 675, 677, 783, 846–865, 910
Starwood Hotels, 863
Steve's, 547
STMicroelectronics (ST), 204
Stowe Mountain Resort, 676
Strategos Consulting, 416
Streamline, 443
Stride Rite Corporation, 625
The Stroh Brewery Company, 504, 506–508, 599
Subaru, 648
Subway Sandwiches, 457, 731, 769, 770, 775, 778–779, 783, 910, 911, 914
Sumitomo Bank, 884
Sumitomo Chemical Company, 808
Sunbeam Corporation, 210, 308, 486
Sun Microsystems, 160, 347, 565, 632
Super-K, 698
Supervalu, 653
Sur La Table, 904
SurModics, Inc., 435
Suzuki, 648
Sweet Tomatoes/Souplantation, 784
Swift and Company, 694

T. Rowe Price Group, 313, 804
Taco Bell, 910, 911, 914
Taco Cabana, 784
Taco Time, 914
Take 2, 538
Tandem Computers, 128
Tandy Corporation, 752
Target Corporation, 171, 172, 869, 876, 879
Tazo, 864
TCBY Yogurt, 547, 770, 914
TechSpace, 447
Tecmo, 749
Tele-Communications Inc., 379
Tengelmann Group, 891, 892

TETCO, 676
Texaco, 382, 383
Texas Air, 127
Texas Instruments (TI), 80, 386, 463, 808
T.G.I. Friday's/Carlson Companies, Inc., 770, 775, 910, 914
Third Millennium Communications, 131
3M Co., 88, 187, 206, 296, 297, 306, 380, 408, 416, 417, 434
Time Inc., 210
Times Digital Company, 637
Times Mirror Company, 187, 191–192
Time-Warner, Inc., 122, 203, 204, 308, 810
Timothy's, 677
Tippett Studio, 795
Tony Roma's, 770
Toro Company, 375
Tosco, 195
Toyota, 63, 74, 158, 228, 296, 343, 644, 646, 648, 663, 664, 884
Toys "R" Us, 866–871
Tradesafe, 632
Travelers/Citicorp, 202
Triangle Industries, 603
Tricon Global Restaurants, 849, 908
Trimble Navigation Ltd., 8
Tsingtao, 683
Tyco International Ltd., 16, 17, 290–291, 309, 312, 382

UBS Warburg, 664, 710
U-Haul, 165, 166
Unilever Ice Cream, 617
Unilever PLC, 173, 616
Uni-Marts, 676
Unisys, 449
United Airlines, 7, 700, 705, 843, 844
United Fruit Company, 590
United Parcel Service (UPS), 30, 133, 458, 562
U.S. Trust Corp., 184
United Technologies (UT), 42
USAA, 128
USA Interactive, 901
US Airways, 705
UST, 819
utrade, 635
UTStarcom, 459

Van Dorn Company, 603, 605, 606
Van Houtte, 677
Verizon Communications, 757, 884, 904
Vertex Pharmaceuticals, 50
VF Corporation, 190
Viacom Inc., 537, 898
ViAir, 131
Viewpoint DataLabs, 90
Village Inn, 770
Virgin Games, 537

Virgin Group, 25, 127, 408, 409, 434
Vivendi Universal, 211
Vodafone/Mannesmann, 202
Vodaphone, 754, 755, 756
Volkswagen, 52, 220, 230, 351, 648

W

Waffle House, 910
Walgreen Co., 31, 80
Walkabout Travel Gear, 443–444
Wal-Mart, 9, 61, 166, 167, 168, 169, 172, 206, 245, 246, 297, 365, 413, 653, 698, 804, 808, 846, 849, 866, 869, 876–894
Walnut Venture Associates, 447
Walt Disney Company, 190, 313, 338, 419, 625, 630, 637, 638, 794, 827
Warner Bros., 210, 629
Warner Communications, 530
Warner-Lambert Co., 203
Washington Mutual, 367, 368
Waste Management, 210
WD-40 Company, 460

WebMD, 474
Wedbush Morgan Securities, 531
Wegman's Food Markets, 75, 678
WellPoint Health Network, 28, 152–153, 155
Wells Fargo, 27, 31
Wendy's, 457, 769, 770, 775, 783, 910, 911, 914
Wertkauf, 878
Western Merchandise, 877
Western Sizzlin', 770, 909
Westinghouse, 346
Weston Presidio Capital, 702
Wetherill Associates (WAI), 387
Whole Foods Market, Inc., 377, 378
Wilshire Associates, 314
The Wine Group, 819
Winn-Dixie, 149
Wipro, 25
Wolfgang Puck Express, 784
Woolworth Corporation, 888

WorldCom, Inc., 6, 7, 17, 210, 211, 312, 384
WorldCom/MCI, 202
World Wrestling Entertainment (WWE), 895–900
WPP Group PLC, 133, 408

X

Xerox, 14, 27, 116, 127, 318, 404, 609, 799

Y

Yahoo!, 448, 621, 629, 635, 636–637, 901–905
Yokogawa, 365
Yoshinoya, 914
Young & Rubicam, 135
YourGrocer.com, 655–656, 657
Yum! Brands, Inc., 907–918

Z

Z Auction, 630
ZDNet, 623
Zurich Financial Services, 235

name index

a

Aaker, D. A., 248
Abell, D. F., 34
Abelson, R., 392
Ackerman, J., 650
Ackerman, R., 415
Ackman, D., 646
Adams, R., 732
Adamson, J., 776
Adler, P. S., 143
Afuah, A., 358
Agee, B., 16, 362–363
Agoos, A., 600
Aguilar, D., 816
Aguirre, F., 589
Aiman-Smith, L., 426
Alahuhta, M., 411
Albrinck, J., 426
Aldag, R. J., 492
Aldrich, H., 467
Alexander, M., 214
Aley, J., 132
Ali-Peitella, P., 751
Allaire, P., 116
Allen, P., 736, 737
Alstead, T., 859
Amabile, T. M., 143
Amar, G., 309
Amburgey, T. L., 357, 358
Ament, K., 786
Amit, R., 101
Amos, K., 842
Amram, M., 215
Anaptyxi, C., 679
Anard, B. N., 215
Anderson, C. J., 100
Anderson, M. J., Jr., 608
Anderson, P., 141
Anderson, S., 654
Andrus, M., 444
Andrus, S., 444
Angwin, J. S., 216
Anslinger, P. A., 214
Ansoff, H. I., 66
Archer, C., 516
Argawal, A., 325
Argyris, C., 323
Arikan, A. M., 34
Armas, G. C., 66
Arnadt, M., 80
Arndt, A., 878
Arndt, M., 49, 179, 326, 735
Arnold, D., 249
Arnold, S. E., 800
Arpey, G. J., 706
Ashkenas, R., 342

Aspelin, D. J., 143
Atkinson, A. A., 34
Attkisson, S., 525
Augustine, N., 11, 180, 299, 344, 350, 358
Ausley, D., 18
Austin, J. E., 20, 35
Austin, S., 898
Avery, W., 607, 609, 614

b

Baatz, E. B., 393
Babcock, C., 782
Bach, R., 741
Bachus, K., 746
Bahrami, H., 352
Baker, S., 324, 688
Bakewell, J., 857
Bakke, D., 387
Baldwin, J., 846
Balmer, S., 381
Bamford, C. E., 66
Barger, D., 704, 708
Barkema, G. G., 35
Barkema, H. P., 215
Barnes, C., 346, 358, 492
Barnevik, P., 311
Barnholt, E. W., 564
Barret, A., 370
Barrett, A., 215, 467, 715
Barrett, C., 840, 842
Barry, T., 458
Bart, C. K., 35
Bartlett, C. A., 142, 180, 248, 249, 336, 357
Bartness, A., 359
Bary, A., 798
Basham, B., 764, 782
Baum, A. C., 35
Baum, C. F., 211
Baumgarter, P., 67, 179
Baysinger, B. D., 325
Bearden, W. O., 180
Beatty, S., 900
Becker, C., 523
Becker, G. S., 142
Beckhard, R., 34, 35, 342, 392, 393
Begley, T. M., 34, 237
Bell, C., 731, 732, 734, 735
Bell, J., 537, 901
Belton, C., 222, 248
Bennet, E., 466
Bennett, N., 325
Bennett, S., 177, 402
Bensaou, B. M., 100

Benton, Philip, Jr., 244
Bergen, M. E., 179
Berger, M., 421
Berggren, E., 100
Berkowitz, E. N., 180, 248
Berle, A., 310
Berman, J., 291
Bernasek, A., 66
Berner, R., 93, 101, 168, 804
Bernstein, A., 25, 67, 321
Besley, S., 216
Bezos, J., 460
Bhagat, R. S., 248
Bhatia, H. (Sue), 453
Bhide, A. V., 426
Bianco, A., 141, 323
Bick, J., 426
Bierce, A., 310
Bilefsky, D., 688
Bills, R., 829
Birch, D., 432, 433, 466
Birkinshaw, J., 249, 426
Bishop, T., 750, 815
Blackley, J., 736
Blank, D., 180
Blenkhorn, D. L., 493
Block, Z., 426
Bloodgood, J. M., 143
Blyler, M., 101
Boehlert, S., 815
Boehm, E. M., 640
Boehm, H., 640
Bogan, C., 420, 427
Boger, J., 50
Bolino, M. C., 143
Bolton, S., 87
Bonnell, B., 530–539
Bonsignore, M. R., 52, 53
Borden, G., 231
Borland, M., 788
Borrus, C. A., 389
Bothe, M., 387
Boulding, A., 750
Bowen, D. E., 393
Bowick, S. D., 562, 563
Bowker, G., 846
Box, T., 646
Boyd, D. P., 34, 237
Boyle, B., 443–444
Boyle, G., 443–444
Brabeck, P., 238
Bradley, D., 900
Bradley, S. P., 597
Brady, D., 641, 644
Brandenburger, A., 60, 61, 67

Brandt, R., 324
Branson, R., 25, 127, 408, 706
Breen, B., 206, 382, 426, 462
Brenneman, K., 474
Brigham, B., 450
Brigham, E. F., 216
Brigham, J., 616
Brinker, N., 782
Briody, D., 467
Briton, B., 357
Brochstein, M., 735
Brock, R., 493
Brockner, J., 392
Brockovich, E., 320
Brokaw, L., 373
Brooker, K., 180
Brown, F., 358, 535
Brown, J., 100, 403
Brown, N., 746
Brown, R., 6–7, 12, 66, 484
Brown, S., 402, 426, 824
Browne, J., 66
Brull, S., 537
Brush, C., 426
Bryant, J., 56, 72
Bubbar, S. E., 143
Buchanan, L., 440, 467
Bucher, M., 456
Buckman, R. C., 143
Budde, K., 47
Buel, S., 631
Buffett, W., 39, 313
Bunderson, J. S., 358
Burgelman, R. A., 426
Burke, J., 388
Burrows, P., 467, 574, 798
Bush, G., 825
Bushkin, N., 537
Butz, H. E., 180
Buzzell, R. D., 215
Bygrave, W. D., 432, 442, 466
Byrne, C., 493
Byrne, J. A., 325
Byrne, J. C., 641
Byrnes, B., 802
Byrnes, N., 18, 49, 323, 325

C

Cabelin, C., 530
Caccott, J., 713
Cadbury, A., 302
Cadbury, S. A., 324
Callahan, B. R., 615
Campbell, A., 214
Canabou, C., 426
Canavor, N., 815
Caney, D., 295
Cantalupo, J. R., 730, 731, 732
Capell, K., 706
Capelli, P., 143
Carbonara, P., 142

Cardin, R., 122, 142
Carey, D., 215
Carey, J., 466
Carley, W. M., 143
Carlson, C., 775
Carlson, D. S., 393
Carney, D., 907
Carney, F., 907
Carruba, F., 344
Carter, R., 785
Carty, D., 312
Caruso, D., 393
Carvell, T., 427
Case, J., 466
Casey, M., 849
Casico, W. F., 215
Cassidy, J. C., 180
Castillo, D., 128
Catmull, E. E., 793–798
Caufield, P., 857
Caulfield, B., 426
Cavanaugh, S. M., 597
Cecil, A. B., 804
Cena, J., 895
Cerkovnik, E., 576
Cerny, K., 359
Chakraborty, A., 211
Challenger, J., 66
Chambers, J., 378, 825
Chambers, S., 382, 456
Champoux, J. E., 392
Champy, J., 354, 359
Chan, P., 180
Chandler, A. D., 357
Chapman, S., 460
Chappt, E., 567
Charan, R., 364, 392, 425
Charitou, C. D., 66
Charples, S. S., 66
Chatterjee, S., 325
Chen, C. Y., 449
Chen, W., 123
Cheney, D., 825
Cherry, C. W., 526
Cherry, N., 857
Chesbrough, H., 404, 426, 441
Chiu, B., 750
Chowdhury, N., 243
Christensen, C. M., 34, 179, 425, 440
Christensen, C. R., 492
Christou, D., 593, 595
Chuanzhi, L., 298
Citrin, J., 311
Clark, A., 683
Clayton, V., 215
Clifford, M. L., 248
Clinton, H. R., 815
Clizbe, J., 519
Close, S., 586
Clymer, S., 474

Cochran, P. L., 324
Coff, R., 101, 143, 326
Cohen, A., 625
Cohen, B., 542–554
Cohen, D., 143
Cohn, L., 51
Colarelli, G., 425
Cole, D., 430, 660
Coleman, D. R., 492
Coleman, G., 904
Collins, A., 127
Collins, G., 554
Collins, J., 296, 324, 417, 427, 453, 454, 467
Collis, D. J., 85, 101, 214, 215, 325, 357, 501
Colvin, G., 23, 24, 35, 66, 161, 162, 180, 364, 392
Comlin, M., 129
Conaway, W., 231
Condit, P. M., 563
Conley, J. H., 393
Connelly, J., 597, 606, 607, 609
Connerty, H., 764–774
Connolly, A., 773
Conyon, M. J., 326
Cook, D., 794
Cook, S., 127, 626, 802
Cookingham, R. W., 562, 563
Cooper, A., 122
Cooper, S., 466, 467
Coors, A., Jr., 505
Coors, A., Sr., 505
Coors, B., 499–513
Coors, J., 508
Coors, P., 508
Copeland, T. E., 214, 216
Corbett, A., 401
Courteney, H., 66
Covey, S., 204, 392, 393
Covin, J. G., 414, 426
Cowger, G. L., 661
Coy, P., 427
Craig, K., 576–588
Crick, F. H. C., 23
Croce, P., 373
Crock, S., 8
Crockett, R. O., 66, 426, 427
Cross, K., 427
Csere, C., 67
Curry, A., 163
Curtis, S., 209
Cusack, M., 215
Cusumano, M., 66

D

Dacin, T., 357, 358
Dae Je Chin, 809
Daft, D., 316
Daft, R., 392
Daily, C. M., 325

D'Alessandro, D., 422
Daley, C., 196
Daley, D., 522, 523
Daly, R., 210
Damanpour, F., 425
Damaraju, N. L., 641, 700, 837
Daniels, J. D., 357
Danko, G., 808
D'Aquanni, L., 449
Darretta, R. J., Jr., 714
Das, T. K., 359
D'Aveni, R., 179, 364
Davenport, C., 474
Davenport, T. H., 426
Davidson, A., 122
Davies, A., 66
Davis, E., 324, 358, 359
Davis, J. E., 179
Davis, P. S., 180
Davis, S., 179, 686, 788
Davis, T., 598
Dawar, N., 248
Dawn, K., 357, 358
Day, C., Jr., 392
Day, G. S., 101, 180
Day, J. D., 426
Day, S., 735
Deal, T. E., 324
Dean, B. V., 180
Dean, T. J., 66
de Carvalho, C., 687
de Carvalho, M., 687
Decker, H., 514, 522
Deephouse, D. L., 101
DeKluyver, C. A., 476
Delaney, K., 533
Dell, M., 345, 565
De Lombaerde, G., 596
DeMaria, R., 750
Demello, T., 443
Dennis, W. J., Jr., 466
Deogun, N., 185
de Pury, D., 22
DeSanctis, G., 358
DeSimone, L. D., 306
DeSio, T., 457
Dess, G. G., 34, 72, 138, 141, 142, 143,
    168, 180, 214, 215, 249, 323, 324,
    357, 358, 359, 366, 392, 393, 414,
    426, 466, 700, 837
Detamore-Rodman, C., 467
Deutsch, C. H., 141
Devine, J., 660
DiCarlo, 704
Dickinson, W., 381
Dickson, P. R., 180
Diller, B., 901
Distelzweig, H., 357
Doerr, J., 132, 832
Dolan, T., 116

Dolida, R. J., 346
Domoto, H., 249
Donald, J., 849
Donlon, J. P., 100
Donnelly, S. B., 706, 841
Donner, F., 660
dos Santos, J. F. P., 66
Douglas, S. P., 248
Dow, H. H., 716
Dowling, G. R., 142
Doz, Y., 66, 249, 358
Driscoll, E. B., Jr., 531
Drucker, P., 39, 43, 66, 400, 423, 426,
    467, 492
Dubini, P., 467
Duffy, J., 831
Duncan, R. E., 357
Dunn, D. L., 562, 563
Durant, H., 514
Durst, L., 819
Dutton, G., 142
Dwyer, P., 18, 389
Dyer, J. H., 100, 143, 249

e

Earl, M., 100
Eastwood, C., 505
Ebbers, B., 211, 312, 384
Echikson, W., 248
Edge, A. G., 492
Edmondson, G., 215, 248, 642
Edvisson, L., 142
Edwards, C., 810
Eickhoff, G., 131
Einstein, A., 482
Eisenberg, A. E., 310
Eisenhardt, K., 191, 325, 402, 426, 467
Eisner, A., 530, 615, 641, 670, 700, 825,
    837, 866
Eisner, M., 191, 313, 338, 794
Elenkov, D. S., 66
Elgin, B., 906
Elliot, S., 651
Ellison, L., 308, 794
Ellison, S., 804
Ellstrand, A. E., 325
Elson, C., 486
Elstrom, P., 574
Elzinga, K. G., 500
Emerson, R. W., 43, 348
Engardio, P., 25, 222, 248, 810
Engen, J., 461
English, M. J., 427
Ensing, I. M., 358
Enz, C., 492
Epstein, J., 44
Eselius, E. D., 215
Esrey, W., 18, 91
Estevez, S., 125
Evans, M., 523, 526

Evans, P., 66, 427
Everhart, T. E., 563
Ewing, J., 688
Eyler, J., 866–871

f

Fahey, L., 66
Fama, E., 325
Farr, D., 201
Fastow, A., 384
Fedele, J., 650
Feldman, A., 732
Fernandez, A., 398
Fery, J. B., 563
Fickenscher, L., 656
Fierman, J., 304
Finkelstein, S., 66, 141, 492
Finnigan, D., 900
Fiorina, C., 79, 559–575
Fisch, J. J., Jr., 685
Fisher, A., 143
Fisher, E., 900
Fisher, G., 381
Fisher, J. W., 603
Fisher, L. M., 654
Fisher, M. L., 100
Fishman, C., 466, 880
Fjeldstad, O. D., 100
Flass, R., 537
Fleisher, C. S., 493
Flint, J., 67, 248
Ford, G., 505
Ford, H., 21, 310, 374, 641
Ford, W. C., Jr., 641–649
Forest, S. A., 180
Forney, A., 764
Forster, J., 358
Forward, G., 377
Fouladpour, T., 220
Foust, D., 323
Franzke, E., 407
Fraser, J. A., 445, 467
Frauenfelder, M., 467
Frederick, J., 750
Frederickson, J. W., 357, 358
Freedman, M., 841
Freeman, M. A., 34
Freeman, R. E., 34, 143, 325, 357
Freibeg, J., 837, 838
Freibeg, K., 837, 838
Friedman, M., 379
Fries, E., 737
Friesen, P. H., 357
Fromartz, S., 466, 467
Frost, R., 348
Frost, T., 248
Fry, A., 297
Fryer, B., 67, 249, 324
Fujii, A., 243
Fuld, L., 41

Funk, K., 35
Furchgott, R., 143

g

Gaal, S., 447
Gadiesh, O., 166, 180
Gaetz, J. R., 700
Gaglio, C. M., 466
Gajilan, A. T., 702
Galbraith, J. R., 331, 357
Gale, B. T., 215
Gallucio, J., 822
Gallucio, V., 822
Galunic, D. C., 191
Galvin, C., 416
Galvin, R., 124
Gamble, J., 799
Gandhi, H., 330
Gannon, T., 764, 765
Garcia, E. R., 849
Garfield, B., 686
Garten, J. E., 35, 248
Gartner, W. B., 466
Gates, B., 120, 160, 736–750
Gatlin, G., 871
Gavetti, G., 425
George, B., 127
Geschke, J., 413
Ghemawat, P., 153, 499
Ghoshal, S., 66, 142, 180, 248, 249, 336, 357
Gibney, F., Jr., 810
Gikkas, N. S., 248
Gilbert, J. L., 166, 180
Gilinsky, A., Jr., 736, 811
Gilley, K. M., 358
Gilliard, D. J., 514, 525
Gillin, A., 804
Gilmartin, R., 125, 367
Gilmore, J. H., 180
Gimon, J-P., 563
Ginn, S., 563
Ginsberg, A., 426
Ginsburg, J., 66
Gladwin, T., 20
Glass, D., 877, 889
Glass, J. T., 358
Glassman, D., 846
Goff, L., 575
Gogoi, P., 735
Goldberg, H. G., 822
Goldberg, M., 393
Goldburg, D., 519
Goldfield, R., 446
Goldin, R. S., 735
Goldsmith, M., 34, 35, 342, 392, 393
Goldstein, A., 30
Goldstein, J., 596
Goldstine, J., 180
Goldwasser, D., 316
Goleman, D., 371, 372, 374, 392, 393

Goll, I., 67
Gonzalez, S., 222
Goodstein, L. D., 180
Goold, M., 214, 215, 323
Goteman, I., 155, 324
Gouldson, T., 575
Govindarajan, V., 130, 248, 249
Gow, D., 646
Graen, G. B., 324
Graham, A. B., 325
Grano, D., 446
Grant, L., 871
Grant, P., 66
Grant, R. M., 83, 101
Graser, M., 798
Grayson, C. J., 723
Green, J., 66
Greenberg, D. S., 523, 524
Greenberg, J. M., 312, 730, 731
Greene, P., 426
Greenfield, J., 542–554
Gregg, F. M., 248
Greising, D., 324
Gren, K., 586
Greulich, J., 159
Gross, D., 531
Grossman, J., 467
Grossman, W., 326
Grove, A., 7, 22, 303, 379
Grover, R., 205, 323, 325, 531, 798, 906
Grow, B., 47, 100
Gruber, P., 27
Gull, N., 467
Gupta, A. K., 130, 248, 249
Gurry, L., 905
Gustin, A., 775
Guth, W. D., 180, 215, 426, 492
Gutierrez, J., 858

h

Habib, M. M., 357
Hackborn, R. A., 563
Haddad, C., 100
Hage, J., 425
Hagmeier, K., 325
Hakim, D., 642, 644, 649
Hall, B. J., 324
Hall, D. J., 358
Hall, R. H., 324, 357
Hall, W. K., 180
Hamaker, S. S., 792
Hambrick, D. C., 180, 325
Hamel, G., 23, 34, 38, 66, 117, 132, 142, 143, 179, 214, 358, 409, 426, 427
Hamermesh, R. G., 608
Hamilton, D. P., 574
Hamm, S., 143
Hammer, M., 354, 359, 375, 393
Hammonds, K. H., 25, 34, 35, 143
Handy, C., 34, 347, 358, 374, 393
Hansen, M. T., 135, 143, 426

Hansen, N., 819, 821
Hansen, S., 440
Hanson, J., 306
Harari, O., 393
Hardwick, J., 51
Hardy, Q., 427, 625, 626
Hargreaves, D., 214
Harmon, M., 513
Harrar, G., 358
Harrigan, K., 214
Harris, J. E., 608
Harrison, J. S., 34, 143, 325, 357, 358
Hart, M., 426
Hartley, S. W., 180
Hartmann, J., 453
Harveston, P. D., 248
Hase, T., 747
Haskins, M. E., 358
Haspelagh, P., 215
Hastings, D. F., 717, 722
Haughton, K., 67
Hax, A. C., 214, 215
Hayes, C., 585
Hayes, R., 425, 426
Hazzard, C., 641
Healey, J., 67, 163
Healy, B., 519
Hearn, R., 815
Hegge, B.-A., 156
Heilemann, J., 825, 832
Helgesen, S., 25, 35, 393
Hellweg, E., 100
Helman, C., 427
Helms, M., 35, 180, 248, 249
Helper, S., 67
Hemp, P., 679
Henkoff, R., 101, 142
Henretta, D. A., 802
Henricks, M., 214
Herbruck, C. G., 717
Herman, L., 750
Herz, J. C., 750
Hesselbein, F., 34, 35, 342, 392, 393
Hesseldahl, A., 750
Hewlett, B., 559, 560, 561, 571
Hewlett, W., 561, 563, 565
Heymann, T., 537
Hill, A., 214
Hill, C. W. L., 357, 358
Hills, G. E., 466
Hilmer, F. C., 358
Himelstein, L., 821
Hinchey, M., 815
Hirshman, P., 135
Hitt, M. A., 34, 35, 83, 101, 143, 214, 249, 325, 326, 357
Hockaday, I. O., Jr., 18
Hof, R. D., 8, 324, 466
Hoff, T., 531
Hofstede, G., 249

Holland, R., 540–544
Holmes, S., 179
Holson, L. M., 798
Holstein, W. J., 427, 810
Holt, J., 381, 393
Holt, R., 446
Hood, M. E., 788
Hopkins, J., 750
Hopkins, M., 452
Hornery, J., 426
Horovitz, B., 735
Horwat, C., 853, 857
Hoskin, R. E., 215
Hoskisson, R. E., 83, 214, 249, 325, 326, 357, 358
Hotard, D., 180
Houghton, A., 815
Hout, T., 249
Howe, T., 694, 695, 697, 698, 699
Howell, R. A., 118
Hrebiniak, L. G., 34, 214, 357
Hume, S., 792
Hutt, M. D., 215
Hutten, C., 320
Huy, Q. H., 35
Hyde, J., 649
Hytner, N., 857

Iams, T., 574
Idei, N., 741, 808, 809
Ihlwan, M., 810
Imperato, G., 100, 393
Inglis, M., 330
Ingram, T. N., 180
Inkpen, A. C., 358
Ireland, R. D., 83, 101, 214, 249, 357
Isaacson, W., 393
Isidore, C., 641, 700, 706, 707
Iverson, K., 305

Jackson, E. M., 325
Jackson, M., 100, 646
Jafari, J., 209
Jager, D. I., 799, 800
Janis, I., 483, 485, 492
Japp, L., Sr., 689–699
Jenkins, D., 80
Jensen, M., 325, 326
Jespersen, F. F., 326
Joachimsthaler, E., 248
Jobs, S., 793–798
Johannessen, J.-A., 425
Johnson, D., 377, 898
Johnson, J. L., 325
Johnson, K., 815
Johnson, R. A., 326
Johnson, S., 24, 392
Johnston, S. J., 421
Jones, C., 615
Jong Yong Yun, 806–810

Jordan, B. D., 102
Joyce, E., 656
Joyce, W. F., 34, 214, 357
Judge, P. C., 143, 466

Kaihla, P., 411
Kale, P., 249
Kalish, I., 413
Kambil, A., 215
Kamen, D., 825–833
Kamen, J., 825
Kananjian, R. K., 357
Kanter, R. M., 358, 398, 426
Kao, J., 398, 426
Kaplan, P., 532
Kaplan, R., 91, 101
Kapur, D., 224, 225
Kasten, T., 380
Katz, J. A., 466
Katzenbach, J. R., 359
Kawamoto, D., 100
Kay, I., 129
Kazanjian, K., 436
Kazanjian, R. K., 331
Kean, J., 474
Keats, B., 357
Kedia, B. L., 248
Keegan, W. J., 678
Keenan, F., 427
Keenan, P. T., 216
Kelleher, H., 7, 87, 837–844
Kelly, B., 474
Kelly, G., 80, 706, 841
Kelly, T., 705
Kemp, S., 320
Kennedy, A. A., 324
Kennedy, J. F., 689
Kent, S. L., 742, 750
Kerin, R. A., 180
Kerr, J., 324
Kerstetter, J., 8, 100
Kerwin, K., 67, 641, 644, 645, 646, 648, 665
Ketner, B., 148
Ketner, R., 148
Kets de Vries, M. F. R., 35, 142, 143, 409
Keynes, J. M., 30
Keyworth, G. A., II, 563
Khandekar, R., 514, 525
Khanna, T., 215
Khermouch, G., 688, 753
Kidd, J. B., 249
Kidwell, R. E., Jr., 325
Kiger, P. J., 393
Killian, K., 304
Killinger, K., 367, 368
Kim, C. R., 649
Kim, E., 808, 809
Kim, H., 358
Kim, L., 180

Kim, S. P., 35
Kintto, L., 596
Kirkland, J., 66
Kirn, S., 101
Kissinger, H., 505
Kletter, D., 426
Kline, D., 35, 101, 249
Kling, K., 155, 324
Knorr, A., 878
Knox, N., 425
Koch, J., 579
Kogut, B., 249
Kolowski, D., 290, 291
Koogle, T., 448, 901
Koppel, B., 357
Koretz, G., 179
Korman, J., 122
Kornblum, W., 870
Korzenowski, P., 575
Kosdere, I., 876
Kosnik, R. D., 326
Kotabe, M., 249
Kotha, S., 846
Kotter, J. P., 392
Koudsi, S., 143, 215
Kovsky, S., 750
Koza, M. P., 249
Kozlowski, D., 211, 216, 312, 382
Kraland, M., 688
Krantz, B., 771
Kripalani, M., 25, 224
Krishnan, D., 751
Krishnan, M. S., 180
Krishnan, V., 837
Kroc, R., 730, 731
Kroll, M., 180
Kromer, E., 66
Krug, J. A., 907
Kruger, I., 733
Kubina, B., 519
Kuedtjam, H., 358
Kulatilaka, N., 215
Kumar, N., 67
Kunii, I., 325
Kupstas, M. J., 788
Kurlantzick, J., 467
Kurtz, R., 449
Kusin, M., 553
Kutaragi, K., 410
Kwatinetz, M., 571
Kwon, S.-W., 143

LaBarre, P., 392
Labarre, P., 136
Lacy, C., 541, 552
Lafley, A. G., 799–804
LaForge, R. W., 180
Lager, F., 552, 554
Lancaster, H., 574
Land, E., 396

Landes, D. S., 248
Lang, N., 602
Langreth, R., 351
Lanier, E., 123
Larsen, R. S., 710
Larson, E., 554
Laseter, T., 650
Lashinsky, A., 82
Lasseter, J., 795–798
Latham, C., 440
Latham, G. P., 324
Lavelle, L., 18, 320, 325, 326
Lavelle, M., 34, 384
Law, J., 857
Lawler, E. E., III, 393
Lawrence, D. M., 563
Lawrence, J., 203
Lawrence, S., 8
Lay, K., 384
Lazarus, C., 866
Lazarus, M., 702
Leach, B., 693
Leana, C. R., 143
Leavitt, H., 344, 345
Lederhausen, M., 730, 732
Lee, J., 324
Lee, L., 214
Lefteroff, T. T., 467
Lei, D., 143, 325
Leifer, R., 425, 426
LeMay, R. T., 18, 91
Lenehan, J. T., 713
Lenzner, R., 143
Leonard, D., 87, 132, 143
Leonard-Barton, D., 377, 393
Leschly, J., 125
Letzelter, J., 407
Leung, S., 735
Levey, N., 100
Levin, G. M., 312
Levinthal, D., 425
Levitt, T., 248
Lewent, J., 367
Lewis, K., 121
Lewis, R., 727–728
Li, J. T., 249
Licking, E., 23
Liebeck, L., 871
Lieber, R. B., 143
Lieberman, D., 368
Lieberman, M. B., 427
Lieberthal, K., 248
Light, L., 180
Lim, Y., 180
Lincoln, J. C., 716–729
Lindemann, K., 852
Linder, K., 591
Lindorff, D., 51
Lipin, S., 185
Lipman-Blumen, J., 345

Lipparini, A., 101
Lipton, M., 35
Littlefield, W., 679, 680, 682
Livengood, S., 436
Livermore, A. M., 563
Locke, E. A., 324
Loeb, M., 34
London, T., 34
Long, W., 466
Loomis, C. J., 34
Lopez, J., 142, 763
Lopez, R. H., 811
Lorange, P., 66, 359, 392
Lorenzoni, G., 101, 358
Lothson, D., 710
Low, C. K., 309
Lowe, T., 441
Lowery, T., 179, 215
Lowry, T., 214
Lu, H. L., 459
Lublin, J. S., 554
Lubove, S., 143, 393
Lucas, G. W., Jr., 793
Luchs, K., 215
Luehrman, T. A., 101, 216
Lukas, P., 417
Lumpkin, G. T., 143, 414, 425, 426, 466
Lundberg, C. C., 492
Luthans, F., 392, 393
Lutz, R., 18, 660, 661, 663

MacArthur, P., 896
MacDuffie, J. P., 430
Machlis, S., 654
MacMillan, I., 179, 180, 248, 426
Madigan, D., 698
Magretta, J., 135, 358
Maguire, J., 788
Maiello, M., 467
Main, J., 393
Majluf, N. S., 214, 215
Makino, S., 248
Malkin, E., 222, 248
Malone, J., 379
Malone, M. S., 142
Mandela, N., 44
Mandelker, G., 325
Mandl, A., 202
Mang, P. Y., 426
Mannix, E. A., 35
Marcial, G., 67
Mardesich, J., 180
Margonelli, L., 155
Mariano, G., 243
Markham, S. K., 426
Markides, C., 66, 180
Martin, D., 678
Martin, J., 142, 249, 466
Martin, R., 44, 804
Martin, X., 249

Martinez, A., 39
Maslen, P., 849, 852, 858, 859, 861
Massouris, J., 441
Mauboussin, M. H., 209
Maurer, J. S., 184
May, R. C., 66
Mayer, J. D., 393
Maynard, M., 100
McAfee, A., 101
McArthur, S., 797, 798
McCarthy, D. J., 540
McCollum, J., 681
McConnell, B., 838
McConville, J., 900
McCune, J. C., 249
McDaniel, T., 841, 843
McDermott, C. M., 425
McDonald, M., 731
McDonald, P. R., 540
McDonald, R., 731
McDougal, R. A., 336
McDougall, P. P., 332
McGahan, A. M., 180
McGeehan, P., 325
McGinnis, C., 706
McGonagle, J. J., 493
McGrath, R., 179, 248, 426
McGuire, J. F., 526
McKenna, M. J., 608
McKnight, W., 380
McLaughlin, D. T., 522
McLaughlin, K. J., 358
McLaughlin, T., 425
McLean, B., 320, 326, 900
McMahon, E., 862
McMahon, L., 895–900
McMahon, V., 895–900
McManus, C., 606
McMullan, W. E., 466
McNamee, M., 18, 320
McNaughton, L., 899
McNealy, S., 565
McTaggert, J., 654
McVae, J., 34
McVey, H., 156
Means, G. C., 310
Meckling, W., 325, 326
Meindl, J. R., 34
Melcher, R., 325, 699
Mellgren, D., 66
Melrose, K., 375, 393
Merchant, H., 249
Merritt, B., 764, 765, 782
Messier, J.-M., 211
Meyer, P., 378, 393
Michaels, N., 448
Mikami, S., 746
Miles, R. E., 352
Miller, A., 34, 179, 215, 357, 392, 393
Miller, D., 324, 325, 357, 414

Miller, J., 493
Miller, K. D., 910
Miller, K. L., 642
Miller, W., 358
Minow, N., 17, 34, 308, 325, 326
Mintzberg, H., 11, 12, 34, 292, 324, 492, 640
Mitchell, R., 324, 417
Mi-Young, A., 249
Mochari, I., 427
Moerk, H., 751
Moldoveanu, M., 35
Monaghan, T., 776
Monahan, T., 457
Monks, A. G., 34, 325, 326
Monks, R., 17, 308
Monteiro, K. A., 215
Montgomery, C., 85, 101, 214, 325, 357
Moody, K. F., 670
Mooney, A. C., 492
Moore, A., 871
Moore, G., 418, 427, 566
Moore, J. F., 359
Moore, P. L., 141, 641, 644
Moreno, F., 773
Morgenthau, R. M., 290
Morris, E., 492
Morris, J., 702
Morrison, S., 293
Morrison, T., 231
Morrissey, C. A., 426
Morse, J., 434
Mortimer, R., 596
Motto, V., 819
Mount, I., 80
Mowery, D. C., 358
Mudambi, R., 67
Mulcahy, A., 116, 117
Mullaney, T. J., 180, 427
Muller, J., 179, 215, 641, 642, 644
Mundt, K., 672, 678
Munk, N., 101, 143
Muoio, A., 215, 366
Murphy, C., 49
Murphy, D., 392
Murphy, K. J., 326
Murray, R., 58
Murray, S., 596
Mussberg, W., 358

Nacher, T., 100
Nader, R., 320, 321
Nahapiet, J., 142
Nalebuff, B. J., 60, 61, 67
Narasimhaiya, G., 25
Narayanan, V. K., 66
Nasser, J., 233, 641, 645
Naughton, K., 642, 645, 646
Navarez, R., 128
Nee, E., 574

Neeleman, D., 700, 702, 703, 704
Neilson, G., 426
Nelson, B., 42, 448
Nelson, L. A., 492
Nelson, M. G., 30
Nelson, R. E., 794
Neuborne, E., 172
Neufville, R. de, 215
Newman, P., 505
Nexon, M., 142
N'Gai, C., 532
Nguyen, B., 451, 452
Niblack, J., 426
Nicely, W., 519
Nixon, J., 681
Nmarus, J. A., 100
Nobel, R., 249
Nohria, N., 135, 143, 426
Nolan, M. J., 788
Nonaka, I., 142
Nordstrom, D., 76
Norton, D., 91, 101
Novak, D., 908
Novak, D. C., 735
Novicki, C., 393
Nuevo, Y., 411

Oakes, P., 730
O'Brien, W., 375
O'Connor, G. C., 425
O'Dell, C., 136
Odlyzko, A., 66
Oestricher, D., 900
Oh Dong Jin, 809
Ohmae, K., 359
Okawara, M., 633
Okie, F. G., 297
Okuda, H., 644
O'Leary-Kelly, A. M., 324
Oliff, M., 641, 700, 751, 876
Olilla, J., 751, 752, 753
Olsen, B., 425
Olsen, D., 850
Olsen, K. H., 43
Omidyar, P., 621–639
O'Neill, H. M., 357
Onstead, K., 842
O'Reilly, B., 392
Ornati, O., 358
Orr, S. P., 563, 565
Orton, R., 895
Osborne, D. M., 467
Oster, S. M., 153
Otero, A., 379
Ouchi, W., 324
Overholt, A., 76, 368
Oviatt, B. M., 332
Owen, J., 705, 708
Owens, T., 445
Owens, W. T., 384

Oxley, J. E., 358
Ozzie, R., 90

Pachter, M., 531
Packard, D., 559, 561, 571
Packard, D. W., 561
Padilla, J., 641
Paine, D., 536
Paine, L. S., 385, 386, 393
Palmer, A. T., 179
Palmeri, C., 389
Palmisano, S., 59
Paltrow, G., 763
Panitz, S., 792
Pare, T. P., 214
Park, A., 34
Parker, J. F., 842
Parkinson, A., 656
Parkinson, T., 656
Pascual, A. M., 179, 215
Patscot, S., 123
Pawlowski, J., 448
Pearce, J. A., 180
Pearl, D., 227
Pearson, A., 392, 632
Pearson, D. R., 301
Peck, S. I., 326
Peckenpaugh, J., 348
Pedroza, G. M., 467
Peel, C., 678
Pepper, J., 382, 385, 800
Pereira, J., 554
Perez, A. M., 562, 563
Perez, F., 304
Perkins, A. B., 142
Perman, S., 427
Perot, R., 6
Perrewe, P. L., 393
Perry, D., 537
Peteraf, M., 67, 143
Peters, L. S., 425
Peters, S., 215, 249
Peters, T. J., 324
Peterson, P. A., 370, 713
Peterson, T., 179
Petry, C., 377
Pfau, B., 129
Pfeffer, J., 34, 79, 120, 124, 143, 344, 358
Phelan, D., 125
Phillips, L., 125
Picken, J., 72, 138, 141, 142, 168, 179, 180, 214, 300, 323, 324, 359, 366, 392, 393
Pickering, C. I., 66
Piesch, F., 220
Pieschala, G., 501
Pinchot, G., 405, 426
Pine, B. J., II, 180
Pink, D. H., 87
Piscitelli, R., 586

Pistorio, P., 205
Pita, J., 632
Pitts, R. A., 143, 325, 357
Pizana, L., 207
Pizzo, V. G., 325
Platt, L., 559, 560, 561, 562, 563, 565–566, 574
Plenge, R., 300, 301
Polanyi, M., 142
Poole, S., 750
Poon, C. A., 714
Porras, J. I., 296, 324, 417, 427
Port, O., 393
Porter, M., 9, 34, 53, 54, 55, 67, 71, 73, 100, 150, 152, 153, 155, 157, 179, 180, 210, 214, 215, 221, 248, 249, 325
Pottruck, D. A., 358
Pound, J., 325
Powell, T. C., 179
Powell, W. W., 351
Prahalad, C. K., 34, 38, 66, 117, 142, 143, 179, 180, 214, 248, 249
Priem, R., 66, 358
Prior, V., 66
Pritchard, D., 303
Procter, W., 799
Prusak, L., 143, 426

Quelch, J. A., 686
Questrom, A., 167
Quigley, J. V., 35
Quinlan, M. R., 730, 731
Quinn, J., 141, 292, 323, 358, 427, 640, 815
Quinn, R., 35, 101, 375, 376, 393

Rabinovitz, J., 407
Rae-Dupree, J., 8
Rahe, A. S., 184
Raisinghani, D., 492
Rajendra, E., 156
Raleigh, T. J., 698
Ramamurti, R., 224, 225
Ramstead, E., 358
Rao, A. R., 179
Rappaport, A., 185, 324
Rasheed, A. M. A., 358
Rasheed, M. A., 67
Raths, D., 474
Rautiola, N., 463
Rechner, P. L., 492
Redmond, W., 750
Reene, M., 131
Reeves, T., 620
Reeves, W. T., 797
Regan, N., 18
Reinemuna, S., 693
Reingen, P. H., 215
Reinhardt, A., 66, 215, 531

Reinhardt, F. L., 101
Reuer, J. J., 249
Revell, J., 34
Rice, M. P., 425
Richter, A., 426
Ridge, G., 460
Ridlen, R., 532
Riechardt, 641
Rigas, J. J., 384
Rigby, D., 101, 215
Rigdon, J. E., 392
Rittenberry, A., 900
Rivette, K. G., 35, 101
Rivlin, G., 829, 832
Robbins, Paul, 450, 451
Roberts, Bari-Ellen, 382
Roberts, D., 248
Roberts, E. B., 425
Roberts, J., 426, 728
Roberts, P. W., 142
Robins, J. A., 101
Robinson, A., 176, 177
Robinson, R. B., 180
Robinson, S. L., 324
Rodengen, J. L., 325
Rodin, R., 366
Rogers, T. J., 27
Roman, J., 795
Roman, M., 76, 837
Romanelli, E., 467
Romeril, B., 116, 117
Rondinelli, D. A., 34
Ronstadt, R., 492
Roos, J., 359
Root, F., 772
Rosenberg, S., 421
Rosenbloom, J., 373
Rosenblum, J. W., 358
Rosendahl, L., 411
Rosenfeld, J., 180
Rosenthal, K., 785
Rosenweig, Daniel, 902
Ross, J., 862
Ross, S. A., 102
Roth, D., 66
Roth, K., 101
Rothstein, K., 792
Rotman, J. L., 804
Rovit, S., 732
Rowland, S., 311
Rowley, T. J., 35
Royer, I., 216, 426
Rucci, A. J., 35, 101
Rudden, E., 249
Ruin, H., 537
Ruisel, I., 393
Rumelt, R. P., 357
Runberg, D., 586, 588
Russell, W. V., 562
Russo, D., 79

Ruys, A., 683, 686, 687
Ryan, L. V., 326
Ryan, P. A., 559

Saber, P., 732
Sabo, R., 722, 725
Sahlman, W. A., 476
Saias, M. A., 357
Salancik, G. R., 34
Salman, W. A., 67
Salter, C., 159
Salvoney, P., 393
Sanborn, S., 523
Sandberg, W. R., 492
Sanders, H., 907
Sanderson, E., 726–727
Sanford, S. H., 66
Sanger, S., 153
Sapet, C., 531, 535
Sargent, R., 76
Savage, R., 895
Savner, M., 797
Schaeffer, L., 152
Schafer, S., 393
Schawlow, A., 127
Schecter, S. M., 180
Scheele, N., 641
Schein, E., 334, 357
Schendel, D., 249
Scherer, F. M., 502
Schmitt, W., 398
Schneid, N., 764, 765
Schneider, M., 326
Schoemaker, J. H., 101
Schoonhoven, C. B., 467
Schreyogg, G., 66
Schultz, H., 438, 677, 846–865
Schumer, C., 815
Schwarz, J., 421
Schweiger, D. M., 492
Scolnick, E. M., 367
Scott, B. R., 357
Scott, F. S., 66
Scott, H. L., Jr., 889
Scott, W., 731
Scrushy, R. M., 384
Seglin, J. L., 467
Seid, M., 730
Seiden, J., 122
Seitz, S., 519
Sellers, P., 324
Semel, T. S., 901–906
Semler, R., 304
Senge, P., 21, 24, 34, 35, 374, 393
Serwer, A., 436, 466
Serwer, B., 837, 841, 844
Sexton, D. A., 35
Shaich, R., 785, 787, 788, 789
Shamsie, J., 660, 683, 710, 730, 793, 799, 806, 895

Shane, S., 426, 466
Shanly, M., 67
Shao, M., 554
Shapiro, C., 67, 72
Shari, M., 248
Sharma, A., 249, 426
Sharplin, A. D., 716
Shaw, R., 193
Sheehan, J. J., 599
Sheff, D., 393, 750
Shepherd, D. A., 432, 466
Sherwood, S., 596
Shhok, C., 143
Shih, S., 381
Shilling, A. G., 214
Shinal, J., 215
Shinn, S., 841
Shirouzu, N., 641, 648
Shrader, R. C., 466
Shultz, H., 626
Siebel, T., 158, 235
Siegl, Z., 846
Siehl, C., 304
Sigiura, H., 249
Silverberg, B., 131
Silverman, B. S., 358
Simmons, C., 445
Simons, R., 295, 323
Simpson, B., 159
Sinclair, C., 831, 832
Singh, H., 143, 249
Sirower, M. L., 185
Skilling, J., 384
Skoll, J., 625, 629, 639
Skow, J., 532
Slabin, A., 793, 798
Slater, R., 126, 142
Slaughter, L., 815
Slevin, D. P., 414, 426
Sloan, A., 21, 374, 663
Sloane, J., 466
Slocum, J., 143
Slocum, J. W., 325
Slocum, J. W., Jr., 324
Sly, L., 600
Slywotzky, A., 82, 413, 678
Smilor, R., 764
Smith, A. R., 793
Smith, D., 142, 353, 359, 457
Smith, F., 460
Smith, G., 66, 393
Smith, H., 204
Smith, J. F., Jr., 660
Smith, O. C., 849
Smith, R., 660
Snow, C. C., 352
Solomon,H., 316
Song Kye-Hyon, 245
Soon Beng Yeap, 857, 858, 859
Sørenson, L., 411

Sorrell, M., 133, 408
Souder, E., 708
Soule, E., 393
Sparks, L., 536
Spear, G., 698
Speight, D., 136
Spencer, J. W., 143
Spielberg, S., 379
Spinelli, S., 442
Spitz, J., 700
Spraggins, M., 300, 301
Sprang, K., 567
Spreitzer, G., 375, 376, 393
Squire, R., 576, 582
Squires, S. L., 563
Stabell, C. B., 100
Stack, J., 376, 393
Stadter, G., 101
Stafford, E. R., 215
Stanton, A., 797
Stanton, S., 375, 393
Staw, B. M., 392
Stearns, T. M., 492
Stecklow, S., 227
Steele, W. H., 799
Steenbuch, F., 52
Steere, W. C., Jr., 426
Stein, N., 596
Stein, T., 407, 426
Steinberg, B., 900
Stern, R. L., 392
Sternberg, R. J., 393
Stewart, B., 726
Stewart, T., 35, 82, 122, 142, 466
Stewart, W. H., 66
Stienmann, H., 66
Stiller, B., 678
Stillman, R., 519
Stipp, D., 50
Stockley, R. L., Jr., 209
Stoughton, S., 172
Stout, H. J., 466
Straus, S., 143
Strickland, A. J., III, 324
Stringer, R., 426
Strong, B., 136
Stross, R. E., 248
Strum, D., 603
Stuart, A., 467
Stuckey, J., 358
Suhr, J., 163
Sull, D., 426
Sullivan, C., 764, 765, 769, 782
Sundaramurthy, C., 211
Sussman, B., 815
Sutcliffe, K. M., 66, 358
Swap, W., 132
Swartz, M., 290
Sweeney, P., 457
Sweo, R., 66

Sylph, J., 320
Symonds, W. C., 179, 180, 323

Takahashi, D., 750
Tallman, J., 134
Tam, P.-W., 798
Tanner, J., 180, 467
Taylor, A., III, 163, 180, 665
Taylor, F., 380
Taylor, H. A., 522
Taylor, M. L., 700, 764
Taylor, W. C., 143, 393
Teather, D., 641
Teitelbaum, R., 143, 324
Teng, B. S., 359
Teramoto, Y., 249
Terman, F., 559
Tesler, L., 427
Tetenbaum, T. J., 35
Thaw, H., 811
Thaw, J., 811–824
Thaw, M., 821
Thaw, N., 811
Thaw, S., 811
Thaw, Stan, 819
Thaw, T., 822
Theodore, S., 688
Theoret, A., 492
Thoman, R., 116, 117
Thomas, J. G., 35
Thompson, A. A., Jr., 324
Thompson, L., 358
Thorndike, E. L., 393
Thornton, E., 179, 642
Thurrott, P., 750
Tibbs, K., 209
Tichy, N. M., 392
Ticknor, C. M., 562, 563, 564
Tierney, C., 649
Tierney, T., 135, 143
Tillman, R., 365
Timberlake, J., 733
Timmons, H., 326
Timmons, J. A., 442, 466
Tinjacha, M., 764
Tischler, L., 67
Toledo, M., 75
Tome, C. B., 302
Torbenson, E., 49, 708, 843
Torode, C., 575
Torre, J., 7
Torres, N. L., 446, 467
Townsend, K., 650, 866
Tracey, A., 825
Trahan, J., 728–729
Trayford, R., 458
Treanor, J., 646
Treece, J., 249
Tretter, M. J., 357
Trevino, L. K., 324

Triandis, H. C., 248
Triantis, A., 216
Trimble, C., 159
Tristram, C., 624, 631
Trotman, M., 842
Trubey, P., 446
Tu, H., 180
Tully, S., 324, 358
Turk, T. A., 326
Turner, F. L., 731
Turnley, W. H., 143
Twohig, P. E., 788
Tyrangiel, J., 523, 524

Uhi-Bien, M., 324
Ulrich, D., 35, 100
Underdahl, B., 750
Useem, J., 168, 206, 425, 466
Useem, M. L., 313
Usinier, J. C., 249
Usry, T., 582, 586

Vadasz, L., 407
Vagelos, P. R., 23, 118, 367
Van Aukun, P. M., 35
Van Buren, H. J., III, 143
Vance, A., 426
van der Minne, F., 685
van der Pool, L., 537
van Putten, A. B., 248
van Putten, N., 685
Varian, H. R., 67, 72
Veitch, M., 427
Vella, C. M., 493
Venkataraman, S., 466
Verdon, J., 871
Vermeulen, F., 215
Veryzer, R. W., 425
Vesper, K., 466, 467
Viault, R., 678
Vicente, J. P., 211
Vickers, M., 325, 427
Victor, B., 357
Viguerie, P., 66
Vogel, C., 467

Wagoner, G. R., Jr., 660–665
Walker, B. A., 215
Wallace, B., 467
Wallace, J., 125
Walsh, F. E., 291
Walsh, J. P., 326
Walters, B. A., 66, 215, 249
Walton, B., 876

Walton, S., 297, 876, 880, 888, 894
Walzer, R., 816
Wan, W. P., 249
Wang, C., 133
Warchol, G., 842
Ward, R. D., 314
Ward, S., 180
Warner, F., 343, 379
Warshaw, S., 591
Wasserman, E., 476
Waterhouse, J. H., 34
Waterman, R. H., 324
Waters, J. A., 12
Watkins, M. D., 66
Watson, J. D., 23
Watson, T., 21, 374
Wayman, P. W., 562
Wayman, R., 563, 564, 567, 575
Weaver, G. R., 324
Weaver, J., 633
Webb, R., 732
Weber, J., 35, 293, 324, 358, 392
Weber, K., 66
Wedel, J., 127
Weiner, B., 522
Weintraub, A., 179, 427
Welch, D., 641, 644, 665
Welch, J., 7, 121, 210, 290, 299, 341
Weldon, W. C., 370, 710, 713, 714
Wells, M., 703
Wells, R. B., 34
Were, M., 596
Wernerfelt, B., 143
Wesley, P., 625, 626
Westerfield, R. W., 102
Weston, J., 293
Weston, J. F., 216
Weston, J. S., 324
Wetlaufer, S., 35, 191, 248, 249, 324, 357, 393
Wexner, L., 148
Whalen, C. J., 179, 215
Whalen, J., 690
Whalen, R. J., 606, 609
Wheatley, J., 66
Wheelwright, S., 425, 426
White, C., 688
White, D., 358
White, G., 306, 325, 357, 641, 642, 648
White, J., 193, 641, 648
White, T., 349
Whitman, M., 625, 626, 629, 639, 804
Whitman, R. A., 204
Wiersema, F., 398, 426

Wiersema, M. F., 101
Wiggett, J., 76
Williams, D., 460
Williams, E., 351
Williams, G., 457, 467
Williamson, O. E., 214
Williamson, P. J., 66
Willis, G., 716, 717, 722, 723
Wilska, K. P., 751
Wilson, C., 618
Wilson, H. J., 426
Wilson, J. L., 750
Wind, Y., 248
Wingfield, N., 216
Winterson, J., 857
Wise, R., 67, 82, 179, 413
Wissman, G., 879
Witkowski, R., 681, 682
Woellert, L., 49, 389
Wolf, A. N., 458
Wolf, C., 809
Wolfenson, J., 66
Wolinsky, H., 398
Wong, W., 100
Wong, Z., 736
Wood, J., 100
Woodley, M., 536
Woods, B., 654
Woodyard, C., 704
Wouk, V., 466
Wright, P., 180
Wriston, W., 21, 374
Wurster, T. S., 66, 427
Wylie, I., 411
Wysocki, B., Jr., 130–131, 143

Yang, C., 466
Yang, J., 901
Yanofsky, N., 788
Yeoh, P. L., 101
Yonekura, H., 808
Yosano, K., 248
Young, J., 561
Young, M., 358
Yu-Bin Chiou, 736

Zacharakis, A. L., 432
Zahra, S. A., 66, 249
Zalla, J., 591
Zellner, W., 80, 324, 700, 708, 841, 842
Zesiger, S., 180
Zganjar, L., 792
Zitzner, D. E., 562, 563, 573
Zwartz, T. A., 698

subject index

a

Acid-test ratio, 106
Actions, and strategic management, 9
Administrative costs, 195
Adolph Coors in the Brewing Industry, 499–513
The Age of Paradox (Handy), 374
The Age of Unreason (Handy), 347, 374
Albany Small Business Development Center, 450
American Business Ethics Award, 386
American Heritage Dictionary, 310
American Red Cross, 2002–2004, 525–529
American Red Cross in 2002 (A), 514–524
Americans with Disabilities Act (ADA), 48
Analysis, and strategic management, 9
Analysis-decision-action cycle, in case analysis, 487–491
Annual Report Collections, 494
Antitakeover tactics, 212
Asset management ratios, 108–109
Asset restructuring, 197
Asset utilization ratios, 479
Atari and InfoGrames Entertainment SA, 530–539
Augustine's Laws (Augustine), 344
Autonomy, 414–416
Average collection period (ACP), 109
Aviation Consumer Action Project, 321

b

Bargaining power of buyers, 56–57
Bargaining power of suppliers, 57–58
Barrier-free organization, 343–346
Behavioral barriers, and change, 368
Behavioral control, 295–307
  motivating with rewards and incentives, 297–299
  setting boundaries and constraints, 299–302
Ben & Jerry's Homemade, Inc.: Passing the Torch, 540–554
Bentley College Center for Business Ethics Award, 386
The Best-Laid Incentive Plans, 555–558
Board of directors (BOD), 17–19
Bootstrapping, 443–444
Boston Consulting Group (BCG) portfolio matrix, 198–201
Boundaryless organizational designs, 341–354
  barrier-free organization, 343–346
  making them work, 352–354

Boundaryless organizational designs—*Cont.*
  modular organization, 347–348, 349
  virtual organization, 348–352
Bribery, abroad, 237
Built to Last (Collins and Porras), 296
Business incubator, 406–407
Business-level strategy, 148–177
  competitive advantage and sustainability, 150–169
  formulating, 14
  industry life-cycle stages, 169–177
  and strategic control, 305–306
Business metasites, 496
Business risk taking, 422
Business Roundtable, 312
Business Week, 7, 41, 93, 167, 204, 308, 320, 379
Buyers, bargaining power of, 56–57

c

CalPERS, 313–315
Capital, types of, 20–21
Capital intensity, 479
Capital intensity ratio, 109
Capital requirements, 56
Capital restructuring, 197
Carly Fiorina: The Reinvention of Hewlett-Packard, 559–575
Case analysis
  analysis-decision-action cycle, 487–491
  conducting, 473–480
  preparing, 484
  reasons for, 472–473
  using conflict-inducing decision-making in, 483–487
Case presentation, preparing, 481
Cash coverage ratio, 108, 479
Cash ratio, 107, 479
Celebrate Your Mistakes (Holt), 381
Census Bureau, 47
Center for Auto Safety, 321
Center for Study of Responsive Law, 321
Challenges Brewing at Breckenridge Brewery, 576–588
Chicago Sun-Times, 398
Chiquita's Global Turnaround, 589–596
Codes of conduct, 387
Coercive power, and leadership, 369
Columbia University, 310
Combination strategies, 164–169
  for new ventures, 462–463
Commercial Alert, 321
Common-size balance sheets, 102, 104

Common-size income statements, 102–103, 105
Company information, sources of, 493–498
Company rankings, 495–496
Competing for the Future (Hamel and Prahalad), 38
Competing on the Edge (Brown and Eisenhardt), 402
Competitive advantage, 150–169
  differentiation, 157–162
  and the five forces, 160, 163–164
  overall cost leadership, 151–156
Competitive Advantage (Porter), 71
Competitive aggressiveness, 414, 419–421
Competitive environment of the firm, 53–63
  and Porter's five-forces model, 54–61
  strategic groups within industries, 61–63
Competitive intelligence (CI), 41–43, 493
Conflict, and decision making, 485–487
Conglomerate, 337
Congress Watch, 321
Consolidation, 174
Consumer price index (CPI), 40
Core competencies, leveraging, 188–189
Corporate credos, 387
Corporate entrepreneurship (CE), 404–414
  approaches to, 405–407
  dispersed approaches to, 408–410
  measuring success of, 410–414
Corporate governance, 307–321
  aligning the interests of owners and managers, 311–317
  external mechanisms, 317–321
  and stakeholder management, 17–21
Corporate-level strategy, 184–212
  achieving diversification, 201–207
  and the erosion of value creation, 208–212
  formulating, 15
  real option analysis, 207–208
  and related diversification, 187–195
  and strategic control, 306–307
  and unrelated diversification, 195–201
Critical Mass Energy & Environment program, 321
Crossing the Chasm (Moore), 418
Crown Cork & Seal in 1989, 597–614
Cultural variations, and international expansion, 231
Culture, building, 296–297

Currency risk, and international
    expansion, 229–230
Current ratio, 105–106, 479

Dartmouth College, 292
David C. Lincoln Award for Ethics and
    Excellence in Business, 386
Days' sales in inventory, 479
Days' sales in inventory ratio, 108–109
Days' sales in receivables, 109, 479
Debt-equity ratio, 107, 479
Decision making, improving, 485–487
Decisions, and strategic management, 9
Demand conditions, and nation
    competitiveness, 222, 223
The Devil's Dictionary (Bierce), 310
Differentiation, 157–162, 164–169
    potential pitfalls, 160–162
    and strategic control, 305–306
Digital business strategy, formulating, 15
Dippin' Dots Ice Cream, 615–620
Distribution channels, 56
Diversification
    achieving, 201–207
    related, 187–195
    unrelated, 195–201
Divisional structure, of organization,
    334–337, 340
Dow Jones Industrial Average (DJIA), 51

eBay: King of the Online Auction
    Industry, 621–639
Ecological capital, 21
Economies of scale, 55–56
Economies of scope, 187–190
EDGAR filings, 494–495
Edward Marshall Boehm, Inc., 640
Egotism, and value creation, 210–211
Electronic Buyer News, 366
Elephants, 434
Emotional intelligence
    creating an ethical organization,
        381–390
    developing a learning organization,
        374–381
    five components of, 371–374
    and leadership, 370–374
Emotional Intelligence (Goleman), 371
Empathy, 372–373
Employees
    empowering, 375–376
    and strategic management, 24–26
Entrants, threat of, 55–56
Entrepreneur Hot 100, 434, 443
Entrepreneurial culture, 408
Entrepreneurial leadership, 450–454
Entrepreneurial orientation (EO),
    414–423
    autonomy, 414–416

Entrepreneurial resources, 442–450
    new-venture financing, 443–447
Entrepreneurial strategy, 454–463
Entrepreneurial ventures, categories of,
    431–435
Entry strategies, 455–459
Environmental forecasting, 43–44
Environmental monitoring, 40
Environmental scanning, 39–40
Equity multiplier, 107
Equity multiplier ratio, 479
Ethics
    individual vs. organizational, 381–383
    integrity-based versus compliance-
        based, 383–386
Euromoney, 228
European Union (EU), 52
Evaluation systems, 388–389
Every Business Needs an Angel
    (Simmons), 445
Excessive product-market diversification,
    317
Exit barriers, 59
Exit champions, 412
Exiting the market, 174
Experience curve, 153
Expert power, and leadership, 369
Exporting, 240–242
External environment of the firm, 14,
    38–63
    competitive environment, 53–63
    creating environmentally aware
        organization, 39–45
    general environment, 45–53
Exxon Valdez, 382

Factor conditions, and nation
    competitiveness, 222–223
Family businesses, 437
Family Firm Institute (FFI), 437
Fast Company, 379
Federal Reserve, 50
Financial leverage ratios, 107–108, 479
Financial ratio analysis, 91–94, 102–112
    asset management ratios, 108–109
    common-size balance sheets, 102, 104
    common-size income statements,
        102–103, 105
    long-term solvency ratios, 107–108
    market value measures, 111
    profitability measures, 110–111
    short-term solvency ratios, 105–107
    standard financial statements, 102
    techniques, 479
Financial risk taking, 422
Financial statements, 102
Firm performance, evaluating, 91–97
Firm strategy, structure and rivalry, and
    nation competitiveness, 222,
    224–225

Focus, 162–164
    potential pitfalls, 164
Forbes, 7, 379
Ford Motor Company in 2004:
    Entering Second Century of
    Existence, 641–649
Foreign Corrupt Practices Act, 237
Fortune, 7, 23, 38, 41, 161, 173, 185,
    320, 362, 379
Franchises, 437
Franchising, 242, 457
Free agent employees, 436
FreshDirect, 650–659
Functional structure, of organization,
    333–334, 340
Funeral Directors Association, 47

Gazelles, 434–435
General administration, 77, 79–80
General Agreement on Tariffs and Trade
    (GATT), 52
General environment of the firm, 45–53
    demographic segment, 45–47, 54
    economic segment, 46, 51, 54
    global segment, 54, 46, 52
    political/legal segment, 46, 48–49, 54
    relationship among elements of, 52
    sociocultural segment, 46, 48, 54
    technological segment, 46, 49–51, 54
General Motors, 660–665
Generic entry strategies, 459–462
Generic strategies, 175
Geographic-area division structures, 339
George Washington University, 80
Glass-Steagall Act, 48
Globalization, 40
    and strategic management, 22
Global strategy, 238
Global Trade Watch, 321
Go Global—or No?, 666–669
Golden parachute, 212, 318
Good to Great (Collins), 453
Government resources, and new ventures,
    448–450
The Great Game of Business (Stack), 376
Greenmail, 212, 318
Green Mountain Coffee Roasters,
    670–678
Groupthink, 483
    symptoms and preventing, 485
Growing for Broke, 679–682

Harvard Business Review, 119, 153, 371,
    372
Harvard University, 50, 132, 210, 221,
    385, 403
Harvesting, 174
Health Research Group, 321
Heineken, 683–688
Hierarchical relationships, 186, 195, 197

Hierarchy of goals, 26
Holding company structure, 337
Home-based businesses, 437
Horizontal relationships, 186, 195
Hot Groups (Leavitt and Lipman-Bluemen), 345
Human capital, 21, 120–129, 447
    attracting, 121–123
    developing, 123–126
    and human resources costs, 129
    leveraging, 133–139
The Human Equation (Pfeffer), 344
Human resource management, 77, 78–79
Hypercompetition (D'Aveni), 364

Inbound logistics, 73, 74
Inc., 434, 452, 500
Incremental innovations, 399
Industry information, sources of, 493–498
Industry life-cycle stages, 169–177
    decline stage strategies, 173–174
    growth stage strategies, 171–172
    introduction stage strategies, 170–171
    maturity stage strategies, 172–173
Information power, and leadership, 369
Innovation and Entrepreneurship (Drucker), 423
Innovation management, 397–404
    challenges, 400–401
    collaborating with partners, 402–404
    defining scope of innovation, 401–402
    managing the pace, 402
    types of innovation, 398–400
Innovativeness, 414, 416–418
Inside Business, 159
Inside Consulting (Rodenhauser), 415
Intangible resources, 83, 84
Intellectual assets, 14, 116–139
    human capital, 120–129
    role of knowledge in today's economy, 117–120
    social capital, 129–133
    using technology to leverage human capital and knowledge, 133–139
Intellectual capital, and strategic management, 22–24
Internal benchmarking, 378
Internal environment of the firm, 14, 70–97
    evaluating firm performance, 91–97
    resource-based view, 81–91
    value-chain analysis, 71–81
International division structures, 339
International operations, and organizational structure, 339–340
International strategy, 220–246
    achieving competitive advantage, 232–239
    entry modes of expansion, 239–246

International strategy—*Cont.*
    formulating, 15
    global economy overview, 220–221
    motivations and risks of expansion, 226–231
    nation competitiveness, 221–226
Inventory turnover, 108–109
Inventory turnover ratio, 479
Investors Business Daily, 320

Jays Foods, L.L.C., 689–699
Johnson & Johnson, 710–715
Joint ventures, 203–206, 242–244
Just-in-time (JIT) inventory systems, 74

Learning organization, developing, 374–381
Legitimate power, and leadership, 369
Leverage ratios, 107–108
Licensing, 242
The Lincoln Electric Company, 716–729
Liquidity measures, 105–107
Liquidity ratios, 479
Long-term solvency ratios, 107–108, 479

Maintaining, 174
Making the Grass Greener on Your Side (Melrose), 375
Malcolm Baldrige National Quality Award, 38
Management restructuring, 197–198
Management risk, and international expansion, 230–231
Marketing and sales, 73, 75
Market-to-book ratio, 111, 479
Market value measures, 111
Market value ratios, 479
Massachusetts Institute of Technology (MIT), 334, 374
Material capital, 21
Matrix structure, of organization, 338–339, 340
McDonald's, 730–735
McGill University, 11, 292
Mergers and acquisitions, 202–203
Mice, 434
Michigan, University of, 20
Microsoft's Battle for the Living Room: The Trojan Horse—The Xbox, 736–750
Mission statements, 28–29
Modular organization, 347–348, 349
Motivation, 371–372
Multidomestic strategy, 236–237, 238

National Association of Home-Based Businesses (NAHBB), 437
National Association of Home Builders, 47

National Association of Purchasing Managers, 50
National Science Foundation (NSF), 449
Net disposable income (NDI), 40
Net present value (NPV) analysis, 209
New-venture financing, 443–447
New venture groups (NVGs), 405–406
New ventures, 431–463
    categories of, 431–435
    characteristics of good opportunities, 440
    entrepreneurial leadership, 450–454
    entrepreneurial strategy, 454–463
    identifying and developing opportunities, 435–442
    and the U.S. economy, 432
New York Times, 371
Nokia's Strategic Intent for the 21st Century, 751–763
North American Free Trade Agreement (NAFTA), 52

Oobeyas, 343
Operations, 73, 74
Oral case presentation, preparing, 481
Organizational capabilities, 83, 84
Organizational design, 330–354
    boundaryless organizational designs, 341–354
    traditional organizational structures, 330–341
Organizational Dynamics, 128, 375
Organizational structures, 330–341
    divisional structure, 334–337, 340
    functional structure, 333–334, 340
    growth of large corporations, 331–332
    and international operations, 339–340
    matrix structure, 338–339, 340
    simple structure, 332–333
    and strategy formulation, 341
Organizational vision, 26–28
Outback Steakhouse Goes International, 764–782
Outbound logistics, 73, 74–75
Outsourcing
    noncore functions, 349
    strategic risk of, 348
Overall cost leadership, 151–156
    and new ventures, 459–462
    potential pitfalls of, 155–156
    and strategic control, 305
    value-chain activities, 152

Panera Bread Company, 783–792
Pension Rights Center, 321
Personal risk taking, 422
Pied Piper Effect, 130–131
Pixar Animation Studios, 793–798
Poison pills, 211, 212, 318
Political barriers, and change, 368

Pooled negotiating power, 190–192
Porter's five-forces model of industry competition, 54–61
Portfolio management, 198–201
Price-earnings ratios, 111, 479
Prime Time Live, 148, 149, 320
Proactiveness, 414, 418–419
Process innovation, 399–400
Procter & Gamble, 799–804
Procurement, 77–78
Product champions, 408–410
Product differentiation, 56
Product innovation, 399
Profitability measures, 110–111
Profitability ratios, 479
Profit margin, 110, 479
Profit pool, 165–166, 168–169
Project definition, 409
Project impetus, 409
Public Citizen, 321
Public Citizen Litigation Group, 321

Quick ratio, 106, 479

Radical innovations, 398–399
Real option analysis (ROA), 207–208, 209
Receivables turnover, 109, 479
Recycling profits, 437
Referent power, and leadership, 369
Related and supporting industries, and nation competitiveness, 222, 223
Resource-based view (RBV) of the firm, 81–91
    generation and distribution of firm profits, 89–91
    and sustainable competitive advantage, 84–89
    types of firm resources, 82–84
Restructuring, 197–198
Retail Merchandiser, 398
Return on assets (ROA), 110–111, 479
Return on equity (ROE), 110–111, 479
Reward power, and leadership, 369
Reward systems, 388–389
Risk taking, 414, 421–423
Robin Hood, 805
Role models, 387

Sales; *see also* Marketing
Samsung Electronics, 806–810
Sarbanes-Oxley Act, 48, 319, 389, 390
Scenario planning, 44
Schoolhouse Lane Estates, 811–824
SEC filings, 494
Securities and Exchange Commission (SEC), 318, 319, 384
Segway: A New Dimension in Human Transportation, 825–833

Self-awareness, 371
Self-regulation, 371
Service, 73, 75–76
Sharing activities, 189–190
Short-term solvency ratios, 105–107, 479
Simple structure, of organization, 332–333
The Skeleton in the Corporate Closet, 834–836
Small Business Administration (SBA), 448, 449
Small Business Development Centers, 448
Small Business Innovation Research (SBIR), 449
Social capital, 21, 129–133, 447–448
    attracting and retaining talent, 130–132
Social responsibility, and stakeholders, 19–21
Social skill, 373
Southwest Airlines: How Much Can "LUV" Do?, 837–845
Southwest Minnesota Initiative Fund (SWMIF), 449
Stakeholder management, and corporate governance, 17–21
Stakeholder symbiosis, 19
Stanford University, 120, 124
Starbucks Corporation: Competing in a Global Market, 846–865
Strategic alliances, 203–206, 242–244
Strategic business unit (SBU), organizational structure, 337
Strategic control, 15–16, 290–321
    attaining behavioral control, 295–307
    ensuring informational control, 291–295
    role of corporate governance, 307–321
Strategic direction, coherence in, 26–31
Strategic implementation, 15–17
Strategic leadership, 362–390
    and emotional intelligence, 370–374
    interdependent activities, 363–370
Strategic management
    defined, 8–10
    key attributes, 10–11
    process, 11–17
Strategic management perspective, 21–26
    driving forces of, 21–24
Strategic objectives, 29–31
Strategy formulation, 14–15
The Structure of Corporation Law (Eisenberg), 310
Substitutes, threat of, 58–59
Suppliers, bargaining power of, 57–58
Switching costs, 56, 59
SWOT analysis, 45, 71, 419–420
    limitations of, 72
Systemic barriers, and change, 368

Takeover constraint, 318
Tangible resources, 82–84
Technology, and strategic management, 22
Technology development, 77, 78
TIAA-CREF, 316, 317
Times interest earned, 107–108
Times interest earned ratio, 479
Time to market, 40
Total asset turnover, 109, 479
Total debt ratio, 107, 479
Toys "R" Us Moving into 2004, 866–871
Transaction cost perspective, 194–195
Transnational strategy, 238–239
Trouble in Paradise, 872–875
Turnaround strategies, 175–177
Turnover measures, 108–109
Turnover ratios, 479

United Steel Workers, 58
U.S. Commerce Department, 437
U.S. Department of Education, 48
USA Today, 294, 295
Utah Microenterprise Loan Fund (UMLF), 449

Value-chain analysis, 71–81
    differentiation, 157–162
    interrelationships among activities, 81
    primary activities of, 73–76
    support activities of, 76–80
Value creation, erosion of, 208–212
Vaporware, 421
Vertical integration, 192–195
Vertical relationships, 195
Virtual organization, 348–352

The Wall Street Journal, 41, 130, 320
Wal-Mart's Strategy for the 21st Century: Sustaining Dominance, 876–894
The Web of Inclusion: A New Architecture for Building Great Organizations (Helgesen), 25
Wholly owned subsidiaries, 244–246
The Wisdom of Teams (Smith), 353
Working with Emotional Intelligence (Goleman), 371
Worldwide functional structures, 339
Worldwide matrix structures, 339
Worldwide product division structures, 339
World Wrestling Entertainment, 895–900

Yahoo!, 901–906
Yum! Brands, Pizza Hut, and KFC, 907–918

Zero sum, 19